The

Longest Night

A MILITARY HISTORY OF THE CIVIL WAR

David J. Eicher

Foreword by James M. McPherson
Maps by Lee Vande Visse

SIMON & SCHUSTER

NEW YORK   LONDON   TORONTO   SYDNEY   SINGAPORE

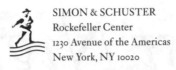 SIMON & SCHUSTER
Rockefeller Center
1230 Avenue of the Americas
New York, NY 10020

SIMON & SCHUSTER and colophon are
registered trademarks of Simon & Schuster, Inc.
For information about special discounts for bulk purchases,
please contact Simon & Schuster Special Sales:
1-800-456-6798 or business@simonandschuster.com
Designed by Edith Fowler
Manufactured in the United States of America

10   9   8   7   6   5   4   3   2   1

Library of Congress Cataloging-in-Publication Data
Eicher, David J., date.
    The longest night : a military history of the Civil War / David J. Eicher ;
foreword by James M. McPherson ; maps by Lee Vande Visse.
        p.   cm.
    Includes bibliographical references and index.
    1. United States—History—Civil War, 1861–1865—Campaigns.   I. Title.
E470 .E35 2001
973.7'3—dc21   2001034153
ISBN 0-684-84944-5

Title Page Photos
61st Pennsylvania Regiment Flag courtesy of the Pennsylvania Capitol Preservation
Committee.

28th North Carolina Infantry Flag courtesy of The Museum of the Confederacy,
Richmond, Virginia; photography by Larry Sherer.

For Lynda and Chris,
who share Father with ghosts from the past.

Contents

List of Maps

From April 12, 1861, to June 2, 1865, the light of the great experiment of democracy burned but dimly as more than 8,700 battles and skirmishes swept across the land and extinguished more than 620,000 lives North and South.

For all Americans, it was the longest night.

Foreword

JAMES M. McPHERSON

THE CIVIL WAR was the most dramatic, violent, and fateful experience in American history. At least 620,000 soldiers lost their lives out of a total population of 32 million. If the same percentage of the American people were to die in a war fought by the United States today, the number of American war dead would be *5.5 million*. An unknown number of civilians in the 1860s also died from disease or malnutrition or exposure brought on by the disruption and destruction of the war in the South. The number of battle casualties in a single day at Sharpsburg, Maryland (September 17, 1862) was four times the number of American casualties on the Normandy beaches on D-Day, June 6, 1944. More Americans were killed in that single day at the battle of Antietam than were killed or mortally wounded in combat in all of the other wars fought by the United States in the nineteenth century *combined*.

Little wonder that the Civil War has produced more books and other publications than any other event in American history—nearly 70,000 titles by one estimate. This outpouring began during the war itself, rose to a flood in the 1880s, ebbed and flowed during the following century, and has increased to an all-time high during the past twenty years. Most of these writings have focused on the war's military campaigns and battles, its commanders and soldiers, strategy and tactics. As early as the 1880s, twice-wounded Union army veteran Albion W. Tourgée complained about this emphasis. Americans, wrote this radical reformer and champion of equal rights for freed slaves, should remember "*not* the courage, the suffering, the blood, *but only the causes that underlay the struggle and the results that followed from it.*"

Tourgée's plea was largely in vain. Although many academic historians today share his sentiments, most readers remain more interested in the stirring call of drum and trumpet, the *Sturm und Drang* of battle. That interest is not entirely misplaced. While it is true that the war's consequences profoundly reshaped the political, social, and economic landscape of the United States, these consequences were largely dependent on the outcome of campaigns and battles—on the results of the courage and suffering and blood of those 3 million weary men in blue and gray who fought it out during four years of violence unmatched in the Western world between the Napoleonic Wars and World War I.

What were the principal consequences of the Civil War? Northern victory in 1865 resolved two fundamental, festering questions left unresolved by the American Revolution of 1776: whether this vulnerable experiment in republican self-government could survive in a world of monarchies, empires, czardoms, aristocracy, and counterrevolutions; and whether this republic, founded on a charter of freedom, would continue to exist as the largest slaveholding society in the world. Appomattox settled these questions: America did not perish from the earth, but experienced a new birth of freedom that ensured the nation's survival as one nation, indivisible and genuinely free. Moreover, the war ended the long contest between contrasting socioeconomic orders that had struggled for more than half a century to determine which order—and which vision of America's future—would prevail: slave-labor, plantation agriculture dominated by a landed gentry, or free-labor democratic capitalism dominated by an entrepreneurial spirit. For better or worse, the fires of civil war forged the framework of the world's only superpower and its economic engine by the end of the millennium.

These are the kinds of questions about the impact of the Civil War that interest most professional, academic historians, many of whom could not care less about the military campaigns and battles. Yet, to deplore the emphasis on these campaigns and battles—as did Albion Tourgée more than a century ago—is to take a view as narrow as that of contemporary Civil War buffs who are interested *only* in the campaigns and battles, and indifferent to the war's causes and consequences. If some of those campaigns and battles had come out differently, the future of the United States—indeed, of the world—might have been quite different.

If General George B. McClellan had been bolder and more aggressive in the spring of 1862, he might have captured Richmond and won the war with only minimal damage to Southern society and slavery. If Robert E. Lee's invasion of Pennsylvania had fulfilled his hopes—if he had won the battle of Gettysburg in the same fashion he had won at Chancellorsville against greater odds two months earlier—the Confederacy might well have triumphed. Even as late as the fall of 1864, if William Tecumseh Sherman had not captured Atlanta, Lincoln probably would not have been reelected and his successor might have been compelled to negotiate peace with an independent Confederacy. Thus, an understanding of how and why McClellan was driven back in the Seven Days battles, how the Army of the Potomac triumphed at Gettysburg, and why Sherman captured Atlanta is important to understanding how and why American history has developed the way it has during the past 140 years.

For all of these reasons, the story of campaigns and battles—and of the commanders, strategy, technology, and other matters necessary to understand those campaigns and battles—that David J. Eicher presents in the following pages is an essential starting point for anyone who wants to know how and why the Civil War came out as it did. *The Longest Night* is almost unique among Civil War books: it is both a narrative and a reference work. Here the reader will find engrossing accounts of all the battles, large and small, linked together in a manner so lucid and logical that the cause-effect relationships among events taking place in several theaters of war in chronological succession—sometimes even simultaneously—emerge with new clarity. The reader will also find detailed descriptions and analyses of many technical aspects of Civil War armies, navies, and armaments: artillery, the Signal Corps, codes and ciphers, intelligence, cavalry, shoulder weapons, and many, many more. In other words, we have here two books in one. You can sit down and read an account of the battle of Shiloh or the Wilderness campaign, or you can go to the shelf and pull down this volume to look up a discussion of different kinds and calibers of artillery. No matter what you are looking for regarding the military history of the Civil War, you are likely to find it in this book—and you will enjoy a good read at the same time.

Introduction

LIKE NO OTHER CONFLICT in our history, the Civil War casts a long shadow onto modern America.

The Civil War means different things to different people: a valiant defense of principle to some, a battle for freedom to others. Americans are still struggling to understand how the Civil War lies behind many of today's problems. Southern state legislators, Civil War reenactors, and others who may know little about the war itself fight to continue flying the Confederate battle flag atop state capitols or as part of state flags. State rights are cited in one matter after another, most recently in the 2000 presidential election controversy.

The war propelled a small economy forward (as wars often do, at least for the victors), establishing the United States as a modern industrial nation. With the martial nature of 1860s society came the American boom in gun production. After the war hundreds of thousands of veterans knew how to use guns, and millions of weapons made their way into society. The postwar era of violence, played out largely in the western states and territories, inaugurated a tradition we still pay for today. As Michael Bellesiles has shown in his book *Arming America: The Origins of a National Gun Culture*, it was in the wake of the Civil War that the "right to own and use weapons" became an assumed constitutional guarantee.

The first income tax in American history passed Congress in August 1861, when the federal government sought to reassure the financial community that it would be paid interest on bonds it was buying. The Legal Tender Act introduced greenbacks into the American monetary system in 1862.

Domestic terrorism became an American concept during the 1850s in "Bleeding Kansas," as pro- and antislavery factions periodically butchered each other on the western plains. It entered small-town America during the

war, as with the burning of Chambersburg, Pennsylvania, and the destruc-
tion of homes and farms in the Shenandoah Valley. Terrorism struck urban
America in 1864 with the Confederate conspiracy to burn hotels in New
York City; it played out in full force with the Lincoln assassination.

Certainly, part of the fascination with the Civil War is the paradox of
both sides being American. Both friend and foe were neighbors, fellow
Americans, sometimes even family members. But there were also important
differences between the sides. Southern soldiers were likely to be farmers or
skilled laborers with the strong preexisting martial tradition common in the
agrarian, rural South. Few cities and factories dotted the landscape, and
Southern boys generally were good horsemen, familiar with the outdoors,
and handy with a gun. By contrast, escalating numbers of immigrants
flocked to factory jobs in the booming Yankee cities. They lacked the martial
tradition of the South—until they acquired it during the war itself. The vast
majority of the boys who fought the war were much younger, skinnier, and
dirtier than the actors who play them on television and in movies. Thankfully, they were a highly literate group who left abundant records of their
experiences in letters, journals, and other documents.

AFTER READING THROUGH numerous battle reports, I am convinced that the
Confederate States of America could not have emerged victorious in the
Civil War. It was beyond the South's capabilities to withstand the hardships
of an extended war. And for the vast majority of Southerners, the war made
life far worse.

The strategic goals faced by each side at the outset of the war could not
have been more different, and they offer a way to interpret the battles. The
Confederate States of America had time on its side in the weeks following
the capture of Fort Sumter and could play a defensive strategy, hoping for
the Yankees to accept secession as a *fait accompli* or to tire of the bloodshed
and suffering and sue for peace. The United States, by contrast, had before it
the task of conquering the South, destroying its armies, and occupying vast
expanses of land and several thousand miles of coastline in order to compel
the rebels to surrender. It did not have time on its side and needed to take the
offensive to quash the rebellion.

To further confuse the early months of the war, few officers on either
side were experienced in leading troops in the field. The most veteran officers had only junior-level experience in the Mexican War. Many of them
were from the South, which had a stronger martial tradition, and nearly all
left the U.S. Army at the outbreak of war to join the Confederacy. Many
other officers were political appointees with no military background what-
soever. Even the "experienced" officers had little understanding of the radi-
cally changing tactics at the outset of the war. Improvements in rifled

muskets and artillery during the 1850s would make many weapons far more effective and deadly at greater range than ever before. The murderous nature of many Civil War battles would result in appalling casualties because even the most visionary field commanders worked with obsolescent concepts that lagged far behind the new developments in weapons, logistics, communication, and tactics. Only during the middle of the war did commanders begin to alter their thinking to respond to the new, deadly technology in the hands of their troops.

The war brought an explosive advance in the invention of things mechanical, particularly in the North. To the despair of his ordnance officers, Lincoln took a particular interest in seeing new gadgets demonstrated, often on what is now Washington's National Mall, or nearby at the Navy Yard.

Lincoln's willingness to experiment with new gadgets went hand in hand with his gradual discovery of the principles of war, which transformed him into a great wartime leader. This development came only after a series of ghastly defeats at the hands of his inexperienced field commanders. As a strategist, Lincoln evolved into the job. By the war's middle year Lincoln and his best general officers began to absorb more modern aspects of tactics and strategy—Grant ahead of many others. Southern leaders remained philosophical conservatives. Jefferson Davis, Robert E. Lee, and others failed to adapt and change significantly with the lessons they learned during the war, as if their aristocratic origins held them in the past, seemingly unable to formulate bold new ideas. Meanwhile, Grant and Sherman applied what they had learned in the West to the eastern theater. Together they successfully embraced the strategic concept that would ultimately win the war: only coordinated movements by several army groups would crush the rebellion. Davis himself commented late in the war that if the Confederacy failed, "there should be written on its tombstone, 'Died of a theory.' "

The story of why the soldiers fought was remarkably similar in the minds of soldiers on each side. Most Confederates fought for liberty and self-determination—many called the war a "second war of revolution" that would bring about the kind of freedom their great-grandfathers had fought for in the 1770s and 1780s. They defended their home territory from what they perceived as "foreign invaders" and hoped to maintain their agrarian lifestyle and economy along with the slaveholding tradition. For most Federals, the struggle was also about freedom and about the preservation of a democratic government. The adherence of many young Northerners to a strong patriotic sentiment—strong enough to die for—baffled many Confederate politicians and soldiers, who couldn't understand why Yankees would care so deeply to keep the Union together.

Only during the war did emancipation redefine the struggle. Prior to that, Lincoln's aim in prosecuting the war had simply been to save the Union.

But on New Year's Day 1863, Lincoln issued the Emancipation Proclamation, declaring that all slaves held in states or territories in rebellion against the United States were "then, thenceforward, and forever free." Although it accomplished little immediately, the psychological impact of the proclamation echoed throughout North and South. As the season of battle began in 1863, the key question became whether black soldiers would fight for their freedom and for the freedom of other black Americans. A flashpoint came at Battery Wagner on Morris Island, within distant sight of Fort Sumter, on July 18. There the 54th Massachusetts Volunteer Infantry, a unit of some 600 black Americans that included former slaves, attacked in headlong fashion, led by its twenty-five-year-old white colonel, Robert Gould Shaw. The assault failed, the regiment suffering more than 25 percent casualties, and Shaw was killed as he shouted "Onward, Fifty-fourth!"

In a larger sense, however, the 54th's deed succeeded. By showing that black Americans would fight for the Union, these soldiers repudiated the racist attitudes that permeated the North as well as the South. Confederate authorities who resisted emancipation began to see it as inevitable—indeed, before the war was over, authorities in Richmond themselves promoted the idea of raising black regiments to fight for the Confederacy, a notion that horrified many Southern conservatives. In reality, however, there was no going back. The Civil War lit the fires of a social revolution that would reach fruition a century later.

Part of the allure of the Civil War is that we can remember the same story in such a variety of different ways. Thus, Robert E. Lee can be remembered as a great commander, revered by many as the greatest American general officer, despite the fact that he lost. Whether it's rooting for the underdog, a fascination with the aberration (the Confederacy) rather than the norm, or simply an affection for lost causes, "when they truly are lost," as Rhett Butler said—or a combination of all of these—our interest in the rebels remains. Conversely, U. S. Grant, who won the war as the triumphant commander, transformed warfare with daring campaigns such as the movements through Mississippi during the Vicksburg campaign, and rewrote old military tactics into more modern form, is often regarded as something of a bumbler. He won by sheer weight of numbers and supplies, goes the popular version, and therefore deserves little credit as a hero. The fact that these erroneous myths about the two leading generals (and many others) have stuck so long says something about how the Civil War has become crucial to America's legend of itself.

The innocent nation that marched into the great Civil War emerged completely different at war's end. The fragile country of localities—many people in the 1850s had not traveled beyond the limits of their own county, let alone outside state borders—was fused by hardship and necessity into a martial society and an industrial monolith that would grow into a super-power. The Civil War amended the Constitution, abolished slavery, and plunged the South into a traumatic Reconstruction in the wake of Lincoln's death. In time, the experience brought the United States together as a nation in every sense of the word, not just a loose collection of somewhat coopera-tive states, at the same time that the country assumed its place on the inter-national stage. As Carl Sandburg remarked, before the war people said, "The United States are . . ." and after the war they said, "The United States is . . ."

Do WE NEED another history of the Civil War? As I began to analyze the lit-erature of the Civil War for my *Civil War in Books: An Analytical Bibliography* (1997), it became clear to me that no modern, single-volume narrative mili-tary history of the war existed of the type I believed readers would enjoy. This is surprising considering that James M. McPherson's stellar *Battle Cry of Freedom* was published to high acclaim in 1988 and won the Pulitzer Prize for history. It certainly stands as the best single-volume introduction to the Civil War era for modern readers. It covers all aspects of the war from causa-tion to the political, economic, and social context of the war and summarizes them brilliantly. By contrast, the present volume is a narrative that describes the strategy and tactics of the battles on land, sea, and river, with the focus on military operations throughout. I have supplemented this military history with the words of the participants themselves, and I have based the narrative on numerous manuscript collections and recently published battle histories, diaries, letter collections, and biographies that I have read. The result is a popular military history that can be thought of as a companion to McPher-son's distinguished work.

My single-volume narrative stands in contrast to the stalwarts of the Civil War bookshelf, the aging classics by Bruce Catton and Shelby Foote, and other more recent volumes that have not incorporated so much fresh material. In *The Centennial History of the Civil War* (three volumes, 1961–1965), his defining work, Bruce Catton, a newspaperman turned Civil War enthusi-ast, helped to determine how the Civil War would be remembered. Catton's work is relatively light on military history and analysis, rich in the political relations between officers, and superb in its biographical glimpses of the characters. He described Allan Pinkerton as "a wildly imaginative, over-grown Tom Sawyer"; declared Roger Taney "frail as a withered leaf"; and believed Isaac Toucey was "an amiable non-entity, a cipher." The writing style is dated, the majority of the important published sources now available weren't available then, and Catton was not immune to error. Oddly, in the third volume, *Never Call Retreat*, his coverage of the main campaigns of 1864 and 1865 is scanty, amounting to a mere 290 pages, in contrast to 1,132 pages that cover the first two years of the war.

Bruce Catton has been portrayed as something of a Yankee apologist. Shelby Foote, in contrast, took a Southern perspective for his work *The Civil War: A Narrative* (three volumes, 1958–1974). Foote offers an engaging, readable style packed with lots of information. He saw no flaws in Jefferson Davis's arguments for secession, but criticized Lincoln's assumption of wartime powers as if these same powers were not assumed by Davis. Foote made the common mistake of equating forces by the numbers of regiments available, as if all regiments, brigades, and divisions were equivalent in size and military potential.

Foote reflected the prevailing sentiment of the time in characterizing Ulysses S. Grant as a drunk, writing that he was "a seedy-looking, round-shouldered slouch with whiskey lines around the eyes showing an overfondness for the bottle." As he railed against Grant, Foote bolstered wherever possible the reputation of his hometown hero, Nathan Bedford Forrest. The Fort Pillow massacre, for example, was no "massacre," and Forrest had "done all he could, first to prevent and then to end the unnecessary bloodshed." Had there been a massacre, Foote posited, the Yankees would have retaliated. "With Sherman in charge," he speculated, "retaliation would have been as prompt as even Grant could have desired."

Foote also blamed Sherman and his drunken soldiers for the burning of Columbia in 1865 and alternatively bolstered the valiant image of the Confederate troops at every opportunity. "The battle [of Wilson's Creek]," for example, "was taken as further proof, if such was needed, of the obvious superiority of the Southern fighting men." In Foote's war the heroic and inspired Southern troops carried out brilliant and stunning victories, while the inept and indecisive Yankees were sullen and disconsolate.

I have attempted a different kind of book. I have drawn on hundreds of sources of several types and have used almost exclusively wartime records and recent analyses to construct a realistic history of what happened on the battlefield. Primary source materials reign supreme in my version of events. With rare exception I avoided postwar reminiscences as sources (the memories of men twenty or thirty years after events are notoriously unreliable) and employed wartime written documents—letters, diaries, journal entries, etc.—wherever possible. I have not credited reports of words spoken on the battlefield unless compelling contemporary evidence from several sources suggested that those phrases were accurately reported. I am interested in what really happened, and I have endeavored to make a story without embellishment. I'm not so naïve as to believe that this book does not include errors, too, of course, but I have tried by careful use of reliable sources to minimize the errors. I have also tried to maintain a balance by using papers, reports, and documents from both sides of the war. Though my own ancestors who fought in the war were Ohioans who served under Grant and Sherman, my fascination with the Confederacy and its military leaders is enormous. I previously composed *Robert E. Lee: A Life Portrait,* a pictorial biography that featured an introduction by Robert E. Lee IV, great-grandson of the general. The scarcity of Confederate materials in some cases, however, invariably tilts the coverage somewhat in favor of Union operations, as historians know. This paucity was in part due to poorer record keeping on the Confederate side but also to the destruction of many Confederate reports and records at the war's end.

Prologue: 1915

ON A SUNNY JULY DAY children played in Central Park and the birds sang sweetly all across New York City. D. W. Griffith's epic motion picture *Birth of a Nation* played in the city's lush theaters, portraying in sweeping grandeur the drama of the American Civil War, which had concluded fifty years ago. But few were focused on the distant war of the past; the "great war" now spread across parts of Europe as Germany was on the march. President Woodrow Wilson protested the sinking of the British ship *Lusitania*, which contained, among others, 128 U.S. passengers, by one of many hostile German submarines. United States troops were about to land in Haiti. W. Somerset Maugham published *Of Human Bondage;* Charlie Chaplin starred in *The Tramp.* Edgar Lee Masters produced the well-received collection *Spoon River Anthology.* And yet as Americans went to the films and read the new books, recalling Wilson's pledge of neutrality of the previous summer, of the American credo of isolationism, the war in Europe grew increasingly hard to ignore.

Every day a little man who was now rarely noticed came out of his door at 3 West 69th Street and took a walk. He was an odd sort of man, with a small frame, an angular jaw, coal-black eyes, and shoulder-length "raven-black" hair. He walked gingerly, at age eighty-seven, traversing the city, through Central Park, watching the children and the birds, and back to his quiet house. (Six years earlier he had even warded off the advances of an assailant on the street.) His wife now deceased, the peculiar man occasionally had visitors and family stop in for lively discussions, and he doted on his young granddaughter, Sara. Otherwise, this relic of an earlier age went to watch trials in court, a favorite pastime, or simply enjoyed the warm summer days and weighed the present-day world against the vast canvas of his past.

The little man was disturbed to see the American nation drawn closer to war in another part of the world. Thinking back to his youth, he recalled the heady events of America's greatest conflict, to him events that were still vivid in his mind's eye. "[N]ever more will you see from Virginia any intimations of hostility to the Union," he had said some years earlier. "She has weighed the alternative of success, and she sees now, every sensible man in the South sees, that the greatest calamity that could have befallen the South would have been the ascendancy of this ill-starred Confederacy." Indeed, it would have been impossible to imagine that this elderly man could have been an important figure in American history. Remarkably, however, the man was so important and pro-Union in his outlook that after the war he had entertained a virtual who's who of Federal general officers, including U. S. Grant, William T. Sherman, Philip Sheridan, Winfield Scott Hancock, George B. McClellan, Henry W. Slocum, Daniel Butterfield, and Fitz John Porter, all of whom visited and paid their high regards in the man's 69th Street house.

Moreover, it would have been impossible to guess that this quiet little man had for years been a successful justice of the New York Supreme Court, respected by virtually all the prominent citizens of the Empire State. He had also been a tough but sensitive lawyer, a newspaper editor, a United States congressman, U.S. minister to Greece, a gifted orator, and a father of seven children. He had also been a soldier. "As an old soldier," he said, "I can say there is nothing in war. I have seen enough of it. The world is not at a stage now where constant killing of men by their fellows can go on. This war will be the great lesson."

The old soldier was Roger Atkinson Pryor. A relative few of those who had heard his name or knew of his record as a New Yorker could have fully described Roger Pryor's amazing past. A staunch Union man since the earliest days following the Civil War, he had been one of the hottest fire-eating secessionists of the South during the war itself. Virginia-born, Pryor was an embodiment of the fact that practically all well-known Southerners in antebellum high society seemed to be at least distantly related: he was a third cousin, once removed, of Robert E. Lee. He had been graduated from Hampden-Sydney College as class valedictorian in 1845, and when the war broke out proceeded to join the Confederate Army after a stint as a Confederate congressman. He served briefly as an aide to Confederate President Jefferson Davis. Commissioned brigadier general in the Provisional Army in 1862, he led a brigade against the hated Yankees during the Peninsular campaign, at Second Bull Run, and at Antietam. Resigning after dissatisfaction with his command in the summer of 1863, Pryor rejoined the Confederate army as a private soldier. Subsequently acting as a volunteer courier and spy, he was captured late in 1864 and confined to Fort Delaware prison until the early spring of 1865, when Abraham Lincoln pardoned him and his great conversion began. He even went so far as to become a legal partner of Benjamin F. Butler, one of the Yankee generals most despised in the South.

In his old age Unionist Roger Pryor held dearly to the hope that the "great war" would not overshadow the more meaningful, more noble war of the past. "I cannot forget the Civil War," he told friends. "But in generations to come people will think of those differences less and less. The words North and South are simply geographical expressions now and have no political significance whatever. You need not ask me why; the word 'union' simply expresses everything." This from a man who fifty years earlier had taken part in the initial action of the Civil War, the bombardment of Fort Sumter. Most of the important players of the American Civil War were long gone now. But Pryor had been all across the spectrum of the conflict, and he had even been offered the opportunity to fire the first shot to open the war, on an island near Fort Sumter, South Carolina.

As he recalled those hazy days, Pryor attached them to one of his favorite verses, a portion of William Shakespeare's *Measure for Measure*, Act II, Scene 2: No ceremony that to great ones longs / Not the king's crown, nor the deputed sword / The Marshal's truncheon, nor the Judge's robe / Become them with one-half so good a grace / As Mercy does.

The War Begins at Sumter

SERGEANT JAMES CHESTER could do nothing but walk out onto the parade ground and wait. The air was cool on this early spring evening as he stood and reflected on his current dilemma, surrounded by the massive three-story brick façade of an unfinished fort. Overhead, the stars twinkled and a waxing crescent moon hung low in the sky; Saturn and Jupiter were paired closely in the constellation Leo, suggesting to some an omen. A chilling breeze passed over the harbor every few minutes, adding to the grim antici-pation. Chester, a youthful Scot, had emigrated to the United States and joined the army in 1854, just as tensions over the expansion of slavery threat-ened to tear the country apart. Now he was standing in the hotbed of seces-sion and all was quiet as could be. "Except that the flag was hoisted, and a glimmer of light was visible at the guardhouse," he later wrote, "the fort looked so dark and silent as to seem deserted."

It was not. In less than two hours Chester would live through a fateful moment in American history. Along with Chester, 75 other Federal soldiers, 8 musicians, and 43 workmen anticipated the start of hostilities from local secessionists this evening in Charleston Harbor. The Federal soldiers' tem-porary home, Fort Sumter, was one of America's coastal forts built following the War of 1812. It was named for Thomas Sumter, a brigadier general of South Carolina militia and hero of the Revolutionary War. Although con-struction on the fort began in 1829, three years before Sumter's death, the fort remained unfinished in the spring of 1861. Fort Sumter was an imposing structure, placed nearly centrally in the harbor, and the powerhouse of the four forts built to protect the city.

Sumter's handsome brick walls, five feet thick, stood 50 feet above the water. The fort's five-sided plan used four sides that ranged from 170 to 190 feet long and a gorge wall containing officers' quarters that faced southwest.

The fort's three stories were designed to hold two primary tiers of casements and a parapet that together would mount 135 guns and hold a garrison of 650. On the evening of April 11, 1861, the men inside the fort were dwarfed by the mammoth size of the structure and chagrined by the fact that only fifteen cannon were fixed in place and ready to fire. To make the garrison even less prepared to face a crisis, its supplies of food were dwindling. On this evening the soldiers had rations to last possibly five days.

Such an unlikely situation was supervised by Maj. Robert Anderson, age fifty-five and a veteran of the regular army. Anderson's Kentucky ancestry and the fact that he favored slavery and married a Georgia girl did not seem to bother his Yankee comrades. He was an expert artillerist and had served gallantly in the Black Hawk, Seminole, and Mexican wars, demonstrating unwavering loyalty toward the United States. Anderson's five principal subordinates would rise to varying degrees of fame and glory in the contest to come. Capt. John Gray Foster of New Hampshire was Anderson's chief engineer, a bearded, balding veteran who had been wounded at Molino del Rey in the Mexican War. Capt. Abner Doubleday, a New Yorker who is erroneously associated with the invention of baseball, was an artillerist from a distinguished family. Capt. Jefferson Columbus Davis was born in Indiana and became a trained artillerist. He would live to kill a fellow officer in cold blood and dodge paying any price for it. Asst. Surg. Samuel Wylie Crawford, the physician at Sumter, was a Pennsylvanian with an elegant mustache and lamb-chop whiskers. First Lt. Truman Seymour, one of the most junior commissioned officers at the fort, was a Vermont-born artillerist with Mexican War experience.

As the evening progressed, Anderson and his men knew that the sparks of war were about to fly and that they were to be the target. As early as the day after Christmas 1860 the storm clouds of war directly threatened Anderson and his companies of the 1st U.S. Artillery. Anderson had arrived at Fort Moultrie on Sullivans Island, the other principal fort guarding the harbor, in November. A fort stood on or near this position, 1,800 yards northeast of Sumter, since guarding against the British in 1776. The present structure, named for Maj. Gen. William Moultrie, who served gallantly during the Revolutionary War, was built in 1809. The other two Federal forts protecting Charleston Harbor were Fort Johnson on the northern tip of James Island, 2,300 yards west of Sumter, and Castle Pinckney on Shute's Folly Island, close to the city and 4,500 yards northwest of Sumter. (The city's wharves themselves lay 5,800 yards northwest of Sumter.) To Southerners, abandonment of these Federal installations seemed a natural implication of the times. The signing of South Carolina's ordinance of secession on December 20 carried with it such an ultimatum. On Christmas Eve, South Carolina Governor Francis Wilkinson Pickens, the grandson of a general in the Revolutionary War, issued a proclamation declaring the state separate, independent, and sovereign.

Six days after the ordinance was signed, Anderson moved his men from Moultrie to Sumter. "I looked anxiously with my glass on the boats and at a preconcerted signal, two heavy guns were fired," wrote the surgeon Crawford in his diary of the abandonment of Moultrie. "I fired the last one. We spiked the guns, and took down the flagstaff." The abandonment and partial destruction of the fort enraged Southerners. On December 27, Anderson raised the U.S. flag over Sumter. The same day secessionists seized Fort Moultrie and Castle Pinckney and began to work on refortifying them. On December 30 the U.S. Arsenal at Charleston was seized. The New Year witnessed a continued decline. On January 2, South Carolinians occupied Fort Johnson. Commissioners from the state had gone to Washington to meet U.S. officials but returned without a resolution. President James Buchanan did absolutely nothing. In the War Department, Secretary Joseph Holt replaced pro-Southern John Buchanan Floyd, who had ordered arsenals in the North to shift weapons into Southern arsenals. During the period November 1859 to February 1860, arsenals in Northern states witnessed a decrease of 115,000 muskets and rifles, while Southern arsenals had their supplies increased by 114,990 muskets and rifles. This shift occurred out of a total pool of 610,292 arms under Federal control. Supplies inside Sumter were scant. On January 5 the *Star of the West*, a merchant vessel, was ordered south from New York to restock the fort.

The pace of secession activity quickened. On January 6 the arsenal at Apalachicola, Florida, was occupied by locals. The following day Fort Marion at St. Augustine was seized by state troops. On the morning of January 9 the *Star of the West* approached Sumter, with 200 infantrymen under 34-year-old 1st Lt. Charles Robert Woods, along with several months' provisions. The ship's captain, John McGowan, steered toward the fort only to receive a sudden bombardment from a masked battery on the northern end of Morris Island, south of the fort, and from Moultrie. Though the ship was only lightly struck, McGowan withdrew his ship. The supply mission had failed. Soldiers on the parapets at Sumter asked Anderson to return fire; he declined but protested the action to Governor Pickens, who proclaimed the supply mission an act of war. Not only did Pickens refuse to let the soldiers replenish their foodstuffs, but in fact two days later demanded the surrender of the fort, which Anderson refused. The next day secessionists demanded the surrender of Fort Pickens in Pensacola Harbor, Florida, which was also refused. In February arsenals were overrun by secessionists at Little Rock and Napoleon, Arkansas, and in March the fledgling government of the Confederate States of America sent a commanding officer to supervise the activities at Charleston.

Pierre Gustave Toutant Beauregard, the first brigadier general in the Provisional Army of the Confederate States, was one of the most colorful military men of the day. Short and slight, he bristled with energy and was expertly trained in a wide variety of subjects. Not only was he a superb engineer, but he had been trained in artillery under none other than Robert Anderson. Beauregard was so liked within the War Department that he had been appointed superintendent of the U.S. Military Academy at West Point in January 1861, an assignment he was relieved of a few days later when his Southern sympathies became starkly clear. With his widespread experience and general popularity—with nearly everyone except the new Confederate President Jefferson Davis—Beauregard was destined to become the first great Southern hero of the conflict.

In Washington, the new president, Abraham Lincoln, ordered another relief expedition, this one departing on April 4. By no means did all Northerners feel at ease with Lincoln's action. "In a great crisis like this, there is no policy so fatal as that of having no policy at all," editorialized the *New York Times* on April 3. Lincoln notified Governor Pickens of the impending arrival of the ships. After debate, the infant Confederate government ordered Beauregard to stop any such supply mission, even if it meant firing on the fort. Beauregard received the news on April 10. By this time the tension among Charlestonians, among Anderson and his men in the fort, and among patriotic Southerners and Northerners had reached a fever pitch. During the first week of April a large crowd gathered at Charleston's waterfront battery. Anderson and his little garrison sat inside the fort and waited. Surrounding them, scattered about the city and the various forts and batteries in the harbor, were more than 6,000 secessionists itching for a fight. Not all Charlestonians agreed with the action. James Louis Petigru, the prominent attorney and statesman, said that South Carolina was too small to be a nation and too large to be an insane asylum. But the majority felt wronged by the North and saw no other way to react to Lincoln and the rest of the Yankees than to fight a war. Roger Atkinson Pryor, the young lawyer, editor, politician, and Virginian, gave a rousing speech in Charleston on April 10. "I thank you especially that you have annihilated this accursed Union, reeking with corruption and insolent with excess of tyranny," he said. "Thank God! It is blasted with the lightning wrath of an outraged and indignant people."

The next day Asst. Surg. Crawford described the dreary condition of the garrison's rations. He recorded the diet as "rice but no bread . . . broken pieces of crackers . . . today we came down to pork and a little rice." The engineer Foster added, "[the rice was] filled with pieces of glass from the window-panes shattered by the concussion of guns fired in practice." Crawford described how at 4 P.M. on this day a boat bearing a flag of truce approached the fort, carrying three staff officers. The three men walked up

Sumter's esplanade, through its sally port, and asked to see Maj. Anderson. They were Col. James Chesnut, Jr., Capt. Stephen Dill Lee, and Lt. Col. Alexander Robert Chisholm. Chesnut was a Princeton-educated lawyer and former U.S. senator who had three days before been appointed an aide-de-camp to Gen. Beauregard. Lee was a young but skilled artillerist whose influence would rise and fall during the war. Chisholm was a South Carolinian who had been educated in New York and now assisted in building the fortifications on Morris Island. The three emissaries met with Anderson in the fort's guard room, where they presented a message from the Confederate commander. "I am ordered by the Government of the Confederate States to demand the evacuation of Fort Sumter," wrote Beauregard. "The flag which you have upheld so long and with so much fortitude, under the most trying circumstances, may be saluted by you on taking it down."

Anderson would not budge. Instead he drew up a formal reply. "I have the honor to acknowledge the receipt of your communication demanding the evacuation of this fort," he wrote, "and to say, in reply thereto, that it is a demand with which that I regret that my sense of honor, and of my obligations to my Government, prevent my compliance." Informally, Anderson told his potential enemies that he was running low on supplies and that he would probably be starved out in a few days if the Southern guns didn't "barter us to pieces." After three hours in the fort, Chesnut, Lee, and Chisholm removed thir white flag of truce and took the boat back out into the harbor with the reply.

Men inside the fort rolled out powder kegs, worked on the guns, and watched the various positions of Confederate guns facing them. The men received orders not to expose themselves on the parapets. Night fell over the fort with the stars overhead and the gleam of lights on the horizon in Charleston. Inside the fort, Anderson had no oil for lamps, and so the three story brick fortress stood in near total darkness. On the morning of April 12 the fort's officers were awakened by another boat bearing a white flag. This time four emissaries came; Chesnut, Lee, Chisholm, and Roger A. Pryor. It was about 1:30 A.M. when these aides brought another letter suggesting that if Anderson agreed to evacuate the fort at a stated time without firing on Confederate forces, the transfer of the fort could be accomplished bloodlessly. Anderson stated that he would abandon Sumter by noon on April 15 but only if his command and flag would not be fired on and unless otherwise instructed by the Lincoln government. By 3:20 A.M. Chesnut and Lee concluded that the terms were not acceptable and that the fort would be fired on beginning in one hour. "By authority of Brigadier-General Beauregard, commanding the Provisional Forces of the Confederate States," wrote Chesnut and Lee, "we have the honor to notify you that he will open the fire of his batteries on Fort Sumter in one hour from this time." If they never again met in this world, God grant that they may meet in the next, Anderson told the Confederates. The emissaries then withdrew. Sleep within the fort was out of the question. "We arose and dressed," wrote Crawford, "and before our arrangements were completed, the firing began."

It was almost exactly 4:30 A.M. on April 12 when the fighting began. "A flash as of distant lightning in the direction of Mount Pleasant, followed by the dull roar of a mortar, told us that the bombardment had begun," James Chester wrote. The mortars at Fort Johnson had the first crack at the Yankees, lobbing shells over and about the fort. Firing also commenced at Fort Moultrie, which was sending cannonballs and shells; from the floating battery near Sullivans Island, which opened up with rifled artillery; from Cummings's Point and elsewhere. In a few minutes' time, the sudden flashes and reports of a surprising number of projectiles, along with the acrid, sulfurous smell of gunpowder and the sight of wafting smoke, cascaded over the fort. After several hours, particularly after daylight, most of the batteries gained an effective range and started throwing some shells and balls into the fort with frightening accuracy. Bricks were smashed, and splinters of wood, brick dust, and mortar chunks cascaded into the air. The soldiers scattered and took cover. "A ball from Cummings's Point lodged in the magazine wall," wrote Doubleday of the first moments of the war, "and by the sound seemed to bury itself in the masonry about a foot from my head, in very unpleasant proximity to my right ear." Suddenly, Fort Sumter had turned into an untenable wreck. What began the day as one of the most magnificent fortifications in North America was disintegrating into a pile of rubble.

The great honor of firing the first shot of the war, coveted by officers at Fort Johnson, was offered the fiery secessionist Roger Pryor, who had retreated to that point by 4 A.M. Oddly, however, he turned down the offer, later saying, "I could not fire the first gun of the war." The first shot, a 10-inch mortar shell sent as a signal round to activate the other batteries, was fired by the fort's commander, Capt. George S. James. At Cummings's Point, the aged Virginian Edmund Ruffin, who would leave one of the war's great diaries behind, participated in revolution with glee by firing a 64-pounder Columbiad shell toward the fort. He had been asked to fire the first shot from this position by Capt. George B. Cuthbert. In a variety of locations, some Southerners stoked hot-shot furnaces to heat their iron balls into fire starters, hoping to ignite Sumter's wooden barracks.

The fire from Southern guns increased in accuracy and frequency after daybreak, when a breeze carried the fumes and sounds of war more effectively into the city. Observers watched the spectacle of smoke and projectiles with amazement as the night turned into day. The youthful Confederacy had struck its first blow. "I do not pretend to go to sleep," confided Charlestonian Mary Boykin Chesnut, wife of Beauregard's aide. "How can

I? If Anderson does not accept terms—at four—the orders are—he shall be fired upon. I count four, St. Michael's bells chime out, and I begin to hope. At half past four the heavy booming of a cannon. I sprang out of bed, and on my knees—prostrate—I prayed as I never prayed before."

The forty-three Confederate guns had been placed well by Beauregard and his subordinates, situated as follows: four mortars and one cannon at Fort Johnson; six cannon and six mortars on Cummings's Point; and on Sullivans Island, eleven guns at Fort Moultrie, six mortars, four guns on the floating battery, four guns on an enfilade battery, and a Dahlgren gun on the tip of the island. With such a small amount of ammunition available, Anderson had no reason to react quickly. After breakfasting on a small amount of farina, some of the Federals mounted a response using several cannon, but only a few guns were brought to bear. Doubleday fired the first Yankee cannon of the war. Crawford reported knocking out a gun in the floating battery. But the volume of shells being fired at Sumter was magnificent. It had already ignited a small fire in the wooden-frame quarters and knocked away a chimney. Doubleday took charge of the guns aimed at Cummings's Point, Davis the pieces directed toward Fort Johnson, and Crawford the cannon aimed at Sullivans Island.

During the afternoon the Confederate bombardment of Sumter continued without pause, raining shot and shell into and over the fort. Because of the activity overhead, Anderson ordered that only the guns in casements be used, eliminating the heavier pieces atop the parapet, and allowing the Federals to respond only with solid shot. Crawford reported in the afternoon that the few guns of Sumter were mostly trained on Fort Moultrie. Some of Sumter's soldiers were wounded slightly by flying debris; most were unscathed, but the fort's walls were becoming pocked with hits and cracks, and brick dust was accumulating on the parade. Pvt. John Carmody tested the Rebels at Fort Moultrie by sneaking up to the parapet and firing the heavier guns in quick succession at the fort; this only prompted the Confederates into returning a heavy fire onto Sumter. With the approach of nightfall the firing from Confederate batteries lessened. Amazingly, there had been no deaths on either side.

On the evening of April 12 rain fell on Charleston. Anderson ordered his firing suspended. On the Confederate side an occasional mortar shell was sent toward Sumter throughout the night. The Federal soldiers finally had the chance to sleep, "well but hungry." Meanwhile, five Federal ships approached, stocked with provisions and offering the opportunity for escape if necessary. Lincoln's special agent Gustavus Vasa Fox attempted to coordinate the movements of the *Harriet Lane,* the *Pawnee,* the *Baltic,* the *Powhatan,* and the *Pocahontas.* Fox was a former naval lieutenant and woolen-goods merchant, a Massachusetts native who would several months hence become the assistant secretary of the navy. The movements coordinated by Fox were impeded by heavy seas and a dense fog that formed before dawn. On the morning of April 13 the storm subsided, but the storm of man would continue.

Anderson's firing was slowed considerably in order to conserve ammunition. The Confederate fire was hot, however, in both senses of the word. By 8 A.M. hot shot fired from Rebel guns started a fire in the officers' quarters, and despite the improvised firefighting efforts, the blaze was slowly spreading. Anderson and his officers worried about the possibility of flames or sparks reaching the magazine, which would be catastrophic. A slightly comic act of moving barrels of powder out of the magazine ensued, the Yankees looking for a safer place to store them.

The shot and shell rained in as heavily as ever, and the fire was now spreading quickly. Sparks, cinders, and burning pieces of debris spiraled upward only to rain down on the spreading fire, which eventually ignited several shells and kegs of powder, causing a few large explosions. Desperate, Anderson had much of the powder thrown into the harbor. It seemed that the whole fort was becoming an inferno; the Federal ships were nowhere in sight, and the sally port and heavy entrance gates had been wrecked by shellfire. The flagstaff had been splintered repeatedly. And then came one more Confederate messenger, who sneaked up to the fort's side in a small skiff. It would be the next odd turn in a surrealistic day.

Col. Louis Trezevant Wigfall was a South Carolina native who had just joined P. G. T. Beauregard's staff as an aide-de-camp. Slightly heavy, black-haired, with intense eyes, Wigfall was a politician who had dabbled in military service but spent most of his energy as a Texas legislator and U.S. senator. Now he came to Anderson on a mission. At 1:30 P.M. the flagstaff in Sumter had fallen, and on Morris Island, James Simons, a brigadier general of South Carolina militia, determined to find out if this act meant surrender. Before he could get an official party off in a nearby rowboat, however, Wigfall demanded that Pvt. Gourdin Young of the Palmetto Guard row him out to the fort. In a bizarre scene, Wigfall and Young moved north amid the hail of shot and shell and, once he reached the esplanade, Wigfall tied a white kerchief to his sword, got out of the boat, and approached the sally port.

Wigfall found Jefferson C. Davis and exclaimed that Beauregard suggested that surrender was inevitable. He then went atop the parapet and waved the white flag in the direction of Moultrie, but the firing continued. Anderson then approached, and said he would capitulate by leaving now rather than on April 15 as he had suggested, if the garrison could take its arms and property, salute its flag, and be transported northward. This was acceptable, said Wigfall. However, astonishingly, Wigfall had no authority from

Beauregard or anyone else to accept such terms. He did so on his own volition.

The South Carolina politician returned to Morris Island in the skiff, which flew a white flag, and firing died down from all points. Now, to confuse the issue further, the authorized emissaries of Beauregard approached the fort: Pryor, Lee, and the politician William Porcher Miles. On reaching the fort, they inquired about Anderson's needs, and all discussed the situation of the fire, which was dying down. They asked Anderson about surrender terms, and he replied that terms had already been agreed on with Wigfall. The three Confederates were dumbfounded, and explained that he had no such authority and that he hadn't even seen Beauregard for two days. Confused, the men stood inside the crumbled and burning fort and discussed the surrender again, this time Anderson becoming upset about the misunderstanding. "Very well, gentlemen, you may return to your batteries," he snapped at the Yankee artillerists. But Pryor, Lee, and Miles convinced him to continue a cease-fire until they could talk again with Beauregard, who accepted all the terms except for allowing the Yankees to salute their flag. After further negotiating, the parties agreed to evacuate and transfer themselves and their supplies on the next morning, Sunday the 14th. The Yankees marched out of the fort "with colors flying and drums beating," Anderson explained. After thirty-four hours of bombardment, the first engagement of the war was over, and the Confederates had won. The battle had been bloodless. Ironically, however, the departure ceremony killed two. One of the cannon fired by Anderson's command produced a spark that was blown into a stand of gunpowder. The resulting explosion killed Pvt. Daniel Hough, who had his right arm blown off, and mortally wounded Pvt. Edward Galloway. They were the first to die in America's greatest conflict.

THE BOMBARDMENT OF SUMTER would begin an unparalleled ordeal for the American people, 1,512 days of darkness that would leave more than 620,000 Northerners and Southerners dead. By inflicting war wounds—physical and psychological—it affected the lives of countless others. It touched every family in the country, many with grave results. It would destroy an old way of life and at the same time remake the young nation into a modern democracy that could emerge as a world leader. The war would bring seemingly endless inventions that accelerated industrial technology. It would revise military tactics and strategy. Because both sides had similar backgrounds, education, religion, and language—and therefore acted on a level playing field more so than in other wars—the strategic and tactical record of the Civil War would be studied meticulously by distinguished European militarists for decades afterward. As wars always do, it would offer the opportunity for greatness to many individuals whose lives would otherwise have been quite ordinary, and it would provide power and glory to many people with less than sterling character. As it unified the nation, so did it abolish the original error of the Constitution, the implied legality of slavery, although more than another century would pass before equal rights for black Americans became a real issue. But no one could have foreseen these outcomes in the days of the Civil War. In the spring of 1861, with Sumter in Confederate hands, all that was clear was that bitter war lay ahead.

Many soldiers initially saw the war as a sweeping adventure, and indeed for most, who were after all quite young men, it eclipsed the remainder of their lives. "A little spice of danger is an excellent thing," wrote Union officer James A. Connolly; "it drives away the blues and gives to the soldier's life that dash of romance which makes pictures on the memory never fade." "You have long before this been made happy by hearing that Fort Sumter has been taken," wrote Lt. Alexander C. Haskell of the 17th South Carolina Infantry, "not only without the loss of any of your sons, but not even one of Carolina's. A glorious day it was, and marked so deeply by the protecting hand of divine Providence that it calls to mind the miraculous victories of the chosen people. . . . Fort Sumter is a terrible wreck." Civilians, too, were boastful and excited over the new adventure about to unfold. "I've often longed to see a war," wrote Louisa May Alcott in Concord, Massachusetts, "and now I have my wish." Yet at the war's outset, virtually no one could see the grim horror or the magnitude of the death and waste to come. For all Americans, whether they knew it or not, it was the start of their longest night.

THE CRISIS that led to the Sumter bombardment had been smoldering for years. And the causes of the war were many, despite the vigorous advancement of old and recent books to promote some over others. For years the North and South had been evolving in different directions. The Southern agrarian economy based in large part on plantation farming supported by slave labor presented a stark contrast to the emerging industrialization and accelerating flow of immigrant free labor into the North. The two sections were in fact like sister countries bound by an economic alliance. The 1850s proved a pivotal decade for the rapidly growing nation. The population increased by 35 percent. The land's wealth in resources began to be tapped in force, including brisk trading in wood, coal, copper, and gold. Production of food skyrocketed, and 30,000 miles of railroads crossed the landscape. Rapid growth and prosperity brought decisions, as well, when Kansas and Nebraska approached statehood and the potential legality of slavery in the new states (and territories) became a hot political issue.

The spread of slavery promoted a riotous disagreement that had its roots in the ambiguous references in the Constitution, the Bill of Rights, and the Declaration of Independence. (Those who now deny that slavery was the paramount issue in the minds of Southerners need only read the papers of the Confederacy's earliest leaders—Jefferson Davis, Alexander H. Stephens, Robert M. T. Hunter, and Howell Cobb included—to educate themselves.) In Charleston, Mary Chesnut worried over the issue in her diary on March 18. "I wonder if it be a sin to think slavery a curse to any land," she wrote. "[Senator Charles] Sumner said not one word of this hated institution which is not true. Men & women are punished when their masters & mistresses are brutes & not when they do wrong. . . . God forgive *us*, but ours is a *monstrous* system & wrong & iniquity."

The flashpoints over the slavery issue extended back decades but boiled over most violently into the territories of Kansas and Nebraska in the 1850s. With the admission of new territories and states, Congress would be faced with deciding the legal status of slavery in them and therefore the balance sheet of slavery versus freedom as factors in governmental representation. The standoff was diametrical: With its agrarian-based economy featuring scattered plantation farming employing blacks as slaves and cotton as the stellar crop, Southern states required the spread of slavery as a legal institution to promote their interests. With its increasing emphasis on industry, growing cities, and cheap immigrant labor, the North's interests had nothing to do with slavery, and indeed many Northerners, chiefly New Englanders, had held out a philosophical hatred of "the peculiar institution" since the earliest days of the Republic.

The contradictions of Southern slaveholders, which many early statesmen felt would solve themselves through the decreasing profitability of slave labor, persisted. Thomas Jefferson, a slave owner, felt that slavery would die out given enough time and that a political war on the issue in his time was not worth the consequences. "As it is," wrote Jefferson, "we have the wolf by the ears, and we can neither hold him, nor safely let him go." Yet just as the economic realities that might have led to the decline of slavery unfolded in Jefferson's lifetime, Eli Whitney, in Massachusetts, invented a device that would inject new life into slavery. Whitney's cotton gin was patented in 1794 and initiated an explosive advance in the efficiency of separating cotton from its seed. By 1800, cotton production in the American South had increased by a factor of twenty-two in just six years—to 35 million pounds annually—and slave labor, now vastly more profitable, gained new life.

The balance between free and slave states sparked fury in 1820, resulting in the Missouri Compromise. When Missouri faced statehood, the balance was equal at eleven slave and eleven free states. Admissions had alternated between slave and free states up to that time; Missouri was admitted as a slave state with the proviso that slavery would be confined within the

Louisiana Purchase territory south of latitude 36°30'. Thirty years later another landmark legislative act occurred in the Compromise of 1850, which contained a mixed bag of legislation that allowed California to enter the Union as a free state in exchange for concessions granted to slaveholders. Four years later the most critical moment of the political war between slavery and freedom came with the Kansas-Nebraska Act. This work, written by Illinois legislator Stephen A. Douglas, virtually ruined the chances for peaceful compromise between the sections. The act concerned the organization of Utah and New Mexico territories and initially upheld the limits of the Compromise of 1850, but pressure from Southern legislators led Douglas to include a nullification of the 36°30' limit set in 1820. The new law took effect on May 30, 1854, and allowed future states admittance into the Union with constitutions that could provide for slavery and preserved the principle of state rights over Federal restrictions. It destroyed the tenuous balance of power that had existed previously and set up a violent border war consisting of guerrillalike skirmishes between Free-Soilers and proslavery men in the western territories.

The situation in Kansas became more violent each day, with factions of proslavery interests and abolitionists battering each other, giving rise to the name "Bleeding Kansas." Arson, mob violence, murder, and terrorism became headlines in papers across the nation in the mid-1850s. In May 1856 a vicious attack occurred at Lawrence, and just two days later a band of abolitionists led by the fanatical raider John Brown massacred five proslavery men at Pottawatomie. Franklin Pierce's administration in Washington failed to deal with the situation and so did the administration of James Buchanan, which took office in March 1857. The violence spilled into the halls of the Capitol itself—in fact, legislators were routinely bringing side weapons into the House and Senate, and when Senator Charles Sumner of Massachusetts denounced the Kansas-Nebraska Act, he was caned and severely injured by Representative Preston Brooks of South Carolina.

The year 1858 brought the issue of slavery forcefully into the national conscience with the senatorial debates between Douglas and one Abraham Lincoln, a Springfield, Illinois, attorney with little national reputation save his single congressional term in the 1840s, who attacked popular sovereignty and slaveholding interests. Lincoln was tall and gaunt, at 6 feet 4, a Kentucky-born, self-educated man who was now 49 years old and impressed those who met him either for his perceptive logic and endless storytelling or for his ungainly, rough appearance. To a packed house in the state capitol in Springfield on June 16, 1858, Lincoln told his fellow politicians, "A house divided against itself cannot stand. I believe this government cannot endure permanently half slave and half free. I do not expect the Union to be dissolved—I do not expect the house to fall—but I do expect it will cease to be divided. It will become all one thing, or all the other." Lincoln lost the Senate race but gained national prominence for his views. He would now be a player in the party politics of the infant Republican party, which had unsuccessfully promoted the military explorer John Charles Frémont as a presidential candidate in 1856.

The political winds of collision seemed to be thick. Most alarming for many slaveholders, however, was the bungled attack by John Brown's "army" of 21 antislavery zealots, armed with muskets and pikes, on the U.S. Arsenal and Armory at Harpers Ferry, Virginia, in October 1859. Connecticut-born Brown spent much of his life in Ohio before moving to Kansas and now, at age 59, lived for a time in the Booth Kennedy Farmhouse at Dargan, Maryland, while plotting his insurrection. Brown felt that his band, which included five black Americans, would capture arms, distribute them to local slaves, and incite a regional rebellion that would liberate tens of thousands and effectively end the Peculiar Institution for good. He had been ordered to do so by God, he claimed, and his long white hair and flowing beard gave him a biblical appearance. Carried out on October 16, 1859, the raid utterly failed. Holed up in the arsenal's engine house, the group was surrounded by a mixture of U.S. infantry, marines, and local militia led by Bvt. Col. Robert Edward Lee, who had been hastily assigned to put down the insurgency. Lee, a Virginian by birth, offered a stark contrast to the rough westerners who would take over the government in Washington fifteen months hence. Aged 52, Lee had been born into an aristocratic family. His father, "Light-Horse Harry" Lee, had been Gen. Washington's cavalry commander and governor of the commonwealth before falling from grace.

Lee, aided by Lt. James Ewell Brown Stuart, surrounded the engine house and captured 10 of Brown's raiders, including Brown himself. Seven of the party were killed during the fiasco. The event sent shock waves through the South, and after a brief trial Brown was hanged in Charles Town on December 2. Before his death he handed a note to the executioner that read, "I John Brown am now quite certain that the crimes of this guilty, land: will never be purged away; but with Blood."

Brown would prove providential in death. A year later the tensions between North and South were palpable and the deep Southern states—particularly South Carolina—were on the verge of secession. For the South the last straw came with the 1860 presidential election. Abraham Lincoln, the Republican candidate who had spoken out for the rights of all men and cautioned against the spread of slavery, was elected in the November contest. Lincoln faced a monumental task in keeping the factions of the nation together and feared this was not possible. Through the end of 1860 and the first two months of 1861, he sat in an office in the state capitol in Springfield and politicked, communicating with as many people as he could about the impending crisis.

On Thursday, December 20, 1860, the American nation began to come unglued. On this day in the "hotbed of rebellion"—Charleston, South Carolina—state legislators passed an ordinance of secession, breaking South Carolina's ties with the United States of America. "We, the people of the State of South Carolina," the ordinance concluded, "in Convention assembled, do declare and ordain . . . that the ordinance adopted by the U.S. in Convention, on the 23d day of May, in the year of our Lord 1788 . . . is hereby dissolved." Other states followed after the New Year. On January 9, Mississippi seceded. A day later Florida left the Union. The next day Alabama went. On January 19, Georgia exited the country. A week later Louisiana seceded. On February 1, Texas, always independent at heart, broke its ties with the United States. It was becoming pandemic in the South.

"All the indications are that this treasonable inflammation—*secessionitis*—keeps on making steady progress week by week," wrote the New York City diarist George Templeton Strong on January 31. Robert E. Lee wrote his son on January 23: "Secession is nothing but revolution. . . . Still, a Union that can only be maintained by swords and bayonets, and in which strife and civil war are to take the place of brotherly love and kindness, has no charm for me. If the Union is dissolved, the government disrupted, I shall return to my native state and share the miseries of my people. Save in her defense, I will draw my sword no more." The nation had lost seven states but gained one when, on January 29, Kansas was admitted to the Union. On February 28, Colorado Territory was organized; March 2 saw the organization of Nevada and Dakota territories.

The actions in Florida in January were especially precipitous. A situation was transpiring that mirrored the difficulties faced by Anderson and his men at Charleston. On the 10th, the day of Florida's secession, 1st Lt. Adam Jacoby Slemmer of the 1st U.S. Artillery, moved his small garrison of 81 men from Barrancas Barracks at Pensacola to Fort Pickens on Santa Rosa Island. He did so after spiking the guns at Barrancas and exploding the munitions at nearby Fort McRee. Slemmer set his men to work on transforming the fort, located out in Pensacola Harbor much as Sumter stands in Charleston Harbor, into defensible shape. Two days later local secessionists took over Barrancas, Fort McRee, and the Pensacola Navy Yard and demanded the surrender of Pickens. Slemmer refused. Unlike his comrades in South Carolina, Slemmer would be successfully reinforced. Some 500 men landed at Fort Pickens on April 12 as the guns opened on Sumter, and on April 18, Col. Harvey Brown arrived and established the Federal Department of Florida at Pickens. Pickens would remain in Union hands, and the importance of the other fortifications and the Navy Yard to the Confederates would be held in check.

Most Americans believed that military conflict was inevitable. All across the nation, and particularly in the South where the martial tradition was emphasized, little units of militia and local defense troops had been organizing, equipping, and drilling. The concept of localism dominated the lives of most Americans in the mid nineteenth century in a way that is hard to appreciate now. Most young Americans (and many older ones) had never traveled outside of their own counties, let alone their own states. They were indeed part of an American nation, but many cared little for what was happening in distant Washington or other locations—the universe existed in a relatively compact region around one's local town. And nowhere would the concept of relativity be more striking than with the secession crisis: Southerners readied themselves to protect their homeland against the onslaught of "foreign invaders"; Northerners would (to the surprise of many Southerners) prepare to fight to preserve the ideals of the Federal Union; Abraham Lincoln would attempt to keep the Union together against the rebellious factions; and a few Northerners—by no means the majority as of early 1861—would fight for the freedom of black Americans. In a peculiarly American way, nearly all who fought on both sides saw themselves as fighting for liberty. For Southerners, the liberty to do as they pleased, unrestrained by Washington's laws. For Northerners, the liberty to carry on with the American democratic ideal of self-government under majority rule, a trailblazing and tenuous experiment at the time that had nothing but failure written all over it.

And yet the crisis that was taking shape was not actually a civil war, a war between two factions of the same government. Nor was it an insurrection to usurp the central government as defined in the famous General Orders No. 100 that would be developed by military jurist Francis Lieber in early 1863. Lieber, a South Carolinian who remained loyal to the Union, codified the Federal rules of the war, and they would be used as a defining document of the U.S. Army until the era of World War I. Lieber's lengthy definition of the conflict outlined it as a rebellion or attempted secession, an act of military aggression against the government by a group of civilians in some of the component states. The rhetoric on both sides ranged from cautionary to vitriolic. "People who are anxious to bring on war don't know what they are bargaining for," wrote Thomas J. Jackson, an eccentric professor at the Virginia Military Institute, to his nephew on January 26. "They don't see all the horrors that must accompany such an event." In Washington, Secretary of the Treasury John A. Dix wrote W. Hemphill Jones, a treasury official in New Orleans, on January 29. "If anyone attempts to haul down the American flag, shoot him on the spot." Such contempt for the secession movement was powerful stuff: on the floor of the U.S. Senate, Tennessee Senator Andrew Johnson spoke plainly: "For myself, I care not whether treason be committed North or South," he said, "he that is guilty of treason is entitled to a traitor's fate!"

Those states in rebellion wasted no time organizing their cause. In February civilian representatives gathered at Montgomery, Alabama, to consult with each other about their common direction and the goals of the Southern states. On February 18 they organized a Provisional Confederacy and appointed Provisional governmental officers. "All Montgomery had flocked to Capitol Hill in holiday attire," wrote Thomas Cooper DeLeon, a Southern journalist, of the festive day. "Bells rang and cannon boomed, and the throng—including all members of the government—stood bareheaded as the fair Virginian [Letitia Tyler, granddaughter of John Tyler] threw that flag to the breeze. . . . A shout went up from every throat that told they meant to honor and strive for it; if need be, to die for it." The self-proclaimed Southern government had chosen as its Provisional president, to serve a single six-year term, Jefferson Davis of Mississippi.

Born in 1808 in Kentucky, Jefferson Finis Davis (the middle name came because he was the last of ten siblings) grew up to be a stylish and highly educated militarist and politician. He attended the U.S. Military Academy at West Point, was graduated twenty-third in his class of thirty-two (in 1828), and spent several years in army duty before resigning to become a Mississippi planter. In 1835, Davis married Sarah Knox Taylor, daughter of the future president Zachary Taylor, but his wife died just three months later from malaria. Ten years later he married again, this time to Varina Howell of Natchez, with whom he would live the rest of his life. Elected to the House of Representatives, Davis resigned his seat to participate in the Mexican War as colonel of the 1st Mississippi Rifles; Davis served gallantly at Buena Vista, where he was wounded in the foot. After the war he began a career as a senator from Mississippi before resigning to make an unsuccessful bid for his home state's governorship. In 1853, Franklin Pierce appointed Davis secretary of war, a position in which he continued to learn a great deal about the U.S. military and about strategy and tactics. He was reelected senator from Mississippi in 1857 and served in that capacity to the brink of war in early 1861.

Davis was a lean man with a cool stare that strangely affected those who faced him because his left eye was partially blind. He had wanted a military commission as a field general of the Confederacy, and probably if that had been the case the South's cause would have been improved considerably. Outwardly stiff, and inflexible on his principles, Davis would not be an easy politician to deal with for the majority of his colleagues. For now, however, all appeared celebratory in the glorious South. "The man and the hour have met," said William L. Yancey of Davis as he introduced the new president to a crowd two days before the inauguration. On the 18th, Davis was inaugurated and delivered his address, a stern and sometimes threatening oration. He spoke of the "wickedness of our aggressors" and stated that if the integrity of the Southern territory be assailed, the Confederacy must "appeal to arms and invoke the blessings of Providence on a just cause." At length, Davis continued: "The right solemnly proclaimed at the birth of the States, and which has been affirmed and reaffirmed in the bills of rights of the states subsequently admitted into the Union of 1789, undeniably recognizes in the people the power to resume the authority delegated for the purposes of government. Thus the sovereign states here represented proceeded to form this Confederacy; and it is by the abuse of language that their act has been denominated revolution."

Davis's vice president was an emaciated Georgia politician named Alexander Hamilton Stephens whose lukewarm involvement with the formation of the Confederate States would lead to out-and-out dissension against Davis. Stephens, who celebrated his 49th birthday by taking the oath as vice president, originally argued against secession and went to Montgomery only after it was clear that his beloved Georgia would not stay in the Union. He came into the series of meetings in Montgomery as a constitutional specialist and without aspirations for office. When the vice presidency was offered him, he accepted only because compromise between Southern states competing for influence in the new national government was necessary. "Little Aleck," who stood 5 feet 7 and never weighed more than 100 pounds, was not only chronically ill with a variety of ailments but also stooped in form and suffered grievous bouts of melancholia. In short, according to one biographer, he "looked like a freak." Moreover, his lukewarm support of Confederate nationalism would mean trouble for Davis as the weeks passed, with an almost nonexistent role for Stephens in much of the war legislation. In the spring of 1861, however, Stephens laid out his philosophical notion of the Confederacy. "Our new government is founded upon exactly the opposite idea [from abolition]; its foundations are laid, its cornerstone rests," he said, "upon the great truth that the negro is not equal to the white man, that slavery—subordination to the superior race—is his natural and normal condition."

The rest of Davis's inaugural cabinet, formed over several days following his inauguration, comprised a crew of varying abilities. Robert Augustus Toombs of Georgia was a former attorney and member of the U.S. House and Senate. South Carolinian Christopher Gustavus Memminger became secretary of the treasury. Leroy Pope Walker of Alabama became the first Confederate secretary of war. Stephen Russell Mallory of Florida was an intelligent choice for secretary of the navy.

Sometimes called "the brains of the Confederacy," the most intellectually gifted of the cabinet was undoubtedly Judah Philip Benjamin, a brilliant lawyer who had been born in 1811 in the Virgin Islands, of English-Jewish parents. His oddities were off-putting, however: he spoke with a lisp, had a sort-of constant smile on his face, chewed on cigars, and had deep black eyes that weren't set quite right. Benjamin's role as attorney general—and later in other positions—would prove an influential force in the new government. Finally, John Henninger Reagan of Texas served as Davis's postmaster general. As the Confederate cabinet assembled and began to organize itself, one prominent Texan issued grave forebodings on the future. "Let me tell you what is coming," said Sam Houston. ". . . Your fathers and husbands, your sons and brothers, will be herded together like sheep and cattle at the point of the bayonet. . . . You may, after the sacrifice of countless millions of treasure and hundreds of thousands of precious lives, as a bare possibility, win Southern independence . . . but I doubt it."

Yet the fever of Southern independence, what amounted to a fundamentally conservative revolution, was taking off like a rocket. Southerners reveled in their new nation, and in many locales songs celebrating the Confederacy sprang up. None was more beloved than the strain of a minstrel tune, "Dixie's Land," concocted by Ohioan Daniel Decatur Emmet in 1859 and first played in Mechanics' Hall on Broadway in April 1859. Sung with mock black dialect, the song went: "I wish I was in de land ob cotton / Old times dar am not forgotten / Look away, look away / Look away, Dixie Land / In Dixie land, I'll take my stan' / To lib an' die in Dixie / Away, away, away down south in Dixie!" The tune captured supreme ranking among Southern war songs before the war even began by virtue of being played at Davis's inauguration.

Davis had departed from his Brierfield Plantation in Mississippi for his appointment with destiny in Montgomery on February 11. On that same day, Abraham Lincoln left Springfield, Illinois, bound for Washington. His inauguration was slated for March 4 on the eastern portico of the Capitol. On the way to Washington, Lincoln spoke in Independence Hall in Philadelphia on February 22. "I have never had a feeling, politically, that did not spring from the Declaration of Independence," said the gaunt Kentuckian, ". . . that *all* should have an equal chance. This is the sentiment embodied in that Declaration of Independence. . . . I would rather be assassinated on this spot than to surrender it." Lincoln then slipped through Baltimore with its Southern sympathizers, avoiding assassination, and on into Washington, whose citizens entered into a remarkable state of anxiety and heightened security.

Lincoln's inauguration day in the city of Washington was a beautiful springtime display for the throngs of bodies surrounding the Capitol. Some 25,000 people had come to the nation's capital to see what would happen on this most uncertain of presidential days. Early in the day the weather was cool but pleasant; later in the day the atmosphere turned "bleak and chilly." Few thought they knew what the new chief executive would say about the tenuous situation the country faced. The nation might be divided without a contest, after all. It was only the day before that Bvt. Lt. Gen. Winfield Scott had written a note to the New York politician William H. Seward, declaring that one of the options available to Lincoln was simply, "Say to the seceded States, Wayward Sisters, depart in peace!" But Lincoln entertained no such notion. He believed firmly in the motto of the United States, *e pluribus unum*—one out of many—reflecting to associates that it embodied all that was America. As he rode from the Executive Mansion to the Capitol beside James Buchanan, he moved along with a military guard that stretched throughout the town, boarding and blocking entrance areas, watching windows along the route of travel, and with sharpshooters strategically posted on buildings about town.

"It is safe to assert that no government proper, ever had a provision in its organic law for its own termination," said Lincoln when he arose to deliver his First Inaugural Address. After a review of the problems faced by the standoff of North versus South, he spoke to the secessionists: "In *your* hands, my dissatisfied fellow countrymen, and not in *mine,* is the momentous issue of civil war. The government will not assail *you.* You can have no conflict, without being yourselves the aggressors." Finally, he concluded with a magic set of phrases. "We are not enemies, but friends," said Lincoln. "We must not be enemies. Though passion may have strained, it must not break our bonds of affection. The mystic chords of memory, stretching from every battle-field, and patriot grave, to every living heart and hearthstone, all over this broad land, will yet swell the chorus of the Union, when again touched, as surely they will be, by the better angels of our nature." "When the address closed and the cheering subsided," wrote the future Union officer Wilder Dwight, "[Chief Justice Roger B.] Taney rose, and, almost as tall as Lincoln, he administered the oath, Lincoln repeating it; and as the words 'preserve, protect, and defend the Constitution' came ringing out, he bent and kissed the book; and for one, I breathed freer and gladder than for months. The man looked a man, and acted a man and a President." Wrote George Templeton Strong of Lincoln's speech: "I think there's a clank of metal in it."

The ceremony was concluded but the standoff far from averted. "The cry to-day is *war,*" wrote the diarist Mary Chesnut on March 6. In much of the North, fear and some measure of shame ruled the day. "The bird of our country is a debilitated chicken," wrote Strong on March 11, "disguised in eagle feathers. We have never been a nation; we are only an aggregate of communities, ready to fall apart at the first serious shock and without a centre of vigorous national life to keep us together."

Lincoln had won the presidency by a combination of factors that elevated the Republican party to prominence (in part because of the fracturing of the Democratic party) and elevated him by circumstance within the party. But many Northerners lacked faith in such a character as Lincoln to pull off the monumental tasks that lay before him. "It is the strangest thing," wrote Nathaniel Hawthorne of Lincoln, ". . . that he, out of so many millions . . . should have found the way open for him to fling his lank personality into the chair of state." Now Lincoln's cabinet would attempt, as had Davis's, to cover the political spectrum. Lincoln's vice president was Hannibal Hamlin of Maine, at age 51 a veteran of the U.S. House and Senate and the governorship of his home state. Of far more significance in the administration would be Secretary of State William Henry Seward, a sharp New Yorker whose own presidential aspirations were snuffed by Lincoln's success and who for some weeks actively conspired to promote a belief in Lincoln's supposed lack of abilities.

The other cabinet members ran the gamut of experience and competency. The exceedingly ambitious and quite religious Salmon Portland Chase of Ohio (a New Hampshire native) was made secretary of the treasury. His somewhat heavy frame, balding crown, and glistening eyes did little to promote social success; his aspirations to sit in the presidential chair frequently brought him into conflict with Lincoln. Even less helpful to the administration was Simon Cameron, chosen as secretary of war. This beady-eyed political boss of Pennsylvania had almost no background in military affairs. More suited to his task was Gideon Welles of Connecticut, secretary of the navy. His imposing presence, white hair and flowing white beard, coupled with his naval pursuits, gave him the sobriquet "Father Neptune."

The secretary of the interior would be Caleb Blood Smith of Indiana, an attorney, newspaperman, and politician. Montgomery Blair of Maryland, scion of a distinguished family that included two famous Frank Blairs, would serve as postmaster general. Finally, Edward Bates of Missouri, another presidential aspirant, would serve as attorney general, which was not legally a cabinet-level position during the war but was important nonetheless.

The Lincoln government was now established, and Davis's upstart Confederate government had Fort Sumter, the first prize of the war, impressively in its hands. Three days after the fall of Sumter, the young Confederacy received a substantial boost when Virginia signed its ordinance of secession. The large, powerful, and strategically placed state was an independent entity, not yet part of the Confederacy. The ex-president and Virginian John Tyler wrote his wife the following day. "Well, my dearest one, Virginia has severed her connection with the Northern hive of abolitionists. . . . The contest into which we enter is one full of peril, but there is a spirit abroad in Virginia which cannot be crushed until the life of the last man is trampled out. . . . The die is thus cast, and her future in the hands of the god of battle."

On April 15, in the wake of Sumter, Lincoln called for 75,000 volunteers. Replies were not always cooperative. "Missouri can and will put one hundred thousand men in the field [for the Confederacy]," wrote the prosecession governor of Missouri, Claiborne F. Jackson, to Jefferson Davis. The governors of Kentucky and Tennessee had similarly hostile sentiments for the Lincoln government. North Carolina troops seized Forts Caswell and Johnston. All-out war was now a reality, and men everywhere began to prepare to go off to the fight, their wives and sweethearts tearfully sending them to an adventure of completely unknown proportion. As the bombardment of Sumter raged, Thomas J. Jackson told his VMI students, "[The time for war] will come and that soon, and when it does come, my advice is to draw the sword and throw away the scabbard."

The first Federal troops to respond to Lincoln's call reached Washington on April 18, five companies of Pennsylvania volunteers. On this same day, Confederate success reached Virginia at Harpers Ferry, at the confluence of the Potomac and Shenandoah rivers. The site of the famous U.S. Arsenal and Armory, where Brown had launched his unsuccessful raid, was threatened by Virginia troops concentrating as close as four miles away at Halltown. At Charles Town, Confederate Capt. John Daniel Imboden moved his battery of six guns toward Harpers Ferry. At nearby Winchester in the Shenandoah Valley, the town had already become a "beehive of military activity," with various companies of militia passing through the town all day. The armory was commanded by 1st Lt. Roger Jones, who had a scant 42 men and who desperately needed reinforcements. Virginia militia commanded by William Henry Harman and Kenton Harper, brigadier and major generals in the militia, respectively, approached the town on the night of the 18th. Jones set a portion of the arsenal ablaze at 10 P.M. to destroy 15,000 crated muskets while a demolition team set bundles of combustible material on fire in the armory's main buildings. Jones then set his men on a march out of town. Jones's fleeing Federal soldiers crossed the Potomac bridge, encountering an angry mob of secessionists, who backed off after the Yankees posed in battle line. The retreating Yankees left the burning arsenal in the hands of the approaching Rebels and could hear several loud explosions as they fled toward Carlisle, Pennsylvania. Much of the arsenal and the armory was destroyed, but a significant amount of matériel, including 4,000 muskets and machinery such as milling machines and lathes, was saved. Again, it was a victory for the South.

On April 19, Lincoln proclaimed a blockade of Southern ports. The Federal navy received a new and startling mission, and, although the blockade would take time to be effective, it would become a major part of the war strategy. However, this day brought more trouble for the North. The largely pro-Southern city of Baltimore lay between Washington and Pennsylvania—hardly Rebel territory. When a full regiment of Federal troops, the 6th Massachusetts Volunteers, passed through Baltimore on this day, a riot between the soldiers and prosecession civilians broke out, producing some of the first casualties of the war. The 6th Massachusetts was changing trains in Baltimore to head for Washington. A crowd around the station grew throughout the morning, many bearing Confederate flags. Four companies of the 6th Massachusetts detrained and had to push their way through the crowd, which began jeering the soldiers and throwing rocks. Shots rang out from soldiers and civilians alike.

"A scene of bloody confusion followed," wrote journalist Frederic Emory, who witnessed the riot. "As the troops retreated, firing, the rioters rushed upon them only to be repulsed by the line of bayonets." At least 4 soldiers and 9 civilians were killed and many were injured. It was another embarrassment for the Lincoln administration, particularly since Maryland's loyalty was much in question. The state teetered on the brink of Confederate support, and a particular song, written by James Ryder Randall, boosted secessionist thinking. Many Southern soldiers would sing "Maryland, My Maryland," to the tune of "O Tannenbaum," while marching in the months to come. "The despot's heel is on thy shore / Maryland! / His torch is at thy temple door / Maryland! / Avenge the patriotic gore / That flecked the streets of Baltimore / And be the battle queen of yore / Maryland! My Maryland!" The poem was first published in the *New Orleans Delta* on April 26 and then worked into the song. Some saw the Baltimore riots as a great tiding, however. "It's a notable coincidence that the first blood in this great struggle is drawn by Massachusetts men on the anniversary of Lexington," George Templeton Strong confided to his diary. "This is a continuation of the war that Lexington opened—a war of democracy against oligarchy. God defend the Right, and confound all traitors." The rioting continued for several days and temporarily isolated Washington.

Frustrated with the isolation and a demand from a Baltimore committee for peace at any price, Lincoln responded. "Our men are not moles, and can't dig under the earth. . . . Keep your rowdies in Baltimore, and there will be no bloodshed. Go home and tell your people that if they will not attack us, we will not attack them; but if they do attack us, we will return it, and that severely."

The following day, April 20, brought yet another disappointing result for the Union. The Gosport Navy Yard near Norfolk, Virginia, was in an endangered position, and the yard's commandant, Capt. Charles Stewart McCauley, decided to abandon it. In the evening McCauley ordered his sailors to burn and evacuate the yard, and they also set fire to five ships. Additionally, four vessels were burned to the water line and then sunk, including the USS *Merrimack,* which would later come back in a different form to haunt its old navy. The old frigate USS *United States* was simply abandoned. The Navy Department was furious with McCauley; the yard's loss set back the Federal navy and coastal strategy for months to come. As at Harpers Ferry, Virginians captured the position and salvaged much of what remained, including an important dry dock, thousands of guns, a naval construction plant, and some of the ships themselves.

With each passing day's news, soldiers and would-be soldiers were grappling with loyalty. Inevitably, many people saw friends and acquaintances move to the other side. Robert E. Lee wrote his sister, Anne Marshall, from Arlington House on April 20: "With all my devotion to the Union and the feeling of loyalty and duty of an American citizen, I have not been able to make up my mind to raise my hand against my relatives, my children, my home." On the same day, he sent a letter of resignation to Union General-in-Chief Winfield Scott: "Save in defence of my native State, I never again desire to draw my sword." The former army officer and clerk in his father's Galena, Illinois, retail store, Ulysses S. Grant, wrote his father on April 21. "There are but two parties now, Traitors & Patriots and I want hereafter to be ranked with the latter, and I trust, the stronger party." Still other soldiers worried that perhaps they wouldn't even see a fight. "We thought the rebellion would be over before our chance would come," recalled Michael Fitch, a soldier in the 6th Wisconsin Infantry.

Events in the West closed the dramatic month of April 1861. On April 23 state troops in Arkansas seized Fort Smith, gaining an important base. On the same day, near San Antonio, a company of troops of the 8th U.S. Infantry under command of 2d Lt. Edwin W. H. Read was captured by state militia. This came two months after Bvt. Maj. Gen. David E. Twiggs surrendered his troops, forts, and barracks in and around San Antonio. Twiggs had been dismissed for treason on March 1 and afterward became a Confederate major general. More U.S. forces surrendered in Texas on April 25, this time at Saluria, where Maj. Caleb C. Sibley, commanding the 3d U.S. Infantry, gave up his command to Confederates under Col. Earl Van Dorn.

At month's end both sides, in fatigued disbelief, struggled to anticipate what lay ahead. For Jefferson Davis the answer seemed clear. "The *creature* has been exalted above its *creators;* the *principals* have been made subordinate to the *agent* appointed by themselves. . . . Under the supervision of a superior race their labor had been so directed as not only to allow a gradual and marked amelioration of their own condition, but to convert hundreds of thousands of square miles of the wilderness into cultivated lands covered with a prosperous people."

In the North, many remained perplexed about the motives of the Southerners and their new nation. "Undoubtedly, thousands of warm-hearted, sympathetic, and impulsive persons have joined the Rebels, not from any zeal for the cause," Nathaniel Hawthorne proclaimed, "but because, between two conflicting loyalties, they chose that which necessarily lay nearest the heart."

CHAPTER 2

Organizing the Struggle

AT THE OUTBREAK of the Civil War, the American nation was an infant among world governments—some of the men and women witnessing its undoing were older than the Federal Union itself. Lincoln stood outside the Capitol and delivered his First Inaugural Address seventy-two years to the day after the ratification of the U.S. Constitution. Such national youth masked growing pains. The nation was in the midst of a rapid shift from a simple agrarian-based society to an industrial and technological trend setter. The year 1861, for example, witnessed the completion of the first transcontinental telegraph line. The actress Adah Menken shocked Boston audiences by appearing on stage unclothed. The aggregate mileage of rail track in the United States rose above 30,000. And with the onset of the war, a Federal income tax of 3 percent for incomes in excess of $800 per year was enacted, beginning a long tradition. In England, still the intellectual grandfather of America, James Clerk Maxwell published his theory on the motions of gases. Charles Dickens topped the bestseller list with his publication of *Great Expectations*, while another English work, Charles Darwin's *Origin of Species*, confused and astounded its readers.

And so the progress of civilization appeared to be moving forward, bringing greater ease and knowledge to the lives of the vast population of Americans. The country's 1860 census shows that 31.4 million human beings were spread across the United States. Some 19 million of these were in the Northern states, about 9.1 million in the Southern states, 3 million in the border states of Missouri, Kentucky, and Maryland, and just under 300,000 were in the territories and the District of Columbia. Of the total, 227,000 Northerners and 4.2 million Southerners were black Americans, nearly all in the South being slaves. The newest state, Kansas, had been admitted to the Union on January 29, 1861. The largest cities in the North were New York

(813,669), Philadelphia (565,529), Brooklyn (266,661), Baltimore (212,418), Boston (177,840), Cincinnati (161,044), St. Louis (160,773), and Chicago (109,260). The largest cities in what would become the war zones in the South were New Orleans (168,675), Charleston (40,522), Richmond (37,910), Mobile (29,258), Memphis (22,623), Savannah (22,292), Petersburg (18,266), and Nashville (16,988).

In 1861 the United States Army was hardly in top form to fight a war. On January 1 the regular army consisted of 16,402 soldiers of which 14,657 were present for duty. Of these, most were scattered in the middle west and west on duty at frontier posts; only about 3,335 were stationed in the Department of the East. Of about 1,080 officers, 286 resigned or were dismissed to enter the Confederate service, while out of about 900 former officers, now civilians, 114 returned to the Union forces and 99 joined the Confederate forces. At the beginning of the war, regulars were not used as leaders and trainers for the volunteers because most officials thought the war would be short, lasting a few weeks to a few months, and because most regular units would be required intact to secure the western frontier and the coastal fortifications, where they alone had previous experience.

The ranks of the U.S. forces swelled in the wake of Fort Sumter, however. On April 15, President Lincoln called for 75,000 volunteers, and when it became clear that the war would last longer than a fortnight, he asked, on May 3, for 500,000 additional volunteers. The patriotic response was strong: On the first call, twenty-one states and territories sent 91,816 men marching off to war, all of whom had enlisted for three months of service, and the second call swelled the ranks such that by July 1 there were 186,751 U.S. soldiers ready for battle, having enlisted for terms of six months, or one, two, or three years. By early summer 1861 the United States had a volunteer army formidable in numbers if consisting of mostly young boys who were entirely green when it came to military matters and who could not imagine what lay in store for them. By year's end the number rose to 575,917.

On the Confederate side, the numbers of soldiers enlisted, active, and serving are incomplete and often, when cited, are suspect for a variety of reasons. Unfortunately, many contemporary records were lost or destroyed during the war. Numbers of enlistments were often inflated to demonstrate patriotism and the efficiency of conscription. They were also often underreported to minimize and conceal losses due to casualties and desertions and to demonstrate superior performance in battle over the enemy. This notwithstanding, two major calls for volunteers and militia came from Jefferson Davis during the war's first weeks: the first, for 100,000, came in March. The second, for 400,000, occurred in August. By year's end the Confederate armies in the field consisted of some 326,768 men.

Private soldiers and noncommissioned officers constituted the overwhelming bulk of the armies, but commissioned officers would lead the armies into the field. In the U.S. Army, three classes of commissioned officers existed. They are given here in decreasing order of hierarchy. General officers included the grades of lieutenant general (Winfield Scott was commissioned brevet lieutenant general on February 15, 1855; the substantive grade was revived on February 29, 1864, for U. S. Grant), major general, and brigadier general; field officers included the grades of colonel, lieutenant colonel, and major; and company officers included the grades of captain, first lieutenant, and second lieutenant. The Federal navy had equivalent grades in three classes. Flag officers included the grades of vice admiral (created on December 21, 1864, for David G. Farragut), rear admiral (legislated on July 16, 1862), and commodore (legislated on July 16, 1862); ship's officers included the grades of captain, commander, and lieutenant commander (legislated on July 16, 1862); and ship's division officers included the grades of lieutenant, master (which in 1883 was renamed lieutenant, junior grade), and ensign (legislated on July 16, 1862, replacing passed midshipman).

The Confederate forces essentially followed the same structure of their old Union, with a few differences. The Confederate States legislated the Provisional Army on February 28, 1861, and a regular army on March 6, 1861. Their grades included general (legislated on May 16, 1861), lieutenant general (September 18, 1862), major general (May 22, 1861), and brigadier general (March 1, 1861), and they followed these with colonel, lieutenant colonel, major, captain, first lieutenant, and second lieutenant. The Confederacy formed its regular navy on March 16, 1861, and its Provisional Navy on May 1, 1863. It had the grade of admiral (although only one was commissioned, Franklin Buchanan, on August 21, 1862), vice admiral (which was never used), rear admiral (only one, Raphael Semmes, was commissioned, on February 10, 1865), and commodore (which was authorized on March 31, 1862, but never used). The grades of captain, commander, lieutenant (which on March 16, 1862, was divided into first and second lieutenant), master (a commissioned officer), and passed midshipman (a commissioned officer) followed.

The types of military commissions in the services and methods by which they were earned, often confused in the literature, deserve an explanation. To obtain a commission in the United States Army, a candidate would often have to accomplish the following ten steps:

1. Proposal by the immediate commanding officer or an important official such as a cabinet member, governor, or congressman.
2. Approbation by the senior officers of the army, especially those of higher rank.
3. Endorsement by the general-in-chief.

4. Appointment by the secretary of war.
5. Acceptance by the candidate together with his oath of allegiance.
6. Nomination by the president.
7. A favorable report by the Senate Committee on the Military and Militia.
8. Confirmation by vote of the Senate.
9. Engrossment and issuance by the Office of the Adjutant General.
10. Signing by the secretary of war and the president.

Steps 1 through 3 were considered routine, steps 4 through 8 were crucial, legal requirements, while steps 9 and 10 were often considered automatic unless the commission was ordered returned to either the Senate or to the president. Often new recommendations, political considerations, or the death of the recipient would interrupt the process, but not always—there were some peculiarities. The navy had an analogous system, and the process worked virtually the same way on the Confederate side.

To further complicate matters, a number of services existed on each side, which may roughly be divided into three classes, regular army, volunteers or provisional army, and militia or state forces. Suppose an officer is commissioned a brigadier general. What is the limit of his authority? From whom does he take orders and to whom can he give orders? This messy business echoes throughout battlefield situations, as we will see. Generally, however, regular army officers outrank volunteers and volunteers outrank militia of a given grade. The term "rank" is often misused to mean "grade"; in fact, it refers to the status of seniority and command within each grade. A brigadier general of volunteers in the U.S. Army, for example, with an earlier date of commission outranks an officer of the same grade who was commissioned later. Moreover, an officer's authority might be affected by his assignment—the task to which he was assigned by the president, the War Department, or a superior officer. An officer might be assigned to command a regiment, brigade, division, corps, army, or military division or department, or to await orders, to serve in a bureau, or on a military commission. These were all assignments, and could affect the relationships between officers significantly. At the time of Gettysburg, for example, George G. Meade was the fiftieth-ranking major general of volunteers, having been commissioned to rank from November 29, 1862. He was outranked, then, in lineal grade by a number of officers in his own army, including John Sedgwick, Henry W. Slocum, and John F. Reynolds. He was also outranked by the commander of the Middle Department, Robert C. Schenck, in Baltimore. However, within the operational area of his own army, Meade was in command of everyone and everything by virtue of his assignment.

The issue of command is further muddled by the often confused subject of brevet commissions. Often considered simply "honorary," brevet commissions were actually provided for three situations in which officers were assigned according to brevet grades. The first and most important reason was to allow the president to assign an outstanding officer to command a unit over those who were his seniors. Thus, if several colonels existed in a brigade but the fifth-ranking one was deemed the best leader, the president could commission him as a brevet brigadier general and assign him to command the brigade in that capacity, outranking the four senior colonels.

Complications in command sometimes arose. For example, John Wool, the most experienced officer in defensive installations, was assigned to Fort Monroe in his rank as brevet major general, thus outranking all other officers in the area. When Maj. Gen. George McClellan arrived on Virginia's Peninsula in 1862 at the head of the Army of the Potomac, he was the highest-ranking substantive general officer in the army. Wool pointed out, however, that McClellan's commission dated from 1861 whereas Wool's brevet commission dated from 1847 and therefore Wool was the highest-ranking officer in Virginia. The War Department was forced to agree and hastily transferred Wool to Baltimore (in another department) to allow McClellan to continue commanding all forces on the Peninsula.

Secondly, brevet grades were issued for purposes of commissioning officers in a grade for which no legal billet existed by statute. The recipient then served as a supernumerary in that grade until such time as a substantive grade became available. Thus, newly graduated cadets from the Military Academy were usually commissioned brevet second lieutenant until a suitable substantive vacancy opened. Likewise, extra staff officers were so commissioned, producing grades and assignments such as brevet captain, assistant adjutant general, until a substantive position was available. Finally, brevet commissions were issued as an accolade for valor in the field or in appreciation of exceptional service. When applicable, brevet commissions were ranked after the substantive commissions of the same grade. Thus, brevet commissions were neither temporary nor honorary.

Although the Confederate army and navy did not issue brevet commissions, its organizational situation was even more complex than that of the Union. Confederate forces consisted of six types of organizations. The first, state militias and state guards, were organizations under state authority regulated by the Militia Act of 1792. The second, the Army of the Confederate States of America (ACSA), the Confederate regular army, was organized by an Act of March 6, 1861, and was to include 15,015 men, including 744 officers, but actually enrolled only about 1,650, as most volunteers preferred the provisional army. Initially, the ACSA included four brigadier generals: Pierre G. T. Beauregard, Samuel Cooper, Joseph E. Johnston, and Robert E. Lee, and later in order to have generals outrank all militia officers, included six generals: Cooper, Albert Sidney Johnston, Lee, Joseph E. Johnston, Beauregard, and Braxton Bragg. The third organization, the Provisional Army of the Confederate States (PACS), was authorized by an Act of February 28, 1861, and organized beginning on April 27, 1861. Most regulars, volunteers, and conscripts entered into this organization.

The fourth important Confederate organization was the Virginia Provisional Army, the largest of the so-called state armies. A call for volunteers was issued on April 17, 1861. A provisional army was organized on April 23, 1861, under a Virginia ordinance of April 27, 1861, consisting of militia units transferred from the individual states, the Virginia State Line, volunteer organizations, and all U.S. soldiers "who have resigned or shall resign with a view to offer their services to this state." The ordinance declared that officers of the Virginia Provisional Army would take rank and precedence over all officers of the same grade of the volunteers and militia, without regard to date of commission. The initial organization comprised five divisions containing 28 brigades of 128 regiments. On June 8, 1861, the Virginia Provisional Army was incorporated into the CSA Provisional Army, but the actual absorption of various units apparently took place over a period of about six months, with some units reverting to militia status. Other states organized militias similar to that of Virginia.

The fifth Confederate organization was the Local Defense Troops (Corps), authorized by an Act of March 27, 1862, which included all men not covered by other calls. The exempted, underage, and overage men were to be activated as needed. The sixth and final important organization was the Reserve Corps, which was established by an Act of February 17, 1864. The Senior Reserves consisted of troops between 45 and 50 years of age, and the Junior Reserves consisted of troops 17 and 18 years of age. By September 1864, conscription had effectively depleted the Reserve Corps troops.

With the growing ranks of soldiers in each of the armies, one reorganizing itself and another at its genesis, officers in Washington and Richmond needed to wrestle with organizational problems. The assignments in the armies in early 1861 consisted of two branches, the line and the staff. The line of the U.S. Army, the combat force organization, was divided into five "arms"—artillery, dragoons, mounted rifles, cavalry, and infantry. These were consolidated into three arms, artillery, cavalry, and infantry, on August 10, 1861. Line officers outranked all staff officers regardless of grade except within the purview of the staff officers' particular staff assignments, wherein the latter took orders from their respective bureau chiefs. Staff officers might serve in one of the many staff bureaus in Washington, which included the Adjutant General's Department, Inspector General's Department, Office of the Judge Advocate, Office of the Military Telegraph, Signal Corps, Quartermaster General's Department, Subsistence Department, Pay De-

partment, Medical Department, Corps of Engineers, Corps of Topographical Engineers, United States Military Academy, and Ordnance Department.
Staff officers could also serve on general staffs, which were headed by a chief
of staff, an assignment often filled by an assistant adjutant general. The staff
also included representatives of the arms such as a chief of artillery and a
chief of cavalry (the infantry arm usually being represented by the commanding officer himself). Finally, the staff included representatives of the
staff bureaus and offices such as adjutant general, inspector general, quartermaster general, commissary of subsistence, medical corps, engineer, ordnance, judge advocate, provost marshal, and signal corps.

In the spring of 1861, the general-in-chief of the U.S. Army was Bvt. Lt.
Gen. Winfield Scott, an aged Virginian whose absolute loyalty to the United
States was strengthened by service in the War of 1812, heroic command in the
Mexican War, and the fact that he had been assigned as general-in-chief
since July 5, 1841. At the outset of the Civil War, Scott was 74 years old and so
overweight, at about 350 pounds, that he had to be hoisted onto a sturdy
horse in the rare event when he rode one. With his slightly cranky demeanor,
loose white hair, and wrinkled face, "Old Fuss and Feathers"—an acquired
sobriquet resulting from his proclivity for military pomp and show—was
hardly the imposing leader he had been twenty years earlier. He sometimes
fell asleep during meetings. He suffered from bouts of vertigo, gout, and
dropsy, and could normally take but a few steps before resting. When in
March and April the Lincoln administration held emergency cabinet meetings about how to handle the probable war, it was immediately clear that although Scott could provide wisdom and insight, he was not long for the job
of guiding the Union army to decisive victory.

Scott was hardly the only important top officer in the army hanging
around Washington, ready to advise the administration. The city housed the
staff bureaus of the army, and these bureau chiefs held an unusual amount of
influence with those who entered wartime Washington. First and foremost
was Bvt. Brig. Gen. Lorenzo Thomas, a regular army officer of long duration
who was chosen to replace Samuel Cooper as adjutant general of the army,
the latter having defected to the Confederacy. Delaware-born Thomas, a
West Pointer and veteran of the Mexican War, began his Civil War tenure
with only moderate success. Second in importance was the aged Col.
Sylvester Churchill, who had been inspector general of the army since the
summer of 1841. A native of Vermont, Churchill was a former carpenter and
newspaper editor who got his start in the military by enlisting in the War of
1812. Military justice had at its helm Capt. John F. Lee of Virginia, judge advocate of the army, whose tenure stretched from 1849.

The administration of many other army duties had to be looked after. A
relatively new branch, the Office of the Military Telegraph, was established

in the War Department on April 25, 1861, under the direction of Col. Thomas A. Scott, a Pennsylvanian. Another new office, that of the Signal Corps, was established in 1860 with Maj. Albert J. Myer in charge. Myer, of New York, had developed the wigwag flag signal code after having invented sign language for the deaf. The duties of the Quartermaster General's Department would be overseen at first by Maj. Ebenezer S. Sibley, after the resignation of the experienced officer Joseph E. Johnston, who went South. By June 1861, however, Sibley's acting role ended and the new quartermaster general, Brig. Gen. Montgomery C. Meigs, took over. Though he was born in Georgia, Meigs (pronounced "Meggs"), a West Pointer, proved loyal to the Union. Before the war he had been active in overseeing the expansion of Federal buildings in Washington. During the war he proved equally effective in supplying the government's troops with the matériel they needed.

Other senior regular army stalwarts filled most of the remaining bureaus. Past his prime, Col. George Gibson of Pennsylvania had served as commissary general of subsistence, ensuring adequate foodstuffs for the army, since 1818. Col. Benjamin F. Larned of Massachusetts had headed the Pay Department since 1854. Virginian Thomas Lawson, surgeon general of the army since 1836, died on May 15, 1861, necessitating a replacement, which brought in Col. Clement A. Finley of Pennsylvania. The army's chief engineer was Col. Joseph G. Totten of Connecticut, so assigned since 1838. The topographical engineers were headed by Bvt. Col. John J. Abert of Maryland, who also held his position since 1838. At the time of the outbreak of war, the U.S. Military Academy at West Point was directed by its superintendent, Maj. Richard Delafield of New York, who had replaced the recently defected P. G. T. Beauregard. On March 1, 1861, Maj. Alexander H. Bowman replaced Delafield as superintendent. The Ordnance Department had as its chief Col. Henry K. Craig, a Pennsylvanian who served as chief of ordnance from 1851 to April 23, 1861, and thereafter Col. James W. Ripley, a Connecticut native.

At war's outset Lincoln had virtually no military background and therefore actively sought and needed the advice of strategists and tacticians. Such was not the case down South. Not only had Davis served as secretary of war in Franklin Pierce's administration from 1853 to 1857 and therefore knew a vast amount about strategy and tactics himself, but he also knew a great deal about the U.S. Army organizationally and was acquainted with many of its officers. Moreover, he had graduated from West Point (although in the bottom third of his class), served in the Seminole Indian wars of the 1830s, and fought in Mexico as colonel of the 1st Mississippi Rifles. Indeed, Davis accepted the nod to be Confederate president reluctantly, preferring a field command as a general officer. (He so wanted to be a general that his tombstone in Richmond's Hollywood Cemetery erroneously reports he was a brigadier general in the U.S. Army.) Davis clearly had military experience and fancied himself a brilliant visionary in terms of military leadership (and with some good reason), such that he established a pattern of micromanaging his officers from the early days of the war. He effectively served as his own general-in-chief throughout the war, although two men, Robert E. Lee and Braxton Bragg, would act as military advisors to the president, and Lee would be appointed general-in-chief in February 1865.

This notwithstanding, a key officer in the formulation of the Confederate army organization emerged in the spring of 1861. He was Samuel Cooper, a somewhat grizzled, 62-year-old West Point graduate. He was a native of New Jersey, a brother-in-law of Virginia's respected military officer Robert E. Lee, and strongly attached to the South because of his wife's Virginia background. He had befriended Jefferson Davis during the latter's tenure as secretary of war, when Cooper was adjutant general of the U.S. Army, an assignment that terminated only when he resigned from the army on March 7, 1861. Now Davis would appoint and encourage the young Confederate Senate to confirm Cooper as adjutant and inspector general of the Confederate States army and also its ranking general officer. (This occurred after a brief stint by George Deas as inspector general in March 1861.) As adjutant and inspector general, Cooper was generally an efficient record keeper for the army, but his potential as a leading light faded rather quickly. He soon established a pattern of staying only hazily informed of details relating to events in various theaters, and his Northern origin and odd habits such as frequently tugging on his shirt collars made his leadership suspect in the minds of many Confederates. That Cooper was not more assertive in formulating Confederate military policy probably didn't matter, as Davis was bubbling over with his own ideas, as were many a field commander who would come under the direction of the president.

Staff bureaus for the Confederate States were slow in evolving. Aside from Samuel Cooper's twin duties, three principal organizations deserve note in the earliest weeks of the war. The Bureau of War was established by an Act of March 7, 1861, and its first chief was the irascible Kentuckian Col. Albert T. Bledsoe. West Point graduate Bledsoe's friendship with Davis helped him become a part of the Confederate inner circle in Richmond. In 1862 he became an assistant secretary of war. The Quartermaster General's Department was established under Col. Abraham C. Myers, a South Carolinian and former regular army officer. Twelve days later Col. Lucius B. Northrop of South Carolina began his tenure as commissary general of subsistence. The Medical Department began its existence in May 1861 under the direction of David C. De Leon, who was acting surgeon general, and was replaced on July 12, 1861, by acting Surgeon General Charles H. Smith, in turn replaced by Samuel P. Moore on July 30, 1861.

The Confederacy's chief engineer was Josiah Gorgas, who served as acting chief from April 8, 1861. Gorgas, a native of Pennsylvania, was a skilled engineer who had graduated high in his West Point class. His primary role during the Confederate war was as the South's chief of ordnance, an assignment that launched his oversight of a vast array of creative inventions of resources brought to bear against the Federal war machine.

The staff bureaus would be crucial to the development and function of the armies, but what of the formulation of the field armies themselves? The sizes of army field components varied widely and are often compared erroneously by authors in terms of similarly titled units on opposing sides. Such comparisons are usually misleading, for the totals of effective combat troops should be used. Thus, one regiment is not necessarily the equivalent of another, nor are five divisions necessarily superior in strength to four divisions in another combat force. Moreover, frequently units are incorrectly named, or the titles are incorrectly used through ignorance or by historical accident. Thus, two regiments might constitute a brigade but not a division, and a battalion is not synonymous with a regiment. Furthermore, units were often consolidated or fragmented while retaining their prior designations. Because army units of similar title may actually vary in size by several orders of ten, unit comparisons are nearly worthless. The military effectiveness of units, even when of equal size, is not necessarily comparable, depending on such diverse factors as leadership, training, morale, readiness, equipment, and support.

The smallest cohesive unit in the Civil War armies was the company, often organized and recruited in a local community as part of the "citizens' army." The company often consisted of from 64 to 83 privates together with 19 officers and/or special members such that the total ranged from 83 to 102 men. Cavalry companies ranged from 79 to 105 men and were often termed a troop. Artillery units ranged from 80 to 156 men and were usually termed a battery (often four to six guns) consisting of gun sections, or pieces. The infantry companies were often subdivided into platoons, squads, sections, patrols, or detachments. Companies were significant in military structure because they reflected the localism that dominated mid-nineteenth-century America. Because they were locally recruited, companies operated psychologically like social clubs with a heightened sense of bonding, communication, and fraternization because the members came from the same community and were often already familiar with each other. Companies often came from one rural county or one ward in a city, and men in a given company normally insisted on electing their own officers, particularly the captain, the officer in charge of the company. Lawyers, sheriffs, firemen, and policemen frequently filled the bill, especially early in the war.

The next-larger unit was the fundamental unit for mustering, training, and maneuvering—the regiment. In the U.S. Army, the size varied from 866 to 1,046 men, usually composed of a regimental staff and ten companies. Nine new regular army regiments raised in May 1861 were to consist of twenty-four companies each but never reached authorized strength. Artillery regiments averaged about 1,800 men. Heavy artillery regiments often consisted of 1,200 men arranged in twelve companies and were frequently converted into infantry units rather than being assigned to garrison duty. Many regiments began with about 1,000 men and often decreased to about 100 men through attrition. Alternative names for infantry regiments included Zouaves or fusiliers (French for elite infantry units), rangers or fencibles (obsolete terms for infantry units), sea fencibles (an obsolete term for the army equivalent of marines), or voltigeurs (an obsolete term for elite foot riflemen). Guards, scouts, pickets, skirmishers, pioneers, and partisans were names given to infantry units on special assignment.

Cavalry regiments were often composed of from four to six squadrons, each squadron of two companies amounting to 660 to 1,168 men. Alternative names for cavalry included dragoons (French for mounted infantry), which were usually dismounted for combat in regular battle lines. All cavalry units preferred to dismount during heavy battle to offer less exposure. Mounted rifles were elite cavalry soldiers equipped with rifles rather than muskets or carbines. Lancers, hussars, and chasseurs were obsolete European terms for cavalry units, but the names were often retained during the Civil War. Vedettes (videttes), pickets, sentinels, and guards described mounted units in terms of their assignments. Comprising regiments were battalions, for which there was no legal size or content, other than "every part of a regiment, composed of two or more companies, will be designated a battalion." A regiment might therefore consist of from two to five battalions, but most frequently a battalion constituted about half the regiment. The battalion originated from the old French notion of a battlefront consisting of 50-man lines, 12 men deep, for a total of 600 men. An American battalion ranged from two to eight companies and was not more specifically defined. Any significant part of a regiment might be called a battalion. The cavalry equivalent was often termed a squadron.

The next-larger unit was the brigade; infantry brigades were composed of from two to twelve regiments, most frequently four, while cavalry brigades were composed of from two to eight regiments, most frequently four. Next came the division, the smallest "self-sufficient" combat unit, composed of from two to five brigades, most frequently three for infantry; and from two to six brigades, most frequently two, for the cavalry. The next larger unit was the army corps, legalized in the U.S. Army by an Act of July 17, 1862, but often used earlier to apply to any large portion of an army. The Confederate army also employed the new organizational principle of army corps. A corps was composed of from two to six divisions, and most frequently three. The next-larger unit was the army, which was the major field unit, and often the entire mobile force within a geographical department. After the creation of corps, an army might be composed of from one to eight corps, most frequently three. The terms "grand division," "wing," "right," "center," "left," and "reserves" were sometimes used to designate portions of armies or corps. The largest primary unit in the field during the Civil War was termed a military division. A military division might include more than one army and/or more than one department. Thus the military division in more modern terminology might be called an army group, a military theater, or both. These large units were so special in organization during the Civil War that they must be individually assessed.

Once the army units were organized, officers—most of them necessarily new and inexperienced—would need to do something with them. The most competent officers at the outbreak of war were schooled in Napoleonic tactics that were regurgitated in numerous textbooks. Some of the best known were Samuel Cooper's *The Concise History of Instruction and Regulation for Militia and Volunteers of the United States* (1836), Henry W. Halleck's *Elements of Military Art and Science* (1846), William J. Hardee's *Rifle and Light Infantry Tactics: For the Exercise and Maneuvers of Troops When Acting as Light Infantry or Riflemen* (1855), and, perhaps most important, Antoine-Henri Jomini's *Précis de l'Art de la Guerre* (1838), translated into *Summary of the Art of War* (1854). A great dilemma of the war would be that the increasing availability of rifled weapons, which began in earnest in the 1850s, made many of these simplistic tactics deadly. Not until the middle of the war would the most forward-thinking field commanders begin to revise their tactics in response to the murderous effectiveness of rifled weapons. And more "modern" and influential manuals such as Karl von Clausewitz's *Von Kriege* (1838), although translated as *On War* in 1854, would not actually become available in English translation until 1873, so its effect on the American Civil War was limited.

Throughout the nineteenth century, texts such as Cooper's, Hardee's, Jomini's, and many others, along with army regulations and military lectures such as those of Dennis Hart Mahan at West Point, stressed various guidelines and principles of warfare that were eventually grouped under nine arbitrary and interrelated headings.

1. Objective: The destruction of the enemy force.
2. Offensive: Only an offensive operation can achieve a decisive result, but an offensive is usually more costly than a defense.
3. Simplicity: Complete organization is required so that directions and orders may be communicated and understood without ambiguity and

difficulty. Responsibility should be compartmentalized and made specific.

4. Unity of Command: For complete cooperation, forces must be coordinated with respect to tactics and logistics. Simultaneous tactical operations were often termed "concentration in time."

5. Mass: Troops and firepower must be concentrated on decisive points of combat, "concentration in space."

6. Economy of Force: Minimum necessary and essential means must be used at all important points except where the maximum force is employed at the decisive point.

7. Maneuver: Forces must be moved to maximum advantage consistent with the terrain. Flanking and envelopment moves are usually superior to frontal attacks, depending on the strength of the defensive positions.

8. Surprise: Striking an enemy force "in detail," or while in motion to change position, or on open terrain, will surprise and confuse a defense.

9. Security: An adequate defense is required to protect bases, camps, fortifications, and supply lines.

At first glance, these principles appear to be obvious truisms, but they are actually complex when applied to large forces, operating with a changing logistical support over an uncertain topography. Early-nineteenth-century tactics stressed the frontal attack, typically a rapid charge by a regiment or battalion before the defense could organize a response. However, by mid-century, improvements in defensive field fortifications, improved artillery, and the introduction of the rifled musket supplied with the "Minié ball" (the cylindroconoidal, hollow-based bullet invented by Claude-Étienne Minié) made most frontal attacks suicidal. Classic frontal attacks that resulted in complete failure included the attack by Ambrose Burnside at Fredericksburg and the attack by Ulysses S. Grant at Cold Harbor. Unsuccessful frontal attacks by Confederates included the attack by John Bell Hood at Franklin, Tennessee, and the attack by Robert E. Lee on the third day at Gettysburg. Frontal attacks during the Civil War were successful only under special circumstances, such as the attack by James Longstreet at Chickamauga (taking advantage of an inadvertent gap in the Union defense line) and the attack by George H. Thomas at Missionary Ridge (taking advantage of steep, undefended terrain). The armies soon favored attempts at flank attacks (turning offenses) to achieve surprise over the direction of the main advance while gaining an advantage of enfilading artillery and rifle fire, analogous to the naval tactic of "crossing the tee." For example, if a broad front advanced, attacking or firing along the ends of the line would greatly favor the attackers.

"Concentration in space" was a principle in which interior lines of communication and transportation made efficient use of limited forces. Robert E. Lee would become a master of this principle in his Virginia and Richmond-Petersburg campaigns. Ulysses S. Grant would use this technique in 1862 in his advance on Forts Henry and Donelson to break the overstretched defenses of the Confederate Department No. 2. Grant would also excel in the "concentration in time" concept as he directed the concurrent campaigns of George G. Meade and William T. Sherman in 1864 along with numerous smaller operations, thereby not allowing the defenders to concentrate in space.

Both sides relied on "cordon" defenses in which strong points such as cities, railroad lines, bridges, and high-elevation geographical positions were defended in strength. This system was risky because it scattered defensive forces such that concentration in space became difficult, as well as opening the weaker portions of the cordon to raiding forces. Likewise, both sides employed administration command in units of geographical departments that stressed autonomy and integrity of the departmental forces. These units then unfortunately operated against cooperation with and strategic support of the adjacent departments. Each department wanted to be its own "kingdom," not to take orders from other departments.

The Union grand strategy was designed to destroy the field armies of the Confederacy, to blockade the Atlantic and Gulf coastlines to prevent foreign commerce with the Confederate States, and to implement the Anaconda Plan of dividing Southern territory by control of the rivers and rail junctions. Winfield Scott communicated the Anaconda Plan to Abraham Lincoln as early as May 2, 1861. Scott realized that the thirteen Southern states could be militarily reduced only by attrition, using the navy to blockade the coast to prevent resupply and then by gaining control of the seaports, river towns, and rail centers to impair internal transportation. Wrote Scott: "In connection with such blockade we propose a powerful movement down the Mississippi to the ocean, with a cordon of posts at proper points . . . so as to envelop the insurgent States and bring them to terms with less bloodshed than by any other plan."

By the spring of 1862 it would become apparent that the Union could not overwhelm the South by a direct invasion. So Federal officers would devise a strategy of attack in detail on weak points in order to occupy points of supply and support. The Confederacy would be reduced, bit by bit, into non-self-supporting sections. This strategy, accomplished by late 1864 by the Virginia and Georgia campaigns, then left only the destruction of the two principal Confederate armies, those of Lee and Johnston, to utterly destroy the Confederacy's ability to fight.

The Confederate States, on the other hand, adopted a strategy of defense, because by the acts of secession, its view amounted to a *fait accompli* in creating a new nation. CSA troops hoped to ward off "invasion" so as to cause discouragement and internal discord in the North. Because two to four times as many resources were required for attack compared with defense, the manpower and matériel advantage of the North would be mitigated.

Occasional offensive raids against Northern strong points such as Washington and Baltimore in the east and St. Louis and Cincinnati in the west would require enormous Union defensive efforts, minimizing the concentration of armies in the North. Cavalry raids and guerrilla attacks helped to disrupt Union supply lines. A few commerce raiders on the high seas would greatly weaken the forces available to enforce a blockade. Moreover, foreign intervention was thought to be probable in order to support cotton and tobacco exports and to improve the importation of arms and munitions from Europe. A slowed or stalled Northern effort to isolate and invade the South would then produce an armistice that would lead to world recognition of the Confederacy. Confederate strategists believed that Kentucky and Missouri were not "divided" states but had seceded and were being held in bondage by the Unionists, hence their thirteen-star flag. They believed that Maryland and western Virginia were pro-Southern and could be liberated by penetration.

But such beliefs were to be tested many times during the summer of 1861 and a great many surprises lay in store for soldiers and civilians on each side. The months of May and June were relatively quiet as the armies organized, stockpiled supplies, and drilled endlessly. "The first thing in the morning is drill, then drill, then drill again," wrote Oliver W. Norton, a young private in the 83d Pennsylvania Infantry. Many of the Northern troops sang a distinctive song as they marched, one which harked back to John Brown's attempted slave insurrection at Harpers Ferry, Virginia, in October 1859: "John Brown's body lies a-mouldering in the grave / John Brown's body lies a-mouldering in the grave / John Brown's body lies a-mouldering in the grave / His soul is marching on." The song may have originated with the Boston Light Artillery and/or the 12th Massachusetts Infantry. The most popular variant words were, "We'll hang Jeff Davis on a sour apple tree."

Myriad troops poured into Washington and concentrated in many small towns North and South to secure the national defense. In May the Union attained an effective army strength of 156,861 and naval strength of 25,000. The regular army—with eight new regiments and one each of artillery and cavalry—numbered 22,714. To the south, Governor John Letcher of Virginia called for additional troops to defend the state's borders, and the

Provisional Army of Virginia, commanded by Maj. Gen. Robert E. Lee, ordered more troops into the field and gathered a force at the captured U.S. Arsenal and Armory at Harpers Ferry.

On May 6, Arkansas and Tennessee passed ordinances of secession, becoming the ninth and tenth states to join the Confederacy. In Montgomery, President Davis approved a congressional bill that recognized a state of war between the United States and the Confederate States. In Missouri local authorities with pro-Southern sentiment challenged Capt. Nathaniel Lyon to remove troops from public buildings, and Lyon refused. At St. Louis a growing assemblage of pro-Confederate Missouri state militia began to threaten the Union's hold on the key border state. Meanwhile, in Maryland, another state with divided loyalties, the state appeared to be solidifying its support for the Union. It was now clear to everyone that at least a somewhat protracted state of war would exist. "The assault on Fort Sumter started us all to our feet, as one man," wrote Horace Binney, a prominent Philadelphia lawyer. "All political division ceased among us from that very moment."

In early May the Stars and Stripes took a minor beating on the remote plains of the Texas frontier. Earlier, at San Antonio, Bvt. Maj. Gen. David E. Twiggs, a Southerner with open sympathies toward the growing Confederacy, had surrendered his garrison along with the forts, supplies, equipment, and funds to Texas troops commanded by Col. Ben McCulloch. This made the Georgia-born Twiggs a traitor of the worst kind in the eyes of most Northerners, as he was the oldest and most senior general officer to side with the Confederacy, which commissioned him a major general. Southerners had solidified their grasp of Texas since the February 18 surrender of Twiggs' and his men. Feeling the sting of a Texas surrender again, on May 9, Bvt. Lt. Col. Isaac V. D. Reeve surrendered his battalion at San Lucas Springs, some fifteen miles outside of San Antonio. Reeve faced a force of about 1,400 and wrote that he had "deemed that stubborn resistance and consequent bloodshed and sacrifice of life would be inexcusable and criminal, and I therefore surrendered."

Another minor surrender took place in St. Louis the following day. Riots broke out, and U.S. regulars and home guards confronted state militia troops with staunch Southern sympathies. On May 6, state militia under Brig. Gen. Daniel M. Frost had gathered at Camp Jackson in the western part of the city. Frost was a former U.S. army officer turned politician whose New York roots did not prevent his taking a stand for the Confederacy. The camp was named for Governor Claiborne F. Jackson, who also had well-known pro-Southern feelings. Some 3,436 soldiers and 70 officers under Col. Nathaniel Lyon planned to attack Camp Jackson, fearing that disguised boxes of mortars and guns discovered coming into the city were bound for the camp. Ultrapatriotic, Lyon determined to seize Camp Jackson on May 10,

surrounding it and forcing Frost's surrender without firing a shot. As the secessionist prisoners (639 men and 50 officers) were marched through the city,
rioting escalated and shots were fired by the U.S. troops against wild and in-
trusive civilians. By the time the violence ended, 29 people were killed or
mortally wounded.

Such early skirmishes and surrenders raised an anxious tone among the
population. "I don't quite understand what we are fighting for, or what defi-
nite result can be expected," wondered Nathaniel Hawthorne. "If we pummel the South ever so hard, they will love us none the better for it; and even
if we subjugate them, our next step should be to cut them adrift. If we are
fighting for the annihilation of slavery, to be sure, it may be a wise object, and
offers a tangible result, and the only one which is consistent with a future between North and South." The fire of secession burned as brightly as ever.
"Those of us who were *the last* to give up the Union, will be *the last* to give up
the principle of *the right of a people to make their own government*," wrote
G. Mason Graham, chairman of the board of supervisors at the Louisiana
Military Academy, to William T. Sherman. "We will live to maintain it, or we
will *die* in defense of it—our 'cities, towns, yea people' *may* be destroyed."
Graham and Sherman had been friends; Sherman had given up the superin-
tendency of the Academy, located at Alexandria, on February 20.

Civil control in all areas continued until May 13 when Maj. Gen. Ben-
jamin F. Butler moved into Baltimore. No repeat of the April riot took place.
A week later North Carolina seceded, the eleventh Confederate state, leav-
ing Kentucky and Missouri with split loyalties but not yet members of the
Confederacy. Meanwhile, the Provisional Congress of the Confederate
States voted to move the capital from Montgomery to Richmond, to support
Virginia's role as the dominant Confederate state and to move the resources
needed closer to the action.

Military-minded men still believed that there might not be any action.
In Richmond, Confederate Col. Daniel Harvey Hill wrote to his wife on
May 20: "There is less war excitement here than in Charlotte, so far as I can
learn. There is a strong possibility that there will be no fighting. Whenever
either party finds a place necessary to its success, it goes out and takes it. A
shot or two is fired in opposition, and there the matter ends." They also often
showed a demonstrable lack of faith in fellow officers. Hill wrote his wife ten
days later: "Col. [John B.] Magruder is always drunk and giving foolish and
absurd orders. I think that in a few days, the men will refuse to obey any
order issued by him."

On May 24, Union troops moved into Virginia, occupying Alexandria.
Federal troops also retained possession of Fort Monroe at Hampton Roads.
A few shots were fired during these movements, but little action resulted.
During the movement to take Alexandria, however, Col. Elmer Ellsworth of

the 11th New York Infantry, the 1st Fire Zouaves, age 24 and a favorite young officer of Lincoln, was killed as he attempted to haul down a secession flag at the Marshall House hotel. The innkeeper, James Jackson, opened on Ellsworth with a shotgun, killing him instantly, and Jackson was in turn shot by Pvt. Francis E. Brownell. Afterward, Ellsworth's body lay in state in the Executive Mansion and for weeks afterward, when Yankee troops confronted the enemy, the chant "Remember Ellsworth!" resonated through their lines. Ellsworth's death again strengthened patriotic fervor in the North. Former officers of the army contacted the adjutant general in Washington, offering their services. One such officer wrote: "Feeling it the duty of everyone who has been educated at the Government expense to offer their services for the support of that Government, I have the honor, very respectfully, to tender my services until the close of the war in such capacity as may be offered.... I feel myself competent to command a regiment if the President, in his judgment, should see fit to intrust one to me." The writer was Ulysses S. Grant of Galena, Illinois.

Minor actions continued during the last days of May. The Union navy established blockades in three important ports, using the USS *Powhatan* at Mobile, the USS *Brooklyn* at New Orleans, and the USS *Union* at Savannah. Federal troops under Col. Benjamin F. Kelley marched into western Virginia and occupied Grafton to protect the Baltimore & Ohio Railroad. The Union navy shelled secession batteries at Aquia Creek, Virginia. The Confederate navy, virtually nonexistent, raised the wreck of the USS *Merrimack* at Norfolk, which had been scuttled when the yard was abandoned by the Yankees, and had curious plans for her ahead. Wrote Confederate Secretary of the Navy Stephen R. Mallory: "Such a vessel at this time could traverse the entire coast of the United States, prevent all blockades, and encounter, with fair prospect of success, their entire Navy."

Yet little would take place in Confederate waters for some time to come. For the moment, the action would occur on land. At Fairfax Court House, Virginia, on June 1, 50 cavalry troopers and 25 dragoons led by Lt. Charles H. Tompkins of the 2nd U.S. Cavalry, a regular army veteran, cut through the town on their way to Germantown. In what was ostensibly the first land battle of the war, Confederates in the Prince William Cavalry and the Warrenton Rifles put up a short fight, opening fire at first from windows in the town. Capt. John Q. Marr of the Warrenton Rifles was killed and Col. Richard S. Ewell, whose fame and influence would rise greatly after he recovered, was wounded in the shoulder. The Confederates in Fairfax Court House greatly outnumbered the U.S. troopers, and Tompkins retreated to safety after the brief skirmish.

Now that blood had been spilled in Virginia, the *New York Tribune* began to print on its editorial page each day the slogan "On to Richmond."

Conversely, the hero of Fort Sumter, P. G. T. Beauregard, wrote Jefferson Davis from Manassas Junction on June 3, telling him "my troops are not only willing, but are anxious, to meet the enemies of our country under all circumstances." Beauregard had just taken command of the Confederate forces on the Alexandria line. On the same day, William T. Sherman contemplated the coming campaigns and their leaders. "As soon as real war begins," he wrote, "new men, heretofore unheard of, will emerge from obscurity, equal to any occasion. Only I think it is to be a long war,—very long,—much longer than any politician thinks."

Yankees and Rebels met again on June 3 at Philippi, Virginia. Maj. Gen. George B. McClellan, in command of the Department of the Ohio, had overall authority in the region. His strategy called for Union forces to march from Grafton through the dark mountain roads during a night rainfall and strike the Confederates under Col. George A. Porterfield at daylight. Union militia Brig. Gen. Thomas A. Morris ordered the attack. The force would be led by Col. Benjamin F. Kelley and would consist of about 2,000 men. At dawn the Union column fired a shell into the midst of the Confederate encampment, stunning and scattering Porterfield's 1,500 troops. Early in the action, Kelley was struck in the chest by a pistol shot and severely wounded, although he subsequently recovered. Thereafter, Col. Ebenezer Dumont of the 7th Indiana Infantry took command. As the secessionists fled, the Yankees pursued until all were exhausted. Although this minor skirmish was glorified in the press, which dubbed it the "Philippi Races," it had little significance. The casualties were slight: 15 Confederates were killed and, aside from Kelley, 2 Yankees wounded. On this same day, the North lost one of its influential politicians. Stephen A. Douglas died in Chicago, having stumped vigorously in support of his old nemesis, Lincoln. On May 1, Douglas had delivered his defining swan song: "Every man must be for the United States or against it There can be no neutrals in this war, *only patriots—or traitors.*"

Fairfax and Philippi were mere skirmishes, tastes of war. The first real land battle of the conflict took place at Big Bethel, Virginia, on June 10. Variously called Great Bethel or Bethel Church, the engagement arose when Maj. Gen. Benjamin F. Butler organized an expedition to strike out from Fort Monroe. Butler was a cantankerous political general from New Hampshire whose career as a lawyer and Massachusetts legislator was filled with controversy. Cockeyed from birth and heavyset, the commander of the Department of Virginia was so hard to get along with that the story of his meeting a cross-eyed general and their "inability to see eye to eye" became a fabled if not invented tale. Butler now ordered his subordinate Ebenezer W. Peirce, a brigadier general in the Massachusetts militia, forward with a force of 2,500 men in seven regiments and one battery, the 1st, 2d, 3d, 5th, and 7th New York infantries, 1st Vermont Infantry, 4th Massachusetts Infantry, and 2d U.S. Ar-

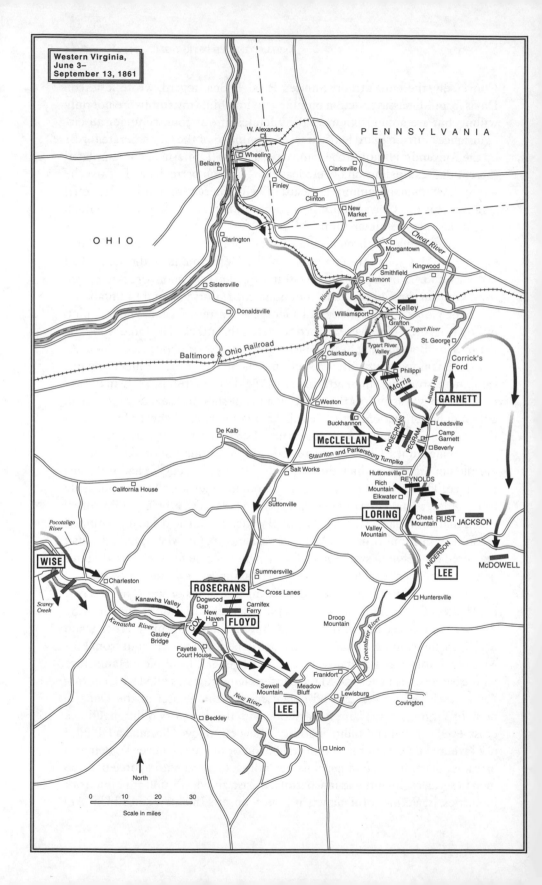

tillery. Facing Peirce's troops was a crafty ex–regular army officer, Col. John B. Magruder of Virginia. A natty dresser and one affected with a peculiar lisp, fancy dress, and somewhat effeminate behavior, Magruder earned the sobriquet "Prince John." Magruder's 1,200 men were clustered around Big Bethel, eight miles north of Hampton. At 1 A.M. the 7th New York Infantry, Duryea's Zouaves, moved out and occupied New Market Bridge, situated on the road between Hampton and Big Bethel. An hour later the rest of the Union regiments began to rendezvous at a position south of Little Bethel, but confusion resulted, shots rang out, and "friendly fire" killed 2 and wounded 19. Peirce moved on, burned Little Bethel, and continued toward Big Bethel.

To make matters worse for the Yankees, Confederates under Magruder observed the oncoming attack and moved out to meet it. Col. D. H. Hill's 1st North Carolina Infantry moved efficiently and stood ready to entrap the Federal attack. "They were all in high glee, and seemed to enjoy it as much as boys do rabbit-shooting," reported Hill. When it came, the attack was poorly coordinated, and it was thrown back in confusion by Hill's troops. Confederate artillery opened briskly and Peirce reported "among the breaks in the hedges the glistening of bayonets in the adjoining field." The Yankees withdrew in disarray. Federal casualties amounted to 76 killed, wounded, and missing, and Confederate losses were only 11.

The most striking aspect of these first minor skirmishes was the almost complete lack of planning, the poor communication, and the confusion that dictated how events unfolded on both sides. Another affair happened in western Virginia on June 13, when Col. Lew Wallace and about 500 men of his 11th Indiana Infantry stumbled into Romney on a raid. Fearing that secessionists were influencing and oppressing pro-Union citizens, Wallace set out from Cumberland, Maryland, on the evening of June 12 and, after traveling part way by rail, marched his men over the mountain roads beginning at about 4 A.M. He would ultimately gain fame as author of the wildly successful novel *Ben Hur*. For now, however, Wallace marched his 500 men over such rough mountain roads that they didn't approach Romney until nearly 8 A.M. After they crossed the Potomac River, small arms fire rang out from a brick house and a minor gun battle ensued, but as the Yankees continued to approach, the secessionists fled in disarray, abandoning the guns. A number of supplies were captured, a few prisoners taken, and two Confederates were killed. The result was almost comically meaningless, as were the results of many small skirmishes. But something more significant did happen while Wallace's force set out for Romney: pro-Union delegates met in Wheeling to organize a loyal Virginia government. Although it would grow slowly, the seed was planted for the creation of West Virginia.

The intrusion of Union forces into Virginia continued throughout mid-month. At Harpers Ferry, site of the ruined Arsenal and Armory, Confederate Gen. Joseph E. Johnston abandoned the town and pulled back into the Shenandoah Valley. At Vienna, Virginia, on June 17, Brig. Gen. Robert C. Schenck was ordered to move most of the 1st Ohio Infantry along the Loudon & Hampshire Railroad to protect the railway and to reconnoiter the area near Falls Church and Vienna. Schenck was an Ohioan, a political general whose friendship with Lincoln created his military position. He detached several companies of the 1st Ohio at various points along the expedition, leaving some 271 men to approach Vienna in the railcars.

"On turning the curve slowly, within one-quarter mile of Vienna," wrote Schenck, "were fired upon by . . . masked batteries of, I think, three guns, with shells, round shot, and grape, killing and wounding the men on the platform before the train could be stopped." Schenck had ridden the train directly into an ambush. The engineer could not move the train away from the line of fire, and so the troops aboard scattered with wild abandon and continued the small arms fight throughout a stand of woods. The Confederate colonel who effectively ensnared Schenck's force was the South Carolinian Maxcy Gregg, a multitalented man who dabbled in astronomy, botany, languages, and law, gaining an impressive amateur education. Gregg's 1st South Carolina Infantry, some 575 strong, heard the distant whistle of Schenck's railroad train with enough time to set two 6-pounder guns on a hill overlooking the fateful bend in the track. At a range of about 400 yards, Gregg's guns opened fire. The result was eight Federal dead and four wounded, and Gregg's boys captured part of the train, which was set ablaze by shells, along with various supplies. Once again, a Federal excursion with undefined goals ended in an embarrassing failure.

On the same day as Vienna, an unusual action took place out west. The energetic warrior for the Union, Nathaniel Lyon, now a brigadier general, had marched into Missouri's capital, Jefferson City, and captured it unopposed on June 15. Lyon pursued the fleeing governor, Claiborne F. Jackson, whose Southern sentiments had been made starkly clear. On the 17th, Lyon moved upriver by boat along the Missouri and landed 1,700 men six miles below Boonville, at a position only two miles south of a Confederate encampment. After moving toward the town, Confederates shortly opened up on Lyon's men with small-arms fire. After a brief but sharp fight the state troops disloyal to the Union dispersed, and Lyon's men continued their advance, occupying Boonville. The Federal loss was 2 killed, 9 wounded, and 1 missing. This action gave Lyon a slight advantage in that it allowed Union troops to control the river in the area and push onward toward southwestern Missouri.

As the month ended, the point of much of this random skirmishing seemed cloudy at best. On June 30 a bright comet was viewed by many as it passed a mere 12 million miles from Earth, glowing as bright as the planet Saturn and producing a tail as long as 100° across the black night sky. The Great Comet of 1861 seemed to many to foreshadow severe calamity associated with the war. Hostility reigned in elements of Lincoln's own cabinet and from all parts of the country. Typical of the many threatening missives received by the president of the United States was a letter from Pete Muggins in Fillmore, Louisiana. A portion read: "God damn your god damned old Hellfired god damned soul to hell god damn you and goddam your god damned family's god damned hellfired god damned soul to hell and god damnnation god damn them and god damn your god damn friends to hell god damn their god damned souls to damnation." Others were more specifically threatening, as with the letter of R. A. Hunt of Lynchburg, Virginia, sent to Lincoln before his inauguration. "I have heard several persons in this place say that if you ever did take the President Chair that they would go to washington City expressly to kill you. . . . resign. if you dont you will be murdered."

The greatest calamity of the early months would not be a pseudoscientific analysis of a misunderstood celestial visitor or threats from a Southern partisan, however, but would come from the lack of clear thinking from many of the military theorists. As spring transformed into summer, commanders worried about the lack of knowledge and experience manifesting itself on both sides. "You are green, it is true, but they are green also," Lincoln told Brig. Gen. Irvin McDowell. "You are all green alike."

CHAPTER 3

Southern Joy
over First Bull Run

IN THE EARLIEST MONTHS of the Civil War, strategy and tactics in the American armies were unrefined concepts. As we have seen, some of the first clashes on land during the war unfolded with no purpose other than to seek out and encounter the enemy. Such unfocused operations would continue for some time. Indeed, three years would elapse before a coordinated Federal grand strategy would come into play, the strategy that would ultimately win the war. Nevertheless, in the first summer of the war, in the sweltering heat and humidity of Washington and Richmond, with the sun beating down on military drills, and pomp, show, and braggadocio still thick in the air, a few theorists and field commanders began to think about what they intended to accomplish with their armies.

Students of the war often confuse the terms "strategy" and "tactics." Strategic goals related to gaining the advantage in one's theater of operations, with one's army, or over the whole course of the war—ideas or events relating to the largest concerns often spread over the time of a whole campaign or even the whole war. Tactical goals related to the fighting of a battle on a single battlefield within the time frame of the action at hand. Although many armchair analysts limit their interpretation of a particular battle to the events that transpired on that ground alone, what was more likely firing off inside the heads of commanders at various levels—particularly army commanders—was driven by strategic concerns. Thus, it's easy to second-guess Robert E. Lee's order to commence Pickett's Charge at Gettysburg in 1863 as foolish and unlikely to succeed on a tactical level. But when one considers that Lee felt the Federal artillery was mostly depleted before the attack and when one considers Lee's strategic objectives and the edgy sense of desperation he must have felt to win a battle on Northern soil, the act is a little more understandable. (Lee's strategic goals included drawing the armies away from war-weary Virginia, foraging from the rich Pennsylvania countryside, easing the tightening noose at Vicksburg, and perhaps gaining foreign recognition for the Confederacy with a battlefield victory—but more on this specific case later.) Time and again during the American Civil War, it's easy to misinterpret the significance of events if one doesn't look at them in proper strategic context. This concept was just beginning to emerge during the hot days of July 1861.

"This is essentially a People's contest," Lincoln told Congress in special session on July 5, one day after the nation's unhappiest birthday, its eighty-fifth. "It is a struggle for maintaining in the world, that form, and substance of government, whose leading object is, to elevate the condition of men—to lift artificial weights from all shoulders—to clear the paths of laudable pursuit for all—to afford all, an unfettered start, and a fair chance, in the race of life." Lincoln asked for 400,000 men and $400 million to put down the rebellion. He made a strong case for the indivisibility of the Union. Three days earlier he had written his aging general-in-chief, Winfield Scott, authorizing Scott to suspend the writ of habeas corpus on or near a military line drawn between New York and Washington. This foreshadowed suspending the writ in a larger way as the war deepened.

Scott, as it happened, was one of the few people thinking strategy. His Anaconda Plan would strike southward in autumn 1861 when the rivers rose and made movement on water possible. The land force would march south and receive supplies along the Mississippi River in order to continue its mission. The Mississippi would be brought back into Union control then, as well as severing its transportation and communication value for Southerners. At first derided by detractors, Scott's brainchild would become an important part of Federal strategy. But during a June 29 meeting, Brig. Gen. Irvin McDowell argued that instead Federal troops should attack overland in Virginia toward Manassas, between Washington and Richmond. In part due to public pressure to move on the Rebels without delay, which echoed the "On to Richmond" sentiment, McDowell won. On July 8 he would assume command of the Army of Northeastern Virginia, the first large eastern army of the Union, and he would lead it south in battle.

But the consequences of the cabinet meeting wouldn't play out for another three weeks. In the meantime, several small actions took place in early July. Yankee troops under Pennsylvania militia Maj. Gen. Robert Patterson crossed the Potomac River at Williamsport, Maryland, on July 2, and moved into the Shenandoah Valley. This initiated the first movement in what would become the First Bull Run campaign, termed Bull Run by the Yankees and Manassas by the Confederates. (The two sides often had their own names for engagements, the Federals preferring geographical names and the Rebels the names of nearby towns.) Patterson began the movement by arguing frequently with Scott and would end it arguing still. Patterson led his force, called the Army of the Shenandoah (USA), consisting of 14,344 men, into the Valley to pin Confederate troops there in position so that the main Union army could strike southward toward Manassas undaunted by Confederate reinforcements. It was simplistic strategy, but strategy nonetheless. Patterson's army was organized into two divisions of equal size commanded by two other major generals of Pennsylvania militia. George Cadwalader, a former regular army officer, commanded the first division. The second division was commanded by William H. Keim.

The Confederate forces in the Valley had a considerable advantage in terms of military education and talent. Brig. Gen. Joseph Eggleston Johnston was assigned by President Davis to command some 10,654 men composing Johnston's division, which would be formally organized as the Army of the Shenandoah (CSA) on July 4. Johnston was a bright and efficient Virginian who was distantly related to Robert E. Lee and whose service in the U.S. army included outstanding performances in the Seminole and Mexican wars. His brief tenure beginning in 1860 as quartermaster general of the army gave him knowledge of supply and logistics. What Johnston lacked was a stable relationship with his president; Davis had unfairly ranked him below the other Confederate generals despite the fact that Johnston had been a brigadier general in the regular army of the United States, while the others had merely been colonels. Rather than grade, however, Davis relied on year of graduation and class standing at West Point to determine seniority of rank.

Johnston's army was divided into four brigades with attached cavalry. The brigades were commanded by Col. Thomas Jonathan Jackson, the eccentric professor from the Virginia Military Institute; South Carolinians Col. Francis S. Bartow and Brig. Gen. Barnard E. Bee, Jr.; and Col. Arnold Elzey of Maryland. The cavalry was ably commanded by a young Virginian, Lt. Col. James Ewell Brown Stuart.

All the movements in the Valley were predicated on what would be happening back near Manassas, where McDowell longed to attack the Confederate forces under the hero of Sumter, Brig. Gen. P. G. T. Beauregard. Beauregard was now assigned to command the Confederate Army of the Potomac, which was stationed at Manassas Junction. The elementary strategy from the Union point of view called for Patterson to move into the Valley and hold Johnston in place so he could not shift his force toward reinforcing Beauregard; the Confederate strategy aimed at preventing just that outcome.

As Patterson moved toward Martinsburg on July 2, his men pushed back Confederate defenders scattered through a series of outposts, and a brief skirmish took place at Falling Waters, Maryland. Patterson's army crossed the Potomac at 4 A.M., and after a five-mile march skirmishers on the front and flanks of the army suddenly were fired upon by Confederates posted in a clump of trees. Soon thereafter the main body of the Confederate troops, "sheltered by fences, timber, and houses," opened on the 1st Wisconsin and 11th Pennsylvania infantries. Confederate artillery fire slowed the Union movement for about half an hour before troops under Col. John J. Abercrombie, Patterson's son-in-law, pressed forward, dispersing the Rebels and overrunning their camps. The casualties were few: 2 killed, 13 wounded, and 1 missing among the Federal soldiers, and some 60 killed and several dozen wounded among the Confederates. The following day Patterson's army entered Martinsburg and Johnston's Confederates retreated toward Winchester. Thus far, the situation was going well for Patterson.

THE WAR OF JULY was also heating up in Missouri. The day after the nation's birthday, at the very time Lincoln delivered his words of hope to Congress, a battle was raging at Carthage. The previous month Brig. Gen. Nathaniel Lyon, the patriotic Federal militarist, had chased pro-Southern Gov. Claiborne F. Jackson over part of the state and attacked him at Boonville. Jackson then withdrew south from the Missouri River to southwestern Missouri, followed by the other units of the Missouri State Guard (CSA). Union soldiers under Thomas W. Sweeny, a militia brigadier general, left St. Louis and moved against the Confederate army. Then Lyon continued his pursuit of Jackson, who was in effect commanding secessionist troops clothed in civilian garb. On July 5, Jackson found himself not only fleeing from Lyon, who was near Springfield, in the direction of Carthage, but also additional Federal troops, mostly German immigrants organized as portions of the 3d and 5th Missouri infantries, commanded by Col. Franz Sigel. They constituted the vanguard of Sweeny's command. The German troops had an appropriate leader: Sigel had been born in Baden and became a revolutionary soldier fighting for Germany's liberalization in 1848 before fleeing to Switzerland, England, and finally New York. Though Sigel demonstrated limited military ability, the U.S. War Department recognized his political influence in motivating German immigrants to stand by Old Glory and fight against the Confederacy. Thus, Sigel was commissioned a colonel and promoted volunteerism among his people so effectively that "I fights mit Sigel" echoed frequently throughout the camps of his soldiers.

Many of the Missouri State Guard were unarmed. They numbered about 4,000 and were headed principally by militia brigadier generals James S. Rains, John B. Clark, Sr., Mosby M. Parsons, and William Y. Slack. As the Confederates approached Sigel's force, deployed near Carthage, they formed a line of battle to await Sigel's attack. About 1,100 Federal soldiers were engaged when Sigel brought his men forward, pushing the poorly outfitted Confederates until they ordered cavalry to strike at Sigel's flanks. "Up to this time the rebellious flag had sunk twice amidst the triumphant shouts of the United States volunteers," Sigel wrote in his report. Though supported by artillery fire, the Yankees were forced to retreat through Carthage, and the Missourians pursued until dark. The Yankees had failed in their objective of pushing the secessionists out of the state. The Union losses were 13 killed and 31 wounded, and the Missourians had about 40 killed and 120 wounded. The dead and wounded were "concentrated along stream beds, the waterways doubling as giant nets that snagged the flotsam of the battle." Sigel retreated back to the main force under Lyon in Springfield, and the Missourians moved southward to meet up with militia Maj. Gen. Sterling Price, who commanded the State Guard.

WITH EACH SMALL ACTION added to the slowly growing list of Civil War battles, commanders on both sides grew either nervous and cautious about their success or brazenly confident despite the dangers that lay ahead. One of those who would err on the side of caution was George Brinton McClellan, the 34-year-old Pennsylvanian who amassed a sterling record at West Point before embarking on an engineering career in the regular army that left most others in his generation far behind. Short of stature, with dark hair, a mustache, penetrating eyes, and no shortage of apparent cockiness, McClellan earned the sobriquet "Little Mac" among the soldiers who would come to know him. He had served gallantly in the Mexican War. He had acted as an official observer for the War Department during the Crimean War and had ably accomplished position and fortune in civil life, serving as chief engineer of the Illinois Central Railroad and president of the Ohio & Mississippi Railroad. Commissioned a major general of Ohio militia at the outbreak of the war, McClellan now found himself a major general in the regular army, commanding the Army of Occupation (of western Virginia). In McClellan's mind he was the military savior of the Union who should supplant the aged Winfield Scott as general-in-chief. Before moving toward such a heady goal, however, McClellan would have to tangle with not only Confederates but his own sense of how to operate as a field general. "Say to [Scott] . . . that I am trying to follow a lesson long ago learned from him— i.e.—not to move until I know that everything is ready, & then to move with the utmost rapidity & energy."

By July 9, McClellan had concentrated three brigades at Buckhannon and one at Philippi, scene of one of the first minor actions of the war. Now he developed a plan to move his force against the small Confederate Army of the Northwest, consisting of mostly Virginia and Georgia troops, commanded by Brig. Gen. Robert S. Garnett. Garnett had most recently served on the staff of Gen. Robert E. Lee, who by now—with the "nationalization" of Virginia's forces into the Confederacy—was acting as an advisor to Jefferson Davis. But following the embarrassing flight of Confederate troops from Philippi in June, the Confederate War Department sent Garnett to take a field command and reorganize the region, one of two strategically important avenues in western Virginia. From the Confederate perspective, this area was vulnerable to attacking forces from Ohio either through the Baltimore & Ohio Railroad and various roads and turnpikes in the northwestern part of the state or through the Kanawha Valley. Garnett would attempt to counter McClellan's threat in the northwest while another Confederate commander, Brig. Gen. Henry A. Wise, former Virginia governor and cantankerous to one and all, was sent to the Kanawha Valley.

Garnett planned to block McClellan's potential advance at two key places near Beverly, Virginia, in the Tygart River Valley, the only supply depot in the area: at Laurel Hill, where the Beverly-Fairmont Pike crosses the Alleghenies, and on the western side of Rich Mountain on the Staunton-Parkersburg Turnpike. Separated by nine miles, the two positions together would cut off the road by which McClellan could advance and seek reasonable ground from which to offer battle. Confederates occupied both places and fortified them with log breastworks. On July 6, skirmishing erupted at Middle Fork Bridge east of Buckhannon. The following day several slight skirmishes took place at Bellington, Laurel Hill, and Glenville. By July 10, McClellan was ready to gain the positions he sought by battle or simply by maneuver. McClellan sent his most trusted subordinate, Brig. Gen. William S. Rosecrans, forward toward Rich Mountain with four regiments and attached cavalry. Rosecrans, dubbed "Old Rosy" by his men, was an Ohioan with military and civil experience. To his credit, McClellan orchestrated one of the first simultaneous movements of the war by also sending militia Brig. Gen. Thomas A. Morris, who had participated at Philippi, from that position toward Laurel Hill. From Middle Fork Bridge on the 10th, McClellan wrote Townsend that his force was "in sight of the enemy," that "this country [is] exceedingly difficult to operate in," and "all my men [are] eager for the fight." He also asked for more troops, reminding the War Department that he had great difficulties to contend with. As it turned out, the skirmish at Laurel Hill on the 10th was a minor affair.

At Rich Mountain, five miles west of Beverly, Rosecrans found a real battle the next day. McClellan was incensed over Garnett's occasional raids that harassed the Federal supply lines. To counter, he sent about 2,000 men led by Rosecrans to attack the entrenched position of Confederate Lt. Col. John Pegram, a Virginia cavalry officer from Petersburg. Rosecrans brought into battle the 8th, 10th, and 13th Indiana and 19th Ohio infantries and 75 cavalry troopers. Pegram had some 1,300 men and four cannon arrayed and ready for battle, and nine miles away at Laurel Hill, sixteen miles north of Beverly, Garnett had about 4,000 men and four cannon ready to resist the

Yankees. Through a vigorous march over difficult country, in a morning rainstorm, Rosecrans's men surprised Pegram by moving up Rich Mountain and assaulting his left. They moved over the mountain "through a pathless forest, over rocks and ravines, keeping far down on the southeastern declivities of the mountain spurs, and using no ax, to avoid discovery by the enemy, whom we supposed would be on the alert." Pegram had to divide his force and, after three hours of fighting, abandoned the summit, leaving two cannon behind as he scurried off to Beverly. While this was underway, at Laurel Hill, Morris's 4,000 Indiana troops encountered Garnett's force and the two armies fired at each other with enthusiasm. The losses for the day were slight: Rosecrans suffered 12 killed and 49 wounded; the Confederate losses were uncertain. By midnight on July 12, Garnett, feeling the pressure from Morris and believing his route to Beverly was untenable, moved over Cheat Mountain into the Cheat River Valley.

The morning of the 12th witnessed the continuance of the Confederate withdrawal following Rich Mountain. Garnett's men continued moving into the Cheat River Valley, concentrating at Kaler's Ford on the Cheat River, with Morris's Yankees in pursuit. A portion of Pegram's command withdrew to Staunton. The town of Beverly received an occupation force of Federals about noon on this day when McClellan himself arrived. At the same time, the Confederate Brig. Gen. Henry A. Wise, in the Kanawha Valley, was about to see his first opposition. The Ohioan Jacob D. Cox moved northeastward with about 3,000 men from the confluence of the Kanawha and Ohio rivers. Brig. Gen. Cox began by boat as well as marching his men on foot, and on this day they moved well upriver and into the difficult, mountainous terrain.

The situation was now ripe for another battle between the mixed group of forces scattered over the Cheat River Valley. On July 13, Garnett continued his retreat through the Valley, pursued by Morris, in a steady rain that began about 6 A.M., turned heavy about 9 A.M., and by 11 A.M., in Morris's words, "became a drenching storm." The Confederate supply train, pulling up the rear, became bogged down in muddy roads, and skirmishing erupted as Morris's men caught up with the wagons. About noon musket fire crackled along Garnett's rearguard at Corrick's Ford, and Garnett directed the action as it flowed across the landscape, throughout the trees, the mud, and the rain. It was a brief affair, the initial fight lasting about thirty-two minutes. After posting a line of skirmishers, Garnett sat on his horse and watched the opening volley from a Federal advance, one bullet of which struck Garnett in the back. He was mortally wounded, hit with a Minié bullet, and bled to death on the field. Garnett became the first general officer to die in battle in the American Civil War. The news was little better for Pegram on this day. He was forced to surrender 555 men. Pegram himself was captured and would not be exchanged until August 1862.

The battle of Corrick's Ford cost 20 Confederate lives; some 50 of Garnett's men were captured. The Federal loss was reported as anywhere from 10 to 53 wounded. It was a small action that nonetheless delighted observers in Washington and made a hero out of McClellan, despite the fact that Rosecrans was more responsible for it. McClellan had done much to take credit, writing Townsend, "Garnett and forces routed; his baggage and one gun taken; his army demoralized; Garnett killed. We have annihilated the enemy in western Virginia . . . our success is complete, and secession is killed in this country." Although Patterson claimed to be eager for a fight against Gen. Joe Johnston in the Shenandoah Valley, when advancing to Bunker Hill on July 15, he failed to attack. The momentum seemed to be running out in western Virginia, and the tide of attention shifted back toward the larger armies, those of McDowell and Beauregard, with their eyes set on Manassas Junction. On July 16, McDowell began moving his 35,000 men southward from Washington through Alexandria and toward Centreville. They would go after Beauregard's 22,000 men, stationed at Manassas Junction since early June. But before anything significant occurred in this largest movement of a Federal army in the war of 1861, more would develop in the Kanawha Valley of western Virginia.

On July 17, Cox continued his advance along the Kanawha River toward Charleston, encountering for the first time Rebel soldiers commanded by Wise. Cox anticipated regrouping at Pocotaligo for several days and rebuilding a key bridge that had been burned by the Confederates. On the morning of the 17th he sent the 12th Ohio Infantry commanded by Lt. Col. Carr B. White (a boyhood friend of Ulysses S. Grant), along the river on the Charleston Road, to reconnoiter. As they approached Scarey Creek, White's men found the enemy and were fired upon by Confederates stationed in an old log house. Cox prepared to attack. At 2 P.M. Federal cavalry found Confederate pickets and drove them back toward Scarey Creek, initiating an infantry skirmish. The Yankees initially drove the Confederate troops through, but the Federal attack faltered and eventually Cox's men retreated, with 10 killed and 35 wounded. "Our generals will resolve never to survive a defeat," wrote the war clerk John B. Jones in his diary. In the end, the action checked Cox's advance through the Kanawha Valley for a week, during which time events elsewhere in Virginia would begin to define the whole character of the early part of the war.

IRVIN McDOWELL'S ARMY of Northeastern Virginia moved westward toward Centreville and Manassas on July 16, some 35,000 strong. Pushed into action largely by public pressure, the movement appeared to many Yankees to be the first indication that any serious attempt to put down the rebellion was underway. Thus, hopes for its success were extremely high, and many believed that a single crushing defeat of the Rebels would end the war in an afternoon. Assisted by Capt. James B. Fry, his assistant adjutant general, Brig. Gen. McDowell had organized his army into divisions on July 8. These were commanded by Brig. Gen. Daniel Tyler, Col. David Hunter, Brig. Gen. Samuel P. Heintzelman, Brig. Gen. Theodore Runyon, and Col. Dixon S. Miles. The competence and experience of his division commanders were generally poor (although they were believed to be good), creating headaches and confusion during the first large battle of the war. As it turned out, Runyon's 4th Division was held mostly in reserve, and Miles's division was entirely in reserve and would help cover what became the Federal retreat. Each brigade had its own attached artillery units, comprising about fifty-three guns.

McDowell's army followed a path based on the ill-formed notion that if it captured the Rebel capital, the strategic objective of the war would be fulfilled. This was an idea that was widely believed and preached by European militarists of the era. It would take months and many bloody battles for commanders on both sides to realize that in order to win they would have to destroy enemy armies rather than simply occupy territory. So in this first campaign McDowell headed south. Patterson was still in the Shenandoah, west of Harpers Ferry, and Maj. Gen. Benjamin F. Butler, even less experienced than most of the other Federal officers and in command of the Department of Virginia, still occupied Fort Monroe.

On the Confederate side, the commands were more complex. Occupying Manassas, and inevitably blocking McDowell's approach to Richmond, was Gen. P. G. T. Beauregard's Army of the Potomac, alternatively designated I Corps, which consisted of about 20,000 men and which was brigaded on July 20. The brigade commanders were Brig. Gen. Milledge Luke Bonham, Brig. Gen. Richard S. Ewell, Brig. Gen. David R. "Neighbor" Jones, Brig. Gen. James Longstreet, Col. Philip St. George Cocke, Col. Jubal A. Early, Col. Nathan G. "Shanks" Evans, and Brig. Gen. Theophilus H. Holmes (Reserve Brigade). In addition to its infantry, Beauregard's army had attached artillery (ten batteries comprising forty guns) and cavalry (four regiments, all from Virginia).

Beauregard's army was not the only one active in the First Bull Run campaign. Out to the west, at Winchester, sat Gen. Joe Johnston's Army of the Shenandoah, alternatively designated II Corps, which consisted of about 12,000 men. Johnston similarly organized his army into brigades, which were commanded by Col. Thomas J. Jackson (1st Brigade), Col. Francis S. Bartow (2d Brigade), Brig. Gen. Barnard E. Bee (3d Brigade), Brig. Gen. Edmund Kirby Smith (4th Brigade), and Col. John H. Forney (5th Brigade). In addition to the infantry, Johnston had five batteries of artillery (20 guns) and attached cavalry commanded by another up-and-coming Virginian, Col.

James E. B. Stuart, who had assisted Robert E. Lee in 1859 at Harpers Ferry. Called Jeb and often "Beauty" due to his fine appearance, Stuart was merely 28 but already developing a reputation as a dashing cavalier and experienced horseman.

As McDowell advanced, Beauregard was ready for him. Holmes was in reserve down along Aquia Creek. Though he was west of the Shenandoah River, if necessary Johnston could quickly march south and take the Manassas Gap Railroad eastward to reinforce Beauregard at Manassas Junction. After two days of marching, McDowell's army reached Centreville on July 18 and was exhausted and hungry. The march was characterized by confused orders, extreme caution, and an utter lack of discipline among many of the troops. It was an inauspicious start to a war in which much longer marches would be made in much shorter times by later, veteran armies. Patterson had moved to Bunker Hill and then to Charles Town and was himself unclear about what the War Department expected of him, despite Scott's frequent messages (some of which were ambiguous). Patterson claimed to be alarmed about the possibility of moving to Winchester and pursuing the Rebels because many of his men had enlisted for three months' service at the end of April. He believed their enlistments might expire during the campaign. Thus, by July 18, Patterson's force sat in confusion at Charles Town and had no idea where Johnston was. Johnston was pulling out and moving southeastward to reinforce Beauregard, Stuart's cavalry having moved up to screen Johnston from any detection of his southward movement. Partly through Confederate maneuvering but mostly through his own ignorance, Patterson had unwittingly taken himself out of the campaign. Johnston's movement resulted from an order from President Davis shortly after midnight on the 18th, asking Johnston to reinforce Beauregard "if practicable." The act was a major first in two ways: it was the first time Davis interposed himself into actively running a campaign, which he would do frequently in the future, and it was the first time that gentlemanly phrases in the Confederate military were used that could open avenues of confusion over subsequent actions. Davis's hedging, couched in the phrase "if practicable," meant the whole notion might be ignored. Fortunately for Davis, Johnston was a highly capable general officer and moved ahead. Others who would repeatedly use this phrase—most notoriously Robert E. Lee—would sometimes be burned by junior commanders who felt that it just wasn't "practicable."

The first great battlefront of the war was arranged on July 18, when Beauregard spread his army along Bull Run from the Stone Bridge of the Warrenton Turnpike in the north to Union Mills Ford on the Orange & Alexandria Railroad in the south. He arranged his seven brigades on the southern bank of the creek with care to block the approaching Federals from crossing, spread over a four-and-three-quarter-mile line oriented from northwest to southeast: Evans protected the Stone Bridge; Cocke scattered his units from Lewis Ford to Ball's Ford and finally Island Ford; Bonham protected Mitchell's Ford; Longstreet occupied Blackburn's Ford; Jones spread over McLean's Ford; and Ewell secured Union Mills Ford where the Orange & Alexandria crossed Bull Run. McDowell, meanwhile, resting his men at Centreville, reduced his number to 30,000 by detaching Theodore Runyon with 5,000 troops to march eastward to guard the army's rear. Just one mile southwest of the Stone Bridge stood Henry House Hill, topographically significant as an artillery position, with Bald Hill behind it, Matthews Hill to the north, Stony Ridge (Sudley Mountain) to the northwest, and Mt. Pone to the south. Few structures stood in the area. About two and three-fourths miles south of Mitchell's Ford lay Manassas Junction, where the railroad lines came together. Some two miles southwest of the Stone Bridge, on the turnpike, stood the little village of Groveton, a small group of tiny houses. North of Stony Ridge lay the little group of buildings at Sudley Springs, one of them a small Methodist Church.

It appeared on this day that Beauregard placed his troops well by guarding the river crossings and readying his men to advance onto high ground if they were pushed back. This excellent preparation, in fact, came with a little help. Washington socialite Rose O'Neal Greenhow, a strong woman with powerful Southern sympathies, lived in the Federal capital and maintained an influential network of friends on both sides of the divided nation. In July 1861 this intelligent, dominating woman of about 56 years developed the knack for simple spying. She sent two messages in cipher—the first on July 9 smuggled in the coiffure of a lady courier—attempting to analyze the strength of the Union armies and announcing their intended movements to Maj. Thomas Jordan, an assistant adjutant general of Beauregard. Although both the predicted strength of the Union army and the timing of McDowell's advance were off, the message alerted Beauregard and shook him into serious preparation. For Greenhow, however, the exercise proved costly when the Washington detective Allan Pinkerton arrested her the following month, consigning her to the Old Capitol Prison.

McDowell, of course, had no idea that the Confederate forces knew he was coming. He also had a reasonably sound plan. He planned to march southward and turn Beauregard's right flank. On the 18th, McDowell sent a force forward toward Blackburn's Ford and Mitchell's Ford to reconnoiter the Confederate position. Dan Tyler moved along a prominent ridge that extended southward from Centreville toward the creek, and when he reached the edge of the formation—after some random artillery fire—he detached a force to scurry down to the water's edge, a distance of about a half a mile, to check both fords. It consisted of his 4th Brigade, troops commanded by Col. Israel B. Richardson, a Vermonter and hard-nosed veteran of the Mexican War called "Fighting Dick" by his men. The reconnaissance did not work well for the Yankees, however. Richardson pushed the movement too far, touching off a brisk engagement with Longstreet's troops at Blackburn's Ford. Skirmishing also erupted at Mitchell's Ford. This went against McDowell's orders. Not only were the fords well defended, Richardson discovered, but what he did not know was even more significant: Early's brigade stood behind Longstreet, ready to counterattack if necessary. As the brisk crackle of musketry opened along the line and several booming cannon belched forth, the enemy opened a heavy fire, causing Richardson's brigade, the 12th New York, to fall back in confusion. After the infantry fight, artillerists continued to fire upon the Confederate lines for some time. "The enemy's intrenchments and batteries appeared to be in rear of a creek called Bull Run," Richardson wrote in his report. It was the first time this name, which would weigh so heavily on Union morale, came to the army's attention. The Union losses in this confused action were 19 killed, 38 wounded, and 26 missing. The Confederate defenders sustained losses of 15 killed and 53 wounded. Beauregard took stock of the fight at his headquarters in the Wilmer McLean House, located two-thirds of a mile south of Blackburn's Ford. "A comical effect of this artillery fight was the destruction of the dinner of myself and staff by a Federal shell that fell into the fire-place of my headquarters at the McLean house," Beauregard later recalled.

The action at Blackburn's Ford forced McDowell to rethink his plan. The creek had steep, muddy slopes leading to its banks and the approaches were untenable under a heavy fire. The scattered retreat of Richardson's force demoralized them and spread fear throughout other elements of the Union army. Conversely, it emboldened Beauregard. "Let to-morrow be their Waterloo," Beauregard told his staff on July 19. The psychological edge would prove significant. McDowell sat in position on this day and did little to prepare except for moving supplies forward and cooking more rations. The hours that ticked away were golden for the Confederacy: Johnston was speeding toward reinforcing Beauregard from the Shenandoah Valley, where Patterson still waited, perplexed by Stuart's screen. On the evening of the 19th, Beauregard held council in the McLean House, and he was startled when Col. Thomas J. Jackson walked in and announced the impending arrival of Johnston's army, as soon as minor delays along the single-track railroad were ironed out. Jackson himself had brought 2,500 troops.

By daybreak on July 20 both sides sensed an imminent major action along Bull Run. During the day, Confederates along the creek worked on fortifying their positions. McDowell's plan evolved into a rather complex one that he optimistically expected his inexperienced army to carry out with precision, and it also required Patterson to prevent Johnston from coming to the aid of Beauregard, something that Patterson had by now already failed to do. The divisions of Samuel P. Heintzelman and David Hunter would cross Bull Run at Sudley Ford and threaten the railroad line leading to the Valley by moving south and occupying it. The coordinated effort would see Tyler's division attacking in force at the Stone Bridge, with his brigade commander Israel Richardson harassing the Confederates at Blackburn's Ford, where they were concentrated, to hold them from moving northwestward and thwarting the main attack. Miles's division was held in reserve. On the Confederate side, the opportunity for battle was strengthened significantly on July 20. Johnston arrived from the Valley with all his force except for Kirby Smith, who was still in transit. His army stood behind Early's position south of the three fords: Mitchell's, Blackburn's, and McLean's. In addition, Holmes arrived on the 19th from Aquia Creek and situated his men behind Ewell at Union Mills Ford. From Beauregard's point of view, the plan was to launch an attack northward to Centreville by way of Blackburn's and Mitchell's fords. Although Johnston ranked Beauregard, he approved of the plan and allowed Beauregard to exercise general field command.

Both plans were sound, and if executed simultaneously might have resulted in both armies dancing in a great counterclockwise circle. Late at night on the 20th a Federal soldier anticipated the great battle to come as he lay on the ground looking skyward. "This is one of the most beautiful nights that the imagination can conceive," he wrote. "The sky is perfectly clear, the moon is full and bright, and the air is as still as if it were not within a few hours to be disturbed by the roar of cannon and the shouts of contending men." At 2:30 A.M. on July 21, McDowell sent his lead columns of Heintzelman and Hunter toward Sudley Ford, and they marched southwestward along the Warrenton Turnpike before turning northwest to march toward their destination. Tyler's column marched straight down the turnpike toward the Stone Bridge. With the plans laid out carefully on both sides, now they came down to a matter of execution.

In the quiet anticipation of early morning on July 21, the First Battle of Bull Run, or Manassas, began. As the Federal army approached the Stone Bridge, a Confederate soldier described the scene: "The stirring mass looked like a bristling monster lifting himself by a slow, wavy motion up the laborious ascent." As elements of Richardson's brigade approached Mitchell's Ford, they unleashed a few stray shots along with some artillery fire. It was 5:15 A.M. and the Confederate commander received a rude announcement that the Yankees had preempted his battle plan. As he stood in the Wilmer McLean House, preparing to eat breakfast with his staff, a shell struck the tent of his engineering and signal officer, Capt. Edward Porter Alexander, announcing the Federal army's arrival. Although the Confederates had been surprised by McDowell's attack, on the northwest side of the field Shanks Evans had identified the threat and moved some of his men out to meet the

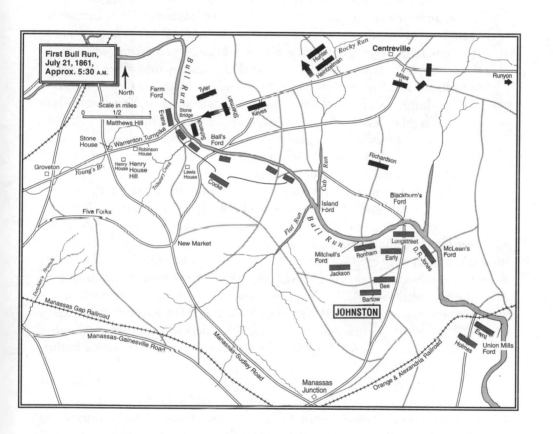

approach of Tyler. Capt. Alexander had spotted the glint of sunlight on a cannon some eight miles away as it was dragged toward Sudley Ford. He sent an immediate message to Evans: "Look out for your left: You are flanked." Evans responded well by leaving some of his force to block the Stone Bridge, which was now being approached by Brig. Gen. Robert C. Schenck of Tyler's division, the Ohioan who had found himself ambushed at Vienna the previous month. But Evans took most of his force and marched it westward to anticipate the Federal advance across Sudley Ford.

With the discovery that Yankees were moving on his left, Beauregard began ordering attacks on the Federal left toward Centreville. Whereas the Federal plan required a precise execution by inexperienced commanders, the new, improvised Confederate plan would be beset by poor communication, bungled orders, and poor staff work by Beauregard's green assistants. Ewell, down at Union Mills Ford, was to lead the attack on Centreville. But he was simply ordered to "hold . . . in readiness to advance at a moment's notice." Neighbor Jones, who was supposed to attack in support of Ewell's advance, moved forward and found himself alone. As the morning continued, Beauregard moved some of Johnston's troops—those of Bee, Bartow, and Jackson—toward the Confederate center.

While Beauregard scrambled to control the battle, Hunter's division reached Sudley Ford about 9:30 A.M. He found the ground south of Bull Run blocked by Evans, however. As the crackle of musketry heated up along the battle line, commanders on both sides were cautious and scared. After firing a volley, a line of men fell back to reload, and officers achieving success in attacking were often slow in hopes of gaining still more ground. At this stage in the war, battle was like holding a branding iron of unknown warmth, as described by Capt. Edward Porter Alexander. Was it just uncomfortably warm or hot enough "to make the flesh sizzle?" Soldiers did not pick up the iron without testing it and dropping it a few times, until it felt comfortable, Alexander explained.

The way the battle was progressing did not feel comfortable to Beauregard. He ordered a demonstration against the Federal left while concentrating his army on Henry House Hill, high ground that would command the Manassas-Sudley Road. The solitary structure near the summit of this hill was the Judith Henry Farmhouse, Spring Hill, the home of an aged widow whose husband had once been a surgeon's mate on the USS *Constellation*. Now Mrs. Henry, ill and unable to flee, was trapped in the clapboard house. As the battle surrounded them, Mrs. Henry's daughter hid inside the chimney, their hired black servant under the bed. Before the day was out, the widow Henry was struck by flying debris from an exploding shell and died inside the house, mortally wounded in the neck, side, and foot. Today she lies buried outside her reconstructed home. On the northern edge of the hill, near the Warrenton Turnpike, stood the James Robinson House, the small home of a free black man. Around the northern edge of Henry House Hill runs a little tributary of Bull Run called Young's Branch. Along this position Evans hammered away at the advancing Federals, succeeding in pushing Hunter northward again.

Meanwhile, an acerbic, red-haired Ohioan, Col. William T. Sherman, led his brigade of Tyler's division across an unguarded ford, Farm Ford, and attacked westward toward Matthews Hill—north of Henry House Hill— where elements of Bartow, Bee, and Evans were posted. Sherman's attack surprised Bartow's right flank and thwarted the line comprised of Bartow, Bee, and Evans, along with pressure from the north—coming chiefly from a brigade commander, Col. Ambrose E. Burnside, and a battalion commander, Maj. George Sykes. Johnston had established his headquarters near the center of the battle line at the M. Lewis Farm, Portici, near which he and Beauregard watched the morning's action unfold from Lookout Hill. Johnston had for some two hours believed that the action to the north was merely a feint. The noise, smoke, and action on the Confederate left only increased as the minutes ticked by, however. By 11 A.M., he could stand it no more. "The battle is there. I am going," he told Beauregard. By 11:30 A.M., the Federal attack by Sherman and firing from the north forced the Confederate battle-front back onto Henry House Hill in what was beginning to appear like a disordered rout. There were signs of hope for the Confederates, however: Capt. John D. Imboden, commanding a battery of four 6-pounder guns positioned on Henry House Hill, valiantly fought off the onrushing Yankees and helped the retreating Confederates regroup. More important, Kirby Smith's brigade was arriving at Manassas Junction and would swing north to reinforce the Rebels already being tested in battle.

By early afternoon the fight at Bull Run was heating up dramatically on Henry House Hill. The temperature had climbed into the low eighties, and there were just a few scattered clouds in the otherwise stark blue sky. The air was still, although this did not prevent the smell of powder and thick clouds of smoke from slowly rising across and over the battlefield. Arrayed on the southern side of the hill, and along part of its crest, was an S-shaped curve of mixed Confederate soldiers who had formed in chaos to hold the position. They consisted of the brigades of Jackson, Bee, Bartow, and Evans. Stuart's cavalry was deployed to the left at the foot of Bald Hill. The Federals leading the attack against Henry House Hill were comprised of the brigades of Sherman and Cols. William B. Franklin, Andrew Porter, Orlando B. Willcox, and Erasmus D. Keyes. Beauregard and Johnston arrived on the hill in time to meet the discouraged veterans of the battle to the north, reforming them into semicoherence. As the fighting continued, Jackson, in the face of a possible collapse of the Rebel line, rallied his troops, prompting the famous comment of Bee, "There is Jackson, standing like a stone wall! Let us determine to die here, and we will conquer! Follow me!" Jackson's sobriquet stuck; he was ever after known as Stonewall.

The man who created the famous phrase, however, would not be destined for fame and glory. A short time later, placed to the left of the 4th Alabama Infantry, Bee led a charge on Henry House Hill and was struck in the abdomen by a Minié bullet. The next day he died in a rude cabin four miles from the front. Bartow was also struck down, hit in the chest as he sat atop his horse; his last words allegedly were, "They have killed me; but, boys, never give it up." Jackson himself was wounded, hit in the middle finger of his left hand with a bullet or piece of shell. Jackson's odd behavior of thrusting his left arm upward, palm facing forward, had exposed his hand, which he had then wrapped in a kerchief. (Several of Jackson's subordinates attributed the gesture to an appeal to the Almighty for good results in battle.) As waves of attacks and countercharges on the hill continued, the fight raged at full caliber to become the most vicious engagement yet seen by most of its participants. "Now for a yellow sash or six feet of ground," said Col. Arnold Elzey, commander of the 1st Maryland Infantry, thinking he would be commissioned a brigadier general or be killed. Johnston retreated to the rear in order to coordinate troops coming from Manassas Junction. Beauregard supervised troops on the spot, as did McDowell and many of his commanders. The Yankee officers Hunter, Heintzelman, Franklin, and Burnside all led regiments, leaving their divisional and brigade duties neglected.

By about 2 P.M. McDowell determined to press with all he could to make the Federal attack a success. The artillery batteries of Capts. James B. Ricketts (Battery I, 1st U.S. Artillery) and Charles Griffin (Battery D, 5th U.S. Artillery) were posted southwest of the main Federal line, as were the 11th New York Infantry (Ellsworth's Fire Zouaves) and the 84th New York Infantry (14th Brooklyn), units outfitted with colorful, European-style uniforms, in support of the guns. McDowell's infantry outnumbered the Confederates on the hill by a factor of two. The battle raged furiously back and forth, appearing that it could go either way. The Federal artillery engaged in a furious cannonade with Jackson's guns. Now one of the great mix-ups of the early part of the war occurred. At this time the uniforms on both sides were hardly standardized: Some Federal troops wore a kind of dark gray while some Southerners wore blue. The 33d Virginia Infantry, led by Col. Arthur C. Cummings, was one of these units clothed in blue. Its soldiers approached the guns of the two Federal batteries, which were holding their fire, believing the 33d Virginia to be Federal soldiers. As Cummings's regiment got close, they opened a murderous volley on the gunners, killing and wounding many of them, and driving the Zouaves away in confusion. Nearly simultaneously, Stuart's cavalry drove against the exposed flank of the

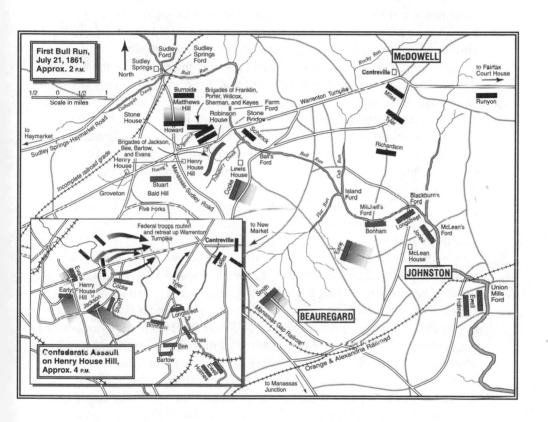

First Bull Run,
July 21, 1861,
Approx. 2 P.M.

North

1/2 0 1/2 1
Scale in miles

McDOWELL

Centreville

to Fairfax
Court House

Sudley
Ford

Sudley
Springs
Ford

Sudley
Springs

Bull Run

Catharpin Creek

Burnside

Matthews
Hill

Brigades of Franklin,
Porter, Willcox,
Sherman, and Keyes

Farm
Ford

Warrenton Turnpike

Miles

Runyon

Stone
House

Howard

Robinson
House

Stone
Bridge

Tyler

to Haymarket

Sudley Springs-Haymarket Road

Branch

Schenck

Richardson

Incomplete railroad grade

Brigades of Jackson,
Bee, Bartow,
and Evans

Henry
House

Henry
House
Hill

Thoroughfare Creek

Ball's
Ford

Bull Run

Club Run

Blackburn's
Ford

Groveton

Stuart

Bald Hill

Five Forks

Manassas-Sudley Road

Young's

Lewis
House

Cocke

Island
Ford

Pitt Run

Mitchell's
Ford

Bonham

Longstreet

Jones

McLean's
Ford

to New
Market

Early

McLean
House

JOHNSTON

Union
Mills
Ford

Smith

Manassas Gap Railroad

BEAUREGARD

Ewell

Holmes

Orange & Alexandria Railroad

to Manassas
Junction

Rocky Run

Federal troops routed
and retreat up Warrenton
Turnpike

Centreville

Miles

Evans

Henry
House
Hill

Early

Cocke

Tyler

Jackson

Stuart

Longstreet

Bonham

Jones

Bee

Bartow

Ewell

Holmes

Confederate Assault
on Henry House Hill,
Approx. 4 P.M.

Zouaves, scattering them and ruining the organization of Yankee troops on the southwestern part of Henry House Hill. The loss of the guns proved disastrous for the Federal side. "The battle was not lost till they were lost," wrote Col. James B. Fry. Of the mix-up with the 33d Virginia, Fry termed it "a fatal mistake."

The tide of battle was now turning. What had been a largely successful attack by the Union army, always a more difficult option than defending ground, was about to unravel. The Yankees counterattacked and retook the position where the guns had been posted, but by this time Confederate reinforcements were arriving on the field. Jackson was rapidly becoming the hero of the day. As he ordered another attack, he told soldiers of the 4th Virginia Infantry, "Reserve your fire until they come within fifty yards! Then fire and give them the bayonet! And when you charge, yell like furies!" For the first time, troops on the field heard the eerie sound of what became known as the "Rebel yell." Although a brigade under Col. Oliver O. Howard was marching southward on the Manassas-Sudley Road, attempting to reinforce the attack on Henry House Hill, it would be too little, too late. None of the other Federal units in the vicinity came to the fight—not Tyler, not Burnside, and not Miles. And of course, Patterson remained in the Shenandoah Valley, out of the way.

By 4 P.M. the momentum seemed securely in Confederate hands. Kirby Smith and Early arrived on the scene to reinforce the strong stand on Henry House Hill. The mixed brigades of Jackson, Bee, Bartow, Evans, and Cocke now commanded the hill. To the south stood Kirby Smith's men (Kirby Smith was wounded and replaced by Elzey), Early, and Stuart's cavalry. The forward Federal line of battle had been pushed north to the foot of Henry House Hill and the larger, secondary line stretched along Young's Branch from Bald Hill in the south to the foot of Matthews Hill in the north. With the pressure of a greater fire of musketry from the reinforcements and artillery placed well on the hill, the Yankee position was untenable, and a withdrawal began. Once begun, with Confederate artillery fire continuing, and the Federal troops demoralized, the withdrawal took on almost comic proportions. Hundreds of spectators had taken wagons laden with picnic supplies out west of Washington City to see the big battle of the war. Newsmen and politicians as well as plain civilians got caught in the accelerating Federal retreat. Initially, much of the army, moving along the Manassas-Sudley Road and across the Stone Bridge on the Warrenton Turnpike, had behaved well. The retreat was poorly supervised by officers, however. When a Confederate shell struck the bridge with troops on it, panic ensued, and many of the troops skedaddled all the way to Washington.

"I perceived several wagons coming from the direction of the battlefield," wrote the English journalist William Howard Russell, "the drivers of which were endeavoring to force their horses past the ammunition carts going in the contrary direction near the bridge; a thick cloud of dust rose behind them, and running by the side of the wagons were a number of men in uniform whom I supposed to be the guard. My first impression was that the wagons were returning for fresh supplies of ammunition. But every moment the crowd increased; drivers and men cried out with the most vehement gestures: 'Turn back! Turn back! We are whipped.' " Near the bridge, watching the scene of confusion, stood a U.S. representative, Alfred Ely of New York. Ely had accompanied the 13th New York Infantry to watch the battle; after his carriage broke down, he hid in the woods for a short time but was soon captured. He spent nearly six months in Richmond as a prisoner, finding his home at Liggon's Tobacco Warehouse in the Rocketts section of the city, which had been designated CSA Prison No. 1. Not only for Ely, but for all of the North, it was a humiliating end to what had almost been a Federal victory.

The casualties and disarray of the Union army shocked Washington and the rest of the nation. The Federal army had lost 460 men, with 1,124 wounded and 1,312 missing; Confederate losses were 387 killed, 1,582 wounded, and 13 missing. The figures stunned all who heard them, although they would pale in comparison to the battles to come. Curiously, Capt. Francis C. Armstrong, known as Frank, fought well with the 2d U.S. Cavalry at First Bull Run, but he would soon have a change of heart. Armstrong defected to the Confederate States on August 13, 1861, and later was commissioned a brigadier general in the Confederate army. He thus became the only high commander of the Civil War to fight on both sides during the conflict.

Much has been made of the disastrous psychological blow First Bull Run caused for the Union army and the Lincoln government, and certainly it was a great disappointment relative to the naïve and grandiose expectations of easy victory and a quick end to the war. Yet the Confederate army gained nothing from the encounter either. The victorious Jackson pushed for a pursuit of the Yankee army, but Johnston and Beauregard knew that their forces were in no shape to do any such thing. The great Southern military analyst Jefferson Davis, president of the Confederate States, had arrived on the field along with his aide and nephew Lt. Col. Joseph R. Davis near the end of the fight. In jubilation, he made what is probably the only real "battlefield promotion" of the war by appointing Beauregard a general in the Army of the Confederate States of America. "Enough was done for glory, and the measure of duty was full," Davis later wrote Beauregard of the battle. The celebration on the Southern side was almost universal. "Whilst great credit is due to other parts of our gallant army, God made my brigade more instrumental than any other in repulsing the main attack," Stonewall Jackson wrote his wife the next day. "This is for your information only—say nothing about it. Let others speak praise, not myself." "I have seen the great and glorious battle of Manassas, which brought a nation into existence," wrote the Confederate doctor J. C. Nott, "and the scene was grand and impressive beyond the power of language. . . . from all accounts, no red fox ever tracks, so fast as did these cowardly wretches. . . . If our men had been equally fresh they would have gone straight into their intrenchments at Arlington."

Sherman wrote his wife of the horrors of the field on July 28. "Then for the first time I saw the carnage of battle, men lying in every conceivable shape, and mangled in a horrible way." Sherman described "horses running about riderless with blood streaming from their nostrils, lying on the ground hitched to guns, gnawing their sides in death." "There is no way I can tell you about the battle so that you get the faintest idea of it," wrote Charles Cheney of the 2d Wisconsin Infantry. "None but those who saw it know anything about it. . . . There were hundreds shot down right in my sight; some had their heads shot off from their shoulders by cannon balls; others were shot in two in the middle, and others shot through the legs and arms. . . . Cannon balls were flying like hail."

In the ranks of the soldiers, the question of future battles and how they would play out now loomed large. "During the day one of the boys brought in a Virginia paper in which it was stated that one 'Southerner could lick five Northern mudsills,' " reported Charles E. Davis, a soldier in the 13th Massachusetts Infantry. "It was not so very comforting to feel that we were to be killed off in blocks of five." "I have no doubt that barring as few lives and legs and arms lost, they'll all like it and be the better for it," suggested Henry Brooks Adams of the experience of soldiers in battle, ". . . One's health is just as likely to be benefited as to be hurt by a campaign, bullets and all."

The meaning of the battle eluded most who attempted to understand it. In Lynchburg, civilian Susan Blackford wrote, "The sound of the cannon were distinctly heard on the hills of Lynchburg, and we well knew that a great battle was being fought from early morn until sunset, and that not only the fate of our country and homes was at stake, but that each boom which stirred the air might be fraught with the dying sigh of those we loved best." Some Southerners were still wrought with apprehension. "Trescot says this victory will be our ruin," wrote Mary Chesnut on July 24. "It lulls us into a fool's paradise of conceit at our superior valor. And the shameful farce of their flight will wake every inch of their manhood. It was the very fillip they needed."

On the Federal side the response was delirium. "Today will be known as BLACK MONDAY," wrote George Templeton Strong on hearing the news of Bull Run. "We are utterly and disgracefully routed, beaten, whipped by secessionists." "Scott's campaign is wholly destroyed and he must now go to work and reconstruct it," wrote the attorney Charles Francis Adams, Jr.—grandson of John Quincy Adams—to his father. "While our army is demoralised, theirs is in the same degree consolidated. Their ultimate independence is I think assured." Patterson was removed from his command. The Federal high command ordered Maj. Gen. George McClellan to come east to take command of the army so humiliated. He assumed command of the Military Division of the Potomac, including all troops in the Washington area, on July 27. "By some strange operation of magic I seem to have become *the* power of the land," he wrote his wife on this day. "I almost think that were I to win some small success now I could become Dictator or anything else that might please me—but nothing of that kind would please me—*therefore* I *won't* be Dictator. Admirable self denial!" Three days later he wrote again. "Who would have thought when we were married, that I should so soon be called upon to save my country?" But McClellan was not yet convinced that he was in a position of sufficient power, nor that the men who surrounded him were as much up to the task as he was. "I am here in a terrible place," he wrote of Washington. "The enemy have from 3 to 4 times my force—the Presdt is an idiot, the old General in his dotage—they cannot or will not see the true state of affairs." McClellan's messianic view of himself as the one predestined by God as the savior of the Union would only increase as the weeks passed. Other major generals assumed new roles: John A. Dix took over the Department of Maryland; William S. Rosecrans now commanded the Department of the Ohio; Nathaniel P. Banks, a Massachusetts politician, replaced Patterson; and John C. Frémont, a celebrated army officer, explorer, and failed first Republican candidate for president, took command of the Western Department in St. Louis.

Despite the shuffling, the blues pervaded the Union cause. "The dreadful disaster of last Sunday can scarcely be mentioned," wrote the politician Edwin M. Stanton. "The imbecility of this Administration culminated in that catastrophe—an irretrievable misfortune and national disgrace never to be forgotten. . . . the capture of Washington seems now to be inevitable."

SUCH A NOTION could not have been further from the truth. The Confederates had neither the strength nor the resources to invade Washington, which was growing more heavily fortified each day. Skirmishing erupted at Gauley Bridge, Virginia, and in Missouri, but was minor; the nation was for the most part quiet during the last days of July 1861. A minor affair took place at Fort Fillmore in New Mexico Territory on July 26–27. The Federal garrison of this fort, the 7th U.S. Infantry, was commanded by veteran regular army Major Isaac Lynde. His force of 500, located near San Augustine Springs, outnumbered the approaching Confederates by a factor of two, yet Lynde pulled out of the fort on July 26 and made tracks for Fort Stanton. The next day the Confederates, commanded by Lt. Col. John R. Baylor, a hard-fighting Texan, received Lynde's surrender without firing a single shot. The U.S. War Department was none too happy: his commission was dropped on November 25. Lynde's surrender left a large tract of New Mexico Territory wide open for Confederate occupation.

The first days of August brought a sense of awakening to both sides of the great American conflict. In the east, minor affairs characterized the early part of the month. Gen. Robert E. Lee left his desk job advising President Davis in Richmond and went to the mountains in western Virginia, hoping to coordinate and oversee the confused commands that had led to several Federal victories. He brought a fighting spirit with him, yet recalled earlier, happier days in 1840 traveling the same road into the mountains. "If anyone had told me that the next time I travelled that road would have been on my present errand, I should have supposed him insane." Tensions rose in the area of Fort Monroe, where Maj. Gen. Benjamin F. Butler was in departmental command. They rose among Butler's own troops because he banned the sale and consumption of liquors, but many of the soldiers won this battle by smuggling and hiding their alcohol inside small containers slipped into gun barrels. More seriously, however, the Confederate Brig. Gen. John B. Magruder, who had fought Butler at Big Bethel, attacked the village of Hampton, Virginia, on August 7. Situated near Fort Monroe, Hampton held a mere 1,848 inhabitants at the time. Magruder brought his force into the town on this Wednesday and burned the village, believing that Butler would use the town as a staging area for concentrating black American refugees, termed "runaway slaves" by Magruder and "contraband" by Butler. Despite his political background and general incompetence as a field general, Butler was on the leading edge of pushing the issues of emancipation and resettlement of freed slaves and black refugees with the Lincoln government. The Confederates fired the town "in a great number of places," Butler reported, and "by 12 o'clock it was in flames, and is now entirely destroyed." Magruder pushed forward with this movement despite the fact that a great percentage of his men was afflicted with measles. And, as Butler put it, "I confess myself so poor a soldier as not to be able to discern the strategical importance of this movement."

In the West, events were heating up with a somewhat more strategic purpose. Brig. Gen. Nathaniel Lyon's Federal "Army of the West" was expecting a serious action with the Rebels in southwestern Missouri. During the first days of August the new departmental commander, Frémont, moved down the Mississippi with supplies, reinforcements, and ships in order to bolster the army's strength. They arrived at Cairo, Illinois, on August 2. While a Federal reconnaissance scouted southeastern Missouri from Ironton to Centerville on this day, so, too, did a skirmish erupt near Springfield at Dug Springs. Lyon's troops, numbering 5,868, were in poor condition when he detected the Confederates moving toward Springfield. They had scant rations except for meat, which caused an outbreak of diarrhea among his troops, and were in need of good-quality water. After marching toward the Confederates under militia Brig. Gen. James S. Rains, they halted on August 2. Rains's men attacked with a force of 1,000 infantry led by cavalry. The Union loss was slight, with four killed and five wounded. The Confederate loss was also slight. During the skirmish a detachment of 150 men under Capt. James McIntosh reconnoitered the Federal position with the intent to aid Rains. But McIntosh found that Rains "had engaged the enemy unadvisedly, and had sent for my small command to re-enforce him, which I respectfully declined, having no disposition to sacrifice it in such company."

The skirmish at Dug Springs was a minor affair that is notable only as a precursor to the battle that followed. On August 9, Confederate troops and state troops loyal to the South moved within ten miles of Springfield along Wilson's Creek. Lyon's army, of course, needed to prevent a capture of the city and wanted to defeat them to oust the Confederacy's influence from Missouri at once.

The battle of Wilson's Creek unfolded on August 10, with Brig. Gen. Lyon's force of about 5,600 outnumbered by about 10,175 Confederates under Brig. Gen. Ben McCulloch and 5,221 troops of the Missouri State Guard under Maj. Gen. Sterling Price. The Confederate commanders offered a distinct contrast. McCulloch was a rough-hewn product of Tennessee who at an early age had traveled with Davy Crockett to Texas. McCulloch had served in the Mexican War, gone to California in search of gold, and received the surrender of Maj. Gen. David E. Twiggs in San Antonio earlier in 1861. Price, nicknamed "Pap," was a Virginian who had moved to Missouri in 1831 before beginning a career as a volunteer soldier in the Mexican War and as a politician, culminating in the governorship of Missouri. The Confederate forces were arranged into three so-called divisions, and although Price held the higher grade, after a fair amount of argument between Price and McCulloch, the two commanders agreed on appointing McCulloch field commander. McCulloch's force consisted of mixed Arkansas, Louisiana, and South Kansas–Texas troops, mostly mounted rifles with cavalry. A second division was commanded by Arkansas militia Brig. Gen. Nicholas B. Pearce. His force now consisted of Arkansas infantry, cavalry, and two four-gun batteries of artillery. Lastly, Price's division was comprised of five "districts," each commanded by a brigadier general of Missouri militia. Price's commanders were James S. Rains, John Bullock Clark, Sr., William Y. Slack, Mosby M. Parsons, and James H. McBride.

Lyon's Army of the West was organized somewhat more straightfor-

wardly into four brigades. His staff included the noteworthy officers Maj.
John M. Schofield, Lyon's assistant adjutant general, who would play a noteworthy role in the war to come, and Brig. Gen. Thomas W. Sweeny, Lyon's
assistant inspector general, who had taken part in the battle of Carthage.
Lyon's brigade commanders were Maj. Samuel D. Sturgis, Lt. Col. George
Lippitt Andrews, Col. George W. Deitzler, and Col. Franz Sigel, who had
been at Carthage, as yet unaware that he had recently been commissioned a
brigadier general.

The battlefield of Wilson's Creek occupied a two-by-three-mile rectangle of rolling hills, farmhouses, and fields, etched by the north-south meanderings of Wilson's Creek itself. The Telegraph Road connecting
Springfield and Fayetteville, Arkansas, runs northeast-southwest through
the field. Near the center stands the Edwards House, south of which may be
found the Sharp House with its corn and stubble fields. Northwest of the Edwards House is the highest point of ground in the area, Bald Knob, which
came to be called Bloody Hill after the fight. East of Bald Knob stands the
Ray House, and on the northern edge of the field Gibson's Mill and the Gibson House near Wilson's Creek.

As the Federals marched toward their enemy, light rain fell after darkness on the 9th and helped suppress the hot daytime temperature and keep
the dust down on the roads and trails. With the Confederates encamped
along Wilson's Creek, Lyon commenced his attack early on the morning of
August 10. At 5 A.M. he struck southward into Rains's Confederates, who were
west of Gibson's Mill, north of Bloody Hill. Initially, this move was highly
successful, as the Yankees pushed their way up Bloody Hill and captured it.
Lyon had also sent Sigel southward to swing around the Confederate right
and attack them from behind, a move that would prove disastrous. Sigel executed his move and captured cavalry camps in Sharp's stubble field. Much of
McCulloch's force was arrayed north of Sigel's position, and Pearce was between McCulloch and the scattering troops of Rains. Shortly after the attacks commenced, McCulloch and Price set themselves to react to the
Federal onslaught. Still early in the morning, Sigel cleared Sharp's cornfield,
blocked the Telegraph Road, and began waiting for Lyon to meet up with
him. He would have a long wait. Lyon, attacking southward through Ray's
cornfield, was stopped cold by a series of hot counterattacks mounted by
Price, nicely supported by the fire of Capt. W. E. Woodruff's Arkansas battery, consisting of four guns, positioned near the Guinn House. Consequently, Lyon sent Capt. Joseph B. Plummer of the 1st U.S. Infantry across
Wilson's Creek in an attempt to silence Woodruff's guns. As the early morning continued, however, with rising temperatures and increasing crackles of
musketry, Plummer found himself attacked by Col. James McIntosh of the
2d Arkansas Mounted Rifles.

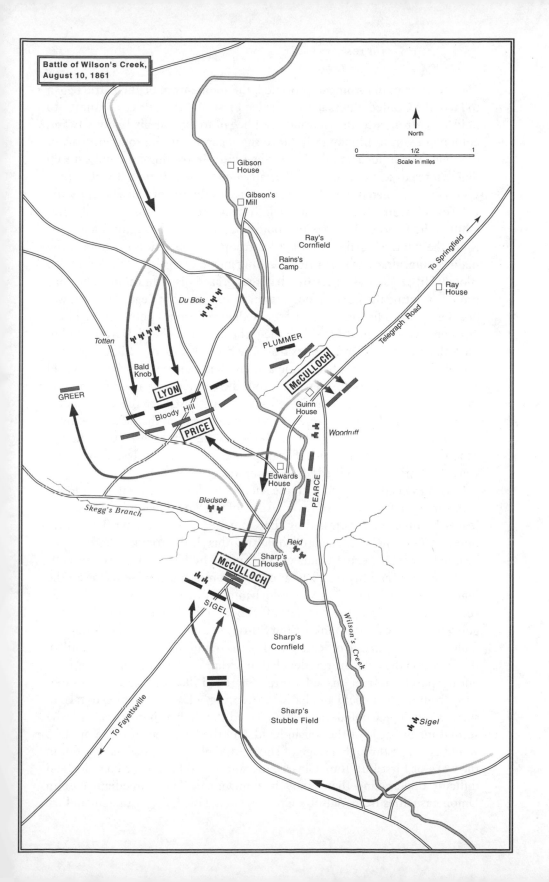

Battle of Wilson's Creek,
August 10, 1861

North

0   1/2   1
Scale in miles

Gibson House

Gibson's Mill

Ray's Cornfield

Rains's Camp

To Springfield

Ray House

Du Bois

Totten

PLUMMER

McCULLOCH

Telegraph Road

Bald Knob

LYON

Bloody Hill

Guinn House

Woodruff

GREER

PRICE

Edwards House

PEARCE

Skegg's Branch

Bledsoe

Reid

Sharp's House

McCULLOCH

Wilson's Creek

SIGEL

Sharp's Cornfield

To Fayetteville

Sharp's Stubble Field

Sigel

Now, as midmorning approached, the momentum of the battle began to favor the Confederates, just as it had at First Bull Run. Price continued to hold Lyon from a further advance and began to extend his line westward, confining Lyon to Bloody Hill. More significantly, on the southern part of the field, McCulloch smashed into Sigel, utterly routing him and causing Sigel's force to scatter in disarray. Cavalry under Col. Elkanah B. Greer, provisionally designated the South Kansas–Texas Regiment (subsequently the 3rd Texas Cavalry), thrust an attack into Lyon's rear that was repelled. After a lull in the fighting during which both sides attempted to reform and continue the fight, McCulloch pulled his troops into position to support the main counterattack against Price. Leading an attack against Price's force on Bloody Hill, Lyon was struck by a ball that grazed his right calf, and he continued directing the fight on foot after his horse was shot dead. The heat was now becoming a factor, and men were exhausted from fighting three hours nonstop. Lyon was next grazed on the right side of his head. Determined to push the attacking Confederates from the crest of Bloody Hill, he ordered the 2d Kansas to join the battle line and climbed onto another horse to lead the charge. A "sheet of fire" erupted from the Confederate lines, and among those hit was Lyon, struck on the left side of his chest, with the bullet piercing his heart and both lungs. He was caught falling from the saddle and lived but a few more moments, his body carried to the Ray House. According to Maj. William M. Wherry, one of Lyon's aides-de-camp, his last, faint words were, "Lehmann, I am killed." (Lehmann was his orderly.)

Lyon's death, coupled with the success of the Confederate counterattack, shattered the morale of Lyon's Army of the West. He was held as a great leader by his men, as attested by the Confederate staff officer Thomas L. Snead. "This mere captain of infantry, this little rough-visaged, red-bearded, weather-beaten Connecticut captain, by his intelligence, his ability, his energy, and his zeal, had at once acquired the confidence of all the Union men of Missouri." As McCulloch joined Price's northward jaunt, they succeeded in pushing the Federals off Bloody Hill. Not only was the battle going badly now for the Yankees, but Sturgis became the commander by default, as higher-ranking officers were not in communication with the bulk of the forces on the field. Sturgis decided to withdraw the army, and an orderly but purposeful retreat ensued. Sturgis marched the army about two miles away from the battlefield and halted at a spring, allowing the men to take in some water. The Confederates again found themselves in victory, with the second major battle of the war in hand, and the Union army and populace would again go through a stage of shock, though not as great as that felt in the wake of First Bull Run. Clearly, the war would be a more complex and difficult undertaking than many had imagined. The immediate cost in Union casualties from Wilson's Creek was 258 killed, 873 wounded, and 186 missing; the Confederates lost 279 men, with 951 wounded. The Springfield area was now in the hands of the Confederates, and Missouri's stand toward the Union appeared to be very much in doubt.

Minor skirmishing on various fields and between the politicians and generals in Richmond and Washington characterized the middle of August. On August 20, Maj. Gen. McClellan was assigned to command the newly organized Department and Army of the Potomac, initiating what would become the greatest Federal army of the war. It had a long way to go at this juncture, however, despite its commander's unbridled confidence. "How does [Secretary of State Seward] think I can save this country when stopped by Genl Scott," McClellan wrote his wife. "I do not know whether he is a *dotard* or a *traitor!* . . . he is a perfect imbecile. He understands nothing, appreciates nothing & is ever in my way." After meeting Lincoln, the writer Nathaniel Hawthorne penned a few thoughts. "Unquestionably, Western man though he may be, and Kentuckian by birth," he wrote, "President Lincoln is the essential representative of all Yankees. His hair was black, still unmixed with gray, stiff, somewhat bushy, and had apparently been acquainted with neither brush nor comb that morning . . . his complexion is dark and sallow . . . he has thick black eyebrows and an impending brow; his nose is large, and the lines about his mouth are very strongly defined." "We are not yet fighting in earnest," observed George Templeton Strong on August 15. "*Not even yet.* Our sluggish, good-natured, pachydermatous Northern people requires a deal of kicking to heat its blood."

Out in western Virginia, troubles continued amid the Confederate commanders. Gen. Robert E. Lee was on the scene and would take part in the autumn campaign. But cantankerous Brig. Gen. Henry A. Wise was still dissatisfied with a great deal of his circumstances and not cooperating effectively with Richmond or fellow commanders. To make matters worse, Brig. Gen. John B. Floyd, the ex–U.S. secretary of war, was placed into command of Southern troops in the Kanawha Valley. "Our enemy is so strong at all points that we can only hope to give him an effective blow by a concentration of our forces," he wrote Wise on August 8, "and, that this may be done surely and rapidly, their movements and actions must be controlled by one head." Rather than confident team play, Lee received a stream of complaints from Wise. "Our teams are shoeless," he wrote on August 11, "and there are but very few blacksmiths. This delays me as much as any other cause." Meanwhile, one Confederate commander was setting his sights on victory in the battles to come. "I am confident from observation that the Northern troops, like other raw soldiers, fear artillery unreasonably," Joe Johnston wrote President Davis on August 10, "and that we shall gain far more by an addition of these guns than by one of a thousand men." One Federal commander in the area, meanwhile, attempted to persuade the locals with a broadside.

"Citizens of Western Virginia," it read, "your fate is mainly in your own hands. If you allow yourselves to be trampled under foot by hordes of disturbers, plunderers, and murderers, your land will become a desolation. If you stand firm for law and order and maintain your rights, you may dwell together peacefully and happily as in former days." It was issued on August 20 by Brig. Gen. William S. Rosecrans.

The Yankee soldiers, although they had yet to win a major battle, were settling into camp life, the rigors of drill, and enjoying their relatively plentiful supplies. A Massachusetts soldier, John Billings, recalled the relative plenty of the early months of the war. "I will now give a complete list of the rations," he wrote. "They were salt pork, fresh beef, rarely ham or bacon, hard bread, soft bread, potatoes, an occasional onion, flour, beans, split pease [sic], rice, dried apples, dried peaches, desiccated vegetables, coffee, tea, sugar, molasses, vinegar, candles, soap, pepper, and salt. It is scarcely necessary to state that these were not all served out at one time."

Squabbling aside, the month would not end with two major Confederate victories unanswered. On the windy Outer Banks of Hatteras Inlet, North Carolina, Confederate forces had constructed two forts made of wood and vast quantities of sand—Forts Hatteras and Clark—to protect the Pamlico Sound from Federal naval forces. The area was critical for the Confederacy to hold because it allowed blockade runners, ships outfitted with supplies, to pass through the Federal flotillas and bring plentiful goods to Confederate ports. Scott's early notions of a grand strategy called for blockading these ports without fail, and so a combined U.S. Army and Navy operation would concentrate on attacking the Hatteras forts and closing them, strangling one of the main blockade-running routes to supply Confederates in Virginia. Altogether, about 900 army troops commanded by Maj. Gen. Benjamin Butler and eight ships with naval personnel under the command of Capt. Silas Horton Stringham would undertake the first combined amphibious operation of the war, the so-called Cape Hatteras Expedition. Stringham was a New Yorker who, at 63, had been a commissioned officer in the United States Navy for 51 years. He brought the USS *Minnesota*, the USS *Wabash*, the USS *Monticello*, the USS *Pawnee*, the revenue cutter *Harriet Lane*, the U.S. tug *Fanny*, and two transports into the action.

On August 27, Stringham's squadron anchored off Hatteras Inlet and prepared to bombard the forts and land the troops. The following day Fort Clark was captured and occupied after a brisk naval bombardment, the Confederate garrison abandoning it. A few shots went back and forth between the ships and batteries at Fort Hatteras, and marines and naval forces were landed by surfboats. The relatively scant defense was joined by Confederate naval officer Samuel Barron, whose two small vessels represented the tiny Confederate Navy. The Confederate fort was forced to surrender unconditionally. The Hatteras victory was much needed for Union morale and made heroes of Stringham and Butler, while the forts were transformed into coal storage facilities. "This was our first naval victory, indeed our first victory of any kind, and should not be forgotten," wrote Comdr. David Dixon Porter.

Before the month ended, however, the prickly issue of what to do with the growing number of black refugees once again came to the fore. Though he personally favored emancipation, President Lincoln would act rigorously within the confines of the U.S. Constitution, and emancipation could only be justified as a military necessity in the face of insurrection. As we have seen, the troublesome political general Benjamin Butler had already been pushing the Lincoln administration over the issue of emancipation and what to do with freedmen, refugee blacks, and army followers coming into his department. Now another troublesome army officer and politician, John C. Frémont, out in Missouri, would cause an even greater problem. On August 30, Frémont, an enthusiastic abolitionist, unilaterally issued an emancipation proclamation that appeared to free all slaves in Missouri. "The property, real and personal, of all persons in the State of Missouri who shall take up arms against the United States," Frémont's proclamation read, "or who shall be directly proven to have taken an active part with their enemies in the field, is declared to be confiscated to the public use, and their slaves, if any they have, are hereby declared freemen." Due to his scrupulous following of the laws of the United States and due to the extremely touchy balance among the border states, Lincoln revoked Frémont's order and the former explorer's long career in the army was sent into rapid decline. But the whole affair created a giant headache for Lincoln, who already had all the headaches he could bear. Finding his friend slipping into a depressive state, Lincoln's confidant, Illinois politician Orville H. Browning, wrote the president. "Be of good cheer. You have your future in your own hands, and the power to make your name one of the most justly revered and illustrious in the annals of the American race."

CHAPTER 4

A Massacre at Ball's Bluff

As THE LONG FIRST SUMMER of the war inched its way toward autumn, Frémont's unilateral emancipation proclamation, made without the advice and consent of Washington, continued to cause quite a stir. Lincoln ordered it modified to conform to existing law, but the damage had been done. While Lincoln the man favored emancipation, Lincoln the politician had to play the cards with tact and perfect timing in order to align the balance of power to favor the Union. This meant, among other things, not upsetting the fragile Border States, and Frémont's proclamation had been issued in Missouri, one of the touchiest spots in the nation. Lincoln wrote Frémont on September 2 that his proclamation might "alarm our Southern Union friends and turn them against us; perhaps ruin our rather fair prospect for Kentucky." On September 8, Frémont wrote Lincoln, still asking for reconsideration. "If upon reflection your better judgment still decides that I am wrong in the article respecting the liberation of slaves," he wrote, "I have to ask that you will openly direct me to make the correction. The implied censure will be received as a soldier always should the reprimand of his chief. If I were to retract of my own accord, it would imply that I myself thought it wrong, and that I had acted without the reflection which the gravity of the point demanded. But I did not. I acted with full deliberation, and upon the certain conviction that it was a measure right and necessary, and I still think so." Frémont found other ways in which to irritate Lincoln. He issued illegal commissions for army officers, handled his troops poorly, mismanaged finances and supplies, and showed a powerful lack of planning for a campaign against the Rebels and guerrilla forces in Missouri. Lincoln was in no mood to placate the troublesome Frémont, or to save face for him, and so he let stand his admonishments of the troubled officer. Frémont would find himself shifted from one insignificant command to another during the coming three years, even though he was the third-ranking officer in the army.

Meanwhile, with a couple of major battles having already occurred, the nation's civilians and the growing numbers in the armies and navies began to wonder where the next engagements would occur. The solidity of the Confederate States amazed many observers, with the seeds of a national Confederate unity sprouting slowly and steadily. The strength of Confederate nationalism, although it may have seemed clear at the time, has more recently become a target for historiographical feuds. Did the Southern populace really develop a strong sense of oneness, or did it simply act as a set of people drawn together only by the act of waging war, never really developing a national purpose or identity? Or does reality lie somewhere in between? Perhaps too much debate about Confederate nationalism has focused on the Richmond government and Southern civilians. The most important aspect of Confederate nationalism in the early days of the war grew within the ranks of the soldiers. Among the most significant ways in which soldiers expressed these feelings of unity, especially while on the march, was in song. And in September 1861 a new song sprang forth that became another Southern anthem that could be heard through the ranks of many of Southern column. Harry McCarthy composed "The Bonnie Blue Flag" in New Orleans, at the Varieties Theater, inspired by the Irish song "The Jaunting Car." Soon the song became the most popular Southern marching song next to "Dixie's Land." "We are a band of brothers, and native to the soil / Fighting for the property we gained by honest toil / And when our rights are threatened, the cry rose near and far / Hurrah for the bonnie Blue Flag that bears a single star! / Hurrah! hurrah! for the bonnie Blue Flag / That bears a single star."

From the many small actions taking place in western Virginia and in Missouri, little resulted in terms of strategic consequence. Confusion, failure, and a desire simply to encounter the enemy without further thought beyond skirmishing ruled the hour on both sides. A growing number of encounters were now taking place on the waters of the Confederacy—all of them minor—both along the coasts and in the rivers, principally the Mississippi. But early in September the first action of significance took place in Kentucky. On September 3, Confederate Brig. Gen. Gideon J. Pillow entered Kentucky, ordered there by his superior, Maj. Gen. Leonidas Polk. The fight for perhaps the most significant of the Border States was begun. Pillow marched his men into Kentucky from Tennessee, moving toward Hickman and Columbus on the Mississippi River. This created a huge, continuous front stretching from the Atlantic Ocean all the way to Kansas. It also aroused pro-Union sentiment in Kentucky, bringing the issue of Kentucky's "neutrality" to the fore, and touching off a fight for the state's citizens and its military value. At first, Secretary of War Walker ordered Pillow to withdraw from the state, but then President Davis reversed that order and allowed him to stay. The struggle over Kentucky in both military and political terms would smolder for months to come. For now, however, a brief shelling of shore batteries erupted on September 4 at Hickman and Columbus, as the Federal gunboats USS *Tyler* and USS *Lexington* opened fire. The fire was returned by the shore batteries, aided by the CSS *Yankee* (also known as the CSS *Jackson*). On this day Ulysses S. Grant arrived at Cairo, Illinois, and established a headquarters there. (Grant's assignment caused a stir when Brig. Gen. Benjamin M. Prentiss objected: "I have this day forwarded you my resignation," Prentiss wrote John C. Frémont. "I see by order from you to Gen. Grant that he is to rank me, that makes me junior whilst I claim to be senior Brigadier Genl from Illinois. I will remain in service but not as junior Brig. Gen.") The flap blew over as Prentiss was assigned to command Mason City, Missouri; he later served under Grant at Shiloh.

The characters now facing off made a striking contrast. Pillow was a planter and lawyer and the former friend of President James Knox Polk. This association allowed him to be commissioned a major general in the regular army during the Mexican War despite having no military training. Pillow was not a competent general. Leonidas Polk—a cousin of the former president—benefited from a close friendship with Jefferson Davis. Polk was a North Carolinian who had attended West Point. At the outbreak of war Polk held the position of Episcopal bishop of Louisiana, a post he held until his death. Like Pillow, Polk's military capabilities were overrated, his influence bolstered by personal connections.

Such was not the case with the Federal commander in the area. Ulysses S. Grant had been born in a rude, one-room house in Point Pleasant, Ohio, and failed at practically every venture in his life except marriage. Though commissioned a brigadier general, he would not rise to anyone's attention for several weeks yet, and only then with a relatively minor victory. For now, he was simply another general officer, age 39, who had attended West Point, where he was graduated twenty-first in a class of thirty-nine. Following competent service in the Mexican War, Grant resigned from the army and became a farmer, a real estate agent, and a clerk in his brothers' leather goods store in Galena, Illinois. His commission as colonel of the 21st Illinois Infantry was short-lived; his commission as brigadier general was typical of many of the early commissions. Issued to him in early September, it was backdated to a much earlier date, "to rank from May 17, 1861." This common practice confuses the issue of exactly who knew they were acting in a particular grade at any given time. Grant's case is well known, however. The new general arrived in Cairo with a typically sloppy uniform (he often wore a private's coat with his correct shoulder insignia sewn on) standing 5 feet 8 inches tall when erect, and with blue eyes and a dark beard that appeared oddly square-cut at this time. Few could have suspected what lay in store for this relatively mild-mannered, quiet soldier who had just received command of the District of Southeast Missouri.

Grant discovered the Confederate invasion of Kentucky on September 5. To neutralize Pillow's movement, Grant immediately concocted a plan to occupy Paducah, located at the confluence of the Tennessee and Ohio rivers, and nearby Smithland, at the mouth of the Cumberland. Realizing that Pillow's Confederates would move swiftly to occupy Paducah, Grant sent a force spearheaded by the USS *Tyler* and USS *Lexington* to move on the city on September 6. Grant departed Cairo at 10:30 P.M. on the 5th with the gunboats, two steamboats, and the 9th and 12th Illinois infantries supported by Smith's artillery. When Grant arrived at Paducah at 8:30 A.M. the next morning, he "found numerous secession flags flying over the city, and the citizens in anticipation of the approach of the rebel army." Grant found that the Confederates in Paducah scattered on his arrival, however, and he took the city without a fight. Although it was not a dramatic start for Grant, this action foreshadowed the ease with which he would coordinate operations with naval forces in the months to come. Grant returned to Cairo, and Brig. Gen. Charles F. Smith was placed in command in western Kentucky.

As NEUTRALITY EVAPORATED in Kentucky, events were heating up again in western Virginia. Slight skirmishing had occurred early in the month at Burlington, Hawk's Nest, Worthington, Rowell's Run, and Shepherdstown. In distant South Carolina, the *Charleston Mercury* editorialized that Confederates in Virginia should press the attack, having rested for six weeks in near view of the Yankee capital. Three primary areas of battle loomed over the western Virginia landscape: Brig. Gen. William S. Rosecrans threatened Confederate forces near Carnifex Ferry on the Gauley River; the Kanawha Valley hosted forces under the command of Brig. Gen. Jacob D. Cox; and at Cheat Mountain, Robert E. Lee headed a Confederate force aiming to push the Yankees from the area. Of all the possible actions growing out of this entanglement of hostile forces, Rosecrans's was the first. His so-called Army of Occupation consisted of three brigades commanded by Brig. Gen. Henry W. Benham, Col. Robert L. McCook, and Col. Eliakim P. Scammon. The Army of the Kanawha under Brig. Gen. John B. Floyd at Carnifex Ferry could not have been more disorganized, in part because of a lack of cooperation between Floyd and fellow Brig. Gen. Henry A. Wise. Wise refused to reinforce Floyd as the battle approached, citing a variety of reasons including measles among his troops, but in actuality because he did not want to weaken his own position at Hawk's Nest or aid Floyd, whom he detested.

Rosecrans moved southward toward Carnifex Ferry, which stood south of the river. Floyd's troops were strongly entrenched. Benham struck first. "Twenty-five minutes after the column left . . . terrific volleys of musketry and the roar of the rebels' artillery told that we were upon them," Rosecrans reported. As they approached the Confederate defenses, the Federals could not see ahead because of dense brush. Benham failed to deploy skirmishers as he spread forward, excited by his first engagement as a brigade commander. The lead regiment was Col. William Haines Lytle's 10th Ohio Infantry, which received a murderous fire as it made contact. Benham ordered his other regiments forward, the 12th and 13th Ohio infantries, and sent word to Rosecrans asking for reinforcements. Lytle was wounded and Floyd hit with a musket ball in his right arm and carried to the rear. The Yankees regrouped and attacked again at about sunset, and Rosecrans planned to continue the movement the following day. But Floyd, who originally vowed not to move at all, withdrew his force across the Gauley River under cover of darkness, giving Rosecrans an apparent victory. Floyd headed for Dogwood Gap and Sewell Mountain. The casualties at Carnifex Ferry were light, amounting to 17 killed and 141 wounded on the Union side and 9 wounded and 23 captured on the Confederate side. The North needed victories, and although this one was small, it held a ray of hope forward that western Virginia could be won over by Federal forces. "Disasters have come, and disasters are coming, which you alone, I fear, can repair and prevent," Wise wrote to Robert E. Lee. As Wise worried on paper, however, Lee was planning to attack the Yankees at Cheat Mountain. Benham, meanwhile, was criticized by Rosecrans for his actions at Corrick's Ford and Carnifex Ferry, and in early 1862 was still trying to live down the scathing attack on his competence.

Robert E. Lee's Cheat Mountain campaign commenced on September 11 and would last for seven days. It was the first military campaign he led. At the time, Lee was a relatively well-known Virginian but had nothing of the kind of fame or success that came later; he was one of many Confederate general officers about whom most of the population knew almost nothing. He had leaned toward holding the Union together until Virginia finally seceded. Lee had been trusted as an excellent military theorist in Richmond by President Davis, and several weeks before Cheat Mountain he had been sent to western Virginia because of the confused state of the bickering commanders in the area, including Wise, Floyd, William W. Loring, and Garnett. Now Lee would direct his own operations against Union forces with a critical area of Virginia hanging in the balance. The outcome in western Virginia was especially critical to the Confederacy because sentiment in this mountainous country, unlike that in the agrarian and tidewater parts of the state, leaned toward support of the Washington government. It was important for Lee and his fellow officers to make a statement about western Virginia by controlling it.

It would not be easy. September brought frequent rains to the area, some of them driving downpours. The roads were muddy and at times impassable, and hauling artillery over them was a challenge. Lee's plan was to divide his forces into five columns and attack the Federals under Brig. Gen. Joseph J. Reynolds, who were encamped at the summit of Cheat Mountain and at Elkwater.

Cheat Mountain rises in a mostly north-south direction southeast of the town of Elkwater. North of the mountain, the Staunton-Parkersburg Turnpike wiggles its way between Huttonsville, north of Elkwater, and the Greenbrier River to the east. Moving south from Huttonsville through Elkwater and on down to Valley Mountain brings into view the intermingled paths of the Tygart Valley River and the Huntersville-Huttonsville Pike. Although Lee's plan was complex, if carried out in a coordinated manner it would almost certainly strike and dislodge the Federals from their defenses on Cheat Mountain, at Elkwater, and along the Staunton-Parkersburg Turnpike.

Lee's columns would be commanded by a diverse group. Two columns would move northward along the Staunton-Parkersburg Turnpike toward the Federal defenses north of the summit of the mountain. They were led by Brig. Gen. Henry R. Jackson and Col. Albert Rust. As Jackson's and Rust's columns marched northward, three columns commanded by Brig. Gens. Samuel R. Anderson and Daniel S. Donelson and Col. Jesse S. Burks would march northward around the western face of Cheat Mountain and up the Huntersville-Huttonsville Pike toward Elkwater.

Lee initiated the movement on the 11th, and by daybreak the following morning Rust was to have been in position on Cheat Mountain, where he would open the attack, firing his guns to signal the other columns. Rain, sometimes heavy, continued to come down on the troops all through the night. Anderson pulled into position first, bringing his Tennessee troops into formation by sunrise, where they were unprotected from the rain. Donelson's men marched along the other side of the valley with even trickier problems through heavy brush, "letting themselves down by the branches of trees and pulling themselves up as occasion might require." Rust had difficulty reaching his position, tangling with thick mountain laurel and crossing his men waist-deep through half a mile of the ice-cold Cheat River. The rain finally let up slightly near dawn, but the awful experience of getting into position for these green troops dampened the chances of seeing them fight with vigor. Nevertheless, the Confederates had executed Lee's plan by getting into their difficult positions by the early morning of September 12.

Now the Confederates scattered from near Elkwater all the way across Cheat Mountain waited for Rust's signal. Soldiers under Rust's command had captured some Federal pickets, however, who exaggerated the strength of the Federal force before them. They suggested the summit held 4,000 men whereas it actually had only 300. Rust immediately got cold feet over his attack, particularly when he heard drums beating in the Federal camp and he felt the element of surprise was lost. His confidence utterly collapsed, and he decided not to carry out Lee's plan after all. As the morning continued, the other Confederate columns grew confused and worried over the lack of the signal. Lee finally ordered Donelson to attack, but the lackluster response caused by the weather and the waiting collapsed the Confederate resolve. Lee's first battle was over before it had even begun.

On September 13, Reynolds sent reinforcements from Elkwater onto Cheat Mountain, and Lee determined to reconnoiter routes by which he could turn the Federal right at Elkwater. He sent one party containing his son, Maj. William Henry Fitzhugh Lee, known as "Rooney," and a favorite aide, Col. John A. Washington, a friend and relative, along the right branch of Elkwater Fork. A Federal picket line opened on the group of horsemen, striking Washington with three Minié bullets, killing him. Rooney's horse was shot out from under him, but he was uninjured and escaped on Washington's horse. With bad weather and roads, supplies and morale low, and the Federals reinforcing, Lee had no choice but to pull back to Valley Mountain. His first battle had been a signal failure, and back at home the newspapers now branded Lee with a derisive epithet, "Granny," mocking his supposed timidity. It was a depressing time for the Southern cause in western Virginia.

Lee had erred in several ways during his first battle, perhaps most significantly by allowing an inexperienced commander without military training to play the crucial role on which all else depended. But he needed to keep the forces together despite the major setback: Yankee generals Jacob D. Cox and William S. Rosecrans were coming together in the Kanawha Valley, and the ever troublesome pair John B. Floyd and Henry A. Wise were still bickering on Sewell Mountain. Before the campaign ended, skirmishing erupted at Princeton on September 16 and near Harpers Ferry on the 17th. The condition of the Confederate troops seemed to be worsening, and Lee was disgusted with the lack of military discipline. "Our poor sick I know suffer much," Lee wrote his wife, Mary Custis Lee, on September 17. "They bring it on themselves by not doing what they are told. They are worse than children, for the latter can be forced." Meanwhile, Lee still hoped for an all-out victory by coordinating all the Southern forces in the area and was preparing to meet Rosecrans in the area of Sewell Mountain. But he could ill afford to have arguments festering between his commanders. "I beg therefore, if not too late, that the troops be united, and that we conquer or die together," he wrote Wise on September 21. Lee and other Confederate commanders clearly anticipated an attack from Rosecrans. McClellan still held overall command; he was beginning to earn his well-deserved reputation for overcaution, however. At a cabinet meeting in Washington on September 27, a heated discussion ensued over the increased cries from the public for action on the various fronts in Virginia. "McClellan consistently thinks no more of attacking the Confederate Army," editorialized the *Richmond Dispatch*, "than of attacking the man in the moon."

Before the snow fell and the season of battle was over, the military meanderings throughout western Virginia would take another step. Federal troops occupied Romney after skirmishing on September 23, and minor affairs took place at Mechanicsburg Gap and Hanging Rock Pass. On the 25th, the Confederate War Department finally made its choice in the dispute between Wise and Floyd, and Wise was relieved of command. Minor actions occurred between the forces of Lee and Rosecrans on this day. On October 3 the last engagement of the season in western Virginia occurred, when at the Greenbrier River, Col. Robert H. Milroy's 9th Indiana Infantry unsuccessfully attacked the Confederate left. The season did leave its imprint on those who helped to command it: Lee found himself at a low point, Wise was out in the cold, McClellan was gaining a reputation as a strong organizer and a weak commander, and Rosecrans's star was on the rise. On October 11, Rosecrans assumed command of the Department of Western Virginia.

THE FIGHTING ALONG ROUGH TERRAIN in western Virginia highlighted the difficult challenge faced by both armies as they grappled with issues of logistics and supply. With the ranks of the armies swelling and the area in which engagements could take place growing, these aspects were becoming critically important. Logistical support of the U.S. Army was entrusted to four bureau chiefs, which made coordination and communication challenging. They were the quartermaster general, the commissary general of subsistence, the chief of ordnance, and the surgeon general, who took care of medical supplies, evacuation of wounded, and hospitals. The Confederate army developed a similar organization and later added a chief of the Bureau of Nitre and Mining.

The odds seemed to be stacked against providing effective supply and logistics from the start. In the Confederacy, political infighting created a daunting lack of coordination and effective planning. The logistical situation in the South was precarious at best; the poor cooperation between parties ensured that faulty execution of supply issues became the norm during the war. To make matters worse, staff officers trained in logistics were perpetually in short supply. On both sides, the newly assigned supply officers were often inexperienced and ignorant of the principles of combat logistics. No supply troops were authorized or trained in either army, so supply troops had to be detached as required from combat forces, which diminished their effectiveness. Such supply troops were employed as laborers, teamsters, ambulance drivers, construction workers, and camp and depot personnel. Both sides employed black Americans in supply and support roles when possible.

For the average individual soldier, the supply issue seemed very different. All that concerned him was how much he had to carry during the march. The typical soldier's supply load often amounted to the following: rifled musket and bayonet (14 pounds), 60 rounds of ammunition (6 pounds), short rations to last two to six days (4 to 12 pounds), canteen (4 pounds), blanket or overcoat (5 pounds), shelter half or poncho (1.5 pounds). The soldier also might carry a knife, fork, spoon, cup, plate, diary, pencil, Bible, skillet, mirror, razor, letters, carte-de-visite photographs, and a "housewife"—a kit with which to mend clothes (1 to 3.5 pounds). The total amount of mass a soldier might haul along, then, might be from 36 to 46 pounds. This was tiring, to say the least, and American soldiers of the Civil War period became notorious for discarding equipment during long marches, in hot weather, and/or approaching battle. The loss of equipment ran as high as 50 percent on some campaigns.

Expecting soldiers to travel miles with heavy equipment and fight battles required providing them with a substantial amount of energy. The basic ration provided to U.S. army soldiers amounted to the following: 20 ounces of salt or fresh beef (or 12 ounces of pork or bacon), 18 ounces of flour (or 20 ounces of corn meal), 1.6 ounces of rice (or 0.64 ounces of beans or 1.5 ounces of potatoes), 1.6 ounces of green coffee (or .24 ounces of tea), 2.4 ounces of sugar, .54 ounces of salt, and .32 ounces of gill vinegar. This amounted to about 3 pounds per day. Peas, fresh potatoes, or hominy could be substituted for rice. Hard or soft bread could be substituted for flour. Vegetables could be substituted for rice, beans, hominy, or potatoes. The short ration, provided on the march, amounted to about 2 pounds per day and was much simpler. It consisted of 1 pound of hard bread ("hardtack"), .75 pound of salt pork or 1.4 pounds of fresh meat, 1 ounce of coffee, and 3 ounces of sugar and salt.

Although the rations were pretty well defined, supplying them was often haphazard at best. There were no "mess sergeants" or trained cooks, and so commissary duty was assigned among the troops by rotation. The mess was usually organized by squad or platoon. With a temporary group of volunteer, inexperienced cooks, one can imagine the quality control problems. A soldier's diet was woefully short on fruits, vegetables, and vitamins. This laid the basis for widespread infectious diseases and brought about a terrible degree of suffering. Realizing the deficiencies of the diet, Union troops often attempted to supplement their diet with onions, pickles, sauerkraut, apples, and peaches. Substitutes such as canned, desiccated vegetables and condensed milk found little acceptance among the men, creating the sarcastic label "desecrated vegetables and consecrated milk." Often men on both sides, but particularly the Union, used some of their pay to purchase additional foodstuffs from sutlers, merchants who traveled with the armies, or they simply received goods from home to help fill in their diet. These included milk, eggs, butter, and chickens. Generally, Confederate troops had less meat, coffee, salt, and vinegar, but had more sugar, molasses, and tobacco. Such inequities led to one of the peculiar aspects of the war, trading between enemy troops even relatively close to the time of battle. The overall supply situation for Confederate troops sometimes became desperate, particularly when the army was on the move in hostile territory. During Robert E. Lee's Maryland campaign, for example, the Army of Northern Virginia subsisted largely on green corn and apples.

Food wasn't the only supply issue on the minds of soldiers, however. Clothing the men was also a major concern, particularly during cold or stormy weather. The standard issue to a U.S. soldier included the following: two caps, one hat, two dress coats, three pairs of trousers, three flannel shirts, three flannel drawers, four pairs of stockings, four pairs of bootees, one blanket (every third year), and one overcoat (every five years). Artillerymen and cavalrymen received jackets and boots instead of dress coats and bootees. The Confederate army officially provided equivalent clothing, but this was seldom achieved. Most Confederate soldiers furnished their own clothing and the standard gray uniform colors soon became replaced by "butternut" (from butternut, walnut, or other plant dyes). The clothing item most frequently in short supply among the Confederacy was shoes and/or boots. In terms of shelter, it was somewhat problematic for both sides. Canvas duck tent fabric was always in short supply. The Sibley tent was patterned after the Indian tepee and designed to shelter twenty people; it was popular early in the war but after two or so years its popularity waned. It had been developed by Henry Hopkins Sibley, a former U.S. army officer who was now a Confederate brigadier general. The U.S. Army adopted the French "Tente d'Abai," or shelter half. The shelter halves could be joined into an inverted V structure that would shelter two soldiers. Thus, two partners on the march would attach their tents at night, crawl inside, and with their heads exposed would often amuse themselves by barking like dogs, giving the whole affair the derisive name "pup tent." Sometimes soldiers also had ground cloths and would build a base of twigs, straw, hay, and leaves and would trench the area to drain away water.

Accompanying animals needed care as well. Each horse required 14 pounds of hay and 12 pounds of grains (oats, barley, or corn) per day. Each mule required 14 pounds of hay and 9 pounds of grains per day. Forage was the most difficult supply to transport. During the campaigns of 1863 and 1864, for example, the U.S. Army required about 50,000 tons of hay and 2.5 million bushels of grains per month.

Transportation was the most difficult of all supply matters. The demands for wagon transportation of supplies by both armies were gigantic. In October 1862, for example, the Army of the Potomac required about 668 tons of resupplies per day. When it was on the move, the army often carried with it 4,204 tons of supplies in about 3,503 wagons, not including weapons, camp equipment, ambulances, medical supplies, sutlers' stores, officers' forage, and headquarters baggage. All the army's supplies could not be moved at once, so trains had to make repeated trips to keep up with requirements.

A six-mule army wagon could carry about 4,000 pounds, but the condition of wagon repair, rough and steep roads, and wet or icy weather reduced the average load to about 2,000 pounds, or a single ton per wagon. Four-mule teams and four-horse teams could pull only about 1,800 pounds. Sometimes two-horse wagons, spring wagons, and/or ambulances were substituted. Pack animals were found to be far less efficient than wagons. Periodically, both the Union and Confederate armies issued orders to reduce the sizes and lengths of their supply trains, particularly to restrict the transport of personal baggage.

Transport by water was much more efficient, and so it was used whenever possible. For example, during the Peninsular campaign of 1862, the Quartermaster General's Department employed 400 ships (113 steamers, 199 sailing ships, and 88 barges) to move 121,500 men, 14,592 animals, and their supplies from the North to the Peninsula. Rivers and canals were also used extensively. One medium-size river steamboat could carry one day's supplies for 70,000 men and 20,000 animals.

Rail transport played a crucial role in supplying the armies, but one that is still debated in terms of its potential. In 1860 some 21,000 miles of railroad existed in the North and 9,000 miles in the South; most of those miles in the South ran along north-south lines. The few east-west Southern rail lines were broken within cities, and frequently changed gauges, making efficient use a real challenge. The South had few railroad shops and supplies. Southern railroad managers were not especially cooperative with the Confederate government, either. By contrast, Northern railroads cooperated very well with the government, and the railroads' operating personnel supervised by Col. Daniel C. McCallum and the railroad construction corps under Brig. Gen. Herman Haupt were very efficient. Although rail movement of troops and supplies was often haphazard, the most dramatic use of rail came in 1863 with the transfer of the 11th and 12th Army corps from the Army of the Potomac to Chattanooga. Alarmed by the stunning defeat at Chickamauga, the War Department initiated on September 25 the movement via Washington, Jeffersonville, Louisville, Nashville, Bridgeport, and Chattanooga, and the trips took from five and a half to eleven days. The transfer involved 23,500 men, 10 batteries of artillery, and 100 cars of baggage and supplies, covering 1,192 miles by rail.

Although the importance of rail supply is still debated by historians, Maj. Gen. William T. Sherman pointed out its critical importance for operations that moved away from oceans and rivers. During the Atlanta campaign of 1864, Sherman estimated that about 160 cars per day were required to supply an army of 100,000 men and 35,000 animals. If the campaign had been supplied by a train of wagons, some 36,800 wagons would have been required, each carrying two tons of supplies and pulled by a six-mule team traveling twenty miles per day. The management and protection of such a supply train, its personnel, wagons, and mules, Sherman reasoned, would have been an impossible task.

Throughout the war, the issues of supplies and logistics would be more troublesome for the Confederacy than for the Union. Even at First Bull Run, for example, jurisdictional disputes between the bureau chiefs in Richmond and the commanders on the field led to a difficult supply situation. Various unit commanders wanted their quartermasters to obtain supplies locally whereas Richmond officials wanted the supplies to come centrally from Richmond. The single-track rail line to Manassas Junction could not have handled such traffic, however, and many rail cars were diverted to sidings for storage rather than being unloaded and returned.

On July 22, the evening following the Battle of Bull Run, Jefferson Davis wanted Beauregard and Johnston to pursue the Federal army. The Confederate commanders, however, with their troops in disarray and their supply situation untenable, did not agree. Beauregard and Johnston could not reasonably supply their armies of about 40,000 men during the late summer and autumn of 1861; despite this, they requested an additional 20,000 men to join them for an advance on Washington. Davis would not approve of moving the reinforcements from other areas because of the potential political repercussions. Moreover, if he had permitted the armies in Virginia to be increased to a strength of 60,000, he probably could not have supplied them for a military advance. During the worst of times, supplies could become a real encumbrance for Southern armies on the run. As Sherman captured Atlanta, for instance, Gen. John Bell Hood resorted to blowing up his huge supply train south of the city about 2 A.M. on September 2, 1864. It consisted of three or four engines and eighty-one cars, twenty-eight cars of which contained almost all of Hood's artillery ammunition.

As THE ARMIES IN THE EAST were worrying about such problems as logistics and supply, the war went on, and not only in Virginia. A concurrent set of actions in Missouri in mid-September held the nation's attention on another of the fragile areas where sentiment could swing in either direction. Emboldened by the Confederate victory at Wilson's Creek in August, Maj. Gen. Sterling Price pressed the Confederate cause in Missouri further, hoping to wipe out the Union forces in the state and swing the civilian psychology clearly toward the South. Price's 7,000 troops of the Missouri State Guard approached the sleepy town of Lexington in northwestern Missouri, population 1,000, on September 13. At Lexington was a force of 2,800 Union infantry commanded by Col. James A. Mulligan. Lexington overlooked the Missouri River, and Mulligan's men were encamped on the campus of a Masonic college just north of town. They were guarding valuables confiscated from the town that included nearly $1 million and the great seal of the State of Missouri. The cash was buried beneath Mulligan's tent. On the 13th a small affair took place at Boonville, but no support yet came to the aid of Mulligan.

A small exchange of fire between Union pickets and skirmishers of the Missouri State Guard opened the engagement at Lexington, which quickly died down and became a siege. A second round of action on the 13th sent the Union defenders reeling back into their entrenchments, which boasted seven cannon and were constructed of 12-by-12-foot ramparts made of dirt and mud. "Finding, after sunset, that our ammunition, the most of which had been left behind on our march from Springfield, was nearly exhausted," recalled Price, "and that my men, thousands of whom had not eaten a particle in thirty-six hours, required rest and food, I withdrew to the fair ground and encamped there." Nearly encircled and hopelessly outnumbered, Mulligan now dug in and waited for reinforcements, which he desperately believed were being sent by Maj. Gen. John C. Frémont, from St. Louis. Not only did Frémont not assist Mulligan, but on September 15 he further hurt his already shaky image by arresting the popular Union politician-officer Frank Blair, Jr. Meanwhile, Price waited for even more volunteers to arrive from other parts of the state and for his ammunition trains to arrive. Each commander waited nearly five days before activity commenced again.

The issue was forced on September 18 when Price surrounded Mulligan's forces and cut off their only water supply. When vigorous action erupted on the following day, it was clear that Mulligan's forces were doomed. Still, they fought valiantly with artillery posted around a single brick structure called the Anderson House, situated on a hill 125 yards from the Union line, which was used as a hospital. The town had been evacuated, and Price fired terrific blasts of artillery into the town and into the Union line, his army having swelled to 18,000 from the many men who came in during the siege. Unknown to Mulligan, a column of reinforcements had indeed been sent by Frémont, commanded by Brig. Gen. Samuel D. Sturgis, another veteran of Wilson's Creek. But it would be too little, too late. Sturgis's men could not even cross the river and enter the battlefield due to well-posted Confederate artillery and a detached column of 3,000 of Price's men.

Hungry, thirsty, exhausted, and demoralized, Mulligan's men were

making a courageous stand. On the morning of the 20th, Price's attack commenced again. At this stage one of the most peculiar events of the war in the
West took place. The lines were so close and so hotly contested that Confederates employed large bales of hemp for cover, moving them slowly toward
the Union ramparts. The hemp absorbed Minié bullets effectively and provided sound cover. Thus, the action came to be called the "battle of the hay
bales." While watching the action, the English newspaper correspondent
Samuel P. Day wrote, "[The Union] men looked at the moving monster in
astonishment. It lay like a large serpent, winding over the hills and hollows,
apparently motionless, yet moving broadside on, to envelop and destroy
them in its vast folds. In vain the cannon were turned upon it. The heavy
bales absorbed the shot harmlessly. . . ." "Our ammunition was about gone,"
wrote Mulligan. "We were out of rations, and had been without water for
days, and many of the men felt like giving up the post, which it seemed impossible to hold longer. They were ordered back to the breastworks, and told
to use up their powder."

After several hours of intense musket fire, several of Mulligan's subordinate officers raised white flags. After some hesitation, Mulligan finally decided to surrender to Price, which was effected at 2 P.M. Mulligan's men had
suffered 259 casualties, lost the money and state seal, the seven cannon, 3,000
rifles, 750 horses, and the surviving members of the garrison. Mulligan himself would be exchanged five weeks later, on October 26. Although the siege
of Lexington was a splendid success for the Confederacy and a personal triumph for Price, he failed to capitalize on it. Price's expanded volunteer army
shrank in size due to lack of enthusiasm on the part of ill-supplied volunteers. Price and the Richmond government could be proud for the moment,
however. Not only had they won both sizable engagements in the area, but
on October 31 a small portion remaining of the Missouri state legislature assembled at Neosho voted the state out of the Union. This in effect made
Missouri a member of both the Union and the Confederacy, and so it was
counted by both sides. Other areas were similarly contested, particularly
Kentucky, while both Tennessee and Virginia contained strong pro-Union
contingencies in their mountainous parts. "The population here is so generally hostile I cannot push spies through," wrote Confederate Brig. Gen. Felix
Zollicoffer in eastern Tennessee to William W. Mackall in Nashville, on
September 26. "The male population has nearly disappeared between here
and Barboursville [Kentucky]." Such areas of mixed sentiment would be
contested for months to come.

ALL THE WHILE, the public on both sides pressured for a decisive fight in the
east. McClellan was busily training the Army of the Potomac, the premier

Federal army, of which he had been assigned command on August 20. He was an excellent organizer and had the ranks of the army drilled thoroughly, eventually molding the army into an effective fighting force with a great love for its commander. The Army of the Potomac was certainly becoming Mc-Clellan's army in terms of spirit, and McClellan's spirit found confidence in himself but not in some of his subordinates or in the administration in Washington. In one of many such letters in the autumn of 1861, McClellan wrote his wife on October 31 that "it is terrible to stand by & see the cowardice of the Presdt, the vileness of Seward, & the rascality of Cameron—Welles is an old woman—Bates an old fool. The only man of courage & sense in the cabinet is Blair, & I do not altogether fancy him!" For now, at least, McClellan was limited to being a great organizer. He seemed hesitant at best to take his army into the field and complained extensively about their lack of preparedness, the shortage of supplies to support offensive operations, and the overwhelming numerical strength of the enemy, all of which were problems exaggerated to greater or lesser degrees in his mind. McClellan's record to come on the battlefield would be so tarnished, in fact, that one of his chief supporters, Louis-Philippe-Albert d'Orléans, comte de Paris, would open a postwar recollection of his commander with, "No one has denied that Mc-Clellan was a marvelous organizer." In the soldier's atmosphere of anticipating some kind of action, a spirit of playfulness emerged among some troops of the opposing sides, particularly those who had been friends before the war. In one such letter, 1st Lt. Orlando M. Poe wrote Confederate cavalryman Jeb Stuart, outside Washington in early September. "My dear Beauty," Poe began, "I'm sorry that circumstances are such that I can't have the pleasure of seeing you although so near you. [Capt. Charles] Griffin says he would like to have you dine with him at Willard's at 5 o'clock on Saturday next. Keep your 'Black Horse' off me if you please." On the verso of the lettersheet, Stuart, who received the letter, penned a reply of sorts. "I have the honor to report that 'circumstances were such' that they could have seen me if they had stopped to look behind—and I answered both at the cannon's mouth. Judging from his speed Griffin surely left for Washington to hurry up the dinner. J. E. B. Stuart."

In the weeks following the Battle of Bull Run, the area stretching from Washington to Harpers Ferry had been placed under the guard of Maj. Gen. Nathaniel P. Banks, who commanded a division of the Army of the Potomac. Banks was a native of Massachusetts, a former machinist and editor of the *Middlebury Reporter*. He had served as a member of the U.S. House, as governor of Massachusetts (just before the war), and as vice president of the Illinois Central Railroad. Devoid of military experience, Banks was a quintessential political general, similar to Benjamin Butler in his early rise to importance. Pickets of Banks's division carefully guarded the northern bank of the Potomac River against possible enemy movements that could signal an invasion of Maryland. Only minor scouting operations and a few rounds of musket fire had passed between the warring sides in this region during the autumn. As the end of October approached, however, the situation was about to change, and it would prove a costly lesson concerning the effectiveness of political generals as field commanders.

Two of the closely watched points of crossing stood along the Potomac near Leesburg, Virginia, a beautiful town with attachments to the early moments of patriotism in America. It was near Leesburg where the Declaration of Independence had been hidden in a barn during the British attack on Washington in the War of 1812. Beauregard had positioned one of the successful Bull Run commanders, Brig. Gen. Shanks Evans, at Leesburg to keep an eye on the Yankee activities in the region. Of special interest were Edwards's Ferry and Conrad's Ferry along the river, across which Confederate armies might move into Maryland or Federal armies into Virginia. Across the river from Leesburg, in Poolesville, Maryland, sat Brig. Gen. Charles P. Stone with a small force of Federal soldiers. When he was mustered into the District of Columbia militia as a colonel and inspector general on January 1, 1861, Stone became the first volunteer mustered into the army during the Civil War period.

On October 19, pressured by the administration and the public, McClellan ordered a forward reconnaissance. On that day Yankee soldiers under Brig. Gen. George A. McCall pushed forward and occupied Dranesville, Virginia, south of the river. Emboldened, McClellan then ordered Stone to watch the force at Leesburg and suggested that "perhaps a slight demonstration on your part would have the effect to move them." Leesburg and Poolesville are separated by about eight miles, Leesburg about two and three-fourths miles west of the Potomac and Poolesville five miles east of it. Drawing a line from Leesburg to Poolesville crosses a position on the river at which the river widens, the water flowing around a prominent island called Harrison's Island. Just north of Harrison's Island is the position of Conrad's Ferry; the western edge of the river at this position slopes down steeply to the muddy banks below and is called Ball's Bluff. Edwards's Ferry stands some four miles south of this position. Receiving his orders at Poolesville, Stone crossed some troops in the area of Ball's Bluff on the 19th but withdrew them in the evening.

The next day, October 20, would witness one of the more celebrated small battles of the war. Called Ball's Bluff, the battle was a minor affair with little strategic significance but would nonetheless cast a long shadow. The numbers of troops on each side were equal for this engagement, with 1,700

Yankees and 1,700 Rebs eager for action. Stone's division consisted of three brigades commanded by three brigadier generals: Willis A. Gorman, Frederick W. Lander, and Edward D. Baker. A close friend of Abraham Lincoln dating back to Illinois legislative years, Baker was so admired by the Lincoln family that they named one of their sons Edward Baker Lincoln, for him. Baker had been born in London in 1811 but moved to Pennsylvania at age four before migrating westward with his family. In his antebellum days Baker had a long and useful career as a legislator from Illinois and as a volunteer officer during the Mexican War. After a stay in California, he moved to Oregon in 1860 and was elected senator from that state. Baker's grade is typically cited as colonel, although he was commissioned brigadier general to rank from May 17, 1861, and he declined the commission on August 17. Despite his declination, the U.S. Senate confirmed Baker in the grade of brigadier general. Thus, he legally held the grade. Baker was also appointed a major general of volunteers on September 21, 1861, but that commission was never confirmed.

As it happened, Baker, the political general, was the one who would cross his men into the heaviest action at Ball's Bluff on October 21. Stone, aided by Gorman, directed operations down south at Edwards's Ferry. The steep, wooded banks of the river at Ball's Bluff greatly favored the defenders on the western shore; Baker's force, with three light field guns, confronted three infantry regiments, one detached company, and three companies of cavalry commanded by Evans. The principal regiments were the 17th Mississippi Infantry (Col. Winfield Scott Featherston); the 18th Mississippi Infantry (Col. E. R. Burt); and the 8th Virginia Infantry (Col. Eppa Hunton). Baker's Yankee regiments were the 15th Massachusetts Infantry (Col. Charles Devens); the 20th Massachusetts Infantry (Col. William R. Lee); the 42d New York Infantry "Tammany Regiment" (Col. Milton Cogswell); and the 71st Pennsylvania Infantry, also called the "1st California" as a compliment to Baker (Lt. Col. Isaac J. Wistar).

After midnight on the 20th, Devens, with 300 men, began the movement by small, inadequate boats across Harrison's Island and onto the western shore of the Potomac. He hoped to capture a Rebel camp and return to the safety of the riverbank. After scaling the muddy banks of Ball's Bluff and being joined by part of Lee's regiment, they halted in a field until daybreak. At about 7 A.M. on the 21st a skirmish erupted on the front as part of Devens's force entered a cornfield "in which the corn had lately been cut and stood in the shocks." The light fighting throughout the morning continued as the remaining troops entered the fray, and the intensity of the gun battle increased during the afternoon. The military inexperience of Baker soon began to show, and it affected the battle. The troops were posted in poor positions, and the artillery could not be used because of the lay of the ground and the heavy woods. The Federal line, disorganized as it was, began to cave in by midafternoon as successful Confederate attacks drove into the stunned Yankees, pushing them back toward the river. "Charge, Mississippians, charge! Drive them into the Potomac or into eternity!" Featherston allegedly told his troops. "The Virginians and Mississippians being accustomed to the rifle, most of them old hunters, rarely missed their man," wrote Randolph Abbott Shotwell, a soldier in the 8th Virginia. "Climbing into the tops of trees, creeping through the tall grass, or concealed in the gullies, they plied their weapons with murderous havoc especially among the Federal officers. It was very poor management to allow this to go on."

Poor management indeed. In the rising confusion among the Federal units, at about 4 P.M., Baker was killed. (It was one of the early and significant personal shocks for the Lincoln family in the war.) Federal soldiers scrambled down the banks of the river followed by triumphant Confederates shooting at them as they retreated. The scene that followed was incredible: boats foundered, men drowned or were shot and floated downstream, and the scene became hellishly emblazoned on the minds of Federal soldiers who survived it. One shocked survivor, Oliver Wendell Holmes, Jr.—the future jurist, at the time a 20-year-old first lieutenant in the 20th Massachusetts—recalled his wounds received during the melee in a letter to his mother: "The first shot (the spent ball) struck me on the belly below where the ribs separate & bruised & knocked the wind out of me— The second time I hope only one ball struck me entering the left & coming out behind the right breast in wh. case I shall probably recover."

Although it involved relatively small numbers, Ball's Bluff became another Union disaster. Cogswell was wounded, as was Wistar. Altogether, 49 Federals were killed, 158 were wounded, and 714 were captured or missing. On the Confederate side, Burt was mortally wounded; the totals were 33 killed, 115 wounded, and 1 missing. The battle was a rout coming at the end of the warm season, and it left a disgusting taste in the mouths of the Northern population and especially in the War Department in Washington. Capt. Robert Garlick Hill Kean, chief of the Confederate Bureau of War, penned that "Friends who were at Leesburg . . . say that Evans is not entitled to any credit whatever for the action there; that he was drunk; that he had timely notice of the crossing of the Yankees in the night, turned in his bed, took another drink and said he did not believe it." For its part, the Northern press blamed Stone, accusing him of treason. He had not been in the heaviest part of the action and had left the inexperienced politician Baker too much responsibility. The government also blamed Stone. (Baker erred significantly in his tactics but could not be further punished, even if he hadn't been Lincoln's close friend.) On January 28, 1862, Stone was ordered arrested by the secretary of war and was imprisoned in Fort Lafayette and then Fort Hamilton until August 6, 1862. Contrary to army regulations, no formal charges were ever pressed against him, but his career was ruined. He later served as chief of staff of the Department of the Gulf and finally resigned in 1864.

As THE WEATHER COOLED and the month of October drew toward a close, the war in America continued. Skirmishes occurred daily, contributing to the number that would eventually swell to more than 8,700 affairs. On October 21 the Confederacy lost a general officer when Brig. Gen. John B. Grayson succumbed to tuberculosis and pneumonia in Tallahassee, Florida. On the 23d small skirmishes took place at Hodgenville, Kentucky—near President Lincoln's birthplace—and at Gauley Bridge in western Virginia. On the 25th a Federal cavalry force attacked Confederates at Springfield, Missouri, capturing the city. Brig. Gen. Benjamin F. Kelley captured Romney in western Virginia on the 26th. A few other minor actions took place in Kentucky, western Virginia, and Missouri during the last few days of the month. As these little encounters were unfolding, technological advances also continued. In the far west, the first transcontinental telegraph was completed on the 24th, linking Denver and Sacramento with the earlier, more easterly line. Although it would often fail due to a variety of reasons, communication from coast to coast was now possible in relatively rapid form. Technology also took a leap forward the next day—although warriors on both sides didn't yet realize it—when the keel of the USS *Monitor* was laid down at Greenpoint, Long Island. The genesis of this little ironclad ship went almost unnoticed; the following spring, however, the ship would help to revolutionize naval warfare.

For now, naval warfare would be a part of the second large combined operation of the war. The Federal navy desperately needed to gain a foothold on the coast of South Carolina, Georgia, and Florida. This had to be accomplished not only to effect a proper blockade along the South Atlantic coast, but to support the army if it were to capture Confederate territory. Altogether, about 16,000 soldiers and sailors departed Hampton Roads, Virginia, on October 29, bound for Port Royal Sound, South Carolina, located strategically between Charleston and Savannah. The so-called Port Royal expedition used seventy-seven ships and was commanded jointly by Brig. Gen. Thomas W. Sherman, in command of the army troops, and Capt. Samuel F. Du Pont, in charge of the naval flotilla. From his flagship USS *Wabash,* Du Pont headed south with the largest naval force ever assembled in United States history. The early hours of activity for the squadron were not encouraging; it encountered a heavy gale off Cape Hatteras, and many of the soldiers and sailors on board ship had a most unpleasant voyage. As he moved southward, Du Pont was only partly confident of success. "We have considerable power to carry on an *offensive* warfare," he wrote Assistant Secretary of the Navy Gustavus V. Fox on October 29. "[But] that of *endurance* against forts is not commensurate. But in so righteous a cause as ours, & against so wicked a rebellion, we must overcome all difficulties."

CHAPTER 5

An Unlikely Hero at Belmont

As THE WEATHER TURNED COLDER during the first days of November, impatience became the operative word on both sides. Nothing of any major military consequence had happened since August, and the major forces in the East seemed to be doing little but drilling. Citizens North and South grew anxious, fearing a prolonged war. They cried out for military action. In the North, the frustration over McClellan's lack of initiative planted the seeds for an opposition to the administration, whether it desired promoting peace or a more vigorous prosecution of the war. The only activity publicly anticipated on any front was that of Du Pont's expedition, and where the captain's ships would go along the South Atlantic coast was unknown to everyone outside of the Navy Department.

Despite McClellan's inaction, on the first day of November he was assigned by President Lincoln as general-in-chief of the army, and Bvt. Lt. Gen. Winfield Scott was sent into retirement at West Point. It was a stunning move to some of the army's old-timers, who were sorry to see one of the most distinguished careers in the army come to an end; at the same time many questioned the competency of the 34-year-old McClellan, a major general in the regular army who now ranked all other officers. The Young Napoleon himself marked the occasion by writing his wife that he arose early "to escort Genl Scott to the depot—it was pitch dark & pouring rain ... it may be that at some distant day I too shall totter away from Washn—a worn out soldier, with naught to do but make my peace with God." At length, McClellan continued describing the transition. "Should I ever become vainglorious & ambitious remind me of that spectacle," he wrote.

A shake-up in Union command in the east would, one day later, echo in a change in command in the west. Troublesome for the administration and the war effort from the beginning, Maj. Gen. John C. Frémont finally saw his time elapse. A messenger from the War Department found one of the general's pickets at Springfield, Missouri, and handed him a dispatch relieving Frémont of command of the Western Department. Although the order from Winfield Scott had been drafted on October 24, Frémont did not receive it until November 2. After some hesitation and frustration voiced toward the War Department and claims that he was about to engage Sterling Price's army near the old battlefield of Wilson's Creek (which was not true), Frémont relinquished command. He wrote his soldiers of their "brave and generous spirit" and told them he anticipated for the army a "brilliant career." In the end, however, Frémont left without much fanfare, although his huge staff of partisan aides claimed for a brief time that they would establish a western empire with Frémont as ruler of his own nation. Even for the second-ranking major general of the regular army and failed presidential candidate, it was an outrageously egotistical notion. Frémont's successor was Maj. Gen. David Hunter, a veteran of First Bull Run and a political favorite of the administration despite his dubious talents as a general officer. The card shuffling brought new doubts about Lincoln and his cabinet. "The President is not equal to the crisis; that we cannot now help," wrote Charles Francis Adams, Jr., to Henry Adams, on November 5. "The Secretary of War is corrupt and the Secretary of the Navy is incompetent; that we can help and ought to."

The Southern armies also witnessed some reassignments during the first days of November. Maj. Gen. Stonewall Jackson assumed command of the Valley District on November 4, with headquarters in Winchester, Virginia, laying the groundwork for what would become an adventurous campaign the following spring. On leaving his old brigade, now called the Stonewall Brigade, Jackson wrote: "In the Army of the Shenandoah you were the *First* Brigade; in the army of the Potomac you were the *First* Brigade; in the second corps of this army you are the *First* Brigade; you are the *First* Brigade in the affections of your General; and I hope by future deeds and bearing you will be handed down to posterity as the *First* Brigade in our second War of Independence. Farewell!" The next day, Gen. Robert E. Lee was assigned to command the newly created Department of South Carolina, Georgia, and East Florida, with headquarters in Coosawhatchie, South Carolina, twenty miles northwest of Beaufort. President Davis, who on November 6 would be elected permanent president of the Confederate States (running unopposed, and winning a single six-year term), needed Jackson to protect and solidify the defenses of the Shenandoah Valley and Lee to shore up the difficult situation along the South Atlantic coast. The two commanders would meet with varying degrees of success in their assignments.

Unfortunately for Gen. Lee, he would arrive too late to do anything about the impending arrival of Du Pont's Union naval flotilla. The seventy-

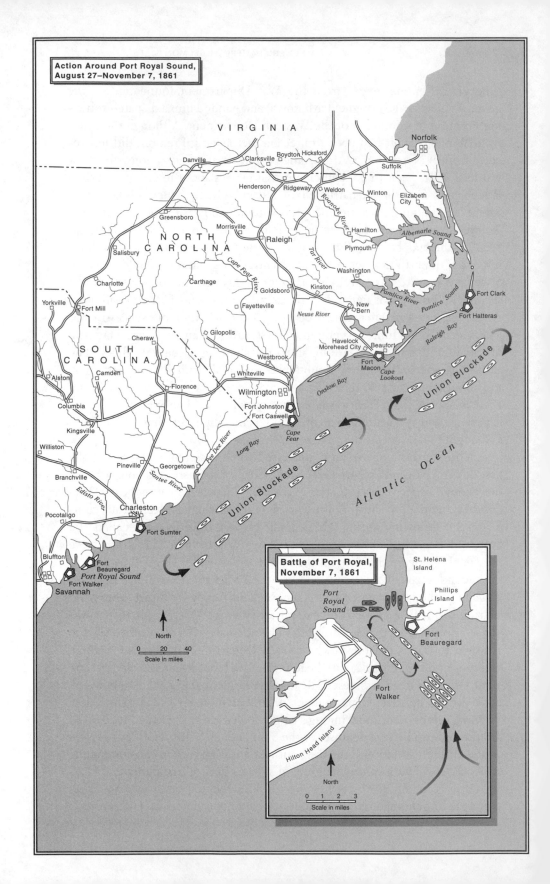

Action Around Port Royal Sound,
August 27–November 7, 1861

V I R G I N I A

Norfolk

Danville Clarksville Boydton Hicksford
Suffolk

Henderson Ridgeway Weldon Winton Elizabeth
City

Greensboro
Roanoke River Hamilton

N O R T H
C A R O L I N A
Morrisville
Raleigh
Plymouth Albemarle Sound

Salisbury
Cape Fear River Tar River Washington
Pamlico River
Charlotte
Carthage Goldsboro Kinston Pamlico Sound Fort Clark

Yorkville Fort Mill
Neuse River New
Bern Fort Hatteras
Fayetteville
Cheraw Gilopolis Havelock Raleigh Bay
Morehead City Beaufort
S O U T H Westbrook Fort Cape Union Blockade
C A R O L I N A Macon Lookout
Alston Camden Whiteville Onslow Bay
Florence Wilmington
Columbia Fort Johnston
Kingsville Fort Caswell
Williston Cape
Pineville Georgetown Fear Long Bay Union Blockade
Branchville Pee Dee River
Edisto River Santee River Atlantic Ocean
Charleston
Pocotaligo
Fort Sumter
Bluffton Fort
Beauregard Port Royal Sound
Fort Walker
Savannah

North

0   20   40
Scale in miles

Battle of Port Royal,
November 7, 1861

St. Helena
Island

Port
Royal
Sound Phillips
Island

Fort
Beauregard

Fort
Walker

Hilton Head Island

North

0 1 2 3
Scale in miles

seven ships in the so-called Port Royal expedition encountered foul weather on November 1 as they sailed southward, and one transport sank. The flotilla was scattered, and in the confusion of the moment many of the ships' captains opened sealed emergency orders prepared in case the vessels were separated. Du Pont had a special sense of urgency about the expedition for two reasons. First, he was the chair of a committee appointed by President Lincoln to study the challenge of blockading Southern ports, and he held a great responsibility for the outcome. (The other members were Maj. John G. Barnard of the Army, Prof. Alexander D. Bache, superintendent of the Coast Survey, and Comdr. Charles Henry Davis, a fellow naval officer.) Second, the exact spot of attack was not certain; the Navy Department wanted Du Pont to capture and secure "one or more important points along our Southern coastline," and the foul weather was seemingly disrupting the clear confidence to make decisions about what to do.

Early in the morning of November 2, Du Pont reported that the ships of the flotilla were so scattered that he could see only five in the relative darkness of the storm and that the skies unleashed a dousing rain. Heavy winds from the southeast rocked the ships, with considerable waves blowing up over some of the smaller vessels. "The fine, ordered fleet, the result of so much thought, labor, and expense, has been scattered by the winds of heaven," Du Pont wrote. By November 3 most of the ships approached a position off Charleston, and the USS *Wabash*, Du Pont's flagship but nominally commanded by Lt. Christopher Raymond Perry Rodgers, arrived at a position twenty-five miles away from the city. The following day many of the ships approached Port Royal Sound, where they concentrated and formed for an attack. Du Pont was losing his nervousness about the storm damage and reported that "the horizon was dotted with uprising sail and all came into focus."

But there had been casualties. The USS *Isaac Smith*, a fourth-rate medium screw combatant, weathered so badly that its crew had to throw the ship's armament overboard to avoid sinking. It assisted a ship in even worse shape, the *Governor*, a transport with a battalion of marines on board. The USS *Sabine*, commanded by Capt. Cadwalader Ringgold, managed to save most of the marines from the *Governor* before the latter ship sank off the coast of Georgetown, South Carolina, on November 2. In the rescue, in which the *Isaac Smith* was also involved, the *Governor* had lines attached and, in the words of Du Pont, "on these [lines] some twenty crazy marines attempted to reach her and were all drowned."

Despite the troubles, the Federal flotilla sailed on. By November 4 the first three ships were placed to enter Port Royal Sound. These were the coast survey ship *Vixen*, a side-wheeler; and the USS *Ottawa* and USS *Seneca*, screw gunboats. By the time the three Federal ships arrived, it had already been clear to the Confederate high command for some three days that the massive Union flotilla was headed for Port Royal Sound. There was little the Confederacy could do in response to such an invasion. The channel through which Du Pont hoped to run his ships was about two miles wide, with the northern end of Hilton Head Island to the south and the southern end of Phillips Island to the north. On the northern tip of Hilton Head Island stood Fort Walker. These Confederate earthworks, although adequately armed and manned, were in positions that could be pounded mercilessly by an overwhelming number of shipboard Federal guns. The Confederate forces in the area were weak at best. Fort Walker had twenty-three guns in place with one additional gun at an outwork to the east; some 622 men were inside the fort to defend it. It was commanded by Brig. Gen. Thomas Fenwick Drayton, whose assignment put him in command of all Confederate army forces in the area. Ironically, Drayton's brother, Comdr. Percival Drayton, commanded the USS *Pocahontas,* one of the attacking Union ships, and would materially participate in silencing his brother's forts. Fort Beauregard contained twenty guns (with an additional five guns in an outwork southeast of the fort) with a garrison of 640, commanded by Col. Richard Gill Mills Dunovant.

The Confederate forts, Walker and Beauregard, were not the only means of defense against the Union navy's onslaught. A small squadron of ships commanded by Capt. Josiah Tattnall would also help. Tattnall was a Georgian who hailed from a wealthy Savannah family; his family's estate, Bonaventure, had burned to the ground and become the site of Savannah's picturesque cemetery. Tattnall's flagship, the CSS *Savannah,* was a side-wheeler with one 32-pounder gun. The other two ships at hand, the CSS *Sampson* and the CSS *Resolute,* were also side-wheel steamers, each with two guns.

The reconnaissance of Port Royal Sound by the Federal ships on November 4 greatly aided the Union cause. Lt. Daniel Ammen commanded the USS *Seneca.* Ammen reported that about noon, U.S. Coast Survey Asst. Charles O. Boutelle, with the steamer *Vixen* and the ships USS *Pawnee,* USS *Ottawa,* USS *Pembina,* USS *Curlew,* and USS *Seneca,* "crossed the bar and went far enough in to have a good view of the faces and embrasures of the earthworks that we were soon to engage." *Vixen,* escorted by the sloop *Pawnee,* surveyed and dropped buoys to mark the channel for the incoming Union flotilla; the gunboats dropped anchor some distance from each other to keep watch over the Sound. By the approach of darkness Tattnall's Confederate ships, positioned in the distance, opened fire. But those ships, no match for the Union gunboats, turned and disappeared up one of the creeks. The following day, November 5, saw a repeat performance of the engagement between the four Union gunboats and Tattnall's ships, which were described by Ammen as "river boats." The four Federal gunboats turned westward toward the Confederate ships, the *Ottawa, Pawnee,* and *Seneca* all firing on the smaller vessels and eventually forcing them again to retreat upstream. At one point the Union ships moved so far in that one of the Confederate ships was in line with Fort Beauregard. One of the Federal shells exploded a caisson inside the fort, and some of the fort's rifled artillery joined in firing back at the Yankee ships along with the smoothbore guns of Tattnall's vessels. At one point the *Seneca*'s 11-inch pivot gun aimed at one of the Southern ships and fired a huge shell that "skipped along the surface of a glassy sea, and, as reported from aloft, struck the vessel abaft the starboard wheelhouse." The Confederate ships were once again sent into retreat.

On November 6, Du Pont and his officers finalized their plan of attack and received approval from the Navy Department. The order of sailing would dictate two columns of ships moving into the Sound; the USS *Wabash* (Du Pont's flagship; Rodgers) would take the lead in the southernmost column, followed by the USS *Susquehanna* (Comm. James L. Lardner), USS *Mohican* (Comdr. Sylvanus W. Godon), USS *Seminole* (Comdr. John P. Gillis), USS *Pawnee*, USS *Unadilla*, USS *Ottawa*, USS *Pembina*, and USS *Vandalia*, towed by the USS *Isaac Smith*. The northernmost, shorter, attack column consisted of the USS *Bienville* (Comdr. Charles Steedman), USS *Seneca* (Ammen), USS *Curlew*, USS *Penguin*, and USS *Augusta*. The plan of attack would be to pass through the fire of Forts Walker and Beauregard while bombarding them as heavily as possible and, after reaching a position two and a half miles north of the forts, turning and attacking Fort Walker from the northwest, its weakest flank. The northernmost flanking attack column would be at the ready to engage Tattnall's ships and put them out of action if possible. They would then concentrate their fire on Fort Beauregard. The weather on November 6 was breezy and "boisterous," according to Thomas Drayton's report; the Federal assault may have gotten underway on this day had it not been for the challenging weather.

As it turned out November 7 dawned "bright and serene; not a ripple upon the broad expanse of water to disturb the accuracy of fire." As soon as morning light permitted, Du Pont signaled his officers to attack. Tattnall's ships were standing ready about midway between the two forts. The Union ships advanced slowly for about half an hour, and at 9:26 A.M. Confederate guns from both forts and from Tattnall's ships opened fire on the leading Union vessels. Soon the Federal navy, gliding slowly forward at about six knots, returned fire and the cumulative sound of many guns erupting at once sent vibrations through the men on the ships. "There was deafening music in the air," wrote Ammen, who watched on board the *Seneca,* "which came from far and near and all around; heavy clouds of dust and smoke, due to our bursting shells and the enemy's fire, partly obscured the earth-works, while our vessels were but dimly seen through the smoke from their own guns which hung over the water."

The battle line took up position north of Fort Walker and delivered an enfilading fire onto the Rebels. Although heavy guns were firing from both Confederate forts, the defenders inside them were withstanding a tremendous pounding from the Yankee ships. "I can conceive of nothing more grand than a view of the main deck of the *Wabash* on this occasion," recorded Ammen. "The hatches being battened down, a faint light only came through the ports, as did the flashes from the discharged guns, which recoiled violently with a heavy thud. As far as the smoke would permit, hundreds of men were visible in very rapid motion, loading and running out the guns with the greatest energy. Such a view, accompanied by the noise of battle, is weird and impressive to the highest degree."

The *Wabash* and the accompanying ships turned again inside the harbor and gave Fort Beauregard a full taste of their broadside guns. Other vessels remained relatively close to Fort Walker and hammered the position with countless shells; the nearness of some of these ships, as close as 600 yards from the fort, meant that many of the rounds fired at them passed harmlessly over the hulls and damaged mostly the riggings and sails. After four hours, Du Pont and his subordinates saw signs of the Confederate resolve crumbling. By 1 P.M. the *Ottawa* signaled that Fort Walker was being evacuated; Rodgers went ashore with a flag of truce a short time later but found no one there. By 2:20 P.M. the Stars and Stripes was hoisted atop the flagstaff at Fort Walker. The cheers among the U.S. forces were so loud and cascaded across the water so effectively that they startled the defenders in Fort Beauregard. Late in the afternoon, as dusk approached, Ammen and the *Seneca* reconnoitered the state of affairs at Fort Beauregard and found the position apparently abandoned. They raised the U.S. flag over the fort the next morning and by noon turned it over to army troops. Indeed, Confederate forces had fled.

The Port Royal expedition had been a success: The United States Navy had secured a beachhead along a critical position on the South Atlantic coast; the navy and the army had worked together in the first large-scale combined operation of the war; and the region of South Carolina about to come under Union occupation—that around Port Royal and Beaufort— would become an important experimental laboratory for a variety of causes over the coming weeks. For citizens in the North, it was great news in a year of war without much to cheer about. "The victory was complete and attended with circumstances which gave it a glare of brilliancy which I never looked forward to," Du Pont wrote his wife after the engagement. For the South, it was disturbing at best. The Yankees indeed were coming. "We

have no guns that can resist their batteries and have no resource but to prepare to meet them in the field," wrote Robert E. Lee to Secretary of War
Benjamin.

THE PORT ROYAL EXPEDITION brought the importance of the Union navy
into the limelight. The navy had been created on April 30, 1798, and served
the early decades of the American nation particularly well although it was
hardly significant compared with European navies. At the outbreak of war in
1860, it had 42 warships. In 1861 the navy possessed 82 ships in operation supported by about 7,600 men. This included about 1,300 officers of which 322
defected to the Confederacy. While these ships were "on the register," most
of them were "in ordinary," that is, laid up for repairs or otherwise decommissioned, while others were in remote foreign stations. Only 16 ships were
stationed on the Atlantic and Gulf coasts. By 1865 about 600 naval ships
were in operation, supported by about 51,500 men. Many hundreds of ships
were chartered or purchased by the army quartermaster corps during the
war, and these acted in the same fashion as naval transports and store ships.

This said, it's important to know that naval forces can't be compared
simply by looking at the numbers of ships employed, nor by the numbers of
guns mounted, for ship and gun types varied enormously as did their efficiency in battle. Ships most often operated in groups that were termed variously forces, flotillas, squadrons, or fleets and consisted of a variable number
of vessels. Naval strategy was based on a blockade of the Southern coastline,
an opening of the Mississippi River to navigation, the suppression of commerce raiders on the high seas, and a support of the U.S. Army. Tactical actions included gunnery contacts such as support for coastal operations and
counterfire against shore-based artillery; temporary contacts such as the interception of commerce raiders, blockade runners, and the supply of shore
installations; and sustained contacts such as the blockading of seaports and
the support of combined operations. The types of ships used for such work
were undergoing changes early in the war. In 1861 the *Naval Register* classified
ships, in decreasing order of tonnage, in the following categories: I. Sailing
ships: A. ships of the line, B. frigates, C. sloops, and D. brigs; II. Steamships: A.
propeller (screw) ships: 1. frigates, 2. sloops: a. 1st-rate, b. 2d-rate, 3. steamers,
3d-rate, 4. tenders, 4th rate; B. Paddlewheel ships: 1. sloops, 1st-rate, 2. steamers, 3d-rate.

By 1865, however, the classification of ships had changed dramatically.
Eight broad classes of ships were developed during the war, as follows: I.
Ironclad steamers: 1st-rate, 2d-rate, 3d-rate, 4th-rate; II. Propeller (screw)
steamers: 1st-rate, 2d-rate, 3d-rate, 4th-rate; III. Paddlewheel steamers: 1st-
rate, 2d-rate, 3d-rate, 4th-rate; IV. Sailing ships: 1st-rate, 2d-rate, 3d-rate, 4th-
rate; V. Purchased propeller (screw) steamers: 2d-rate, 3d-rate, 4th-rate; VI.

Purchased paddlewheel steamers: 2d-rate, 3d-rate, 4th-rate; VII. Receiving ships: 3d-rate; VIII. Supply and store ships: 4th-rate.

The total of about 769 ships in service in the U.S. Navy during the Civil War may be classified by type: 54 monitor steamships, 26 ironclad steamships, 275 screw steamships, 271 wheel steamships, and 143 sailing ships. Only 29 of the 82 ships originally in service at the outbreak of war were still in commission at war's end. The majority of the naval losses were through decommissioning. During the war the Federal navy captured about 1,149 Confederate ships and destroyed about 351.

In terms of organization of officers, captains and lieutenants were the earliest grades in the navy, the captains being equated to army colonels, lieutenant colonels, or majors, depending on their assignments to 1st-, 2d-, or 3d-rate ships, respectively. The naval lieutenants were equated to army captains. As ship designations were altered from time to time and as varying assignments of ship commanders were made, the status of naval captains became blurred and the distinctions became based on seniority of service rather than assignment. Commanding officers of ships were termed "captain" regardless of their substantive grades. Commanders of small ships were often called "masters" or "commandants," which, by the beginning of the nineteenth century, had developed into a third, intermediate grade of master commandant. This title was simplified to the grade of commander in 1837. The title "commander" was also used as a courtesy title in both the army and navy as a contraction for "commanding officer." A lieutenant in charge of a small ship was often called a "lieutenant commanding," a title which led to the grade of lieutenant commander by 1862.

Commanding officers of yards, bases, or ports were often titled "port captain" or "post captain" regardless of their substantive grades. The ranking officer of a multiple ship group might be titled "commodore," "senior captain," or "flag officer" after the custom of his flying a flag or broad pennant from a mast of his flagship for identification. The terms "commodore" and "flag officer" were used loosely and sometimes interchangeably until 1862, when commodore became a grade and "flag officer" was replaced by the grade of rear admiral. "Sailing masters" were warranted officers in charge of handling navigation on sailing ships. By 1837 this position became the grade of master, to rank next after lieutenant. The title was retained until 1883, when it was changed to lieutenant, junior grade.

Most Civil War high-command naval officers began their careers as midshipmen prior to the establishment of the Naval Academy. They were assigned to study under naval officers in an apprentice relationship until they completed their training as junior officers and could be recommended for sea duty, or after 1819 they were promoted to passed midshipmen by a board of naval examiners. This grade was roughly the equivalent of the army brevet second lieutenant and was superseded by the grade of ensign in 1862. The grades of vice admiral and admiral were introduced in 1864 and 1866 respectively to match the army grades of lieutenant general and general.

The so-called commander-in-chief of the U.S. Navy early in the war was Senior Flag Officer Charles Stewart, the eldest of President Lincoln's military advisors. Stewart, age 83, was born in Philadelphia during the Revolutionary War. He was commissioned a captain in the navy three years prior to Lincoln's birth, and he commanded the USS *Constitution,* "Old Ironsides," among other ships in the War of 1812. By late 1861, however, it was painfully clear that Stewart was even less able to do his job than was Winfield Scott, and so Lincoln appointed a new senior flag officer, David Glasgow Farragut, on December 21. Farragut was born in Campbell's Station, Tennessee, and became a seasoned veteran of naval service; orphaned as a child, he was adopted by the accomplished naval officer David Porter, who raised Farragut along with his own sons, David Dixon Porter and William D. Porter. Farragut, age 60, would help to revolutionize naval combat tactics. He had quite some time to study naval strategy: he was a commissioned officer in the navy by age nine. Fighting in the War of 1812, he was wounded on the USS *Essex* at Valparaiso. Despite his Southern birth and marriage to a Southerner, Farragut remained staunchly loyal to the Union as the secession crisis approached.

Various bureaus and offices kept the U.S. Navy moving forward as it expanded from a small size in 1861. The source of naval thought since its founding in 1845 was the U.S. Naval Academy at Annapolis, Maryland, the brainchild of then–Secretary of the Navy George Bancroft. Because of military pressures, the Academy moved during the war from Annapolis to Newport, Rhode Island. The superintendent of the Academy during the war was Capt. George S. Blake, a Massachusetts native who excelled at administration. In Washington, the U.S. Naval Observatory and Hydrographic Office specialized in timekeeping and charting the oceans and rivers; it provided maps and logistical support for the burgeoning navy. Its chief during most of the war was James M. Gillis. Although small numerically during the Civil War, the United States Marine Corps contributed materially to the Union war effort; it was headed through the first three years of war by John Harris and thereafter by Jacob Zeilen.

The Bureau of Ordnance and Hydrography was headed by Capt. Andrew A. Harwood, a Pennsylvanian. The Bureau of Construction, Equipment, and Repair was under the direction of John Lenthal. The Bureau of Provisions and Clothing was headed by Horace Bridge. The Office of Detail, which amounted to the equivalent of the "adjutant general" of the navy, was under the authority of Capt. Charles Henry Davis, one of the great scientific minds of the navy, until mid-1862. Davis was a Bostonian who would appear prominently in a variety of places during the war.

Among the most important bureaus was the Bureau of Yards and Docks, headed by the aged Capt. Joseph Smith of Massachusetts, which co-ordinated the important activities such as shipbuilding, refitting, training, and supplying out of the nation's naval yards and facilities. The preeminent yards were the Boston (Charlestown) Navy Yard (at this time commanded by William L. Hunson), the New York (Brooklyn) Navy Yard (Capt. Hiram Paulding), the Philadelphia Navy Yard (Capt. Garrett J. Pendergrast), the Portsmouth (Kittery) Navy Yard, Maine (Capt. George F. Pearson), the San Francisco (Mare Island) Navy Yard (Capt. William H. Gardner), and the Washington Navy Yard (Comdr. John A. B. Dahlgren).

The Navy's most important early squadrons or flotillas were the Gulf Blockading Squadron (commanded at this time by Capt. William W. Mc-Kean; in 1862 it would be divided into two components), the Mississippi River Squadron, or Western Flotilla (Capt. Andrew H. Foote), the North Atlantic Blockading Squadron (Capt. Louis M. Goldsborough), the Pacific Squadron (Capt. John B. Montgomery), the Potomac Flotilla (Capt. Thomas T. Craven), and the South Atlantic Blockading Squadron (Capt. Samuel F. Du Pont).

The Confederate navy faced an even more formidable task at the out-set of war. The Navy Department was established by an act of February 21, 1861, and the regular navy was established by an act of March 16, 1861. The main difficulty for the naval officer corps was that too many of the new officers were high-ranking, having been transferred from the U.S. Navy, including at least ten captains, twenty-five commanders, and seventy lieutenants, all qualified for command of ships, while the navy had few ships available. Moreover, both promotion and assignment depended mainly on seniority in the old navy, which was slowly corrected as Navy Secretary Stephen Mallory took personal responsibility for new assignments based on merit.

An act of May 1, 1863, established the Provisional Navy, into which qualified officers could be appointed or transferred, without jeopardy to their rank in the regular navy. The advantage of the Provisional Navy was to allow promotion and assignment of competent officers over the heads of their regular navy seniors for the duration of the conflict. There remained, however, too many high-ranking officers and too few junior commissioned and warrant officers. A volunteer navy was established to provide for more junior officers as well as to register Confederate merchant officers and privateers. The volunteer navy status added legitimacy to the ship crews in the eyes of foreign governments.

But throughout the war the Confederacy faced the difficult task of acquiring ships. At the beginning of the war no Confederate ships existed. Each Southern state owned a few ships and acquired a few more by purchase, gift, or seizure. Most of these were turned over to the Confederate navy, which also constructed, purchased, chartered, or seized more. Many additional ships under army control were employed as transports, store ships, freighters, receiving ships, guard ships, dispatch boats, barges, and/or launches. Still other privately owned ships carried on international trade as privateers or blockade runners.

The Confederate navy acquired between 100 and 150 ships annually until 1865 when the number dropped off rapidly. The number of naval ships in registry at any one time was fairly constant at about 130. The total number of naval ships during the war was about 485 of which about 7 percent were sunk in action, about 33 percent were captured, about 25 percent were destroyed to prevent capture, about 12 percent were decommissioned or sold, about 7 percent were lost outside of combat, and about 16 percent were not accounted for in the contemporary records. The 485 naval ships were classified as: 22 ironclad steamers, 72 screw steamers, 321 wheel steamers, and 70 sailing ships. During the war Confederate commerce raiders captured or destroyed about 255 Union ships, mostly accounted for by the three raiders CSS *Alabama*, CSS *Florida*, and CSS *Shenandoah*.

The most important bureau of the small Confederate navy was the Bureau of Orders and Detail, commanded in late 1861 through early 1862 by the ranking officer of the Confederate navy, Capt. Franklin Buchanan. Born in Baltimore in 1800, Buchanan was an experienced sailor, having been an officer in the U.S. Navy since 1815 and a former commandant of the Washington Navy Yard. The Bureau of Ordnance and Hydrography was headed principally by George B. Minor throughout the first two years of war and by John Mercer Brooke, a Virginian and one of the most distinguished Confederate naval officers, during the final two years. Naval ordnance works in the South were located at Atlanta, Georgia (abandoned in 1864); Augusta, Georgia; Charlotte, North Carolina; Columbia, South Carolina; Columbia Naval Powder Works, South Carolina; Columbus, Georgia; Gosport Naval Yard, Virginia (abandoned in May 1862); New Orleans, Louisiana (surrendered April 25, 1862); Petersburg Powder Works, Virginia; Richmond, Virginia; and Selma Naval Gun Factory, Alabama. The Torpedo Bureau worked on a particularly ingenious program of developing special naval weapons; it was headed by Matthew Fontaine Maury, the Virginia-born hydrographer called the "Pathfinder of the Seas," during the first part of the war. In 1862, Brig. Gen. Gabriel J. Rains directed the bureau; he was succeeded by 1st Lt. Hunter Davidson. Other bureaus included the Bureau of Provisions and

Clothing, the Bureau of Medicine and Surgery, and the Confederate States Marine Corps, which was established on March 16, 1861, and commanded by Col. Lloyd James Beall.

The Confederate navy's squadrons or flotillas were the Charleston Squadron (South Carolina, created in 1862), the European Squadron (created in 1863), the Galveston Squadron (Trans-Mississippi), the James River Squadron (Virginia), the Mississippi River Squadron, the Mobile Squadron (Alabama, created in 1862), the North Carolina Squadron (created in 1862), the Red River Squadron (Mississippi River area, created in 1863), and the Savannah River Squadron (Georgia). The Confederacy's most important naval yards and stations were located at Charleston; Charlotte, North Carolina; Columbus, Georgia; Mobile, Alabama; New Orleans; Norfolk, Virginia; Pensacola, Florida; Richmond Naval Yard (Rocketts); Savannah, Georgia; Selma, Alabama; and Wilmington, North Carolina.

NOVEMBER 1861 would be a milestone month for the U.S. Navy not only because of the successful combined operation off the Atlantic coast, but because of a combined operation on the inland rivers as well. On the same day of Du Pont's battle for Forts Beauregard and Walker, Brig. Gen. Ulysses S. Grant carried off what was in essence a large-scale amphibious raid on the Kentucky-Missouri border, hundreds of miles to the west. Six days before his "battle," on November 1, Grant had been directed by the War Department to make a demonstration southward from his headquarters at Cairo, Illinois, while his fellow officer, Brig. Gen. Charles F. Smith, made a similar stab toward Paducah, Kentucky, to keep the Confederate defenders off guard. The only sizable enemy force in the area was that of Maj. Gen. Leonidas Polk, situated at Columbus, Kentucky, consisting of about 5,000 troops. This force was termed the 1st Division of the Western Department and included reinforcements from Brig. Gen. Gideon J. Pillow. Grant's so-called Expeditionary Command, consisting of 3,114 men, disembarked by transports downriver, escorted by the gunboats USS *Tyler* and USS *Lexington*. Grant's army was organized into two brigades under Brig. Gen. John A. McClernand and Col. Henry Dougherty.

What resulted was less valuable for the Federal cause in terms of the outcome than it was as a training exercise for Grant. On the evening of November 6, Grant left Cairo with his troops and moved by transport to a position nine miles south, where the expedition paused until the following morning. The idea was to "distract the enemy," as Grant put it, and make them believe they were to be attacked at the strongly held position of Columbus, which effectively gave them control of the river. However, at 2 A.M. on the 7th, Grant learned that Confederate troops had been crossing the Mississippi River from Columbus to Belmont, Missouri, attempting to cut off U.S. infantry commanded by Col. Richard J. Oglesby. What became the battlefield at Belmont and Columbus was a peculiar, sparsely inhabited region lying along a gentle bend in the nearly north-south direction of the Mississippi. To the east, on the Kentucky shore, was Columbus, where the Confederates were encamped and had two batteries of artillery. Some 2,000 feet to the west, across the river, stood Belmont, a smaller town with a single significant road heading north along the shore. By the time Grant approached Belmont, he would find a camp and battery of Rebel soldiers there as well. Grant now deemed it prudent to attack to prevent the Confederates from reinforcing the nearby Confederate forces of Maj. Gen. Sterling Price or militia Brig. Gen. M. Jeff Thompson, both operating in Missouri, and to prevent Oglesby's exposed left flank from attack.

At 6 A.M. Grant's force proceeded downriver and disembarked on the Missouri shore, just out of range of the six Rebel batteries placed at Columbus. At Belmont, Polk had established a camp of observation, as his son, Capt. William M. Polk, later wrote. "In order to command the approaches to this position by the batteries on the high ground at Columbus, the trees had been felled for some distance along the west bank, and the fallen timber had been placed as to form an abatis capable of obstructing the advance of an enemy," Polk wrote. "This camp Grant decided to attack." The camp and battery of the Confederates at Belmont, dubbed Camp Johnston, stood just north of the town; along the northward shore road were several cornfields and two ponds between the town and the Federal point of disembarkation. From the transports (*Aleck Scott, Chancellor, Keystone State, Belle Memphis, James Montgomery,* and *Rob Roy*), Federal troops marched southward along the road and deployed skirmishers, moving about a mile toward the town before forming a battle line. There, arrayed in front of a cornfield, they struck into the Confederates.

The Federal battle line, north to south, consisted of the 22d Illinois Infantry, the 7th Iowa Infantry, the 31st Illinois Infantry (Col. John A. Logan), the 30th Illinois Infantry, and the 27th Illinois Infantry (Col. Napoleon B. Buford). Interposed within the Federal force was a company of cavalry. Facing this Federal approach in Belmont, thrown up on a low ridge northwest of the Confederate camp, was a north-south battle line consisting of the 12th Tennessee Infantry, 13th Arkansas Infantry (Col. James C. Tappan), 22d Tennessee Infantry, 21st Tennessee Infantry, and 13th Tennessee Infantry. One daunting problem facing the Yankees was the amazingly high degree of fortification at Columbus. Polk's men had constructed heavy water batteries that featured 10-inch Columbiads and 11-inch howitzers, and one gun placed near the shore was the largest gun in the Confederacy, a 128–pounder Whitworth rifle nicknamed the "Lady Polk."

Despite the cannonading that bore down on the approaching Union troops, they moved toward Belmont. By late morning the Confederate skirmish lines had been driven back and a general collapse of the line of battle seemed imminent. The principal Federal line fought stubbornly through a cornfield, along a low ridge, east of the junction of two roads leading to the shore. The Confederate musketry fire was hot. For a time Grant sat on his horse behind the solid fire of Logan's Illinois soldiers. The Federals made brief advances followed by short retreats, covering the same parcels of 100 yards or so, each side alternately tasting joy and frustration. Bandmaster Thayer of the 7th Iowa was outraged when his regiment's position was overrun and his men lost their instruments. Sometime later he rejoiced when the 7th Iowa recaptured the ground they had surrendered and he retook "our instruments except one fife and drum head busted." Col. Jacob G. Lauman commanded the 7th Iowa Infantry at Belmont. Lauman told his men to "fall to the ground" so the musket balls would pass over their heads. "Crawl, boys," he commanded. Then his regiment got close enough to fire a devastating volley into the Confederate line. They arose, and fired at will with great success.

By 2 P.M. the savage fighting was becoming one-sided. Pillow's Confederate line was collapsing, the Confederate units withdrawing toward Camp Johnston. In pulling back, Southern units lost their order and a panic began to spread through the ranks. Four Federal guns manned by Chicagoans bombarded the Confederates relentlessly. Meanwhile, columns of Yankee infantry were closing in and the Rebels scattered back across the abatis and into the camp. The savagery of the small-arms fire increased: As Confederates fled in disarray, Yankee soldiers with adrenaline surging loaded and fired en masse, as when the 31st Illinois poured a savage fire into the retreating 12th Tennessee. Dozens of Confederates were shot in the panic. The pursuit became even more vigorous as Federals, attacking from three sides, surged into the camp and set tents on fire. The Confederates abandoned their colors, their guns, and made a trail northward along the river toward two transports, the *Prince* and the *Charm*, by which many could escape. Lauman led the pursuit. "A strange scene followed," wrote Eugene Lawrence of the initial foray into the Confederate camps. "Grant's troops, carried away by the joy of the moment, having taken several hundred prisoners and the enemy's camp, broke into disorder. Speeches were delivered by excited orators; the captured camp was plundered; in the midst of their enemies the inexperienced soldiers believed themselves secure."

Grant's soldiers showed their inexperience. Brig. Gen. McClernand walked to the center of the camp, near the flagstaff that flew the Stars and Stripes, and asked for three cheers. A bizarre, carnival-like atmosphere prevailed among the troops. Grant said his soldiers had become "demoralized from their victory." To regain control of the rampant plundering and partying, Grant ordered the camp set ablaze. Torches lit the tents and camp supplies, and scattered burning debris littered the ground, with great clouds of black smoke spiraling skyward. Wounded men placed in some tents in the camp may have been accidentally burned to death, giving the appearance to later Confederates that they had been purposefully murdered.

The Federal soldiers soon began a march back to their transports. They dragged two cannon, guarded 106 prisoners (all of whom were soon exchanged), and brought captured horses with them. (Four more cannon could not be suitably transported and were spiked and left on the road.) Polk and Pillow had a surprise in store for Grant, however. Confederates had been reinforced from Columbus by the *Prince* and the *Charm* and rallied along the riverbank, under cover of woods north of the camp, appearing to cut off Grant's avenue of withdrawal. Fresh troops moving south toward Grant's men now comprised the 15th Tennessee Infantry, the 11th Louisiana Infantry, and mixed infantry under Pillow and Col. Benjamin F. Cheatham. As the Yankees marched northward, a bellowing boom rang forth and a shell struck a tree near the marching column, sending dirt cascading upward and raining down on all. The "Lady Polk" had issued a protest, and numerous other Confederate guns opened fire. Maj. Gen. Polk described what resulted: "The route over which we passed was strewn with the dead and wounded . . . a heavy fire was opened on [the enemy] . . . riddling them with balls. . . . Our fire was returned by heavy cannonading by his gun-boats, which discharged upon our lines showers of grape, canister and shell."

When it was over, the Yankees escaped, aided by the fire from the *Lexington* and the *Tyler*. The battle had accomplished little and Grant's soldiers had acted in an embarrassing fashion once they believed they had tasted victory. Smith's stab toward Columbus from Paducah also was ineffective. As the smoke lifted above Camp Johnston, the Federals tallied their losses at 120 dead, 383 wounded, and 104 captured or missing. Confederate casualties were 105 killed, 419 wounded, and 117 missing. Although no one would have called Grant a hero at Belmont—he acted on weak intelligence and had no reason to hold Belmont—the action provided a test that would reset his thinking; Grant, after all, was the only Union commander who had literally followed Lincoln's order to advance on all fronts.

THE DAY AFTER GRANT'S EPISODE at Belmont brought the first international political uproar of the Civil War. At 11:40 A.M. the officers and men of the USS *San Jacinto*, cruising along the Old Bahama Channel, caught a glimpse of their prize target, the British mail packet *Trent*. The sailors of *San Jacinto* cared little for capturing a British ship but did wish to take her passengers: James Murray Mason of Virginia and John Slidell of Louisiana, Confederate commissioners to Great Britain and France. They were in transit to their new posts in Europe, having escaped the blockade in Charleston on October 12. The high-ranking yet troublesome naval Capt. Charles Wilkes, a famed explorer, commanded the *San Jacinto*. Wilkes was a native New Yorker who began service in the U.S. Navy as a midshipman in 1818; his career included leading the famed Wilkes Expedition from 1838 to 1842. But Wilkes had long been known as a hothead and a potential political nightmare. On November 8, 1861, his time for trouble arrived. The Lincoln administration had not authorized Wilkes to stop the *Trent*.

Wilkes began his entrapment of the Confederate commissioners by bringing the *San Jacinto* to Havana, Cuba, on October 31. There he learned that Mason and Slidell were present and would depart on November 7 on the *Trent*, bound for St. Thomas and then Europe. Before trailing the ship, however, Wilkes traveled to Key West to enlist a second ship, the USS *Powhatan*, to aid him. The *Powhatan* was gone, however, so he returned to Havana to undertake the mission alone. Smoke from the *Trent* appeared in the distance; it was nearly noon on November 8. Clearly, in Wilkes's mind, he was about to become a great Union hero. The Navy Department and the Lincoln administration would celebrate the capture of the commissioners as well. But none could foresee the firestorm it would provoke.

"We were all prepared for her," wrote Wilkes, "beat to quarters, and orders were given to Lieutenant D[onald] M. Fairfax to have two boats manned and armed to board her and make Messrs. Slidell, Mason, Eustis, and Macfarland prisoners, and send them immediately on board." (George Eustis and James E. Macfarland were the commissioners' secretaries.) The ships were about 240 miles from Havana, within sight of the Paredon Grande Lighthouse. "The steamer approached and hoisted English colors," Wilkes continued. "Our ensign was hoisted, and a shot fired across her bow; she maintained her speed and showed no disposition to heave to; then a shell was fired across her bow, which brought her to." Fairfax was Wilkes's executive officer. He boarded the *Trent* alone at first, argued with the ship's captain, James Moir, over seeing the passenger list, and as the argument began to heat up, Slidell, who heard his name mentioned, walked in and asked Fairfax what the trouble was. Mason, followed by the two secretaries, joined them. The four men all protested against Fairfax's intrusion and his legal right to do anything with them.

At about 1:35 P.M. Fairfax brought several armed marines on board from two small cutters, attempting to induce the four men to come with him. After a few minutes two men placed their arms strongly on Mason's shoulders and moved him into one of the cutters. Soon Macfarland followed. Fairfax again asked for more marines, and, as recorded by one of the boarding party, Lt. James A. Greer, "At that time I heard some one call out, 'Shoot him!'" Slidell attempted to escape from his stateroom into another cabin through a window but was caught; shortly thereafter Eustis turned himself over to the Federal marines. It was a "most ungraceful movement out of the window of his cabin, which opened into a small gangway," according to R. M. Hunter. Greer reported some of the disturbed outrages of the passengers on the *Trent.* "Why, this looks devilish like mutiny," people said. "This is the best thing in the world for the South." "Did you ever hear of such a piratical act?" "Why, this is a perfect Bull Run."

For its part, the Navy Department couldn't have seemed happier. Secretary Welles wrote Wilkes, thanking him for the "great public service you have rendered in the capture of the rebel emissaries." Those captured immediately lodged a protest. They were taken to Fort Warren in Boston Harbor as the *Trent* sailed on to England. Every day newspapers North and South contained news about the *Trent* affair. The outraged reactions of the Mason and Slidell families were reported, as were the fiery reactions of the *Trent*'s crew. Fairfax reported that Slidell, as he left his wife on the *Trent,* told her, "Goodbye, my dear, we shall meet again in Paris in 60 days."

In the end, Slidell was only off by twenty days. The firestorm of publicity inflamed the possibility of an intervention by Great Britain on behalf of the Confederacy and made many in Washington nervous over war with England. It also induced sympathy for the Confederate cause with many British citizens. The French government called for a joint intervention with the British to end the war, with support thrown behind the Confederacy. In December the British government accused the Lincoln administration of violating international law; it demanded an apology and the return of the men. Lincoln, Seward, and Minister to Great Britain Charles Francis Adams—who feared that calming the crisis might also require lifting the blockade of Southern ports—spent tense and busy days trying to quell the storm. On December 26 the administration decided to release the two men, terming them "personal contraband," and claiming that Wilkes had erred by not capturing the *Trent* as well. When Mason and Slidell were freed on January 1, 1862, many felt the settlement was merely a "reprieve" from British recognition of the Confederacy. Wilkes's career was over.

WHILE THE DISRUPTIVE WORRY over foreign intervention hovered over the Union cause, cold weather meant little activity on the battlefront. Scattered actions of minor consequence marked the period. In eastern Tennessee, mountaineers loyal to the Union created havoc against Confederate Brig. Gen. Felix K. Zollicoffer by burning railroad bridges and terrorizing Confederate outposts, but the support they expected to receive from approaching Union troops would not come for some time yet. In Savannah, the citizens began to panic fearing the might of a major Federal invasion to the north; on November 9, Federal forces captured Beaufort, South Carolina, without firing a shot. On the same day, the Yankees again reorganized some of their commands, this time with far-reaching consequences. Maj. Gen. David Hunter took command of the new Department of Kansas. Col. Edward R. S. Canby assumed charge of the Department of New Mexico. The Department of the Missouri, a large area consisting of Missouri, Arkansas, Illinois, and Kentucky west of the Cumberland River, was taken over by Maj. Gen. Henry W. Halleck. Believed to be one of the intellects of the U.S. Army and author of some influential military manuals, Halleck now had the job of restoring order to the area once under Frémont's direction.

The new Department of the Ohio (Ohio, Indiana, Michigan, and Tennessee) came under the command of Maj. Gen. Don Carlos Buell, who replaced Brig. Gen. William T. Sherman. The latter left under the suspicion of a nervous breakdown; the *Cincinnati Commercial* reported that "The painful intelligence reaches us . . . that Gen. William T. Sherman, late commander of the Department of the Cumberland, is *insane*. It appears that he was at the time while commanding in Kentucky, stark mad." Sherman had ruffled feathers and opened the question of his sanity as an issue in part by claiming that to win the war in Kentucky would take more than 200,000 men and require months of difficult campaigning. This, coupled with sickness and a degree of paranoia about spies and newspapermen, created doubts about Sherman in the minds of his superiors. Sherman's estimate may have seemed vast, but in the end it would be judged accurate.

While assignments were changing rapidly, President Lincoln on November 13 visited his commanding general, George McClellan, at the general's home in Washington. The president and his secretary, John Hay, along with Secretary of State Seward, waited for about half an hour after arriving, after which they found that McClellan had retired after Lincoln arrived and would not see the president. Such an indignity was characteristic of the relationship between McClellan and his superiors, and Lincoln could only joke about it afterward. Growing frustration with McClellan's inactivity spurred Lincoln to urge others to move. "He who does *something* at the head of one Regiment, will eclipse him who does *nothing* at the head of a hundred," he wrote Hunter, who was grumbling about the clout of his assignment, by year's end. Many field commanders were also growing exasperated with the quality of their commands. "The men are good material, and with good officers might readily be moulded into soldiers," wrote Brig. Gen. George G. Meade to his wife, "but the officers, as a rule, with but very few exceptions, are ignorant, inefficient, and worthless. . . . We have been weeding out some of the worst, but owing to the vicious system of electing successors which prevails, those who take their places are no better."

Frustration over poor officers, raw troops, and slow progress was growing in the Confederate Army as well. "What are they sending me unarmed and new recruits for?" wrote Brig. Gen. William H. C. Whiting to Adjutant General Cooper. "Don't want them. They will only be in my way. Can't feed them nor use them. I want re-enforcements, not recruits." James Henry Hammond, a South Carolina aristocrat and plantation owner, wrote his son Harry, a soldier in the 14th South Carolina Infantry the following day. "This miserable scheme of carrying on a war by Volunteers is utterly suicidal," wrote Hammond. "The Chivalry go at the tap of the first drum and get badly cut up and physicked out the first campaign. Little remains for a second."

Despite the anxiety over all things related to combat and the unknown time frame of the conflict, eyes on both sides turned toward Kentucky in mid-November 1861. On the 18th, soldiers of the Confederate army met at Russellville and voted on an ordinance of secession; two days later the state seceded in part and was thereafter counted by both the United States and the Confederate States. The Confederacy was thus justified in decorating its flags with thirteen stars. With its pro-Confederate governor, Beriah Magoffin, and a pro-Union legislature, the state headed for confusing times, to say the least, and its standing and influence as a border state would ultimately be decided on the battlefield. Later in the month, a convention at Wheeling, Virginia, in the loyal, mountainous part of the state, adopted a constitution for a new state that would be called West Virginia. The breakaway of part of Virginia would not occur right away, but the seeds were sown.

PURELY MILITARY ACTIONS crept along through the final weeks of the year. Brig. Gen. Lloyd Tilghman of the Confederate army was named to command Forts Henry and Donelson on the Tennessee and Cumberland rivers, which now appeared to be obvious targets for the Union invasion of Southern waterways. On November 22, Union soldiers and sailors began a two-day coordinated bombardment of Confederate installations around Pensacola, Florida. The Federal shelling came from Fort Pickens and the screw frigate USS *Niagara* (Capt. William W. McKean) and the screw sloop USS *Richmond* (Capt. Francis B. Ellison) and concentrated on the Pensacola Navy Yard, Fort McRee, and Fort Barrancas. The attack also shelled the Confederate steamer *Time*. At 9:55 A.M. the guns at Fort Pickens commenced firing; half an hour later the two Federal ships joined the bombardment and Confederate batteries returned fire. Col. Harvey Brown, inside Fort Pickens and commanding the Department of Florida, reported that he opened his batteries on the Confederates to find a four-mile line of Rebel guns respond, with many 10-inch Columbiads and 13-inch seacoast mortars. A "spirited fire" was kept up during the whole day. The rate of fire from Pickens amounted to one shot per gun every fifteen or twenty minutes until it was "too dark to see." By noon the guns at Fort McRee had been silenced, and by day's end the batteries at Barrancas were perceptibly lessened and the *Time* abandoned in partial ruin.

During the action a portion of the town of Warrington caught fire, as did several structures inside the Confederate forts. The two Union ships did not move close in on the second day due to the prevailing winds. The Confederate commander of the Army of Pensacola, Maj. Gen. Braxton Bragg, embellished his after-action report. "Their ships, both crippled," he wrote, "are withdrawn to their former anchorage, a miserable failure being their reward for commencing an engagement without notice and firing into houses they knew to be occupied by women and children and closing it by disgracefully violating the hospital flag, in accordance with a former barbarous threat." In the end, the action resulted in little except for a small number of casualties on each side. For a time, however, the heavy destruction of guns at Fort McRee forced Bragg into considering its abandonment, and his emotional report may reflect a case of nerves.

On November 24, Union forces took another step toward controlling more of the South Atlantic coast by landing on Tybee Island, Georgia, giving them a starting point for attacking Fort Pulaski, the massive brick fort that helped protect the city of Savannah. Cotton planters burned much of their cotton along the coast, near Savannah and Charleston, to prevent its capture. Small fires could be seen along parts of the shore from ships on various nights. The military action itself had reached a "droning stage," with many small skirmishes taking place almost every day in Missouri, Kentucky, Virginia, and Tennessee, but none of these amounting to much. Federal and Confederate ships, intermingling with blockade runners, encountered each other every few days on the high seas, near the Leeward Islands, or on inland rivers, resulting in a few captures but little of consequence. On December 9, the renewed session of the U.S. Congress and anxiety over the spare progress of the war and "disasters" of the army led to the creation of the Joint Committee on the Conduct of the War. Its origin was tied mainly to the Ball's Bluff fiasco and sparked by the burning desires of radical Republicans to prosecute the war vigorously.

One of the worst disasters for Confederate citizens came about accidentally when on December 11–12 a great fire swept through the business district of Charleston, the emotional center of the Confederacy, ruining much of the city east of King Street and along the Cooper River. Alarms sounded at 8:30 P.M. and the flames eventually burned 540 acres, 575 homes, and some of the city's great buildings, such as the Circular Congregational Church, Institute Hall (where the ordinance of secession had been signed), and St. Andrews Hall. Robert E. Lee was among those who witnessed the fire, watching it from the roof of the Mills House. "In general . . . the whole space in S.W. direction from the foot of Hasell Street on the Cooper River side to the Ashley River at a point between Tradd and Gibbs Street is one smoking ruin," the attorney James L. Petigru wrote his daughter. "Hour after hour of anxiety passed," wrote Emma Holmes, age 22 and a resident of Charleston, "while flames raged more fiercely and the heavens illuminated as if it were an Aurora Borealis—it was terrifically beautiful. The tide was rising & every wave crested with foam, while beyond the rosy clouds floating overhead was the intense blue of the sky & Sirius sparkling like a brilliant diamond.... The terror! the misery, & desolation which has swept like a hurricane over our once fair city will never be forgotten as long as it stands."

Amid the din of skirmishing, two more significant military actions would provide fire for the armies North and South. On December 13, Brig. Gen. Robert H. Milroy led his Federal force at Cheat Mountain in western Virginia against a Confederate encampment commanded by Col. Edward Johnson at Camp Baldwin on nearby Alleghany Mountain. Johnson had about 1,200 men encamped at Alleghany and nine cannon, and Milroy brought some 1,760 toward the camp, with skirmishers deployed, aided by a loyal Virginian who knew the camp's position. The 25th Ohio Infantry led the way up a steep, rocky mountain road and ran into Confederate pickets instead of waiting for the other regiments to form for attack. The result was that the Confederates attacked several times, being repulsed often but pouring a hot volley into the Yankees. After sharp fighting, both armies retreated from the summit, the Federals with 137 casualties and the Confederates with 146. "The enemy were totally routed," wrote Johnson. "I hear from citizens on the line of their retreat that they carried numbers of dead and wounded by the houses, and acknowledged that they had been badly whipped." The Federals indeed retreated to Cheat Mountain, but Johnson's men also retreated, to Staunton in the Valley. Afterward, Johnson would be called "Old Alleghany."

One week later a severe action erupted at Dranesville in northern Virginia, about midway between Alexandria and Leesburg. Both McClellan's army and Joe Johnston's army were much in need of hay during this winter season, and they by chance sent foraging parties out to the same place. At daybreak on December 20 the Rebel party took nearly every wagon in Johnston's army, escorted by Brig. Gen. Jeb Stuart's cavalry, and moved north from Centreville. They also brought four regiments of infantry and a battery of artillery—it was a heavily armed foraging expedition. At about the same time, Union Brig. Gen. Edward Otho Cresap Ord moved five infantry regiments, a four-gun battery, and a squadron of cavalry from Camp Pierpont in the same direction as Stuart.

Ord's Yankees entered Dranesville about noon after a twelve-mile march, and after rebuffing a few scattered Confederates, they occupied the town. An hour later the lead elements of Stuart's horse troopers approached the town, and Col. Thomas L. Kane, commanding the 1st Pennsylvania Reserve Rifles, moved his regiment onto a hill, deploying his men and notifying Ord of the Confederates. Both Ord and Stuart were briefly uncertain about what to do next but soon moved units forward into the fight. Ord moved three more regiments south of the Leesburg Turnpike, on Kane's right, and moved the battery into position, enabling it to begin to lob shells toward Stuart's men. The 11th Virginia Infantry (Col. Samuel Garland, Jr.) and 10th Alabama Infantry (Col. John H. Forney) then attacked headlong into the Union line, part of which was protected by a two-story brick house; a vicious fight with heavy musketry fire ensued for a thirty-minute period. Stuart withdrew about 3 P.M., taking his wagons and suffering a total of 194 casualties; Ord had lost only 68 men. "Our artillery did terrible havoc," wrote Ord of the fight, "exploding one ammunition wagon, and some of their men whom we brought in say the slaughter was terrible. Several dead lay around the exploded caisson, three of whose blackened corpses were headless."

TOWARD THE END OF THE YEAR both presidents struggled to sum up what the war meant thus far and how their nation had responded to the challenges that lay before it. "Liberty is always won where there exists the unconquerable will to be free," said Jefferson Davis to the Confederate Congress. "A succession of glorious victories at Bethel, Bull Run, Manassas, Springfield, Lexington, Leesburg, and Belmont has checked the wicked invasion which greed of gain and the unhallowed lust of power brought upon our soil, and has proved that numbers cease to avail when directed against a people fighting for the sacred right of self-government and the privileges of freemen." Lincoln, on the other hand, told the U.S. Congress in his State of the Union message that "the insurrection is largely, if not exclusively, a war upon the first principle of popular government—the rights of the people." He concluded by describing how the United States would grow to a country of 250 million people and how "the struggle of today, is not altogether for today— it is for a vast future also." At the same time, the leading military man in the nation, George McClellan, still showed no signs of initiating action. Lincoln wrote him a memorandum around December 1. "If it were determined to make a forward movement of the Army of the Potomac . . . how long would it require to actually get in motion?" Lincoln inquired. In reply, McClellan stalled and mentioned having another, undisclosed plan.

"All quiet along the Potomac" became the operative phrase of the end of 1861, a term occasionally scribbled into telegrams by McClellan and printed in many newspapers. At first the phrase was a boast, meaning that none in Washington need be alarmed at the possibility of a Confederate approach. As time wore on, however, and certainly by year's end, the phrase became a jab at McClellan's inactivity. Ethel Lynn Beers immortalized the phrase in her poem "The Picket Guard," published in *Harper's Weekly* on November 30 and later set to music presumably composed by James Hewitt. "All quiet along the Potomac tonight / No sound save the rush of the river / While soft falls the dew on the face of the dead / The picket's off duty forever."

CHAPTER 6

Grant Moves into Tennessee

THE YEAR 1862 DAWNED with no particular glow on the American landscape. The war was still in its infancy, the armies and navies relatively unorganized, and the political will of North and of South to carry on a protracted struggle uncertain. In America life went on despite the war. Congress authorized the first U.S. legal tender banknotes; by war's end more than $400 million in "greenbacks" would be issued. The Pacific Railway Act authorized the Union Pacific Railroad to construct a line from Nebraska to Utah to meet the Central Pacific coming eastward from the West Coast. British and French troops withdrew from Mexico, where Napoleon III established French rule.

The slow progress of the American Civil War, now frustrating North-erners who wished they would not lose any more sons and Southerners who felt the same plus the added sting of shortages caused by the blockade, would accelerate in the coming year. Slowly, the chaos of tactics and strategy would cohere into structure; some farsighted field commanders would begin to appreciate the deadliness of the rifled muskets many of their soldiers now used; the concepts of troop concentration in time and space would begin to make themselves known; and a new motivation for fighting the war would come into play.

This year the sizes and organizations of the armies and navies would undergo significant changes. On January 1, the U.S. adjutant general reported his army's size as 527,204 present and 48,713 absent for an aggregate strength of 575,917. By year's end the figure would rise to an aggregate strength of 918,191, although only 698,802 were present for duty. By contrast, the Confed-erate Army consisted of approximately 318,011 at the beginning of 1862 and 449,439 by year's end. While the numbers seem greatly to favor the Union, it must be remembered that the Federal army's aims were much loftier. While the Confederates could fight in large part a defensive war on their own ground, the Yankees most often needed to attack (offensive operations normally require at least two to four times the number of men relative to defensive operations), had to operate without the advantage of interior lines, and had the formidable task of holding and occupying ground they had taken, including vast miles of coastline, railroads, and western territories. So the strategic goals of the Federal side required many more men. The navies grew slowly during this transitional year, but they would undergo changes in the way they fought.

The officers who commanded the troops in the field and those who occupied staff offices in Washington and Richmond would also change materially over the war's second year. On top of the general climate of inactivity—attributable to inexperience, the winter weather, timid field commanders, poor planning, and many other complexities of war—the public, the politicians, and senior officers themselves lamented the pitiable condition of the officer corps. "I am in the condition of a carpenter who is required to build a bridge with a dull ax, a broken saw, and rotten timber," Maj. Gen. Henry W. Halleck wrote Lincoln on January 6, concerning his subordinates. The greatest series of changes relating to any officer during 1862 would concern George McClellan, whose inactivity on the battlefront caused Lincoln to begin issuing a series of war orders to force him and others to move forward. Lincoln and McClellan also disagreed on the plan that should be used once the army did begin to move, McClellan favoring a movement down the Chesapeake, up the Rappahannock to Urbana, and then toward the railroad terminus along the York River. Lincoln favored a direct approach across land toward the railroad south of Manassas.

On March 11, Lincoln's exasperation over McClellan led to the termination of his assignment as general-in-chief. Thereafter, for four months, the army was directed by Lincoln and the gruff secretary of war, Edwin McMasters Stanton, who had replaced the corrupt Cameron on January 15, assisted by a "war board." The board consisted of Maj. Gen. Ethan Allen Hitchcock, who represented the line, and the bureau chiefs Lorenzo Thomas, Montgomery C. Meigs, Joseph G. Totten, James W. Ripley, and Joseph P. Taylor. The board functioned as a general staff, operations office, and coordination group. Stanton was an Ohioan, age 47, whose balding head and flowing dark beard gave him an odd appearance; he had briefly served as attorney general before the outbreak of war.

Later in the year new faces would show up in a variety of assignments. In September, Col. Joseph Holt, a Kentuckian and former secretary of war and postmaster general, became the army's judge advocate general. The newly established Provost Marshal General's Department, created in October, would be headed by Simeon Draper. The following month Hitchcock, who had chaired the president's war board, took charge of the Office of the Commissioner for Exchange of Prisoners. In the Pay Department, Col. Timothy Patrick Andrews became paymaster general. Brig. Gen. William A. Hammond of Maryland became surgeon general of the army.

On the Confederate side, 1862 would bring adjustments in personnel in other ways. Despite his lackluster performance in western Virginia in the autumn of 1861 and inability to prevent the Federal capture of Hilton Head and other points along the South Atlantic coast, Gen. Robert E. Lee was held in great esteem by President Davis. In March, Lee would be called to Richmond to act as an advisor to Davis and was "charged with the conduct of military operations in the armies of the Confederacy," making Lee more or less a temporary general-in-chief of the Confederate armies (although he did not hold such a title at this time). In the Bureau of War, Robert Garlick Hill Kean took charge. The Bureau of Indian Affairs, which was already receiving considerable support by Indians because of soured relations with the Federal government, was now headed by Sutton S. Scott. William Norris was assigned command of the newly created Signal Bureau. The Bureau of Nitre and Mining, created to assist the Bureau of Ordnance, was headed by Maj. Isaac Munroe St. John, a Georgian. Robert Ould, a native of the District of Columbia, headed the Bureau of Prisoner Exchange. Worries over the strength of the army forced the creation of the Bureau of Conscription at the end of 1862; it was assigned to Gabriel J. Rains, which was actually a cover for his work in sabotage and the development of land mines.

Some personnel had petty, but nagging, problems. One Union colonel, Justus McKinstry (often misidentified as a brigadier general; his commission as such was never confirmed) spent the first autumn of the war as an assistant quartermaster in the Department of the West. Described by one writer as "one of the most thoroughgoing rogues ever to wear a United States uniform," McKinstry was caught stealing a wide variety of supplies and subsequently court-martialed for graft, corruption, and fraud. "My accounts would have been rendered long since if I had not been prevented from so doing by officers & agents of the Government," the embattled officer attempted to explain in February 1862. "The books & papers as I have been credibly informed were taken from the cases in which they had been appropriately placed & were rudely thrust into boxes in a heterogeneous mass without regard to their character or value. . . . I now again respectfully ask that my limits of arrest may be enlarged so that I may be permitted to go to my office where my books & papers are said to be & be enabled to make up & render my accounts." The explanation didn't stick, and McKinstry was finished in the army.

As both sides were shifting personnel, Lincoln began to think about military strategy. Frustrated with his commanders, he had been borrowing large numbers of books on militarism from the Library of Congress and educating himself about what McClellan and others refused to impart to him. "I state my general idea of this war to be that we have the *greater* numbers," Lincoln wrote Maj. Gen. Don Carlos Buell, on January 13, "and the enemy has the *greater* facility of concentrating forces upon points of collision; that we must fail, unless we can find some way of making *our* advantage an over-match for *his;* and that this can only be done by menacing him with superior forces at *different* points, at the *same* time; so that we can safely attack, one, or both, if he makes no change; and if he *weakens* one to strengthen the other, forbear to attack the strengthened one, but seize, and hold the weakened one, gaining so much."

Lincoln was beginning to understand the principles that would help him achieve victories, and the character of the capital city was transforming around him. "Washington was then a military camp," explained Noah Brooks, a California reporter, "a city of barracks and hospitals. The first thing that impressed the newly arrived stranger . . . was the martial aspect of the capital. Long lines of army wagons and artillery were continually rumbling through the streets; at all hours of the day and night the air was troubled by the clatter of galloping squads of cavalry; and the clank of sabers, and the measured beat of marching infantry, were ever present to the ear." It was in this martial atmosphere that the author and activist Julia Ward Howe, wife of the Bostonian reformer Samuel Gridley Howe, visited Washington in November 1861. As she awoke from a dream in the middle of the night at Willard's Hotel, a block from the Executive Mansion, Julia Howe scrawled some lines on hotel paper with a pencil. When the poem was finished, she had written one of the masterpieces of the era, "The Battle Hymn of the Republic."

The piece was published in the *Atlantic Monthly* in February 1862 and was soon set to the same music used for "John Brown's Body." "Mine eyes have seen the glory of the coming of the Lord / He is trampling out the vintage where the grapes of wrath are stored / He hath loosed the fateful lightning of His terrible swift sword / His truth is marching on." Following stanzas focused Howe's message more concretely. "I have seen Him in the watch fires of a hundred circling camps / They have builded Him an altar in the evening dews and damps / I can read His righteous sentence by the dim and flaring lamps / His day is marching on." Finally, the concept of the Civil War as a holy war for freedom was stated clearly. "In the beauty of the lilies Christ was born across the sea / With a glory in His bosom that transfigures you and me / As He died to make men holy, let us die to make men free / While God is marching on." In several weeks' time observers would hear the song sung in Union camps, and its lyrics embraced the direction the war would take later in the year, toward emancipation as a moral crusade. Already the pressure from some abolition groups was mounting to use black Americans in battle against the Confederacy. One of the most eloquent advocates of this idea was Frederick Douglass, about 44 years old, the articulate former slave who mesmerized audiences with his ideas and his form of expression. "We are striking the guilty rebels with our soft, white hand, when we should be striking with the iron hand of the black man," Douglass said in Philadelphia on January 14. He believed firmly that "The destiny of the colored American . . . is the destiny of America," as he said in a speech at the Emancipation League in Boston on February 12. Douglass also said a loyal black man would serve the Union Army "with a pickaxe if he cannot with a pistol, a spade if he cannot with a sword."

FOR THE MOMENT, however, no black Union troops would be employed, and emancipation seemed to many of its ardent supporters an unimaginably distant goal. On the very first day of the year, military action erupted at Port Royal Ferry, South Carolina, along the Coosawhatchie River, as the Federal beachhead on the South Atlantic coast took hold. The objective for Brig. Gen. Thomas W. Sherman's expeditionary corps was to attack the Confederate batteries erected at Port Royal Ferry and those opposite Seabrook, South Carolina, northwest of Beaufort. The attack itself was to be led by Brig. Gen. Isaac I. Stevens, Massachusetts born, a brilliant soldier. Stevens stood only 5 feet 1 inch tall and has been described as a "swarthy little man." His attack force of about 3,000 men would be supported by Federal gunboats under the command of Comdr. Christopher R. P. Rodgers. For this combined operation, the naval flotilla would consist of the screw gunboat USS *Ottawa* (Lt. Thomas Holdup Stevens), screw gunboat USS *Pembina*, four armed boats from the USS *Wabash*, the screw gunboat USS *Seneca* (Lt. Daniel Ammen), the tug *Ellen*, and the armed tug *E. B. Hale*.

On December 31, Stevens's force departed from Beaufort after he left a small detachment to guard the town. This consisted of two companies of the 100th Pennsylvania Infantry ("Roundheads"), while the remaining companies struck out with Stevens's expedition. Scattered companies of the 79th New York Infantry ("Highlanders") would also occupy outposts as well as participate in the coming attack. The remaining land force, seven companies, would operate against the Confederate left. At the break of dawn on January 1 the Federal forces, supported by the navy and carried by many flatboats, were underway.

Opposing the Federal force was a small contingent of Confederates under the overall command of Brig. Gen. John C. Pemberton, who was then commanding the 4th Military District in South Carolina. More immediately, Brig. Gen. Daniel S. Donelson was in command of the 1st Brigade of his district and Col. James Jones of the 14th South Carolina Infantry was in immediate command of the troops on the field. About 7 A.M. on January 1, Jones was informed that Federals were landing in force on Chisholm's Island, near Port Royal Ferry. About noon the Federal gunboats opened fire with barks and claps of artillery shells thundering over the Confederates. The Federals advanced toward Port Royal Ferry. Instead of advancing along the Kean's Neck Road, the enemy "left his artillery in his rear, and advanced creeping along opposite his gunboats, five of which steamed slowly on, throwing shells in advance of and over his troops," according to Jones's report. The Federal force crossed the Coosawhatchie River successfully, in the words of Stevens, "having caused the buildings in the vicinity of the fort to be burned and the fort to be leveled sufficiently for all practical purposes."

The engagement at Port Royal Ferry was a Federal success that widened the enclave of the Yankee army and navy on the South Atlantic coast. The casualties were light: 2 killed and 13 wounded or missing on the Union side and 8 killed and 24 wounded on the Confederate side. This action helped to increase the alarm among the Confederate strategists over the Union invasion of the South. "Wherever his fleet can be brought no opposition can be made to his landing, except within range of our fixed batteries," Robert E. Lee wrote Samuel Cooper on January 8. "We have nothing to oppose his heavy guns, which sweep over the low banks of this country with irresistible force." Meanwhile, the strategic importance of precisely operated naval operations was becoming clearer in Washington. "The importance of a rigorous blockade at every point under your command cannot be too strongly impressed or felt," Gideon Welles wrote Samuel F. Du Pont on January 25. "By cutting off all communications we not only distress and cripple the States in insurrection, but by an effective blockade we destroy any excuse or pretext on the part of foreign governments to aid and relieve those who are waging war upon the Government."

A succession of minor affairs unfolded in a multitude of places during the cold first days of 1862. Maj. Gen. Stonewall Jackson's Confederates in the Shenandoah Valley moved north from Winchester on January 1, instigating a series of operations sometimes called the Romney campaign. To threaten the Baltimore & Ohio Railroad and destroy dams along the Chesapeake and Ohio Canal, Jackson's men created a minor skirmish at Bath, Virginia, on January 3, which he occupied the next day. On the 5th he followed the retreating Federals to the Potomac opposite Hancock, Maryland, and Jackson bombarded the town for two days. By January 10, Yankees at Romney evacuated the town rather than fight, and here Stonewall's men settled in for a time. But Jackson was furious with Brig. Gen. William W. Loring, one of his subordinates, and the War Department's ill-advised communications. After receiving a telegram ordering Loring's force back to Winchester, effectively negating the gains of the Romney campaign, Jackson submitted his resignation: "With such interference with my command I cannot expect to be of much service in the field . . . I respectfully request that the President will accept my resignation from the Army." Jackson wrote Governor Letcher of Virginia regarding Secretary of War Benjamin's "interference," on February 6. He explained, "I am in active service not because it is more congenial to my taste, but from a sense of duty. The moment that my services are not required in the field I desire to return to the [Virginia Military] Institute." The trouble was smoothed over, Jackson was placated, and he went on to make Confederate history.

Much of the Federal effort was focused on eastern Tennessee. In Kentucky, Brig. Gen. Don Carlos Buell listened only vaguely to Lincoln's call for the movement into Tennessee. Neither Buell nor Maj. Gen. Henry W. Halleck had responded to Lincoln's request to name a day on which they would move forward. Despite this, action was heating up in eastern and in southern Kentucky. Buell was in command of the Department of the Ohio, and he detached his 18th Brigade, commanded by Col. James A. Garfield of Ohio, to harass the Confederate troops under Brig. Gen. Humphrey Marshall, concentrated at Paintsville. Marshall was a Kentuckian; Garfield, age 30, was a teacher, lawyer, and politician who had served as president of Hiram College as a relative youth and would one day become president of the United States.

Garfield set out to find Marshall's force near Paintsville. Garfield's force numbered about 3,000. Marshall's Army of Eastern Kentucky had desired a battle around Hagar's Farm, near Paintsville, but Marshall intercepted a letter of Garfield's. On learning of the advance of Col. Jonathan Cranor's 40th Ohio Infantry, Marshall decided to fall back to a strong position on a ridge near the forks of Middle Creek, near Prestonsburg, where he waited for Garfield. By January 10 the Yankees had moved up into position facing Marshall and were ready to attack.

Marshall had about 2,000 men ready for battle, deploying the 5th Kentucky Infantry ("Ragamuffin Regiment," Col. John S. Williams), 29th Virginia Infantry, and a portion of a mounted regiment of riflemen along the ridge. The 54th Virginia Infantry occupied high ground along with an artillery battery. Skirmishing erupted about 10 A.M., and a full-fledged attack led by Union cavalry began at noon. Confederate guns opened fire and devastated the charge, throwing the horsemen back and taking them out of the action for the rest of the battle. Garfield next ordered an infantry attack on Marshall's right. The fight went on until dark, with each side claiming a victory afterward. The casualties were about 25 killed and wounded on each side. "It was growing dark and I deemed it unsafe to pursue him," Garfield wrote of the action's termination, "lest my men on the different hills should fire on each other in the darkness."

Garfield's tactics were unsatisfactory, but Marshall withdrew nonetheless a day later. It was a harsh winter and some of the men were "nearly naked." A single regiment had 350 men without shoes and not more than 100 blankets for 700 men.

A greater Kentucky battle with farther-reaching consequences would come in little more than a week's time. In the southern part of the state, forces were drawing closer to the town of Somerset. Confederates were encamped at Beech Grove with their backs facing the Cumberland River, and they were hearing sporadic reports of a Union advance by troops under Brig. Gen. George H. Thomas, commanding the 1st Division of the Department of the Ohio. Confederate Maj. Gen. George B. Crittenden, commanding the Military District of East Tennessee, faced the prospects of a strengthening Federal advance into eastern Tennessee. Crittenden's 1st Brigade was commanded by a colorful politician, Brig. Gen. Felix K. Zollicoffer, who had previously commanded the district. Zollicoffer had placed his men at Mill Springs, south of the Cumberland, but had recently moved them into an exposed position north of the river. Crittenden ordered Zollicoffer to move back south of the river, an order that Zollicoffer ignored.

What resulted on January 19 was the battle of Mill Springs. Thomas's force consisted of the 2d Brigade (Col. Mahlon D. Manson), 3d Brigade (Col. Robert L. McCook), 12th Brigade (Col. Samuel P. Carter), and attached artillery; Brig. Gen. Albin F. Schoepf rejoined Thomas's army with his 1st Brigade from Somerset after the fighting had ceased. Altogether, Thomas had about 4,000 men on the field. On the Confederate side, Crittenden's force of about 4,000 consisted of the 1st Brigade (Zollicoffer), 2d Brigade (Brig. Gen. William H. Carroll), with a reserve consisting of the 5th Battalion of Tennessee Cavalry.

The hot-tempered Confederate commander, Crittenden, held a council of war at Zollicoffer's camp and decided to attack Thomas before the Federal commander could concentrate his forces and be rejoined by Schoepf. Crittenden ordered an advance at Mill Springs on January 18 and formed the column of attack with Zollicoffer followed by Carroll with artillery. Despite gloomy darkness and heavy rain, Crittenden's army began marching over nine miles of muddy roads at midnight on January 19, finally reaching the pickets of the Federal 1st Kentucky Cavalry about 5:30 A.M. Thus began the second-largest battle to be fought in Kentucky during the Civil War, a relatively small affair militarily that would nonetheless have significant fallout. The pickets fell back and were supported in the early morning rain by the 10th Indiana Infantry. The busiest Yankee officer of the moment was Col. Manson, who ran through several camps calling for support and warning of the action.

The Confederate attack came up from the south along the Mill Springs

Road, past a blacksmith's shop and a log house, into the Federal lines and camps scattered across both sides of the road and through some woods and fields. To the north was the camp of the 10th Indiana Infantry, near the Logan House, and the east-west road that connected Columbia with Somerset. Manson yelled at Col. Speed S. Fry of the 4th Kentucky Infantry, who clambered out of his tent and got his men into order in jig time. Kentucky-born Fry was a lawyer and volunteer soldier. Fry raced his men toward the sound of the firing and deployed them along a fence at the edge of the woods.

Fry's regiment, with the 2d Minnesota Infantry (Col. Horatio P. Van Cleve) and the 10th Indiana behind, along with cavalry, faced the oncoming rush of the 15th Mississippi Infantry (Lt. Col. Edward C. Walthall) and the 20th Tennessee Infantry (Col. Joel A. Battle). Fry's 4th Kentucky almost at once received a blistering fire from the front and from Confederates who were sheltered in a deep ravine through the open field in front of Fry's regiment. Other Confederates were posted on a hill about 250 yards away. Fry considered the placement of his Confederate foes unsporting and, mounting the fence, "in stentorian tones denounced them as dastards, and defied them to stand up on their feet and come forward like men."

After a lull in the firing, Fry mounted his horse and rode to the front to get a better view of the situation. The visibility was poor: the ground was soaked with rain, the sky cloudy and the woods dark, and the whole scene pervaded by a gloomy smoke that settled low to the ground. As Fry turned back toward the Federal line, he suddenly encountered a mounted officer clad in a white raincoat. The other fellow on horseback approached so suddenly that for a moment the two men's knees touched; the officer murmured that "we must not fire on our own men," and then nodded toward the left, saying "those are our men." As Fry wheeled his horse back, he told the man that of course he would not fire on the Federal troops. Just then, another officer rode toward the pair on horseback and fired a pistol shot at Fry's horse. Fry immediately fired at the suspicious officer in the raincoat, and a number of other shots rang out from Federal men behind Fry. The officer in the raincoat, who fell wounded and died at the base of a tree, was Zollicoffer. He had been struck by a pistol shot in the chest and by two musket balls. It was the first such instance in the war of a general officer being killed by such a high ranking officer; Fry himself would later become a general. The tree under which Zollicoffer died, known as "the Zollie tree," stood on the battlefield until it fell in 1995.

The death of Zollicoffer and the hot firing from Fry's regiment that followed resulted in the center of the Confederate line falling back for a time in confusion. Thomas arrived on the field to lead the Union center. A period of intense fire now erupted across the line as Thomas ordered the 9th Ohio Infantry (Maj. Gustave Kammerling) up in support and the 2d Minnesota kept up a furious fire in the front line. At this time a position of the lines was so close that the "enemy and the Second Minnesota were poking their guns through the same fence," wrote McCook. The 9th Ohio's ability to turn the Confederate left served as the battle's hinge. Thomas pursued most of the fleeing Confederates as they scrambled back to the area of Beech Grove. By nightfall the battle was clearly a rout, the Confederates leaving scattered debris in their wake for miles as they made paths to Crittenden's small stern-wheel ship and two tiny flatboats. By the morning, much of Thomas's army had passed or captured numerous items in the abandoned Confederate camps, including 12 guns, a vast quantity of small arms, 150 wagons, and more than 1,000 horses and mules. Not only had Crittenden's senior brigade commander been killed, but his whole army had been so demoralized that many deserted in the coming days.

The casualties were relatively light. Thomas reported 39 killed and 207 wounded, and the Confederate casualties were 125 killed and 404 wounded and missing. Strategically and psychologically, the battle was a big boost for the Union cause in Kentucky and a blow to Confederate morale. Excuse making pervaded the reports of Southern officers. "Perceiving the fortunes of the day were against us, and that we could not longer maintain the unequal contest," wrote Carroll, "I reluctantly permitted my entire command to retreat in the direction of our works at Mill Springs." Carroll also invoked the tools of war. "The repulse of the regiments of my command that gave way in confusion during the battle is attributed (besides the superior numbers with which they were contending), in a great measure, to the inefficient and worthless character of their arms, being old flint-lock muskets and country rifles, nearly half of which would not fire at all."

WHILE SUCH ACTION was transpiring in the West, inactivity continued in the East. Partly, this was a reflection of legitimate concerns such as the horrible winter weather and muddy roads. "Mud, mud. I am thinking of starting a steamboat line to run on Penn. Avenue," wrote Elisha Hunt Rhodes, a soldier in the 2d Rhode Island Infantry, in Washington, on January 31. "If I was owner of this town I would sell it very cheap. Will the mud never dry up so the army can move? . . . I want to see service and have the war over so that I can go home." A good part of the inactivity came from the continued timidity of the Federal commanders, too, chiefly George McClellan. The new secretary of war, Edwin Stanton, was growing embittered day by day with the lack of aggressiveness, and he let his favorite correspondents know this. "This army has got to fight or run away. . . . the champagne and oysters on the Potomac must be stopped," he wrote his friend Charles A. Dana, managing editor of the *New York Tribune,* on January 24. Several days later he wrote Dana again: "We have had no war; we have not even been playing war." And by late February, Stanton wrote a letter to the *Tribune* that contained the sentence, "Battles are to be won, now, and by us, in the same and only manner that they have ever been won by any people since the days of Joshua—by boldly pursuing and striking the foe."

One of the few Federal commanders with a bold idea of how to strike at the Confederacy would ultimately prove one of the least bold. Brig. Gen. Ambrose E. Burnside, who had fought at First Bull Run, concocted a plan in the late autumn of 1861 to organize a special expeditionary force to operate along the South Atlantic coast. Burnside had become a favorite officer of President Lincoln and enjoyed political prestige due to his friendship with McClellan, which extended back into the antebellum days when Burnside worked for McClellan at the Illinois Central Railroad. The plan was based in part on the well-received suggestion by Union Col. Rush C. Hawkins, that North Carolina's Roanoke Island ought to be captured as a Federal base of operations, along with an occupation of the Neuse and Pamlico rivers. Burnside took up the plan and vigorously promoted it to the Lincoln administration, which approved the idea. Not only would such a position lead to inland operations in eastern North Carolina, but by occupying the coast it would impede blockade running and cut off harassment of Union shipping by Confederate vessels. Moreover, the sentiment of many citizens in eastern North Carolina leaned against the Confederacy. Burnside would lead the next great combined operation that would see a considerable army force supported by a naval flotilla. By early January the armada and the army organization for what became the Albemarle Sound expedition, or the Burnside expedition, gathered at Annapolis, Maryland, ready to strike into North Carolina.

The Burnside expedition departed for the Atlantic coast on January 12 with "colors flying and bands playing." It consisted of a total force of about 15,000 men deployed on about one hundred naval vessels of a variety of sizes and types. Burnside had been freshly assigned to command the newly created Department of North Carolina; his was termed the so-called Coast Division, comprising three brigades, commanded by Brig. Gens. John G. Foster, Jesse L. Reno, and John G. Parke. Additionally, there were nine army gunboats, five floating batteries, a huge armada of army transports, and naval forces. The naval flotilla was commanded by Capt. Louis Malesherbes Goldsborough, a career naval officer who had been born in the District of Columbia in 1805. For those who believed that many army officers received commissions when they were young, Goldsborough, a large man with a large temper, demonstrated that the navy could be even more inviting for youngsters. He had been warranted a midshipman in the U.S. Navy at age seven. The naval forces consisted of twenty gunboats plus additional ships operating off Beaufort.

As Burnside, Goldsborough, and their fighting men approached Albemarle Sound, they would find a scattered group of Confederate defenders in their path. Nearly 2,500 men were arrayed on Roanoke Island, a sandy island laden with trees. They were commanded by Brig. Gen. Henry A. Wise, who commanded the District of Albemarle and had, the previous autumn, contributed to the Confederate failure in western Virginia by quarreling with various officers. Not only was Wise an ineffective commander, but he was also ill, and so turned over command of the island's forces to Col. Henry M. Shaw of the 8th North Carolina Infantry. Wise, at Nag's Head, was suffering from pleurisy. The island's defenders consisted of six regiments and were supplemented by a naval squadron of nine vessels commanded by Capt. William F. Lynch. Confederate forces to the south at New Bern were under Brig. Gen. Lawrence O'Bryan Branch, who commanded the District of Pamlico; various river batteries were also brought to bear as the Yankees approached.

With the Federal armed forces already establishing bases in South Carolina, the task at hand was now to establish a beachhead along the North Carolina coast. By late January the delicate task of moving vessels over the shallow sand bar at Hatteras Inlet began. Mismanagement and poor planning, which became hallmarks of Burnside's army career, began to show. The separation of command for the army and navy troops and vessels resulted in a lack of overall coordination. Cape Hatteras holds dangerous currents as well as areas with shallow water—as little as six feet—and many ships had to be tugged, dragged, or lightened to get across the bar, while some had to use their propellers to gouge out a trough through the muck. To make matters worse, a gale swept over the flotilla and scattered, damaged, or beached vessels, so the whole force had to be reassembled. Three army vessels were lost. Fortunately for Burnside and Goldsborough, the small number of Confederates in the area could do virtually nothing against the armada despite its troubles.

On Roanoke Island, the Confederates were able to defend themselves at five positions. Three of these positions were on the western side of the island. Fort Huger stood to the north at Weirs Point, with Fort Blanchard and Fort Bartow to the south, stretching down to Pork Point. Between Fort Bartow and Fort Forrest, which stood on the mainland, across Croatan Sound, stretched a line of piles and sunken vessels. On the eastern side of the island, artillery was placed at Ballast Point, which commanded Roanoke Sound and Nag's Head to the east. At Ashby Harbor, on the western side of the island's midsection, stood more guns. As Confederate defenders watched the Burnside expedition slowly come across the bar at Cape Hatteras, they issued an ever more alarming call for reinforcements from New Bern and other parts of the state. The calls fell largely on deaf ears, however, and when Jefferson

Davis ordered Maj. Gen. Benjamin Huger, at Norfolk, to reinforce the area of Albemarle Sound, it was too late. The only option for Confederate authorities was to hope that Wise's small force could turn back the invasion.

On February 5 the Union ships formed into three divisions and began their movement toward Roanoke Island. Fog, wind, and rain stalled the movement, however, and the attack was set for the morning of February 7. As the fog lifted, Goldsborough moved his flag from the USS *Philadelphia,* a side-wheeler, to the USS *Southfield,* an ex-ferryboat converted into a side-wheel steamer. Goldsborough's nineteen active gunboats, mounting fifty-seven guns, moved toward the island at about 11 A.M., with the steamers USS *Ceres,* USS *William G. Putnam,* and USS *Underwriter* taking the lead. Seven Confederate vessels opposed the onslaught, with merely eight guns ready to fire.

The first loud reports came from the *Underwriter,* which opened fire on Ashby Harbor at 11:25 A.M. By noon a general bombardment opened up from many Union ships, which pummeled the small Confederate fleet and concentrated a good deal of fire on Fort Bartow. Meanwhile, the northernmost Confederate forts, Blanchard and Huger, were effectively out of the action because their shells could not reach the Union ships. Two ships were put out of action by early afternoon—the CSS *Curlew* was knocked out of action and run aground, and the CSS *Forrest* was forced to abandon the fight and seek refuge in Elizabeth City. The remaining Confederate vessels ran out of ammunition by midafternoon and withdrew from the fight. "Repeatedly in the course of the day I feared that our little squadron of seven vessels would be utterly demolished, but a merciful Providence preserved us," wrote Lynch in his report.

Now came the army's opportunity. At 4:30 P.M. the Confederate fire was weak enough that Burnside decided to begin landing his troops just north of Ashby Harbor. Some 10,000 men stepped through sticky mud and sandy shore and moved inland. By 6 P.M. the Federal ships ceased firing altogether, and by midnight the Yankee troops were bivouacked for the night, mostly in a clearing and cornfield around the Hammond House on the north side of the harbor. The night was uncomfortable at best; soldiers stripped wood from fences to make plank "roads" to haul artillery and to make small fires to warm coffee. Cold rain began to fall before midnight, producing mud everywhere. Col. Shaw withdrew to Suple's Hill and tried to regroup.

By 7:30 A.M. the lead regiment of the Union attack, the 25th Massachusetts Infantry, was ready to move. It was followed by the 23d Massachusetts Infantry, the 27th Massachusetts Infantry, and the 10th Connecticut Infantry. After an advance of a mere half mile, the Federal troops found in their path a deep gulch of cold water, and as they crossed it, Confederate pickets opened fire. The battle of Roanoke Island had begun. Col. Shaw deployed his men around a three-gun battery positioned in the middle of the island alongside the north-south road. He held most of the Confederate units behind this position in reserve and stationed several scattered companies of his own regiment, the 8th North Carolina Infantry and the 31st North Carolina Infantry at the battery itself. The ground was swampy, and some of the soldiers sank appreciably as they tried to fire; preserving unit organization was nearly impossible.

A series of volleys opened and grew hotter as more units came into the fight and as artillery was better positioned on both sides. The road was opened up finally so that Reno's brigade could move forward and enter the fight. Union commanders began to move their men through the swampy ground and then to attempt to turn the Confederate right. Much of the Union fire had been high and ineffective on the entrenched Confederate line. But by 11 A.M. this began to change: Reno's men increased the rapidity of their fire and Lt. Col. Alberto C. Maggi and his 21st Massachusetts Infantry charged and stormed the works.

As the battle developed, the 9th New York Infantry, dressed in colorful Zouave uniforms and led by none other than Col. Rush Hawkins, who had suggested the expedition in the first place, moved through the swampy ground toward the Confederate position. (Hawkins, a respected soldier, had said that he did not wish promotion because "Brigadier-generals are made of such queer stuff nowadays, that I should not esteem it a very great honor to be made one.") Just as they anticipated joining the charge, the 10th Connecticut Infantry—dressed in gray overcoats—stood up and fired a volley. Confused by the uniforms, the chaos of the battle, and the charge by others underway, many of the 9th New York scattered and fled; elements of the regiment attacked after the enemy had retreated. Most of the Confederates in the end were captured; Shaw surrendered 2,488 officers and enlisted men. The Confederate casualties were 24 killed and 222 wounded and missing. On the Federal side the losses were 41 killed and 242 wounded and missing.

Despite the sloppy start, Burnside's Expedition could score an impressive gain by capturing Roanoke Island, and again a combined operation had resulted in a Federal strategic victory. The Lincoln administration had something to be truly happy about, and a base of operations here would allow Burnside and others to probe more deeply into North Carolina in the weeks to come. "The mission of our joint expedition is not to invade any of your rights," Burnside decried to the population on February 16, "but to assert the authority of the United States, and thus to close with you the desolating war brought upon your State by a comparatively few bad men in your midst." Most Confederates staved off alarm about such losses. "We must give up some minor points, and concentrate our forces, to save the most important ones, or we will lose all of them in succession," wrote P. G. T. Beauregard. In summarizing his army's achievement, Burnside wrote: "No body of troops ever had more difficulty to overcome in the same space of time. Its perils were both by land and water. Defeat never befell it. No gun was lost by it. Its experience was a succession of honorable victories."

WHILE CONVENTIONAL NAVAL OPERATIONS resulted in Union success in North Carolina, Virginia was witnessing what would become the transformation of naval history. With blockade runners multiplying in number and the small but burgeoning Confederate navy promising to pose a threat, Federal naval authorities looked for ways to stiffen the strength of the Union navy. Despite the fears and ill faith of some conservatives in the Navy Department, Federal forces explored a variety of novel ideas that would modernize the Union flotilla, including ironclad warfare—a concept that would help to redefine warfare on the water. On January 30 a crowd gathered at Greenpoint, Long Island, New York, to see the launching of the startling USS *Monitor,* the ironclad gunboat created by Swedish inventor John Ericsson. The vision of an ironclad gunship had percolated in Ericsson's mind since 1826, but he had been unable to sell the idea to the British and French governments. During the early months of the war it had become clear that the Confederate navy was retrofitting the hull of the old USS *Merrimack,* captured at Norfolk, into an ironclad gunboat—it would be renamed the CSS *Virginia*—and that a similar ironclad warrior, a floating battery, ought to be created by the Union navy.

The *Monitor*'s design was revolutionary and odd. The hull spanned a mere 124 feet and was just 6.5 feet deep, with an "upper hull" or deck mounted on top that measured 172 feet long and 41 feet across. On this deck was mounted a single turret some 9 feet high and about 20 feet in diameter, containing two 11-inch smoothbore Dahlgren guns. The hull was constructed of solid oak beams covered by two 1-inch-thick iron plates, and aside from the turret, the whole ship stood above the waterline by a mere foot. An iron skirt protected the rudder, propeller, and the hull. The ship incorporated some forty inventions and was well-nigh impossible to destroy by conventional means; to penetrate the lower hull below the armor belt, a cannonball might have to travel through more than 25 feet of water before striking, and no gun on earth could accomplish this feat. The queer appearance of the ship gave rise to the epithet "cheesebox on a raft."

ON JANUARY 28, Brig. Gen. Ulysses S. Grant, commanding the District of Cairo, wrote his superior, Maj. Gen. Henry Halleck, in charge of the Department of the Missouri, with a plan. "With Permission I will take Fort McHenry [*sic*] on the Tennessee and hold & establish a large camp there," wrote Grant. He referred to Fort Henry, one of three forts protecting Tennessee from a southward invasion. At Cairo, Illinois, Grant's force had recovered fully from its baptism by fire at Belmont and was ready for further action. In January four separate plans of action were proposed by Union authorities—Buell, Halleck, McClellan, and Lincoln—but none was agreed upon. The victory at Mill Springs resulted from the partial implementation of Buell's idea of attacking toward Nashville. Frustrated with the lack of communication, Halleck finally authorized Grant to proceed with his action to move on Fort Henry without coordinating any movement with Buell, who was commanding the Department of the Ohio and was currently in central Kentucky. (Halleck and Buell were in essence equals, who each received commands directly from the War Department.) The commander who faced this potential southerly movement was Gen. Albert Sidney Johnston, who oversaw Confederate Department No. 2, charged with Confederate forces from Arkansas to the Cumberland Gap.

Although the weather was cold, the time was ripe for a clash in the West. Halleck's 91,000 soldiers were mostly in Missouri, with nearly half his force in St. Louis. Buell's 45,000 men were arrayed across Kentucky from Louisville to Munfordville, with detachments at Lebanon, Columbia, and Somerset. Grant had approximately 20,000 men from Cairo through Paducah to Smithland, Kentucky. The Confederate forces of Johnston's, about 43,000, stretched across most of western Tennessee and parts of southern Kentucky. At Columbus, Kentucky, Maj. Gen. Leonidas Polk faced Grant's line with some 12,000 men. About 22,000 Confederate troops under Maj. Gen. William J. Hardee occupied Bowling Green and Hopkinsville, Kentucky, and Clarksville, Tennessee. Confederate strongholds existed at Forts Henry and Heiman on the Tennessee River, Fort Donelson on the Cumberland River, and—well to the west—Forts Pillow, Randolph, and at Island No. 10 along the Mississippi.

What became the Henry and Donelson campaign began on February 2 as Grant moved his force, about 12,000 men altogether, south from Cairo. Grant's Army of West Tennessee consisted of three divisions, commanded by Brig. Gens. John A. McClernand, Charles F. Smith, and Lew Wallace. Supporting the infantry units were two regiments of cavalry and eight batteries of artillery. Grant's force was assisted by the Mississippi River Squadron under Capt. Andrew H. Foote. For the movement on Fort Henry, Foote's squadron of seven iron- and timberclad gunboats consisted of the flagship USS *Cincinnati*, the USS *Essex* (Comdr. William D. Porter), the USS *Carondelet* (Comdr. Henry Walke), the USS *St. Louis*, the USS *Conestoga*, the USS *Tyler*, and the USS *Lexington*. The plan called for Foote's squadron to steam south and open fire on Forts Henry and Heiman, pounding them into submission before Grant's men overran and captured the positions.

Forts Henry and Heiman stood on opposite banks of the Tennessee

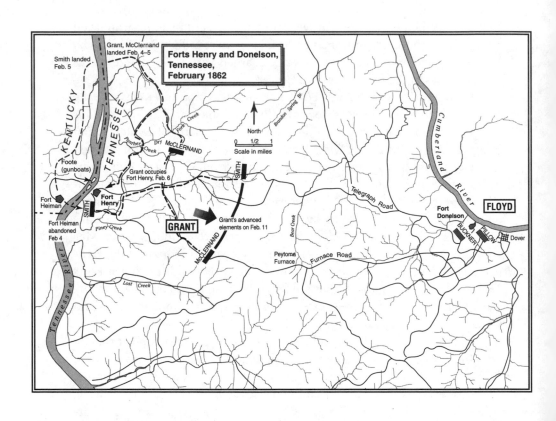

Forts Henry and Donelson, Tennessee, February 1862

Smith landed Feb. 5

Grant, McClernand landed Feb. 4–5

KENTUCKY

TENNESSEE

North

0   1/2   1
Scale in miles

Fork Creek

Panther Creek

Dry Creek

McCLERNAND

Foote (gunboats)

Grant occupies Fort Henry, Feb. 6

Fort Heiman

SMITH

Fort Henry

Fort Heiman abandoned Feb 4

Piney Creek

GRANT

Grant's advanced elements on Feb. 11

McCLERNAND

SMITH

Tennessee River

Lost Creek

Bear Creek

Bowton Spring Br.

Telegraph Road

Peytoma Furnace

Furnace Road

Cumberland River

Fort Donelson

FLOYD

BUCKNER

PILLOW

Dover

River near the Kentucky-Tennessee border, and almost on the line that sep-arated the departmental commands of Halleck and Buell, nearly fifty miles southeast of Smithland. Fort Henry stood on the east bank of the river, in a considerably marshy area, while smaller Fort Heiman stood on the western shore about one mile away. (In modern times the creation of Kentucky and Barkley lakes has altered the riverbanks and placed the sites of Forts Henry and Heiman under water.)

During the first days of February the Confederate garrisons at Forts Henry and Heiman consisted of a relatively small number of men. Fort Henry's commander was Brig. Gen. Lloyd Tilghman. Tilghman's two brigades, comprising 3,000 men total, were commanded by Cols. Adolphus Heiman and Joseph Drake. Forts Henry and Heiman were relatively weakly defended: Henry mounted only seventeen guns, including a dozen that fronted the river. Heiman was defended chiefly by field guns and small arms, hardly adequate to help bolster Fort Henry's ability to ward off a major attack from Grant's army or the gunboats. Fort Henry was also built at a tactically vulnerable position, being relatively low in elevation and open to enfilading fire. It was also filled partly with water, having been flooded by recent icy rains. In addition to the 3,000 men around these two forts, 1,956 Confederate defenders were garrisoned at Fort Donelson. As Grant received his approval to proceed upriver toward Forts Henry and Heiman, snow was falling in the region. Despite this, the Union troops were eager to have the chance to dis-place Tilghman's men and perhaps open a gateway into Tennessee.

Grant's movement would take place in two columns on either side of the river. Beginning at 4:30 A.M. on February 4, Grant began to disembark McClernand's division well north of Fort Henry along the eastern shore of the river. (McClernand, a political troublemaker who had received his com-mission in part because he had known Lincoln in Illinois before the war, named his headquarters Camp Halleck after Gen. Halleck, attempting to in-flame perceived differences between Halleck and Grant.) The men had to be shuttled to the position due to a shortage of water. The return fire from the Confederates was persistent, however. At one point during the action a ball passed through one of the boilers of the *Essex,* seriously wounding 29 officers and men, scalding most of them, including Porter. "*Essex* then necessarily dropped out of line, astern," wrote Foote, "entirely disabled and unable to continue the fight, in which she had so gallantly participated until the sad ca-tastrophe." The *Carondelet* knocked out one of the Confederate guns early in the contest and so some of the Rebel cannon concentrated their fire on it throughout the fight.

But the shelling of Foote's gunboats overwhelmed the small garrison and its few guns, and by 1:50 P.M. Tilghman raised a flag of truce that was not seen, as the firing continued, due to the dense smoke that surrounded it. A few minutes later Tilghman succeeded in surrendering, with the condition that officers could retain their side arms and that the men would be treated with respect. Tilghman, along with the other 11 officers, 66 enlisted men, and 16 men on the hospital boat *Patton,* were taken prisoner by Foote and his naval subordinates. Tilghman would be imprisoned for six months until being exchanged. McClernand and Smith, slowed by the muck and mire of the icy roads, failed to capture the retreating columns moving east to Fort Donelson. The Confederates would now concentrate there. Drawing on the *Nashville Union and American,* Foote could proudly quote the Southern feeling about the operation: "We had nothing to fear from a land attack, but the gun boats are the devil."

Tilghman's ineffective defense of Henry and Heiman cost the Confederacy dearly, as it gave the Federal navy control of the upper portion of the Tennessee River. Grant continued his penetration much more deeply into Tennessee. Union gunboats could move farther upriver to destroy the Memphis & Ohio Railroad Bridge, thus severing Johnston's line of communication between the two portions of his army. It so threatened Johnston that he had to withdraw along the line he had established or attack Grant himself, and in the confused series of actions he took during the second and third weeks of February, he decided to try both options. Johnston moved his right wing under Hardee from Bowling Green and environs south to Nashville, enabling Buell to enter the fray more effectively, and at the same time he sent reinforcements to Fort Donelson to attempt to ward off Grant. The reinforcements came in the form of 12,000 men commanded by Brig. Gen. John B. Floyd, who had fought in the western Virginia campaign the previous autumn.

As Johnston was maneuvering, Grant was encamped with most of his force in the vicinity of Fort Henry until February 11. The weather was harsh, with blowing winds and floodwaters from the heavy rains that prevented resupply. Grant was anxious to move on Fort Donelson before the Confederates could conduct further work on the structure, but the high water, inadequate supplies, and poor roads blocked a movement. Grant advocated quick action, against the wishes of Halleck, who advised him to "hold onto Fort Henry at all hazards. Picks and shovels are sent, and large reinforcements will be sent immediately." Grant was the opposite of Halleck in strategic planning, however, so he pushed on toward Donelson in earnest on February 12, marching across the land between the rivers. McClernand's command was divided, with a portion taking the Telegraph Road and the other portion taking the Furnace Road, while Smith's division took the Telegraph Road. By nightfall on the 12th, most of Grant's force was in position on a high ridge opposite the entrenchments constructed by the defending troops of Floyd. James A. Connolly, a major in the Federal army, described the trip from Fort Henry to Fort Donelson in a letter written to his wife. "The ground was strewn with . . . coats, pants, canteens, cartridge boxes, bayonet scabbards, knapsacks, . . . raw pork, broken guns, broken bayonets, . . . all sorts of things that are found in the army."

Floyd had built a partial ring of trenches from a position south of the town of Dover west and north to a position west of Fort Donelson. Floyd's army, consisting of approximately 20,000 men, was formed into three major divisions, garrison troops, and attached cavalry. The divisions were those of Floyd himself (commanded by Col. Gabriel C. Wharton when Floyd took command of the whole force) and Brig. Gens. Gideon J. Pillow and Simon B. Buckner. The garrison troops, from Tennessee, were commanded by Col. John W. Head. The cavalry was led by Col. Nathan Bedford Forrest, who would become one of the more remarkable figures of the war. Tennessee-born, Forrest had moved to Mississippi, received a scant education, but nonetheless became a wealthy planter and slave trader.

The Confederacy employed a better design at Fort Donelson than it had had at Henry and had tactical advantages, too. The fort itself was in a much stronger position for defense, and the artillerists at Donelson had constructed formidable water batteries for insurance. Floyd's ring of trenches had Pillow's troops south of the fort and town and Buckner's men west of it. As Smith's Federal division made its way eastward, it settled due west of Buckner's line. McClernand, who had halted south of Smith, moved his way over to a position south of Pillow's line by February 14. On the night of the 13th, Grant's missing division—that of Brig. Gen. Lew Wallace—landed on the west bank of the Cumberland at a point four and a half miles north of the fort and marched its way south to move in between Smith and McClernand by the 14th. Meanwhile, Grant had urged Foote to bring his gunboats into position in the Cumberland and repeat the heavy bombardment that had so easily overwhelmed the Confederates at Henry.

On February 13 the two principal Union divisions, those of Smith and McClernand, tested the defenses of Donelson. After limited action, little of consequence resulted other than the Yankees finding that they had a tough line in their front. By nightfall Foote's ships were in place and ready for action the next day, but a terrific winter storm began to dump snow on the region, and all that most of the troops could do was to dig in and hope for the best. The experience was miserable, and the cold added much to the suffering of those on both sides—in and out of the fort—who had relatively meager supplies. It was especially grim for those who were already sick. The next morning Grant turned his attention to the gunboats. On February 14, Foote's gunboats moved in and unleashed a terrific fire, but this time the result was completely different than it had been at Henry. The Confederate water batteries returned a steady and pounding fire, inflicting great damage on the

Union squadron and forcing Foote to withdraw. The fight commenced at 3 P.M. and lasted about ninety minutes, with the six Union vessels moving to within 400 yards of the fort. Foote reported that the *St. Louis* alone had received fifty-nine shots and that a rifled gun burst on the *Carondelet*, causing great damage.

The *Louisville* also received a Columbiad shot that carried away the heads of three crewmen. After an hour, only the *Pittsburg* and the *Carondelet* remained in the action. During the height of the firing from Confederate cannon, the always excitable Bedford Forrest turned to his chaplain, David C. Kelley, and screamed, "Parson! For God's sake, pray. Nothing but God Almighty can save that fort." The Federal naval force had lost 54 dead and wounded in the attack. Foote himself was wounded, struck in the left foot by a fragment of shell. Although he lived another sixteen months, Foote died in June 1863 from complications caused by the Fort Donelson wound, along with Bright's disease. The suffering from this wound was much on his mind: in a routine letter of July 17, 1862, Foote, sending an admirer his autograph, mentioned that "the effects of my wound at Fort Donelson compels me to be brief."

The naval bombardment of Donelson didn't work. Seizing the fort would be a task for Grant's infantry, and the bitter cold on the morning of February 15, accompanied by fresh snow on the ground, did little to promote a feeling of confidence among the Yankee troops. The fort was much stronger than Henry, being placed along an elevated ridge. Moreover, Donelson was garrisoned adequately, had a larger number of cannon, and was generally well supplied with ammunition at the fight's outset. Little action occurred between the armies on the 14th, as the Confederates occupied the entrenchments strengthened in the wake of Henry's fall. Floyd now had about 21,000 Southern soldiers in the fort and around the ring of trenches. The water battery mounted eight 32-pounder guns and two 32-pounder howitzers. The Confederate lines stretched from Buckner to the west, on a high position between the fort and Hickman Creek, to Pillow south of the fort on a high ridge between the town of Dover and Indian Creek. Pillow's left was placed along the edge of the town of Dover.

Meanwhile, McClernand, now reinforced with the returning brigade of Col. John McArthur, had spent part of the 14th extending his right flank up to a position near the Cumberland River. McClernand's line stretched southward through scattered timber and undergrowth along Wynn's Ferry Road, terminating at a point between Pillow's right and the Rollins House. Smith concentrated his force southwest of Buckner, between Hickman Creek and the terminus of the southern road to Fort Henry, and east of the Crisp House. Wallace posted his men into a smaller area between McClernand and Smith. Meanwhile, Grant was let down by the failure of the naval operation, demoralized by Foote's wounding, and resigned to the very thing he dreaded—a siege operation. The welfare of his troops under such a circumstance was a major concern as well, as both rations and clothing were scant for some soldiers, and the thermometer indicated a mere 12°F temperature on the morning of the 15th. This was hardly ideal for any kind of fighting.

On the Confederate side, the psychology was even more grim. Suffering, want of supply, and a feeling that Grant's force was considerably larger than it was all contributed to a sense of panic in Floyd. He decided to hold a council of war on the evening of February 14 and polled his subordinates about what to do. He decided to abandon the fort. This shocking turn of events was partly fueled by a feeling that the Federal navy would also be back to shell his position again and perhaps fueled as well by a fleeting sense of personal fear. Floyd had been secretary of war under James Buchanan, and he feared that if captured he would be hanged as a traitor to the United States. These factors produced another unwise decision in the Confederate chain of command as Floyd decided to cut his way out of the Union onslaught. He wanted to preserve his army by escaping to Nashville.

By 5:30 A.M. on February 15, Floyd commenced the Confederate attack by sending Pillow to lead a breakout on the Union right, smashing into McClernand. The idea was to push McClernand southward and open a route of escape upriver to the vicinity of Clarksville, and then on to Nashville. As Pillow pushed McClernand out of the way, Buckner was assigned to move his division across Wynn's Ferry Road and scatter it slightly, acting as a rearguard for the remainder of the army as it pulled out and moved northeast. A single brigade of Buckner's force would stay in the trenches and act as a thwart to any Federal movement. Pillow's attack began well, and the fighting that erupted along the line was heavy throughout most of the morning. For two hours Pillow's men fought savagely against those of McClernand without the Confederates advancing substantially; by midmorning Pillow was pushing McClernand away and opening the escape route successfully.

Pillow's attack was succeeding, considerably aided by Brig. Gen. Bushrod R. Johnson, his second-in-command. After noon the Federal line was south of the Charlotte Road, the attack being successfully supported by Forrest's cavalry. Everything was going well for the planned escape; McClernand's right flank was exposed and disorganized, Forrest had a significant cavalry force in place to assist the Confederate retreat, Buckner was moving into position to cover the movement, and a route of escape was open. The threshold of Confederate success had been achieved despite the fact that several of the Confederate commands were fighting in relative isolation, without much overall coordination of attacks. By 1:30 P.M. Pillow believed the first phase of the attack was successful and that he should regroup before pushing forward. Astonishingly, he ordered his men back to their trenches. At first Buckner and Floyd were outraged; a short time later, after Pillow had tried to justify his move to Floyd, the two men were standing together looking at the scene with field glasses. They saw what appeared to be immense activity in the area of C. F. Smith's lines. They heard false reports about Grant receiving 20,000 reinforcements.

Floyd now had one of those moments of the worst kind for a field commander, a moment that many others would share during the war—the McClellans, Popes, Burnsides, and Hookers. He froze. Panicked by his lack of confidence in the breakout, alarmed by the increasing action by skirmishers under Smith's division, and rattled by the possibility of what might happen to him if captured, he ordered *all* of his troops back into their trenches.

Grant, all the while, had been absent for much of the crisis. Foote's wound of the previous day meant that Grant had to go to visit him rather than the reverse. So early in the morning of the 15th, Grant went to see the naval commander, hoping to coordinate further action, and ordered Smith, McClernand, and Wallace not to bring on a general engagement. He did not anticipate any such action as Pillow's and left the divisions as they were, and his headquarters in the hands of his chief of staff, Col. Joseph D. Webster. Grant rode back toward the sound of booming cannon not knowing exactly what was taking place and encountered the headquarters tent of his friend Smith, who briefed him on the attack. Although alarmed to learn that McClernand was engaged in a hot fight, and believing part of his army at least was in a state of demoralization, Grant dispatched Foote to make a show of force and believed that the Confederates, who had moved back, were in an even poorer state. He regrouped and ordered Smith to press an attack along his front. Then he rode by about 3 P.M. to the Union right and pushed McClernand and Wallace to counterattack and retake the ground they had lost earlier in the day. By now Grant had found that Confederates were fighting with filled haversacks and knapsacks, which suggested they were going to break out. Floyd had offered the initiative to the Federal army, and Grant wasted no time in accepting it. He coolly told Smith that "all has failed on our right—you must take Fort Donelson," to which Smith replied, "I will do it."

About 2:15 P.M. Smith moved his men off the ridge and toward the old works constructed by Buckner. Three battalions of the 30th Tennessee Infantry were left here, armed with shotguns, and they could not match the attack put on by Smith. The Federal movement toward this position forced them to retreat in haste; by the time Grant rode to the right of the line, Smith had already cleared out the outer defense ring without firing a shot. Floyd now ordered Buckner's division back to stop the movement on the Federal left, and just as Smith's men took aim at the inner defense line, Buckner's

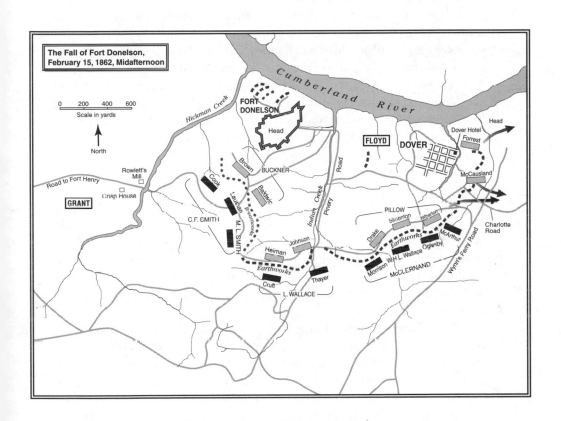

The Fall of Fort Donelson,
February 15, 1862, Midafternoon

0   200   400   600
Scale in yards

North

Cumberland River

Hickman Creek

FORT
DONELSON

Head

FLOYD

DOVER

Dover Hotel

Forrest

Head

McCausland

Rowlett's
Mill

Road to Fort Henry

Crisp House

GRANT

Brown

BUCKNER

Cook

Baldwin

Laubian

Breastworks

M. L. SMITH

C.F. SMITH

Indian Creek

Pilney Road

PILLOW

Simonton

Wharton

Drake

McArthur

Earthworks

Charlotte
Road

Heiman

Johnson

Morrison

W.H.L. Wallace Oglesby

McCLERNAND

Earthworks

Cruft

Thayer

L. WALLACE

Wynn's Ferry Road

men—exhausted though they were—filled in and stopped Smith's advance. Likewise, Pillow fell back into his position along the inner defense line, and the investment and siege of Fort Donelson fell back into place. However, McClernand failed to block the Charlotte Road, thereby leaving an escape route wide open. After an hour of intense fighting during the evening, the battlefield slowly quieted down and the men were vaguely positioned where they had been the previous morning. Campfires sprang up to warm the troops from the freezing cold; the moans of the wounded mingled with the subtler sounds of nature. Across the fields some 3,000 men had become casualties throughout the day, and Maj. James A. Connolly noted with morbid fascination of having picked up more than twenty hats with bullet holes containing pieces of flesh, skull, or blood and hair matted inside. He also saw the oddity of pools of frozen blood and many dead horses littering the ground.

To mark the occasion of another night, Floyd unceremoniously held another council of war at about 1 A.M. on February 16. Now Floyd, Pillow, and Buckner came to the conclusion that they must surrender the fort, and Floyd and Pillow—both fearful of treason charges—determined to escape and leave Buckner holding the bag. Despite this, Buckner had been the loudest in terms of panic and had argued with the other commanders that the position was untenable. Floyd also ignored Albert Sidney Johnston's order to evacuate the command to Nashville. The council now approached madness: Buckner and Floyd went to great lengths to rationalize that Johnston should be happy with the army's performance because it bought him time; Pillow, angry and wanting to fight his way out, finally caved in to the pressure but would not entertain a personal surrender. During the night Floyd and Pillow both fled, two steamboats having arrived and the generals climbing aboard the *General Anderson*.

They left the overwhelming bulk of the force behind to surrender to Grant. Not so with all the soldiers, however. Forrest led a daring escape with his whole cavalry command traversing a flooded, frozen road that ran parallel to the river, moving past the Federal line fifteen minutes before the road was closed by McClernand's sluggish action. Forrest and his whole command arrived safely in Nashville by 10 A.M. on February 18. Men of the 20th Mississippi Infantry formed a guard around the riverboats, and many eventually climbed aboard; Cols. John McCausland and Wharton and their men were successfully ferried across the river. One soldier, Pvt. Thomas J. Riddell, was so mortified at the thought of being captured that he waded through neck-deep, freezing-cold water in the river to reach one of the boats.

Meanwhile, Grant received a note from Buckner requesting terms of surrender, which arrived about daybreak. Bugle calls from the fort and a large white flag were now attracting attention all across the Federal lines. At the Crisp House, Grant consulted with Smith, his old teacher at West Point, who suggested no mercy toward the Rebels. Grant's reply shocked Buckner and made Grant a hero of the war overnight. "No terms except an unconditional and immediate surrender can be accepted," Grant wrote. "I propose to move immediately upon your works." In the papers that covered the surrender, particularly in the North, where good news from the war front was much needed, Grant now acquired a new name to match his somewhat unusual initials, "Unconditional Surrender" Grant. Causing Buckner to feel the sting even further was the fact that he had been Grant's prewar friend. Now he replied, "The distribution of forces . . . and the overwhelming force under your command compel me . . . to accept the ungenerous and unchivalrous terms which you propose." The formalities of the surrender took place in Dover at the Dover Hotel.

What resulted was the largest capture of troops to date. About 11,500 men were taken as prisoners, along with forty cannon, the fort itself, and large quantities of supplies. The casualties of killed and wounded were about 2,000 on each side, such that what remained of Floyd's army was a mere shadow of its former self. This obviously failed to please Johnston and the Confederate authorities in Richmond, and investigations of the actions by Floyd, Pillow, and others extended for months. Northern prisons had hundreds of new customers, and among the notables captured was Head. The campaign was a serious loss for the Confederacy. Johnston's defensive line was now penetrated. Although Johnston himself was at Murfreesboro, Tennessee, Beauregard at Jackson, Tennessee, and Polk at Columbus, Kentucky, the final days of February extended the Union movement into Tennessee. With Grant at Dover and Buell moving toward Nashville, the potential for Union movement southward could be felt all the way toward Florence, Alabama. Grant had not only taken the forts but had cut Johnston's east-west communications by holding the Memphis & Ohio Railroad. Federal gunboats under the command of the wounded Foote now could patrol the Tennessee River as far south as the Alabama border, seriously jeopardizing a variety of Confederate options for resisting Grant, who was now commissioned a major general of volunteers.

Grant's success at Fort Donelson was not a unilateral action. Although McClellan had advised Buell to move toward eastern Tennessee, Halleck had strongly pressed him to move to the area of Clarksville and Nashville to cover Grant's operations. Buell somewhat sluggishly moved south and as Buckner was surrendering to Grant, Buell found his force occupying Bowling Green, Albert Sidney Johnston's old stomping grounds. As Johnston continued retreating southward, Buell pursued slowly. He detached one division, that of Brig. Gen. Ormsby M. Mitchel, which moved by water and arrived at Nashville on February 24, about 9,000 strong. At this time Nashville was a town of 16,988 citizens, all of whom were startled and perplexed at the Confederate evacuation and the arrival of the Yankees. Brig. Gen. William Nelson's division of 7,000 men also arrived during the night of the 24th, so that the Union occupation force equaled in number the civilian inhabitants of the city. The Federal forces captured a large number of cannon and stores within the town. Meanwhile, Grant's force occupied Clarksville. Tennesseans loyal to the Confederacy watched the developments with hearts sinking rapidly. "We have backed far enough," wrote George E. Eagleton, chaplain of the 44th Tennessee Infantry. "If we yield this grain-growing state to the foe, where will we get bread for the army? If we yield this state with its important railroads and tributaries to the Ohio River, we only have built and surrendered the best avenues to the heart of the Confederacy."

As always, Grant was restless to continue, but he was stalled momentarily by Halleck, who worried over a Confederate attack by Polk. Halleck did save enough energy to write McClellan, asking for command of the whole western theater of operations. "Make Buell, Grant, and Pope major-generals of volunteers, and give me command in the West. I ask this in return for Forts Henry and Donelson," he penned, despite not having had anything to do with the conquest of the forts. He got his wish, however. On March 11 he was assigned to command the newly created Department of the Mississippi, which comprised a vast western area.

On the Southern side, alarm spread in Richmond over Albert Sidney Johnston's situation. Beauregard arrived at Jackson on the day Donelson fell, but he was ever more out of favor with Jefferson Davis and was essentially transferred west because of his poor relations with Joe Johnston. After consulting with Sidney Johnston, he took command of the troops and geographical area between the Mississippi and Tennessee Rivers. In another of his odd maneuvers, Sidney Johnston gave up much of the control of his Department No. 2. The two Confederate commanders began to concentrate what force they had in the vicinity of Corinth, Mississippi. Grant remained positioned near the vanquished forts, Buell remained at Nashville, and Pope was at Commerce, Missouri.

MATTERS WERE NOT SO TRANQUIL in the Far West, either. For several weeks Louisiana-born Confederate Brig. Gen. Henry Hopkins Sibley had been carrying on a campaign of sorts in Arizona and New Mexico territories. Sibley was a career army officer who had been graduated low in his West Point class before serving in the Mexican War. Now 45, he looked older, with a worn but distinguished face, graying locks, and a thick mustache and sideburns. He was widely recognized in the service due to his invention of the Sibley tent, a conical affair built around a single pole that would accommodate twelve soldiers. Though much in use during the war's first year or so, its popularity faded thereafter. Sibley would be celebrated for another achievement during the campaign under way, his predilection for drink. Not that the campaign's strategic goals needed further confusion: The intentions of Sibley's 2,600 men as they marched up the Valley of the Rio Grande were hazy at best. Sibley hoped to preserve New Mexico Territory for the Confederacy, but what the Confederacy would do with New Mexico Territory was not certain.

Nonetheless, Sibley advanced his Army of New Mexico toward Fort Craig, New Mexico Territory, which stood just southwest of Valverde Ford on the Rio Grande. Sibley's force was organized into four regiments and attached artillery, as follows: 2d Texas Mounted Infantry, 4th Texas Mounted Infantry (Lt. Col. William R. Scurry), 5th Texas Mounted Infantry (Col. Tom Green), and 7th Texas Mounted Infantry, and some artillery. Fort Craig held a garrison force of about 3,810 under the command of Col. Edward Richard Sprigg Canby, who also was graduated low in his West Point class but went on to serve with some distinction in the Mexican War. Canby, 44, was a native Kentuckian whose Civil War service would be varied and who would become remembered for his tragic murder at the hands of Modoc Indians in California in 1873. For now, however, he commanded the Department of New Mexico; the troops at Fort Craig consisted of the 1st New Mexico Infantry (Col. Christopher "Kit" Carson), 2d New Mexico Infantry, 3d New Mexico Infantry, 4th New Mexico Infantry (Col. Gabriel Paul), 5th New Mexico Infantry (Lt. Col. Benjamin S. Roberts), and attached artillery, cavalry, and militia.

Early on the morning of February 21, Sibley moved northward, and by 8 A.M. the two forces detected each other and began skirmishing. The battle of Valverde began at about 11:30 A.M. Canby initiated what became a two-hour conflict as he twice ordered Roberts to attempt to turn the Confederate left, failing both times. An organized Confederate attack force consisting of the Texans, armed with lances, charged into the Federal line. This was repulsed successfully by Canby's troops, and the Confederate forces looked for an alternative plan. Sibley was "ill," as he later reported, but it became widely known that he had been drinking to excess. ("The Commanding General was an old army officer whose love for liquor exceeded that for home, country, or God," reported one of his soldiers.) Finally, by about 4:15 P.M., Tom Green led the Confederates into a frontal attack in which they captured a battery and routed the Federal line, throwing Canby's men into disarray and forcing many of them to retreat into the fort by about 5 P.M. The Yankee losses were 68 killed, 160 wounded, and 35 missing; the Confederate casualties were about 36 killed and 160 wounded. Curiously, the night before the battle, Capt. James Graydon attempted a covert action by putting twelve 24-pounder howitzer shells onto the backs of two mules, which he led to within a short distance of the Confederate picket line; the mules exploded without endangering any Confederate lives. The battle was a definitive Confederate victory in a campaign that seemed hazily conceived at best. Sibley continued his northward march toward Santa Fe, bypassing Fort Craig, where Canby's men holed up.

As THE DISTANT EVENTS in the West were taking place, a black pall hung over Lincoln's Executive Mansion. On February 20, William Wallace Lincoln, "Willie," died at age 12. The doctors described the illness as "bilious fever." The death shook the Lincolns badly, especially Mary Todd Lincoln, who was inconsolable and felt that it had occurred as God's punishment for being "so wrapped up in the world, so devoted to our political advancement." Casualty lists from the action at Fort Donelson deepened the sadness North and South. In Richmond, on February 22, Jefferson Davis was inaugurated as permanent president of the Confederate States of America. "The tyranny of an unbridled majority, the most odious and least responsible form of despotism, has denied us both the right and remedy," he said as rain poured down in Richmond. Already, however, there were doubts among the Confederate populace as the Yankees moved into cracks all along the geography of the Southern States. An editorial in the *Washington Telegraph* in Arkansas said it plainly: "We have despised the enemy and laughed at their threats, until, almost too late, we find ourselves in their power."

CHAPTER 7

Clash of the Ironclads

THE SPRING OF 1862 brought a milestone to the American landscape. The War of the Rebellion, the Great Civil War, the War of Northern Invasion—whatever Americans called it, had been going on for a calendar year. At its outset, few could have imagined the scale of violence that would wash across the landscape. In the South, armies and a small navy had come together and focused on defensive operations, aided by the strategic difficulty of the Northern military operations. To many in the South, time appeared to be on the side of the Confederacy, despite the loss of Forts Henry and Donelson, the huge Federal armies encamped near northern Virginia, the Yankee forces at Fort Monroe, approaching Mobile and New Orleans, along the Mississippi, and threatening the southeastern coast, targeting Charleston and Savannah. Nevertheless, Southern soldiers remained defiant and boastful. "The next summer will probably be the most eventful in a century," James E. B. Stuart wrote his wife on March 2. "We must plant our feet firmly upon the platform of our inextinguishable hatred to the northern confederacy, with a determination to die rather than submit."

McClellan, though unwilling to march forward, had successfully managed to pull together and efficiently train a mammoth army, preparing it for later actions. If there was a worrisome crack in the armor of the Confederacy, it certainly lay in the West, where Grant had plunged into Tennessee. Northerners who wished for peace were outraged at the escalation of violence over broad fronts, and those who wanted the war to incorporate emancipation as one of its goals were dissatisfied as well. "In my judgment, gradual, and not sudden emancipation, is better for all," said Lincoln in his annual message to Congress on March 6. The Lincoln administration was gaining critics across a broad spectrum. Despite the widespread reasons for pessimism on both sides, the will to fight was strong. It would be tested again during the spring of 1862 with what was by far the largest and deadliest battle to date in American history.

March 1862 began with a scattering of small actions. Operating from Port Royal, South Carolina, Capt. Samuel F. Du Pont continued his movement to capture positions along the South Atlantic coast by steaming a flotilla toward Fernandina, Florida. The expedition would secure Cumberland Island along the southern coast of Georgia, move through Cumberland Sound and St. Andrew's Sound, attack the Confederate position at Fort Clinch on Amelia Island, Florida, and secure the island and the town of Fernandina for the Union. Twenty vessels were involved; Du Pont issued his orders on March 1. Three days later the flotilla moved into position, with Du Pont on board the flagship USS *Mohican* (Comdr. Sylvanus W. Godon). Additionally, six transports carried a brigade of soldiers under the command of Brig. Gen. Horatio G. Wright.

Du Pont anticipated a great battle but in fact carried off the movement to Fernandina in an almost bloodless fashion. Anchoring in Cumberland Sound on March 2, Du Pont learned that the Confederates were abandoning their defenses in haste and that most of them had already left Amelia Island. Given this change of events, Du Pont ordered Comdr. Percival Drayton, with the steam sloop USS *Pawnee,* to push through the channel at high speed, to "save public and private property from threatened destruction, to prevent poisoning the wells, and to put a stop to all those outrages by the perpetration of which the leaders in this nefarious war hope to deceive and exasperate the Southern people."

The Confederate defenders of Fort Clinch were commanded by Col. Edward Hopkins, who was ill at the time of the appearance of the Federal navy. The batteries were under the direction of Col. Charles H. McBlair and amounted to thirty-three heavy guns within all the emplacements on Amelia Island, Cumberland Island, and Talbot Island (south of Amelia). At about 2:30 A.M. on March 3, Hopkins ordered his men to retreat and take as many of their supplies with them as possible, passing through Fernandina and heading toward Jacksonville. They took eighteen guns, leaving fifteen for the Yankees, but five more were captured when they were left at St. John's Bluff between Talbot Island and Jacksonville.

The resistance to Du Pont's movement was slight. Fort Clinch was the first fort to be captured by Confederate forces and then retaken by Federals. Fernandina, Amelia Island, Cumberland Island, the nearby town of St. Mary's, and other locales were now under Federal occupation. "The victory was bloodless," recalled Du Pont, "but most complete in results." The success of the Fernandina operations would bring more success at nearby positions along the coast as well. During the next several days, Yankees occupied St. Simon's Island, Jekyll Island, and Brunswick, Georgia; reconnoitered the

Savannah River and moved to Elba Island in Georgia; temporarily occupied Jacksonville, Florida; and moved onto Santa Rosa Island, Florida, and Edisto Island, South Carolina. On Cumberland Island, naval officers ordered U.S. soldiers and sailors to respect and protect Dungeness, the former mansion of Revolutionary War hero Nathanael Greene. The men were instructed not to "disturb or take away any article without a special order from Commodore Du Pont or General Wright." One of the things they would not be disturbing was the grave of Henry "Light-Horse Harry" Lee, Robert E. Lee's father, who had died at the house on his way back to America from the West Indies in 1818.

WHILE THE FEDERAL NAVY slowly increased its hold on parts of the southern coastline, armies out west were set to clash in more direct fashion. In December 1861 the War Department created the Army of the Southwest and assigned command to Brig. Gen. Samuel R. Curtis. A New Yorker by birth, Curtis had been a lawyer and U.S. representative. On February 10, 1862, Curtis had advanced toward Springfield, Missouri, hoping to push Confederate Brig. Gen. Sterling Price, who had fought at Wilson's Creek and at Lexington, out of the region. Price's force of about 8,000 Missourians had established winter quarters near Springfield; rather than being pushed, Price offered little resistance and simply moved into northwestern Arkansas. Price's plan was to join with the forces of Brig. Gen. Ben McCulloch, another veteran of Wilson's Creek, who was retreating from Keetsville, Missouri. Price and McCulloch were both subordinate to Maj. Gen. Earl Van Dorn, who was in January assigned to command the Trans-Mississippi District. Van Dorn stopped both Price and McCulloch in the Boston Mountains, south of Fayetteville, Arkansas, and began to collect reinforcements so that they could form one large force to coordinate an attack on Curtis.

Curtis's Army of the Southwest was organized into four divisions, with Brig. Gen. Franz Sigel acting as a sort of second-in-command, overseeing both the 1st and 2d divisions. Curtis's division commanders were Brig. Gen. Alexander S. Asboth and Cols. Peter J. Osterhaus, Jefferson C. Davis, and Eugene A. Carr. Osterhaus's brigades were commanded by himself and Col. Nicholas Greusel. Asboth's division had a brigade commanded by Col. Frederick Schaefer and the 3d Missouri Infantry and two cavalry units, which were unbrigaded. Davis's division contained brigades commanded by Cols. Thomas Pattison and Julius White, and attached cavalry. Carr's division had brigades led by Cols. Grenville M. Dodge and William Vandever.

Van Dorn's Army of the West was organized into the two primary divisions of McCulloch and Price, but also included Missouri State Guard troops in six divisions as follows: 2d Division (Brig. Gen. Martin E. Green), 3d Division (Col. John B. Clark, Jr.), 5th Division (Col. James P. Saunders),

6th Division (Maj. D. Herndon Lindsay), 7th and 9th Divisions (Brig. Gen. Daniel M. Frost), and 8th Division (Col. James S. Rains). McCulloch's division consisted of the infantry brigade of Col. Louis Hébert, the cavalry brigade of Brig. Gen. James M. McIntosh, attached artillery, and the Indian Brigade of Brig. Gen. Albert Pike, consisting of mostly Cherokees, Choctaws, Chickasaws, and Creeks. Price's division contained the brigades of Col. Henry Little (1st Missouri Brigade), Col. William Yarnel Slack (2d Missouri Brigade), and Col. Colton Greene (3d Missouri Brigade).

By March 5, Van Dorn decided to attack what he perceived as the overextended Federals. He grouped his forces beyond Fayetteville and Elm Springs, and by the late afternoon of March 6 events were gravitating toward battle. The strength of the Yankee force was about 11,000; those conglomerations of units under Van Dorn amounted to about 18,000. Curtis's army was entrenched along Little Sugar Creek, north of Fayetteville, waiting for an attack. Van Dorn wished to push northward and capture St. Louis, allegedly saying, "I must have St. Louis and then Huza!" Curtis hoped to move Van Dorn southward and crush his force, securing northwestern Arkansas for the Union. The local geography created an unusual meeting place. North of Bentonville stood a rocky plateau called Pea Ridge, and a single significant building stood in the immediate area of Pea Ridge, called Elkhorn Tavern, where travelers would stop on the Telegraph Road that connected Fayetteville with southern Missouri. On February 17, elements of the two armies had skirmished along Little Sugar Creek in the battle of Dunagin's Farm; the results were inconclusive.

Now Van Dorn faced the issue of making a frontal attack. He decided against it. Late on March 6, after some moderate skirmishing erupted between elements of the two armies, Van Dorn decided to make a night march around part of the Federal army and attack from the north at Pea Ridge. The battle of Pea Ridge, or Elkhorn Tavern, was the result.

Clear but cold weather prevailed on the field when the two forces met. The weather conditions hardly favored Van Dorn's army in its difficult, fifty-five-mile march, made under low temperatures and with a wet, heavy snow falling. In February, Van Dorn fell into an ice-cold stream and suffered chills and fever for several weeks; he directed the advance from the comfort of an ambulance and took to the saddle on occasion but was weak and feverish. During the night of the 6th, the Indian brigades of Cols. Stand Watie, John Drew, and Daniel N. McIntosh arrived. The Confederates were now mostly bivouacked at Camp Stephens, on the southwestern edge of what would become the battlefield, while Curtis's men were about three miles to the east along Little Sugar Creek Valley.

In his tactical vision Van Dorn believed that Curtis was preparing to move away from a fight; in fact, Curtis was digging in to prepare for one.

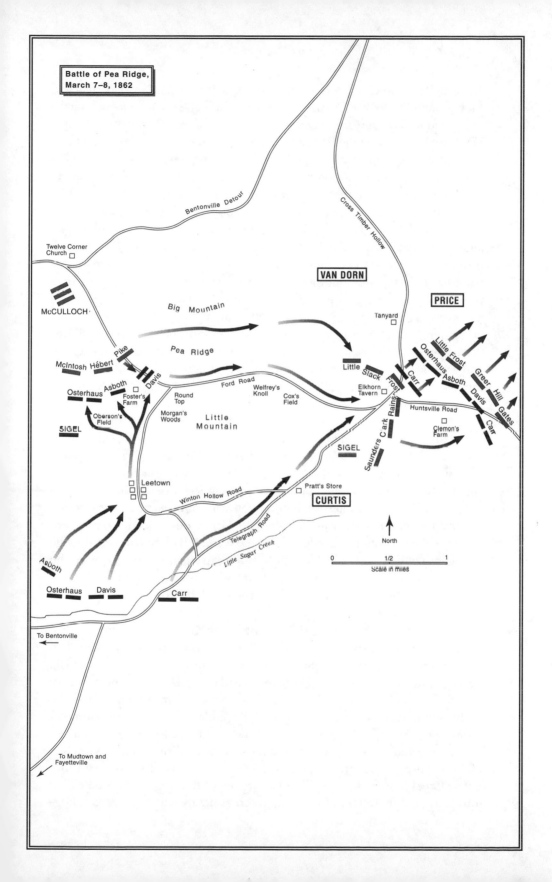

**Battle of Pea Ridge,
March 7–8, 1862**

Twelve Corner
Church

Bentonville Detour

Cross Timber Hollow

VAN DORN

McCULLOCH

Big Mountain

Tanyard

PRICE

Pike

Pea Ridge

Little Frost

McIntosh Hébert

Davis

Osterhaus

Little

Slack

Carr

Greer Hill

Asboth

Davis

Asboth

Osterhaus

Foster's
Farm

Ford Road

Welfrey's
Knoll

Cox's
Field

Elkhorn
Tavern

Frost

Gates

Oberson's
Field

Round
Top

Morgan's
Woods

Little
Mountain

Rains

Huntsville Road

Carr

SIGEL

Clemon's
Farm

Saunders Cark

Leetown

SIGEL

Winton Hollow Road

Pratt's Store

CURTIS

Telegraph Road

Little Sugar Creek

North

Asboth

0   1/2   1
Scale in miles

Osterhaus   Davis

Carr

To Bentonville

To Mudtown and
Fayetteville

Nevertheless, the Confederate commander met with McIntosh, Price, and McCulloch. At first Van Dorn embraced McCulloch's idea of moving northward around the Bentonville Detour and moving on the enemy's right flank. When he learned that the Bentonville Detour extended all the way to Telegraph Road, he altered the plan to focus on enveloping Curtis; by marching over to Cross Timber Hollow and blocking Telegraph Road in Curtis's rear, Van Dorn would have the Yankees trapped. He pressed for the movement to begin that night, with a first-quarter moon hanging in the constellation Taurus. "For God sake to let the poor, worn-out and hungry soldiers rest and sleep that night... and then attack the next morning," McCulloch protested. But Van Dorn would not relent. Despite the fact that many of his troops were in terrible condition, the past three days witnessing great effort throughout the terrible cold and occasional snow. The army's food and forage were largely depleted, and morale was sinking, with desertions rising to an epidemic level. Van Dorn ordered that campfires be left burning to deceive Curtis's men, and set the whole operation in motion despite the length and complexity of the maneuver, the dangerous conditions of night marching, the poor shape of his army, and his misgivings over the competence of his subordinates.

Van Dorn ordered that the primary attack on the enemy be made against the position at Elkhorn Tavern, with Van Dorn and Price moving southward along Telegraph Road into the area. McCulloch would make a diversionary advance on Leetown to scatter and confuse the Yankee response. Van Dorn then wanted the envelopment to move around the southern edge of Pea Ridge and stretch into Leetown. For his part, Curtis fortified his position with new arrivals and sent Col. Grenville M. Dodge out to reconnoiter the Bentonville Detour and to blockade it with felled trees. Dodge moved out with a portion of the 4th Iowa Infantry and one company of the 3d Illinois Cavalry and began to implement the blockading plan. Dodge's men heard a fair amount of noise from the other side of the first blockade, northeast of Twelve Corner Church.

At 8 P.M. the enveloping movement began. It was one of the hardest nights of the war for some of the soldiers present. It was becoming clear that, even in the best of times, fighting a battle in the Civil War was a hellish, nerve-shattering experience. With the weather against you, and when ill supplied, it was dramatically worse. The temperature plummeted. "The night was one of intense severity and the men suffered immeasurably," wrote the surgeon of the 4th Arkansas Infantry. "For my own part I shall retain a lively and an unpleasant recollection of my suffering on that wretched night, for my whole natural lifetime." The absence of a bridge over Little Sugar Creek on the Bentonville Detour meant that logs had to be rolled into place and thousands of men had to cross slowly and haphazardly, bogging down the initial phase of the movement. Hours were spent moving Price's, Hébert's, McIntosh's, and Pike's men across the crude substitute for a bridge.

The icy cold, clear morning of March 7 brought sunlight and the revelation to the Federal command that the Rebels had abandoned their camps. At 7 A.M. Missouri cavalry units found their way into Cross Timber Hollow and reconnoitered Telegraph Road, seeing no sign of Yankees. Van Dorn split his force, sending Price south along Telegraph Road toward Elkhorn Tavern, and McCulloch south on Ford Road. The division would last a short time, Van Dorn hoped, and a reunited army would be able to smash Curtis near Elkhorn Tavern. Curtis, meanwhile, breakfasted at his headquarters at Pratt's Store.

The initial skirmish escalated into a major, rolling fight that lasted all day as the Federals discovered and responded to Van Dorn's envelopment. At 9 A.M. Curtis held a council of war; he still believed that he faced one Confederate force in Little Sugar Creek Valley and another near Twelve Corner Church, about to move around his right flank. After an inconclusive council, Curtis ordered Osterhaus, aided by Cols. Greusel and Cyrus Bussey (3d Iowa Cavalry), to assemble a legion and take it northwest through Leetown toward Twelve Corner Church. Osterhaus headed to Little Sugar Creek to initiate the movement. Meanwhile, by 10.30 A.M., Curtis received the alarming news that a column of Confederate cavalry and infantry had initiated a skirmish along Telegraph Road about one mile north of Elkhorn Tavern. He then sent Dodge's brigade, which was conveniently out of place, north toward Elkhorn Tavern to encounter the Rebels. Carr accompanied and supervised the movement. Confused, Curtis by 11 A.M. had nearly one-third of his army moving against the Confederates, whose positions he was mostly uncertain about. Due to the uncertainty, most of Curtis's men were kept behind in defensive positions along Little Sugar Creek.

On their way north, Osterhaus and Greusel passed through Oberson's Field north of Leetown, and Osterhaus decided to deploy Greusel's infantry in the field as a precaution. As he rode into Foster's Farm, north of Oberson's Field, Osterhaus was stunned by suddenly seeing McCulloch's Confederate division moving eastward along Ford Road. Osterhaus realized that the Confederate column was flanking the Federal right, and advancing directly into the rear of the Yankee army, endangering its trains and moving on a completely undefended position. In a panic, just before noon, Osterhaus sent Bussey on the attack, which opened the battle of Leetown, one portion of the Pea Ridge fight. McCulloch was completely surprised by the Yankee cannon and small-arms fire. Three Federal cannon repeatedly fired into McCulloch's right, killing and wounding a substantial number of men, who were now scattering and returning fire. McCulloch ordered McIntosh to strike into the Yankees. Texas and Arkansas cavalry swarmed toward the Federal position, with carbines and sabers drawn. The Federal artillerists were completely overrun by the Southern horsemen, and although some Federal cavalry counterattacked, the Confederate horse charge overwhelmed the Yankees and forced Bussey to retreat toward Oberson's Field. At this time the large Indian force, about half of whom were on foot, attacked and routed the Iowans on Foster's Farm. Back at Oberson's Field, the morale of the Union force was not improved when a dozen riderless horses spattered with blood rode into the Yankee lines, several with their saddles soaked in blood and body parts hanging underneath their bellies.

A lull now occurred in the battle of Leetown, although all the officers and men could hear the booming of cannon and crackle of musketry in the distance, in the direction of Elkhorn Tavern. Greusel began shelling the Confederate positions with fresh artillery salvos, which terrified the Indians. McCulloch and McIntosh, meanwhile, began assembling their force into two lines of attack. McCulloch's plan was to launch a frontal attack against the Federal position and sweep the Yankees clean. As he reconnoitered on horseback at about 1:30 P.M., however, McCulloch was struck by a volley of musket fire from Co. B of the 36th Illinois Infantry and killed instantly, hit at a distance of only 40 yards. McCulloch's horse was struck by four bullets before galloping away, leaving McCulloch dead on the field. Later, McCulloch's body was found with a single shot through the chest.

Now McIntosh effectively commanded the forces at Leetown, but he reverted to the thought processes of a regimental commander. As the fight on Foster's Farm heated up again, McIntosh rode out to a rail fence in front of his old regiment, the 2d Arkansas Mounted Rifles, and was shot through the heart with a musket ball, falling dead to the ground. Arkansas and Texas troops that had attacked southward moved back to the north, and the Confederate assault west of the Leetown Road ended. Now the final hope for Confederate victory at Leetown lay in the hands of Hébert, who was in Morgan's Woods encouraging his men to get ready for battle. By the time he advanced south with his command—the 4th Arkansas Infantry, 3d Louisiana Infantry, 14th Arkansas Infantry, and 15th Arkansas Infantry—Hébert still had no idea that his two fellow officers had been killed. His movement through Morgan's Woods began sloppily, with lines drifting and falling behind, and after he regrouped a couple of times, disarray returned with several well-placed Yankee cannon shots. By 2 P.M. Col. Jefferson C. Davis reached Osterhaus's position with reinforcements. He marched his 1,400 men up into the path of Hébert in Morgan's Woods. For an hour a thick fight rolled back and forth between Illinois and Indiana troops and Hébert's men, in a tangle of woods lined with scrubby brush. The Yankees were outnumbered, and for some time it appeared that Hébert's men might overwhelm them. After heavy fighting, during which both sides became exhausted and caked with powder, the Union force disengaged and pulled back, affording Hébert's men the opportunity to pour into Oberson's Field.

Confederates counterattacked into Morgan's Woods with disastrous results when the Yankees cut into them and dealt Hébert's command heavy casualties, effectively knocking it out of the fight. Among the many prisoners taken in Winton Springs Hollow during the Confederate withdrawal was Hébert himself. Later in the afternoon Sigel arrived with his command near the Leetown battlefield, but by then it was too late to be of much help.

Since morning, heavy action had been taking place around Elkhorn Tavern. Carr had assured Curtis that when he left at 10:30 A.M. he would "clean out" Cross Timber Hollow "in a very short time." Carr arrived at Elkhorn Tavern and realized its tactical value in terms of the surrounding ground. Instead of cleaning out the hollow, he would deploy his men around the tavern and wait for the Rebels to show up. Carr set up the 24th Missouri Infantry, and the 35th Illinois Infantry north of the tavern and ordered Dodge to deploy the 4th Iowa Infantry north of Clemon's Farm along the Huntsville Road. Facing off with the men of Carr and Dodge was the force under Van Dorn and Price, coming southward. It consisted of the brigades of Slack, Little, Greene, and the State Guard troops.

The Confederates formed a line of battle across Telegraph Road. Federal and Confederate artillery sent a few shells back and forth, and many of the Confederates, tired from the rigors of march, lay down and fired at the masses of Yankees in the distance. Price directed the formulation of Confederate forces on the left, while Slack and Little set up the order of battle on the right. Soon after the fight began, Confederate artillery opened fire on the Federals, one shell of which tore open an ammunition chest, sending a blast of debris into the surrounding Yankee soldiers. Because the air was so cold and due to the physical conditions of the hollow, thick clouds of smoke simply hung low in the air, obscuring practically everything along the ground, and making Pea Ridge one of the murkiest battlefields of the war.

Soon Illinois and Iowa units slowly pushed forward and forced Price and Van Dorn to abandon the initiative, checking the Confederate tactical plan. Instead of taking the high ground along the ridge and crushing the Federal army, now the Southerners would need to fight their way out of Cross Timber Hollow, from a poor position. Federal reinforcements arrived about 12:30 P.M. Twice, troops under Vandever attempted to break through the Confederate lines and force them back in disarray, ultimately failing each time. During this phase of the battle a Federal bullet struck Slack in the left hip, nearly in the same place he had been wounded at Wilson's Creek. This time the wound was fatal: he died on March 21. About 2 P.M. Van Dorn received the distressing news that McCulloch's movement had stalled; a short time later Price was hit in the side with a bullet, causing a contusion. An hour later the two Confederate commanders decided that perhaps the Federal right was vulnerable, and they determined to attack it. They erroneously believed that Curtis was pulling his force away from Elkhorn Tavern to reinforce the Yankees near Leetown. Van Dorn and Price were once again wrong.

At 4:30 P.M. a barrage of artillery belched from Confederate guns from the hollow, signaling the start of the Confederate advance. A tremendous assault started forward over the whole line, with units under Little and Col. Thomas L. Rosser leading the way. For a time, in the vicious, smoky musketry fire, it appeared that the Yankees would ward off the Confederate onslaught. But a surge of Rebels pushed their way into the Union line, into the weakened position of Vandever's front. The whole line of battle erupted into a series of uncoordinated attacks, waves that rushed forward and then back over the same parcels of ground. As units were mixed and commands not heard above the din of battle, confusion grew among the attacking Confederates. Capt. Henry Guibor's battery helped push Vandever back across Ford Road and onto Pratt's Store. Carr made a desperate attempt to coordinate forces and launch a counterattack that would hold some of the ground around the tavern.

The scattered fighting went on until the sun set. Despite the dusk and the cold, Curtis mounted a counterattack after 6:30 P.M. featuring two dozen Federal cannon and a bayonet attack from the 4th Iowa Infantry, which had run out of ammunition. The Yankee advance stalled out shy of the tavern, however, and there was no more to be done on this day.

Dawn broke on March 8 with a pall of smoke from cannon and small-arms fire still hanging over the battlefield. Van Dorn simply reorganized his forces but for the most part left them where they were at the close of the previous day's battle. The most significant change on the Federal side was Brig. Gen. Franz Sigel's participation on the second day. Quiet on the battle's first day, Sigel on the morning of the 8th formed his command to pass through Cox's Field and over Welfrey's Knoll, south of Big Mountain, and slam into the Confederate right, held up by Rosser, west of Elkhorn Tavern. Sigel attacked with great vigor, believing that the Confederate army was near surrender. Federal guns opened a heavy bombardment on the Confederate lines, joined by guns on the Union right, and a terrific artillery barrage lasted about two hours. By the time it was over, it was the greatest artillery bombardment in North American history until then. It was the prelude to a stinging Confederate retreat that left Van Dorn and the wounded Price utterly defeated. The scattered Confederate forces fled in disarray from Pea Ridge to the Arkansas River, with the sight of nearly 10,000 men in the Federal army fresh in their minds, and Van Dorn subsequently received orders from the War Department to abandon Arkansas and support operations in defense of the Mississippi River. The Confederate army marched from Pea Ridge with heavy hearts. For his part, Van Dorn could at least look for scapegoats. "In the recent operations against the enemy on Sugar Creek," he wrote, "I found the want of military knowledge and discipline among the higher officers to be so great as to counteravail their gallantry and the fine courage of their troops."

The battle would be costly for the Confederates. McCulloch, McIntosh, and Slack were killed, Price wounded, and Hébert captured. Confederate casualties were about 800. On the Union side, Asboth, Carr, and Dodge were wounded. The Federal casualties amounted to 1,384. Wrote Curtis in a letter to his brother: "The scene is silent and sad—the vulture and the wolf now have the dominion and the dead friends and foes sleep in the same lonely graves."

The chaos in the wake of Pea Ridge might be summarized in the journal of a Confederate soldier, William Watson of the 3d Louisiana Infantry. "The effects of an army passing over a country distracted by war were now clearly to be seen," wrote Watson of the retreat. "Be that army friend or foe, it passes along like a withering scourge, leaving only ruin and desolation behind. . . . [When they rejoined part of their regiment] they were actually staggering from want and fatigue. Their shoes were worn off their feet, from passing over rocks and boulders, and through creeks. . . . Their eyes were bleared and bloodshot, from want of sleep and the smoke of the woodfires, and their bodies were emaciated by hunger."

ON THE LAST DAY of the battle of Pea Ridge, a new era of naval warfare began far to the east at Hampton Roads, Virginia. When Confederates captured the Norfolk Navy Yard in the spring of 1861, one of the prizes acquired was the damaged but salvageable hull of the USS *Merrimack*, a 4,636-ton frigate built in 1854 that carried 48 guns. Burned to the waterline and scuttled to prevent capture at Norfolk on April 20, 1861, the *Merrimack* was nonetheless rebuilt as a new type of warship by the Confederate navy. Christened the CSS *Virginia*, she was designed by John Mercer Brooke, the Virginian who would direct the Bureau of Ordnance and Hydrography for the last two years of the war. The armored ram was the forerunner of a formidable new type of warship. The *Virginia* displaced 3,200 tons, had a single screw with two horizontal back-acting engines, four boilers, and a cruising speed of 9 knots. Her sides were constructed of wooden panels 2 feet thick faced with 2-inch-thick iron plates and a 2-foot iron ram at the bow. She measured 263 feet by 51 feet 4 inches by 22 feet and had a crew of 320. Her armament consisted of two

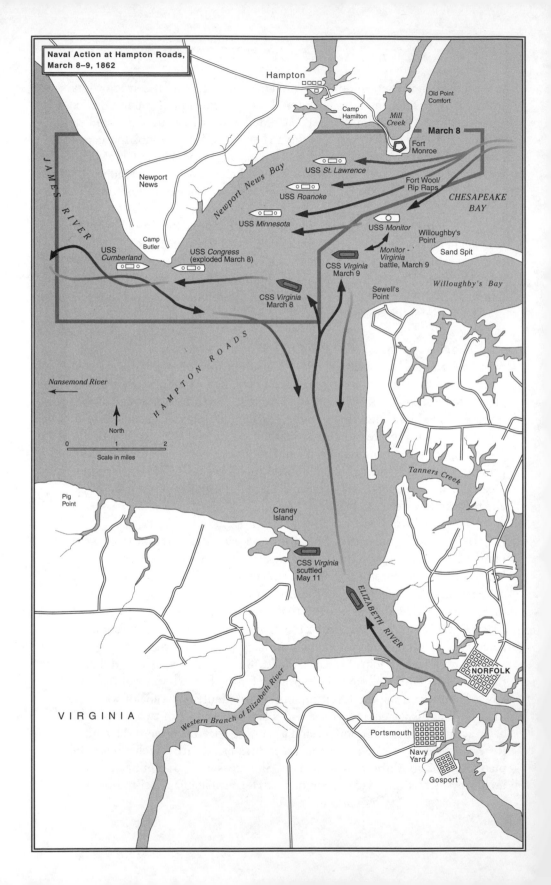

Naval Action at Hampton Roads, March 8–9, 1862

Hampton

Old Point Comfort

Camp Hamilton

Mill Creek

March 8

Fort Monroe

Newport News

USS *St. Lawrence*

Fort Wool/ Rip Raps

CHESAPEAKE BAY

Newport News Bay

USS *Roanoke*

JAMES RIVER

USS *Minnesota*

USS *Monitor*

Willoughby's Point

Sand Spit

Camp Butler

USS *Cumberland*

USS *Congress* (exploded March 8)

CSS *Virginia* March 9

Monitor - Virginia battle, March 9

Willoughby's Bay

CSS *Virginia* March 8

Sewell's Point

HAMPTON ROADS

Nansemond River

North

0   1   2

Scale in miles

Tanners Creek

Pig Point

Craney Island

CSS *Virginia* scuttled May 11

ELIZABETH RIVER

NORFOLK

VIRGINIA

Western Branch of Elizabeth River

Portsmouth

Navy Yard

Gosport

7-inch Brooke rifles, six 9-inch Dahlgren smoothbores, and two 6.4-inch Brooke rifles. The CSS *Virginia* was commissioned on February 17, 1862, as the most sophisticated and well equipped ship in any navy.

The CSS *Virginia* steamed out of Norfolk Harbor and arrived at Hampton Roads to face several Federal ships on March 8. She had bypassed shipboard training and sea trials. She was under the command of Capt. Franklin Buchanan, age 61, a Baltimore native who had served with distinction in the Federal navy from an early age. He had been superintendent of the U.S. Naval School during the Mexican War, had overseen the Washington Navy Yard, and made a serious blunder at the outset of the Civil War. Buchanan resigned his U.S. Navy commission in April 1861 only to ask for its reinstatement when he learned that Maryland would not secede; this was denied.

During the engagement of the next two days in Hampton Roads, the CSS *Virginia* was accompanied by five smaller gunboats: the CSS *Beaufort*, CSS *Jamestown*, CSS *Patrick Henry*, CSS *Raleigh*, and CSS *Teaser*. The five principal Federal ships facing this onslaught of hostile vessels were the USS *Cumberland* (Lt. George U. Morris), USS *Congress*, USS *St. Lawrence* (Capt. Hugh Y. Purviance), USS *Minnesota* (Capt. Gershom J. Van Brunt), and USS *Roanoke* (Capt. John Marston).

The layout of the Hampton Roads area is complex. Hampton Roads connects the wide expanse of Chesapeake Bay to the east with the James, Nansemond, and Elizabeth rivers to the west and south. In the spring of 1862 the Federal forces held the northern shoreline and its towns and camps while Confederates occupied the shore to the south. In Federal hands, then, were the town of Hampton and, near the water, Old Point Comfort and Fort Monroe, the post where Robert E. Lee had spent part of his engineering career before the war. Southward from Fort Monroe stood the Rip Raps, also known as Fort Wool, a pile of rocks laid into the channel that supported a small Federal battery, and Willoughby's Point farther south. To the west lay Federal batteries and Camp Butler near Newport News. Southerners established batteries and camps at Norfolk, well to the south on the Elizabeth River, and at Sewell's Point along the southern shore of Hampton Roads. They also established batteries at Craney Island to the south and at Pig Point near the mouth of the Nansemond.

At about 2 P.M. on March 8 the CSS *Virginia*, along with the CSS *Beaufort* and the CSS *Raleigh*, made its appearance in Hampton Roads. In plain view of the Federal shore batteries and a large number of Union army troops, who were watching in disbelief, *Virginia* opened fire less than a mile from the frigate *Cumberland*, which had 400 men on board and an armament of twenty-two 9-inch, one smoothbore, and one 70-pounder rifles. The engagement spread rapidly, with blockaders and shore batteries joining in and firing wildly. After a short time the *Virginia* rammed the *Cumberland* below the water line, and the old sailing vessel sank rapidly, firing her guns hotly but to little avail. "At 3:35 [P.M.] the water had risen to the main hatchway," wrote Morris, "and the ship canted to port, and we delivered a parting fire, each man trying to save himself by jumping overboard." The *Cumberland* sank into the turgid water with its colors flapping in the breeze, and 121 men were killed in the action or drowned with the ship.

Meanwhile, the *Virginia*, which had lost its ram stuck in the side of the mortally wounded *Cumberland*, turned toward the *Congress* and initiated an intense fire from its broadside guns. Ramming hot shot and incendiary shells into the smoothbore guns, the gunners on board the *Virginia* soon set the *Congress* ablaze. This veteran frigate had a crew of 480 and mounted ten 8-inch smoothbores and forty 32-pounder guns, many of which fired back in haste at the *Virginia*, but with little effect. "The shot from the *Congress* glanced from her iron-plated sloping sides without doing any apparent damage," wrote Van Brunt. The *Congress* had run hard aground and sat help-lessly as it was pounded by the *Virginia*, the flames towering up through its masts and all along the ship. At about 4:30 P.M. the *Congress* struck her colors and surrendered, with heavy casualties. Among the dead was the ship's com-mander, Lt. Joseph B. Smith. Many prisoners, including wounded men, were hauled aboard the CSS *Beaufort*. All was not glorious for the *Virginia*, how-ever: Buchanan had been wounded severely in the left thigh and was suc-ceeded in command by Lt. Catesby ap Roger Jones, his executive officer. Jones was a Virginian, age 40, who would in 1863 be sent to the Confederate Naval Iron Works at Selma, Alabama, to supervise the manufacturing of Confederate naval cannon. Jones broke off the action about 5 P.M. and re-turned to Sewell's Point, hoping to wreck the other Federal ships the next day. The tide had receded, running two more Federal ships aground, but Jones could not reach them with the *Virginia*, which was developing several leaks.

Some five hours following the retreat of the *Virginia*, under cover of darkness a curious vessel made its way into Hampton Roads. It was John Er-icsson's invention, the USS *Monitor*, with its amazing set of technological ad-vances and two-gun turret. At first glance, the soldiers on shore were not impressed with the "cheese box on a raft." The *Monitor* was the first ironclad warship built without rigging or sails. It had been launched at New York in January and was now ready to stand up to its fearsome adversary, the *Vir-ginia*. Under command of Lt. John Lorimer Worden, much beloved by his men, the *Monitor* readied that night for the return of the great Confederate ironclad. Worden, 43, was a New Yorker who served in the Federal navy be-fore the war and whose main Civil War experience was as a captive during a return from Fort Pickens, Florida. Exchanged in November 1861, he now sought glory with the innovative ship. The USS *Monitor,* a mere 987 tons and measuring 172 feet by 41 feet 6 inches by 10 feet 6 inches, appeared much smaller because the single deck extended just over the waterline. The only portion that stuck out substantially was the 140-ton, spindle-mounted revolving cylindrical turret that contained two 11-inch smoothbore Dahlgren guns firing 170-pound shot. The crew numbered 59 men. The armor plating consisted of eight layers of 1-inch iron plates on the turret, five layers of 1-inch plates on the sides, two layers of 1-inch plates on the deck, and 9-inch-thick blocks on the pilothouse; the single screw was driven by a double-piston Ericsson vibrating-lever engine equipped with a jet condenser and two horizontal fire-tube boilers. As the *Monitor* readied for battle, a reminder of the disastrous Federal results of the first day came about when the *Congress* exploded about 12:30 A.M. on March 9.

Later that morning the *Virginia* moved back into Hampton Roads. At first light, Jones could see from the deck of the *Virginia* the still-burning hull of the *Congress* to the north, the *Minnesota,* imprisoned by the tide, and the other Federal ships. They would be destroyed by the *Virginia* on this second day of battle. Jones did not know that the *Monitor* was present when he moved the *Virginia* northward into action. The battle that altered naval history opened about 9 A.M. Jones steered his ship toward the *Minnesota* and the strange craft, which looked like a barge with a water tank on top, appeared nearby. Midshipman H. Beverly Littlepage of the *Virginia* believed it to be a raft carrying one of the *Minnesota*'s boilers. Jones knew about the new ship but was determined to destroy the *Minnesota* before turning on the *Monitor.* A mile from the *Minnesota,* Jones opened with the 7-inch rifle and set a small portion of the frigate ablaze. Before the *Virginia* could steam closer to the *Minnesota,* however, Worden directed his little ship midway between the two vessels. The "duel of the ironclads" began as both ships opened fire at close quarters, circling, ramming, firing broadside into each other with relatively little effect. The battle raged on for three hours. Jones reported frustration with trying to maneuver the *Virginia* and had to position the ship with one side exposed in order to fire. The *Monitor,* on the other hand, could rotate its turret from any position and fire at will, but could use only one gun at a time because of the need to reposition the gunport shutters.

Sixteen gunners and three officers crowded into the *Monitor*'s turret. Although their ship remained relatively undamaged by the numerous shots striking it, each Confederate salvo rang the turret like a gigantic, amplified bell, causing those inside substantial temporary deafness. The ships were separated throughout much of the fighting by a mere few yards. Despite its great success against the larger foe, the *Monitor* did experience frustrating problems. The speaking tube between the pilothouse and the turret broke down, and officers had to run back and forth to relay messages between

Worden, in the pilothouse, and Lt. Samuel Dana Greene, the executive officer (and son of Union general officer George S. Greene), in the turret. The turret was difficult to move and nearly impossible to stop once motion had begun. Sighting from the turret was incredibly challenging. Aboard the *Monitor,* Act. Lt. William F. Keeler recorded that "the sounds of the conflict at this time were terrible. The rapid firing of our own guns amid the clouds of smoke, the howling of *Minnesota*'s shells, which was firing whole broadsides at a time just over our heads (two of her shot struck us), mingled with the crash of solid shot against our sides & the bursting of shells all around us."

The two ironclads hammered away at each other with shot after shot, to the utter amazement of observers on shore. Shortly after 10 A.M. the *Virginia* accidentally ran aground and the tiny *Monitor* circled it for some time, pounding away with her two guns. Finally, the *Virginia* dragged herself off the shoal and attempted to ram the *Monitor.* The attempt resulted in a mere graze. The *Monitor*'s guns struck the aft guns on the *Virginia,* knocking out and badly wounding some of the gunners. Artillerists on both ships worried about using so much powder so quickly. The *Minnesota* and the *Virginia* exchanged angry belches of smoke and fire, and the *Monitor* momentarily moved away to take account of her condition. At this point a shot from the *Virginia* struck the pilothouse squarely, temporarily blinding Worden and severely wounding him. Greene came from the turret to see his commanding officer "with his eyes closed and the blood apparently rushing from every pore in the upper part of his face." "I cannot see, but do not mind me," Worden said. "Save the *Minnesota* if you can."

Greene took command of the ironclad. During the momentary confusion the *Virginia* turned from the scene of the action, and Greene believed this to be a sign that she was breaking off the engagement and had been beaten. The ship was actually taking account of its own leaks and minor damages, and Greene directed the *Monitor* back to the vicinity of the *Minnesota.* At about 12:30 P.M. the *Monitor* dropped anchor beside the *Minnesota,* and Worden, in his cabin, asked if the *Minnesota* was saved. When told that it was, he responded, "Then I can die happy."

Worden would not die soon, but would outlive both of the revolutionary ships. The *Virginia* moved off and accomplished little else before being scuttled off Norfolk on May 11, 1862, to prevent capture by Federal forces. The *Monitor* foundered sixteen miles south-southeast of Cape Hatteras, North Carolina, on December 31, 1862, during a storm. The ship went down quickly into 220 feet of water; 2 officers and 14 sailors lost their lives, and 47 officers and crew were rescued. "The *Monitor* is no more," wrote Keeler a few days after the sinking. "What the fire of the enemy failed to do, the elements have accomplished." The wreck was discovered in 1973; during the 1990s divers brought up small numbers of *Monitor* artifacts. In 2000 large pieces of the ship, including the turret, were planned for recovery before they deteriorated completely in the hostile sea. Perhaps the final casualty of the battle of the ironclads was Greene. Chastised for years after the war for breaking off the engagement and not finishing off the *Virginia,* Greene finally had enough. After writing an article about the affair, which undoubtedly refreshed his memories, he shot himself in 1884.

Despite the inconclusive nature of the famous battle, it ushered in a new era of naval warfare. Many descendants of the *Monitor* fought throughout the war. "Now comes the reign of iron," wrote naval officer John A. Dahlgren; "the cased sloops are to take the place of wooden ships." Perhaps Van Brunt phrased the oddity of the new era best in his after-action report. "The contrast was that of a pygmy to a giant," he wrote. "Gun after gun was fired by the *Monitor,* which was returned with whole broadsides by the rebels, with no more effect, apparently, than so many pebble-stones thrown by a child."

As THE IRONCLAD WARRIORS were revolutionizing naval history, Brig. Gen. Ambrose Burnside continued his successful expedition along the North Carolina coast. Following the capture of Roanoke Island in February, Burnside concentrated his men and moved southwestward toward New Bern. This small town of 5,432 citizens represented a gateway for the Yankees from which to strike eastward into the heart of North Carolina, demolishing the railroads, and to move southward on Beaufort, which was protected by Fort Macon. Moreover, New Bern hosted the Confederate headquarters of the District of the Pamlico and offered the opportunity to attack directly into the center of the Confederate organization within the eastern part of the state. After leaving a garrison at Roanoke Island (Col. Rush C. Hawkins's 4th Brigade), Burnside's expedition proceeded apace with the aid of the Federal navy. The organization of forces was pretty nearly the same as it had been at Roanoke. Burnside, commanding the Department of North Carolina, led the army force of about 11,000. The Federal naval force, the North Atlantic Blockading Squadron, was commanded by Capt. Louis M. Goldsborough, but he was summoned to Hampton Roads and Comdr. Stephen Clegg Rowan substituted. The Confederate force at New Bern consisted of about 4,000 troops under the command of Brig. Gen. Lawrence O'Bryan Branch. His most notable subordinate was Col. Zebulon B. Vance, who later would become governor of the state and much celebrated for his lack of cooperation with President Davis.

As early as March 3, Federal soldiers in Brig. Gen. Jesse L. Reno's 2d Brigade marched onto transports and readied for the journey south. Those of Brig. Gens. John G. Foster and John G. Parke followed, but rough weather and inadequate supplies necessitated delays. It was the morning of

March 11 before the flotilla moved away from Roanoke Island, and then the movement was made under a dismal rainstorm. Thirteen gunboats moved alongside the army transports, with Rowan aboard his flagship, the USS *Philadelphia*.

Awaiting the Federal expeditionary force were well-positioned shore batteries alongside the Neuse River. Burnside believed he could minimize the potential risk by landing his men at the mouth of Slocum's Creek, about thirteen miles south of the city, and marching them northward. Just before darkness on March 12 the flotilla moved into position up the Neuse River and dropped anchor, ready to disembark their cargoes of infantry. Oddly, some of the soldiers found the Federal flotilla anything but military in appearance. Many of the transports were decorated with patriotic bunting, and to some the expedition "appeared more as a pleasure outing than a Union attack force." By 8 A.M. on March 12 the first of Burnside's troops climbed into small surfboats and were towed in toward shore. Before bringing in the men, the boats raked the shoreline with grape and canister. The landing was unopposed, but Burnside's men did not know what faced them on the march to New Bern.

The Northern soldiers marched slowly up to the Beaufort–New Bern Road, while their gunboats steamed up the Neuse and shelled the woods to ward off Confederate soldiers and artillery. The roads were muddy to begin with and by late morning rain began to fall. Rain continued to fall sporadically throughout the soggy, chilly morning hours. Still, the discomforts faced by the Federals were relatively minor compared with the problems facing Branch and his Confederates. Poor muskets, a shortage of gunpowder, and inadequate communications gave Branch considerable concern. Moreover, many of the civilians in the region did not support the Confederacy. And Branch's cavalry commander, Col. Samuel B. Spruill of the 2d North Carolina Cavalry, was an incompetent officer, and the two were barely on speaking terms.

The first shots of the battle of New Bern rang out at about 7:30 A.M. on March 13. Branch's troops were deployed in a line of battle from Fort Thompson on the Neuse westward across the Beaufort Road and the Atlantic & North Carolina Railroad to a position across a small creek and the Weathersby Road. Foster's brigade moved out in front of the bulk of Branch's troops east of the creek. Parke's brigade moved northward behind Foster, and Reno's brigade moved north up the railroad cut. A general series of volleys was unleashed from the guns of Northern and Southern regiments, and shells were lobbed from the Union gunboats, some of which fell short and caused great consternation among the Yankee troops. After some hard fighting, the Union troops found it difficult to advance on the Confederate positions, which had been partly fortified. The fighting raged on for a short time before Confederate retreat.

The losses at New Bern were relatively minor. Confederate casualties amounted to 68 killed, 116 wounded, and 425 missing. The Yankees lost 90 killed, 385 wounded, and 1 missing. "With such soldiers advance is victory," Ambrose E. Burnside wrote of his men. Indeed, Burnside had reason for great joy. He had captured the second-most-important commercial city in North Carolina, along with nine forts with forty-one heavy guns, six 32-pounder guns, more than 300 prisoners, more than 1,000 small arms, tents and barracks for 10,000 men, and large amounts of ammunition and supplies. Moreover, with New Bern in Federal hands, the Confederate policy of lightly defending the coastal positions ended in utter failure. Now the city of Beaufort and its protector Fort Macon were vulnerable to attack from Burnside's movement. For their part, the Confederates, who burned a bridge and scattered mostly into Kinston on their retreat, seemed stunned.

The Burnside expedition was not quite over. On April 11 the Federal troops laid siege to Beaufort, some forty miles southeast of New Bern. Beaufort stands on a thumb of land protected by several outer banks. Fort Macon is south of Beaufort on the eastern tip of Bogue Banks. Morehead City stands west of Beaufort and represents the terminus of the Atlantic & North Carolina Railroad. Burnside ordered Parke's 3d Brigade to undertake the final mission of the expedition, reducing Fort Macon. The fort was commanded by Col. Moses J. White, a young ordnance officer with a garrison of some 450 men and fifty-four guns. In addition to Parke's brigade, the Federal forces near Fort Macon included four gunboats under the direction of Comdr. Samuel Lockwood. On April 19 minor exchanges of gunfire flared.

On this same day a skirmish broke out at South Mills, in the northeast-ernmost corner of the state. In this action, Reno's brigade was sent to South Mills from Elizabeth City to destroy locks on the Dismal Swamp Canal, thereby preventing the passage of rumored ironclad Confederate gunboats into North Carolina waters. The Federal navy's inability to destroy the locks set up a combined army-navy action that followed. Heavily outnumbered, the Southern troops opposed a charge of Col. Rush Hawkins's 9th New York Zouaves up Sawyer's Lane. There were fearsome casualties, one of whom was Hawkins, hit in the left arm. The Confederates, running low on ammu-nition, abandoned the field and retreated toward North West Locks during the night. Of the 3,000 Yankees engaged, 13 were killed, 101 wounded, and 13 missing. Wright had a mere 400 infantrymen engaged, and lost just 7 killed, 18 wounded, and 4 captured. Despite the Confederate abandonment of the field, the action at South Mills prevented the Yankees from destroying the locks. However, the Confederate program to create ironclads amounted to virtually nothing, and in the coming weeks they would abandon Norfolk and scuttle the CSS *Virginia.*

Meanwhile, the siege of Fort Macon continued. Parke's men attempted to get closer to the fort by building earthworks on April 21 but were pounded by grapeshot, ending the attempts to belly up to the fort. The following day a terrific fire from the guns of Fort Macon scattered Yankee soldiers from a rifle pit, throwing up sand and debris high into the air. Burnside determined to attack the fort early on the morning of April 25. A correspondent from the *New York Tribune* witnessed the bombardment and wrote that the fort "looked like a volcano belching fire and smoke. The noise of the cannonade . . . seemed as if a dozen tropical thunderstorms" were unleashing their fury over the region.

By 8 A.M. the four ships under Lockwood's command cruised into position and opened up with repeated salvos. They were the screw combatant USS *Daylight* (Lockwood), the side-wheel combatant USS *State of Georgia* (Comdr. James F. Armstrong), the screw gunboat USS *Chippewa,* and the bark USS *Gemsbok.* The naval fire increased the fury of the Federal attack, but most of the shots inflicting damage in the fort were from Parke's batteries. After 11 A.M. more than half the shells from Parke's guns were landing squarely in the fort and beginning to reduce the fort. The danger of exploding the fort's magazine, and a well-placed hit that knocked down every man in three gun crews, began to show the hopelessness of White's task. By 4:30 P.M. White hoisted a white flag. After the surrender, Burnside inspected the fort. Of 1,150 projectiles fired, 560 had struck within Fort Macon.

WHILE BURNSIDE WAS BATTLING a weakly defended series of positions in the east, another Federal movement was assisted by the inland rivers. In April 1861, Confederate troops began constructing fortifications at New Madrid, Missouri, and nearby Island No. 10 to block the Federal flotilla from moving farther south along the Mississippi River. New Madrid stands near the southeastern base of Missouri—close to the borders with Kentucky and Tennessee—and just north of a reversed S-shaped bend in the river called Madrid Bend. Southbound river traffic at this point has to turn sharply northward and then turn southward again. Such a circuitous route allows for placing many heavy guns along the shore and on Island No. 10, at the base of the northernmost sharp curve in the river, that would make passage by hostile ships a very hazardous affair indeed.

The strategic relevance of New Madrid and Island No. 10 came into play in the earliest stage of what would become the Shiloh campaign. At the beginning of March, Maj. Gen. Leonidas Polk withdrew his force from Columbus, Kentucky, and sent Maj. Gen. John P. McCown, along with 5,000 men, to reinforce these positions, which already had 2,000 Confederates present. McCown was a Tennessean who was incompetent as an army commander. Island No. 10 held three batteries of five guns, four guns, and six guns. A floating battery of nine guns stood just northwest of the island. A redoubt and shore batteries stretched along the south of the island, amounting to an additional 18 guns. New Madrid, which featured two forts mounting twenty-one guns, stands at the northwestern tip of the bend.

McCown's Confederates at Madrid Bend consisted of four brigades, some artillery, and unbrigaded men amounting to a force of 7,432. They would be approached by the Federal Army of the Mississippi under Brig. Gen. John Pope. A Kentuckian by birth, Pope had a commission as brigadier general that may have been influenced by his illustrious connections, which included a collateral descendancy from George Washington, an uncle who was a U.S. senator from Kentucky, and a connection by marriage to the family of Mary Todd Lincoln. Pope's substantial army consisted of some 25,059 men organized into five regular divisions plus artillery and cavalry, commanded by Brig. Gens. David S. Stanley, Schuyler Hamilton, John M. Palmer, Eleazer A. Paine, Joseph B. Plummer, and Gordon Granger (Cavalry Division), and artillery plus a flotilla brigade commanded by Col. Napoleon B. Buford.

By March 3, Pope had moved down to a position confronting New Madrid. Not only did he find the heavy guns manned by Confederates, but he also discovered that the Southerners had a flotilla of six ships. They were led by Comm. George N. Hollins, with the flagship CSS *McRae* in the lead and the CSS *Livingston*, CSS *Polk*, CSS *Pontchartrain*, CSS *Maurepas*, and CSS *Jackson*. Pope resigned himself to a siege operation, sent for siege artillery, and began bombarding New Madrid heavily on March 13, at about the same time McCown ordered the town and nearby gun emplacements evacuated. He moved his Confederates across the river, and for this action he was soundly condemned. "I abandoned New Madrid because it involved a constant loss of life to hold it," McCown wrote. The explanation did not satisfy Richmond authorities, and McCown had to ward off accusations that he had been drinking during the engagement as well.

The Confederate War Department placed Brig. Gen. William W. Mackall in command. Mackall (pronounced "Make'all") was a Maryland-born soldier who had served on the staff of Gen. Albert Sidney Johnston before being commissioned brigadier general. Mackall's force was divided into two brigades commanded by Brig. Gen. Lucius M. Walker and Col. Edward W. Gantt.

Pope's next move was to cross the Mississippi south of New Madrid and turn against the defenses of Island No. 10. But his troop transports and supporting ships were still north of the bend and would have to run the guns to move southward. Rather than risk having his transports blown apart, Pope determined to have his engineers cut a canal north of the bend and its defenses, from the Mississippi to Wilson's Bayou, a distance of about twelve miles through the swampy timberland and soggy cornfields and bayous. It was hard going as engineers worked with submersible saws that cut each tree under water near the bottom of the swamp. Amazingly, the canal project was completed by April 4.

On April 4, the *Carondelet* ran the batteries under cover of darkness as an intense storm bellowed above, dropping sheets of rain into the river. The whole scene was made surrealistic by intensely bright flashes of lightning that illuminated the ship like a strobe light. The gunboat fired and the shore batteries fired back with savagery, but in the end the Yankee ship got south of the batteries and now posed a huge threat to the Confederate defenders. The next night, under similar circumstances, the USS *Pittsburg* repeated the *Carondelet's* successful passage. On April 7 the gunboats fired mercilessly into the Confederate defensive batteries as transports moved through the canal—it was one of the few times during the war that such an improvised canal actually worked. Pope's force began landing near Watson's Landing on the western peninsula and moved southward toward the Confederates at Tiptonville. The Federal ships were bombarding the Confederate gunners with full force, and soon Mackall had no choice but to surrender. The surrender on April 8 was a large one: some 4,538 troops gave themselves up to the Yankees, some 1,500 of them being sick, and some 1,000 soldiers escaped into the swamps. Mackall himself was among the prisoners. To summarize the operation, one might simply observe that Mackall's report on his surrender made it to President Davis's desk by August 1862. Davis simply marked it "read/unsatisfactory."

On the Federal side, jubilation ruled the day. "I congratulate you & your command on your splendid achievement," Halleck wrote Pope on April 8. "It exceeds in boldness & brilliancy all other operations of the war. It will be memorable in military history, and will be admired by future generations. You deserve well of your country." On the same day, Halleck wrote Stanton: "Our victory is complete and overwhelming. We have not lost a single man."

On behalf of Pope, Illinois Governor Richard Yates wrote the president asking for Pope's promotion. On April 10, Lincoln replied: "I fully appreciate Gen. Pope's splendid achievements with their invaluable results; but you must know that Major Generalships in the Regular Army, are not as plenty as blackberries."

OTHER ACTIONS FLARED in the West during March. At Pound Gap, Kentucky, on the 16th, Brig. Gen. Humphrey Marshall's Confederates faced a Union force commanded by Brig. Gen. James A. Garfield. These two forces had clashed at Paintsville in January; now they were again coming to grips, this time in the Cumberland Mountains along the Kentucky-Virginia border near the present-day town of Jenkins. On March 13, Garfield left Pikeville with a force of 600 infantry and 100 cavalry troops. The Confederates entrenched along Pound Gap consisted of some 500 men of the 21st Virginia Battalion of infantry. The Confederates had constructed crude breastworks and blocked the road to the gap on the Kentucky side with fallen trees. Nevertheless, on the morning of the 16th, Garfield advanced during a snowstorm. After a sharp fight lasting about half an hour, the Confederates broke and fled in disorder, having been struck by several heavy volleys of musketry.

Way out west, in New Mexico Territory, Maj. Gen. Henry Hopkins Sibley continued his ill-conceived campaign to bring the territory under Confederate influence by marching northward along the Rio Grande. Though Sibley's strategic goals were fuzzy, his military successes on the surface seemed pleasing, particularly to a commander who experienced much of his campaign under the influence of liquor. Near the end of February he had beaten the force under Col. Edward R. S. Canby at Valverde, near Fort Craig, and by March 2 the approach of the Rebels forced the evacuation of Albuquerque by Federal troops. The following day minor actions erupted at Cubero (where Confederates captured supplies) and Comanche Pass, and by March 4, Sibley marched into Santa Fe, forcing the Yankees to withdraw to Fort Union northeast of the city.

The situation was complicated for Sibley in early March when a second Federal force entered the picture, that of Col. John P. Slough, a Denver attorney who had been an Ohio legislator before being expelled for fighting. Slough brought his 1st Colorado Infantry, consisting of 884 men, south toward the Confederate invasion. As the middle two weeks of March expired, both sides strengthened for a coming fight. Slough relieved the garrison commander at Fort Union, Col. Gabriel R. Paul of the 4th New Mexico Infantry, and believed that Canby would be marching northward to meet up and consolidate Federal forces in the area. Meanwhile, Sibley's men enjoyed their occupation of Santa Fe.

On March 22, Slough's force, 1,342 strong, left Fort Union in pursuit of the Confederates. Four days later the first of three clashes resulted, which together are termed the battle of Glorieta Pass, New Mexico Territory, the decisive series of actions in the campaign. (The action carries the alternative names Apache Canyon, Glorieta Canyon, Pigeon's Ranch, and Johnson's Ranch.) Slough dispatched his second-in-command, Maj. John Chivington, with 200 cavalry and 180 infantry, to move toward Santa Fe. Meanwhile, Sibley had concocted his own plan: He would send three distinct columns toward Fort Union, the northernmost led by Maj. Charles Pyron (2d Texas

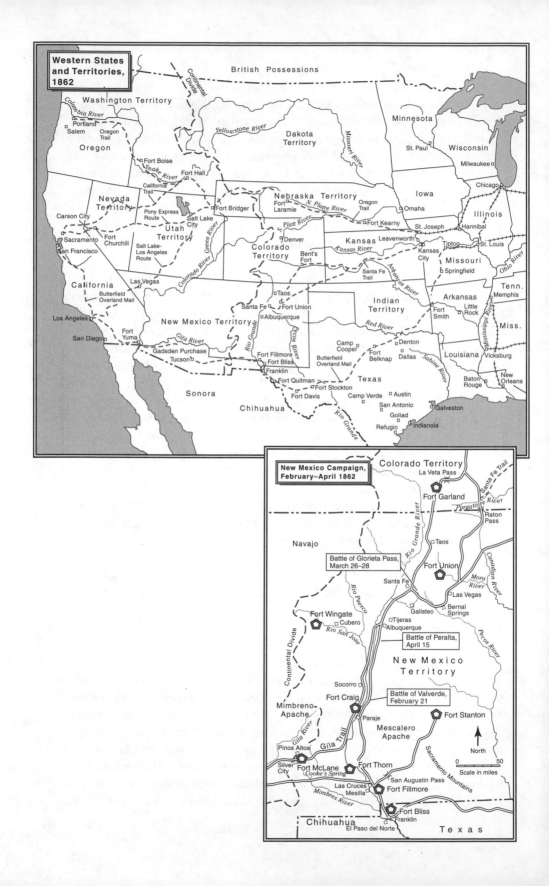

Western States and Territories, 1862

British Possessions

Continental Divide

Washington Territory

Columbia River
Portland
Salem
Oregon Trail

Oregon

Fort Boise
Snake River
Fort Hall

California Trail

Yellowstone River

Dakota Territory

Minnesota

St. Paul

Wisconsin

Milwaukee

Nevada Territory

Pony Express Route

Fort Bridger

Nebraska Territory

Fort Laramie
N. Platte River

Oregon Trail

Missouri River

Omaha

Iowa

Chicago

Illinois

Carson City
Sacramento
San Francisco

Salt Lake City
Utah Territory
Fort Churchill
Salt Lake-Los Angeles Route

Green River

S. Platte River
Denver

Colorado Territory

Platt River

Fort Kearny

St. Joseph

Kansas

Leavenworth

Bent's Fort

Kansas River

Leavenworth
Kansas City
St. Louis
Tipton

Hannibal

Missouri

Springfield

Ohio River

California

Butterfield Overland Mail

Las Vegas

Colorado River

Taos
Santa Fe
Fort Union
Albuquerque

Santa Fe Trail

Arkansas River

Indian Territory

Red River

Fort Smith

Arkansas

Little Rock

Tenn.

Memphis

Miss.

Los Angeles

San Diego

Fort Yuma

Gila River

Gadsden Purchase
Tucson

New Mexico Territory

Rio Grande

Pecos River

Fort Fillmore
Fort Bliss
Franklin

Camp Cooper

Butterfield Overland Mail

Fort Belknap

Denton
Dallas

Louisiana

Vicksburg

Baton Rouge

New Orleans

Sonora

Fort Quitman

Fort Stockton
Fort Davis

Camp Verde

Texas

Austin
San Antonio
Goliad
Refugio

Galveston
Indianola

Chihuahua

Rio Grande

New Mexico Campaign, February–April 1862

Colorado Territory

La Veta Pass

Santa Fe Trail

Fort Garland

Purgatoire River

Raton Pass

Navajo

Rio Grande River

Taos

Canadian River

Battle of Glorieta Pass, March 26–28

Santa Fe

Fort Union

Mora River

Las Vegas

Fort Wingate
Cubero

Rio Puerco

Galisteo
Tijeras
Albuquerque

Bernal Springs

Pecos River

Rio San Jose

Battle of Peralta, April 15

New Mexico Territory

Continental Divide

Socorro

Fort Craig
Paraje

Battle of Valverde, February 21

Fort Stanton

Mimbreno-Apache

Gila River

Mescalero Apache

Pinos Altos

Gila Trail

Silver City
Fort McLane
Cooke's Spring

Fort Thorn

Sacramento Mountains

North

0   50
Scale in miles

Las Cruces
Mesilla

San Augustin Pass

Fort Fillmore

Fort Bliss
Franklin

Mimbres River

Chihuahua

El Paso del Norte

Texas

Infantry), the middle column by Col. William R. Scurry (4th Texas Infantry), and the southernmost by Col. Tom Green (5th Texas Mounted Infantry). The actions unfolded in a lengthy valley comprised of Apache Canyon and the elevated terrain of Glorieta Pass, through which the Santa Fe Trail stretches eastward past three ranches—sprawling western equivalents of taverns, military supply depots, and farms rolled into one—termed Johnson's Ranch, Pigeon's Ranch, and Kozlowski's Ranch.

On March 26, Chivington's force of 418 men encountered Pyron's 300 Confederates at Apache Canyon. After brief, intense fighting in the valley, the Yankees emerged triumphant but retreated eastward to Pigeon's Ranch. The Federal losses were 5 killed, 11 wounded, and 3 captured; Confederate losses were 3 killed, 1 wounded, and 71 captured. Scurry arrived during the night and reinforced Pyron, and Slough made his appearance at Kozlowski's Ranch by the 27th. On the morning of the 28th, the forces gravitated together once again. Slough moved westward about 11 A.M. toward Apache Canyon, undeterred by the horrible nature of the battlefield, which contained a deep, narrow gorge surrounded by hills, its bottom cut by the furrowed path of the Trail, and clumps of knotty cedars clustered around groups of boulders. The first of two phases of the battle occurred at Pigeon's Ranch. Slough's 844 men faced approximately 600 Confederates under Scurry. A general engagement began between infantry and artillery on both sides; within a short time Slough learned that Confederate baggage and ammunition trains were nearby at Johnson's Ranch, so he sent Chivington off to destroy them. Some sixty wagons stood in the valley along with a single gun; Chivington's men picked off some of the guards and attacked the 200 men at that position before spiking the gun and moving toward the wagons. "[They were] heavily loaded with ammunition, clothing, subsistence, and forage, all of which were burned upon the spot or rendered entirely useless," wrote Chivington. "We also took 17 prisoners, and captured about 30 horses and mules, which were in a corral in the vicinity of the wagons."

Sibley now had a serious problem—his supplies were gone. In the action at Johnson's Ranch, Chivington's Federals had lost 2 killed and 5 wounded; Confederate losses were about 2 killed, 2 wounded, and 17 captured. The casualties at Pigeon's Ranch were also about equal: 47 killed, 78 wounded, and 13 captured or missing on the Federal side and 42 killed, 61 wounded, and 14 captured of the Rebels. Scurry and the other Confederates rushed back to Santa Fe, their battle fatigue and loss of supplies crushing Sibley's further hopes for a conquest of New Mexico Territory. Slough and his troops returned to Fort Union believing, correctly, that they had stopped the Confederate campaign. A final action took place at Peralta, south of Albuquerque, on April 15, as Canby's Union soldiers struck Green and fought during an intense dust storm. By early May the remnants of Sibley's men marched back into Mesilla, north of El Paso, their hopes shattered. The New Mexico campaign of 1862 was over.

FOR THE ARMIES IN THE EAST, the focus of the military operations, however, was twofold. In the Shenandoah Valley, Maj. Gen. Stonewall Jackson, in command of the Valley District, was in Winchester preparing to move as the left wing of the army under Gen. Joe Johnston, who was still encamped in the vicinity of Manassas Junction near the old Bull Run battlefield. To Jackson, the Valley was paramount: "If this Valley is lost, Virginia is lost," he wrote Col. Alexander R. Boteler, a staff member. As far as the Confederate War Department was concerned, Jackson's primary mission was to guard against the army of Maj. Gen. Nathaniel P. Banks, spread over four positions at Cumberland and Frederick, Maryland, and Bath and Romney in western Virginia. Jackson's force in the Valley consisted of some 13,759 men, but widespread sickness reduced the number of effectives in the field to a mere 5,000. He was not well equipped for offensive operations against Banks. Nonetheless, events during the first days of March 1862 would make Jackson a legend.

Southern military planners valued the Shenandoah Valley because it offered a screen of mountains behind which Confederate armies could travel unscouted by Union forces—and they would use this route later in the war for two raids into the North. They also valued it highly because such abundant foodstuffs were produced in the Valley that it came to be known as the "breadbasket of the Confederacy." Jackson respected the Valley even more because he felt some ownership in it, having grown up northwest of the area in the mountainous region of Virginia. Jackson remained realistic about his army's size, however. "If we cannot be successful in defeating the enemy should he advance," he told Johnson on March 8, "a kind Providence may enable us to inflict a terrible wound and effect a safe retreat in the event of having to fall back."

While Jackson was formulating a course of action, he dispatched Col. Turner Ashby, a trusted Virginian and skilled cavalryman, on a series of raids to harass the Baltimore & Ohio Railroad and the Chesapeake & Ohio Canal. During the first half of March, Banks was in command of a detached division of the Army of the Potomac. During the last half of March he headed the detached 5th Corps of the Army of the Potomac. By April 4 he commanded the Department of the Shenandoah. Banks moved south of the Potomac in response to Ashby's raids. Nathaniel Prentiss Banks was a former governor of Massachusetts and member of the U.S. House of Representatives who had begun life in Waltham, Massachusetts, as a machinist and later became editor of the *Middlebury Reporter*. Banks turned out to be one of those political generals who never made much of himself on the battlefield. His first lesson in humility was about to be delivered by Jackson's much smaller force.

Banks's movement forced a small Confederate force under Brig. Gen. D. H. Hill to evacuate Leesburg on the Potomac, and on March 9, Johnston pulled the entire Army of the Potomac (CSA), some 40,000 strong, out of Manassas Junction on a retreat south to Culpeper Court House. This left Jackson's command at Winchester exposed. Banks occupied Winchester on March 12, pushing Jackson into Strasburg. Ashby acted as a rearguard, screening with 600 cavalry. Banks now continued south, driving Jackson up the Valley, and planning to turn toward Washington after accomplishing that goal.

Banks's force moved south of Winchester on March 17, sending 6,000 infantry, 750 cavalry, and 24 field guns under the command of Brig. Gen. James Shields in pursuit of Jackson. Shields was a colorful character in a war of many colorful characters. A soldier, legislator, judge, and governor of Oregon Territory, Shields was most celebrated for his encounter with Lincoln: in 1842 the playful Lincoln wrote a letter terming Shields "a conceity dunce" under the pseudonym "Rebecca" and sent it to the *Sangamo Journal*, where it was published. When Shields discovered the authorship, he challenged Lincoln to a duel, and Lincoln accepted the much shorter man's challenge after suggesting "large cavalry broadswords" as the weapons. Across the Mississippi from Alton, Illinois, the duel nearly took place, but friends persuaded the two to call it off at the last moment. Shields's force of 9,000 was organized into three brigades commanded by Cols. Nathan Kimball, Jeremiah C. Sullivan, and Erastus B. Tyler. The cavalry was commanded by Col. Thornton F. Brodhead. Jackson's force of about 4,200 consisted of three brigades with attached cavalry. The brigade commanders were Brig. Gen. Richard B. Garnett (who had the celebrated "Stonewall Brigade," Jackson's old unit), Col. Jesse S. Burks, and Col. Samuel V. Fulkerson. Ashby headed up the cavalry. As the two armies were about to tangle in the Valley, McClellan's great force began an embarkation to the east.

A game of cat and mouse now unfolded in the Valley. Shields pursued Jackson to Strasburg, forcing Jackson to move south to Woodstock. Shields further pursued to Woodstock, driving Jackson back to Mount Jackson. The Yankee cavalry under Brodhead raced after Ashby, attempting to drive through his screen, but shortly returned to Shields and erroneously reported that Jackson was fleeing and retiring outside of the Valley. This allowed Banks to pursue the second phase of his mission, moving eastward toward Washington. What he did not know was that Jackson had not fled. On March 20, Banks left Shields at Winchester and began moving most of his force toward the capital city. Jackson began to panic because he had been specifically ordered not to allow Banks to escape and reinforce Maj. Gen.

Irvin McDowell, who was massing troops near Fredericksburg in preparation for reinforcing McClellan. On March 22, Ashby skirmished with Federal pickets at Kernstown, two miles south of Winchester, and concluded
that the Yankee forces in the area were relatively scant. Shields was wounded
when a shell fired during the skirmish struck his left arm above the elbow;
Kimball took command.

Jackson saw an opportunity to strike Shields's force. On March 23 he
moved north and arrived in front of the Union line at Kernstown by 1 P.M.
The resulting battle would be known as Kernstown, or alternatively, First
Winchester. Discovering that Ashby had been pushed back, Jackson reinforced him with Burks's brigade, positioned behind two guns just south of
Kernstown. Jackson now devised a plan to turn the Federal right flank, and
he sent the brigades of Garnett and Fulkerson northwestward from the Valley Turnpike, across Middle Road, and up on several rises east of Opequon
Creek. The 23d Virginia Infantry and 37th Virginia Infantry took a more
northerly, parallel route. The Yankee forces were deployed as follows: Sullivan north of Hogg Run and Kernstown, east of the turnpike, and Kimball
to Sullivan's right. Tyler was back closer to Winchester. Yankee infantry
was posted on both sides of the Valley Turnpike, and artillery stood on
Pritchard's Hill, west of the road and a short distance north of Kernstown.

Jackson plucked a resident out of Kernstown, Maj. Frank B. Jones of the
2d Virginia Infantry, and employed him as a temporary aide because he
knew the countryside so well. "He ordered me to lead . . . across the open
fields & take positions on the high & long ridge overlooking the back road,"
Jones recalled. "The Enemies batteries had full play upon us but they did little damage & we soon reached the cover of the woods." A brief, reasonably
heavy barrage of artillery between the Federal guns on Pritchard's Hill and
the Confederate guns near Burks's brigade and along Sandy Ridge, west of
the turnpike, led to a general movement of Confederate infantry to the left
in the attempt to turn the Yankee right.

Kimball at once recognized the sweeping movement to the west and
promptly took countermeasures. He shifted Tyler's brigade, which had been
posted at the toll gate between Kernstown and Winchester on the turnpike,
ordering them along the Cedar Creek Road to anchor the extreme Federal
right. He moved Sullivan to the northernmost edge of the ridge, where it
supported the center of the Federal line. Savage attacks of heavy musketry
fire erupted along the line, particularly between Fulkerson's and Tyler's
brigades, and the 110th Pennsylvania Infantry (Col. William D. Lewis, Jr.)
took a heavy pounding. The focus of fire soon shifted to Garnett's portion of
the Confederate line, where the action of musket and other small-arms fire
surged for nearly two hours. Garnett desperately awaited more reserves that
could not be found. By now it was nearly 6 P.M. and Garnett felt he had no op-

tion but to order a retreat. Jackson, who had been reconnoitering when Garnett fell back, found his subordinate moving to the rear and asked him why he had not halted and rallied his men. It was too late, though, with Confederates scattering, dust rising, and daylight waning. Jackson was furious. He relieved Garnett of his assignment and had him placed under arrest for "neglect of duty," replacing him with Brig. Gen. Charles S. Winder. But the court-martial of Garnett desired by Jackson never came about. The Yankees held the field, and this further enraged Jackson. Ironically, however, he had nothing to fear. Confederate losses from the battle were 80 killed, 375 wounded, and 263 missing; Federal losses amounted to 118 killed, 450 wounded, and 22 missing.

Kernstown ensured that Banks would come back into the Valley and not reinforce McDowell. The Federals also believed that Jackson must have been much stronger in force than he was to attack as he did, and this caused future errors by Federal commanders in the Valley. Shields, lying in Winchester, requested reinforcements from Banks, and the Massachusetts politician reinforced the Yankees personally by returning to Strasburg, and then southward to Woodstock by April 2, where he remained for the first half of the month. Jackson stayed put at Mount Jackson and attempted to deduce Banks's next move. "Our gallant little army is increasing in numbers, and my prayer is that it may be an army of the living God as well as of its country," Jackson wrote his wife on April 7. Indeed, Jackson was a man on a mission, charged with a fervent religious doctrine that overshadowed all else. "The religious element seems strongly developed in him," wrote observer Garnet Wolseley, "and though his conversation is perfectly free from all puritanical cant, it is evident that he is a person who never loses sight of the fact that there is an omnipresent Deity ever presiding over the minutest occurrences in life, as well as over the most important." On April 11, Jackson again wrote his wife, with a message again about religion, recalling that the battle of Kernstown had taken place on a Sunday. "You appear much concerned at my attacking on *Sunday*. I was greatly concerned, too; but I felt it my duty to do it. . . . I hope and pray to our Heavenly Father that I may never again be circumstanced as on that day."

Jackson wouldn't necessarily need help from God as long as he opposed Nathaniel Banks. Banks's 15,000 men in Woodstock faced 6,000 under Jackson. The apparent considerable size of Jackson's force in the minds of Federal strategists had a long shadow, however, as did other effects of Kernstown. Lincoln did not allow McDowell to reinforce McClellan with his 30,000 men, keeping McClellan's burgeoning effort to move along the Virginia Peninsula weaker than it might have been. The Valley was becoming a dumping ground for Federal political generals as well: Maj. Gen. John Charles Frémont, the tarnished warrior of Missouri fame, now headed the

Mountain Department, which scattered its 8,000 men along various posts—McDowell, Franklin, Moorefield, and Romney. Brig. Gen. Louis Blenker's division of 7,000 was also ordered away from McClellan to reinforce Frémont. Banks stalled out at Woodstock fearing that if he attacked Jackson, the Confederate commander would slide down the Luray Valley (on the eastern side of Massanutten Mountain) and attack Banks's lines of communication at Front Royal. Banks finally devised a strategy to move upon Jackson without imperiling his communications and on April 17 marched his men south to New Market and then Harrisonburg. This forced Jackson to retreat to Conrad's Store. By month's end, McClellan was operating with a major movement southward toward the Peninsula, though weakened by scattered elements; Johnston had swung south to head off McClellan's movement; Jackson occupied the area of Conrad's Store to Swift Run Gap; and Maj. Gen. Richard S. Ewell brought his division of 8,000 up from Gordonsville to bolster Jackson. By April 30, Jackson could rejoice in the victory at Kernstown, but he also began to perceive justifiable fears. Frémont threatened Staunton, which held a supply base, and a joining of Frémont and Banks could throw the balance of power off throughout the Valley. Meanwhile, major events were transpiring down South.

"I NOW PROCLAIM . . . that unless a chief of proven military prestige—success under fire with troops—is put in command of the Army of the Potomac, leaving to McClellan the staff duties of General in Chief, we will come in for some awful disaster." These words of Brig. Gen. Phil Kearny mirrored the attitudes of many officers in the premier eastern army of the United States. To be sure, many of the soldiers and officers of the Federal Army of the Potomac adored McClellan, and he drilled the army almost to perfection in his quest to make it a well-oiled military machine. But the poor performance of McClellan in terms of making use of the army exasperated not only Lincoln but the majority of the civilian population, which wanted quick action, and many members of the army itself, which after a time preferred action to endless life in camp. When McClellan came to consider his course of action for the spring of 1862, he blundered. Originally, the Young Napoleon planned a direct movement on Centreville; this was abandoned when McClellan feared the vast numbers that he believed existed in Johnston's Confederate force—far more than actually existed. (To be fair, the overestimates of Confederate strength were based on inaccurate reports by "intelligence agents" such as Allan Pinkerton, but McClellan further exaggerated most of them in his own mind after the reporting had ceased.)

McClellan now made one of the greatest mistakes in strategy during the war: Rather than attacking the opposing army, McClellan would make Richmond, the enemy capital, his target. He planned to move his army by water south to a point of disembarkation at Urbana on the Rappahannock River and then move southwestward toward Richmond, beating Johnston to the Confederate capital city. The plan was debated, sometimes with gentlemanly decorum and other times with hot tempers, in Washington for three months. Lincoln preferred the land approach both from a logical standpoint and because it favored a defense of Washington; McClellan argued for a Peninsular campaign. He believed that roads were too poor to permit a movement toward Centreville and that the defenses of Washington were adequate. By early March the parties agreed to allow McClellan to move south and approach Richmond by way of the Peninsula. Johnston and his Army of the Potomac (CSA), some 43,000 strong at Centreville, withdrew on March 9 to Culpeper Court House, anticipating a Union advance through Maryland that never came. Following Johnston's move, McClellan's planned movement was now outmoded, and so he redirected his strategy, calling for a landing at Fort Monroe on the eastern tip of the Peninsula and a northwestward movement toward Richmond, aided by naval bombardment. After feverish discussion, Lincoln again acquiesced.

But he did so with reservations. On March 11, Lincoln's War Order No. 3 relieved McClellan as general-in-chief of the Federal armies and he was reassigned to command the Department and Army of the Potomac. This created something of a command dilemma for the Union War Department. Fort Monroe had a garrison of 12,000 under the command of Maj. Gen. John E. Wool, a New Yorker and veteran of the War of 1812. Wool, the most experienced officer in defensive installations, was assigned to Fort Monroe in his rank as brevet major general, thus outranking all other officers in the geographical area. When McClellan arrived on the Peninsula, he was the highest-ranking substantive general officer in the army. Wool pointed out, however, that McClellan's commission dated from 1861, whereas Wool's brevet commission dated from 1847, and therefore Wool was the highest-ranking officer in the field. The War Department was forced to agree and hastily transferred Wool to Baltimore (in another department) to allow McClellan to continue commanding all forces on the Peninsula.

McClellan had to contend with more than Wool. He faced the task of moving several tens of thousands of men by transport to Fort Monroe and then organizing artillery, animals, forage, communications, and other logistics. He also faced Johnston's force at Culpeper (43,000), 6,000 troops under Maj. Gen. Theophilus H. Holmes at Fredericksburg, a force of 13,000 under Maj. Gen. John B. Magruder at Yorktown, and a contingent of 9,000 under Maj. Gen. Benjamin Huger at Norfolk. To ready his men, McClellan marched to the now-abandoned Centreville, where the army discovered that the Confederate positions were much weaker than had been supposed, with some positions even containing "Quaker guns"—false cannon constructed from logs painted black—and imaginary men consisting of shirts stuck on poles. The perceptive New Yorker George Templeton Strong commented, "We have been humbugged by the rebels. . . . their works . . . were flimsy and armed with logs painted black instead of heavy guns." The soldiers had encountered a scattered few of the enemy, and one young aide-de-camp named George Armstrong Custer wrote his sister about the peculiar nature of the American war. "At night, when it is too dark to shoot or be shot at, both [sides] come out of hiding-places, holler at each other, calling names and bragging what they intend to do. Then, when daylight appears, the party which sees the other first, fires, and that puts a stop till night comes, when the same thing is repeated."

The command structure on each side was evolving dramatically. Lincoln himself, supplied with numerous military books and frequent advice, would take over the position of general-in-chief for the coming four months. In Virginia, on March 13, Robert E. Lee was called to Richmond for a new assignment. Despite relative unpopularity during the first year of the war, the veteran of the western Virginia campaigns was a great favorite and distant relative of Jefferson Davis. Now Davis, through his secretary of war and adjutant general, would appoint Lee to a new position. "General Robert E. Lee is assigned to duty at the seat of Government," General Orders No. 14 began, "and under the direction of the President, is charged with the conduct of military operations in the armies of the Confederacy. By order of the Secretary of War."

As he prepared to move his force southward, McClellan circulated a message to his army. "For a long time I have kept you inactive," it read, "but not without a purpose: you were to be disciplined, armed, and instructed. . . . I shall demand of you great, heroic exertions, rapid and long marches, desperate combats, privations, perhaps. We will share all these together; and when this sad war is over we will all return to our homes, and feel that we can ask no higher honor than the proud consciousness that we belonged to the ARMY OF THE POTOMAC." Many soldiers were supercharged with the electricity of this message, including Custer, who wrote his parents on March 17. "I have more confidence in General McClellan than in any man living," wrote Custer. "I would forsake everything and follow him to the ends of the earth. I would lay down my life for him."

For the time being, Custer and his fellow soldiers followed McClellan only to Fort Monroe. On March 17 the movement began and proceeded slowly; by April 2, when McClellan arrived at Fort Monroe, some 50,000 men under his command were ready for action. In the first phase of the Peninsula campaign, the Army of the Potomac had present three army corps plus one division and reserve forces; they were the 2d Corps (Brig. Gen. Edwin V. Sumner; divisions of Brig. Gens. Israel B. Richardson and John

Sedgwick); 3d Corps (Brig. Gen. Samuel P. Heintzelman; divisions of Brig. Gens. Fitz John Porter, Joseph Hooker, and Charles S. Hamilton); 4th Corps (Brig. Gen. Erasmus D. Keyes; divisions of Brig. Gens. Darius N. Couch, William F. Smith, and Silas Casey); and the 1st Division of the 1st Corps, commanded by Brig. Gen. William B. Franklin. The reserve infantry was commanded by Brig. Gen. George Sykes. On the Confederate side, Johnston's army—freshly christened the Army of Northern Virginia on March 14—during the first phase of the Peninsula campaign was organized into three wings, each containing several brigades. The Left Wing was Maj. Gen. D. H. Hill's, and contained the brigades of Brig. Gens. Robert E. Rodes, Winfield S. Featherston, Jubal A. Early, and Gabriel J. Rains, as well as two detached, smaller commands; the Center was Maj. Gen. James Longstreet's, and contained the brigades of Brig. Gens. A. P. Hill, Richard H. Anderson, George E. Pickett, Cadmus M. Wilcox, Raleigh E. Colston, and Roger A. Pryor; the Right Wing was Maj. Gen. John B. Magruder's, and contained the division of Brig. Gen. Lafayette McLaws (consisting of the brigades of Brig. Gens. Paul J. Semmes, Richard Griffith, Joseph B. Kershaw, and Howell Cobb, and the division of Brig. Gen. David R. Jones, which held the brigades of Brig. Gens. Robert A. Toombs and George T. Anderson. The Confederate reserve forces were commanded by Maj. Gen. Gustavus W. Smith.

But most of the Confederate force was not down on the Peninsula when McClellan arrived. Only Magruder's 13,000 troops were posted along a series of fortifications constructed on opposite sides of Yorktown, the old Revolutionary War battle site. Magruder's line stretched along the Warwick River, past Lee's Mills, and on up to Yorktown itself and across the York River to Gloucester Point. With the lack of naval support for an amphibious assault on Yorktown, which rather than investigating beforehand McClellan discovered in situ as a "surprise," he now ordered an assault up the Peninsula to begin on April 4. (The difficulty for the naval ships was twofold: the heavy Confederate batteries at the mouth of the York River and the lurking presence of the CSS *Virginia* on the James River.)

McClellan's plan called for Heintzelman's 3d Corps to occupy the Confederate troops in the trenches along the river while the 4th Corps, under Keyes, enveloped the Confederate right, moved around its rear, and cut off Magruder's pathway of retreat at the Halfway House, between Yorktown and Williamsburg. Heintzelman and Keyes, both veterans of First Bull Run, seemed aglow at the prospects of destroying a portion of Johnston's magnificent army. The problem was that McClellan and his corps commanders misread the situation badly. They believed that Magruder's line of entrenchments was concentrated around Yorktown itself but would soon discover that the line stretched along the whole width of the Peninsula and that fording the Warwick River under fire was a nearly impossible task. On the morning of April 5, Heintzelman's force marched on the road toward Yorktown and Keyes's men marched toward Lee's Mills, both under the discouraging conditions of a rainstorm. The good roads each commander had hoped for were not to be found, and already transporting artillery became a challenge. Moreover, the Federal commanders found that their maps were poor and gave them false indications of what they would find. Maj. Charles S. Wainwright, commanding the artillery in Hooker's division, noted the peculiar nature of the roads. He found that the topsoil consisted of about a foot of light, sandy loam atop a bed of shell marl, which rested on heavy clay deep below. Water sank directly into the marl, which converted it into something like "soft mortar." A heavy object such as a wagon broke through the surface crust and there was "nothing to stop its sinking until it reached the hard clay," Wainwright observed. The movements along roads on the Peninsula were slow and challenging at best.

McClellan's surprise on April 5 was twofold. Not only was his army stopped, particularly alarming in the case of the enveloping move by Keyes, but he was informed that Lincoln had stopped the planned movement of Brig. Gen. Irvin McDowell's troops to Fort Monroe. Rather than leaving in excess of 40,000 men in place to defend Washington, which he had reported, McClellan had in actuality, the War Department found, left slightly more than 26,000 behind. No one in Washington was amused. Authorities in the administration also continued to show concern over the somewhat startling activities of Stonewall Jackson in the Valley.

Rather than running around Magruder in lightning fashion, McClellan now faced a much harder decision of how to handle the two corps that were bogged down. "Prince John" Magruder, with an odd, somewhat dandy behavior, seemed to enjoy thwarting the Young Napoleon. Rather than drilling back in the North, McClellan was now in "enemy territory" and Johnston was already sending reinforcements to Magruder, the first of which would arrive on April 10. Little Mac could surmise that Magruder's hastily constructed line of entrenchments, spanning ten miles across the Peninsula, must be extremely thin.

Faced with a clever adversary, McClellan froze. Magruder at once employed a sophisticated and exhausting ploy to make it appear to the Yankees that he had far more men than he did. He frantically shifted troops around from one part of the line to the next, pulling them out and reinserting them elsewhere. The result was an accumulation of reports that mentioned "a column of 2,000 Rebels" at one spot and "a large force of heavy firing from the Reb line" at another, and this was all the warning that McClellan needed to back off. With a timidity that would become legendary, the Federal commander decided to lay siege to Yorktown. The siege began on April 5 and would last more than a month, giving Johnston and Davis all the time they would require to reinforce and prepare their army to fight on the Peninsula. In his first major move as an army commander, McClellan had lost the initiative.

McClellan repeatedly wrote the War Department that his army was not being properly sustained. On April 6, Lincoln replied, "You now have over one hundred thousand troops, with you independent of Gen. Wool's command. I think you better break the enemies' line from York-town to Warwick River, at once. They will probably use time, as advantageously as you can." "The country will not fail to note—is now noting—that the present hesitation to move upon an intrenched enemy, is but the story of Manassas repeated," Lincoln wrote three days later. "I beg to assure you that I have never written you, or spoken to you, in greater kindness of feeling than now, nor with a fuller purpose to sustain you. . . . *But you must act.*" Astonishingly, McClellan was so committed to a siege that when Brig. Gen. William F. Smith's reconnaissance in force to Lee's Mills on April 16 broke the Confederate line, the Federal commander called him back rather than reinforcing the breach.

Transporting the army, altogether some 121,500 men, 14,592 animals, and 1,150 wagons, to Fort Monroe and the Peninsula had taken an enormous effort. Participating in the movement were 113 steamers, 188 schooners, 88 barges, 74 ambulances, a number of pontoon bridges, cattle, supplies, and food. McClellan kept his men busy erecting heavy fortifications, hauling big siege guns, and erecting batteries and lines of entrenchments. But only sporadic shots were fired from time to time. "Some men seem born to be shot," wrote 1st Lt. Charles B. Haydon of the 2d Michigan Infantry after seeing an isolated man hit by a shell. For most, however, the weeks of April reinforced opinions about McClellan. The Federal commander wrote Lincoln on April 20 regarding the Confederate high commanders. "I prefer Lee to Johnston," he penned, "the former is *too* cautious & weak under grave responsibility— personally brave & energetic to a fault, he yet is wanting in moral firmness when pressed by heavy responsibility & is likely to be timid & irresolute in action." Privately, Lincoln repeated the comment he had first made in January by saying that if McClellan was not going to use the Army of the Potomac, "he would like to *borrow* it, provided he could see how it could be made to do something."

On the Confederate side, disdain of George McClellan was widespread. "No one but McClellan could have hesitated to attack," Johnston wrote Robert E. Lee, military advisor to Davis, on April 22. Yet the Confederates on the Peninsula and in Richmond knew that McClellan's army was growing and that they would have to throw everything they could at him to prevent the capture of the Confederate capital. At the end of the month, Johnston again wrote Lee, this time with somber undertones. "We are engaged in a species of warfare at which we can never win. It is plain that General McClellan will . . . depend for success upon artillery and engineering. We can compete with him in neither. We must therefore change our course, take the offensive, collect all the troops we have in the East and cross the Potomac with them." Johnston's sense of panic reflected a growing nervous tension among the Davis administration about the military action to come.

CHAPTER 8

A Bloodbath at Shiloh

IN THE WESTERN THEATER, the military situation for the Confederacy seemed as worrisome. There, another Johnston, Gen. Albert Sidney Johnston, commanded the sizable Confederate Department No. 2, as well as the newly organized Army of Mississippi, sometimes called the Army of the West. The disposition of troops in the current campaign resulted from the fallout of the Forts Henry and Donelson campaign in February, which had been disastrous for the South. Maj. Gen. U. S. Grant's army (the Army of West Tennessee; the name was changed to the Army of the Tennessee about March 11) had opened a pathway into middle Tennessee and Brig. Gen. Don Carlos Buell had taken Nashville, the state capital. The great danger for the Confederate armies in the west was their separation: Johnston was at Murfreesboro in central Tennessee at the end of February and Gen. P. G. T. Beauregard migrated southward to Corinth, Mississippi. Beauregard suggested to Johnston a heavy concentration of forces at Corinth, just south of the Mississippi-Tennessee border, and Johnston marched his force of 17,000 southward to Huntsville, Alabama, and then westward to Corinth, arriving there between March 18 and 24. In the meantime, Beauregard ordered Maj. Gen. Leonidas Polk and his 8,000 troops southward from Columbus, Kentucky, and they arrived between March 15 and 24. Additionally, Maj. Gen. Braxton Bragg brought his force of 10,000 north from Mobile, and Brig. Gen. Daniel Ruggles shifted 5,000 men to Corinth from Memphis. By the end of March, Johnston had a force of 40,000 concentrated in Corinth, ready to face the Union onslaught from the north.

The Federal preparations for the coming campaign in the west were marked by the peculiar personality traits of Maj. Gen. Henry W. Halleck. This skilled student of military tactics demonstrated such an appetite for political gain during the period that he squandered many opportunities for striking at the isolated Confederate forces before they were concentrated at Corinth. Instead, Halleck focused his energies primarily on a long series of communications with the War Department, lobbying for more power and control of the forces in the western theater. Halleck was buoyed by the success of Grant and yet threatened by it, too. He wanted Grant to remain in the field as an aggressive commander but also wanted to keep him in check. So Halleck attempted to plant enough seeds of doubt about Grant to counterbalance his successes in the field. On March 4, for example, Halleck wrote McClellan a famous letter implying that Grant was drinking and informing McClellan that Grant had repeatedly ignored Halleck's requests for reports on the strength and position of Grant's command. "A rumor has just reached me that since the taking of Fort Donelson General Grant has resumed his former bad habits," Halleck wrote. "If so, it will account for his neglect of my oft-repeated orders." Two days later Halleck wrote Grant one of a series of stern warnings: "Your going to Nashville without authority, and when your presence with your troops was of the utmost importance, was a matter of very serious complaint at Washington, so much so that I was advised to arrest you on your return."

"It has been reported that soon after the battle of Fort Donelson, Brigadier General Grant left his command without leave," wrote Lorenzo Thomas on March 10. "By direction of the President, the Secretary of War desires you to ascertain and report whether General Grant left his command at any time without proper authority."

Halleck entertained removing Grant from the scene and placing Grant's old teacher, Brig. Gen. Charles F. Smith, in command of the movement toward Corinth. Halleck was upset and posturing with McClellan and the War Department in part because Buell had been made a coequal of Halleck's in the West, and the two commanders could not agree on courses of combined action. Halleck dispatched Grant's force up the Tennessee River from the area of Fort Donelson on March 5, and ordered Smith to lead an expedition to destroy the railroad bridge over Bear Creek between Florence, Alabama, and Corinth and the railroad lines along Polk's lines of communications at Corinth, Humboldt, and Jackson, Tennessee. Under Smith's overall command, a division of Brig. Gen. William T. Sherman's troops moved toward Eastport, Mississippi, to accomplish the bridge-burning mission but found the countryside too flooded with rainwater to carry out the plan. (In February, Sherman had felt so useless at finding something meaningful to do that he wrote Halleck: "I beg of you to consider if you may not use me at Cairo, Paducah, or some place where I would have a limited but clearly defined duty.") On learning of this failure plus the movement of Polk southward, Halleck now fixed his plan to concentrate the army northeast of Corinth, along Pittsburg Landing on the Tennessee River, joining with Buell in a cooperative move to cut the Memphis & Charleston Railroad, or perhaps move against the city of Memphis itself.

Though Grant was temporarily out of favor, some of his fellow officers supported him vigorously. "We have heard with deep regret of your having been disposed from your authority as commander in the field of the forces in this district," wrote John A. McClernand, William H. L. Wallace, Leonard F. Ross, Mason Brayman, and seven other officers on March 9. "As our commander at Belmont and Forts Henry and Donelson, besides in numerous mere skirmishes, you were successful. Under your lead the flag of the union has been carried from the interior further towards the seaboard than by any other hands. You have slain more of the enemy, taken more prisoners and trophies, lost more men in battle and regained more territory to the Union than any other leader. . . . We place this spontaneous tribute at your disposal for such use as you may think proper to make of it."

The situation changed again on March 11 when Lincoln's Presidential War Order No. 3, the same document that relieved McClellan as general-in-chief, assigned Halleck his prize of overall command in the West. Halleck wasted no time in ordering Buell to move south from Nashville to reinforce Smith's force. (On March 21, Buell and Smith were commissioned major generals of volunteers.) Buell was sluggish in moving south, however: he took thirteen days simply to make it to Columbia, Tennessee, and delayed again because a bridge over the Duck River was out. On both sides of this theater of operations small numbers of troops were left in position: a Confederate garrison at Island No. 10 under Maj. Gen. John P. McCown, necessitating leaving Maj. Gen. John Pope's force of 25,000 at New Madrid. In the mountains of East Tennessee, several small Confederate garrisons under Maj. Gen. Edmund Kirby Smith spread from Chattanooga in the south to Cumberland Gap in the north. North of Cumberland Gap, in Kentucky, was the 8,000-man force under Union Brig. Gen. George W. Morgan. In Nashville the new military governor of Tennessee, Andrew Johnson, gave a rousing speech on March 13 that struck fire into the pro-Union civilians on hand. Though born in North Carolina, Johnson, age 53, was a Tennessean who had started as a tailor and served as mayor of Greeneville, Tennessee. Before being appointed military governor of Tennessee, Johnson was commissioned a brigadier general of volunteers. "I return to you with no hostile purpose," he told the Nashville crowd. "I come with the olive branch in one hand and the Constitution in the other, to render you whatever aid may be in my power, in re-erecting, upon her rightful domain of Tennessee, the Star Spangled Banner." In closing, Johnson remarked that "traitors should be punished and treason crushed."

Bickering along the Federal chain of command wasn't over. "To-day, at 11 o'clock A.M., I had the honor to receive your special order No. 36, which is as follows," Maj. Gen. John A. McClernand wrote Grant on March 27. " 'Maj. Gen. C. F. Smith the senior officer of the forces at Pittsburgh [*sic*], is appointed to command that Post, during the continuance of headquarters at this place (Savannah), or until properly relived [*sic*]. He will be obeyed and respected accordingly.' This order is evidently founded upon the idea that Genl. Smith is my senior and hence ranks me. Lately, I was Genl. Smith's senior, as a Brigadier. I wish to be advised how he became *my* senior." Grant docketed the verso: "I shall move my Hd Qrs. to Pittsburg on Monday which will obviate present difficulty on the subject of rank, but I would like to know if Maj. Gen. McClernand or Maj. Gen. Smith are commissioned on the same day to guide me in future." McClernand did rank Smith as a major general, and such arguing about seniority only grew as the complexity and numbers of the officers did. McClernand hardly stopped letting his superiors know he was unhappy. "Since your reorganization of the forces of this Department my position in the Army of the Tennessee has been one of actual inferiority if not practical subordination to that of other officers inferior to me in rank," he wrote Halleck on June 1.

By April the gloomy tidings of an insecure superior had begun to lift for U. S. Grant. Now firmly in command of the West, Halleck restored Grant to command of the force now named the Army of the Tennessee. On April 4, Grant suffered a fall and his leg was pinned under his horse's body. Grant's ankle was so injured that the boot had to be cut off and he needed crutches for walking for several critical days. By April 5, Grant had most of his army of 48,894, five of its six divisions, encamped on the western edge of the Tennessee River near Pittsburg Landing. The area was known as "Shiloh" after the small log church that stood in the area. "Shiloh" was a Hebrew word meaning "place of peace."

Grant's divisions were commanded by Maj. Gen. John A. McClernand, Brig. Gen. William H. L. Wallace, Maj. Gen. Lew Wallace, Brig. Gen. Stephen A. Hurlbut, Brig. Gen. William T. Sherman, and Brig. Gen. Benjamin M. Prentiss. What would become the Shiloh battlefield was a roughly triangular tract of land measuring about fifteen by seventeen miles bordered by the river on the east, the winding form of Snake Creek on the north, Owl Creek on the northwest, and a network of roads and fields—some slightly swampy—throughout. On the night of April 5–6, Grant's troops were encamped on the field with Wallace to the northeast, nearest the river, Hurlbut south of him, and the 2d Brigade of Sherman's division under Col. David Stuart south of Hurlbut. To the west, McClernand's division and Prentiss's division filled another north-south corridor, while Sherman, minus one brigade, was encamped around the area of Shiloh Church itself. The missing division was that of Lew Wallace, which was left five miles downstream at Crump's Landing. His mission was twofold: to prevent the placement of

Confederate river batteries and to strike out at the railroad line at Bethel Station. Meanwhile, Buell's Army of the Ohio, some 17,918 strong, was still a long way from Shiloh.

The disposition of the Federal troops at Shiloh was random. Grant and his subordinates had not made any defensive plan in case of attack. In one of the few incidents of the war for which Grant can be squarely criticized, despite his postwar writings about the affair, the evolving commander was deficient in terms of his army's security. Only a few scattered pickets were posted to warn of any oncoming troops, and the communications network in the newly assembled army was weak. A small skirmish had taken place between Confederate cavalry and Union forces on April 4, but even after this Grant and his friend Sherman—who consulted each other during a battle for the first time at Shiloh—were caught largely unaware by what was about to happen.

Grant, Sherman, Halleck, and the other Union officers in the region were soon surprised in a big way. Johnston's army of some 44,699 was encamped only two miles away from the divisions of Sherman and Prentiss and had already set in motion an attack for the morning of April 6. "I have put you in motion to offer battle to the invaders of your country," Johnston informed his army in a circular. "Remember the dependence of your mothers, your wives, your sisters, and your children on the result. Remember the fair, broad, abounding land, the happy homes, and the ties that would be desolated by your defeat."

Johnston's army consisted of four very large army corps commanded by Maj. Gen. Leonidas Polk (division commanders were Brig. Gen. Charles Clark and Maj. Gen. Benjamin F. Cheatham), Maj. Gen. Braxton Bragg (divisions under Brig. Gens. Daniel Ruggles and Jones M. Withers), Maj. Gen. William J. Hardee (organized into three brigades under Brig. Gens. Thomas C. Hindman, Patrick R. Cleburne, and Sterling A. M. Wood), and the reserve corps of Brig. Gen. John C. Breckinridge (three brigades under Col. Robert Trabue, Brig. Gen. John S. Bowen, and Col. Winfield S. Statham, plus attached cavalry). Beauregard was assigned by Johnston as nearly a coequal; it was the hero of Sumter who urged attacking the apparently unprepared Grant. The Confederate troops used two narrow dirt roads to march north from Corinth and came together at Mickey, where they turned and moved toward Pittsburg Landing. This convergence caused a two-day delay from the original plan to attack on April 4. On the evening of April 5, the exhausted Confederates, tired from the march, encamped and prepared for attack, with Hardee's and Bragg's corps taking the lead and planning to stretch into one huge battle line on the advance.

"I have scarsely [sic] the faintest idea of an attack, (general one,) being made upon us," Grant wrote Halleck on the evening of April 5, "but will be prepared should such a thing take place." But prepared he wasn't. Neither Sherman nor Prentiss anticipated an attack from the south, and Grant himself was at Savannah, Tennessee, north of Crump's Landing. He received word from Lew Wallace that Confederates were in the vicinity of Purdy, near Bethel Station, but that was just Cheatham's detached division rather than Johnston's army. The Army of the Tennessee, now being approached in heavy force from the southwest, and in a position to be pushed against the Tennessee River, awaited circumstances and wondered about being reinforced by Buell, whose lead element, the division of Brig. Gen. William Nelson, reached Savannah and held up as the bulk of the Army of the Ohio followed.

Johnston and Beauregard planned to strike the left of Grant's army hard, pushing the Union battle line in retreat against Snake and Owl Creeks, pinning them and eliminating the possibility of reinforcement by troops landing along the Tennessee River. But the nearly seven-mile-long battle line of Hardee's and Bragg's troops didn't allow for the kind of heavy concentration of effort on the Union left that Johnston desired. Without anticipating this problem, Johnston set the troops into action. At 5:15 A.M. on April 6, the 25th Missouri Infantry sent a scouting party forward into Fraley Field near the southern end of the field, spurred on by Prentiss's nervousness about potential scattered forces; Confederate pickets fired a volley into the approaching Yankees and the battle of Shiloh began. For an hour, mostly in the darkness, flashes of musketry fire illuminated small portions of the woods as each side slowly escalated its activity. Around 6:15 A.M. the Yankees sounded retreat, and the 21st Missouri Infantry supported the return. This gave Sherman and Prentiss a slight amount of time to get ready and wake up before the onslaught of a major Confederate assault was on them.

"Suddenly, away off on the right, in direction of Shiloh Church, came a dull, heavy 'Pum,' then another, and still another," recalled Leander Stillwell, a private in the 61st Illinois Infantry, of the early morning action. "Every man sprung to his feet as if struck by an electric shock, and we looked inquiringly into one another's faces. . . . off to the southwest, came a low, sullen, continuous roar. There was no mistaking that sound. That was not a squad of pickets emptying their guns on being relieved from duty; it was the continuous roll of thousands of muskets, and told us that a battle was on."

Although many Union units were surprised by the attack, the Confederates had problems of their own. The long, unwieldy lines of Bragg's and Hardee's corps became intermingled and the coordination of command began to unravel early in the morning. Thus, unit commanders spread along the long battle line had trouble issuing commands and took over mixed groups of soldiers in small areas. The problem was worsened when at 7:30 A.M. Beauregard ordered the corps of Breckinridge to the Confederate right

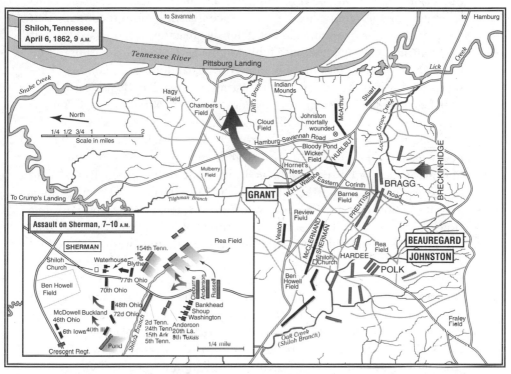

Shiloh, Tennessee, April 6, 1862, 9 A.M.

to Savannah

to Hamburg

Tennessee River   Pittsburg Landing

Snake Creek

Hagy Field

Chambers Field

Dill's Branch

Indian Mounds

Cloud Field

Johnston mortally wounded

McArthur

Stuart

Lick Creek

Locust Grove Creek

← North

1/4 1/2 3/4 1   2
Scale in miles

Hamburg-Savannah Road

Bloody Pond
Wicker Field

HURLBUT

Mulberry Field

Hornet's Nest

To Crump's Landing

Tilghman Branch

GRANT

W.H.L. Wallace Eastern Corinth

Review Field

Barnes Field

PRENTISS

BRAGG

BRECKINRIDGE

Corinth Road

McCLERNAND

Veatch

SHERMAN

Shiloh Church

HARDEE

Rea Field

BEAUREGARD
JOHNSTON

POLK

Ben Howell Field

Fraley Field

Oak Creek (Shiloh Branch)

Assault on Sherman, 7–10 A.M.

SHERMAN

Shiloh Church

Waterhouse

Blythe

154th Tenn.

Rea Field

Ben Howell Field

77th Ohio

70th Ohio

48th Ohio

72d Ohio

Cleburne

Anderson

Russell

McDowell Buckland
46th Ohio

6th Iowa   40th Ill.

2d Tenn.
24th Tenn.
15th Ark
5th Tenn.

Bankhead
Shoup
Washington

Anderson
20th La.
9th Texas

Pond

Crescent Regt.

Shiloh Branch

1/4 mile

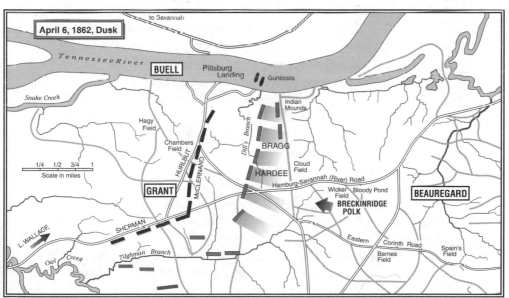

April 6, 1862, Dusk

to Savannah

Tennessee River

BUELL   Pittsburg Landing   Gunboats

Snake Creek

Indian Mounds

Dill's Branch

Hagy Field

Chambers Field

BRAGG

Cloud Field

1/4 1/2 3/4 1
Scale in miles

HURLBUT

McCLERNAND

HARDEE

Hamburg-Savannah (River) Road

Wicker Field   Bloody Pond

GRANT

BEAUREGARD

SHERMAN

BRECKINRIDGE
POLK

L. WALLACE

Owl Creek

Tilghman Branch

Eastern

Corinth Road

Barnes Field

Spain's Field

and Polk to the left to support the attack. By midmorning the assault formation came unglued and what resulted was a frontal attack, with many Confederate units forging ahead into the confused Union regiments that
attempted to organize some kind of defensive reaction. Beauregard was left
in command of the field because Johnston made the foolish decision to ride
forward and lead attacks himself, effectively abandoning his command assignment during the battle. Before thrusting command on Beauregard, however, he had with characteristic bravado remarked to a staff officer, "Tonight
we will water our horses in the Tennessee River."

Sherman's division bore the brunt of the initial attack. Despite the
heavy cannon fire on his position and constant volleys of musketry,
Sherman's men fared reasonably well for a time despite their Right Wing
crumbling badly. Supported on the left by McClernand, Sherman's men
fought stubbornly against the mixed forces of Bragg, Hardee, and Polk, but
slowly lost ground and fell back to a position behind Shiloh Church. Prentiss, on the extreme left of the early morning battle line, was compelled by
midmorning to fall all the way back along Eastern Corinth Road to a field
that would become known as the Hornet's Nest for the ferocity of fire that
occurred there. Grant, meanwhile, arrived on the field about 8:30 A.M. from
Savannah and began to consult with Sherman and others about how to handle the Confederate attack. He dispatched William H. L. Wallace to secure
the Snake Creek Bridge, enabling the hoped-for advance of Lew Wallace
from Crump's Landing, and forged a bond with Sherman as they contemplated what to do next.

Prentiss's withdrawal into the Hornet's Nest created a tenuous situa-
tion for McClernand, who by late morning had an exposed left flank. By 10:30
A.M. Sherman, now on the Federal right, was pushed back, too, forcing Mc-
Clernand to back up toward Tilghman Creek. Hurlbut's position left of the
Federal center was also pushed back by heavy Confederate fire, collapsing a
salient into a smoother Yankee line of battle. By noon the Yankee line consisted of Sherman on the right, with McClernand, W. H. L. Wallace, Prentiss,
Hurlbut, Brig. Gen. John McArthur's brigade of Wallace's division, and
Stuart's brigade of Sherman's division. Facing this line, and having success in
easing it backward, was the Confederate line, which still consisted of heavily
mixed units that were further intermingled during the afternoon hours.
They generally followed a west-east line of Hardee, Polk, Bragg, and Breckinridge.

Grant, meanwhile, rode along the line and attempted to calm his men,
sending reinforcements to the center of activity in McClernand's command
and again dispatching urgent requests to Lew Wallace and Buell asking
them to speed to the field of battle. As the battle raged, its intensity flared
throughout pockets of the lines. "Fill your canteens, boys," said Isaac C.

Pugh, colonel of the 41st Illinois Infantry. "Some of you will be in hell before night and you'll need water!" Prentiss had been ordered to hold the area of the Hornet's Nest at all hazards. He deployed most of his command in a sunken farm lane and fired back viciously against the Confederate guns posted at the other side of the field. This struggle carried on with rattles of musketry for hours, then Confederate artillery was brought to bear on the position. The Confederate attack seemed on the verge of achieving a victory, but some of the Confederate soldiers stalled portions of the attack on various parts of the line by dropping out to scavenge the overrun Union camps. Casualties mounted, creating chaotic action in improvised field aid stations. Despite the mounting confusion amid the intermingled Confederate units, the field officers pushed onward and looked for a decisive victory against the Yankees. Grant hoped desperately for the reinforcements that might come from only a few miles beyond the battlefield.

During the afternoon hours the Federal commanders pulled back their lines, creating an impending sense of doom among some of the Yankee troops, but they also inflicted heavy casualties against the attacking Confederate units. Confederates under Bragg and Breckinridge on the Union left were now pushing this area of the Yankees back on itself, with Hurlbut's division beginning to crumble and break in disarray. By midafternoon the detached brigades of McArthur and Stuart found themselves enveloped and withdrew in a panic toward Pittsburg Landing, the first Union troops to make tracks for the river. The Confederate forces on the extreme right, those of Bragg, could now move around the Union left and wreak havoc along the whole line, but there were not sufficient Confederate troops to do this. The hottest part of the fight during the afternoon was unfolding in the Hornet's Nest, where Prentiss and W. H. L. Wallace withstood twelve major charges from the Confederate line and repeated artillery bombardment, suffering heavy casualties but steadfastly holding their ground as ordered. One of those leading the charges in this area of the field was none other than Albert Sidney Johnston. Early in the afternoon he led a charge on horseback and was struck by a ball behind the right knee. Johnston perhaps did not realize the severity of the wound, but allegedly blood filled up much of his boot before he fell off his horse and was carried to relative safety. By about 2:30 P.M. he was dead. Johnston's physician later found that he not only had suffered the apparently fatal wound behind his knee, but he also was hit with a spent ball on the right thigh, a shell fragment above the right hip, and a Minié bullet that cut the sole of his left boot. Johnston had received a series of relatively minor wounds, and if he had been treated at once rather than after riding for at least fifteen minutes, his life might have been saved.

Word of Johnston's startling death spread among many of the Confederate troops. Command devolved upon Beauregard. It may be too much to say that this period marked a turning point in the battle, but the death of Johnston also coincided with something of a Federal reinforcement of the Hornet's Nest. Union units moved back to support Prentiss and Wallace, despite the fact that Confederate artillerists rolled sixty-two field pieces into position to continue bombarding the stubbornly held Yankee salient. Grant frantically repeated his instructions to Lew Wallace and to Buell, whom he met near the river, to get their men onto the battlefield as fast as possible. The reinforcements still did not occur, and by late afternoon most of the Federal army was forced to withdraw to a position along the Hamburg-Savannah (River) Road and the Pittsburg Landing Road, leaving Prentiss and Wallace exposed and isolated in the Hornet's Nest. The bulk of Grant's army reinforced the new position and anticipated making something of a last stand along the roads if not joined by the missing forces of Wallace and Buell. This permitted the Confederate forces of Hardee and Polk to push inward toward the Hornet's Nest and increase the already significant fire on the Yankees there.

Though the Confederate soldiers were running low on energy and food, the Yankees were in the same physical state and also were increasingly panicked by the minute. Wallace recognized the hopelessness of holding out in the Hornet's Nest and turned his regiments around, hoping to break out and rejoin the bulk of the Union army along the roads toward the north. Two of the regiments under Wallace's command pushed northward and joined Hurlbut, who was reorganizing his men on the ridge west of Pittsburg Landing. Others did not fare so well and remained in the Hornet's Nest; Wallace himself, a field officer on the rise in the regard of many, including Grant, was mortally wounded, struck by a musket ball behind his left ear, which passed through his head. An Ohioan by birth and Illinois attorney by profession, William Harvey Lamb Wallace lingered for four days with his terrible wound before dying in Savannah. The other commander trapped in the Hornet's Nest, Prentiss, held on well before he was forced to surrender 2,200 men at about 5:30 P.M.

Although it ultimately failed for the Union, the fight in the Hornet's Nest bought Grant time. All along the roads, "Grant's last line" was being assembled as Col. Joseph Dana Webster, Grant's chief of staff, directed more than fifty guns into position and the tattered remnants of Hurlbut's command, some 4,000 strong, filed into position behind them. As the evening of April 6 began, the Confederate officers on the field could almost feel a decisive victory against Grant, and they were eager for it in return for Forts Henry and Donelson. Bragg, eager to lead a charge on the new Union line, could only muster about 2,000 troops. Again a lack of reserves thwarted a potential Confederate victory. Beauregard was not so eager to attack the position, and he suspended the Confederate attack all along the line, but Bragg failed to receive the order in time and so launched an assault anyway. A brave bayonet attack from troops without much ammunition, mostly Brig. Gens. John K. Jackson's and James R. Chalmers's brigades of Withers's division, drove for the Union line under heavy artillery fire. The efforts of both officers to storm the ridge on which the Union batteries unleashed a storm of shot and shell stalled before they could reach the guns, ending in a ravine below the Union position.

The battle was now dying down as night approached, and Col. Jacob Ammen's 10th Brigade—the lead unit of Nelson's 4th Division, which in turn was the first element of Buell's army—arrived. By about 7:15 P.M. Lew Wallace finally arrived, only to meet with Grant's fury. Most of the delay by Wallace was caused by his poor understanding of the orders given him, causing Wallace's men to march and countermarch along the wrong roads. The USS *Tyler* and the USS *Lexington*, gunboats out in the Tennessee, took a position off Pittsburg Landing and blasted eight-inch shells in the direction of the Confederate lines. Their effectiveness was limited by the very high angle of fire necessitated by the bluffs above the landing.

Exhausted and faint with hunger, most of the soldiers on both sides settled in for a terrifying night. The size and calamity of the battle was so much larger than anything most of the participants had ever seen before that many were in a state of shock. "Seeing the elephant" was never again something that most of these young men wished for. The night was bleak when a rainstorm began, drenching everyone on the field. With soldiers in bivouac, the shrill cries and piercing, dull moans of the wounded and dying carried across the battlefield. Wounded soldiers from both sides, caked with powder and as thirsty as they could be, made their way to a small pond near a peach orchard, staining the water from their wounds and giving it the name "Bloody Pond." There could be no more fighting now, as both sides were fatigued. Beauregard crawled into a captured tent and informed Richmond that he had won a great victory. Grant, whose army had been substantially hurt, remained as calm as ever, despite the fact that most of his force was pushed up against the Tennessee River. At midnight, Sherman, rattled and nervous as he could be, told his friend, "Well, Grant, we've had the devil's own day, haven't we?" Grant puffed a cigar in the dim lantern light and replied, "Yes, lick 'em tomorrow, though."

The second day at Shiloh indeed brought a reversal of fortunes. The spark that turned around the Union effort was the arrival during the night of 25,000 fresh troops from Buell's Army of the Ohio, who marched down to the opposite bank of the Tennessee River and were ferried across the river using a variety of steamboats and transports. Grant and Buell each decided to attack the Confederate line early in the morning. The action began at daybreak. About 5 A.M. Brig. Gen. William Nelson began the advance by moving south along the Hamburg-Savannah Road. Slight skirmishing erupted, but before major action began, Buell stopped the movement to give Brig. Gens. Thomas L. Crittenden and Alexander M. McCook time to place their divisions in line. Buell's force consisted of four divisions, those of Nelson, Crittenden, McCook, and Brig. Gen. Thomas J. Wood. Buell started the advance on the Confederate lines at about 9 A.M., giving the Confederates ample time to organize for the day's fight.

The new Yankee line of battle was composed, east to west, of Nelson, Crittenden, McCook, Hurlbut, McClernand, Sherman, and Lew Wallace. Sherman began his advance early in the morning but had to wait for the resumption of Crittenden's movement in order to press on. By late morning, about 10 A.M., the whole Federal line erupted with sheets of fire coming from well-coordinated volleys and from the field pieces set atop the last line position. For the remainder of the morning, the opposite result from the previous day occurred, with Federal brigades moving southward and pushing the Confederate line into a retreat. After noon Wood's division arrived and joined the fight between McCook and Crittenden, supporting the line near its center.

The suddenness of the Federal attack swept the field. Beauregard decided he had had enough and ordered a retreat to Corinth about 2:30 P.M. An hour and a half later the whole Confederate army was in motion southward across the same narrow muddy roads they had used to approach the field with such high hopes. The attack on Grant turned into a miserable failure for the South after what seemed like the crest of glory. The army was now reduced to about 34,000, and even the men who were not wounded were exhausted, hungry, and dispirited. The Confederate casualties at Shiloh amounted to 1,728 killed, 8,012 wounded, and 959 missing. It left a sad legacy for Albert Sidney Johnston. The celebrated commander, much of whose reputation was built on his perilous journey back to the Confederacy from California at the war's start, not only lost the only battle he commanded in the field but lost his life in the process. His body was brought back to Corinth. In addition to Johnston's death, Brig. Gen. Adley Hogan Gladden was struck with a cannonball, necessitating a battlefield amputation. He lived six days after the battle, perishing in Corinth. "I cannot describe the field," Polk wrote his wife on April 10. "It was one of great carnage, and as it was the second battle I have been in—the other being a bloody one also—I felt somewhat more accustomed to it. This one was on a large scale, and a magnificent affair."

The scale of the death at Shiloh, by far the largest battle fought in America to date, stunned the nation. The Federal casualties amounted to 1,754 killed, 8,408 wounded, and 2,885 missing. To depress the western soldiers even further, on April 25, Maj. Gen. Charles F. Smith died near Savannah. Grant's old teacher had missed a step on a gangway on the Tennessee River on March 7, injuring his shin. The wound became infected, then worsened such that by late April the spreading disease, along with chronic dysentery, killed him. "If I am not too feeble, I trust in a few days more to move to the only climate where I have the best hope of recovery," Smith wrote Halleck while ailing on April 21. "At my period of life I can scarcely anticipate the strength necessary for active service in many months; which is a subject of great regret that I cannot lend a helping hand to entirely crush this rebellion whose days are over or so evidently numbered." Four days later Andrew C. Kemper, an assistant adjutant general, informed the soldiers that "The Major General commanding announces with deep regret, to the troops of this Department, the death of Major General Charles F. Smith, who at 4 o'clock, P.M., to-day, departed this life at Savanna [sic] on the Tennessee River."

In the wake of the battle, gloom spread throughout the surviving troops on both sides. "You have bravely fought the invaders of your soil for two days in his own position," Beauregard told his soldiers. "Fought your superior in numbers, in arms, in all the appliances of war. Your success has been signal. His losses have been immense, outnumbering yours in all save the personal wealth of the slain." But words could not undo the obvious, with Beauregard's army having abandoned the field and their wounded, failed in the strategic objectives of the campaign, and allowed Grant's army to move still farther south. Halleck now commanded a department of U.S. forces that could drive deep into the Southland.

Grant himself remarked that "I saw an open field . . . so covered with dead that it would have been possible to walk across the clearing, in any direction, stepping on dead bodies, without a foot touching the ground." Despite the magnitude of the horror at Shiloh, however, despite the realization that the war could last a long time and produce more Shilohs, and despite the criticism Grant had received from Halleck and from battlefield critics who pelted him with fury for being caught unaware on the first morning of the battle, Lincoln's faith in Grant did not waiver. Of the western general, Lincoln said simply, "I can't spare this man; he fights."

Down South in Georgia, along the coast near Savannah, the springtime war was about to take a strategic turn. After the fall of the forts along Port Royal Sound in November 1861, Federal army and navy officers had been organizing an operation toward Savannah, one of the great seaports of the South Atlantic coast and the oldest city in Georgia. With its wartime population of 22,922, it was a sizable city as well. For several weeks in early 1862,

Union Brig. Gen. Quincy A. Gillmore had been supervising the erection of batteries facing Fort Pulaski, the principal fort guarding the river approach to Savannah. The fort stood on muddy, marshy Cockspur Island.

Gillmore undertook one of the most important actions of the period along the coastal islands. The Savannah River, which served as the waterway entrance into the city, was divided into north and south channels, between which stood a thin strip of land called Long Island and, close to the Atlantic Ocean, Cockspur Island, which measured about 4,000 yards by 1,200 yards. Fort Pulaski stood squarely in the middle of Cockspur Island. Close to the south channel were Tybee Island, on which Gillmore directed his Federal troops, and McQueen's Island to the west. Near the north channel were Turtle Island and Jones Island.

Fort Pulaski was one of the most formidable coastal forts in the nation. It was a pentagonal fort consisting of brick masonry walls 7.5-feet thick, backed by massive masonry piers, deemed by its constructors unbreachable. The fort "could not be reduced in a month's firing with any number of guns," wrote Bvt. Brig. Gen. Joseph G. Totten, chief engineer of the U.S. Army, of the formidable work. Named for the Revolutionary War soldier of fortune Casimir Pulaski, who died during the 1779 siege of Savannah, the fort was constructed beginning in 1829 and finished in 1847, after Congress had spent $1 million on the work and 1 million bricks had gone into the walls. By late 1860 the fort's armament was still incomplete, and no garrison was assigned.

In early 1861, Governor Joseph E. Brown of Georgia ordered seizure of the fort, and so the Confederacy established a garrison in the structure that they exploited for more than a year before Gillmore approached. In December 1861, Yankee troops cut the line of communications from Cockspur Island to the city. The 46th New York Infantry arrived on Tybee Island and began to plan the reduction of Pulaski. In February the lone regiment was reinforced by the 7th Connecticut Infantry (Col. Alfred H. Terry), two companies of New York engineers, and two companies of the 3d Rhode Island Artillery, and Terry took overall command of the troops on the island, while Gillmore was assigned as chief engineer of the expedition. For two months the engineers and soldiers toiled under the guidance of Gillmore and Terry to construct heavy batteries along the northern coast of Tybee Island, with their 36 guns and mortars aimed at Pulaski. The work was nothing short of heroic, particularly that of the 7th Connecticut Infantry. Much of the hauling of the very heavy guns (the siege mortars weighed 17,000 pounds apiece) had to be done at night, in virtual silence, across a muddy crust that broke through to a "quicksand" below. The flies and filth were incredible, and the soldiers had to construct skids attached to sling carts that created crude "wagons" that could be pulled slowly by units of 250 men at a time. All the while, the battery positions were screened from the Confederates by discrete changes made with trees and brush. The batteries stretched from Goat Point near the mouth of Lazaretto Creek eastward with ranges from 1,650 to 3,400 yards, and included two 84-pounders, two 64-pounders, and one 48-pounder James rifle; five 30-pounder Parrott rifles; six 10-inch and four 8-inch Columbiads; and twelve 13-inch and four 10-inch siege mortars.

For its part, the garrison in Fort Pulaski, consisting of 385 men under the command of Col. Charles H. Olmstead, was relatively serene. The fort was well armed with guns in casements and barbettes as follows: five 10-inch and nine 8-inch Columbiads; three 42-pounders and twenty 32-pounders; one 24-pounder and two 12-pounder Howitzers; one 12-inch and three 10-inch mortars; and two 4.5-inch Blakely rifles, with approximately 130 rounds of ammunition per gun. Twenty of the guns could be trained on Tybee Island. Moreover, virtually every defender who discussed the Federal movement on Pulaski knew the fort could not be breached. The generally accepted consensus among artillerists and engineers was that beyond a distance of about 700 yards smoothbore cannon and mortars would not impart enough force to break through brick masonry walls.

By early April the first transports with ammunition arrived on Tybee Island, and Gillmore and his engineers, assisted by the infantry troops and skilled artillerists, were ready for the great experiment to begin. Two batteries had also been constructed north of Pulaski, one at Venus Point on Jones Island and the other on Bird Island, northwest of Long Island. Another small contingent of Union forces under Brig. Gen. Egbert L. Viele occupied a part of Daufuskie Island, northeast of Turtle Island. By April 9 the Union forces were ready to open a bombardment on Pulaski. First Lt. Horace Porter, a young Pennsylvania artillerist who would later join U. S. Grant's staff, wrote, "so much were the preparations hurried for opening the bombardment, that we could not wait for many of the ordnance stores that had been ordered from the North. Powder-measures were made out of copper from the metallic cases in which the desiccated vegetables are received. Columbiad shells were strapped with strips of old tents, rough blocks being used for sabots."

After daybreak on April 10, time had nearly run out for the Confederate garrison in Pulaski. Maj. Gen. David Hunter, commanding the Department of the South, sent a summons to Olmstead asking for surrender. Olmstead refused, and the first Union shell was fired at 8:15 A.M. By 9:30 A.M. each of the guns at the eleven Federal batteries had opened fire. Thus began the first encounter in warfare between rifled cannon and a brick masonry fort. What the Confederates could not have easily anticipated was that many of Gillmore's guns were rifles and fired from the relatively great distances with devastating accuracy and effect. The Confederate guns answered back with great vigor, firing shells mainly at Batteries Burnside and Sherman, which had not been well hidden. The bombardment toiled on relentlessly. By 1 P.M., as Gillmore wrote, it became clear that "a breach would be effected: With a glass it could be seen that the rifled projectiles were surely eating their way into the scarp of the pan-coupé and adjacent south-east face." When the firing ceased at nightfall, after nine and a half hours, the breach on the fort's southeast corner was plain to see. The mortars were also observed to be wildly inaccurate. An assault by land was impossible, so that Gillmore's best option was to pound the fort's walls with his rifled cannon.

The exchange of fire resumed after sunrise on April 11. By noon it was clear that the fort's brick walls were being knocked down piece by piece. Two casements were opened fully, leaving the fort's nearby magazine in the northwest corner vulnerable. The Yankee guns began directing their fire on the next casement in line, with "puffs of yellow smoke marking the effect of shot and shell," when at 2 P.M. a white flag was hoisted inside the fort. Gillmore received Olmstead's surrender, and the soldiers on opposing sides joked with each other as the affair concluded. The damage inside the fort was extensive: 16 of the 20 guns trained on Tybee had been knocked out of action; the fort's walls were crumbling in several spots, particularly at the breach on the southwest corner; one Confederate soldier was killed and several more wounded. One Union soldier was killed in an accident. After two months of preparation the siege and reduction of Fort Pulaski came to an abrupt end. Gillmore's guns had fired a total of 5,275 shots—an average of one shell every sixteen seconds—expending only one-fifth of the ammunition they had on hand. Many of the shells fired from rifled guns had penetrated the walls to depths of 11 to 26 inches. A span of thirty hours witnessed the end of an era at Fort Pulaski. Rifled cannon now relegated brick masonry forts, the backbone of the coastal defense system, to obsolescence. Gillmore became a hero, and Fort Pulaski was in the hands of the Union army.

Elsewhere in Georgia the early days of April witnessed one of the strangest and least predictable episodes of the war. The day after Pulaski fell, a curious group of 20 men boarded a train on the Western & Atlantic Railroad at Big Shanty (now Kennesaw), near Marietta, northwest of Atlanta. It was breakfast time, and the men were on a train pulled by the *General*, a Western & Atlantic engine. The party appeared to be rural Southerners but actually consisted of Union soldiers in disguise, planning to hijack the locomotive, run it northward, and destroy the rail and communications lines between Atlanta and Chattanooga. The sabotage operation had been the brainchild of Brig. Gen. Ormsby M. Mitchel, the astronomer-soldier who had been at Nashville and who commanded a division in Buell's Army of the Ohio. Mitchel and many civilians in the Lincoln administration longed for a Union occupation of eastern Tennessee, where sentiment ran toward the Union, and Mitchel proposed that wrecking these rails and communications could help the Federals advance toward Chattanooga.

Following Shiloh, Mitchel had detached a force that seized Huntsville, Alabama, and moved with 2,000 men to within thirty miles of Chattanooga. Buell employed a civilian spy, James J. Andrews, whom he trusted to execute the most daring underground operations. In March, Andrews had been sent with a party of eight to burn bridges between Chattanooga and Bridgeport. This failed, and Andrews ended by secretly exploring Atlanta and its environs before returning to Buell. The soldiers for the new raid, which became known as Andrews's raid, or the Great Locomotive Chase, were volunteers from three regiments (2d Ohio Infantry, 21st Ohio Infantry, and 33d Ohio Infantry) in Col. Joshua W. Sill's brigade of Buell's army. In deep twilight on April 7, the soldiers met Andrews near Shelbyville, Tennessee. They then broke into groups of three or four who would travel southward and meet again in Marietta to proceed with the mission. If questioned, they were to be Kentuckians traveling south to join the Confederate army.

The band assembled early in the morning of the 12th in Andrews's room at the Marietta Hotel (Kennesaw House), finding that two men failed to show up, two others had been discovered and forced to join the Confederate army (though the plan was not discovered), and two who reached Marietta failed to find Andrews and the other raiders. Twenty men remained, including Andrews. The conditions at Big Shanty were not ideal, the men found when they boarded. Big Shanty had been made into a Confederate camp, with many soldiers around, and the tracks were busy with rail traffic. The plan would require capturing the locomotive surrounded by lounging Confederate soldiers before running it northward 200 miles as they tore up track and telegraph poles along the way. To say the plan was daring would be an understatement.

The morning at Big Shanty was dull and gloomy, and a misty rain that would last all day began to fall. At the station the engineer and conductor left for breakfast, and the *General* was unguarded. Andrews rushed into the engine and, assisted by the others, uncoupled it along with the tender and one boxcar. An armed Confederate sentinel stood nearby without responding. Andrews pulled the valve and the *General*'s wheels squeaked and spun for a moment before grabbing the rail and rolling the train forward toward Chattanooga. The raiders left Big Shanty station, leaving the Confederates bewildered, some shouting and preparing after a short time to send an engine in pursuit.

The raiders steamed ahead, planning to stop periodically to tear up track, cut telegraph wires, collect crossties (with which to burn bridges), and take on water and wood to keep the engine fueled. After they passed through Chattanooga, the raiders would try to find Mitchel in Huntsville or wherever they needed to go. Along the way, Andrews coolly told station managers that he was on a mission from General Beauregard to get a train full of impressed powder on to Corinth. It worked beautifully.

The raiders kept their mission moving along quickly, through the rain, to Etowah Station and on to Kingston, where they encountered a southbound train hoisting a red flag, indicating another train behind. The minutes ticked by tensely as the raiders had to wait, and when the expected train arrived, it, too, held a red flag. For sixty-five minutes the raiders sat at Kingston, sixteen of the men stuffed inside the boxcar and unable to distinguish events outside. Andrews sent word to the men in the car to be ready for a fight, but soon thereafter the southbound train arrived and they were again on their way.

The raiders had slipped out of danger at Kingston, but not for long. The *General*'s conductor, William A. Fuller, along with Anthony Murphy of the Western & Atlantic Railroad, had started on foot after the captured engine and subsequently found a handcar. At Etowah they impressed the engine *Yonah* into service, pursuing more quickly. Four miles from Kingston, the Yankee spies were tearing up a section of track when suddenly they were startled by the whistle of a pursuing engine. They scurried back into the car and took off at top speed. At Calhoun, Andrews and his men faced suspicious questions before they could move out again. Near Adairsville, Fuller met a train being pulled by the engine *Texas* and convinced Peter J. Bracken, its conductor, to pursue the stolen *General*. The whole episode now turned into a desperate race as the Yankees could see the pursuing *Texas* with armed Confederates on board. The race teetered back and forth, with the *General* gaining and losing a substantial lead, and finally the engine running out of fuel north of Ringgold. They had thrown off all the debris they could onto the track behind, moved the men up and set the boxcar ablaze, uncoupling it, but still the *Texas* came on. "With no car left, no fuel, the last scrap having been thrown into the engine or upon the burning car, and with no obstruction to drop on the track, our situation was indeed desperate," wrote William Pittenger, one of the raiders. "A few minutes only remained until our steed of iron which had so well served us would be powerless."

The Union raiders scattered into the woods. Several of the raiders were soon captured, and all were eventually found and imprisoned in Chattanooga. Eight men, including Andrews, were executed. Their graves can be seen at Chattanooga National Cemetery. Six of those who survived and were exchanged were the first to be awarded the newly created Medal of

Honor, the nation's highest military honor. They received the medals in Washington from President Lincoln on March 25, 1863.

THE ANDREWS RAID was a mere distraction in the Confederate war effort, but a campaign that had been building for several weeks on the Mississippi River threatened more far-reaching consequences. By mid-April it was clear that a Federal attack on the forts guarding the Confederacy's largest city, New Orleans, was coming. With its population of 168,675, the Crescent City was a booming seaport with vast trading in cotton, shipping of war supplies, and manufactured goods. Losing the city and its port would be a devastating blow to the Confederacy in real and psychological terms. A joint army-navy plan was adopted on November 15 to capture the city and control the entrance into the lower Mississippi. The plan of attack was conceived by Comdr. David Dixon Porter, who convinced Navy Secretary Gideon Welles and then–General-in-Chief George McClellan of its practical likelihood to succeed. After sorting out the details for such a large combined operation, the administration settled on Capt. David G. Farragut, Porter's foster brother and the commander-in-chief of the U.S. Navy, to lead the expedition. At the time the expedition commenced, Porter was assigned to command the Mortar Boat Flotilla of the West Gulf Blockading Squadron. The army force designated to participate in the action was being raised in New England by the politician-general Maj. Gen. Benjamin F. Butler, whose Army of the Gulf would consist of about 15,000 men. The combined operation employed the names Department of the Gulf and West Gulf Blockading Squadron, in part believing they would help fool the Confederates into thinking that the planned operation would strike at Pensacola, Mobile, or some other gulf port.

But the ruse didn't last long. New Orleans was clearly the target, and it was defended by green militia troops under Maj. Gen. Mansfield Lovell, a native of Washington, D.C. Lovell's force was dispersed throughout the small set of river forts that guarded the city, with emphasis on the two masonry forts about seventy miles downriver, Forts Jackson and St. Philip, which afforded the heaviest firepower and best position to prevent river traffic from moving toward the city. Fort Jackson stood on the west bank of the Mississippi and Fort St. Philip on the east bank, about 800 yards to the north. Fort Jackson mounted 59 guns, 12 howitzers, and three mortars, while St. Philip was protected by 44 guns, 1 howitzer, and 7 mortars.

Lovell ordered the river barricaded with a massive chain strung together with a series of floating barges that crossed the river from a position east of Fort Jackson. The heavy chain was secured by fifteen anchors weighing from 2,500 to 4,000 pounds each. Rising water partly wrecked this obstruction in February and during the second week of April, diminishing its value as a blockade. Lovell's garrison troops within the forts amounted to some 1,000 men in Forts Jackson and St. Philip; Fort Macomb, near the entrance to Lake Pontchartrain, held 250 men and 30 guns. Fort Pike, nearby, had 350 men and 33 guns. Fort Livingston, on the other side of the Delta, near Barataria Bay, had a garrison of 300 men and 15 guns. Lovell also had 3,500 men manning entrenchments built near the city, and some 6,000 men in New Orleans itself. The Confederate navy had a presence in the area. Under Comdr. John K. Mitchell, it had six ships carrying about 30 guns: the ironclad ram CSS *Manassas,* the screw gunboat CSS *McRae,* the center-wheel ironclad ram CSS *Louisiana,* and the cottonclad side-wheeler gunboats CSS *Jackson,* CSS *General Quitman,* and CSS *Governor Moore.* Cottonclad rams were fitted with compressed bales of cotton to strengthen their wooden and iron rams; the cotton could also be ignited when ramming to set enemy ships ablaze.

Lovell had the River Defense Fleet, commanded by Capt. John A. Stevenson. It consisted of five side-wheeler cottonclad rams: the CSS *Warrior,* CSS *Stonewall Jackson,* CSS *Resolute,* CSS *Defiance,* and CSS *General Lovell.* There were also the CSS *General Breckinridge,* a cottonclad stern-wheeler, and the CSS *Mississippi,* an unfinished ironclad ram, without armament. In early naval operations in the area, the outcome seemed to favor the Confederacy. On October 11, 1861, the ram *Manassas* alone had moved down to Head of Passes, Mississippi, and attacked the USS *Richmond,* USS *Vincennes,* and USS *Preble* in a night action, during which the *Manassas* rammed the *Richmond.* In late February 1862, Lovell seemed confident of his success against the mounting Federal attack. "I regard Butler's Ship Island expedition as a harmless menace so far as New Orleans is concerned," he wrote Secretary of War Benjamin.

Farragut's fleet was a far more powerful force than that at Lovell's disposal. The Union fleet consisted of one screw, one side-wheeler, and two sail frigates; six screw and three sail sloops; seventeen screw and five side-wheeler gunboats; two sail schooners; three barks; one brig; and twenty-five mortar schooners carrying a total of 523 guns, including nineteen huge 13-inch mortars. The principal ships included the screw frigate USS *Colorado;* the side-wheeler frigate USS *Mississippi;* the screw sloops USS *Brooklyn,* USS *Hartford* (Farragut's flagship), USS *Iroquois,* USS *Oneida,* USS *Pensacola,* and USS *Richmond;* the screw gunboat USS *Varuna;* and the side-wheeler gunboat USS *Harriet Lane* (Porter's flagship of the mortar boat force).

With the surprising Federal naval buildup becoming known, the Confederates shifted all their faith onto Forts Jackson and St. Philip, beyond which New Orleans would be indefensible. Brig. Gen. Johnson K. Duncan, in charge of the forts, would have little time to prepare. At 9 A.M. on April 18, Porter's mortar boat fleet opened fire on the two forts, pounding away incessantly as the day matured. The heavy rumblings of the mortars startled everyone who heard their voluminous fire, and they poured out great quantities of shells—on this day alone, after ten hours of firing, the mortars had thrown 2,997 shells into and around the forts. The hope was that if the fort's gunners were weakened enough, Farragut's wooden ships could run the gauntlet and speed upriver into New Orleans. Despite the heavy dropping of shells, however, the mortars inflicted scant damage on the forts, and after nearly a week of bombardment the forts remained essentially intact. During the night of the 20th, sailors from the gunboats USS *Itasca* and USS *Pinola* attacked the river obstructions, attaching explosives to them in hopes of blowing them up. Despite the failure of the explosives, the men managed to open a breach in the hulks and chain that lessened the value of the blockade.

On April 23, Farragut came to a decision. Rather than land Butler's army troops in the marshy swampland or hope the mortar firing would somehow reduce the forts' garrisons, he would under cover of darkness during the morning of the 24th speed his wooden sloops and gunboats past the forts and into New Orleans. At 2 A.M. Farragut ordered his fleet forward, signaled by two red lanterns raised to the mizzen peak of the *Hartford*. The movement, though full of fire and danger, worked. On this dark, cold night, the ships slid forward in the glassy water and by 3 A.M. the expedition was off. The first division, ending with the *Wissahickon*, sailed and steamed ahead through the obstruction without being discovered. By about 3:40 A.M., however, the moon was on the rise, low in the sky, and the gunners at Forts Jackson and St. Philip opened fire. The center and third divisions, including the flagship *Hartford*, came under heavy fire from the cannon on the shore. Before dawn the Yankee ships had moved upstream and out of range of the forts' guns, with the exception of three small vessels, although many of the ships were struck repeatedly and subjected to a din of whistling shells, small fires, the booming of Porter's mortars, and the hot flashes of cannon on the horizon. The Federal flotilla lost the *Varuna*, which was run against the riverbank and sank after being rammed by the *Stonewall Jackson*. Farragut's casualties were 37 killed and 149 wounded. Once upriver, Farragut paused at Quarantine, where Butler's army was approaching. He regrouped and then faced more action upstream as Confederate gunboats pursued and the ram *Manassas* attempted to destroy Yankee ships. The *Manassas* rammed both the *Brooklyn* and the *Mississippi* but caused little damage.

Some of the Confederate ships fought well while others seemed confused in action and after a time sped out of the scene. The Confederate garrison within the forts suffered relatively light casualties, but the naval forces were badly mauled. Thirteen Confederate ships were lost. Of this great naval calamity, Stephen R. Mallory, Confederate navy secretary, simply wrote, "The destruction of the Navy at New Orleans was a sad, sad blow."

Farragut speeded ahead. The forts were now lost to the Confederacy,

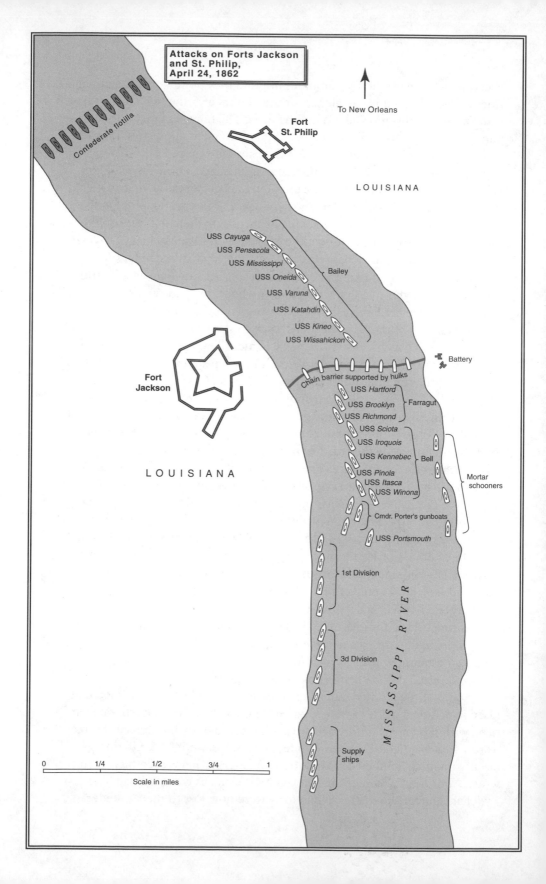

**Attacks on Forts Jackson
and St. Philip,
April 24, 1862**

To New Orleans

Fort
St. Philip

Confederate flotilla

LOUISIANA

USS *Cayuga*
USS *Pensacola*
USS *Mississippi*
USS *Oneida*
USS *Varuna*
USS *Katahdin*
USS *Kineo*
USS *Wissahickon*

Bailey

Battery

Chain barrier supported by hulks

Fort
Jackson

USS *Hartford*
USS *Brooklyn*   Farragut
USS *Richmond*
USS *Sciota*
USS *Iroquois*
USS *Kennebec*   Bell
USS *Pinola*
USS *Itasca*
USS *Winona*

Mortar
schooners

LOUISIANA

Cmdr. Porter's gunboats

USS *Portsmouth*

1st Division

M I S S I S S I P P I   R I V E R

3d Division

Supply
ships

0   1/4   1/2   3/4   1

Scale in miles

isolated and with Butler's army fast approaching. Many within their garrisons were captured, Duncan included. His inglorious future held only death from typhoid fever the following December. For Farragut the city of New Orleans, one of the great prizes of the territory in rebellion, lay straight ahead. To the utter despair of the Confederate authorities in Louisiana and in Richmond, Lovell—unable to defend his position—withdrew the 4,000 men he had left and abandoned the city, leaving it to the civilian authorities. This after Lovell had claimed that he would "never surrender." Mayor John Monroe said that he did not have the authority to surrender the city to Farragut. After a short skirmish with Confederate gunners at English Turn, Farragut's eleven ships anchored at the city's waterfront on April 25 only to witness a portion of it blazing with fire, set by the horrified populace. "A gloom has settled o'er my spirit, a gloom envelopes our dearly-beloved city," wrote Clara Solomon, a young girl living in the Crescent City. "My breaking heart but aches the more, when I am prepared to record events, which can never fade from my memory." Another New Orleans resident, Julia LeGrand, penned: "These people have complimented us highly. To quell a small 'rebellion,' they have made preparations enough to conquer a world." Mary Chesnut, the Charleston diarist, simply wrote, "New Orleans gone— and with it the Confederacy. Are we not cut in two?" Farragut recorded, "That we did our duty to the best of our ability, I believe; that a kind of Providence smiled upon us and enabled us to overcome obstacles before which the stoutest of our hearts would have otherwise quailed, I am certain."

Lovell was ruined. A court of inquiry investigated his unsuccessful defense of New Orleans and he was eventually relieved of duties by the Confederate War Department. Farragut was a hero, perhaps the first Yankee naval hero of the war. And now a troublesome political general was introduced in a personal way to the South: Butler became military governor of Louisiana and offered a vindictive set of rules and restrictions on the civilian population. Butler's harsh rule of the Confederacy's largest city over the coming weeks would become legendary. When a 42-year-old New Orleans gambler, William B. Mumford, was caught desecrating a U.S. flag raised over the Mint, Butler wrote Stanton. "This outrage will be punished in such a manner as in my judgment will caution both the perpetrators and abettors of the act so that they shall fear the *stripes* if they do not now reverence the stars of our banner." Mumford was executed on June 7, 1862. Butler's famous "woman order" of May 15, General Orders No. 28, suggested that U.S. officers were repeatedly subjected to insults from women on the city's streets. Warning the city's women not to speak lightly toward occupation troops, Butler suggested any lady insulting a Yankee soldier would be considered as "plying her avocation," suggesting that she was a prostitute, a terrible insult in the times. In no time Butler's image appeared on the bottom of porcelain chamber pots all over the state, and soon all over the South. Jefferson Davis denounced him as a felon. His behavior led to his reassignment by year's end.

WITH THE MOUNTING BATTLES on land and water, the military situation of the Confederacy appeared to be bleak. Heads were held high, however, even in New Orleans, in the hope that somehow a military victory could yet be won. For many in the North, why the South would fight so fanatically seemed inexplicable. "We woo the South 'as the Lion wooes his bride,'" wrote Nathaniel Hawthorne, in Concord, Massachusetts. "It is a rough courtship, but perhaps love and a quiet household may come a bit at last."

CHAPTER 9

Jackson's Valley Campaign

AS THE WAR CONTINUED, the value of ordnance was of increasing importance, particularly as evidenced by such operations as the siege at Yorktown. Knowing the value and range of artillery types employed during the Civil War is important in the story to come. "Artillery" was the common term used for all projectile weapons larger than small arms (handheld weapons). While "artillery" was usually used as a plural or collective term, the near synonym "cannon" was used for both singular and plural designations. Descriptions of artillery may be both complicated and confusing, as there were at least fifteen methods of classification that may be used separately or in various combinations. They are:

1. Metal. The weapon tube may be either bronze or iron. Bronze (gunmetal) is usually 90 percent copper and 10 percent tin. Bronze is golden yellow in color but tarnishes to gray with a blue-green patina. Bell metal (78 percent copper and 22 percent tin) was frequently substituted, but brass (averaging 70 percent copper and 30 percent zinc) was inferior and seldom used. Iron (or steel) was usually gray or white cast iron or wrought iron and varied from silver-gray to black in color with from 94 to 99 percent iron content plus small amounts of carbon, silicon, and/or manganese, which tarnished from red-brown to gray-black.

2. Tube type. Weapons might be smooth-bored or rifled (grooved) within the tube.

3. Tactical use. The army had field, siege, seacoast, and garrison-fortification weapons, including casement, embrasure, barbette, and parade-ground types. The navy had boat, broadside, pivot, and turret types.

4. Trajectory. Weapons designed to send projectiles in nearly a straight line were classed as guns, while those that projected in a high parabolic arc were termed mortars. Small mortars were often called "Coehorns" after the Dutch inventor, Menno van Coehoorn. Howitzers were weapons with intermediate trajectories. A carronade was a lightweight howitzer, usually produced at the Carron Iron Works in Scotland. The ranges of fire for all weapons depended on several factors, such as weapon construction, weight, dimensions, elevation, powder charge, atmospheric conditions, and topography. The true range and effectiveness of the fire was mostly determined by trial and error.

5. Caliber. The diameter of the bore was usually expressed in inches. For rifles the measurement was made on the flats rather than on the grooves.

6. Tube length. The tube length was usually measured in inches from the back of the projectile chamber to the muzzle. Sometimes the length was expressed in calibers. Thus, the Napoleon, a 4.625-caliber gun, was 14.27 calibers long ($4.625 \times 14.27 = 66$ inches).

7. Weight. The tube weight was usually measured in pounds and the value was often stamped on the tube. Sometimes the Old English units of hundredweight (cwt. = 112 pounds) and quarterweight (qwt. = 28 pounds) were employed.

8. Loading. Weapons were either muzzle-loaded or breech-loaded.

9. Shot weight. An old classification was based on the weight of the usual solid spherical iron cannonball used as a projectile. The system fell apart when alternative kinds of ammunition were introduced, often for the same weapon. Solid shot varied from 0.5 to 300 pounds. The Napoleon was often called a 12-pounder.

10. Manufacturer. The name or initials of the maker might be stamped on the lip of the muzzle or on the end of a trunnion.

11. The year or date of manufacture might also be stamped on the muzzle or trunnion.

12. Ownership. The letters "USA" or "CSA" or various state designations might be stamped on the top of the tube. Weapons belonging to the Union or to Confederates often cannot be segregated because both armies and both navies acquired and used the other's weapons. The Confederate army especially employed many captured weapons.

13. Year of approval or adoption. A portion of the description often included a model year number. Model years ranged from 1776 to 1864. The American Napoleon was a model 1857.

14. Nationality of manufacture. Many imported weapons were in use. Common countries of origin were England, France, Austria, Spain, and Mexico. Some pieces were purchases, gifts, or trophies from previous wars.

15. Construction characteristics. Tubes might be homogeneous as seen with the Columbiad (developed by George Bomford), Dahlgren (John A. B. Dahlgren), Napoleon, ordnance rifle (John Griffin), or Rodman (Thomas J. Rodman) designs. Or they might be built up with reinforcing bands or sleeves as seen in the Armstrong (William G. Armstrong), Blakely (Alexander T. Blakely), Brooke (John Mercer Brooke), Parrott (Robert P. Parrott), and Whitworth (Joseph Whitworth) designs. Some weapons showed prominent knobs or buttons on the cascabel (breech end of a muzzle-loader); some might have fillets (bands) or astragals (molded rings) around the tube, or might exhibit muzzle flair (a bulge to strengthen the muzzle portion).

Additionally, many types of mounts and carriages were supplied to support the various gun tubes.

A survey of the major types of Civil War artillery weapons shows that there were 11 types of bronze smoothbore mortars (from 2.25- to 16-caliber), 10 iron smoothbore mortars (5.52- to 16-caliber), 12 bronze smoothbore howitzers (3.67- to 18-caliber), 12 iron smoothbore howitzers (3.50- to 10-caliber), 15 bronze smoothbore guns (2.02- to 8-caliber), 68 iron smoothbore guns (0.45- to 20-caliber), 7 bronze rifled guns (2.25- to 5.30-caliber), and 90 iron rifled guns (1.50- to 13-caliber). Altogether, then, there were 225 types of artillery pieces used during the war, of which about 25 might be called experimental and another 25 might be considered to be seldom used.

Well-known individual examples of artillery spring up throughout Civil War literature. For example, the large Cochorn was a 5.82-inch bronze 24-pounder mortar. The principal siege mortar was the 10-inch iron 125-pounder. The "Dictator," made famous on the railroad lines at Petersburg during the siege, was a 13-inch, 17,120-pound mortar often mounted on a railroad flatcar; it could hurl a 200-pound shell or 770-pound shot. (The actual "Dictator" is believed to be the one on the grounds of the Connecticut State Capitol at Hartford, while the gun on display at Petersburg National Battlefield is a substitute.) The navy used 13-inch mortars to send more than 8,000 rounds into Forts Jackson and St. Philip from their position on the Mississippi River.

Other examples of artillery included the 4.62-inch bronze 12-pounder mountain howitzer, a favorite for use over rough terrain because it weighed just 200 pounds. The 5.82-inch bronze 24-pounder boat howitzer was the best light naval weapon. The Napoleon, a 4.625-inch bronze 12-pounder smoothbore gun with a tube weight of 1,200 pounds, was a celebrated and heavily used field artillery piece. The 10-inch iron 125-pounder smoothbore Rodman gun was often the preferred weapon for fortifications. The 11-inch iron smoothbore Dahlgren gun was the choice for the innovative turret in the

USS *Monitor.* The gun weighed 15,700 pounds and fired a 136-pound shell. The famous Gatling gun was an iron 0.58-caliber smoothbore with either six or ten revolving barrels; the precursor of the machine gun, the piece was used only rarely and with difficulty during the Civil War. Much-used field artillery pieces were the 2.9-inch iron 10-pounder and the 3.67-inch iron 20-pounder Parrott rifles. Favorite siege and fortification rifles were the 4.2-inch iron 30-pounder, the 6.4-inch iron 100-pounder, and the 8-inch iron 200-pounder Parrott guns. One of the latter size, named the "Swamp Angel," shelled Charleston from Morris Island but burst after thirty-six rounds. The best-liked field gun was the 3-inch iron ordnance rifle. A well-known Confederate gun on a river battery at Vicksburg was a 7.44-inch iron Blakely rifle, which burst on April 22, 1863, blowing off a two-foot section at the nozzle. The gun was used thereafter as a heavy howitzer and was named the "Widow Blakely." The most-publicized gun of the Confederate river defenses at Vicksburg was called "Whistling Dick" and was reputed to be either a 7.5-inch iron 100-pounder Blakely rifle, a 9-inch iron Brooke rifle, or a 10-inch iron 100-pounder smoothbore Columbiad. (Considerable mystery of identification surrounds the legendary gun.)

Munitions required various natural resources that depended on the mining of coal, iron, copper, tin, lead, mercury, sulfur, and nitrates. Considerable quantities of these materials were imported and some were obtained by salvage and reclamation. Gunpowder was composed of two fuels, graphite (charcoal or lampblack) and sulfur (sulphur), together with an oxidizer, potassium nitrate (nitre) or rarely other nitrates or chlorates. The Confederates had only about 30 tons of gunpowder at the beginning of the war and had to depend heavily on imports and also on various ingenious manufacturing techniques including the leaching of nitre from cave deposits of bat guano.

Detonators required compounds such as mercury fulminate, a particularly scarce commodity. Special weapons included "torpedoes" (land and naval mines), petards (demolition explosives), grenades, flares, rockets, bombs, and incendiaries such as "Greek fire," which consisted of various mixtures of petroleum, sulfur, and phosphorus.

Ammunition included solid shot in the forms of cannonballs and various cylindrical shapes (bolts). Sometimes two solid shots were connected to produce chain or bar shot, but these were rarely and almost always unsuccessfully employed. Shells were hollow spheres or cylinders filled with explosives and fitted with a fuze. Case shot (encased projectiles) included three basic types. First, grapeshot, a nearly obsolete charge, consisted of iron balls (typically nine) held together by end plates, rings, and a central iron rod that would break apart after hitting a target. Second, shrapnel (spherical case shot) consisted of a shell filled with lead or iron pellets and a fuzed explosive, devised by English general officer Henry Shrapnel. Third, canister, which was an iron, cylindrical can loaded with small iron or lead balls (usually forty-eight with a sawdust filler, acting when fired like a giant shotgun shell. Cannonballs and canister were most often used—cannonballs to fire into ranks at a distance and canister at close range.

Special types of ammunition and projectile-propellant packages were available for particular weapons under the names of Amsterdam, Armstrong, Blakely, Brooke, Dahlgren, Dimmick, Dyer, Hotchkiss, James, Parrott, Reed, Sawyer, Schenkl, and Wiard.

Field guns were often served by a gun crew of eight plus four other men to handle the horses and equipment. Six horses pulled a limber with the gun in tow. Six more horses pulled a second limber with a caisson attached. Each limber was equipped with an ammunition chest and the caisson carried two chests. A chest for the 12-pounder Napoleon usually contained 32 rounds while a chest for the 10-pounder Parrott or the ordnance rifle contained 50 rounds. The total ammunition carried for the Napoleon was therefore 128 rounds and for the Parrott, or ordnance, rifle 200 rounds.

A single gun was often called a "piece" and two guns were termed a "section." Usually four to six gun units with their auxiliary equipment—sometimes including artillery wagons and a forge—constituted a "battery," often commanded by a captain. Additional ammunition and supplies were furnished by brigade, division, and reserve commands.

All cadets from the U.S. Military Academy as well as some volunteer and militia officers were trained in the fundamentals of the artillery arm, in addition to infantry and cavalry, and thus had some contact with the management of artillery.

During the war, the United States Army had arsenals, armories, or ordnance depots at the following locations:

> Allegheny Arsenal, Pa.
> Apalachicola Arsenal, Fla.
> Augusta Arsenal, Ga. (seized by Florida troops, Jan. 5, 1861; seized by Georgia troops, Jan. 24, 1861)
> Baton Rouge Arsenal, La. (seized by Louisiana troops, Jan. 10, 1861)
> Bellona Arsenal, Va. (seized by Virginia troops, Apr. 17, 1861)
> Benicia Arsenal, Calif.
> Champlain Arsenal, Vt.
> Charleston Arsenal, S.C. (seized by South Carolina troops, Dec. 30, 1860)
> Columbus Arsenal, Ohio
> Detroit Arsenal, Mich.
> Fayetteville Arsenal, N.C. (seized by North Carolina troops, Apr. 22, 1861)
> Fort Monroe Arsenal, Va.
> Fort Union Arsenal, N.M. Terr.

Frankfort Arsenal, Pa.
Harpers Ferry Arsenal and Armory, Va. (abandoned Apr. 18, 1861)
Indianapolis Arsenal, Ind.
Kennebec Arsenal, Me.
Liberty Arsenal, Mo. (seized by secessionists, Apr. 20, 1861)
Little Rock Arsenal, Ark. (seized by Arkansas troops, Feb. 8, 1861)
Louisville Ordnance Depot, Ky.
Mt. Vernon Arsenal, Ala. (seized by Alabama troops, Jan. 4, 1861)
Nashville Ordnance Depot, Tenn.
New York Arsenal, N.Y.
Pikesville Arsenal, Md.
Rock Island Arsenal and Armory, Ill.
Rome Arsenal, N.Y.
San Antonio Arsenal, Tex. (seized by Texas troops, Feb. 16, 1861)
Springfield Arsenal, Mass.
St. Louis Ordnance Depot, Mo.
Vancouver Arsenal, Wash. Terr.
Washington Arsenal, D.C.
Watertown Arsenal, Mass.
Watervliet Arsenal, N.Y.

Note that eleven of the thirty-three installations were seized by forces of the Southern States, which were able to acquire about 429 artillery pieces and about 154,000 small arms.

Union naval ordnance yards operated at Portsmouth, Boston, New York, Philadelphia, and Washington. Navy ordnance depots were located at Baltimore, Norfolk, Port Royal, Key West, Pensacola, New Orleans, Mound City (Ill.), and San Francisco.

Confederate States ordnance facilities were located at:

Apalachicola Arsenal, Fla. (ex-USA)
Athens Armory, Ga.
Atlanta Arsenal, Ga.
Augusta Arsenal and Powder Works, Ga. (ex-USA)
Baton Rouge Arsenal, La. (ex-USA)
Bellona Arsenal, Va. (ex-USA)
Charleston Arsenal, S.C. (ex-USA)
Clarksville Ordnance Harness Shops, Va.
Columbia Armory, S.C.
Columbus Arsenal, Ga.
Columbus Arsenal, Miss.
Dalton Ordnance Depot, Ga.
Danville Ordnance Depot, Va.

Fayetteville Arsenal and Armory, N.C. (ex-USA)
Greensboro Ordnance Depot, N.C.
Holly Springs Armory, Miss.
Jackson Arsenal, Miss.
Little Rock Arsenal, Ark. (ex-USA)
Lynchburg Ordnance Depot, Va.
Macon Armory, Ga.
Macon Central Laboratory, Ga.
Memphis Ordnance Depot, Tenn.
Milledgeville State Armory, Ga.
Mt. Vernon Arsenal, Ala. (ex-USA)
Nashville Arsenal, Tenn.
New Orleans Arsenal, La.
Petersburg Lead Smelter, Va.
Petersburg Powder Works, Va.
Raleigh Powder Works, N.C.
Richmond Armory, Va.
Richmond Arsenal, Va.
Richmond Laboratory, Va.
Salisbury Arsenal, Va.
San Antonio Arsenal, Tex. (ex-USA)
Savannah Arsenal, Ga.
Selma Arsenal, Ala.
Selma Powder Works, Ala.
Tallahassee Armory, Fla.
Tredegar Iron Works, Va.
Tyler Arsenal, Tex.
Virginia Military Institute, Va.

Confederate naval ordnance facilities existed at:

Atlanta, Ga.
Augusta, Ga.
Charlotte, N.C.
Columbia, S.C.
Columbia Naval Powder Works, S.C.
Columbus, Ga.
Gosport Navy Yard, Va. (ex-USA)
New Orleans, La.
Petersburg Powder Works, Va.
Richmond (Rocketts), Va.
Selma Naval Gun Factory, Ala.
Tredegar Iron Works, Va.

The amount of artillery employed during the war was dizzying. The records of the U.S. Army are complete and accurate, allowing a clear look at the way artillery progressed during the war. On April 1, 1861, just days before Sumter, the U.S. Army had 2,283 guns, only about 10 percent of which were field pieces. At that time it had 364,191 artillery projectiles of all types and some 555 tons of gunpowder and 318 tons of lead metal. At war's end, on June 30, 1865, the army had 3,325 guns, of which 53 percent were field pieces, and some 1,690,504 artillery projectiles, 1,683 tons of gunpowder, and 19,831 tons of lead metal. The army reported as "supplied to the army during the war" the following quantities: 7,892 guns, 6,335,295 artillery projectiles, 2,862,177 rounds of fixed artillery ammunition, 45,258 tons of lead metal, and 13,320 tons of gunpowder. In another chapter we'll explore the quantities and use of small-arms weapons and projectiles.

OF THE MANY PLACES in the field where commanders fretted over artillery and a galaxy of other matters, one important place was Corinth, Mississippi. Maj. Gen. Henry W. Halleck, having received command in the west, concentrated a vast army at Pittsburg Landing, near the Shiloh battlefield. By April 29 his force of about 100,000, consisting of the Army of the Tennessee (Grant), the Army of the Ohio (Buell), and the Army of the Mississippi (Pope), was ready to move on the rail center of Corinth. Facing Halleck was Beauregard's Army of Mississippi and other forces, comprising some 70,000 men. In the wake of Grant's strategic victory at Shiloh, which made Halleck envy Grant's success, Grant was placed in a position of second-in-command without direct authority over any portion of the army in the field. Brig. Gen. George H. Thomas was assigned to command the Army of the Tennessee. This decision was also influenced heavily by the attacks from the press on Grant over his surprise at the start of the battle at Shiloh and of its bloody cost, and by the communications mishaps between Grant and Halleck. Grant wrote Halleck, suggesting that his position in the army differed "but little from that of one in arrest," and he requested to be relieved of duty or to have his position defined so "that there can be no mistaking it." He considered resigning his commission but was persuaded not to by Brig. Gen. William T. Sherman. Of Sherman, Grant wrote his wife Julia that "In Gen. Sherman the country has an able and gallant defender and your husband a true friend."

At Corinth, Beauregard's Army of Mississippi consisted of the 1st Corps ("First Grand Division," Maj. Gen. Leonidas Polk), 2d Corps ("Second Grand Division," Gen. Braxton Bragg), and 3d Corps (Maj. Gen. William J. Hardee). Also present was the Army of the West, commanded by Maj. Gen. Earl Van Dorn, the veteran of Pea Ridge. Halleck's twenty-mile advance on Corinth was executed with the kind of caution that made Mc-

Clellan appear bold by comparison. He began on April 29 and by May 3 encountered Confederate forces at Farmington, Mississippi, creating a series of skirmishes that lasted a week, despite the fact that Halleck reported to the War Department on May 3 that he would occupy Corinth the following day. Halleck's force entrenched with the onset of each night, inching its way along. On May 3, Pope encountered a force of about 4,500, consisting of some artillery and cavalry, and he reported that the enemy left 30 dead on the field and was driven "in wild confusion." Despite this, he wrote, his forces "are all returning, and will bivouac tonight 2 miles this side of Farmington." The most significant fighting at Farmington came on May 9 when Van Dorn's force struck into Pope's advancing line along Seven Mile Creek, and a five-hour skirmish, often marked by bloody sheets of fire, resulted. The Union casualties were 16 killed, 148 wounded, and 14 missing, while partial Confederate returns indicated 8 killed, 89 wounded, and 2 missing in Ruggles's division, and allegedly 9 killed and wounded in Van Dorn's force.

Halleck continued his glacial advance. The next skirmish came at Russell's House on May 17. Here Sherman's 5th Division of the Army of the Tennessee determined to drive Confederates from their entrenched position before Corinth. Sherman ordered a multiple advance with regiments under Brig. Gens. James W. Denver and Stephen A. Hurlbut and Col. Morgan L. Smith. On reaching a causeway and small bridge on the approach to Russell's House, which stood on a ridge, Smith deployed skirmishers toward the Confederate line and spread his advance guard forward. By midafternoon four guns opened on the Confederates, who hid in Russell's House and the surrounding outbuildings. The Federal artillery fire scattered the Rebels in confusion and after a time the Union force took the position. "From Russell's we could hear distinctly the drums beating in Corinth," Sherman recalled. He reported the Union loss as 10 killed and 31 wounded, and stated that the Confederates lost "12 dead on the ground, whom we buried."

Although the Union forces were approaching and moving to surround Corinth—and greatly outnumbered Beauregard's Confederates in and around the town—Halleck was reluctant to press the attack and began siege operations against the rail city. A few small skirmishes resulted, and Halleck rolled up his heavy guns and prepared to bombard the town by May 25. He had taken more than three weeks to march his force a distance of twenty miles. Beauregard polled his subordinates on the matter of evacuation, anticipating a heavy shelling of his rather weak defensive lines.

On the evening of May 29 the evacuation sprang into action as many trains ran back and forth along the southern rail line, and each time a series of cars arrived the Confederate soldiers cheered mightily, leading Halleck's men to believe the Southerners were being reinforced. Before sunrise on May 30, virtually all of Beauregard's army was on its way south, and Pope,

Halleck, and the other Union commanders were fooled completely. Beauregard regrouped and took up a defensive line to the south along the Tuscumbia River. Pope's troops pursued for several days, capturing abandoned stores and supplies and moving thirty miles south of Corinth. Troopers commanded by a little-known Ohioan, Col. Philip H. Sheridan, rode furiously after the Rebels. At Booneville on May 30, Sheridan's men captured or destroyed 10,000 small arms, three artillery pieces, large quantities of clothing and ammunition, and paroled 2,000 prisoners who could not march fast enough to keep up with Sheridan's horsemen. On June 11, Halleck halted the pursuit of Beauregard, who had sped toward Tupelo, some fifty-two miles south of Corinth.

WITH THE WARM WEATHER there were actions on and along the Mississippi River. After the fall of New Madrid and Island No. 10, the greatest stronghold along the river south of that position was Fort Pillow, which stood on the eastern bank of the river some thirty-five miles north of Memphis, Tennessee. Several Federal actions over the coming weeks would focus on taking Fort Pillow and moving on Memphis, whose wartime population was 22,623. On May 10, a flotilla of Federal mortar boats moved on Fort Pillow, resulting in the battle of Plum Run Bend, about four miles north of Fort Pillow. Due to the failing health of Capt. Andrew H. Foote, who had been wounded at Fort Donelson, Capt. Charles Henry Davis was assigned command of the Mississippi River Squadron. The Federal ships and boats were faced by the small, makeshift River Defense Fleet, at this time commanded by Capt. James E. Montgomery, who had eight cottonclad rams at his disposal: the CSS *Colonel Lovell,* CSS *General Beauregard,* CSS *General Bragg,* CSS *General M. Jeff Thompson,* CSS *General Sterling Price,* CSS *General Sumter,* and CSS *Little Rebel* (Montgomery's flagship). Merriwether Jeff Thompson, a brigadier general in the Missouri State Guard, accompanied the naval expedition. Thompson was a Virginia-born guerrilla and veteran of Belmont who would become notorious for his exploits later in the war.

The seven ships in Davis's squadron were tied to the banks around 7 A.M. when Montgomery's Confederate flotilla appeared on the water around the bend and made for the Union vessels. Several of the Federal mortar boats were anchored in the river and had begun the process of shelling Fort Pillow, lobbing heavy shells across the four-mile span, and Mortar Boat No. 16 was exposed and closest to the approaching Confederate rams. Almost at once some of the Confederate ships opened fire and the river ironclad gunboats USS *Cincinnati* and USS *Mound City* steamed to intercede. The *Cincinnati* was rammed and finally sunk. The *Mound City* was rammed by the *General Sterling Price* and the next day run aground. The *General Bragg* was damaged by ramming. The *General Sterling Price* was extensively damaged by gunfire.

When it ended, Plum Run Bend was a victory for the North—the unarmored Southern flotilla retreated southward, but not before fighting valiantly in the face of a more heavily armed and armored foe. Montgomery withdrew first to Fort Pillow and then all the way downriver to Memphis. Events now accelerated in conjunction with Beauregard's evacuation of Corinth. That maneuver meant losing the east-west Memphis & Charleston Railroad and exposing Memphis to an almost undefended status. Davis's ships and mortar boats began pouring a heavy rain of shells into the fort. By June 3 nervous Confederate gunners at Fort Pillow, commanded by Brig. Gen. John B. Villepigue, readied for an evacuation to Grenada, Mississippi. As the pullout was underway, he reported a great many desertions and informed Ruggles that the "enemy captured 4 men this morning; fear they understand my situation." By the night of June 4, the earthworks and bluffs of Fort Pillow were empty, and the Confederates did the best they could to haul away anything of value. On the morning of June 5, when Lt. Col. Alfred W. Ellet went ashore with a flag of truce, he found after a laborious journey to the fort that it had been abandoned. "The people express a desire for the restoration of the old order of things," wrote Col. Charles Ellet, Jr., commanding the Ram Flotilla, "though still professing to be secessionists."

The excitement wasn't over, for Montgomery's River Defense Fleet still offered some protection to the city. Citizens of Memphis assembled on the river shores to watch the impending battle of Memphis, which began at 4:20 A.M. on June 6 when Davis's five ships and Charles Ellet's four rams moved downriver toward the levee where the Confederate ships lay. Davis's ships were the ironclad gunboats USS *Benton*, USS *Louisville*, USS *Carondelet*, USS *Cairo*, and USS *St. Louis*. The two rams that engaged first were the USS *Queen of the West* (Ellet's flagship) and the USS *Monarch*. The Federal ships mounted a total of sixty-eight guns.

Montgomery had the same flotilla he had used at Fort Pillow, and it was weak, mounting only twenty-eight guns. The battle erupted into a close-quarters melee right away, with broadsides firing and shells and balls arcing wildly through the air. Ellet's *Queen of the West* took a leading role in ramming several of the Confederate vessels, and soon heavy cannon fire from the gunboats pounded away at the Confederate ships. For Montgomery the situation was nearly hopeless. After two hours of intense fighting the growing list of casualties for the Confederate river navy was daunting: only the *General Earl Van Dorn* escaped. On the Union side, the *Queen of the West* and the *Carondelet* were damaged. Charles Ellet was mortally wounded, dying fifteen days later. By 11 A.M. many of the city's civilians went home from the river in shock, and the mayor, John Park, surrendered Memphis to the Union army and navy. The United States now had possession of the Mississippi River except for that territory inside the state of Mississippi, and they had another important Southern city in their hands. They also would find Memphis to be a convenient launching point for driving farther into the South. Now the strategic target would become the Confederate stronghold at Vicksburg, Mississippi.

WARM-WEATHER ACTIONS sprouted across the American landscape in 1862 much faster than they had a year earlier. In early May, Confederate forces prepared to evacuate Pensacola, Florida, a town of only 2,876 civilians but protected by several important forts. They had been ready to pull out of the important supply and shipping base for several weeks, ever since the Union successes on the Mississippi River necessitated redeploying the Confederate resources. Still, moving out of the area was a bitter pill for many Confederate strategists to swallow because Pensacola Bay provided such a good position for creating a base on the Gulf. Forts Barrancas and McRee had been captured by Confederates in January 1861; but thanks to the heroics of Lt. Adam J. Slemmer, the Yankees held on to Fort Pickens. On May 9, Confederate forces burned and destroyed matériel at the Pensacola Navy Yard, Forts Barrancas and McRee, two Confederate steamboats, and an ironclad building on the Escambia River. The following day they withdrew, and a combined Union operation salvaged what it could of the smoking ruins. On May 12, Federal troops under Brig. Gen. Lewis G. Arnold marched from Fort Barrancas into the city and—interrupted only by sporadic gunfire from a few Confederate pickets—planted the Stars and Stripes on the flagstaff in the city's central plaza.

"The most painful duty it ever fell to my lot to perform was accomplished," wrote Col. Thomas M. Jones, charged with evacuating the town's fortifications, "namely, the signalizing for the destruction of the beautiful place which I had labored so hard night and day for over two months to defend, and which I had fondly hoped could be held from the polluting grasp of our insatiate enemies."

Other actions in a scattering of places yielded less well defined results. At Searcy Landing in north-central Arkansas, a portion of Maj. Gen. Samuel R. Curtis's Army of the Southwest skirmished with Confederates along the Little Red River. Near Searcy Landing, Capt. Francis Wilhelmi of the 17th Missouri Infantry explained that a battalion departed camp with him and foraged for corn at a farmhouse nearby when they heard firing, deployed in a line, and encountered about 150 enemy troops. A brisk skirmish resulted in 10 dead and 5 wounded Federals.

On the Mississippi, Union eyes were turning toward Vicksburg. On May 12, Comdr. James S. Palmer requested surrender of the city of Natchez from its mayor, John Hunter. The city of 6,612 fell to Union occupation. On May 18, Comdr. Samuel Phillips Lee on board the USS *Oneida* submitted a demand of surrender to the mayor of Vicksburg. The town had only 4,591 citizens, but its position high atop a bluff made it a formidable fortress. Mayor L. Lindsay refused, writing that "I will state that neither the municipal authorities nor the citizens will ever consent to a surrender of the city." This refusal set into motion a year-long operation to take the city. One stepping-stone toward that goal was the fortification built by Confederates near the hamlet of Grand Gulf, Mississippi, about twenty-five miles south of Vicksburg, on the eastern shore of the river, near where the Big Black River joins the Mississippi.

On his way steaming upriver during May on board the USS *Brooklyn,* Capt. Thomas T. Craven sent a long letter to his wife that captures the haunting despair of the citizenry along the river and the racist attitudes still permeating many of the Northern soldiers and sailors. "It was interesting and sometimes exciting, as we steamed along inshore, to witness the dense crowds of spectators," he wrote. "As we passed the groups of darkies, particularly if they were hidden from their masters' view by intervening trees or houses, such demonstrations of joy, such jumping and bowing, and such antics and grins as could only be imagined by those who are familiar with the monkey traits of the negro character." Craven described a junior officer's first encounter with Southern citizens on shore. A plantation owner, "with his wife and two or three grown-up daughters, appeared to be terribly frightened, but after learning that we were not on a nigger-stealing expedition, and that all their property was safe, or not to be molested, they gradually calmed down, and as their reserve wore off they became quite cheerful and friendly."

In this pivotal year of the war, attitudes about slavery and emancipation among the ranks of the Federal soldiers and sailors had for the most part not yet developed. "The boys think it *their* duty to put down rebellion and nothing more," wrote Wilbur Fisk, a private in the 2d Vermont Infantry, "and they view the abolition of slavery in the present time as saddling so much additional labor upon them before the present great work is accomplished." Public opinion was in flux, however. "Every gun fired in this struggle, no matter on which side, no matter what else it hits or misses, lodges a ball in the carcase [*sic*] of the writhing monster," editorialized Horace Greeley's *New York Tribune.* "Man may hesitate or vacillate, but the judgment of God is sure, and under that judgment Slavery reels to its certain downfall."

At the end of May, expeditionary forces under Brig. Gen. Thomas Williams, along with the screw gunboat USS *Kineo,* shelled the town and battery at Grand Gulf and after its temporary abandonment captured a single gun. From June 7 through 10, Williams and the Federal navy made forays into the vicinity of Vicksburg with a force of two screw gunboats, the USS *Wissahickon* and the USS *Itasca.* These ships were near Grand Gulf when the shore batteries, manned by some 500 artillerists, opened suddenly and vigorously on June 9 at about 4 A.M., sending a barrage of balls from rifled cannon toward the Federal vessels. After a two-hour fight, during which the ships fired numerous shells with 5-second fuzes, the batteries on shore were silent. There were several casualties on ship; the *Wissahickon* took twenty-five shots through her side and the *Itasca* seventeen. Confederate forces began erecting batteries at Rodney and fortifying those at Grand Gulf, Vicksburg, and elsewhere.

On the other side of the western theater, in East Tennessee, efforts were made during the first warm weeks to gain a foothold on that part of the state containing many people loyal to the Union. The critical gateway for operations was Cumberland Gap, on the Kentucky-Tennessee-Virginia border, where Col. James E. Rains had about 4,000 men guarding the pass and a sizable quantity of stores. A standoff of sorts transpired between Rains and Brig. Gen. George Washington Morgan. In April, Morgan brought a force of 8,000 to Cumberland Ford; several skirmishes resulted. Morgan's 7th Division (Army of the Ohio) consisted of four brigades commanded by Brig. Gens. Samuel P. Carter and James G. Spears and Cols. John F. De Courcy and John Coburn. The Confederate authority in the area was Maj. Gen. Edmund Kirby Smith, who commanded the Department of East Tennessee. Though blocked by obstructions and having to work his way through a series of narrow defiles, Morgan by early June was ready to move toward the gap. Buell made several demonstrations toward Chattanooga, and Kirby Smith was forced to pull away because of the threat. Morgan's men quickly occupied the heights, and the news seemed a spark in the progress of liberating Tennessee.

On June 16 a battle erupted near Secessionville, South Carolina, on James Island, in the vicinity of Charleston. Brig. Gen. Quincy A. Gillmore, strategist of the successful reduction of Fort Pulaski, positioned a force on James Island. The idea was to move against Charleston and perhaps recapture the symbolically vital Fort Sumter, but by mid-June Gillmore decided to keep his force in place without moving against Charleston. The Confederate defenses were commanded by Brig. Gen. Nathan G. Evans, who had served memorably at First Bull Run and at Ball's Bluff despite his cantankerous attitude and addiction to drink. "Shanks" Evans was the district commander; Brig. Gens. William D. Smith and States Rights Gist, along with Col. Johnson Hagood, had more immediate command of the troops in the field. The action took place near Secessionville, a hamlet on James Island, south and west of Charleston. About 9,000 Federal troops of Brig. Gen. Henry W. Benham (divisions of Brig. Gens. Horatio G. Wright and Isaac I. Stevens, and Col. Robert Williams) attacked the Confederates without orders or sound planning.

A skirmish took place at Thomas Grimball's plantation on the west coast of the island on June 10. The major action came on the 16th, when elements of Wright's brigades attempted to move northward to Secessionville. Here was located the Tower Battery, a fortification constructed in the shape of an M and with a front wall measuring 175 feet across, defended by the 1st South Carolina Artillery, consisting of 500 men, mostly of the Pee Dee Battalion with an 8-inch Columbiad, several 18-pounder guns, two 24-pounder rifled guns, and a mortar battery.

The fighting began at about 4:30 A.M. The Federal attack bogged down, however, with heavy cannon fire taking its toll. Second Lt. Thomas Hooton of the 7th Connecticut "spun around and fell with a projectile lodged deeply in his body." He was conscious as aides carried him rearward, and he spoke to his comrades, asking them to continue the fight. A soldier "bitterly noticed afterward that the Confederate projectile that killed [Hooten] was a 'junk bottle.'" The three assaults that took place over six hours that morning all failed, and Benham's career was ruined. He was relieved of command, his commission as brigadier general was revoked (although this revocation was suspended the following year), and Benham spent the rest of the war executing routine engineering duties.

For many soldiers on both sides, Secessionville marked a bitter experience of battle. "Well I was in the fight on the 16th & got slightly wounded in the right arm just below the shoulder," wrote Henry Cooley, a soldier in the 7th Connecticut. "The enemy had very strong batteries & rifle pits & we had to march right up in front of them. . . . It was a regular slaughter pen to march us up in the way they did but our boys stood it nobly & bravely. . . . It was a regular hornet's nest & I never expected to come out of it alive."

LATE SPRING 1862 marked the culmination of Stonewall Jackson's brilliant Valley campaign. Following the battle of Kernstown in late March, Jackson waited and watched as the Peninsular campaign got underway to the south. Jackson had two major concerns at this time: preventing the capture of the supply base at Staunton and blocking Maj. Gens. John C. Frémont and Nathaniel P. Banks from uniting. Jackson also wanted to keep Banks in the Valley rather than reinforce the Federal army on the Peninsula. On April 30, Jackson initiated a complex series of plans. He sent Col. Turner Ashby to make a feint toward Harrisonburg while Maj. Gen. Richard S. Ewell would occupy Swift Run Gap in the Blue Ridge to block possible routes of advance for Banks's army. To further confuse Federal scouts, Jackson then moved by a circuitous route from Conrad's Store to West View, west of Staunton, southwest to Port Republic, southeast through Brown's Gap to Mechum's River Station, and west along the Orange & Alexandria Railroad across Rockfish Gap. Jackson joined the division of Brig. Gen. Ed "Alleghany" John-

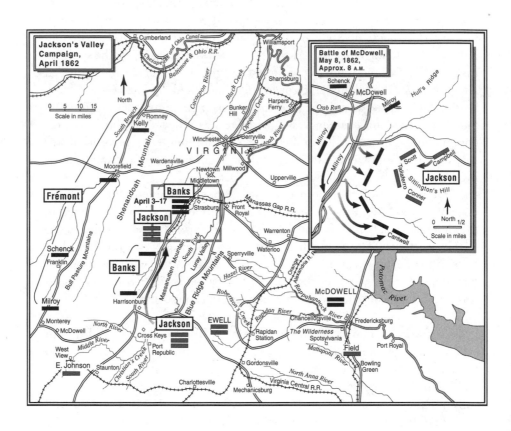

Jackson's Valley Campaign, April 1862

Cumberland
Williamsport
Chesapeake and Ohio Canal
Baltimore & Ohio R.R.
Cacapon River
Black Creek
Sharpsburg
North
Scale in miles
0 5 10 15
Romney
Kelly
Bunker Hill
Harpers Ferry
Opequon Creek
Shenandoah River
Moorefield
South Branch
Shenandoah Mountains
Wardensville
Winchester
Berryville
VIRGINIA
Newtown
Millwood
Upperville
Middletown
Frémont
Banks
April 3–17
Strasburg
Front Royal
Manassas Gap R.R.
Jackson
Warrenton
Schenck
Franklin
Banks
Sperryville
Waterloo
Hazel River
Bull Pasture Mountains
Massanutten Mountain
Luray Valley
South Fork
Blue Ridge Mountains
Robertson Creek
Milroy
Harrisonburg
Orange & Alexandria R.R.
Rappahannock River
Rapidan River
McDOWELL
Potomac River
Monterey
McDowell
North River
Middle River
Jackson
Cross Keys
Port Republic
Chrisman's Creek
EWELL
Rapidan Station
Chancellorsville
The Wilderness
Spotsylvania
Fredericksburg
Port Royal
West View
E. Johnson
Staunton
South River
Gordonsville
Mattaponi River
Field
Bowling Green
Charlottesville
Mechanicsburg
North Anna River
Virginia Central R.R.

Battle of McDowell, May 8, 1862, Approx. 8 A.M.

Schenck
McDowell
Hull's Ridge
Milroy
Crab Run
Milroy
Milroy
Scott
Campbell
Taliaferro
Jackson
Sittington's Hill
Conner
North
Cantwell
Scale in miles
0   1/2

son and proceeded to McDowell, arriving on May 7. During the late afternoon Johnson's lead skirmishers encountered outposts of Union Brig. Gen. Robert H. Milroy's brigade. On the other side of Bull Pasture Mountain, a long ridge west of the Shenandoah, the Federal brigade commanded by Brig. Gen. Robert C. Schenck had been ordered to move south quickly to come to Milroy's aid when Jackson's movement became known; Schenck's men marched thirty-four miles in twenty-three hours. Jackson's own men, now being celebrated in some Confederate circles as the "foot cavalry," had marched ninety-two miles in four days and ridden twenty-five miles on train cars from Mechum's River Station to Staunton.

On May 8, these movements resulted in the battle of McDowell. Jackson's force of 9,000 formed in a C-shaped defensive line along the top of Sitlington's Hill, east of Bull Pasture River. The hamlet of McDowell stood at a crossroads west of the river's confluence with Cub Run, north of Sitlington's Hill. Jackson's force consisted of the Army of the Valley and Johnson's Army of the Northwest. Col. Z. T. Conner's 1st Brigade held the southern flank of the hill, and the line bent around in a clockwise direction consisted of the brigades of Brig. Gens. William B. Taliaferro and Charles S. Winder and Cols. William C. Scott and John A. Campbell. On the Federal side, Schenck commanded the field at McDowell because he outranked Milroy. Schenck's brigade consisted of mostly Ohio infantry along with Connecticut cavalry; Milroy's brigade was composed of Ohioans and men from western Virginia. During the early afternoon hours of May 8, Jackson busied himself by searching for a position by which he could flank Schenck's army. Simultaneously, Schenck moved south from McDowell, forded the river, and formed for an uphill attack.

The fighting at McDowell was severe during periods and was difficult going for the Yankees. The hill was so steep, Schenck wrote, that the only way to bring ammunition up to the troops was "by hand or in haversacks." The Union plan was poor, but Confederate troops had some trouble, too. Seeing skulkers lying down in the rear, Col. William C. Scott found a successful method of recharging their participation. "Observing that some men retired farther to the rear than necessary," he wrote, "and were lying on their faces and taking no part in the battle, I attempted to rouse them by words, but finding that neither harsh words nor threats were of any avail, I commenced riding over them, which soon made them join the line of battle." The action began in midafternoon and continued until about 9 P.M., when it became clear that with darkness falling the Federal position was untenable and Schenck withdrew. Jackson engaged about 5,000 and Schenck employed about 2,500 on the attack; Union casualties amounted to 26 killed, 227 wounded, and 3 missing, while Confederate losses were 75 killed and 423 wounded. Schenck moved back toward Franklin, with Jackson in pursuit, who encountered small pockets of burning forest set by the retreating Yankees to stall Jackson's men. Jackson reached the vicinity of Franklin on May 12 and left Col. Turner Ashby's cavalry in place there as a screen before returning to the Valley to organize the next phase of his campaign. For Jackson, it was his first clear victory in battle during the Valley campaign, and it emboldened him.

Just as he decided how to fight the Yankees, however, Jackson experienced a series of frustrating episodes involving the Confederate high command. For two weeks following McDowell, little action occurred in the Valley. Gen. Robert E. Lee revealed alarm at the possibility that Banks might move down to join Maj. Gen. Irvin McDowell at Fredericksburg and together they might move on Richmond simultaneously with McClellan's advance up the Peninsula. On May 13, Lee advised Ewell, without communicating with Jackson, to endanger Banks's lines of communication. This ran counter to what Jackson had ordered Ewell to do, and Ewell justifiably became confused. To aggravate the situation, Gen. Joe Johnston, who commanded the Army of Northern Virginia that was facing McClellan, reminded Lee that he held authority over Jackson and had not been consulted.

Noting by mid-month that Banks's troops at New Market and Harrisonburg appeared to be gearing up to depart, Ewell gave up the idea of raiding Banks's communications. Instead, he simply informed Jackson about Banks and did nothing. Jackson immediately moved toward Harrisonburg. Meanwhile, Banks, afraid of a possible surprise attack, moved his 8,000 troops northward to Strasburg. He then detached 1,000 men under Col. John R. Kenly eastward to Front Royal, east of Massanutten Mountain, to reconnoiter the Luray Valley. By May 17, Ewell was again confused. Jackson had ordered Ewell to shadow Banks. On May 14, Lee had ordered him not to move until Jackson returned to the Valley. The following day Johnston's orders arrived in which Ewell was told to move eastward if Banks moved east first; the same day, Jackson ordered him to go to New Market. Two days later Ewell learned that Brig. Gen. James Shields had moved out of the Valley, suggesting that he should move eastward also. Instead he decided to visit Jackson for clarification. By May 20 Ewell was at Luray with 6,000 men; Jackson had another 10,000 south of New Market. Banks's position at Strasburg was now fortified, but he was still there. Jackson consulted Lee and suggested that with Shields gone, a great opportunity to strike a blow at Banks existed if Ewell were kept in Jackson's command.

Jackson wanted to capture Front Royal, thereby turning Banks's position. Jackson's men marched across Massanutten Mountain and joined Ewell at Luray, creating a force of about 17,000 with fifty guns. Jackson now marched rapidly northward to strike at Kenly, cut Banks's line of communication with Harpers Ferry, and force him to pull out of the fortified line at Strasburg. Ashby's cavalry had performed such a highly effective job of screening the Confederate movements that the Yankees hardly realized what was coming. The men in Jackson's "foot cavalry" did not know where they were going, as their commander was secretive about the army's intentions. Kenly had not made things easier on himself by failing to post pickets on all the roads in the Luray Valley. On May 23 the battle of Front Royal occurred as elements of Jackson's army bolstered by Brig. Gen. Richard Taylor's brigade of Ewell's division swept onto the scene and opened fire.

Union troops fired out the windows of a hospital as gray-clad soldiers swept forward. They soon learned that soldiers of the 1st Maryland Infantry (Kenly) lay ahead of them. In a fight consisting largely of Marylanders on both sides, Col. Bradley T. Johnson's 1st Maryland Infantry (CSA) surged forward and pushed Union troops out of the town, across bridges, and scattering for the hills. Kenly attempted to make a stand. By 5 P.M. he retreated, however, giving up the town. When Union artillery opened fire on a group of guns and officers that included Ewell, the Confederate general asked an artillerist, "What do you mean, sir, by making a target of me with these men?" "Why, general," the officer said, "you told me to stay near you, and I'm trying to do it." "Clear out, sir, clear out," Ewell replied. "I didn't tell you to get all your men killed and me too."

Jackson next moved to get around Banks's position. The main force moved on Winchester, while cavalry rode off to Newtown and Middletown. At this phase Jackson's army consisted of the divisions of Jackson and Ewell, plus attached cavalry commanded by Col. Thomas S. Flournoy. Jackson's division had the brigades of Brig. Gen. Charles S. Winder and Cols. John A. Campbell and Samuel V. Fulkerson, and an artillery brigade led by Col. Stapleton Crutchfield. Ewell's division held the brigades of Col. William C. Scott and Brig. Gens. Arnold Elzey, Isaac R. Trimble, Richard Taylor, and George H. Steuart (Maryland Line, attached to the 2d Brigade), and artillery.

At Strasburg, Banks couldn't believe that Jackson had struck with force at Front Royal. The day after the battle, Banks assessed Jackson's character. He wrote to the War Department over Jackson's "adherence . . . to the defense of the valley and his well-known purpose to expel the Government troops from this country if in his power. . . . There is probably no one [of] more fixed and determined purpose in the whole circle of the enemy's plans." Banks's force now consisted of the division of Brig. Gen. Alpheus S. Williams, with the brigades of Cols. Dudley Donnelly and George H. Gordon, and cavalry and artillery; a cavalry brigade (Brig. Gen. John P. Hatch); and unattached troops. On the 24th, Banks began a withdrawal from his fortified position, lacking faith in his ability to protect the Valley Turnpike, the railroad bridges, supplies and wagons, and themselves. The only factors preventing Jackson from intercepting Banks at Middletown were the fatigued condition of Jackson's footsore troops and the effective rearguard action staged by Gordon. Heeding Gordon's advice, Banks ordered his main body to Winchester, where he hastily began a defense, preparing to face Jackson. The battle of Winchester occurred the next day and is often called First Winchester, to differentiate it from later actions.

The battle was again a lopsided Confederate victory. During the early morning hours of May 25, Ashby's cavalry and Maj. C. Roberdeau Wheat's 1st Louisiana Battalion, the "Louisiana Tigers," got bogged down with looting a wagon train along the pike. Jackson pushed his troops hard down the turnpike after this incident, while Ewell moved on Winchester from Front Royal. Strategic heights south of the town, among them Apple Pie Ridge, had to be taken by Jackson before they were occupied by Banks, and Jackson attacked headlong by dawn, crossing Abraham's Creek and encountering Yankee pickets. Quick work by the Federal guns and by Hatch's cavalry kept the Union left intact, but after a time of heavy action Jackson determined to maneuver Taylor's Louisianans to the Yankee right flank and rolled guns up to soften Banks's defenses. While Taylor moved into position, Ewell took the initiative to do the same on the left flank. At 7:30 A.M. Jackson ordered an attack by Taylor and the center and Ewell's flank soon followed; the Federals withstood the attack for a short time before crumbling. Just as at Front Royal, however, Jackson was unable to organize a competent pursuit of the enemy. He could not reach Ashby to issue orders to the cavalry. "Maryland" Steuart would not move on any orders unless they came from his immediate superior, Ewell. So the opportunity for defeating Banks decisively was lost, but Banks had been pushed from the Valley, across the Potomac to Williamsport, and a defensive force was hastily assembled at Harpers Ferry under Brig. Gen. Rufus Saxton. Confederate casualties were 68 killed, 329 wounded, and 3 missing; Union losses were 62 killed, 329 wounded, and 1,714 missing or captured. For Banks, it was tough going. After telling a group of retreating soldiers, "Stop, men! Don't you love your country?" Banks was met with the reply, "Yes, by God, and I'm trying to get back to it just as fast as I can."

Banks's sudden departure from the Shenandoah Valley cast a long shadow. In Washington, President Lincoln canceled the plan of sending McDowell to the Peninsula to support McClellan. Instead, he wanted to destroy Jackson's army, and so he ordered Frémont to move toward Harrisonburg, and McDowell was asked to send 20,000 troops to Front Royal. Continuing his ineffective generalship, however, Frémont moved to Moorefield instead of Harrisonburg. Now Lincoln's plan altered to a rapid concentration at Strasburg to block Jackson from moving up the Valley Turnpike. As Frémont approached from the west with 15,000, Shields marched a force of 10,000 from the east, along the railroad line. On May 29, Jackson discovered the situation and maneuvered up the Valley. The next day Shields startled the Confederate garrison at Front Royal, capturing the town, and then faltered by stalling there and not pressing onward to ensnare Jackson. To make matters worse, Frémont pursued sleepily from the west, and both commanders strung their lines out along muddy roads. Jackson moved his men systematically southward through Strasburg and by May 31 Jackson had escaped. McDowell reached Front Royal and sent a reconnaissance into Strasburg that was turned back by Ewell. A critical opportunity for the Federal high command was handled foolishly by both Frémont and Shields.

On the late afternoon of the first, as events were transpiring down South, Jackson's old Stonewall Brigade, now commanded by Winder, marched south again through Strasburg, along the Valley Turnpike, and Ewell quickly followed. The following day McDowell's cavalry, and infantry commanded by Frémont, attempted to trap Jackson's force, but instead of being cut off from the south Jackson was now speeding southward along the Valley Turnpike. By contrast, the Federal forces used poor, often muddy roads in pursuit, lacked the aggressive marching tactics practiced so routinely by Jackson, and failed to coordinate their movements with any degree of skill. Therefore, on June 3, Jackson's army was making a beeline toward Harrisonburg with the Yankees following.

The lead element of pursuers consisted of a portion of Frémont's 15,000 men, specifically cavalry commanded by Brig. Gen. George D. Bayard, loaned by McDowell. Part of McDowell's corps, Shields's division, also moved in parallel up the Luray Valley. Having been pushed out of the Valley a week earlier, Banks returned from Harpers Ferry to occupy Winchester with 11,000 men. Down South, Jackson destroyed bridges effectively, thereby delaying the Union pursuit, although several small clashes between the lead elements of Frémont's army and the Confederate rearguard erupted during the first days of the month. In the action near Harrisonburg on June 6, a cavalry force under Col. Turner Ashby, who nominally commanded the 7th Virginia Cavalry, attacked a Union force spread before them. His horse shot, Ashby dismounted and approached the battle line on foot. He was struck by a Minié bullet that entered on his right side above the hip, passed through his body diagonally, and exited near his left arm. Ashby died instantly and the Confederacy lost a promising cavalry leader, although not a brigadier general as most sources report; his commission as such was never confirmed by the Confederate Senate. Jackson himself wrote of Ashby that "as a partisan officer I never knew his superior."

By June 7, Jackson had cleverly destroyed the bridges over the flooded south fork of the Shenandoah River, which cut off communications between Frémont and Shields. His force of 15,000 had now withdrawn to the tiny farm

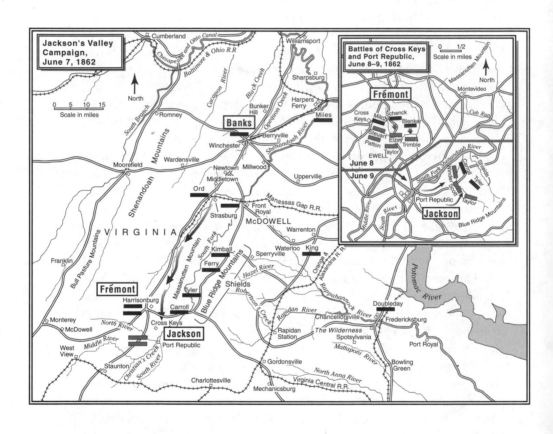

Jackson's Valley Campaign, June 7, 1862

Battles of Cross Keys and Port Republic, June 8–9, 1862

communities of Cross Keys and Port Republic, southeast of Harrisonburg, and he arrayed his forces along the roads and controlled the intact bridge between the two hamlets. Now Jackson faced one of the momentous decisions of his campaign: He might have simply marched southeast through Brown's Gap toward Charlottesville and safety, moving down to the Peninsula, where he was needed. Jackson, characteristically, decided not to take the easy way out but rather determined to try to defeat in detail the separated Union forces. Jackson originally planned on drawing Frémont into attacking Ewell on the 7th, but Frémont's temerity unraveled such a plan.

Events on June 8 reversed Jackson's plan and resulted in the battle of Cross Keys. A raid on Port Republic led by Col. Samuel S. Carroll set about from Conrad's Store with a cavalry force of 150 and infantry mostly consisting of the 7th Indiana. About 9 A.M. Carroll's force burst into the small town and completely surprised the Rebels, nearly capturing Jackson in the process. Jackson was on the western side of town at his headquarters, the G. W. Kemper House, Madison Hall, accompanied by a small number of staff officers. Federal artillery opened fire on the town shortly before the raiders entered, and to the startled Confederates, "Yankees seemed to be everywhere." Jackson hurriedly mounted his horse, Little Sorrel, dashed through the town, crossed the bridge over the North River, and made his way toward Cross Keys. Three of Jackson's staff officers—Ned Willis, Stapleton Crutchfield, and Hunter Holmes McGuire—were captured.

About this time, Jackson's plight was complicated further because Frémont attacked at Cross Keys, his battle line facing southward east of the town. Jackson suddenly had to contend with the possibility of that most unwanted of military situations, a battle on two fronts. As it turned out, Jackson's destruction of the bridges prevented the Union coordination that could have brought that event about. Frémont's 10,500 men were organized into the Germanic division of Brig. Gen. Louis Blenker, consisting of the brigades of Brig. Gens. Julius Stahel, Adolph W. A. F. von Steinwehr, and Henry Bohlen, along with three brigades commanded by Brig. Gens. Robert H. Milroy, Robert C. Schenck, and George D. Bayard. Ewell's 6,500 men faced Frémont and were organized west-east in a double line, with the front consisting of the brigades of Brig. Gens. George H. Steuart, Arnold Elzey, and Isaac R. Trimble; the secondary line consisted of the brigades of Col. John M. Patton and Brig. Gen. Richard Taylor. The battle of Cross Keys began with an artillery barrage, after which Blenker's division attempted to flank Ewell's right, which consisted of Trimble's brigade. Blenker's largely German regiments, composed almost entirely of New Yorkers, approached closely enough to open a short musketry fight before falling back. Trimble's men pursued the retreating Yankees over a mile of ground before being ordered to halt by about noon. Jackson forbade pressing the counterattack further, concerned about the scattered Federal forces around him. No more action occurred on this unusual day of battle.

Just after 7 A.M. the next morning Winder brought the old Stonewall Brigade into action just south of the south fork of the Shenandoah, and the battle of Port Republic was underway. The action was anything but well coordinated. Piecemeal attacks were thrust against the Union line, and heavy Federal artillery barrages inflicted casualties on Winder's brigade. In danger of a rout, Winder's men were finally supported by reinforcements from Ewell before their attack was halted. This reinforcement nearly arrived too late after troops encountered problems crossing the improvised bridge over the south fork of the Shenandoah. It was Taylor's brigade that came up in support on the right and fought through heavy thickets of laurel to focus fire on one of the most intensely active Federal batteries. The situation for the Confederate attack was teetering on disaster both on Winder's front and with Taylor's brigade, which had been struck heavily by artillery during three successive assaults. At a critical moment, Ewell ordered reinforcements forward with the 44th Virginia Infantry and 58th Virginia Infantry, which by 11 A.M. broke a portion of the line and captured 450 prisoners, 1 field piece, and about 800 small arms.

On the western side of the field, danger came anew in the form of lead elements from Frémont's force, which approached the south fork of the Shenandoah but were unable to cross because Trimble had burned the improvised bridge on his retreat. By late morning Tyler's men withdrew and the Confederates followed for only a short distance. Jackson then pulled out and concentrated his force at Brown's Gap, where he encamped until June 17, when he was ordered to move south to the Peninsula. The Union losses at Cross Keys and Port Republic were 181 killed, 836 wounded, and 685 missing, while Confederate losses were 139 killed, 951 wounded, and 60 missing. Thus, the last action of Jackson's storied Shenandoah Valley campaign of 1862 came to an end. Jackson's double victory at Cross Keys and Port Republic caused the Lincoln administration to cancel the movement of McDowell's Corps south in support of McClellan.

Curiously, Banks wrote on June 10 that "a dispatch from W[ashington] assures me that the President is engaged upon a plan for the defence of the Valley. Otherwise nothing new." At New Market a small fight erupted on June 13, but Jackson's brilliant campaign was over. In thirty-eight days Jackson's men had marched about 400 miles and confounded the Federal commanders in the Valley, thwarting Lincoln's plans for sending Banks and/or McDowell southward. Despite the fact that he was outnumbered, Jackson remained victorious throughout five battles. Jackson's sobriquet may have been coined at First Bull Run, but it was the Valley campaign that made him a legend. The campaign was followed daily with great emphasis in the

Southern papers, and Jackson became the preeminent hero among Southern generals. "I would rather be a private in such an Army than a Field Officer in any other Army," wrote one soldier. The English industrialist W. C. Corsan traveled through the South during this period and remarked on Jackson and his men. "Such heroism will inflame even cowards," he wrote, "and it falls on the fiery and reckless Southern soldiers like a spark on gunpowder. They may be annihilated, but the force does not exist on earth that can subdue them." The campaign produced fallout in the Union circles, as with Shields, who resigned. "I beg leave to tender my resignation as Brig. Genl. in the volunteer service of the United States," Shields tersely wrote the adjutant general on June 24. On the verso of the letter, Edwin Stanton simply wrote: "Accepted."

The Peninsular Campaign

Simultaneously with the Valley campaign, the Peninsular campaign was developing to the south. In front of Yorktown, Maj. Gen. George B. McClellan's long siege continued. McClellan had spent the entire month of April preparing to make a huge bombardment against Yorktown, where the Confederates were entrenched. The timid Federal commander planned the cannonade for May 5. He also waged war with his own War Department, asking for more reinforcements and additional ammunition and artillery and for naval support for a large combined operation that would follow the fall of Yorktown, the latter something he had failed to plan for before coming down to the Peninsula.

By the time McClellan made his final preparations to test the heavy siege guns he had brought down and placed in front of Yorktown, it was too late. The cagey commander of the Confederate Army of Northern Virginia, Gen. Joe Johnston, hastily pulled his men and matériel out of the Yorktown lines on May 3, withdrawing toward Richmond and covering his rear with the skilled cavalry of Brig. Gen. James E. B. Stuart. Chaos now prevailed. Scattering northwestward from the Warwick River line, Stuart's cavalry was chased by horse soldiers commanded by Union Brig. Gen. George Stoneman. Stoneman's pursuit reached fruition near the Halfway House, midway between Yorktown and Williamsburg, where Maj. Gen. James Longstreet's division, assembled as a rear guard, filed into a line of defenses that had been constructed earlier by Maj. Gen. John B. Magruder.

On May 5 the lead elements of Hooker's infantry division closed up in front of this line and attacked its center, Fort Magruder, from the east. In McClellan's absence from the field until late in the day, Brig. Gen. Edwin V. Sumner commanded the Yankee forces. Hooker's attack was forceful but after a short time was repulsed by Longstreet. Despite the muddy, nearly im-

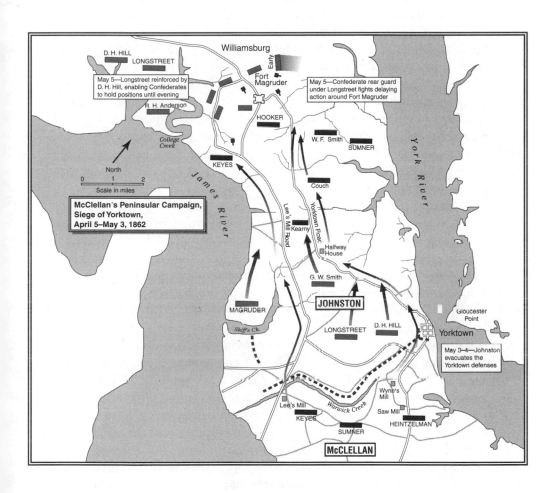

McClellan's Peninsular Campaign, Siege of Yorktown, April 5–May 3, 1862

D. H. HILL
LONGSTREET

May 5—Longstreet reinforced by D. H. Hill, enabling Confederates to hold positions until evening

R. H. Anderson

Williamsburg

Early

Fort Magruder

HOOKER

May 5—Confederate rear guard under Longstreet fights delaying action around Fort Magruder

College Creek

North

KEYES

W. F. Smith

SUMNER

York River

Scale in miles
0   1   2

James River

Lee's Mill Road

Couch

Kearny

Yorktown Road

Halfway House

G. W. Smith

MAGRUDER

JOHNSTON

Skiff's Ck.

LONGSTREET

D. H. HILL

Gloucester Point

Yorktown

May 3–4—Johnston evacuates the Yorktown defenses

Wynn's Mill

Warwick Creek

Lee's Mill

KEYES

Saw Mill

SUMNER

HEINTZELMAN

McCLELLAN

passable roads, Brig. Gen. Philip Kearny marched his brigade up in support of Hooker, and Maj. Gen. D. H. Hill's division swung over in support of Longstreet. About noon, Smith's division attacked Hill. Bloody fighting raged without either side gaining an advantage. "Well, I'm a one-armed Jersey son of a gun, follow me!" Kearny shouted above the din of battle. Nearby, Brig. Gen. Samuel P. Heintzelman, the 3d Corps commander, shouted vigorously at the passing men: "Give them hell God damn them, give the steel, don't wait to shoot." The decisive moment came early in the afternoon when the brigade of Brig. Gen. Winfield Scott Hancock enveloped the Confederate left, capturing two isolated redoubts and issuing an enfilading fire southward down Longstreet's line, holding the redoubts against Confederate counterattacks. As the fighting wound down with the approach of darkness, Longstreet pulled out and marched northwest toward Richmond along the Chickahominy River. He withdrew in good order and preserved the supply trains and artillery, which, given the almost impassable nature of the roads, was a heroic feat. Of the 40,768 Union men engaged in the battle, the losses were 456 killed, 1,410 wounded, and 373 missing. The Confederates employed 31,823 men, losing a total of 1,603 casualties.

McClellan claimed a victory in telegrams sent to the War Department, and he celebrated Williamsburg in a letter to his wife written the following day. "As soon as I came upon the field the men cheered like fiends," he wrote, "and I saw at once that I could save the day. I immediately reinforced Hancock and arranged to support Hooker, advanced the whole line across the woods, filled up the gaps, and got everything in hand for whatever might occur. The result was that the enemy saw that he was gone if he remained in his position, and scampered during the night." Yet in actuality McClellan had fumbled again. Rather than accompanying his army on the march and supervising the action, he had remained at Yorktown to oversee the organization of the amphibious movement to West Point up the York River. One at a time, the divisions of Brig. Gens. William B. Franklin, Fitz John Porter, John Sedgwick, and Israel B. Richardson would move by water and cut off Johnston's retreat up the Peninsula. McClellan's absence at the critical area of battle left sole direction to the senior corps commander, Sumner, who held at least half of his force out of the action, in true McClellan style.

Sound in concept, the notion of moving the divisions by water did not work in reality. McClellan's poor planning doomed the maneuver. Johnston learned about the movement and on May 7 sent the division of Maj. Gen. Gustavus W. Smith to head off Franklin's approach. The battle of West Point was a tactical victory for Smith and stalled the plan of moving more divisions for a glorious landing at West Point. McClellan had pushed past the Yorktown siege and could now move on Richmond. Continued rains made muddy roads worse than ever. The maps in the hands of the Federal army

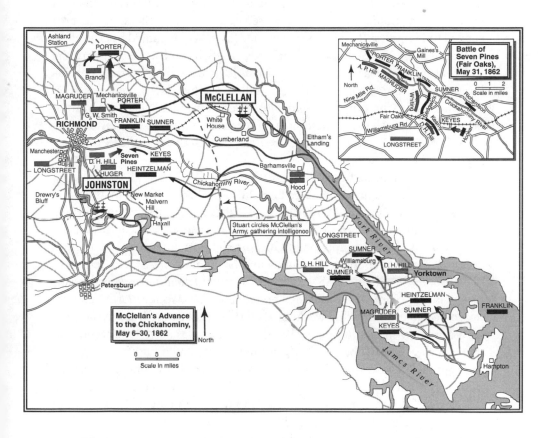

Ashland Station

PORTER

Branch

MAGRUDER   Mechanicsville
                PORTER
            G. W. Smith
RICHMOND   FRANKLIN   SUMNER

Manchester
                    Seven   KEYES
LONGSTREET D. H. HILL Pines
            HUGER   HEINTZELMAN
JOHNSTON
Drewry's   New Market
Bluff   Malvern
             Hill
             Haxall

Petersburg

McCLELLAN

White
House

Cumberland

Eltham's
Landing

Chickahominy River

Barhamsville
            Hood

Stuart circles McClellan's
Army, gathering intelligence

LONGSTREET
York River
        SUMNER

D. H. HILL   Williamsburg   D. H. HILL
        SUMNER   Yorktown

                    HEINTZELMAN
        MAGRUDER   SUMNER
            KEYES
                                FRANKLIN

James River

Hampton

**McClellan's Advance
to the Chickahominy,
May 6–30, 1862**

North

0   5   0
Scale in miles

**Battle of
Seven Pines
(Fair Oaks),
May 31, 1862**

Mechanicsville   Gaines's
                  Mill
        PORTER FRANKLIN
    A. P. Hill MAGRUDER
North
                        SUMNER
Nine Mile Rd.
                        Richardson
                    Chickahominy River
        Fair Oaks
        Williamsburg Rd.   KEYES
                    D. H.

LONGSTREET

0   1   2
Scale in miles

were poor. McClellan displayed his ability as an organizer but failed as a tactician. The troops still showed great affection for their commander, but by now they certainly must have wondered what was going on.

On May 9, Confederate forces evacuated the strategically crucial naval base at Norfolk, Virginia, near the site of the battle of the ironclads that had occurred in March. Faced with an increasingly menacing Federal force on the Peninsula across Hampton Roads, the Confederates found holding the increasingly isolated position untenable. Its loss was a significant blow for the Confederate operations in Virginia and northern North Carolina that would follow. Lincoln himself witnessed this action of the war. He proceeded to Hampton Roads by steamer on May 5, accompanied by Secretary of War Stanton and Secretary of the Treasury Salmon P. Chase, aboard the U.S. revenue cutter *Miami*. Lincoln wished to provide input to the Peninsular campaign, which appeared to have stalled. For five days Lincoln acted as commander-in-chief in the field and directed some operations toward Sewell's Point, such as the shelling of Confederate batteries on May 8 by the USS *Monitor,* USS *Dacotah,* USS *Naugatuck,* USS *Seminole,* and USS *Susquehanna.*

Lincoln identified a landing position near Willoughby Point, and on May 10, Yankee troops under Maj. Gen. John E. Wool, assisted by the naval forces of Capt. Louis M. Goldsborough, landed, and arrived in Norfolk, which contained 14,620 residents, late in the afternoon. The capture of the city and subsequent occupation of Gosport and Portsmouth forced another crisis for the Confederacy. The following day at about 5 A.M. Confederates blew up the formidable CSS *Virginia* off Craney Island to prevent its capture; without Norfolk, the ship had no tenable port. Wool reported capturing some 200 cannon in the works around the city. The facilities at the navy yard were in ruins, including the dry dock, which was partially burned, and many of the guns had been spiked, although a large amount of ammunition was captured. These operations "are regarded by the President as among the most important successes of the present war," wrote Stanton. "Thus perished the *Virginia*," Josiah Tattnall lamented, "and with her many highflown hopes of naval supremacy and success." The loss of the *Virginia* was not as serious as was the opening of the James River to Federal gunboats as far upriver as Drewry's Bluff, where Confederates had constructed fortifications and sunk a stone fleet to obstruct enemy ships from threatening Richmond, only seven miles to the north.

Taking advantage of the free river navigation, a Federal flotilla of five vessels, a small portion of the North Atlantic Blockading Squadron, steamed upriver to Drewry's Bluff near dawn on May 15. The ships were the ironclad gunboats USS *Monitor* (Lt. William N. Jeffers), the USS *Galena* (Comdr. John Rodgers), the screw gunboat USS *Aroostook,* the side-wheel gunboat USS *Port*

Royal, and the twin-screw ironclad USS *Naugatuck.* Awaiting any Federal penetration on the water were heavy batteries placed around the forts at Drewry's Bluff as well as gun pits manned by Confederate marines, sailors, and army troops. For nearly four hours a brisk battle between the Federal ships and batteries on land tested the mettle of each side. The *Galena* anchored about 600 yards away from Fort Darling at Drewry's Bluff and exchanged heavy fire with the fort's guns, which were elevated about 600 feet above the river and so could drop shells down with heavy force. The fort's guns consisted of heavy caliber pieces, some of the best long-range guns in the Confederacy. The fort's guns were sufficiently high that the naval pieces on shipboard could not be elevated enough to fire on them. Moreover, Jeffers found in attempting to maneuver the *Monitor* upriver "at the foot of the bluff in the river, an obstruction formed of sunken steamers and vessels secured with chains." The Confederate defenses were supervised by Comdr. Ebenezer Farrand and by Capt. Augustus H. Drewry of the 2d Virginia Artillery, for whom the bluff was renamed. The *Galena,* which fought heavily and was more or less stationary during much of the fight, took heavy damage. Rodgers reported that troops could be landed within ten miles of the city, a fact that was almost certainly true and if heeded by McClellan might have made a difference in the remaining part of the campaign. Instead, the Confederates would control this approach until the end of the war.

But a measure of alarm spread through the city. The heavy booming of the guns could be heard plainly, and life in Richmond already was becoming difficult due to shortages of supplies and common goods. "Oh, the extortioners!" noted the war clerk John B. Jones on May 23. "Meats of all kinds are selling at 50 cts. per pound; butter, 75 cts.; coffee, $1.50; tea, $10; boots, $30 per pair; shoes, $18; ladies' shoes, $15; shirts, $6 each." Joe Johnston was busy moving his army back across the Chickahominy and at some positions retreated to within three miles of Richmond. Few civilians were showing outright alarm, despite the close approach of the Yankees. The diarist Mary Chesnut, now living in Richmond, simply wrote, "Hope springs eternal in the Southern breast."

This tenuous situation for Southern morale and even for the Southern army received support from Jackson's activities in the Valley. Jackson's actions on May 23 at Front Royal and Banks's subsequent retreat nullified Lincoln's proposed movement of McDowell to reinforce McClellan. Lee, serving as military advisor to Davis, had foreseen this danger and worked with Jackson to effect a happy outcome. It marked a significant moment in the solidification of the Lee-Jackson relationship.

By the third week of May, McClellan had 105,000 men in position northeast of Richmond, and he outnumbered his enemy significantly; Johnston had about 60,000 defending the city. Still, McClellan handed away the initiative once again and was in typical fashion thwarted by the exaggerated intelligence figures provided by his network of scouts and spies, including the renowned Allan Pinkerton (who went by the alias Maj. E. J. Allen). McClellan typically received inaccurate reports of the enemy's strength, which were invariably raised rather than lowered relative to the facts, and the general commanding embellished the figures in his own mind when reporting to Washington. A convenient excuse was then established to delay further action.

Well to the west in the mountainous country of Virginia, an action occurred on May 16 and 17 at Princeton and along Wolf Creek, midway between Beckley and Wytheville. Confederate Brig. Gen. Humphrey Marshall brought 2,195 men and a single battery of artillery forward to cut the Union line of communication at Princeton, attempting to force the Federals away from their movement against the railroad. Marshall's force consisted of the 54th Virginia Infantry, the 29th Virginia Infantry, the 5th Kentucky Infantry (Brig. Gen. John S. Williams), and Bradley's Mounted Kentucky Rifles. The Federal commander, Brig. Gen. Jacob D. Cox, commanded the District of the Kanawha and was outside Princeton with a force of about 1,000. About noon on the 16th a detachment of Marshall's force skirmished with Col. Augustus C. Moor's 2d Provisional Brigade, inflicting heavy casualties on them, which consisted of the 28th Ohio Infantry, the 34th Ohio Infantry, and the 37th Ohio Infantry. The battle raged for three hours before the Confederates flanked the Union line and forced its withdrawal.

Cox ordered the town of Princeton held for as long as possible. By the morning of the 17th, Cox arrived with most of Moor's brigade and attacked the enemy's force south of Princeton, driving back Marshall's troops. The Confederates withdrew to an elevated and timbered ridge on which they placed the artillery battery, making a Federal attack difficult. By late in the day Cox learned that Williams had arrived, reinforcing Marshall. "I did not think it prudent to push the attack farther," wrote Cox, "but took my position on the outskirts of town, and awaited the arrival of Colonel [Eliakim P.] Scammon's brigade." By midevening Scammon arrived with the 1st Provisional Brigade, but early in the morning of the 18th, Cox slipped his force out of the area. The victory was celebrated by Marshall and Williams, who had lost only 4 killed and 12 wounded, and gained four wagons with assorted supplies at Princeton. The Federals, on the other hand, lost 23 killed, 69 wounded, and 21 missing in Moor's brigade alone.

Back on the Peninsula, skirmishing broke out between the lines at Bottom's Bridge, Turkey Island Creek Bridge, Mechanicsville, Hogan's, and Buckton Station on May 23. The following day minor actions erupted at New Bridge, Seven Pines, Mechanicsville, and Hanover Court House. On

May 26, Lincoln wrote McClellan: "What impression have you, as to in-trenchments—works—for you to contend with in front of Richmond? Can you get near enough to throw shells into the city?"

McClellan extended his line north of Richmond primarily because he anticipated McDowell joining him. This influenced him to select as a base of operations the White House on the Pamunkey River, a home owned at the time by Col. William Henry Fitzhugh "Rooney" Lee, Robert E. Lee's second son. The house and region surrounding was transformed into a supply base near which a railroad passed between West Point and Richmond and which afforded landings from the Pamunkey. Later on, McClellan offered a parcel of logic regarding his strange troop movements: He had wished to hold his army near the James River, but McDowell's long delays in moving down from Fredericksburg gave him no choice but to march north and spread a line of corps strung along the Chickahominy, a delicate assignment of posi-tions that placed his army in a relatively precarious and exposed state. Dur-ing the campaign, incidentally, Rooney Lee's White House would be burned by the retreating Yankees.

On May 27 preliminary skirmishing intensified, particularly with the set of actions known as Hanover Court House, Slash Church, Peake's Sta-tion, and Kinney's Farm. Two days earlier McClellan had ordered Brig. Gen. Fitz John Porter to take his 5th Corps on a movement north to Hanover Court House because McClellan believed a Rebel force there might endan-ger the right flank of the Union line. At 4 A.M. Porter departed from New Bridge with a force consisting of his 1st Division (Brig. Gen. George W. Morell), the 3d Brigade of Sykes's 2d Division (Col. Gouverneur K. Warren), and a composite brigade of cavalry with some artillery in tow led by Brig. Gen. William H. Emory. Opposing this Federal movement was the brigade of Brig. Gen. Lawrence O'Bryan Branch, consisting of 4,500 men, which had moved down from Gordonsville to protect the Virginia Central Railroad. Branch's force included the 18th North Carolina Infantry, the 28th North Carolina Infantry, the 37th North Carolina Infantry, and the 45th Georgia Infantry. During a driving rainstorm, the Federal column moved northward with Morell's division in the lead. They encountered Confederate resistance at Peake's Station, about four miles south of Hanover Court House, where Porter threw forward a line of skirmishers consisting of the 25th New York Infantry and the 1st U.S. Sharpshooters (Col. Hiram Berdan) to engage the enemy. The Confederates retreated toward Hanover Court House, and Porter ordered Brig. Gen. John H. Martindale forward with his 1st Brigade of Morell's division to push up the railroad, while Warren scattered cavalry forward to destroy bridges across the Pamunkey. When by midafternoon Porter approached Hanover Court House, however, he received the alarming news that Confederates were approaching to his rear. One Federal soldier recalled marching through "one broad mass of plastic mud knee deep, while the rain pelted us in torrents."

On returning to the battlefield south of town, by 5 P.M., Porter found Martindale's Brigade in heavy action, along with brigades of Col. James McQuade and Brig. Gen. Daniel Butterfield, engaged in a hot fight with the Confederates under Branch. Together, the brigades drove the Rebel forces south toward Ashland by darkness, and the next day they simply took stock of the battle, cared for casualties, and buried a reported 200 Confederate dead left on the field. The Federals also captured 730 prisoners, while they lost 62 killed, 223 wounded, and 70 missing.

The action at Hanover Court House was a mere prelude to the major engagements to come. Johnston knew that with McDowell on his way (he had no way to know anything but to anticipate McDowell's arrival as a logical consequence of Federal strategy), time was not on his side. He should strike at McClellan's army soon, and particularly while it was in an exposed, somewhat illogical disposition. So Johnston planned to attack McClellan on May 29 north of the Chickahominy rather than await further developments. The day before the attack, however, Johnston learned that McDowell was on his way to the Shenandoah Valley. This now caused a quick reassessment of his own tactical plans, and Johnston now decided to attack the most vulnerable isolated corps of the Federal army, the 4th Corps.

The result was the battle of Fair Oaks, also called Seven Pines, which took place over two days, May 31 and June 1. It was the largest and costliest action yet in the Peninsular campaign. At this time McClellan's Army of the Potomac had the following organization: 2d Corps, Brig. Gen. Edwin V. Sumner (divisions of Brig. Gens. Israel B. Richardson and John Sedgwick); 3d Corps, Brig. Gen. Samuel P. Heintzelman (divisions of Brig. Gens. Joseph Hooker and Philip Kearny); 4th Corps, Brig. Gen. Erasmus D. Keyes (divisions of Brig. Gens. Darius N. Couch and Silas Casey); 5th Corps, Brig. Gen. Fitz John Porter (divisions of Brig. Gens. George W. Morell and George Sykes); and 6th Corps, Brig. Gen. William B. Franklin (divisions of Brig. Gens. Henry W. Slocum and William F. Smith). Heintzelman had been given joint command of the 3d and 4th Corps. Johnston's Army of Northern Virginia consisted of the Right Wing, Maj. Gen. James Longstreet (divisions of Brig. Gen. Richard H. Anderson, commanding Longstreet's division, Maj. Gen. D. H. Hill, and Brig. Gen. Benjamin Huger); and Left Wing, Maj. Gen. Gustavus W. Smith (divisions of Brig. Gen. William H. C. Whiting, commanding Smith's division, and Maj. Gen. A. P. Hill); Maj. Gen. John B. Magruder commanded the reserve (divisions of Brig. Gens. Lafayette McLaws and David R. Jones).

McClellan moved his corps into position along the northeastern bank of the Chickahominy with Porter to the north, along Beaver Dam Creek, Franklin to his left, then Sumner, and finally Heintzelman down across the Richmond & York River Railroad with the Federal left near the confluence of the Chickahominy and White Oak Swamp Creek. Keyes had taken the 4th Corps out in advance of the Union line and exposed it to attack, marching up to Fair Oaks Station on the rail line. Keyes deployed the division of Casey in front and Couch in the rear. About a mile south of this position was the lush area known as Seven Pines, named for seven pine trees that distinctly stood together in a clump. Distinctive twin houses stood on the battlefield, a sight that many a soldier would recall for years to come. Johnston planned to strike Keyes with Longstreet's Right Wing, while A. P. Hill and Magruder kept the forces north of the river distracted and lightly engaged. Longstreet would attack from three sides, with his own division commanded by Anderson approaching from the west along the Nine Mile Road, from the southwest, Huger's division would strike from the Charles City Road, and from the west, D. H. Hill would attack along the Williamsburg Road. This pincer movement would crush Keyes's isolated corps and allow Johnston to turn to the other corps later, defeating them in detail. Also playing a role was Whiting, whose division was posted at Old Tavern, between Fair Oaks Station and the right flank of the Union army, to thwart any attempt by Yankee infantry from crossing the river and aiding Keyes. To make matters worse for the Yankees, McClellan was ill with dysentery and confined to bed at New Bridge, "not thinking clearly," and recent heavy rains had swollen the Chickahominy and other rivers and made roads difficult to use.

What began on May 31 as an excellent opportunity for the Army of Northern Virginia turned into a series of mistimings and misunderstandings. A. P. Hill and Magruder faced the right of the Federal line, Porter and Franklin. But Longstreet took the wrong road, marching part of his command down the Charles City Road away from Keyes. This threw off the timing of D. H. Hill's and Huger's advances toward Seven Pines along the Williamsburg Road, intermixing some of the units into a large area between the Williamsburg and Charles City roads and delaying any coherent attack until about 1 P.M. By then Union forces were in part aware of a large Confederate movement, and when D. H. Hill attacked headlong into Keyes's line, the Federals were partly ready for it. The attacks that took place during the afternoon were largely piecemeal affairs that were poorly coordinated: Of the 13 brigades on the Confederate right flank, no more than four were engaged at any given time, and seven were not used on the battle's first day. Hill's attacks through soggy, forested landscape slowly made progress against the Yankee lines, especially the brigades of Brig. Gens. Samuel Garland, Jr., Robert E. Rodes, and Gabriel J. Rains, and Col. George B. Anderson. Despite the Union intelligence and steadfast fighting, however, Keyes's isolated corps appeared to be losing the fight as the afternoon waned. Longstreet supported Hill's attack, pushing back Keyes and the hard-fighting division of Phil Kearny. But the issue wasn't yet decided. As he moved up in support of Hill, Whiting was assaulted with heavy force between Fair Oaks Station and the Chickahominy by the fresh division of John Sedgwick, which had crossed Grapevine Bridge and joined the fight after being ordered forward by Sumner.

The Confederate attack received a boost from Col. Micah Jenkins's Brigade (Anderson), which successfully supported Hill's position, and Longstreet effectively deployed the brigades of Brig. Gen. Cadmus M. Wilcox and Col. James L. Kemper along the Williamsburg Road, with the brigades of Brig. Gens. Raleigh E. Colston and Roger A. Pryor on the Confederate right flank. Large-scale maneuvering also characterized the Federal side of the fight at Fair Oaks. A large portion of Brig. Gen. Henry M. Naglee's brigade commenced a strong attack with bayonets that eased the fire against the artillery of Casey's division and enabled the creation of a secondary line of battle. With the right flank endangered, Couch led an attack comprised of the 7th Massachusetts Infantry and 62d New York Infantry to bolster the sagging defensive line of the 23d Pennsylvania Infantry and the 61st Pennsylvania Infantry. Confederate attacks collapsed this flank, however, sending Couch reeling back to Fair Oaks to avoid capture. Kearny's division supported the attack by moving across Bottom's Bridge to support the line. Now Casey attempted a significant attack to regain some of the ground lost earlier, supported by the brigades of Brig. Gens. Hiram G. Berry and Charles D. Jameson, but this assault failed in the face of a stinging counterattack. Keyes attacked across a field with the 10th Massachusetts Infantry, enabling the tenuous third Yankee line to stay in place. But by nightfall the action ceased, with only scattered musket shots ringing out across the rain-soaked landscape, disaster for Keyes's corps having been narrowly averted.

What might have been a strong Confederate victory was poorly carried out, and the confusion stemmed primarily from Longstreet's actions as Right Wing commander. It was one of the few times during the war in which this officer displayed poor leadership. About dusk, another calamity struck the Confederate effort. While mounted on his horse, Johnston was struck in the right shoulder by a musket ball, and moments later a shell fragment hit him in the chest. He fell unconscious from his horse and was taken to an aid station about a quarter mile away from the front, where it was determined that his right shoulder blade and two ribs had been broken. After a surgeon dressed the commanding general's wounds, Johnston was taken to Richmond to recover. The wound caused protracted illness, and that evening Maj. Gen. Gustavus W. Smith was placed in command of the Army of Northern Virginia. Near the same time as Johnston's wounding, another noted Confederate officer was struck, but this time with grave results. Col. Robert H. Hatton, a native Ohioan who had led Tennessee troops through western Virginia during the early days of the war, was killed instantly when struck by a Minié bullet as he led a charge. (Hatton is often termed a brigadier general, but his nomination as such was not confirmed by the C.S. Senate.) Brig. Gen. J. Johnston Pettigrew and Col. John Bratton were both wounded and captured.

One of the Union casualties was Brig. Gen. Oliver O. Howard, who received a wound in the right arm that necessitated amputation. "I hereby certify that ... he is unfit for duty," wrote Surg. Gideon S. Palmer at Fair Oaks about Howard. The same day Howard sought time to recover, writing, "I have the honor to apply for a leave of absence for sixty days, on account of a severe wound received in the action of yesterday," and signing the manuscript with a shaky, left-handed signature.

Smith's command of the army led him to order an attack for the next morning, but this action was weakly supported and resulted in no gain for the Confederate forces. Two new faces arrived on the battlefield on June 1, those of McClellan and, from his office in Richmond, Gen. Robert E. Lee. McClellan now considered himself sufficiently recovered to supervise activities in the field. The action of the previous day had been managed in an amateurish way, however, with the exception of Sumner's bold move to send Sedgwick across the river. Concerned over the impending disaster that lay before the Confederate nation, Lee assumed command of the army from Smith, who had directed it for less than one day. Lee's assignment as commander of the Army of Northern Virginia would begin a partnership that established the core of Confederate legend. "General Lee had up to this time accomplished nothing to warrant the belief in his future greatness as a commander," as Col. Evander M. Law, who commanded Whiting's brigade at Fair Oaks, wrote. "The general tone, however, was one of confidence, which was invariably strengthened by a sight of the man himself."

Each side claimed victory. "The heroism shown at Seven Pines has had a most wonderful influence upon the subsequent battles around Richmond," D. H. Hill wrote in his report of the engagement. "After this decisive victory, under such disadvantageous circumstances, not a brigade in the ranks seemed to entertain the remotest doubt of our ultimate success over the besieging army of the Yankees." For McClellan's part, the day after he arrived on the field, he sent this comment to his wife, "I am tired of the sickening sight of the battlefield, with its mangled corpses & poor suffering wounded! Victory has no charms for me when purchased at such cost."

Astonishingly, given the chaos and accidental development of the battle, almost the same number of men fought on each side—41,797 Federals and 41,816 Confederates. Over the two days of battle, 790 Union soldiers were killed, 3,594 wounded, and 647 missing; Confederate casualties amounted to 980 killed, 4,749 wounded, and 405 missing. After all the blood-shed, virtually nothing had changed. McClellan was still within a few miles of Richmond, and his force greatly outnumbered that of the defending Confederates, who now found themselves under the command of Gen. Robert E. Lee. This was not the Lee of legend yet, but an officer who had been a failure in western Virginia early in the war, unable to stop the Federal successes on the Carolina coast, and a veteran of his desk job advising President Davis for only a few weeks.

Following the battle, McClellan moved nearly all his army to the south side of the Chickahominy, probably where he should have been to begin with, except for Fitz John Porter's 5th Corps, which was detached to guard the line of communications running to the White House on the Pamunkey. The weather remained bad, with frequent rains keeping the roads in poor shape until about June 20. Though he was goaded by the War Department and by President Lincoln, McClellan initiated no attack during the first three weeks of June. The soldiers dug in and tried to get used to life in a swampy rain forest in an alien land, making the best of it.

A characteristic pattern of aggressive Confederate leadership—one that would mark the Army of Northern Virginia for months to come—now emerged from Robert E. Lee. Correctly believing himself significantly out-numbered, Lee took the initiative because he believed the situation was desperate enough to require it. Lee planned a series of offensive operations that would dislodge the groggy McClellan from his position close to Richmond, and to pull this off he would need to bring Jackson south from the Valley to unite him with the Army of Northern Virginia. Lee tentatively planned to attack McClellan south of the Chickahominy while Jackson moved to surprise Porter on the north bank. On June 12, Lee sent his cavalry commander, Brig. Gen. James E. B. Stuart, now known throughout the army as "Jeb," on a mission to gather intelligence by riding northward. Stuart took it upon him-self to ride circuitously around the entire Union army; after reaching a point near Hanover Court House he turned eastward, harassed only slightly by Federal cavalry under Brig. Gen. George Stoneman, and rode his troopers hard along the south bank of the Pamunkey to New Kent Court House, where he turned south, crossed the Chickahominy, turned west and rode through Charles City Court House, south of Malvern Hill, through New Market, and back within the Richmond lines. The spectacular ride around the Federal army accomplished little, however, and this first celebrated raid of the war offered little of military value. Nonetheless, it provided a psycho-logical edge in the newspapers of the day when Stuart and his 1,000 horse-men returned to his army on June 15. Stuart's troopers did capture some prisoners and destroy some property during their 150-mile odyssey. They also alerted McClellan that he needed to change his base. On June 18 the

Federal commander ordered transports loaded and began to move his supply base south to the James River.

This unexpected result forced Lee to alter his plan of attack significantly and made it even riskier than it had been. Lee now set most of his army into motion across the Chickahominy and devised a plan to attack McClellan's north flank, and he ordered Jackson south from the Valley. Jackson halted briefly at Ashland Station, north of the city, on June 25. Lee now embraced the doctrine by which he would maneuver his army; time did not favor his cause. He would need to act quickly and avoid a war of attrition. Lee's boldness in attacking a superior force was viewed as a necessity, especially with the opposing army so close to his political and psychological epicenter. He left Magruder and Huger in front of the main Federal line; their danger would in reality be minimal, he reasoned, because of the undue caution displayed by McClellan.

When on June 24 it became clear that Jackson had moved south out of the Shenandoah Valley, the entire Federal high command believed that he was about to launch an attack against Porter's relatively isolated corps. Once again, McClellan approached action before retreating. He had organized a small-scale attack in the vicinity of the Fair Oaks battlefield for June 25, but now, with Jackson posing imminent danger, he reflected on whether he should reinforce or protect Porter by launching a grand assault against the Confederate lines to his west. Again McClellan waited, this time another day, and once again, as he had during the whole campaign, he handed the initiative to his Confederate counterpart.

The next phase of the campaign would become the decisive one, and it would offer to Gen. Robert E. Lee the first test of bringing the Army of Northern Virginia into battle. Beginning on June 25 and carrying over the following week was a series of battles known as the Seven Days. Though confused and poorly executed at turns on both sides, these critical actions would decide the fate of Richmond. They offered the Union the opportunity to close the war rather quickly. The tactical and strategic decisions to come, as well as the quality of execution on the field, would play into the fortunes of nearly 180,000 men on both sides and the whole civilian population on each side. The Seven Days battles represented a critical turning point of the war.

Lee's army consisted of Maj. Gen. Thomas J. Jackson's command, fresh from the Valley, which in turn held the divisions of Jackson himself, commanded by Brig. Gen. Charles S. Winder, those of Maj. Gen. Richard S. Ewell, Brig. Gen. William H. C. Whiting, and Maj. Gen. D. H. Hill. The second primary component of Lee's army was Maj. Gen. A. P. Hill's so-called Light Division, a large, crack division that was so named because it traveled light and prided itself on quick marches and heavy action. It held the brigades of Brig. Gens. Charles W. Field, Maxcy Gregg, Joseph R. Anderson, Lawrence O'Bryan Branch, James J. Archer, and William Dorsey Pender. Comprising an experienced portion of the army was Maj. Gen. James Longstreet's division, which consisted of the brigades of Brig. Gens. James L. Kemper, Richard H. Anderson, George E. Pickett, Cadmus M. Wilcox, Roger A. Pryor, and Winfield Scott Featherston. (Longstreet was also in command of A. P. Hill's division.) Maj. Gen. John B. Magruder's command consisted of the divisions of Maj. Gen. Lafayette McLaws, Brig. Gen. David R. Jones, and Magruder's own division, commanded by Brig. Gen. Howell Cobb. Maj. Gen. Benjamin Huger's division held the brigades of Brig. Gens. William Mahone, Ambrose R. Wright, Lewis A. Armistead, and Robert Ransom, Jr. Lastly, Maj. Gen. Theophilus H. Holmes's division consisted of the brigades of Brig. Gens. Junius Daniel, John G. Walker, Henry A. Wise, and the cavalry brigade of Brig. Gen. Jeb Stuart.

McClellan's organization had changed little since Yorktown and Fair Oaks. Brig. Gen. Edwin V. Sumner's 2d Corps consisted of the divisions of Brig. Gens. Israel B. Richardson and John Sedgwick. The 3d Corps, commanded by Brig. Gen. Samuel P. Heintzelman, held the divisions of Brig. Gens. Joseph Hooker and Philip Kearny. Brig. Gen. Erasmus D. Keyes's 4th Corps comprised the divisions of Brig. Gens. Darius N. Couch and John J. Peck. The 5th Corps, commanded by Brig. Gen. Fitz John Porter, had the divisions of Brig. Gens. George W. Morell and George Sykes, and the 3d Division of Pennsylvania Reserves commanded by Brig. Gen. George A. McCall. Brig. Gen. William B. Franklin's 6th Corps consisted of the divisions of Brig. Gens. Henry W. Slocum and William F. Smith. Troops held in reserve included the cavalry reserve (Brig. Gen. Philip St. George Cooke, Jeb Stuart's father-in-law) and a command at White House under Brig. Gen. Silas Casey.

The battle lines defending Richmond stretched in a north-south direction with Jackson to the north, below which were arrayed Longstreet, D. H. Hill, A. P. Hill, Magruder, and Huger. Lee dispatched some 65,500 men on the northern side of the Chickahominy to meet an attack from that area, leaving only 25,000 south of the river. Again, Lee, feeling the desperation of the moment, employed unusual tactics. The Federal lines consisted of Porter's 5th Corps to the north, and in southward order Franklin's 6th Corps, Sumner's 2d Corps, Heintzelman's 3d Corps, and Keyes's 4th Corps. Porter had about 30,000 men in the northern sector of the Federal lines; McClellan's remaining 60,000 were scattered to the south. While these dispositions were being made in anticipation of the major battles to come, the first of the Seven Days' battles took place on June 25 and was known as Oak Grove. The battle resulted from McClellan's order to Heintzelman to drive the pickets out of his front. The action began at about 8 A.M. when Hooker's division marched westward along the Williamsburg Road, led by the brigades of Brig.

Gens. Daniel E. Sickles and Cuvier Grover, with Col. Joseph B. Carr's brigade held in reserve. McClellan ordered the pickets of Kearny's and Richardson's divisions to assist the movement on either side of the column. The attack was pushed forward but stopped after some heavy opposition from Huger's men. The brigade of Brig. Gen. David B. Birney came to Hooker's assistance but was unable to break the Confederate resistance.

McClellan's chief of staff (and father-in-law), Col. Randolph B. Marcy, arrived on the field and ordered Hooker to pull out to his previous position. About 1 P.M., however, McClellan himself arrived on the field and with un-characteristic boldness ordered the attack repeated, this time supported by Brig. Gen. Innis N. Palmer's brigade and the 3d Corps artillery batteries of Capt. Gustavus A. De Russy, which struck Huger's men with repeated firings of canister at close range. This last attack drove away Huger's pickets and Federal troops flooded into the vacant battlefield, but by now it was nearly dark and the action was halted for the day without decisive results. The Federal casualties at Oak Grove were 51 killed, 401 wounded, and 64 missing, while Huger's Confederates suffered 40 killed, 263 wounded, and 13 missing. In the end, McClellan's attack accomplished little change in the battle lines and did not thwart Lee's plan to attack on a larger scale the next day.

Lee's attack was planned on June 23 at a council with his subordinates. He would assign Jackson to attacking Porter's right flank early on the morning of June 26 and A. P. Hill would simultaneously move from Meadow Bridge, evacuate any scattered Union forces or pickets from the area of Mechanicsville, and then move to Beaver Dam Creek, which flows into the Chickahominy, to move up to the line of Federal trenches. Following this spearhead by A. P. Hill, Longstreet and D. H. Hill would pass through Mechanicsville in support of the previous movements and offer battle. Simultaneous with these actions, Huger and Magruder would produce enough flurry on their fronts to distract McClellan from divining Lee's real intentions. The result would be that Porter would be overwhelmed from two sides, his right flank crushed, and the two leading divisions would then move on Cold Harbor and cut McClellan's communications with White House Landing, seriously jeopardizing his ability to continue the campaign. As with many of his battle plans, and perhaps understandably since it came from a skilled engineer, Lee's plan was complex and required a capable execution on all fronts in order to work successfully. It also anticipated a certain amount of failure on the part of Porter; Lee expected him to pull out of his trenches when attacked on the flank rather than to dig in and force the Confederates to assault the Union position. In theory, the plan was masterful if overly complex; in practice, it was horribly bungled. The result was the second action of the Seven Days, the battle of Mechanicsville.

On the morning of June 26 McCall's division was arrayed along Beaver

Dam Creek with the brigade of Brig. Gen. John F. Reynolds to the north, that of Brig. Gen. George G. Meade in the center, and the brigade of Brig. Gen. Truman Seymour to the south, terminating at the junction of the creek and the Chickahominy River. The line stretched over about two and a half miles. Spread along a distance of about three miles on the north bank of the Chick-ahominy, adjoining the end of Seymour's line, was Sykes's division. Morell's division was held in reserve, although one brigade had been posted opposite New Bridge, north of the river.

The Confederate maneuvers were to begin at 3 A.M., with Jackson leaving Ashland and meeting up at Half Sink with Branch's brigade. But at this crucial time Jackson was, uncharacteristically, not equal to the task. His lead columns got underway so late that they didn't reach Merry Oaks on the Virginia Central Railroad, a rendezvous point, until about 9 A.M., which was nearly six hours behind schedule. About 3 P.M. Jackson's lead elements began to arrive near Totopotomoy Creek, still north of the action. A. P. Hill, meanwhile, had grown impatient for the missing Jackson and began his attack without orders. Heavy combat resulted by late afternoon, with small-arms fire crackling through the swampy terrain, and where it was possible to post guns on the still unmanageable roads, Hill fired heavy cannonades. McCall's division fought briskly against Hill's attack, with some of the heaviest action yet on the Peninsula erupting by about 5 P.M. Porter threw in as reinforcements the brigades of Brig. Gens. John H. Martindale and Charles Griffin and extended and strengthened his right flank, now the focus of the action. But he fell back and concentrated along Beaver Dam Creek and at Ellison's Mill.

Astonishingly, Jackson with his command arrived at Pole Green Church, a mere three miles northeast of where the battle was now furiously underway, but failed miserably at improvising the details of the day. He did not find A. P. Hill or D. H. Hill, and so inexplicably did nothing. Late in the afternoon, with a major battle raging within earshot, he ordered his command to bivouac for the evening. Longstreet and D. H. Hill had moved into position behind A. P. Hill, and shortly thereafter Lee himself arrived on the field and ordered A. P. Hill to hold his ground and stop any further advance. A. P. Hill misinterpreted the spirit of this order, however, and attacked on his left with the brigades of Pender and Brig. Gen. Roswell S. Ripley; this desperate attempt was beaten back with heavy casualties. Musketry rattled through the woods and along the creeks for another three hours, dying down by about 9 P.M., and artillery fire harassed each side's redistributed troops until 10 P.M., when the battle ended. The Confederates held most of their ground; Morell was ordered back to Gaines's Mill, north of his position during the battle. About 15,631 Federal soldiers and 16,356 Confederates had been actively engaged this day. The Union casualties at Mechanicsville were 49 killed, 207 wounded, and 105 missing; Confederate losses were 1,484 combined. The day was not a Confederate fiasco, however: on the southern part of the line, Huger and Magruder fought creditably, and convinced McClellan they must have been far more than the 25,000 they actually were. Although Hooker and Kearny were ripe for further action, the Confederate fighting to the south altered McClellan's thinking about his available options on the following days. The weak link was Jackson, whose performance was derelict, and historians have proposed a variety of explanations for it, although it remains difficult to justify. Perhaps mental and physical exhaustion from his triumphs in the Valley remains the safest line of reasoning. Jackson's poor performance on the Peninsula would not be limited to a single day or action, however: three more times during the Seven Days battles Stonewall Jackson would exhibit lethargic, incompetent command behavior.

Porter's outcome at Mechanicsville seemed a nominal victory, yet he was still heavily outnumbered, and Lee hoped to reopen the attack the following day. The third of the Seven Days battles, fought on June 27, would be known as Gaines's Mill, alternatively as First Cold Harbor, or the Chickahominy. It would be the heaviest-fought battle yet on the Peninsula. The Federal line now was concentrated into a semicircle with the forces south of the Chickahominy essentially holding their positions but Porter collapsing his line into an east-west salient north of the river, with McCall east of Duane's Bridge, Morell and Sykes to his north. Porter was now ordered to hold Gaines's Mill at all costs to enable McClellan to change his base to the James River. McClellan ruminated over the possibilities after being urged by several subordinates to attack Magruder, but in the end he did nothing once again, fearing vast numbers in the Confederate army before him.

Early on June 27, A. P. Hill resumed his attack against the Federal positions along Beaver Dam Creek but he now found them lightly defended, with a small force that delayed his motion toward the bulk of Porter's corps. Gregg's brigade fought stubbornly through the thickets and approached Gaines's Mill, where a determined regiment, the 9th Massachusetts Infantry, fought and stalled Gregg's onrushing Confederates. By early afternoon Hill's main battle line was stopped cold by a considerable force of Porter's deployed along Boatswain's Creek, near the Sarah Watt House, which served as Porter's headquarters. The swampy terrain in this area posed a major obstacle for coordinating Confederate attacks. Assaults made by the brigades of Gregg, Pender, Anderson, and Branch all failed after pressing partially into the difficult terrain under heavy fire of musketry.

Longstreet arrived to A. P. Hill's south, foresaw the difficulty of attacking into such ground, and delayed on Lee's orders until Jackson could come up on Hill's left. Again, however, Jackson was late and his delay complicated the plan for Confederate success. D. H. Hill attacked the Federal right, en-

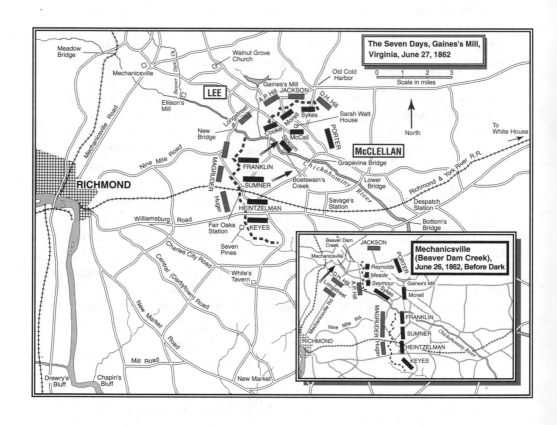

The Seven Days, Gaines's Mill, Virginia, June 27, 1862

0 1 2 3
Scale in miles

North

Meadow Bridge

Mechanicsville

Walnut Grove Church

Old Cold Harbor

Gaines's Mill

LEE

Ellison's Mill

A.P. Hill

JACKSON

D.H. Hill

Sarah Watt House

Morell

Sykes

Cooke

McCall

New Bridge

Slocum

PORTER

To White House

Beaver Dam Ck.

Mechanicsville Road

MAGRUDER

Longstreet

Nine Mile Road

FRANKLIN

Chickahominy River

McCLELLAN

Grapevine Bridge

Richmond & York River R.R.

RICHMOND

Huger

SUMNER

Boatswain's Creek

Lower Bridge

Despatch Station

Williamsburg Road

HEINTZELMAN

Savage's Station

Bottom's Bridge

Fair Oaks Station

KEYES

Seven Pines

White's Tavern

Charles City Road

Central (Darbytown) Road

New Market Road

Mill Road

Drewry's Bluff

Chapin's Bluff

New Market

Mechanicsville (Beaver Dam Creek), June 26, 1862, Before Dark

Beaver Dam Creek

JACKSON

PORTER

Mechanicsville

Reynolds

Meade

Seymour

Gaines's Mill

D.H. Hill

A.P. Hill

Sykes

Morell

Longstreet

Mechanicsville Rd.

MAGRUDER

FRANKLIN

Huger

SUMNER

Chickahominy

Nine Mile Rd.

RICHMOND

HEINTZELMAN

KEYES

countering hardy soldiers under Sykes, and backed off also awaiting Jackson's assistance in strengthening the assault. The intensity of the fight along the Confederate right was increasing, and so Longstreet was ordered to conduct a diversionary attack to stabilize the lines until Jackson could arrive and attack from the north. In Longstreet's attack, Pickett's brigade attacked headlong but was beaten back under severe fire with a considerable loss. Jackson, meanwhile, was still en route. Having left Walnut Grove Church on his way to Old Cold Harbor, Jackson's enlightenment that he would pass through Gaines's Mill caused him to order a countermarch of four miles away from that position. He finally reached the position of D. H. Hill by 3 P.M., and then only in total confusion. He believed Longstreet's attack was under way or imminent, and so pulled his own command and those of D. H. Hill out of the fight so they would not be struck by friendly fire. Jackson finally attacked by 4:30 P.M., after he received a series of messages from Lee. Again, Jackson botched his assignment.

On the Federal side, Slocum's division moved into position and helped to bolster Porter's line, staving off disaster. "Dashing across the intervening plains, floundering in the swamps, and struggling against the tangled brushwood, brigade after brigade seemed almost to melt away before the concentrated fire of our infantry and artillery," wrote Fitz John Porter. But shortly before darkness fell, the Confederates mounted another semicoordinated attack that unleashed a heavy barrage of musketry and artillery fire, and the Federal line collapsed. Brig. Gen. John Bell Hood's Texas Brigade smashed into the Federal line, punching a gap, as did Pickett's brigade, which had failed earlier in the day. As Porter considered his routes of retreat, the brigades of Brig. Gens. Thomas F. Meagher and William H. French arrived, but too late to help. They did assist in acting as a rear guard during the withdrawal, an action in which Sykes's regulars fought with great valor, and in which Capt. Charles J. Whiting's battalion of 5th U.S. Cavalry was cut to pieces and mostly surrendered.

As with the previous day, diversionary attacks were made south of the Chickahominy to continue fooling McClellan. Magruder again skillfully pulled off this feat, with only minor fighting at Fair Oaks and elsewhere, holding 60,000 Yankee troops fixed in place while the heavier action occurred north of the river. By 4 A.M. on June 28, Porter had withdrawn across the Chickahominy, burning the bridges behind him. For the Confederacy, the victory at Gaines's Mill seemed to mark a real turning point in the psychology of the Peninsular campaign. The skedaddle by the Federal troops to a position south of the river seemed to signal a relief of the pressure on Richmond, and despite the uncoordinated tactics, the failure of Jackson, and the inability to follow up and pursue Porter after breaking his line, a weight seemed to be lifted from the shoulders of the Army of Northern Virginia.

The fighting at Gaines's Mill had been intense. Of 34,214 engaged, Federal casualties amounted to 894 killed, 3,107 wounded, and 2,836 missing (mostly captured), while of 57,018 engaged, Confederate losses were about 8,751 total. The scale of the fight had also been larger than ever before for most participants. "Going on to the field, I picked up a tent and slung it across my shoulder," remembered Oliver W. Norton, a soldier in the 83rd Pennsylvania Infantry. "The folds of that stopped a ball that would have passed through me. I picked it out, put it in my pocket, and, after firing sixty rounds of my own and a number of wounded comrade's cartridges, I came off the field unhurt, and ready, but not anxious, for another fight."

Another fight would indeed come the next day. This time the circumstances would be different, and Porter would not be expected to fight alone for two days while McClellan held the bulk of his army in place. As the fighting was winding down at Gaines's Mill, McClellan ordered his base of operations changed to the James River. He then panicked, perhaps hearing of the inevitable retreat of Porter across the river, ordering the entire Army of the Potomac to pull out of their trenches and move toward the new base. It marked a new and heightened level of illogical thinking for George McClellan. The situation in fact still favored McClellan greatly. He had not even brought four of his five army corps into action, and Porter's corps had fought extremely well against long odds. Moreover, the War Department created a new assignment for Maj. Gen. John Pope, commanding the newly formed Army of Virginia, and ordered it to be organized (with the forces of McDowell, Banks, and Frémont) and sent to McClellan to reinforce him further. By solidifying his base on the James and turning to fight Lee, McClellan would have put himself in a position of strength; instead, he again surrendered the initiative to the Confederates. On the day of this decision, McClellan, now clearly in psychological turmoil, sent a famous message to Edwin M. Stanton updating the secretary of war on his movements, and included the astonishing statement: "If I save this Army now I tell you plainly that I owe no thanks to you or any other persons in Washington—you have done your best to sacrifice this Army." Fearing the secretary's reaction, the supervisor of military telegraphic messages, Edward S. Sanford—the chief censor—deleted this sentence before giving it to Stanton. Also on this day, Lincoln wrote to Seward, stating: "I expect to maintain this contest until successful, or till I die, or am conquered, or my term expires, or Congress or the country forsakes me."

The contest had a long way to go. McClellan now ordered Erasmus Keyes's 4th Corps to move west of Glendale and protect the Federal army's withdrawal. McClellan ordered Porter to move to the high ground at Malvern Hill to secure a key defensive position north of the C-shaped bend in the James. The supply trains were then ordered to move south toward the river, and McClellan himself departed without assigning any officer to command in his absence and without specifying any exact routes of withdrawal. McClellan vacated his position of command on the Peninsula with more major battles to come, wherein he would neither be present nor direct the action. The first such action was a relatively minor one, the fourth in the Seven Days group, designated Garnett's Farm or Golding's Farm. Fought on June 28, the engagement was a continuation of the battle of Gaines's Mill. As an outgrowth of Magruder's diversionary attacks, Col. George T. Anderson was sent forward to attack the Union right flank while, on Anderson's right, Brig. Gen. Robert Toombs would follow with a second prong of the attack. After brief, sharp fighting, Anderson was stopped, but Toombs marched his brigade forward into heavy fighting that lasted until dark, when the Confederate line of battle was sent reeling back by a forceful musket attack by Brig. Gen. Winfield Scott Hancock.

Demonstrating the uncoordinated system of poor communication that was now plaguing the Confederate command, Toombs attacked again the following morning. This time he had more success, however, having deployed a battery of artillery during the night and now using the 7th and 8th Georgia infantries to good effect; Smith's division of the 6th Corps was forced to withdraw under heavy cannon fire from Garnett's Farm. The total losses for these actions over the two days were 368 Union troops and 461 Confederates. The action now swirling pell-mell around soldiers on both sides developed the core of veteran soldiers who would emerge in coming months. "The army is a great place to learn philosophy, I find, and in it you not only get careless of danger, but indifferent as to what disposition is made of you," wrote Federal 1st Lt. Charles Francis Adams, Jr.

On the Confederate side, Lee occupied himself with trying to divine McClellan's motives. Unfortunately, Stuart had gone south and east to scout and was of almost no use for the coming three critical days. Additionally, Lee sent Ewell down the Chickahominy to Dispatch Station on the Richmond & York River Railroad in an attempt to ascertain McClellan's movements. Was McClellan actually retreating, and if so, in what direction? Without his cavalry, Lee was faced with determining where he should move his army, and without knowing about McClellan's movement crossing his force south of the Chickahominy, any movement would be a risky event, even for the risk-taking Lee. Late on June 28, Lee decided that McClellan was indeed moving south and could be pursued to the south, enabling Lee to cross his army over the river. Lee quickly ordered Longstreet and A. P. Hill to cross the New Bridge and pursue McClellan in haste via the Central (Darbytown) Road. Jackson was ordered to move south and strike the Union rear. Magruder and Huger were both instructed to march southeast along the Williamsburg and Charles City roads.

Simultaneous with these movements, the bulk of McClellan's army, each corps directing its own affairs, retreated to positions near Savage's Station on the Richmond & York River Railroad, readying for the problematic journey through and around the White Oak Swamp. The plan called for Keyes's 4th Corps to guard the Union left flank during the withdrawal as Porter's 5th Corps followed. Sumner's 2d Corps, Heintzelman's 3d Corps, and Franklin's 6th Corps assembled as a rear guard. This set up the situation for the fifth of the Seven Days battles, Savage's Station, which occurred on June 29. Magruder began the pursuit early on the 29th, after Lee solidified his idea about the direction the Federal corps were moving. Orders were given to Stonewall Jackson to rebuild Grapevine Bridge, which had been rebuilt and destroyed several times, and move along the divisions of D. H. Hill, Ewell, and Whiting between the Chickahominy River and the White Oak Swamp. Magruder was supposed to move east along the railroad line and attack as the Federals retreated. Huger was assigned the most challenging task of cutting off the Yankees, moving to the south and blocking their line of retreat west of the White Oak Swamp. He would march his division down the Charles City Road and strike at the columns of Federals he encountered on June 30. Again, the plan relied on a complex set of maneuvers by Lee's subordinates. Longstreet and A. P. Hill were to cross their divisions at New Bridge and move southeastward along the Darbytown Road to strike at the Yankees south of Huger. Lastly, Holmes, at Drewry's Bluff, would cross the river and join Longstreet in his pursuit.

Though Magruder was initially suspecting a Federal attack, he soon learned that Longstreet had crossed the river and moved in pursuit as well. The old Federal line stretching from New Bridge in the north down along the old battleground of Fair Oaks and south of Seven Pines had been abandoned early in the morning. Magruder pressed forward past Fair Oaks and by 9 A.M. struck the Union forces of Sumner near Allen's Farm. The division of William F. Smith was scattered just north of Sumner's corps. Brisk fighting erupted and lasted for more than two hours, by which time Sumner pulled back to Savage's Station, meeting up with Franklin's 6th Corps in that area. To avert disaster, the Federal commanders devised a plan to use Heintzelman's 3d Corps to block the Williamsburg Road and prevent a Confederate penetration into the southern flank of Sumner, but Heintzelman determined it was too risky and marched southward across the White Oak Swamp without communicating his decision to Sumner and Franklin. Amazingly, Slocum also withdrew his division from Franklin's corps without Franklin's knowledge, but only because he had begged McClellan to allow him to pull out of formation and retreat because of his division's battered state.

The Confederate commanders were having troubles, too. For the third time during the campaign, Jackson inexplicably failed and delayed his participation. He used the entire day to rebuild Grapevine Bridge and allow his soldiers to rest, despite the fact that the Chickahominy was fordable downstream. Magruder himself now adopted a cautious attitude and waited to attack further, believing he might be struck hard by the Federal forces, but after hesitating he finally attacked again in force by about 4 P.M. In doing so, he committed only a small portion of his available men. A mere two and a half brigades went into the attack, and the results were predictable. Brig. Gen. Joseph B. Kershaw's brigade attacked south of the railroad line and ran into heavy fighting against the brigade of Brig. Gen. William W. Burns along with the 1st Minnesota Infantry. A similar lack of success resulted on Kershaw's right when the brigade of Brig. Gen. Paul J. Semmes attacked, supported by the 17th Mississippi Infantry and 21st Mississippi Infantry (Col. Benjamin G. Humphreys). This attack met stiff resistance from the brigade of Brig. Gen. William T. H. Brooks, particularly through the heroics of the 5th Vermont Infantry (Lt. Col. Lewis A. Grant). The battle fizzled out with the approach of nightfall and a vigorous thunderstorm that grew in intensity as the evening hours progressed. The Federal casualties at Savage's Station were 1,590 and the Confederate losses 626; the Union forces left 2,500 men behind in a field hospital and large stores of supplies that were captured by Magruder. Among the Confederate casualties was Brig. Gen. Richard Griffith, who had been struck in the thigh by a piece of artillery shell that may have ricocheted off the railroad section house; Griffith fell from his horse mortally wounded and died in Richmond the same day.

Long after the battle, Jackson crossed Grapevine Bridge by about 2:30 A.M. on June 30. During the chaotic, rain-soaked night, Jackson was not the only one on the move. The Federal corps, artillery and supply trains, and rear guard marched rapidly southward in retreat. Most of the army had cleared White Oak Swamp Creek by noon on June 30, but McClellan's army was still in a precarious position, largely due to a delay in moving wagons through the muddy roads near Glendale. Rather than make a beeline for the James, again the Union rear guard had to prepare for another battle in anticipation of the onrushing Confederates. The sixth of the Seven Days battles resulted on June 30 in the action known as White Oak Swamp, Frayser's Farm, or Glendale. Lee's plan was to move his divisions together to strike at the retreating Union columns in a mass attack, and he ordered Holmes to capture Malvern Hill. Again, however, poor performance plagued the Confederate commanders. Jackson was unable to perform the task he was assigned; Huger was afraid of a counterattack and unable to maneuver across abatis placed in the Charles City Road and failed to take an alternative path, so he sat out the action; and Magruder could not decide whether he should come to the aid of Longstreet or Holmes and ended up marching in circles and coming to the aid of neither.

With McClellan in full retreat toward Harrison's Landing on the James, the opportunity for Lee was now running out. His orders to staff members were vague and unhelpful, and Lee can be faulted for not directing this effort clearly. When Jackson arrived before White Oak Swamp Creek by about 11 A.M., he encountered a bridge that was out and resistance from the divisions of Richardson and William F. Smith. Jackson deployed artillery and lobbed shells across the creek, but again faltered, although he easily might have found suitable fords nearby. The inexperienced troops under Holmes, some 6,000 strong, could not contend effectively with Porter's 5th Corps in the area of Malvern Hill; they took hot fire from Federal cannon before backing off and abandoning their attack. As Longstreet and Lee sat astride their horses, accompanied by none other than President Davis, they anticipated "fruitful results" from the day's action. "It was impossible for the enemy to see us as we sat on our horses in the little field," Longstreet wrote, "surrounded by tall, heavy timber and thick undergrowth; yet a battery by chance had our range and exact distance, and poured upon us a terrific fire. The second or third shell burst in the midst of us, killing two or three horses and wounding one or two men. Our little party speedily retired to safer quarters. The Federals doubtless had no idea that the Confederate President, commanding general, and division commanders were receiving point-blank shot from their batteries."

Despite the faulty execution and poor communications on the Confederate side, Lee ordered an all-out attack from the divisions of Longstreet and A. P. Hill, a movement which only occurred at about 4:30 P.M. The attack came south of the White Oak Swamp Creek, along the Long Bridge Road, and into the area of Frayser's Farm. McCall's division was on the receiving end and stood up well to heavy artillery and musketry action; the brigades of Brig. Gens. Truman Seymour, John F. Reynolds, and George G. Meade fought vigorously against the Confederate attack, with the divisions of Hooker to the south and Kearny and Slocum to the north. The lead brigades in the Confederate attack were those of Col. Micah Jenkins (Anderson's Brigade) and Brig. Gen. James L. Kemper. Hot fighting ensued during the late afternoon with calamitous situations on both sides; six companies of the 12th Pennsylvania Reserves were captured nearly in their entirety. Steady artillery fire from the 1st Battalion New York Artillery prevented a breach of the Federal line, but eventually this position broke and the Confederates pushed on, only to be counterattacked.

The Confederate attack then shifted and intensified along the line composed of Meade's and Kearny's positions, where the 55th Virginia Infantry and the 60th Virginia Infantry (Col. William E. Starke) struck viciously into the line, resulting in hand-to-hand fighting with muskets, pistols, and even swords. A brief stand was made by the 4th Pennsylvania Reserves before they too were pushed back. With the approach of darkness, Brig. Gens. George A. McCall and John F. Reynolds each rode into Confederate lines and were captured. To avoid a catastrophic break in the Federal line, by nightfall Brig. Gen. George W. Taylor's brigade moved into position near the attack of the Virginians, but by 9 P.M. darkness halted the battle.

The fighting had again bloodied both sides considerably. The Union casualties were 297 killed, 1,696 wounded, and 1,804 missing, and the Confederate losses 638 killed, 2,814 wounded, and 221 missing. On the Union side, Meade and Sumner were wounded, while Confederate general officers wounded were Joseph R. Anderson, Featherston, and Pender. The Federal retreat continued, as on that night the final corps moved into position on Malvern Hill.

This time the situation was different, however. No longer would Lee have a reasonable opportunity to inflict serious damage on McClellan's isolated corps. The Union army was on high ground with a large number of cannon deployed in good position and concentrated reasonably well. The final battle of the Seven Days took place on July 1 and was known as Malvern Hill. The hill not only served as a fine artillery position but was relatively clear of timber and offered a good lookout position. Located within two miles of the James River, Malvern Hill witnessed a concentration of the Federal corps during the night, with the whole army present save for Keyes's 4th Corps, which had moved south toward Harrison's Landing to contact the navy.

Lee's attempt to strike at the Union army at Malvern Hill was poorly planned and badly executed. Porter's 5th Corps had prepared for a possible action there, and Col. Henry J. Hunt, McClellan's chief of artillery, had positioned 250 cannon. Thus, when Lee attacked Malvern Hill, one of the greatest artillery barrages of the war resulted, and Lee attacked headlong into the fire of the Union guns despite warnings about the defensive strength of the position. Lee not only failed to avoid one of the primary pitfalls of infantry attack—a frontal assault on a position well defended by artillery—but he believed that his own army was in much better shape than it was (exhausted by the six days of previous fighting) and thought McClellan's men in worse shape than they were.

Lee believed that his own artillery could outdo the Federal guns. He asked Jackson, with Ewell, D. H. Hill, and Whiting, to continue his march down the Quaker Road to strike Malvern Hill from the north. Magruder was ordered to follow Jackson's route of march and to deploy to his right on approaching the new battlefield. Huger would receive his orders on the march

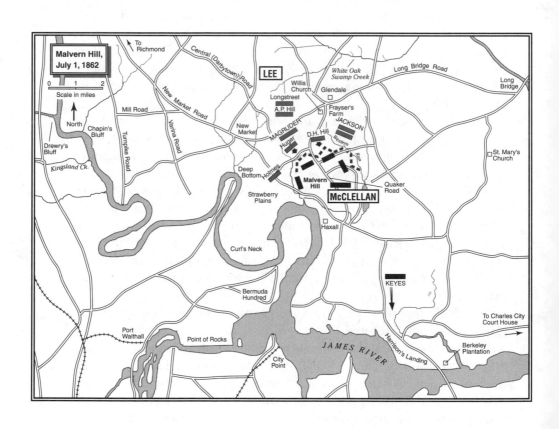

so that Lee could place him where most needed, and the troops that had fought heavily the previous day—those of Longstreet and A. P. Hill—were to be held in reserve so they could rest.

Again poor execution entered the fray. Both sides had terrible problems during the whole campaign with muddy, nearly impassable roads and poor maps, but one would expect the Union army to have had the lion's share of trouble since they were on unfamiliar terrain. Jackson soon arrived along Western Run, a swampy creek, and stopped abruptly to analyze the situation before him. Magruder's guides misdirected him entirely, sending him down the Long Bridge Road to the southwest, away from the battlefield, and down a local farm road that they thought was the Quaker Road. Huger's division soon came to the rescue, however, as the brigades of Brig. Gens. Ambrose R. Wright and Lewis A. Armistead arrived on the Confederate right and took up positions north of the Crew House. To their left on the Quaker Road, D. H. Hill's division organized a battle line that formed the Confederate center, and on the Confederate left were the brigades of Hood and Col. Evander M. Law, while Jackson was held behind the lines.

As they formed a battle line, however, it became clear to Lee and his subordinates that the position on Malvern Hill could not be taken without an initial pounding by artillery. Confederate batteries were concentrated on a hill some 1,200 yards north of the Crew House and at Poindexter's Farm, near the position of Whiting to the northeast. Armistead was assigned the task of determining the time at which the Confederate fire had dispersed the Union guns sufficiently well to launch an attack. But before the Confederate guns opened, Hunt began a bombardment about 1 P.M. with the Union field pieces, sending the front ranks of the Confederate soldiers reeling and causing great confusion among the Southern artillerists. As the Rebel guns were brought into position, many of the Federal pieces fired mercilessly into them, and the Union gunners outdid their foes; by 2:30 P.M. it was apparent that the Confederate artillery could not contribute substantially to the battle.

Despite the risk involved, Lee pressed for an infantry attack, having lost all but a few of his guns by 3:30 P.M. It was a whirlwind of battle. By late afternoon Armistead made something of an advance, driving into some of the sharpshooters of Col. Hiram Berdan's elite unit, and three Confederate regiments approached the Crew House but could not move any farther due to the return fire. By about 4 P.M. Magruder, having been lost for several hours, finally arrived and took up a supporting position behind Huger's brigades, awaiting developments to enter the battle. Dissatisfied with the way the battle was unfolding, Lee decided to put in the veteran troops of Longstreet and A. P. Hill, though they had fought hard the day before, but then reconsidered and ordered Magruder forward instead in support of Armistead. Magruder's advance was like many of the others on the Confederate side—a confused attempt that lacked organization. A mere third of Magruder's men joined in the attack, and they were beaten back with many casualties. "Magruder's report is very like a romance," wrote the artillerist Maj. Alexander S. Webb, "but bold as his final charge was, and far as it was pushed, his determined men were never near enough to threaten seriously the safety of the main Union batteries."

Meanwhile, confusion continued on the field. D. H. Hill believed the time had come for the general attack he anticipated, so he pushed forward an attack along the Quaker Road, past Willis Church, and into the Union line. Joining in on the attack were the brigades of Brig. Gens. Ambrose R. Wright and William Mahone. So costly was this advance that Hill later wrote that "it wasn't war; it was murder." The whole line of battle erupted as the brigades of Toombs, Kershaw, Ransom, Semmes, Cobb, and Col. William Barksdale surged forward to within a couple of hundred yards of the Union center; they were hurled back with heavy losses by nightfall. "It is not my desire to indulge in criticism or crimination," Brig. Gen. Samuel Garland, Jr., reported. "It is enough to say that there was somehow a want of concert and co-operation in the whole affair that made a successful attack impracticable and the consequent disorder and straggling of the troops most lamentable. . . . The whole division became scattered."

The casualties at Malvern Hill were terrific. Federals lost 3,214 and Confederates 5,355. The following day the Federal corps commanders withdrew toward Harrison's Landing and their waiting army commander while Lee decided, wisely, that he was too bloodied to pursue further. He moved his army back to Richmond. Over the whole course of the Seven Days, both armies lost great numbers, the Federals about 16,000 and the Confederates 20,000.

The Peninsular campaign was brought to a close. There was much to be concerned about on both sides. Lee had stopped McClellan's onslaught and preserved the Southern capital. He had turned back an opponent who fought to within just a few miles of Richmond. The Confederate commander and his subordinates would need to fight much more effectively in the future, however. Repeated instances of poor coordination, nebulous tactics, and incompetent execution could have proved disastrous for their cause. McClellan had fought a campaign with a huge army that was also poorly led. When McClellan wasn't vacillating, he was absent from the army entirely. The Federal army might have regrouped and turned back toward Richmond to take up the fight again, but remained static. With McClellan in command, the Army of the Potomac encamped around Berkeley Plantation, birthplace of William Henry Harrison, at Harrison's Landing. It remained there until August, squandering still more time. Though they pushed Mc-

Clellan back, many Confederates were stunned by the bloodiness of the campaign. "This fight beggars description," Lt. Col. James K. Edmondson (27th Virginia Infantry) wrote his wife on July 5. "It has been most horrible.... On the battlefield men are lying in great piles dead, mangled horribly in every way, hundreds and thousands of the Yankees lie upon every field yet unburied and many of our men and decomposition has gone on so far that it is almost if not impossible to go upon the fields.... I have never felt so gloomy and low spirited as I do now."

Confederate Triumph at Second Bull Run

AN OFTEN OVERLOOKED ASPECT of the Civil War began to emerge as an important factor in the summer of 1862. Communications by telegraph, signal flags, and ciphered messages flashed across the American landscape increasingly as the number of armies grew and complexities of geographical departments multiplied. Communication in the Civil War is worth investigating before we return to the story of the midsummer battles.

The logical place to start for the United States Army is with the Signal Corps, which begins with Albert James Myer, born in 1828 in New York. Myer became a telegrapher, an assistant surgeon USA, studied Indian signals, and developed sign language for the deaf. Myer also created the system of flag signaling used during the Civil War. Whereas semaphore signaling employed two flags, Myer's "wigwag" system used one flag by day and a torch or lantern by night. The flag was held overhead between signals and was then dipped from one to four times to the right, left, or front of the signalman to indicate letters of the alphabet. On June 27, 1860, Myer was assigned as signal officer of the Army in the grade of major. He accompanied the Army of the Potomac in the field from August 1861 to November 1862. The U.S. Army Signal Corps was organized on March 3, 1863, with Myer as the chief in the grade of colonel. Myer also wrote the influential treatise *A Manual of Signals: For the Use of Signal Officers in the Field*, published in 1864.

Even before the Signal Corps was established, however, military intelligence had to contend with encryption and interception of enemy messages. To discourage interception, a cipher disk consisting of two concentric circles was distributed. It contained an alphabet spaced around the edges of each circle. The circles could be rotated so that letters on each would correspond to a predetermined code. An "adjustment" letter on one circle was set opposite "A" on the other so as to shift the first alphabet to a substituted alphabet. The substitute alphabet could then be used by the wigwag, which was then not as easily read by the enemy. Call letters and signature letters were added to authorize the messages.

The Signal Corps also operated by wire from time to time, frequently using the Beardslee magneto-electric field telegraph. This brought them into competition with the U.S. Military Telegraph, a bureau established in 1862 to oversee telegraphic communications. Arguments between Col. Myer and Col. Anson Stager of the USMT led to Myer's removal on November 10, 1863, by order of Secretary of War Stanton. Maj. William J. L. Nicodemus took command of the Signal Corps from November 15, 1863, to December 3, 1864, when he was in turn suspended for releasing the information that his signalmen could read Confederate field signals. (Actually, both armies read each other's flag signals frequently.) Col. Benjamin F. Fisher, signal officer of the Army of the Potomac until June 1863, when he was captured at Aldie, Virginia, escaped from Libby prison in Richmond in February 1864, made his way to Washington, and was appointed chief of the Signal Corps on December 3. Fisher gave up his assignment on November 15, 1866, and was succeeded by Capt. Lemuel B. Norton as acting chief until August 21, 1867, when Myer was restored to his office in the grade of brevet brigadier general.

Union telegraphic communications evolved slowly. Thomas A. Scott, a one-time telegrapher and vice president of the Pennsylvania Railroad, on April 25, 1861, was placed in charge of the railroad and telegraph lines between Washington and Annapolis by a worried Federal administration. Scott secured communications with the North and by May 23, 1861, was made director of all Union wire and rail lines. By August 3, 1861, Scott had become assistant secretary of war, and on November 25, 1861, he installed Stager, former superintendent of the Western Union Telegraph Co., as general manager of telegraphs, which were allowed to remain under private ownership as long as military traffic was given priority and the civilian operators were under military supervision.

After Edwin M. Stanton became secretary of war on January 15, 1862, Stager was appointed superintendent of the supervisory organization, the USMT, established on February 22, 1862. Stager was known to have worked efficiently with Maj. Gen. George McClellan during the campaign in western Virginia. Stanton also appointed Edward S. Sanford, president of the American Telegraph Co., as superintendent of telegraphic messages, a euphemism for chief military censor; Thomas T. Eckert (postwar assistant secretary of war and president of the Western Union Telegraph Co.) as assistant superintendent; and David Homer Bates as chief operator for the Washington office.

Fearing that McClellan, as general-in-chief of the army, might act independently of the War Department, Stanton at once installed Eckert and Bates into a two-room suite adjacent to his own offices in the War Department, so that in this central location most communications to and from field armies, geographical departments, and bureau chiefs would pass under his scrutiny.

Stager brought to the USMT a cipher he had devised for Governor William Dennison of Ohio for interstate messages in the North, which had also been adopted by McClellan. It was a simple word transposition in which a "commencement" code word was first transmitted. This code word gave knowledge of the numbers of columns and lines into which the words of the message were to be arranged, and also the route through the resulting network or matrix that was to be used to copy the text of the message. Thus, the commencement "marine," by a predetermined plan, indicated arranging the words in nine lines by six columns, and copying the fifty-four-word message up the sixth column, down the first, up the fifth, down the second, up the fourth, and down the third. The cipher message was then transmitted line by line.

As the system was later elaborated, many variations in numbers of lines, columns, and routes were introduced, the messages were interspersed with nulls ("checks" or "blinds" that were distracting, nonsense terms) and with special, previously assigned code words ("arbitraries" such as "Adam" for President Lincoln or "Egypt" for George McClellan) that were supplied to disguise particularly sensitive terms. When the cipher was received, a corresponding procedure would yield the deciphered plain language communication. Only the USMT operators, Stager, and Stanton were privy to the codebooks.

As the word-transposition route cipher code gained acceptance, a series of twelve families of ciphers was produced during the war years to replace the original Stager cipher, each with a vocabulary of commencements, nulls, and code words. To protect the system further, homophones (multiple code words for one ordinary word) and polyphones (a code word that could have multiple meanings depending on the context) were introduced. For example, Cipher No. 9 (January 1863) contained 72 commencements and 792 arbitraries, while Cipher No. 4 (March 1865) contained a twelve-page list of commencements and 1,608 arbitraries. During the war, four of the twelve cipher families were captured in their entirety, and several cipher transcripts were taken from couriers or operators. However, the Confederates were apparently never able to decipher a Union telegraphic message, even though this should have been possible. An estimated 6.5 million Union telegrams were sent in cipher during the war. Demonstrating the importance of ciphered military messages, Abraham Lincoln was said to have spent more time in the War Department telegraph office than anywhere else outside the

Executive Mansion during the war years. Bates wrote that when Lincoln saw the code words "husband" and "hunter" for Davis and Lee, he invariably read them aloud as "Jeffy D." and "Bobby Lee."

The Confederate States Signal Bureau followed a markedly different path from that of its Union counterpart. It began on April 19, 1862, under the supervision of Adjutant and Inspector General Samuel Cooper until the assignment of Maj. William Norris as chief of the bureau on July 31, 1862. The Signal Bureau managed all signal and telegraphic communication, courier services, and numerous clandestine operations including military intelligence, espionage, and cryptology. Most telegraphic traffic was handled by private companies, while most of the covert activities were directed by the president's office, the State Department, the War Department, and/or various field commanders. Communications and message security were compromised by an overall lack of planning, coordination, and control.

Many Confederate field signals were patterned after the Federal system, beginning with the Signal Service of Beauregard's Army of the Potomac in July 1861, under the direction of Capt. Edward Porter Alexander, a former assistant to Albert Myer. Like the Yankee signalmen, the Confederates used brass concentric circle alphabet devices to yield substitution cipher alphabets. Curiously, sometime between 1858 and 1861, Porter Alexander signed a document asserting that he would not "disclose, discover, or use the plan for signals communicated to me, without the written consent of Dr. Meyer [*sic*] & the consent of the U.S. War Department."

The Confederate telegraphic cipher was a polyalphabetic letter substitution originally created in 1587 by the Frenchman Blaise de Vigenére (pronounced Veezh-nair). For the Vigenére, a table or matrix of alphabets was constructed in which the complete alphabet was written across a line and then repeated on twenty-five successive lines wherein each alphabet was shifted to the right one letter position from the previous line. The completed matrix then consisted of a square, twenty-six letters wide and twenty-six letters long.

A key phrase was memorized that dictated which column of letters was employed along the top line, using each letter of the key in succession and repeating the letters of the key as often as needed. The letters contained in the plain message were selected in succession from the first column on the left of the matrix. Where the key-letter column and the corresponding plain-letter line met within the body of a matrix, a substitution letter was found. Thus, a message might begin:

Key (first line) MANCHESTERBLUFFMANCHESTERB . . .
Plain (left column) LIEUTENANTJONESWILLPROCEED . . .
Cipher (matrix body) XIRWAIFTRKKZHJXIIYNWVGVIVE . . .

A reversal of the process using the same matrix and key will yield the plain. The advantage of the system was that no cipher codebooks are required, so capture of the system is impossible, but the disadvantage in requiring the telegraphic transmission of large numbers of jumbled letters led to frequent transmission errors that often ruined the whole message. Moreover, only a few key phrases were used during the war, and they were deduced by Federal cryptanalysts, such as "Manchester Bluff," "Complete Victory," "My Old Kentucky Home," and "Come Retribution." Transmission errors, poor handwriting, letter reversals, and misspellings could destroy a ciphered message, making repetitions necessary.

In order to simplify transmission efforts, usually only selected words and phrases in a message were enciphered and the results were usually preserved in the letter groups of the plain words. These two simplifications allowed Union cryptanalysts to guess at the ciphered words, both from their length and from their positions in context. A good number of Vigenére ciphers were broken by this process.

In attempting to preserve the doctrine of state rights, Southern leaders also devised many private cipher codes for delivery by courier or by mail that were not often shared with other states, offices, or military units, thereby limiting communication. Some of these were dictionary cipher codes in which references were made to words or phrases by indicating their locations by page, column, line, and item in a secret dictionary, the sender and receiver each having a copy of the book. Jefferson Davis, Confederate diplomats, naval officers, and foreign agents used dictionary cipher codes extensively. Simple substitution ciphers or cipher codes employing alphabets and various symbols were used by many officers and spies in the field.

Remarkably, the Civil War has been judged a "clean and honest" war with little or no hard evidence that Federal agents infiltrated the Confederate Signal Bureau, and conversely, little or no evidence that Confederate agents entered the U.S. Signal Corps or USMT. However, both sides were sometimes able to tap each other's telegraph lines, capture their stations, intercept mail, obtain each other's military orders, catch each other's couriers and spies, and read each other's flag signals.

The summer of 1862 brought a shift in the psychology of the war front. The joy of battle triumphs and clear confidence on the Federal side seemed to have been checked. In the Shenandoah Valley, Stonewall Jackson stalled the Federal forces and actually helped to unravel the reinforcement of McClellan's huge force on the Peninsula. Lee had taken command of the Army of Northern Virginia only to see it pushed to within the doorsteps of Richmond but he fought off the invading Northerners despite a clumsy set of uncoordinated actions. Halleck was still in the vicinity of Corinth, and the vital rail city of Chattanooga was still in Confederate hands. For Southerners there seemed to be a turn in momentum; a few things of importance seemed to be going their way.

McClellan still found time to carp at the administration during the retreat and buildup at Harrison's Landing on the James. "Never did such a change of base, involving a retrograde movement, and under incessant attacks from a most determined and vastly more numerous foe, partake so little of disorder," he wrote Lincoln on July 4. Later on the same day he again telegraphed, reporting, "Our whole Army is now drawn up for review in its positions, bands playing, salutes being fired & all things looking bright." Three days later he described for the president how the course of the war should be exercised. "It should not be, at all, a War upon population," wrote McClellan, "but against armed forces and political organizations. Neither confiscation of property, political executions of persons, territorial organization of States or forcible abolition of slavery should be contemplated for a moment." Six days after lecturing the commander-in-chief, McClellan confided to his wife a few lines about the secretary of war. "I think that he is the most unmitigated scoundrel I ever knew, heard, or read of," wrote McClellan. "I think that (& I do not wish to be irreverent) had he lived in the time of the Saviour, Judas Iscariot would have remained a respected member of the fraternity of the Apostles, & that the magnificent treachery & rascality of E. M. Stanton would have caused Judas to have raised his arms in holy horror." The administration had long ago lost faith in McClellan, particularly those who were in power and opposed to McClellan's political stance. While they were being attacked by McClellan in his letters to his wife, Lincoln's cabinet radicals were plotting to oust him. In August, Stanton, Salmon Chase, Caleb B. Smith, and Edward Bates drafted a memorandum and sent it to the president requesting McClellan's removal from command of "any army of the United States."

JULY 1862 BEGAN with a minor cavalry action at Booneville in Mississippi. At the end of May, Union Col. Philip H. Sheridan had raided Booneville, a station on the Mobile & Ohio Railroad, and captured supplies; now about 4,700 Confederate troopers led by Brig. Gen. James R. Chalmers thrust into Sheridan's pickets and stood poised to annihilate Sheridan's tiny force of 827, which consisted of the 2d Michigan Cavalry (Sheridan) and 2d Iowa Cavalry (Lt. Col. Edward Hatch). (The estimate of 4,700 Confederates may have been far too high; the real number may have been as little as 1,200.) Nonetheless, Sheridan's outnumbered troopers performed well. Several of his companies of the 2d Michigan were armed with Colt six-shot repeating rifles, which helped immensely. When Chalmers contacted the pickets about 8:30 A.M., they immediately informed Sheridan, who reinforced the pickets with four companies. A withdrawal began through a heavy woods, but Sheridan sent a telegram that morning stating, "I am holding my camp." Two regiments of Chalmers's cavalry took up positions on opposite sides of the approach road and began firing into the small Federal force, but the 2d Iowa came up in support and sent a blistering fire across an open field. Chalmers next determined to flank Sheridan's position, attempting to place his troopers between the Federal line and its camp.

Sheridan seized the offensive, however, sending four companies under Maj. Russell A. Alger with sabers drawn to thwart the Confederate plan, and Alger's horsemen circuitously moved around their enemy, charging into the Confederates and forcing a retreat. Simultaneously, Hatch's portion of the 2d Iowa charged the Confederate left. The attack worked beautifully, aided by the surprise element of the saber charge and the firepower of the Colt repeaters, and Chalmers's men were scattered back. The Yankee casualties were 1 killed, 24 wounded, and 16 missing, and among them was Alger, who was captured but escaped the same day.

Other actions occurred in Mississippi this month. On July 3 a minor bombardment of Vicksburg took place. On July 10 and 11 a Federal expedition set out to Guntown under a flag of truce, and they exchanged goods with Confederates. On the 11th a major change in command took place when Maj. Gen. Henry W. Halleck was assigned by President Lincoln as general-in-chief of all U.S. armies, which position he assumed on July 23. This brought Halleck out of the field, where his judgment was sometimes questionable, and sent him to Washington to undertake in reality what would be a new administrative role. An excellent organizer, Halleck would act as a sort of filter through which commanders in the field would communicate to the secretary of war and the president. Of the assignment, McClellan wrote his wife, "I see it reported in this evening's papers that Halleck is to be the new Genl in Chief. Now let them take the next step & relieve me & I shall once more be a free man." But for George McClellan, difficulties continued apace.

The major activity in Mississippi came at midmonth. On the morning of July 15 the newly completed Confederate casemate ironclad CSS *Arkansas* set out on the Yazoo River in search of Federal ships in the area. Commanded by Lt. Isaac N. Brown, the *Arkansas* spanned 165 by 35 by 11.5 feet, ran on two screws turned by low-pressure engines, and had an armament of two 9-inch smoothbore guns, two 8-inch guns, two 6-inch rifles, and two 64-pounder smoothbores. It was a formidable ship and faced a flotilla of Union ships that included the ironclad gunboat USS *Carondelet* (Comdr. Henry Walke), the ram USS *Queen of the West* (Lt. Col. Alfred W. Ellet), and the timberclad gunboat USS *Tyler*. The *Arkansas* opened fire on the three Federal ships and a hot fight ensued in which the *Carondelet* and the *Tyler* were considerably damaged; the Federal ships withdrew. The *Arkansas* ran past them into the Mississippi River, where it turned southward toward Vicksburg and passed through heavy fire from the Union ships downstream to the relative safety of the shore batteries about Vicksburg. The ship had been struck repeatedly, however, and was substantially damaged. On the Mississippi, Rear Adm. David G. Farragut's fleet pursued, but, as Farragut wrote, "it was so dark by the time we reached the town that nothing could be seen except the flashes of the guns."

On the *Arkansas,* 10 had been killed and 15 wounded. Among the Federal ships, 18 were killed, 50 wounded, and 10 missing. In a singular event, this running of the *Arkansas* downriver, the psychology of the Mississippi River war had changed. To the Lincoln administration, it pointed up the extreme importance of reducing and capturing Vicksburg. To the Confederacy, the ship's run was nothing short of supreme victory. Brown was commissioned a commander and given the thanks of the Confederate Congress, and Navy Secretary Stephen R. Mallory wrote that "Naval history records few deeds of greater heroism or higher professional ability than this achievement of the *Arkansas.*"

In Virginia the major naval action of the month took place on July 4. On this day Independence was celebrated widely in the North despite the less than encouraging war news from the Virginia front. "This is the 4th of July," wrote Charles Francis Adams, minister to Great Britain, to his son, cavalry officer Charles Jr. "Eighty-six years ago our ancestors staked themselves in a contest of a far more dangerous and desperate character. . . . Had they then consented to follow Thomas Jefferson to the full extent of his first draught of the Declaration, they would have . . . saved the present trials from their children." To bolster volunteerism on the Union side, James Sloan Gibbons even composed a poem following Lincoln's call for 300,000 additional soldiers that came on July 2. The poem was published two weeks hence in the *New York Evening Post* and was later adapted into a song. Its first two familiar patriotic bars went, "We are coming, Father Abraham, three hundred thousand more/From Mississippi's winding stream and from New England's shore."

On Independence Day in the James River, the gunboat CSS *Teaser,* commanded by Lt. Hunter Davidson, steamed forth near Haxall's Landing, above City Point, and was engaged by the side-wheel gunboat USS *Maratanza,* commanded by Lt. Thomas Holdup Stevens. After a brief fight in which a shell from the *Maratanza* exploded *Teaser*'s boiler, the Confederate gunboat was captured. The Union sailors discovered that not only had Davidson and his crew been placing mines in the river, but a deflated balloon was on board. The Rebels had gone downriver to launch a balloon and reconnoiter McClellan's withdrawal at City Point and Harrison's Landing. Balloons had been used periodically and infrequently to spy on the opposing army but with limited success. The most active proponent of aerial warfare was Thaddeus S. C. Lowe, a pioneering balloonist who had made a long test flight from Cincinnati to South Carolina in 1861. He took a small group of balloons into service with the Army of the Potomac, seeing the height of his activity with his balloon *Intrepid* and others during the Peninsular campaign at such actions as Fair Oaks. Lowe and other balloonists made a real contribution on a few occasions by sketching enemy positions or signaling from the balloon using flags or a telegraph wire, and sometimes the balloons drew heavy fire from the enemy. Their gear was extremely heavy and cumbersome, involving the transportation of hydrogen generators as well as the balloons themselves. Among the early supporters of such aeronautics in the Union army was Maj. Gen. Fitz John Porter, who on one occasion, at Yorktown, was aloft in a runaway balloon and nearly captured. The Confederate balloon was sent to Washington along with insulated wire and mine equipment captured on board and shells with "peculiar fuzes" that were forwarded to Capt. John A. B. Dahlgren at the Washington Navy Yard.

A NEW TYPE OF WARFARE was developing rapidly in the western theater under the direction of Col. John Hunt Morgan. This cavalry officer had been born in 1825 in Alabama and was a brother-in-law of fellow Confederates A. P. Hill and Basil W. Duke. Morgan had been a merchant in Kentucky before being commissioned a captain in the 2d Kentucky Cavalry in September of the war's first year. This background hardly hinted of the things that would follow: Morgan would become one of the greatest cavalry raiders of the war. His first significant raid began on July 4 when he commenced a ride throughout parts of Kentucky and Tennessee; two days later another raid, this one directed by Forrest, another Confederate legend in the making, began in Tennessee. The diversions were fueled by Maj. Gen. Don Carlos Buell's movement toward Chattanooga. By midmonth Buell was at Huntsville, hoping to move eastward. The loss of Chattanooga would be disastrous for Confederate strategy in the western theater.

Morgan led two companies of his 2d Kentucky Cavalry, numbering 867 troopers (and an advance force of 60 scouts), from Knoxville northwestward toward Kentucky. (His force grew to 1,200 by recruitment along the way.) It consisted of Morgan's regiment, Georgia partisans, two companies of Tennessee cavalry, and Texas Rangers commanded by Maj. Richard M. Gano. For twenty-five days the raiders blazed a trail of guerrilla tactics spread across portions of two states. They left Knoxville, crossed the Cumberland River, and moved into Kentucky through Tompkinsville, Glasgow, Horse Cave, Lebanon, Springfield, Harrodsburg, Versailles, Midway, and Georgetown. After a brisk action at Cynthiana, the most intense fighting of the expedition, Morgan's raiders turned south and went through Paris, Winchester, Richmond, Crab Orchard, Somerset, Monticello, and back into

Tennessee to Sparta. They rode more than 1,000 miles, interrupted Buell's movement on Chattanooga, lit panic into the hearts of Cincinnatians, captured and paroled 1,200 prisoners, wrecked railroad supplies, and left Buell with a major headache. All this came at a cost of fewer than 100 casualties for Morgan. He began a great tradition of guerrilla raids during the Civil War, particularly on the Southern side.

Morgan's raid worked in large part because of superb intelligence. He attacked when he knew that he could win by surprise and overwhelming numbers. At Tompkinsville on July 9, Morgan reported that he "surprised the enemy, and having surrounded them, threw four shells into their camp, and then carried it by a dashing charge." Maj. Thomas J. Jordan of the 9th Pennsylvania Cavalry remembered the day with less enthusiasm. "As day broke . . . my officers were all at their posts, when a faint discharge of fire-arms was heard far out on the Salina [Celina] Road," he reported. "Within a minute the head of Colonel Morgan's command began to deploy from the woods into an open field some 300 yards from me. . . . I soon found that re-sistance would be madness and surrendered myself a prisoner of war. After I had surrendered, I was fired upon at the distance of but a few feet, the charge, happily for me, missing its mark, but blackening the side of my face with the powder." Morgan's troops left 22 dead and 30 wounded, captured 300 prisoners, and destroyed a baggage train. After attempting to escape on horseback, Maj. Jordan refused to sign a parole, insisting that legitimate Confederate soldiers would not be operating in such a manner behind the Federal lines.

At Glasgow, Morgan's men stopped for a brief reunion, as some of the men lived there and had not seen their families since before Shiloh. The next day they set off for Horse Cave, on the railroad, thirty-three miles northeast of Bowling Green, and a tremendous thunderstorm unleashed itself over the huddled troopers. One of the riders, a Canadian telegraph operator named George A. Ellsworth, tapped into the telegraph line despite the thunder-storm, frequent flashes of lightning, and sitting in water up to his knees, earning himself the nickname "Lightning." With intelligence gathering ac-complished, the raiders reached the Rolling Fork River near Lebanon on July 11. A volley of Federal musketry fire across the river forced the Confed-erates to roll out their two guns, and two sharp bursts of the cannon sent the Yankees in retreat back to Lebanon. Again, Morgan's swift encirclement of the small Federal force resulted in a capture of the town, and this time, in Lebanon, about 200 prisoners were paroled. The supplies captured in town were either taken or thrown into a nearby creek. The raiders entered Har-rodsburg at 9 A.M. on July 12. They were received warmly in this prosecession town and enjoyed a picnic. They also recruited some additional soldiers.

By this time the Federal command in the region was alarmed, particularly Brig. Gen. Jeremiah T. Boyle in Louisville, military governor of Kentucky. "It is certain Morgan cannot be caught without cavalry," Boyle wrote Capt. Oliver D. Greene in Nashville on this day. "He will lay waste to large parts of the State. He is aiming at Lexington. I have no force to take him. If Buell would save Kentucky it must be done instantly." On the same day, Buell, not aware of how this affair was tarnishing his reputation, replied from Huntsville. "Morgan ought not to escape without a severe blow," he wrote Boyle, "but he will effect no doubt a good deal of harm, and the mischief will be done before troops could arrive from here to prevent it." Meanwhile, with Confederate raiders approaching the area, George Hatch, the mayor of Cincinnati, received an alarming telegram from Boyle asking for as many men as possible to be sent to Lexington along with artillery. This caused concern in Cincinnati and other Ohio cities, as well as Lexington.

The intelligence gathering of Morgan's telegrapher Ellsworth enabled Morgan to taunt the Federals with messages. He harangued George Prentice, pro-Union editor of the *Louisville Journal,* who had belittled Morgan in print and called him a "misguided young man." Morgan telegraphed Prentice on July 22 from Somerset, "Good morning, George D! I am quietly watching the complete destruction of all of Uncle Sam's property in this little burg. . . . I expect in a short time to pay you a visit and wish to know if you will be at home. All well in Dixie." On the same day he sent the following message to Boyle himself: "Good morning, Jerry. This telegraph is a great institution. You should destroy it as it keeps me posted too well. My friend Ellsworth has all your dispatches since July 10 on file. Do you wish copies?"

Morgan's raiders passed through Versailles and Georgetown. By this time Boyle had calmed down somewhat and written Buell, "I am persuaded Morgan has not over 1,000 men and two brass [*sic*] howitzers. . . . The secessionists have lied for Morgan and magnified his forces." But another major skirmish was to come on July 17 at Cynthiana, where Morgan met stiff resistance from a Federal garrison larger than he had anticipated. Still, Morgan won the day.

By the time Morgan reached the Licking River north of Cynthiana and decided to turn around and go back to Tennessee, Boyle was panicking again. "The state is in danger of being overrun by Morgan and those joining him," he wrote Stanton. "If he should succeed in a fight with our forces there is danger of an uprising of the traitors in our midst." But there would be no such uprising. By July 29 the raid was over, and it helped to spark a new kind of warfare in America, to diminish the confidence of the Lincoln administration concerning Kentucky, and to unhinge Buell's intentions completely. And another raid was taking place in Tennessee during these same days.

The second raid was led by Col. Nathan Bedford Forrest, who had escaped narrowly at Fort Donelson and solidified his role as a cavalry tactician.

Forrest's raid began on July 6 and set out from Chattanooga with about 1,000 troopers. The brigade consisted of the 8th Texas Cavalry (Col. John A. Wharton), the 1st Louisiana Cavalry, the 2d Georgia Cavalry, and Helm's Kentucky Cavalry. The Confederates pressed hard, soon passed through McMinnville, northwest of Chattanooga, and kept on until they reached Murfreesboro, a railroad town containing Union supplies guarded by a Federal garrison of 1,040 men under the command of Brig. Gen. Thomas T. Crittenden. Forrest swept into town so briskly that he surprised and captured the entire Federal command, including Crittenden, Lt. Col. John G. Parkhurst of the 9th Michigan Infantry, and other field officers. "I must demand an unconditional surrender of your force as prisoners of war or I will have every man put to the sword," Forrest wrote Parkhurst. Forrest also seized military stores worth almost $1 million, and he wasted no time in appearing to threaten Nashville to the northwest.

"It was Forrest's birthday," wrote Garnet Wolseley later, "and the evening before, when he told his men this, he begged they would celebrate it by their courage. His appeal was not in vain; for they never fought better or against greater odds." Thomas Jordan and journalist J. P. Pryor described the initial action. "Led by their Colonel, the gallant Texans ... in a few moments were in the very heart of the Federal cantonment, the occupants of which were at the instant for the most part in their tents, but from which they speedily emerged. Many, undressed and seeking all possible means of shelter from their fierce-smiting adversaries, rushed in with confusion through the mazes of the encampment." Crittenden was ruined by the affair. Of the surrender, Buell said simply, "Few more disgraceful examples of neglect of duty and lack of good conduct can be found in the history of wars."

Moving back to McMinnville, Forrest and his horse soldiers departed again on July 19, this time moving on Lebanon, east of Nashville, and pursuing the Yankee garrison from that place westward toward the capital city. As a Federal force commanded by Brig. Gen. William "Bull" Nelson was dispatched to catch Forrest, the Confederate cavalryman wrecked two bridges south of the city to thwart Nelson's approach. This action alarmed the military governor of Tennessee, Brig. Gen. Andrew Johnson, and with good reason. Buell's planned operation against Chattanooga was again delayed, the railroad line between Nashville and Stevenson, Alabama, was out of operation for the final week of the month, and Johnson had to deploy two Federal divisions, those of Nelson and Brig. Gen. Thomas J. Wood, to protect the railroads. Forrest's first raid had halted the Union army's plans in Tennessee. In discussing the action with John Hunt Morgan, Forrest explained, "I just took the short cut and got there first with the most men." This legendary comment would be remembered by many raiders as a maxim of this new type of warfare, and would later be corrupted by some historians into the phrase "git thar fustest with the mostest men." Following the raid, Bull Nelson proclaimed, "I will have about 1,200 cavalry, and Mr. Forrest shall have no rest. I will hunt him down myself." Nelson and others would find out in the coming months just how difficult a task that could be.

Meanwhile, cavalry greats were beginning to be made in the East. "The bearer, John S. Mosby, late 1st Lt. 1st Va. Cavalry, is en route to scout beyond the enemy's line toward Manassas and Fairfax," wrote Jeb Stuart to Stonewall Jackson on July 19. "He is bold, daring, intelligent and discreet, the information he may obtain may be relied upon, and I have no doubt that he will soon give additional proof of his value." At about the same time, Stuart heard from the army commander himself, having been commissioned a major general. "I congratulate you on your promotion," wrote Robert E. Lee. "It is deserved though has been somewhat tardy. Tell Fitz Lee the same. You two must make good my recommendation. [Wade] Hampton I hope will make a good officer too. I am endeavoring to put the cavalry on a good footing."

SCATTERED ACTIONS in the western theater occurred during the warm months of July and August. On July 6, as Forrest pulled away from Chattanooga, a Federal infantry brigade under Col. Graham N. Fitch, numbering about 2,000 men, encountered Confederates along the White River in Arkansas. The casualties amounted to 84 killed, wounded, and missing on the Confederate side and 22 on the Federal side. In other places, minor actions might have been more consequential, according to those involved, at least. "I have the honor to report that Gen. [Robert B.] Mitchell reached Bay Springs yesterday morning at 7 o.c.," wrote Brig. Gen. Jefferson C. Davis from Jacinto, Mississippi, on August 6. "The rebels have escaped with their baggage. The small cavalry force Mitchell had with him overhauled their rear guard & after some skirmishing abandoned the pursuit. They have brought us several (10) prisoners. . . . Had not the heat been so intense the infty. troops would have in my opinion succeeded in capturing this party, *five hundred* in number."

Few military actions occurred during the Civil War north of the Ohio River. One of them took place on July 18, however, when Confederate raiders occupied Henderson, Kentucky, and then crossed the Ohio and moved on Newburgh, Indiana, southeast of Evansville and just north of the river. Union authorities were outraged because the actions appeared to be those of guerrillas, with unidentified "soldiers" in no particular uniform firing at Union soldiers. The action involves one of the more assertive ploys of the war, in which Confederate Capt. Adam R. Johnson showed great ingenuity. (In August 1864 he would be accidentally shot in the eyes and blinded.) For now, however, Johnson's raid into Indiana temporarily captured a hospital

with 80 sick and wounded soldiers and succeeded in destroying a large number of hospital supplies. The amazing feat for Johnson was that he rode into
town with 12 men on a wagon loaded with two quaker guns—false cannon—
made from sections of stovepipe. As Johnson recalled it, "from two pairs of
old wagon wheels, with their axles, and a stovepipe and a charred log, I soon
had manufactured two of the most formidable-looking pieces of artillery
into whose gaping mouths a scared people ever looked."

Johnson further bluffed by maneuvering his horses around on the other
bank of the river, threatening soldiers who held cocked guns at his face, and
after traveling to meet the town's commanding officer, who owned an expensive house in Newburgh, threatening to "shell this town to the ground" if
he did not cooperate. Johnson's ruse worked magnificently and he was ever
after known as "Stovepipe Johnson." Two Union citizens were shot and
killed by the Federal soldiers for ferrying the Confederate raiders across the
river. The casualties were mounting in terms of the high command, too. On
July 5, in Augusta, Georgia, Confederate Maj. Gen. David E. Twiggs, age 72,
who had surrendered Texas to Confederate forces in the spring of 1861, died
of pneumonia before Federal authorities caught up with him, hoping to
punish Twiggs for treason. Near Plevna, Alabama, on August 5, Union Brig.
Gen. Robert L. McCook, one of the "fighting McCooks" of Ohio, who had
fought at Carnifex Ferry, was mortally wounded by guerrillas while sick and
riding in an ambulance.

Along the Mississippi River, combined actions resumed on August 5–6
with the attack on Baton Rouge by Confederate infantry commanded by
Maj. Gen. John C. Breckinridge. Yankees had occupied the city on May 12
before commencing operations toward Vicksburg. After their failure there,
they retreated to Baton Rouge by July 26. During this period some changes
took place among the Confederate commanders. After being commissioned
a general ACSA in April, for example, Braxton Bragg, who held President
Davis's favor, was assigned to replace P. G. T. Beauregard as commander of
the Army of Mississippi and actually assumed permanent command on August 15. "The great changes of command and commanders here has well nigh
overburdened me," Bragg wrote his wife on July 22, "but I hope yet to mark
the enemy before I break down."

Set against this background of change, Breckinridge attacked at Baton
Rouge. Maj. Gen. Earl Van Dorn ordered the attack with about 5,000 men
under Breckinridge and another 1,000 under Daniel Ruggles. The force consisted of two divisions, commanded by Brig. Gen. Charles Clark (with the
brigades of Brig. Gens. Benjamin Hardin Helm, 2d Brigade, and Lt. Col.
Thomas B. Smith, 4th Brigade), and Ruggles (with two brigades). Of the
more colorful characters involved, Daniel Ruggles had fought at Shiloh; Ben
Hardin Helm was President Lincoln's brother-in-law, his wife being Emily

Todd Helm, Mary Lincoln's younger sister. Helm was a Kentuckian, age 31, who had declined a commission in the U.S. Army at the outbreak of the war. Two companies of partisan rangers and three batteries of artillery were also attached to Breckinridge's command.

The movement was an outstanding example of a Confederate joint operation. The casemate ironclad CSS *Arkansas,* which had fought so well in engaging and passing the Yankee flotilla on the Yazoo River, would move from Vicksburg and attack the naval ships as Breckinridge assaulted the Federal troops on land from the east. In Baton Rouge, Brig. Gen. Thomas Williams commanded seven regiments comprising about 2,500 men, and attached cavalry and artillery. Williams had fought at Grand Gulf; now he faced a terrible onslaught.

He did have help from the Navy. The Federal converted ironclad gunboat USS *Essex* (Comdr. William D. "Dirty Bill" Porter, brother of David Dixon Porter), the cottonclad USS *Sumter,* which had been captured at the battle of Memphis, and the screw gunboats USS *Cayuga,* USS *Kineo,* and USS *Katahdin* lay offshore. The CSS *Arkansas,* now commanded temporarily by Lt. Henry Stevens, experienced engine trouble, but Stevens pressed on nonetheless. On the morning of August 5, Breckinridge spread his force into two columns, with Clark to the north, and attacked headlong into the Union picket line through a dense fog. Over several hours of bloody fighting, the Confederate attack overran the Federal camps, killing many soldiers and capturing and burning supplies. Among the dead was Brig. Gen. Williams. To worsen matters for the grief-stricken family, the transport carrying the general's corpse was struck and sank, and Williams's body was recovered only after a considerable search.

With the battle going solidly well for the Confederates, the *Arkansas* arrived despite starboard engine failure, but soon the gunboat lost its ability to steer and ran aground, allowing the Federal ships to pulverize it with repeated heavy fire. The ship was fired and destroyed on August 6, and the poor coordination of the battle in its later stages the previous day led to a Confederate withdrawal. The Federal Navy and army troops pounded out a victory, leaving 84 killed, 315 wounded, and 57 captured Confederates. The total Federal losses were 84 killed, 266 wounded, and 33 missing. Among the captured Confederates was Brig. Gen. Clark.

Elsewhere in the west, fighting erupted along the Nueces River near Fort Clark, Texas, on August 10. During a routine scouting operation, a detachment of Confederate horsemen under Lt. C. D. McRae, 2d Texas Mounted Rifles, picked up the trail of "60 to 100" Federal soldiers. At daybreak the Confederates charged and routed the encampment, capturing 83 horses and finding 38 men killed on the ground. The Confederates lost 2 killed and 18 wounded. The remainder of the Yankee troops "fled," in

McRae's words, "scattering in all directions.... From the many signs of blood I infer many of those escaping were seriously wounded."

At Chattanooga, Maj. Gen. Edmund Kirby Smith was preparing an invasion of Kentucky that would retake much of the territory captured and occupied by Federal troops. Much was at stake: The armies of Maj. Gen. Don Carlos Buell and Gen. Braxton Bragg were maneuvering toward the rail-center prize of Chattanooga itself. This created a theater of war in eastern Tennessee and Kentucky. The Confederate plan called for Bragg to concentrate at Chattanooga while Kirby Smith should move against Cumberland Gap to open a thoroughfare into central Kentucky. Then the two Confederate armies would unite to destroy Buell and push him from Tennessee, reducing the threat to the Deep South and regaining the territory that had been lost. It was an audacious plan strategically, but one that might work if the timing were perfectly handled and if preliminary events favored the South.

Col. John Hunt Morgan's raiders sprang into action again in August. Morgan was assigned the task of preventing the anticipated retreat of Brig. Gen. George W. Morgan, who was presently at Cumberland Gap. Beginning a forced march from Sparta, Tennessee, Morgan's men moved out to cut the Louisville & Nashville Railroad and on August 12 attacked Gallatin, northeast of Nashville, skirmishing with a Union garrison and destroying an 800-foot-long railroad bridge over the Cumberland River and a railroad tunnel between Gallatin and Bowling Green. The Federal force consisted of the 28th Kentucky Infantry, commanded by Col. William P. Boone, who left his camp to visit his wife, lying ill in a hotel in town. On leaving his hotel room, Boone was surrounded and captured. Morgan's men infiltrated the town so quietly that most of the pickets and guards were asleep and surprised as well. The result was, in the words of Capt. Walworth Jenkins, "a shameful and complete surprise within two hours after Colonel Boone had left his guards 'on the alert and doing their duty,' and the surrender of the whole camp, on guard, and at the tunnel and bridges without a shot being fired for the defense of their position, the reputation of their State, or the honor of their country."

On August 13 bad news again befell the Union when the Federal garrison, the 71st Ohio Infantry under Col. Rodney Mason, surrendered Clarksville, Tennessee, northwest of Nashville, to Kentucky cavalry under Lt. Col. Benjamin H. Bristow. Mason's command totaled 320 men and faced more than 800 horse soldiers, some armed with Sharps carbines. After conducting an interview under flag of truce with the enemy, Mason surrendered without a fight, and nine days later he was cashiered from the service by President Lincoln for "repeated acts of cowardice in the face of the enemy."

For Morgan the situation went swimmingly. At Hartsville, just seventeen miles east of Gallatin, Morgan struck again at the Louisville & Nashville Railroad on August 21 and succeeded again in every respect. To head off Morgan's raiders, Brig. Gen. Richard W. Johnson had taken his force of 640 cavalry from McMinnville and encountered Morgan along the Hartsville Road. Johnson's force consisted of troopers chosen from the 2d Indiana Cavalry, 4th Kentucky Cavalry, 5th Kentucky Cavalry, and 7th Pennsylvania Cavalry. Johnson reached Hartsville looking for Morgan only to find his old camp littered with debris captured from Boone's camp at Gallatin, but kept moving quickly on hearing reports that Col. Nathan Bedford Forrest might be approaching from the rear. After a brisk fight with heavy rifle fire on each side, Johnson's men fell back three miles, reformed, and offered a battle line again. Morgan's attack was overpowering, however, and Johnson was compelled to surrender.

Morgan's was not the only Confederate cavalry brigade active during this period. Col. John S. Scott's brigade, the "Kirby Smith Brigade," left Kingston, west of Knoxville, on August 13, preparing to lead the way for the Cumberland Gap operation. The brigade consisted of the 1st Georgia Cavalry, the 1st Louisiana Cavalry, and a Kentucky company, the Buckner Guards. On August 17, Scott captured London, Kentucky, in the southeastern part of the state, after a 160-mile ride. Scott's brigade captured 75 prisoners and killed or wounded 50 in the Yankee garrison, suffering only 2 killed and 4 wounded themselves. The remaining 65 Federal soldiers retreated to the mountains after an hour's fight, reaching Cumberland Gap after five days of wandering through the wilderness. On August 23, at Big Hill, southeast of Richmond and east of Berea, Scott's cavalry again clashed with Federal troops, this time the 7th Kentucky Cavalry (Col. Leonidas Metcalfe) and a battalion of the 3d Tennessee Infantry. Metcalfe led an attack on the Confederate position on Big Hill, but found that only about 100 horse soldiers of his regiment followed him. "The remainder," recalled Capt. J. Mills Kendrick, "at the first cannon-shot, turned tail and fled like a pack of cowards, and are now dispersed over a half-dozen counties, some fleeing as far as Paris." It was a humiliating loss for the Federal regiments, and Scott continued on, blazing a trail for the Kentucky invasion.

Kirby Smith had assembled his Army of Kentucky and marched 9,000 men under the divisions of Brig. Gens. Patrick R. Cleburne, Thomas J. Churchill, and Henry Heth. Kirby Smith directed another 9,000 men under Brig. Gen. Carter L. Stevenson to approach the 8,000 soldiers of Brig. Gen. George W. Morgan at Cumberland Gap. Kirby Smith had marched northward to Barboursville by August 18 but found the position too intimidating for an attack, and he kept on the march northward toward Richmond. On August 29, Kirby Smith encountered Yankees in force and the battle of Richmond took place the following day. Scott's cavalry, now reinforced by the 3d

Tennessee Cavalry, aided Kirby Smith with valuable reconnaissance the day before the battle but joined the Confederate battle line after encountering the Federal cavalry.

On the Federal side, something of a growing panic was ensuing after some of the setbacks in the wake of Morgan's successes and the approach of a substantial army into central Kentucky. Commanding the Department of Ohio with headquarters in Cincinnati, Maj. Gen. Horatio G. Wright ordered Maj. Gen. William "Bull" Nelson, commanding the Army of Kentucky and headquartered in Lexington, to hold a position along the Kentucky River, where steep, high bluffs afforded a naturally formidable defense. But neither Nelson nor his most trusted subordinate, Brig. Gen. Mahlon D. Manson, believed that the river would offer such a sound defense, so they decided to ignore Wright's order. In the resulting battle, Confederate forces utterly routed the hapless Yankee troops, and Nelson decided to blame Manson, even alleging that Manson had not followed Nelson's orders, which was untrue.

Meanwhile, the Confederate forces were spread. Heth was well in the rear at Barboursville, awaiting supplies. The lead element of Kirby Smith's force was the division of Cleburne, who had fought so well at Shiloh that he was building a reputation as one of the most intelligent soldiers in the West. Churchill's reputation wasn't far behind. The 6,500 Federal troops south of the river, Nelson's men under the command of Manson, had been sent from Louisville to protect the state from the invasion. Manson's force consisted of his own brigade, that of Brig. Gen. Charles Cruft, and Metcalfe's cavalry. They were poorly instructed and led, most being recruits quickly assembled by Nelson. On August 29, Manson positioned Cruft at Richmond and moved south toward the enemy, a skirmish of small-arms fire erupting a mile and a half south of his camp at Rogersville, also known as White's Farm. The Confederates were pushed back and Manson survived a counterattack, holding his command in position near Rogersville as he dispatched cavalry forward.

The next morning brought the real action. The Federal battle line was formed across the Lexington Turnpike near the Mount Zion Christian Church, a brick building barely ten years old. Soldiers awaited a Confederate attack. Kirby Smith did not disappoint. At 6 A.M., Manson ordered Cruft forward in support. An hour of brisk skirmishing began during which casualties accumulated on both sides, though the Federals were positioned on a wooded hill that afforded a reasonable defensive stand. The action was hottest on the Confederate right among the 154th Tennessee Infantry. Cleburne soon decided to attack the Union left and attempt to turn it, and he launched a formidable assault west of the pike, led by Col. T. H. McCray's brigade of Arkansas and Texas men. The attack struck into the positions held by the 16th Indiana Infantry and 55th Indiana Infantry, and then moved into the 71st Indiana Infantry. Of Cruft's men, the 95th Ohio Infantry formed in line behind the battered right flank and charged a battery that held the Union position in check. The charge was repulsed with heavy casualties, however, and the majority of the Union line began to waver. The 18th Kentucky Infantry moved into position and commenced firing but was also repulsed with a stinging loss.

The Union line now in a disorganized retreat, a portion of the command attempted to reform a line at White's Farm a mile behind the original battlefield. It was merely 10:30 A.M. and the day seemed won by the Confederates, but there was still fighting to come. The Rebels attacked until they reached a fence running alongside a ditch about 200 yards shy of the Federal line. There, according to McCray, "finding the air literally filled with bombshells and Minié balls, I ordered the troops to lie down under cover." Nelson communicated his desire to retreat, but Manson found the regiments too heavily engaged to pull away quickly, and the Union troops actually charged the resting Confederates. The attack was a bloody disaster, and Cruft's and Manson's men all retreated northward toward the camps near Richmond.

Kirby Smith arrived on the field and had to be cautioned by his chief of staff, Col. John Pegram, not to lead an attack himself. By this time the third position for the Federal army was established near the city cemetery on the south side of Richmond itself. Nelson arrived and helped to establish the line, which was spread along a low ridge running through the cemetery. This time, Kirby Smith deployed Churchill on his left and the brigade of Col. Preston Smith on the right. By about 5 P.M. the exhausted Confederates approached, and through heavy fighting in the cemetery the Confederates again emerged triumphant. The battle of Richmond ended a complete Confederate victory, with casualties on the Federal side of 206 killed, 844 wounded, and an astonishing 4,303 captured or missing; Confederate losses were 78 killed, 372 wounded, and 1 missing. Among the Federal prisoners was Manson, who would be exchanged the following December, and Nelson, who had been wounded twice and who was captured but escaped the same night by sneaking into a cornfield. Having routed the Federal troops at Richmond, Kirby Smith had only to march northward to enter Lexington, which he did on September 1. The invasion of Kentucky was progressing better than the Richmond authorities could have hoped.

THESE ACTIONS in the western theater, in the critically important border state of Kentucky, were fought against a politically volatile backdrop of coming emancipation. On July 17, President Lincoln signed the Second Confiscation Act, after considerable debate in Congress. The act stated that slaves held by those in rebellion against the government of the United States could be set free after coming into regions of Federal control or occupation.

Vigorously supported by the radical Republicans, criticized by many abolitionists for not going far enough, the act was highly controversial and regarded as radical by most of the North. In addition to authorizing the confiscation of slaves, it suggested that other types of property could be seized, and allowed the government both to employ freedmen in various tasks as well as to establish a provision for colonization somewhere outside the United States, an idea that had been proposed for several decades as a compromise solution to the slave problem. Although Lincoln was not satisfied with all parts of the act, and many elements were never enforced (as is the case with many complex laws), Lincoln signed it. It signaled another step toward transforming the character of the war, and it upset nearly everyone in one way or another.

"We think you are strangely and disastrously remiss in the discharge of your official and imperative duty with regard to the emancipating provisions of the new Confiscation Act," implored the powerful, radical, eccentric editor Horace Greeley in an open letter to the president. The letter, titled "The Prayer of Twenty Millions," was published in the *New York Tribune* on August 20. "We think you are unduly influenced by the councils," continued Greeley, "the representations, the menaces of certain fossil politicians hailing from the Border Slave States. . . . The Rebels from the first have been eager to confiscate, imprison, scourge, and kill; we have fought wolves with the devices of sheep."

In response to this public stab at his policy, Lincoln sent a reply to the editor two days later. "My paramount object in this struggle *is* to save the Union," Lincoln wrote, "and is *not* either to save or to destroy slavery. If I could save the Union without freeing *any* slave, I would do it; and if I could save it by freeing *all* the slaves, I would do it; and if I could do it by freeing some and leaving others alone, I would also do that. . . . I intend no modification of my oft-expressed *personal* wish that all men, everywhere, could be free." Greeley printed the text of Lincoln's letter on August 25. While Lincoln was stepping into considerably more controversial waters as the chief executive, Secretary of State Seward wrote off concerns about the violent war spilling over into politics. "Assassination is not an American practice or habit," he wrote John Bigelow, the U.S. consul in Paris, on July 15, "and one so vicious and so desperate cannot be engrafted into our political system."

"I HAVE COME TO YOU from the West, where we have always seen the backs of our enemies," wrote Maj. Gen. John Pope, addressing his new soldiers, "from an army whose business it has been to seek the adversary, and to beat him when he was found; whose policy has been to attack and not defense. . . . Let us look before us, and not behind. Success and glory are in the advance; disaster and shame lurk in the rear." On June 26, Pope was assigned command of the newly created Army of Virginia, which Lincoln had created to comprise the forces of Banks, Frémont, McDowell, the troops in and around Washington's forts (commanded by Brig. Gen. Samuel D. Sturgis), the western Virginia division of the Ohioan Brig. Gen. Jacob D. Cox, and several lesser forces. This reorganization resulted from the unsuccessful operations in the Shenandoah Valley against Stonewall Jackson. Lincoln chose Pope because of his successes at New Madrid, Island No. 10, and Corinth.

Because Pope was a western officer who was junior to all the officers who would serve as his corps commanders, his appointment was controversial and objectionable to many. Pope aggravated the situation with boastful dispatches, as with his address to the new troops, in which he showed something of a contempt for eastern soldiers and for the leadership of George McClellan. So struck by the perceived injustice of the assignment was Frémont, who was after all the second-ranking major general in the regular army, that he refused to serve under Pope and resigned, which resignation the Lincoln administration quickly and gladly accepted. What would have been Frémont's corps fell under the command of Maj. Gen. Franz Sigel. All cavalry in the Army of Virginia—the troopers of Brig. Gens. John P. Hatch and George D. Bayard—was attached to the 2d and 3d Corps, so that Pope would not command any cavalry directly, and this would come back to haunt him during the ensuing campaign. At the time of Pope's order the *Richmond Inquirer* printed an old military joke that it attributed to Robert E. Lee: The newspaper offered a supposed communication from Pope and provided his address as "headquarters in the saddle." The *Inquirer* erroneously quoted Lee as saying, "If so, his headquarters are where his hindquarters ought to be." Others stated their feelings for Pope more directly. On August 23, after stopping a train and attempting to use it for transporting his brigade, and hearing that Pope might object, Sturgis uttered the famous line "I don't care for John Pope one pinch of owl dung."

Like him or not, Pope now commanded about 47,000 men spread from the Shenandoah Valley to Fredericksburg. He was given a threefold task: to assist McClellan, who was fighting on the Peninsula, by moving along the Orange & Alexandria Railroad toward Gordonsville, a critical railroad junction for the Confederate armies; to protect Washington from any Confederate military threat; and to preserve the occupation of the Shenandoah Valley. Pope did not move southward quickly to aid McClellan, for by the time his command was organized, the Seven Days were underway and Pope watched and waited to ascertain McClellan's intentions.

By mid-July, with McClellan encamped at Harrison's Landing, the situation began to develop into the Second Bull Run campaign, termed by Southerners Second Manassas. With Halleck now general-in-chief, Pope finally organized his army and began to move it east of the Blue Ridge Mountains and southward toward Gordonsville. Pope's army was now organized as follows: Sigel's 1st Corps consisted of the divisions of Brig. Gens. Robert C. Schenck, Adolph W. A. von Steinwehr, and Carl Schurz, with the independent brigade of Brig. Gen. Robert H. Milroy and cavalry brigade of Col. John Beardsley, and attached artillery; Banks's 2d Corps comprised the divisions of Brig. Gens. Alpheus S. Williams and Christopher C. Augur, with the cavalry brigade of Brig. Gen. John P. Hatch and attached artillery; McDowell's 3d Corps consisted of the divisions of Brig. Gens. Rufus King and James B. Ricketts, the cavalry brigade of Bayard, and attached artillery, along with the Pennsylvania Reserves, commanded by Brig. Gen. John F. Reynolds; and the Reserve Corps commanded by Sturgis, which contained the brigade of Brig. Gen. Abram S. Piatt and other attached troops.

On July 14, Banks sent his cavalry forward to wreck the railroad that connected Gordonsville with Charlottesville and Lynchburg. Hatch commanded the expedition, taking artillery along and moving so glacially that he did not arrive within the vicinity of the town until five days later, when he suddenly discovered with alarm that Stonewall Jackson, from the Peninsula, occupied the town. What of the movements of the large armies in force facing off near Richmond? Halleck visited McClellan at Harrison's Landing and after considerable discussion decided to order Little Mac to withdraw to a point along Aquia Creek, north of Fredericksburg—this in the face of McClellan's contention that the army should continue to threaten Richmond or move on Petersburg. As a commander who had taken a huge army up the Peninsula to within a few miles of the Confederate capital only to be beaten back in inglorious defeat, McClellan must be given credit for wanting to carry on the campaign. But again his notion of continuance was based on receiving more reinforcements from Washington. He believed firmly that Lee had in excess of 200,000 men in front of Richmond, and McClellan now had a mere 90,000 left. In reality, Lee had fewer men than the Army of the Potomac.

At meeting's end, Halleck had concluded that if the Federal armies were to take Richmond or move on Petersburg (as they would do two years later) then McClellan was not the general to lead them. By contrast, Lee was emerging as a bold leader for the Army of Northern Virginia, partially by nature and partially because with so much at stake and with limited resources, he had little choice. Pinned into his Richmond defenses by the continued nearby presence of McClellan, he nonetheless sent Jackson to delay Pope's movement toward Gordonsville, searched for reinforcements for the badly outnumbered Jackson, and rebuilt and strengthened the fortifications and entrenchments in front of Richmond.

At the end of July, Lee decided to make his bold move. He dispatched Maj. Gen. A. P. Hill's "Light Division," 12,000 strong, to join Jackson and head off any threat posed by Pope, bringing Jackson's corps to an effective strength of 24,000. Simultaneously, Lee created a diversion by sporadic firing at Federal positions at and near Harrison's Landing, which was all that was needed to hold McClellan in check. Meanwhile, Maj. Gen. Ambrose E. Burnside's 9th Corps (14,000), which had come north from North Carolina to Fort Monroe, by August 5 pressed on to Falmouth and began to move westward toward Pope's forces, located near Culpeper Court House. Lee now contemplated a major northward movement but reconsidered when on August 5 a small number of McClellan's troops moved north from Harrison's Landing back to Malvern Hill, where skirmishing occurred, but they returned to the Federal base two days later. By August 7, not waiting any longer for orders from Lee, Jackson took the initiative to march northward and defeat the separated corps of Pope's army before they could concentrate.

To muddy the waters on the Federal side, Pope was told that McClellan's army would move north and unite with the Army of Virginia, giving the Confederates battle in northern Virginia. He moved into position near Cedar Mountain, west of the railroad and between Rapidan Station to the south and Culpeper Court House to the north, hoping to await McClellan's arrival and build a defensive line from which he could launch raids, if necessary. This decision was partly affected by Halleck's desire to maintain a base on Aquia Creek. With McClellan pulling out of the Peninsula, Lee would certainly follow, and Pope hoped that he would not be overwhelmed by united Confederate forces before McClellan's arrival. But as with most strategic plans of the Civil War, Pope's ideas during the early phases of the Second Bull Run campaign would not go the way the commander had envisioned them.

Jackson's Corps consisted of the divisions of Brig. Gen. Charles S. Winder, Hill (the "Light Division"), and Maj. Gen. Richard S. Ewell, with attached cavalry commanded by Maj. Gen. Jeb Stuart. Jackson arrived before Cedar Mountain about noon on August 9, and a battle resulted (sometimes called Slaughter Mountain). Jackson deployed Winder on the left and Ewell on the right, with Hill behind them. Jackson first encountered George Bayard's cavalry and forced it back with artillery fire beginning about 2 P.M., the decisive movement coming from Brig. Gen. Jubal Early's brigade. It was an incredibly hot day, the temperature reaching near 100°F by early afternoon. For an hour and a half, beginning at 3:30 P.M., the battlefield witnessed a duel of artillery fire, with Federal guns firing an amazing 3,213 rounds during the afternoon, and the Confederate pieces firing a similarly high number. One of the shells mortally wounded Winder, commander of Jackson's old division, who was directing the fire of his artillery batteries, standing in his shirtsleeves. A shell fragment ripped through his left arm, tearing the arm and lacerating his left side as deeply as his spine. He died a few hours later.

By 5:30 P.M., action was beginning to unfold over the enormous rectangle of ground north of Cedar Run that had witnessed such heavy artillery fire. Col. Edward L. Thomas's brigade of Georgians came up to support the brigades of Early and Brig. Gen. William B. Taliaferro and encountered the sweeping division of Brig. Gen. Christopher C. Augur, sent into battle as Banks's lead element. Augur led a savage attack into the fields north of Cedar Run, spearheaded by the brigades of Brig. Gens. Henry Prince and John W. Geary. Of the attack, Col. Charles Candy of the 66th Ohio remarked that it was "the hottest day I ever experienced in the field," and that he "never knew troops to suffer more for water." By 6 P.M. Brig. Gen. Samuel Wylie Crawford's brigade was attacking into a wheatfield against the Confederate left, dissolving it into confusion. Crawford next struck southward along the Confederate line and, with Prince and Geary, drove the exhausted Confederates of Early and Taliaferro back in disarray. Writing from "headquarters under a cedar tree," Crawford addressed McClellan "My dear Mac," informing him that "the enemy's cavalry is still around us. Send rations for the men. I do not know how long we will be in this line but we must fight before long. I took up a strong position & he has been moving here & there to find out our strength."

But after a dinnertime verdict of a Federal victory, fortunes changed. Brig. Gen. Lawrence O'Bryan Branch arrived with his North Carolinians and helped Jackson to rally the retreating troops; the counterattack necessitated a withdrawal of Crawford. An hour later, a Confederate cavalry charge across Brushy Field failed miserably as Brig. Gen. George H. Gordon's brigade made a stand and fired heavy volleys of musketry into the Southern horsemen. By early evening a full-scale counterattack of A. P. Hill's division pushed the Yankees into a scramble, the brigades of Brig. Gens. James J. Archer and William Dorsey Pender taking the most aggressive roles in routing the Federals. To add insult to injury, Brig. Gen. Isaac R. Trimble brought his brigade down from the mountain and struck artillery positions as the Yankees retreated.

The casualties at Cedar Mountain for the Union forces were 314 killed, 1,445 wounded, and 594 missing; the Confederate losses were 231 killed and 1,107 wounded. Banks was compelled to retreat across Cedar Run, so the battle was a tactical Confederate victory, another feather in Jackson's cap, and revived his image after the damage it sustained during the Peninsular campaign. But Jackson's advance was arrested by the division of Brig. Gen. James B. Ricketts, and the coordination of orders on both sides had been poorly handled. Jackson's disposition of troops on the field had been poorly organized: His now famous secrecy, a reluctance to divulge intentions even to his senior subordinates, had frustrated Hill and led to poor coordination. The withdrawal of Jackson from the battlefield was all that Lee needed to believe

Jackson could not handle facing Pope with his current force, and so Lee took a big risk again on August 13 by sending Longstreet's corps to further bolster Jackson's numbers. The next day McClellan, Lee learned, was pulling out of the Peninsula. Now Lee launched into a race to move northward himself, join with Jackson, and strike Pope before McClellan's probable slow movement would create a single huge Federal army. The dramatic movements that would lead to the battle of Second Bull Run were underway.

By now both Lee's and Pope's armies counted about 55,000 effectives each, and by August 15, Lee arrived at Gordonsville. Lee had to attack quickly to avoid McClellan's reinforcement but also to cut off Pope from his lines of communication. He massed the Army of Northern Virginia south of Clark's Mountain—southeast of Cedar Mountain—and planned to send Jeb Stuart's cavalry, followed by the whole army, north to the Rapidan River, screened from view by Clark's Mountain. Stuart would cross at Somerville Ford and destroy the railroad bridge, then move on Pope's rear to distract and destroy as much of the Federal supplies as he could, also blocking the route of Yankee retreat. The plan for a turning movement on Pope's left was sound and the timetable was established for August 18. Pope, meanwhile, sent telegrams to Washington asking for a speedier movement of McClellan's troops up the Potomac River, and he began to panic slightly, leaving his army in a relatively exposed position around Cedar Mountain.

Lee's timing failed him and ruined the excellent plan to turn Pope's left. Stuart's tardiness in carrying out his orders didn't help. By the time Lee crossed the Rapidan on August 20, Pope had already pulled away from his position and moved behind the Rappahannock River along the Orange & Alexandria Railroad, by which he was now receiving supplies from Manassas, the supply landing at Aquia Creek having wound down to naught. Poor staff work and the capture on August 17 by marauding Yankee cavalry of one of Jeb Stuart's assistant adjutant generals, Maj. Norman R. Fitz Hugh, sealed the fate of Lee's plan. Stuart was not exactly thrilled that he narrowly escaped capture himself and that his favorite uniform coat and plumed hat were taken along with Fitz Hugh. He retaliated on August 22–23 with a raid on Pope's headquarters, termed the battle of Catlett's Station, or Rappahannock Station, in which he captured Pope's dress coat and a cache of papers that gave the Confederates specific information about the planned routes of the Federal reinforcement. This information alerted Lee that within five days the Union army's ranks would grow to nearly 130,000. Another minor action had occurred at Brandy Station on August 20, resulting from an attempt by Lee to turn Pope's position, which failed. The prospects for Lee's aggressive plans were worsened by incessant rains on the 22d and 23d, which made roads muddy.

Rising waters in rivers and creeks thwarted plans on both sides. Pope hoped to strike at two exposed brigades of Confederates that had been isolated by high water at Waterloo. Before he could send Sigel and Banks into action, however, Jackson pulled them out, assisted by slowly falling water levels on the river. Time favored only Pope. After all of Lee's superb marching and planning, he had failed to attack and the Federal reinforcements were getting closer. Now a new plan, sanctioned by Jackson, emerged. Lee would divide his army, once again risking a lot for the proposed gain, sending Jackson upriver with Stuart's cavalry, endanger Pope's line of communications and supply, and force him to retreat. The bulk of Lee's army would attack Pope to create a major diversion and rapidly follow Jackson's route, unite with him, and offer battle in force if necessary—he hoped while Pope was retreating—allowing a decisive Confederate victory.

To say Lee's plan was risky is an understatement, but Lee was growing comfortable with excessive boldness, and he felt the other options, particularly those involving waiting for McClellan to show up, would be far costlier. Lee was not only confident in the abilities of his army, which had stopped McClellan at Richmond and marched handsomely northward, but he was motivated by a sense of desperation. The alternative to boldness might be certain, eventual defeat. So on August 25, Jackson began his northward movement, marching relentlessly and reaching Salem on the railroad the first night before sending Stuart off eastward to Thoroughfare Gap through the Bull Run Mountains the next day. Jackson's force drove eastward and by nightfall on August 26 encamped at Bristoe Station, on the Federal line of communications, where he learned that the Union supply base was a short distance away at Manassas Junction, just south of the old Bull Run battlefield. Jackson dispatched Stuart and the infantry brigade of Trimble to capture the supply depot before reinforcements arrived from Alexandria, where troops under Union Maj. Gen. William B. Franklin (6th Corps) and a portion of Maj. Gen. Edwin V. Sumner's command (2d Corps) were landing; Longstreet had by now completed the first leg of the maneuver in Jackson's wake, arriving at Orleans on the railroad line.

The forces were now rapidly converging and a major battle was certain to result. The command situation in the Northern army was unclear. Halleck had failed to specify the seniority of command assignments, and McClellan believed he would command all the forces, including Pope's, whereas Pope believed the two armies would be directed by Halleck. Pope knew that Jackson was on the march, but the Federal horse soldiers lost the rapidly moving Confederate columns and Pope believed the Confederates were moving into the Shenandoah Valley. Then, on August 26, the situation grew even more confused. There were skirmishes at Bristoe Station, Manassas Junction along Bull Run, at Gainesville and Haymarket. At Manassas Junction the Confederates captured several hundred prisoners and substantial supplies. "What a prize it was!" remembered Allen C. Redwood of the 55th Virginia Infantry. "Here were long warehouses full of stores; cars loaded with boxes of new clothing *en route* to General Pope, but destined to adorn the 'backs of his enemies.' . . . one was limited in his choice to only so much as he could personally transport." At 8 P.M. the telegraph to Manassas Junction went dead. Two hours later Pope's confusion grew when scouts reported that Jackson occupied Manassas Junction and Bristoe Station. At dawn on the next morning Pope discovered that Jackson's presence at Manassas meant that Lee's army was divided, and any military man would surely grasp the chance that was offered for defeating the Southern force. For the moment, it appeared that John Pope held all the cards.

The composition of the armies for the battle of Second Bull Run was altered and expanded from those at Cedar Mountain. Pope's Army of Virginia remained similar in organization with the exception that Brig. Gen. George S. Greene was assigned to command the 2d Division of Banks's 2d Corps, in the place of Augur. Additionally, two army corps from the Army of the Potomac arrived in time to participate in parts of the battle. These included the corps of Maj. Gen. Samuel P. Heintzelman (3d Corps; divisions of Maj. Gens. Philip Kearny and Joseph Hooker); and Maj. Gen. Fitz John Porter (5th Corps; divisions of Maj. Gen. George W. Morell and Brig. Gen. George Sykes). From North Carolina came Maj. Gen. Jesse L. Reno (9th Corps; divisions of Maj. Gen. Isaac I. Stevens and Reno).

Lee's Army of Northern Virginia now consisted of two enormous corps, sometimes called "wings," led by Maj. Gens. James Longstreet and Thomas J. Jackson. Longstreet's divisional commanders were Maj. Gen. Richard H. Anderson and Brig. Gens. David R. Jones, Cadmus M. Wilcox, John Bell Hood, and James L. Kemper, with attached artillery. Jackson's divisional commanders were Brig. Gen. William B. Taliaferro, Maj. Gen. A. P. Hill, Maj. Gen. Richard S. Ewell, and the cavalry division under Maj. Gen. Jeb Stuart.

Realizing that his position along the Rappahannock was untenable and, more significantly, that he could strike at the separated corps of Lee's army and defeat them in detail, Pope rearrayed his forces on August 27 and acted well. On this day, skirmishing erupted at Kettle Run near Bristoe Station, Cub Run, Bull Run Bridge, Broad Run, Buckland Run, Salem, and Waterford. At 10 A.M. Pope urgently requested aid from Halleck, expecting to retake the railroad at Manassas Junction and reopen communications with Washington by nightfall. But Col. Herman Haupt, the army's chief of railroad construction, was ahead of him. Haupt had anticipated the critical need for holding the railroad bridge over Bull Run at Union Mills, and he had thrown together a brigade and two small regiments to protect it. The force was led by Brig. Gen. George W. Taylor. Rather than protecting the bridge with his rather small force, Taylor marched toward Jackson and encountered A. P. Hill, who stopped the Federal approach. In the action, called Bull Run Bridge, Taylor was struck in the left leg, which damaged the bone substantially, and on September 1 he died. By the evening of August 27, Pope's redisposition of troops was as follows: Sigel and McDowell's corps were at Gainesville, Reno's corps to the south at Greenwich, Porter and Banks were farther south at Warrenton Junction, and Hooker's division (fresh from the Peninsula and running low on ammunition) occupied Bristoe Station. Hooker had been ordered to march on Bristoe, recapture it, and open the communication with Alexandria, but in moving to do so he found Ewell there in force. But Ewell had been ordered not to engage heavily and so abandoned Bristoe, moving back to Manassas Junction. A Union cavalry brigade led by Brig. Gen. John Buford, who had replaced Hatch, scouted against Longstreet's approach from White Plains, while Jackson was concentrated at Manassas Junction. By nightfall nearly half of Lee's army—Jackson's corps—stood between the Federal force and Washington.

Although Pope had made logical decisions about where to move his troops, he failed to follow up with the second requirement—how to use them. He did not order McDowell to move westward to guard the mountain passes through which Longstreet could move to reunite with Jackson, particularly along the railroad at Thoroughfare Gap, and he did not exercise control over the cavalry, losing touch with it. Jackson, meanwhile, rejoiced in the abundant captured Federal supplies. He ordered the men to fill wagons with four days' rations and then burned the remaining goods. He then moved closer to the old Bull Run battlefield to take up a defensive position along Stony Ridge, expecting an imminent attack by Pope and hoping that Longstreet would arrive soon.

By the morning of August 28, Pope began to lose confidence and grow anxious. Expecting that Jackson might characteristically attack, he feared for Hooker, the closest force to Jackson, whose men had an average of only five rounds of ammunition each. In response, Pope ordered his commanders to concentrate at Manassas Junction. He sent Porter to reinforce Hooker at Bristoe Station. But he had forgotten about Longstreet. Exercising clear independent thinking, McDowell dispatched a small force toward Thoroughfare Gap that consisted of the cavalry brigades of Buford and Bayard plus the infantry division of Brig. Gen. James B. Ricketts. Having left this small force behind, McDowell then proceeded to move toward Manassas Junction. Longstreet approached the gap, accompanied by Lee, and by 3 P.M. dispatched troops northward to break through the gap at Hopewell, defended lightly by Buford, bypassing Thoroughfare Gap altogether and flanking Ricketts. Pope, at Bristoe Station, faced the increasingly perplexing situation. Meanwhile, Jackson's ill-defined and secretive orders confused Ewell and A. P. Hill, and they took illogical routes northward, Hill marching all the way to Centreville and then westward again, delaying their presence on Stony Ridge until early afternoon. Reconnaissance reported Hill's division at Centreville and Pope believed it to be Jackson's concentration. Without any control over cavalry to provide him with accurate information, Pope ordered Sigel and the division of reserves under Brig. Gen. John F. Reynolds to countermarch northward to the Warrenton Turnpike. Heintzelman and Reno, meanwhile, were ordered to turn north as well, with Porter and Banks following. With Pope essentially blind to what was actually happening, only one division was in the vicinity of Jackson's army. It was the division of Brig. Gen. Rufus King, which had moved eastward along the turnpike and approached the hamlet of Groveton, south of Stony Ridge, by late afternoon.

Jackson continued to reap good fortune. He received a captured copy of Pope's General Orders, so that he now knew that Pope wished to concentrate at Manassas Junction. But Jackson believed that Pope's intention was to retreat across Bull Run to hook up with the trailing elements of McClellan's army. Fearing a united, large Yankee force, Jackson decided to take the initiative and attack. King's division arrived in force before Jackson about 5:30 P.M., and a blistering attack resulted with heavy fighting on both sides. The battle, known as Groveton or Brawner's Farm, was a prelude to the large-scale battle the following day. King's division fought stubbornly against the divisions of Ewell and Taliaferro, and the Union brigade commanded by Brig. Gen. John Gibbon, consisting of the 2d Wisconsin Infantry (Col. Edgar O'Connor), 6th Wisconsin Infantry (Col. Lysander Cutler), 7th Wisconsin Infantry (Col. William W. Robinson), and 19th Indiana Infantry (Col. Solomon Meredith) fought so bitterly against a larger Confederate wave that it earned the name "Iron Brigade." With heavy casualties mounting around the John C. Brawner Farm, the fighting continued apace until about 9 P.M. The intensity of the fight here was remarkable. "Our men on the left loaded and fired with the energy of madmen," wrote Maj. Rufus Dawes of the 6th Wisconsin, "and a recklessness of death truly wonderful, but human nature could not long stand such a terribly wasting fire. It literally mowed out great gaps in the line, but the isolated squads would rally together and rush right into the face of Death." The cries of the wounded were fierce, and among them was Ewell, who was hit in the right kneecap with a Minié bullet, which necessitated amputation of his right leg. His health was seriously jeopardized, but Ewell wore a wooden leg and returned to field duty in May 1863.

At daybreak on August 29, Pope's forces were still spread considerably and he did not adequately understand where Jackson and Longstreet were. Moreover, McClellan's communications entered the fray with more force, the Army of the Potomac's chief believing that Jackson alone had 100,000 men, despite hearing the accurate figure of 24,000 reported to him. Reno's 9th Corps and Heintzelman's 2d Corps were northeast of Jackson at Centreville. Sigel's 1st Corps, with Reynolds's division in tow, was approaching Jackson from the south and marched up the southern slope of Henry House Hill, in the center of the Bull Run battlefield of the previous summer. McDowell's 3d Corps, Porter's 5th Corps, and Banks's 2d Corps were spread to the south from Manassas Junction to Bristoe Station, and were joined by the divisions of Ricketts and King. The cavalry brigades of Buford and Bayard were scattered near Haymarket, and little now opposed Longstreet's approach from the west.

Pope's orders issued during the night called for Sigel and Reynolds to attack at dawn, with Heintzelman and Reno in support; McDowell was supposed to march eastward; and Porter would move north to Centreville, creating a pincer movement on Jackson that would crush him before he could be reinforced by Longstreet. But Pope's ignorance of what was actually happening continued; as his orders suggest, he didn't realize where Ricketts and King were, and the seeds of failure were planted by the Federal commander's foolish assumptions. Moreover, Pope made no plans for the possibility of facing Longstreet should he join the action, somehow believing that half of the Army of Northern Virginia had been thrust back to the west by two small cavalry brigades. Longstreet had actually moved through the gaps by now and was approaching Jackson's position on Stony Ridge in front of Catharpin Creek, southwest of Sudley Springs. Early on August 29, Pope discovered where McDowell actually was, and so it dawned on him that the plan set forth was no longer sensible.

Thus, the stage was set for one of the major battles of the eastern theater, Second Bull Run, also known as Second Manassas. Early on the morning of August 29, Pope had about 62,000 in the field and Lee about 50,000. Pope wished to attack Jackson from both sides, despite Longstreet's approach, so he ordered Porter to change direction, turning southward and then westward, toward Gainesville, along with King's battered division. McDowell presumed he should go, too, so he followed the same path, taking his corps along with Ricketts's division.

By 7 A.M., during their march, Porter and McDowell received a telegram from Pope with still more confusing (and confused) news. He worried over the impending arrival of Longstreet and ordered Porter and McDowell to stop their march after joining Sigel's 1st Corps, so that Pope could then reassess the situation and tell them where they should go—to Gainesville or elsewhere. Pope also worried openly about a perceived lack of supplies and suggested that perhaps Jackson was retreating and he should not be allowed to escape unharmed. Although Pope recognized now that Longstreet was coming, he felt that his corps would not arrive on the field until the end of the following day, which was significantly wrong. Pope also allowed Porter and McDowell to exercise their judgment. "If any considerable advantages are to be gained by departing from this order it will not be strictly carried out," declared Pope, which could be interpreted as meaning practically anything.

Longstreet was long gone from Gainesville, however, and had deployed his troops as the southern half of a Confederate battle line that stretched from Jackson to the north, along Stony Ridge, south through Groveton, across the Warrenton Turnpike, and along a chain of hills, terminating west of Dawkins's Branch. By 11 A.M. the faithful cavalry officer John Buford had composed a telegram and sent it to McDowell to forward on to Pope; in the missive Buford reported that Longstreet had passed through Gainesville. McDowell, however, inexplicably failed to forward the communication to the army commander, and what was shaping up as a very badly directed battle on the Federal side grew worse.

During the late morning hours the corps of Reno and Heintzelman attacked headlong into Jackson's well-fortified position on Stony Ridge, and a thick blanket of smoke and haze settled over parts of the field as artillery fire heated up and musket volleys rang throughout the old battleground. Pope, arriving at 1:30 P.M. and establishing headquarters at the John Dogan House in Groveton, coordinated his attacks very poorly, sending unit after unit into the fray, smashing into the Confederate lines, in piecemeal fashion and without proper support. Still, he seemed outwardly confident, declaring of the Rebels, "We shall bag the whole crowd." Late in the morning, attacks against Jackson by Schurz's division and Milroy's brigade had failed. At times the Confederate line nearly broke in disorder, especially on the left flank, but it held stubbornly as units fired savagely into the onrushing bluecoats. To the south, McDowell and Porter could see smoke rising and hear the cannon booming but did not march toward the action. McDowell sent Porter on a resumption of his march toward Gainesville, wherein he eventually met resistance from Jeb Stuart's cavalry along Dawkins's Branch and stopped. Late in the afternoon Porter received a telegram from Pope that ordered him to "push forward into action at once on the enemy's flank, and, if possible, on his rear, keeping your right in communication with General Reynolds."

Reynolds, however, was considerably north near Bald Hill, facing the northern flank of Longstreet's command, near the Confederate center. Carrying out both parts of Pope's orders was impossible, Porter found, and so he failed. The order clearly demonstrated that Pope did not understand or appreciate the situation his army faced. Nonetheless, when the battle turned from confusion into Union disaster, Pope needed a scapegoat, and the nonresponsive Porter, a McClellan loyalist who distrusted Pope, became the target. Shortly after the battle, he was brought up on charges of disobedience and misconduct. Arrested on November 25, Porter was tried and on January 21, 1863, cashiered from the army. Porter was in fact a great soldier, age 39, New Hampshire–born and a cousin of the naval officers David Dixon Porter, William D. Porter, and David G. Farragut. His military career ruined, Porter became police commissioner of New York City and, on review of the case, was reinstated by President Chester A. Arthur on August 5, 1886, as a colonel in the regular army to rank from May 14, 1861.

Jackson, meanwhile, was attacked about 3 P.M. by the brigade of Brig. Gen. Cuvier Grover, with the Yankees maneuvering in retreat after hard fighting. Initially, an attack of Col. James Nagle's brigade into the unfinished railroad cut achieved some success, but eventually it came crashing back. While the guns were booming loudly and Jackson was engaged to the north, Longstreet failed to participate substantially on the battle's first day. Several times Lee firmly suggested that his senior corps commander ought to strike at the Yankees' left flank, but Longstreet repeatedly begged off and wanted more time to coordinate an attack. Finally, about 7 P.M., Longstreet sent the division of Brig. Gen. John Bell Hood forward to reconnoiter a position from which to attack the next morning; Hood instead encountered the Federal division now commanded by Brig. Gen. John P. Hatch (formerly Augur's). After a short fight Hood retreated to the safety of the Rebel battle line.

Pope now made still another misjudgment on the progress of the battle. Early on August 30, the battle's second day (sometimes called Groveton Heights in addition to day two of Second Bull Run), he convinced himself that the Confederate army was withdrawing from the position along Stony Ridge and south of it, partly inspired by Hood's retreat and partly by wishful thinking. This caused Pope to order the corps of McDowell, Heintzelman, and Porter to pursue the fleeing enemy and offer battle. But Lee's army was not retreating. Lee's plan for the day called for sweeping around to the Federal right and placing his force between Pope's army and the supply and communications source at Alexandria, thus forcing Pope to withdraw. Another set of misunderstandings and misdirections then took place. Pope was informed by John F. Reynolds that Jackson's corps was not retreating; he then ordered an attack on Jackson with Porter's corps striking him on the right and Heintzelman's corps along with the divisions of Hatch and Ricketts on the left. Reno's and Sigel's corps were held in reserve. Reynolds's division of Pennsylvania reserves occupied Bald Hill to the south of the battle lines and were to be called up later. Porter's corps attacked savagely and with good co-ordination at about 1:30 P.M., initially sending Jackson's somewhat wearied soldiers on the right of his line into a mild panic. Longstreet's corps, with artillery placed on high ground south of Groveton, responded to the attack on Jackson by opening a thunderous cannonade on Porter's attacking columns. The attack was fully under way by 3 P.M., but ultimately Longstreet's artillery

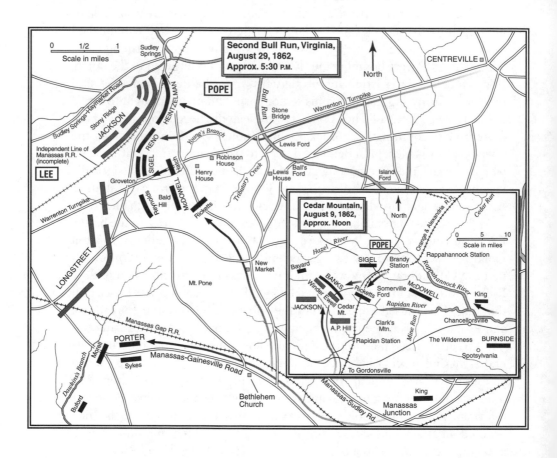

Second Bull Run, Virginia, August 29, 1862, Approx. 5:30 P.M.

North

CENTREVILLE

Scale in miles
0   1/2   1

Sudley Springs

POPE

Sudley Springs–Haymarket Road

Stony Ridge

JACKSON

HEINTZELMAN

Bull Run

Stone Bridge

Warrenton Turnpike

Lewis Ford

Young's Branch

RENO

SIGEL

Hatch

Robinson House

Lewis House

Ball's Ford

Island Ford

Independent Line of Manassas R.R. (incomplete)

LEE

Groveton

Henry House

Tributary Creek

Warrenton Turnpike

Reynolds

Bald Hill

McDOWELL

Ricketts

LONGSTREET

Mt. Pone

New Market

Cedar Mountain, August 9, 1862, Approx. Noon

North

Hazel River

SIGEL

Brandy Station

Orange & Alexandria R.R.

Cedar Run

Rappahannock Station

Scale in miles
0   5   10

POPE

Bayard

BANKS

Ricketts

Somerville Ford

Winder Ewell

JACKSON

Cedar Mt.

Rapidan River

McDOWELL

Rappahannock River

King

A.P. Hill

Clark's Mtn.

Mine Run

Chancellorsville

Rapidan Station

The Wilderness

BURNSIDE

Spotsylvania

To Gordonsville

Manassas Gap R.R.

PORTER

Morell

Sykes

Manassas-Gainesville Road

Manassas-Sudley Rd.

Buford

Doubkins's Branch

Bethlehem Church

King

Manassas Junction

fire devastated the Yankees and sent the attack reeling back in retreat. At times, with men on both sides running low on ammunition—particularly along the unfinished railroad in an area known as the Deep Cut—soldiers on both sides resorted to throwing rocks at each other. Support by Reynolds's division, swinging up from Bald Hill, was too little too late to assist in regrouping the assault.

Longstreet now sent a solid, well-coordinated attack forward into the retreating left flank of the Federal army, striking with five fresh divisions. Brig. Gen. John Bell Hood struck eastward into the brigades of Col. Gouverneur K. Warren and Lt. Col. Martin D. Hardin. Longstreet's men pushed forward, enveloping Chinn Ridge, Kemper's division capturing the ground around the Chinn House and pushing off the brigades of Cols. John A. Koltes and Wladimir Krzyzanowski. Longstreet's attack captured Bald Hill with ease, and counterattacks by Sigel's corps were beaten back several times. Pope now played his own army's line against itself. By pulling troops out of the right flank for fear that the left might crumble, he weakened the right enough such that a renewed attack by Jackson pushed it back. The whole Yankee battle line was slowly retreating back to old familiar ground such as Henry House Hill, where the first large battle of the war had similarly ended in Union defeat. The landmarks or ruins of the landmarks from First Bull Run surrounding them—the Henry House ruins, the Robinson House, the Stone Bridge, the Stone House—the Federals must have had a sense of déjà vu. In a humiliating repeat of history Federal soldiers on Henry House Hill once again withdrew from the battlefield at dark, Pope feeling outwitted, upset, and unaware of how to combat the Confederate counterattack. The search for the scapegoat now began.

In a panic, Pope issued the orders to withdraw his army toward Centreville at 7 P.M. During the early hours of the night the entire Federal army marched in relatively good order, the last elements, Sigel's corps, arriving at Centreville by midnight on August 31. On crossing the old Stone Bridge on the Warrenton Turnpike, under which Bull Run quietly flowed, Sigel's troops wrecked the bridge. Lee's army was much too wearied and depleted of ammunition and other stores to pursue Pope's army, and such a pursuit at night would have been unusual at the time. To make matters even messier, a rain started to fall and became heavy by morning, ruining roads and creating rain-swollen creeks. Lee sent Jackson around to the north to position himself behind the Federal force at Centreville; on this day Pope's dispatches took on an especially alarming quality; McClellan, meanwhile, was even more panicked, fearing for the safety of Washington as well as Pope's army and in a snit because Halleck would not order Pope to fall back from Centreville.

By late on August 31, Pope had begun to regain his senses, envisioning the turning movement that was underway by Lee and Jackson (Longstreet

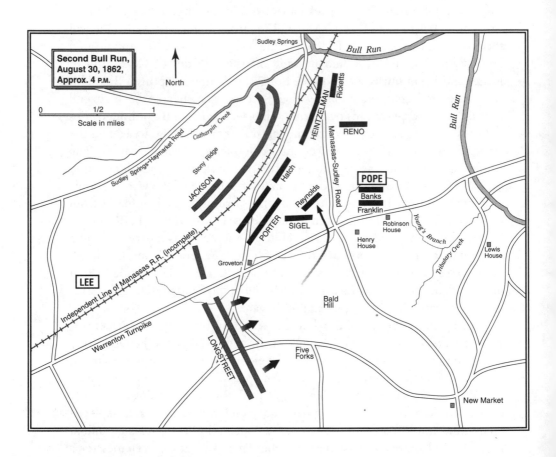

Second Bull Run,
August 30, 1862,
Approx. 4 P.M.

North

0   1/2   1
Scale in miles

Sudley Springs

Bull Run

Ricketts

HEINTZELMAN

RENO

Bull Run

Catharpin Creek

Sudley Springs–Haymarket Road

Stony Ridge

JACKSON

Hatch

Reynolds

Manassas-Sudley Road

POPE

Banks

Franklin

PORTER

SIGEL

Robinson House

Henry House

Young's Branch

Lewis House

LEE

Independent Line of Manassas R.R. (incomplete)

Groveton

Bald Hill

Tributary Creek

Warrenton Turnpike

LONGSTREET

Five Forks

New Market

would stay in place for a day, helping to deceive Pope, then march in support of the operation). Jackson spent the night at Pleasant Valley, three miles north of Centreville, and pondered the coming day. Early the next morning, September 1, Pope ordered a brigade from Sumner's corps northward to scout for Jackson, the cavalry being too depleted of energy for the mission. Pope's mood shifted to the positive when he agreed on a plan with Halleck to fall back toward Washington and also to block Jackson. He ordered McDowell back toward the city, to Fairfax Court House, and two brigades of infantry under Brig. Gen. Isaac I. Stevens toward Chantilly, northwest of Fairfax Court House. A brigade of infantry commanded by Maj. Gen. Philip Kearny joined Stevens early in the afternoon.

The result was the battle of Chantilly, the final action of the campaign and a rearguard engagement that accomplished little except for accruing casualties, two of whom were important and respected Federal generals. Jackson's soldiers marched southward at an extremely slow pace, making just three miles by midafternoon, and they struck the brigades of Stevens and Kearny. Stevens's men made up the Federal left and faced the soldiers of A. P. Hill, while Kearny's men on the right opposed those of Ewell, now commanded by Brig. Gen. Alexander R. Lawton. The attacking Confederates sent musket volleys into the defensive positions of the Yankees, and although they outnumbered the Northerners, they could not break the Yankee line by dark.

During the intense fighting, Kearny mistakenly rode into the Confederate lines and was shot and killed instantly by a musket ball that entered near his hip and caused extensive internal injuries and bleeding before lodging in his chest. Charles F. Walcott, a captain in the 21st Massachusetts Infantry, described Kearny's death. "I watched him moving in the murky twilight through the corn, and . . . saw his horse suddenly rear and turn, and half-a-dozen muskets flash around him: so died the intrepid soldier, Gen. Philip Kearny!" Several weeks later McClellan received a letter from Robert E. Lee over the effects of Kearny. "I have the honor to acknowledge the receipt of your letter of the 4th inst. enclosing a letter to Mrs. Philip Kearny, and at the same [time] committing to my care the sword, horse, and saddle of Maj. Gen. Kearny to . . . Mrs. K.," Little Mac responded. "I shall be happy to reciprocate the courtesy when circumstances shall place it in my power to do so."

Stevens, who had fought so well and in such a variety of situations, beginning with his participation in the Port Royal expedition, also was killed. After passing his son, Capt. Hazard Stevens, who was wounded and on the ground, he took a stand of colors and waved it in front of his troops, receiving a bullet through the brain that killed him instantly. Two Federal commanders of significance were gone in this action that meant little.

The cost of Second Bull Run was enormous. The Union army had engaged about 75,000 effectives; the Confederates 48,500. Over the course of the campaign, the Union army lost 1,724 killed, 8,372 wounded, and 5,958 missing; Confederate losses were 1,481 killed, 7,627 wounded, and 89 missing. Robert E. Lee had been painfully injured during the campaign by an accident, at Stewart's Farm, Virginia, on August 31. He had been wearing a poncho, standing in the rain with Traveller and holding the horse's reins, when someone shouted "Yankee cavalry!" and a number of prisoners rushed across a nearby embankment, startling the horse. Lee stumbled and fell, partly catching the reins, and when he arose his hands had been injured. He had sprained one hand and broken several bones in the other. Both hands went into splints, one into a sling, and he could not ride a horse for nearly two weeks.

But the pain was even greater on the Federal side. Despite being outnumbered as he had been on the Peninsula, and despite poor and confused leadership on the Federal side, as was the case in the Peninsula, Lee had beaten back the Union army and now was poised on the doorstep of Washington. The Federal forces retreated into the city's forts; Lee would consider his options for a new campaign. In response to the defeat Lincoln told his secretary John Hay, "Well, John, we are whipped again."

CHAPTER 12

The War's Bloodiest Day

WITH THE FIRST DAYS OF SEPTEMBER 1862 came a bothersome milieu of uncertainty on both sides of the military effort. The news from the Virginia front seemed unclear: Where was the Army of Northern Virginia? How badly whipped was Pope's Army of Virginia at Second Bull Run? Certainly, the momentum now seemed to have shifted toward the Confederacy in that McClellan's and Pope's efforts had failed and Lee's army was reasonably close to Washington. In the wake of the debacle at Second Bull Run, the Army of Virginia by September 12 was disbanded, its forces rolled back into the Army of the Potomac, and Pope was left without a command. This was exactly as McClellan had wished, many officers believing he had hoped that Pope would fail. Lincoln now handled Pope as he did other fallen commanders, by shuffling him into a trivial assignment. Pope was ingloriously sent to command the Department of the Northwest in St. Paul, Minnesota. Soldiers and civilians alike were breathing far easier in Richmond, awaiting a continued upturn in news from the Southern armies. On hearing Lee's report on Second Bull Run, the war clerk John B. Jones responded, "That is glory enough for a week. When Lee says 'signal victory,' we know exactly what it means, and we breathe freely. *Our* generals *never* modify their reports of victories."

The pressure on Vicksburg seemed to have been relieved somewhat, too, as the Federal navy had withdrawn its flotilla of gunboats to Helena, Arkansas, to the north and Baton Rouge to the south. U. S. Grant's force still menaced northern Alabama and Mississippi, but Kirby Smith's and Bragg's efforts in Kentucky would help to reduce the Yankee threat to the deeper South. At the start of September, Lincoln wrote a document he titled "Meditation on the Divine Will." He said that "in great contests each party claims to act in accordance with the will of God. Both *may* be, but one *must* be, wrong. God can not be *for*, and *against* the same thing at the same time. . . . He could have either *saved* or *destroyed* the Union without a human contest. Yet the contest began. And having begun He could give the final victory to either side any day. Yet the contest proceeds." It was the seed of an idea that would come back to haunt religious Southerners in a huge way later when it became clear that they were losing the war.

Meanwhile, the war was transforming in deeper ways. The cries from abolitionists to end slavery were growing louder, although a large majority of citizens even in the North wasn't primarily concerned with this principal cause of the conflict. Still, on August 25, War Secretary Stanton authorized Maj. Gen. David Hunter, commanding the Department of the South, to receive into the service of the United States Army as many as 5,000 black soldiers to be used as guards on plantations and in towns. A small step toward emancipation, it was nonetheless somewhat remarkable for the time. Opposed to the war and its expanding list of casualties, the anti-Lincoln factions in the North, called Copperheads or peace advocates, began to organize themselves into a semisecret movement to end the war. (The term Copperhead resulted from the practice of excising the Indian bust from a one-cent piece and pinning it on members' shirts as a badge.) Moreover, violence was spreading into actions entangling citizens with the war in ever more complicated ways. On August 17 an uprising of Sioux Indians occurred in southwestern Minnesota. With dwindling amounts of food on their reservation, the Sioux revolted by murdering several settlers near Acton, then ambushing Union soldiers near Redwood Ferry. The uprising lasted a week and was countered by troops directed by the former governor of Minnesota, Henry Hastings Sibley—a distant cousin of the Confederate general officer Henry Hopkins Sibley. At New Ulm and Fort Ridgely, Federal troops captured more than 1,000 Indians and during the uprising between 450 and 600 Indians died; ultimately, the worst murderers and rapists in the group were identified and 38 Sioux were executed at Mankato.

THE MONTH'S MAJOR ACTIVITY would result from Gen. Lee's strategic plans. "We cannot afford to be idle," Lee wrote Jefferson Davis on September 3, "and though weaker than our opponents in men and military equipments, must endeavor to harass, if we cannot destroy them." On September 4, Lee began moving his army northward across the Potomac and three days later had it concentrated about Frederick, Maryland, having decided for obvious reasons that demonstrating toward Washington itself would accomplish nothing. Furthermore, he believed strong strategic interests justified a raid to the north. First, he could buy time for war-ravaged Virginia by shifting the action away from his beloved soil. Second, he could retain the bold initiative; keep the momentum going for his tired, undersupplied, but recently victorious army. Third, and looming large in his mind, a victory on Northern soil might spark foreign recognition for the young Confederate States, particularly from Britain and/or France, which might shift the weight of the war considerably. Fourth, Lee's army might do some recruiting along the way and certainly would be received well in Maryland, with its Southern sympathies. Screened by Maj. Gen. Jeb Stuart's cavalry on its eastern flank, Lee's giant raid would move out toward Harrisburg, Pennsylvania, and strike at the major east-west line of the Pennsylvania Railroad. With initial success, perhaps Lee could even reciprocate for the Peninsular campaign by bringing the war to the doorsteps of the Northerners in Philadelphia, Baltimore, or Washington. This would certainly inflame the rising peace movement in the North and would offer severe political problems for Lincoln. It was a bold and risky plan, but Lee was growing accustomed to great risks, with much justification—they often paid off for him. Moreover, time was not on the South's side.

The result, over the coming two weeks, was the Antietam campaign, also called the Sharpsburg, or Maryland, campaign, which would become one of the most furious periods of fighting in the war. Gen. Lee's Army of Northern Virginia, consisting of about 55,000 effectives in early September, was organized as usual into two corps. Maj. Gen. James Longstreet's corps held the divisions of Maj. Gen. Lafayette McLaws (brigades of Brig. Gens. Joseph B. Kershaw, Howell Cobb, Paul J. Semmes, and William Barksdale); Maj. Gen. Richard H. Anderson (brigades of Cols. Alfred Cumming, W. A. Parham, and Carnot Posey, and Brig. Gens. Lewis A. Armistead, Roger A. Pryor, and Ambrose R. Wright); Brig. Gen. David R. Jones (brigades of Brig. Gens. Robert A. Toombs, Thomas F. Drayton, Richard B. Garnett, James L. Kemper, and Cols. Joseph T. Walker and George T. Anderson); Brig. Gen. John G. Walker (brigades of Col. Van H. Manning and Brig. Gen. Robert Ransom, Jr.); Brig. Gen. John Bell Hood (brigades of Cols. William T. Wofford, Evander M. Law, and Brig. Gen. Nathan G. Evans); plus attached artillery. Maj. Gen. Thomas J. "Stonewall" Jackson's corps consisted of the divisions of Brig. Gen. Alexander R. Lawton (brigades of Col. Marcellus Douglass, Brig. Gen. Jubal A. Early, Col. James A. Walker, and Brig. Gen. Harry T. Hays); Maj. Gen. A. P. Hill (Light Division, brigades of Brig. Gens. Lawrence O'Bryan Branch, Maxcy Gregg, James J. Archer, and William Dorsey Pender, and Cols. J. M. Brockenbrough and Edward L. Thomas, plus attached artillery); Brig. Gen. John R. Jones (brigades of Cols. A. J. Grigsby, E. T. H. Warren, Bradley T. Johnson, and Brig. Gen. William E. Starke, plus attached artillery); Maj. Gen. D. H. Hill (brigades of Brig. Gens. Roswell S. Ripley, Robert E. Rodes, Samuel Garland, Jr., George B. Anderson, and Col. Alfred H. Colquitt, plus attached artillery); and reserve artillery commanded by Brig. Gen. William N. Pendleton, along with Stuart's cavalry.

Having absorbed Pope's force, McClellan happily worked on his re-constituted army that now numbered about 84,000. "Again I have been called upon to save the country," he wrote his wife on September 5. He com-manded a huge staff and six full army corps, as follows: Maj. Gen. Joseph Hooker (1st Corps; divisions of Brig. Gens. Rufus King, James B. Ricketts, and Brig. Gen. George G. Meade); Maj. Gen. Edwin V. Sumner (2d Corps; divisions of Maj. Gens. Israel B. Richardson and John Sedgwick and Brig. Gen. William H. French); Maj. Gen. Fitz John Porter (5th Corps; divisions of Maj. Gen. George W. Morell and Brig. Gens. George Sykes and Andrew A. Humphreys); Maj. Gen. William B. Franklin (6th Corps; divisions of Maj. Gens. Henry W. Slocum and William F. Smith and the attached division of Maj. Gen. Darius N. Couch from the 4th Corps); Maj. Gen. Ambrose E. Burnside (9th Corps; divisions of Brig. Gens. Orlando B. Willcox, Samuel D. Sturgis, and Isaac P. Rodman, and Brig. Gen. Jacob D. Cox's Kanawha Divi-sion attached); and Maj. Gen. Joseph K. F. Mansfield (12th Corps; divisions of Brig. Gens. Alpheus S. Williams, George S. Greene, and the cavalry division of Brig. Gen. Alfred Pleasonton). McClellan was elated because Franklin's and Sumner's corps were fresh, not having fought at Second Bull Run, and some thirty-five new regiments arrived and were inserted into the army to replace units battered and depleted in the recent campaigns. Brig. Gen. John F. Reynolds had been relieved of command of a division in Hooker's Corps and ordered to command reserves and militia in Pennsylvania. "I request that the Major General commanding will not heed this order," penned Hooker to Seth Williams, adjutant general of the Army of the Potomac. "A scared Governor ought not to be permitted to destroy the usefulness of an entire Division of the Army on the eve of important operations. . . . It is sat-isfactory to my mind that the Rebels have no more intention of going to Harrisburg than they have of going to heaven." Pennsylvania Governor An-drew Curtin carried the day and Reynolds stayed in command of reserves for the time being.

Many now had grave reservations about McClellan's abilities. Secre-taries Stanton and Chase wanted him sacked. "McClellan is an intelligent engineer and officer, but not a commander to head a great army in the field," wrote Navy Secretary Gideon Welles on September 3. "To attack or advance with energy and power is not in him; to fight is not his forte. . . . The study of military operations interests and amuses him. It flatters him to have on his staff French princes and men of wealth and position; he likes show, parade, and power."

Lee decided to divide his army in the face of a hostile, changing situa-tion. He sent Longstreet to Boonsboro to await Jackson, who would have the difficult task of invading and capturing the strategically located town of Harpers Ferry, site of the old John Brown raid and the burned-out arsenal and armory. Exactly why Lee went after Harpers Ferry in such a risky way is not clear; he may have felt that he needed to hold it to maintain his line of communications into the Shenandoah Valley. But as the operation got underway Lee received news of Pennsylvania militia troops gathering at Chambersburg, in the southern part of that state, and this influenced him to direct Longstreet to Hagerstown, Maryland, even though the militia turned out to be a mere 20 men. Thus, only the thinly spread cavalry of Jeb Stuart and the division of D. H. Hill were positioned in front of McClellan's approach.

The Confederate plan did not go as envisioned from the beginning. Not only was Lee's army dangerously scattered and therefore vulnerable to attack in detail, but the reception the Army of Northern Virginia looked for in Maryland didn't materialize, either. The starkness of this failure, as Southern infantry sang "Maryland, My Maryland" on the march and were met with a notable lack of enthusiasm, stunned many of them.

Moreover, the conditions of life in the Southern army were becoming terrible. Supplies were growing increasingly scarce, especially shoes, and marching along the rocky roads cut up the feet of the many shoeless Southern infantrymen. "Posterity will scarcely believe that the wonderful campaign which has just ended with its terrible marches and desperate battles, was made by men, one fourth of whom were entirely barefooted, and one-half of whom were as ragged as scarecrows," reported the *Richmond Dispatch*. "We cease to wonder at the number of stragglers, when we hear how many among them were shoeless, with stone bruises on their feet." The foodstuffs available to the army during this campaign were horrible; supplies ran low, the ability to move food to the railhead and on to the army was weak, and many of the soldiers foraged liberally from the countryside. The result was that the diet for many soldiers in the Army of Northern Virginia during this period consisted largely of green corn and apples. The number of cases of diarrhea was astronomical. The commissary supplies for the Northern army were sometimes not markedly superior. "What in Heaven's name it was composed of, none of us ever discovered," lamented Abner R. Small of his rations. "It was called simply 'desiccated vegetables.' ... Still, it was a substitute for food. We ate it, and we liked it, too." Many of the Confederate army's soldiers were an especially ragged lot, as evidenced by a famous surviving photograph of the army marching through a street in Frederick, Maryland, past the J. Rosenstock Dry Goods & Clothing Store, probably during this campaign but possibly in 1864. Lee counted on his boldness and McClellan's lack of initiative to allow him to move swiftly northward through the Cumberland Valley to the Susquehanna River and Harrisburg before McClellan organized a pursuit that would overtake him.

Predictably, McClellan reacted lethargically to the news that Lee had crossed the Potomac River. He succumbed to the old delusion of a vastly superior army, at least in order to justify his behavior. On September 11, he wrote Halleck, "All the evidence that has been accumulated from various sources since we left Washington goes to prove most conclusively that almost the entire Rebel army in Virginia, amounting to not less than 120,000 men, is in the vicinity of Frederick City." Faulty intelligence from a variety of sources, mostly Pleasonton's cavalry, and magnified postreporting anxiety in McClellan's mind, created this erroneous evaluation. Additionally, McClellan was disgusted with the assignment of Maj. Gen. Samuel P. Heintzelman to command the defenses of Washington—he insisted that he have command of those troops, too—even as Halleck fired off telegrams fretting over the security of Washington and McClellan worried that Halleck's attentions were spread too wide. With so many arguments erupting in the command structure of the U.S. army, Brig. Gen. James A. Garfield of Ohio wrote simply, "If the Republic goes down in blood and ruin, let its obituary be written thus: 'Died of West Point.' "

Then, on September 13, an event happened that might have turned around the whole campaign. The 27th Indiana Infantry (Col. Silas Colgrove) was bivouacked on the outskirts of Frederick, in the camp used by D. H. Hill's division on September 12. While resting with his friend Sgt. John M. Bloss, Cpl. Barton W. Mitchell discovered an envelope lying in the field, picked it up, and pulled out three cigars wrapped in a manuscript copy of Special Orders No. 191, issued by Lee on September 9 and addressed to D. H. Hill, which provided his corps and division commanders with the strategic plan for the Maryland campaign. By late morning, the order was in the hands of McClellan himself; after seeing it, he boasted to John Gibbon, with prophetic and ironic foresight, "Here is a paper with which if I cannot whip Bobbie Lee, I will be willing to go home." The document was judged genuine because it was in the handwriting of Lee's chief of staff, Col. Robert H. Chilton. But rather than acting quickly on this amazing stroke of luck—with the entire blueprint of Lee's movements in hand—McClellan waited half a day. Why McClellan reacted in such an unbelievably neglectful manner after receiving this document has been debated for decades. Suffice it to say it may have marked the lowest point of his mental peculiarities to abandon the opportunity to strike briskly at Lee's army, thus sealing his fate in history as a great planner but a poor tactician and strategist.

Strangely, this failure came only days after McClellan had seemingly reached the high point of his career by vigorously reorganizing and preparing the Army of the Potomac for a campaign. Only very late on the night of September 13 did McClellan order Burnside and Franklin to proceed toward the mountain gaps west of Catoctin Creek, along South Mountain, the former marching toward Turner's Gap south of Boonsboro and the latter

Crampton's Gap to its south, east of Rohrersville. The stage was set for the preliminary actions in the Maryland campaign, the battles for South Mountain, also known as Turner's Gap, Fox's Gap, Crampton's Gap, Boonsboro, and Boonsboro Gap. Nonetheless, the recovered document had its effect. "It is evident from General Lee's movements from the time he left Frederick City," observed Colgrove, "that he intended to recross the Potomac without hazarding a battle in Maryland, and had it not been for the finding of this lost order, the battle of South Mountain, and probably that of Antietam, would not have been fought."

As it happened, McClellan had made another blunder. A Southern sympathizer was among a group of Frederick citizens to witness McClellan's jubilant attitude when he received the copy of the order. Security, it seemed, was lacking in McClellan's army that morning. The Frederick citizen informed Lee's army by 10 A.M. the following morning, and so Lee had to recalculate his plan. Two brigades of D. H. Hill's corps were blocking the approach to Turner's Gap, using a stone inn called the Mountain House as a lookout, and Lee directed the remainder of Hill's force and whatever else Longstreet could spare to reinforce that strategic position. The battle of South Mountain resulted, as Hill's line stretched from Fox's Gap along the Old Sharpsburg Road to the south, along the three crests atop the mountain in this area, to the National Road at Turner's Gap in the center and to the Frosttown Road north of it. On this day McClellan placed Burnside in command of both the 9th Corps (Reno) and the 1st Corps (Hooker), effectively making him commander of the Union army's Right Wing; Sumner was placed in command of the Center (2d and 12th corps); and the Left Wing was commanded by Franklin (6th Corps and Couch's division of the 4th Corps). But this arrangement did not prevail during the whole campaign.

The Confederate center was anchored with the brigades of Brig. Gens. Alfred H. Colquitt and Samuel Garland, Jr. The 5th Virginia Cavalry and Capt. John Pelham's horse artillery stood firm at Fox's Gap. On the approach up the Old Sharpsburg Road was Jacob D. Cox, and the lead brigade in scouting the Confederate position was that of Col. Eliakim P. Scammon, who was ordered to move on the Confederate right flank. Before the action began, D. H. Hill described spying the Federal approach from the Mountain House. "The marching columns extended back as far as the eye could see in the distance," wrote Hill. "I had never seen so tremendous an army before, and I did not see one like it afterward . . . here four full corps were in full view, one of which was on the mountain and almost within rifle-range."

Burnside's wing approached cautiously because of McClellan's belief in the fantastic numbers of his opponent. Pleasonton's cavalry had discovered Hill's position on the morning of September 14. Scammon, accompanied by Cox, reached a point on the main road where they saw a solitary

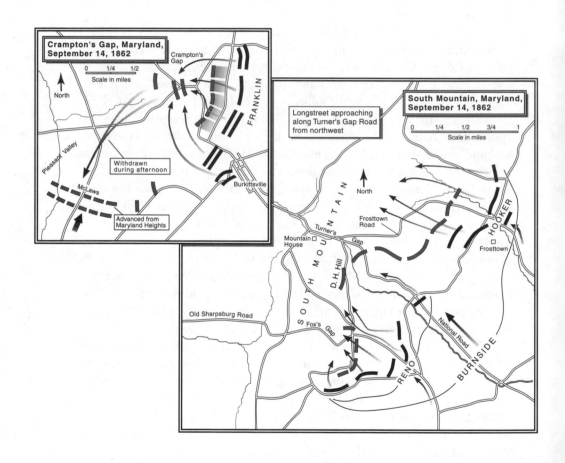

Crampton's Gap, Maryland, September 14, 1862

Crampton's Gap

0   1/4   1/2
Scale in miles

North

FRANKLIN

Pleasant Valley

Withdrawn during afternoon

McLaws

Burkittsville

Advanced from Maryland Heights

South Mountain, Maryland, September 14, 1862

Longstreet approaching along Turner's Gap Road from northwest

0   1/4   1/2   3/4   1
Scale in miles

North

SOUTH MOUNTAIN

Frosttown Road

Frosttown

HOOKER

Mountain House

Turner's Gap

D.H. Hill

Old Sharpsburg Road

Fox's Gap

National Road

RENO

BURNSIDE

blue-clad figure walking toward them. It was Col. Augustus C. Moor of the 28th Ohio Infantry, who had been captured the day before. Paroled on his word of honor that he would not divulge information on the Confederate positions, he simply told Scammon and Cox, "My God! Be careful." Cox worked his way up the mountain and attacked by 9 A.M., struck by fire from Col. Thomas L. Rosser's cavalry. Cox ordered the 11th Ohio Infantry and the 23d Ohio (Lt. Col. Rutherford B. Hayes, the future president) to deploy and attack the North Carolina troops commanded by Garland. Hand-to-hand fighting ensued, during which Garland was killed, struck by a Minié bullet just after being urged to take cover. Garland was a great-grandnephew of James Madison. Cox had attempted the difficult assignment of attacking uphill, and after an hour of fighting he succeeded in gaining enough ground to turn the Confederates and attack northward along the ridge toward Mountain House.

Colquitt's brigade made a vigorous stand, however, and by 11 A.M. Cox was resting his men. It was after noon when Reno's 9th Corps began to move toward Fox's Gap. Heavy fighting resulted, and Hooker soon arrived and joined in the fight about a mile north of Reno. From Hill's division, the brigades of Brig. Gens. George B. Anderson, Robert E. Rodes, and Robert Ransom, Jr. deployed, with Anderson's North Carolinians on the right and Rodes's Alabamians on the left. The approach of Union Brig. Gen. Orlando B. Willcox's division was delayed by a wrong turn long enough to allow Longstreet's men to come up in support. Through thickly forested ground, with haphazardly placed artillery, and using a number of stone walls for cover, the soldiers fought on in the late afternoon hours. Burnside arrived on the field to coordinate the whole affair, and by late evening the Federals, after savage effort, succeeded in enveloping the Confederate flanks and taking most of the high ground from which they could command the pass at Turner's Gap. During a lull in the fighting, Maj. Gen. Jesse L. Reno, a native of western Virginia who had moved to Pennsylvania and adopted strong Union sentiment, was mortally wounded. He rode out to reconnoiter the position near where Garland had been killed and was struck by a volley from Confederates in the deep woods, falling from his horse and rolling down the eastern slope to the base of an oak tree. The bullet hit Reno's scabbard and glanced into his chest, penetrating just below the heart. When Brig. Gen. Samuel D. Sturgis, a friend, approached, Reno lifted his head and simply said, "Hallo, Sam. I'm dead." Sturgis replied that he must be joking. "Yes, yes, I'm dead. Goodbye," said Reno, in a calm, strong voice. He expired a short time later.

While the fighting continued, Burnside ordered a brigade sent straight up the National Road to create a diversion. It was that of Brig. Gen. John Gibbon, the Iron Brigade, which had fought stubbornly at Brawner's Farm—

the Wisconsin and Indiana men known as "those damned black hat fellers" by the Confederates. They proceeded to strike Colquitt's line, but both sides were running low on ammunition and daylight was waning. By about midnight on September 15, Hill's weary and bloodied Confederates began withdrawing to the west. The farmstead of Daniel Wise with its spread of fields stood in the thick of the fighting at Fox's Gap; after the battle, burial details worked in the area and, faced with the task of disposing of bodies in such a mountainous country, resorted to a grisly solution: They dumped several dozen bodies down Wise's well, and when farmer Wise discovered the well had been ruined, he took over the task, asked for $1 per body, and sealed the well, earning $60.

While the action at the central and northern gaps unfolded, Franklin attacked five miles to the south at Crampton's Gap. Having moved through Burkittsville, he proceeded headlong into the pass with the orders that he should move through and support the Federal garrison at Harpers Ferry, under attack by Jackson. In the process of moving up onto Maryland Heights to support Jackson, Maj. Gen. Lafayette McLaws had his division and that of Maj. Gen. Richard H. Anderson place artillery into position there but had to break off and turn northward to meet the threat of Franklin's approach. By noon the battle of Crampton's Gap had begun, with heavy, sporadic fighting lasting until dusk, when McLaws retreated into a lower-elevation position in Pleasant Valley to the south. Still timid from McClellan's instructions, however, and fooled by McLaws's bluff by clever positioning of troops, Franklin did not pursue further but held the pass. He did not further damage McLaws's two divisions or come to the aid of Harpers Ferry. The forces engaged on this day amounted to some 28,000 Federals and 18,000 Confederates; the Union casualties were 443 killed, 1,807 wounded, and 75 missing; Confederate losses were 325 killed, 1,560 wounded, and 800 missing. The battlefield was a horribly sad sight on the day following. A farmer and his son walked up the farm road between the Mountain House and Wise Farm on September 15 and found a dead Confederate soldier in an upright sitting position. His head lowered and rifle propped on his knees, the soldier had a bloody head wound, they discovered, on raising his chin. A short distance away they found another corpse with half the head missing. It was a disturbing sight for anyone not accustomed to living with death every week as a soldier in the armies.

Meanwhile, Jackson was moving on Harpers Ferry. Halleck had ordered the town held, which was virtually impossible in the face of a strong enemy force, as it lay in a triangular valley with rivers on two sides and with the high ground of Maryland Heights, Bolivar Heights, and Loudoun Heights surrounding it. Assigning the garrison as a Union defense force was an outright error, yet by drawing the Federal force from Martinsburg into

Harpers Ferry, Halleck also unwittingly slowed down and hampered Lee's operation. Lee had ordered the town taken by September 12, but it was only by late on September 13 that Jackson's Confederates drew up in position around the town. Harpers Ferry was currently held by a force of 12,737 Federal soldiers under the command of Col. Dixon S. Miles, an aged Marylander who had spent more than forty years in the army despite the fact that he was a hard drinker. He had irritated his superiors, and had acquired a reputation for annoying his troops to the point that they conspired to do him harm. In the wake of First Bull Run, a court of inquiry was convened and found that Miles had been drunk during the battle. The gray-haired warrior now faced his toughest moment in the sun, as his troops in Harpers Ferry, spread along Bolivar Heights and down in the town near the confluence of the rivers, were virtually surrounded. Jackson's three divisions had moved from Fredericksburg on September 10, proceeded to Williamsport, across the Potomac River, and then traveled down the Baltimore & Ohio Railroad to Harpers Ferry. By late on the 13th, Jackson, with the divisions of John R. Jones to the north, Alexander R. Lawton in the center, and A. P. Hill to the south, was little more than a mile west of the town. Across the Shenandoah on Loudoun Heights, the division of Maj. Gen. John G. Walker commanded the town with artillery, as did the divisions of McLaws and Richard H. Anderson.

On September 14, as the guns boomed on South Mountain, the Confederate forces around Harpers Ferry began to bombard the town. Halleck's decision to leave Miles's garrison in place doomed it to capture; McClellan had wanted to pull the force out of Harpers Ferry and absorb it into the Army of the Potomac. Unfortunately for his men, Miles continued to show poor judgment in every respect. A Federal force of 2,500 from Martinsburg, commanded by Brig. Gen. Julius White, had escaped Jackson and joined Miles before the Confederates closed in. Miles concentrated virtually his whole force in the low-elevation parts of the town and in a vulnerable position on Bolivar Heights, and he drew the exposed troops along the heights down into the town after the shelling started. This bottled up the entire force and sealed its fate.

The Confederate guns, perched high on three sides surrounding the town, opened up with heavy fire of shells early on the morning of September 15. Miles now considered the situation hopeless, and he was correct. He had not been told that Franklin, in the wake of his action at Crampton's Gap, was assigned to come to Miles's relief. But it would make little difference. The Federal command in town consulted on their dilemma and White, Col. Benjamin F. "Grimes" Davis (8th New York Cavalry), and Lt. Col. Hasbrouck Davis (12th Illinois Cavalry) determined that taking infantry or artillery out of the town would be impossible, but that a force of 1,200

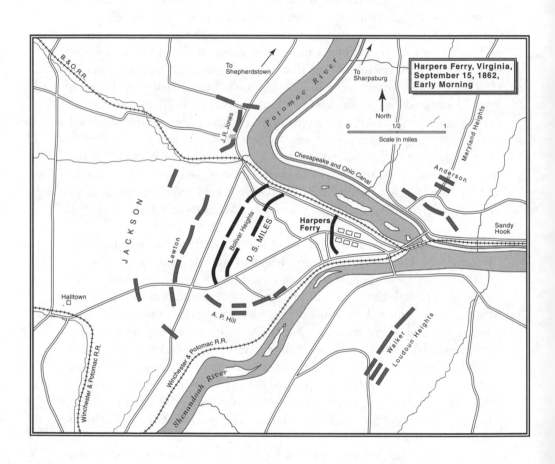

Harpers Ferry, Virginia, September 15, 1862, Early Morning

To Shepherdstown

To Sharpsburg

North

Scale in miles

0   1/2   1

B. & O. R.R.

Potomac River

J. R. Jones

Chesapeake and Ohio Canal

Maryland Heights

Anderson

Sandy Hook

JACKSON

Lawton

Bolivar Heights

D. S. MILES

Harpers Ferry

Halltown

A. P. Hill

Winchester & Potomac R.R.

Winchester & Potomac R.R.

Shenandoah River

Walker

Loudoun Heights

cavalrymen could try to dash for safety. During the night of September 14, the two Davises and Col. Arno Voss (12th Illinois Cavalry) led the cavalry force on a hard ride out of the town, capturing one of Longstreet's ammunition trains of 97 wagons and its escort of 600 soldiers, en route to the Union line at Greencastle, Pennsylvania. But such good fortune would not come to the remainder of the Federal force. By 9 A.M. Miles decided the garrison's position was untenable and he called a brief council of war. Together with White and Cols. Frederick G. D'Utassy and William H. Trimble, brigade commanders, he decided to capitulate. Thus, confused and possibly drunk again, Miles surrendered, hoisting white flags. It was one of the largest surrenders of U.S. troops during the war, and a court of inquiry again came together in Washington. This time Miles would not be present, however.

Miles suffered contempt from his men for his incompetence, his arrogant behavior, and his drunkenness. It cut so deeply that Capt. Philo Phillips of the 126th New York Infantry argued with Miles after learning of the proposed surrender, saying "For —'s sake, Colonel, don't surrender us. Don't you hear the signal guns? Our forces are near us. Let us cut our way out and join them." Miles replied, "Impossible. They will blow us out of this [place] in half an hour." Phillips angrily disagreed, and Miles asked, "Do you know who I am?" To which Phillips replied, "You are Colonel Miles." The captain turned around, started to walk away, and a shell exploded. He turned back and saw Miles on the ground, his left leg shattered, and he openly said, "Good." He later wrote that "the rest felt it if they did not say it. It was difficult to find a man who would take him to the hospital." He was mortally wounded at least ten minutes after the white flags of surrender were raised and died a day later; ever since, debate has raged over the possibility that Miles was deliberately struck by fire from a Federal, rather than a Confederate, cannon. Whether or not Miles was killed by his own angry Union troops will perhaps never be known, but there does not seem to be evidence to make that case definitively.

Lee had gained Harpers Ferry but lost the South Mountain passes, and so he determined to regroup his army before McClellan could defeat its scattered divisions in detail. Lee decided to pause near Sharpsburg and await the regrouping, but when he received news of the fall of Harpers Ferry, Lee's boldness reemerged and he established a defensive position at Sharpsburg, behind the winding banks of Antietam Creek, to await McClellan's approach. The battle of Antietam, or Sharpsburg, the bloodiest single day of the entire war, was the result.

The position was tactically a questionable one. With McClellan pursuing from the east, the major obstacle in Lee's rear was the Potomac River itself, which flowed through a series of twists and curves west of the town of Sharpsburg, a village of about 1,200 residents. About three miles west of

Sharpsburg on the Boonsboro Turnpike was the smaller village of Shepherdstown, Virginia, on the west bank of the Potomac. Antietam Creek itself
offered a relatively minor line of defense, as it could be crossed with relative
ease. Perhaps Lee's greatest limitation was that his only route of escape in a
major crisis was also his route of supply, Boteler's Ford, a poor crossing on
the Potomac that lay south of Shepherdstown. Four bridges offered quick
crossings over Antietam Creek. They were the Upper Bridge near Pry's Mill,
west of the hamlet of Keedysville; the Middle Bridge where the turnpike
crossed the Antietam; the Lower or Rohrbach Bridge, southeast of the town;
and the Antietam Bridge near the juncture of Antietam Creek and the Potomac. North of Middle Bridge, the eastern bank of the Antietam offered a
fine position for Federal artillery; south of it the western banks of the creek
were high, sloping, and rugged, and would offer a good defensive position for
Lee's posted troops.

By the time Harpers Ferry had capitulated on September 15, the ever
cautious McClellan had pursued slowly to positions near Keedysville,
Porterstown (east of Middle Bridge), and Rohrersville (south of Porterstown). His disposition of troops was evolving out of the semiofficial "wing"
concept of grouped commands to the official organization of independent
corps, in which capacity the battle of Antietam would be fought. The northern group, near Keedysville, consisted of Hooker's 1st Corps, the 9th Corps
(now commanded by Brig. Gen. Jacob D. Cox, vice Reno), Sumner's 2d
Corps, and Mansfield's 12th Corps, along with Pleasonton's cavalry. Sykes's
division of the 5th Corps was positioned near Porterstown. Franklin's
6th Corps and Couch's division of the 4th Corps lay at and south of
Rohrersville. With this arrangement of his force approaching an unknown
enemy, McClellan decided it was too late in the afternoon to attack on September 15. The next day he spent entirely in skirmishing with the forward
defenses of Lee's army and weighing his options. Again, lacking the initiative, McClellan abandoned a golden opportunity. Had he struck hard into
Longstreet's corps on that day, he certainly would have overwhelmed it.
Longstreet's 19,000 troops, consisting of the divisions of Stuart's cavalry,
Hood, D. H. Hill, and David R. Jones were all the force the Southern army
had in Sharpsburg during the early part of September 16. Later in the day
Jackson's divisions of Lawton and John R. Jones sped northward from
Harpers Ferry, along with the cavalry brigade of Col. Thomas T. Munford,
and later still John G. Walker moved northward to join Lee's Sharpsburg
force, amounting to a reinforcement of 11,000 men. The divisions of A. P.
Hill, McLaws, and Richard H. Anderson—some 10,000 troops altogether—
stayed put in Harpers Ferry for the time being, overseeing the parole proce-
dures for many of the Federal prisoners and reequiping themselves with
captured matériel.

Finally, McClellan determined to make an attack, but the plan was ill defined, to say the least. He announced an intention to "make the main attack upon the enemy's left—at least to create a diversion by assailing the enemy's right—and, as soon as one or both of the flank movements were fully successful, to attack their center with any reserve I might then have in hand." By midnight on September 16, McClellan ordered Franklin to maneuver northward to join the other corps. He made various tactical blunders in the hours that followed, such as failing to reconnoiter properly Lee's positions, again overestimating the size of the Confederate army before him, going into action with only a vague idea of the fords by which the creek could be crossed, and reorganizing the locations and commands of his forces so as to confuse his subordinates. Moreover, he issued no written orders to the corps and division commanders for the action to come.

On the afternoon of September 16, McClellan nonetheless initiated his plan for battle by sending Hooker's 1st Corps marching past the Samuel Pry Mill, the Jacob Cost House, and across the Upper Bridge toward Sharpsburg. They would begin the battle by attacking the Confederate left the following morning. Lee discovered the movement, however, and Longstreet deployed Hood's division to stop the approach. Hot skirmishing ensued on the 16th, after which Hood withdrew and Hooker encamped for the night along the Hagerstown Pike, among some rocky rises north of the North Woods. About midnight Maj. Gen. Joseph K. F. Mansfield received orders to follow Hooker and support him for the planned daylight attack. Arriving so late, Mansfield was thus unfamiliar with the ground his corps would march across the following morning.

At dawn on the morning of September 17, McClellan had some 75,316 effectives arrayed as follows: Hooker's lead divisions, closest to the North Woods, were those of Brig. Gens. Abner Doubleday and James B. Ricketts; Brig. Gen. George G. Meade's division followed behind. Mansfield's 12th Corps was north and east of Hooker. Well to the south and east, south of Pry's Mill, were deployed Pleasonton's cavalry division and Sumner's 2d Corps. Maj. Gen. Fitz John Porter's 5th Corps enveloped an area from Porterstown to near Keedysville. In this area McClellan established his headquarters at the stately Philip Pry House on a hill near the Boonsboro Pike, some one and a half miles from what would turn out to be the center of the action. To the south, east of the Lower Bridge, was the 9th Corps, now commanded by Maj. Gen. Ambrose E. Burnside, who was Cox's senior.

The Confederate dispositions stretched from Stuart's cavalry division in the north near the Potomac River, which held the Confederate left, and moving south included Jackson's corps between Sharpsburg and the river and Longstreet's corps in the town and south of it. Lee established headquarters in a series of tents in a field on the west side of Sharpsburg. The northern units included the divisions of John R. Jones and Hood in the West Woods, near the little whitewashed building called the Dunkard Church—named for the German sect of Baptist Brethren who immersed their converts—Lawton in front of Hood, D. H. Hill's division spread from near the church and the Roulette and Mumma farmsteads to the north, southward to the Henry Piper Farmhouse and a nearby sunken farm lane, to a position east of Sharpsburg itself. The division of David R. Jones was spread from south of town to a position opposite the Lower Bridge, and Munford's cavalry screened the Confederates along Snavely's Ford, near a sharp bend in Antietam Creek. John G. Walker's division supported Jones's rear, and the divisions of McLaws and Richard H. Anderson had just arrived from Harpers Ferry.

Rain overnight had left the field damp, but as daylight approached and camp fires smoldered all across the landscape surrounding Sharpsburg, the rain stopped. A foggy mist covered the field, and sporadic single shots of musket fire rang out starting about 3 A.M. Suddenly, before dawn, the heavy barking of four Federal cannon on the eastern bank of the Antietam initiated the real action. By 6 A.M. Hooker's 1st Corps had set out from its bivouac around the Joseph Poffenberger Farm and marched southward toward a most unusual day, with cool, breezy, overcast weather dominating the scene, though the temperature would rise to 75 degrees. Hooker's movement would carry his soldiers past the North Woods and between the East and West Woods, toward the Dunkard Church, defended by Jackson. The ground over which the 1st Corps would attack was a relatively flat 30-acre cornfield attached to the David R. Miller Farm, along the Hagerstown Pike. Before midmorning, the cornfield would transform into one of the most savage areas of fighting during the whole war. Hooker's nearly 9,000 men faced about 5,500 in the divisions of Jones and Lawton. Hooker himself described the opening of the battle: "We had not proceeded far before I discovered that a heavy force of the enemy had taken possession of a corn-field . . . in my immediate front, and from the sun's rays falling on their bayonets projecting above the corn could see that the field was filled with the enemy, with arms in their hands, standing apparently at 'support arms.' "

Confederate fortunes were shining as Jeb Stuart's artillery was posted to the right of Hooker's line, occupying Nicodemus Heights, which offered a fine perch for gunnery that would command the turnpike and environs. As Gibbon's "Iron Brigade" approached cautiously through the corn, unable to see much of anything in its front, the Confederate guns opened on them with great blasts and Lawton's division screamed forth on the attack with a high-pitched Rebel yell. Musket volleys from several Confederate brigades unleashed a fire of balls through the air, with the brigades of Brig. Gens. Jubal A. Early and Isaac R. Trimble joining in. Hooker brought up thirty-six guns, posted them on a ridge between the North Woods and the Miller Farm, and pounded the Confederate line with artillery fire, but the stubbornly resistant Rebels simply dug in and returned fire for what seemed like an eternity. Soon a thunderous storm of sound and a pall of heavy black smoke hung over the battlefield, and it became difficult to see what was happening and where units were—something that in the days before smokeless powder was a particular problem on hazy, foggy mornings.

Maj. Rufus R. Dawes of the 6th Wisconsin Infantry recorded his impressions of the early morning fight. "There is a rattling fusillade and loud cheers. 'Forward' is the word. The men are loading and firing with demoniacal fury and shouting and laughing hysterically, and the whole field before us is covered with rebels fleeing for life, into the woods. Great numbers of men are shot while climbing over the high post and rail fences along the turnpike. . . . A sharp cut, as of a switch, stings the calf of my leg as I run. . . . As I entered the field, a report as of a thunderclap in my ear fairly stunned me. This was Gibbon's last shot at the advancing rebels. The cannon was double-charged with canister. The rails of the fence flew high into the air."

The Confederates fought savagely and suffered large numbers of casualties early on because of their aggressive spirit. Many of Lawton's men were Virginians and Georgians. Jones's men, those of Stonewall's old division, were mostly Virginians with some Louisiana troops as well. The severe casualties suffered by these units early this morning put them into precarious command status; one-third of the brigades of Col. Marcellus Douglass and Brig. Gens. Harry T. Hays and Isaac R. Trimble were already casualties, and Douglass had been killed along with some other officers. John R. Jones was disabled by a shell that exploded over his head, and aides led him from the field. Lawton was seriously wounded in the leg, and he was borne from the field and sent to Virginia for treatment. In the West Woods, Brig. Gen. William E. Starke was struck by three Minié bullets and died within an hour.

To launch a counterattack, the Confederates looked to the tenacious fighter Brig. Gen. John Bell Hood, whose division composed of Texans, Alabamians, and Mississippians had a burgeoning reputation for toughness. After 7 A.M. Hood launched a stinging assault from the West Woods that succeeded in recapturing the cornfield in such a vicious fight that the Federals were driven back to intersperse with their artillery, firing sporadically at the oncoming Southerners. The ferocity of this part of the action was legendary, and it represents some of the heaviest action of the war. "In the time I am writing every stalk of corn in the northern and greater part of the field was cut as closely as could have been done with a knife," recalled Hooker, "and the slain lay in rows precisely as they had stood in their ranks a few moments before. It was never my fortune to witness a more bloody, dismal battlefield."

Hooker's 1st Corps lost about 28 percent of its men in this initial attack alone; the Confederates spread across the Miller Farm suffered 50 percent casualties. By about 7:30 A.M. the situation changed slightly with the arrival of the 12th Corps, commanded by Joseph King Fenno Mansfield. A Connecticut native, Mansfield had the responsibility of turning the tide and restoring a sense of order to the Federal battle line. Mansfield led the movement himself and had the division of Brig. Gen. Alpheus S. Williams as the spearhead of his counterstroke. Thick smoke covered the field, and troops were scattered in confusion from the previous and ongoing action. As Mansfield rode ahead to reconnoiter, a bullet struck his horse. He led the animal to cover, but as this was occurring, a Minié bullet hit Mansfield in the stomach.

Lt. John Mead Gould of the 10th Maine Infantry described the scene. "The General imagined [Confederates nearby] to be Union troops into which we had commenced firing by mistake. . . . his horse was shot in the right hind leg, and became unruly. . . . the General was shot a few seconds afterward, but it was not observed by the men, who thought only the horse was wounded. Passing still in front of our line and nearer to the enemy, he attempted to ride over the rail fence which separated a lane from the ploughed land where most of our regiment were posted. The horse would not jump it, and the General dismounting led him over. He passed to the rear of the regimental line, when a gust of wind blew aside his coat, and I discovered that his whole front was covered with blood. . . . I ran to him and asked if he was hurt badly. He said, 'Yes,' 'I shall not live,' 'shall not live,' 'I am shot,' 'by one of our own men.' . . . [The shooters] are now known to have been the Twentieth Georgia Regiment."

Mansfield was taken by ambulance to the George Line House in the rear of the action, where he died the following day. Williams took over command of the 12th Corps. Hooker was also injured, shot in the right foot as he sat astride his horse. He lost a fair amount of blood on the field before being taken to the Philip Pry House for recovery. "I have the honor to request that leave of absence for twenty days may be granted me," Hooker wrote Seth Williams, adjutant general of the army, two days after the battle, but he did not return to duty until November 1862. The hospitals around Washington being full, he was for a time a resident of the city's insane asylum. Brig. Gen. George G. Meade assumed command of the 1st Corps. "I go into action to-day as the commander of an army corps," Meade warned his wife the day after the battle. "If I survive, my *two* stars are secure, and if I fall, you will have my reputation to live on."

Hood stubbornly resisted a fresh attack from the bloodied 1st Corps, and east of the pike the division of Brig. Gen. George S. Greene pushed on successfully into the area east of the Dunkard Church, along the Smoketown Road. But no one was in a position to provide Federal coordination on the northern part of the field. McClellan had failed to regroup his forces successfully after the woundings of two corps commanders. Greene's movement petered out with no support behind it. Nonetheless, Meade successfully gathered the survivors of the 1st Corps attacks in the area of the North Woods while Williams and Greene continued to fight southward.

By about 7:20 A.M., with scant knowledge of how the attack was progressing, McClellan ordered the 2d Corps under Maj. Gen. Edwin V. Sumner forward to assist in the Union assault. A cantankerous Massachusetts cavalry officer, Sumner, 65, the oldest corps commander in the Union army, had been wounded at Cerro Gordo during the Mexican War, where a spent ball bounced off his head, giving him the name "Bull Head." Sumner marched the 2d Corps westward completely unaware of the condition of the fight going on to his west and without reconnoitering the ground. He deployed his leading division under Maj. Gen. John Sedgwick, which approached the East Woods by 9 A.M., for battle. Sumner's other division commanders, following, were Brig. Gen. William H. French and Maj. Gen. Israel B. Richardson. Sumner foolishly marched his men forward in columns as if they were in a parade. The approach was such a spectacle that Gen. Robert E. Lee, his hands bandaged from the accident at Stewart's Farm, was brought forward to a ridge to watch along with staff officers. As this attack unfolded, Confederate Col. Stephen Dill Lee carried a message forward for Robert E. Lee, finding him about halfway between the town and the Dunkard Church. "Don't be excited about it," R. E. Lee told the artillerist. "Go tell General Hood to hold his ground, reinforcements are now rapidly approaching between Sharpsburg and the ford."

The columns reached the Samuel Mumma Farm and Sedgwick deployed them for attack. Stonewall Jackson had been preparing for the onslaught, and the newly arrived divisions of Brig. Gen. John G. Walker and Maj. Gen. Lafayette McLaws, both from Longstreet's corps, took up positions to thwart the Union assault. The situation now favored the Confederate defense, suddenly, for even if the Federal columns did succeed in penetrating the West Woods, they would be in the unenviable danger of being encircled and captured or completely routed. Attacks and counterattacks had so cut up the front-line troops on both sides that the field now quieted considerably, and Sumner's approach again promised to unleash a fresh fusillade of small arms and artillery fire. On the Confederate side, units had been so hastily thrown into the defensive positions that they were considerably intermingled, which led to some command and supply problems, but they stood fast against the oncoming blue wave. As Sedgwick's men advanced through the cornfield, they had to step lightly to avoid crushing the wounded or trampling corpses that lay scattered throughout.

Sedgwick's lead brigade was that of Brig. Gen. Willis A. Gorman. After

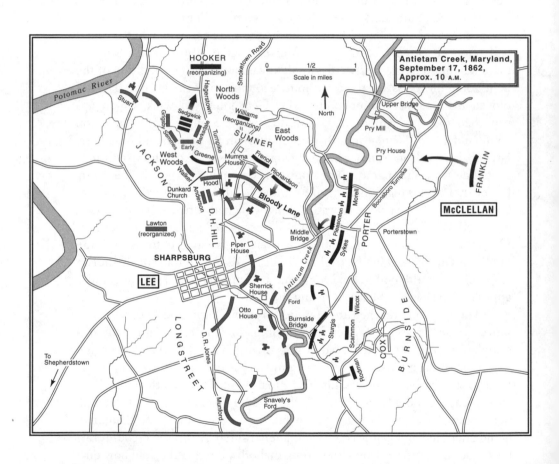

Antietam Creek, Maryland,
September 17, 1862,
Approx. 10 A.M.

trudging through the cornfield they suddenly came into the open and saw Lee's weakened left flank before them. As other Federal units emerged, a thunderous boom along with nerve-shattering crackles of musketry exploded into the air. For the next twenty minutes some of the most intense fighting of the war erupted around them as the Confederates resisted Sedgwick's attack. The suddenness of the Confederate surge into the Union advance astonished many of the Yankees because of the nonexistent reconnaissance prior to launching the attack. Two months after the battle Stephen D. Lee described Antietam as "artillery hell," and several key Southern batteries pounded the Union attack during this period, forcing it into doom. Supported by this artillery, Jackson sent his stinging counterattack forward from three directions, which drove Sedgwick's assault to the rear in great disorder and with 2,200 casualties. Many of the Confederate units pursued vigorously, the Rebel yell echoing into the air, until they retook much of the ground they had occupied earlier in the morning. Heavy fighting emerged from the soldiers in the brigades of Brig. Gens. Howell Cobb, Joseph B. Kershaw, William Barksdale, and Paul J. Semmes. A gap now existed between Jackson's men in the West Woods and the position of D. H. Hill in the field's center, and Col. John R. Cooke took two regiments to fill it. The Confederate cavalryman Heros von Borcke, of Jeb Stuart's staff, wrote that it was "astonishing to see men without shoes, whose lacerated feet stained their path with blood, limping to the front to conquer or fall with their comrades." Running out of ammunition, Cooke sent a message to Longstreet declaring that "we will stay here, by J.C., if we must go to hell together."

Jubal Early's brigade reformed in the West Woods and came back out to fight about the time the 34th New York Infantry and 125th Pennsylvania Infantry approached the Dunkard Church, threatening the Confederate position. Both Early and Kershaw launched a movement that sent the Union regiments reeling, and the converging Confederates nearly ran into each other. Kershaw's South Carolinians were badly struck by artillery fire in the ensuing melee, acquiring frightful casualties. The Sedgwick attack was a Federal disaster, and the fighting quieted by about 10:30 A.M. The action left the division of George S. Greene exposed, and so he had to pull back to avoid catastrophe.

A second, semi-independent Federal attack resulted from a mistake. Sumner's other division, that of French, missed following Sedgwick down the Smoketown Road, and so it swung into a line of attack farther to the south. French wheeled into position, attacking southwestward, and struck into the troops of D. H. Hill that anchored the Confederate center. The action centered on the areas occupied by the Henry Piper Farmhouse, the surrounding fields and an adjacent orchard, and a sunken farm lane to the northeast. French's troops marched southward past the Roulette and Clipp farms, east of the Mumma Farm, which had been set ablaze by retreating Confederates early in the morning, and approached D. H. Hill's Confederates, the northernmost of whom were lying down in the sunken road, transforming it into a trench. McClellan's movement of his men into battle was at the very least fragmented. The right had been committed to action, the center was still east of Antietam Creek, with small parts of it entering the battle in piecemeal fashion, and the left, under Burnside, had not yet been taken into action at all—it was also on the eastern side of the creek.

The sunken farm lane was situated some 600 yards south of the Dunkard Church and east of the pike. The lane left the pike, ran 500 yards along a downslope, and then 500 yards up to a little ridge. Here the lane turned abruptly southward, again eastward, and then south again to rejoin the ridge, where it met the Boonsboro Pike. Hill's veterans of the action at Turner's Gap were posted along the lane, awaiting the approach of French's troops, and—after a time—Richardson's. The casualties that would pile up in this natural trench would transform the road's name from the sunken road to "Bloody Lane."

French's men moved southward from the East Woods and encountered sporadic fire from skirmishers in the area of the Roulette Farm. The Confederates were part of the brigade of Col. Alfred H. Colquitt. Lee, meanwhile, was visiting the troops posted in the sunken road, and there Col. John B. Gordon of the 6th Alabama Infantry told Lee, "These men are going to stay here, General, till the sun goes down or victory is won!" Shortly thereafter, a shell took off the forelegs of Hill's horse, and the animal collapsed into an awkward position, forcing Hill to disentangle himself. As French's men approached, a Confederate shell burst open a beehive on the Roulette Farm and members of the 132d Pennsylvania Infantry scattered with bullets and bees pursuing. The Federals formed for attack north of the sunken road, however, and wave after wave of attack fell back, cut to pieces from volleys of musketry from the Confederate gunners in the lane. Maj. Gen. Richard H. Anderson arrived with his men on the field and joined in, directed by Longstreet to support D. H. Hill. The line of defense now consisted of Brig. Gen. Robert E. Rodes's brigade of mostly Alabamians posted from the Hagerstown Pike eastward to the bend in the lane, where Anderson's brigade of mostly North Carolinians were placed. The Confederate position was so impenetrable that Longstreet ordered an attack, and Rodes set out on a charge with his brigade and a part of Colquitt's on an attack that reached the Roulette Farm, after which counterattacks drove the Confederates back south. Richardson arrived and deployed his division, assigning his brigades as follows: Brig. Gen. Thomas F. Meagher with the Irish Brigade on the right,

Brig. Gen. John C. Caldwell's brigade on the left, and Col. John R. Brooke's brigade in the rear.

Richardson's force slammed into the right side of Anderson's line in the sunken road and was forced to halt and offer battle from a distance because of the galling fire. Meagher was wounded and carried from the field. Vicious fighting ensued, and once more during the Antietam battle the caliber of action surged to one of the hottest fights of the war. Tremendous, rolling surges of musketry fire snapped back and forth from both lines. Dick Anderson was wounded in the thigh, fell from his horse, and was taken to the rear, and the Confederate system of command faltered on the right. Commanders screamed orders that were rarely heard in the chaos; great billowing clouds of white smoke belched from cannon; shells ripped trenches into the plowed fields; and men were dying at a great rate on both sides of the fight. Brig. Gen. George B. Anderson was mortally wounded, struck in the ankle by a Minié bullet. He was taken back to Raleigh, North Carolina, where eventually his foot was amputated, and he died on October 16, never recovering from the operation.

Nearby, Gordon and Rodes were both injured. Gordon, helping to direct the Confederate regiments huddled in Bloody Lane, was wounded five times this day. He was shot through the calf of the right leg; higher up in the same leg; in his left arm; his shoulder, and finally in the face, narrowly missing his jugular vein on exit. "I fell forward and lay unconscious with my face in my cap," recalled Gordon, "and it would seem that I might have been smothered by the blood running into my cap from this last wound but for the act of some Yankee, who, as if to save my life, had at a previous hour during the battle, shot a hole through the cap, which let the blood out." Later, the Alabamian recalled the sensation of being struck in the head and lying senseless, in a haze. "I have been struck on the head with a six-pound solid shot," he felt. "It has carried away my head. On the left side there is a little piece of scull [sic] left, but the brain is gone entirely; therefore, I am dead. And yet I am thinking. . . . I may have consciousness while dead, but not motion. If I can lift my leg, then I am alive. I will try that. Can I? Yes, there it is; lifted up! I'm all right!"

Caldwell, meanwhile, made progress against George Anderson's and Brig. Gen. Ambrose R. Wright's brigades and pushed portions of each southward into the Piper Cornfield. Rodes's brigade was left in the road, but the Union position, inching southward, was working toward achieving an enfilading fire on the Confederates in the once-strong entrenchment; any men left in the road would soon be victims of a crossfire from both sides that would send bullets down the length of the road, creating murderous casualties. Rodes's brigade was now commanded by Lt. Col. J. N. Lightfoot, who made a desperate attempt to save the position. Rodes's men regrouped and tried to make a stand, but the Union penetration took over Bloody Lane and Caldwell captured 300 prisoners in the process. Hill himself took a musket and helped lead a movement against Caldwell's left, stricken with fear of the closeness of the Union forces to the hill to the south that would command the town of Sharpsburg. Hill's Confederates moved on a hill that was contested by the 5th New Hampshire Infantry, led by Col. Edward E. Cross, and Cross, wounded in the head, streaked his face with black powder and led his men forward to occupy the position. Desperate, Hill located Capt. M. B. Miller's battery of the Washington Artillery, posted near the Piper Barn. Longstreet himself desperately directed the fire from this battery, which held off the Federal surge. After a time, a caisson was directly hit and several gunners wounded; Longstreet and his staff themselves manned and fired the gun, Longstreet wearing carpet slippers over his chafed heel, which had been irritated by rough boots.

The Federal advance southward ran out of steam, but only after three and a half hours of intense fighting. Near the Sunken Road, Richardson had been mortally wounded, hit by spherical case shot while astride his horse, directing the Federal gunners to silence the Confederate batteries firing northward. He was taken to McClellan's headquarters at the Pry House, where he was visited by many officers and even by President Lincoln after the campaign, but Richardson died of complications from the wound.

The battle for Bloody Lane was the costliest part of the most violent day of the war. More than 3,000 Union soldiers were casualties during this action, and the Confederate losses were not known. "I was astonished to observe our troops moving along the front and passing over what appeared to be a long, heavy column of the enemy without paying it any attention," wrote Lt. Col. David Hunter Strother, a volunteer aide of McClellan's, at the Pry House. "I borrowed a glass from an officer, and discovered this to be actually a column of the enemy's dead lying along the hollow road. . . . Among the prostrate mass I could easily distinguish the movements of those endeavoring to crawl away from the ground; hands waving as if calling of assistance, and others struggling as if in the agonies of death."

The loss of the Confederate center had a devastating effect on Lee's tactical position. Fleeing, demoralized troops filled the town of Sharpsburg. The Confederate artillery had been decisively handled by the superior firepower of the Northern guns. The attacks on the Confederate left and center had resulted in the utter destruction of some of the veteran units of Lee's army. Virtually every portion of this force was or had been engaged, while McClellan had not yet fought with anything like his entire available army. The situation was beginning to look desperate for the Army of Northern Virginia.

Rather than continuing an offensive, however, McClellan made a weak response. Instead of throwing in his reserves in force, which included the elite 5th Corps of Maj. Gen. Fitz John Porter, now held in reserve, he made a demonstration only on the Confederate right, again in a piecemeal, uncoordinated way. McClellan left the portion of his plan to "assailing the enemy's right" as a diversion to Burnside, who began his maneuvering at 7:30 A.M. but only received an order to attack by 10 A.M. In the tradition of his commanding general, Burnside was sluggish even after receiving orders and had failed to reconnoiter before moving his force.

Finally, Burnside moved his 9th Corps, consisting of the divisions of Willcox, Sturgis, Rodman, and Cox, to positions from which they could make a movement toward crossing the creek. Without any reconnaissance, however, Burnside sent Rodman south to cross at Snavely's Ford, which he knew about, but concentrated crossing the bulk of his divisions at the Lower Bridge, also called Rohrbach Bridge—a structure that would later become known as Burnside's Bridge because of the struggle to cross it. Burnside, meanwhile, was upset over his assignment (he no longer commanded the 1st Corps, as he had in the quasi-official "wing" arrangement) and so was miffed at his old friend McClellan as he went into action. Consequently, he took a distant role in leading the southernmost actions on the field and passed on his orders to Cox.

With the exception of Rodman's division to the south, Burnside's corps approached the area of the Lower Bridge cautiously, deploying Sturgis's division in front, followed by the spread-out Kanawha Division, commanded by Col. Eliakim P. Scammon, and lastly Willcox's division. The ground they faced in attempting to capture and cross the Lower Bridge was formidable—much more so than the weaker defensive ground to the north. The primary road coming out of Sharpsburg to the southeast wound around a few gentle curves before passing the farmhouses owned by Joseph Sherrick and John Otto, then approached the creek where it crossed over Lower Bridge, passing near the Rohrbach farm to the east. The ground gently sloped upward to the east, but on the western side of the creek a high bluff overlooked the bridge, and afforded an excellent position to post sharpshooters. This is exactly what the Confederate defenders at the Lower Bridge did, their regiments consisting of men from Brig. Gen. David R. Jones's division, specifically the 2d Georgia Infantry, 20th Georgia Infantry, and 50th Georgia Infantry, primarily from Brig. Gen. Robert Toombs's brigade.

It is one of the great unanswered questions of the eastern battles: why did Burnside fail to note that Antietam Creek could be forded at a variety of places out of enemy range? The action that resulted at the Lower Bridge was a combination of faulty communications on both McClellan's and Burnside's parts and poor tactical thinking by Burnside. Early in the morning, when skirmishing and sporadic artillery fire crossed the creek at several points, Cox deployed the 9th Corps into position and waited. What the Union attackers did not understand, besides the easy fordability of the creek, was that, at that time, the whole of the Confederate right—the sharpshooters posted on the bluffs—amounted to only 450 men, supported by two artillery batteries.

Sometime about 10 A.M. Cox directed the initial movement on the Lower Bridge, and it accomplished nothing. Cox wished to advance Crook's brigade to the front and order its men to rush the bridge and cross it. Crook, however, emerged in a position from which he received a constant fire from the Rebels, and he was pinned down for some time. With Crook thus engaged, Cox ordered Sturgis to move to the front and make a charge toward the bridge, which he did, but the narrow columns of men filing toward the bridge were shot to pieces by the crack Georgia riflemen. The batteries firing down upon the blue-clad men employed everything available, including what was later determined to be scrap railroad iron. Sturgis was ordered to take the bridge and cross it at all costs, and he assembled four of his best regiments, the 51st New York Infantry (Col. Robert B. Potter), 51st Pennsylvania Infantry (Col. John F. Hartranft), 35th Massachusetts Infantry, and 21st Massachusetts Infantry to do it. Potter's and Hartranft's regiments were ordered to take the bridge, and Brig. Gen. Edward Ferrero—who had quite a reputation for drinking—offered whiskey to those soldiers who would make it across. Still pinned down, Crook opened a terrific fire, and in forming near the bridge, the 51st New York and 51st Pennsylvania were being shot up severely. But the "two 51sts" made it up and across the bridge and finally, after noon, succeeded in scattering the Georgians from the hillside beyond. The 9th Corps had received terrific casualties in the process.

By 1 P.M. the Federal regiments were on the western bank of Antietam Creek and Toombs's Georgians were withdrawing into the cornfields toward Sharpsburg. Rodman, meanwhile, finally waded through waist-deep water at Snavely's Ford, lost a few men to enemy pickets, but crossed basically intact. On the right of the movement, Crook finally crossed, too, and moved toward the west. A slow movement characterized by scattered fighting, hauling of supplies in wagons westward, coordination of mixed units, and other problems delayed any definitive push westward for about two hours. It was the middle of the afternoon by the time the Federals could aim for capturing the town of Sharpsburg and perhaps pinning Lee against the Potomac. David L. Thompson, a private in the 9th New York Infantry, described the intensity of fighting that followed Rodman's advance westward. "The mental strain was so great that I saw at that moment the singular effect mentioned, I think, in the life of Goethe on a similar occasion, the whole landscape for an instant turned slightly red." Despite the great flurry of bullets in the air during this phase of the battle, not all soldiers feared for the worst. "How natural it is for a man to suppose that if a gun is discharged, he or some one is sure to be hit," wrote Frank Holsinger, a Federal soldier. "He soon finds, however, that the only damage done, in ninety-nine cases out of a hundred, the only thing killed is the powder! . . . I have frequently heard the remark that it took a man's weight in lead to kill him."

Despite that assessment, many men died on this day. By 3 P.M. Burnside himself went to the bridge that soldiers were already calling his, and the divisions of Willcox on the right, Rodman on the left, and Scammon in the rear were moving relentlessly westward toward Sharpsburg. Sturgis's division was held back with Burnside at the bridge, and Porter's 5th Corps was still inactive, east of Antietam Creek. By 4 P.M. the situation brightened considerably for the 9th Corps when it had occupied nearly all the high ground south and east of the town and began to deploy artillery, and Lee faced a nearly desperate situation in that every single available man had been thrown into the battle. Pleasonton's cavalry and a small force from the 5th Corps, commanded by Brig. Gen. George Sykes, explored the ground over Middle Bridge and detected the weakness of Lee's center. Then fate again helped the Southern cause. Willcox's batteries ran out of artillery, causing a delay in the Federal push toward the town, and McClellan did nothing when advised to attack strongly through the center.

Then up came Hill. Through a hard-driving march from Harpers Ferry, A. P. Hill's Light Division arrived on the scene and at the critical position to stop the Federal advance just when they were most sorely needed. From Boteler's Ford, Hill's 3,000 men were creating a low cloud of dust on the horizon at 4 P.M.; a short time later they arrived in force south of town and counterattacked savagely into the Federal advance. The situation was confused because of the unexpected nature of any such force slamming into the Yankees, and because many of Hill's men wore blue uniforms captured at Harpers Ferry. At an especially hot part of the front line, the inexperienced 16th Connecticut Infantry was being shot to pieces by the 1st South Carolina Infantry and 12th South Carolina Infantry of Brig. Gen. Maxcy Gregg's brigade, when Rodman himself decided to spring them from the predicament. Rodman brought the 4th Rhode Island Infantry into position and was then struck by a ball that passed through his lung. He died on September 30 in a field hospital near Sharpsburg. Their division commander down on the field, the Northern boys panicked and the Southern attack pushed the Yankees back in confusion. On the Confederate side, Brig. Gen. Lawrence O'Bryan Branch stood in consultation with A. P. Hill, Maxcy Gregg, and Brig. Gen. James J. Archer on the ridge between Sharpsburg and the Lower Bridge. A Federal sharpshooter fired into the group and struck Branch in the right cheek, killing him instantly.

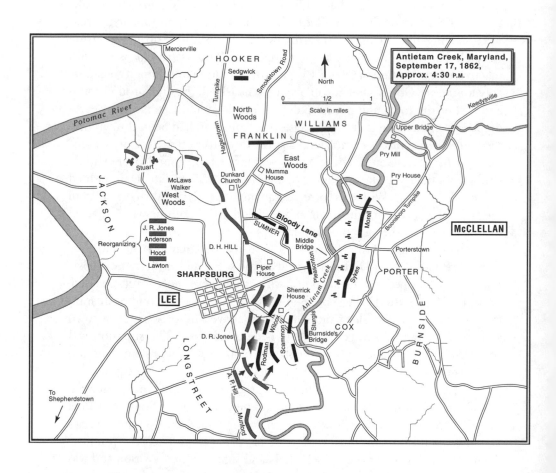

Antietam Creek, Maryland,
September 17, 1862,
Approx. 4:30 P.M.

Mercerville

HOOKER

Sedgwick

North

0   1/2   1
Scale in miles

Potomac River

North
Woods

FRANKLIN

WILLIAMS

Keedysville

Upper Bridge

Pry Mill

Hagerstown Turnpike

Smoketown Road

Stuart

McLaws
Walker

East
Woods

Dunkard
Church

Mumma
House

Pry House

JACKSON

West
Woods

J. R. Jones

Anderson

Hood

Lawton

Reorganizing

D. H. HILL

SUMNER

Bloody Lane

Middle
Bridge

Morell

Boonsboro Turnpike

McCLELLAN

Porterstown

SHARPSBURG

LEE

Piper
House

Sherrick
House

Pleasonton

Sykes

PORTER

Antietam Creek

Wilcox

Sturgis

D. R. Jones

Scammon

Burnside's
Bridge

COX

LONGSTREET

Rodman

A. P. Hill

BURNSIDE

To
Shepherdstown

Munford

The bloodiest day of the war came to an end. In a single day McClellan's army of 75,500 had lost 2,010 killed, 9,416 wounded, and 1,043 missing; of about 38,000 men engaged, Confederate losses were about 2,700 killed, 9,024 wounded, and 2,000 missing. Some 4,810 men lay dead on the fields surrounding the village of Sharpsburg. The scale of the carnage shocked all Americans, particularly because photographers arrived on the scene shortly after the battle and made gruesome images of the dead that were displayed in Northern cities. The battle transformed forever what Americans thought about war.

On the evening of September 17, Lee called his subordinates together for a council. "Here is my old war horse at last!" he reputedly said when Longstreet arrived. When Lee asked about the status of Hood's division, the rough Texan allegedly told him, "I have no division, General Lee." Despite the appalling state of his army, Lee stayed in position on September 18, almost taunting the inactivity of McClellan. For Lee the battle and campaign had been a loss in every respect, and most important by the strategic measuring sticks—none of his strategic goals for the campaign had been accomplished. For McClellan, the battle had been horribly mismanaged. Still, on September 18, McClellan was reinforced with fresh troops, had not utilized either the 5th or 6th Corps in the battle, and had Pleasonton's cavalry in excellent condition to scout a follow-up attack on Lee, who could still have been pinned against the Potomac River. But McClellan, in affirmation of Lee's lack of concern, did nothing. "O, why did we not attack them and drive them into the river?" wrote 2d Lt. Elisha Hunt Rhodes. "I do not understand these things. But then I am only a boy."

Lee's army limped back across Boteler's Ford, where Porter slowly crossed after Lee on September 19, only a small skirmish resulting. The next day Porter crossed again but came reeling back when he encountered A. P. Hill. McClellan had demonstrated a disastrous ability to allow his army to be used in an uncoordinated fashion, without engaging major portions of it, issuing abysmal communications from a distance by which he could be called more of a spectator than a commanding general. If anyone needed further proof of McClellan's incompetence as a field commander, they received it with full force at Antietam. One simply wonders what good might have resulted for the Union cause in the early days of the war if McClellan had been taken out of the field and transformed into a chief of staff in Washington, as had happened with Halleck.

With the armies bloodied and disengaged, the men and officers, their families, and the sick and wounded struggled to comprehend the awful suffering at hand. Many families read newspaper casualty lists or received awful letters such as the following, addressed to "Mr. Parmalee" and written by Benjamin S. Calef of the 2d U.S. Sharpshooters. "To me is given the painful task of informing you that your son, Lewis C. Parmalee, was killed in the battle near this place on the morning of the 17th," Calef wrote. "He had been leading on the remnant of our little band after the Col. was wounded, & had just succeeded in taking a Rebel color, when he was struck by a ball in the right arm & breast—he could not have lived but a short time. His body was recovered this morning & interred near the field. The place will be marked so it may be known where he lies."

Others simply had wounds to contend with. The celebrated nurse Clara Barton helped to ease the suffering of Northern and captured Southern wounded on the Antietam battlefield. She would later help to found the American Red Cross. Hannah Ropes, a nurse in Washington tending to some of the Antietam wounded, noted how many of them slipped through a gripping delirium as they lay in pain. "The young man who was shot through the lungs," she penned to her mother in late September, "to our surprise and, as the surgeons say, contrary to all 'science,' lived till last night, or rather this morning. . . . The pressure of blood from the unequal circulation had affected the brain slightly, and, as they all are, he was on the battlefield, struggling to get away from the enemy. I promised him that nobody should touch him, and that in a few minutes he would be free from all pain. He believed me and, fixing his beautiful eyes upon my face, he never turned them away; resistance, the resistance of a strong natural will, yielded; his breathing grew more gentle, ending softly as an infant's."

The battlefield of Antietam was transformed in a day into a terrible spectacle. "At last, night came on, and, with the exception of an occasional shot from the outposts, all was quiet," Robert Gould Shaw wrote his father of the field. "The crickets chirped, and the frogs croaked, just as if nothing unusual had happened all day long, and presently the stars came out bright, and we lay down among the dead, and slept soundly until daylight. There were twenty dead bodies within a rod of me."

Two days after the battle of Antietam, Assistant Secretary of War Peter H. Watson wrote Maj. Gen. John A. Dix, in command of the Department of Virginia. "The Secretary of War directs me to acknowledge the receipt of your communication of the 15th instant," wrote Watson, "in which you state that 'the contraband negroes,' which have been permitted to collect at Fort Monroe and in its vicinity, have been and now are a very great source of embarrassment to the troops in the garrison and neighboring camps, and in the event that the fort should be invested or approached by the enemy's forces, you should be obliged to ship them north." The request was granted.

Dix's dilemma was symptomatic of the growing question of what to do with freed, abandoned, runaway, and refugee slaves. The whole question was beginning to transform the war, taking it from simply a struggle to preserve the Union to one that would reconstruct the Union into the nation it should have been without slavery. Whereas dusty histories of the Civil War period describe Reconstruction as if it began in 1865, reconstructing the Union actually began in 1861. The key question was how to handle the slavery issue, the most explosive of the war's causes. Why Abraham Lincoln handled the matter as he did warrants some examination.

Though his beliefs and actions have been questioned in modern times from all angles, Lincoln believed in the abolition of slavery as a moral imperative. He was also politically expedient: Viewed as slow to act by the New England abolitionists such as William Lloyd Garrison and Wendell Phillips, Lincoln was enough of a politician and realist to know he had to bide his time to abolish slavery. The Constitution, after all, specifically protected slavery in states where it existed, and Lincoln, in his First Inaugural Address, wondered aloud why Southerners would bring on war when that was the case.

For much of the early part of the war, Lincoln supported ideas to colonize blacks and return them to Africa. On a realistic level, colonization never could have taken place. There weren't enough ships to move 4 million slaves in such a way—it was logistically preposterous. Lincoln grew to support the idea of compensated emancipation. This scheme proposed Federal aid to each state that adopted a policy of gradual emancipation. Lincoln's hope was that the Border States would adopt it first and the more southern states would see its positive effects and this would help to erode their allegiance to the Confederacy. The monetary cost would be trivial compared with the cost of fighting the war. Compensated emancipation was used successfully in April 1862 to abolish slavery within the District of Columbia. The change came when it was clear that abolition in the rebellious states was a military necessity, and this approach was also Constitutionally valid.

By August 1862, when Lincoln exchanged letters with Horace Greeley over the "Prayer of Twenty Millions," he had already weeks earlier finished a draft of the Preliminary Emancipation Proclamation, a document declaring all the slaves free within states rebelling against the United States. On July 22 he read a draft of the text to his cabinet. Secretary of State William Seward declared the president should wait until a later time to issue it, however, since it might appear in the light of recent military defeats as "the last measure of an exhausted government, a cry for help."

So Lincoln decided to wait for a military victory to issue the document, and Antietam was it. He had been emboldened slightly by the book *The War Powers of the President,* freshly written and published by William Whiting, a solicitor in the War Department. The preliminary proclamation, issued on September 22, stated, "On the first day of January in the year of our Lord, one thousand eight hundred and sixty-three, all persons held as slaves within any state, or designated part of a state, the people whereof shall then be in rebellion against the United States shall be then, thenceforward, and forever free." Lincoln provided a grace period, asserting that states had until January 1, 1863, to comply, and on that date the formal Emancipation Proclamation would be issued. It was a powerful document and instantly drew praise and criticism worldwide. "I desire to express my undissembled and sincere thanks for your Emancipation Proclamation," wrote Lincoln's vice president, Hannibal Hamlin, on September 25. "It will stand as the great act of the age."

Others were less courteous, and the document outraged many Southerners, who confidently predicted that Northern soldiers would not stand and fight in the field for the cause of liberating slaves. But the door had been opened now to end slavery, as Lincoln called again for a restoration of the Union and Congressional support to enact compensated emancipation. True, many soldiers and civilians in the North did not believe they were fighting a war for emancipation, at least at first, but they were not about to leave the field. The Emancipation Proclamation has been criticized as a document without spirit, lacking the glorious style that could have made it a truly momentous edict in human history. But Lincoln wrote the document in a dry, lawyerlike style for a purpose. It was in effect a legal notice directed at the attorney Jefferson Davis, and it was written with the terse precision of a document intended for a specific effect. It left no legal loopholes for the opposition to criticize. In its own workmanlike way, the Emancipation Proclamation is a masterpiece.

In at least one community it failed to surprise anyone. Along the sea islands of South Carolina, the proclamation did not "seem to have made a great deal of stir," according to Edward S. Philbrick, one of the New England Freedmen's Aid Society members sent down to help the black Americans who had been freed in the wake of Du Pont's expedition. "Here the people don't take the slightest interest in it. They have been free already for nearly a year, as far as they could see, and have so little comprehension about the magnitude of our country and are so supremely selfish that you can't beat it into their heads that any one else is to be provided for beyond St. Helena Island."

On September 24, as if to buttress the impact of the proclamation, Lincoln issued a new suspension of the Writ of Habeas Corpus, providing for military trials of anyone rebelling or assisting in a rebellion against the government. "The Writ of Habeas Corpus is suspended in respect to all persons arrested, or who are now, or hereafter during the rebellion shall be, imprisoned . . . by any military authority or by the sentence of any Court Martial or Military Commission."

THE WAR IN THE FIELD, meanwhile, was bristling along out west. At Clarksville, Tennessee, which had been surrendered to the Confederacy, Union forces led an expedition from Fort Donelson that resulted in two skirmishes. Col. William W. Lowe (5th Iowa Cavalry) brought a portion of his regiment together with companies of the 11th Illinois Infantry, 13th Wisconsin Infantry, 71st Ohio Infantry, and attached artillery, a force numbering about 1,030 men. Confederates about three miles outside Clarksville met Lowe's force and decided to give battle. Engagements near Clarksville at New Providence on September 6 and at Riggin's Store the following day left Clarksville in Union hands. The Federals burned supplies and brought pro-Union families back to Fort Donelson with them.

The war in Kentucky heated up around Munfordville, between Elizabethtown and Bowling Green. This continuation of Bragg's invasion of Kentucky, which had commenced in August with the actions of Kirby Smith and the cavalry raids of Morgan and Forrest, was now spearheaded by the brigade of Brig. Gen. James R. Chalmers. Up to now, the contest had consisted of maneuvering. "This campaign must be won by marching, not fighting," wrote Bragg. Chalmers's Confederates moved on Munfordville, defended by the earthwork dubbed Fort Craig. The town's defensive force consisted of 4,133 Union troops commanded by Col. John T. Wilder, a native New Yorker who had moved to Indiana and become an industrialist. On September 14, Chalmers attacked the Union line without Bragg's orders or permission. After three days Wilder surrendered the fort, its garrison, artillery, and 5,000 small arms. The Union force had lost 15 killed and 57 wounded; the Confederates, 35 killed and 253 wounded. Now the situation in the critical border state grew even more complex. On October 1, Maj. Gen. Don Carlos Buell advanced his Army of the Ohio, 60,000 strong, from Louisville to face Bragg's Army of Tennessee, which consisted of 22,500, and Maj. Gen. Edmund Kirby Smith's Army of Kentucky, with about 10,000 troops located near Lexington.

The resulting battle on October 8, fought southwest of Harrodsburg, would be called Perryville or Chaplin Hills, and would be the largest Civil War action in Kentucky. In this engagement Buell's army consisted of three corps, as follows: Maj. Gen. Alexander M. McCook (1st Corps; divisions of Brig. Gens. Lovell H. Rousseau and James S. Jackson); Maj. Gen. Thomas L. Crittenden (2d Corps; divisions of Brig. Gens. William Sooy Smith and Thomas J. Wood); and acting Maj. Gen. Charles C. Gilbert (3d Corps; divisions of Brig. Gens. Albin F. Schoepf, Robert B. Mitchell, and Philip H. Sheridan). The portion of Bragg's army that fought at Perryville, Polk's Army of Mississippi, was divided into two "wings." Maj. Gen. Benjamin F. Cheatham's Right Wing held the division of Brig. Gen. Daniel S. Donelson (brigades of Col. John H. Savage, Brig. Gen. Alexander P. Stewart, Brig. Gen. George Maney, and the cavalry brigade of Col. John A. Wharton). Maj. Gen. William J. Hardee's Left Wing consisted of the divisions of Brig. Gen. J. Patton Anderson (brigades of Brig. Gen. John C. Brown, Brig. Gen. Daniel W. Adams, Col. Samuel Powell, and Col. Thomas M. Jones); and Maj. Gen. Simon B. Buckner (brigades of Brig. Gens. St. John R. Liddell, Patrick R. Cleburne, Bushrod R. Johnson, and Sterling A. M. Wood); and a cavalry brigade commanded by Col. Joseph Wheeler.

Buell approached Bragg's army cautiously, separating his corps so they might converge upon Bragg at Bardstown, west of Harrodsburg and Perryville. Two detached divisions, those of Brig. Gens. Joshua W. Sill and Ebenezer Dumont, approached elements of Kirby Smith's forces near Frankfort, between Lexington and Louisville. Bragg misinterpreted this movement as that of Buell's main army and ordered Polk to move up and attack Sill's flank, while Kirby Smith assaulted Sill frontally. Shortly after this happened, however, Polk discovered the actual disposition of Union forces and then moved southeast to Harrodsburg, while Hardee moved in force to Perryville, establishing the position from which the battle would occur.

Buell's army approached Perryville on October 7. The Federal army lacked water, and so spread out its corps along Doctor's Creek and Wilson's Creek. In the lead was Sheridan's division of Gilbert's corps. In the meantime, Bragg arrived at Harrodsburg and ordered Polk forward to reinforce Hardee and attack Gilbert's corps. He sent another of Polk's divisions, that of Maj. Gen. Jones M. Withers, to march to the aid of Kirby Smith. On the evening of October 7 it was becoming clear that a battle was developing at Perryville and the respective commanders deployed their troops into position. The Federals established their line of battle northwest of Perryville along the Benton Road, between the two creeks. The line stretched southward all the way to the H. P. Bottom House, where Doctor's Creek crossed under the Mackville Pike. The corps of Crittenden and McCook marched toward positions on the left and right of Gilbert.

The battle of Perryville began quietly, with only scattered skirmishing on the morning of October 8. Col. Daniel McCook's Union brigade moved out to secure high ground that guarded pools of water along Doctor's Creek. The divisions of Jackson and Rousseau finally arrived late in the morning and skirmished briefly with Wheeler's cavalry and the Southern infantry of St. John R. Liddell. The battle surged into high gear as Cheatham's division moved around to the right and by about 2 P.M., led by Maney's brigade, struck hard into the Union flank, Alexander McCook's men. The surprise attack stunned the Union soldiers. The Confederates had simply walked through the tiny amount of water in the creek, marched up a bluff, and opened fire. South of Maney's attack, Donelson attacked, with Stewart's division fighting

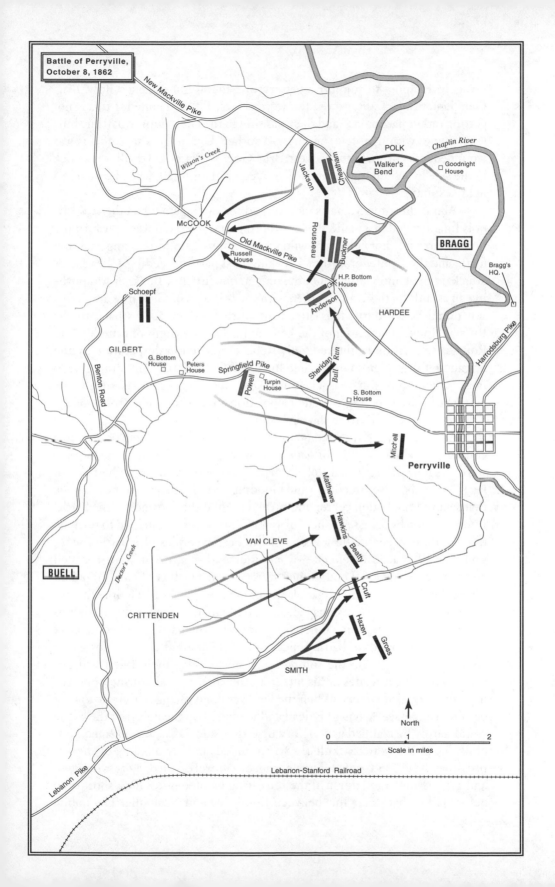

Battle of Perryville,
October 8, 1862

New Mackville Pike

Wilson's Creek

POLK

Chaplin River

Walker's
Bend

Goodnight
House

Jackson

Cheatham

McCOOK

Old Mackville Pike

Rousseau

Buckner

BRAGG

Bragg's
HQ.

Russell
House

H.P. Bottom
House

Anderson

HARDEE

Schoepf

Harrodsburg Pike

GILBERT

G. Bottom
House

Peters
House

Springfield Pike

Sheridan

Bull Run

Benton Road

Powell

Turpin
House

S. Bottom
House

Mitchell

Perryville

Matthews

BUELL

Doctor's Creek

VAN CLEVE

Hawkins

Beatty

Cruft

CRITTENDEN

Hazen

Gross

SMITH

North

0   1   2
Scale in miles

Lebanon Pike

Lebanon-Stanford Railroad

savagely. Helping to support a battery of Federal guns firing wildly, Brig. Gen. James S. Jackson uttered the words "Well I'll be damned if this is not getting rather particular," and then was shot in the chest with two Minié bullets, dying within a few minutes. Another Union general officer was wounded in a cornfield to the west. Brig. Gen. William R. Terrill was struck in the side by a shell fragment. He survived until nightfall, when he died in a field hospital.

About this time Maney's men surged forward again when the 123d Illinois Infantry fled in a panic. The northern part of the field was transforming into an intensely hot fight, with wild sheets of musketry fire blazing back and forth, and the Confederate attack for the most part succeeding. Cheatham's attack on the Union left was not the only action. By now Buckner was pushing an assault on the Union center, with the brigades of Cleburne and Johnson doing heavy duty. This attack drove the Federal forces back to the Russell House. The center of the Federal line showed signs of crumbling as Rousseau's division splintered, only to be supported in desperation by the brigades of Brig. Gen. James B. Steedman and Col. Michael Gooding. Due to faulty communication on Buell's part, Crittenden's corps arrived during the battle but halted and regrouped at a position about three miles south of the fighting and took no part in the day's action.

As Union troops teetered on the brink of disaster, Sheridan organized a counterattack that sent the brigade of Col. William P. Carlin in the lead toward the now disorganized Rebels, driving them back through the town of Perryville. Likewise, Steedman and Gooding combined for a vigorous attack that secured the Union center and turned around the fortunes of the battle. Intense action by Rousseau and Col. John C. Starkweather helped to turn the tide. Curiously, Perryville was one of the best examples of a battle fought under peculiar acoustic effects—what nineteenth-century militarists called an "acoustic shadow." Though they were within a radius of two and a half miles, Buell, Gilbert, and McCook all failed to realize for some time that elements of the army were engaged, and Buell failed to realize the battle was on until about 4 P.M., some ninety minutes after the battle reached its peak intensity. The sounds of battle appear to have been muffled by atmospheric conditions, foliage, and the rolling landscape. Oddly, then, Buell had engaged only nine brigades of his fifteen in the area, and he lost the opportunity for a decisive victory. When the day was done, Bragg withdrew toward eastern Tennessee, leaving his dead and wounded on the field, but the battle could hardly be claimed as a victory by either side. Of 36,940 engaged Federals, the losses were 845 killed, 2,851 wounded, and 515 missing; of the approximately 16,000 Confederates engaged, 510 were killed, 2,635 wounded, and 251 missing. Buell pursued the retreating Confederates for a short time before falling back on a line between Louisville and Nashville. The public

outcry against Buell was so voluminous that a military investigation ensued—the "Buell Commission"—and although he was a relatively competent soldier and Perryville was at least a strategic victory due to Bragg's
retreat, Buell's career in the wake of Perryville was essentially ruined. The
commission found no action against him, but he was superseded in command of the Army of the Ohio by Maj. Gen. William S. Rosecrans. Buell
awaited orders for more than one year, by which time he resigned from the
army. The investigative entries of the Buell Commission's reports are astonishing in their volume.

After Perryville, hopes for glory in Kentucky diminished for both sides.
Maj. Gen. Edmund Kirby Smith's Army of Kentucky retreated southward
from Lexington. Col. John Hunt Morgan ordered his men to commence a
second great cavalry raid from Crab Orchard on October 17. This time it
would last nineteen days. His brigade of 1,800 troopers circled eastward, capturing Lexington on the 18th and some of the 4th Ohio Cavalry stationed in
the town, following a skirmish with a portion of the 3d Ohio Cavalry. A cavalry force under Maj. Gen. Gordon Granger pursued. Capturing and destroying supplies and knocking down some railroad bridges characterized
the remainder of the raid, which saw Morgan's men circle west through Versailles, Lawrenceburg, and Bardstown by October 19. Five days later the
raiders made it to Morgantown, north of Bowling Green, and the following
day they created a stir at Hopkinsville, northeast of the old battleground at
Fort Donelson. By November 17 the raid had concluded, and Morgan and his
men were safely back in Gallatin, Tennessee, with their reputation growing
again for freely riding throughout Kentucky.

Toward the end of October the Kentucky campaign was winding down.
By October 19, Bragg was approaching Cumberland Gap, dragging grain and
captured supplies with him, and he passed through the gap and into Tennessee on October 22 and 23. On the day of the Perryville battle, Jefferson
Davis wrote the Confederate Congress. "Tender consideration for worthless
and incompetent officers is but another name for cruelty toward the brave
men who fall sacrifices to defects of their leaders," he wrote. Some militarists
and citizens in the Confederacy felt such sentiments toward Bragg, but the
grizzled North Carolinian enjoyed a favored relationship with Jefferson
Davis, although not with many of his fellow officers.

THE WAR IN MISSISSIPPI produced two battles of consequence in the late autumn of 1862. While Buell was facing Bragg's threat in Kentucky, Confederate operations farther south aimed at preventing Buell's reinforcement by
Grant. The action concentrated just a scant few miles south of the old Shiloh
battlefield, south of the border into Mississippi. On September 14, Maj. Gen.
Sterling Price moved his Army of the West, some 17,000 strong, to Iuka, in

the extreme northeastern corner of the state, about twenty miles east of the rail center of Corinth. Price had come from Tupelo and was awaiting Maj. Gen. Earl Van Dorn's Army of West Tennessee (7,000) before acting further. The original plan of simply preventing Buell's reinforcement was partially abandoned as Van Dorn suggested the two commanders unite to attack Grant's lines in western Tennessee. Price, however, scattered the small Union force at Iuka as he moved into town and waited. At Corinth, Grant determined not to wait but to attack. This situation led five days later to the battle of Iuka, as Grant sent the Army of the Mississippi, commanded by Maj. Gen. William S. Rosecrans, east toward that town.

Grant wanted a combined effort with Maj. Gen. Edward O. C. Ord leading about 8,000 men in one column of three divisions along the Memphis & Charleston Railroad line, passing through Glendale and Burnsville, while Rosecrans, with about 9,000 men in two divisions, would drop south along the Mobile & Ohio Railroad, then cut east to Davenport's Mill, Jacinto, and Barnett's Crossroads, before turning northward to eliminate any route of escape for Price's army. The plan was a sound one, but did not come off as intended. As circumstances dictated, the composition of the armies actually engaged at Iuka was as follows: Price's army consisted of the division of Brig. Gen. Lewis Henry Little (brigades of Col. Elijah Gates, Brig. Gen. Louis Hébert, Brig. Gen. Martin E. Green, and Col. John D. Martin), and cavalry commanded by Brig. Gen. Frank C. Armstrong. The Confederate forces engaged amounted to 3,179 men. Rosecrans's Federal forces engaged amounted to about 4,500, organized into two infantry divisions and one cavalry division, as follows: Brig. Gen. David S. Stanley (brigades of Cols. John W. Fuller and Joseph A. Mower), Brig. Gen. Charles S. Hamilton (brigades of Col. John B. Sanborn and Brig. Gen. Jeremiah C. Sullivan), and the cavalry division commanded by Col. John K. Mizner.

By the night of September 18, Ord's column was in place about two miles west of Iuka. But Rosecrans was late. By late afternoon Rosecrans arrived within about two miles of the town when his leading element, Sanborn's brigade, was struck suddenly by a Confederate attack by Little's division. The battle commenced about 4:30 P.M. Sanborn reported: "As I came back through my own line . . . I gave the command as loud as I was able to both infantry and artillery to commence firing, and the battle opened as fiercely as it is possible to conceive. Leaves, twigs, men, horses—everything—was falling." By 5:15 P.M. Little and Hébert organized an attack that sent five infantry regiments and cavalry into the center of Sanborn's line along Mill Road, with the six guns of the 11th Ohio Artillery the primary focal point, situated near the front of the Union line between the 48th Indiana Infantry and the 5th Iowa Infantry. As nightfall approached, after vicious fighting that swayed the lines in several places, the Confederates succeeded

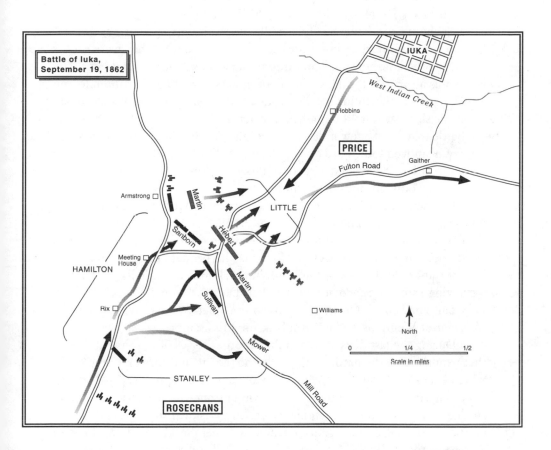

Battle of Iuka,
September 19, 1862

IUKA

West Indian Creek

Hobbins

PRICE

Fulton Road

Gaither

Armstrong

Martin

LITTLE

Sanborn

Hebert

Meeting
House

HAMILTON

Martin

Rix

Sullivan

Williams

North

Mower

0   1/4   1/2
Scale in miles

STANLEY

Mill Road

ROSECRANS

in taking the 11th Ohio's guns, and Sanborn's line collapsed. But the oncoming Confederates pulled up and stopped on the ground the Federals had held during much of the afternoon. Smoke and darkness created confusion. To make matters worse, Price had arrived and found his division commander, Henry Little, who was on his horse behind the 3d Texas Cavalry position, watching the battle. Little had served as a staff officer of Price's in the first summer of the war. As the two talked, Price outstretched his arm to show Little an area of the field. Just then, a Minié bullet passed under Price's arm and struck Little over the left eye, killing him instantly.

At about 7 P.M. Federals under Sullivan counterattacked. It was so dark, however, that soldiers on both sides could barely see what they were shooting at, and the last shots rang out through the woods about an hour later. The battle was a surprise for the Union participants. Grant had not intended on attacking until the following day, and in another strange instance of an "acoustic shadow," Ord did not hear the action. His men stood idly by while the battle raged just a few miles away. When Price learned that Ord was also nearby, he moved southward during the night. The Federal losses for the day were 144 killed, 598 wounded, and 40 missing; Confederate losses were 263 killed, 692 wounded, and 561 missing.

Following Iuka, Van Dorn moved his Army of West Tennessee to Ripley, between Corinth and Holly Springs, hoping to join Price at that place. Rosecrans moved to the rail town of Corinth, and Ord moved to Bolivar in southern Tennessee, northwest of Corinth. This brought the force at Bolivar to 12,000 under Ord and Maj. Gen. Stephen A. Hurlbut, while Rosecrans had a growing force of 23,000 at Corinth. Van Dorn had a total of 22,000 men. Grant also had control of 7,000 troops commanded by Maj. Gen. William T. Sherman at Memphis, and 6,000 at Jackson, Mississippi.

During the last days of September another series of movements began that would set up the battle of Corinth, the second such action in the town, which had already survived Halleck's slow advance of the previous spring. Preliminarily, on September 25, a reconnaissance of cavalry to Davis's Bridge, Tennessee, on the Hatchie River, led to a skirmish, also called Pocahontas. This small action occurred when Lt. Col. John McDermott's force of 200 troopers (11th Illinois Cavalry) was surprised and scattered by Confederates who acted as guerrillas; the Federal horsemen suffered a loss of about 70 men.

Not satisfied with allowing Grant the opportunity to reinforce Rosecrans and believing that Rosecrans had fewer men than he did, Van Dorn decided to attack Rosecrans at Corinth. On September 29, Federal scouts detected Van Dorn's movements, but they could not predict where he was going. When he reached Pocahontas on the evening of October 2, Van Dorn turned his force eastward, and he pulled up at a position just nine miles from

Corinth. The stage was now set for a battle, and the participants would be largely different from those at Iuka. They now consisted of Rosecrans's Army of the Mississippi, with two divisions, those of Brig. Gen. David S. Stanley (brigades of Cols. John W. Fuller and Joseph A. Mower), and Brig. Gen. Charles S. Hamilton (brigades of Brig. Gens. Napoleon B. Buford and Jeremiah C. Sullivan), and the cavalry division of Col. John K. Mizner, with the brigades of Cols. Edward Hatch and Albert L. Lee. Secondly, Rosecrans had two divisions loaned from the Army of the Tennessee, commanded by Brig. Gen. Thomas A. Davies (brigades of Brig. Gen. Pleasant A. Hackleman, Brig. Gen. Richard J. Oglesby, and Col. Silas D. Baldwin), and Brig. Gen. Thomas J. McKean (brigades of Brig. Gen. John McArthur and Cols. John M. Oliver and Marcellus M. Crocker). On the Confederate side, Van Dorn's Army of West Tennessee consisted of two major elements. The first was Price's corps, or the Army of the West, organized into two divisions as follows: Brig. Gen. Louis Hébert (brigades of Col. Elijah Gates, Col. W. Bruce Colbert, Brig. Gen. Martin E. Green, and Col. John D. Martin), and Brig. Gen. Dabney H. Maury (brigades of Brig. Gen. John C. Moore, Brig. Gen. William L. Cabell, and Col. Charles W. Phifer). The second component, the 1st Division of the District of the Mississippi, was commanded by Maj. Gen. Mansfield Lovell and held the brigades of Brig. Gen. Albert Rust, Brig. Gen. John B. Villepigue, Brig. Gen. John S. Bowen, and a cavalry brigade commanded by Col. William H. Jackson.

At 10 A.M. on October 3, Van Dorn attacked the Federal line of battle, largely built up inside old abandoned Confederate earthworks from the previous spring. The Union line stretched about four miles west to east, with McArthur's brigade of McKean's division securing the left flank along the Memphis & Charleston Railroad, Oglesby's brigade near the center, and Davies's division, with Hackleman and Sullivan prominently arrayed, to the right. The Confederates approached spread east-west with the divisions of Lovell, Maury, and Hébert. Lovell opened the battle with an attack on McArthur that struck the Federal troops from three sides, and which succeeded marvelously save for Brig. Gen. Albert Rust discovering stubborn resistance for a time from the 21st Missouri Infantry. Severe fighting erupted all along the line, with many regiments receiving a galling fire from the attacking Rebels, as with the 14th Wisconsin Infantry (Col. John Hancock), which was stuck in the midst of a heavy crossfire. Pvt. J. M. Vandoozer was found two days after being shot through the head in this attack, a plug of tobacco still clenched in his hands.

To the north, meanwhile, Oglesby's men were being pushed back south along with the scattering troops of Hackleman. By early afternoon much of the Federal line had condensed into a semicircle around the Federal camps on Chewalla Road north of the Memphis & Charleston Railroad. McArthur

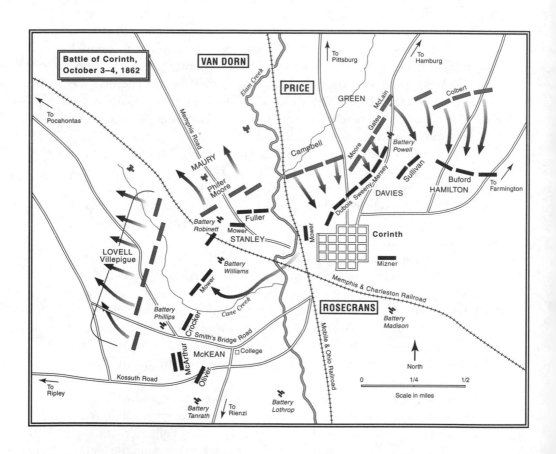

**Battle of Corinth,
October 3–4, 1862**

VAN DORN

PRICE

To Pittsburg

To Hamburg

To Pocahontas

Memphis Road

Elam Creek

GREEN

McLain

Colbert

MAURY

Moore

Gates

Campbell

Battery
Powell

Phifer
Moore

Sullivan

Buford

HAMILTON

Battery
Robinett

Fuller

Dubois

Sweeny

Mersey

DAVIES

To Farmington

Mower

STANLEY

Mower

Corinth

LOVELL
Villepigue

Battery
Williams

Mizner

Mower

Battery
Phillips

Crocker

Cane Creek

Memphis & Charleston Railroad

Smith's Bridge Road

ROSECRANS

Battery
Madison

McKEAN

College

Mobile & Ohio Railroad

North

To
Ripley

Kossuth Road

Oliver

McArthur

0   1/4   1/2

To
Rienzi

Battery
Tanrath

Battery
Lothrop

Scale in miles

compressed his badly suffering men, positioned artillery, and with the assistance of Crocker's brigade, readied for attack into the Confederates of John C. Moore's brigade, who occupied the camps. Lovell's men were approaching from the northwest, meanwhile, and Oglesby and Hackleman's soldiers retreating southward toward Corinth along the Memphis Road. By 2 P.M. the hot sun beat down and water was scarce, many of the men exhausted and near fainting from their efforts. McArthur nonetheless drove northward in a well-coordinated attack that scattered Moore's Confederates from the camps. Shortly thereafter Moore counterattacked, and drove back some of the Federal force but was too exhausted to pursue further. Tired, hungry, and sick from battle, the Southern soldiers did not resume the attack after midafternoon. The rest of the day was spent nursing injuries and regrouping. Van Dorn and Price consulted, and ordered their men to move west along the railroad. The battle was not yet over, though.

Renewed action came around 4 P.M., when Brig. Gen. Richard J. Oglesby, a well-liked Illinois politician who would be governor of that state before war's end, was seriously wounded, shot through the lungs. The fighting continued through dusk, and Brig. Gen. Pleasant A. Hackleman, another of Davies's brigade commanders, was hit too. A ball struck him in the neck. He was taken to the finest facility in Corinth, the Tishomingo Hotel, but died the same night.

The night of October 3, the troops on both sides attempted to repair the damages of the day and get some food and water, which was aggravatingly scarce, while Van Dorn was so intent on crushing Rosecrans that he considered a moonlight attack. During the night the Confederates, Van Dorn and Price included, could hear the rumble of wagons and the felling of trees. Rather than evacuating, as some Confederates had hoped, Rosecrans's men were building up their ammunition and supplies and the fortifications north and west of the city. Seven artillery positions around the town helped to protect it. By 4 A.M. a Rebel cannonade began and lasted nearly an hour, firing shot and shell toward the Federal positions—mostly over them—with nothing of a response. Finally, by midmorning, the Confederate attackers assembled with Lovell to the west, Maury to his north, and Green still farther north. By 10 A.M. Green launched an attack that wheeled the brigades of Cols. Gates, Robert McLain (replacing Martin), Colbert, and William H. Moore (replacing Green) into motion against the Union positions at Battery Powell, north of the town. Illinois and Iowa troops scattered in helplessness. Thomas Sweeny's brigade fought well, as did the gunners in Battery Powell. Similarly, an intense attack on Battery Robinett ensued by 11 A.M. This area marked the greatest, hottest action of the battle, as the 63d Ohio Infantry, 27th Ohio Infantry, and 39th Ohio Infantry fought off a frontal attack in and around the battery by the brigades of John C. Moore and Phifer.

Among the critical units attacking most savagely into this area was the 2d Texas Infantry led by Col. William P. Rogers. Rogers was an accomplished Texas attorney well known in political circles; he had led a company of Jefferson Davis's Mississippi Rifles in the Mexican War. Heavy casualties mounted in the fighting around and north of Battery Robinett; in one of the charges at the battery, Rogers rode into action on his black horse, perhaps attempting to surrender, and was shot dead. A famous wartime image shows Rogers's body propped on that of a fellow officer; it is one of the few images of a deceased important officer in the field during the war. The attacking Confederates burst into the streets of Corinth in front of the Tishomingo Hotel but were beaten back.

The fight at Battery Robinett and in the town was decisive in that Confederates were cast out of the town. Grant's reinforcements, consisting of troops under Brig. Gen. James B. McPherson, arrived from Jackson about 4 P.M., and the following day Rosecrans and McPherson pursued the fleeing enemy. A portion of Ord's troops also arrived from Bolivar, bringing 6,500 men into position at Pocahontas, and they struck Van Dorn along the Hatchie River on October 5. It was a skirmish, really, in which Van Dorn lost still more men as some 300 prisoners were taken, and he had to hurry southward to cross the river safely. The Yankees discontinued their pursuit at Ripley, and Van Dorn reached the relative safety of Holly Springs, the battle of Corinth concluded. The Union losses were 355 killed, 1,841 wounded, and 324 missing; Confederate losses were 473 killed, 1,997 wounded, and 1,763 missing.

Smaller, scattered actions occurred in the western theater during the fall. These included an engagement at Newtonia, Missouri, on September 30. In this action Col. Douglas H. Cooper's Confederate division, numbering some 4,000, many of them Indians, resisted attacks from Federal troops under Brig. Gen. Frederick Salomon. On October 22–23, in Pocotaligo, South Carolina, Federal troops under Maj. Gen. Ormsby M. Mitchel reconnoitered along the railroads and fought briefly around the Caston and Frampton plantations, in what was known as the engagements of Coosawhatchie, Pocotaligo, or Yemassee. Mitchel's men cut telegraph lines, destroyed portions of the Charleston & Savannah Railroad, and fought three times, primarily against the forces of Col. William S. Walker. The expedition accomplished minimal gains.

Some commanders expired in unusual ways. On September 29, while drinking with fellow officers at the Galt House in Louisville, Kentucky, Maj. Gen. William Nelson was assassinated. Nelson, a Kentuckian, was a lieutenant commander in the U.S. Navy and had been "loaned" to the army. Nelson was not well liked, to be sure, but the identity of the murderer surprised everyone. Brig. Gen. Jefferson Columbus Davis of Indiana, "the other Jeff Davis," had engaged Nelson, his former commander, in an argument. After

Nelson slapped Davis in the face and walked off, Davis met the Kentuckian in the lobby and shot him once with a pistol. The ball entered Nelson's chest and he died shortly afterward. Davis was never punished or prosecuted for the crime—he was a friend of Indiana Governor Oliver P. Morton—and indeed he became a corps commander during Sherman's March to the Sea.

AS THE WARM WEATHER that made war possible chilled in the autumn, soldiers and civilians alike tried to make sense out of where the war was going, especially with Lincoln's proclamation of freedom. Mostly, still, civil warriors worried about their own world. "Do not make any calculations after my promotion, nor my election," Lt. Col. Edward S. Bragg of the 6th Wisconsin Infantry wrote his wife after Antietam. "Col. [Lysander] Cutler is living, and still holds his commission. That prevents me being made a Col. no matter which I may do. . . . Attesting to, I think, the sentiment in general that should one be appointed from this Brigade, I am entitled to it, being the highest-ranking officer who was present at all the battles, and in command of the regiment during all of them. . . . 'Uncle Abe' came out here yesterday & we marched out to see him—& he *was not there!* My hand pained me so I had to come back. . . . Stay at home and say but little. I do not want anyone to be able to say that I took an active part & that my wife was disappointed in the calculations! I am only 35!"

Maj. Gen. William T. Sherman, acting as military governor of Memphis, worried constantly on paper about the course of the war and how to achieve success as early as possible. "We cannot change the hearts of those people in the South," he wrote Grant on October 4, "but we can make war so terrible that they will realize the fact that, however brave and gallant and devoted to their country, still they are mortal and should exhaust all peaceful remedies before they fly into war." One of the seeds of the Sherman strategy for success was growing, at least in the Ohioan's mind. "If, as you threaten in your letter, you hang an officer, a prisoner in your hands, in retaliation of some act of ours, conjured up by false statements of interested parties, remember that we have hundreds of thousands of men bitter and yearning for revenge," Sherman bitterly wrote Confederate Maj. Gen. Thomas C. Hindman on October 17. "You initiate the game, and my word for it [is that] your people will regret it long after you pass from earth."

And still Lincoln wondered about his commander, McClellan, who had seemed so bright and had done such good work organizing the Army of the Potomac but also often failed to engage it or employ proper tactical thinking when he did. "Are you not over-cautious when you assume that you can not do what the enemy is constantly doing?" Lincoln wrote his baffling general on October 13. He went to visit McClellan on the battlefield of Antietam in October and took a measure of the man and the militarist, Lincoln himself continuing to learn more about militarism each day. It appeared that in the wake of Antietam, even with the issuance of the Preliminary Emancipation Proclamation, time was running out for Little Mac. "I have just read your despatch about sore tongued and fatiegued [*sic*] horses," Lincoln wrote on October 25. "Will you pardon me for asking what the horses of your army have done since the battle of Antietam that fatigue anything?"

Fredericksburg's Appalling Loss

COLD WEATHER SLOWED military activity in the winter of 1862, the war apparently grinding to a halt. In the wake of Antietam, McClellan's Army of the Potomac continued a slow rebuilding as the commander played with the idea of a movement on Richmond despite the oncoming poor weather. Lee's Army of Northern Virginia was back safely in Virginia, out of harm's way for the moment. Although his Army of Tennessee was intact, Bragg had withdrawn from Kentucky, his strategic aims for the celebrated invasion failed. But he was not far from Rosecrans's newly organized Army of the Cumberland. In the strategically important Mississippi River corridor Grant was commencing his campaign on Vicksburg. Van Dorn's efforts in the Corinth area amounted to nothing but lost Southern soldiers. In Kentucky and Tennessee the major activities were raids, which had proved so successful thus far, by the cavalry leaders Morgan and Forrest. The naval blockade pre scribed by the Federal strategists in Washington was slowly growing tighter, making life on the home front less and less comfortable.

The shock of the Preliminary Emancipation Proclamation was beginning to wear off, although this document was highly controversial even among Northern civilians. Most important for the South, the hopes of recognition by foreign governments, particularly England and France, were dimming. The gamble that England would come to the Confederacy's aid rested with King Cotton. Warehousers and merchants even burned bales of cotton on Southern wharves to increase its scarcity and make it more valuable to English textile mills. But Britain and other industrial countries found other sources for cotton. The Confederacy magnified its own importance vastly and miscalculated its place in the world economy.

November 1862 began quietly on the battlefields of America. A naval action occurred in the Deep South at Bayou Teche, Louisiana, when Federal gunboats moved up the Atchafalaya River. The idea was to support the movement along the railroad line by troops under Brig. Gen. Godfrey Weitzel, an Ohioan assigned command of the Military District of LaFourche, a region in the Department of the Gulf, which was commanded by the much-hated Maj. Gen. Benjamin F. Butler. By midmonth, however, Butler would be removed from this assignment and Maj. Gen. Nathaniel P. Banks named his successor. The small Union flotilla consisted of the side-wheeler gunboats USS *Calhoun*, USS *Diana*, and USS *Kinsman*; the screw gunboat USS *Estrella*, and the transport USS *St. Mary's*, which contained the army troops of the 21st Indiana Infantry. Facing this assemblage were the gunboats CSS *J. A. Cotton* and CSS *A. B. Segar*.

On November 1 the ships encountered each other in Berwick Bay, off Brashear City. On that evening the USS *Estrella* and USS *Kinsman* engaged a steamer that turned out to be the partially ironclad CSS *J. A. Cotton*, which had apparently signaled surrender before opening with casemated guns. The CSS *A. B. Segar* was run aground, abandoned, and captured. The USS *Calhoun* and USS *Diana* arrived up the Atchafalaya, moving into Bayou Teche, and on to Franklin. About three miles from the mouth of Bayou Teche, Confederate artillery opened fire on the Union ships. The troops posted there belonged to Brig. Gen. Jean-Jacques Alfred Alexander Mouton. The river was obstructed by the Confederates above this point, and the CSS *J. A. Cotton* blasted the Union flotilla when it attempted to come within range of this position. A fight occurred on November 3 in which the USS *Kinsman* anchored at near point blank range of the eleven Confederate guns ashore and within range of the CSS *J. A. Cotton*. Inconclusive as this little engagement was, it would precede a more decisive battle that would come after the first of the New Year, nearly in the same place.

Little happened back east during the month's first days. On November 5 a minor echo of the Antietam campaign sounded when a cavalry skirmish erupted at Chester Gap, Virginia, in an action also called Barbee's Crossroads. The Federal cavalry largely had its hands full during the early parts of the war, not being nearly the equal of the Southern horsemen. Southern soldiers really had much more riding experience than their Northern counterparts. This action at Chester Gap provided a glimpse of hope and respect for the Yankees, however. Brig. Gen. Alfred Pleasonton's force of 1,500 cavalry attacked Maj. Gen. Jeb Stuart's 3,000 horsemen and, supported by artillery, scattered Stuart's cavalry after several attacks. The Southerners left 10 dead on the field and 20 prisoners, while Pleasonton lost 5 dead and 8 wounded.

More momentous events occurred in Washington, however. Finally reaching his limit with George McClellan, Lincoln removed him from command again, this time for good. (Lincoln allegedly told friends afterward that he enjoyed McClellan because he had the pleasure of firing him twice.) After months of buildup, frustration, pressure, and poor battlefield performance, McClellan was to be sent to New Jersey to await orders, in effect in purgatory. "By direction of the President it is ordered that Major General McClellan be relieved from command of the Army of the Potomac; and that Major General Burnside take the command of that Army," Lincoln's order read. The day before, Democrats had made strong gains in the national elections, and McClellan was a Democrat—he would eventually resign from the army and oppose Lincoln in the 1864 presidential election. For now, however, he was simply shocked. On November 7, Brig. Gen. Catharinus P. Buckingham, a distinguished Ohio soldier and assistant adjutant general of Secretary Stanton's, who had been dispatched specially from the War Department to carry a copy of the order, arrived at McClellan's tent at Rectortown, Virginia. At 11:30 P.M. McClellan received the copy, read it, and told his close friend, "Well, Burnside, I turn the command over to you." The soldiers were equally shocked, as the majority of them adored their commander.

Rough roads lay ahead for the Army of the Potomac. Despite Lincoln's apparent confidence in him, Ambrose Everett Burnside was hardly a sterling soldier, and he would shortly demonstrate his inabilities at the first opportunity. "Poor Burn feels dreadfully almost crazy," McClellan wrote his wife. A native of Liberty, Indiana, graduate of West Point, railroad officer, engineer, inventor of the Burnside breech-loading carbine, major general in the Rhode Island militia, and genuine hero of the Burnside expedition of the war's first autumn, Burnside nevertheless lacked confidence in his ability to handle the job of leading the Union's premier eastern army. He even told people so. Nonetheless, he assumed command of the army at Warrenton, Virginia. Joseph Hooker, who had been wounded opening the battle of Antietam, took charge of the 5th Corps in place of the discredited Fitz John Porter.

Mid and late November witnessed mostly a succession of small engagements. Yankees took over the rail center of Holly Springs, Mississippi, after a skirmish on November 13. Minor actions took place near Nashville, along a portion of the Georgia coast, outward from New Bern, North Carolina, to Little Creek and Rawles's Mill. Among the Federal soldiers participating in the Georgia expedition was Col. Thomas Wentworth Higginson's 1st South Carolina Infantry (African Descent), still in the process of forming and only semiofficial, which became the first black regiment in the Union army. To Southern soldiers and civilians alike who might see such a regiment of black troops in Federal blue, the sight would be as stunning as a spacecraft from another galaxy might be today. Of Brig. Gen. Rufus Saxton's request that abolitionist and historian Higginson take command as colonel of the regiment, Higginson wrote: "Had an invitation reached me to take command of a regiment of Kalmuck Tartars, it could hardly have been more unexpected. I had always looked for the arming of the blacks, and had always felt a wish to be associated with them. . . . But the prevalent tone of public sentiment was still opposed to any such attempts; the government kept very shy of the experiment, and it did not seem possible that the time had come when it could fairly be tried."

More small actions erupted at Piketon, Kentucky; Lamar, Missouri; and Charles Town, Virginia. Of great consequence for the Confederate cause was the commissioning of Stonewall Jackson and James Longstreet as lieutenant generals in the Confederate army and their assignments in the Army of Northern Virginia as corps commanders, Longstreet being the senior. Questioning the direction of an expected Union approach, Robert E. Lee communicated with Jackson on November 12. "It would be grievous for the Valley & its supplies to fall into the hands of the enemy unnecessarily," he warned, "but we can only act upon probabilities and endeavor to avoid greater evils." Jackson had to worry over not just the enemy but his own subordinates, as with A. P. Hill, whom Jackson had arrested in the wake of the Shepherdstown fight "for neglect of duty," according to Jackson. "I suppose I am to vegetate here all the winter under that crazy old Presbyterian fool," Hill wrote Jeb Stuart of Jackson. "I am like the porcupine—all bristles, and all sticking out too, so I know we shall have a smash up before long."

Most of the rest of the November actions were small. Federals undertook a reconnaissance from Edgefield Junction, Tennessee, toward Clarksville. Skirmishes near Suffolk, Virginia, included minor actions at Providence Church and Blackwater Bridge. A Union reconnaissance set out from Helena, Arkansas, toward Arkansas Post, also known as Fort Hindman. Grant tested the defenses of Vicksburg with an expedition from Grand Junction, Tennessee, to Ripley, Mississippi. Two more small expeditions near the end of November were those of the Federal forces moving from Sharpsburg, Maryland, to Shepherdstown, and from Summerville, Virginia, to Cold Knob Mountain. The surprise of the month for the South came with the sudden resignation of George Wythe Randolph, the Secretary of War, who had exercised a troublesome command of his department with frequent micromanagement by Davis, who was quick to intercede in small affairs. The well-liked Richmond attorney and former U.S. Congressmen James A. Seddon replaced Randolph on November 21. Capt. Robert G. H. Kean, chief of the Bureau of War, sided with a friend who "used to think Davis a *mule,* but a *good mule,*" but had by now come to think of the Confederate President as a "jackass." Kean, whose sharp eye and wit were quick to judge nearly anyone, felt that Seddon "staggers under his load. He is physically weak, seems to be a man of clear head, strong sense, and firm character but from long desuetude, wanting in readiness and dispatching business."

The last real engagement of the month occurred on November 28 at Cane Hill, Arkansas. With about 5,000 men fresh from a minor victory over the Rebels in a skirmish at Old Fort Wayne, Indian Territory, in October, Brig. Gen. James G. Blunt looked toward attacking Confederates in the area of the Boston Mountains. Blunt's command consisted of the 1st Division of the Army of the Frontier. In bivouac at Lindsey's Prairie, Blunt learned that a Confederate cavalry force of 8,000 under Brig. Gen. John S. Marmaduke was nearby. Blunt went on the attack before Marmaduke's force could reunite with Maj. Gen. Thomas C. Hindman's Trans-Mississippi Army for a possible raid into Missouri. Blunt marched his column thirty-five miles, attacked at Cane Hill at 10 A.M., and surprised and scattered the Confederates, who after three hours of fighting retreated into the Boston Mountains. Blunt's army followed briefly but broke off and retreated after a short time because of the dangers of fighting in a forested mountain setting. On the Confederate side, Col. Joseph O. Shelby organized a brief counterattack. The Union losses were 40 and the Confederates 435. The action was potentially important because the region of Cane Hill afforded some of the best food supplies in the area, and the army that held it had a supply advantage.

As the final month of 1862 opened, Confederate military fortunes still seemed buoyant, but the Southern armies were on the defensive. In Virginia, Maj. Gen. Ambrose Burnside's Army of the Potomac was readying itself for a movement against Gen. Robert E. Lee's Army of Northern Virginia, at Fredericksburg. In Arkansas, along the coasts of Georgia, the Carolinas, and Texas, Union naval forces were continuing the blockade and threatening further gains. At New Orleans, Federal troops still held the largest city in the Confederacy. So despised was Butler's regime in the city that when he departed this month, Jefferson Davis put a price out for his head. "Now, therefore, I, Jefferson Davis, President of the Confederate States of America, and in their name, do pronounce and declare the said Benjamin F. Butler to be a felon, deserving of capital punishment," Davis penned. "I do order that he shall no longer be considered or treated simply as a public enemy of the Confederate States of America, but as an outlaw and common enemy of mankind, and that, in the event of his capture, the officer in command of the capturing force do cause him to be immediately executed by hanging."

Davis failed to stop with Butler, however. The same proclamation raged over confiscation of property in occupied territories of the South, and of inciting a slave insurrection generally over the South. Davis continued to proclaim that black soldiers captured in arms against the Confederacy would be returned to the respective states from which they came for reenslavement, and that Federal officers serving in a military capacity with black troops would be executed. This destructive seed, planted as a response to emancipation, would engender a breakdown of the program of prisoner exchange between the two governments. If black soldiers and the white officers serving with them would not be treated as equals to be exchanged, reasoned Lincoln and Grant, then the basis for prisoner exchange was disallowed.

Butler had no intention of being captured and executed. "I saw that this Rebellion was a war of the aristocrats against the middling men, of the rich against the poor," he told the people of New Orleans in a farewell address. "I therefore felt no hesitation in taking the substance of the wealthy, who had caused the war, to feed the innocent poor, who had suffered by the war."

IN MIDDLE TENNESSEE Gen. Braxton Bragg's Army of Tennessee at Murfreesboro readied itself for a confrontation with the Army of the Cumberland, led by Maj. Gen. William S. Rosecrans, at Nashville. Haunted by the legacy of McClellan's inactivity and ever anxious for action, Lincoln worried about Rosecrans's preparation to attack Bragg. "The President is greatly dissatisfied with your delay, and sent for me several times to account for it," Halleck wrote Rosecrans on December 5. "He has repeated to me time and again that there were imperative reasons why the enemy should be driven across the Tennessee River at the earliest possible moment."

Along the Mississippi River, Maj. Gen. Ulysses S. Grant was organizing a drive toward Vicksburg. At Coffeeville, Mississippi, on December 5, cavalry forces of Grant's Army of the Tennessee operated along the Mississippi Central Railroad and precipitated a skirmish with infantry under Brig. Gen. Lloyd Tilghman. The horsemen, led by Col. T. Lyle Dickey, attacked the Confederates in town and an artillery duel ensued before musketry crackled along improvised battle lines. The Confederate infantry pushed the cavalrymen three miles outside of town before darkness ended the engagement. The Federals lost 34 killed and about 200 wounded; the Confederate losses were 7 killed and 43 wounded.

Army troops weren't the only participants in the campaign for Vicksburg, however. Many ships were engaged in the movement on Vicksburg, and among them was the USS *Cairo,* one of naval inventor James Eads's city-class ironclad gunboats. On patrol duty in the Yazoo River, the ship was commanded by Lt. Comdr. Thomas O. Selfridge, Jr., a Massachusetts native and son of Comm. Thomas O. Selfridge, Sr., who headed the navy at San Francisco. Dispatched on December 12 to find torpedoes (naval mines) up the Yazoo River north of Vicksburg, the USS *Cairo* proceeded along after its 8 A.M. departure without great caution, as few of these torpedoes, although placed plentifully in the rivers, had actually damaged gunboats. The torpedo technology in the Yazoo resulted from the experiments of Confederate Lt. Beverly Kennon, who devised a torpedo that was experimentally used on Lake Ponchartrain in the war's first year. In the summer of 1862, Kennon described the design to Acting Masters Zedekiah McDaniel and Francis M. Ewing, and they obtained five-gallon glass demijohns from Vicksburg, filled them with black powder, attached copper wires, buoyed the contraption with a wooden log float, and anchored it to the bottom so that it would float in proximity to the bottoms of riverboats. The copper wires led to a "torpedo pit" behind the nearby levees, and volunteers would man them, waiting for prey to approach, and exploding the torpedoes with a galvanic battery.

The ships comprising the expedition were the tin-clad stern-wheelers USS *Marmora* and USS *Signal*, the Ellet ram USS *Queen of the West*, and the ironclad gunboats *Cairo* and *Pittsburg*. The light gunboats moved out in front of the two ironclads, ready to return fire from any shore batteries that might initiate artillery fire. The small flotilla arrived near the position where they were to search for torpedoes when Selfridge heard heavy musketry firing ahead, as *Marmora* disappeared around a bend in the river. Rather than Confederate infantry, however, the firing came from the *Marmora's* own guns firing at a floating block of wood. Selfridge approached, lowered a boat, and found the wood was a portion of a previously exploded torpedo.

The *Marmora* was ordered ahead and Selfridge backed the *Cairo* before turning it to proceed ahead. Two thunderous explosions suddenly ripped into the *Cairo*, one under the port quarter and the other under the port bow. The explosion under the bow was severe enough to "raise the guns under it some distance from the deck," Selfridge wrote. The ship began sinking so rapidly that after three minutes the water covered her foredeck; Selfridge maneuvered the *Cairo* toward shore, but it was useless. In a scramble the crew of 251 officers and men hurried to help the sick and some of the arms onto the *Queen of the West*, which came up alongside the sinking vessel. It was a spectacle to see one of the technological naval wonders of the age slip into six fathoms of water. The 512-ton ship measured 175 feet by 51 feet 2 inches by 6 feet and was armed with three 8-inch smoothbore guns, three 42-pounder rifles, six 32-pounder rifles, one 30-pounder rifle, and one 12-pounder smoothbore. The massive iron hull slipped into the river in only twelve minutes. The sailors who couldn't make it onto the *Queen of the West* climbed into the *Cairo's* lifeboats and made it ashore. No one lost his life. The odd sight that remained was the tops of the *Cairo's* smokestacks and jack staffs, one of which still displayed Old Glory flapping in the breeze. Though no Federal commanders were happy with the loss of the *Cairo*, particularly Capt. Henry Walke, the senior officer in the area, her loss was a blessing for later naval historians. Because the ship went down so quickly, it became a virtual time capsule of river naval fighting in the Civil War, with a complete set of goods on board, many of which were preserved relatively well in the cold mud of the Yazoo. Between 1960 and 1965 historians worked with the National Park Service to raise the *Cairo* and catalog her contents, eventually building a museum to house them at Vicksburg National Military Park. Despite a tragic breakup of the ship as it was being raised, the partially reconstructed ship, along with hundreds of artifacts, portrays naval life during the Civil War like no other exhibit.

Other actions occurred during these early phases of the Federal movements on Vicksburg. Gen. Braxton Bragg ordered Brig. Gen. Nathan Bedford Forrest to embark on his second great raid, this time with 2,500 troopers, to strike Grant's supply base at Columbus, Kentucky. On December 11, Forrest left Columbia, Tennessee, moved westward rapidly, crossing the Tennessee River at Clifton between December 13 and 15, and clashed with Yankee cavalry at Lexington, Tennessee, on the 18th. The action at Lexington was brisk and resulted in a victory for Forrest. Col. Ralph G. Ingersoll had 200 horse soldiers and a battery of artillery before being reinforced by 200 soldiers of the 5th Ohio Cavalry and 272 men of the 2d West Tennessee Cavalry (Col. Isaac R. Hawkins) prior to the battle. Ingersoll's troopers discovered approaching Confederate cavalry near Beech Creek and withdrew toward Lexington, the Union horsemen demolishing bridges in their wake. On the morning of the 18th, Forrest approached along the Stage Road from Beech Creek and was met by a battalion of cavalry of the 5th Ohio under Maj. Otto Funke, which offered a sharp musketry fight. But the Yankees had failed to destroy a bridge on the Lower Road and the defensive force there under Hawkins was hit hard; they repulsed two attacks before being overrun by Forrest's experienced soldiers. Meanwhile, the 11th Illinois Cavalry charged and gained a measure of success before also being turned back. The Yankees fled toward Lexington, and Forrest's men captured 124 prisoners, including Ingersoll.

The following day, Forrest struck again at Jackson, in a battle that also came to be known as Salem Church or Salem Cemetery. Alarmed by the results of the skirmish at Lexington, Brig. Gen. Jeremiah C. Sullivan, commanding the District of Jackson, rushed reinforcements toward the town, held by the remaining elements of the three cavalry regiments that had fought the previous day, along with the 43d Illinois Infantry (Col. Adolph Englemann) and the 61st Illinois Infantry. On the morning of December 19, Englemann's infantry briefly skirmished with Forrest's advanced elements before moving back to Jackson. At Salem Cemetery, on the edge of town, Englemann's men concealed themselves near a woods and fired hotly into the Confederates, after a time driving them from the field. Forrest's losses amounted to 73 killed and wounded and the Federals lost one killed and five wounded. Of the climactic moment of the fight in the cemetery, Englemann wrote, "As they approached they were received by a well-directed fire, some of the foremost horses falling and obstructing the road, those immediately behind came to a halt, while half a dozen riderless horses rushed madly through our lines."

Following this setback, Forrest turned north, destroying sections of the railroad between Jackson and Humboldt, and approached Trenton on December 20. Trenton was a Union post weakly held by a detachment of the 7th Tennessee Cavalry, the 126th Illinois Infantry, and a number of convalescents. The majority of regular troops from the town's garrison had been sent to Jackson and were not yet back in the town when Forrest attacked. Thus, a meek defense of 130 wounded men made a short stand at the city's railroad depot, barricaded behind bales of cotton, before surrendering the town to the cavalry raider. On December 21, Forrest gathered what supplies he could make use of and set out again on a ride northward, moving into and capturing Union City, and after plundering and capturing supplies, retired back to Dresden. Approaching Lexington again, this time from the north, Forrest found his way blocked at Parker's Crossroads, where Union Col. Cyrus L. Dunham's brigade established a roadblock. Heavy skirmishing erupted on December 31, during which Forrest successfully extricated himself from the surprise melee, when he was struck in force from the rear by the brigade of Col. John W. Fuller. "The ground was soft and miry," wrote Col. John W. Sprague of the 63d Ohio Infantry, "but notwithstanding this and the long and rapid march made by my command the men responded with cheers, and at a double-quick rushed forward to engage the enemy, who seemed to be panic stricken. They fled in the utmost confusion and so rapidly that we could not get but a few telling shots at them." Due to this secondary phase of the action, Forrest's troopers were smashed; his command scattered in retreat, losing 300 prisoners, 350 horses, 6 field guns, and most of the matériel captured during the raid. Forrest escaped across the Tennessee River once again at Clifton after a brief skirmish on January 3, 1863.

While Forrest was raiding to the north, Maj. Gen. Earl Van Dorn left Grenada, Mississippi, planning to attack Grant's secondary supply base at Holly Springs and to disrupt Grant's operations along the Mississippi Central Railroad. Van Dorn's force of 3,500 swiftly approached the town, which was commanded by Col. Robert C. Murphy (8th Wisconsin Infantry). Although Grant and even Murphy had been alerted to Van Dorn's movements, Murphy failed to inform his subordinate officers of the threat. As a result, on December 20, most of the garrison in Holly Springs was completely surprised and captured, many of the 1,500 soldiers awakened in their bedclothes. Van Dorn captured and paroled the whole garrison, took $1.5 million in war matériel, and disrupted Grant's plans. "General Van Dorn burned up all the stores, depot buildings, armory, and ordnance buildings," claimed Murphy. "There are no supplies here for the paroled prisoners and the sick, and what shall be done for them? My fate is most mortifying." Grant was forced to withdraw to La Grange and Grand Junction, Tennessee, from Oxford, Mississippi. He also was cautioned against pushing an offensive toward Vicksburg too early by Halleck and was unable to support successfully Sherman's movement from Memphis, down the Mississippi toward Chickasaw Bayou, north of Vicksburg. In the wake of the Holly Springs fiasco, Murphy was dismissed from the army. But for the Yankees, the damage was done: Van Dorn's raid unhinged the timing of the planned coordination between Grant and Sherman and therefore cast a shadow over their strategic plans.

Sherman's expedition to Chickasaw Bayou represented one of the early attempts to move on Vicksburg. Sherman wanted no time lost in winning the war. "Thousands will perish by the bullet or sickness; but war must go on," he wrote his brother, Senator John Sherman, on November 24. "It can't be stopped. The North must rule or submit to degradation and insult forevermore." While Grant moved overland toward the Confederate stronghold, Sherman's force of 32,000 moved downriver along the Yazoo by transport, planning to disembark above Vicksburg and attack the city from the north. Sherman commanded what was, during this operation, termed the "Right Wing," 13th Corps, which was redesignated as the 15th Corps, Army of the Tennessee, on December 22, 1862. His division commanders were Brig. Gens. Andrew J. Smith, Morgan L. Smith, George W. Morgan, and Frederick Steele. On the Confederate side, Lt. Gen. John C. Pemberton commanded the Department of Mississippi and East Louisiana. Maj. Gen. Martin L. Smith oversaw the defenses of Vicksburg; his brigade commanders were Brig. Gens. Seth M. Barton, John C. Vaughn, John Gregg, and Edward D. Tracy. Additionally, a provisional division was commanded by Brig. Gen. Stephen D. Lee, with brigades commanded by Cols. William T. Withers and Allen Thomas. The total Confederate force in opposition to Sherman's movement was approximately 25,000.

Sherman landed his first troops on the Yazoo, opposite Steele's Bayou at Johnston's Plantation, on December 26. Van Dorn's raid on Holly Springs allowed Pemberton to shift 6,000 men from Grenada to help block Sherman's approach. The battle that followed was known as Chickasaw Bayou, Chickasaw Bluffs, or Walnut Hills. Sherman nearly immediately deployed the brigades of Col. John F. De Courcy and Brig. Gens. David Stuart and Francis P. Blair, Jr., to reconnoiter the enemy, and they moved slowly through the swampy mire that lay ahead. Sherman spread A. J. Smith's division to the right, to move directly south, M. L. Smith to his left, Blair to his left, and Morgan on the right, along the western shore of the bayou. For two days this plan unfolded slowly, hampered by the almost impassable terrain, with skirmishing between the advance elements of Sherman's men and the Confederate pickets. By the early morning of December 28 the Federal soldiers had advanced to the obstacles of McNutt Lake and Chickasaw Bayou. Confederates posted high on the bluffs had a perfect position from which to rain down small-arms fire onto the Yankees, making further movement difficult. The battle was fought on a triangular wedge of land, the apex consisting of the junction of the bayou's two branches and the base consisting of the high bluffs with the Confederate infantry line.

The talented Confederate artillerist Stephen D. Lee coordinated the defensive position until Maj. Gen. Carter L. Stevenson arrived late on December 29 and took command. Sherman reconnoitered this strong position and soon found two sandbars, four miles outside Vicksburg, which were protected by abatis but offered an avenue of attack. He ordered an assault for noon on December 29. At the time the battle commenced, with a cannonade at 10 A.M. and the Federal infantry moving an hour later, Pemberton had essentially thrown everything he had outside the city against Sherman; Vicksburg itself was occupied by a single regiment, the 27th Louisiana Infantry, commanded by Col. Leon D. Marks. De Courcy's brigade attacked first, under musketry fire from above, and fought its way to the foot of Chickasaw Bluff. "Notwithstanding the destructive fire from all sides . . . ," De Courcy wrote, "the brave men nearly composing these corps had nearly crossed the large open space of more than half a mile which lay stretched out before them glacis fashion, when the enemy increased his fire of small arms and grape to such a degree as to render a farther advance impossible." Blair's brigade also advanced to the base of the bluff, to the east, where the lake and bayou joined, and the brigade of Brig. Gen. John M. Thayer was ordered forward but lost its way and only one regiment, the 4th Iowa Infantry was engaged. In the center, along M. L. Smith's line, the 6th Missouri Infantry fought vigorously before stalling out by nightfall. By evening on the 29th, Sherman's attack had essentially failed, halted by the impenetrable defenses of the high bluff before it, and inadequately supported along the line. The highly effective Confederate artillery fire from above doomed any notion of returning fire from artillery located below. "The enemy left in great confusion," Lee wrote, "leaving their dead and wounded on the field. . . . Immediately after the battle the fire of their sharpshooters was redoubled. They would not allow my command to care for their wounded."

There had been 30,720 Federals and 13,792 Confederates engaged. The Federal losses were 208 killed, 1,005 wounded, and 563 missing. Confederate losses were 63 killed, 134 wounded, and 10 missing. The beaten Union troops huddled in a driving, cold rain, opposite their old positions, while Sherman and Comdr. David Dixon Porter devised a plan to renew the campaign. "Complete military success can only be accomplished by an united action on some general plan embracing usually a large district of country," Sherman had written his division commanders five days before the battle. But that proposition was becoming difficult for Sherman at Chickasaw Bayou. He conceived a plan to move up the Yazoo River to attack the Confederate right at Drumgould's Bluff, just a mile south of Haines's Bluff, with a force of about 10,000 men, consisting mostly of Steele's division. On the night of December 31, however, Sherman found his operation terminated by dense fog that enveloped the area. His troops continued to suffer in chilled, rainy conditions. The following night the sky cleared and a bright moon eliminated any hope of surprise on the part of the Federals. Sherman abandoned his campaign, moving down to the mouth of the Yazoo River by January 2, 1863, and prepared to take command of the 2d Corps, Army of the Mississippi, as Maj. Gen. John A. McClernand arrived and assumed command of the new Army of the Mississippi. Union forces in the area concentrated on a planned attack against Fort Hindman on the Arkansas River.

In Arkansas a battle for control of the state shaped up on December 7 at Prairie Grove, west of Fayetteville. Union Brig. Gen. James G. Blunt's Army of the Frontier, with 7,000 men, consisted of three divisions: Blunt's own (brigades of Brig. Gen. Frederick Salomon and Cols. William Weer and William F. Cloud together with the cavalry brigade of Col. Dudley Wickersham). These were encamped south of Fayetteville. The other two divisions were located near Springfield, Missouri, under Brig. Gen. Francis J. Herron, and consisted of the division of Col. David Huston, Jr. (brigades of Cols. John G. Clark and William M. Dye) and Herron's own division (brigades of Col. William W. Orme and Lt. Col. Henry Bertram).

At Van Buren, Maj. Gen. Thomas C. Hindman positioned his detachment of the Trans-Mississippi Army of 11,000 men, preparing to drive the Yankees from Arkansas. The detachment consisted of the division of Brig. Gen. Francis A. Shoup (brigades of Brig. Gen. James F. Fagan and Col. Dandridge McRae); Brig. Gen. Daniel M. Frost (brigades of Brig. Gen. Mosby M. Parsons, Col. Robert G. Shaver, and Brig. Gen. John S. Roane); and Brig. Gen. John S. Marmaduke (cavalry brigades of Cols. James C. Monroe, Joseph O. "Jo" Shelby, and Emmett MacDonald).

On the evening of December 6, Hindman approached the Federal army, skirmishing with the Yankee pickets at Reed's Mountain. He then discovered that Herron's Federal divisions were moving toward Fayetteville. This dramatically altered Hindman's plan of battle. He suddenly ordered Monroe's cavalry brigade to screen against Blunt and took the bulk of his force to defeat the Union forces in detail. Led by a cavalry force under Marmaduke, the Confederate column marched rapidly to turn the Union forces, interposing itself between Blunt and Herron before the Yankees could unite into a single army. The idea was to strike the approaching Herron first, then turn on Blunt. Herron arrived at Fayetteville near midnight of December 7, after a forced, twenty-five-mile march. The weather conditions hardly helped: Harsh, freezing temperatures characterized northwestern Arkansas for a stretch until December 2, a storm passed through the following day, dumping icy rain and snow, and on December 4 the hard freeze returned, chilling everyone to their bones. One soldier recalled that "the men were so sore that they limped and stumbled along in the dark, until the continued exercise produced a better circulation in their almost worn out legs which, while it enabled them to walk with a freer step, increased the pain in their bleeding feet."

The turning movement began before dawn on December 7 as Marmaduke's cavalry set out with Shelby's brigade in the lead. Among the horse soldiers approaching the Federal horsemen were Col. William C. Quantrill's notorious bushwhackers (confusingly clad in blue uniforms), who would be celebrated in the coming year for their guerrilla tactics and destruction in Kansas. Federal cavalry encamped around Prairie Grove Church were surprised and scattered by this attack after a short fight, Maj. Eliphalet Bredett's 7th Missouri Cavalry (U.S.) receiving the brunt of Shelby's attack. After a half hour's engagement this unit and other Federal horsemen—the 1st Arkansas Cavalry (U.S.), 6th Missouri Cavalry, and 8th Missouri Cavalry—were all routed. Confederates captured a large store of supplies as well as 200 prisoners, who were directed back to the graveyard at Prairie Grove Church. The Confederates now found themselves with a grand opportunity. Eight miles away, at Cane Hill, Blunt could hear the skirmishing but decided to stay put and await further developments. Herron's men were so exhausted from their march that they were vulnerable. Instead of attacking the separated forces as he had planned, Hindman discussed the situation with Parsons and Shoup. After the consultation, he surrendered the initiative and established a defensive line. He anticipated Blunt to attack from Cane Hill. Thus, from 8 A.M. to about 11 A.M., Confederate infantry occupied and strengthened positions along Prairie Grove Ridge.

Herron set the next phases of the battle in motion. Having recovered only slightly from its hard, cold march, Herron's division readied for further movement from its position at Walnut Grove Church. Around 10 A.M. Herron ordered artillery fire to probe the Confederate positions and shortly afterward let loose an outright assault by the 94th Illinois Infantry and other units of Orme's brigade. The attack crossed the Illinois River, passed the Thompson House, and moved southwestward toward the Confederate lines along the ridge. After some intense fighting Orme's attack was repulsed. By noon a furious artillery duel began with dozens of rounds being fired between the batteries for more than an hour. At one point one of the shells crashed so close to Orme that the Union colonel was knocked off his horse, but he remounted it, unhurt. While this was taking place, Blunt's men were finally ordered to move toward the battle. All was "inextricable confusion,"

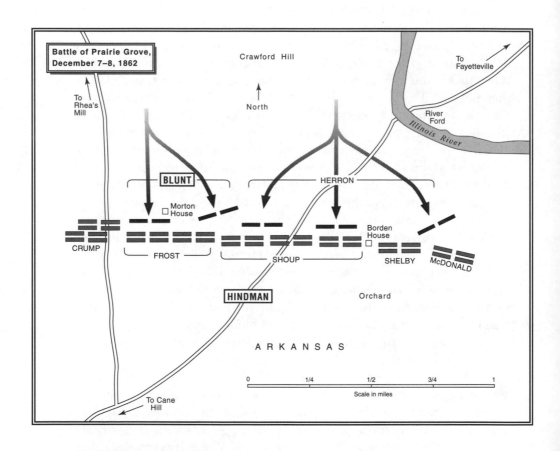

Battle of Prairie Grove, December 7–8, 1862

Crawford Hill

To Fayetteville

To Rhea's Mill

↑
North

River Ford

Illinois River

BLUNT

HERRON

☐ Morton House

☐ Borden House

CRUMP

FROST

SHOUP

SHELBY

McDONALD

HINDMAN

Orchard

A R K A N S A S

To Cane Hill

Scale in miles

0   1/4   1/2   3/4   1

according to one Federal soldier. "Infantry filled the road in spite of all command to the contrary, cavalry rushed in, knocking them right and left in frightful manner, and the artillery in turn rode both and beat its way through."

The artillery barrage wound down by about 2 P.M., the Federal gunners firing most of the rounds. For Herron, the technique apparently worked in keeping the battle at long range until Blunt arrived. On the Confederate side, Hindman simply continued waiting. Shifting troops on the Union left produced a response by Marmaduke, however, which in turn induced Herron to advance so his gunners would have a more advantageous position. This set of maneuvers led to what became an all-out infantry assault, the lead units being the 94th Illinois Infantry, 20th Wisconsin Infantry, and 19th Iowa Infantry. The attack succeeded marvelously, capturing a battery of Confederate guns, until running headlong into Fagan's Arkansas infantry. The attack pushed into the Borden House and grounds. Dismounted, Shelby's men helped with a blazing fire into the oncoming Yankees. The stinging Southern counterattack pushed the Yankees back. By midafternoon a fresh attack led by the 26th Indiana Infantry and the 37th Illinois Infantry led a new set of troops toward the ridge.

Blunt deployed his troops and between 3 and 4 P.M. made a major southward attack all along the Confederate line. The attack was successful for a time, but by 4 P.M. Parsons's Confederates counterattacked, with heavy small-arms and artillery fire erupting all along the fronts. By nightfall both sides considered their options, neither side having gained any sort of advantage that could be considered a victory. In the wake of the battle, wounded men who had died of exposure were found on various parts of the field, and others were found burned to death huddling near burning haystacks, attempting to stay warm. The Federal losses were 175 killed, 813 wounded, and 263 missing; Confederate casualties were 164 killed, 817 wounded, and 336 missing. About 9,546 Yankees and 12,051 Confederates fought in the battle. Confederate forces held their ground along the ridge during the first hours of the night and then withdrew, undetected by Blunt, allowing the Union forces to continue their control of northwestern Arkansas.

IN THE EAST, the war focused on the small town of Fredericksburg, Virginia, population 5,022, where George Washington had played as a boy. Fredericksburg stood on the western bank of the Rappahannock River, between Washington and Richmond, on the line of the Richmond, Fredericksburg & Potomac Railroad. The town became the focus because of the combined movements following Antietam. Robert E. Lee had moved his Army of Northern Virginia to the nearest area of security and subsistence, along Opequon Creek, southwest of Sharpsburg and in the northern corridor of the Shenandoah Valley. Lee regrouped, rested, and strengthened his army, building it and restoring stragglers to their original units, so that by November the army had nearly 85,000 men. Burnside, the new commander of the Army of the Potomac, fumbled for a time before devising a plan for operations of his army of 120,000. Burnside was a dedicated soldier who had shown competence in directing the North Carolina campaign early in the year. How could he possibly perform any *worse* than McDowell, McClellan, or Pope?

On November 9, Burnside communicated his plan to Halleck to oppose Lee. Burnside's scheme relied on quick movement and deceit. He would concentrate the Federal army in a showy fashion near the railroad town of Warrenton, feigning a movement on Culpeper Court House, Orange Court House, or Gordonsville—a southward movement along the railroad—and outfit his army with several days' rations. Then, abruptly, he would shift the army southeast to Fredericksburg, leaving Lee perplexed, and make a rapid movement on Richmond south along the railroad from that historic town. By mid-November, Jackson's corps was in the Valley near Millwood, south of Winchester; Longstreet was at Culpeper Court House. Burnside settled on his plan feeling that he would be exposed to attack from Jackson if he were to move directly south from Warrenton, and that as a supply route the Orange & Alexandria Railroad from Warrenton to Gordonsville would be inadequate. Burnside reasoned that moving to Fredericksburg and south from there would be far easier to support, as supply and communication lines could reach from Washington south to Aquia Creek and southward along the more stable railroad line at Fredericksburg. This movement might bottle up Lee against Richmond, repeating the conditions that had developed during the Peninsular campaign, this time with better results anticipated.

Burnside began assembling a supply base at Falmouth, a small town opposite Fredericksburg on the eastern bank of the Rappahannock, along Aquia Creek, and at nearby Belle Plain Landing. After considerable debate Lincoln approved Burnside's plan but cautioned his new commander to move with great speed in order to boost the chances for success.

During the Fredericksburg campaign, Burnside divided his Army of the Potomac into three so-called grand divisions. The Right Grand Division was commanded by Maj. Gen. Edwin V. Sumner. It consisted of the corps of Maj. Gen. Darius N. Couch (2d Corps; divisions of Brig. Gens. Winfield Scott Hancock, Oliver O. Howard, and William H. French) and Brig. Gen. Orlando B. Willcox (9th Corps; divisions of Brig. Gens. William W. Burns, Samuel D. Sturgis, and George W. Getty). A cavalry division was commanded by Brig. Gen. Alfred Pleasonton. The Center Grand Division was commanded by Maj. Gen. Joseph Hooker. It consisted of the corps of Brig.

Gen. George Stoneman (3d Corps; divisions of Brig. Gens. David B. Birney, Daniel E. Sickles, and Amiel W. Whipple) and Brig. Gen. Daniel Butterfield (5th Corps; divisions of Brig. Gens. Charles Griffin, George Sykes, and Andrew A. Humphreys. A cavalry brigade was commanded by Brig. Gen. William W. Averell. The Left Grand Division was commanded by Maj. Gen. William B. Franklin. It consisted of the corps of Maj. Gen. John F. Reynolds (1st Corps; divisions of Brig. Gens. Abner Doubleday and John Gibbon, and Maj. Gen. George G. Meade) and Maj. Gen. William F. Smith (6th Corps; divisions of Brig. Gens. William T. H. Brooks, Albion P. Howe, and John Newton). A cavalry brigade was commanded by Brig. Gen. George D. Bayard. Maj. Gen. Franz Sigel's 11th Corps was held in reserve in the area of Fairfax Court House.

Robert E. Lee's Army of Northern Virginia was organized into army corps commanded by Lt. Gen. James Longstreet (1st Corps; divisions of Maj. Gens. Lafayette McLaws, Richard H. Anderson, George E. Pickett, and John Bell Hood, and Brig. Gen. Robert Ransom, Jr.) and Lt. Gen. Thomas J. "Stonewall" Jackson (2d Corps; divisions of Maj. Gens. D. H. Hill and A. P. Hill, and Brig. Gens. Jubal A. Early and William B. Taliaferro); reserve artillery was commanded by Brig. Gen. William N. Pendleton, and cavalry was commanded by Maj. Gen. James E. B. Stuart.

Burnside set his army into motion on November 15; two days later the first elements arrived in Falmouth. The risky aspect of Burnside's plan was that it required suitable pontoon bridges to be sent to the front and assembled to enable the Federal army to cross the Rappahannock. Scheduled to arrive before the troops did, the pontoon bridges were late. Matters became even more frustrating because the weather turned bad with icy rains soaking everyone. Sumner arrived and desperately wanted to cross immediately and scatter the relatively small force of Confederates (about 500) in the town, commandeering the tactically important ridges that stood west of the city. The rains swelled the river, decreasing the amount of time Sumner had to decide whether or not to ford it. For his first large command decision in the field, Burnside began to panic. He worried that if Sumner crossed and then the rains made the fords unusable for the remaining elements of the army, Sumner might be caught exposed without aid and destroyed by the Confederates. So in the mold of McClellan, he took the cautious route and held Sumner in Falmouth to await the rest of the army.

Like McClellan, Burnside had already squandered the initiative. By November 21, Longstreet's corps had arrived near Fredericksburg, with McLaws in the lead. Jackson's corps was in rapid motion toward the city as well. Lee at first anticipated an armed conflict with Burnside northwest of the city; when it first seemed that Burnside was moving toward Fredericksburg, he still felt it probably necessary to drop back behind the North Anna

River. But when Burnside's movement unfolded with such slowness, exactly what Lincoln had warned Burnside against, Lee moved his forces directly toward Fredericksburg. By November 25 the first pontoon bridges arrived at Falmouth, much too late to enable the Federal army to cross the river without opposition. With the opportunity for quick, unopposed action eliminated, Burnside still had an opportunity. He now faced only half of Lee's army, and if he acted during the last days of November, he could engage Longstreet before Jackson arrived.

But he didn't. The needed pontoon bridges did not arrive until month's end, and by that time Jackson was present. During the final days of November, Burnside's plan became clear in Lee's mind, and the Southern commander maneuvered his troops into position to exploit it. Originally, Burnside planned to cross his army east of Fredericksburg at Skinker's Neck, ten miles downstream, but Early's Confederates arrived there. So he changed his mind and would cross the army at Fredericksburg itself. By Thanksgiving Day, Early's division occupied Skinker's Neck and D. H. Hill's division held Port Royal, twenty miles downstream from Fredericksburg. Showing an inept grasp of his command duties, Burnside failed to move the pontoon bridges effectively, reconnoitered the Confederate position only weakly by using a balloon for observation (which failed to reveal much where the terrain was heavily wooded), and misunderstood his enemy thoroughly. On December 9 he wrote Brig. Gen. George W. Cullum in Washington, Halleck's chief of staff, that "I think now the enemy will be more surprised by a crossing immediately in our front than in any other part of the river. . . . I am convinced that a large force of the enemy is now concentrated at Port Royal, its left resting on Fredericksburg, which we hope to turn."

Burnside could not have been more wrong. On December 10 his engineers began laying six pontoon bridges, two in close proximity north of the town's center, a third on the southern end of the town, just south of the Richmond, Fredericksburg & Potomac Railroad bridge, and three in close proximity to the south, just south of the intersection of the Rappahannock with Deep Run. Burnside had 220 cannon posted on Stafford Heights opposite the town to assist in silencing Confederate fire from Fredericksburg. As the bridges were being laid, cannon overlooked the town from a position east of Falmouth, where the river bends southward, to Falmouth itself, where Burnside occupied the Phillips House as headquarters, allowing the more elegant J. Horace Lacy Estate, Chatham, to be occupied by Sumner. The cannon were placed along the eastern shore of the river across from the town and all the way south to a position opposite Hamilton's Crossing. Confederate snipers had a field day firing at the engineers, however—most of them from Brig. Gen. William Barksdale's brigade of Mississippians—and many Union soldiers were picked off, despite the sometimes heavy artillery fire into the town. "The pontoon bridges had been pushed nearly to the opposite shore under cover of darkness, and ere the faintest ray of dawn had streaked the east, the quick, sharp rattle of musketry broke the stillness," recalled Pvt. William Maxson of the 23d New York Infantry. "The engineers laying the last plank were charged upon and a bloody struggle followed. . . . A shaft of flame leaps out from the opposite shore, the earth trembles, the air breaks with a deafening roar and a huge shell, with a shriek like a demon, speeds out its errand of destruction. Another followed and another, till the storm of iron crushed through the walls and set the town on fire." Near the onset of darkness on December 10, some Union soldiers crossed in boats and completed the task, but it was too late in the day to move elements of the army across. Lee decided to back off from a stiff resistance to the Union crossing because of the heavy artillery fire that could be brought to bear from Union cannon in front and to the left.

Burnside's plan was a tactical nightmare, and it was ill defined. It called for attacking across a river, in part through a town, uphill to steep ground on which Confederates had posted artillery and could fire down onto the attackers. It was the first major Civil War battle that would cut right through a town. It would have been an illogical plan even if carried out with great skill. When the Union army finished crossing the Rappahannock in icy weather on December 12, under the cover of a dense fog, its soldiers could not fully perceive what a hellish trial of fire lay before them. Union artillerists sent more than 5,000 shells crashing down into the town and the ridges beyond, and many of the town's buildings were smoldering or burning. Longstreet's corps was spread along the ridges behind the town, comprising the Confederate left and center, with Anderson's division to the north, on Taylor's Hill, Stansbury's Hill, and Cemetery Hill; the remaining portion of this rise, known as Marye's Heights, held the divisions of McLaws and Ransom, on Cemetery Hill and Marye's Hill. Marye's Hill was the location of the John L. Marye House, Brompton. South of Hazel Run, parallel and east of Telegraph Road, stretched the divisions of Pickett and Hood, east of what became known as Lee's Hill and on Howison's Hill, on which stood the Howison House, Braehead. To the south was the second corps of the Army of Northern Virginia, Jackson's, which was clustered along Mine Road and on Prospect Hill, west of a portion of the railroad line. A. P. Hill's division was out in front, Taliaferro behind and to the left, Early to his right, and D. H. Hill in reserve to the rear. Anchoring the right of the Confederate line was Stuart's cavalry and Maj. John Pelham's horse artillery down at Hamilton's Crossing.

Burnside's attack would commence on December 13, beginning the battle of Fredericksburg. Burnside ordered Franklin to make the primary attack to the south, near Hamilton's Crossing, assisted by Hooker. While this was taking place, Sumner would attack through the town and assault Marye's Heights by route of Telegraph Road. Somehow, Burnside deceived himself into believing that these two attacks would dislodge the entire Confederate army from its tactically defensive high ground. It seems clear that, as he had written Cullum, he believed that only a fraction of the Confederate army lay before him. For Union soldiers the battle would be among the most brutal of the war and certainly engendered the bitterest memories for many participants. Fought less than two weeks before Christmas, the action seemed senseless to many of the soldiers. It began following a brutally cold night during which many soldiers bivouacked without campfires. A deep chill stayed with them during the whole affair.

The lead elements of Franklin's Grand Division moved up into place for an attack by about 8:30 A.M. By 10 A.M. the thick fog was beginning to lift, and movements began in earnest. The opening and main attack at Fredericksburg was made by Meade's division, which moved toward the Hamilton House and was supported by the divisions of Doubleday and Gibbon. Two guns of Maj. John Pelham's Virginia Horse Artillery initially stalled Meade's attack, and a blistering artillery duel commenced and lasted about an hour. Pelham, age 24, was observed by General Lee, who simply said, "It is glorious to see such courage in one so young." Pelham was eventually forced back, however, and Meade's division advanced south of the railroad line, to Military Road, where it crashed into Brig. Gen. Maxcy Gregg's brigade, routing and temporarily scattering it. Gregg's brigade was in bivouac in the Confederate second line of defense, and was surprised; Gregg himself was shot and mortally wounded by a Minié bullet that injured his spine. He fell from his horse, pulled himself up near a tree, and later was carried from the field on a litter. Two days after the battle Gregg died.

To Meade's right, Gibbon advanced with some success against the brigades of Brig. Gens. William Dorsey Pender and Edward L. Thomas. Fighting through the wooded ground of Prospect Hill, however, Gibbon's and Meade's men were separated and their efforts uncoordinated; by about 1:30 P.M. a heavy Confederate counterattack was unleashed that pushed them back in disarray. Because of the foggy nature of the day, the Federal artillery fire on the heights could support the movements only sporadically, which didn't help. Meade's and Gibbon's men were driven back and chased by Confederate infantry, alarming Meade to the point that he worried over a possible capture of the Federal pontoon bridges. Franklin's Grand Division was so scattered that units could not come to the assistance of the fleeing bluecoats. Smith's 6th Corps was closer to the river, behind the Old Richmond Road, and Doubleday was deployed to the south. Eventually, the divisions of Sickles and Birney came to the aid of the weakened Federal line, stopping the Confederate counterattack with volleys of musketry fire.

Jackson's attempt at a reorganized attack northeastward was a nonstarter after a clear view from the heights permitted Union artillery to pummel the ground in his front.

With the heavy battle of Fredericksburg occurring south of the town, what has come to be known as the "slaughter" of Fredericksburg took place inside the town. Sumner infiltrated the smoldering town and advanced westward; by 11 A.M. French's division made the initial assault. They moved westward along the Plank Road and parallel streets, across a wide, open plain of 400 yards that held only a few houses, across a drainage ditch, and into a heavily fortified position. Only two bridges crossed the drainage ditch, and so Union infantry had to file across in column, repeating the disadvantageous situation that occurred at Antietam with Burnside's Bridge. Confederate defenders, those of Col. Thomas R. R. Cobb's brigade and others, stood in a sunken lane behind a stone wall that ran along the base of Marye's Heights, near the Innis House and the Martha Stevens House and below Brompton. Such a stone wall combined with a sunken road provided a natural trench for the Confederate defenders, much as the sunken lane had at Antietam. This one also afforded the protection of a stone wall. Many charges were ordered against the position, and death came suddenly to the ranks of Union soldiers who approached it. The position was attacked by the divisions of Hancock, Howard, and Sturgis, all without success, all of them by 1:30 P.M. having lost any hope of taking the position.

The horror of the stone wall was typified by the assault on it by Brig. Gen. Thomas F. Meagher's Irish Brigade. As Meagher's soldiers advanced, Confederate guns on the ridge raked it, producing "red flashes in the white gloom of a pearly powder cloud," and then followed the "crackle of rifles like a thousand packs of Chinese crackers, and from that ghastly gulf of flame but few of the boys in blue reappeared." Watching the battle from Marye's Heights, Confederate Col. Edward Porter Alexander remarked to Longstreet, "A chicken could not live in that field when we open on it." But the casualties were not limited to Union soldiers on the attack. Confederates also died, one of them being Col. Cobb, who was hit by a shell fragment that struck him in the thigh. Knocked to the ground and bleeding severely from his femoral artery, Cobb was taken to an aid station where he died a short time later. Cobb is frequently termed a brigadier general, but his commission as such was not confirmed by the Confederate Senate.

Franklin now settled into a period of inactivity, even after receiving orders to renew an attack. He later claimed that the orders were vague, and in the style of McClellan he simply requested more troops to initiate any further assaults. The badly mishandled attacks on the stone wall by Sumner could not be supported by artillery from Stafford Heights because it was out of range. By early afternoon, despite the horrible outcome of the battle thus

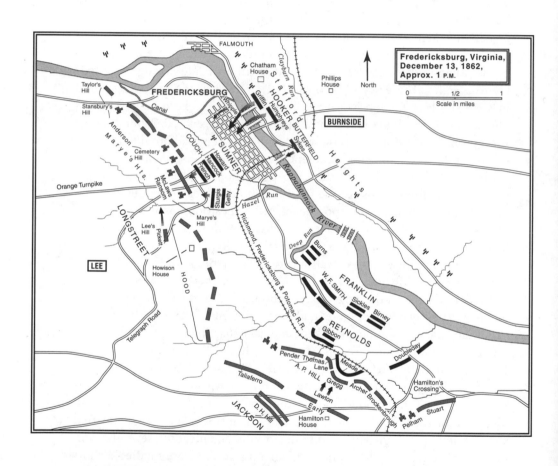

FALMOUTH

Chatham House

Clayburn Run

Phillips House

North

**Fredericksburg, Virginia,
December 13, 1862,
Approx. 1 P.M.**

0   1/2   1
Scale in miles

Taylor's
Hill

FREDERICKSBURG

Stansbury's
Hill

Canal

Stafford

Griffin Humphreys

HOOKER BUTTERFIELD

BURNSIDE

Anderson

Whipple

COUCH

SUMNER

Howard

Hancock

Heights

Cemetery
Hill

Marye's Hts.

McLaws Ransom

French

Skel

Rappahannock River

Orange Turnpike

Sturgis

Getty

Hazel Run

LEE

Lee's
Hill

Pickett

Marye's
Hill

Richmond Fredericksburg & Potomac R.R.

Deep Run

Burns

LONGSTREET

Howison
House

HOOD

FRANKLIN

W. F. SMITH

Sickles Birney

Telegraph Road

REYNOLDS

Gibbon

Doubleday

Pender Thomas
Lane

Meade

Hamilton's
Crossing

A. P. HILL

Gregg

Archer Brockenbrough

Taliaferro

Lawton

JACKSON

D. H. Hill

Early

Hamilton
House

Pelham

Stuart

far, Burnside ordered both Franklin and Hooker, now in position in the town, to resume attacks. Franklin continued to remain inactive, with Reynolds's 1st Corps deployed out in front and Smith's 6th Corps behind and to the north. Franklin's inactivity allowed Lee to shift Pickett's division and other scattered units northward to reinforce the line along Marye's Heights. Incredulous at the prospect of attacking the base of Marye's Heights yet again, and destroying his men uselessly, Hooker nonetheless eventually complied with the order. The divisions of Griffin and Humphreys attacked headlong into the stone wall again at 3:30 P.M. and 4 P.M., and each was hurled back with ghastly losses, as the earlier Union units had been. Watching the struggle from a position now called Lee's Hill, Gen. Lee commented, "it is well that war is so terrible, or we should grow too fond of it." As darkness approached and temperatures plunged, Getty's division attacked the wall again, to no avail. Hooker disengaged, withdrew, and awaited orders.

The night that came was one of the most horrifying of the war, with the ground frozen, the sky clearing, and the otherworldly screams and cries of the chilled victims permeating the air. Somewhat unusual for latitudes as southerly as Virginia's, a prominent and active aurora showed itself and was taken by many of the Confederate soldiers as an omen of military glory to come. "The light streamed up from the northern horizon," wrote Pvt. David Holt of the 16th Mississippi Infantry, "and also from the southern. At one time the two streams met and broadened out, then contracted and disappeared, only to suddenly flare up again more brilliantly. The landscape lit up with a weird kind of light that brought an uncanny feeling, but out of it all one thing was apparent. The enemy had withdrawn their skirmish line to a position nearer the city, which assured us a quiet night." Conversely, the Federal soldiers were greatly demoralized by the day's action. "At last, out wearied and depressed with the desolate scene," reflected Joshua L. Chamberlain, lieutenant colonel of the 20th Maine Infantry, "my own strength sunk, and I moved two dead men a little and lay down between them, making a pillow of the breast of a third. There was some comfort even in this companionship."

"It will scarcely be believed that the force of folly could further go," wrote Col. G. F. R. Henderson, "and that the bloody lesson taught by the defenders of the stone wall should have been utterly lost; yet, on the night of the 13th, Burnside 'as one of sense forlorn,' announced to his generals in council that he intended, on the morrow, to attack Marye's Hill with the Ninth Corps in column of regiments." Fortunately for the battered Union army, Burnside's Grand Division commanders were able to talk him out of this action. Both armies remained in place on December 14 and used the opportunity to strengthen their defenses. In the single competent action of the campaign, Burnside withdrew his army on the night of the 14th, pulling back

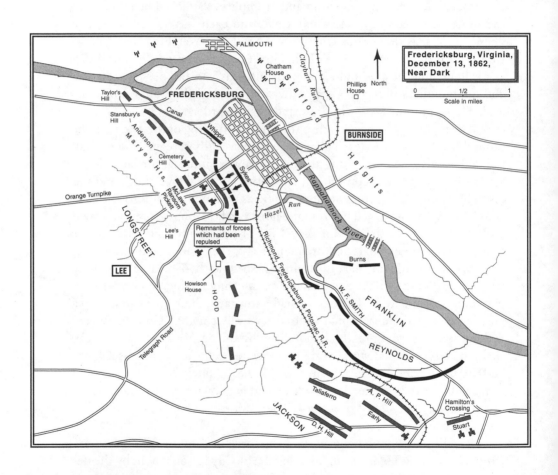

Fredericksburg, Virginia,
December 13, 1862,
Near Dark

North

0   1/2   1
Scale in miles

FALMOUTH

Chatham House

Clayburn Run

Phillips House

Taylor's Hill

FREDERICKSBURG

Stafford

Stansbury's Hill

Canal

Anderson

Whipple

BURNSIDE

Marye's Hts.

Cemetery Hill

Sykes

Heights

Orange Turnpike

McLaws
Ransom
Pickett

Hazel Run

Rappahannock River

LONGSTREET

Lee's Hill

Remnants of forces which had been repulsed

LEE

Howison House

HOOD

Richmond, Fredericksburg & Potomac R.R.

Burns

W. F. Smith

FRANKLIN

REYNOLDS

Telegraph Road

Taliaferro

A. P. Hill

Hamilton's Crossing

JACKSON

D. H. Hill

Early

Stuart

all units across the pontoon bridges, taking the entire quantity of supplies back, and bringing all the wounded the army could transport with it. Fredericksburg was an utter disaster for the Union and a signal triumph for the Confederacy. As at Malvern Hill, the armies had learned the perils of a frontal attack.

Casualties were severe. Of the approximately 114,000 Federal soldiers engaged, 1,284 were killed, 9,600 wounded, and 1,769 missing; Confederate losses were 595 killed, 4,061 wounded, and 653 missing out of about 72,500 engaged. Among the Union dead was Brig. Gen. George D. Bayard, 26, a New York cavalryman who was mortally wounded by a round shot. He died in Mansfield, the Bernard House, which was used as a hospital, the day after the battle. Another Union brigadier general, Conrad F. Jackson, was shot in the head and died shortly afterward during the initial southern attack. "I paid him much attention," wrote Capt. Ujanirtus Allen of the 21st Georgia Infantry. "He gave me two of the finest blankets I ever saw if I would go upon the field after them. I got them and placed them under him to keep him warm. He was sent back to our hospital and I do not suppose I will ever see him or them again."

During the final month of the year, a few lesser actions in the east occurred in addition to the terrible carnage at Fredericksburg. They included an engagement at Kinston, North Carolina, on December 12, and another at Kelly's Ford, Virginia, on December 22. They were skirmishes. At this holiday time the attention in America focused more and more on the increasing numbers of deaths by battle and especially disease, which continued at a frightening pace. Wounded the previous summer at Seven Pines, Union Brig. Gen. Charles D. Jameson had been recuperating at his home in Old Town, Maine. Jameson's horse had fallen on his leg, and he came away from the injury suffering from a high fever. On November 6, Jameson died in his bed of typhoid fever. Closer to the action, South Carolinian John B. Villepigue expired on November 9 at Port Hudson, Louisiana. Brig. Gen. Villepigue had received a sick leave in August but declined to use it, instead fighting at Corinth. He succumbed to pneumonia. In the east, on November 22, a probable accident took the life of Brig. Gen. Francis E. Patterson, son of Robert Patterson, the commander found so controversial during the First Bull Run campaign. Young Patterson was found dead in his tent at Fairfax Court House, Virginia, apparently killed by the discharge of his own pistol. Charges were pending against Patterson, brought by the irascible officer Daniel E. Sickles, and writers have suggested that Patterson committed suicide, but the evidence is not convincing. Further, on December 18, Confederate Brig. Gen. Johnson K. Duncan died at Knoxville, Tennessee. This Northern-born officer was serving as Gen. Braxton Bragg's chief of staff at the time of his death, which came by typhoid fever. Duncan's wife, expecting a child when he died, wore mourning attire for the following fifty-six years and never visited his grave in the Carnton Cemetery at Franklin, Tennessee. Death seemed to be consuming the thoughts of civilians on the home front as well as those of the soldiers, doctors, and nurses. "The first thing I met was a regiment of the vilest odors that ever assaulted the human nose, and took it by storm," wrote nurse Louisa May Alcott. "I must bear it. I did, armed with lavender water, with which I so besprinkled myself and premises, that . . . I was soon known among my patients as 'the nurse with a bottle.' "

Deaths of generals and common soldiers alike were much for both sides to bear, but for the Confederacy, the thought of assistance from abroad was always a paramount, if not realistic, hope. Losing this possibility, as now seemed to be the case—it was clear that England and probably France, too, would not side against emancipation—was almost a greater despair than death on the battlefield. "In the course of this war our eyes have often been turned abroad," Jefferson Davis told the Mississippi state legislature on December 26. "We have expected sometimes recognition and sometimes intervention at the hands of foreign nations, and we had a right to expect it. Never before in the history of the world had a people for so long a time maintained their ground, and showed themselves capable of maintaining their national existence, without securing the recognition of commercial nations. I know not why this has been so, but this I say, 'Put not your trust in princes,' and rest not your hopes in foreign nations. This war is ours; we must fight it ourselves, and I feel some pride in knowing that so far we have done it without the good will of anybody."

For black Americans, some of whom were about to feel emancipation or at least the promise of it, joy was about to spring eternal. "This is scarcely a day for prose," wrote Frederick Douglass. "It is a day for poetry and song, a new song. These cloudless skies, this balmy air, this brilliant sunshine, (making December as pleasant as May) are in harmony with the glorious morning of liberty about to dawn upon us."

At the end of 1862 the architect of emancipation, Lincoln, struggled with the military setbacks that had befallen the Union since late summer. In his annual message to Congress, delivered on December 1, Lincoln tried to summarize the progress of the war and its shifting goals. "Fellow citizens, *we* cannot escape history. We of this Congress and this administration will be remembered in spite of ourselves. No personal significance, or insignificance, can spare one or another of us. The fiery trial through which we pass, will light us down, in honor or dishonor, to the last generation. We *say* we are for the Union. The world will not forget that we say this. We know how to save the Union. The world knows we do know how to save it. We—even *we here*—hold the power, and bear the responsibility. In *giving* freedom to the *slave,* we *assure* freedom to the *free*—honorable alike in what we give and what we preserve. We shall nobly save or meanly lose, the last best, hope of earth."

Privately, Lincoln was not so certain of success. At month's end he told his friend Andrew G. Curtin, governor of Pennsylvania, "If there is a worse place than hell, I am in it."

Stalemate at Stones River

THE YEAR 1863 WITNESSED many changes in the Civil War, especially in the grim situation for black Americans. The event on everyone's mind in America was the issuance of the final Emancipation Proclamation by President Lincoln on January 1. "I do order and declare that all persons held as slaves within said designated States, and parts of States, are, and henceforward shall be free," wrote Lincoln. Though it would take another hundred years before African-Americans would truly be free, the country had taken its first steps down that long, tortuous highway. There would be no going back to a life of bondage for future generations.

At the start of 1863, life in the United States for the soldiers was alternately boring and terrifying, and the numbers of families that had been touched by war was growing steadily. If a family had not lost a son, it certainly knew members of other families who had died in the service. There were rising prices for goods, continual sacrifices to support the war effort, and, in the South, scarcity of materials that led to an experimental market in creating substitute goods—coffee made from ground corn, and the like.

The Civil War had taken on a new degree of bloodiness in the year 1862, particularly with the battles of Shiloh, Antietam, and Fredericksburg. The coming year of 1863 would be bloodier still, would witness an alarmingly high number of men dying from disease, and, although no one could know it at the time, would contain some of the most strategically important battles of the war. Many changes came about in the armies in the year 1863. In the U.S. Army, the ranks swelled to 918,191 by January 1, 1863. (The army would report a slight decrease in its aggregate strength by January 1, 1864, to 860,737.) New assignments in late 1862 and 1863 were plentiful. Col. Joseph Holt, former secretary of war, was now judge advocate general of the army. In the spring of 1863, Col. James B. Fry was named provost marshal general of the army. The U.S. Army Signal Corps was organized; Col. Albert J. Myer became its chief. Due to a lengthy inspection tour in the field by Brig. Gen. Montgomery C. Meigs, Col. Charles Thomas acted as quartermaster general from August 1863 to January 1864. A Cavalry Bureau was established in Washington in July 1863; Maj. Gen. George Stoneman was assigned as director. Col. Timothy P. Andrews assumed command of the Pay Department. In the absence of Surg. Gen. William A. Hammond on inspection tours, Col. Joseph K. Barnes took over as acting surgeon general beginning in September 1863. During the same month, Brig. Gen. George D. Ramsay was assigned command of the Ordnance Department.

The strength of the Confederate army grew to 465,584 on January 1, 1863. It grew slightly during the year before falling to 464,646 by December 31, 1863. There were a few new faces in the Confederate command structure, too. Brig. Gen. Alexander R. Lawton was assigned as quartermaster general in August 1863. In that same month Lt. Col. Alfred L. Rives became acting chief of the Engineer Bureau. In November 1863, Lt. Col. Julius A. de Lagnel was assigned as inspector of arsenals in the Bureau of Ordnance.

By the war's third year, it was beginning to dawn on some of the field commanders that the ancient tactics generally practiced in the field—frontal attacks, coordinated volleys at close range, and anachronistic marching techniques—were contributing toward the monstrous casualties in large part because of the new technology of small arms. These tactics were Napoleonic in heritage, described on paper and disseminated by Antoine-Henri Jomini. Civil War commanders had studied them at West Point and later taught them to their men on the field. But those tactics were outmoded by a greater number of rifled muskets, rifled cannon, and high-tech weapons like repeating rifles that were adopted to replace smooth bore muskets as the war developed.

The U.S. Ordnance Department furnished 3,477,655 small arms (rifles, muskets, carbines, revolvers, and pistols); 544,475 swords, sabers, and lances; 2,362,546 sets of combat accouterments for the men; and 539,544 sets of horse equipments during the war. Of the small arms, 2,687,450 were rifles and muskets, 407,734 were carbines, and 373,471 were revolvers and pistols. Of the edged weapons, 124,676 were swords and 415,232 were sabers. The Ordnance Department supplied a total of 1,022,176,474 rounds of small-arms ammunition. Ideally, about 200 rounds per man were carried by infantry units. Brigade and division trains carried about 200 rounds per man additionally. The department supplied 1,220,555,435 percussion caps and 23,450 tons of lead bullets.

To demonstrate the type of destruction and loss that occurred during a large battle, it's astonishing to reflect on the report of Lt. John R. Edie, acting chief of ordnance of the Army of the Potomac, on the matériel collected from the battlefield at Gettysburg after the three-day engagement. Edie reported that ordnance officers had collected 24,064 muskets and rifles, 114 carbines, 10,591 bayonets, 366 sabers, 1,834 cartridge boxes, 246 cap pouches, and a variety of other items from the field, either wrecked or simply discarded in the chaos of battle. They were shipped to the Washington Arsenal. More recent successes by relic hunters excavating rusted weapons from hundreds of battlefield sites show that not all of the discarded guns were brought back into service.

Of the types of rifles and muskets in circulation, the most plentiful in the U.S. Army were the Springfield rifle (54 percent) and the imported Enfield rifle (16 percent). Many other types existed and were used on both sides, but the Springfield was the principal weapon for both armies. Manufactured at the Springfield Arsenal in Massachusetts, which began production of arms in 1795, the Civil War Springfield was a .58-caliber percussion rifle that fired a Minié bullet and was officially designated the United States Rifle Musket, Model 1861. About 800,000 were produced in Springfield during the war, and other factories produced 900,000 more of the same design. It was a muzzle-loader, used percussion caps (rather than an earlier, Maynard percussion tape that never worked well), had an overall length of 56 inches, and weighed about 9.75 pounds with its triangular bayonet attached. Slight modifications to the design were introduced in 1863, creating the United States Rifle Musket, Model 1863, types I and II, type I being a slight simplification to aid in manufacturing and type II bringing the design slightly closer to the 1861 model. Confederates ultimately captured and used about 150,000 Springfields. The Springfield had an effective range of about 500 yards; it could hit targets at twice that distance but without any accuracy. The gun could effectively be loaded and fired, at maximum, once every twenty seconds. Various contractors aided in producing this popular gun, chiefly Colt Arms Co., Amoskeag, and Lamson, Goodnow, & Yale. Still in heavy use were the United States Rifle Musket, Model 1855, produced chiefly at Springfield and using the disliked Maynard tape system, and the variant Model 1855 produced at the Harpers Ferry Arsenal that featured a shorter barrel, the so-called Artillery Model.

Other prewar U.S. rifles played important roles in the war. The United States Rifle, Model 1841, often called the Mississippi Rifle or the Jäger Rifle, was often employed. It was the first U.S. Army rifle specifically designed for use with percussion caps. It was a .54-caliber gun measuring 48.75 inches long and weighing 9.75 pounds. It employed a paper cartridge with a spherical ball, but by the time of the Civil War many of these guns were converted to .58-caliber weapons and adapted to accommodate Minié bullets. The original had no mount for a bayonet, but this was also often altered. Some 101,096 of these guns were produced, and many alterations used during the

Civil War, having been named Mississippi rifles during the Mexican War in honor of Jefferson Davis's 1st Mississippi Regiment. The name Jäger derived from the legendary German hunters.

Many older weapons were also used, particularly during the first months of the war, when long arms were in short supply. For a time, a popular gun was the United States Flintlock Musket, Model 1822. This Revolutionary War–style gun was a .69-caliber smoothbore muzzle-loader that employed a paper cartridge and required a powder flask to fill the pan before firing. Its effective range was limited to about 100 yards, and it often misfired. Its cumbersome loading technique limited its frequency of fire to about twice per minute at best. The United States Percussion Musket, Model 1842, was widely used during the war, with about 150,000 having been produced. It signaled a great advance over flintlock weapons by employing percussion caps, but its .69-caliber smoothbore barrel limited the gun's accuracy. Many Confederate units employed this gun during the first two years of the war, and it wasn't until after Gettysburg that the Army of Northern Virginia was extensively equipped with rifles.

Second only to the Springfield in numbers employed was the English Enfield Rifle Musket, which had been used by the British Army since 1855. This weapon was imported by both the U.S. and C.S. armies in great quantities; more than 500,000 were imported by the North and it was probably the most widely used single rifled gun in the Confederate armies. A muzzle-loader, the Enfield fired a .577-caliber bullet similar to the Minié bullet and had an effective range of about 1,000 yards with reasonable accuracy. Fitted with its bayonet, the Enfield weighed 9 pounds 3 ounces. Other imported long arms included a variety of models from Austria and Belgium, often referred to as simply Austrian and Belgian rifles. One such popular gun was the Austrian Lorenz Rifle, a .54-caliber gun that was often rebored to the standard .58 caliber. Federal ordnance officers purchased 226,924 of these guns, while Confederates acquired at least 100,000 of them.

Other popular rifles in Civil War use included the Remington Percussion Contract Rifle (.58-caliber muzzle-loader, 1862–1865), Sharps Military Rifle (.52-caliber breechloader, 1859–1865), Whitney Contract Rifle Musket (.58-caliber muzzle-loader, 1861–1863), Moore-Enfield Rifle Musket (.58-caliber muzzleloader, 1861–1863), Greene Rifle (.53-caliber breechloader, 1859–early 1860s), and Merrill Rifle (.54 caliber breechloader, 1862–1865). Repeating rifles represented new technology during the war, and they often presented problems by not working efficiently or correctly. Nonetheless, a considerable quantity saw their way onto Civil War battlefields. Made first by the Samuel Colt Co., the repeating rifle adopted the multicylinder principle of the revolver. But the Colt 1855 Military Rifle and Rifled Musket (.44 [6-shot] and .56 [5-shot] calibers, 1856–1864) were plagued by problems of gas and flame leaks between the cylinder and the barrel and by the unexpected displeasure of all chambers occasionally firing together. Other repeating rifles in wartime use included the Henry Rifle (.44-caliber rimfire with 15-shot magazine, 1860–1866), the most successfully adapted repeating weapon in the U.S. Army's arsenal, which was popular with cavalry and confounded Confederates who faced it. About 10,000 were used during the war after its development by B. Tyler Henry at Oliver Winchester's New Haven Arms Co. Also popular was the Spencer Repeating Rifle (.52-caliber 7-shot magazine, 1862–1867), produced in Boston, and deadly on the field of battle.

A vast array of carbines also was available to the Civil War soldier. Carbines were light shoulder rifles originally designed for, and favored by, cavalry. They were virtually all breechloaders (loading from the rear) so that cavalrymen could load them while mounted, and for a time they faced an odd disadvantage. Many of the old-timers in the Ordnance Department—primarily Ordnance Chief James W. Ripley—disfavored new inventions, worried over the necessity of supplying ammunition of different calibers, the complexity of the mechanism in the hands of simple soldiers, and so put off attempts to introduce the more efficient system of breech-loading until the middle of the war. Lincoln appreciated the fact that breechloaders were the way of the future early on, as he witnessed a demonstration of their effectiveness in the Treasury Park, south of the Executive Mansion, one day in 1861. Gunfire had been banned within the capital, but Lincoln, accompanied by his secretary William O. Stoddard and soldiers of the 150th Pennsylvania Infantry ("Bucktails"), who guarded the White House, set up some targets and fired away. Lincoln was impressed with the breech-loading guns, although startled by angry soldiers who rode up wondering who had violated the firearms ordinance. After the angry lads saw that it was the President, they skedaddled. "Well," said Lincoln "they might have stayed and seen the shooting."

The battle over the breechloaders finally resulted in their adoption, but it took a long time. The three most significant carbines used during the war were the Spencer Repeating Carbine (.52-caliber, 7-shot repeater, 1863–1865), Sharps Carbine (.52-caliber breechloader, 1859–1865), and Burnside Carbine (.54-caliber breechloader, 1857–1865). Others included the Cosmopolitan Carbine (.52-caliber breechloader, 1859), Gallager Carbine (.50-caliber breechloader, 1860), Gibbs Carbine (.52-caliber breechloader, 1856–1863), Gwyn & Campbell Carbine (.52-caliber breechloader, 1862), Joslyn Carbine (.52-caliber rimfire breechloader, 1862–1864), Lindner Carbine (.58-caliber breechloader, 1859–1865), Maynard Carbine (.35-1 and .50-caliber breechloader, 1857–1865), Merrill Carbine (.54-caliber breechloader, 1858–1865), Remington Carbine (.46- and .50-caliber rimfire, 1863–1865), Smith Carbine (.50-caliber breechloader, 1857–1865), Starr Carbine (.54-caliber breechloader, 1858–1865), and Triplett & Scott Carbine (.50-caliber rimfire, 7-shot magazine, 1864–1865).

The cavalry had a special need for light, efficient, breechloading weapons. An even more elite group, sharpshooters, had special needs, too. The most celebrated unit of Civil War sharpshooters, Col. Hiram Berdan's 2d United States Sharpshooters, employed custom-built Sharps rifles, fitted with oversized octagonal barrels, heavy rifle stocks, globe sights, and double triggers.

Revolvers and pistols were also used heavily during the war, and were typically carried by officers and cavalrymen as well as some common soldiers. The Colt revolver was overwhelmingly the favorite type during the war. Manufactured by the Samuel Colt Co., in Hartford, several varieties saw heavy use, principally the Colt Model 1851 Navy Revolver, the Colt Model 1860 Army Revolver, and the Colt Model 1861 Navy Revolver. These pistols were .36-caliber, 6-shot revolvers with octagonal barrels measuring 7.5 inches; they had an attached loading lever. Second in popularity to the Colt was the Remington revolver, which was produced in a variety of models, chiefly the Remington New Model Army Revolver (1863–1875), a .44-caliber, 6-shot revolver with an 8-inch octagonal barrel. Not as widely used, the Remington 1861 Army Revolver ("Old Model Army") was a .44-caliber, 6-shot cylinder with an 8-inch octagonal barrel, produced in relatively small quantity in 1861–1862.

Many other pistols and revolvers were manufactured and carried along to the war. They included the Adams Patent Revolver (.31- and .36-caliber, 5-shot cylinder, 1857–1861), Allen & Wheelock Center Hammer Army Revolver (.44-caliber, 6-shot cylinder, 1861–1862), Benjamin F. Joslyn Army Model Revolver (.44-caliber, 5-shot cylinder, 1861–1862), Manhattan .36-Caliber Model Revolver (.36-caliber, 5- and 6-shot models, 1859–1868), Savage Revolving Fire Arms Co. Navy Model (.36 caliber, 6 shot cylinder, 1861–1865), Starr Arms Co. S.A. 1863 Army Revolver (.44-caliber, 6-shot cylinder, 1863–1865), and Whitney Navy & Eagle Co. Revolver (.36-caliber, 6-shot cylinder, late 1850s–early 1860s). Imported revolvers in Civil War service included the Lefaucheux Pinfire Revolver (French, .47-caliber, 6-shot cylinder, 1853–1865), Perrin Centerfire Revolver (French, .45-caliber, 6-shot cylinder, 1860–1865), and Kerr Percussion Revolver (English, .38- and .44-caliber, 6-shot cylinder, 1859–1866).

The situation was very different in the Confederacy because of the lack of manufacturing facilities. This, coupled with a lack of trained personnel to produce weaponry, plus a shortage of raw materials, posed a significant problem for supplying Confederate armies adequately throughout the war. Early in the secession crisis Raphael Semmes, Caleb Huse, and other agents acting on behalf of the proto-Confederacy purchased a large number of arms, mostly from abroad, and Huse eventually secured more than 100,000 Enfields for service in the Confederacy. But they were slow in coming, and early Confederate units had ever-present problems of being undersupplied with guns. At the outbreak of war the South had about 150,000 small arms, only 20,000 of which were rifles. What they could not purchase, however, Confederate soldiers sometimes captured: more than 100,000 Northern small arms were taken throughout the first two years of the war. But by mid 1863 losses began mounting and a small-arms shortage plagued the Confederacy until war's end.

Hand weapons for the Confederacy were in even worse supply. During the war Southern factories produced only about 10,000 revolvers, nearly all of which were "imitations" of the .36-caliber Colt Navy Revolver. Nonetheless, some were produced and used on the battlefield. These included the Griswold & Gunnison Revolver (.36-caliber, 6-shot cylinder, 1862–1864), Leech & Rigdon Revolver (.36-caliber, 6-shot cylinder, 1863–1864), LeMat Two-Barrel Revolver (manufactured in Paris, France, and Birmingham, England; .42-caliber, 9-shot cylinder, plus single-shot .63-caliber barrel on swivel for firing buckshot, 1856–1865), Rigdon & Ansley Revolver (.36-caliber, 6-shot cylinder, 1864–1865), and Spiller & Burr Revolver (.36-caliber, 6-shot cylinder, 1862–1865). Other Confederate handgun manufacturers included the Palmetto Armory in Columbia; Samuel Sutherland in Richmond; George Todd in Austin; Tucker, Sherrard & Co. in Texas; J. & F. Garrett & Co. in Greensboro; and the Dance Brothers in Texas. By the summer of 1863 the logistics of maintaining an operating factory had nearly put Spiller & Burr out of business. The firm "prepared to throw in the sponge," and suggested that "it might be more profitable for all concerned if the Confederate States of America would step in and buy their plant, lock, stock, and barrel." Not only did Confederate arms makers have great difficulties with production, but as Federal troops drew closer, they had to contend with "keeping out of the way of the Union Army."

Long arms produced in the Confederacy suffered from many of the same problems. They included the J. B. Barret Rifles and Carbines, which were rebuilt from Hall rifles and carbines, from breechloaders into muzzle-loaders (.54-caliber, rebuilt 1862–1863), Cook & Brother Rifles and Carbines (.58-caliber muzzle-loaders, 1861–1864), Davis & Bozeman Muzzle-Loading Rifle (.58-caliber muzzle-loader, early wartime), Dickson, Nelson Carbine and Rifle (.58-caliber muzzle-loader, 1863–1865), Fayetteville Armory Rifles (.58-caliber muzzle-loader, 1862–1865), H. C. Lamb Muzzle-Loading Rifle (.58-caliber muzzle-loader, early wartime), Morse Carbine (.50-caliber breechloader, middle wartime), J. P. Murray Percussion Carbines and Rifles (.58-caliber muzzle-loaders, 1862–1864), Richmond Armory Carbines and Rifle Muskets (.58-caliber muzzle-loaders, 1861–1865), Sharps Type Carbines

(.52-caliber breechloader, 1862–1864), and Tyler Texas Rifle (.57- and .54-caliber muzzle-loaders, 1863–1865). Additionally, many soldiers carried older weapons off to war, particularly in the Confederacy. These included a wide range of hunting rifles and shotguns.

Of lesser importance but present during the war in tremendous numbers were edged weapons—swords, sabers, bayonets, lances, knives, cutlasses, and pikes. Swords were omnipresent in the dress code of most officers, and although they were rarely used in battle, they provided the crowning symbol of an officer's authority over his men; they were often drawn and waved or pointed to lead attacks. But of the 246,712 wounded treated in Federal hospitals during the war, 922 causes were reported as traceable to wounds from edged weapons of any kind. Most of those resulted from personal arguments or use by camp guards rather than by fighting on the field. Often swords were produced with engraved blades and fancy guards, frequently as presentation tokens to officers. The most common sword was the so-called Model 1850 Foot Officer's Sword, which came in very plain to extremely fancy varieties and was standard issue to field-grade officers such as majors, lieutenant colonels, and colonels. General officers had fancier swords. An odd variety of sword, the Artillery Short Sword, was a stubby broadsword offered to artillery batteries early in the war for assaulting cavalry that had overrun their guns; rarely used, these weapons were relegated to the scrap heap of relics even during the war. More utilitarian were cavalry sabers—heavy, curved blades resembling scimitars that were carried by horsemen and could in theory be used to swipe at ground troops or enemy riders in battle. During the early months of the war these weapons typically had blades spanning 42 inches, and they were so heavy that they were extremely difficult to swing effectively. Later reduced to 36 inches in blade length, they were easier to handle but still infrequently used in action during the era of rifled muskets.

Even less valuable were pikes and lances, which correctly seem more appropriate to the Middle Ages than to the Civil War. In 1859, John Brown conspired to arm his hoped-for army of freed slaves with pikes, and these weapons were delivered into the field during the first naïve months of the war. Largely driven by a relative shortage of small arms, the Confederate government considered arming whole regiments with pikes, and on April 10, 1862, the Confederate Congress passed an act allowing for the supply of two companies of soldiers carrying pikes in each regiment. In Georgia, Gov. Joseph E. Brown initiated production of Confederate pikes, which consisted of a 12-inch double-edged blade on a 6- or 7-foot pole. Though thousands were produced at a cost of $5 each, they were rarely or perhaps never used in battle. Equally impractical were lances, technologically updated spears, which were offered to cavalry as an alternative weapon. At least one Federal unit, the 6th Pennsylvania Cavalry, carried lances until nearly the middle of 1863. Commanded by Col. Richard H. Rush, the regiment was dubbed "Rush's Lancers."

Personal edged weapons saw slightly more use, but their value in battle is questionable. Bayonet attacks occurred occasionally during the war, usually as a measure of last resort when ammunition for guns ran out. Among the few successful and publicized bayonet attacks that occurred were those of the 17th Wisconsin Infantry at Corinth, Mississippi, on October 3, 1862, and that of the 5th Wisconsin Infantry and 6th Maine Infantry at Rappahannock Bridge, Virginia, on November 7, 1863, which took place at night. Smaller-edged weapons such as Bowie knives, named for Col. James Bowie, and pocketknives were often carried by soldiers and perhaps used from time to time in action. Among collectors the celebrated Confederate "D-guard" Bowie knife is a treasure, though its significance as a weapon may be slight. Manufacturers of edged weapons were many. In the North the leading producer was the Ames Manufacturing Co. of Chicopee, Massachusetts, which during the war produced 155,240 edged weapons, or about 34 percent of the U.S. Ordnance Department's purchases. Producers and importers of swords and sabers in the South included James Conning of New Orleans, Thomas, Griswold & Co. in New Orleans; Kraft, Goldschmidt & Kraft of Columbia, South Carolina; the Memphis Novelty Works; and the Tredegar Iron Works in Richmond.

EQUIPPED WITH BETTER WEAPONS, the soldiers in the cold trenches commenced another year of bloody war. As the first big failure at Union capture of Vicksburg occurred, the celebrated Confederate raider Brig. Gen. John Hunt Morgan began his third raid in Kentucky. Morgan's two brigades were commanded by Col. Basil W. Duke, Morgan's brother-in-law, and Col. Adam R. "Stovepipe" Johnson. With 4,000 troopers, Morgan left Alexandria, Tennessee (east of Nashville), on December 21, 1862, to strike out at the lines of communications supporting Maj. Gen. William S. Rosecrans in Tennessee. Morgan's raiders moved north into Kentucky, striking Tompkinsville the following day, Glasgow on December 24, and Cave City on Christmas Day. At Glasgow, a skirmish occurred between Morgan's men and a battalion of the 2d Michigan Cavalry, creating slight losses. On December 26, Morgan's men moved past Munfordville to Bacon Creek, where a small skirmish took place, and they passed a short distance west of the cabin birth site of Abraham Lincoln at Hodgenville. On the same day, the stockade at Nolin and the town of Upton were captured. The following day the raiders moved into Elizabethtown, where Federal authorities offered a flag of truce and suggested they were surrounded and ought to give themselves up. Morgan countered that the Union troops instead ought to surrender. After they refused, Morgan "immediately began to shell the houses in which the enemy had taken refuge," as he recorded in his report, and "after a brisk firing of three-quarters of an hour . . . the place was surrendered." Morgan captured and paroled 800 prisoners.

Morgan and his men continued their northward raid, and on December 28 approached perilously close to Louisville, fighting a small action at Muldraugh's Hill near the present-day site of Fort Knox. Passing through Lebanon Junction and then turning northwestward, Morgan's men destroyed stockades, trestles, army supplies, and captured about 700, which they paroled. Receiving shellfire from Federal artillery on the evening of the 28th, Morgan advanced his command eastward to Bardstown by the next day. A skirmish occurred at Johnson's Ferry (Hamilton's Ford) on the Rolling Fork near Boston, and minor action at New Haven, wherein fire was exchanged between Morgan's men and the 78th Illinois Infantry guarding the stockade. Of the affair at Johnson's Ferry, Col. John M. Harlan of the 10th Kentucky Infantry (U.S.) invoked faulty train engines and a lack of shoes and socks to explain his inability to stop Morgan. "It is for you to determine what is to be done," he wrote Brig. Gen. Jeremiah T. Boyle, the military governor of Kentucky.

On December 30, Morgan continued eastward to Springfield, where he learned that a large Union force was assembling at Lebanon. Now pursued by several brigades, Morgan speedily retreated southward to Campbellsville during the night. Morgan's command reached Burkesville by January 2 and slipped back into Tennessee, to Smithville, on the same day. The raid had been highly successful, Morgan's two brigades having destroyed and disrupted much of the Louisville & Nashville Railroad between Munfordville and Shepherdsville, captured and paroled 1,877 prisoners, and seized $2 million in Federal property.

Confederates were not the only raiders in Tennessee and Kentucky at this time, however. Morgan tried to thwart the movements of Union Maj. Gen. William S. Rosecrans. But Tennessee-born Brig. Gen. Samuel P. Carter set out on a raid to support Rosecrans. On December 26, 1862, Carter departed Manchester, Kentucky, with a force consisting of the 9th Pennsylvania Cavalry, two battalions of the 2d Michigan Cavalry, and one battalion of the 7th Ohio Cavalry, crossed the high mountains east of Cumberland Gap, and brought Federal cavalry into southwestern Virginia and the eastern Tennessee Valley. Carter had the unusual background of a Princeton University education. He was a lieutenant commander in the U.S. Navy and acting "on loan" to the army as a brigadier general with active operations under way.

Carter's raid was as important psychologically to the Union war effort in eastern Tennessee as any other early action. Carter planned to strike the

East Tennessee & Virginia Railroad at two points a hundred miles apart and bring his divided brigade together, thereby destroying the whole stretch of railroad. But second thoughts compelled Carter to keep his force united. Moving swiftly, he brought his horse soldiers southward toward Moccasin Gap, south of Estillville, Virginia, which they discovered was defended by Confederates. At his headquarters some thirty miles east of the gap, at Abingdon, Virginia, Confederate Brig. Gen. Humphrey Marshall, commanding the District of Abingdon, learned of Carter's approach. Marshall was alarmed because of large quantities of Confederate supplies stored at Bristol, on the Tennessee-Virginia border southwest of Abingdon, and over a possible raid on the saltworks at Saltville, Virginia, northeast of Abingdon. On the approach of the 2d Michigan Cavalry, meanwhile, the Confederates in Moccasin Gap retreated and opened the door for Carter's approach to Blountville, southwest of Bristol.

Carter's raiders reached Blountville by dawn on December 30. There they were greeted with the hysterical screams of a Confederate woman who chanted, "The Yankees! The Yankees! Great God, we are lost!" Carter's men took the military hospital in town, captured and paroled 30 prisoners, and turned their attention toward Union, to the east, which marked the approximate positions of two railroad bridges Carter wished to destroy. Two companies of the 62d North Carolina Infantry guarded the town; their commander, Maj. B. G. McDowell, was captured by Carter's raiders as he calmly rode up to investigate a wild rumor that Yankees were approaching the town. The North Carolinians surrendered, too, and Carter arrived and had the soaked wooden bridge at Union burned by ordering substantial quantities of dry wooden beams stacked against it. The bridge over the Holston River spanned 600 feet. The Federals also destroyed the railroad depot, a nearby wagon bridge, three railroad cars filled with supplies, telegraphic equipment, and more than 700 muskets and rifles.

In the afternoon, a portion of Carter's brigade set off for Carter's Depot (Carter's Station), ten miles south of Union. A significant railroad landmark, Carter's Depot stood on the northern end of the Watauga Bridge, a wooden trestle 400 feet long. The depot also was a major refueling and telegraph stop on the railroad line. A company of the 62d North Carolina Infantry, commanded by Col. Robert G. A. Love, defended Carter's Depot. Col. Charles J. Walker led the Union force approaching the depot. An evenly matched, brisk skirmish erupted between the 150 Federals and 130 Confederates in the gloom of deepening twilight. Finally, a mounted charge by horsemen of the 9th Pennsylvania Cavalry broke the Confederate center, and the Southerners retreated. Carter's men burned the depot, burned a cache of supplies, and fired the bridge, which created a sensational sight. The whole structure caught aflame and, with a wrecked Confederate train on board, collapsed into the Watauga River sixty feet below, producing a shower of sparks blowing upward along with hissing steam escaping from the locomotive.

Though its value was limited, Carter's Raid marked the first successful Union cavalry raid in the western theater. The men left Watauga and Jonesville, Virginia, by January 2. There they skirmished with Confederates again. Carter's men reached Richmond, Kentucky, by January 9, separated, and seemed satisfied with the results.

As the Morgan and Carter raids were progressing, the major military movement in the west was drawing toward a pitched battle in Tennessee. The chief combat forces in central Kentucky and Tennessee in late 1862 were those of Gen. Braxton Bragg, who had some 38,000 troops in the Confederate Army of Tennessee, and Maj. Gen. William S. Rosecrans, with 47,000 men in the Army of the Cumberland. Following the battle of Perryville, Maj. Gen. Don Carlos Buell had been replaced by Rosecrans, victor of Iuka and Corinth, who the War Department hoped would show a greater sense of urgency to attack the enemy than had Buell. Halleck wanted Rosecrans to occupy eastern Tennessee.

Rosecrans at first concentrated his army at Nashville, which was secure despite being threatened occasionally by Morgan's and Forrest's cavalry. With Bragg at Murfreesboro and Morgan raiding Rosecrans's communications, the commander the troops called "Old Rosy" finally marched south in pursuit of Bragg on December 26. The resulting action would be called the campaign and battle of Stones River, or Murfreesboro. Rosecrans moved his wings south by different routes, and they were effectively harassed by Brig. Gen. Joseph Wheeler's cavalry, which delayed their movements. Maj. Gen. Thomas L. Crittenden's wing paralleled the Nashville & Chattanooga Railroad, passing through La Vergne and south of Smyrna on the approach. Maj. Gen. Alexander M. McCook marched south along the Nolensville Turnpike to Nolensville, south to Triune, and then east toward Murfreesboro. Thomas moved south along the Wilson (Wilkinson) Turnpike and the Franklin Turnpike, parallel to the Nashville & Decatur Railroad, then eastward through Nolensville and along the same route used by Crittenden south of the Nashville & Chattanooga Railroad. The separation of the wings afforded Thomas and McCook the opportunity to launch a turning movement against Hardee, who was at Triune when the Federal march began. But with the Federal soldiers on the move, Bragg moved Hardee back to Murfreesboro and solidified his defense.

The organization of the armies at Stones River differed greatly on each side. Rosecrans divided the Army of the Cumberland (14th Army Corps) into three "wings" commanded by Maj. Gens. Alexander M. McCook, George H. Thomas, and Thomas L. Crittenden. McCook's Right Wing held the divisions of Brig. Gens. Jefferson C. Davis, Richard W. Johnson, and Philip H. Sheridan. Thomas's Center Wing held the divisions of Maj. Gen. Lovell H. Rousseau and Brig. Gens. James S. Negley and Speed S. Fry. Crittenden's Left Wing contained the divisions of Brig. Gens. Thomas J. Wood, John M. Palmer and Horatio P. Van Cleve. The cavalry was commanded by Brig. Gen. David S. Stanley.

Bragg's Army of Tennessee consisted of two corps plus cavalry. Lt. Gens. Leonidas Polk (Polk's corps) and William J. Hardee (Hardee's corps) were the corps commanders; the cavalry was commanded by Brig. Gen. Joseph Wheeler. Polk's corps contained the divisions of Maj. Gens. Benjamin F. Cheatham (brigades of Brig. Gens. Daniel S. Donelson, Alexander P. Stewart, and George Maney, and Col. Alfred J. Vaughan, Jr.) and Jones M. Withers (brigades of Col. J. Q. Loomis, Brig. Gens. James R. Chalmers and James Patton Anderson, and Col. Arthur M. Manigault). Hardee's corps consisted of the divisions of Maj. Gens. John C. Breckinridge (brigades of Brig. Gen. Daniel W. Adams, Col. Joseph B. Palmer, Brig. Gens. William Preston, Roger W. Hanson, and John K. Jackson) and Patrick R. Cleburne (brigades of Brig. Gens. Lucius E. Polk, St. John R. Liddell, Bushrod R. Johnson, and Sterling A. M. Wood). Additionally, McCown's division, loaned from Kirby Smith's corps, was temporarily attached to Hardee's division. It was commanded by Maj. Gen. John P. McCown and held the brigades of Brig. Gens. Matthew D. Ector, James E. Rains, and Evander McNair. Wheeler's cavalry division consisted of Wheeler's own brigade and those of Brig. Gens. Abraham Buford, John Pegram, and John A. Wharton.

Bragg established his defensive line along the West Fork of the Stones River, which meandered through graceful arcs and curves west of Murfreesboro, a town of 2,861 residents. The geography of the battlefield contained a matrix of elements. The Nashville & Chattanooga Railroad entered the field from the northwest, skirted the southwestern edge of the town, then angled more sharply to the south. West of the town the Nashville Turnpike, the major road of the area, ran alongside the railroad. At least six fords were available at various points along Stones River. A series of hills stood north of the town and east of the river. Most of the land west of Bragg and east of the oncoming Union soldiers consisted of woods, cultivated farmland, and farmhouses.

By the evening of December 30, Bragg established a line that stretched more than four miles long and for the most part was logically defensible. Polk occupied the west bank of the river and the bulk of Hardee's force was on the eastern bank. Confederate cavalry had completely circled around the Union force, creating considerable havoc with supply and communications. Bragg expected Rosecrans to attack, but as the Union army built up a line and no attack came, Bragg ordered his commanders to attack early on De-

cember 31. The plan would be simple. Hardee would leave Breckinridge behind, to remain on the hills north of town in reserve, and swing south swiftly,
attacking the Union right and enveloping it. Polk would then join the attack,
crushing Rosecrans's right flank. The Federal communications would be disrupted, and Rosecrans's men might be encircled and pushed against the river
and routed.

There was only one problem. Simultaneously, Rosecrans anticipated
attacking the Confederate right, turning it, disrupting Bragg's communications, and pinning him against the river. The two battle plans, conceived at
and planned for the same time, were exactly complementary. Having them
unfold as such would produce two armies both turning clockwise, doing a
large dance with tens of thousands of men in sync with each other across the
Tennessee landscape. Crittenden would send two divisions eastward across
Stones River, into the hills to attack Breckinridge, and establish an artillery
position that would dominate the battlefield. McCook would attack the
Confederate center and left with the divisions of Sheridan, Davis, and Johnson. Thomas (and John M. Palmer's division) would make light assaults on
the northern segment of the Confederate center until he could support
Crittenden. McCook constructed dozens of campfires along the Union right
to suggest large numbers of men on that side of the line.

Bragg ordered the movement on the evening of December 30, and during the night that followed, Cleburne's division shifted southward, supporting McCown's division, already in place on the Confederate left. Wharton's
cavalry spread south of the end of the infantry line, to assist in turning the
Union right. At the same time, on the Union left, engineers and pioneer
troops prepared several fords along Stones River for crossing, ordered to
prepare the Federal turning movement. But the initial units to move, the divisions of Van Cleve and Wood, only received orders on the morning of December 31. By this time parts of the Union army, one of Wood's brigade
commanders included, learned about the shift of Cleburne. At this point security and intelligence faltered in Rosecrans's army. Rosecrans did not adequately reconnoiter the advanced Union positions prior to the planned
attack; Crittenden learned of Cleburne's movement but failed to respond or
alert Rosecrans; and McCook did not reconnoiter the end of the Union line.
The plan was established effectively, but the Union commanders neglected
looking after the details that might have made it work.

Despite the many fires burning in McCook's increasingly vacated
camps, Hardee and Wharton launched a vigorous attack on the Federal right
about 6 A.M. on December 31. The weather was cold and wet, and McCook's
men faced a bleak landscape of dark cedar thickets and seasonally abandoned cotton and cornfields to gaze upon before the attack. McCown's blistering surprise attack seemed at first like a repetition of Shiloh, with many

Federal soldiers caught completely off guard, slumbering or eating breakfast in camp. Despite the startling blow, however, many of the Federal troops quickly went on the defensive and offered stiff resistance. The sudden, heavy firing of muskets signaled "an overwhelming force," recalled Capt. Gates P. Thruston, an aide of McCook's. Seeing the onrushing Confederates was "a thrilling spectacle that a soldier might see once in a lifetime of military service." The ground was suddenly covered with wounded men and dead horses, and the shrieks of shattered lives echoed throughout the stands of timber and open fields. One of the first soldiers injured in the fight was Brig. Gen. Edward N. Kirk, an Ohioan who had gone to Illinois and become a lawyer and a soldier. The Minié bullet that struck Kirk entered the side of his spine, injuring his hip, and lodged next to the sacrum. He lingered for seven months before dying in Chicago at the Fremont House Hotel.

Cleburne soon joined in the attack, and despite parts of this action seeming like a "tidal wave" to soldiers in the brigades of Kirk and Brig. Gen. August Willich, Davis's men helped to defend against an overall rout. Polk joined the attack by sending his initial battle line, formed by Withers's division, racing in and firing volleys of musketry against the left end of Davis's division and the right end of Sheridan's division. This attack initially succeeded but then was repulsed by the Federals, and so Polk sent Cheatham reeling into the fight, and then added the brigade of Brig. Gen. John K. Jackson, marching from Breckinridge's reserve position, past the W. Murfree House, and across the river to support the Confederate assault. The Federal right itself, the troops under Johnson, had been pushed back and scattered in confusion. Wharton's cavalry had penetrated into the Union rear, pushing back the smaller Union cavalry brigade of Col. Louis Zahm and endangering McCook's ammunition train, in the vicinity of the General Smith House on the Wilkinson Turnpike. But Polk seemed unable to send a thrust through the Union center, which would have been triumphant. On the Union left, meanwhile, Van Cleve finally advanced after 7 A.M., crossing Stones River at McFadden's Ford and maneuvering toward Breckinridge and the hills, and Wood was preparing to do the same slightly farther south. Before 8 A.M., however, Rosecrans began to panic and had second thoughts. He ordered Wood to halt without crossing the river and instructed Thomas to move Rousseau's division to support Sheridan, bolstering the defense against Polk's repeated attacks. He also ordered Van Cleve to abort his mission of attacking Breckinridge. Instead, Van Cleve was now instructed to guard the nearby fords along the river and withdraw to the vicinity of the railroad to await further orders.

During the heavy fighting created by Polk's attacks, Sheridan's artillery fired hotly into the rebel lines, helping to prevent a successful Confederate sweep of the Union center. One of the key figures in helping to coordinate the Union counterattack along this part of the line was Brig. Gen. Joshua Woodrow Sill. As he led a spirited counterattack against the Rebels in this area, Sill was shot in the head and killed.

Hardee's continued forceful attacks, along with solid pressure from Polk's unit, soon pushed the Federal right flank back. By late morning the divisions of Davis and Sheridan scrambled northward past the Harding and Griscom houses, near the Blanton House north of the Wilkinson Turnpike. Davis's retreating men continued to be harassed by Wharton's cavalry, spread to the west. Zahm's Union cavalry brigade had been sent fleeing from the field and was headed toward La Vergne on the Nashville Turnpike. Sheridan's division launched a stinging counterattack against Hardee's right, inflicting heavy casualties before retreating back to a new position in the woods north of the Wilkinson Turnpike. Now lodged between Rousseau to his right and Negley to his left, Sheridan's men kept up a terrific fire against the oncoming soldiers of A. P. Stewart's brigade. Lucius Polk's Confederate brigade captured a key Federal battery. Sheridan's soldiers remained brave but their ammunition began to run out. Rousseau and Negley both defended against further attacks, solidifying the Union line, but the ammunition train had to be moved eastward to prevent its capture by Wharton and so could not be used effectively for resupplying the front-line troops such as Sheridan's. Wharton did succeed in capturing stragglers and an artillery battery, and he caused considerable alarm in the Union rear, although he was stopped by a regiment of Zahm's cavalry and portions of other cavalry units that returned to the fight by late morning. The rapid action of the Confederate soldiers had stunned some Union boys. "The line in advance of us, a brigade that had passed us only a few minutes before, had been crushed and beaten back, and were drifting toward us in utter confusion," recalled Cpl. Ebenezer Hannaford of the 6th Ohio Infantry. "Organization and discipline were forgotten; they were fleeing for their lives ... and almost before I had time to comprehend its meaning, the rebel bullets were hissing all about us. We were in action."

Breckinridge continued to be isolated during the late morning. John Pegram's cavalry was spread in a north-south line along the Lebanon Turnpike and failed to reconnoiter the approach or subsequent retreat of Van Cleve, who had withdrawn by now back across the river, following Rosecrans's changed orders. By late morning the furious attacks by Hardee and Polk were running out of steam as units and commanders were intermingled, reducing their effectiveness in coordinating action, and as the Confederates, who had attacked repeatedly, tired. By late morning Bragg was growing frustrated with the lack of tactical success of Polk's and Hardee's attack. He ordered his reserves up. Breckinridge first protested that he was about to be attacked and could not move, unaware of the actual dispositions of Union troops. He finally complied and moved southward, only to find no Union troops in the vicinity. To further confuse coordination on the Confederate side, Bragg believed that a large Union force might be moving southward on the Lebanon Turnpike, toward Murfreesboro. Afraid of the possibility of an attack from behind, he ordered Breckinridge to stay put and not to cross Stones River.

Hardee now resumed several northward attacks into what was fast becoming a disorganized, clustered Union "line." Many of the Union brigades were attempting to reform along the Nashville Turnpike; the holdouts, in the divisions of Sheridan, Negley, and Rousseau, were grouped in the woods west of the Cowan House and south of the turnpike. Rosecrans desperately tried to regroup his army and rally his men to fight with great force. Rosecrans's chief of staff, Lt. Col. Julius P. Garesché, worried over his commander's exposure to small arms and shellfire. "Never mind me," said Rosecrans, a fatalistic Roman Catholic. "Make the sign of the cross and go in. This battle must be won." But it was Garesché who should have been more careful. Early in the afternoon, while riding with Rosecrans and staff along the railroad line, Garesché was struck squarely by a cannonball and decapitated. Rosecrans was shaken at his best army friend's gruesome, sudden death, which splattered some of Garesché's brains onto Rosecrans's overcoat, and he muttered something to the effect that "good men must die in battle." At other times Rosecrans's religious nature could be less forgiving. Spotting Sheridan walking back from his line, covered in gunpowder and swearing over the shortage of ammunition, Rosecrans admonished his fellow Ohioan, declaring, "Watch your language. Remember, the first bullet may send you to eternity."

By II A.M. Sheridan's division had exhausted its ammunition, and Hardee plunged units into the gap created by Sheridan's northward movement. A measure of chaos now infused the Union line; Rousseau and Negley fought off vicious attacks from the front even as Negley was exposed to fire from his left and rear, as Polk's line was extending northward past the Cowan House, past the railroad, and to Harker's Crossing on the river. Though his division fought stubbornly for a time, Negley ultimately had to withdraw, and this forced Palmer to pull back as well. Palmer's toughest brigade, posted on his left flank, dug in and fought savagely in the Round Woods. It was the brigade of Col. William B. Hazen, and the ground it fought to hold during the early afternoon came to be called "Hell's Half Acre." Hazen described the off-and-on fight in his after-action report. "The enemy now took cover in the wood," he wrote, "keeping up so destructive a fire as to make it necessary to retire behind the embankments of the railroad. . . . A sharp fight was kept up from this position until about two P.M., when another assault in regular lines and in great force, supported by artillery, was made upon this position."

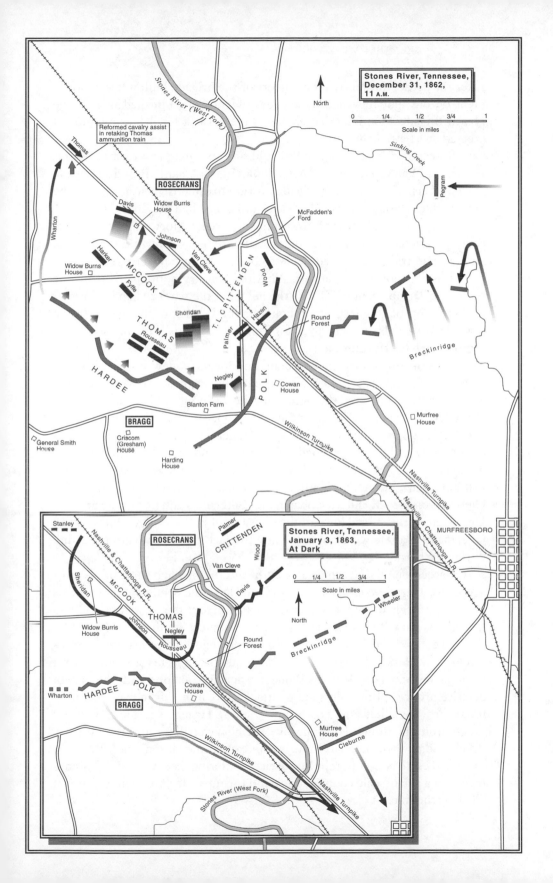

Stones River, Tennessee,
December 31, 1862,
11 A.M.

North

0 1/4 1/2 3/4 1
Scale in miles

Stones River (West Fork)

Sinking Creek

Reformed cavalry assist
in retaking Thomas
ammunition train

Thomas

Pegram

ROSECRANS

Davis
Widow Burris
House

McFadden's
Ford

Wharton

Johnson

Van Cleve

Wood

Harker

Widow Burns
House

Fyffe

McCOOK

Hazen

Breckinridge

Sheridan

THOMAS

Round
Forest

Rousseau

HARDEE

Palmer

POLK

Negley

Cowan
House

Blanton Farm

Murfree
House

BRAGG

Wilkinson Turnpike

Nashville Turnpike

General Smith
House

Griscom
(Gresham)
House

Harding
House

Nashville & Chattanooga R.R.

MURFREESBORO

Stanley

Palmer

Stones River, Tennessee,
January 3, 1863,
At Dark

Nashville & Chattanooga R.R.

ROSECRANS

CRITTENDEN

Wood

Sheridan

Van Cleve

0 1/4 1/2 3/4 1
Scale in miles

McCOOK

Davis

Wheeler

Johnson

THOMAS

North

Breckinridge

Widow Burris
House

Negley

Rousseau

Round
Forest

Wharton

HARDEE

POLK

Cowan
House

BRAGG

Murfree
House

Cleburne

Wilkinson Turnpike

Stones River (West Fork)

Nashville Turnpike

After the battle, the surviving members of the brigade built a stone monument on the spot they had defended so vigorously. Finished in 1863, the Hazen Brigade Monument is famous as the earliest Civil War monument erected on a battlefield.

Rosecrans desperately tried to hold his crumbling and retreating line. He ordered Van Cleve into the fight, deploying Col. James P. Fyffe's brigade and Col. Charles G. Harker's brigade forward to establish a position near the Widow Burns House, across which McCook's men had previously retreated. Col. Milo S. Hascall's brigade was similarly ordered forward but found its route obstructed by confused and retreating troops. Meanwhile, the Federal ammunition train, which had made a circuitous journey across the battlefield, was still not out of danger. Wharton's cavalry approached it on the Nashville Turnpike, northwest of the field, but the scattered and disorganized segments of Union cavalry fought him off. What appeared to be leaning toward a Union disaster stabilized for a time, with Davis's and Johnson's men regrouping by early afternoon.

Early in the afternoon Rosecrans solidified his new line, which now consisted of a convex arc along the railroad line northwest of Murfreesboro. Davis's division anchored the right, with the divisions of Sheridan, Johnson, Van Cleve, Rousseau, Palmer, and finally Wood (on the left) in succession, and Negley's division in reserve behind Palmer. Arriving at noon, the Union cavalry of David S. Stanley finally reorganized and spread northwest of the battle line, facing Wheeler's and Wharton's Confederate troopers. (Wheeler had also arrived at noon.) Hardee faced the Union right and center, with Cleburne on the left and McCown in the center. Polk squared off against the Union left, with a mixed force of the divisions of Breckinridge, Withers, and Cheatham. Matters were not helped by the fact that Cheatham was drunk during the battle.

Hardee's high tide came early in the afternoon when some of his most aggressive brigade commanders—Liddell, Johnson, Vaughan, and Lucius Polk—approached Rosecrans's headquarters first at the Cowan House and later the Widow Burris House, both short distances south of the Nashville Turnpike. By midafternoon, however, Hardee had received stinging counterblows by Harker, Fyffe, and by Col. Samuel Beatty's brigade, along with Capt. James St. Clair Morton's Pioneer Brigade. Unhappy with the lack of decisive progress, Bragg decided to attack the Union left in overwhelming force, throwing all of Polk's corps into the fray. Hazen's brigade stubbornly fought from the Round Forest despite the heavy artillery fire, and by 4 P.M. Breckinridge was ordered to come into line opposing Hazen's men. Breckinridge attacked and was repulsed twice, suffering heavy losses. Thomas launched a small-scale counterattack and the musketry fire then died down all along the line.

Despite the failed last attack, Bragg felt that he had won a decisive victory. It's difficult to comprehend how he reckoned this, but he told his subordinates the fact and had his soldiers dig in. Rosecrans, nervous about the shattered condition of his army, held a council of war on the final night of 1862 and polled his wing and division commanders about what should be done. Some felt the army had been "whipped" and ought to retreat during the night. Thomas, Crittenden, and Rosecrans himself felt this was wrong, and that the army should stay and fight. Rosecrans reorganized his forces and early in the morning of January 1 sent Van Cleve's division across McFadden's Ford once again to occupy the high hills north of the town, preparing them for artillery use.

By coincidence, each army spent New Year's Day 1863, reorganizing, repositioning, and awaiting further developments from the enemy. Skirmishes erupted along the lines at scattered points but amounted to little. Both sides entrenched. Wheeler's cavalry tested troops in the Union rear, raiding supply trains and even escorting wounded soldiers. Because of the movements of Federal wagons along the Nashville Turnpike, Wheeler felt Rosecrans was readying for a withdrawal, and he let Bragg know. Rosecrans, meanwhile, spent the day strengthening Van Cleve's position on the hills east of the river. Van Cleve's division, commanded by Beatty (Van Cleve had been shot in the right leg and sent back to Nashville), consisted of the brigades of Fyffe, Col. Samuel W. Price, and Col. Benjamin C. Grider. Breckinridge had recrossed to face him from the south.

After the quiet came the storm. Early on the morning of January 2, Bragg ordered Breckinridge to attack. At 4 A.M., under protest that the assault would be suicidal, Breckinridge brought the brigades of Hanson, Brig. Gen. Gideon J. Pillow, Col. Randall Lee Gibson, and Preston forward. Initially, Breckinridge's attack succeeded marvelously, striking the Union soldiers like thunder, but massed artillery across Stones River opened with a horrendous boom and concentrated a tremendous shelling onto Breckinridge's hapless soldiers. The attack was forced back, and the Southerners were severely cut up. "My poor Orphan Brigade torn to pieces," Breckinridge allegedly said, with tears in his eyes, referring to his special brigade of Kentuckians who "couldn't go home" because their homes were in Federal occupation. Two Confederate generals were lost in the final attack. Tennessee-born Brig. Gen James E. Rains was struck by a Minié bullet that passed through his right hand and into his chest, killing him. Brig. Gen. Roger W. Hanson of Kentucky was struck by the lead strap of a shell, injuring his thigh. Breckinridge himself held on to the wound to decrease the bleeding, but Hanson died in a nearby house on January 4.

The Confederate assault was wrecked by Union cannon fire and stopped by Federal infantry, who crossed the river and blocked the advance.

Supplies finally reached the exhausted Federal commander on the morning of January 3. Thomas attacked later in the day, driving back a portion of the Confederate line, and Wheeler's cavalry unsuccessfully attempted to disrupt the ammunition bound for Rosecrans via the Nashville Turnpike. The battle was finished. Bragg moved his units south through Murfreesboro, with cavalry covering the withdrawal. Hardee moved out on the evening of January 3; Polk followed during the night, and Cleburne and Breckinridge acted as a rear guard, finally departing the battlefield early on the morning of January 4. Rosecrans moved his army into Murfreesboro but did not follow Bragg.

In the end, both sides claimed a victory of sorts, and neither had actually achieved one. Bragg, solidly befriended by Jefferson Davis, found virtually no other support in the battle's wake. His fellow officers and subordinates in Confederate service all lost faith in him, believing the victory should have been forceful and decisive. Bragg adopted the tactic of blaming everyone but himself. "It has come to my Knowledge that many of these accusations and insinuations are from Staff officers of my Generals who persistently assert that the movement [from Murfreesboro] was made against the opinion and advice of their chiefs and while the enemy was in full retreat," Bragg asserted in a circular sent to his corps and division commanders. "False or true the soldiers have no means of judging me rightly or getting the facts and the effect on them will be the Same, a loss of confidence and a consequent demoralization of the whole army." Bragg would continue to have such command problems for months to come.

Union and Confederate troops alike professed shock over the carnage at Stones River. "An awful battle," penned Col. Nicholas Longworth Anderson of the 6th Ohio Infantry. "Thank God for my merciful preservation! Terrible fire all day. Jones, Terry, Foster, and others killed. Ordered early in line of battle as reserve. . . . Sixth Ohio met the enemy unsupported. . . . The regiment behaved nobly and worthy its reputation." The losses at Stones River were large. Of about 41,400 effectives, Union losses were 1,677 killed, 7,543 wounded, and 3,686 missing; Confederate casualties were 1,294 killed, 7,945 wounded, and 2,500 missing out of about 35,000 engaged.

THEN CAME THE MUD MARCH. Following the disaster at Fredericksburg, Maj. Gen. Ambrose E. Burnside moved his Army of the Potomac up along the Rappahannock River, hoping to turn Robert E. Lee's left. The movement began on January 20. The weather was so bad, with nearly constant, heavy, icy-cold rains, that the roads became almost impassable for marching soldiers, let alone wagons, artillery, and equipment. The dubious maneuver was quickly dubbed the "Mud March." Burnside had hoped to cross his main force at Banks's Ford and move south toward Salem Church, taking Lee by surprise. He would be assisted by a diversion at Muddy Creek, southeast of Fredericksburg, and a feint at United States Ford, north of Chancellorsville. In the end, Burnside's army was simply coming apart at the seams. The commander quarreled extensively with his subordinates, and morale among the common soldiers—after being whipped at Fredericksburg and marching endlessly in freezing mud—was at its lowest point during the war.

Finally, Lincoln again had had enough. He removed Burnside from command of the Army of the Potomac and assigned Maj. Gen. Joseph Hooker as his replacement. A brash, sometimes hard-drinking egotist, Hooker was well known for criticizing his superiors and for believing that he could do a better job as army commander than any of the previous generals. Despite these facts, Lincoln needed an aggressive fighter who had some strategic vision. "I have heard, in such a way as to believe it, of your recently saying that both the Army and the Government needed a Dictator," he wrote Hooker on January 26. "Of course it was not *for* this, but in spite of it, that I have given you the command. Only those generals who gain successes, can set up dictators. What I now ask of you is military success, and I will risk the dictatorship. . . . And now, beware of rashness. Beware of rashness, but with energy and sleepless vigilance go forward and give us victories."

In the wake of Fredericksburg and the Mud March, confidence from Southern soldiers and civilians was rising rapidly. "Well, let them come! They will be annihilated," challenged the Richmond war clerk John B. Jones of an anticipated offensive toward the city. "If Hooker had 300,000, he could not now come to Richmond! "Our generals, I think, have less dread of 'Fighting Joe Hooker' than anyone they have yet to contend against," wrote Maj. Thomas J. Goree, an aide of Longstreet's. But Lee was concerned about a variety of practical matters in the army, despite its magnificent performance at Fredericksburg. "More than once have most promising opportunities been lost for want of men to take advantage of them, and victory itself has been made to put on the appearance of defeat, because our diminished and exhausted troops have been unable to renew a successful struggle against fresh numbers of the enemy," he wrote the secretary of war on January 10, asking for more men. "The lives of our soldiers are too precious to be sacrificed in the attainment of successes that inflict no loss upon the enemy beyond the actual loss in battle."

A FEW ACTIONS HAPPENED in the Trans-Mississippi theater early in the year. At Helena, Arkansas, on New Year's Day, a small band of Texas Rangers attacked the pickets of Brig. Gen. Willis A. Gorman's Federals. A more significant operation came a few days later when Maj. Gen. John A. McClernand launched his operation against Vicksburg. McClernand somewhat deviously discussed the expedition with Lincoln and received his tentative approval but informed neither Henry Halleck nor U. S. Grant, and instead of attacking Vicksburg, he set out from the Mississippi River to reduce Fort Hindman on the Arkansas River. McClernand's Army of the Mississippi consisted of about 32,000 infantry, 1,000 cavalry, and 40 pieces of artillery. They had some 50 transports and 13 gunboats under the command of Comdr. David Dixon Porter. McClernand's force was organized into two army corps led by Brig. Gen. George W. Morgan (13th Corps) and Maj. Gen. William T. Sherman (15th Corps). Morgan's corps was composed of the divisions of Brig. Gens. Andrew J. Smith (brigades of Brig. Gen. Stephen G. Burbridge and Col. William J. Landram) and Peter J. Osterhaus (brigades of Cols. Lionel A. Sheldon and Daniel W. Lindsey). Sherman's corps contained the divisions of Brig. Gens. Frederick Steele (brigades of Brig. Gens. Frank P. Blair, Jr., Charles E. Hovey, and John M. Thayer) and David Stuart (brigades of Cols. Giles A. Smith and Thomas Kilby Smith).

On the Arkansas, some forty-five miles downriver from Pine Bluff, stood Fort Hindman, a bastioned fort with heavy guns and an eighteen-foot ditch that protected this approach to the Mississippi. Inside the fort, also called Arkansas Post, were about 5,000 men commanded by Brig. Gen. Thomas J. Churchill. His troops, consisting primarily of Texas cavalry and Arkansas infantry, were organized into three brigades commanded by Cols. Robert R. Garland, James Deshler, and John W. Dunnington.

McClernand not only failed to consult the department commander, Grant, but he reorganized troops that had been used in Sherman's unsuccessful Chickasaw Bluffs expedition the previous month and, before Sherman could object, assumed command by virtue of the seniority of his commission. McClernand began his move on January 4, and five days later Lindsey's brigade disembarked on the west bank of the Arkansas River to block a possible Confederate retreat. The bulk of McClernand's force landed on the east side of the river. On January 10 the assault on Arkansas Post commenced. By 11 A.M. the brigades of Sheldon, Landram, and Burbridge took a leading position in the assault; Steele's division became disoriented in the swampy ground and did not participate in the attack on the first day. Porter's gunboat fleet consisted of his own tinclad USS *Black Hawk;* the ironclads USS *Baron de Kalb,* USS *Louisville,* and USS *Cincinnati;* the timberclad USS *Lexington;* and the stern-wheelers USS *Signal,* USS *New Era,* USS *Romeo,* USS *Rattler,* and USS *Glide.*

By 3 P.M. McClernand decided to launch a full infantry assault on the fort. Porter's gunboat fleet shelled the fort with great force, softening its defenses considerably and enabling the Union attack to work effectively, eliminating most of the fire from the Confederate guns in the fort. "You can't expect men to stand up against the fire of those gunboats," a captive Confederate soldier reportedly told Porter. But Porter's fleet moved back out of

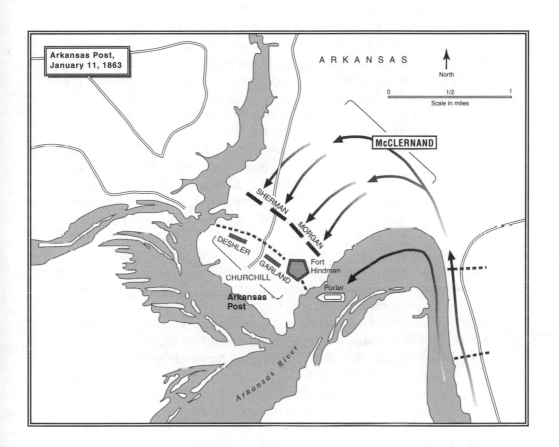

Arkansas Post,
January 11, 1863

ARKANSAS

North

0   1/2   1
Scale in miles

McCLERNAND

SHERMAN

MORGAN

DESHLER

GARLAND

CHURCHILL

Fort
Hindman

Porter

Arkansas
Post

Arkansas River

range of the Confederate guns after the infantry attack did not take place on time. By the morning of January 11, after Churchill had received orders that he should hold the fort at any cost, a well-coordinated attack by both the army and navy forces finally occurred. By 3 P.M., twenty-four hours after Mc-Clernand had planned, Arkansas Post had surrendered. Churchill exaggerated the numbers just slightly in his after-action report, excusing his surrender. "In no battle of the war has the disparity of forces been so unequal," he claimed. "The enemy's force was full 50,000, when ours did not exceed 3,000, and yet for two days did we signally repulse and hold in check that immense body of the enemy." Losses at Arkansas Post were relatively light. The Union army lost 134 killed, 898 wounded, and 29 missing. Churchill reported 60 killed and 80 wounded, and Sherman reported that 4,791 prisoners were embarked on Federal transports. The operation was a success for the Union, although it didn't help the campaign for Vicksburg in any substantial way. Grant ordered McClernand back to the planned operations on Vicksburg, thereby terminating the Army of the Mississippi on January 12.

Grant, however, had blundered by issuing a highly controversial order. Equating Jews with peddlers and speculators that plagued his army, Grant issued General Orders No. 11 on December 17, 1862, at Oxford, Mississippi. A portion of the document read: "The Jews, as a class, violating every regulation of trade established by the Treasury Department, and also Department orders, are hereby expelled from the Department." Although the controversial order was later revoked by Lincoln, the damage was done. Grant's anti-Semitic order spread noxious social and political effects over the American landscape for years. A month after Grant's issuance of the order, newspaperman Charles A. Dana, who had been dispatched to do some scouting for Secretary Stanton, tried to summarize the situation. "The mania for sudden fortunes made in cotton, raging in a vast population of Jews and Yankees scattered throughout this whole country," he reported, "has to an alarming extent corrupted and demoralized the army. Every colonel, captain, or quartermaster is in secret partnership with some operator in cotton; every soldier dreams of adding a bale of cotton to his monthly pay."

Most soldiers in the western theater of war simply wondered what they were doing there. Near Vicksburg, 1st Lt. Cyrus F. Boyd of the 34th Iowa Infantry couldn't believe his surroundings. "The flat space between the River and the levee is knee deep in black mud," he penned. "Then comes the levee which is about ten feet high and twenty feet wide at the base and this is all the dry ground we can find. . . . Saw many hospitals along the levee and there are thousands of sick men here. The levee for long distances is full of *new made graves*. This is a hard place for a sick man. He must have plenty of *grit* or *die*."

IN THE CHILLY FIRST WEEKS OF 1863, naval and combined actions outnumbered land engagements. At Galveston, Texas, fighting erupted on January 1. Confederate Maj. Gen. John B. Magruder, veteran of the Peninsular campaign, attacked the Union-held garrison and the surrounding Federal flotilla with improvised gunboats and army troops termed the Army of Galveston. Magruder surprised the town's soldiers at dawn and a four-hour fight ensued, during which the Confederates used the cottonclads CSS *Neptune* and CSS *Bayou City* to carry sharpshooters and artillery to bombard the city and attack the Federal gunboats USS *Harriet Lane,* USS *Westfield,* and USS *Clifton;* the screw gunboats USS *Owasco* and USS *Sachem;* and the schooner USS *Corypheus.* The *Harriet Lane* was captured and the *Westfield* grounded and exploded. The garrison of 260 soldiers of the 42d Massachusetts Infantry was dispersed. The Confederate ships were completely victorious, driving away the remaining Union ships, and Galveston was again in Southern hands and would stay that way, although blockaded, until June 1865. Magruder commended his troops: "You have repossessed yourselves of your beautiful 'Island City,'" he wrote, "and made its hostile garrison, intrenched behind inaccessible barricades, surrender to you at discretion. . . . Your general is proud to command you."

Ten days later, near Galveston, ships clashed again when the famed cruiser CSS *Alabama,* commanded by Capt. Raphael Semmes, attacked and sank the schooner USS *Hatteras.* The Federal ship, commanded by Lt. Comdr. Homer C. Blake, spotted a peculiar ship and approached it, only to find the fearsome *Alabama.* When Comm. Henry H. Bell's USS *Brooklyn* passed the wreck of the *Hatteras,* Bell saw only "two masts of a sunken vessel standing out of water. The tops and yards were awash, topmasts up, and a United States naval pennant gaily flying from the main truck. . . . She lies in 9½ fathoms water about 20 miles south, true, from Galveston lighthouse."

At Sabine Pass, Texas, on January 21, two Federal blockading ships were captured by Confederate steamers. The USS *Morning Light* and the USS *Velocity* were attacked by the cottonclads CSS *Josiah Bell* and CSS *Uncle Ben.* At Charleston on January 31, the rams CSS *Chicora* and CSS *Palmetto State* attacked the Union blockading fleet off the Carolina coast in a dense, early morning fog. The USS *Keystone State* was crippled; the USS *Memphis* towed her off as she began to sink. The USS *Mercedita* was rammed and sank. The USS *Quaker City* was badly damaged. The USS *Augusta* was hit near the boiler. The USS *Housatonic* fought back with heavy cannonfire, forcing the Confederate rams to withdraw. A degree of Union naval success came at Bayou Teche, Louisiana, on January 14. Here Federal gunboats joined with army troops to attack Confederate defenses, and they brought to bear a flotilla comprising the USS *Kinsman,* USS *Estrella,* USS *Calhoun,* and USS

Diana. The heavy shelling of these ships forced the Southern artillerists on shore to withdraw. The Confederate gunboat CSS *Cotton* engaged the larger Union ships but was forced to evacuate its position, was set ablaze, and burned and sank.

A few more scattered actions marked the first weeks of 1863. At Fort McAllister, Georgia, south of Savannah, Federal gunboats attacked on February 1. The ironclad gunboat USS *Montauk,* under Comdr. John L. Worden, who had commanded the USS *Monitor* at Hampton Roads, assaulted the Rebel guns. In the early morning mist, the *Montauk* took position 600 yards from the fort, assisted by the ships USS *Seneca,* USS *Wissahickon,* USS *Dawn,* and the mortar schooner USS *C. P. Williams.* During a four-hour engagement, the *Montauk* was struck forty-eight times. The blockade runner CSS *Rattlesnake* exchanged fire with the Union ships. The Confederate troops inside Fort McAllister were commanded by Col. Robert H. Anderson, who later wrote that "the enemy fired steadily and with remarkable precision. Their fire was terrible. Their mortar fire was unusually fine, a large number of their shells bursting directly over the battery." At month's end, at Ossabaw Sound, Georgia, once again near Fort McAllister, the same ships encountered each other and this time the *Montauk,* supported by the other Federal ships, shelled and destroyed the *Rattlesnake.* Under heavy fire from McAllister, the Federal ships nonetheless pounded the *Rattlesnake* and set her ablaze, exploding the magazine "with terrific violence, shattering her smoking ruins."

Back out west, the Navy helped to support the skirmishing that accompanied U. S. Grant's renewal of a campaign toward Vicksburg. By February 19 the river ironclad gunboat USS *Indianola* ran past the Vicksburg batteries and engaged three Confederate ships south of Warrenton, Mississippi. The action occurred on February 24. The CSS *William H. Webb,* CSS *Queen of the West,* and CSS *Beatty,* the squadron commanded by Maj. Joseph L. Brent, attempted to overtake the Union gunboat with their greater speed. The *Webb* and the *Queen of the West* rammed the *Indianola,* crushing the starboard wheel, disabling the starboard rudder, and starting onboard leaks. Powerless, the *Indianola* ran aground and surrendered. Afterward, Porter ended his attempts to blockade the Red River, writing that the loss of the *Indianola* was "the most humiliating affair that has occurred during this rebellion. . . . My only hope is that she has blown up."

As THE WAR CONTINUED, political gains were made and losses were suffered. In December 1862, after six months of discussion, the U.S. House of Representatives passed a bill creating the state of West Virginia. On December 31, Lincoln signed the act, making West Virginia the thirty-fifth state in the Union (it was admitted on June 20, 1863). If all of Virginia would not yet come back, at least its loyal mountain counties would. Congress organized Arizona

Territory on February 24, 1863. On March 3, Congress made Idaho a territory. Various officers weathered storms of criticism from their fellow officers and civilians alike. In Missouri, Col. Lewis Merrill was not exactly worshiped. "I am an old soldier, was with General Macelelan [*sic*] at Williamsburg and before Richmond, was wounded at Fair Oaks now discharged a cripple for life, but in my time, never saw such behavior as this regiment of Genl. Merrill," wrote Thomas Schrader of Warrenton, Missouri. "He is drunk and insulting, no discipline, never had a picket guard round the camp. Soldiers get drunk, brake in family houses. They have stold so many nigers they and they are pulling down fences, throwing rocks again houses, brakin windows, killing all the farmers hogs and every thing mean that on Union men too. Unless something is done soon I will try head quarters at Washington. They are not here for any good, so please send them to some place where they may be used." Other officers were more straightforward, as with Nathan Bedford Forrest's comment to Joseph Wheeler: "I will be in my coffin before I fight again under your command."

To lift the spirits of Northern soldiers who were suffering in the cold and with the whistles of bullets in the air, the composer George F. Root issued a new song that caught on with instant popularity. Called "The Battle Cry of Freedom," it was issued for a rally in Chicago. It became such a hit that Southern soldiers created substitute lyrics to enable their side to sing the tune as well. On the march, as the weather slowly warmed toward the spring of 1863, many trails echoed with the song's words: "Yes, We'll rally round the flag / Boys, we'll rally once again / Shouting the battle-cry of Freedom / We will rally from the hillside, we'll gather from the plain / Shouting the battle-cry of Freedom / The Union forever / Hurrah! boys, Hurrah! / Down with the traitor, up with the star / While we rally round the flag boys, rally once again / Shouting the battle cry of Freedom."

CHAPTER 15

The Campaign for Vicksburg

SPRINGTIME IN 1863 brought a blend of hope and trepidation on each side concerning the new campaigns. In the east, Hooker continued to ready the Army of the Potomac to face Lee again. In Tennessee, the armies of Bragg and Rosecrans were idle, swelling the chorus of discontent on the home fronts North and South. It was becoming increasingly clear to the government in Richmond that a military concentration was being made toward Vicksburg, the bastion on the Mississippi River, by a variety of forces under the command of U. S. Grant. The Northern officers were much criticized during this period, with Rosecrans and Hooker attacked in the press and even Grant, with his few initial forays toward Vicksburg unsuccessful, coming under criticism. The first Federal draft was enacted on March 3 by President Lincoln; it called for all healthy males between 20 and 45 to enter the draft unless they purchased their exemption by hiring a substitute or paying commutation of $300. This led to the sarcastic phrase "a rich man's war but a poor man's fight." But the draft was not significant; only 162,535 men were raised by it throughout the war, a mere 6 percent of the enlisted men of the U.S. Army. Some 116,188 furnished substitutes, and 86,724 paid commutation. The first draft of the war had actually come from the Confederacy. The First Conscription Act was enacted in Richmond on April 16, 1862, and required men between ages 18 and 35, "to meet exigencies of the country and the absolute necessity of keeping in the service our gallant army. . . ." Altogether, a total of 81,993 men were reported in camps of instruction and 76,206 in service without attending camps. The Second Conscription Act was enacted on September 27, 1862, affecting Southern men ages 18 to 45, although its implementation was delayed until July 1863.

The push by elements of the abolition movement to commit the United States Army to employ black combat troops gained momentum now that the Emancipation Proclamation had been issued. "I urge you to fly to arms, and smite with death the power that would bury the government and your liberty in the same hopeless grave," proclaimed Frederick Douglass in his famous broadside "Men of Color to Arms." "The day dawns," he continued, "the morning star is bright upon the horizon! The iron gate of our prison stands half open. One gallant rush from the North will fling it wide open, while four millions of our brothers and sisters shall march out into liberty." Soon the 1st South Carolina Infantry, led by the famous Massachusetts abolitionist Col. Thomas Wentworth Higginson, would become the first African-American regiment. Others would follow, notably the "national" regiments (containing black soldiers recruited from around the country), the celebrated 54th and 55th Massachusetts infantries. "The bare sight of fifty thousand armed, and drilled black soldiers on the banks of the Mississippi, would end the rebellion at once," Lincoln wrote Andrew Johnson that spring.

But for the present only white soldiers would fight. On March 4, Federal troops sent to Franklin, Tennessee, moved on Spring Hill and Thompson's Station to the south. They had been ordered by Acting Brig. Gen. Charles C. Gilbert, commanding at Franklin, to reconnoiter toward Columbia. As Confederate forces of Maj. Gen. Earl Van Dorn closed in, the two-day action at Thompson's Station resulted. It was alternatively termed Spring Hill or Unionville. The Union force consisted of a brigade of infantry and a brigade of cavalry from the Army of the Cumberland. At Spring Hill the Federal forces, 2,837 strong, were surrounded by Van Dorn's infantry and the cavalry division of Brig. Gen. William H. Jackson, including the hard-fighting brigade of Brig. Gen. Nathan Bedford Forrest. After more than a day of periodic severe fighting, the Union infantry surrendered, along with the 18th Ohio Artillery, badly outnumbered by the Southerners. The Union casualties were 173 dead, 204 wounded, and 1 missing; Confederate losses were 56 killed, 289 wounded, and 12 missing. Van Dorn's men captured 1,306 prisoners. Col. John Coburn later bitterly complained of their treatment, describing his incarceration in Richmond's Libby prison. "Food consisted of a scanty ration," he wrote, "half a pound a day of bread and of putrid, starveling meat, totally unfit for use, filling the room with a foul stench . . . two wretched blankets were given to each officer and one to each man; they were lousy, filthy, fetid. The prison swarmed with vermin. . . . Scurvy, erysipelas, inflammatory sore throat, rheumatism, fever, lockjaw, delirium, and death in its most horrid forms were the legitimate results."

The war in central Tennessee flared again with Forrest's raid on Brentwood and Franklin on March 25. Located between Nashville and Franklin, Brentwood was a small town garrisoned with the 22d Wisconsin Infantry (Lt. Col. Edward Bloodgood). Forrest, commanding a cavalry division, dispatched a cavalry brigade to cross the Little Harpeth River east of Franklin and proceed to Brentwood, cutting telegraph wires and destroying a railroad as well as attacking the Union forces he encountered. Bloodgood's 400 men received a flag of truce from Forrest demanding surrender, to which Bloodgood replied that he would have to be captured by force. After about half an hour of action, Bloodgood was forced to surrender. Rosecrans's subsequent reports showed that "Colonel Bloodgood and his command were captured with such feeble resistance as to reflect disgrace on all concerned." Maj. Gen. Gordon Granger, commanding the Army of Kentucky at Franklin, sent Brig. Gen. Green Clay Smith's cavalry brigade to assist in defending against Forrest, and for several hours in the afternoon the Federal horse soldiers fought with Forrest's mounted troops, for a time gaining back some ground before being pushed back to Brentwood. Smith's losses were 4 killed, 19 wounded, and 4 missing; Forrest's for the whole day were 4 killed, 16 wounded, and 39 missing.

THE MAJOR STRATEGIC FOCUS in the early spring of 1863 centered on Vicksburg. The city's position was naturally defensible, on the eastern shore of the Mississippi River, astride a portion of the waterway that arced sharply eastward, forcing ships to pass within long fields of fire from the Confederate batteries. Grant's ablest lieutenant, William T. Sherman, was now recognized as possessing an astute military mind even by most of his critics. In early March, Sherman pondered the difficulties of capturing Vicksburg. "To invest [the city] we should have a vastly superior force, and should be on the levee side of the River," he warned his father, "but thus far we have not superior forces. . . . Our plan thus far was to prepare three lines of approach; by the main River, by the Yazoo entering at its head, and by the Tensas and Red Rivers, by which we turn Vicksburg and all the Bluffs which lie on the east bank of the River. The latter is the only one which solves all the problems."

Along with his perceptive analysis of the necessities for Federal success at Vicksburg, Sherman continued to worry over security concerns caused by newspapermen. "As you say we have much to fear from anarchy among our people," he opined. "We have long been drifting that way. I would gladly escape it, and will do so if the President can manifest the least impotence with me, or if my command is unshaken by the Press that regard me as their enemy. I do think that the Free Press has done as much to lower our national character and pull down our government as slavery. It is our cause, and this war cannot end until it is brought within proper restraint & limits. I want to see a government so strong that a weak one will not defy it anywhere or at any time, and it makes little difference whether it be South or North."

On March 7 the secondary force along the Mississippi, Maj. Gen. Nathaniel P. Banks's Army of the Gulf, began a move upriver from New Orleans to Baton Rouge. Banks's mission was to support Grant's movements on Vicksburg. Following Sherman's unsuccessful movement via Chickasaw Bluffs in December, Grant ordered several expeditions up various bayous from February through April 1863. He did this despite the relatively high water levels that made military movements a challenge. Grant first ordered a mile-long canal dug across the peninsula of land opposite Vicksburg, hoping that this short circuit would allow ships and army transports to move past the Confederate batteries unscathed, permitting Grant to attack the city from the south. Commenced by Sherman's corps in January, the project was abandoned by March. Next, Grant ordered a more substantial canal excavated at Duckport, about 20 miles downriver from Vicksburg, but this project was abandoned when low water made it untenable. Grant ordered Maj. Gen. James B. McPherson's corps to undertake a 400-mile march from Lake Providence, Louisiana, southward through the swamps and bayous, to swing southward and eventually attack eastward and northward from along the Mississippi. But this plan was abandoned after others were formulated. The Yazoo Pass expedition aimed at opening the levee into the Yazoo Pass, 150 (as the crow flies) miles north of Vicksburg. This would enable Federal transports to enter the Coldwater and Tallahatchie rivers and move toward Vicksburg. This allowed a more secure, albeit much longer, approach for Grant, as it enabled him to employ the Federal navy and permitted protecting the lines of communication along the water, rather than having them raided on land by Confederate cavalry.

In late February the Yazoo Pass expedition got underway. Lt. Comdr. Watson Smith led the naval flotilla, which consisted of the stern wheelers USS *Rattler,* USS *Forest Rose,* USS *Romeo,* USS *Signal,* and USS *Marmora;* the ironclad gunboats USS *Chillicothe* and USS *Baron de Kalb;* and the tugboat USS *S. Bayard.* The army troops along on transports were commanded by Brig. Gen. Leonard F. Ross. From Vicksburg, Lt. Gen. John C. Pemberton, commanding the Army of Mississippi, dispatched one of his divisional commanders, Maj. Gen. William W. Loring, to construct a protective fort. The resulting structure, Fort Pemberton, was built between the Tallahatchie and Yazoo rivers, near the town of Greenwood, Mississippi. Its position blocked the Yazoo Pass approach some ninety miles north of Vicksburg. Positioned on flooded terrain and made from earth and cotton bales covered with sand, Fort Pemberton was hardly the best-designed fortification.

The clash of arms first came to Fort Pemberton on March 11, when the fort's Whitworth rifle, four other heavy guns, and several field pieces opened on the approaching Union ships. The ironclads USS *Chillicothe* and USS *Baron de Kalb* led the attack. During a four-hour fight, the *Chillicothe* maneuvered within 800 yards of the fort and blasted away with her guns, receiving a heavy fire, moving away and returning again to engage the Confederate artillerists. The *Chillicothe* had one gun crew taken out instantly when a Confederate shell ignited a shell inside the muzzle of the gun, exploding the heavy piece and killing 3 sailors and disabling 15 others. "Give them blizzards, boys! Give them blizzards!" Loring allegedly said as he encouraged the Confederate gunners, and the name stuck. Loring was thereafter known as "Old Blizzards." Loring had ordered the steamer CSS *St. Philip* (ex–*Star of the West*) sunk as an obstruction in front of the fort, and this prevented Smith from deploying more than one ship at a time at close range. So Smith removed a field gun from the USS *Rattler* onto shore to aid in shelling the fort. This resulted in a slight improvement, but the Confederate artillery was still too severe to allow the Federal ships to pass.

Two days later the USS *Chillicothe* and the USS *Baron de Kalb* engaged the fort again, and in a severe action the *Chillicothe* sustained thirty-eight hits. The fort was again damaged but withstood the naval assault handsomely. "The *Chillicothe* is an inglorious failure," declared Lt. Col. James H. Wilson, a young engineer along with the army troops on the expedition. "The wooden backing to her armor is of only 9-inch pine, and shivers into pieces every time the plating is struck; her bolt flies off at a terrible rate." On March 16 the attack was again renewed and the Federal ships forced to withdraw. The following day the expedition was called off and the Confederate defenders of Fort Pemberton celebrated a huge psychological victory. But other areas of the Vicksburg campaign now began to overshadow Fort Pemberton in prominence.

In Vicksburg, citizens and soldiers alike—many living in dugout shelters or caves—received a slow shelling from gunboats that periodically tested the city's defenses. The small town had a population of only 4,591, despite its distinctive, high-altitude Court House and towering bluffs overlooking the water. In March an unknown civilian who happened to be a Northerner caught in the city had written a diary entry: "The slow shelling of Vicksburg goes on all the time, and we have grown indifferent. It does not at present interrupt or interfere with daily avocations, but I suspect they are only getting the range of different points; and when they have them all complete, showers of shot will rain on us all at once." The same diarist later reported, "To sit and listen as if waiting for death in a horrible manner would drive me insane."

Banks's movement on Port Hudson was assisted by a naval flotilla moving upriver, commanded by Rear Adm. David G. Farragut. This flotilla included the screw sloops USS *Hartford*, USS *Richmond*, and USS *Monongahela*; the side-wheel frigate USS *Mississippi*; the ironclad gunboat USS *Essex*; the side-wheel gunboat USS *Genessee*; and the screw gunboats USS *Sachem*, USS *Albatross*, and USS *Kineo*. On March 14, Farragut issued orders for the ships to attack the heavily fortified Confederate positions, which consisted of seven

forts south of the city. Farragut hoped that his flotilla could run the guns and
head upstream toward Vicksburg, and he issued orders to move forward at
9 P.M. The USS *Essex* was given the assignment of protecting the wooden
ships if necessary, because of her heavy iron plate. Two ships were late in
maneuvering into position, however, and a tug soon pulled up alongside Farragut's *Hartford,* carrying the information that Banks felt his army troops
could not provide a land diversion as had been planned. A short time after 10
P.M. the squadron moved north.

Awaiting Farragut's flotilla was a large assemblage of Confederate gunners ready for action, alerted by the high daytime activity and the initial firing of Federal mortar boats. The Southerners ignited large piles of pine logs
along the riverbanks to illuminate their targets effectively. One of the batteries featured a hot-shot oven that heated solid shot far past the temperature at
which it would ignite wooden ships. Maj. Gen. Franklin Gardner supervised
the defenses of Port Hudson, as commander of District No. 3 in the Department of Mississippi and East Louisiana. The USS *Hartford,* with the USS *Albatross* lashed alongside, passed the lower batteries under heavy fire. On
board, Farragut's son Loyall, who acted as a signal officer, panicked when a
shot passed close by. "Don't duck, my son," said Farragut, "there is no use in
trying to dodge God Almighty." The current was so strong that several of the
ships nearly careened out of control, and the flashes of light from Confederate batteries, illuminating ghostly, rising columns of smoke, did little for the
confidence of some of the Federal sailors. The USS *Richmond* took a disabling hit. The *Monongahela* ran aground and stayed in position for half an
hour, taking multiple hits. Capt. James P. McKinstry's bridge on the *Monongahela* was shot out from under him, injuring him severely and killing three
others on board. The *Mississippi* was also run aground accidentally and suffered brutally from the Rebel batteries, later being abandoned. By 3 A.M. the
following morning the ship was "seen floating downstream on flames," and
still later the ship exploded with a terrific thud. Lt. Comdr. Andrew B. Cummings, Capt. James Alden's executive officer on the *Richmond,* was killed. The
attempted passage of the batteries at Port Hudson was a disaster for Farragut's flotilla. The *Hartford* and the *Albatross* had run the gauntlet; the others
had failed miserably and with great loss of life and machinery.

Grant had also scouted a circuitous water route that would use Steele's
Bayou, necessitating a 200-mile trek that would enter the Yazoo River north
of Vicksburg and threaten the city from the rear. The naval force that would
undertake the Steele's Bayou expedition was commanded by Capt. David
Dixon Porter, and consisted of the Eads ironclad gunboats USS *Louisville,*
USS *Cincinnati,* USS *Carondelet,* USS *Pittsburg,* and USS *Mound City,* along
with four mortar boats and four tugs. On March 14, Porter launched the difficult operation, which maneuvered to Black Bayou only to be obstructed by

thick forest. From that position Porter hoped to enter Deer Creek and move on the city. But the thick growth of trees meant the ships were stalled to a virtual standstill as the sailors pulled up trees or tried pushing them over with the ironclads. After two days of hard work, Grant dispatched army troops of Sherman's corps to assist Porter. "The ironclads," Sherman reported, "push their way along unharmed, but the trees and overhanging limbs tear the wooden boats all to pieces."

By March 19 the Steele's Bayou expedition had reached within one and a half miles of Rolling Fork, the point from which the ships could turn south toward the city. By this time, the backdoor entrance of Porter's flotilla had been discovered by the Confederates, who sent sharpshooters to the shores and felled hundreds of trees to block Porter's squadron at Rolling Fork. Had the ships been able to move swiftly, they might have gotten through as planned, but Confederates now began to harass the operation. Porter dispatched 300 men and two boat howitzers to the shore to fight off the Confederates, who were forcibly employing blacks to obstruct the river. "After working all night and clearing out the obstructions," wrote Porter, "we succeeded in getting within 800 yards of the end of this troublesome creek." Now the expedition took on an air of entrapment, however. Porter reported that more obstructions had been laid ahead, cutting through the naturally existing trees was highly troublesome in itself (stumps often had to be cut underwater with special saws), and by now 800 Confederate troops had landed ahead of the Federal ships and begun a sporadic fire, assisted by seven cannon. Moreover, Porter had heard that a large Confederate force had embarked at Haines's Bluff on the march toward his ships and that logs were being laid in Steele's Bayou behind the ships. The trap seemed to be closing. The Union sailors were exhausted, too, having worked nearly around the clock for six days and nights.

On March 21 some of Sherman's troops reached Porter's gunboats. But the situation had already eroded miserably. The soldiers brought no provisions nor any artillery. With Confederate troops growing in the area, Porter's only option seemed to be retreat. On March 22 he ordered the gunboats and the ironclads near Rolling Fork all the way downstream to a bend in the river that was supposedly obstructed. The *Louisville* began work clearing the blockade when a report of some 3,000 Confederate infantry nearby reached the ship, and suddenly artillery from the shore opened fire. The gunboats replied with heavy booming of their guns, and coupled with an attack by Sherman's troops, the Union response soon scattered the Confederate infantry. Fighting their way through, the ships reached Hill's Plantation, near Black Bayou, where they had started out eight days earlier. The Steele's Bayou expedition had failed, and yet another inventive route to strike at Vicksburg was unsuccessful. The day before the Steele's Bayou expedition ended, two Federal rams attempted to run the Vicksburg batteries from the north, to link up with and support Farragut. The USS *Switzerland* and the USS *Lancaster* were badly mauled by Confederate fire; the *Lancaster* sank after being struck thirty times and the *Switzerland* was crippled by gunfire and floated downstream, out of control. The latter ship was salvaged and put back into service, however.

The next action in the Vicksburg campaign began on March 29, when Maj. Gen. John A. McClernand, now commanded to follow Grant's orders (McClernand desperately wished to operate independently), was instructed to open a pathway from Milliken's Bend—northwest of Vicksburg and west of Steele's Bayou—to a position along the river south of Vicksburg. To enable McClernand to make this movement, Porter was ordered to run the Vicksburg batteries with his ironclads and move south to rendezvous with McClernand below Vicksburg. The ships would be required to ferry McClernand's infantry across the river and to bring the needed supplies southward for the expedition that would result. On April 16, Porter brought his twelve vessels into position. The shore of the Mississippi was aglow from burning tar barrels the Confederate gunners had erected, anticipating the event. Shortly before midnight, Porter ordered his ships forward, each towing a coal barge. For almost two and a half hours the Confederate batteries opened a heavy fire on the ships, and each was hit repeatedly, often with destructive results. The transport USS *Henry Clay* was sunk; the USS *Forest Queen*, another transport, was disabled but assisted by sailors from the USS *Tuscumbia*. The eleven ships that passed through the hail of shells arrived soon thereafter at Hard Times, south of Vicksburg, joining Grant. On April 21 six more transports attempted passage to reinforce the ships already below, but only three made the journey safely.

As an interlude to the primary Vicksburg operations, Banks continued his move into Louisiana. With his Army of the Gulf, Banks decided to advance northward along the Atchafalaya River and Bayou Teche to Alexandria, scattering the Confederate defenders from the west shore of the Mississippi River and turning the defenses of Port Hudson. This signaled the beginning of Banks's Red River campaign of 1863, which resulted in three days of actions known collectively as Irish Bend, Fort Bisland, and Bayou Teche. The Confederate forces in the region were those of Maj. Gen. Richard Taylor, in command of the District of West Louisiana. Taylor protected the approach up Bayou Teche with Fort Bisland, west of Brashear City (now Morgan City), which had about 2,700 infantry troops in its vicinity. The Confederates also protected Grand Lake (north of Bayou Teche) with the Ellett ram CSS *Queen of the West*, which had been captured at Fort de Russy in February. Similarly, Bayou Teche itself was protected by the ironclad CSS *Diana*, formerly the USS *Diana*, which had been captured in Bayou

Teche at the end of March. Banks ordered the division of Brig. Gen. Cuvier Grover up Grand Lake to cut off Taylor's possible route of retreat at Irish Bend, an arc in Bayou Teche north of the village of Franklin. The division of Brig. Gen. William H. Emory and the brigade of Brig. Gen. Godfrey Weitzel were ordered to attack Fort Bisland while Grover maneuvered around to flank Taylor's force.

With 15,000 infantry, Banks set his plan into motion on April 12. Grover had been delayed slightly because one of the four accompanying gunboats, the USS *Arizona,* grounded. Finally, by 4 P.M. on April 13, Grover got under way after stumbling in confusion over roads and managing the difficulties of maneuvering ships to within a reasonable distance of shore. Grover's awkward attempts at landing his troops at Madam Porter's Plantation finally allowed his men access to the defending Confederates after they built a bridge with rafts to disembark. By 2 P.M. on the afternoon of April 12, the main column of Federal infantry, Emory's and Weitzel's men, engaged the Confederates at Fort Bisland. After heavy fighting, with significant artillery fire, the Union troops pushed to within 400 yards of the fort by nightfall on April 13. "The contest raged during the whole afternoon," wrote Col. Halbert E. Paine of the 4th Wisconsin Infantry. "My brigade was constantly swept by the enemy's projectiles, which, but for the shelter afforded by the ditches, would have inflicted upon me a fearful loss." The Confederate commander within the fort was Col. Henry Gray, who determined by now that the situation was hopeless. Attacking anew on the morning of the 14th, the Federal troops discovered that the Confederates had pulled out, abandoning Fort Bisland.

On the same morning, Taylor consolidated his forces and attacked the brigade of Union Col. Henry W. Birge near Irish Bend. Grover deployed his division and the action heated up intensely, with the brigade of Confederate Brig. Gen. Alfred Mouton coming into the fore. On board the *Diana,* Confederate Capt. Oliver J. Semmes, son of the renowned naval officer Raphael Semmes, attempted to hold off the Federal infantry by shelling them. The young Semmes was captured, however, and the *Diana* was destroyed along with the CSS *Hart* on April 18 to prevent their capture. Moreover, the *Queen of the West* was blown up and burned in the action. Taylor withdrew his forces with great aplomb, moving them out of the planned entrapment, but the losses suffered along the way by the Confederate naval vessels and the ground vacated stung the Confederate cause in Louisiana. The Confederate troops engaged amounted to about 5,000; Banks claimed to have captured more than 2,500 prisoners, a figure that was probably exaggerated. The Union losses were about 350. Although Grant was supposed to coordinate his movements with Banks, the latter's absence nullified this plan. Grant renewed his movement against Vicksburg unassisted, and Banks moved to assault Port Hudson, the heavily defended area north of Baton Rouge.

Grant did not order the movement southward to concentrate at Hard Times without well-considered diversions. With a force of 1,700 cavalry troopers, Col. Benjamin H. Grierson left on a diversionary raid from La Grange, Tennessee, bound for Baton Rouge. The raid would cover 600 miles in sixteen days; Grierson's force consisted of the 6th and 7th Illinois cavalries and the 2d Iowa Cavalry, plus an attached two-gun battery. Grierson, age 36, was a Pennsylvania-born music teacher who had moved to Ohio and volunteered as an aide to Benjamin M. Prentiss during the first weeks of the conflict. Valued as a horse soldier, Grierson came to the attention of Grant, who assigned him to the raid. At dawn on April 17, Grierson's raiders left La Grange, early the next day encountering Rebel cavalry near Ripley, Mississippi. The Southern horsemen belonged to the 1st Mississippi Cavalry (militia). Such a harassment by swift-moving Federal cavalry was the last thing that Southern officers expected at this time. Maj. Gen. Samuel Gholson had three regiments of militia troops undergoing organizational drills in the area. On the 19th the raiders reached Pontotoc, and by April 20 the raiders had made it to Houston, Mississippi; the same day Grierson detached 175 raiders who seemed too fatigued to continue and sent them back to La Grange, along with 12 prisoners captured during the initial skirmish. Capt. Hiram Love commanded this "Quinine Brigade." On the fifth day, April 21, Col. Edward Hatch was ordered to move against the Mobile & Ohio Railroad and feint northward to draw the Confederates away from Grierson's main force. The Confederates caught up with Hatch's 2d Iowa Cavalry and a skirmish at Palo Alto resulted; this holding action enabled Grierson to move southward with the main force.

On April 22 the raiders reached Starkville; here, Capt. Henry Forbes's company of horsemen detached from the main body, cut telegraph lines, and confused the Confederates about where Grierson was headed. On this day Hatch raided the town of Okolona, writing afterward that his men "charged into the town just before sunset, where we burned thirty barracks filled with Confederate British stamped cotton. This done we moved five miles out of town and camped for the night on a wealthy plantation, which afforded everything we needed both for animals and men." The next day the raiders reached Louisville. South of this place Sgt. Richard Surby led a detachment of several men who termed themselves the "Butternut Guerrillas," and they captured a bridge on the flooded Pearl River, allowing the raiders to cross. Gholson arrived in the area, and on April 24 a skirmish took place at Birmingham, outside Okolona. Hearing of Grierson's presence at Newton's Station on the Vicksburg Railroad, Pemberton ordered troops sent eastward to annihilate him.

The Confederate response to Grierson's raid escalated. Maj. Gen. William W. Loring, at Meridian, took charge of the operation. Brig. Gen.

Abraham Buford's infantry force halted at Meridian. Three infantry regiments and attached artillery were sent to Morton, west of Newton's Station, under the command of Col. John Adams, with instructions to guard against a westward movement. To block Grierson's possible northward escape, Brig. Gen. James R. Chalmers was sent to Okolona, while Brig. Gen. Lloyd Tilghman was ordered to transfer troops to Carthage to block an escape route to the northwest. At Port Hudson, Maj. Gen. Franklin Gardner dispatched cavalry to block any attempted linkage of Grierson with Banks's force in Louisiana.

This heightened activity signaled that Grierson's raid was working magnificently as a confusing distraction. At Newton's Station, Grierson captured two trains and destroyed several miles of track and telegraph wires, wrecking communications between Vicksburg and the east. To the south, a skirmish erupted at Garlandville. On April 25 the raiders turned sharply westward, entered the Piney Woods country, and rested in relative seclusion while the Confederates searched for them to the east. As the raiders approached the Pearl River, having to cross westward, Col. Edward Prince stole a ferry boat to enable the movement. By now Pemberton was completely baffled about Grierson's intentions and believed that the Northern raider might be headed for Grand Gulf, south of Vicksburg. Pemberton ordered Brig. Gen. John S. Bowen to send a large cavalry force under Col. William Wirt Adams to intercept Grierson. On April 28, Adams established an ambush, expecting the Northern horsemen to ride into it, near Union Church. But Grierson learned about the trap and circled back to Brookhaven on the New Orleans & Jackson Railroad, leaving the expectant Confederates all alone. Though they were nearly surrounded now by pursuing Confederate cavalry, Grierson's raiders destroyed the southern supply route into Vicksburg at Brookhaven before turning south again and moving on to Summit. West of Magnolia at Wall's Bridge, on May 1, the raiders clashed with Confederate cavalry commanded by Maj. James De Baun in the harshest engagement of the raid. They continued on, crossing the Amite River at Williams's Bridge, and made it to safety in Baton Rouge on May 2.

Grierson's raid was a complete success. In sixteen days the colonel's men had killed 100 Confederates, captured 500 prisoners, wrecked 50 miles of rail and telegraph lines, seized or destroyed 3,000 small arms, and captured 1,000 horses and mules. The Confederates were completely confused by the movement, at a critical time in the early phase of the Vicksburg campaign. Grierson lost 3 killed, 7 wounded, and 9 missing. Grant summarized the raid by simply writing, "Grierson has knocked the heart out of the state!" Grierson reflected on the poor state of civilian life in the region. "Much of the country through which we passed was almost entirely destitute of forage and provisions," he wrote. "It was but seldom that we obtained over one meal per day. Many of the inhabitants must undoubtedly suffer for want of the necessities of life, which have reached most fabulous prices."

Two other raids of significance occurred concurrently. On the same day that Grierson left La Grange, Confederate Brig. Gen. John S. Marmaduke began a cavalry raid through Missouri. Marmaduke's division totaled about 5,000 men organized into brigades commanded by Cols. G. W. Thompson, John Q. Burbridge, and George W. Carter and comprised mostly Missouri, Arkansas, and Texas troopers. Ten artillery pieces were attached. Marmaduke anticipated striking at and capturing the force of 2,000 under Brig. Gen. John McNeil, at Bloomfield, which would not only provide Marmaduke with a victory but resupply his poorly outfitted division. About 1,200 of Marmaduke's men were unarmed and 900 marched along with no mounts.

As he converged on the town of Patterson, south of St. Louis, Marmaduke divided his force into two columns, one led by Col. Jo Shelby and the other by Marmaduke himself. On April 20, Marmaduke's cavalry approached Patterson only to find the 400 Union cavalry under Col. Edwin Smart (3d Missouri Militia Cavalry) fleeing westward to Pilot Knob after a brief skirmish. Two days later Shelby's men proceeded to Fredericktown, where they surprised the Federal garrison and captured telegrams ordering McNeil to move to Ironton. Marmaduke deployed his troops such that if McNeil stayed at Bloomfield, Carter's men would press an attack, and if he moved to Ironton, Shelby's column would assault him there.

By the 25th, Carter's pursuit of McNeil pushed the Union force to within a few miles of Cape Girardeau. There McNeil's Union soldiers occupied fortifications that had been erected, and Shelby attacked the following day before withdrawing to Jackson. On the same night, Col. Robert C. Newton's 5th Arkansas Cavalry was attacked by Brig. Gen. William Vandever's division, sent in pursuit to destroy Marmaduke, near Cape Girardeau. Under moonlight, a rare night attack occurred in which the 1st Iowa Cavalry drew sabers and scattered Newton's regiment, capturing prisoners and horses. Vandever pursued Marmaduke with great energy, and each force moved south while McNeil positioned himself to cut off Marmaduke's retreat. Crossing the Castor River on April 29, the Union forces skirmished repeatedly with elements of the Confederate force on the 30th, but by May 1 and 2, Marmaduke's exhausted troopers reached Chalk Bluff, Arkansas, after which the Union pursuit was called off. The fruits of Marmaduke's raid were tenuous at best: "My loss in the expedition is some 30 killed, 60 wounded, and 120 missing (stragglers), perhaps captured," recorded Marmaduke. "I gained on the raid about 150 recruits and a great improvement in the number and quality of horses."

Another raid occurred at the same time as those of Grierson and Marmaduke. In Tennessee, Maj. Gen. William S. Rosecrans conceived a plan to send raiders deep into Georgia to cut the Georgia Railroad south of Dalton, thereby preventing a reinforcement of Gen. Braxton Bragg. Rosecrans assigned Col. Abel D. Streight, a native New Yorker who was colonel of the 51st Indiana Infantry, to lead the expedition. Streight (pronounced "Straight") was a volunteer soldier who had been a lumber merchant, manufacturer, and publisher before hostilities began. Streight's independent brigade of 1,700 cavalry departed Nashville on April 11; the raid actually commenced in force on April 26, when the cavalry left Tuscumbia, Alabama, near Florence, and headed east. Delays had resulted from acquiring all the horses necessary for the raid. Streight was ordered to rendezvous with Brig. Gen. Grenville M. Dodge's division of the Army of the Tennessee and appear to be joining this unit for an expedition, but then to split off and push south and eastward into Georgia.

On April 28 none other than Brig. Gen. Nathan Bedford Forrest discovered Streight's cavalry moving toward Blountsville, north of Birmingham. On the 30th, Forrest's two regiments caught up with Streight's raiders and fought them savagely at Day's Gap and Sand Mountain. Hard rains and terrible muddy roads did not help either side to maneuver or fight effectively. Streight's men continued a heavy fire into the Confederate ranks, and soon the Confederates gave way, but they reformed and attacked again. The fighting lasted all day and moved slowly over a distance of ten miles from the initial encounter. By about 10 P.M. the fighting ceased, the Confederates retreating and leaving a large number of dead and wounded on the field.

Streight's raiders continued their march and reached Blountsville on the morning of May 1. There Forrest struck Streight's rear guard, and a rolling, guerrillalike fight ensued during portions of this day as small bands of Streight's men hid in brush along the roads and fired back at dismounted Confederates of Forrest's command. The following morning Forrest again attacked as the last elements of Streight's command attempted to cross Black Creek, bound for Gadsden. Reaching Gadsden on May 2, Streight paused briefly, long enough to destroy the quantity of arms and stores he found in the town. Resuming the march, Streight's raiders rode again despite the fact that both animals and men were now "completely worn out," according to the expedition's commander. By 4 P.M. on May 2, Streight's raiders reached Blount's Plantation, where another skirmish took place. Halting to feed the animals, Streight's command found its rear guard struck abruptly by Forrest's cavalry. By the onset of darkness one Confederate attack had been repulsed but another massed attack was ready to be launched, and Streight felt that nearly all his remaining ammunition was "worthless." He chose 200 men to carry on to Rome, Georgia, to secure the bridge until the remainder of the command could catch up.

Discovering that Forrest was attempting to flank him, Streight moved on to Centre, where another skirmish occurred, the main body of the raiders continuing to the south. Hopeful that they could secure a crossing of the Chattooga River, Streight's exhausted men carried on, too fatigued to "keep awake long enough to feed the horses," the commander reported. Matters soon deteriorated even further, and the command separated and scattered, trying to find a way to Rome, and crossing at Cedar Bluff. They discovered that Forrest was closer to Rome than they were, and on May 3, Streight reported that "a large portion of my best troops actually went to sleep while lying in line of battle under a severe skirmish fire." Forrest sent a flag of truce, and Streight's raiders were captured. Streight and the other officers went to Libby prison in Richmond, where Streight and others escaped on February 9, 1864. Streight's raid was a Union disaster.

IN THE EYES OF MOST SOLDIERS, the war in the east remained quiet during March and April 1863. Not so for the youthful Federal officer Edwin H. Stoughton, however. Born in Vermont, the 24-year-old soldier had been graduated low in his West Point class before being commissioned colonel of the 4th Vermont Infantry in the autumn of 1861. The ambitious Stoughton was appointed brigadier general of volunteers in late 1862, but the appointment expired without a commission; contrary to most accounts, Stoughton was no general. The young colonel suffered a second embarrassment on March 8. On that quiet evening Stoughton and his garrison were asleep in Fairfax Court House, Virginia, on the outskirts of Washington. Also in the area were 29 men commanded by Capt. John S. Mosby, who had fought in the east as a private soldier before scouting for Jeb Stuart. In January, Mosby, age 29 and a Virginia attorney prior to the war, had organized a battalion of partisan rangers who would become famous for their guerrillalike exploits in Virginia. Stoughton had been looking for Mosby to eliminate this pesky cavalry soldier and his followers. But on this night, Mosby's 29 rangers entered the town, amid a large Union force, and captured 33 men and 48 horses. The Confederates escorted Stoughton outside in his bedclothes after Mosby allegedly slapped him on the behind. Stoughton was disgraced and sought no further command after he was exchanged in May, resigning from the army.

Southern anxiety was growing over a probable Federal advance of the Army of the Potomac under Maj. Gen. Joseph Hooker. Increasing shortages of supplies and foodstuffs were beginning to worry many in the Confederacy. "Unless our farmers and planters put forth their utmost endeavors, there will be something like a famine in the land," editorialized the *Southern Illustrated News* on March 14. Two weeks later Richmond experienced a "bread riot," in which a mob commenced disorder by crowding a wagon in the street, demanding bread. The scene quickly turned ugly as hungry citizens broke into shops and looted a wide variety of goods—edible and otherwise. Finally, Jefferson Davis himself addressed remnants of the angry mob as he stood in a wagon near the Capitol. Pathos reigned supreme as Davis ended his plea for order by throwing the change he had in his pockets into the crowd. The relatively short-lived riot amounted to little actual damage, but psychologically it alarmed both citizens and soldiers alike. Wondering about the inability of the Confederate Congress to deal with such difficulties, the South Carolina planter James Henry Hammond informed his acquaintance, Confederate Senator Robert M. T. Hunter, on April 9. "Some malign influence seems to preside over your councils. Pardon me, is the majority always drunk?"

Militarily, Southern commanders worried about the state of the Army of Northern Virginia. "The greatest difficulty I find is in causing orders & requisitions to be obeyed," Robert E. Lee said in a dispatch to Jefferson Davis. "This arises not from a spirit of disobedience, but from ignorance. We therefore have a need of a corps of officers to teach others their duty, see to the observances of orders, & to the regularity & precision of all movements." In serious times, Lee could retain his playfulness, however. He wrote his wife on March 19, ending with a postscript about fame seekers and referring to his nephew. "You can give Fitzhugh's autograph to those persons desiring mine," he wrote. "It is worth more."

Other Southerners were Southerners no more. In Houston, Sam Houston, the deposed governor of Texas, who had argued against secession, gave a futile speech on March 18, hardly able to believe what had become of his country. "Once I dreamed of an empire for an united People," Houston declared. "The dream is over." Houston died four months later, laying blame for the Confederacy's poor state on the doorstep of Jefferson Davis, whom he called "cold as a lizard and ambitious as Lucifer." Unruffled by the determination of the rough Texans, the British traveler Lt. Col. Arthur J. L. Fremantle of the elite Coldstream Guards, observing the American Civil War on a three-month trip with various Confederates in mid-1863, enjoyed the westerners. "In spite of their peculiar habits of hanging, shooting, &c., which seemed to be natural to the people living in a wild and thinly-populated country," he wrote, "there was much to like in my fellow-travelers."

The first notable eastern action in the spring of 1863 occurred on March 17, at Kelly's Ford, Virginia. The action ranked as one of the most significant cavalry engagements of the war to date. The Cavalry Corps of the Army of the Potomac had just been organized, and its commander was Maj. Gen. George Stoneman. On March 16, Hooker ordered Brig. Gen. William W. Averell with his 2d Division, Cavalry Corps, to cross the Rappahannock River and attack the Confederate cavalry thought to be near Culpeper Court House. At Culpeper the brigade of cavalry detached from the Army of Northern Virginia, consisting of five Virginia regiments, 800 men strong, was commanded by Brig. Gen. Fitzhugh Lee. Fitz Lee, age 27, was an accomplished horseman and Robert E. Lee's nephew. Averell assembled a force of about 3,000 horse soldiers and six artillery pieces and set off to cross the river. After detaching various troops to cover his movements and to drive the enemy's pickets at Rappahannock Station, Averell had 2,100 men in three brigades commanded by Col. Alfred N. A. Duffié, Col. John B. McIntosh, and Capt. Marcus A. Reno.

Averell's advance guard reached Kelly's Ford early on the morning of March 17 and found a small outpost of the Confederate cavalry, some 60 troopers strong. After a fight that lasted about ninety minutes, Averell's advance elements, led by Maj. Samuel E. Chamberlain, Averell's chief of staff, forced a crossing. This occurred after a portion of the 1st Rhode Island Cavalry scattered the defenders and captured 25 Confederates in the process. After the skirmish Averell could count his losses: Chamberlain had been wounded in the head, 3 men were killed, 6 others wounded, and 15 horses lost. Thereafter, Averell crossed his force slowly, taking two hours to ford the swift currents of the Rappahanock.

By 7:30 A.M. Fitz Lee was notified of Averell's crossing and sent 800 troopers forward to block the Yankees from approaching the perceived target, Brandy Station on the Orange & Alexandria Railroad. Near the ford, Averell's men had deployed themselves, many behind a stone fence, others clustered near the C. T. Wheatley House. Confederate skirmishers approached the dismounted Federals and were followed by the 3d Virginia Cavalry, which charged the stone fence expecting to find a gap in it, which they did not locate. This caused the men to rush along the fence, exposed to a murderous fire from the Union line. In this action one of the beloved young Confederates of the Army of Northern Virginia, Maj. John Pelham, age 24, was mortally wounded in the back of the head by a small piece of an exploded shell. Ironically, Pelham was simply there along with Stuart to observe the battle rather than to participate. Pelham had caught the notice of Robert E. Lee, Jeb Stuart, and others at Fredericksburg and on other fields, and his loss was a shock, as he represented the vigorous youth of the Southern armies. "The gallant Pelham—so noble, so true—will be mourned by the nation," wrote Jeb Stuart after the battle.

A Union counterstrike now developed as the blueclad horsemen of the 4th and 16th Pennsylvania cavalries moved up toward the Wheatley House, and the 3d and 5th Virginia cavalries moved out to meet this new threat. After heavy fighting, the Virginians had to withdraw from this position. Along the main road leading westward from Kelly's Ford, near the Federal left, Duffié organized and led a charge that employed the 4th Pennsylvania Cavalry, the 1st Rhode Island Cavalry, and the 6th Ohio Cavalry. Heavy fighting resulted, and the Union troops made a steady, slow movement into a stubblefield, which the Confederates set ablaze to thwart the Federal progress. "My men rushed forward," remarked Averell, "and beat it out with their overcoats." After reporting a steady advance, Averell next focused on the shoddy quality of his ammunition; by 5:30 P.M., he invoked a steady stream of excuses for his advance sputtering out: exhausted men and horses, poor posting of men in the front, and he "deemed it proper to withdraw." Fellow officers believed Averell went stone cold over the imagined possibility of Confederate infantry pinning him against the river, and so he abandoned his plan and recrossed. The Federal expedition had moved about two miles over more than twelve hours, lost 6 killed, 50 wounded, and 22 missing, and inflicted 11 dead, 88 wounded, and 34 captured Confederates, as well as killing 71 Rebel horses and capturing 12.

In February, Maj. Gen. D. H. Hill led an expedition against New Bern, North Carolina, fighting a two-day skirmish at Deep Gully, eight miles from New Bern, beginning on March 13. Col. Josiah Pickett (25th Massachusetts Infantry) resisted the Confederate attack at Deep Gully and found "the city being attacked in our rear, the regiments supporting me were withdrawn for its defense, and I was left, with my regiment and two pieces of artillery, to take care of the enemy as best I could." The two-day fight at Deep Gully transformed into an artillery assault on the Federal-held Fort Anderson on March 14. Brig. Gen. James Johnston Pettigrew, leading the attack, shelled the position extensively, hoping to capture it and thereby bombard the town and the Federal gunboats on the Neuse River. But the attack failed, and the city and Fort Anderson remained in Union hands.

Lincoln had ordered the 9th Army Corps to shift from Fredericksburg to Fort Monroe, and this established a concern in Robert E. Lee's mind over the safety of Richmond, which might be approached from Yorktown or Suffolk. Lee thus dispatched Longstreet with the divisions of Maj. Gens. George E. Pickett and John Bell Hood to obstruct any possible advance of the Federal 9th Corps. The division of Brig. Gen. George W. Getty was stationed at Suffolk. Longstreet began a siege of the Federal garrison at Suffolk that would last from April 11 to May 4. The post was now commanded by Maj. Gen. John J. Peck. This lengthy and detailed operation amounted to essentially nothing. The Federal force at Suffolk slowly escalated from 15,000 to 25,000, and by late April, Longstreet wavered in his commitment to capture the position. At first Longstreet assembled his force for a vigorous thrust. The first few days witnessed an attack on Peck's right and an assault on the Federal gunboats and river batteries on the Nansemond by Brig. Gen. George T. Anderson's men, which was repulsed. The Federal forces engaged consisted of the divisions of Brig. Gen. Michael Corcoran, Brig. Gen.

George W. Getty, and Col. William Gurney. On April 17, Longstreet wrote the secretary of war, James A. Seddon. "I am very well convinced that we could reduce [Suffolk] in two or three days," the Confederate commander suggested, "but doubt if we can afford to expend the powder and ball." The considerable presence of the Federal Navy seemed to provide quite an obstacle for Longstreet. "We will beat the enemy or sink at our post," declared Lt. William B. Cushing, engaging Confederate batteries near Suffolk. On April 19, Getty's men, assisted by the navy, stormed one of the key Confederate batteries, Fort Huger, capturing 6 guns and 200 prisoners. After the sword of a Confederate commander was sent to Getty, the army man kept it. "I have never seen men so devoid of Common justice," wrote navy Lt. Roswell H. Lamson, "and of all generosity as these army Generals."

The capture of Fort Huger was a major success in the Suffolk operation. Conversely, its loss was a blow to Longstreet's aspirations. Never one to be accused of excess brilliance, Confederate Maj. Gen. Samuel G. French offered the following explanation: "It appears to me that if the garrison was surprised, they were negligent; if not surprised, they did not offer a sufficient resistance." By late April and early May, Longstreet seemed resigned to foraging in the fertile farming region surrounding Suffolk and calling it quits on further military operations. Federal casualties suffered during the siege of Suffolk amounted to 41 killed, 223 wounded, and 2 missing; Confederate losses were about 900, 400 of whom were missing or captured.

A two-pronged eastern raid unfolded during late April. In West Virginia, Confederate Brig. Gen. William E. "Grumble" Jones commenced a raid on the Baltimore & Ohio Railroad that resulted in a variety of small skirmishes over the following month. Jones commanded a cavalry brigade of Stuart's corps from the Army of Northern Virginia, as well as holding temporary command of the Valley District. Jones set out on April 20 to move to Mount Jackson and the Northwestern Turnpike and then attack the rail line between Oakland, Maryland, and Rowlesburg, West Virginia. Operating in concert with Jones would be Brig. Gen. John D. Imboden, who would depart Monterey, Virginia, on April 20 to capture Beverly, West Virginia, and reunite with Jones near Grafton or Clarksburg. The two Confederates wanted to prevent Col. James A. Mulligan from adding his force to the other Yankee units in the area while they disrupted as much of the important east-west rail line as they could.

Jones began his raid with about 2,100 men altogether—including 350 infantry and 1,600 cavalrymen—and five 6-pounder rifles. The infantry units were comprised of the celebrated "Maryland line," and the cavalry force consisted almost entirely of Virginians with some Maryland horse soldiers. Imboden had a mixed brigade of 3,500 that included 700 cavalry. Imboden marched his men seventy miles over four days to reach Cheat Mountain, scene of the old campaigns by Robert E. Lee, where his men had to march or ride over 18 or 20 inches of snow and "a pelting storm of sleet." On the morning of April 24, Imboden's force approached Beverly and initiated a rolling skirmish through the woods that covered about two miles of ground; during this action the Federal garrison set a portion of the town ablaze and abandoned it, retreating under the command of Col. George R. Latham. "The attack was so sudden that the enemy could not remove his stores nor destroy his camp," wrote Imboden. "His loss was not less than $100,000." By May 4, Jones reunited with Imboden, and the raid carried on. Jones, meanwhile, had fought several skirmishes. On April 25 his men clashed at Greenland Gap, West Virginia, where the Confederates set a church ablaze to drive out Union snipers, and the following day skirmishes occurred at Altamont, Oakland, and Cranberry Summit, Maryland. Mulligan's men got into the action on April 29 at Fairmont, West Virginia, where a three-hour firefight pushed the Union soldiers back to Grafton.

On April 30, Jones's men fought the Federals at Bridgeport, West Virginia, and on May 6 and 7 affairs developed at West Union and Cairo Station. On May 9, in the final action of the raid, Jones's men destroyed the wells and set boats, tanks, and barrels on fire, creating a blazing inferno. "A burning river, carrying destruction to our merciless enemy," boasted Jones, "was a scene of magnificence that might well carry joy to every patriotic heart." The raid was a success, Jones having destroyed a large number of bridges on the railroad line between Rowlesburg and the Alleghenies. He briefly alarmed citizens in Pittsburgh and Wheeling before returning to Virginia. Imboden's success was not as general, although he adequately carried out his part of the mission.

OTHER, SCATTERED ACTIONS also occurred during March and April. On March 3 another Federal naval attack targeted Fort McAllister near Savannah. Capt. Percival Drayton commanded a flotilla that consisted in part of the ironclad monitors USS *Passaic,* USS *Nahant,* and USS *Patapsco,* along with mortar boats and the screw gunboat USS *Seneca,* the medium screw combatant USS *Dawn,* and the screw gunboat USS *Wissahickon.* After six hours of heavy bombardment the assault failed. On March 10, at Jacksonville, Florida, Federal troops disembarked a regiment from the small screw gunboat USS *Norwich* and took possession of the town. They were not ordinary troops, but included Col. Thomas Wentworth Higginson's 1st South Carolina Infantry, comprised of black Union soldiers. On March 29 the troops evacuated and burned much of the city, unable to hold it permanently.

A major series of naval actions occurred in Charleston Harbor on April 7. There a flotilla of Union ships attacked Fort Sumter and the other strong Confederate forts guarding the city. Rear Adm. Samuel F. Du Pont led the attack squadron of nine vessels that included the monitors USS *Catskill,* USS *Nahant,* USS *Montauk,* USS *Nantucket,* USS *Passaic,* USS *Patapsco,* and USS *Weehawken;* and the ironclad gunboats USS *New Ironsides* and USS *Keokuk.* By noon Du Pont signaled the order to attack, but it wasn't until about 3 P.M. that the ships opened on Fort Sumter, *Weehawken* taking the lead, followed by the other monitors. *Weehawken* became heavily engaged and a torpedo exploded near her, lifting the ship momentarily. Artillery fire from Forts Sumter and Moultrie splashed about the ships and struck them, doing considerable damage throughout the afternoon. The *Weehawken* took fifty-three hits during forty minutes of action; the *Passaic* had thirty-five hits and had her 11-inch gun knocked out, and the *Patapsco* lost headway and became a sitting duck, receiving forty-seven hits. After heavy fighting over the whole afternoon, with all the Federal monitors receiving heavy batterings, the *Keokuk* ran ahead of the crippled *Nahant* and was blasted by more than ninety hits from a range of less than 600 yards from Sumter. Anchored overnight, the gunboat filled with water and sank the next morning. The *Keokuk*'s guns were salvaged by the Rebels, who mounted them in what is now Battery Park in Charleston and used them during future operations. "The monitors are not intended to lose life except by sinking as a general rule," Du Pont lamented to his wife. "They are iron coffins; once perforated they go down." The quest for control of Charleston Harbor would be delayed indefinitely.

THE WAR CONTINUED to effect a vast toll on the soldiers who fought it and the notable persons who promoted or opposed it. On March 9, the celebrated Charleston attorney James Louis Petigru, deeply respected in the city despite his staunch pro-Union stance, died at age 73. His nephew, James Johnston Pettigrew, had since become one of the more intellectual of the Confederate officers. He had just attacked Fort Anderson at New Bern and would soon help to lead a notable charge across the Pennsylvania soil. Anti-secessionist though he was, Petigru's funeral and burial drew throngs of saddened Charlestonians. His famous epitaph in Charleston's St. Michael's Churchyard reads in part: "In the great Civil War he withstood his People for his Country / But his People did homage to the Man / Who held his conscience higher than their praise / And his Country heaped her honors on the grave of the Patriot / To whom, living, his own righteous self respects sufficed / Alike for motive and reward."

General officers on both sides continued to expire. On March 21, Edwin Vose Sumner, one of the higher-ranking Union volunteer major generals, died from fever and congestion of the lungs. In the autumn of 1862, after participating in the Peninsular campaign (and being hit twice by spent balls), and at Fredericksburg, the 65-year-old Sumner was assigned to desk duty. He died in Syracuse before taking command of the Department of the Missouri. He was survived by Edwin Vose Sumner, Jr., who would be commissioned a brevet brigadier general of volunteers before war's end. A week after Sumner's death Union Brig. Gen. James Cooper died in Columbus, Ohio. Assigned as commandant of Camp Chase prison, which housed vast numbers of captured Rebels, Cooper contracted "congestion of the lungs," the same symptomatic illness that claimed Sumner. On April 17, far to the south, a celebrated but unruly Confederate commander died. At Montvale Springs, Tennessee, Maj. Gen. Daniel Smith Donelson perished from chronic diarrhea after several months of poor health. Donelson had served in western Virginia, South Carolina, and eastern Tennessee. He was the nephew of Andrew Jackson.

By 1863 the soldiers increasingly wanted to go home. They missed their sweethearts, so much so that they popularized many songs to remember them by. One such song was embraced by soldiers, particularly in the South during the spring of 1863. It was so powerfully sad that some commanders allegedly forbade it to be sung by the troops. It was "Lorena," attributed to H. D. L. Webster. So began its haunting verses of love once precious but now lost: "The years creep slowly by, Lorena / The snow is on the grass again / The sun's low down the sky, Lorena / The frost gleams where the flowers have been / But the heart throbs on as warmly now / As when the summer days were nigh / Oh, the sun can never dip so low / Adown affection's cloudless sky."

CHAPTER 16

Lee's Master Stroke

THE ONSET OF WARM WEATHER in 1863 brought about a flurry of activity in all theaters of war. In the west, Maj. Gen. Ulysses S. Grant's campaign for Vicksburg resumed in earnest during the last days of April. Grant now planned to move his entire army south of the city, using transports and barges, cross the Mississippi River, and attack Vicksburg from the south and east. It was a daring and risky plan, one that Halleck left up to Grant (as long as Grant did not neglect Banks at Port Hudson). Sherman and Capt. David Dixon Porter—whose transports and gunboats would have to make and assist the movements—worried about the plan. The land and water over which the Army of the Tennessee would need to pass was difficult, to say the least. Most of the planned route, over a wide bottomland, much of it swampy, bayou-choked terrain, lacked suitable roads for transporting heavy equipment. Sandy streams crisscrossed the area, and the stagnant, algae-filled bayou water would not be particularly healthful to drink. Army engineers would become busy constructors of corduroy roads.

The tactical approach in this phase of the Vicksburg campaign was bold and risky. Grant would undertake a long, complex, and hazardous set of actions with relatively tenuous lines of communications and supply. "We must live upon the enemy's country as much as possible and destroy his supplies," Halleck wrote Maj. Gen. Stephen A. Hurlbut. "This is cruel warfare, but the enemy has brought it upon himself." By April 29, Grant had moved the corps of McClernand and McPherson to Hard Times. There, Porter brought his flotilla of gunboats and transports to meet them, and the combined force prepared for the springtime offensive.

Grant's Army of the Tennessee was composed of five army corps, commanded by Maj. Gen. John G. Parke (9th Corps; joined the army from June 14–17 and contained the divisions of Brig. Gens. Thomas Welsh and Robert B.

Potter); Maj. Gen. John A. McClernand (13th Corps; containing the divisions of Brig. Gens. Peter J. Osterhaus, Andrew J. Smith, Alvin P. Hovey, and Eugene A. Carr; on June 19 Maj. Gen. Edward O. C. Ord assumed command of this corps); Maj. Gen. William T. Sherman (15th Corps; divisions of Maj. Gens. Frederick Steele and Frank P. Blair, Jr., and Brig. Gen. James M. Tuttle); Maj. Gen. Cadwallader C. Washburn (a detachment of the 16th Corps; divisions of Brig. Gens. William Sooy Smith, Jacob G. Lauman, and Nathan Kimball); Maj. Gen. James B. McPherson (17th Corps; divisions of Maj. Gens. John A. Logan and Francis J. Herron, and Brig. Gens. John McArthur and Marcellus M. Crocker); and troops detached from the District of Northeast Louisiana, commanded by Brig. Gen. Elias S. Dennis.

Pemberton's Army of Mississippi consisted of five divisions, commanded by Maj. Gen. William W. Loring (brigades of Brig. Gens. Lloyd Tilghman, Winfield Scott Featherston, and Abraham Buford); Maj. Gen. Carter L. Stevenson (brigades of Brig. Gens. Seth M. Barton, Edward D. Tracy, and Alfred Cumming, and Col. Alexander W. Reynolds; Texas Legion commanded by Col. Thomas N. Waul); Maj. Gen. John H. Forney (brigades of Brig. Gens. Louis Hébert and John C. Moore); Maj. Gen. Martin L. Smith (brigades of Brig. Gens. William E. Baldwin, John C. Vaughn, Francis A. Shoup, and Jeptha V. Harris); and Maj. Gen. John S. Bowen (brigades of Col. Francis M. Cockrell and Brig. Gen. Martin E. Green). The Vicksburg river batteries were commanded by Col. Edward Higgins. Gen. Joseph E. Johnston's forces, engaged at Raymond and Jackson, consisted of forces of the Department of the West, which were the brigades of Brig. Gen. John Gregg, Col. Peyton H. Colquitt (Gist's Brigade), and Brig. Gen. William H. T. Walker.

Grant's movements included a feint by Sherman, who remained on the river opposite Vicksburg. Pemberton firmly believed the attack would come from a position north of the city. Still, Pemberton perceived the threat against Grand Gulf—opposite Hard Times—when it was almost too late, and the beleaguered Confederate sent 5,000 troops to reinforce Brig. Gen. John Stevens Bowen, who commanded the batteries there. Some forty feet above the river stood Fort Cobun, where most of the heavy guns were situated, and a secondary stronghold, Fort Wade, stood behind the town of Grand Gulf, which had been devastated by fire. At 7 A.M. on April 29, Porter's squadron, including the ironclad gunboats USS *Carondelet,* USS *Louisville,* USS *Mound City,* USS *Pittsburg,* USS *Tuscumbia,* USS *Benton,* and USS *Lafayette,* commenced a blistering fire at the two forts, hammering away for five hours. The guns of Fort Wade were silenced, but heavy cannon at Fort Cobun continued to lob a parade of shells and hot-shot cannonballs raining back down on the Federal ships, sending great plumes of smoke into the air and splashes of water high into the sky above the river. Grant stood watch on a tug, chewing on the stub of a cigar, and Porter disengaged his vessels in disgust, declaring that "Grand Gulf is the strongest place on the Mississippi." Porter's men suffered 18 killed and 57 wounded, a third of which occurred aboard the flagship *Benton*.

Following the stiff resistance at Grand Gulf, Grant moved McPherson's and McClernand's men south to Bruinsburg, where he used the transports and barges to cross about 24,000 men to the eastern shore of the river by April 30. There was no Confederate opposition. Grant sent word to Sherman to begin moving his corps south. After an incompetent delay, McClernand began moving his men eastward toward the town of Port Gibson, population 1,453, where about midnight on May 1 he encountered forward pickets of Bowen's force. In an engagement that lasted nearly all day, McClernand and McPherson attacked half a mile west of Port Gibson, in an area of swampy land with three creeks and two roads, Magnolia Church, and a half dozen small houses. At dawn the divisions of Brig. Gen. Peter J. Osterhaus attacked northward into Brig. Gen. Edward D. Tracy's brigade, spread along the Bruinsburg Road. Many of Tracy's men were exposed to a galling fire from the onrushing Yankees. Tracy himself was struck in the chest by a Minié bullet and killed instantly. Col. Isham W. Garrott assumed command of the brigade. At the same time, the Federal division of Brig. Gen. Eugene A. Carr pressed an eastward attack, sweeping Brig. Gen. Martin E. Green's brigade past Magnolia Church. As additional units arrived from Bruinsburg, McClernand deployed them, making Confederate resistance more difficult as the hours passed.

By noon Bowen had brought his brigade forward to aid the Confederate defense, and after noon McPherson arrived and deployed his divisions. A major fight ensued. Osterhaus, meanwhile, continued an attack northward into the troops of Garrott. After being reinforced on the left by Green, Garrott successfully held off some of the Federal attacks, but Brig. Gen. John E. Smith reinforced Osterhaus and created a collapse of that Confederate portion of the field. To the southeast, for more than two hours, Carr pounded the defensive units deployed by Brig. Gen. William E. Baldwin to block him, assisted by the Federal infantry division of Brig. Gen. Alvin P. Hovey. With the tactical situation deteriorating, Baldwin moved the brigade of Col. Francis M. Cockrell along with two additional regiments to turn McClernand's right. "Their artillery opened on us with great rapidity," reported Capt. George W. Covell of the 3d Missouri Infantry (CSA) of the Federal onslaught. "As soon as we got within range the infantry poured the Minié balls into our ranks as thick and fast as hailstones from a thundercloud or rain drops in an April shower." Reinforcements arrived in the form of Brig. Gen. Andrew J. Smith's division, and by late afternoon the Confederate hopes for success dwindled with the envelopment of the Confederate right. At sunset

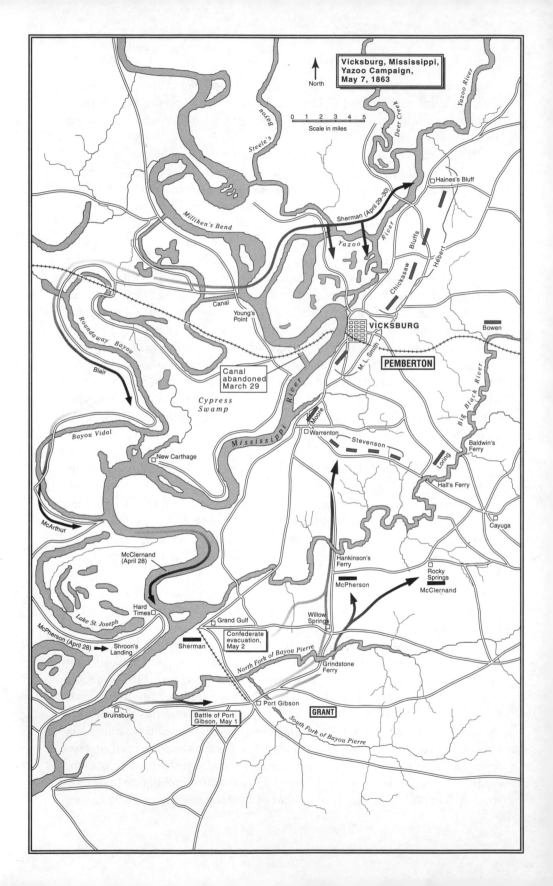

Vicksburg, Mississippi,
Yazoo Campaign,
May 7, 1863

North

0 1 2 3 4 5
Scale in miles

the grayclad soldiers withdrew, crossing the South Fork of Bayou Pierre and burning the bridge behind them. The exhausted Federals did not pursue. The Federal casualties at Port Gibson were 131 killed, 719 wounded, and 25 missing; Confederate losses were 68 killed, 380 wounded, and 384 missing. Grant's bold tactical movement into Mississippi was underway.

Sherman, meanwhile, fought his own action north of Vicksburg at Haines's Bluff on April 30 and May 1. Sherman made a small demonstration along with a flotilla of several Union gunboats that shelled the bluff, and the ships took a few hits from the heavy Confederate batteries there under the command of Brig. Gen. Louis Hébert. The action resulted in slight casualties on both sides.

The increasingly imperiled Trans-Mississippi, now chiefly held by means of Vicksburg and Port Hudson, also saw fighting. On May 7, Banks advanced his Army of the Gulf into Alexandria, Louisiana, occupying this town without opposition. The Confederate forces in the area withdrew to Shreveport.

Grant's expedition into Mississippi now accelerated. In Vicksburg, Pemberton began to panic over the prospects that were shaping up, and by May 9, Confederate Gen. Joseph E. Johnston was directed to assume command of the forces scattered throughout the Department of the West, which included Mississippi. Pemberton would continue to command the Army of Mississippi, with some 32,000 men spread defensively around Vicksburg. A garrison of about 1,000 troops held the capital at Jackson. Johnston would soon arrive on the scene and attempt to bring order back into the defense of Mississippi. By contrast, Grant's 44,000 troops had now crossed the river and were at Rocky Springs (McClernand), Hankinson's Ferry (McPherson), and Grand Gulf (Sherman).

Grant had promised Halleck to send one army corps southward to assist Banks with his operations. But by early in the first week of May, Grant discovered that Banks had moved up the Red River and would not be ready to combine forces for a coordinated operation until May 10 and, further, that he would only have about 15,000 men available—much less than originally anticipated. The failed timing exasperated Grant; the whole campaign against Vicksburg required fast action, and Banks's meaningless expedition now jeopardized the whole Federal operation in the state. Grant now found himself with several options, each of them distasteful: If he waited for Banks, Pemberton might solidify his defenses and fortify Vicksburg into one giant bastion that would make Grand Gulf seem weak by comparison. Moreover, the longer he waited, the greater the chances that his long, tenuous lines of supply might be destroyed. If he moved quickly, without Banks, he would have less manpower than anticipated. Grant now made one of the most daring moves of the war: He moved his army quickly into the state, decided to fight the necessary pitched battles, and would turn and attack Vicksburg from the east, all without a supply line. The army simply took all the matériel it could carry and abandoned the route of supply altogether. The decision marked from a strategic sense a new mode of warfare, and one that foreshadowed and laid down the theory for Sherman's March to the Sea the following year. The army brought forward all the available wagons it could muster. Sherman gathered some 120 and loaded them with "army bread" (hardtack), sugar, coffee, and salt; all the wagons available, about ten per brigade, were loaded with ammunition.

McPherson sent a reconnoitering party north of the Big Black River and discovered Pemberton's heavy concentration south of Vicksburg. Federal reports also indicated a Confederate presence at Jackson. So Grant moved quickly to interpose his army between the two smaller forces, aiming to move on Jackson first, defeat the small force there, and then turn back on Vicksburg—defeating the separated forces "in detail." Pemberton now had a real dilemma. Northern-born and mistrusted by many of the Southern civilians, defended almost solely by his friend Jefferson Davis, and beset with a difficult task in holding Vicksburg against Grant's powerful army, his days were numbered. To make matters more difficult, Johnston was not the sort of commander who would risk a great many of his men. So careful was Johnston (many Confederate soldiers and civilians thought his caution bordered on cowardice relative to bolder, less experienced officers) that the Confederate officer Charles Minor Blackford wondered in a letter about his mental state. "He is a very able man, I doubt not, but seems to so doubt the ability of his troops to carry out the plans his skill devises that he will not test it. No victory has ever been won without bringing about a fight." Perhaps the gravest problem Pemberton faced was a relative lack of support from Richmond. With the easy brilliance of hindsight it seems clear to many observers of the war that it was won in the western theater, and that the loss of Vicksburg was perhaps the single most crucial blow to the Confederate war in the west—it separated the Trans-Mississippi from the rest of the Confederacy for the duration. In Richmond, Davis definitely held an east-centric view of the importance of war resources, swayed by many officers, none more prominent than Robert E. Lee, who garnered all the resources he could for his own Army of Northern Virginia and shared little with others. Historians have sometimes argued that Lee was simply mustering the best effort he could in the arena in which he operated. But viewed in retrospect, more resources deployed toward Vicksburg might have made quite a difference in the strategy and psychology of the war of 1863.

In any event, Grant now had his work before him. Pemberton believed that Grant might strike toward Jackson but that any such movement might be short-lived and weakly supplied; both Pemberton and Johnston underestimated the Federal army's ability to subsist away from a supply base. On May 9, McPherson's advancing soldiers clashed briefly with Confederate cavalry at Utica, east of Rocky Springs. The advanced division of Brig. Gen. Marcellus M. Crocker marched forward as Col. Clark Wright's 6th Missouri Cavalry dashed out ahead into Utica and clashed with Confederate cavalry in the town before scattering it into a retreat. As Grant continued to move his elements northeast toward Jackson, Pemberton deployed his forces along the Vicksburg & Jackson Railroad that ran east-west between the two cities, and in particular he concentrated them along the Big Black River at Edwards's Station. On May 11, Grant commenced moving from Rocky Springs, and by day's end McPherson's corps was on the Telegraph Road north of Cayuga, Sherman's corps was at Auburn, and McClernand's corps was northeast of Utica. Pemberton's concentration of troops at Edward's Station continued, with Bowen's division forming its anchor.

On May 12 the first battle of the campaign occurred, near Raymond, a town at the southern terminus of a rail spur, located fifteen miles southwest of Jackson. Anticipating the approach of Federal troops, Confederate Brig. Gen. John Gregg established a defensive line with his brigade two miles southwest of the town, along Fourteen Mile Creek. The advanced division of McPherson's corps, that of Maj. Gen. John A. Logan, clashed with Gregg's Tennessee and Texas infantry. The battle commenced about 2 P.M. and lasted about three hours. The brigade commanders of Logan's division, Brig. Gens. John E. Smith, Elias S. Dennis, and John D. Stevenson, committed their troops to the attack. "The line was ordered forward and charged," recalled Smith, "which they did handsomely, completely routing the enemy, who fled precipitately through Raymond, leaving their dead and wounded on the field." Gregg reported about 2,500 engaged and casualties of 73 killed, 251 wounded, and 190 missing. McPherson's corps suffered 66 killed, 339 wounded, and 37 missing. The casualties attest to the high intensity of the fighting at Raymond, and the serious, stubborn defense of the outnumbered Confederates before they broke and fled. On this evening it occurred to Grant that Pemberton was concentrating forces at Edwards's Station. Johnston, meanwhile, had arrived at Jackson, which had 3,199 highly concerned residents. Sherman and McPherson now set off on their mission of attacking and defeating Johnston, while McClernand's corps remained at Raymond and Clinton (on the main east-west rail line) to block any Confederate reinforcements that might attempt to arrive from the west.

The resulting action on May 14 was the battle of Jackson. Approaching the town by midmorning in a driving rainstorm, McPherson's corps used the road from Clinton, Sherman's corps the approach from Raymond. Johnston's 6,000 men faced potential disaster attempting to hold off Grant's 44,000, and no one appreciated this fact better than Johnston. By the time

Johnston arrived in Jackson he could not affect the situation. Finding the brigades of Gregg and Brig. Gen. William H. T. Walker there, and a faint promise of two more brigades on the way, Johnston wired the news of hopelessness to Secretary of War Seddon. "I arrived this evening [May 13], finding the enemy's force between this place and General Pemberton, cutting off communication. I am too late."

Sherman's corps made first contact about 10 A.M. and savagely cut into Gregg's brigade, routing the Southerners. Despite the muddy roads, hard rain, and swollen streams, Sherman's men pushed on and laid down a heavy fire into the entrenchments that had been quickly erected by Gregg's men. They emerged from a woods into heavy fire; artillery somehow managed to throw projectiles back and forth between the two lines. About 1 P.M. Sherman's hard-fighting men found after a brief reconnaissance by the 95th Ohio Infantry that the entrenchments had been abandoned and that Gregg's men had scattered behind the railroad line west of the city. McPherson delayed his attack for an hour, concerned about damp ammunition, but finally struck Walker's brigade late in the morning. Heavy fighting erupted along the lines, and Walker's resistance was initially brisk; McPherson's men made repeated attacks before weakening the Confederates and only broke the Rebel line with a final assault in the afternoon. Walker's brigade had been bolstered slightly by the addition of a portion of the brigade of Brig. Gen. States Rights Gist, which was commanded by Col. Peyton H. Colquitt.

By 4 P.M. Federal forces entered Jackson, and Johnston, completely overwhelmed, took his forces on a northward retreat in great haste, along the Canton Road toward Richland. Sherman's predilection for destroying enemy supplies, stores, and objects of military value—much celebrated and exaggerated during accounts of the later March to the Sea—now emerged. "The railroads were destroyed by burning the ties and warping the iron," reported Sherman, describing the technique that produced the twisted segments of rail that came to be called "Sherman's hairpins." "In Jackson the arsenal buildings, the Government foundry, the gun-carriage establishment, including the carriages for two complete six-gun batteries, stable, carpenter and paint shops were destroyed," he wrote. "The penitentiary was burned, I think, by some convicts who had been set free by the Confederate authorities." The Federal casualties at Jackson were 42 killed, 251 wounded, and 7 missing; Confederate losses were incompletely reported as "200" by Gregg and 17 killed, 66 wounded, and 118 missing by Colquitt. Following the battle, McPherson supplied Grant with a copy of an intercepted message from Johnston to Pemberton, which ordered Pemberton eastward from Vicksburg to Clinton so that the Confederate armies could join to defeat Grant. The Federal commander boldly wasted no time in turning back to the west to face the approach of Pemberton, blocking him from reaching Johnston.

Amazingly, Grant—with a large force in enemy territory, isolated from his supply line—was winning battles exactly as he had planned, and found himself in a strong position. The Confederates, with the crucially important key to the Mississippi River at stake, were in disarray. Johnston's force was scattering northeastward from Jackson. Elements of Pemberton's army, unaware that they were about to be blindsided, wandered out of their defenses at Vicksburg hoping to cut the Federal supply line (which didn't exist) and somehow expel Grant from the state.

Pemberton's council of war on May 14 reflected his feeling of lost confidence. Johnston, too, had committed the grievous blunder of imprecision in his orders, dictating that Pemberton should move out to unite the armies "if practicable," using the same vague phrase often employed by Robert E. Lee. Such wide latitude in interpretation was disastrous at this critical time, and when Pemberton polled his subordinates, he preferred the minority view of Maj. Gens. Carter L. Stevenson and William W. Loring, that the army should move out to attack the enemy's supply line rather than vigorously marching to Clinton to join Johnston. Pemberton later justified his decision in a hazy way: "My own views were strongly expressed as unfavorable to any advance which would separate me further from Vicksburg, which was my base," wrote the commander. "I did not however, see fit to put my own judgment and opinions so far in opposition as to prevent a movement altogether, but believing the only possibility of success to be in the plan of cutting the enemy's communications, it was adopted."

Pemberton delayed his movement toward Raymond in search of Grant's supply line until May 15. By this time Grant's forces were converging on Edwards's Station, and the two movements in direct opposition created the most important of the small actions during the campaign. At this moment Pemberton received another order from Johnston, directing him again to join Johnston at Clinton—a movement that was now impossible. With frequent, nearly continuous rains, muddy roads, and bulging creeks before him, Pemberton now altered his plan, deciding to countermarch through Edwards's Station to unite with Johnston at Brownsville, northwest of Clinton. But as it had been for Johnston at Jackson, it was already too late for Pemberton at Edwards's Station. At 7:30 A.M. on May 16 the skirmishing had already begun, and Pemberton found his forces engaged with the enemy on a seventy-five-foot rise east of Edwards's Station (and west of Bolton's Depot) called Champion Hill. The action would also be termed Baker's Creek and Edwards's Station, but it was fought on the hill that provided a good position for artillery to block the roads to Vicksburg from the east. Pemberton's force, with Stevenson on the north, Bowen in the center, and Loring on the south, moved out east of Baker's Creek and to a point near Champion Hill sluggishly, after finally locating fords over which they could cross the creek, which was filled with muddy brown water. Pemberton's force consisted of about 20,000 men. Simultaneously, the Union corps of McPherson (to the north, with the divisions of Logan, Hovey, Crocker, and Osterhaus) and McClernand (to the south, divisions of Carr, Blair, and A. J. Smith) approached westward, also arriving near Champion Hill and bringing some 29,373 men toward the impending action.

Stevenson's Confederates held the high ground on Champion Hill, while their comrades in Bowen's and Loring's divisions occupied a mile-long ridge to the south. Hovey's soldiers attacked into the densely wooded hill, and by 11 A.M. a severe musketry battle resulted in the Federals capturing some of the ground on Champion Hill. McClernand delayed without good reason and might have jeopardized the outcome of the battle if not for the actions of McPherson's corps. Logan attacked with great skill and penetrated a portion of Stevenson's line. Although the Southerners fought stubbornly, they had great difficulty slowing the onslaught of Union infantry attacks. "Under a heavy charge we were run over, our infantry breaking, and our horses being shot down by the charging troops and by our own infantry," wrote Capt. John W. Johnston of the Boutetort Artillery, who was Joe Johnston's nephew. Pemberton vainly attempted to support the caving left flank and reestablish the right by ordering Bowen and Loring to counterattack in support of Stevenson. These orders went unheeded, until Col. Francis M. Cockrell struck the Federal line.

Cockrell's attack was repulsed with a bloody loss, however, and by midafternoon the whole Confederate army seemed in great peril. Bowen's division had fallen back in confusion, and Stevenson's division had been shattered in the morning. Loring's division now had the task of salvaging the operation, but it was useless. The best the Confederate army could hope for by midafternoon was to withdraw without being badly mauled. By 4 P.M., as most of the army withdrew in haste to the southwest, Bowen's and Stevenson's divisions turned sharply westward on the Raymond Road and crossed Baker's Creek, bound for Edwards's Station. Loring escaped southward along the eastern bank of the creek, his preferred route of retreat blocked by Logan, who had crossed the creek toward Edwards's Station. South of the Ratliff House, on the southern end of the field, Brig. Gen. Lloyd Tilghman's brigade of Mississippians, part of Loring's division, fought a rearguard action attempting to secure time for the fleeing Southern forces. Tilghman was struck by a shell and killed instantly. Sherman, coming from Jackson, arrived only after the battle was over.

Champion Hill was a disaster for Pemberton, who placed the blame squarely on Loring (with some justification) for failing to follow orders. It marked another solid victory in Grant's bold plan. The Federal casualties at Champion Hill were 410 killed, 1,844 wounded, and 187 missing; Confederate losses were 381 killed, 1,800 wounded, and 1,670 missing. Confederate losses also included 27 field guns, several thousand small arms, and several stands of captured battle flags. It was a shattering defeat for Pemberton and his men.

The action wasn't over. McClernand and McPherson encamped between Champion Hill and Edwards's Station on the night of May 16, and Sherman wasn't far behind at Bolton Depot. The majority of Pemberton's army had skedaddled west toward Vicksburg, but about 5,000 men held a bridge on the Big Black River where the Vicksburg & Jackson Railroad crossed it. On the morning of May 17, McClernand's and McPherson's corps aggressively approached the bridge while Sherman crossed his corps to the north at Bridgeport in order to reconnoiter and to block that part of Pemberton's force from returning to Vicksburg. Some of the 5,000 were left on the river's western bank, while others were along the eastern bank, all prepared for a fight. At the battle of the Big Black River, when McClernand's men approached and began firing, the Confederates set the bridge ablaze, abandoning their comrades on the eastern shore, leaving them prisoners, and scattering at high speed toward Vicksburg. Cavalry attached to Sherman's corps settled into the old forts at Haines's Bluff and reestablished lines of communication along the Mississippi River. Johnston, meanwhile, fled northward to Livingston, well north of Jackson and out of the way of the current operations. The Union losses at the Big Black River were 39 killed, 237 wounded, and 3 missing. About 1,700 Confederates were captured.

The following day Grant's army of 35,000 moved to within a mile and a half of Vicksburg and faced the heavily fortified ring of trenches that Confederate defenders had elaborately constructed over the previous months. The importance of Vicksburg as a bastion on the Mississippi had been recognized since the earliest days of the war, when Winfield Scott had proposed the Anaconda Plan to split the Confederacy in two. The Confederate entrenchments and fortifications at Vicksburg were large, scattered, and formidable. The Confederate defensive lines encompassed a ring around the city that stretched two miles from the northwestern edge of the city (on the river) to a point northeast of the city, then wound southwestward over a distance of two and a half miles before slicing westward and continuing southwestward another two miles to a position on the river two miles south of the city. Along the perimeter were many gun pits, forts, redoubts, and lunettes. The whole landscape was roughly variable in elevation, such that many hills and knobs featured into the line, making it exceedingly difficult to attack, aside from the heavy artillery placed at points along the line. Steep approaches toward well-defended gun pits or infantry breastworks transformed the land surrounding Vicksburg into one of the greatest challenges for any attacking troops during the war. In order to capture the city and Pemberton's remaining army, the Union troops would need to capture the strongholds along the line: Fort Hill, perched atop a high bluff north of the city overlooking the Yazoo City Road; the Stockade Redan, northeast of the city on Graveyard Road; the 3d Louisiana Redan, northeast of the city near the James Shirley House; to its south, the Great Redoubt; the Railroad Redoubt, east of the city along the railroad line; the Square Fort to the southeast; and a salient along Hall's Ferry Road south of the city.

On May 19, Grant, hoping to strike the Confederates before they were reorganized at Vicksburg, ordered an attack on the Stockade Redan. The attack point was difficult at best: Soldiers of the 1st Battalion, the 13th U.S. Infantry, the 116th Illinois Infantry, the 8th Missouri Infantry, and other units assaulted the position by cutting through a steep ravine partially barricaded by abatis, encountering a split-rail fence, passing across Graveyard Road, moving across the glacis, and attempting to cross a 6-foot-deep, 8-foot-wide ditch before attacking the 17-foot-high walls of the Redan, all while under heavy small arms and artillery fire. It was a suicidal attack. The Stockade Redan was defended by the 36th Mississippi Infantry, which anchored the left of Brig. Gen. Louis Hébert's brigade. About 9 A.M. Grant ordered an artillery bombardment to soften the defenses and began massing the troops of Blair's division of Sherman's corps to support the attack, with Col. Thomas Kilby Smith's brigade on the left, along Graveyard Road, Col. Giles A. Smith's brigade in the center, and Brig. Gen. Hugh Ewing's brigade on the right. At 2 P.M. the Federal artillery opened a barrage that signaled the start of the attack, and the U.S. regulars and other troops pressed forward into a tangled scene of dense brush, cane, felled trees, abatis, holes covered with grass, and tree stumps. Confederate artillery shells exploded all around them, and Minié bullets filled the air. The attack lost momentum quickly, and only a small number of men cleared the fence and entered the ditch at the base of the Redan—some 10 brought the colors of the 13th U.S. Infantry into the ditch; all but one of them was killed or wounded. A brutal melee witnessed the use of hand grenades that were lobbed back and forth as Federal soldiers shouted demands of surrender and were ignored. Musketry fire spread all along the line outside the fort.

The May 19 assault was a Federal failure. It was costly in lives and morale. Grant knew that his men were riding high emotionally following their unprecedented series of victories during the approach to the city. The last thing he wanted was a long siege during the swelteringly hot and humid Mississippi summer. The Federal commander established headquarters north of the city, employed Sherman's corps in that vicinity, McPherson's corps in the center, and McClernand's corps south of McPherson. Before resorting to siege operations, which would of course be very costly in terms of time, resources, and lives, Grant ordered that one more attack be launched to crack the Vicksburg defenses. This time he enlisted the aid of the Federal

Mississippi River gunboats under Capt. David Dixon Porter. The attack would be a more general one across wide sectors of the Confederate defenses. At 10 A.M. on May 22 the Union troops marched with their battle flags waving toward the Confederate strongholds along the defensive line. The Confederate resistance was stubborn, however, and the strong Confederate artillery and small-arms fire withering. By 11:30 A.M. it was clear that the assault—defended by Martin L. Smith in the north, Forney in the center, and Carter L. Stevenson to the south, with Bowen sending in troops where needed—had failed. But a short time later exaggerated messages of success from McClernand suggested the attack might succeed if renewed with further support. So Grant ordered Sherman and McPherson to redouble their efforts. But by nightfall it was clear that McClernand was mistaken and that the assault had failed by noon and continued to fail throughout the afternoon. The two assaults had cost the Union army 659 killed, 3,327 wounded, and 155 missing. After a brief truce to recover and bury bodies of the slain, it was clear to all that a protracted siege lay ahead. The army's chief engineer, Capt. Frederick E. Prime, ordered his engineers to design and construct approaches consisting of mines, trenches, tunnels, or batteries. Capt. Andrew Hickenlooper, chief engineer of McPherson's corps, worked energetically on a series of mines and approaches in the vicinity of the James Shirley House, which soldiers simply called the White House, with an aim toward taking the 3d Louisiana Redan.

Sherman, meanwhile, attempted to reduce Fort Hill by enlisting the aid of gunboats. On May 27 the river ironclad USS *Cincinnati,* packed with logs and hay, proceeded downstream and opened fire on the fort. Heavy cannon fire from the fort struck the ship repeatedly, perforating the ship entirely and sinking her in short order. "Two shots entered the shell room," reported Bache, ". . . it was immediately filled with water. A third shot entered the magazine and flooded it almost instantly, thereby preventing us from returning (any more) the enemy's fire." Not only was the ironclad lost, but 25 sailors were killed or wounded and 15 drowned. At Milliken's Bend on June 7, Confederates under Maj. Gen. John G. Walker attacked Union forces but were repulsed with the aid of the ironclad gunboat USS *Choctaw* and the timberclad USS *Lexington.*

Engineer operations dominated the next few weeks around the Vicksburg trenches, although sniping and scattered fighting erupted. Hickenlooper's engineering work turned all the soldiers in the area into gophers with "a spade in one hand and a gun in the other," and by the end of May his approach reached the Jackson Road and turned westward. By June 8, Hickenlooper's approach reached within seventy-five yards of the redan, and an observation tower was constructed with railroad ties east of Battery Hickenlooper. Confederate sharpshooters took a heavy toll on exposed Union troops, and even Grant climbed the tower one day and was recognized by a Confederate marksman who yelled obscenities at Grant; the private's commanding officer sternly reprimanded the man for using such language. Grant climbed down quickly before any of the Confederates had the notion to shoot him.

By June 23, Hickenlooper commenced constructing a mine within twenty-five yards of the 3d Louisiana Redan, planning to pack it with explosives and blow it up. The digging sounds were clearly audible to Confederates within the redan. On June 25, Hickenlooper exploded 2,200 pounds of black powder set along the mine, as a prelude to a massive attack. Later, Hickenlooper recalled the scene. "At the appointed moment it appeared as though the whole fort and connecting outworks commenced an upward movement," he wrote, "gradually breaking into fragments and growing less bulky in appearance, until it looked like an immense fountain of finely pulverized earth, mingled with flashes of fire and clouds of smoke, through which could occasionally be caught a glimpse of some dark objects—men, gun-carriages, shelters, etc."

As dozens of Federal soldiers ran into the resulting crater, hoping to punch a hole into the Confederate line and collapse its defenses, a horrifying hand-to-hand melee ensued, with soldiers using clubbed muskets, firing pistols and long arms at point-blank range, and fighting on the ground with knives and their bare hands. The spectacle continued on past dusk and throughout the night into the next morning; only during the midmorning hours of June 26 did Grant order McPherson to recall the exhausted troops. After some twenty hours of fighting, the Federal casualties were 34 men killed and 204 wounded; Confederate losses in the crater were 21 killed and 73 wounded.

The Vicksburg operations were proving difficult and discouraging for the Union forces, after such a tremendously impressive start. The situation was becoming even worse for Pemberton, his army, and the citizens of Vicksburg. Despite the success at staving off Federal attacks, the city was cut off from the rest of the world. The inhabitants of the Confederate lines, including the city, would if nothing else be slowly starved out. For all his ineffectiveness with the small force at Jackson, Joe Johnston had warned Pemberton to get his army out of Vicksburg after the action at the Big Black River Bridge. Vacillating, Pemberton had again conducted a council of war and decided to stay and defend the city. This he did knowing that help from other theaters was not likely to come, given the condition and psychology of Bragg and Lee and their armies. "Vicksburg contains many of my old pupils and friends," cautioned Sherman near the end of June. "Should it fall into our hands I will treat them with kindness, but they have sowed the wind and must reap the whirlwind." Some of them did reap it. On June 17, Col. Isham

W. Garrott, a North Carolina native, was shot dead through the heart while aiming a rifle from the Square Fort along the southern part of the defense line. Although he is often claimed to have been a brigadier general, Garrott's commission as such was not confirmed. On June 27 the Virginian Brig. Gen. Martin E. Green was struck in the head by a Minié bullet and killed instantly as he looked out over a parapet, allegedly having said that "the bullet has not yet been made that would kill me."

The siege ground on, with the approaches worked and reworked. The one soldier who seemed above it all was the troublesome McClernand. He issued a congratulatory order to his men, and he took credit for the genius of the Vicksburg campaign. The order vastly exaggerated the accomplishments of McClernand's corps and cast a subtle air of inferiority over the other corps. Of the attack on June 22, McClernand claimed that his men "within thirty minutes had made a lodgment and planted your colors on two of his bastions . . . it . . . was the first and largest success achieved anywhere along the whole line of our army. . . . How and why the general assault failed, it would be useless now to explain." In reality, however, McClernand's performance during the campaign had been the only shaky one among an otherwise solid group of commanders, and despite Lincoln's friendship with McClernand, Grant had had enough. On June 18, Grant relieved him of command and assigned Maj. Gen. Edward O. C. Ord in his place. The press and the public would in part celebrate and in part overlook the tremendous accomplishments of the campaign to date and would focus on the unhappy aspect of the continuing siege. Disgusted with both press and public, Sherman simply told his wife, "Vox populi, vox humbug."

As Grant continued to concentrate on Vicksburg, Banks moved into a siege of Port Hudson. Banks's Army of the Gulf (also termed the 19th Corps) consisted of four divisions commanded by Maj. Gen. Christopher C. Augur (brigades of Col. Edward P. Chapin, Brig. Gen. Godfrey Weitzel, and Col. Nathan A. M. Dudley); Brig. Gen. Thomas W. Sherman (brigades of Brig. Gens. Neal Dow and Frank S. Nickerson); Brig. Gen. Halbert E. Paine (brigades of Cols. Timothy Ingraham, Hawkes Fearing, Jr., and Oliver P. Gooding); and Brig. Gen. Cuvier Grover (brigades of Cols. Richard E. Holcomb, William K. Kimball, and Henry W. Birge). The cavalry was commanded by Col. Benjamin H. Grierson. The Federal force held about 13,000 effectives when the siege began. On the Confederate side, Maj. Gen. Franklin Gardner's garrison was comprised of approximately 4,500 defenders whose line officers were Brig. Gen. William Nelson Rector Beall and Cols. William R. Miles and I. G. W. Steedman.

For three days beginning on May 8 a Federal mortar flotilla under Comdr. Charles H. B. Caldwell, with the screw sloop USS *Richmond* (Capt. James Alden) in support, pounded the Confederate batteries at Port Hudson almost continuously during daylight. Then Banks's army advanced through the swampy ground and attacked the Confederate defenders along the Bayou Sara Road, four miles outside of Port Hudson, on May 27. The timbered lay of the battlefield was interspersed with rolling ravines, making it difficult country to march across. Banks's attack was not coordinated well, thwarted by thick sheets of Confederate small-arms fire and hampered by the difficult terrain. Weitzel began the advance about 6 A.M., and by noon a number of regiments darted out toward Commissary Hill, where the Confederates waited. Lt. Col. Willoughby Babcock challenged the 75th New York Infantry to follow him, drawing his sword and running headlong toward the Rebels. "Come on," shouted a corporal, "Here goes the Colonel, boys, we won't leave the Colonel! Charge!"

A severe fight raged throughout the morning and early afternoon, and the Federals failed to secure the Confederate works along the Little Sandy Creek, in the Confederate center. The majority of the attacks were piecemeal affairs that could not have hoped to achieve success. This being the case, the Yankees now looked to the flanks. Some of the units who fought at Port Hudson consisted of black American soldiers, giving the "Corps D'Afrique" one of its first tastes of battle, and Confederate soldiers one of the first opportunities to fight black soldiers. The African-American troops fought generally well despite some confusion, but were overwhelmed by Confederate artillery fire. Capt. Andre Cailloux, a free black from New Orleans, led an advance even after being struck by a canister ball. His arm dangling, he led his brethren forward, shouting orders in English and French, until a shell struck him squarely, killing him on the spot.

By late in the day Banks realized that his attack would not succeed, and in an echo of the events transpiring at Vicksburg, a siege of Port Hudson resulted. Banks conducted two more serious attacks against the fortifications at Port Hudson, on June 11 and 14. By the time these took place the relatively weak entrenchments Confederates had fought behind in late May were strengthened considerably, and again these attacks failed, although a few Confederate outposts were captured on the 11th. In most instances, severe cannon and small-arms fire thwarted the assailants long before they reached the Confederate positions. During the June 14 attack a large number of Union troops cowered in a deep ravine, unwilling to move farther. "I started out this morning with the determination to be a hell of a man," said Lt. Nicholas Day. "I've been a hell of a fellow long enough. If anybody else wants to be a hell of a fellow, I've no objections! But it's too damned risky."

The casualties at Port Hudson mounted; Federal losses on May 27 amounted to 293 killed, 1,545 wounded, and 157 missing; Confederate casualties were about 235 total. On June 14 the Federal casualties amounted to 203 killed, 1,401 wounded, and 188 missing; Confederate losses were 22 killed and

25 wounded. Brig. Gen. Neal Dow was wounded, shot in the left thigh, and captured. He would spend the next seven months of the war in Richmond's Libby prison until being exchanged for Robert E. Lee's son "Rooney." In Brashear City, Louisiana, on June 23, 275 Union soldiers surrendered to Confederates commanded by Col. James P. Major. The Southern soldiers took four field guns, huge stores of ammunition and supplies, and "about 3,000 Negroes." And so the siege at Port Hudson would continue on into July unresolved. So, too, would important questions hanging in the balance at Vicksburg. Both places were vital to the Confederacy's strategic war aims. Richmond's attitude toward helping them out of apparent doom would not change, either, as the focus of war shifted back to the eastern theater.

FOLLOWING BURNSIDE'S AWFUL LOSS at Fredericksburg, the pointless Mud March, and the assignment of yet another suspect commander to lead the Army of the Potomac (Hooker had not only a reputation for unparalleled egotism but also for hard drinking), the soldiers of the primary eastern Union army were virtually demoralized. Hooker, 48, added to his Massachusetts roots a moderately successful record at West Point, a Mexican War record, and time as a California farmer before reentering the service, first in the California militia and later as a brigadier general of volunteers. Though his army may well have had more than its share of less than pure "camp followers"—ladies who made a fair fortune following the officers and offering their services, the term "hooker" as slang for prostitute most certainly existed long before Joe came onto the scene. Gone forever, it was now clear, was McClellan, who was popular with the troops if no one else. The soldiers faced an uncertain future being commanded by generals who did not seem to be experienced enough to command an army, had vague plans of what to do, and squared off against a foe that seemed at the height of confidence. Yet for a time Hooker rose to the occasion. He organized his army into seven corps, eliminating the "grand division" scheme employed by Burnside, which suggested an improvement in communications. He cleaned up and organized the hospitals, food supplies, and quartermaster logistics to better serve the soldiers in the field. His creation of a cavalry corps under Maj. Gen. George Stoneman centralized the command aspects of the Federal horse soldiers, who had previously been attached to the corps. This made increases in fighting efficiency possible. But Hooker failed to do the same with his artillery, keeping those units attached to corps, which would not help the struggles to come.

During late winter and early spring Lee's emboldened Army of Northern Virginia had fortified the ground along the southern bank of the Rappahannock River very effectively. The protection against a potential Federal crossing of the river extended from Port Royal in the east all the way to

Banks's Ford, west of Fredericksburg, and Lee's engineers had constructed detached defenses as far west as United States Ford north of the crossroads of Chancellorsville, which consisted of a tavern and several scattered farms. Lee's strength (in defending rather than attacking and in a psychological superiority after the great victory at Fredericksburg) would be tempered by his caution over the Union 9th Corps's movements at Hampton Roads, however. Alarmed by this development, Lee sent Longstreet with the divisions of Pickett and Hood to move south to the Virginia-Carolina coast to guard against any movement there. This in fact almost evened the table prior to what became the Chancellorsville campaign because it gave Hooker a superiority in numbers.

With the weather warming and the government, soldiers, and general populace yearning for action, Hooker decided to move upstream north of the Rappahannock and attempt to turn Lee's left. Hooker had the idea of dispatching Stoneman on a raid to disrupt Lee's lines of communication, thereby drawing him away from Fredericksburg. He would then pursue with infantry, which would smash Lee's army before it caught up with the Union horsemen. An abortive attempt at this plan began late in April, but after poor weather set in, it was called off. The plan that actually unfolded was then devised by the Federal commander.

Hooker's corps were commanded by Maj. Gen. John F. Reynolds (1st Corps; divisions of Brig. Gens. James S. Wadsworth, John C. Robinson, and Abner Doubleday); Maj. Gen. Darius N. Couch (2d Corps; divisions of Maj. Gens. Winfield Scott Hancock and William H. French, and Brig. Gen. John Gibbon); Maj. Gen. Daniel E. Sickles (3d Corps; divisions of Brig. Gen. David B. Birney and Maj. Gens. Hiram G. Berry and Amiel W. Whipple); Maj. Gen. George G. Meade (5th Corps; divisions of Brig. Gens. Charles Griffin and Andrew A. Humphreys, and Maj. Gen. George Sykes); Maj. Gen. John Sedgwick (6th Corps; divisions of Brig. Gens. William T. H. Brooks and Albion P. Howe, Maj. Gen. John Newton, and Col. Hiram Burnham); Maj. Gen. Oliver O. Howard (11th Corps; divisions of Brig. Gens. Charles Devens, Jr., and Adolph von Steinwehr, and Maj. Gen. Carl Schurz); and Maj. Gen. Henry W. Slocum (12th Corps; divisions of Brig. Gens. Alpheus S. Williams and John W. Geary). The cavalry corps was commanded by Maj. Gen. George Stoneman and held the divisions of Brig. Gens. Alfred Pleasonton, William W. Averell, and David M. Gregg.

Gen. Robert E. Lee's Army of Northern Virginia was organized into two army corps with reserve artillery and cavalry attached. The majority of Lee's first corps, commanded by Lt. Gen. James Longstreet, was detached on duty in southeastern Virginia, as mentioned. Longstreet's absent force included the divisions of Hood and Pickett and two artillery battalions. This left two divisions of Longstreet's corps, plus attached artillery. Maj. Gen.

Lafayette McLaws's division held the brigades of Brig. Gens. William T. Wofford, Paul J. Semmes, Joseph B. Kershaw, and William Barksdale. Maj. Gen. Richard H. Anderson's division contained the brigades of Brig. Gens. Cadmus M. Wilcox, Ambrose R. Wright, William Mahone, Carnot Posey, and Edward A. Perry. The second army corps of Lt. Gen. Thomas J. Jackson contained the divisions of Maj. Gen. A. P. Hill ("Light Division"; brigades of Brig. Gens. Henry Heth, Edward L. Thomas, James H. Lane, Samuel Mc-Gowan, James Jay Archer, and William Dorsey Pender); Brig. Gen. Robert E. Rodes (D. H. Hill's division; brigades of Col. Edward A. O'Neal and Brig. Gens. Alfred H. Colquitt, Stephen Dodson Ramseur, George P. Doles, and Alfred Iverson); Maj. Gen. Jubal A. Early (brigades of Brig. Gens. John B. Gordon, Robert F. Hoke, William Smith, and Harry T. Hays); and Brig. Gen. Raleigh E. Colston (Trimble's division; brigades of Brig. Gens. Elisha F. Paxton, John R. Jones, and Francis R. T. Nicholls, and Col. E. T. H. Warren). The reserve artillery was commanded by Brig. Gen. William N. Pendleton; the cavalry was commanded by Maj. Gen. Jeb Stuart and contained the brigades of Brig. Gens. Fitzhugh Lee and William Henry Fitzhugh "Rooney" Lee. The cavalry brigades of Wade Hampton and William E. Jones were detached.

The campaign for Chancellorsville got underway on April 27, following skirmishes at Kelly's Ford and Port Royal. On that day Maj. Gen. Slocum marched with the 5th, 11th, and 12th corps northwestward to Kelly's Ford, where they crossed the Rappahannock on April 29. Simultaneously, Sedgwick marched the 1st and 6th corps to a crossing just south of Fredericksburg, not far from the costly battlefield of the previous December. Sickles's corps was left in reserve, while two divisions of Couch's marched to Banks's Ford and dug in there so as not to be observed.

This great blitz after so many weeks of utter inactivity caught Lee off guard, as he had been planning an offensive toward the Shenandoah Valley that was now out of the question. The off-balance army strengths were 42,000 in the main enveloping Federal force (Slocum's), 12,000 under Couch, 40,000 led by Sedgwick, 19,000 under Sickles, and 5,000 detached from the 2d Corps under Brig. Gen. John Gibbon at Falmouth, yielding 118,000 effectives. Lee's army, on the other hand, with Longstreet's two divisions absent, had a mere 53,000, plus 6,500 cavalry under Stuart, approaching 60,000 effectives on the battlefield as the campaign commenced. As the battle of Chancellorsville actually began, several days later, the numbers would rise to about 133,868 Federals and 60,892 Confederates present over the whole area of operations, a more than two-to-one advantage for Hooker. Lee was anything but clear in reading Hooker's intentions. Thinking Slocum might move toward Gordonsville, he wished for immediate, detailed intelligence reports from Stuart, whose position was temporarily cut off by the Federal advance. On April 29, as the Federals were maneuvering, Lee could wait no longer and he deployed three divisions on his right in a line close to that of the old defensive one at Fredericksburg, preparing to block Sedgwick's movement. He sent the division of Maj. Gen. Richard H. Anderson westward to Chancellorsville, who after a short time withdrew at high speed. Stuart reentered the picture on the southern flank of the field, watching Slocum's movement carefully as he detached one brigade to go after Stoneman, who had embarked on a fruitless "raid" that accomplished little.

Stoneman's raid sent the columns of horsemen under Brig. Gens. William Woods Averell and John Buford away from the main army, southward—Averell toward Gordonsville, and Buford to break up the Richmond, Fredericksburg & Potomac Railroad. On April 30 a skirmish occurred at Raccoon Ford; the next day, Brig. Gen. Rooney Lee's brigade of Southern horsemen was pushed back to Rapidan Station. Ordered back to the army, Averell's column returned by May 2. Following Averell's unsatisfactory report that the countryside was ill suited to cavalry operations, Averell was dismissed from his assignment by Hooker and replaced with Brig. Gen. Alfred Pleasonton. Buford, meanwhile, assisted primarily by the brigade of Brig. Gen. David M. Gregg—whose long beard made him the "hairiest general in the Army of the Potomac"—proceeded to Louisa Court House, where they skirmished with the rebels. A detachment under the eccentric soldier of fortune Col. Percy Wyndham destroyed part of the James Canal at Columbia; a column led by Col. H. Judson Kilpatrick, one of the nattiest, most egocentric and trouble-prone officers in the army, went to Hungary to destroy a section of the Fredericksburg railroad and approached the doorstep of Richmond. A third detachment, under Col. Benjamin F. "Grimes" Davis, wrecked the railroad line between the South Anna River and the outskirts of Richmond. The cavalry corps suffered casualties of 17 killed and 75 wounded by the time it concluded the raid on May 7. By accomplishing the minor feats to the south, it succeeded in sitting out the whole of the major action at Chancellorsville, failing to help Hooker when he needed help.

By midafternoon on April 30, back in the vicinity of Fredericksburg, Hooker's plan was solidifying. He had moved three army corps into position near Chancellorsville. Couch's divisions had moved out from Banks's Ford and were en route to Chancellorsville. Sedgwick solidified his major force at Fredericksburg and, although Hooker had separated his army, the two halves were each nearly as strong as Lee's entire force and so could reasonably look forward to moving from two sides and crushing the Southern army with a pincer movement. The opportunity, with Longstreet absent, seemed grand. On this last day of April, Hooker made no secret of his pretensions. Hooker issued General Order No. 47 to his troops, which read: "It is with heartfelt satisfaction the commanding general announces to the army that the operations of the last three days have determined that our enemy must either ingloriously fly, or come out from behind his defenses and give us battle on our own ground, where certain destruction awaits him." Hooker also allegedly told the newspaper reporter William Swinton, "The Rebel army . . . is now the legitimate property of the Army of the Potomac. They may as well pack up their haversacks and make for Richmond." Faith in the movement as it had been made also existed among the army and the corps commanders. "This is splendid, Slocum!" George Meade allegedly said. "Hurrah for old Joe! We're on Lee's flank and he doesn't know it."

The hamlet of Chancellorsville stood at the junction of the Orange Turnpike and Ely's Ford Road, which continued southward as the Orange Plank Road. The whole area west of Fredericksburg was one vast forest, with secondary growth oak and pine having produced a thicket of brush so dense it was called the Wilderness. The brick tavern that stood at Chancellorsville was an imposing structure of the time, inhabited by the Frances Chancellor family. The two-and-a-half-story tavern was built in 1816 and served as a stopover for many travelers before being converted into a large house with outbuildings before the war. Despite the thick woods dominating the region, other landmarks peppered what was about to become a battlefield: across the Turnpike, to the southwest, stood Fairview, another prominent house, and a nearby cemetery. Southwest of Fairview was a clearing called Hazel Grove. Some one and a half miles south of Fairview stood Catharine Furnace, constructed in 1837 as the only manufacturing operation in the area, which produced iron until the end of the Mexican War, when the furnace fell into disrepair. West along the turnpike stood a variety of structures including Dowdall's Tavern, Wilderness Church, and Wilderness Tavern. East along the pike were the Zoan Church and, halfway back to Fredericksburg, the prominent brick Salem Church. The peculiarity of the area made it impossible to fight a battle that followed prescribed tactics, with well-formed units marching and deploying in order, and artillery and cavalry operating effectively by scouting and viewing long-range sights. The poor visibility and inability of both sides to deploy troops conventionally or move them around effectively would characterize the coming fight.

Hooker approached the Confederate army cautiously on May 1, moving the lead corps of Slocum's forward by 11 A.M., despite his good intelligence of Lee's movements as provided by Thaddeus S. C. Lowe's observation balloons. As Slocum moved southeastward along the Plank Road, with Howard's 11th Corps behind him, the divisions of Sykes and Hancock struck eastward along the turnpike. Lee's peculiar range of options baffled him for a time, as he did not know which flank of Hooker's attacking force to strike. Initially deploying Stuart's cavalry to the south, and the divisions of Anderson, Rodes, and McLaws across the battlefront, this deployment had come only after a major reconnaissance of the Federal force at Fredericksburg, made along the railroad line south of the city, where Jackson had fought so valiantly the previous winter. Lee and Jackson soon concluded that Sedgwick posed no serious threat, at least immediately, and so withdrew most of their force back to Chancellorsville except for an effective screen by Early. Hooker, meanwhile, pressed the attack despite the absence of most of his cavalry and seemed to be organizing a relatively sound movement. At first Sykes's men pushed back McLaws, but a coordinated Confederate counterattack pushed him back into Hancock's division. As the main battle raged across the turnpike, Meade marched the remainder of his corps, the divisions of Humphreys and Griffin, in a flanking maneuver north of Duerson's Mill, and nearly around to a position from which he might attack the enemy's rear.

Almost inexplicably, with the attack going reasonably well, Hooker committed an almost surrealistic blunder. With his corps commanders protesting, Hooker ordered the infantry to return to the positions it had held the previous night. "From character of information have suspended attack," he wrote at 2 P.M. A short time later he recorded, "After having ordered an attack at 2 o'clock, and most of the troops in position, I suspended the attack on the receipt of news from the other side of the river. Hope the enemy will be emboldened to attack me. I did feel certain of success. If his communications are cut, he must attack me. I have a strong position." The news that Hooker received from balloon observers and from Sedgwick could hardly have given him reason for such caution. Later writers ascribed Hooker's astonishing pullback to drunkenness during the battle, or simply because he "lost confidence in Joe Hooker," as he allegedly told Doubleday. Neither of these seems to be the case. A more credible version of the facts appears to be put forth by claims that because he often found courage to attack from a bottle, and because he was *not* drinking on this day, Hooker was bedazzled and overly cautious because his head was too clear. Independent of this oblique difficulty, if it existed, many historians have cited the probability that Hooker simply appeared to be overawed by the scale and complexity of that which he had to direct; both earlier and later he performed well as a corps commander.

Hooker's puzzled army withdrew to a C-shaped inner ring of defensive works surrounding Chancellorsville by the evening of May 1, and even more confused Confederates followed them. Hooker's men began constructing trenches fortified with abatis constructed from logs and fallen trees, with Slocum forming the midportion of the line, Couch and Sickles behind him, Howard spread to the right and Meade to the left along the Turnpike, and Pleasonton's cavalry to the north. Lee, meanwhile, was with some justification continuing to have problems trying to ascertain what Hooker was likely to do next. His army remained in serious peril, despite the sloppy and peculiar actions of Hooker's force. The Federal army now occupied a strong defensive position that could not be attacked headlong, and if Sedgwick moved vigorously westward, he would find only a thin force of Early's in his path. The situation gave rise to another legendary aspect of the campaign. On the evening of May 1, Lee and Jackson met along with other officers at the intersection of the Furnace Road and the Orange Plank Road, which had become the Confederate headquarters. After Stuart arrived and informed them that the Union right was exposed and vulnerable to a surprise attack, they discussed what might be done the following day. The following morning, before dawn, Jackson and Lee met again and discussed their plans by a small fire, sitting on discarded Federal cracker boxes. Lee and Jackson had agreed on an audacious move to be made by Jackson—to take half the Southern army and move on a circuitous march around the Federal right. Charles C. Wellford, the proprietor of Catharine Furnace, would act as guide. Topographical engineer Capt. Jedediah Hotchkiss recalled spreading a map on another cracker box as the meeting continued, and hearing Jackson speak. "I propose to go right around there," said Jackson, showing the route. "What do you propose to do it with?" asked Lee. "With my whole command," replied Jackson. "What will you leave me here to hold the Federal army with?" inquired Lee. "The two divisions that you have here," replied Stonewall. After a pause, Lee said, "Well, go ahead." It would be the last time the two great commanders ever saw each other.

The Lee-Jackson plan (no one has ever settled how much credit each of the commanders gets for originating the idea) would allow Stonewall to march 26,000 men around the Federal flank and attack it eastward, using Stuart's cavalry as a screen. To say that it was bold is an understatement: the mere 17,000 men left to Lee might have been crushed while Stonewall's march took place. But they weren't, and Jackson's flank march indeed did work. The risk taker who wins is a genius, and the one who fails is a fool—so go the fortunes of war. The maneuver surely does show the desperation felt by Lee and Jackson in the face of a superior numerical force. Already divided in two, the army now separated into three components, violating the most sacrosanct of Napoleon's maxims.

By 6 A.M. on May 2, Jackson began his celebrated flank march, taking his men past the stone stack of Catharine Furnace, turning sharply south along Furnace Road, crossing the route of an unfinished railroad, and turning sharply northward along the Brock Road, marching diligently across the Orange Plank Road, and finally turning eastward onto the turnpike. It was a march of fourteen miles over narrow roads, across small fords, and in peril of being spotted by elements of the Federal army. In the end, the march consumed eight and a half hours, Jackson's men taking position and pulling into formation by 2:30 P.M. The slowly moving Confederates had indeed been spotted. Under different circumstances, such an event might easily have proved disastrous. Hooker, who took position on the high ground at Hazel Grove, was advised of Jackson's maneuver by about 9 A.M. He rightly suspected that Jackson might be attempting to turn his right flank, and informed Howard, commanding the 11th Corps (on the flank) of the movement. The unlikely visionary of the moment was Sickles, who immediately urged an attack. This temporarily inconvenienced Jackson's march but failed to disrupt it. With Sickles making some progress, his commanding general stepped in once again. Inexplicably, Hooker now brought himself to believe that Jackson, attacked by Sickles, was not flanking Howard but instead retreating to Gordonsville. In his last message to Lee, Jackson sent a telegram at 3 P.M. that read, "The enemy has made a stand at [Melzi] Chancellor's [another name for Dowdall's Tavern] which is about 2 miles from Chancellorsville. I hope as soon as practicable to attack. I trust that an ever kind providence will bless us with great success."

By midafternoon Jackson's men were forming for a large-scale attack, with the division of Rodes in front, followed by the divisions of Colston and A. P. Hill, with Stuart's cavalry spread to the south. The attack would commence from the thick undergrowth brush of the Wilderness and strike eastward along the turnpike, hitting the Federal flank that consisted of Howard's 11th Corps. Jackson's soldiers occupied about three hours arranging their men and equipment over the difficult landscape, and during this time both Howard and Hooker received reports of a troubling buildup where Jackson's 26,000 were. Amazingly, they both disregarded the danger from such reports. The Federal units on the right flank were posted along the turnpike, between Dowdall's Tavern and a position well west of Wilderness Church. They consisted of the divisions of Devens, Schurz, and Steinwehr. The front ranks of the Confederate battle line contained the brigades of Colquitt, Doles, O'Neal, and Iverson. To the south, along the Orange Plank Road, was Paxton's brigade. Near the Luckett House south of the turnpike, Jackson issued orders for an attack that would commence shortly after 5:15 P.M., telling his brigade commanders that once the attack began, "under no circumstances was there to be any pause in the advance."

Caught unaware of a major attack even though he knew about activity in the area, Howard, headquartered at Dowdall's Tavern, turned in a shameful performance at Chancellorsville. Jackson's massive attack struck the right-flank brigades of the Union army like a swarm of hornets, with great sheets of fire emanating from the woods, chasing deer bolting out from the tree line and into the mad scramble of soldiers lounging around in camp, cooking dinner and playing cards. The men in the ranks were essentially unaware of any enemy approach, and they were routed in utter chaos. They

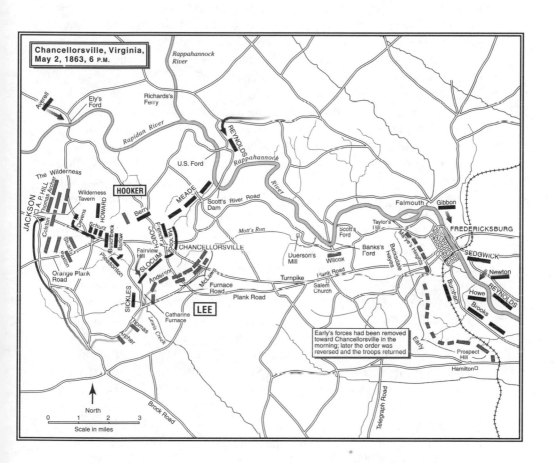

Chancellorsville, Virginia,
May 2, 1863, 6 P.M.

Rappahannock
River

Averell

Ely's
Ford

Richards's
Ferry

Rapidan River

REYNOLDS

U.S. Ford

Rappahannock

The Wilderness

River

A. P. HILL
Thomas Archer

Wilderness
Tavern

HOWARD

HOOKER

MEADE

Scott's
Dam

River Road

Falmouth

Gibbon

JACKSON

Devens

Schurz

Berry

FRENCH

COUCH

Hancock

Mott's Run

Scott's
Ford

Taylor's
Hill

FREDERICKSBURG

Colston

Stuart
Paxton

Pleasonton

Burschick

Barlow

CHANCELLORSVILLE

Mayre's Heights
Barksdale
Hayes

SEDGWICK

Fairview
Hill

SLOCUM

Duerson's
Mill

Wilcox

Banks's
Ford

Newton

Orange Plank
Road

Anderson

McLaws

Turnpike

Plank Road

Salem
Church

REYNOLDS

SICKLES

Furnace
Road

Plank Road

LEE

Howe

Brooks

Thomas

Catharine
Furnace

Lewis Creek

Early

Early's forces had been removed
toward Chancellorsville in the
morning; later the order was
reversed and the troops returned

Archer

Prospect
Hill

Hamilton

North

Brock Road

Telegraph Road

0   1   2   3

Scale in miles

knocked down tents, clanked pots and pans, and ran through campfires to grab weapons and defend themselves. Many of the soldiers were Germans who spoke poor English, and the language barrier only added to the perilous alarm quickly spreading through the Union right. Col. Leopold von Gilsa's brigade was hit by heavy small-arms fire and could only send a few disoriented volleys back before fleeing to the east. The majority of the Federal rifle pits were quickly taken by the onrushing Confederates, but Col. Adolphus Buschbeck's brigade held their position for more than thirty minutes, allowing some of the surrounding units to scatter without being overrun. Howard sat atop his horse with a flagstaff tucked underneath the stump of his right arm, which he had lost at Fair Oaks. Despite his words of encouragement to rally the fleeing men, he saw only "blind panic and great confusion."

The remnants of the Federal right retreated and Howard, aided by Hooker, attempted to establish a new line with all available troops. Reynolds ordered his men forward to help plug the collapsing line. With darkness approaching, the Confederate attack had been severe and punishing but not devastating; confusion on the Confederate side, along with the rough thickets and poor decisions by junior commanders, stalled the attack by the time it reached a position west of Fairview. By dusk the 8th Pennsylvania Cavalry rode out from its position at Hazel Grove and blundered into the flank of Doles's brigade, drawing sabers and slicing its way through elements of the brigade after seeing so many grayclad bodies ahead. Though it has been described as a gallant, lengthy charge, "the whole affair was accidental," lamented Capt. Andrew B. Wells of the 8th Pennsylvania. "We were on our way to report to General Howard." Jackson's first two attack waves now intermingled. By 9 P.M., A. P. Hill's brigades, advancing along the turnpike, came under an artillery barrage from Sickles's guns at Fairview.

Then, under the cold moonlight, a fateful event happened. Believing that the fighting had all but died out, Stonewall Jackson rode out ahead of Lane's brigade along the turnpike, reconnoitering the prospects for positioning his troops. He wanted to find a route by which he could block Hooker from retreating via United States Ford. Jackson rode on, followed by some of his staff, telling them at one point that "the danger is all over; the enemy is routed. Go back and tell A. P. Hill to press right on." Hill indeed was close, and he shouted as horsemen approached to cease firing, that the soldiers in the front ranks were firing into their own men. "It's a lie! Pour it into them, boys!" shouted Maj. John D. Barry of the 18th North Carolina Infantry. A line of Confederate infantrymen opened fire with two volleys into the approaching horsemen, cutting them apart, sending horses reeling and men bleeding. Sitting atop his horse Little Sorrel, Stonewall was hit three times, his left arm hanging limp, and Little Sorrel bolted, dragging Jackson through the rough branches of a tree, which scraped his face, knocked off his cap, and nearly dragged him off the horse. Capt. R. E. Wilbourn assisted Jackson at first, and urgent word was sent to Jackson's medical director, Hunter Holmes McGuire.

Jackson had been shot at close range, two bullets mangling his left arm, one fracturing the humerus and the other striking the forearm an inch below the elbow. The third projectile lodged under the skin of his right hand. So dazed was the celebrated Confederate commander that his feet needed to be taken out of his stirrups. Placed on a litter, he was once dropped so hard as to cause a chest contusion. As described by Jackson's chaplain, James Power Smith, "Under this volley, when not two rods from the troops, the general received three balls at the same instant. . . . The large bone of the upper arm was splintered to the elbow-joint, and the wound bled freely." Jackson was carried far westward to an aid station along the turnpike, where McGuire amputated his left arm with a simple circular operation, the arm being buried nearby at Ellwood, the J. Horace Lacy House in the Wilderness owned by the same Confederate major—and friend of Jackson's—who occupied Chatham, a mansion at Falmouth. Members of Jackson's staff initially thought he might die on the spot. Jackson was taken by ambulance over a series of poor roads to recuperate at Richmond. "Could I have directed events, I should have chosen for the good of the country to be disabled in your stead," Lee wrote Jackson on May 3. Jackson was too weak to go as far as Richmond, as it turned out. He was taken to the Thomas C. Chandler House at Guinea's Station, on the Richmond, Fredericksburg & Potomac Railroad.

On the night of May 2, Hooker ordered Sickles to attack the Confederate right from his position at Hazel Grove. Terrific artillery fire from Hazel Grove and a halfhearted advance by Sickles produced only chaos in the night as units were intertwined and confused, finally pulling back to Hazel Grove and aborting any forward movement. It had been a hellish, disastrous day for the Federal army under the weight of Jackson's stunning attack. "The events of the few hours of this afternoon and evening are imprinted on my memory in a grand picture," reflected Capt. Thomas L. Livermore of the 18th New Hampshire Infantry. "I can now, and probably always shall be able to again bring before my eyes the dusty plain bounded by long lines of men on all sides; the smoke of musketry and batteries, whose thunders still reverberate in my ears." The cost in commanders had been enormous. Not only was Jackson badly injured—a calamity for the Confederacy, which adored him over all other generals at this time—but others had been lost, too. A. P. Hill had been struck in the legs by a ball a short time after Jackson was hit, and command of Jackson's Corps was assigned temporarily to Jeb Stuart.

Though Jackson's flank march and massive attack had stunned the Federal army, dawn broke on the third day at Chancellorsville without any decision; the battle could still go either way. Alarming to the Federal army was

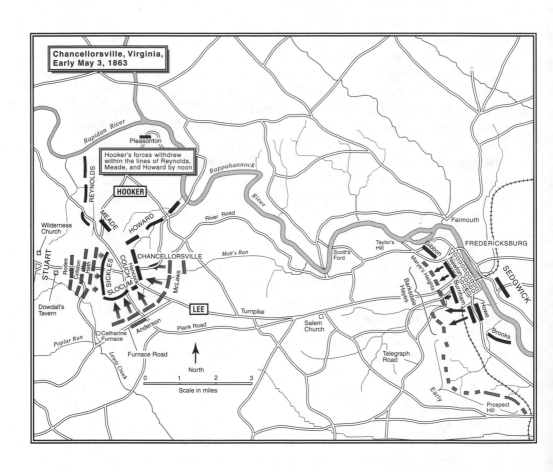

**Chancellorsville, Virginia,
Early May 3, 1863**

Rapidan River

Pleasonton

Hooker's forces withdrew
within the lines of Reynolds,
Meade, and Howard by noon

REYNOLDS

Rappahannock

HOOKER

MEADE

HOWARD

River

River Road

Falmouth

Wilderness
Church

Taylor's
Hill

FREDERICKSBURG

STUART

Rodes

Colston

Heth

SICKLES

CHANCELLORSVILLE

Mott's Run

Scott's
Ford

Gibbon

Newton

SEDGWICK

COUCH

SLOCUM

Hancock

McLaws

Marye's Heights

Burnham

Dowdall's
Tavern

LEE

Turnpike

Barksdale

Hayes

Howe

Anderson

Plank Road

Salem
Church

Brooks

Catharine
Furnace

Poplar Run

Furnace Road

Telegraph
Road

Lewis Creek

North

Early

0   1   2   3

Scale in miles

Prospect
Hill

that its formation, a crunched semicircle, now had a pronounced salient that was surrounded by elements of Stuart's corps on two sides. The Confederate army was still divided, however, with Early's force still in the trenches behind Fredericksburg, awaiting some action on Sedgwick's part. The Federal army at Chancellorsville was reinforced by Reynolds's 1st Corps on the right flank, and Howard's 11th Corps, shattered the day before, reorganized into a wing acting as the left flank stretching toward United States Ford. As the opportunities for the Federal army should have made themselves clear, Hooker's friend Sickles took his turn in making a nonsensical decision. Although his men held the plateau at Hazel Grove, from which artillery might dominate the surrounding area—and from which an attack could hit either wing of Stuart's Corps—Sickles withdrew to Fairview, leaving Hazel Grove wide open for occupation by Confederate artillery.

Not only would Stuart order artillery placed at Hazel Grove, but he discovered that a road was now opened so that the two halves of the army could be reunited conveniently. At dawn Stuart advanced elements of his corps, placing thirty-one field guns on Hazel Grove and opening a withering fire on Sickles, Slocum, and Couch, whose corps occupied the salient at the center of the Union line. Stuart managed the early phase of the third day's battle superbly, bringing up more guns to increase the number posted at Hazel Grove to fifty and launching waves of attacks into the Union breastworks, the western surges being led by the brigades of Pender, Thomas, Lane, Paxton, McGowan, and Cols. John M. Brockenbrough and Thomas S. Garnett. In one of the morning attacks Paxton led the Stonewall Brigade, Jackson's old command, forward into battle. Brig. Gen. Elisha F. "Bull" Paxton, a Virginia native, was killed almost instantly by a Minié bullet that penetrated his chest. His friend Garnett was mortally wounded a short time later. The air was furiously thick with fire during this phase.

A tremendous artillery battle raged between the Confederate guns at Hazel Grove and the Union pieces at Fairview. While this intensely horrifying third morning of battle was progressing, Joe Hooker was at his headquarters at the Chancellor Tavern. Inside, surgeons frantically worked to piece together badly mauled casualties; piles of arms and legs grew outside the sitting-room window. Several couriers raced back and forth on horseback, presenting the general fragmentary reports from the battlefront. A short time after 9 A.M. Hooker stood leaning against one of the tall pillars of the front porch. Suddenly, a Confederate solid cannonball struck the pillar squarely, splintering it and sending portions of it raining down on the commanding general. Dazed and confused, Hooker for a time could not be brought to his senses. He soon lay down inside his tent, and rumors began to circulate that Hooker had been killed. "General Hooker was lying down I think in a soldier's tent by himself," reported Maj. Gen. Darius N. Couch, the senior corps commander, of the period following the incident. "Raising himself a little as I entered, he said: 'Couch, I turn the command of the army over to you.' . . . This was three-quarters of an hour after his hurt. He seemed rather dull, but possessed of his mental faculties."

Hooker, in painful agony in his tent and temporarily paralyzed, now had even less to do with the battle than the minimal direction he had given it when alert. Although battered by the morning attacks, the Federal army could still turn the tide against the exhausted Confederates and continue the fight. Couch, however, in consultation with the groggy Hooker, decided to pull the army northward in retreat to the line of defenses that had been established by the army's rear north of Chancellorsville. Sedgwick, simultaneously, had decided to attack after receiving orders to do so from Hooker early in the morning. In a haunting repeat of the tactics employed so unsuccessfully by Burnside during the battle of Fredericksburg, Sedgwick this time succeeded. By 5 A.M. his force crossed the river and occupied the town of Fredericksburg, aiming to fight uphill into Marye's Heights just as they had last time. The Confederate trenches along the heights west of town had been strongly built up following Burnside's attack, but Early's slim force of 10,000 was not up to defending against 28,000 soldiers led by Sedgwick. With the brigades of Barksdale and Hays on Marye's Heights and Early to the south, the Confederates fought back the first three morning assaults. Wilcox's brigade arrived and aided the defense on the northern flank, but Gibbon's Union division also arrived and attacked there, with the divisions of Newton, Burnham, Howe, and Brooks in the center and left. The fourth Union assault accomplished the long-awaited goal of pushing the Confederates out of their trenches at Fredericksburg. After so much blood had been spilled in the little town, Early's men scrambled westward by early afternoon.

Hooker's men, meanwhile, were scattering northward, leaving Chancellorsville in the hands of Lee. Lee's army, much of it under the command of young Stuart, was now fully united along a front that stretched across the turnpike from north of Hazel Grove to a position south of Scott's Ford on the Rappahannock. The men in Lee's army were absolutely exhausted from hard fighting. Hooker's army, demoralized, with a wounded, frightened commander, stood in lightly fortified positions between their adversary and the Rapidan and Rappahannock rivers, in a tactically vulnerable position. Artillery and supplies were running low on both sides, and the ghastly shrieks of the wounded did little to keep up men's spirits. Despite the limitations, Lee moved north to batter Hooker's army still more. And then he received a courier's report that Sedgwick was moving west from Fredericksburg. The Confederates in the east, alarmed by Sedgwick's success, came unglued. Early retreated southward along Telegraph Road away from both fields of battle. Wilcox retreated in haste toward Lee's main force, hoping to connect with it. Sedgwick pursued diligently, leaving Gibbon's division spread along Marye's Heights at Fredericksburg. For some of the Federal soldiers who had fought at Fredericksburg and now stood guard atop the hideous rebel fortress, the feeling was nearly overwhelming.

Lee dispatched four brigades under the command of Maj. Gen. Lafayette McLaws to move quickly to stop Sedgwick's advance. By 3 P.M. the Confederates were in position near Salem Church, where an hour later Sedgwick approached and immediately, aggressively, surged into an attack on McLaws. The battle of Salem Church, fought around the same brick structure that had housed civilians fleeing Fredericksburg the previous December, was initially a Federal success. Strong counterattacks by McLaws pushed Sedgwick back, however, and as night fell, both armies stayed put, looking for action the following day.

On May 4, the final day of action transpired at Chancellorsville. Hooker solidified his line and, although his army was pinned against the rivers, the line of retreat through United States Ford was secure and able to accommodate large numbers of troops if necessary. Hooker now had 75,000 men in a final battle line; Lee determined to operate against the ominous threat of Sedgwick, leaving a force of 25,000 with Stuart and taking 21,000 to shatter the threat from the east. Early first struck against Gibbon's force along Marye's Heights, and the Federals were pushed back into the town. "For two miles we saw not a Yankee," recalled Adj. William C. Matthews of the 38th Georgia Infantry, "but on ascending a hill near the old plank road we got a sight of them in line of battle behind the road that afforded some protection to them." Sedgwick now cleverly established a convex defensive line from Scott's Ford to Taylor's Hill that disabled the Confederate lines of communications and delayed Lee's attack until 5:30 P.M., by which time the Union infantry units could repel most of the poorly organized attacks. After nightfall Sedgwick withdrew his men northward across Scott's Ford. With the major action occurring between Fredericksburg and Salem Church, neither Hooker nor Stuart moved out to join the engagement.

On May 5 the inevitable Union retreat was taking shape. Gibbon withdrew to Falmouth, while Sedgwick was now safely on the north bank of the Rappahannock. Hooker held a council of war after midnight on May 6, polling his corps commanders, who were slightly unsure of his behavior or whether he had recovered enough to make sense of anything. Howard, Reynolds, and Meade wanted to attack, while Sickles and Couch suggested retreating, and Slocum did not participate. Couch seemed to be angrily holding a grudge because Hooker did not turn over the command to him. Deciding to withdraw, Hooker moved the artillery across United States Ford during the night, and the infantry followed starting at 5 A.M. Swollen currents on the river made the crossing difficult, even threatening to ruin the pontoon bridges, but by midday the Federals had crossed, and Lee, surprised by the action, was disappointed that the campaign terminated so abruptly.

The cost of Chancellorsville had been staggering. Pvt. Rice C. Bull of the 123d New York Infantry had been wounded at Chancellorsville and left in a hospital overtaken by Confederates. "By May 8th our wounds had all festered and were hot with fever," he wrote, "our clothing which came in contact with them was so filthy and stiff from the dried blood that it gravely aggravated our condition. Many wounds developed gangrene and blood poisoning; lockjaw caused suffering and death. . . . Finally, not the least of our troubles were the millions of flies that filled the air and covered blood-saturated clothing when they could not reach and sting the unbandaged wounds."

Altogether, the Federal casualties during the campaign were 1,606 killed, 9,762 wounded, and 5,919 missing; Confederate losses were 1,665 killed, 9,081 wounded, and 2,018 missing. Among the dead were Federal general officers Hiram G. Berry, struck in the arm with a Minié bullet that passed into his chest; Edmund Kirby, struck in the left thigh with two spherical case shot (the leg was amputated but Kirby died on May 28); and Amiel W. Whipple, who was on his horse, writing an order, when he was struck in the spine and mortally wounded, dying on May 7. As chief engineer of the Army, Brig. Gen. Joseph G. Totten sent a circular as follows: "It has become the painful duty of the Department to announce to the Corps the death of a brother officer, Major Amiel W. Whipple, Corps of Engineers, Maj. Gen. of Volunteers, who died at Washington on the 7th instant, from the effects of a wound received on the 4th instant, while commanding his Division at the battle of Chancellorsville, Virginia."

For the South, however, the greatest calamity came on May 10 when Stonewall Jackson succumbed to pneumonia at Guinea's Station, dying with his wife and members of his staff present, in a small room in the Chandler Farm Office building. Abram Fulkerson summed up the feelings of many: "We feel that his death is a national calamity. The poorest soldiers among us appreciated his worth—loved the man, and mourn his loss. . . . Could his life have been spared till the close of this cruel war, the unanimous voice of a grateful people would have proclaimed him chief ruler of the nation."

The general's last words were reportedly, "Let us cross over the river and rest under the shade of the trees," delivered in delirium after calling out incoherent commands to William N. Pendleton. The inconsolable reality of his death was too costly a price to pay for a victory such as Lee's at Chancellorsville. The leading hero among general officers, he would leave an immense void to fill. "There was the stuff of Cromwell in Jackson," editorialized the *Richmond Examiner* the day following his death. "Hannibal might have been proud of his campaign in the Valley, and the shades of the mightiest warriors should rise to welcome his stern ghost." "The Lord has crowned our arms with another glorious victory although many a gallant officer and soldier was made the Victim of Death," penned Confederate soldier Derastus E. W. Myers, "amongst them was Lieut. Gen. Jackson. . . . But we cannot expect to fight and loose no men. I feel sorry for the loss of them all but the Lord gave them to us and He saw proper to take them away."

Lee, unhappy with the inability to damage more of Hooker's army, yet pleased with his overall victory, swelled with pride in his foot soldiers. "I agree with you in believing that our army would be invincible if it could be properly organized and officered," he informed John Bell Hood on May 21. "There never were such men in an army before. They will go anywhere and do anything if properly led. But there is the difficulty—proper commanders. Where can they be obtained?" "Numbers have now no terror for the Southern people," wrote the war clerk John B. Jones in Richmond. "They are willing to wage the war against quadruple their number." This feeling of invincibility might prove a dangerous thing.

Facing a firestorm of criticism, Hooker might have sensed that his days as commander of the Army of the Potomac were numbered. "He who survived the thunder-burst of Stonewall Jackson and the terrific rains of May is likely to be demolished by the critics of New York and Philadelphia," recorded the correspondent Noah Brooks. In the wake of Fredericksburg, the largest disaster yet in the portfolio of Federal eastern troubles, Chancellorsville seemed like a signal of impending doom to the North. Lincoln could only utter, "My God! My God! What will the country say?"

AFTER CHANCELLORSVILLE, Hooker's 115,000 troops and Lee's 75,000 resumed their old strategic dispositions along the Rappahannock River. The victory had boosted Lee's confidence and the morale of the Army of Northern Virginia to its greatest level of the war. Lee reorganized his army into three giant corps commanded by Longstreet, Ewell (replacing Jackson), and A. P. Hill. The army was strengthened by the addition of more troops from the Carolinas, and greater means were taken to improve staff work and communications. The Confederate armies seemed in a strong position, but somewhat deceptively so. The feeling of invincibility was aided by Hooker's weakness. In terms of confidence, Hooker was nearly destroyed, and the War Department ordered him to protect Washington and Harpers Ferry.

Far to the south, at Charleston, Gen. Beauregard seemed to be holding the line against Federal combined operations. In middle Tennessee, Bragg and Rosecrans were deadlocked after a series of inconclusive operations. In Arkansas and Louisiana, Lt. Gen. Theophilus H. Holmes and Maj. Gen. Richard Taylor were holding their own, involved in a guerrilla war in which criminal actions erupted by various "armies" that consisted of little more than armed thugs. Along the Mississippi River corridor, however, the Confederates were in desperate trouble. Grant had encircled Vicksburg, and the siege there was slowly starving out the military and civilians within the city; loss of the important bastion would be disastrous for Southern war aims because it would effectively cut off the Trans-Mississippi from the rest of the Confederate States. Port Hudson was under siege by Banks.

Lee faced a critical decision during early June 1863. Longstreet, his senior and most trusted lieutenant, offered a solution to the growing seriousness of the Federal successes in the west. Why not leave a defensive force in the trenches facing Hooker and take the bulk of his army westward to strike Rosecrans in middle Tennessee? This would panic the whole Northern populace, draw the war away from beleaguered Virginia, and possibly force Grant to evacuate his position at Vicksburg to support the war in the center. It might be a decisive turning point in the conflict, Longstreet reasoned. But after serious contemplation, Lee refused. He was the commander of the Army of Northern Virginia and had gone to war primarily to protect his home state from the "foreign invaders." Lee had always shown a relative selfishness when it came to asking for vast quantities of men and supplies for his own army, and he wasn't about to risk it all now to go fight in Tennessee. At this critical moment in the war the conservatism and nineteenth-century localism that dominated Lee's thinking dictated his actions. Refusing to fight the contest as a whole, he looked inward to Virginia at the expense of Vicksburg, Tennessee, and everywhere else.

Thus began the Gettysburg campaign. Though he would not assist the war as a whole, Lee had to act in some way. "There is always hazard in military movements," he wrote Secretary of War Seddon on June 8, "but we must decide between the positive loss of inactivity and the risk of inaction." Even without the unwavering risk-taking Stonewall Jackson at his side, Lee felt emboldened as he never had before by the impressive confidence of his men, his newly reorganized army, and the victories at Fredericksburg and Chancellorsville. Determining that he could never win the war defensively, Lee decided to take the initiative and launch a second Northern raid; he could not attack Hooker directly because of the Federal army's strong position. A raid would enable his troops to draw the war away from Virginia and to resupply in Maryland and Pennsylvania. Moreover, by fighting and winning a battle on Northern soil, the army could prove its superiority, frightening the Yankee civilians and perhaps igniting the burgeoning peace movement in the North. With a stunning victory perhaps the waning ember of foreign intervention would even reignite. Whichever way it occurred, a major victory in the North—coupled with a Confederate military threat to Harrisburg, Philadelphia, Baltimore, or even Washington—might bring the end of this long and dreadful war by such a resolution. Lee clearly saw the possibility of a negotiated peace as a driving factor. "We should neglect no honorable means of dividing and weakening our enemies that they may experience some of the difficulties experienced by ourselves," he alerted Jefferson Davis on June 10. "It seems to me that the most effectual mode of accomplishing this object, now within our reach, is to give all the encouragement we can, consistently with truth, to the rising peace party of the North. Nor do I think we should in this connection make nice distinctions between those who declare for peace unconditionally and those who advocate it as a means of restoring the Union, however much we may prefer the former."

During the first days of June, Lee moved his troops westward, planning to advance northward down the Shenandoah Valley, using the Blue Ridge and South mountains as a screen. A. P. Hill's corps was kept along the Rappahannock line and was organized and shifted to make Hooker's scouts believe that the whole army was still in position. But Hooker and his army intelligence network deciphered Lee's activities and began responding by June 5, when he sent Maj. Gen. John Sedgwick across the Rappahannock to attack a portion of Hill's line. The resulting reconnaissance in force came to be known as Franklin's Crossing. The 26th New Jersey Infantry and 5th Vermont Infantry struck into the Confederates at the crossing, firing from well-constructed gunpits, forcing infantry to cross with great hazard on pontoon bridges before driving away a portion of the defenders, taking 35 prisoners and suffering 6 dead and 35 wounded. The stiff resistance convinced Sedgwick that the whole Confederate army still lay before him. Hooker next proposed moving straight upon Richmond, but Lincoln dismissed this notion, now having firmly learned the lessons that Grant and Sherman had perfected—that the real objective was not the capture of a city with a civilian government but the destruction of the enemy army. After learning of Lee's movements, Lincoln playfully wrote Hooker on June 14. "If the head of Lee's army is at Martinsburg and the tail of it on the Plank Road between Fredericksburg and Chancellorsville, the animal must be very slim somewhere. Could you not break him?"

Unhappy with Sedgwick's outcome, Hooker sent his cavalry corps under Brig. Gen. Alfred Pleasonton on a reconnaissance toward Culpeper Court House. The Confederate cavalry division of Maj. Gen. Jeb Stuart was situated at Brandy Station, northeast of Culpeper on the Orange & Alexandria Railroad. On June 9, Pleasonton's troops rode up into Brandy Station and clashed with Stuart, creating a large cavalry and infantry action. The battle of Brandy Station was a turning point in the role of Federal cavalry during the war. Pleasonton divided his cavalry into two wings commanded by Brig. Gens. John Buford and David M. Gregg. Buford's right wing included the 1st Division and the reserve brigade, along with the infantry brigade of Brig. Gen. Adelbert Ames. Gregg's left wing comprised the 2d and 3d divisions and Brig. Gen. David A. Russell's infantry brigade, so that the entire Federal force comprised about 8,000 cavalry supported by 3,000 infantry. The Confederate cavalry force consisted of the brigades of Brig. Gens. Fitzhugh Lee, Wade Hampton, William H. F. "Rooney" Lee, Albert G. Jenkins, Beverly H. Robertson, and William E. "Grumble" Jones, plus attached horse artillery.

Pleasonton planned to attack at dawn on June 9, and he formed Buford's cavalry brigade, supported by Ames, at Beverly Ford on the Rappahannock. The Federal force would cross the river and attack southwestward into Grumble Jones's horse soldiers. Six miles downstream, at old familiar Kelly's Ford, Gregg and Col. Alfred N. Duffié (2d Division) would attack, supported by the infantry of Russell, and the recipient of this attack would be Robertson, with the cavalrymen of Hampton positioned close by. Duffié was to go to Stevensburg while the rest of the force united at Brandy Station, where a long open ridge named Fleetwood Hill allowed horsemen to operate more freely. As the Federal soldiers prepared for attack, Stuart was on June 8 proudly displaying his cavalry division to Robert E. Lee in a grand review on Fleetwood Hill, a spectacle of 10,000 troopers with sabers gleaming and ready for admiration if not battle.

When the two columns of Federal horsemen attacked at 4 A.M. on the hazy morning of June 9, the Confederate horsemen were oblivious to the threat. Buford's troopers pushed Jones back toward Brandy Station; intense fighting raged over Fleetwood Hill, with charges and countercharges unleashing a complete pandemonium over the landscape. During normal Civil War operations, horses were used for rapid transport to the battlefield and for reconnaissance. Once at the engagement, cavalry typically dismounted and fought on foot. But Brandy Station was different. The utter surprise and chaos that erupted led to a mounted contest. Brandy Station was an antiquated cavalry battle, with mounted saber attacks along with firing guns. The 1st New Jersey Cavalry made six charges throughout the ten hours of fighting, and the action over the battlefield at Brandy Station raged for more than twelve hours. Gregg pushed Robertson back from Kelly's Ford and soon attacked from the south.

At Stevensburg, Duffié clashed with a force of the 2d South Carolina Cavalry and the 4th Virginia Cavalry, causing him to be late. Gregg moved forward in attack, but Fleetwood Hill was held firm by Hampton, and the shocked Confederates thus retained the battlefield. But Stuart paid a heavy price, receiving attacks in the Southern newspapers for being startled and for being subjected to such manhandling by the Federal horsemen, who were supposed to have been much inferior to their Confederate counterparts. The embarrassment Stuart experienced in the immediate wake of his boastful grand review would help to shape his actions over the remainder of the campaign. The Union casualties at Brandy Station were 69 killed, 352 wounded, and 486 missing (taken as prisoners); Confederate losses were 523 total. Among the casualties were Robert E. Lee's son Rooney, who commanded a brigade and was shot in the thigh. He was sent to Hickory Hill, an estate near Hanover Court House, where he was captured on June 26. Among the Federal dead was Col. Benjamin "Grimes" Davis, who had taken such an active role at Harpers Ferry during the Antietam campaign.

In response to the Confederate movements, Hooker began shifting his troops slowly northwestward. He moved into the old area of battle near Manassas and sent Pleasonton's cavalry farther westward as a reconnoitering force. By midmonth the Confederate forces had finally pulled out entirely from Fredericksburg. A. P. Hill followed the movement of the rest of the Army of Northern Virginia. The Gettysburg campaign now accelerated. The advanced portion of Lee's army was Ewell's 2d Corps, which drove into the Shenandoah Valley at high speed. At Berryville, on June 13, the division of Maj. Gen. Robert E. Rodes, assisted by Jenkins's cavalry brigade, moved to capture the Union brigade of Col. Andrew T. McReynolds. Alerted to the danger, McReynolds skillfully withdrew to Winchester, where his force occupied the star fort there; Confederates captured portions of a Federal supply train at nearby Bunker Hill and 75 prisoners. Alarmed by the Confederate "raid," Maj. Gen. Robert H. Milroy was ordered to fall back from Winchester to Harpers Ferry. Far to the north, the Federal garrison at Martinsburg, Virginia, was attacked on June 14. Commanded by Col. Benjamin F. Smith, the brigade stationed there was struck by Rodes's Confederate infantry and cavalry under Jenkins about 8 A.M. A short time later Brig. Gen. Daniel Tyler arrived but took only an advisory role in what followed. By sunset the Federal regiments broke in confusion under the weight of Confederate artillery fire; they fled to Harpers Ferry. Confederates did not pursue in the darkness. Rodes took 700 prisoners, five field guns, and great quantities of supplies.

At Winchester, meanwhile, the second battle of Winchester had begun and was fought on June 14 and 15. Ewell planned to attack the defenses spread west of the town, namely the Star Fort and the Main Fort. Milroy's garrison consisted of about 6,900 men. Ewell ordered Maj. Gen. Jubal A. Early's division to attack, and after a short time it captured some earthworks and damaged the two main forts with heavy artillery fire. Two Union outposts northwest of the town were commanded by Col. Joseph W. Keifer; about 6 P.M. Confederate guns opened on these positions, too. Union artillery answered back, and an artillery duel ensued for about forty-five minutes. Thereafter, the outposts were attacked by Brig. Gen. Harry T. Hays's Louisiana brigade, which captured them. Milroy then withdrew most of his force into the main fort and started a panicked consultation with his subordinates, holding a formal counsel of war about 9 P.M. and deciding to withdraw after spiking his guns and burning his supply wagons. About 1 A.M. on June 15 the Union force began a withdrawal, but a fierce battle erupted two hours later at Stephenson's Depot, four miles northwest of Winchester, between Brig. Gen. Washington L. Elliott's brigade and Confederates of Maj. Gen. Edward Johnson's division. What resulted was a catastrophe for the Federal soldiers: Milroy attempted an envelopment, but just as he moved out, the brigade of Col. Jesse M. Williams (Nicholls's brigade) joined the battle and crushed the Union movement. Federal casualties were 95 killed, 348 wounded, and about 3,358 captured; Confederate losses were 47 killed, 219 wounded, and 3 missing. Ewell had also captured 23 field guns, 300 horses, and more than 300 wagons filled with supplies. The Confederate idea of resupplying during their campaign seemed to be working. The number of Union troops captured stunned the Lincoln administration, and Secretary of War Stanton called for additional militia to be federalized.

By midmonth Confederate troops were on the move, stretching more than 100 miles in a huge line from Chester Gap, Virginia, to Hagerstown, Maryland, with some cavalry forces having crossed the Pennsylvania border. More cavalry actions took place. On June 17, at Aldie, Virginia, west of Washington and south of Leesburg, a skirmish occurred. Col. Thomas T. Munford's Southern horsemen (Fitz Lee's brigade) rode to Aldie to help screen Longstreet's right flank while Col. John R. Chambliss, Jr. (Rooney Lee's brigade) scouted toward Thoroughfare Gap, and Brig. Gen. Beverly H. Robertson moved to Rectortown. Kilpatrick's brigade (of D. M. Gregg's division) pushed back the Confederate scouts successfully at Aldie until Munford's 5th Virginia Cavalry mounted a charge with drawn sabers and stunted the Federal success. Munford's Confederates then established a line supported by horse artillery and resisted a series of Union attacks that lasted until darkness. Union losses were 305 and Confederate casualties about 100.

Seven miles to the west, at Middleburg, the 1st Rhode Island Cavalry (Duffié) was chopped to pieces and 160 of its men captured. At first the action transpired well, and Duffié scattered Stuart and his staff after pushing through Thoroughfare Gap. But the regiment was then surrounded, and Duffié hammered his way through the encirclement with only 31 others in tow. For the following two days, June 18 and 19, more substantial fighting erupted at Middleburg. On the 18th, Pleasonton dispatched Col. J. Irvin Gregg's brigade to Middleburg, but he arrived too late to assist Duffié and withdrew to Aldie. The following day Gregg's brigade again advanced on Middleburg and this time sent the 4th Pennsylvania Cavalry charging through the town, securing it for the Union. This leading attack was followed by the far more substantial assault of Brig. Gen. David M. Gregg's division, which pushed Stuart's troopers back half a mile from the town. The Union casualties were about 99 and the Confederate losses approximately 40. Minor skirmishing continued throughout the region, with the largest such clash coming at Upperville—six miles northwest of Middleburg and east of Ashby's Gap—on June 21. The Union cavalry was successfully driving Stuart back toward the main Confederate army, and here Stuart was attacked along Goose Creek. Gregg's division, along with the infantry brigade of Col. Strong Vincent, struck into Hampton's and Robertson's cavalry, driving them into Upperville. In heavy fighting throughout much of the day, Buford's Federal cavalry attempted to turn Stuart's left, but was stopped by Grumble Jones and Chambliss. The flamboyant Brig. Gen. H. Judson Kilpatrick, nicknamed "Kill Cavalry" for his recklessness, attacked twice and the second time achieved success, helping to push Robertson back through Upperville. Hampton's counterstrikes enabled Stuart to evacuate in relative order, but the disturbing feeling of being whipped by "inferior" horsemen continued in Stuart's mind. Stuart's mission of reconnoitering and supplying Lee with information had not worked because of the Federal cavalry's harassment. The Southerners retreated to Ashby's Gap, with losses of 180; Union casualties were 209.

By June 24 the situation was becoming clear to Hooker, and he started the Army of the Potomac in motion toward Frederick, Maryland. Hooker's scouts by now had a fair idea of where the Confederate units were and where they might be going. Not only had Stuart's Confederate cavalry failed to serve as the "eyes of the army" for Lee, but a cavalry expedition under Confederate Brig. Gen. John D. Imboden sent westward along the Baltimore & Ohio Railroad had not resulted in gathering intelligence or disrupting the Yankees. Alarm was certainly beginning to spread in Pennsylvania, however. Gov. Andrew G. Curtin called out the Pennsylvania militia and homespun volunteers to ward off the Confederates who were entering the state.

THE WAR CONTINUED ELSEWHERE as well. On June 17 a fierce naval battle erupted when the casemate, an iron-hulled ship built with a bombproof deck housing cannon, CSS *Atlanta* (Comdr. William A. Webb) along with the gunboat CSS *Isondiga* and the steamer CSS *Resolute* attacked a Federal flotilla in Warsaw Sound, near Savannah. The *Atlanta* had been constructed from the hull of the blockade runner *Fingal* and was one of the finest iron ships of the Confederacy. The Federal squad consisted of the ironclad monitors USS *Weehawken* (Capt. John Rodgers) and USS *Nahant*. Webb fitted the *Atlanta*'s bow with a percussion torpedo with which he hoped to sink the *Weehawken*. But coming into the channel, the *Atlanta* grounded and was only able to move again after some difficulty, thereafter experiencing steering trouble. Five heavy shots boomed forth from the *Weehawken;* the *Nahant* moved into position, and the two wooden Confederate ships fled. After a two-hour fight, Webb could only surrender, and the formidable *Atlanta* was captured and out of action.

A towering political action also took center stage during this month. On June 20, West Virginia officially became the thirty-fifth state in the Federal Union when Abraham Lincoln signed his proclamation. The splintered loyalties in Virginia had in part taken their place in history; Confederate sympathizers were disheartened by the outcome of this question; and the Reconstruction of what would become the new Union took another major step.

The war in Tennessee heated up in June. On the 4th, Confederates began a reconnaissance along the Shelbyville Pike near Murfreesboro, and fighting erupted at Franklin and Snow Hill. At Franklin, Col. John P. Baird (85th Indiana Infantry) was attacked by the cavalry and mounted infantry of Brig. Gen. Nathan Bedford Forrest; Baird was reinforced by Col. Ferdinand Van Derveer and Federal cavalry fought a brisk action that scattered the Confederate forces. After many such skirmishes across middle Tennessee and much prodding by the administration, Rosecrans finally decided to do something in the area late in the month. On June 23 he set into motion the week-long Tullahoma campaign, so named because he moved his Army of the Cumberland, 56,000 strong, south from Murfreesboro toward Tullahoma, where Bragg's army was centered. The conditions for marching and fighting were poor, with frequent rains and muddy roads. (The soldiers' legend that Tullahoma was derived from the Greek *tulla*, meaning "mud," and *homa*, meaning "more mud," was untrue.)

Though it didn't produce significant action or materially harm Bragg's force of 44,000, the Tullahoma campaign would be a feather in Rosecrans's cap. In the span of a week he would relieve some of the pressure from Grant's Vicksburg operations by forcing Bragg to retreat behind the Tennessee River. From Bragg's point of view he simply had to block a possible advance by Rosecrans toward Chattanooga, which prevented Bragg from sending reinforcements to Mississippi. At the start of the campaign, Bragg's Army of Tennessee was spread relatively thin, with Lt. Gen. Leonidas Polk's corps at Shelbyville; Lt. Gen. William J. Hardee's corps to Polk's northeast at Wartrace; Forrest's cavalry along the Duck River to the west, near Columbia; and Maj. Gen. Joseph Wheeler's cavalry to the northeast at McMinnville. From Murfreesboro, Rosecrans sent Brig. Gen. Gordon Granger's reserve corps toward Polk, while he dispatched the corps of Maj. Gens. George H. Thomas and Thomas L. Crittenden southeastward to Manchester, to threaten Bragg's right flank; and the corps of Maj. Gen. Alexander M. McCook a short distance southward as a ruse before moving toward Wartrace.

As the forces moved slowly toward the swollen Duck River, heavy rains

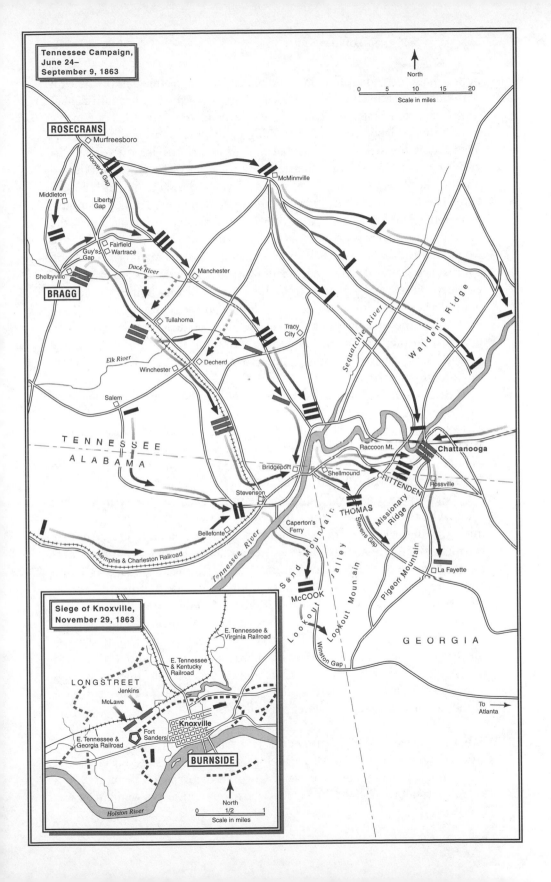

Tennessee Campaign, June 24– September 9, 1863

North

0 5 10 15 20
Scale in miles

ROSECRANS
◇ Murfreesboro

Hoover's Gap

Middleton

Liberty Gap

McMinnville

Fairfield
Guy's Gap
Wartrace
Shelbyville

Duck River
Manchester

BRAGG

Tullahoma

Tracy City ◇

Elk River
Winchester ◇
Decherd ◇

Walden's Ridge

Sequatchie River

Salem

TENNESSEE
ALABAMA

Raccoon Mt.

Chattanooga

Bridgeport
Shellmound

CRITTENDEN

Rossville

Memphis & Charleston Railroad

Bellefonte ◇

Stevenson

Tennessee River

Caperton's Ferry

THOMAS

Missionary Ridge

McCOOK

Sand Mountain

Lookout Valley

Stevens Gap

Lookout Mountain

Pigeon Mountain

◻ La Fayette

GEORGIA

Winston Gap

To Atlanta

Siege of Knoxville, November 29, 1863

E. Tennessee & Virginia Railroad

E. Tennessee & Kentucky Railroad

LONGSTREET
Jenkins

McLaws

E. Tennessee & Georgia Railroad

Knoxville

Fort Sanders

BURNSIDE

North

0 1/2 1
Scale in miles

Holston River

pelted the soldiers day after day, making the campaign almost intolerable for both sides. The rain converted "the whole surface of the country into a quagmire," reported Maj. Gen. David S. Stanley, and "rendered this one of the most arduous, laborious, and distressing campaigns upon man and beast I have ever witnessed." Four principal skirmishes occurred, mostly involving cavalry forces. On June 24 an engagement took place along the Middleton-Shelbyville Pike, involving Stanley's cavalry. On the same day, at Hoover's Gap, Thomas's corps struck into Confederate defenders on the mountainous approach to Manchester. Col. John T. Wilder's brigade led the attack, the 72d Indiana Infantry (Col. Abram O. Miller) driving the rebel pickets into a wooded hillside where the battle commenced. Wilder's men pushed on and approached the well-defended gap, deploying his regiments along with six artillery pieces and opening into the rebel position. Miller's regiment poured a heavy fire into the gap, and Wilder reported that it "caused them to first fall to the ground to escape the tornado of death which was being poured into their ranks. But finding no cessation of our leaden hail, they crawled back as best they could, under cover of the hills, and made no further attempt to take our left."

Brig. Gen. William B. Bate, commanding the defending brigade of Confederates, put the best spin he could on losing the gap by nightfall. "It was a bright day for the glory of our arms, but a sad one when we consider the loss of the many gallant spirits who sealed with their blood the devotion to our cause." The Confederate losses were 19 killed and 126 wounded, while Wilder's brigade lost 14 killed and 47 wounded.

McCook's corps also fought a battle in the gap, a day later and farther south. On their approach to Tullahoma, McCook's lead elements skirmished with the Confederate defenders at Liberty Gap on June 25. Another skirmish took place at Guy's Gap and Shelbyville on June 27. Bragg's ineffective defense of these positions sent Polk retreating through Guy's Gap and Hardee's pickets scrambling back from Liberty Gap. When it became clear that Rosecrans's force was concentrating at Manchester, Bragg recalled his entire army to Tullahoma, and shortly thereafter he determined to retreat southward across the Elk River. Wilder moved his brigade to destroy the bridge between Tullahoma and Decherd, but Forrest's cavalry prevented the Yankees from hindering the Confederate escape. On June 30, Bragg's army sped southward and destroyed the Elk River bridges, and the next stage of the war in Tennessee was about to begin.

THE LATE SPRING and early summer of 1863 was a time of troubles for many officers great and small. On May 7, in Spring Hill, Tennessee, Maj. Gen. Earl Van Dorn, commander of the Cavalry Corps of the Army of Tennessee, was killed by a jealous husband. Van Dorn, whose reputation as a womanizer was well known, had established headquarters at the Martin Cheairs House, a lovely square brick mansion on the town's main street. Van Dorn had been spending late nights in the company of Mrs. Jessie Peters, an attractive brunette married to one of the town's doctors, George B. Peters. The doctor had heard a variety of rumors about his wife and the visiting general officer and issued warnings about them. When he traveled to Nashville on business for several days and returned to hear convincing evidence that Van Dorn had visited his wife every night during his absence, Peters went to the Martin Cheairs House and, concerned about his wife's honor, asked Van Dorn to sign a statement exonerating his wife of guilt. The next day, when he was to pick up the statement, Van Dorn had not prepared it. Peters returned half an hour later, and Van Dorn then balked at signing anything, saying it would "hurt the cause." Enraged, Van Dorn allegedly shouted, "You damned cowardly dog, take that door or I will kick you out of it," whereupon Peters drew a Deringer and shot Van Dorn in the head, killing him instantly.

In dishonor, the Confederacy had lost a corps commander. Discreetly, Van Dorn was buried with a simple, small headstone in a corner of the family plot in the cemetery at Port Gibson, Mississippi, his hometown. Of the many indictments of Van Dorn's sloppy behavior, one of the most vitriolic appeared in the *Atlanta Confederacy*. "Van Dorn has been recognized for years as a rake," editorialized the writer, "a most wicked libertine—and most especially of late. If he had led a virtuous life, he would not have died—unwept, unhonored, and unsung. . . . The country has sustained no loss in the death of Van Dorn. It is a happy riddance."

Some officers deplored what they had to do in the name of orders from superiors. Col. Robert Gould Shaw, the youthful leader of the 54th Massachusetts Infantry, the soon-to-be-famous black unit, regretted deeply having to set fire to the town of Darien, Georgia, on June 11. Darien, on the Darien River, was Georgia's second leading port and home to a number of wealthy prewar slave owners. The eccentric Kansas jayhawker Col. James Montgomery led a reconnaissance to the town on that day, with Shaw's regiment a part of Montgomery's brigade. After encouraging his soldiers to loot the town, Montgomery turned to the less experienced Shaw and simply said, "I shall burn this town," explaining that the Southerners "must be made to feel that this was a real war, and that they were to be swept away by the hand of God like the Jews of old." Shaw was humiliated to have to engage in such destruction as his first military act with the new regiment of black soldiers. "For myself, I have gone through the war so far without dishonor, and I do not like to degenerate into a plunderer and robber—and the same applies to every officer in my regiment," he declared to his wife. A few days earlier, Federal troops in Mississippi had sacked and burned Jefferson Davis's Brierfield Plantation.

But no one suffered more harassment by everyone imaginable than the Union commander-in-chief. The newspaper correspondent Noah Brooks wrote about Lincoln being besieged about this time by an applicant for a pass conveying him to Richmond. "My dear sir," said the president, according to Brooks, "I would be most happy to oblige you if my passes were respected; but the fact is I have within the last two years given passes to more than two hundred and fifty thousand men to go to Richmond, and not one of them has got there yet in any legitimate way." The applicant withdrew, "with a rush of blood to the head."

The war by now was taking a heavy toll on Lincoln, visible even to casual acquaintances and strangers. "He has a face like a Hoosier Michael Angelo," wrote the poet and war nurse Walt Whitman that spring, "so awful ugly it becomes beautiful, with its strange mouth, its deep cut, criss-cross lines, and its doughnut complexion. . . . He has shown, I sometimes think an almost supernatural tact in keeping the ship afloat at all. . . . I say never yet captain, never ruler, had such a perplexing dangerous task as his, the past two years. I more and more rely upon his idiomatic western genius, careless of court dress or court decorum."

CHAPTER 17

Three Days at Gettysburg

BY THE LAST WEEK OF JUNE, the two great eastern armies were converging on Pennsylvania. Southern soldiers relished marching onto Northern ground to resupply and perhaps to terrorize the Yankee populace. They crossed to the north bank of the Potomac River, passed farms, encountered citizens (who again, like last autumn, failed to demonstrate support for the Confederacy), foraged in the fertile fields and woods, plundered stores and wrecked property, and in a couple of rare cases, even hurt civilians. Little opposed the Confederate advance, as Hooker was cautious and largely ignorant of Lee's whereabouts. A small contingent of Pennsylvania and New York militia troops was hastily assembled by Pennsylvania Governor Curtin.

At the head of the Army of the Potomac, Joe Hooker was in a difficult spot. Still stinging from the disaster at Chancellorsville, he was ordered by Lincoln and Halleck to keep a close watch on the danger toward Washington, yet to move out and prevent Lee from ransacking Maryland and Pennsylvania as well. Mostly, however, the powers in Washington were seriously questioning Hooker's ability to lead the army, and this was the worst possible time to have an army commander in the field whose competence was suspected by even the private soldier. Hooker had planned an operation toward the Confederate lines of communications but by June 27 had not sent orders to his corps commanders. Following terse and testy telegrams between Hooker and the War Department, mostly over Hooker's newly acquired, McClellan-like fears of immense Confederate strength, and the War Department's insistence that the Union garrison on Maryland Heights, opposite Harpers Ferry, be left in place, Hooker requested to be relieved of command. Lincoln quickly accepted and initiated plans to replace him. At 3 A.M. on June 28, Col. James A. Hardie, the feared assistant adjutant general attached to Secretary Stanton's office, arrived at Maj. Gen. George Gordon

Meade's tent at Frederick and said he brought "trouble." In actuality, Hardie brought an order assigning Meade to the command of the army. Among the candidates for command at this time were John Sedgwick, Winfield Scott Hancock, Darius N. Couch, and John F. Reynolds. The last, well liked by everyone, declined an offer to command the army reportedly because the offer did not include a "free hand."

But Meade would make a good choice, although he has been treated harshly by historians ever since. Described by one of his soldiers as a "damned, goggle-eyed snapping turtle," the general's most famous fearsome attribute was his occasional fierce temper. But he was a careful and considerate commander whose bookish knowledge matched his battlefield experience in tactics and strategy. Meade was a Pennsylvanian, although he had been born in Cadiz, Spain, of American parents. He was graduated in the West Point class of 1835 and, backed by his engineering training, served gallantly in the Mexican War. Wounded at Glendale and at Antietam, his Civil War service was impressive to date. "By direction of the President of the United States, I hereby assume command of the Army of the Potomac," Meade wrote on June 28. "As a soldier, in obeying this order—an order totally unexpected and unsolicited, I have no promises or pledges to make. The country looks to this army to relieve it from the devastation and disgrace of a hostile invasion. . . . let each man determine to do his duty, leaving to all controlling providence the decision of the contest." Rather than being exiled into a meaningless sphere, Hooker, like Burnside, would return to significant actions as a skilled and thoughtful corps commander in battles to come, redeeming his tarnished reputation.

The organization of the armies changed, then, from the days of Chancellorsville. Meade's Army of the Potomac consisted of the corps of Maj. Gen. John F. Reynolds (1st Corps; divisions of Brig. Gens. James S. Wadsworth, and John C. Robinson, and Maj. Gen. Abner Doubleday); Maj. Gen. Winfield Scott Hancock (2d Corps; divisions of Brig. Gens. John C. Caldwell, John Gibbon, and Alexander Hays); Maj. Gen. Daniel E. Sickles (3d Corps; divisions of Maj. Gen. David B. Birney and Brig. Gen. Andrew A. Humphreys); Maj. Gen. George Sykes (5th Corps; divisions of Brig. Gens. James Barnes, Romeyn B. Ayres, and Samuel W. Crawford); Maj. Gen. John Sedgwick (6th Corps; divisions of Brig. Gens. Horatio G. Wright and Albion P. Howe, and Maj. Gen. John Newton); Maj. Gen. Oliver O. Howard (11th Corps; divisions of Brig. Gen. Francis C. Barlow, and Adolph von Steinwehr, and Maj. Gen. Carl Schurz); Maj. Gen. Henry W. Slocum (12th Corps; divisions of Brig. Gens. Alpheus S. Williams and John W. Geary); and Maj. Gen. Alfred Pleasonton (Cavalry Corps; divisions of Brig. Gens. John Buford, David M. Gregg, and H. Judson Kilpatrick). The artillery was commanded by Brig. Gen. Henry J. Hunt. Altogether, the Army of the Potomac had about 93,500 men on the field.

Lee's Army of Northern Virginia consisted of three corps, that of Lt. Gen. James Longstreet (1st Corps; divisions of Maj. Gens. Lafayette McLaws, George E. Pickett, and John Bell Hood). McLaw's brigade commanders were Brig. Gens. Joseph B. Kershaw, Paul J. Semmes, William Barksdale, and William T. Wofford. Pickett's brigade commanders were Brig. Gens. Richard B. Garnett, Lewis A. Armistead, and James L. Kemper. Hood's brigade commanders were Brig. Gens. Evander M. Law, George T. Anderson, Jerome B. Robertson, and Henry L. Benning. A newer corps commander was Lt. Gen. Richard S. Ewell, who had replaced Jackson (2d Corps; divisions of Maj. Gens. Jubal A. Early, Edward Johnson, and Robert E. Rodes). Early's brigade commanders were Brig. Gen. Harry T. Hays, Col. Isaac E. Avery (Hoke's brigade), and Brig. Gens. William "Extra Billy" Smith and John B. Gordon. Johnson's brigade commanders were Brig. Gen. George H. Steuart, Col. Jesse M. Williams (Nicholls's brigade), and Brig. Gens. James A. Walker (Stonewall Brigade) and John M. Jones. Rodes's brigade commanders were Brig. Gens. Junius Daniel, Alfred Iverson, George P. Doles, Stephen Dodson Ramseur, and Col. Edward A. O'Neal. Third in line was the corps of Lt. Gen. A. P. Hill (3d Corps; divisions of Maj. Gens. Richard H. Anderson, Henry Heth, and William Dorsey Pender). Anderson's brigade commanders were Brig. Gens. Cadmus M. Wilcox, William Mahone, Ambrose R. Wright, Carnot Posey, and Col. David Lang (Perry's brigade). Heth's brigade commanders were Brig. Gens. James Johnston Pettigrew, James J. Archer, Joseph R. Davis, and Col. J. M. Brockenbrough. Pender's brigade commanders were Brig. Gens. James H. Lane, Edward L. Thomas, Alfred M. Scales, and Col. Abner Perrin. The cavalry was commanded by Maj. Gen. Jeb Stuart and included the brigades of Brig. Gens. Fitz Lee, Wade Hampton, Albert G. Jenkins, Beverly H. Robertson, William E. Jones, and Col. John R. Chambliss (Rooney Lee's brigade); and Brig. Gen. John D. Imboden led a semiautonomous brigade. Altogether, the Confederate strength at Gettysburg amounted to about 70,200.

The march of the Army of Northern Virginia behind the screen of the Blue Ridge had been smooth and without incident. The defense of Pennsylvania's capital was entrusted to Maj. Gen. Darius N. Couch, who assisted Governor Curtin as best he could with arming militia units. Primitive forts were constructed hastily along the river at Harrisburg and Wrightsville, and most of the volunteers who quickly enlisted to stem the Rebel tide were shopkeepers, clerks, or government employees from Harrisburg and its environs. By midmonth Couch had organized Pennsylvania and New York militia outfits and dispatched troops to the area of Chambersburg, where the

Confederate advance was then directed, receiving valuable assistance with railroad logistics such as prefab, "portable" bridges from Col. Thomas A. Scott and Brig. Gen. Herman Haupt. A few days later the 8th and 71st New York Militia regiments took their places at Fort Washington, near Harrisburg. The tough task of delaying Ewell's oncoming Confederates at Chambersburg fell onto Brig. Gen. Joseph F. Knipe, a Harrisburg resident on leave from the Army of the Potomac due to wounds, who took the two small New York militia regiments forward and led them to Chambersburg.

The 71st New York Militia arrived in Chambersburg on June 22 and prepared to block Jenkins's cavalry as it approached. On that day, local citizen Jacob Hoke reported, "A person supposed to be a woman came into camp. She was attired in mourning apparel, with her face almost concealed in a black bonnet of somewhat antiquated style. She went about the camp pretending to be silly, and inquired where a certain farmer lived who no one knew." The Federal soldiers in town soon learned that the person was a Confederate scout, and probably a male. A detachment of Jenkins's cavalry and Rodes's infantry moved ahead to a position near Greencastle, between Chambersburg and Hagerstown, where a skirmish occurred. One of the men struck, Union Cpl. William F. Rihl (1st New York Cavalry), was shot in the face, becoming the first soldier to die north of the Mason-Dixon line in the campaign; thousands more would meet the same fate in the ensuing days.

Ewell approached the Susquehanna River line at midmonth, bringing 25,000 men toward the frightened but festive camps of militia set up along the riverbanks. Wrightsville became an obvious target, for it held the Columbia Bridge over the Susquehanna, a 5,620-foot structure that was alleged to have been the longest wooden span in the world at the time. The 27th Pennsylvania Militia protected the western bank of the river and other units, including black laborers who took up rifles, readied for a defense of the bridge. In case of heavy attack the Federals would withdraw across the bridge and then blow it up with prearranged powder charges. Brig. Gen. John B. Gordon, the brave Alabama soldier who had been so badly wounded at Antietam's Sunken Road, led the Confederate approach on Wrightsville. Gordon set up two captured Federal cannon and began bombarding the town and the Union defensive works. The Union militia troops withdrew rapidly eastward across the bridge into Columbia and exploded the charges, but the bridge did not fall. Instead, the kerosene-soaked timbers caught fire and the blaze spread into the town of Wrightsville, creating an inferno visible as far away as Harrisburg.

By June 28, Lee's men were scattered through southern Pennsylvania, with Longstreet's corps at Chambersburg, A. P. Hill at Fayetteville and Greenwood, Ewell with Rodes and Johnson at Carlisle, Early at York, with Gordon at Wrightsville, threatening Lancaster, and Jenkins's cavalry across

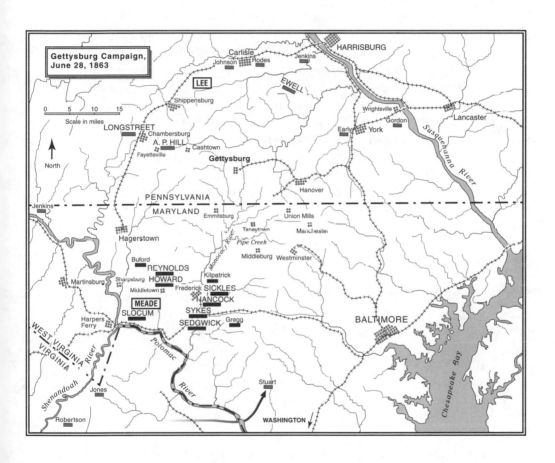

Gettysburg Campaign,
June 28, 1863

the Susquehanna from the capital, Harrisburg. The Army of Northern Virginia foraged and gathered supplies liberally from the countryside and forced purchases of materials from farmers' stores, providing Confederate currency in exchange. At York, Early demanded $100,000 in U.S. currency as he threatened destruction; he let the town stand after receiving the sum of $28,000. Lee wanted Ewell chiefly to replenish his corps's supplies and remedy its hunger; he had permitted Ewell to strike toward Harrisburg, but did not order it outright.

Lee had been rather vague about his intentions for the campaign, preferring to see how the situation might develop before issuing specific orders. During the last week of June, Lee was much hampered by the absence of Jeb Stuart, who failed to remain in touch with Lee; therefore, Lee had little information about the whereabouts of the Union forces. But Stuart's absence was supported by Lee's note to Stuart of June 22, which Stuart received the next day. "If you find that [the enemy] is moving northward," ordered Lee, "and that two brigades can guard the Blue Ridge and take care of your rear, you can move with the other three into Maryland, and take position on General Ewell's right, place yourself in communication with him, guard his flank, keep him informed of the enemy's movements, and collect all the supplies you can for the use of the army." In an accompanying letter, Longstreet wrote of Lee speaking of "leaving, via Hopewell Gap, and passing by the rear of the enemy. If you can get through by that route, I think that you will be less likely to indicate what our plans are than if you should cross by passing in our rear."

What if Stuart *didn't* find those things to be the case? Armed with a vague set of suggestions and ample latitude for interpretation, Stuart took full advantage of his embarrassment in the Southern press following Brandy Station. He set out to restore his name as the most dashing and heroic cavalry commander in the war by interposing between the Federal army and Washington, capturing as many supplies as he could, and raiding northward into Maryland via Rockville toward Westminster before pushing into Pennsylvania. The action was designed to restore Stuart's ego as well as to aid the current campaign. He left the brigades of Beverly Robertson and Grumble Jones behind to guard the gaps of South Mountain and soon discovered that precious little forage lay ahead of him in the picked-over countryside. He also found that he would have to contend with passing close to many scattered columns of Federal infantry. Slowed by these circumstances, Stuart crossed the Potomac only on June 27 (following a skirmish at Fairfax Court House), after which he struck out for Hanover, late in the eyes of his commanding general. A 125-wagon supply train he captured was, in Lee's words, a "liability" for the army when Stuart finally arrived at Gettysburg. On July 1, Stuart reached Carlisle, looking for Ewell. He ordered the town surrendered; Brig. Gen. William F. "Baldy" Smith commanded the place, and he evacuated the civilians and prepared to fight. Stuart shelled the town with one cannon and burned the cavalry barracks, but then broke off toward Gettysburg.

Lee planned a movement on Harrisburg, believing the Union army was still south of the Potomac River. On the evening of June 28, however, one of Longstreet's scouts, probably 2d Lt. Henry Thomas Harrison, informed Longstreet and Lee that the Union corps were rapidly moving northward. This occurred near Chambersburg, and Harrison let Lee know that the Union army was concentrated around Frederick, Maryland, and now commanded by the cautious, bookish Meade. In Stuart's absence, Lee determined to trust the spy's information, which turned out to be accurate. So Lee altered his plan, ordering his troops to converge on Gettysburg and Cashtown, the former a hub of eight significant roads, and the latter merely a crossroads with several structures, standing about seven miles northwest of Gettysburg, on the other side of Marsh Run.

Meade was a risky command choice in some senses, given the enormous responsibility afforded him. He assumed command of a vast army, the largest Federal force in the war, on the virtual eve of battle with a vast enemy army operating in Pennsylvania, and without previous experience commanding an army. He ordered the seven Union corps to move northward from the Frederick area on June 29, at 4 A.M., not knowing where Stuart's cavalry was or, thanks to the secrecy of his predecessor, the details of how the army communications worked. Given the studious caution that characterized Meade, he moved quickly, which reflected the gravity of the situation. Meade's orders from the War Department were as vague as those Lee gave his subordinates: "Your army is free to act as you may deem proper under the circumstances as they arise," wrote Halleck on June 27. "You will, however, keep in view the important fact that the Army of the Potomac is the covering army of Washington as well as the army of operation against the invading forces of the rebels. You will, therefore, maneuver and fight in such a manner as to cover the capital and also Baltimore, as far as circumstances will admit." Due to the exigencies of the crisis, all Union forces in the area were placed under Meade—including those commanded by Maj. Gen. Robert C. Schenck (Middle Department), Darius Couch (Department of Pennsylvania), Samuel P. Heintzelman (Department of Washington), and those of three of his own corps commanders, John F. Reynolds, Henry W. Slocum, and John Sedgwick, all of whom ranked him.

Gettysburg was a sleepy village of 2,390 residents, unique as an interchange of roads. Indeed, the Southern armies initially formed at nearby Cashtown, and the resulting battle might easily have become the battle of Cashtown. At this stage it seems reasonable to believe that Lee was still developing a plan of operations, and with Stuart absent, the formulation percolated more slowly than usual. The cavalry forces that were north of the Mason-Dixon line were essentially ignored by Lee, including those of Jenkins and Imboden, and Lee ordered only the cavalry brigades of Jones and Robertson forward from the Shenandoah Valley as if by an afterthought, on June 29. Meade, meanwhile, began to show signs of stress, and altered his plans from attacking Lee to establishing a defensive line. On June 30, Meade ordered his engineering staff to construct a defensive line along Big Pipe Creek near Union Mills, Maryland; by now, the coming battle might have been fought along Pipe Creek. Two orders issued within a few hours of each other late on June 30 and early in the morning of July 1 reveal a vacillation on Meade's part. On the afternoon of June 30, Meade planned to "push on tomorrow in the direction of Hanover Junction and Hanover"; in his celebrated "Pipe Creek circular," issued early on July 1, Meade wrote that the present objective of the army in advancing into Pennsylvania, to relieve Harrisburg and parry an invasion above the Susquehanna, had been achieved. He further stated that if the enemy attacked he meant to withdraw his army "from its present position, and form line of battle with the left resting in the neighborhood of Middleburg, and the right at Manchester, the general direction being that of Pipe Creek." Meade wrote that he would not undertake an offensive operation "until the enemy's movements or position should render such an operation certain of success."

While Meade attempted to dictate events, the events would actually end up dictating to Meade. He did order Reynolds to advance with his own corps and those of Howard and Sickles, leaving Sedgwick's corps as an anchor at Manchester. "Major Gen. Reynolds will upon receipt of this order assume command of the three corps forming the left wing in the present position of the army. . . . He will make such dispositions & give such orders as circumstances may require & report from time to time to the comdg. general," Meade ordered on June 30. Brig. Gen. John Buford's Federal cavalry, meanwhile, rode into Gettysburg on June 30 and scouted toward the Cashtown Gap. A brief skirmish erupted west of the town between Buford's troopers and infantry of Johnston Pettigrew's brigade. After Pettigrew retreated to Cashtown and informed Heth of the enemy cavalry's presence, Heth determined to move to Gettysburg the following day to deal with the Union horsemen before Federal infantry could march northward in support. The stories of Confederate expeditions into Gettysburg to "search the town for army supplies (shoes especially)" appear to be spurious, postbattle extrapolations, which may have been concocted by Heth to cover himself for advancing such a heavy force to Gettysburg without orders. One wonders why a force of 2,400 soldiers would be required to find shoes and why Heth expected that a vast store of shoes would exist in a small town such as Gettysburg. Moreover, the town had previously been inspected by Early. Despite the chaotic action that lasted but a brief time on June 30, Buford's reconnaissance demonstrated that potentially heavy forces of Confederates were in the vicinity, west of Gettysburg, and that high ground around Gettysburg, particularly east and south of the town, might afford a strong defensive position.

Finally, on June 30, Stuart crossed the Mason-Dixon line into Pennsylvania and proceeded to smash into a portion of Kilpatrick's cavalry at Hanover. After a confused melee, Stuart broke off and headed for York, having heard of Early's presence there. He would be further delayed from assisting Lee, who, in camp at Greenwood, wondered where his "eyes" were, despite the fact that he had issued such poorly defined orders to his Southern horsemen.

At Cashtown, A. P. Hill sent word to Lee that Federal cavalry had appeared in Gettysburg and that he intended to reconnoiter the town the next morning to find out what force was there. The Confederates had no notion that the following day might spark a great battle. Neither did the Federal army, moving northward under Reynolds, who had his headquarters at the Moritz Tavern, Maryland, along Marsh Creek, nor the army's headquarters under Meade, also en route north and approaching Taneytown. But Buford began to have his suspicions. The lay of the land around Gettysburg worried Buford, should the Confederates seize control of the high ground and entrap the Federals in the town. Fredericksburg still haunted the Union soldiers and their officers.

Constructed on a plat of land with gridded streets in the middle of a basin, Gettysburg was surrounded by north-south ridges of land to the west (Herr Ridge and Seminary Ridge), to the northwest (Oak Ridge), and to the south (Cemetery Ridge). Roads diverged from the town square like spokes from the hub of a wheel, and the hills surrounding the town, speckled by granite outcrops, gave the region a New England flavor. Northward, roads departed for Heidlersburg, Carlisle, Mummasburg, and Harrisburg. Running to the west was the important Chambersburg Pike, just north of which lay an unfinished railroad that stood trackless west of the town. The Gettysburg & Hanover Railroad came into the city from the east. To the southwest was the Fairfield Road; southward ran the Emmitsburg Road, Taneytown Road, and Baltimore Pike. Eastward, the Hanover Road and York Pike completed the complex tangle of access roads running through this small community.

The high ground that both worried and intrigued Buford would hold the secret to unfolding action at Gettysburg. Seminary Ridge was marked by the Lutheran Theological Seminary half a mile west of town and offered a solid artillery position. South of town stood Cemetery Hill, the highest point along Cemetery Ridge, so named because the city's burying ground, Evergreen Cemetery, was positioned on the hill. East of Cemetery Hill stood the much higher and more formidable Culp's Hill, at an elevation of 615 feet. The most impressive hills stood two miles south of town, however— Big Round Top and Little Round Top. Big Round Top, or simply Round Top, peaked at 767 feet. To its north, the lesser Round Top crested at 655 feet. Big Round Top was heavily wooded, but Little Round Top had in recent times been cleared of much of its timber on its western side, exposing a vista over the landscape south of the town. The whole area contained a network of streams, most oriented approximately north-south, the greatest of which was Rock Creek, east of the town, which flowed along the eastern base of Culp's Hill. Also prominent were Plum Run, which drained the land west of the Round Tops and then joined Rock Creek, Willoughby's Run and Pitzer Creek, west and southwest of the town, and Marsh Creek, farther west of Gettysburg. Numerous landmark buildings would play into the struggle as Gettysburg transformed from a Pennsylvania town into a battlefield. Among the principal ones were the seminary, whose cupola atop what is now called Samuel Simon Schmucker Hall afforded an excellent observation post, the buildings of Pennsylvania College (now Gettysburg College) on the northwest edge of town, the County Home, or Almshouse, north of the city, and many scattered farmhouses.

The battle of Gettysburg, the largest and costliest act of warfare played out in the Western Hemisphere, began primarily as an accident in the sense that neither Union nor Confederate forces planned for a battle. At 5 A.M. on July 1, Heth ordered the brigades of Archer and Davis eastward toward Gettysburg, along the Chambersburg Pike. Some two hours later the Confederate infantry reached a position about three miles west of Gettysburg, along Herr Ridge, where it encountered the dismounted troopers of Buford's division. Some 7,600 Confederate infantry marched toward the Union cavalry force of only 2,748 men. The Federal horsemen used trees, fence rails, or simply ground for cover as best they could, and although they were badly outnumbered, Buford employed his breechloading carbines well enough to buy time until more of the Federal army might arrive and relieve his two brigades. A weak defensive line was established straddling the turnpike, east of Willoughby's Run, from McPherson's Woods on the south, across the unfinished rail line, and north toward Oak Hill. Col. William Gamble's brigade was spread along much of the line; with two regiments under Col. Thomas C. Devin anchoring the Union right. By 7:30 A.M. the two forces approached within distant sight of each other; Lt. Marcellus Jones of the 8th Illinois Cavalry fired his carbine and the first shot of the engagement echoed along the swale containing Willoughby's Run.

By 8 A.M. the Confederates advanced and engaged the horsemen in battle. The fight opened with great savagery. The horse soldiers of Gamble and Devin, supported by six guns from Tidball's battery, commanded by Lt. John H. Calef, held the Confederate infantry at bay. The cavalry sought refuge behind a stone wall and demonstrated the brilliance of their breechloaders in combat, firing and loading three times faster than the Confederates with their conventional muskets. But many of Buford's troopers were holding the horses while they fought like infantrymen, and the numerical superiority of the Southern force began to show. By 9 A.M. the Federal cavalry fell back to a line along McPherson's Ridge, midway between Willoughby's Run and the Lutheran Seminary, on which was the farmstead of Edward McPherson, who had earlier served as a volunteer aide on the staff of John F. Reynolds. About 9:30 A.M. Reynolds arrived on the field, much to the relief of Buford, who had received intelligence that not only would he need to contend with Heth's advance from the west but also with that of Ewell from the north, who was reported advancing from Heidlersburg. At the seminary, Reynolds and Buford briefly discussed the situation (although the authenticity of their meeting at the cupola has been questioned); with the crackling musketry fire and spurts of cannon booming a short distance away, they determined to stay and fight. Reynolds rode to the rear and ordered fences torn down along the Emmitsburg Road so that the advancing Union infantry could, on reaching the scene, cut across the fields to the action on Seminary Ridge. Until about 10:45 A.M. the Union cavalry fought stubbornly, holding off the greater number of Rebels.

The advancing Union infantry did not know what awaited it, although the soldiers could see whitish puffs of smoke off in the distance and hear the faint booms of cannon. Wadsworth's division advanced swiftly up the Emmitsburg Road, with Brig. Gen. Lysander Cutler's brigade in the lead. "We were being hurried at the utmost speed along the road on that hot July morning," wrote the chaplain of the 147th New York Infantry, "sweltering from every pore, as for me, my clothes could not have been wetter if I had fallen into a pond of water." Following Cutler's brigade was Brig. Gen. Solomon Meredith's unit, the so-called Iron Brigade, consisting of the hardy Wisconsin, Indiana, and Michigan troops who had fought so stubbornly at Brawner's Farm and South Mountain. An unfounded rumor broke out in the line of march that McClellan, still much adored by the boys, had retaken command of the army. It instilled new confidence in the soldiers even if McClellan was actually cooling his heels in New Jersey.

With Buford's men hanging on perilously and so many troops on the march toward the fight, Reynolds could only decide to counterattack. He had a stiff, fighting spirit and had no indication of Meade's notion to pull the action back to the Pipe Creek line. So he threw the divisions of Wadsworth and Doubleday toward the fight, brought Robinson up from the rear, and ordered Howard's 11th Corps forward as quickly as possible to stem the threat from Ewell. Cutler's brigade formed a line bisected by the railroad cut and, supported by artillery, faced Davis's men to the north and the left flank of Archer's line in McPherson's Woods. To the south the Iron Brigade, its soldiers characterized by their distinctive black hats, slammed into Archer's line, flanking and crushing the 13th Alabama Infantry (Col. Birkett D. Fry), the 1st Tennessee Infantry, and other regiments. The movement at once convinced Heth that elements of the Army of the Potomac lay in front of him in force—this was no militia. In the attack of the Iron Brigade, the 2d Wisconsin Infantry (Col. Lucius Fairchild) captured about 75 Confederates. Among those taken were Col. Fry, who was wounded, and Archer himself. After surrendering his sword so quickly on the morning of July 1, Archer would not be easily forgiven by his friends in Richmond. He spent more than a year in Federal prison before being exchanged; in 1864 he died from the effects of pneumonia.

As the Iron Brigade moved forward in triumph, however, tragedy also struck the Union command. During the attack Reynolds was killed by a gunshot wound to the head, making him one of the highest-ranking Union officers killed during the war. Struck by a bullet, Reynolds collapsed in his saddle, and only after he was placed on the ground by aides was a wound discovered. Reynolds gasped a single time, smiled slightly, and died from the ball that entered behind his right ear. His body was taken into the town of Gettysburg and readied for transport home to nearby Lancaster. Among the soldiers who confronted the onrushing Rebels at this position was a citizen of Gettysburg, John L. Burns, age 69 and a spur-of-the-moment volunteer. He took up arms alongside the 150th Pennsylvania Infantry, and later with the 7th Wisconsin Infantry during three hours of the afternoon fight on July 1. Other civilian residents also fought in the action. Following Reynolds's death, the unremarkable Maj. Gen. Abner Doubleday assumed command of the Federal forces.

A short time later most of Cutler's brigade was forced into a retreat to Seminary Ridge, but the 147th New York Infantry held fast along the unfinished railroad bed. "The line of the [regiment] was lying in a [wheat]field at and below the ridge," wrote Capt. James Coey. ". . . The fire of the enemy, the zipping of their bullets, cut the grain, completely covering the men, who would reach over the ridge, take deliberate aim, fire and then slide back under their canopy or covering of straw; reload and continue their firing. Those of the regiment wounded here were wounded in the head or upper part of the body, consequently more fatal." The 147th New York also withdrew to Seminary Ridge. The withdrawal exposed the Union artillery and the right flank of the Iron Brigade. By 11 A.M. a furious counterattack commenced along the Chambersburg Pike, with the 84th New York Infantry driving across the Pike northward toward the 42d Mississippi Infantry, positioned along the railroad cut; to the east, the 95th New York Infantry similarly attacked along with the 6th Wisconsin Infantry (Lt. Col. Rufus R. Dawes) of the Iron Brigade, which speared the 2d Mississippi Infantry in a brutal melee.

The Confederates were driven back into the cut, which served as a natural rifle pit for a time, and the 6th Wisconsin, led by Dawes, fought hand to hand with the 2d Mississippi Infantry and the 55th North Carolina Infantry. Amid shouts of "Throw down your muskets!" the Wisconsin men fought stubbornly against the Mississippians, clubbing them with musket stocks, firing down into the cut, and grappling with Confederates in a desperate contest to see who might surrender. "My color guards were all killed and wounded in less than five minutes," wrote Cpl. W. B. Murphy of the 2d Mississippi, who carried the colors that morning. "My colors were shot more than one dozen times, and the flag staff was hit and splintered two or three times. . . . There were over a dozen shot down like sheep in their mad rush for the colors."

A lull now passed over the field. Stunned by the ferocity of the Union fight, Archer's and Davis's brigades retreated to Herr Ridge, so named for its prominent stone Herr Tavern, to regroup. Heth wanted reinforcements from Pender's division to move up and take a position to support another attack, especially given the poor condition of Archer's brigade. By about noon, Union Maj. Gen. Oliver O. Howard arrived on site and assumed command of the field from Doubleday; Howard immediately sent messages asking Slocum and Sickles to move their corps into battle as fast as possible. He assigned Maj. Gen. Carl Schurz to the command of his own 11th Corps. Howard positioned the division of Brig. Gen. Adolph von Steinwehr along Cemetery Hill, recognizing it as a naturally strong position. He also warned about the approach of Ewell's men from the north. The leading division, that of Rodes, was moving fast on Oak Hill, and there Howard posted a line of defenders with Brig. Gen. John C. Robinson's division in the center.

The afternoon battle of the first day erupted about 1:30 P.M., as Rodes's division, some 8,600 men strong and supported by sixteen field pieces, sent a deadly fire into the Union line along Oak Hill, south of the Mummasburg Road and along the southeastern edge of Forney's Field. Rodes planned to send the brigade of Col. Edward A. O'Neal obliquely into the right flank of the Federal line, rolling it up as it was attacked by his other brigade, that of Brig. Gen. Alfred Iverson. The numerically inferior force of Robinson, about 4,100 men, consisted of the brigade of Brig. Gen. Henry Baxter, which occupied a position behind the stone fence alongside Forney's Field, and Cutler's brigade to the south. Rodes's initial attack was a failure, for Iverson did not participate and O'Neal's regiments found a galling fire returned at them as

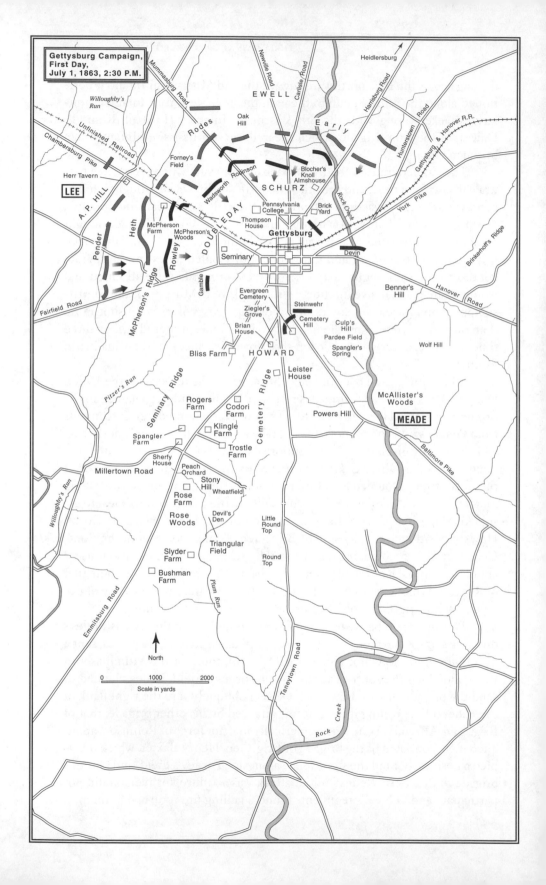

they approached the Yankees. At 2:30 P.M. Iverson's brigade finally did attack, again in uncoordinated fashion, with O'Neal to his left and the brigade of Brig. Gen. Junius Daniel on his right. Iverson stayed behind the assault rather than joining it, raising allegations of cowardliness and even drunkenness. The commander and his men failed to realize the Yankees waited for them behind a stone wall.

"When we were in point blank range," a Southern soldier later recalled, "the dense line of the enemy rose from its protected lair and poured into us a withering fire." The Yankees sent "a sheet of fire and smoke . . . from the wall, flashing full in the faces of the Confederates, who at once halted, and, though their men were falling like leaves in a storm . . . attempted to make a stand and return the bitter fire." The attack of Iverson's brigade was a Confederate disaster, and Baxter's men rushed onward and captured more than 300 Southern soldiers. Poor leadership by Iverson and O'Neal would account for most of the Confederate loss in this area, one of the greatest brigade losses of the war. Next, Daniel's brigade attacked Col. Roy Stone's brigade, resulting in several bloody counterassaults. The brigade of Brig. Gen. Gabriel R. Paul joined the fight, and in the intense action that ensued, Paul, a regular army, Mexican War veteran who was much liked by the Washington authorities, was hit in the head.

By midafternoon, despite sloppy tactical performance by Confederates at Oak Hill, the overwhelming Southern force was having its effect. A. P. Hill began attacking from the west anew, supported by well-placed Confederate cannon, with Pender's fresh division now facing the Iron Brigade. Rodes threatened Oak Ridge, and Maj. Gen. Jubal A. Early arrived with his division, some 6,300 strong, from York, endangering the Union right flank. A short time after 3 P.M. the stout regiments of the Iron Brigade were forced back from McPherson's Woods by Pender's strong, coordinated sheets of musketry fire. On Seminary Ridge, Federal artillery fired canister into Pender's approaching ranks. After engaging along six lines of battle between late morning and late afternoon, the Iron Brigade was ordered to fall back to Cemetery Hill at about 3:45 P.M. Gamble's Union cavalry attempted to cover the retreat, firing hotly into Pender's men. Ramseur's brigade led an attack that speared into and scattered the Union regiments still on Oak Ridge. The resulting movement back through the town of Gettysburg, which still had plenty of civilians hiding in cellars and wondering which way the battle was moving, reflected a sense of panic. Pender attacked fiercely at 4 P.M., driving the Union retreat into further chaos. He sent Col. Abner Perrin's brigade thrusting into the Union brigade of Col. Chapman Biddle, west of the seminary, sending it into retreat. Finally, believing that the Yankees were utterly routed, his men exhausted after six hours of fighting, Hill halted the attack.

Ewell, moving southward toward the town, attacked headlong into the unfortunate, outnumbered 11th Corps, which had been so mauled at Chancellorsville by Jackson's flank attack. Schurz initially occupied a position just north of town, posting the divisions of Brig. Gen. Alexander Schimmelfennig along the Carlisle Road and Brig. Gen. Francis C. Barlow northeast of town. Barlow pushed on past the Almshouse to occupy a slight rise on the ground known as Blocher's Knoll, subsequently as Barlow's Knoll. He sent the brigade of Col. Leopold von Gilsa to post his 900 men on the knoll, which had an elevation of 519 feet. Von Gilsa deployed his men in a skirmish line to engage the Confederates already spread across the area. By 3:15 P.M. Early launched an all-out attack on the 11th Corps, sending the brigades of Brig. Gen. Harry T. Hays, John B. Gordon, and George P. Doles forward toward Gettysburg. The intensity of fire into Blocher's Knoll was incredible, with the Union soldiers taking heavy casualties. Gordon's men charged into Barlow's position, routing the Yankees and sending them scurrying. Numerous wounded covered the knoll after the desperate struggle, including the badly wounded Barlow, who was shot in the left side. Age 29, Barlow was a well-liked New Yorker who had been a lawyer and newspaperman. As he lay alone, after surviving Yankees fled, he was struck in the back by a second ball that bruised him. Another bullet grazed a finger; a fourth struck his hat. Barlow was captured and taken to a house on the Blocher Farm, expecting to die. He survived, however, and was recaptured by Union troops when the Confederate army retreated from the field. Years later Gordon, the Confederate general who attacked Barlow's position, spun a story about taking Barlow's possessions to his wife should he die; this appears to be an invention of Gordon's for the sake of selling his autobiography.

Pressed by the southward attack of Early, Col. Wladimir Krzyzanowski's Union brigade collapsed and began a chaotic retreat toward the town. Early's second line was established and he continued to push his men forward and regularly pierce the Union battle lines with volleys of musketry. Amid the Federal chaos, a supporting battle line was established by Col. Charles R. Coster's brigade, which formed on the northern part of town along a brickyard operated by John Kuhn. As the divisions of Schimmelfennig and Brig. Gen. Adelbert Ames were falling back into the town, Coster made a last stand at the brickyard, deploying the 154th New York Infantry in the center, flanked by the 27th Pennsylvania Infantry on the left and the 134th New York Infantry on the right. At the brickyard Coster's brigade came under attack by Hoke's brigade (Col. Isaac E. Avery) by 3:45 P.M. After vicious hand-to-hand fighting erupted between the soldiers, the Union regiments were cut to pieces and numerous prisoners were taken. "I got up and went as fast as any of them," explained Pvt. Janus Quilliam of the surrounded 154th

New York, "but when we got to the road, it was full of Rebels and they were coming up behind us, so there we had to stay, and few got away."

Finally, Confederates secured the town. Fleeing Union soldiers raced through the streets to the relative safety of Cemetery Hill; casualties were strewn all over; gunshots rang out through the streets; civilians fled or hid at the sight of Rebel soldiers inside their town. Men were laid out all over as makeshift hospitals immediately sprang into action. A chaplain, Horatio M. Howell (90th Pennsylvania Infantry), was killed on the steps of the Lutheran church. Schimmelfennig made the unfortunate decision to run down an alleyway that dead-ended at a barn in the yard of the Garlach family. There he hid between a barrel and a woodshed for three days before Union troops retook the town and liberated him. The Garlach family, while the town was in Confederate occupation, brought the young general bread and water in a bucket supposed to be used for feeding pigs. The danger in town would continue. Inside the McClellan House on Baltimore Street, on the morning of July 3, Mary Virginia Wade, 20, was struck by a Minié bullet while baking bread and killed instantly. She would be the only civilian death during the battle.

Lee, having observed the battle for a time, saw the critical importance of Cemetery Hill and Culp's Hill, both of which rose to 615 feet. By 4:30 P.M. Lee sent Ewell one of his famously ambiguous orders, asking Ewell to take the high ground of Cemetery and/or Culp's Hill "if practicable," a phrase that left open the widest possible range of interpretation. Lee might have gotten away with this in ordering Ewell's predecessor, Stonewall Jackson, who was naturally aggressive. Ewell, however, was another type. Ewell believed that he could not position his artillery effectively to provide support for an infantry attack, felt that his troops were exhausted by fighting and marching, lacked one of his divisions (that of Maj. Gen. Edward Johnson), and had more than 4,000 Federal prisoners to contend with. Moreover, the troops he did have at hand had been intermingled due to the chaotic fighting through the narrow streets of the town as the Yankees scattered southward. Early in the fight Ewell had been knocked to the ground when his horse was killed by a shell fragment near Oak Hill; that incident must have been alarming enough to caution him. By 5 P.M. Ewell made his way into the town square and saw masses of Confederate troops mingling with many Union prisoners and virtually no citizens in sight. Johnson, meanwhile, with his missing division, finally reached Cashtown and heard the sounds of battle. In the town Ewell rode forward with Rodes and Early to examine Howard's Union line on Cemetery Hill. Although it was clear that artillery could not be placed to advantage in the town, Ewell finally determined to make an attack on Cemetery Hill. A messenger from Lee, however, made it clear that no support would be available on the right, and so Ewell first decided not to attack, worrying more with each passing minute about the condition of Rodes's men. Ewell then determined to move against Culp's Hill ("the wooded hill to my left") only when Johnson came up.

Ewell's decision to halt the battle stunned many of the subordinate officers who had been accustomed to Stonewall Jackson's brashness. In typical oversimplification, claims after the war hinged the whole of the Confederacy on this moment, as with Lt. Col. H. C. Jones's postwar statement that "there was not an officer, not even a man, that did not expect that the war would be closed upon the hill that evening, for there was still two hours of daylight when the final charge was made, yet for reasons that have never been explained nor ever will be . . . someone made a blunder that lost the battle of Gettysburg, and humanly speaking, the Confederate cause." Exaggeration aside, Ewell's hesitation was costly, even if tempered by real concerns. Attacking or seizing Culp's Hill and the adjoining portions of Cemetery Hill plainly would yield valuable ground for any fighting to come. And like Lee, Ewell failed to make effective use of the cavalry he did have to scout the roads east of town. So Ewell judged an attack on the high ground south of the town "impracticable," much to the aggravation of some of his subordinates, who favored aggressively attacking Culp's and/or Cemetery Hill.

By late afternoon the Union command was finally stabilizing. From Taneytown, Meade had sent Maj. Gen. Winfield Scott Hancock forward to Gettysburg, having issued orders for him to assume command of the troops on the field. Hancock arrived about 4:30 P.M. and was stunned to see the 1st and 11th corps "retreating in disorder and confusion." Howard and other officers had great trouble attempting to hold a line south of the town, particularly when the loud whine of musketry fire began to erupt from buildings in Gettysburg. Although Howard knew of Hancock's approach, it isn't clear whether he realized Hancock had been given command of the army on the field. After a hasty salute, Howard instantly reminded Hancock that he was the senior officer in rank. Hancock replied that he was aware of that fact, but that he had been ordered by Meade to assume command, and he would show Howard the document if necessary. Howard allegedly replied that it wasn't necessary, and after a brief, civil argument amid the bullets whizzing by in the surrounding airspace, Howard and Hancock agreed that this was a good place to fight the battle north of Pipe Creek, and that they would commence fighting the Rebels rather than each other. Beginning at about 5 P.M., some 12,000 Union soldiers on Cemetery Hill began constructing a fortified line of defense. Hancock and Howard now held the Union center, with Doubleday's battered 1st Corps stretching southward a little way along Cemetery Hill, save Wadsworth's division, including the tattered survivors of the Iron

Brigade, which protected the northern base of Culp's Hill. Buford's cavalry was posted along the Emmitsburg Road to the south. The first elements of Maj. Gen. Henry W. Slocum's 12th Corps came slowly up, with Brig. Gen. Thomas H. Ruger's division to the east, south of Wolf Hill, and the division of Brig. Gen. John W. Geary marched southward along the Taneytown Road, passing nearby Birney's division of the 3d Corps. As portions of the 12th and 3d corps approached the already bloodied town, they saw odd sights. Col. Ezra A. Carman (13th New Jersey Infantry) witnessed a crowd of citizens who had fled the town, seeking refuge behind a rail fence along the Taney-town Road. "They seemed to fear that the 'rebs' would prove too much for us," he commented. ". . . Our arrival in the town, however, was the cause of great rejoicing by the inhabitants, and from every house we received tokens of gratitude and delight in the shape of cooked provisions, biscuits, bread and butter, cakes, pies, and other luxuries which were keenly relished."

The battle of Gettysburg had thus far favored Lee's Army of Northern Virginia, but mostly because it had fought an outnumbered enemy. Division and brigade commanders had escalated the fight into a major pitched battle throughout the day, something that neither side desired. Lee's army was scattered throughout southern Pennsylvania and his cavalry mostly absent from the scene. Lee now faced continuing this escalating engagement on ground that might greatly disadvantage his soldiers and with the bulk of the Federal army rapidly approaching. Johnson's tardy division finally arrived about 7:30 P.M. and pulled into position north of Culp's Hill; Early occupied the town itself, Rodes was positioned on the northwest edge of town, and Pender stretched southward along Seminary Ridge. The divisions of Heth and Anderson were still scattered west of town. Finally, with darkness approaching, Ewell ordered Lts. Robert D. Early and Thomas T. Turner to reconnoiter the summit of Culp's Hill. Almost miraculously, they reached the summit without detection by the nearby Union troops. They reported the enemy's line of battle to Ewell, who halfheartedly and finally asked Johnson to move toward Culp's Hill and occupy it "if you find no enemy troops there." Early urged that it be done because "if you do not go up there tonight, it will cost you ten thousand men to get there tomorrow." Ewell was also repeatedly pushed by Brig. Gen. Isaac R. Trimble, who claimed that "if we don't hold that hill, the enemy will certainly occupy it, as it is, the key to the whole position about here." Ewell responded that he didn't require advice from Trimble.

Johnson approached Culp's Hill by a peculiar route, forming east of the town, fording Rock Creek, and moving toward Benner's Hill first. A small reconnaissance party moved out ahead of the division, and as it approached the base of Culp's Hill, encountered the pickets of the 7th Indiana Infantry, who opened fire and caused the advancing Confederates to retreat in panic and report that an overwhelming Yankee force lay ahead. Ewell nervously backed off. At Ewell's headquarters, a short time later, none other than Robert E. Lee arrived to consult with the general. Present also were Early and Rodes. After considering several options, Lee decided to leave Ewell's corps in position for the night. Ewell later rode to Lee's headquarters near the Mary Thompson House along the Chambersburg Pike, west of town, for more consultation. By 2 A.M. on July 2, Ewell ordered Johnson's division to reform southeast of the town and await further orders. The opportunity to attack Culp's Hill, which probably had existed only about 6 P.M. the previous evening, was lost. Heavy fortification of the Union line and support from fresh troops on the hill occurred during the night.

Lee's menu of choices late on July 1 was limited. As Longstreet's fresh corps marched toward the battlefield, Lee and Longstreet contemplated the best strategy for the morning. Cautious about the Federal battle line that was forming along the ridges of high ground extending southward from Gettysburg, Longstreet warned against attacking but instead suggested interposing the Confederate army between Meade's army and Washington. This would force Meade to take the initiative away from the formidable high ground. As many of Lee's subordinate officers observed during the last half of the first day's fight, however, the Confederate commander appeared to "have his blood up," and was determined to make a stand and show his army's ability on Northern soil; he was desperate also not to disengage and possibly appear to be in retreat. Lee, therefore, formulated an offensive strategy after observing the Union line from Culp's Hill, Cemetery Hill, and Cemetery Ridge south to the Round Tops. With his 70,200 men and 262 field guns, Lee would attack on July 2 with a three-pronged movement, sending Longstreet around on the right flank to lead the assault, A. P. Hill in the center on Cemetery Ridge and southern Cemetery Hill, and Ewell into the Union right on Culp's Hill and eastern Cemetery Hill. Ewell's movement would be mostly a demonstration that would force the Union right to stay in position rather than shift in support of the defense against Longstreet.

Arriving after his journey from Taneytown about 11:30 P.M. on July 1, Meade walked about the Federal line on Cemetery Hill. Near the brick gatehouse of Evergreen Cemetery, he spoke with generals Slocum, Howard, Sickles, and Warren, formulating an opinion on the battlefield. One of the officers mentioned that they occupied good ground, and Meade replied that it was just as well, as they could not now abandon the field. Meade soon established his headquarters at the Lydia A. Leister House on the Taneytown Road and set to work formulating a tactical plan. The night remained hot and a bright moon hung overhead, which "presented a scene of weird, almost spectral impressiveness," wrote an observer to the *National Tribune.* "The roads south and southeast of the town flowed with unceasing, unbroken rivers of armed men, marching swiftly, stolidly, silently. Their garments were covered with dust, and their gun barrels gleamed with a fierce brilliance in the bright moonlight. The striking silence of the march, the dust-gray figures, the witchery of the moonbeams, made it spectral and awesome. No drum beat, no trumpet blared, no harsh command broke the monotonous stillness of the steady surge forward."

As more Federal troops marched piecemeal into the battlefield area, Meade deployed them into a form that began to resemble a fishhook with its barb on Culp's Hill, curving through Cemetery Hill, and with a straight shank extending southward along Cemetery Ridge. This defensive line was established for four reasons: such high ground offered a natural bastion from which to ward off expected attacks from Lee; two subordinate officers, Slocum and Warren, strongly opposed taking the offensive; Meade's entire army was not yet present; and the troops on the field were exhausted from the march.

The second day at Gettysburg, July 2, would transform into one of the hottest, most intense days of fighting in the war. It would also be decisive for Gettysburg, although another day of battle lay after it. The many waves of attacks and counterattacks that flowed across the battlefield south of Gettysburg were so complex, so numerous, and involved so many intermingled units that in many cases took heavy casualties, that the full story of the regimental positions on this second day is not known. But it's clear that from his headquarters of the Army of Northern Virginia, Lee envisioned his attack would commence sometime in the morning. Lee and Longstreet were both awake very early, perhaps as early as 3 A.M. Though his headquarters tents were pitched across the Chambersburg Pike from the Thompson House, north of the Theological Seminary, Lee spent a great amount of time on a tree stump or fallen log north of the largest seminary building, talking with various officers and writing out orders. Though much has been made of Lee's health during the battle of Gettysburg, and he certainly was suffering to some degree from diarrhea and possibly a recurrence of the malaria he had picked up while supervising work at Baltimore's Fort Carroll in 1849, he was anything but incapacitated. He walked, discussed orders at length, rode the battle lines, and although somewhat weakened, performed his duties.

Longstreet was in attendance at Lee's headquarters from the early morning hours up until about 11 A.M. Also present for extensive consultation that morning were Hood, A. P. Hill, McLaws, and other officers. From this vantage point, Lee might have spied Federal cannon on Cemetery Hill one and a quarter miles away on his right front. Still formulating his plans in the morning, Lee believed the route to the right offered the greatest opportunity, and he sent scouting parties off to explore that direction, led by staff officers Col. Armistead L. Long, Lee's military secretary, artillery chief Brig.

Gen. William N. Pendleton, and engineer Capt. Samuel R. Johnston. Pendleton moved down to Spangler's Woods and saw little except for capturing two stray Yankees drinking from a stream. Long explored potential artillery positions. Johnston set out at 4 A.M., moved south along Willoughby's Run, turned eastward and climbed the slope of Seminary Ridge, and near the Peach Orchard explored the ground but reported seeing no Union troops, an oddity considering that many should have been visible from that position. Even more strangely, Johnston's party moved to the Round Tops, exploring the base of Little Round Top, and reported seeing no Federal soldiers in that area. After three hours and a convoluted path that miraculously prevented them from spotting the enemy, they returned to Lee and reported their reconnaissance. Longstreet was asked to move into position and ready for an attack on the Federal left.

Lee next took off to explore the preparations for battle on the Confederate left. Leaving his headquarters about 9 A.M. and moving through the town, he could not find Ewell on his arrival at the 2d Corps headquarters on the east side, near Rock Creek, but he did find Trimble. Lee and Trimble visited the cupola at the Almshouse for a view of the surrounding terrain and allegedly lamented that they could not yet "pursue our advantage of yesterday." Lee next returned to his headquarters and supposedly remarked to Long, "What *can* detain Longstreet?" suggesting already his impatience with a tardy attack. The implication sparked a firestorm of controversy after the war. Longstreet supposedly told Hood that "the General [Lee] is a little nervous this morning; he wishes me to attack; I do not wish to do so without Pickett. I never like to go into battle with one boot off." If Longstreet did say this, it suggests that an early attack was on Lee's mind. Certainly, many of Lee's supporters later claimed he had ordered an attack by Longstreet at sunrise; this is clearly not the case. But perhaps Lee wanted an attack as early as "practicable," when intelligence could be sorted out, troops positioned, and organizational details minded. But Longstreet and others claimed that Lee gave no orders to attack until after he returned from his visit to Ewell's headquarters. Indeed, the written order of II A.M. instructs Longstreet to "move with the portion of [his] command that was up, around to gain the Emmitsburg Road, on the enemy's left." Therefore, preparations for the attack did not get underway until between II A.M. and noon. Longstreet, already not a believer in attacking at Gettysburg, readied his corps for an assault on the Union left by late morning. How the Confederate command structure worked and whether it broke down by failing to initiate an attack sooner and how much of the blame should rest on Lee as army commander or Longstreet as a sullen subordinate really isn't quite as relevant as some might wish. The attack happened the way it happened, and might-have-beens in war are meaningless.

Longstreet was certainly grumpy. He marched his corps over the unfamiliar Pennsylvania ground, with its rises and swales, stands of trees and granite outcrops, following orders but perhaps without urgency. It was a hot, sunny day, and the wool uniforms and heavy equipment made the soldiers uncomfortably warm. From Herr Ridge, Longstreet took his men to a position south of the Black Horse Tavern on the Fairfield Road, turned the column around, proceeded south along Willoughby's Run, turned southeastward toward Pitzer's Schoolhouse, and finally positioned them along the southern stretch of Seminary Ridge. All the while, Longstreet's columns kept avoiding detection by the Federal signal station atop Little Round Top. At times the march was a model of confusion and inefficiency. Anderson's division, to the north, had been in position since noon, although A. P. Hill had been tardy in posting it. Longstreet's divisions of McLaws (center) and Hood (south) took much longer to deploy and organize than anyone had hoped. Certainly, Longstreet's crankiness didn't help. The unfolding of Lee's plan was fraught with delays, clarifications, and wasted time. By 4 P.M. the wings of the army were in position along Seminary Ridge, ready for the day's battle.

Confusion and poor subordination also characterized a portion of the Federal side of battle preparations on this day. In fact, the obfuscation couldn't have come much closer to where Longstreet's men were lining up for their attack. The Union 3d Corps, commanded by the irascible Maj. Gen. Daniel E. Sickles, had marched out into a salient far in front of the rest of the Union army, to a position reasonably close to the Confederate lines. Sickles advanced his men to the Sherfy Peach Orchard along the Emmitsburg Road, with the divisions of Humphreys on the north and Birney on the south, without any justification to do so. Although the ground was somewhat higher along the Peach Orchard (591 feet) than that inside the southward line along Cemetery Ridge (perhaps 550 feet), which Meade understood Sickles would hold, Sickles believed the forward ground might offer a better artillery position and allow guarding the Emmitsburg Road for the passage of artillery trains. Sickles discussed the proposed movement with Meade's chief of artillery, Brig. Gen. Henry J. Hunt, and asked for authority to make it, but Hunt begged off and referred Sickles to Meade. After Hunt rode off to check on artillery, Sickles ordered Birney to make a reconnaissance on the woods in front of the Peach Orchard, and Birney dispatched four companies of the 1st United States Sharpshooters (Col. Hiram Berdan), with the 3d Maine Infantry in support. Berdan's men moved out of the Peach Orchard, crossing the road, and sweeping north through Pitzer's Woods, encountering Confederate skirmishers. After a sharp, twenty-minute firefight with Wilcox's brigade of Alabamians, during which the men saw numerous Confederates marching through the open fields beyond, Berdan's group withdrew.

When McLaws's men advanced from the woods about 3 P.M. and gazed out over the countryside in their front, they were more than slightly alarmed. Instead of finding an open route to the Yankee line posted in the distance, they stood in front of a formed line of battle supported by artillery. "The enemy was massed in my front and extended to my right and left as far as I could see," recalled McLaws. Longstreet soon grew impatient and asked McLaws why he did not attack at once. He discovered that the whole 3d Corps blocked his path and ordered McLaws not to attack. While Hood's division deployed to McLaws's left, Longstreet discovered that the Union line extended nearly all the way to the Round Tops and that attacking up the Emmitsburg Road, as originally instructed by Lee, would expose the Confederate right. Scouts reported no Union troops near Little Round Top, however, and so Longstreet realized that a movement around the Federal left might position troops in the rear of the Federal line, potentially collapsing it. But Lee's orders to Longstreet allowed no discretion. Between 3:30 P.M. and 4 P.M., the artillery of Col. Edward Porter Alexander, commanding Longstreet's reserve guns, opened fire on the Federal position; shortly afterward, by 4:30 P.M., Hood's men fired volleys and marched forward, and the attack was underway.

By 3 P.M. Sickles had unilaterally decided to block the Confederate approach and moved his corps out into the exposed salient. At this time the final corps on the approach to Gettysburg, the 6th Corps of Maj. Gen. John Sedgwick, was sighted approaching the battlefield along the Baltimore Pike. Meade summoned his corps commanders to the Leister House for a meeting, and all showed up except for Sickles. About this time the group heard cannon fire in the direction of the 3d Corps, and an aide of Brig. Gen. Gouverneur K. Warren, Meade's chief engineer, rode up and reported the situation was "not all straight" along Sickles's front. (Warren was commissioned a major general only in 1864, and it was then backdated to the time of Gettysburg.) Meade then mounted his horse, Old Baldy, and rode with Warren toward Sickles's position, ordering Maj. Gen. George Sykes to move the 5th Corps over to the Federal left as quickly as he could. Along Cemetery Ridge, the generals found a gap where the 3d Corps was supposed to be. Behind the Peach Orchard, Meade finally caught up with Sickles and asked for an explanation and a description of his lines. Meade, known for his quick temper, bristled with anger after Sickles explained, and the chagrined corps commander suggested he would withdraw to the assigned position. Meade, however, pointed out that the enemy would not allow it without attacking, and just about this time the Confederate line exploded with artillery fire. With this the agitated Meade rode back to his headquarters to reorganize the situation. In the so-called Meade-Sickles controversy that would boil over in the years following the battle, the army commander was clearly right and Sick-

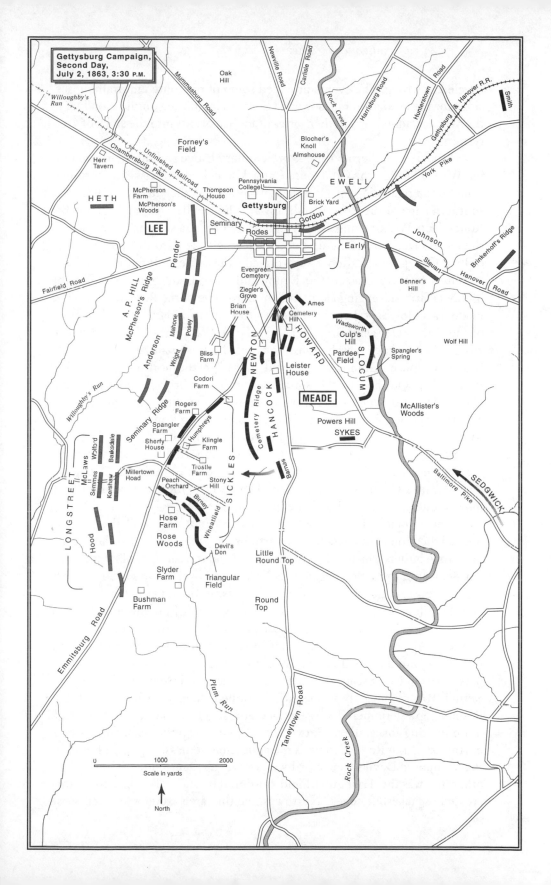

Gettysburg Campaign,
Second Day,
July 2, 1863, 3:30 P.M.

les clearly wrong. The events provided some of the more entertaining sessions for the ill-starred but powerful Senate Committee on the Conduct of the War and added yet another series of foolish events into the story of Gettysburg.

From the southern terminus of Seminary Ridge and the nearly adjoining Warfield Ridge, the Confederate attack struck eastward with determination. Southern soldiers of Hood's division fired as they headed toward the southern edge of the Rose Woods, toward the Devil's Den, and toward Big Round Top. Withdrawing, Birney's division formed a skirmish line north of the Devil's Den, stretching up to the Wheatfield. Toward this position, half of Brig. Gen. Jerome B. Robertson's brigade, the 1st Texas Infantry and the 3d Arkansas Infantry crossed the Emmitsburg Road, and marched past the Timbers farm, advancing along the southern edge of the Rose Woods. They made tracks for Capt. James E. Smith's 4th New York Battery (posted north of the Devil's Den) and Brig. Gen. John H. H. Ward's brigade. The 4th and 5th Texas infantries marched just north of the Bushman Farm, passed the J. Slyder House (Granite Farm), and moved to the northern end of Big Round Top. On the assault's southern end, Law's brigade moved straight eastward toward Big Round Top, with the exception of the 44th and 48th Alabama infantries, which, on reaching the base of Big Round Top and Plum Run, moved around northward to the Devil's Den, shifting to Law's left. As the attack proceeded, Benning's brigade, in support, advanced toward the Devil's Den and Anderson's brigade later moved on Rose Woods. Along the left of Ward's Union line north of the Devil's Den, the 4th Maine Infantry moved southward to block a Confederate advance through Plum Run Valley.

The ferocity of the attack was evident. Not only had the soldiers hugged the ground during the fierce artillery duel that preceded the assault, but Minié bullets whistled by the advancing and retreating ranks with equal zip. Soon after the action began, a shell exploded over Hood's head, wounding him severely and causing the loss of the use of his left arm. Law's brigade and the 4th and 5th Texas regiments crossed Plum Run and found themselves moving around the northwestern slope of Big Round Top. The 44th and 48th Alabama regiments, meanwhile, began to shift northward along Plum Run into the Devil's Den. The lay of the ground was incredibly complex here, and viewscapes from place to place were severely limited. Big Round Top was heavily timbered and sloped steeply; to its north, Little Round Top's detimbered western face and shallower slope made it much more inviting for artillery. Between the Round Tops was a shallow swale; northwest of Big Round Top was the collection of massive granite boulders that composed Devil's Den. Northwest of Devil's Den, along the base of another hill, was the Triangular Field, bordered by stacked granite rocks that created a makeshift fence. Northwest of this area stood the thick Rose

Woods, and north of the woods was the exposed Wheatfield, which sloped gently down to a branch of Plum Run. Another rise, Stony Hill, stood west of the Wheatfield. Plum Run ran through the whole scene, one branch emanating at the Peach Orchard and the other along Cemetery Ridge; the two joined along the base of Big Round Top. The Rose Farm stood west of Stony Hill and the Triangular Field.

The chaotic series of fights throughout this area escalated rapidly during the waning, hot hours of the afternoon of July 2. The 1st Texas and 3d Arkansas regiments attacked savagely into Ward's brigade, firing on Smith's battery, to open the assault at the Devil's Den. A "fierce, charging yell" opened the first of two assaults on the line, with Smith's artillerists firing like mad in return and beginning to run low on ammunition. With their case shot expended Smith shouted "Give them shell! Give them solid shot! Damn them, give them anything!" Posted at a rock wall between the Wheatfield and the Rose Woods, the 17th Maine Infantry opened a withering fire on the attacking Confederates, and the 4th Maine blocked the advance of the Alabama regiments into Plum Run Valley (an area that came to be called the "Valley of Death"). Benning's brigade of Georgians now attacked Ward's line; a counterattack by the 4th Maine and 99th Pennsylvania infantries anchored Smith's position for a time until Benning's and Robertson's brigades together struck the position, which unhinged the Federal line. Covering the position along Plum Run, the 6th New Jersey Infantry permitted the Yankees to retreat in reasonable order. The fighting at the Devil's Den had been severe, with "roaring cannon, crashing rifles, screeching shots, bursting shells, hissing bullets, cheers, shouts, shrieks, and groans." At one point when the Confederates attacked strongly, Smith simply stated, "For God's sake, men, don't let them take my guns away from me!" Among the dead during this phase was Col. Augustus van Horne Ellis (124th New York Infantry), a New York fireman who had been struck in the head with a Minié bullet and was posthumously commissioned a brevet brigadier general for his valor.

As the fierce fighting witnessed the rattle of musketry and booming echoes of cannon fire throughout the southern end of the field, Warren, who had been investigating the Federal left, discovered the open nature of Little Round Top and the fact that no one occupied it. Warren sent a dispatch to Meade asking for a division to defend the tactically crucial hill. Meade initially assigned Humphreys to the task but quickly found that Sykes's 5th Corps was coming up into position. Col. Strong Vincent, one of the 5th Corps brigade commanders (in Brig. Gen. James Barnes's 1st Division), on his own initiative moved his four regiments onto the crest of Little Round Top, using an old logging path to avoid drawing artillery fire.

The crest of Little Round Top held a Federal signal station. To its south, along the craggy ridge, the hill's southwestern slope, were then posted the 16th Michigan Infantry, 44th New York Infantry (Col. James C. Rice), 83d Pennsylvania Infantry (Vincent's old regiment), and, on the extreme left of the Union line, the 20th Maine Infantry (Col. Joshua L. Chamberlain). The 20th Maine Infantry had the toughest part of the assignment, as its position would surely be the one to be attacked most heavily should the Confederates attempt to get around the Union left and collapse the line, assaulting it from the rear and forcing a withdrawal. To minimize that potential, Chamberlain, age 34 and a former professor of languages and religion at Bowdoin College, spread his 386 men along the ridge of Little Round Top and detached 42 men under Capt. Walter G. Morrill eastward in a skirmish line. Morrill's Co. B moved to a rock wall between and slightly east of the Round Tops, some 400 feet away from the regiment's left flank. The 20th Maine was an unlikely regiment to be holding such a critical position; indeed, it was relatively inexperienced and had achieved only a modest record during the year of its existence. But war is chaos, and the chaos of the moment placed this unit, led by a lightly experienced officer, here at an important position.

By 5 P.M. the Alabama regiments began their attack on the left of Little Round Top. As the 4th Alabama Infantry and 4th and 5th Texas infantries moved forward from the northwest face of Big Round Top against Vincent's battle line, the 15th Alabama Infantry (Col. William C. Oates) and the 47th Alabama Infantry (Lt. Col. Michael J. Bulger) made their way to the summit of Big Round Top and climbed down again to assault the left flank of Vincent's line, the 20th Maine. The 4th Alabama Infantry opened fire into the right of Vincent's line from the base of Little Round Top, and minutes later the 47th Alabama and 15th Alabama attacked the 20th Maine in a confused hillside fight with both sides ducking behind cover (trees and rocks) and popping out to fire at will. "Soon we found the enemy flanking us," reported Cpl. William T. Livermore of the 20th Maine, "and ere making fearful havoc in our ranks as every one who dared raise his head was sure of his man, but many lost their brains in the attempt." The Confederates attacked headlong twice and were repulsed both times. The 4th Maine Infantry meanwhile, continued to block the foot of Little Round Top by protecting access via Plum Run Valley.

The fighting for Little Round Top intensified as both sides came to appreciate its tactical value, and volleys between the 20th Maine and the 15th Alabama created large numbers of casualties as they depleted ammunition. Benning's brigade finally dislodged the protection from the base of Plum Run Valley, taking possession of Devil's Den, and posting two regiments between it and the Triangular Field. The Federal line atop Little Round Top also solidified, with four regiments of Acting Brig. Gen. Stephen H. Weed's brigade added north of the 16th Maine—the 140th New York Infantry (Col. Patrick H. "Paddy" O'Rorke), 91st Pennsylvania Infantry, 146th New York In-

fantry (Col. Kenner Garrard), and 155th Pennsylvania Infantry. Violent fighting ensued along Little Round Top; both musketry volleys and cannon fire
raked the shelf of rocks atop the hill and were sent down into the oncoming
Confederates. Law's and Robertson's brigades now attacked Vincent's line
for a third major thrust, threatening the Union ability to hold the hill, which
regimental commanders such as Chamberlain had been told to do at "all
hazards." Oates and his brother John led the right wing of the 15th Alabama
in a particularly savage thrust against the left of the 20th Maine, momentarily taking the crest of the spur that held most of the regiment. During savage,
hand-to-hand fighting, with some soldiers firing guns point-blank into the
bodies of combatants who then fell into them, the 20th Maine rallied and retook the spur. Oates now turned about in horror and saw the enemy behind
him—it was Capt. Morrill's Company B, which had risen from behind the
rock wall between the Round Tops and delivered a volley into the backs of
the Alabamians. Confederate junior officers panicked and believed that "two
regiments" might be closing in from behind; it was enough to convince Oates
that he was being surrounded.

Running low on ammunition, Chamberlain was also in a panic. "At this
moment my anxiety was increased by the great roar of musketry from my
rear, on the farther or northerly slope of Little Round Top." Chamberlain
believed the Union artillery atop the hill might be overrun and turned
against his men. Both Oates and Chamberlain decided their time had run
out. For the former, retreat seemed the only option. For the latter, downhill
attack with bayonets if necessary seemed the only way out. "It was imperative to strike before we were struck by this overwhelming force in a hand-to-
hand fight," penned Chamberlain. "At that crisis I ordered the bayonet. The
word was enough. It ran like fire along the line from man to man, and rose
into a shout, with which they sprang forward upon the enemy, now not thirty
yards away. The effect was surprising; many of the enemy's first line threw
down their arms and surrendered. An officer fired his pistol at my head with
one hand while he handed me his sword with the other." Aided by Lt. Holman Melcher's forward movement and Lt. Col. Ellis Spear's instinct to follow it, the 20th Maine swung downhill. "Suddenly, in the midst of the noise
of musketry," wrote Spear, "I heard a shout on the center, of 'Forward,' & saw
the line & colors begin to move. I had received no orders. . . . But there was
no time to seek explanation. The center was going ahead, apparently charging the enemy, if any, then all of course, and we all joined in the shouts and
movement, and went in a rush over the boulders and down the slope." Oates
finally signaled retreat, and the 15th Alabama fled in confusion. The 20th
Maine and the other regiments had held the high ground on Little Round
Top as instructed, and although this was critical ground, the fate of the
whole nation hardly rested on this one action, as some recent histories might

suggest. Had Confederates made their way behind the left, Sedgwick's 6th Corps awaited them behind the hill.

The fight for Little Round Top had been costly, however. Col. Strong Vincent, age 26, a well-liked Pennsylvanian who had become a Harvard-educated lawyer, was mortally wounded during the fight by a Minié bullet, which fractured his left thighbone and lodged in his right thigh. He died in a nearby farmhouse five days later. Sometimes the bad news came abruptly, in the haste of war. After the battle an assistant adjutant general, Lt. Col. Frederick T. Locke, wrote the War Department simply: "B. G. Strong Vincent died July 7th." Vincent was posthumously commissioned a brigadier general of volunteers. Also in the fight, Acting Brig. Gen. Stephen H. Weed, a thirty-one-year-old New Yorker, and a regular army man, was mortally wounded in the spine and paralyzed below the shoulders. "I'm as dead a man as Julius Caesar," said the young soldier. Carried behind some boulders, Weed died within a few hours. Additionally, the youthful artillerist Lt. Charles E. Hazlett was killed, struck in the head as he was speaking to his mortally wounded friend Weed. Also dead was Paddy O'Rorke, age 27, a beloved, Irish-born engineer who had been shot through the neck while shouting orders to his troops.

While the action was occurring on Little Round Top, other parts of the battlefield were also flaring with fire. By 5 P.M. activity commenced in the Wheatfield. Union Col. Philippe Régis Denis de Kerenden de Trobriand, French-born, a skilled attorney, poet, novelist, and publisher who had been titled "Baron" in 1840, led his brigade into action. His opponent was Brig. Gen. George T. Anderson, nicknamed "Tige," a hard-fighting Georgian. Establishing a line along a rock wall bordering the southern edge of the Wheatfield, de Trobriand's brigade along with the 115th Pennsylvania Infantry and the 8th New Jersey Infantry held this area as well as Stony Hill, which was occupied by the brigades of Cols. William S. Tilton and Jacob B. Sweitzer. As the attacks on Ward were taking place to the south, near the Devil's Den, Tige Anderson's brigade advanced through the Rose Woods and the right of Ward's line and de Trobriand's brigade. Although the 115th Pennsylvania Infantry and the 8th New Jersey Infantry withdrew, Anderson's initial attack failed, but he regrouped and the second attack brought support from the brigade of Brig. Gen. Joseph B. Kershaw. Originating from the edge of Biesecker's Woods, this assault moved swiftly southward across the Rose Farm and into Stony Hill, causing the brigades of Tilton and Sweitzer to withdraw to the Trostle's Woods, east of the Wheatfield. Fighting a brief delaying action, de Trobriand's men fell back to beyond the Wheatfield, and the Confederates advanced onto Stony Hill and the Rose Woods as well as the Devil's Den.

Known as the "whirlpool," the Wheatfield (527 feet) and surrounding woods witnessed attacks and counterattacks by at least eleven Union and Confederate brigades during a two-hour period on the early evening of July 2. As the intense fighting progressed, Brig. Gen. John C. Caldwell's division (consisting of the brigades of Brig. Gen. Samuel K. Zook and Cols. Edward E. Cross, Patrick Kelly with his famed "Irish Brigade," and John R. Brooke) formed in Trostle's Woods and moved into the Wheatfield, attacking the right side of Anderson's battle line. Prior to the attack, Cross, a hard fighter but not one particularly well liked by his troops, talked over the attack with his corps commander, Winfield Scott Hancock. "Colonel Cross, this day will bring you a star," said Hancock. "No, General," replied Cross, shaking his head, "this is my last battle." A short time later the aggressive colonel was shot in the abdomen with a ball, which mortally wounded him. The Union attacks were roughly handled by Confederate musketry volleys. "The Rebs had their slight protection," noted Lt. Charles A. Fuller, "but we were in the open without a thing better than wheat straw to catch a minnie bullet that weighed an ounce. Of course our men began to tumble." Following the initial movement, Zook's brigade moved out from its attack point toward Kershaw's position on Stony Hill. Zook was an unusual character. A Pennsylvanian by birth who moved to New York, he had been a militia soldier and superintendent of the Washington & New York Telegraph Co. before the war. "If you can't get out of the way, lie down and we'll march over you," Zook shouted at Barnes's retreating men as he commenced his movement.

As Zook rode along to lead his men into the fight, he suddenly felt a severe burning in his left chest, and his head fell back and grew light. A Minié bullet had struck him in the left side of the stomach, perforated his sword belt, and lodged near his spine. He died in a field hospital the next day. As Zook's brigade attacked, Kelly's Irish Brigade struck the southern end of Stony Hill, causing Kershaw's men in the 3d and 7th South Carolina infantries to retreat to the yard surrounding the Rose farmhouse. With the Union attack apparently gaining momentum, Brooke's brigade pushed Anderson's Confederates from the Rose Woods. But a Confederate counterattack was in the making; Anderson and Kershaw reformed, and supported by vigorous thrusts by the brigades of Brig. Gens. Paul J. Semmes and William T. Wofford, they struck through the Wheatfield, scattering the Federals, including Sweitzer's brigade, sent in to support Caldwell. Caldwell's attack, so successful for a short time, was shattered. In the process, numerous dead and wounded were left littered across the Wheatfield, making it one of the most awe-inspiring areas of the field. Semmes, a Georgian, cousin of Confederate naval Capt. Raphael Semmes, was struck in the thigh with a Minié bullet and died a week later in West Virginia.

The savage fighting in the Wheatfield was not over yet. The next division to form in support of Caldwell was that of Brig. Gen. Romeyn Beck

Ayres. His brigade commanders were Cols. Hannibal Day, Sidney Burbank, and Kenner Garrard, who took over for the mortally wounded Stephen H. Weed (the 3d Brigade was up on Little Round Top). The going was difficult for Ayres's two brigades in the Wheatfield: As Burbank's brigade marched into the fight about the time Sweitzer's men were being roughly handled, they moved into the Wheatfield hoping to maneuver into the Rose Woods. But Burbank's men were struck with severe force by Anderson on the left and Kershaw and Wofford on the right, forcing Ayres's men to retreat hastily eastward across Plum Run and assemble again north of Little Round Top. Wofford, meanwhile, pushed the Union division of Brig. Gen. James Barnes out of Trostle's Woods, effectively clearing this sector of the battlefield of Federal soldiers—none remained west of Plum Run.

As the fighting on Little Round Top and in the Wheatfield contributed toward America's most costly battle, heavy fighting erupted in the Peach Orchard, east of the Emmitsburg Road, beginning about 5:30 P.M. McLaws's division struck hard into the Union divisions of Barnes, Birney, and Andrew A. Humphreys. Not only was the fight characterized by murderous sheets of musketry fire, but the area witnessed some of the hottest artillery action of the war. Though Antietam has been described as "artillery hell," Porter Alexander described the artillery battle at Gettysburg's Peach Orchard by recalling, "I don't think there was ever in our war a hotter, harder, sharper artillery afternoon than this." The initial Confederate attack on the Peach Orchard commenced after a blistering artillery barrage and witnessed Kershaw's brigade advancing eastward, its right toward Stony Hill and its left across the Emmitsburg Road and toward the Peach Orchard near the Sherfy House. It then turned left, moving against the Union artillery batteries posted along the Wheatfield Road. After a short delay, Brig. Gen. William Barksdale's brigade struck out across the road and passed directly beside the Sherfy House on its way to attacking Brig. Gen. Charles K. Graham's brigade. The two commanders now facing each other offered quite a contrast. Barksdale was a true old-time Southerner, a Mississippi attorney and politician who in 1859 had assisted Preston Brooks in his Senate-floor caning of Massachusetts Senator Charles Sumner. Barksdale's men first attacked Graham's brigade between the Peach Orchard and the Sherfy Barn. With a hot musketry battle testing the limits of both battle lines, the 73d New York Infantry shifted leftward to support the 114th Pennsylvania Infantry. At the Wentz Farm, south of the Sherfy House on the Emmitsburg Road, Barksdale's men collapsed Graham's line, the 21st Mississippi Infantry (Col. Benjamin G. Humphreys) pushing the blueclad soldiers away from the Peach Orchard. To protect the Union retreat, artillery commanded by Lt. Col. Freeman McGilvery and Capt. John Bigelow was ordered to keep a heavy fire going as long as it could. "I then saw Confederates swarming on our right flank," wrote Bigelow, "some standing on the limber chests and firing at the gunners, who were still serving their pieces; the horses were all down; overhead the air was alive with missiles from the enemy." Supported by Kershaw's left, the 21st Mississippi then drove the Union batteries out from their positions along the Wheatfield Road.

Barksdale's fierce attack next defeated Graham's soldiers who were lodged around the Sherfy buildings, sending them reeling back in confusion. The victorious Mississippians broke down Sickles's salient, exposing Andrew A. Humphreys's left flank and forcing a Union withdrawal. Not only did Sickles's salient collapse, but the Federal corps commander himself was struck in the process. Sitting in the saddle near the Abraham Trostle House, north of Stony Hill, Sickles was hit in the right knee by a low-velocity round shot. The knee was mangled and Sickles was placed on a stretcher next to Trostle's Barn, where despite loss of blood and the onset of shock, he continued talking in rather good spirits with various officers, asked to have himself propped high enough so that his men could see that he was alive, and then requested and smoked a cigar. Taken to a makeshift field hospital at the Daniel Sheaffer Farm in the rear, Sickles had his right leg amputated, wrapped and placed inside a small coffin, and eventually sent to the Army Medical Museum in Washington, where he visited it each year. In some measure the unruly 3d Corps commander had the last laugh: Effectively taken out of the war at his most controversial moment, he continued to aid the Lincoln administration in valuable ways and by losing his leg made himself into an instant hero in his mind and the minds of many others. After the war he served as minister to Spain and used the position as an opportunity to have an affair with Queen Isabella, former ruler of the country. This only added to his prewar notoriety, which came from his having shot and killed on a Washington street his wife's paramour, Washington District Attorney Philip Barton Key, the son of the author of "The Star Spangled Banner." In a sensational murder trial prosecuted by Robert Ould (who would flee under a cloud of treason to become an assistant secretary of war for the Confederacy) and defended by Edwin M. Stanton (who became Lincoln's secretary of war), Sickles was acquitted by reason of temporary insanity—the first such successful defense in America. Even more shockingly to Victorian morals, he took his unfaithful wife back. Sickles outmaneuvered his detractors. He lived until 1914 and presided over many Gettysburg reunions. When asked why no monument was erected to him, he claimed "the whole damn battlefield is my monument."

The movement from the Peach Orchard to Cemetery Ridge also claimed Barksdale and Graham as casualties. As Barksdale's men surged eastward, northeast of Trostle's Farm, it was supported by a simultaneous attack by the brigade of Brig. Gen. Cadmus M. Wilcox. The charge of the Mississippians was a success. In the aftermath of the charge, however, Barksdale was spotted lying on the ground, and a private, Joseph C. Lloyd of the 13th Mississippi Infantry, gave the fallen general a drink of water from his canteen. Union Brig. Gen. Joseph B. Carr had first given an order to fire at a Confederate officer mounted on a white horse, believed to be Barksdale. Struck above the left knee, Barksdale nonetheless continued the fight. He was then hit in the left foot by a cannon shot. Still, Barksdale continued on. Only the third wound, a Minié bullet delivered to the chest, knocked him from his horse onto the ground, where he was found by Lloyd. The young private was shaken when the water Barksdale drank began oozing out of his chest. In the oncoming milky twilight, the general was captured and taken to the Jacob Hummelbaugh House in the rear, where he died the following day.

The next series of events unfolded quickly as Maj. Gen. Richard H. Anderson's division attacked along the Emmitsburg Road north of the Peach Orchard. Wilcox's brigade attacked across the Spangler Farm and into the Rogers Farm, while Perry's brigade of Floridians commenced its movement from the Spangler Woods and struck Joseph B. Carr's brigade, north of the Klingle House. Wright's Confederates, meanwhile, prepared to attack toward the Codori Farm. Barksdale's brigade pushed northward against the left of Andrew A. Humphreys's division and inflicted severe damage to its leftmost regiments, to which Humphreys responded by pulling back two batteries placed along the road and by moving his left to meet the advance of Barksdale's brigade. Wilcox's brigade, meanwhile, shifted leftward and formed a line behind the Spangler House. After vicious fighting, Humphreys was compelled to pull his division back to Cemetery Ridge.

The center of the Union line was now well formed along Cemetery Ridge, running from Ziegler's Grove, a wooded area around the Brian (or Bryan) House, the home of a free black, southward to a prominent, isolated stand of trees afterward called the Copse of Trees, northeast of the Codori House and Barn. The Confederate attack that now jeopardized the Federal center late on the second day emanated from Seminary Ridge. Skirmishers from the brigade of Confederate Brig. Gen. Carnot Posey and Union Cols. Thomas A. Smyth's and Samuel S. Carroll's brigades battled around the buildings comprising the Bliss Farm, west of the Brian House. On Perry's left, Brig. Gen. Ambrose R. Wright's brigade advanced toward the Codori homestead, pushing the 82d New York Infantry (Lt. Col. James Huston) and the 15th Massachusetts Infantry (Col. George H. Ward) back in utter disarray and killing a large number of men, including Huston and Ward. For the advanced portion of the Union center, the tragedy continued. Wright's men scrambled forth to capture Lt. Gulian V. Weir's battery south of the Codori House and two guns of Lt. T. Fred Brown's Rhode Island battery between the Codori farm and the Union line on Cemetery Ridge. On Cemetery Ridge itself, Wright's attack struck Hancock's 2d Corps line with a thrust into Col. Norman J. Hall's and Webb's brigades; intense fighting along the line erupted as Posey's men finally captured the Bliss Farm and the 48th Mississippi Infantry moved toward the Emmitsburg Road.

By dusk, the situation seemed to be shaping into a grim vision for the Federal high command. The high point had come when Vincent's and Weed's men saved Little Round Top for the Union, preserving tactically critical ground that would afford an invaluable artillery perch for fighting to come. Dangerously, however, Confederate brigades had almost systematically swept away the Federal presence from the fields and swales west of Little Round Top, forcing most of the Union troops back into the original fishhook-shaped battle line along Cemetery Ridge. On the southern end of the field Confederate brigades of Robertson and Benning held the ground at the Devil's Den and along the western base of Big Round Top; the brigades of Kershaw, Semmes, and Tige Anderson concentrated along Plum Run. Wofford's brigade settled along the northern side of the Wheatfield, west of the John Weikert House. Though night was fast coming on, the action was not yet over. The Union troops of Brig. Gen. Samuel Wylie Crawford's division, consisting of Pennsylvania Reserves, formed north of Little Round Top for a counterattack. In particular, Col. William McCandless's brigade, along with the 98th Pennsylvania Infantry, launched an assault into the Wheatfield as soon as stunned and defeated Union troops on the retreat cleared the way. The charge of the Pennsylvania reserves pushed the Confederates back through the Wheatfield, and to the north, Brig. Gen. Frank Wheaton's brigade similarly charged and pushed Wofford's men back away from the area. Local citizen Tillie Alleman, 15 years old, described the thrill of seeing the charge of the reserves. "The Confederates faced toward them, fired, halted, and then began to retreat. I saw them falling as they were climbing over a stone wall and as they were shot in the open space. The fighting lasted but a short time, when the Confederates were driven back in the direction of Little Round Top." Sedgwick's 6th Corps now began to enter the scene not only in supporting attacks but by securing this ground with fresh troops. A portion of Sykes's 5th Corps, the brigades of Vincent (now commanded by Col. James C. Rice) and Col. Joseph W. Fisher, the heroes of the Little Round Top struggle among them, now moved to scale and secure Big Round Top, occupying the summit in darkness.

At sunset the fight raged along the Union center. North of the Round Tops, the Confederate attack was repulsed. East of the Trostle Farm, Lt. Col. Freeman McGilvery established a line of cannon to harass the Confederates approaching via that route. Through sharp, often hand-to-hand fighting, Confederates of the 21st Mississippi Infantry captured Lt. Malbone Watson's battery, which was then retaken by the 39th New York Infantry. Two Union brigades, those of Brig. Gen. Henry H. Lockwood and Col. George L. Willard, recaptured some of the valuable ground lost earlier in the day. Lockwood recaptured the area surrounding the Trostle Farm and four guns of Bigelow's battery; Willard's men pushed Barksdale's advance back to the Emmitsburg Road and retook some Federal artillery, although Willard was killed in the process. Desperate for troops with which to counter the Confederate surge, Hancock had located the 1st Minnesota Infantry (William Colvill, Jr.). Hancock pointed toward Wilcox's Confederate line and simply shouted at Colvill, "Advance, Colonel, and take those colors!" Of the 262 soldiers of the 1st Minnesota who attacked, 215 lay dead or wounded after they charged, one of the highest casualty rates of any unit during the war. The attack worked, however, stalling Wilcox's Confederates and pushing them westward to the other side of the Emmitsburg Road. Perry's Florida brigade, meanwhile, south of the Codori Farm, received a substantial fire from units along the Federal center, and when the officers learned of Wilcox's withdrawal, Col. David Lang, commanding the brigade, pulled his men back too. In the deepest Confederate penetration of the day, Wright's right wing fought its way onto the crest of Cemetery Ridge and fought stubbornly with the brigades of Hall and Brig. Gen. Alexander S. Webb, which repulsed the assault in a whirlwind of bullets and cannon fire, assisted by the stubborn fighting of the 13th Vermont Infantry. Rallying behind their sudden counterattack, Union regiments of the 2d and 3d Corps, chiefly those of Gibbon's and Humphreys's divisions, advanced to the Emmitsburg Road and reclaimed more guns lost during the afternoon.

In the evening of July 2, Ewell finally planned and launched an attack on the Union right, centering on the high ground at Culp's Hill. The Union defensive line along the area had been established throughout the first night and reinforced during the afternoon of the second day. The hill's topography afforded a naturally strong position, and Union engineers incorporated the granite outcrops as best they could, as well as felling trees to use as makeshift defensive barriers. The Federal positions in the area were concentrated between the Baltimore Pike and Rock Creek, along the high ground, and consisted of Wadsworth's and Geary's divisions along Culp's Hill and Ruger's division to the south. Many of the troops on the hill came from the latecomers to the battlefield, Slocum's 12th Corps, which finally positioned itself and erected breastworks. In Geary's division, which manned the main portions of the hill, the brigade of Brig. Gen. George S. Greene formed a principal line along the southern slope of the hill. Held in reserve to the rear were the brigades of Col. Charles Candy and Brig. Gen. Thomas L. Kane. Ruger's men held the southern slope of the hill, the area around Spangler's Spring, and McAllister's Woods. East of the main battlefield, meanwhile, an action erupted near Brinkerhoff's Ridge. The 9th Massachusetts Infantry, on picket duty near the Deardorf House, skirmished with elements of the Stonewall Brigade throughout the afternoon. The Massachusetts men were then relieved by the 10th New York Cavalry, which formed along the Hanover Road and accelerated the fight against the Virginians. Frustrated with the continuing fire, the 2d Virginia Infantry moved north of the road and pushed forward into the Federal cavalrymen. By 7 P.M. the 10th New York Cavalry was relieved by elements of the 3d Pennsylvania Cavalry, the 1st New Jersey Cavalry, and Purnell's Legion, which kept up a heavy fire. After bitter fighting between the 2d Virginia Infantry and the 3d Pennsylvania Cavalry along a fence line, the Pennsylvania troops captured the area and held it, and the fight in this sector died out at dusk.

To support his long-awaited attack on Culp's Hill, Ewell positioned artillery on Benner's Hill and on Seminary Ridge north of Fairfield Road. The corps of A. P. Hill also deployed a large number of guns, mostly positioned along Seminary Ridge south of Fairfield Road. These Confederate positions held a total of 73 serviceable cannon prior to the attack. In response, the Union guns of the 11th Corps comprised 43 pieces inside or near Evergreen Cemetery, 33 oriented toward Seminary Ridge, and 10 facing Benner's Hill. The 1st Corps guns amounted to 25 pieces pointed toward Benner's Hill.

The Confederate attempts to take Culp's Hill began as Maj. Gen. Edward Johnson's division attacked about 7 P.M. As units of the 12th Corps shifted their lines, Greene's Union brigade moved rightward to cover the area between the summit of Culp's Hill and the lower hill, to the south. As dusk approached, a well-coordinated Confederate thrust witnessed the brigades of Brig. Gen. John M. Jones, Col. Jesse M. Williams (Nicholls's brigade), and Brig. Gen. George H. "Maryland" Steuart attacking the left, center, and right of Greene's position. The furious start of the assault stunned the soldiers waiting in line for action. So thick were the woods and poor the visibility that skirmishers waited nervously, hoping not to be shot by their own men. "Moments passed which were years of agony," recorded one soldier. "The pale faces, starting eyeballs, and nervous hands grasping loaded muskets, told how terrible were those moments of suspense." Soon the smoke filled the woods so thickly that soldiers could not see what they were firing at but merely had to fire in the direction of sounds. On the lower hill, Col. Archibald L. McDougall's brigade vacated a line of works that was soon taken over by advancing Confederates from Steuart's brigade. Attacking the right side of Greene's line, Maryland Steuart's men spun around to attack Greene's right and threaten the whole Union position, but this line was reinforced successfully, despite the abandonment of their position by the 137th New York Infantry. The fighting shortly subsided, and later the brigades of Candy and Kane moved back into their former positions.

Ewell's assault heated up substantially by 7:30 P.M. when Early's division attacked headlong into the Union position and batteries atop East Cemetery Hill. The movement was spearheaded by the brigades of Brig. Gen. Harry T. Hays and Col. Isaac E. Avery (Hoke's brigade). The defensive situation for the Union army was complicated by the fact that Brig. Gen. Adelbert Ames, worried over the attack by Johnson to the east, shifted two regiments eastward into Culp's Meadow and moved the 17th Connecticut Infantry to the right, which strengthened the line atop the hill but created a gap near the Federal left flank on the hill. As soldiers of Hays's brigade advanced across the Brickyard site and fanned out to attack uphill into the Union position, small-arms fire rang out from both battle lines and the advanced Union infantry fell back to a concentrated line atop the hill. Strengthening their position around the core of New York regiments posted in Col. Leopold von Gilsa's line, the Yankees readied for a major assault. Hays's Louisianans "moved forward as steadily, amid this hail of shot and minnie ball, as though they were on parade far removed from danger," recorded Col. Andrew L. Harris, who held the Union left flank on the hill. Hays's Louisiana Tigers initially struck into Harris's Ohioans, scattering them in bloody fighting and pushing up the hill toward several batteries including that of Capt. Michael Wiedrich, which fired canister rounds and, when the canister was depleted, "rotten shot," spherical case shot loaded without fuzes, which would explode just outside the muzzle and send balls screaming forward like poor man's canister. Together, in the confused, chaotic darkness, Hays's Tigers and Avery's Tarheels scrambled up East Cemetery Hill piecemeal, fighting at close range and scattering the center of von Gilsa's line. Despite the Confederate success, however, four Union regiments—the 75th Ohio Infantry (Harris), 17th Connecticut Infantry, 41st New York Infantry, and 33d Massachusetts Infantry held their positions at the base of East Cemetery Hill, in the Brickyard Lane. One of the casualties was Col. Avery, who was struck at the base of his neck by a ball and knocked from his horse. Alone and unrecognized in the darkness, as battle raged around him, the North Carolinian pulled a pencil and scrap of paper from his pocket and, in a scrawl, wrote, "Tell my father I died with my face to the enemy. I. E. Avery." The bloodstained paper was found with his dead body.

The attack on Cemetery Hill developed further as Rodes's division entered the fray. Though the Confederate thrust of Hays and Avery had succeeded in part by pushing many of the Union soldiers away from the main line on East Cemetery Hill and endangering the Union batteries posted near the Cemetery Gatehouse, many of the scattered Union men rallied near the guns and reformed after a short time. The Union batteries were seriously jeopardized, however. One oft-repeated story mentions a Confederate in the charge of the Louisiana troops who placed his torso across the muzzle of a

Federal cannon and declared, "I take command of the gun." The cannoneer, still holding the lanyard, replied, *"Du sollst sie haben!"* and pulled away, blasting the Rebel to pieces. The 11th Corps regiments west of the Baltimore Pike moved into support of the crumbling Union line, and from Cemetery Ridge, Col. Samuel S. Carroll's brigade marched in reinforcement. After savage fighting atop the hill, Hays's and Avery's men were driven back from the hill and reformed in the darkness along Winebrenner's Run, considerably north of Brickyard Lane and near Gordon's brigade. Following the failed attack by Early, Rodes swung his division southward into position for an attack from the west, with the brigades of Doles, Iverson, and Ramseur in front. But this tardy movement accomplished nothing as Rodes halted his men along Long Lane.

Nightfall ended the day's desperate struggles. When an officer mentioned to Meade that the situation seemed to be tenuous, the goggle-eyed general replied simply, "Yes, but it is all right now; it is all right now." At about 9 P.M. Meade met with his wing commanders (Hancock and Slocum), chief engineer Warren, and corps commanders inside the tiny Leister House on the Taneytown Road, wanting to poll them on a course of action for the next day. Meade's chief of staff, Dan Butterfield, created a memoir of the event that was found in the general's papers in 1881. Its questions and answers read:

1. Under existing circumstances, is it advisable for this army to remain in its present position, or to retire to another, nearer its base of supplies?
2. It being determined to remain in present position, shall the army attack or await the attack of the enemy?
3. If we await attack, how long?

The replies followed.

Gibbon: 1. Correct the position of army, but would not retreat. 2. In no condition to attack, in his opinion. 3. Until he moves.

Williams: 1. Stay. 2. Await attack. 3. One day.

Birney, same as Williams.

Sykes, same as Williams.

Newton: 1. Correct position of army, but would not retreat. 2. By all means not to attack. 3. If we wait, it will give them a chance to cut our line.

Howard: 1. Remain. 2. Await attack until 4 P.M. tomorrow. 3. If they don't attack, attack them.

Hancock: 1. Rectify position without moving so as not to give up field. 2. Not attack unless our communications are cut. 3. Can't wait long, can't be idle.

Sedgwick: 1. Remain. 2. Await attack. 3. At least one day.

Slocum: Stay and fight.

Newton thinks it a bad position, Hancock puzzled about practicability of
retiring, thinks by holding on [illegible] to mass forces and attack.
Howard in favor of not retiring. Birney don't know. 3rd Corps used up
and not in good condition to fight. Sedgwick [illegible]. Effective
strength about 9,000, 12,5000, 9,000, 6,000, 8,500, 6,000, 7,000. Total,
58,000.

Meade's decision, bolstered by the prevailing opinions of his subordinates, was to stay and fight for a third day. Slocum maneuvered his 12th Corps
throughout the night, preparing to mount an attack that would recapture all
of the positions he formerly held on and around Culp's Hill. Though one
more grisly day of battle lay ahead at Gettysburg, the actions of the third day
evolved from the second day's affairs. It was July 2 on which the decisive
movements and engagements took place.

Early on the morning of July 3, at daybreak, Johnson's division attacked
again at Culp's Hill. Union batteries opened fire for a fifteen-minute period
at dawn, hoping to stave off the encroaching Confederate line. But after the
artillery bombardment, Johnson attacked with Jones's, Nicholls's, and
Steuart's brigades, concentrated toward Greene's line from the summit of
Culp's Hill down to lower Culp's Hill. The rattle of men moving at the double quick melded with the zipping of Minié bullets through the air along
both lines and the occasional thuds of a bullet into a tree or a human being.
Tree canopies were sometimes briskly splintered by artillery fire, sending a
shower of debris down onto the men. Johnson's attack stalled, as some Union
defenders hid among the boulders and poured out a heavy fire. The 1st
Maryland Potomac Home Brigade Infantry attacked from the Baltimore
Pike, thrusting into the area of Spangler's Spring and toward the 2d Virginia
Infantry, but without support behind it, withdrew after a short fight. The
heavily engaged 2d Virginia, holding the left of the Confederate line of attack, was finally relieved by the brigade of Extra Billy Smith.

Unwilling to accept the outcome of the first attack, Johnson attacked a
second time. As midmorning approached, the 2d Virginia Infantry and the
1st North Carolina Infantry moved out as skirmishers east of Rock Creek,
south of the Taney House. As the Stonewall Brigade moved out of the battle
line, seeking replenished ammunition, O'Neal's brigade moved forward in
the place of Avery's men, to face Greene's center. Now, to support Greene,
the brigades of Candy and Brig. Gen. Henry H. Lockwood moved forward to
take positions in the breastworks atop Culp's Hill. On the lower part of the
hill, Geary left two key regiments in place along Spangler's Lane to face a
possible Confederate strike; they were the 5th Ohio Infantry and the 147th

Pennsylvania Infantry. Moving in from the right, the 20th Connecticut Infantry began a skirmishing action that would occupy the next several hours. The initial thrust of the second attack, formed by O'Neal and Steuart, struck into Greene's right but failed after severe fighting. By late morning a third Confederate attack was hatched for seizing Culp's Hill. Having failed to take the summit of Culp's Hill, so ably defended by Greene, the attack point now shifted to the open field near the top of Lower Culp's Hill. Steuart's brigade moved into position here, with the Stonewall Brigade relieving O'Neal and moving on Greene's center. The brigade of Brig. Gen. Junius Daniel moved into position to assault the area between the summit and the lower hill.

A prominent stone wall had been constructed along the northeastern side of the open field, and a vicious fight ensued then throughout the field. During this engagement, Lt. Col. Ario Pardee, Jr., directed his 147th Pennsylvania Infantry to recapture the stone wall, which they did to subsequently employ as a natural rifle pit. This action ensured that later historians would call the area Pardee Field in honor of the 23-year-old Pennsylvania engineer who led his men heroically that day. The attack of the Stonewall Brigade and Steuart's men into Pardee Field failed miserably. During the charge of Steuart's men a dog raced forward from the Confederate line. "At first— some of the men said, he barked in valorous glee; but I myself first saw him on three legs between our own and the men in Gray on the ground as though looking for a dead master, or seeking on which side he might find an explanation of the Tragedy he witnessed, intelligible to his canine apprehension. He licked someone's hand, they said, after he was perfectly riddled." Kane had the dog buried after the battle as "the only Christian minded being on either side." The brigade of Brig. Gen. Alexander Shaler joined the fight midway through, and the 122d New York Infantry fought stubbornly in the line for a time. The detached 20th Connecticut Infantry, skirmishing west of Spangler's Spring, tangled with the 10th Virginia Infantry.

On the Union far right, amid a continuous fire by the 12th Corps artillery, Slocum dispatched the brigade of Brig. Gen. Thomas H. Neill to hold the right of the Federal line, causing Neill to post several regiments on a hill near the Tancy House. A brisk, brief skirmish erupted in this area with the 2d Virginia Infantry. On Powers Hill, well to the southwest, Slocum established headquarters and ordered the 77th New York Infantry to guard the Union guns on the hill.

In the aftermath of the third failed attack by Johnson on Culp's Hill, Federal units in the area mounted a counterattack through Spangler's Spring. Col. Silas Colgrove was ordered to assault the Confederate left, led by Extra Billy Smith, with the 2d Massachusetts Infantry and the 27th Indiana Infantry. Though this counterattack failed, so had the Confederate assaults on Culp's Hill; Ewell's movements were disastrous to the Confederate cause at Gettysburg, piling up immense casualties and resulting in no tactical or strategic gains.

Addled by these developments, Lee had few options left for the third day. His only fresh forces were Maj. Gen. George E. Pickett's division of Longstreet's corps and Jeb Stuart's cavalry, which had finally arrived on the battlefield on the afternoon of July 2, too late to contribute much. Accounts of the exchange between Lee and Stuart vary wildly, many being concocted long after the war, but certainly Lee must have been disappointed with Stuart's ride around the Union army and absence, despite Lee's own latitude granted for making it. By one account Lee snapped at Stuart, claiming that the 125 captured wagons "are an impediment to me now" and declaring that he needed Stuart's help and would not discuss the matter any further with the cavalryman. Longstreet again on July 3 urged his commander to move around the Union left, endanger or cut Meade's communications, and force the Union army to attack the Confederates. Lee would have no part of it, however; as we have seen, his "blood was up," and he could not bear to break off the engagement and appear to be retreating. This point is often discussed as one of the great mysteries of Civil War history, but it makes perfect sense if one recalls the strategic goals of the Gettysburg campaign and how, as yet, none of them had been met. The key word for Lee, strategically—and general officers thought in strategic terms—was desperation. He had to win a battle on Northern soil to reawaken the hallmarks of Confederate success, including the Northern peace movements and/or foreign recognition, and he had to do so *now*. Based on the near success his men had had the previous evening engaging the Union center, Lee firmly believed it could be won here.

Lee had attacked both flanks unsuccessfully on July 2 and on the morning of the 3d. The unsuccessful but momentarily promising attack had occurred as Rans Wright's men had assaulted the Union center. For Lee, the solution seemed to be to attack the center again. Ignoring Longstreet's counsel, Lee ordered a frontal attack on the Union center, beginning at the Confederate lines along Seminary Ridge and attacking nearly a mile eastward toward Cemetery Ridge. By early morning, when Lee hoped to initiate the attack, he found Longstreet planning for a movement around the right. A defining moment occurred between the commander of the Army of Northern Virginia and his chief subordinate as Longstreet proclaimed words to the effect that, "General, I have been a soldier all my life. I have been with soldiers engaged in fights by couples, by squads, companies, regiments, divisions, and armies, and should know, as well as anyone, what soldiers can do. It is my opinion that no fifteen thousand men ever arranged for battle can take that position." Lee would not hear of it, though. "The enemy is there, and I am going to strike him," Lee replied. As Longstreet recalled, "Nothing was left but to proceed." What Lee did not know was that the relatively weak Union center that was attacked by Wright had been reinforced on the night of July 2 by troops that had shifted away from the line earlier in the evening, and that 1st and 3d corps veterans were placed in support in the rear of the line.

As the battle for Culp's Hill wound down by late morning, Brig. Gen. Henry J. Hunt initiated an inspection tour of the Federal cannon posted along Cemetery Ridge. As he checked the status of his guns and ammunition, he observed with field glasses an amazingly long line of Confederate cannon stretching from a point just south of the town, southward along Seminary Ridge, to a position near the Peach Orchard. By 11 A.M. it wasn't clear whether this display was to protect against a Union attack or simply to reinforce the main battle line and free up more men who could support Ewell's attack. Or perhaps the artillery was being massed to prepare for a major Confederate attack on the Union center, with a barrage that would precede the attack so that Federal artillery would answer in kind and deplete its ammunition before the infantry approached. Should this be the case, Hunt determined to hold much of his ammunition in reserve so that he would be able to open fire as troops approached within close range. Hunt called the display of Rebel guns "an unbroken mass" that covered an amazing amount of ground, and he believed they constituted "a magnificent display." Evander M. Law thought: "The cannonade in the center . . . presented one of the most magnificent battle-scenes witnessed during the war. Looking up the valley toward Gettysburg, the hills on either side were capped with crowns of flame and smoke, as 300 guns, about equally divided between the two ridges, vomited their iron hail upon each other."

Invited by Gibbon to sit and rest after a long morning of observing the conditions of the battle, George Meade sat on a cracker box between 11 A.M. and 12 noon near the Leister House. Also present were Hancock, Newton, Pleasonton, and staff officers of the 2d Corps. The group lunched on stewed chickens and discussed the afternoon's possibilities. Lee, meanwhile, did not issue the anticipated orders to advance all through the morning. By 1 P.M., finally, came an order to start the artillery bombardment that would precede the charge. The 159 Confederate guns commenced firing. To the soldiers in the Union lines, the sudden cannonade was like a thunderstroke. Meade had ridden off to Powers Hill to consult Slocum, and then proceeded on the East Cemetery Hill and cautioned Maj. Thomas W. Osborn's gunners not to exhaust their ammunition. To the Union artillerist Charles Wainwright, the noise from the barrage was "as continuous and loud as that from the falls of Niagara."

After a short time, despite Hunt's self-proclamation to reserve as much ammunition as he could, the Federal guns answered in kind. It was during this period that country people as far away as Pittsburgh claimed to have heard the booming of cannon from the distant battle of Gettysburg, many miles away. Hunt had some 175 cannon in line, including 132 posted between Little Round Top and Cemetery Hill. Additionally, he had 95 more pieces waiting in reserve that could be brought up to the front lines. The Union artillery lines were separated into three parts, the south Cemetery Ridge line (or McGilvery's line), which commanded Plum Run Valley; the Cemetery Ridge line (Hazard's line), commanding the area at the Union center and from south of the Codori Farm north to the Bliss Farm; and the Cemetery Hill line (Osborn's line), which was commanded by Osborn and Wainwright and swept the position from northern Seminary Ridge to the Codori Farm. As Hunt, Howard, Osborn, and Carl Schurz stood talking on East Cemetery Hill during the barrage, Osborn proposed suddenly ceasing fire to simulate running out of ammunition, hoping that Lee might take the bait and attack with infantry (while the Federal cannon would in actuality be well supplied with canister). "Hunt said that he thought I was correct," wrote Osborn, "and if Howard agreed to it, he would give the order. Howard thought the suggestion a good one and said that he would like to see the experiment tried. . . . [Hunt] then gave the order to stop firing and said that he would ride down the line and stop all the batteries."

The lure worked. Soon after the Union guns fell silent, the Confederate infantry ranks appeared from the woodline. And so began the celebrated Pickett's charge, or the Pickett-Pettigrew-Trimble charge, as it has become known. The attack force consisted of troops from Longstreet's corps and from A. P. Hill's corps, comprising some 10,500 to 13,000 men. To the north, west of the Bliss Farm, was arrayed the division of Henry Heth, a part of which had opened the battle on July 1, now commanded by Brig. Gen. Johnston Pettigrew (Heth had been wounded on the first day when a Minié bullet struck his hatband, which fractured his skull but did not endanger his life). Pettigrew was the highly educated North Carolinian who was the nephew of the Charleston Unionist James L. Petigru. Pettigrew's brigades, right to left, were those of Cols. Birkett D. Fry (Archer's brigade), Col. James K. Marshall (Pettigrew's brigade), Brig. Gen. Joseph R. Davis, and Col. J. M. Brockenbrough. Lined up behind Pettigrew's division were two brigades commanded by Isaac R. Trimble, the argumentative Marylander who had so criticized Ewell for lackadaisical soldiery regarding Culp's and Cemetery hills. (Ewell received not only criticism on this day, but to add insult to injury, was also shot in his wooden leg.) Trimble was assigned to command Pender's division after William Dorsey Pender had been struck in the thigh by a shell fragment on the second day; Pender appeared to improve for a time before his leg was amputated on July 18 and he died several hours later.

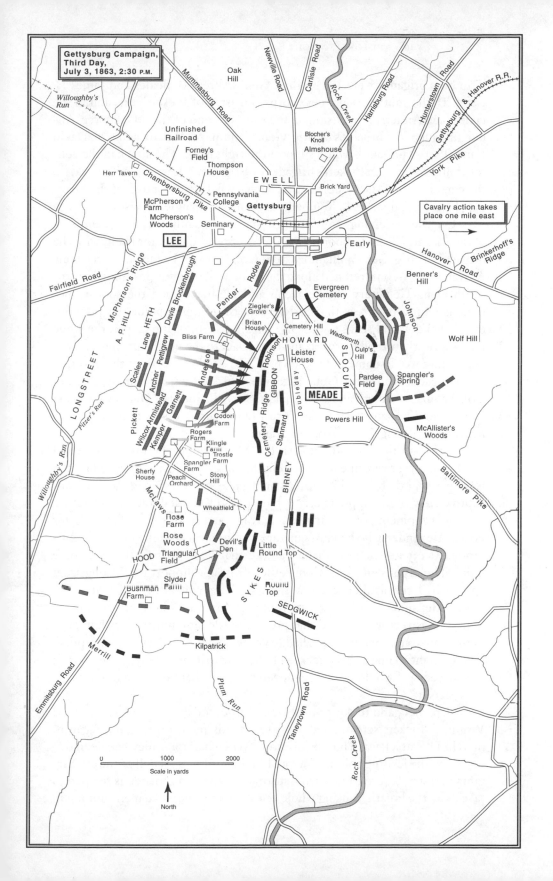

Gettysburg Campaign,
Third Day,
July 3, 1863, 2:30 P.M.

Trimble's brigades were led by Brig. Gens. Alfred M. Scales and James H. Lane. To the south, Longstreet's corps consisted of Pickett's division in the center and Anderson's division on the southern end of the attack force. Anderson's men, the brigades of Brig. Gen. Cadmus M. Wilcox and Col. David Lang (Perry's brigade), would support the right flank. The attack in the center would come from Pickett's brigades of Brig. Gens. Lewis A. Armistead (in the center, west of the Codori Farm), Richard B. Garnett (north of the Spangler House), and James L. Kemper (south of the Spangler House).

On the receiving end of this massive assault was the center of Hancock's 2d Corps. Gibbon's division comprised the center itself, with the brigades of Brig. Gen. William Harrow, Col. Norman J. Hall, and Brig. Gen. Alexander S. Webb stretched along the stone wall that was positioned north-south along Cemetery Ridge. Webb and Hall straddled the soon-to-be-famous Copse of Trees that had served as an attack point the previous evening and would serve as the target again. North of the Copse, the stone fence abruptly turned eastward and then again to the north, making a pair of angles that would come to be known as "the Angle." North of this position were brigades from Brig. Gen. Alexander Hays's division; namely, those of Col. Thomas A. Smyth and Col. Eliakim Sherrill. South of Harrow's brigade were posted brigades of the 1st Corps, Doubleday's division, most prominently that of Brig. Gen. George J. Stannard.

Although the ground between the woods along Seminary Ridge and the Copse of Trees appears relatively flat on casual inspection, in fact the terrain is slightly rolling in nature, which gave observers along the line a deceptive view of the approaching parade lines of Confederate infantrymen. The final moments of the artillery barrage had been nerve-wracking for Porter Alexander, who had lost guns and was himself running low on ammunition. At 1:35 P.M. he sent Pickett a note that read, "For God's sake come quick. The 18 guns are gone. Come quick or I can't support you." Longstreet approached the artillerist a few minutes later and after suggesting that Porter Alexander halt Pickett and replenish his ammunition before the assault, Longstreet was advised that precious little ammunition was left, even in the trains, and that an attack had to come now if ever. Longstreet replied, "I don't want to make this attack—I believe it will fail—I do not see how it can succeed—I would not make it even now, but that Gen. Lee has ordered & expects it."

"Up, men, and to your posts! Don't forget today that you are from old Virginia," Pickett screamed about 3 P.M. as his men formed and began to march. The attack was a bloody disaster. "When half the valley had been traversed by the leading column," wrote Pvt. Randolph Shotwell of the 8th Virginia Infantry, "there came such a storm of grape and canister as seemed to take away the breath, causing whole regiments to stoop like men running in a violent sleet. Shower upon shower of the fatal shot rattle through the ranks, or scream through the air overhead till one wonders that a single human being can escape. But there is no pause, scarcely a waver; on, on on! Within six hundred yards of the Yankee breastworks!" The reawakened Federal artillery sliced into the oncoming Confederates with fury, many guns creating an enfilading fire that chopped down whole rows of soldiers in line with a single shell. The oncoming Confederate ranks closed up and proceeded toward the Union line gallantly, despite the booming and smoke-filled pall that hung over them on this hot, sunny day. After the Confederates crossed the fence along the Emmitsburg Road, Federal guns loaded canister and sent giant clouds of balls flying through the air, hitting immense numbers of men. As the Confederates approached closer, Federal soldiers behind the stone wall cried out cheers of "Fredericksburg, Fredericksburg," hoping to exact revenge and cast off their uncomfortable memories. "The moment I saw them I knew we should give them Fredericksburg," asserted Henry Livermore Abbott of the 20th Massachusetts Infantry. "So did every body. We let the regiment in front of us get within 100 feet of us, & then bowled them over like nine pins, picking out the color first. In two minutes there were only groups of two or three men running around wildly, like chickens with their heads off. . . . The rebels behaved with as much pluck as any men in the world could; they stood there, against the fence, until they were nearly all shot down."

The furious attack lasted for about an hour, as the brigades of Garnett and Kemper sliced into the Union center (with Armistead just behind) near the Angle and the Copse of Trees, with Stannard's Vermonters attacking northward from their part of the Union line. A crazed melee of hand-to-hand fighting ensued, with a few hundred of Pickett's men momentarily fighting along the stone wall, surging over the crest of the line. Grisly noises emerged from the fusillade of cannonfire, crackles of musketry, and musket stocks smashed into heads and torsos. The whole scene of carnage was wrapped in an almost impenetrable blanket of thick white smoke. As Lt. Col. Edmund Rice recalled "Voices were lost in the uproar; so I turned partly toward them, raised my sword to attract their attention, and motioned to advance. They surged forward, and just then, as I was stepping backward with my face toward the men, urging them on, I felt a sharp blow as a shot struck me, then another; I whirled round, my sword torn from my hand by a bullet or shell splinter. My visor saved my face, but the shock stunned me." Col. Frank A. Haskell of Gibbon's staff remembered the chaos: "The line springs—the crest of the solid ground with a great roar, heaves forward its maddened load, men, arms, smoke, fire, a fighting mass. It rolls to the wall—flash meets flash, the wall is crossed—a moment ensues of thrusts, yells, blows, shots, and indistinguishable conflict, followed by a shout universal that makes the welkin ring again, and the last and bloodiest fight of the great battle of Gettysburg is ended and won."

Indeed, Gettysburg had been won. The grayclad wave of Confederates were chopped to pieces, either wounded, killed, captured, or they slowly retreated back to the Confederate lines, many retreating facing the enemy so they wouldn't be shot in the back. Kemper's brigade took the heavy toll from the counterattack by the two Vermont regiments, the 13th and 16th Vermont infantries. Amid the horrifying casualties, the Virginia politician Kemper, age 40 and former Speaker of the House of the Virginia legislature, fell from his horse, grievously wounded. The ball struck Kemper in the thigh, passing through his body and lodging near his spine. Captured by Federal troops, he was retaken by Confederates, conversed with Robert E. Lee, believing himself to be mortally wounded, and was again captured by Federals during the Confederate retreat. He survived imprisonment and was exchanged after three months.

Others were not as fortunate as Kemper. The survivors of Garnett's and Armistead's brigades pierced the Angle, briefly skirmishing with Union soldiers who received support from fresh troops in the rear. Soldiers from the 69th Pennsylvania Infantry, 71st Pennsylvania Infantry, and 72d Pennsylvania Infantry aided in the vicious fight; Garnett, cousin of the first Confederate general officer to die in the war, a Virginian who had mounted his bay horse because he was too sick to walk, was killed as he approached the stone wall, both horse and rider going down. The ferocity of the struggle here is reflected by the fact that Garnett's body was never identified, despite Hunt's efforts to locate the body of his friend the following day. Garnett's sword, curiously, did show up in a Baltimore pawnshop many years later and was purchased by ex-Confederate general officer George H. Steuart. Armistead was the son of U.S. Bvt. Brig. Gen. Walker K. Armistead. Dismissed from West Point for breaking a dinner plate over Cadet Jubal A. Early's head, he nevertheless amassed a great record as a soldier. Leading his men with a chant, "Give them the cold steel!" with his hat on his sword, Armistead was mortally wounded during the charge as he led his men over the wall. Struck in the chest and arm, he fell at the base of a Union cannon and died two days later at the nearby George Spangler Farm. Trimble, too, was wounded and captured, but survived. Pickett, watching in horror in the rear, was criticized for not materially participating in the attack, but this would have been highly unusual for a division commander because it almost certainly would have cost Pickett his life.

Union casualties also mounted during the charge. The most celebrated was the death of the young regular army artillerist, Lt. Alonzo H. Cushing, who kept firing his battery's cannon at the Angle after being wounded. The Wisconsin-born artillerist was only 22 at the time of his death but had already garnered a reputation as a hard, smart fighter. His brother, moreover, was the celebrated young naval officer William B. Cushing. Alonzo Cushing was hit beside his guns, lunging forward as his knees buckled, falling to his knees, blood cascading out of his nose and mouth, splattering a fellow officer's boots, trousers, and blouse. Cushing had been struck squarely below the nose, and the bullet lodged in his brain. Waiting atop his horse along the lines during the attack, Hancock was admonished to get down and seek shelter, but allegedly responded with, "There are times when a corps commander's life does not count." Later, Hancock was seriously wounded, struck in the right thigh; the shot carried wooden and metallic pieces of his saddle pommel into his thigh muscles, necessitating a slow, painful recovery. Thus, Hancock and Armistead, close prewar friends, each lay dangerously wounded within a hundred yards of each other. Altogether, more than 7,000 soldiers were killed or wounded during the charge. In the wake of the disaster, Lee was quick to accept responsibility as he rode past his Confederate survivors. "All this has been my fault," he told Cadmus Wilcox. Other, similar statements came from Randolph A. Shotwell, who wrote that Lee stated: "I am very sorry—the task was too great for you. But we mustn't despond. Another time we shall succeed." Longstreet recalled that Lee said, "It's all my fault. I thought my men were invincible." Pickett, who complained to Lee that "I have no division now," was told by the army commander, "Come General Pickett, this has been my fight and upon my shoulders rest the blame." As the spotlight for failure typically shines brightly on the Confederate attackers, one prominent historian reminds us with keen logic and analysis that "the Union army had something to do with it."

As the Pickett-Pettigrew-Trimble charge resulted in Confederate disaster, the Federal and Southern horsemen were busy to the east. Stuart's 6,000 horsemen rode around the Union right only to be intercepted by the cavalry of Brig. Gen. David M. Gregg's Union horse soldiers. After a hand-to-hand contest, with charges and countercharges (no doubt Brandy Station was fresh on the minds of all involved), the Union troops pushed the Confederate horsemen from the field. One of the distinguished participants in this action was the young Brig. Gen. George A. Custer, who was now accumulating quite a reputation as a cavalryman despite his poor record at West Point. Finally, at 5:30 P.M. near Big Round Top, Col. Elon J. Farnsworth's cavalry brigade was ordered by the reckless officer Judson Kilpatrick to form and charge the Confederate right. Farnsworth, age 25, was a Michigander by birth who enlisted in the 8th Illinois Cavalry and rose to brigade command. Farnsworth strongly protested that the cavalry charge would be suicidal, but was ordered to commence. Kilpatrick later wrote that the charge set off "through a piece of woods, and drove the enemy from one position to another until a heavy stone wall was reached, behind which the enemy was gathered in great numbers." The charge failed miserably and Farnsworth was shot five times and killed. Reports of Farnsworth drawing a pistol and committing suicide rather than subjecting himself to capture are postwar propaganda. Although often described as a brigadier general, Farnsworth's appointment as such was never confirmed.

The losses at Gettysburg were staggering and particularly appalling for the South. Of the 93,534 engaged in the Army of the Potomac, the losses were 3,149 killed, 14,503 wounded, and 5,161 missing; Confederate casualties among the 70,274 engaged were reported as 4,637 killed, 12,391 wounded, and 5,846 missing, but probably actually totaled 28,000 or more. About 163,808 men had come together by accident and made war on the plains of Pennsylvania during three sweltering July days; afterward, at least 45,687 were dead, wounded, or missing—28 percent of those who fought and more than the total of American casualties in the Revolutionary War, War of 1812, and Mexican War combined.

Gettysburg was a strategic loss for the Confederacy, and because many Civil War buffs have believed it so large and crucial a battle, it is often called the "High Water Mark of the Confederacy." Satisfied with Lee's strategic failure, Meade determined not to attack on July 4 despite the urgings of the wounded Hancock to do so, using the 6th Corps, which had been held in reserve, along with elements of the 5th and 12th corps. But Meade showed no willingness to continue the fight and had scattered the 6th Corps rather than concentrating it for a fight. Lee's line, established on the night of July 3, stretched from Oak Hill to the Peach Orchard; despite the mauling of his Army of Northern Virginia, Lee demonstrated his aggressive nature again by staying in place on July 4, awaiting a possible Federal attack. As rains set in, transforming into a heavy downpour on the night of the United States's 87th anniversary, the Army of Northern Virginia began to pull out of Pennsylvania, the supply and ammunition trains by way of Cashtown and Chambersburg and the bulk of the army by way of Fairfield.

Much has been made of the slowness of the Federal pursuit, and speculators have made a virtual business out of declaring how Meade might have ended the war in mid-1863 by smashing into Lee's army as it scurried away. Lincoln was visibly upset during the final days of the Gettysburg campaign, viewing the lost opportunity to smash the Southern army as a failing of the new commander. But to be fair, both armies were seriously battered and hardly capable of coherent fighting after the three-day affair in the Pennsylvania hills. The Confederates had lost nearly one man out of every three, and the Federals one out of four. On both sides, ammunition and other supplies were almost entirely depleted. The suddenly dismal weather on July 4 did not help pursuit on the bogged-down roads. (Curiously, many soldiers mentioned that heavy rains almost invariably followed major battles.) Al-

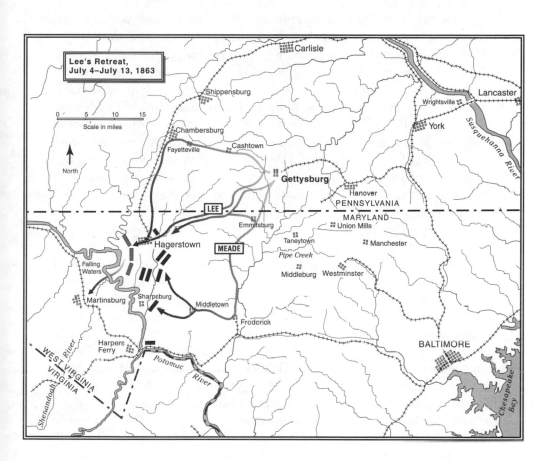

Lee's Retreat,
July 4–July 13, 1863

0   5   10   15
Scale in miles

North

Carlisle

Shippensburg

Lancaster

Chambersburg

Wrightsville

Fayetteville   Cashtown

York

Gettysburg

Hanover

LEE

PENNSYLVANIA

MARYLAND

Emmitsburg

Union Mills

Hagerstown

Taneytown

Manchester

MEADE

Falling
Waters

Pipe Creek

Middleburg   Westminster

Martinsburg   Sharpsburg

Middletown

Frederick

BALTIMORE

Harpers
Ferry

WEST VIRGINIA
VIRGINIA

Potomac   River

Susquehanna River

Shenandoah   River

Chesapeake
Bay

though Lee had been whipped at Gettysburg, marking his poorest performance on the field, he did not yield the initiative to Meade. The Federal commander reorganized and took stock of his army on July 4. He planned a
reconnaissance for the following day, but by then Lee's army was gone.

On July 6, minor fighting erupted at Hagerstown and Williamsport,
Maryland, but no major pursuit was organized by Meade. The great danger
for Lee was that his route of retreat relied on a single pontoon bridge on the
Potomac River at Falling Waters, Maryland; without this bridge over the
river, now swelling with the rains, Lee's men might be trapped. Indeed,
Union cavalry under Maj. Gen. William H. French was ordered to destroy
the bridge on July 3. The retreat through Pennsylvania was a disaster for the
Confederacy in terms of straggling and desertion, which pared the army
down to nearly 35,000. Alarmed, Lee ordered his hungry, soaked, and demoralized men to entrench a position along the river as the army tore down
warehouses and barns for use in constructing a pontoon bridge. At Hagerstown, he wrote Ewell, anticipating a possible attack. "Strengthen your
line, rectifying your position as circumstances require, & do every thing in
your power to ensure success."

On July 12, Meade cautiously approached the Potomac River and held
another council of war, wherein this time the conservative heads prevailed
and Meade decided not to attack. Amazingly, Halleck had telegraphed
Meade that same day, warning him: "Call no council of war. It is proverbial
that councils of war never fight. . . . Do not let the enemy escape." Meade
wasn't the only one receiving harsh criticism: In Washington, Gideon Welles
and many others thought little of Halleck, too. "He has suggested nothing,
decided nothing," criticized Welles of the general-in-chief. "Done nothing
but scold and smoke and scratch his elbows. Is it possible the energies of the
nation should be wasted by the incapacity of such a man?" On the night of
July 13 and the early morning of the 14th, Lee began moving his army back
into West Virginia. Buford's cavalry detected the move on the 14th and
fought an action at Falling Waters that took 500 prisoners and inflicted a
number of casualties, including Brig. Gen. Johnston Pettigrew, who was
struck by a pistol shot in the left abdomen, dying three days later.

In Washington, Lincoln was dissatisfied by his army's performance. "I
was deeply mortified by the escape of Lee across the Potomac," Lincoln informed Oliver O. Howard a week after Falling Waters, "because the substantial destruction of his army would have ended the war, and because I
believed, such destruction was perfectly easy—believed that Gen. Meade
and his noble army had expended all the skill, and toil, and blood, up to the
ripe harvest, and then let the crop go to waste. . . . A few days having passed,
I am now profoundly grateful for what was done, without criticism for what
was not done. Gen. Meade has my confidence as a brave and skillful officer,

and a true man." Lee, shamed by his performance, offered to resign. On August 8 he wrote Jefferson Davis, "I . . . request Your Excellency to take measures to supply my place. . . . I cannot even accomplish what I myself desire. How can I fulfill the expectations of others? In addition I sensibly feel the growing failure of my bodily strength. . . . Everything, therefore, points to the advantages to be derived from a new commander, and I the more anxiously urge the matter upon Your Excellency from my belief that a younger and abler man than myself can readily be attained." Davis would have no part of it. "Were you capable of stooping to it, you could easily surround yourself with those who would fill the press with your laudations, and seek to exalt you for what you had not done, rather than detract from the achievements which will make you and your army the subject of history and object of the world's admiration for generations to come," he wrote Lee three days later. "To ask me to substitute you by some one in my judgment more fit to command, or who would possess more of the confidence of the army, or of the reflecting men in the country, is to demand an impossibility."

The repercussions of Gettysburg were huge. On the battlefield, following the third day's action, the scene was indescribable. "Our brigade moved to the front in order to feel and develop the enemy," wrote Capt. Francis A. Donaldson of the 118th Pennsylvania Infantry. "On reaching the slope and foot of the hill—what a sight presented itself. The ground was literally covered with shattered and shot torn limbs of trees, whilst there was scarcely room to move without treading upon the dead body of an enemy. As far as the eye could see the dead lay in all manner of shapes, some upon their faces, others upon their backs, others still kneeling behind the rocks where they had taken shelter, some of them with their muskets still poised and supported by the rocks in readiness to fire." "I spent the night in the middle of the battlefield with the dead and wounded that still remained," recorded Régis de Trobriand. "This morning, I saw all around me, the most terrible piles of bodies that I never [*sic*] saw before. In some places and in front [of] our batteries they were piled up." After walking across the battlefield, Union Pvt. Wilbur Fisk described the scene. "Their bodies were swollen, black, and hideously unnatural. Their eyes glared from their sockets, their tongues protruded from their mouths, and in almost every case, clots of blood and mangled flesh showed how they had died, and rendered a sight ghastly beyond description. My God, could it be possible that such were lively and active like other people so shortly previous, with friends, parents, brothers and sisters to lament their loss. It certainly was so, but it was hard to realize it."

Although recent historians have demonstrated to a degree that after Gettysburg a huge sense of loss and panic did not exist within the Confederate armies, much of the Southern press was disgusted with the turn of events. "It is impossible for an invasion to have been more foolish and disastrous," editorialized the *Charleston Mercury.* Wishful thinking pervaded many early accounts of the battle and campaign. "You have full account of Gen Lees glorious exploits in the North," wrote Confederate Capt. Thomas Henderson. "We have dispatch to day that he has whipped Genl Meade at Gettysburg & taken 40,000 prisoners. Most too many to be true, I have no doubt he has whipped him & may get Baltimore & threaten Washington, but avails but little if [Vicksburg] has fallen." Other Confederates, even some principally involved in the campaign, seemed lighthearted about the whole affair. If Jeb Stuart was admonished by Lee during the late stages of the battle, he certainly didn't show it in writing his wife, Flora Cooke Stuart, ten days later. "I am all right thus far, and all the staff have thus far escaped," wrote Jeb. "I had a grand time in Penna. and we return without *defeat* to recuperate and reinforce. . . . I crossed near Drainesville [*sic*] and went close to Georgetown and Washtn. cutting 4 important railroads and joining our army in time for the battle of Gettysburg, with 900 prisoners and 200 wagons and splendid teams. . . . I have been blessed with great success in this campaign and the accidents and loss in the way of captures are in no way chargeable to my command." Stuart actually seemed to believe the whole operation a grand success. "We must invade again," he continued. "It is the only way to peace. . . . If they had only sent 10,000 reinforcements *and plenty of ammunition* to join him here, our recrossing would have been under banners of peace."

As Lee was slipping away across the flooded Potomac, the greatest civil unrest of the war took place in New York and other cities. The new Federal draft had commenced on the 11th, and broiling unrest among the underprivileged exploded, particularly reflecting resentment toward provisions for substitutes and exemptions. The situation was made worse by the actions of Peace Democrats and other politicians who wanted to fuel the antiwar movement. In New York City a mob consisting mostly of immigrants concocted a riot in which the draft headquarters were stormed, businesses looted, and hooliganism reigned supreme throughout the largest U.S. city's streets. "The fury of the low Irish women . . . was noteworthy. Stalwart young vixens and withered old hags were swarming everywhere, all cursing the 'bloody draft' and egging on their men to mischief," recalled the New York diarist George Templeton Strong. An account from *Harper's Weekly* described how "one of the first victims to the insane fury of the rioters was a negro cartman residing in Carmine Street. A mob of men and boys seized this unfortunate man on Monday evening, and having beaten him until he was in a state of insensibility, dragged him to Clarkson Street, and hung him from a branch of one of the trees that shade the sidewalk by St. John's Cemetery. The fiends did not stop there, however. Procuring long sticks, they tied rags and straw to the ends of them, and with these torches they danced around their victim, setting fire to his clothes, and burning him almost to a cinder."

Led by Irish immigrants who resented the wealthy population's ability to buy their way out of military service, the draft protesters extended their riots into a second day. After numerous fires, damage inflicted to black churches, and nearly 1,000 casualties and property losses of $1.5 million, the New York City draft riots were put down by exhausted veterans who were speeded along from the Gettysburg battlefield. Less destructive riots occurred in Boston, Portsmouth, New Hampshire; Wooster, Ohio; Troy, New York; and Rutland, Vermont. Ultimately, Northern civilians adjusted to the draft, but its commencement offered one of the most intense periods of civil unrest in U.S. history.

Actions in the eastern theater over midsummer were minor and scattered in the wake of the bludgeoning both armies received at Gettysburg. As Longstreet's corps arrived at Culpeper Court House, in advance of slowly pursuing Yankees, a skirmish erupted at Battle Mountain, Virginia, on July 24. The Gettysburg campaign concluded with another cavalry action at the now much-fought-over battlefield at Brandy Station, from August 1 to 4. This affair, also termed Culpeper or Second Rappahannock Station, amounted to minor skirmishing without important results.

THE CONFEDERATE RETREAT from Gettysburg would not be the only alarming news for the South during the first days of July. At Vicksburg, Maj. Gen. Ulysses S. Grant's siege was progressing steadily, tightening the noose around the Confederate soldiers and civilians in the town. Throughout the Confederate defensive lines, Pemberton's soldiers were reduced to a state of near starvation. The soldiers hollowed out what ground they could sleep in, some digging and inhabiting bunkers and bombproofs. Food was scarce and many small mammals—former pets such as cats and dogs—met their end during the Vicksburg siege, and rats and other creatures became routine sources of nourishment for some of the besieged.

Inhabiting one of the area's many natural caves, Mary Ann Loughborough delighted in sharing some of the mule steaks offered to Confederate soldiers by their commissary officers. "A certain number of the mules are killed each day by the commissaries," she wrote during the siege, "and are issued to the men, all of whom prefer the fresh meat, though it be of mule, to the bacon and salt rations they have eaten for such a long time without change." The Federal shelling continued all the while. Out of boredom many of the town's residents tried humor. FOR RENT: INQUIRE OF DAVIS & PEMBERTON read a sign posted on a vacant house on one of the hills. During the Federal flotilla's heavy mortar fire one night, a shell ripped through the house, and someone changed the sign to read, RENTED, BY GRANT AND

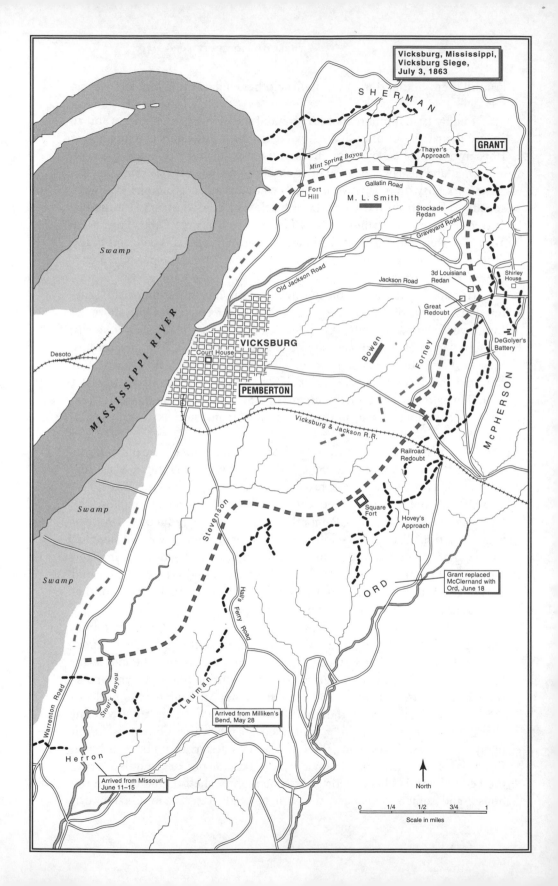

Vicksburg, Mississippi,
Vicksburg Siege,
July 3, 1863

SHERMAN

GRANT

Thayer's
Approach

Mint Spring Bayou

Gallatin Road

Fort
Hill

M. L. Smith

Stockade
Redan

Graveyard Road

Old Jackson Road

Jackson Road

3d Louisiana
Redan

Shirley
House

Great
Redoubt

DeGolyer's
Battery

Desoto

MISSISSIPPI RIVER

Court House

VICKSBURG

Bowen

Forney

McPHERSON

PEMBERTON

Swamp

Vicksburg & Jackson R.R.

Railroad
Redoubt

Stevenson

Square
Fort

Hovey's
Approach

Swamp

ORD

Grant replaced
McClernand with
Ord, June 18

Hall's Ferry Road

Swamp

Warrenton Road

Stout's Bayou

Lauman

Arrived from Milliken's
Bend, May 28

Herron

Arrived from Missouri,
June 11–15

North

0   1/4   1/2   3/4   1

Scale in miles

McPHERSON. Humor supported the "Hotel de Vicksburg," created by civilians looking to their past and future as a way out of the current stress. Longhand menus for the "hotel" advertised ten-course dinners from soup to desserts with about one of three items consisting of mule parts, as with "Mule Ears fricasseed ala Gotch," "Mule Rump stuffed with rice" as a roast, and "Mule Beef jerked ala Mexicana," perhaps to be followed by a dessert course consisting of beech nuts, white oak acorns, and blackberry leaf tea.

Relief for the Rebels came too little and too late. Southern forces attacked Helena, Arkansas, on July 4, in an attempt to undo the siege. Gen. Joe Johnston commenced a march to relieve Pemberton, and by July 1 reached a position along the Big Black River, with the divisions of Loring, French, Walker, and Breckinridge spread from Birdsong's Ferry to Edwards's Station. But it was too late for Johnston's 31,000 men to have any effect on Vicksburg. Sherman moved toward Johnston's divisions and chased them as they retreated back to Jackson, where they dug in temporarily after skirmishing at Birdsong, or Bolton Ferry on July 5 and near Jackson two days later. Preparing to invest the city, Sherman sent the corps of Parke, Steele, and Ord forward, but Johnston, fearing another siege, eventually retreated from the area by July 16. Skirmishing erupted again on July 19 at Brandon. At Vicksburg, the situation having spun completely out of control, his men starving to death, Pemberton determined to surrender by July 3. Northern-born and knowing his adversaries quite well, however, he believed that better terms awaited him if he were to capitulate on July 4. Under an oak tree Grant and Pemberton conferred on the parole of prisoners. Grant's 71,000 troops ceased their battle action and received the surrender of about 29,000 of Pemberton's Confederates; about 6,000 were sent north as prisoners. (Grant has been criticized for paroling so many Confederates, but transporting them was logistically impracticable.) "As soon as our troops took possession of the city, guards were established along the whole line of parapet, from the river above to the river below," wrote Grant. "The prisoners were allowed to occupy their old camps behind the intrenchments. No restraint was put upon them, except by their own commanders." "The great Ulysses—the Yankee Generalissimo, surnamed Grant—has expressed his intention of dining in Vicksburg on Saturday next, and celebrating the 4th of July by a grand dinner," editorialized the *Vicksburg Daily Citizen,* composed by Confederates on July 2 and printed by Union soldiers early on Independence Day. "Ulysses must first get into the city before he dines in it. The way to cook a rabbit is 'first catch the rabbit.' " After the city's fall, Federal soldiers with printing experience composed a new message: "The banner of the Union floats over Vicksburg. Gen. Grant has 'caught the rabbit.' " Grant was an instant hero, of much larger stature than he had become following Forts Henry and Donelson, and he was supremely proud of his army. "It is a striking feature of the present volunteer Army of the United States that there is nothing which men are called upon to do, Mechanical or Professional," he reflected, "that accomplished adebts cannot be found to perform in almost every regiment."

Following the sullen mood of the North in recent months, the double victory of Gettysburg and Vicksburg set off waves of celebration, and the interval really did mark a great psychological turning point of the war. "Was ever the Nation's Birthday celebrated in such a way before[?]" inquired New Englander Elisha Hunt Rhodes. "This morning the 2nd R. I. was sent out to the front and found that during the night General Lee and his Rebel Army had fallen back. . . . At 12 M. a National Salute with shotted guns was fired from several of our Batteries, and the shells passed over our heads toward the Rebel lines." Five days later he wondered on paper, "I wonder what the South thinks of us Yankees now. I think Gettysburg will cure the Rebels of any desire to invade the North again." Near month's end, Henry Brooks Adams, in London, wrote his brother with expressions of his reaction on first hearing the news. "I wanted to hug the army of the Potomac," he proposed. "I wanted to get the whole of the army of Vicksburg drunk at my expense. I wanted to fight some small man and lick him."

The casualty figures for the Vicksburg campaign had been monstrous, though. On the Federal side, some 9,362 men had been killed, wounded, or captured. Confederate casualties were large, but mostly unreported. Indeed, Pemberton's career was ruined by the outcome, and Independence Day was not celebrated in Vicksburg until eighty-six years after the surrender. "I have no heart to write," penned Confederate diarist Catherine Ann Devereux Edmondston. "Vicksburg has fallen! It is all true. No lying speculator has imposed upon us. Pemberton has surrendered! As yet it is all dark. We are told they were reduced to the verge of starvation & yet 200 mounted men of the garrison have been paroled & have reached Jackson, the officers allowed to march out with their side arms, retain their *horses* & private property. Now who ever heard of a beleaguered city starving with horses and mules in it?" Many Southerners were simply transformed into refugees because of the military activities. "Our home is gone—everything there destroyed & Reuben, Maria & Elizabeth all free—Susan & her children are with us yet, *But I would rather have my home,*" wrote Tryphena Blanche Holder Fox, a Northerner who had gone south to teach and had adopted Southern political alliances. She referred to her lost slaves and plantation house, which was overrun by Federal soldiers after the fight at the Big Black River.

Grant's stunning victory led to his commission as major general in the regular army, meaning that he was now ranked only by McClellan and Frémont, who had both been sent into oblivion, Halleck, and the soon-to-retire John E. Wool. His path to greatness took a major step forward. "General, allow me to observe to you that the entire people of the loyal states are filled

with admiration & gratitude to you & your army for the glorious achievements of your arms," wrote the old Jacksonian politician Frank P. Blair.
"Among the best & most intelligent people especially does this feeling pre-
dominate." Grant, meanwhile, was quick to assign success to others. "The
Navy under Porter was all that it could be during the entire campaign," he
wrote. "Without its assistance the campaign could not have been successfully made with twice the number of men engaged." Lincoln, however, knew
better. "I do not remember that you and I ever met personally," he wrote
Grant following Vicksburg's fall. "I write this now as a grateful acknowledgment for the almost inestimable service you have done the country. . . . I
never had any faith, except a general hope that you knew better than I, that
the Yazoo Pass expedition and the like could succeed. When you got below
and took Port Gibson, Grand Gulf, and vicinity, I thought you should go
down the river and join General Banks and when you turned northward, east
of the Big Black, I feared it was a mistake. I now wish to make the personal
acknowledgment that you were right as I was wrong." Lincoln finally had a
major event to celebrate. "The Father of Waters again goes unvexed to the
sea," he wrote his friend, the Illinois politician James C. Conkling, echoing
Grant's praise of the Navy. "Nor must Uncle Sam's web feet be forgotten. At
all the watery margins they have been present. Not only on the deep sea, the
broad bay, the rapid river, but also up the narrow muddy bayou, and wherever the ground was a little damp, they have been and made their tracks."

The situation for the Confederates was no better at Port Hudson,
which had been under siege by Maj. Gen. Nathaniel P. Banks since May 24.
In the wake of Vicksburg's capitulation, Maj. Gen. Franklin Gardner saw his
own hopes vanish. Gardner surrendered unconditionally on July 8; the following day a ceremony was held at Port Hudson and some 7,000 Confederates, the entire garrison, were taken as prisoners and sent north. The attacks
by black troops at Port Hudson impressed Banks, the New Englander who
commanded the army. In his official report, Banks stated that "they answered every expectation. In many respects their conduct was heroic. No
troops could be more determined or more daring. . . . Whatever doubt may
have existed heretofore as to the efficiency of organizations of this character,
the history of this day proves conclusively . . . that the Government will find
in this class of troops effective supporters and defenders."

Western skirmishing erupted along a wide range of locations during
the summer of 1863, mostly paling in strategic or tactical importance to
Vicksburg and Port Hudson, however. On July 13 an engagement took place
at Bayou La Fourche, Louisiana, also called Second Donaldsonville or Cox's
Plantation. On the same day, the Federal ironclad gunboat USS *Baron de Kalb,*
the transport USS *New National,* and the stern-wheel tinclads USS *Kenwood*
and USS *Signal* aided a movement on Yazoo City, enabling Union soldiers to

capture the town and also to occupy Natchez without firing a shot. On August 17, actions erupted at Grenada, Mississippi, and Sparta, Tennessee, as expeditions created clashes between wandering bands of soldiers. On August 31, Federal forces skirmished around Fort Smith, Arkansas, and the following day they captured the fort and town and proceeded on a quest to move against Little Rock.

THE SUMMER OF 1863 also brought one of the most curious events of the war north of the Ohio River. On July 2, as the fighting raged at Gettysburg, Confederate Brig. Gen. John Hunt Morgan launched another raid. This time he set out from southern Kentucky to cross the Cumberland River at Burkesville and bring to reality a dream he had frequently entertained—a raid north of the Ohio. With 2,500 cavalry organized into ten regiments in two brigades, Morgan set off supported by two 3-inch Parrott rifles and two 12-pounder howitzers. Though he was well equipped, Morgan's "Great" raid into Kentucky, Indiana, and Ohio was far more ambitious than anything he had previously done, and some of his soldiers believed he had lost his mind. He described how the horsemen might link up with Lee in Pennsylvania or operate in Illinois for a month or two, and even Morgan's brother-in-law, Col. Basil W. Duke, was gravely apprehensive. Without such spectacular visions, though, the officers agreed that they could at least operate north of the Ohio for a time and reemerge into the Confederacy via West Virginia.

In Cincinnati, Maj. Gen. Ambrose Burnside shifted into a new command after his disastrous tenure with the Army of the Potomac and was busy overseeing the Department of the Ohio. Burnside was planning an offensive movement into eastern Tennessee. Notified of Morgan's movements, Burnside ordered the Federal infantry of Brig. Gen. Henry M. Judah and the cavalry of Brig. Gen. Edward H. Hobson to harass the dangerous Southern horsemen. On July 2 a skirmish erupted near Burkesville, Kentucky, sending Hobson's 300 troopers scurrying back to Marrowbone. Morgan's men pressed on and encountered, on the late evening of July 3, Col. Orlando H. Moore's 25th Michigan Infantry erecting a makeshift fort on the opposite bank of the Green River near Tebb's Bend. Morgan demanded Moore's surrender on Independence Day. The Federal colonel replied that "it is a bad day for surrender, and I would rather not." Morgan attacked, but his dismounted cavalrymen ran into heavy fire from the new fort and had trouble navigating around debris from newly felled trees. After a half-hour contest, Morgan withdrew his men. The Southerners had lost 35 killed and 40 wounded, and among the Michiganders were 6 killed and 23 wounded.

By July 5, Morgan's men reached the outskirts of Lebanon, Kentucky, where they demanded the surrender of the 380 men of the 20th Kentucky Infantry (Lt. Col. Charles S. Hanson). Morgan ignored the hastily established

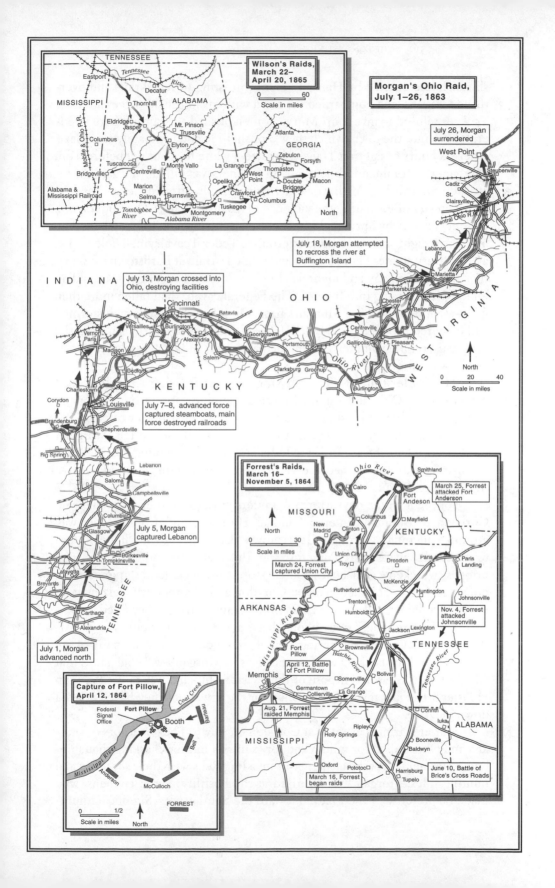

Wilson's Raids, March 22– April 20, 1865

Scale in miles 0 60

TENNESSEE
Eastport
Tennessee River
Decatur
MISSISSIPPI
Thornhill
ALABAMA
Mt. Pinson
Trussville
Eldridge
Jasper
Atlanta
Columbus
Elyton
GEORGIA
Zebulon
Forsyth
Tuscaloosa
Monte Vallo
La Grange
Thomaston
Bridgeville
Centreville
West Point
Macon
Double Bridges
Alabama & Mississippi Railroad
Marion
Selma
Burnsville
Opelika
Crawford
Columbus
Tombigbee River
Montgomery
Tuskegee
Alabama River
North
Mobile & Ohio R.R.

Morgan's Ohio Raid, July 1–26, 1863

July 26, Morgan surrendered
West Point
Steubenville
Cadiz
St. Clairsville
Central Ohio R.R.
Lebanon
Marietta
July 18, Morgan attempted to recross the river at Buffington Island
Parkersburg
Chester
Belleville
INDIANA
July 13, Morgan crossed into Ohio, destroying facilities
Cincinnati
OHIO
Batavia
WEST VIRGINIA
Vernon
Paris
Versailles
Burlington
Alexandria
Georgetown
Centreville
Madison
Portsmouth
Gallipolis
Pt. Pleasant
Salem
Bedford
Clarksburg
Grohup
Ohio River
North
Charlestown
KENTUCKY
Burlington
0 20 40
Scale in miles
Corydon
Louisville
July 7–8, advanced force captured steamboats, main force destroyed railroads
Brandenburg
Shepherdsville
Big Spring
Lebanon
Saloma
Campbellsville
Columbia
July 5, Morgan captured Lebanon
Glasgow
Burkesville
Tompkinsville
Lafayette
Breyards
TENNESSEE
Carthage
Alexandria
July 1, Morgan advanced north

Forrest's Raids, March 16– November 5, 1864

Ohio River
Smithland
Cairo
Fort Anderson
March 25, Forrest attacked Fort Anderson
MISSOURI
Columbus
Mayfield
North
New Madrid
Clinton
KENTUCKY
0 30
Scale in miles
Union City
Paris
Paris Landing
March 24, Forrest captured Union City
Troy
Dresden
McKenzie
Huntingdon
Johnsonville
ARKANSAS
Rutherford
Trenton
Humboldt
Nov. 4, Forrest attacked Johnsonville
Mississippi River
Jackson
Lexington
TENNESSEE
Fort Pillow
Brownsville
Hatchie River
Bolivar
Tennessee River
April 12, Battle of Fort Pillow
Memphis
Somerville
Aug. 21, Forrest raided Memphis
Germantown
Collierville
La Grange
Corinth
Iuka
ALABAMA
Ripley
Booneville
MISSISSIPPI
Holly Springs
Baldwyn
Oxford
Pototoc
Harrisburg
June 10, Battle of Brice's Cross Roads
March 16, Forrest began raids
Tupelo

Capture of Fort Pillow, April 12, 1864

Coal Creek
Fort Pillow
Federal Signal Office
Booth
Barteau
Bell
Mississippi River
Anderson
McCulloch
FORREST
0 1/2
Scale in miles
North

skirmish line erected by Hanson's men, consisting of fence rails and over-turned wagons, and bombarded the town with his four field pieces after the Yankees refused to give it up. Morgan's men pushed the outnumbered Federals back into the town, which they kept shelling and ultimately set ablaze. After six hours of fighting, Hanson hoisted a white flag, but not before Tom Morgan, the commander's 19-year-old brother, was killed. Morgan's bitter attitude toward the North worsened considerably after this event, and he spoke openly of escalating the violence in his future raids. The raiders took prisoners to nearby Springfield and entered Bardstown on July 6, where they had a brisk fight with a surrounded group of Federal cavalrymen holed up in a brick livery stable. They stopped and robbed a train at Bardstown Junction, then marched all day and night heading for Brandenburg, Kentucky, and an Ohio River crossing into Indiana. The Federal cavalry had fallen more than forty-eight hours behind Morgan's pace. On July 7, Morgan's men stormed and captured the steamer *John T. McCombs,* and they similarly captured the *Alice Dean,* robbing and terrorizing the passengers of both vessels before securing them for a crossing.

The whole of July 8 witnessed Morgan's men ferrying across the broad expanse of the Ohio, interrupted by a small demonstration from a company of Indiana militia and a short-lived firing of the side-wheeler tinclad USS *Springfield,* which after a time exhausted its ammunition and left. Morgan's raiders moved northward from the Indiana shore after burning the *Alice Dean* but sparing the *McCombs* because Morgan knew its captain. The raid north of the Ohio had begun.

For the next ten days Morgan's raiders crossed southern Indiana from Corydon to Sunman, entered Ohio at Harrison, and wound their way around Cincinnati, through Georgetown (U. S. Grant's boyhood hometown), and eastward to Pomeroy and Buffington Island. They burned bridges, wrecked canal boats, looted stores, grabbed food supplies from houses and farms, opened banks at Corydon and Georgetown (seizing government monies), and extorted cash from manufacturers. They filled wagons with books, groceries, silks, hoops, hats, and female undergarments. Although the days were sweltering, one of the raiders tied seven pairs of ice skates around his neck. One of the farmers in Morgan's wake declared that "they eat as if the sole purpose of their visit to Indiana was to get fat upon Hoosier bread and meat, and make up for the privations they have endured down in Dixie."

A brief skirmish erupted at Corydon on July 9. The governors of Indiana and Ohio called for militia and for "squirrel hunters," asking that able-bodied farmers meet the challenge of invading Rebs with their shotguns and hunting rifles. Morgan was surprised at the hostility of the civilians, who made no pretense of their hatred toward the Southerners. Significant numbers of militiamen turned up, many of them felling trees to block Morgan's routes so that the tardy Union cavalry might catch up. Once he approached Ohio, Morgan anticipated that Burnside would concentrate his force at Hamilton, northwest of Cincinnati, along the Hamilton & Dayton Railroad. On July 13 he began an ambitious, lightning-paced ride around Cincinnati that originated near Harrison and did not let up for thirty-two hours and ninety-five miles. The next day the raiders passed near Camp Dennison, Cincinnati's principal training and recruiting post. They galloped across Ohio, usually moving for twenty-one hours per day, but the swelling ranks of the Ohio amateur soldiers began taking their toll. More than 50,000 militia were operating to slow down Morgan, and in Meigs County the Home Guards established rifle positions in the hills above Buffington Island. By midmonth Morgan's overconfidence began to get the best of him. Knowing that Hobson was approaching (and without the knowledge that Judah was also nearby), he failed to deploy scouts. Judah disembarked his men from transports and interposed himself between Morgan and the river. Morgan now headed into a peninsula of land from which there appeared to be no escape. Lt. Comdr. Leroy Fitch brought his stern-wheel tinclad USS *Moose* and five other ships forward, reaching Buffington Island about when Morgan approached. Stunned, Morgan's men fought a short action with the Federal cavalry before Duke and half the command surrendered. Morgan escaped northward with some of his men, and Brig. Gen. James M. Shackelford pursued with a group of cavalrymen who vowed to stay in the saddle "without eating or sleeping" until Morgan was caught. He was surrounded on July 26 near West Point, Ohio. Morgan and his men were imprisoned in the Ohio State Penitentiary in Columbus, where after elaborate construction of a tunnel was completed (and dummies left in their beds), Morgan and six others escaped on November 26. Morgan returned to Kentucky posing as a cattle buyer or government mule purchaser.

In August another celebrated raid occurred, this one considerably more brutal than Morgan's. Few men in the Trans-Mississippi war were as bitter as the young guerrilla leader William Clarke Quantrill. Twenty-six years old, Quantrill was Ohio-born, but he moved west to teach and quickly became a gambler and outlaw. Heavily embroiled in the Kansas border wars prior to the outbreak of the Civil War, Quantrill garnered a reputation for brutally attacking pro-Union communities. After serving at Wilson's Creek, the fiery Confederate subsequently captured a Union wagon train and executed everyone in it; he honed his vicious style of war throughout the early months of 1863. On August 21, Quantrill led a band of about 450 men, Confederates and Missouri militia, into Lawrence, Kansas, a town boasting Union sympathies, and commenced a murderous pillaging of the community. Quantrill's men were just as devoted as he. A number of Southern girls accused of aiding guerrillas and bushwhackers had been held in a three-story brick building in Kansas City; on August 13 the building had collapsed, killing several and injuring others of the girls and inciting the already considerable fury of Quantrill and his raiders. In particular, "Bloody" Bill Anderson had an attitude: Three of his sisters were injured in the building collapse. His mind "became insane because of the injury to his sisters, and his attitude toward all men who supported or served the Union was that of a homicidal maniac." As he led his men into the town, Quantrill shouted at them: "Kill! Kill and you will make no mistake! Lawrence should be thoroughly cleansed, and the only way to cleanse it is to kill! Kill!"

After Quantrill's three-hour sacking and burning of the town, about 150 men and boys lay dead and $1.5 million in property was lost. Only women and very young children were spared; Quantrill's men looted the town, taking everything they could get their hands on. Quantrill's scout, John McCorkle, recorded how the party came upon a small unit of black soldiers in tents near the town. "Immediately the negroes and white men rushed out of their tents, the majority of them starting in the direction of the river and some going in the direction of town. The command was given to break ranks, scatter, and follow them. A few of the negroes reached the river, plunging into it, but none succeeded in reaching the opposite shore."

As LEE'S ARMY retreated toward the Potomac, the campaign for Charleston, South Carolina, heated up. The recapture of Fort Sumter and occupation of Charleston had been high on the priority list of Union military planners ever since the fall of Sumter had sparked the war. Holding the very city in which the secession movement began would surely be psychologically damaging to the Confederacy, but the task was complex. Concentrating on Sumter would require first capturing Morris Island, to its south, from which heavy batteries could concentrate fire toward the fort and the city. The attack on Morris Island had been anticipated for weeks. In early June the marginally competent political Maj. Gen. David Hunter, commanding the Department of the South, was replaced by the highly capable engineer Brig. Gen. Quincy A. Gillmore. It was Gillmore's sound planning and effective use of rifled artillery that had moved Fort Pulaski to surrender in April 1862. Now Gillmore's job was tactically more difficult because of the nature of Charleston Harbor, the batteries on Morris Island, and the Confederate defenses spread around the city. Gillmore would be aided by Rear Adm. John A. B. Dahlgren, the expert in naval ordnance who enjoyed Lincoln's friendship and had recently replaced Rear Adm. Samuel F. Du Pont as commander of the South Atlantic Blockading Squadron.

The prime target on the northern end of Morris Island was powerfully gunned Fort Wagner (also called Battery Wagner), an isolated redoubt that covered nearly the width of the narrow strip of sand that composed a portion of the island's northern side, in view of Sumter. On the northern tip of the island stood Fort (Battery) Gregg, also necessary to capture but more lightly equipped. To the southeast, on Folly Island, Union troops commanded by Brig. Gen. Israel Vogdes had been in place since April 1863. West of Morris Island was the substantial form of the far larger James Island, which contained numerous Confederate troops as well as Forts Johnson and Pemberton, and Union plans included forays onto James to reduce its solidity. Preliminary actions in the area occurred during June 1863, when Federal troops raided plantations along the Combahee River and took part in the raid and destruction of Darien, Georgia; the Federal navy destroyed the fearsome CSS *Atlanta*. Now, under Gillmore's direction, the division of Brig. Gen. Truman Seymour would attempt to take parts of James Island and all of Morris Island, providing artillery positions from which to bombard Sumter. One of Seymour's brigade commanders was Brig. Gen. George Crockett Strong, age 30, a Vermont native who had moved to Massachusetts and later graduated fifth in his West Point class before becoming skilled with ordnance. Already, on the northern end of Folly Island, Federal batteries consisted of thirty-two rifled guns and fifteen mortars, and Dahlgren's naval force would participate forcefully in bombardments prior to most of the Federal attacks.

Among the regiments waiting for a chance to fight was Col. Robert Gould Shaw's 54th Massachusetts Infantry, the black regiment that shamefully was required to torch Darien. It now operated under the rumors that its armament would soon be changed to pikes rather than guns and the fact that its private soldiers were paid $10 per month rather than the $13 the army's white privates received. (This injustice was not rectified until months later.) "Now the main question is, Are we *soldiers*, or are we *Labourers?*" African-American soldier and newspaper correspondent James Henry Gooding appealed to President Lincoln. "The patient, trusting Descendants of Africa's Clime have dyed the ground with blood, in defense of the Union, and Democracy.... Now your Excellency, we have done a soldier's duty. Why can't we have a soldier's pay?"

Still, Shaw and his lieutenant colonel, Edward Needles Hallowell, longed for a fight so they could show how the black troops would fare. Col. Thomas Wentworth Higginson and others had raised black troops earlier than Shaw, and other black regiments had fought already in such locations as the siege of Port Hudson, but Shaw had a burning desire to show that his men could fight, in this midsummer of the "Year of Jubilee." On July 2, Shaw wrote Gov. John A. Andrew, a friend of his influential parents, describing how Strong "seems anxious to do all he can for us, and if there is a fight in the Department will no doubt give the black troops a chance to show what stuff they are made of." The 54th Massachusetts Infantry saw its first taste of battle on James Island but would not yet be commanded by Strong. Brig. Gen. Alfred H. Terry was ordered to make a demonstration against James Island with the brigades of Cols. William W. H. Davis and James Montgomery and Brig. Gen. Thomas G. Stevenson, while other troops readied for a major attack on Morris Island and Higginson's 1st South Carolina Infantry cut a nearby railroad line.

Gillmore's force consisted of 10,000 troops, 36 field guns, and 60 siege guns and mortars. Still under command of Montgomery, the oddball Kansas Jayhawker, Shaw's men departed on July 9 from the northern end of Folly Island on transports as the ironclad monitor USS *Nantucket,* the screw sloop USS *Pawnee,* the side-wheel combatant USS *Commodore McDonough,* and the mortar schooner USS *C. P. Williams* plunged upriver, firing heavily on James Island. In command of the Department of South Carolina, Georgia, and Florida, Gen. P. G. T. Beauregard considered the approach to Charleston via James Island dangerous, and so he ordered 2,926 Confederate troops posted in fortifications there, with 927 men on Morris Island, 1,158 men on Sullivans Island (to the north, mostly at Fort Moultrie), and 850 men in the city. He had heavy artillery posted on James and Morris islands, as well as the guns at Sumter, Moultrie, and at Battery Park along the city waterfront. Brig. Gen. Roswell S. Ripley commanded the 1st Military District, which included the islands, and during these first days of the renewed attack on Charleston, the Confederate defenses on James Island were commanded by Brig. Gen. Johnson Hagood, those on Morris Island by Col. Robert F. Graham and later by Brig. Gen. William B. Taliaferro.

As the 54th Massachusetts Infantry and other regiments were moving by boat, they heard heavy cannonading early on July 10, toward Morris Island. It was Strong's brigade, which pushed forward under heavy thunderclaps of cannon fire from forty-seven Federal guns on the northern tip of Folly Island; surprised Confederates returned fire from Morris Island as best they could. By 7 A.M. Strong thrust his skirmish lines forward and established a foothold on the southern part of Morris Island. "The two columns now moved forward," he wrote, "under a lively discharge of shell, grape, and canister, converging toward the works nearest the southern extremity of the island, and thence along its commanding ridge and eastern coast, capturing successively the eight batteries, of one heavy gun each, occupying the commanding points of that ridge, besides two batteries, mounting, together, three 10-inch seacoast mortars." On July 11 a major attack on Fort Wagner failed after briefly gaining the parapet but having to retreat after exposure to heavy fire from the fort's cannon and musketry.

On James Island, Shaw's regiment landed on the 11th and indeed, in the early morning mist five days later, they tasted battle. An attack on the Union line near Secessionville was planned by Brig. Gen. Alfred H. Colquitt's Confederate brigade of South Carolinians and Georgians, some 1,400 men, supported by the 54th Georgia Infantry. As many of the bivouacked men of the 54th began to awake on July 16, distant flashes of fire were suddenly visible among the outposts on the horizon, and "sharp, metallic explosions" of cannon fire followed. The regiment quickly fell in and readied for the attack. The assault struck squarely into the 10th Connecticut Infantry, and the quick firing of the 54th Massachusetts Infantry helped to spring the Connecticut troops from their predicament. After a brief, heavy engagement, the Confederates retreated.

Two days later came the second and most celebrated assault on Fort Wagner. On July 18, Brig. Gen. Truman Seymour organized an attack that would employ 6,000 men and place Strong's brigade in the lead. Brutal, heavy cannonades preceded the attack, both from the Federal batteries on the southern part of Morris Island and from the naval flotilla, and of course Confederate guns inside the fort returned fire. On a bright, breezy afternoon, the Federal batteries poured heavy rounds of shot and shell into the fort, driving most of its soldiers into the bombproofs and twice knocking down the Confederate flag flying above the parapet. Showers of sand leaped high into the air with every shot that exploded. Inside the fort, Taliaferro dug in with the rest of the men and occasionally watched as Confederate batteries from Forts Gregg, Sumter, and Moultrie barked back to the Union guns. After noon Gillmore reconnoitered the scene and Shaw found Strong, who informed the young colonel that the works would be stormed that evening. Shaw immediately volunteered his regiment to participate and, as it turned out, take the lead in the assault.

Seymour's attack force would consist of three brigades commanded by Strong, Col. Haldimand S. Putnam, and Stevenson. Formed in the lead with five other regiments behind them, the 54th Massachusetts was instructed to lie down in the sand and await nightfall. The attackers would need to conform to a narrow strip of beach on the approach, allowing the Confederate gunners within Fort Wagner to concentrate their heavy fire onto this location. Though the attack would be suicidal, and many realized it, Shaw and the men of the regiment had much to prove, and Seymour approved of the black soldiers leading the charge because "it was believed that the Fifty-fourth was in every respect as efficient as any other body of men; and as it was one of the strongest and best officered, there seemed to be no good reason why it should not be selected for the advance. The point was decided by General Strong and myself." The regiment numbered barely 600 men on this day. With twilight deepening, Shaw handed a package of personal effects and letters to a friend, the correspondent Edward L. Pierce, and Strong mounted a gray horse and rode ahead of the formed columns. Shaw told

Hallowell that he would keep the regiment's national colors with him if Hallowell would keep the state flag at close hand, and that they would "take the fort or die there." Strong asked, if the color bearer should fall, who would take up the flag? Shaw took a cigar from his lips and said that he would take it, producing loud applause from the regiment.

In the darkness the attack commenced. The regiment marched 1,000 yards under heavy fire at the double-quick and then broke into a helter-skelter charge, screaming and firing and attempting to grab cover on the beach as shells exploded around them, showering many with blasts of sand. The walls of Wagner shook every few seconds with explosions and cannon flashes, and Shaw led his men furiously, sword drawn. The lead elements of the regiment passed through the defile under heavy musket fire, and great holes caused by shell explosions slowed their progress as the incessant rattle of long arms sparked all along the face of the fort. As the surviving men approached the fort, they were struck with enfilading fire from the flanks, cutting down many of them. Both flags were planted on the parapet, the national colors by Sgt. William H. Carney, who later said "the old flag never touched the ground, boys." Shaw, much beloved as a promising officer (and almost certainly a future general), stood up atop the parapet, shouting "Forward, Fifty-fourth!" and was shot in the chest, falling dead instantly. In one of his last letters home, written to his mother, he had described abolitionists meeting on a South Carolina plantation and penned the phrase, "God isn't very far off." Shaw was buried in the sand with his dead soldiers, and when Confederate authorities finally offered to disinter his body and send it North, Shaw's parents responded by writing that Shaw would have preferred to be buried with his men.

Though men of the 54th fought briefly inside the fort, the assault failed and was beaten back with miserable casualties. When the rest of Strong's brigade attacked, they failed, too, and Strong himself was mortally wounded, hit in the right thigh by a shell. The shelling of the fort continued for several days, after which the situation transformed into a siege. On July 24, Union artillery pounded the fort with more than 2,500 shells, and Maj. Edward Manigault recorded in his journal that "the discharges really did not appear to average more than 28 seconds apart. If it had not been for the flag of truce [to bury the dead and exchange prisoners], it would have been necessary to evacuate or surrender Battery Wagner."

The war around Charleston heated up again in mid-August with the first great bombardment of Fort Sumter. Union batteries erected on the southern half of Morris Island, along with Dahlgren's Union naval guns, opened a withering fire, aiming 938 shots at Fort Sumter on August 17 alone. They also targeted Forts Wagner and Gregg. Gillmore's heavy Parrott guns sent shells that crumbled the brick masonry walls of Sumter, repeating the effect pioneered at Fort Pulaski. Yet with crushing shellfire and debris and desolation growing about them, the Confederate defenders of Sumter held on. Six days of operations meant that by August 22 only four serviceable guns were left inside Fort Sumter. Five Union ironclad monitors attacked on August 22, and some of the Federal batteries shocked Southern sensibilities (and notions of "civilized" war) by opening fire on the city of Charleston. Also on this day the most celebrated cannon in Gillmore's growing Federal arsenal, the "Swamp Angel," a 200-pounder (8-inch) Parrott rifle, exploded on firing only its thirty-sixth round. The behemoth lobbed incendiary shells a distance of up to 1.5 miles and produced a few minor fires in Charleston before it exploded. Thereafter, the massive gun was used for a time as an improvised "mortar" with a far shorter range. Confederate naval operations didn't help their cause. On August 29 the submarine *H. L. Hunley* sank in Charleston Harbor, drowning its crew of five.

"The part of the Confederacy we still hold is in the shape of a boot," wrote War Bureau chief Robert G. H. Kean in Richmond, "of which middle Virginia, North Carolina, South Carolina, and, Georgia to the gulf is the leg and Alabama and part of Mississippi the foot; besides this, the Trans-Mississippi. Nearly half the whole area is in the hands of the enemy, or outside of our lines. We have never substantially recovered any territory once occupied." Some Confederate soldiers, in light of the Northern victories, fatigue, poor supplies and food, were growing morose. "The soldiers has a by word when any body dies or anything lost saying its gone up the spout," wrote Pvt. W. Lawrence Barrett, near Richmond, on July 18. "Tell Washington that I say the Confederacy is on her way up the spout. Nothing more."

CHAPTER 18

Visiting the River of Death

AT THE CLOSING CREDITS of the otherwise brilliantly produced motion picture *Glory*, which chronicles the attack of the black soldiers of the 54th Massachusetts Infantry on Fort Wagner, the writers inform us that "the fort was never taken." But of course it was. Brig. Gen. Quincy A. Gillmore continued his assaults on Morris Island after the failed attack of July 18. The bombardment of Confederate forts around Charleston continued apace. On September 1 mortar fire took aim at Wagner while ironclads and Gillmore's massive Parrott gun batteries took aim at Fort Sumter, continuing to transform the glorious bastion into a pile of brick dust. On this day 627 shells and shot were thrown into Sumter; the fort's magazine was endangered, but the small garrison inside withstood the pounding and remained unwilling to surrender. The following day Yankee soldiers approached and dug in on the beach within eighty yards of the parapets of Fort Wagner. Although the fort's garrison fought sporadically, they generally stayed well within the bombproofs and out of danger. By September 5 entrenching Union soldiers had scratched their way to within a few paces of the ditch at the fort's perimeter. The Federal navy tried to attack Battery Gregg on the northern end of Morris Island by boat; this failed. On September 6 it was clear that a major attack was imminent.

Desperate from the swelling Federal presence, Southern Col. Jeremy F. Gilmer appealed to the Confederate navy secretary for assistance. (Gilmer is often misidentified as a major general; his appointment as such was never confirmed by the Confederate Senate.) "To enable us to hold Morris Island to the last extremity," wrote Gilmer, "I appeal to you for the services of as many sailors as you can possibly give us from Richmond, Wilmington, Savannah, and other points, not less than 200, to be employed as oarsmen to convey troops and *materiél* to and from that island. I earnestly ask for assistance at once." But signs of desperate times were beginning to show, with the Confederacy's resources stretched too thin to meet many emergencies in many places. As Union batteries found their range on Cummings's Point and other areas of supply, Confederate operations on Morris Island were coming to a close. The constant bombardment of Morris Island and Fort Sumter for nearly two months had taken its toll, and Col. Lawrence M. Keitt, now commanding Fort Wagner, decided to withdraw. Some 900 men had remained within Wagner on September 5, but on that day alone 100 of those Confederate defenders had been killed or wounded. "The parapet of salient is badly breached," Keitt wrote. "The whole fort is much weakened. A repetition tomorrow of today's fire will make the fort almost a ruin. The mortar fire is still very heavy and fatal, and no important work can be done. Is it desirable to sacrifice the garrison?" Sgt. William H. Johnson of the 7th Connecticut Infantry termed the bombardment "a thousand New Haven Fourth of Julys each day and night."

Rather than withstand more punishment, Keitt ordered an evacuation of Fort Wagner under the cover of darkness, by boat, during the night of September 6. Confederate transports assembled between Fort Johnson (on James Island) and Sumter and were aided by the ironclad gunboat CSS *Charleston.* As the final squads of Confederate soldiers arrived at James Island, Union officers discovered the movement, and they captured three barges loaded with Rebel soldiers and sailors. On September 7, Union soldiers finally occupied Fort Wagner and found it deserted, with broken debris scattered on the sandblown landscape everywhere, and the junk and waste of war littering the ground where the 54th Massachusetts Infantry had fought seven weeks earlier. "The enemy now holds Cumming's Point," editorialized the *Richmond Sentinel,* "in full view of the city."

With the stubborn defenders of Fort Wagner gone, Union engineers could place cannon on the northern end of Morris Island. They could also focus on more aggressive operations against Fort Sumter. Because the artillery had been so heavily damaged inside Sumter, Gen. P. G. T. Beauregard replaced most of the artillerists within the fort with infantrymen. The Federal naval flotilla, commanded by Rear Adm. John Dahlgren, now concocted a plan to surprise the fort's garrison by storming it at night by boat to capture the prized ruin. On September 7, Dahlgren demanded that Sumter surrender, to which Beauregard replied that Dahlgren should be welcomed to "take the fort if he could." An observer of Fort Sumter on this day described the structure as so battered from the prolonged Union bombardment that its appearance "from seaward was rather that of a steep, sandy island." A force of naval ships prepared to support the coming attack; the ironclad monitor USS *Weehawken* moved out to reconnoiter but grounded on the narrow channel and could not be moved again until the following day. Other ships, meanwhile, moved into position near Fort Moultrie and exchanged heavy fire with the Confederate fort to weaken its ability to fire at the Federal boats during the planned attack on Sumter. The ironclad monitors USS *Nahant*, USS *Lehigh*, USS *Montauk*, and USS *Patapsco*, and the ironclad gunboat USS *New Ironsides* (Capt. Stephen C. Rowan) all shelled Moultrie on the evening of the 7th and morning of the 8th, after Moultrie's guns opened on the stranded *Weehawken*. "Moultrie fired like a devil," wrote Dahlgren, "the shells breaking around me and screaming in chorus." The *Weehawken* replied with its guns as best it could, but the stuck ship took a battering, and the *New Ironsides* positioned itself between Fort Moultrie and the stranded ship. Struck more than fifty times, the *New Ironsides* finally retreated after running low on ammunition, and the *Weehawken* eventually broke free and withdrew. She had been signaled by Dahlgren, "Don't give up the ship."

The following night Dahlgren mounted his "surprise" attack on Fort Sumter. Having assembled 400 soldiers and marines in 30 landing boats, Comdr. Thomas H. Stevens would lead the assault. Unfortunately for the Federals, however, Confederates in Charleston and within the fort knew all about the planned attack. The USS *Keokuk*, wrecked in the April assault on Confederate forces in Charleston Harbor, contained a key to Union signal codes that was recovered by Confederates and which they employed to monitor the attack. Readied and supplied as well as they could be, Sumter's defenders opened a withering small-arms fire on the approaching boats, lobbed hand grenades into them as they drew near the fort's base, and watched as the heavy guns of the casemate ironclad CSS *Chicora* poured a heavy fire into the Union boats and encircled them to prevent reinforcements. The attack was disastrous for the Federals; they accumulated 125 casualties before withdrawing and temporarily abandoning their plans to storm Sumter or capture the city of Charleston.

Operations around Charleston Harbor turned quiet, despite the heavy Union presence. On September 15 a magazine at the Confederate Battery Cheves exploded, killing six soldiers. A minor bombardment of Sumter was resumed on September 28 and lasted six days without producing results. After 560 shots, sporadic return fire was received. An amazing, isolated incident did occur on October 5, however. Commanding a four-man crew, 1st Lt. William T. Glassell set a secret weapon of the Confederate navy into motion against the formidable Federal armada. Cigar-shaped, steam-driven, and barely visible above the water on this hazy night, the submarine CSS *David* set out armed with 60 pounds of powder rigged to its spar torpedo, hanging 10 feet ahead of her bow. Built in Charleston during the early autumn, the *David* stretched 50 feet long and was the first of several spar-torpedo submarines to succeed with an attack. (The submarine torpedo boat *H. L. Hunley*, built in Mobile, had sunk at its dock in August, was raised, and sank again on October 15, killing its crew of nine before being raised yet again. Other submarines had attempted attacks on Federal ships but without much success.)

At a speed of only 7 knots, the *David* moved stealthily through the water toward the USS *New Ironsides*. Lookouts on the *New Ironsides* spotted the mysterious ship (or at least her port hatch gliding through the water) and fired on her. But *David* continued on, its torpedo striking the ship under the starboard quarter. The sudden and unexpected explosion, a huge blast and upward fountain of water, created havoc on the *New Ironsides*, which sustained heavy damage but stayed afloat. The explosion bathed the *David's* engines in water, putting her out of action. After the explosion damaged the *New Ironsides*, Glassell and another crewman were captured; the other two managed to restoke the *David's* fires and pilot her away to safety. Asst. Engr. James H. Tomb, who helped bring back the *David*, reported that "the enemy fired rapidly with small arms, riddling the vessel, but doing us no harm. The column of water thrown up was so great that it recoiled upon our frail bark in such force as to put the fires out and lead us to suppose that our little vessel would sink." Tomb wrote that he and the pilot escaped by passing through the Federal ships again, "within 3 feet of a monitor, being subjected the whole time to one continuous fire of small arms, the *Ironsides* firing two XI-inch shot at us." The *David's* escape ensured that it would fight another day. The bombardment of Charleston's forts would resume during the final days of October.

MANY SMALL AND SCATTERED ACTIONS erupted in the Trans-Mississippi theater during late summer and early autumn 1863. On the Texas-Louisiana border, a Union naval force moved into Sabine Pass on September 8, intending to launch an attack into the Houston and Beaumont region. The operation resulted from the post-Vicksburg mission of Union Maj. Gen. Nathaniel P. Banks to "raise the flag in Texas." With the French regime in Mexico, the Lincoln administration wished to demonstrate its force in the area not only to defeat the Confederacy but to thwart any ideas that French authorities might harbor to invade Texas. In Washington, General-in-Chief Halleck chose the Red River as a route by which Banks could attack, but the field commander won the dispute and instead moved on Sabine Pass. In the naval escort that accompanied Maj. Gen. William B. Franklin's 4,000 men who set out from New Orleans were the gunboats USS *Arizona*, USS *Clifton*, USS *Granite City*, and USS *Sachem*. Franklin had planned the attack as a surprise, but once again Union officers were caught off guard during naval operations.

The Federal ships tried to draw the fire of the Confederate fort guarding Sabine Pass as well as that of the cottonclad steamer CSS *Uncle Ben*. At

3:30 P.M. the Union ships entered the pass and attacked the fort, which was defended by only about 46 Confederate troops under Lt. Richard W. Dowling and which held only a few guns. Maj. Gen. John B. Magruder, now in command of the District of Texas, New Mexico, and Arizona, had no more men or supplies. Though the Federal gunboats opened on the fort, Dowling's men replied with the artillery they had and struck the Union ships heavily, crippling the *Sachem* by a shot through its boiler and tearing away the wheel rope of the *Clifton,* thus grounding her in close range of the Southern guns. Both lead ships were forced to surrender with heavy casualties on board. The Sabine Pass expedition was a disaster, with the other ships and troop transports turning around and heading back to New Orleans.

The Confederate Congress termed the victory "one of the most brilliant and heroic achievements in the history of this war." Aboard the *Sachem,* 38 of its crew were taken prisoner, 7 killed, and 16 missing; aboard the *Clifton,* 10 were killed, 9 wounded, and 28 missing. Others were captured, too. "Thus it will be seen that we captured with 47 men two gunboats, mounting thirteen guns of the heaviest caliber," remarked Dowling, "and about 350 prisoners. All my men behaved like heroes; not a man flinched from his post. Our motto was 'Victory or death.' "

Federals had more success at Little Rock, Arkansas, two days later. Shudders of fear and hopelessness struck many of the loyal Southerners in the state when Maj. Gen. Frederick Steele led the Army of Arkansas, 12,000 strong, forward from Helena to capture the state's capital. Encamped near Little Rock, Maj. Gen. Sterling Price, commanding the District of Arkansas, also had about 12,000 troops. After a series of cavalry skirmishes that mainly consisted of scattering Confederate Brig. Gen. John S. Marmaduke's horse soldiers, Steele forged on and Price retreated southward to Rockport and Arkadelphia. (Marmaduke had on September 6 mortally wounded his fellow brigadier general Lucius M. Walker in a duel, after Marmaduke had criticized Walker's ability.) The fall of Little Rock put the squeeze on the whole Confederate Trans-Mississippi Department, making life difficult for its commander, Lt. Gen. Edmund Kirby Smith.

After the fall of Little Rock, Col. Jo Shelby set out with his light horse Confederates on a raid of sorts through Arkansas and Missouri. On September 22 the horsemen commenced their movement from Arkadelphia, beginning a series of actions that would last until late October and cover 1,500 miles with 600 troopers. Shelby's men rode hard for the Arkansas River, ready to retreat into the Boston Mountains if Federal units pressed them too hard. They approached Moffat's Station on September 27 and encountered the 1st Arkansas Infantry. About 200 of the Federal soldiers took cover among timber and fired heavy volleys into the Southerners. Dismounting, Shelby's men formed for a charge that "scattered them like chaff," Shelby re-

ported, "and our rough riders rode them down like stubble to the lava tide."
By October 4 the raiders were safely into Missouri, making their way to
Neosho, southwest of Springfield, where they found and scattered some 300
Union cavalry—"a terror to the country, the insulters of unprotected
women, and the murderers of the old and infirm men," in Shelby's words.
Continuing north, the raiders moved through Sarcoxie, finding "bare and
fire-scarred chimneys [which] point with skeleton fingers to heaven for
vengeance." Passing through the town of Oregon, or Bowers's Mill, claimed
to be an outpost for Union cavalry, Shelby's men "sacked [the town] and then
swept [it] from the face of the Earth, to pollute it no more forever."

By October 9, Shelby's raiders passed through Cole Camp, capturing
vast numbers of horses, "Union steeds . . . changed into Rebel chargers," and
the following day surrounded the town of Tipton, west of Jefferson City.
Driving out about 100 militia troops, they captured the town, destroyed the
nearby railroad bridge at La Mine Bridge, and skirmished at Syracuse. The
railroad blockhouse guarding the bridge, after a short, sharp fight, stood
against the midnight sky, "one mass of hissing, seething, liquid fire," Shelby
wrote. The raiders fought briefly with Union cavalry before heading north
through a driving rain to Boonville. The town and its few defenders quickly
surrendered. "They knew their evil course," recalled Shelby. "The night before our arrival all the citizens had been armed and resistance determined
on, but daylight brought sober reason, and the trembling mayor was only too
glad to take the oath of allegiance." Brig. Gen. Egbert B. Brown now pursued
with a sizable force of Union cavalry from Jefferson City. On October 13 the
two commands fought a skirmish at Arrow Rock, northwest of Boonville,
nearly surrounding Shelby's command before it broke free and escaped,
moving quickly southward to the safety of Arkansas. Some 600 Union soldiers had been killed or wounded during the raid, another 500 captured and
paroled, and numerous stores and railroad property and supplies taken or
damaged.

While this raid was underway, the notorious Col. William C. Quantrill
set off on another expedition, this time headed for Baxter Springs, Kansas, in
the extreme southeastern corner of the state. From Carthage, Missouri,
Quantrill's 600 raiders struck westward and encountered an encampment
(of the 3d Wisconsin Cavalry) belonging to nearby Fort Baxter, which had
recently been constructed and garrisoned with black troops. Striking hard
into the camp, Quantrill's men scattered the soldiers and sent them reeling
for cover behind the encampment's buildings. Quantrill next took three
companies, about 150 men, out to the position of a stopped railroad train,
which turned out to be carrying Union Maj. Gen. James G. Blunt, his staff,
and an escort of about 125 troops. Blunt was in the process of moving his
headquarters from Fort Scott, Kansas, to Fort Smith, Arkansas. Later, as a

battle erupted at the main fort, Quantrill formed 250 men and charged the train, forcing its passengers to flee while Quantrill slaughtered as many bluecoats as he could; only about 40 men from the train were left alive. "As soon as Quantrill was informed of the approach of General Blunt's escort, he posted several men to observe it pass over a ridge in the prairie," wrote Wiley Britton of the 6th Kansas Cavalry. "General Blunt, and several of his staff, quickly got out of his carriage and commenced to direct the movements of his men. . . . But the enemy were closing around him on all sides, it was impossible to keep them firm under the galling fire. . . . General Blunt and fifteen to twenty men cut their way through and escaped, but not without bullet holes in their clothing. All the rest of the escort, members of the band, and teamsters, were killed or wounded, and lay on the field within the radius of half a mile."

"We continued the chase about 4 miles," reported Quantrill, "when I called the men off. . . . On returning, we found they had left us 9 six-mule wagons, well loaded; 1 buggy (General Blunt's); 1 fine ambulance; 1 fine brass band and wagon, fully rigged." Blunt was unhurt, at least physically. Quantrill's men were dressed in Union blue, which afforded great covert value to the start of their attack. The aftermath was hideous. "On looking over the ground for the wounded," wrote Blunt, "I soon discovered that every man who had fallen, except 3, who had escaped by feigning death, had been murdered, all shot through the head."

THE CENTER OF ACTIVITY was now in Tennessee. Relatively inactive since the Tullahoma campaign, the middle war reshaped itself as Maj. Gen. William S. Rosecrans's Army of the Cumberland grappled strategically with Gen. Braxton Bragg's Army of Tennessee. Threatened by a Union southward movement following the Tullahoma campaign, Bragg withdrew his force in mid-August to the area of Chattanooga, strengthening its defenses dramatically. Clearly, a major battle was shaping up between the armies, as the lead elements of the Federal army moved close to the city near Stevenson, Alabama, staying on the opposite bank of the Tennessee River. By September the composition of the armies had changed considerably since earlier in the year. Rosecrans's force now consisted of the corps of Maj. Gen. George H. Thomas (14th Corps; divisions of Maj. Gens. James S. Negley and Joseph J. Reynolds and Brig. Gens. Absalom Baird and John M. Brannan); Maj. Gen. Alexander M. McCook (20th Corps; divisions of Maj. Gen. Philip H. Sheridan and Brig. Gens. Jefferson C. Davis and Richard W. Johnson); Maj. Gen. Thomas L. Crittenden (21st Corps; divisions of Maj. Gen. John M. Palmer and Brig. Gens. Thomas J. Wood and Horatio P. Van Cleve); Maj. Gen. Gordon Granger (Reserve Corps; division of Brig. Gen. James B. Steedman and an attached brigade of Col. Daniel McCook); and Brig. Gen. Robert B.

Mitchell (Cavalry Corps; divisions of Brig. Gen. George Crook and Col. Edward M. McCook).

Bragg's army comprised a right wing commanded by Lt. Gen. Leonidas Polk, which contained the division of Maj. Gen. Benjamin F. Cheatham, Maj. Gen. D. H. Hill's corps (he had been named a lieutenant general in July 1863 but the appointment was not confirmed; divisions of Maj. Gens. Patrick R. Cleburne and John C. Breckinridge), and the reserve corps of Maj. Gen. William H. T. Walker (divisions of Brig. Gens. States Rights Gist and St. John R. Liddell). The army's left wing would be commanded by Lt. Gen. James Longstreet (who would be detached from the Army of Northern Virginia on September 9) and contained the division of Maj. Gen. Thomas C. Hindman, Maj. Gen. Simon B. Buckner's corps (divisions of Maj. Gen. Alexander P. Stewart and Brig. Gens. William Preston and Bushrod R. Johnson), and Longstreet's corps (commanded by Maj. Gen. John Bell Hood and consisting of the divisions of Maj. Gens. Lafayette McLaws and Hood). A cavalry corps, commanded by Maj. Gen. Joseph Wheeler, contained the divisions of Brig. Gens. John A. Wharton and William T. Martin. Lastly, Brig. Gen. Nathan Bedford Forrest's corps held the divisions of Brig. Gens. Frank C. Armstrong and John Pegram.

Rosecrans's movement on Bragg was designed to flank him, forcing the Confederate commander to evacuate Chattanooga. The Tennessee city, population 2,545, was not only an important rail center, with the East Tennessee & Georgia Railroad running to the east, the Western & Atlantic Railroad to the south, and the Memphis & Charleston Railroad to the west, but whichever side held it would occupy a formidable base ringed by mountains. Bragg was ordered by his friend Jefferson Davis not only to stop Rosecrans from investing the city, but to reverse the assault and crush the Army of the Cumberland, reigniting the Southern spirit in the wake of the grim defeats in Pennsylvania and Mississippi. By September 4, Rosecrans, though poorly outfitted with too few pontoon bridges, rafts, and boats, crossed most of his army (save for Granger's reserve corps) to the eastern bank of the Tennessee River. Most of McCook's corps crossed at Caperton's Ferry, south of Stevenson, Alabama; Crittenden crossed at Shellmound, Tennessee, northeast of Bridgeport; Sheridan crossed at Bridgeport; and Thomas employed all these sites. Using all three roads that passed over the high mountains to the east, the corps of McCook (to the south, via Winston's Gap), Thomas (in the center, at Stevens's Gap), and Crittenden (to the north, via Wauhatchie) approached the Confederate army. By September 6, Thomas's men were positioned in the valley of Lookout Creek. The Federal cavalry covered the flanks, particularly that of McCook's to the south, with heavy horse reconnaissance moving forward through Alpine and into Georgia. To the north Crittenden had a small cavalry force in his front along with the brigade of

Col. John T. Wilder, whose men were heavily equipped with Spencer repeating rifles. Thomas, approaching in the center, had no cavalry force
screening his movements. In eastern Tennessee, a simultaneous movement
of Maj. Gen. Ambrose Burnside's Federals moved on Knoxville (this will be
described in the following chapter).

Bragg, meanwhile, concentrated his army after learning that Rosecrans's force had crossed the river and moved southward to strike the Confederate rear. (Bragg had anticipated that Rosecrans would move to the
north side of the city so that help might arrive if needed from Union forces
in eastern Tennessee.) On September 6, Bragg decided to withdraw from the
city, concentrate at La Fayette, Georgia, twenty-two miles to the south, and
fight Rosecrans's men as they came down from the high mountain passes. On
September 8, Bragg evacuated the city (thus abandoning one of his missions
right away), moving his entire force, save for the screening cavalry of Forrest
and Wheeler, to La Fayette. As Forrest harassed Crittenden near Chattanooga itself and Wheeler grappled with the Union cavalry in McCook's
front, D. H. Hill assigned infantry to move forward into the mountain gaps
facing Thomas in the center. Hill moved to La Fayette first and was soon
joined by Walker; Polk moved south to Lee and Gordon's Mill, a few miles
south of Chattanooga, and Buckner placed his men into an intermediate position. On September 9, Federal troops marched into Chattanooga, victori-
ously holding the town without entirely appreciating the imminent danger
they were in, being spread over forty miles of mountain passes. Despite the
threat, Confederate authorities in Richmond were in a near panic over the
thrust of Union soldiers so deeply into the heart of the South. Davis considered sending Robert E. Lee to Chattanooga but then reconsidered when he
feared for Virginia's safety; instead, Longstreet would be detached and sent
to assist Bragg. Buckner was also assigned to operate under Bragg's command. Longstreet's men would not arrive in the field until September 18.

With a golden opportunity to strike at isolated corps, Bragg prepared
for major assaults. The chance to wreak havoc on Rosecrans's army was
heightened by the fact that Rosecrans believed that because Bragg withdrew
southward, his army must be hungry, ill supplied, and demoralized. Rosecrans surmised that Bragg was on a straight escape to Dalton, Georgia. He
ordered the Union cavalry to ride ahead and disrupt the railroad line at Resaca, south of Dalton, and sent Crittenden forward from Chattanooga to follow up the enemy's positions and push him farther to the South. Faulty
intelligence added to the delusion Rosecrans embraced, and so on the verge
of a major battle in which his corps were spread thin, Rosecrans believed he
held the upper hand, when in fact a trap awaited him. In the Federal center,
Negley's division pushed out from Stevens's Gap on the evening of September 9 and raced toward Dug Gap, west of La Fayette. The Confederate plan

of battle now began to take shape. Bragg ordered Hindman to attack Negley through McLemore's Cove (from the "rear"), but Hindman, starting from Lee and Gordon's Mill, moved slowly on September 10 and halted before reaching Negley's force, sending out only a small reconnaissance toward the enemy. D. H. Hill was next ordered to attack the exposed division of Negley, pinning the Federals between the two Confederate forces. But Hill failed to set up his attack properly. After considerable vacillation, Hill moved toward Dug Gap by 1:30 P.M. and formed for attack. Despite the fact that Negley's force was nearly surrounded, neither Hill nor Hindman attacked, though the latter was now reinforced by Buckner, and Bragg failed to press his orders. The opportunity was squandered.

Bragg next ordered the three commanders to attack Negley on the morning of September 11. This time Hindman's judgment collapsed as he called a council of war and decided not to attack until more was known about Union forces that might be arriving through Stevens's Gap. Bragg angrily denied Hindman's request to instead attack Crittenden and ordered Hindman again to attack Negley on the morning of September 12. Inching his way toward Negley's division, Hindman began to see the walls closing around him. He believed that some 15,000 Yankee soldiers lay in his front (only 8,000 were there), and Bragg had cautioned him about the possible approach of Crittenden and McCook. Hindman's behavior now took on a reflection of George McClellan's anxious character as he suddenly ordered a withdrawal northward, only to change his mind and march southward again toward battle. But with all these possible attacks and hours passing, Negley finally realized that danger lay ahead and retreated to Stevens's Gap. The result was that nothing happened, due mostly to Hindman's sudden fears but also to Bragg's and Hill's indecisiveness.

The cavalry legend Nathan Bedford Forrest, meanwhile, had been keeping Bragg well informed of the movements of Crittenden's corps. Bragg held on to the plan of defeating Rosecrans's army in detail by turning his sights upon Crittenden, who had deployed his divisions southward into Georgia to Reed's Bridge and Lee and Gordon's Mill. On September 12, Crittenden discovered the whereabouts of the Southern army and quickly concentrated at Lee and Gordon's Mill, where Brig. Gen. Thomas J. Wood's division was encamped. Bragg next ordered Polk and Walker to attack this position on the morning of September 13. He directed Polk to make the attack "quick and decided," requesting that "no time be lost." But Polk also resorted to the standard failure of the Army of Tennessee, hesitating after orders were received and holding a council of war to think things over with the subordinates. Moreover, before the attack could be launched, on the evening of September 12, the Confederates learned that Crittenden had concentrated his force and that an attack would no longer be feasible. By 9 A.M.

on the 13th, Bragg arrived on the scene and found that Polk had not yet attacked, despite the numerical superiority Polk had over Crittenden. Bragg was outraged. For the second time in three days Bragg failed to capitalize on a grand opportunity to damage isolated portions of the Federal army.

Rosecrans, slow to realize the danger his army faced, finally began to appreciate the situation. For as many as three days now Rosecrans could see that Bragg was not in full retreat but might be assembling his army for an attack. Rosecrans ordered McCook to move northward to Stevens's Gap, placing his corps closer to Thomas in the center. Rosecrans's corps were less scattered by September 17, although they were still not disposed well for the coming battle. The Federal commander strung his cavalry force along a line in front of Wheeler's cavalry to the south and Forrest's to the north. By September 18 the tactical situation had evened; either army might have an opportunity to strike at the other in a turning movement, but it was the angry, exhausted Bragg who retained the initiative to fight. Reinforced now by Hood's division arriving from Virginia, and with the remainder of Longstreet's corps due the following day, Bragg was emboldened to strike. He determined on the 18th to move on Crittenden's left, interpose his army between the Federal corps and Chattanooga, and thus cut off their routes of supply and retreat. Granger's reserve corps was stationed to the north at Rossville, just south of Chattanooga, but its small size (6,000) posed a minimal threat. Bragg now had a force of 47,500 infantry and 14,500 cavalry relatively well concentrated, facing Rosecrans's three corps, placed from Lee and Gordon's Mill (Crittenden) southward to Pond Spring (Thomas) to Stevens's Gap (McCook), totaling 50,000 infantry and 9,000 cavalry.

Thus the stage was set for the largest battle of the western theater, the two-day affair at Chickamauga, Georgia. Fought along the meandering West Fork of Chickamauga Creek, the battle would again severely test the Northern spirit, despite the two recent victories to the north and west. The word Chickamauga is Cherokee for "river of death," an appellation, according to legend, derived from illnesses contracted from drinking its muddy brown water. The creek would see greater death over the two-day battle than it had ever witnessed before, however. The battlefield surrounding the creek's west fork consists of a ten-by-six-mile rectangle of land southeast of Rossville, along the foothills of one portion of Missionary Ridge, an area marked by many rolling hills, sandy, ruddy loam, fields punctuated by cabinlike farmhouses, and lush forests of pine. A crisscross of minor roads bespeckled the landscape, the most important of which was the north-south La Fayette Road. Over this picturesque landscape, Bragg planned to send Hood, Walker, and Buckner across Chickamauga Creek at Reed's Bridge, Alexander's Bridge, and Thedford's Ford, to strike Crittenden's left and flank him. Hill, meanwhile, would block the exit via McLemore's Cove (to the south) so that Crittenden could not be reinforced by that route. Polk would cross the creek to the south at Lee and Gordon's Mill, on Crittenden's right. But all along the front, Confederate theory and execution once again separated, as the poor roads delayed marches and communications broke down. Late in the afternoon of the 18th, Hood, resisting the sporadic fire of the Union cavalry, finally pushed through and crossed at Reed's Bridge; Walker, however, could not cross at Alexander's Bridge and had to move northward to cross at Lambert's Ford, delaying his participation in the engagement. By nightfall Hood and Walker had encamped on the west bank of the creek, and the remaining Confederate units had moved up to their positions along the eastern bank.

By now Rosecrans, slow to grasp the situation, realized fully the Confederate plan. He sent Thomas and McCook to reinforce Crittenden, and Thomas arrived in Crittenden's rear late on that night. By the following morning the Federal troops were repositioned, with Crittenden concentrated around Lee and Gordon's Mill, Thomas spread over a wide line behind him, from Negley south at Crawfish Springs, Reynolds to his north at the Widow Glenn House (with Wilder's brigade in his front), Baird's division farther north in Kelly's Field, and Brannan still farther north. To Brannan's east, Col. Robert H. G. Minty's cavalry brigade scouted near Dyer's Ford. Approaching from the north was Granger's reserve corps, which had spread eastward from Rossville to McAfee's Church. Given every advantage to this point, Bragg now faltered by moving his forces so slowly. The corps of Buckner, Hood, and Walker would make the initial attack on September 19, Bragg ordered, with Forrest's cavalry screening to the north, Cheatham's division held in reserve in the center, Cleburne's division in reserve at Thedford's Ford, Hindman facing Crittenden at Lee and Gordon's Mill, and Breckinridge to the south opposite Negley. What Bragg did not count on was the relatively rapid reinforcement of Crittenden, and he was unaware of the three Yankee divisions north of Crittenden; as if to achieve parity, the Federal commanders were unaware of the Confederate troop positions as well. The battle lines were about six miles long.

Early on the morning of September 19 the battle of Chickamauga commenced as Thomas sent Brannan to scout toward Alexander's Bridge, believing that a Confederate brigade was positioned across the creek. Instead, Brannan slammed into Forrest's dismounted cavalry and the battle escalated throughout the morning with confused, poorly coordinated assaults. Many of the attacks were hopelessly crude, frontal affairs that were launched in piecemeal fashion. By 9 A.M., near Jay's Mill, along the Reed's Bridge Road, Col. John T. Croxton's Union brigade fought stubbornly against Brig. Gen. Henry B. Davidson's Confederate horsemen; to their north, Col. Ferdinand Van Derveer's Ohio and Indiana troops fired volleys into Col. George G.

Dibrell's Tennessee horse soldiers. Though the Confederates were being roughly handled, Forrest darted around encouraging his men, shouting, "Hold on boys, the infantry is coming," "Stay by the battery, men; support the battery. General Walker will be here in five minutes to help us."

The fighting raged extensively around the Jay's Mill area, with both sides accumulating numerous casualties, and by 11:30 A.M. heavily reinforced Union troops were fighting with spirit when they received shocking news. The brigades of Brig. Gen. John C. Starkweather and Col. Benjamin F. Scribner, posted south of the rest of the Federal units, along Winfrey Field, received a northward surprise attack from the infantry of Col. Daniel C. Govan and Brig. Gen. Edward C. Walthall's brigade of Mississippians. In Scribner's brigade, Col. Oscar Moore and Scribner were stunned after their brigade surgeon approached with the news that he had just been in the hands of the enemy. Dr. Miller told them that "I mean to say that the enemy is in your rear and on your right. They have taken my field hospital with all the wounded. They have captured the provost guard and all the prisoners and are coming down upon you like a pack of wolves." A bitter fight ensued at close range, with heavy musketry fired and artillery discharging as the Rebels stormed into the front. Four hundred men surrendered in Scribner's brigade alone, and many of the Federal troops in the area simply scattered at breakneck speed.

At 1 P.M. heavy action flared in Brock Field, west of the Winfrey House and east of another cabin-farm, the George Brotherton House. In Brock Field, Brig. Gen. William B. Hazen's brigade of mostly Ohio and Indiana boys squared off with the Confederates of Brig. Gen. Preston Smith's Tennesseeans, both groups of regiments scrambling for the corn-covered plot. Soldiers fired in line and as they marched, leaving trails of the shrieking wounded behind. Pvt. Jacob Miller of the 9th Indiana Infantry had just fired a shot when he was struck in the forehead by a ball and three buckshot, which shattered his left eye, leaving it dangling. "I . . . tried to place it back," wrote Miller, "but I had to move the crushed bone back as near together as I could at first. Then I got the eye in its proper place. I then bandaged the eye the best I could with my bandanna." North of the field, the Union brigades of Brig. Gen. August Willich and Col. Joseph B. Dodge approached the Mississippi and Georgia boys of Brig. Gen. John K. Jackson. South of the Brotherton Road, another battle front was established as Col. William Grose's Ohio and Indiana troops marched into the Tennesseeans of Brig. Gen. Marcus J. Wright. Confused fighting followed, with both sides slugging it out and gaining little advantage. At 2 P.M. the action around Brock Field continued to rage, and to the south along La Fayette Road, north of Viniard Field, Col. Hans C. Heg's brigade approached a portion of the Confederate line formed by the divisions of Brig. Gens. Bushrod R. Johnson and Evander M. Law.

Rosecrans had established his headquarters to the west near the Widow Glenn House, and Bragg was far to the east near Thedford's Ford. The desperate, disorganized fighting would continue.

By 2:30 P.M. a vicious battle line raged along Brock Field, with eight Union brigades forming an arc-shaped battle front and witnessing more artillery brought in support of the battle. In Brock Field itself, Tennessee men fighting for Brig. Gen. Otho F. Strahl opposed the brigades of Hazen and Brig. Gen. Charles Cruft; to the north, Dodge and Willich contested the attacks of Brig. Gen. George Maney's Tennesseeans. Dibrell's Confederates were scattered after being beaten savagely. The Confederate line along this area was becoming a patchwork, yet the flashes of musketry continued, with booming artillery in the rear, and the Confederates held their position. As the 11th Ohio Infantry prepared to march toward the field, the regiment's chaplain, William Lyle, spoke to the men in loud tones, over the cannon and small-arms fire, telling them that "it is but little I can do for you in the hour of battle, but there is one thing I will do—I will pray for you. And there are thousands all over the land praying for you this morning, and God will hear them. . . . Be brave—be manly! . . . if any of you fall this day in battle, may you not only die as brave soldiers for your country, but die as soldiers of the Lord Jesus Christ."

By 3:30 P.M. not only had the fierce fighting continued raging throughout Brock Field, with the Confederate brigades eventually breaking on the retreat, but the intense action shifted northeastward into Winfrey Field, with the brigades of Willich and Col. Philemon P. Baldwin's Ohioans fighting Walthall's Mississippi men and with Govan's Arkansans just to the north. Maney's brigade, meanwhile, had been utterly routed and sent into retreat along Alexander's Bridge Road. About this same time, far to the south, action heated up in Viniard Field. There the Union brigades of Brig. Gen. William P. Carlin and Col. Sidney M. Barnes met soldiers of Florida and Virginia in Col. Robert C. Trigg's brigade and the Texas and Arkansas troops of Brig. Gen. Jerome B. Robertson. Confusion reigned on the Federal side as Barnes's men cut across the front of Carlin's brigade, necessitating a cease-fire, during which Trigg's men fired heavy volleys into the Yankees, causing them to fall back from the southern part of the field. The fighting in this area raged for more than two hours, during which neither side gained appreciable ground. At 5:30 P.M. the western edge of Viniard Field was still held by Union brigades, now those of Cols. Luther P. Bradley and George P. Buell. Robertson and Trigg were still in place, with the brigade of Georgians under Brig. Gen. Henry L. Benning in support.

To the west, meanwhile, fighting raged around the Brotherton House on La Fayette Road. At first the action in this area reflected the struggles in the Viniard and Brock fields, with brigade and even regimental commanders

ordering attacks, waves of musketry fire, and retreats on their own, uncoordinated by a larger hand. Brig. Gen. Henry D. Clayton, a lawyer and politician leading Alabama troops, ordered his troops, lying in the thick brush, to
cease firing in preparation for a charge against the brigades of Brig. Gen.
Samuel Beatty and Cols. William Grose and George F. Dick. Clayton's boys
took a heavy pounding as small-arms fire clattered and artillery boomed,
sending shells falling near and behind the brigade. Clayton reconsidered the
idea of a charge and withdrew to regroup, pursued for a time by Beatty and
Dick. Disorganization only increased. "Confusion reigned even before the
battle began," wrote Lt. Albion Tourgée of the 105th Ohio Infantry. "Communications between the flanks was almost impossible. The winding roads
were full of lost staff officers. The commander of a regiment rarely saw both
flanks of his command at once. . . . The enemy determined our movements
for us."

In Grose's front, south of Brotherton Road, Brig. Gen. William B. Bate's
Tennesseeans withdrew to check their ammunition and regroup, and Col.
Edward A. King's Yankees unleashed a fearful fire to his front but after heavy
fighting was flanked by regrouped Tennessee boys. King's Indiana and Ohio
men were struck on the flanks, retreating wildly past the Brotherton House
to the safety of the woods to the west. Other Federal units collapsed as the
Confederates attacked toward La Fayette Road, with deadly consequences
for some of the Union troops who were swept up in the fight. Near the
Brotherton House, the 75th Indiana Infantry (Col. Milton Robinson) determined to counterattack; its ranks pushed forward, striking the right flank of
Brig. Gen. John C. Brown's brigade, but Robinson was struck down by a bullet through the shoulder; his lieutenant colonel was struck about the same
time. The Confederate movement turned into a "stampede" and appeared to
be overwhelming the whole line running along La Fayette Road. As Brig.
Gen. Charles Cruft's Union infantry retreated, Brig. Gen. John B. Turchin's
men passed them, heading for the Confederates. Turchin (Ivan Vasilovitch
Turchinov) was a Russian-born soldier of fortune who had fought as a
colonel in the Crimean War before receiving his commission as colonel of
the 19th Illinois Infantry. In 1862, Turchin allowed his men to pillage the
countryside at will, following an old Russian custom. Court-martialed, his
conviction was set aside by the War Department and he simply returned to
the field. This high-spirited fighter, the "Russian Thunderbolt," passed his
retreating comrades and at his men screamed words to the effect of, "Damn
you, get out of our way—if you can't fight, give them a chance that can." In-
vigorated by Turchin's spirited charge, reformed Federals struck Col. James
L. Sheffield's Alabamians and scattered them in disarray. Fresh from his encounter with Chamberlain's 20th Maine at Gettysburg, Col. William C.
Oates took charge of the retreating men after Sheffield was thrown from his

horse, and Turchin met up with his men back at the Brock Field, following the charge. "Bully for mine brigade!" he shouted in his broken English.

Back in Winfrey Field, fighting raged on into the evening. By 6 P.M. the Union brigades of Baldwin, Willich, and Dodge struck again into the Confederates of Col. James Deshler and Brig. Gens. Lucius E. Polk and Sterling A. M. Wood. The division commander, Pat Cleburne, sent his Alabama, Tennessee, and Arkansas troops forward into Winfrey Field, north of the Winfrey House, supported by well-placed guns to the rear. In dwindling sunlight, Wood's men were the first to cross the field and strike into the Yankees in the dusky woods. A dirty, bludgeoning fight resulted, with officers and men of both sides simply shooting wildly, not really seeing anything in the darkness. Bullets zipped all around with the lead thudding into the bark of trees, knocking splinters high into the air. To some of the men, veterans of Shiloh and Stones River, this end-of-the-day fight seemed as intense as any of the western theater. "For half an hour the fighting was the heaviest I had ever heard," Cleburne wrote. "Accurate shooting was impossible. Each party aimed at the flashes of the other's guns, and few of the shots from either side took effect." The Confederate attack faltered. Deshler was an Alabama-born colonel who had served as a staff officer before being captured at Arkansas Post and exchanged just two months before Chickamauga. He was struck squarely in the chest with a shell while he was examining cartridge boxes during the attack, and killed instantly. Despite claims of brigadier generalship for this young officer, his appointment as such was never confirmed. Union Col. Philemon P. Baldwin had also been killed, shot dead from his horse.

During one of the early evening melees Confederate Brig. Gen. Preston Smith accidentally rode into the midst of a Union brigade and a volley rang out, mortally wounding him. One of the rounds struck a gold watch worn on his chest, crushing it. Smith died within the hour. The fighting across the battlefront at Chickamauga sputtered out as the darkness deepened, characteristically leaving only the organization of troops, care of the wounded and dying, resupply for the morning, and councils of war to be looked after during the night. Rosecrans held a council and, urged by George H. Thomas, planned to keep his left flank as strong as he could for the morning's fight. Thomas had his engineers erect log breastworks around Kelly Field, near the Federal left, and the remaining portions of the army, jumbled after the first day's fight, would concentrate northward to a line stretching from Kelly Field southward to Viniard Field, abandoning the position of Lee and Gordon's Mill.

Bragg's army, having finally crossed to the western bank of Chickamauga Creek by 11 P.M., was now reorganized by Bragg into two wings, commanded by Leonidas Polk and Longstreet. Bragg's plan for attack, to commence the following morning, would revive the intention of enveloping Rosecrans's left. Breckinridge would strike first, followed progressively by Cleburne, Stewart, Hood, McLaws, Bushrod Johnson, Hindman, and Preston.

But the attack, slated for early morning on September 20, developed too slowly. D. H. Hill and Polk failed to communicate throughout the night, and as often happened with operations in the Army of Tennessee, plan and reality did not meet. A comedy of errors occurred as Polk, who should have been preparing for attack, interrupted his schedule for breakfast. Then Hill's corps was in the midst of receiving rations when Polk inquired about starting the attack. So instead of a dawn attack, which had been clearly ordered (as opposed to the fabled dawn attack at Gettysburg), the action got underway only by around 9:30 A.M. Breckinridge's men slammed into the division of Absolom Baird. The attack stretched over a mile-wide front as Brig. Gen. Daniel W. Adams's men fired volleys into the Hoosiers surrounding the Mc-Donald House, sending them scurrying back. To the south Brig. Gen. Marcellus A. Stovall's Floridians emerged from the wood line to attack the Illinois men in an open field along La Fayette Road. Farther south, on the northern end of Kelly Field, numerous Federal units manning the log breastworks received an attack from Brig. Gen. Benjamin Hardin Helm's Kentuckians. In the hail of bullets exchanged during the first minutes of the attack, Helm, mounted for the charge, was struck in the right side and wounded mortally. Age 32, Kentuckian Helm was a regular army man who had married Mary Todd's sister and thus become brother-in-law to Abraham Lincoln. Helm died about midnight in a field hospital behind the lines.

The attack raged to the south, all the way to the Poe House and Field, as Cleburne and Stewart entered the fray. By 11 A.M. Union units in Kelly Field had been battered significantly but held on to their positions with the aid of a heavy return fire and the fortified position. Stovall's men swept southward into the northern fringe of the field, supported by Adams's men to the west. As the men of Grose's and Van Derveer's brigades defended the attack, with the Kelly House and Barn ablaze behind them, sending black smoke skyward, the fight raged back and forth without significant resolution. After many rounds loaded and exchanged, Stovall's brigade finally retreated about 11:15 A.M., leaving Adams dangerously exposed. While the Confederates in Kelly Field began a northward retreat, the Southern attack would fare much more favorably to the south.

By late morning Rosecrans, without much sleep, began to lose control of the situation. Thomas was greatly concerned about being attacked by Cleburne over such a wide front and requested support in the form of Brig. Gen. John M. Brannan's division. Brannan had moved up, unknown to Thomas, to plug a gap between the divisions of Brig. Gens. Thomas J. Wood

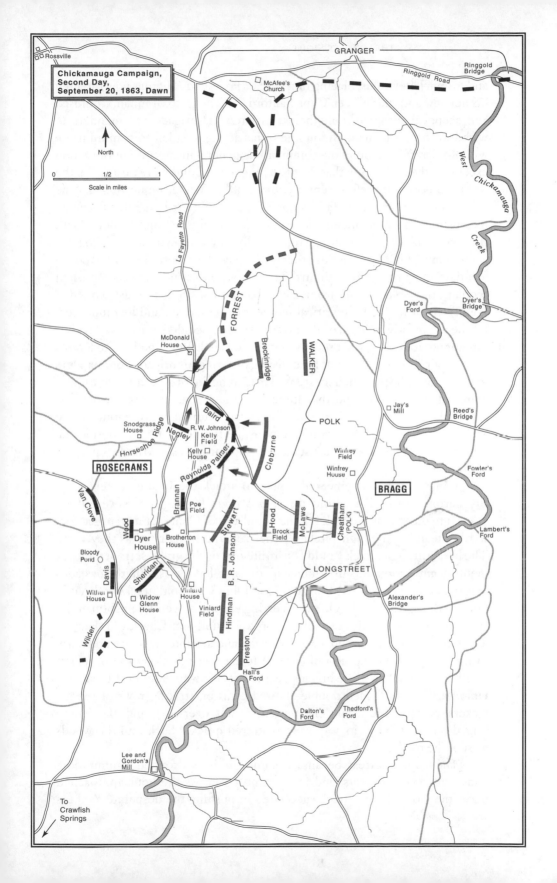

**Chickamauga Campaign,
Second Day,
September 20, 1863, Dawn**

North

0   1/2   1
Scale in miles

Rossville

GRANGER

McAfee's Church

Ringgold Road

Ringgold Bridge

West Chickamauga Creek

FORREST

La Fayette Road

McDonald House

Breckinridge

WALKER

Dyer's Ford

Dyer's Bridge

Jay's Mill

POLK

Reed's Bridge

Snodgrass House

Horseshoe Ridge

Negley

Baird

R. W. Johnson

Kelly Field

Cleburne

Winfrey Field

Winfrey House

Fowler's Ford

ROSECRANS

Kelly House

Reynolds Palmer

BRAGG

Van Cleve

Brannan

Poe Field

Hood

McLaws

Cheatham (POLK)

Lambert's Ford

Wood

Dyer House

Brotherton House

Stewart

Brock Field

LONGSTREET

Bloody Pond

Wilder House

Davis

Sheridan

B. R. Johnson

Alexander's Bridge

Widow Glenn House

Viniard House

Viniard Field

Hindman

Wilder

Preston

Hall's Ford

Dalton's Ford

Thedford's Ford

Lee and Gordon's Mill

To Crawfish Springs

and Joseph J. Reynolds, placing him west of Poe Field. Thomas now directed his nephew and staff officer, Capt. Sanford C. Kellogg, to Brannan. Confused and skeptical, Brannan nonetheless ordered his brigade commanders to withdraw from the main Union line of battle. Kellogg left to communicate with Rosecrans and found the commanding general in approval of the action except for the realization that Brannan's movement might create a gap in the lines. Rosecrans therefore sent a courier off to Wood, requesting that he "close up on Reynolds as fast as possible, and support him." But Brannan, meanwhile, countermanded the orders to his brigade commanders. With Brannan in place, the order to Wood to close up on Reynolds was illogical. "Gentlemen, I hold the fateful order of the day," he reportedly said. Wood, a few days short of his fortieth birthday, was a Kentuckian, an accomplished regular army soldier (and ironically, a second cousin of the just-wounded Helm). He now faced the critical moment of his career, and he blundered. But he was mostly a victim of Rosecrans, who had scolded him a few days before for not following what seemed a vague order. Determined not to let this occur again, Wood pulled out his division, ordering his brigade commanders to withdraw (despite their current skirmishing in Brotherton Field), and marched around to the north. Although the idea seemed crazy, they complied. The result was to set up one of the grandest moments of Confederate advantage of the war. Rosecrans, responsible for the army and perplexed, might have ridden the short distance of 600 yards to see Wood to prevent confusion.

Longstreet had engineered a plan to attack the Union center at the Brotherton House that unfolded just as Wood's last regiments were filing away. Into the gap of the Federal line, hundreds of Confederates surged forward, screaming the high-pitched Rebel yell and firing away as they went. The breakthrough attack would constitute one of the greatest frontal movements in any action. Bushrod Johnson's division led the assault, the brigades of Brig. Gen. Evander McNair and Col. John S. Fulton attacking directly into the Brotherton Field. On the receiving end of this central portion of the attack were the brigades of Cols. George P. Buell and Charles G. Harker. The Confederates swarmed across the road and around the house and barn, swayed only by the zigzag rail (worm) fence that ran along the property. Buell wrote that "my little brigade seemed as if it were swept off the field." Union artillerists loaded double-shotted canister, striking rows of the attackers, but to little avail. The onslaught was overwhelming, the Union brigades that stood in its way were scattered quickly back into the woods west of the road.

The Union retreat became a panic; soldiers dropped ammunition, guns, and accoutrements, and many simply ran. As the hour approached noon, the Confederate attack succeeded in pushing the desperate Yankees south of the Brotherton House, collapsing the whole southern part of the battle line. Brig. Gen. Arthur M. Manigault's brigade of Alabamians and South Carolinians struck into a conglomeration of Federal units spread over the Widow Glenn House area, where Rosecrans had held his council. To the north the brigades of Brig. Gens. James Patton Anderson and Zachariah C. Deas attacked the Union brigades of Col. Nathan H. Walworth and Brig. Gen. William H. Lytle. Other Federal units had been crushed by the stinging wave and sent reeling westward and northward from the Robert Dyer House area; these included the brigades of Brig. Gens. William P. Carlin and Samuel Beatty and Cols. Bernard Laiboldt and John A. Martin (Martin assumed command of Heg's brigade after the Norwegian-born Wisconsin colonel had been shot down). Col. John T. Wilder's "Lightning Brigade," armed with Spencer repeating rifles, fought off Confederate assaults stubbornly, but soon the position had to be abandoned. The focus of the current attack fell on what came to be known as Lytle Hill, between the Dyer and Widow Glenn houses. There the pride of Cincinnati, Brig. Gen. William Haines Lytle, held off the Confederate onslaught as best he could.

Thirty-six-year-old Lytle was a well-educated career soldier, politician, and poet. Wounded badly at Perryville and left for dead, he had nonetheless recovered to lead his men again. Their position in jeopardy, Lytle's brigade fought stubbornly although they were surrounded with dead and wounded from Laiboldt's brigade and had Confederate soldiers shooting at them in droves. First Lt. Alfred Pirtle of the 10th Ohio Infantry, beside Lytle, witnessed the fight as the noise and smoke of the battle rose to such a degree that the whole scene was surreal; Lytle suddenly leaned over and shouted that he had been hit. He had been struck in the spine, chewing a plug of tobacco as his men comforted him, when suddenly a bullet struck him in the cheek, spattering Pirtle with blood. Shot through the head, Lytle was suddenly dead. "The remains of Genl. Lytle reached us yesterday and are now lying in state in our chapel tent," Pirtle wrote Phil Sheridan, his division commander, three weeks after the fight. "Not knowing how long they may remain, I send you this word, unofficially, so that you may, if you desire it, see the last of our gallant friend."

By noon the Union cause at Chickamauga seemed all but lost. At Dyer Field, Confederate brigades were routing all the Yankees in sight. Sheffield's Alabamians struck squarely into the Ohio and Indiana troops at the field's northwest edge, and the beaten survivors of Cols. John M. Connell and John T. Croxton's brigades were shuffling northwest toward a semicircular hill named Horseshoe Ridge. The routed elements of Van Cleve's division scrambled westward to a position north of Dyer Road, and sporadic fighting occurred in the deep woods as far west as a little watering hole that, just as at Shiloh, came to be called Bloody Pond. By early afternoon the majority of

Rosecrans's army had pulled out in a panic, along with Rosecrans himself. The divisions of Phil Sheridan and Jefferson C. Davis, separated from the rest of the army, retreated via McFarland's Gap. The corps of McCook and Crittenden followed. By the (at the time) unexplained absence of Rosecrans, Thomas, strengthening the position on Horseshoe Ridge, was left in command of the field by default. He received an order from Rosecrans, hastily written during his flight, to pull out and head north to Rossville. But the situation would not be quite as simple. Granger's reserve corps, to the north at McAfee Church, came into play when Granger heard the firing and sent Brig. Gen. James B. Steedman southward to support Thomas. "There's nothing in our front but ragtag, bobtail cavalry," Granger told his chief of staff. "I am going to Thomas, orders or no orders!"

By 2:15 P.M. a raging fight had erupted along Horseshoe Ridge near the George Washington Snodgrass House, on a knob also called Snodgrass Hill. Thomas, having established headquarters on the hill, posted the remnants of Harker's brigade around him and the brigades of Brig. Gen. Walter C. Whitaker and Cols. John G. Mitchell and William Stoughton to the south and west. Horseshoe Ridge was attacked strongly by the Confederate brigades of Anderson, Fulton, Brig. Gen. Joseph B. Kershaw, and Col. Cyrus A. Sugg. The Union defense line, nominally held by Brannan and established by Thomas, held. By 4 P.M. Longstreet had reorganized his remnants and made a last attack on Horseshoe Ridge, sending Brig. Gen. William Preston's division forward (which had been protecting against a possible attack by Wilder). After bitter fighting that culminated on the hill about 4:15 P.M. and involved frontal assaults by the brigades of Brig. Gen. Archibald Gracie, Jr., Kershaw, and Col. John H. Kelly, the Confederate attack stalled. "It was unquestionably the most terrific musketry duel I have ever witnessed," Wood wrote. Thomas heroically earned the sobriquet "Rock of Chickamauga" for his coolheadedness and stubborn defense of Horseshoe Ridge although his army commander had already fled. Of the action on the hill, Lt. Col. Gates P. Thruston, a Federal staff officer, recalled, "The Union line held the crest. Longstreet was stayed at last. Gathering new forces, he soon sent a flanking column around our right. We could not extend our line to meet this attack. . . . For a time the fate of the Union army hung in the balance. All seemed lost, when unexpected help came from Gordon Granger and the right was saved." Rosecrans, predictably, would be essentially ruined. At Kelly Field, the Federals tightened their defensive ring and prepared to withdraw. Thomas moved north during the night and the two-day battle of Chickamauga was over.

But only after a frightful cost. Of about 58,000 Union soldiers engaged, 1,657 were killed, 9,756 wounded, and 4,757 missing; of 66,000 Confederate effectives, losses were 2,312 killed, 14,674 wounded, and 1,468 missing. The

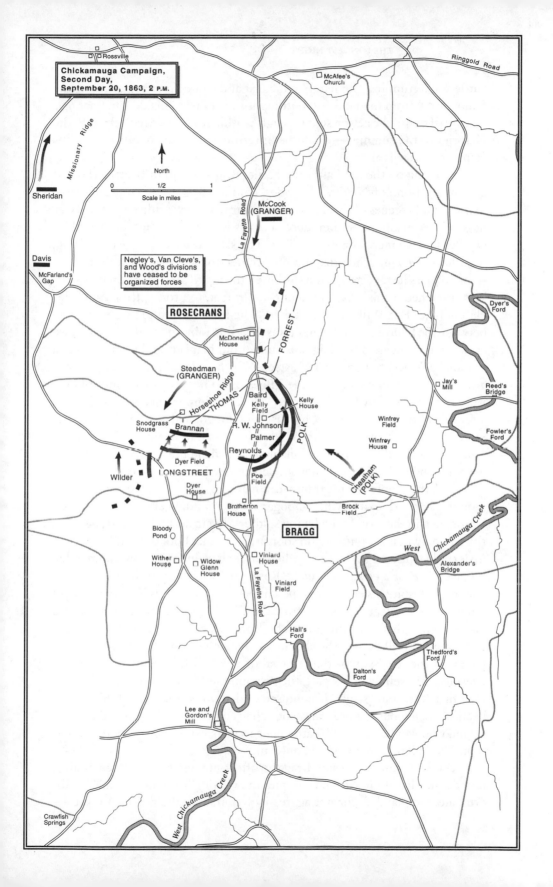

battle was a stunning Confederate tactical and strategic victory, driving the Union army from the field and bottling it in confusion inside Chattanooga. The terrific chill the action sent through Washington—particularly after the victories of the summer—would be bitter indeed for army officers, politicians, and citizens alike.

Sleeping on the field after the battle, Brig. Gen. John Beatty, who had commanded one of Negley's brigades, couldn't forget the savagery. "How many terrible scenes of the day's battle recur to us as we ride on in the darkness. We see again the soldier whose bowels were protruding, and hear him cry, 'Jesus, have mercy on my soul!' . . . The sky was darkening, earth fading; wealth, power, fame, the prizes most esteemed to men, were as nothing." For some soldiers lesser aggravations followed the fight. "We spread on two blankets, stretched a small fly tent about 5 × 7 feet, to protect from rain," declared Texas Pvt. William A. Fletcher. "The horses cared for, we were soon between the blankets and the night was drizzling rain, and twilight. When we crawled in we heard a buzzing noise under our blankets and we were over a bumblebee's nest but were soon asleep—for how long, I don't know. I was awakened by the bees stinging me." Bees or no bees, Confederate soldiers were reinvigorated by Chickamauga. "The most important battle of the war, after that of the first Manasses, has just been fought and won by the Confederate arms," wrote a private whose identity is lost to history. "The result is told in a few words; There is no longer an armed enemy on the soil of Georgia; Only the Federal dead and wounded and prisoners remain."

And the Confederates tramped northward and occupied some of the mountains overlooking Chattanooga, further endangering the battered Union men in the city. As the Union soldiers dug in around the city, near the river, hoping that supplies would soon arrive so that both they and their animals could continue to eat, the verdict was long in on the Union commander. Judged a fool or a coward by most, Rosecrans appeared to simply be overwhelmed, despite his earlier, competent performance. "It is hard to give up a popular idol," reflected Noah Brooks, the Washington reporter. "It is sad and disheartening that such things must be, but yet they must be, and it is a sufficient answer to all cavils to be able to say that no man in the nation was more pained at the necessity of the removal of General Rosecrans than was the President himself." For his part, the disappointed Lincoln simply told John Hay that Rosecrans seemed "confused and stunned like a duck hit on the head." On October 19 Rosecrans would be removed from command by U. S. Grant, who would come to Chattanooga to turn around the desperate situation. Thereafter, Rosecrans held only minor assignments.

On the Confederate side Bragg, gruff, argumentative, and demanding, found himself with few friends despite the victory. Ridiculed by many subordinate commanders for not aggressively pursuing the fleeing Yankees—

especially by Polk and Longstreet—Bragg found that as he moved his force into position around Chattanooga, few soldiers or officers in his army held any confidence in him. Yet as was almost always the case, the army was too depleted to further pursue the enemy, in terms of manpower and matériel.

Bragg blamed D. H. Hill for not following orders, and Buckner emerged as an anti-Bragg ally of Longstreet. On October 4, furious over what they envisioned as Bragg's incompetence, this core of general officers launched a cabal against Bragg by sending a petition to President Davis for his removal as commander of the Army of Tennessee. Written by Buckner, the document was signed by eleven general officers. Breckinridge hated Bragg so thoroughly that he declined to sign, believing his signature might actually dampen the chances of the petition taking effect. In the end, however, the signers decided not to submit the document to Davis, and it was filed with Longstreet's papers. Instead, Bragg held a council of war and listened as his corps commanders denounced his ability to lead the army. Polk assumed temporary command of the army, Hill was singled out and removed from his command, and Bragg resumed command of the Army of Tennessee by November 7.

Bickering among generals aside, the dead were now buried, albeit temporarily, on the battlefield, and the wounded survivors were shuttled into makeshift hospitals scattered across the land in the vicinity of the Chickamauga battlefield. Perhaps the most difficult job in the wake of a major battle was to deal with the wounded, whose suffering marked the true human specter of the battles. Confederate nurse Kate Cumming recorded her impressions of the wounded left behind at one field hospital. "As we rode out of the yard, I tried to look neither to the right nor the left, for I knew that many eyes were sadly gazing at us from their comfortless sheds and tents," she wrote. "I could do nothing for the poor fellows, and when that is the case, I try to steel my heart against their sorrows."

Fighting following the Chickamauga campaign and in eastern Tennessee (where Burnside thus far had accomplished little) continued. As the third autumn of war commenced, the Confederates were still besieged; the tremendous tactical success at Chickamauga did not turn around what was coming to be a desperate situation. Union armies, though exhausted, held Chattanooga. In Washington, continuing alarm over the battered condition of Rosecrans's army led to the largest reinforcement of troops in U.S. military history. In Chattanooga, during the last week of September, Assistant Secretary of War Charles A. Dana was greatly alarmed over the condition of the Federal army and its ability to hold the city. He telegraphed Stanton, who met with Lincoln and ordered the entire 11th and 12th Army corps (commanded by Maj. Gens. Oliver O. Howard and Henry W. Slocum, respectively), 23,300 men, 10 batteries, and all their equipment, horses, and mules, to move quickly by rail to Chattanooga. The Federal movement proceeded smoothly, for the most part, the troops moving from Virginia through Maryland to the Ohio River, through central Ohio to southern Indiana, and southward through Kentucky and Tennessee. By October 2 the first Federal troops from the Army of the Potomac would arrive at Bridgeport, Alabama, having traveled 1,159 miles in seven days. Longstreet, meanwhile, would move his force to eastern Tennessee to face Burnside, a second-rate assignment that nonetheless would be preferable to remaining with Bragg.

As the armies jockeyed for position in eastern Tennessee, a skirmish took place at Blountville, north of Johnson City, on September 22. Real activity commenced on September 30, however, when the Confederate cavalry Maj. Gen. Joseph Wheeler launched a raid to disrupt Rosecrans's lines of communications. Having pushed to within a few miles of Chattanooga and reported back to Bragg the condition of the Union army, Wheeler was strengthened before setting off on his raid and hearing that Bragg would settle into a siege of Chattanooga over the coming days. Among the many subordinates Bragg had frequently argued with was Nathan Bedford Forrest. At this critical time, Bragg ordered Forrest to turn his command over to Wheeler for the raid.

The raid began despite the shabby condition of the cavalry, and Wheeler's men skirmished on October 1 at Decatur, midway between Chattanooga and Knoxville. On October 2 skirmishing occurred at Anderson's Crossroads and the raiders reached the top of a high ridge over which they would need to pass. Wheeler then divided his command, taking 1,500 men into the valley below and sending the bulk of his men westward to McMinnville, where most of the gathering Federal stores were reported to be. Now pursued by Brig. Gen. George Crook's Union cavalry, Wheeler sped forward and captured 32 six-mule wagons loaded with supplies; many other wagons were abandoned, and the mules ran wild, overturning wagons and blocking roads for miles in complete chaos. At least 500 wagons were lost to the Federal resupply operation. This disaster for the Yankees considerably worsened the conditions of starving soldiers in Chattanooga because now a perilous sixty-mile route through the Sequatchie Valley had to be used to bring supplies. While Wheeler wreaked havoc on the supply train, Brig. Gens. Henry B. Davidson and John A. Wharton threatened the Union garrison at McMinnville, commanded by Andrew Johnson's son-in-law, Maj. Michael L. Patterson. Wharton threatened the town and demanded surrender, which he got, Patterson turning over 600 soldiers and $2 million worth of munitions and stores. The Rebels then took "boots, watch, pocket-book, money, and even finger-rings, or, in fact, anything that happened to please their fancy," reported Patterson. One Confederate horse soldier so liked the boots worn by a Union officer that he forced the man at gunpoint to sit down, strip them off, and hand them over.

Wheeler now headed for Murfreesboro, with Crook in hot pursuit. Wheeler sacked the town of Shelbyville on October 6, burned bridges (including one over Stones River), and ordered Davidson's division to fall back and unite with Brig. Gen. William T. Martin's infantry if threatened. Instead of accomplishing this, Davidson fell back to Farmington, a few miles west of Shelbyville, where he fought a five-hour engagement with Yankee cavalry. The Confederate horsemen then scattered quickly to the Tennessee River, where they crossed on October 9 near the head of Muscle Shoals. As he had at Fort Donelson, Wheeler again led Forrest's troops to an unsuccessful conclusion. Forrest, far away and already in a foul mood, could not muster kind thoughts about his fellow cavalryman.

Although the campaign for Knoxville really heated up in November, preliminary actions occurred during the two previous months. In early September, Burnside's Army of the Ohio occupied Knoxville and dispatched a column to attack and secure Cumberland Gap from the south. Simultaneously, from Kentucky, advance elements of the Federal 9th Corps (Brig. Gen. Robert B. Potter) were ordered to move on Cumberland Gap. On September 9 a Confederate brigade commanded by Col. John W. Frazer, 2,000 strong, surrendered. The Union 23d Corps (Maj. Gen. George L. Hartsuff), meanwhile, moved eastward to meet the threat from Maj. Gen. Samuel Jones's Confederate force in western Virginia. At Blue Springs, Tennessee, on October 10, elements of the 9th Corps scattered the Confederates, who had to withdraw in haste. Potter's 9th Corps then returned to duty at Knoxville and guarded railroads leading into the city, as the 23d Corps protected the Tennessee River southwest of the city, between Loudon and Kingston. The division of Brig. Gen. Orlando B. Willcox was sent to Jonesborough to protect against another Rebel intrusion from western Virginia.

Rainy weather and long, difficult routes of supply were taking a toll on the soldiers in Chattanooga. Many of the men were sick; all were discouraged, heartbroken over the crushing loss at Chickamauga, and depressed over the lack of food and sloppy conditions. None had much faith left in Rosecrans after his hasty retreat from the field. Horses within the city began dying of starvation. The majority of Hooker's men who shifted from the east arrived at Nashville by October 4 and began guarding the railroad line to Stevenson, Alabama. Dissatisfied with the entire scheme before him, Lincoln ordered a reorganization of the command in the west. He assigned Maj. Gen. Ulysses S. Grant command of the sprawling Military Division of the Mississippi, which gave Grant sway over all troops from the Mississippi River to the Alleghenies, with the exception of Banks at New Orleans. Grant advised Lincoln to replace Rosecrans with Maj. Gen. George H. Thomas, the hero of Chickamauga. Thomas was ordered by Grant to hold Chattanooga at all costs, and Grant himself set out for the place, arriving to take charge of the situation on October 23. Grant was probably relieved to be in a new location: while reviewing Banks's troops near Carrollton, Louisiana, on September 4, his horse reared in the presence of a locomotive and fell on him, injuring his leg. Painful bed rest in Vicksburg followed, and he walked only with crutches. As he arrived at Chattanooga, he again fell from his horse, reinjuring the leg. Maj. Gen. Gordon Granger was assigned command of a new 4th Corps, which replaced those units of the discredited Crittenden and McCook. Maj. Gen. John M. Palmer was assigned command of Thomas's 14th Corps.

The situation was indeed desperate, with men as well as animals now starving in the city. By the last days of October the Federal soldiers were reduced to "four cakes of hard bread and a quarter-pound of pork" every three days. The tomblike city saw little action, with a few Confederate shells occasionally raining down from the heights ringing the city, a few crackles of musketry lighting the ridges with flashes at dusk and dawn. But mostly the pickets watched each other warily and even wandered close to trade stories or coffee or tobacco as they could, and took no shots at all.

IN THE EAST the armies were on the move again in a campaign that would result in relatively little action. Following Gettysburg, the Army of Northern Virginia moved slowly back up the Shenandoah Valley to its old familiar ground. Both armies had been battered at Gettysburg; neither was in shape for a major fight again without significant rebuilding and resupplying. Meade's Army of the Potomac crossed the Potomac and pursued southward very slowly, the Federal commander constantly on the watch for Lee's 50,000 men to be reinforced by Bragg or other forces. Meade's 83,000 men rapidly marched across the Blue Ridge and southward past Upperville and along the Manassas Gap Railroad, positioning themselves by the end of July along a wide line north of the Rappahannock River from Jefferson, Virginia, in the west, to east of Rappahannock Station. Meade's elements were in place along this line before Lee's men were fully in position to the south at Culpeper Court House; for a time, near Manassas Gap, Meade considered an attack on Lee's flank, but he sent Maj. Gen. William H. French ahead to lead the expedition, and French, overcautious, backed away from the initiative. Despite the military setbacks of the period, heads were held high in Richmond. "The hour now seems a dark one," proclaimed the war clerk John B. Jones. "But we must conquer or die. . . . It is said a deserter has already gone over from our lines and given information to the enemy of the large number of troops detached from the Army of Virginia. No doubt Gen. Meade will take advantage of their absence, and advance on Richmond again. Yet I am told the very *name* of Richmond is a terror to the foe."

The principal eastern army of the Confederacy, now back on its home ground, faced a critical dilemma during the early autumn of 1863. Lee badly wanted to seize the initiative and launch an offensive operation, but this time President Davis and other commanders won out, and Longstreet had gone off to support Bragg while other units of the army were sent to Charleston. Thus, during the time frame of the Chickamauga campaign, the Army of Northern Virginia was mostly in a holding pattern. But Meade discovered Longstreet's absence and sent his cavalry across the Rappahannock on September 13, driving Jeb Stuart's troopers southward. Meade surged forward with his infantry, now 77,000 strong (versus Lee's 47,000), occupying Culpeper. This forced Lee southward across the Rapidan to his new concentration east of Clark's Mountain. On the eve of Meade's planned turning movement against Lee's army, designed to cave its line and inflict heavy casualties, came word of Rosecrans's disastrous defeat at Chickamauga. With the midnight conference in Washington carrying away the 11th and 12th Army corps, so went Meade's ambitions for a major attack to be carried out in this way. On October 9, Lee, not Meade, moved advanced elements of his army out around the western edge of Cedar Mountain and then turned northward, hoping to turn Meade's right and perhaps even move on Washington. Thus began the Bristoe campaign, which lasted through late October and amounted to little save for positioning and skirmishing.

Union troops probing the advancing columns of Lee's men skirmished extensively along the Rapidan River on October 10. Meade believed the Confederates were moving into the Shenandoah Valley and only after several days surmised their intention of falling back to strike his flank. The major action of the campaign came on October 14 at Bristoe Station, along the Orange & Alexandria Railroad, south of Manassas. Approaching the Union rear guard and believing the 3d Corps (French) was isolated, A. P. Hill attacked it without knowing of the Federal 2d Corps, commanded temporarily by Brig. Gen. John C. Caldwell, which had taken up entrenched positions behind the railroad embankment.

A Confederate advance by the brigades of Brig. Gens. John R. Cooke and William W. Kirkland met galling musketry fire and artillery; charging the Union position, the brigades were cut to pieces, 700 men in Cooke's brigade alone becoming casualties. Both Cooke and Kirkland were wounded, and altogether Lee lost 1,900 men in the action. The Mississippi Brig. Gen. Carnot Posey was struck in the left thigh by a shell fragment and died in Charlottesville a month later. Following the debacle, Lee, grown hardened by the war and feeling his age with increasing severity, simply told A. P. Hill, who would take a beating over the battle as evidence that he could not rise to the level of competence of a Jackson or Longstreet, "Well, well, General, bury these poor men and let us say no more about it."

Simultaneous fighting also occurred nearby at Catlett's Station. This cavalry skirmish took place as the Union infantry brigades of Brig. Gen. Joshua T. Owen and the 12th New Jersey Infantry thwarted an attack of Jeb Stuart's cavalry. On the 18th, Lee's army began to withdraw from the area, and a final significant action of the campaign occurred the following day when cavalry clashed at Buckland Mills. Stuart regained some measure of confidence in this action by routing Brig. Gen. Judson Kilpatrick's cavalry and capturing as many as 250 prisoners. (Confederate sources termed the Union retreat the "Buckland Races.") Small skirmishing accompanied the return to former positions along the Rappahannock and Rapidan rivers, as musketry flared along the Rappahannock Bridge on October 22.

Lee's men had exhausted their supplies midway through this ill-executed campaign. After his army's return southward, Lee and his fellow officers seemed embittered. He had a severe cold in early September, which aggravated his rheumatism, and he felt old. In October he was confined to his headquarters tent during most of the month, and he could neither mount nor ride Traveller; the pain was too severe. His hair and beard were turning from gray to white. His admonition from Davis to stay in command after Gettysburg aside, Lee must have felt that his days as a field commander were dwindling.

AGAIN THE CHANCE OF ENDING the war under the spell of warm weather vanished. Cold temperatures ushered in more despair, and the dying and killing continued for common soldiers and officers alike. On October 31, in Rockland County, New York, Brig. Gen. Louis Blenker died. The eccentric Bavarian commander had never recovered from his fall in early 1862 when the full weight of his horse slammed down on his body. His liver function was impaired and Blenker's trouble with his hepatic system only worsened until he passed away. Angered by the waste and death, other commanders were sharpening their vision of the responsibility for the war and its growing, as yet uncounted, casualties. William T. Sherman brooded over such questions and, when asked about possibilities for Reconstruction, grimly determined that the war must be carried out to the extreme in order to preserve the American nation. "The young Bloods of the South, sons of Planters, Lawyers about Town, good billiard-players and sportsmen," Sherman wrote Halleck, "men who never did work, or never will. War suits them, and the rascals are brave, fine riders, bold to rashness, and dangerous subjects in every sense. . . . They must all be killed, or employed by us before we can hope for Peace. . . . In accepting war it should be pure & simple as applied to the Belligerents. I would Keep it so, till all traces of the war are effaced; till those who appealed to it are sick & tired of it, and come to the emblem of our Nation and Sue for Peace. I would not coax them, or even meet them half-way, but make them so sick of war that Generations would pass away before they would again appeal to it."

CHAPTER 19

The Battles for Chattanooga

As THE WEATHER TURNED COLDER over the last days of October 1863, the situation for the Union army in Chattanooga, bottled up amid the hills ringing the city, was still desperate. The long and imperiled supply line established through the hamlet of Anderson's, north of the city, was ineffective at routing supplies to the hungry troops. Under Grant's supervision, George Thomas, celebrated since his defensive maneuver at Chickamauga, came into action again. He determined to devise and open a route of supply from Confederate-occupied Bridgeport, Alabama, pushing supplies eastward across the Memphis & Charleston Railroad to Wauhatchie, where they would be unloaded, brought north to Brown's Ferry, west of the city, and ferried across the Tennessee River and a peninsula of land called Moccasin Point into the Union garrison. It was an ambitious plan, and required seizing control of Bridgeport as well as the railroad line; but desperate times call for desperate measures, and Thomas rose to the occasion.

The Federal army in Chattanooga had been holed up for nearly a month, and, as their Confederate brethren had been at Vicksburg, was now on the brink of starvation. When the rare bit of salt pork or beef was issued, every few days, most of the specimens were rancid and full of worms. The men were suffering, lethargic, thinning down from a lean start even when they were "healthy." The early onset of autumn also brought cold downpours of rain, and barely adequate clothing increased the suffering. As men held on to life as best they could, the rates of disease growing day by day, animals died off more quickly and had even less to eat. Capt. Jeremiah Donahower of the 2d Minnesota Infantry described seeing the horses of Battery I, 4th U.S. Artillery, slowly succumbing. They became "too weak to walk to the usual watering place, and as they stood day after day in line along their picket ropes with their noses near the ground, growing leaner and weaker, they drew on our sympathies, but we could do nothing for them."

The situation on October 25 saw Thomas's Army of the Cumberland inside the city of Chattanooga (altitude about 750 feet), down near the river, mostly inhabiting a series of defensive lines collectively termed Fort Wood. The wide Tennessee River made a U-shaped curve past the city, around Moccasin Point, and aimed north again up to Brown's Ferry, west of the city. Near Brown's Ferry, Brig. Gen. Evander M. Law's Confederate brigade guarded the river approach; rugged Raccoon Mountain stood to the west. A tad less than five miles south of the ferry was the railroad junction at Wauhatchie; Lookout Creek ran alongside a portion of the rail line. Wauhatchie stood in a valley between Raccoon Mountain and Lookout Mountain (2,146 feet), a sharp promontory south of Moccasin Point, on which a tiny village, Summertown, had existed in stillness to this point in its history. A prominent house stood on the northern shoulder of Lookout Mountain, the residence of Robert Cravens, a gleaming clapboard structure visible from the city and called by the soldiers the "White House on the Bench." East of the city ran the formidable form of Missionary Ridge (1,128 feet), another north-south mountain, which towered over the city. Longstreet's Confederates occupied the valley between Lookout Mountain and Missionary Ridge; the divisions of Breckinridge and Cheatham were spread along the face of Missionary Ridge, with the Confederate picket line extending down into the valley to a prominent, stubby hill, Orchard Knob, between the outer limits of Fort Wood and Missionary Ridge.

The opposing forces in operation over the following month, in what would come to be termed the battles for Chattanooga, were reorganized somewhat from the Chickamauga campaign. The heavy action came in late November, and the forces are given for this time interval. Grant was now in overall command of the Federal forces in the area and was present for the Chattanooga operations. Thomas led the Army of the Cumberland; his corps commanders were Maj. Gen. Gordon Granger (4th Corps; divisions of Maj. Gen. Phil Sheridan and Brig. Gens. Charles Cruft and Thomas J. Wood), and Maj. Gen. John M. Palmer (14th Corps; divisions of Brig. Gens. Richard W. Johnson, Jefferson C. Davis, and Absalom Baird); Maj. Gen. Joseph Hooker commanded the 11th and 12th corps together (as well as portions of the 4th, 14th, and 15th corps). The 11th Corps was led by Maj. Gen. Oliver O. Howard (divisions of Maj. Gen. Carl Schurz and Brig. Gen. Adolph von Steinwehr), and the 2d Division of the 12th Corps by Brig. Gen. John W. Geary. In addition, Maj. Gen. William T. Sherman's Army of the Tennessee participated in some of the fighting at Chattanooga, comprising the corps of Maj. Gen. Frank P. Blair, Jr. (15th Corps; divisions of Brig. Gens. Peter J. Osterhaus, Morgan L. Smith, and Hugh Ewing) and the 2d Division of the 17th Corps, led by Brig. Gen. John E. Smith.

Bragg, still despised by most of his subordinates and not communicating with most of them, established headquarters on Missionary Ridge. His force consisted of Hardee's corps (Lt. Gen. William J. Hardee, divisions of Maj. Gens. Carter L. Stevenson and Patrick R. Cleburne, and Brig. Gens. John K. Jackson [Cheatham's division] and States Rights Gist [Walker's division]) and Breckinridge's Corps (Maj. Gen. John C. Breckinridge, divisions of Maj. Gen. Alexander P. Stewart and Brig. Gens. J. Patton Anderson [Hindman's division] and William B. Bate [Breckinridge's division]). Longstreet's corps fought early in the campaign but was detached on November 4 for operations in eastern Tennessee. It consisted of the divisions of Maj. Gen. Lafayette McLaws and Lt. Gen. John Bell Hood (who was absent, having lost his leg at Chickamauga, being replaced by Brig. Gen. Micah Jenkins).

Thomas's creative solution to open the new route of supply came from his chief engineer, Brig. Gen. William F. Smith. A Vermonter by birth, "Baldy" Smith, age 39, had fought with some distinction on the Peninsula at White Oak Swamp and at Antietam, and now his engineering background led him to envision opening the so-called Cracker Line across Moccasin Point. As a heavy fog enveloped the area on the night of October 26, Thomas sent the brigade of Brig. Gen. William B. Hazen downstream on bridge pontoons, around Moccasin Bend, toward Brown's Ferry. The brigade of Brig. Gen. John B. Turchin moved westward across Moccasin Point. At 4:45 A.M. the following morning Hazen's regiments landed at the ferry, surprising Evander Law's brigade. The Ohio and Kentucky troops scattered the Confederates, and even the efforts of Col. William C. Oates's 15th Alabama Infantry, moved into the fight from the valley beyond, did not help. Small ferryboats carried Turchin's men across the river, and once the west bank was reached, the Union column advanced. Hazen told his men that "we had knocked the cover off the cracker box and plenty to eat was in sight if we would hold the ground we had gained." Though the movement was a success, Smith embroiled himself in a controversy over who could claim credit for the idea that smoldered for years, launching various attacks at Rosecrans and Grant for claiming the concept. In any case, aided by the steamboat *Chattanooga*, a tenuous line of supply was soon to be opened to relieve the 40,000 men and several thousand animals still in the city. On the 26th, the *Chattanooga* brought 40,000 rations and 39,000 pounds of forage to Hooker's force, which had only half a breakfast ration left in its haversacks. "In Chattanooga there were but four boxes of hard bread left in the commissary warehouses," wrote Capt. William G. Le Duc, an assistant quartermaster of the 11th Corps. The news of the arrival of new rations, Le Duc reported, "went through the camps faster than [a] horse, and the soldiers were jubilant, and cheering, 'The Cracker line open. Full rations, boys!' " While the Brown's Ferry skirmish occurred, Hooker detached a portion of the 12th Corps to guard the railroad and moved the remainder of his command westward to Bridgeport. By October 28 the route from Bridgeport was open and protected by Hooker.

Though the arrival of rations took place only three miles from Longstreet's headquarters, the Confederate commander remained oblivious to the action. South of the main body of Hooker's force, however, the division of Brig. Gen. John W. Geary was posted at Wauhatchie, and this was detected by Longstreet. After consultation, Bragg ordered a night attack at Wauhatchie, a rare event in the American Civil War. Longstreet ordered Evander Law to block the Brown's Ferry-Wauhatchie Road, preventing a movement back to the ferry by Geary, while Jenkins's (Hood's) division conducted the southward attack. In one of the most confused actions of the war (so chaotic that reconstruction on a regimental level defies description), Jenkins struck into Geary at Wauhatchie in the late evening of October 28. Col. John Bratton's (formerly Jenkins's) brigade led the assault, striking into Geary's picket line about midnight. Bratton's six regiments, some 1,800 men altogether, mostly South Carolinians, hit Geary's Pennsylvanians and New Yorkers hard along the Nashville & Chattanooga Railroad, near the Rowden House. The Palmetto Sharpshooters, meanwhile, were ordered to work around to the south and launch an enfilading fire into the Yankees. In the confused melee of darkness, with thick, oblong clouds rolling over the moon and casting odd shadows across the Wauhatchie Valley, the fighting intensified. Visibility was 100 yards at best, when beams of moonlight struck through; nominally the only real light visible over distance was the flash of musket barrels or cannon. Several Confederate attacks directed into the brigades of Brig. Gen. George S. Greene and Col. George A. Cobham, Jr., were driven back. In the process Greene one of the heroes of Gettysburg, received a ghastly wound when he was struck in the face with a ball that carried away all of his upper teeth, portions of his right cheek, and mangled the upper jawbone.

Several miles to the north, Hooker heard the firing and sent the fresh divisions of Steinwehr and Schurz on a southward march in support of Geary. As it marched southward near what came to be known as Smith's Hill, Brig. Gen. Hector Tyndale's Union brigade was fired on out of the darkness by Law's division of Alabama, Arkansas, and Texas men. Following brigades were halted and failed to reach Geary, but Tyndale's men struck into the Southerners near the Ellis House, east of Brown's Ferry Road. Repeated, ill-coordinated attacks failed in this region, accumulating numerous casualties on both sides. Col. Orland Smith's brigade struck frontally and then flanked the Confederate line, charging forward and springing the Confederates in a rout. A few minutes before 4 A.M., as the battle drew to a climax on Smith's Hill, Confederates suddenly found themselves endangered. "We gave a most unearthly yell," wrote Sgt. George Metcalf of the 136th New York Infantry. "It was a yell of fright, of terror. We were face to face with death. We fired our guns and yelled, and roared and screamed. If the rebels were not frightened, I was." Longstreet, outraged over the failure by Law, proffered charges against his subordinate that kept Law on the hot seat until the next year, when they were dropped.

Bludgeoned repeatedly and unable to push Geary or to flank him, despite the posted sharpshooters, Bratton's Confederates withdrew from their southward position at Wauhatchie. By dawn the fight was over and a bloody double battlefield emerged. Federal casualties were 78 killed, 327 wounded, and 15 missing; Confederate losses were 34 killed, 305 wounded, and 69 missing.

Following the senseless clash at Wauhatchie came a period of inactivity as both armies strengthened themselves—physically, organizationally, and emotionally—for the further battle action sure to come. The weather chilled. Bragg sent Longstreet off to attack Burnside at Knoxville. Sherman, newly in command of the Army of the Tennessee, was requested by Halleck to repair the damaged Memphis & Decatur Railroad on his way east, but Grant soon ordered Sherman forward at the quick and the latter arrived in Bridgeport by November 15. The division of Brig. Gen. Grenville M. Dodge was halted at Athens, Alabama, and proceeded with this important repair work. While Bragg waited, Grant unfolded a plan to dislodge him from the hills and push the Union movement southward into Georgia, simultaneously reducing the danger to Burnside. He ordered Sherman to speed toward Brown's Ferry, cross, and attack at Tunnel Hill on Missionary Ridge by November 21. As Sherman maneuvered southward, Thomas would attack northeastward, join forces with Sherman, and the two would sweep the Confederates off of Missionary Ridge and into northern Georgia. Hooker, positioned near Wauhatchie, would guard the Lookout Valley and would keep Howard in reserve near Brown's Ferry. The theory was sound, but the execution did not unfold as Grant had hoped, largely due to heavy, cold rains that characterized the third week of November. Sherman crossed at Brown's Ferry late, with the rains falling, and the bridge constructed for the purpose failed before the final division, that of Osterhaus, could cross. Grant simply detached Osterhaus to Hooker's command and ordered Hooker to prepare for the attack as well.

By the time Sherman's force was in position to attack, well north of the city and on the opposite bank of the Tennessee River, it was the night of November 23. Sherman had the division of Jeff C. Davis closest to the river; Osterhaus and Cruft were positioned near Brown's Ferry, Geary still down in the Lookout Valley, and the forward divisions of Thomas's army, the eastern-most, were those of Wood, Sheridan, and Baird. Confederate forces were scattered from Lookout Mountain to the south, where Stevenson's division was posted, eastward through the Lookout Valley (divisions of Jackson and Stewart) to a line stretched along Missionary Ridge, containing the divisions of Bate and Anderson. The weakened lines along Missionary Ridge pre-sented an opportunity for the aggressive Grant, and on November 23, Grant ordered Thomas to send forward divisions to reconnoiter the Confederate front to see whether Bragg's army might be preparing to withdraw. The ob-jective for Wood's division, consisting of mostly midwestern boys from Ohio, Indiana, Illinois, and Kentucky, would be the steep knoll known as Orchard Knob, 2,000 yards east of Fort Wood. Some 8,000 men formed as if marching in a parade drill, with bands playing and flags unfurled, and the Confederate pickets at Orchard Knob looked on with puzzlement. "Flags were flying; the quick, earnest steps of thousands beat equal time," expressed Lt. Col. Joseph S. Fullerton of Granger's staff. "The sharp commands of hundreds of com-pany officers, the sound of drums, the ringing notes of the bugles, companies wheeling and counter-marching and regiments getting into line, the bright sun lighting up ten thousand polished bayonets till they glistened and flashed like a flying shower of electric sparks—all looked like preparations for a peaceful pageant, rather than for the bloody work of death."

All along the Confederate line this amazing display of Federal bravado halted actions as officers gazed through their field glasses and privates scratched their heads. Atop Missionary Ridge, Bragg and his chief subordi-nates guessed that the distant exercise was certainly a review staged for Grant's entertainment; the work simply didn't have the appearance of a mil-itary reconnaissance waiting to happen. At 1:30 P.M. Union troops blew the bugle command to start their forward march, and Yankees marched toward Orchard Knob at the double-quick, unharassed by Confederate fire until they had marched 800 yards and come to within close range of Orchard Knob, emerging from a patch of nearby woods. The resulting action, termed Orchard Knob or Indian Hill (another rise south of Orchard Knob), amazed those within it and provided many stories for later telling and retelling after the great war. Musketry shots rang out as Confederates atop Orchard Knob suddenly sprang to action and were greeted with a brisk small-arms fire from the onrushing Yankees; this brought into action the field guns on Missionary Ridge, which belched plumes of smoke and sent shells lobbing down toward the Union columns. Union artillery answered from Forts Wood and Negley in the city, and soon some 600 Confederates on Orchard Knob discovered the uncomfortable fact that they stood in the path of 14,000 approaching bluecoats. Two Confederate regiments, the 24th and 28th Alabama in-fantries, were so arrayed that a gap existed between the two. Hazen's Union brigade struck fast at the Alabamians and scurried the Rebels away from the position as the Union men rushed onto Orchard Knob.

The attack was a stunning success, sending waves of excitement through the Federal command. Observing the movement, Grant was in turn observed by others. One such writer William Wrenshall Smith, noted that Grant seemed "well pleased with what was accomplished" and seemed "perfectly cool, and one could be with him for hours and not know that any great movements were going on. It is a mere matter of business with him." Charles A. Dana, the newspaperman and special assistant to the War Department (dispatched to serve as Stanton's mobile eyes and ears) was in town keeping a watchful eye on the ever more powerful Grant. Dana believed that with Orchard Knob and Indian Hill in possession of the Federals, it was now impossible for Bragg to mount a counterattack toward the northern end of Missionary Ridge. Bragg, meanwhile, fell into a panic after failing to anticipate any such move by the Federal army. He sent repeated messages to Cleburne, whom he had just ordered to eastern Tennessee, calling him back to the city. He fussed over the structure of Hardee's command, which had replaced Longstreet in guarding a possible flanking movement at Lookout Mountain. He now impulsively ordered Hardee to take most of his force and harass the strong, forward Federal position, in effect reducing the defense of Lookout Mountain to just a brigade.

Even before the now hapless Bragg contemplated shifting strength from his left to his right, Sherman had initiated his movement toward the northern end of Missionary Ridge. Sherman crossed the Tennessee River and by 1 P.M. drove his four divisions toward Tunnel Hill, a spur of mountain detached from the main part of Missionary Ridge, south of which stood a prominent railroad tunnel. By 4 P.M. his force had secured the northernmost end of Missionary Ridge without firing into anything more formidable than scattered Confederate pickets. But faulty "intelligence"—poor maps and lack of reconnaissance—came into play and stalled Sherman's driving movement when the grizzled Ohioan and his subordinate officers found a wide gully separating the rise they occupied from Tunnel Hill. Another unexpected surprise came in the form of Cleburne's division, which after the alarming recall from Bragg had deployed itself along the crest of Tunnel Hill. Stopped cold, Sherman ordered his men to entrench.

On the other Union flank, Hooker moved his three divisions into the valley east of Lookout Mountain to occupy Rossville Gap. With a battle underway, Hooker's previous mission of protecting lines of communication through Lookout Valley had evaporated, and Howard was withdrawn into the city. Bridging difficulties near the city precluded Hooker's three divisions from moving in that direction and so they were ordered on November 24 to attack the remaining Confederate forces at Lookout Mountain. Thus the stage was set for one of the most curious actions of the war, and one that has been overdramatized. Though fog hugged the mountain that day, the battle of Lookout Mountain's claim as "the battle above the clouds" is romanticized lore—it was more like the battle with fog and mist. Confederates had mostly withdrawn from the mountain and continued holding it simply to protect against a Union advance from Trenton, on the rail line southward into Lookout Valley. Certainly, the terrain was dramatic: Lookout Mountain's summit features a relatively flat area that drops sharply some 1,100 feet to the valley floor and river below.

Only two Confederate brigades occupied the summit of Lookout Mountain, that of Brig. Gen. Edward C. Walthall on the northern slope and to the south, Brig. Gen. John C. Moore's brigade. Farther south on Lookout Mountain were the brigades of Brig. Gens. John C. Brown and Edmund W. Pettus. Hooker deployed his men about 8 A.M., sending Geary's division across Lookout Creek with Osterhaus and Cruft following. Attacking northward, along the mountain's western base and marching steadily upward, Hooker's men struck into Walthall's brigade about 10:30 A.M., pushing the pickets into the area of the Cravens Farm, the "White House on the Bench." Crackles of musketry rang out across the face of the mountain's northern slopes and echoed throughout the valley below. Footing was uncertain at best; thick stands of timber, mostly cedar and spruce, covered the mountainside, and as Yankee troops climbed higher, they stumbled on rocky outcrops and found the fog only thickened. As Geary advanced, he saw a cloud bank "hovering above us," and "fogs darkening the hills below." Yet between the two apparitions was clear sky, as if "our path [was] a well-defined stratum," he recorded. As the mostly New York front line of soldiers charged and fired, the Mississippi troops withdrew in haste to the north. Dozens of Confederates were struck by bullets from the sudden attack, which seemed to emerge out of the ether, and many dropped their rifles and fled, stunned by the Yankee onslaught.

After noon the Union assault succeeded in driving the Confederates about 400 yards from the Cravens House, which had been struck by artillery and knocked to pieces, and the Confederates held fast until after midnight. They were then ordered to withdraw, yielding Lookout Mountain to Hooker's victorious attack. By 3 P.M. Hooker halted, running low on ammunition and yielding to the increasingly blinding fog. Shrouded in fog for most of the rest of November 24, the mountain gave up its secret the next day, when a party from the 8th Kentucky Infantry scaled the heights and planted a large national standard atop Lookout Mountain; the crisp, cool morning air, cleared for a time of fog, allowed vast numbers of the Union troops in Chattanooga to see their colors flying from the mountain, which at intervals produced wild cheers of joy.

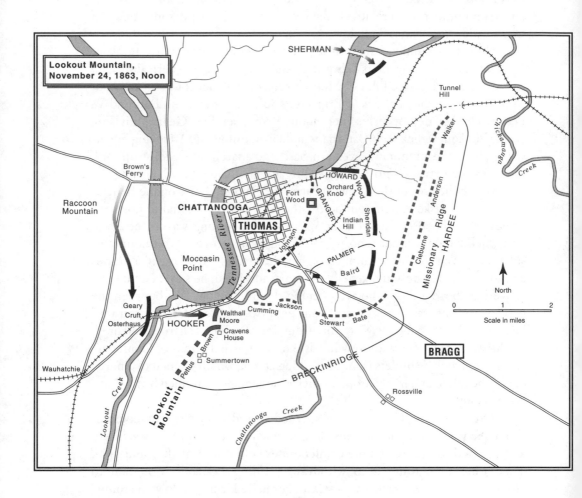

Lookout Mountain,
November 24, 1863, Noon

SHERMAN

Tunnel
Hill

Brown's
Ferry

Raccoon
Mountain

CHATTANOOGA

THOMAS

Moccasin
Point

HOWARD

Fort
Wood

Orchard
Knob

GRANGER

Wood

Sheridan

Indian
Hill

Johnson

PALMER

Baird

Cleburne

Anderson

Walker

Missionary Ridge

HARDEE

Chickamauga

Creek

North

0   1   2

Scale in miles

Geary
Cruft
Osterhaus

HOOKER

Cumming

Jackson

Walthall
Moore

Cravens
House

Pettus

Brown

Summertown

Stewart

Bate

BRECKINRIDGE

BRAGG

Rossville

Wauhatchie

Lookout
Mountain

Lookout

Creek

Chattanooga

Creek

Tennessee River

On the night of November 24, Bragg withdrew Cheatham's and Stevenson's divisions eastward across Chattanooga Creek, attempting to solidify his increasingly formidable line along the crest of Missionary Ridge. Chewing on his customary cigar, Grant now altered his battle plan for the following day, November 25. He now conceived of an envelopment on both ends of the Rebel line, Hooker on the south and Sherman on the north, while Thomas, in the center, would advance frontally only when Hooker reached the southern end of Missionary Ridge above Rossville. A twin line of entrenchments was constructed along Missionary Ridge (one line of rifle pits along the mountain's western base and another at its crest), with Breckinridge (divisions of Stewart, Bate, and Anderson) along the main body of the ridge and Hardee (divisions of Walker and Cleburne) facing off Sherman to the north. A third, central line of entrenchments—halfway up the mountain's western face—had been partially constructed between the two occupied lines. Grant, accompanied by an assortment of subordinate generals, onlookers, and official observers from Washington, established headquarters at Orchard Knob. By midnight he sent word to Sherman to attack at dawn, similarly ordering Hooker forward, pushing onward as soon as morning light came to reach Rossville Gap.

"No firing at the front," Charles Dana recorded at 7:30 A.M. "This makes it pretty certain Bragg retreated." But that could hardly have been further from the truth. By midmorning the division of Sherman's foster brother and brother-in-law, Brig. Gen. Hugh B. Ewing, attacked southward. Brig. Gen. John M. Corse's brigade of Illinois, Iowa, and Ohio boys spearheaded the movement toward Tunnel Hill, with Brig. Gen. Joseph A. J. Lightburn's brigade following over Billy Goat Hill and south toward the railroad tunnel. Brig. Gen. Morgan L. Smith's division proceeded in support, along the eastern slope of the hill, and several brigades moved along the hill's western slope in support of Corse.

Corse moved his midwesterners out under a galling musketry fire to a position about 80 yards shy of the Confederate battlefront north of the railroad tunnel, a position held by the mostly Texas troops of Smith's and Lewis's brigades. For more than an hour Corse sent repeated attacks forward, only to be met by heavy musketry volleys from the Confederate front, and accruing casualties. Union regiments on Corse's right and left temporarily gained some ground but were only weakly supported by artillery because of the difficult terrain, and Corse was shot in the leg and taken from the field. Sherman's attack on the tunnel was getting nowhere. The fighting along this area raged on until 3 P.M. with little positive result for the Union cause. Numerous Federal men were killed, wounded, and captured in the melee that washed back and forth near the tunnel. First Lt. Samuel H. M. Byers of the 5th Iowa Infantry was one of those captured. "In a moment I reflected that I was a prisoner," he recalled, "and horrible pictures of Libby and Andersonville flashed through my mind—and with them the presentiment of evil I had had the night before the assault."

Hooker, meanwhile, was encountering as much trouble as the stymied Sherman. Delayed by nearly five hours by bridge troubles (the retreating Confederates had wrecked the span across Chattanooga Creek), Hooker's men were not even close to posing a threat to the Confederate left until late afternoon. As Sherman's bludgeoning attack continued, Bragg reinforced his right so that Cleburne had little trouble continuing his defense against Sherman, who had perhaps his worst experience as a commander, first miscalculating the terrain and then stumbling through a prolonged, unsuccessful, and needless attack. Grant, meanwhile adapted skillfully to the emerging crisis. He shifted Howard's divisions into support of the failing Sherman assault and held Thomas back from launching the frontal movement without initial success on the wings. Bloody fighting continued on Sherman's front throughout the early afternoon, and Grant ordered Baird's division to move from Indian Hill to support the action. By late afternoon Hooker began to contact the Confederate left, sending skirmishers from the 27th Missouri Infantry forward into Rossville Gap and the remainder of Wood's brigade forward, pushing the Confederates in the area away and capturing numerous stores and supplies. Surmounting his bridge troubles, Hooker then sent Cruft, Geary, and Osterhaus forward into a driving movement that struck the Confederate left along Missionary Ridge, resuscitating Hooker's reputation as a corps commander (if not an army commander). As it advanced, the battle line formed by the 9th and 36th Indiana infantries fired hotly into the soldiers of Clayton's brigade. Though the Confederate left was endangered, it was now 3 P.M., and Grant began to show great concern over achieving more success by nightfall; Sherman's attack was still a nonstarter. Grant ordered a general assault over the center that would push the divisions of Baird, Wood, Sheridan, and Johnson forward to seize the rifle pits along the base of Missionary Ridge. A short time after 3 P.M. six cannon shots were fired to signal the advance, and what followed would astonish observers on both sides like few events of the war.

Arrayed in position for an assault, Thomas's army set out marching eastward toward the base of Missionary Ridge in full view of the enemy, with their bayonets glistening in the daylight and shells bursting above them in the expansive valley. As they marched, the pace quickened. On Missionary Ridge, the sight was quickly emblazoned onto the memories of many officers and men as one of the grand spectacles of the war. "Such a sight I never saw either before or after," recollected Brig. Gen. Arthur M. Manigault, "and I trust . . . never to see again." Many Civil War battles, as we have seen, were tightly constricted by regimental, brigade, or division commanders, scripted

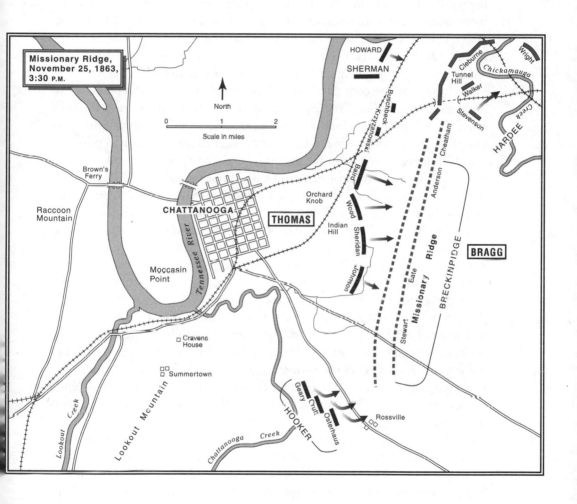

Missionary Ridge,
November 25, 1863,
3:30 P.M.

North

0   1   2
Scale in miles

HOWARD
SHERMAN
Cleburne
Chickamauga
Tunnel Hill
Walker
Stevenson
HARDEE
Wright

Buschbeck
Krzyzanowski

Brown's
Ferry

Baird

Orchard Knob

CHATTANOOGA

THOMAS

Indian Hill

Wood

Anderson
Cheatham

BRAGG

Raccoon
Mountain

Sheridan

Eate

Missionary Ridge

BRECKINPIDGE

Johnson

Moccasin Point

Stewart

Tennessee River

Cravens House

Summertown

Geary
Cruft
Osterhaus

Rossville

HOOKER

Lookout Creek

Lookout Mountain

Chattanooga Creek

and controlled within reason by a plan that was if not always followed exactly, at least adhered to in principle. But the battle of Missionary Ridge was a soldier's battle in the truest sense of the word, an action that occurred not as planned but by the fortitude of the individual soldiers in the ranks. As the soldiers moved forward with Grant, Thomas, and other officers observing them with field glasses on Orchard Knob, they surged into the rifle pits, firing wildly and scattering most of the Confederates, and then—to everyone's utter amazement—started scurrying up the steep, rocky face of Missionary Ridge itself. Part sheer determination and courage, part an avoidance of remaining at the mountain's base where they would continue to be exposed to small-arms fire, the Union soldiers scaled the face of the ridge.

Present at the command post along with the two commanders were Thomas J. Wood; Gordon Granger; Baldy Smith; Charles Dana; Grant's chief of staff, Brig. Gen. John A. Rawlins; and the army's quartermaster general, Brig. Gen. Montgomery C. Meigs. The bedazzled Grant reportedly asked Thomas who ordered the men up the hill and stated that there would be explaining to do if "it turned out badly." Grant wondered if Thomas ordered the men up. No, answered the Rock. Was it Granger? He also denied responsibility, replying to Grant, "When those fellows get started all hell can't stop them." "The line ceased to be a line," Meigs recalled of the Federal advance. "The men gathered toward the points of least difficult ascent, for very steep is this hill-side, a horse cannot ascend or descend except by the obliquely graded roads. The three colors approach the summit, another mass, gathered gradually into a confused column or stream, at another point directly, in our front, reaches the summit, the color bearer springs forward and plants his flag upon the crest, a gun gallops wildly to the right, cheer upon cheer rings out from the actors and spectators. The men swarm up, color after color reaches the summit, and the rebel line is divided and the confused, astonished and terrified rebels fly this way and that to meet enemies, every way but down the rear slope of the ridge and by this way they mostly escape."

The Confederates scurried into a retreat, having lost the crest of Missionary Ridge, 37 field guns, about 2,000 prisoners, and numerous casualties in an hour-long final assault. The attack was instantly memorable, but it had been unplanned and benefited from another round of Bragg's mistakes. The Confederate commander had posted the riflemen along the base of Missionary Ridge and informed some but not all that he wanted them to fire when Union troops approached within 200 yards *and then retreat*; many Confederate gunners held their position long enough to be overrun and captured. By dividing his army into two widely separated lines, Bragg ensured its weakness after the first line had been conquered. The artillery posted along the crest of Missionary Ridge could successfully lob shells onto the approaching

Yankees, but once the Yankees got close, at the base of the mountain, the guns could not be aimed low enough to strike them and they were effectively useless against the hill-climbing infantry. The weirdly disorganized Union advance created, by chance, pockets of concentration from which Federal soldiers unleashed enfilading rifle fire into the staggered Confederates. It was an entirely unplanned brilliant move. Sheridan was in essence the only Federal commander to maintain any cohesion as his men moved up the hill, and he nearly captured Bragg and Breckinridge in addition to other high-ranking Rebel officers as his men overran the position of Bragg's headquarters. "The disaster admits of no palliation and is justly disparaging to me as a commander," wrote Bragg, in a letter to Jefferson Davis. "I trust, however, you may find on full investigation that the fault is not entirely mine." Once again, Bragg had stumbled and raised the distrust and anger of much of the Confederacy against him, and again his friendship with the Confederate president would save him from fallout. In fact, the following spring Bragg would be "charged with the military operations of the Confederate States," becoming a live-in special advisor to the president.

But Bragg's loss of Chattanooga was a terrible blow to the Confederacy. Grant was unable to mount an effective pursuit, and during the night Bragg withdrew toward Dalton. Of the approximately 56,000 Union troops engaged, losses amounted to 753 killed, 4,722 wounded, and 349 missing; of 46,000 Confederates engaged, casualties were 361 killed, 2,160 wounded, and 4,146 missing (mostly prisoners). Tired of the death and destruction, asked by a chaplain whether or not the dead should be sorted and buried by state, Thomas, who had again showed himself to be an able army commander, replied, "Mix 'em up. I'm tired of States' Rights."

As the action at Chattanooga unfolded, so did the machinations of Burnside and Longstreet in eastern Tennessee. The campaign that was now unfolding in the pro-Union portion of the Volunteer State was considered critically important by the Lincoln administration, principally because of the strong Union backing in the state's mountainous counties. The roots of this action went back to March 1863, when Maj. Gen. Ambrose Burnside had taken command of the Army and Department of the Ohio. Burnside's orders were to move as swiftly as possible toward an attack on Knoxville, while Rosecrans was urged to move against Bragg (resulting in the Chickamauga and Chattanooga campaigns). By the end of May, Burnside had organized two corps (the 9th and 23d) and was ready for a movement but suddenly had to dispatch the 9th Corps to aid Grant's late stages of the Vicksburg campaign. While he waited for his 9th Corps's return, Burnside dispatched Brig. Gen. William P. Sanders forward with a brigade to strike at Knoxville with a force of cavalry and infantry. On June 14, Sanders's men moved forward and disrupted communications over a wide area as well as destroying railroad bridges.

Confederate response to Burnside's threat was initially handled by Maj. Gen. Simon B. Buckner, commander of the Department of East Tennessee, who had surrendered Fort Donelson to Grant. After a month-long temporary command by Brig. Gen. William Preston in July, the department was folded and the District of East Tennessee created, which was commanded by Buckner (until early September), Maj. Gen. Samuel Jones (through early December), and Lt. Gen. James Longstreet (from December 1863 until the following March).

By August 15, Burnside began a cautious advance into eastern Tennessee. At the start of the Chickamauga campaign, Buckner was ordered south to Chattanooga. By September 2, then, Burnside was able to occupy Knoxville. Following the Union victories at Cumberland Gap in September and Blue Springs in October, Longstreet was detached from the Chattanooga campaign to head off the threat from Burnside. Due in part to the fact that Longstreet simply couldn't bear to be near Bragg any longer (he felt just as the majority of Bragg's comrades did), Jefferson Davis unwisely dispatched the easterner to eastern Tennessee. This weakened Bragg considerably, helping to set up the probability for failure at Chattanooga, just as it led to a trail of futility in Tennessee. As Longstreet readied his troops for movement by rail, a skirmish erupted at Rogersville, northwest of Andrew Johnson's hometown of Greeneville, on November 6. A brisk attack by forces commanded by Maj. Gen. Robert Ransom, Jr., scattered and demoralized the Union cavalry and infantry in the area. Most of the 7th Ohio Cavalry and the 2d East Tennessee Mounted Infantry was shot to pieces or captured by Confederates under Ransom and by Brig. Gen. Grumble Jones's horsemen.

Longstreet's force reached Loudon, southwest of Knoxville, by November 12. As he had at Chickamauga, Longstreet commanded the divisions of McLaws and Hood (led by Micah Jenkins), and he was assigned the cavalry of Maj. Gen. Joe Wheeler, giving him about 10,000 infantry and 5,000 cavalry. Wheeler first struck at the city by dispatching two of his brigades to guard the railroad at Athens and then crossing the Little Tennessee River, scattering the Federal horsemen in his path. On November 15 he approached Knoxville from the south and aimed at occupying the heights overlooking the city from the south bank of the Holston River. Knoxville was a town of just 3,704 citizens, many of whom were huddled in the city; some had already left as refugees. But the Federal horsemen of William Sanders thwarted Wheeler's plan, assisted by the gun embrasures in the forts on the river's southern bank. Abandoning his initial plan, Wheeler rejoined Longstreet on the river's northern side.

On November 14, Longstreet began his own movement against Burnside's men. He erected a bridge across the Tennessee River west of Loudon and crossed his infantry and two battalions of artillery. Moving swiftly, the Confederates pursued Burnside, who withdrew hastily into the Knoxville forts. At Campbell's Station the Union 9th Corps (Brig. Gen. Robert B. Potter), one division of the 23d Corps, and Sanders's cavalry fought a delaying action that covered the Federal withdrawal. Both sides raced toward the crossroads at Campbell's Station (southwest of the city), securing the route of march, and Col. John F. Hartranft's division beat the Confederate division of McLaws to the punch, as Col. William Humphrey's brigade resisted Jenkins's pursuit. Federal supply trains moved swiftly by as the Confederates fought hard to break the route, but after brisk skirmishing Burnside succeeded in his retreat. Union casualties at Campbell's Station were 29 killed, 202 wounded, and 75 missing; Confederate losses were 174. The well-liked Union cavalryman Sanders, a native Kentuckian, was mortally wounded on November 18 in another, minor delaying action. His horse was first shot out from under him and then Sanders was struck in the stomach and spleen, dying the next day in the Lamar House in Knoxville.

The movement on Knoxville then transformed into a siege, and it would extend from November 17 to December 4. After Campbell's Station the spirits of the outnumbered pro-Confederates in eastern Tennessee surged; Ellen Renshaw House, age 20, wrote that "We whipped them twice below here today, terribly down at Campbell's Station. Longstreet is down there. . . . Such running and racing was never seen."

Longstreet was not equipped or supplied for a siege operation. The defenses of Knoxville had been laid out quickly and expertly by an array of engineers headed by the young and exceptionally skilled regular army Capt. Orlando M. Poe, a 31-year-old Ohioan who would later ascend to fame on the staff of William T. Sherman. A series of forts protected the city superbly, and one of these—located on a hill on the northwest corner of the city's earthworks—was selected as a target by Longstreet. The position had just been renamed Fort Sanders in honor of the fallen cavalryman. Longstreet planned an assault on the fort for November 20 but delayed for days waiting for reinforcements in the form of Brig. Gen. Bushrod Johnson, who would add 3,500 troops, and picking up the cavalry brigades of Grumble Jones.

Longstreet's attack on Fort Sanders (called Fort Loudon by the Southerners), commenced on November 29, was poorly planned and badly executed. The fort was about 70 feet higher than the surrounding plateau and was protected by a ditch 12 feet wide and 8 feet deep. From the ditch, a high, almost vertical wall rose 15 feet; it was a formidable position under any circumstances. Some 12 guns were placed within the salient at Fort Sanders when the attack commenced, and about 440 Federal infantry were at the ready, consisting of a mixture of Michigan and New York troops. Rather than using his artillery to soften the position, Longstreet ordered a surprise infantry assault at sunrise on the 29th. Three brigades were selected to make the assault—the Mississippians of Brig. Gen. Benjamin G. Humphreys, and Georgians commanded by Brig. Gen. Goode Bryan and Col. S. Z. Ruff (Wofford's brigade).

A freezing night preceded the attack. The men, huddling for warmth, crawled forward into position, some 150 yards short of the salient. As dawn approached, the hardy Southern troops surged forward in an attack that must have seemed cruel and gruesome by nineteenth-century standards. The ditch was an impossible obstacle; wire strung around tree stumps and wooden stakes netted many approaching men in a hopeless tangle, and they were shot trying to wiggle free. The frozen ground made a slippery surface for many men, who hobbled about with ghastly wounds, dripping steamy blood onto the ground. As a thick tangle of Minié bullets whizzed and popped through the air, the men warming only through the wickedly paced action of loading and firing, supreme chaos reigned on the ground embracing the attack force. "For fully twenty minutes the men stood around the ditch unable to get at their adversaries but unwilling to retreat," remarked Col. Edward Porter Alexander, Longstreet's acting chief of artillery. For a brief time some Southern soldiers vainly attempted to stand on each other's shoulders to rise up to the parapet, and a succession of color bearers was shot down trying to plant Southern banners on the fort. For a time, during the intense melee, three Confederate flags, those of the 16th Georgia Infantry, 13th Mississippi Infantry, and 17th Mississippi Infantry were sunk into the fort's wall.

The bullets continued unabated. Orlando M. Poe recalled, "Meanwhile those who remained in the ditch found themselves under a deadly flank fire of musketry and canister, supplemented by shells thrown as hand-grenades from inside the fort, without the slightest possibility of returning a blow." After the Confederates began a retreat, Union troops surged after them and captured at least 200 men in the ditch. The attack was a complete disaster, and Longstreet was alarmed. Just 8 men had been killed and 5 wounded inside the fort, whereas the Confederate casualties were 813.

Further worrying Longstreet was the intelligence report of Bragg's defeat at Missionary Ridge. Longstreet intended to move south to relieve Bragg, but Washington authorities found themselves in a mild panic over Burnside just as they had been over Rosecrans after Chickamauga, although to a lesser degree. Thus, they ordered Sherman and Granger to move to Knoxville and reinforce Burnside. Longstreet, on hearing of Sherman's approach, moved his supply trains away and disengaged from the city, ending his operations on December 4. He moved into winter quarters at

Greeneville, while Sherman, learning of Longstreet's movements, sent Granger ahead and returned to Chattanooga with his own army.

But Longstreet wasn't stopped entirely by the cold. A final action in the campaign occurred on December 14–15 at Bean's Station, northwest of Greeneville. When he found that three Union cavalry brigades held Bean's Station, Longstreet decided to attack. Moving from Rogersville, the Confederate force under Maj. Gen. William T. Martin would cross the Holston River near the junction while Grumble Jones cut off a possible route of retreat through Bean's Station Gap. Martin's attack was mismanaged and succeeded in capturing only a few wagons, while Brig. Gen. James M. Shackelford's Union horsemen rode away with ease. Longstreet was not amused, and he accused McLaws and Evander M. Law of not ordering their men forward until their lunch had been served. Settled in camp, Longstreet now attacked his subordinates for the season's failures. He had already drawn up charges against Law, and now he sent paperwork through asking for a court-martial of McLaws and of Brig. Gen. Jerome B. Robertson. All charges were eventually dropped, as Jefferson Davis opted to hang onto as many commanders as he could (those who were still alive and unwounded were becoming scarce), and they were simply shifted elsewhere.

ACTIONS IN THE EAST were smaller in size and significance as the cold weather arrived. In western Virginia the Federal cavalry of Brig. Gen. William W. Averell was on the move. On November 1 he led a mixed brigade out of Charleston, West Virginia, hoping to unite with Brig. Gen. Alfred N. A. Duffié at Lewisburg. After this juncture the two forces were to cut the East Tennessee & Virginia Railroad in support of the Knoxville operation. On November 6, Averell's force of 3,000, united with Duffié, clashed with a mixed force of 7,000 under the command of Brig. Gen. John Echols at Droop Mountain near Lewisburg. Averell split his force, sending the infantry (commanded by Col. Augustus Moor) and one company of horse soldiers around to the right to ascend a series of hills, permitting them to get around the enemy's rear. "At 3 P.M. the enemy were driven from the summit of the mountain," reported Averell, "upon which they had been somewhat protected by rude breast-works of logs, stones, and earth." Moor's effective infantry attack was starting to crumble the Confederate left and center, and soon some of the Confederate artillery batteries were overrun. Droop Mountain was abandoned by the Confederates in full-scale retreat and Averell joined his troops the following day in Lewisburg. Too exhausted to pursue or accomplish the railroad destruction, Averell's men followed the battle of Droop Mountain by simply holding their position.

While this was taking place, another action flared at Rappahannock Station and Kelly's Ford on November 7–8. Following the inaction after Gettysburg, the two principal eastern armies resumed their normal positions along the Rapidan and Rappahannock rivers. Along his front Lee maintained a built-up bridgehead at Rappahannock Station where the Orange & Alexandria Railroad bridge spanned the water. This was held in support of Kelly's Ford, four miles to the southeast, the weakest position along Lee's front.

Maj. Gen. Jubal Early's division was given the task of holding Rappahannock Bridge, and posted in front was Brig. Gen. Harry T. Hays's Louisiana brigade. Maj. Gen. Robert E. Rodes was given the task of holding Kelly's Ford. At the end of the first week of November, Meade determined to attack both positions. About noon on November 7 elements of the Federal 3d Corps moved across the river at Kelly's Ford, and the Confederate defenders made a weak attempt at blocking them. The Union 5th and 6th corps, meanwhile, moved into position opposite Early's front at Rappahannock Bridge, and after consultation and reinforcement, Lee and Early guessed that the position could be held. At dusk, however, another night attack commenced as Sedgwick pushed two brigades forward. A brutal bayonet attack at the bridge by the 6th Maine Infantry and 5th Wisconsin Infantry overwhelmed the Louisiana men as infantry led by Col. Emory Upton swarmed in over the bridgehead behind the fixed bayonets. Col. Archibald C. Godwin, commanding the final group of Confederates, was captured along with 65 withered holdouts.

Embittered, feeling increasingly ill, and emotionally stilled by the icy weather, Lee withdrew his army to behind the Rapidan River. While Lee had nothing more than winter quarters in mind, Meade geared up for a wintertime offensive. The Mine Run campaign, which lasted for a week from November 26 to December 1, resulted. Meade theorized that he could march downstream and cross the Rapidan and Germanna Ford and Ely's Ford before Stuart's cavalry would be alarmed, and then turn west to strike the unsuspecting corps of A. P. Hill and Dick Ewell. While reasonably sound in concept (and clearly unsuspected), the plan unfolded poorly. In calculating the last details of the plan, in what today might be termed command micromanagement, Meade failed to provide room for error.

Successfully crossing, mostly at Germanna Ford, Meade promptly maneuvered his five corps westward toward Orange Court House. The movement was immediately detected by Stuart, however, who alerted Lee to post heavy infantry along Mine Run, a little creek flowing southward from the Rapidan near Morton's Ford (between Germanna Ford and Clark's Mountain). Lee ushered Ewell back and moved Hill forward, solidifying the Mine Run line. Skirmishing erupted at many little points near the front, at Payne's Farm on November 27, for example. Meade then initiated a series of reconnoitering movements to feel out weak spots in the Confederate line. He dispatched Maj. Gen. Gouverneur K. Warren's 2d Corps to the southern flank while Sedgwick explored the north. Massing infantry on both flanks (one can see visions of Lee's Gettysburg strategy replaying itself in Meade's mind), the Federal commander prepared for a grand assault to be launched at 8 A.M. on November 30. The northern flank attack began as artillery opened a brisk bombardment, but to the south, Warren had witnessed the Confederate lines strengthening and called off the artillery bombardment and infantry assault. When Meade arrived, he agreed with Warren's assessment. As Lee was preparing for an attack of his own, which might have repeated Jackson's flank march tactics of Chancellorsville, Meade pulled away and began recrossing the Rappahannock. When Lee launched his attack on December 2, there were no Yankees to be found. The whole affair brought some visions of Burnside's infamous Mud March, a grand, glorious, wet, miserable affair, with a great deal of energy expended for no purpose. "The country of course overrated Meade after Gettysburg," declared one skeptic, Capt. Samuel W. Fiske of the 14th Connecticut Infantry who employed the pseudonym "Dunn Browne," "concluding that *the* great military hero had now made his appearance on the stage in the chief part, and all we should have more to do would be to clap our hands and shout 'Encore!' (at each new victory) till the curtain dropped." But the great eastern armies would need to wait at least another season for their chance at the decisive battle of the war.

THE PROLONGED ACTION during these weeks of cold weather was the interminable bombardment of Fort Sumter by the Federal guns placed on the islands around Charleston Harbor. Maj. Gen. Quincy A. Gillmore's engineers had been constructing Federal batteries all around the sandy islands ever since the attack on Fort Wagner the previous September. From the final days of October through December 11, Federal guns blasted Fort Sumter nearly every day, sending thousands of shells and balls onto the increasingly demolished fort, the symbol of the war's start. When President Davis visited Charleston on November 2, he witnessed a portion of the day's attack that sent 793 Union shells exploding above, in, and around the battered brick walls. The following day, 661 rounds were fired into the fort. By the 5th, Union batteries slowed to a more steady, less intense battering. A four-day bombardment opened on November 12. The bombing sharpened on November 20, when 1,344 rounds were dropped onto Sumter. An intense period again raked the fort over the last days of November and first days of December. On December 11, after which the bombardment ceased for a time, only 220 shells were thrown onto the fort. Still, Sumter's garrison did not raise the surrender flag. "She deserves it all," recorded New York diarist George Templeton Strong of Sumter's fate. "Sowing the wind was an exhilarating pastime. Shelling Anderson out of Sumter was pleasant; resisting the whirl-wind is less agreeable; to be *shelled back* is a bore." On Christmas Eve an en-gagement flared as Confederates attempted to stop Union troops from pulling down houses in Lagareville, gathering the wooden planks, and trans-porting them to Kiawah Island to erect huts there. "The night was a bril-liantly clear Moonlight night," wrote the Confederate artillerist Maj. Edward Manigault. Early on Christmas morning the battle raged. "After about ¼ of an hour the enemy's fire became so hot that Col. [Delaware] Kem-per determined to withdraw the guns. Private [William H.] Ancrum of Co. 'A' had his leg shot off by a shell which killed both the horses he was driving. . . . Private [James W.] Zorn was shot through the hand by [a] fragment of shell." The Confederate assault ebbed away and the uninjured soldiers tried to enjoy what remained of the holiday.

MILITARILY, the pendulum seemed to have swung toward the Federals, al-though Southern hearts—despite horrific losses of life on the battlefield and depressing shortages and substitutions on the homefront—could wistfully look forward to a Southern nation, despite the setbacks. The coming year would be an election year for the Union, and a political election had never been held in such a country in the midst of civil war. If the faint echo of for-eign intervention was not to be heard, killed by emancipation's rising sound, then perhaps the love of peace in the North would put in office candidates who would settle the war without further bloodshed and let the South leave for good. All this was possible, if not probable, late in the year 1863. Although Federal armies and navies controlled much of the territory of the Confeder-ate States, the war had not yet been won.

Although few had yet considered backing away from their principles—"giving up"—fighters and civilians alike on both sides were growing more than weary by this time in the war. Private soldiers were dying and being mutilated by the scores, and both sides were continuing to lose their officer corps. On November 24, Confederate Brig. Gen. Claudius C. Wilson died of "camp fever," or dysentery, at Ringgold, Georgia. On December 16, in Wash-ington, Brig. Gen. John Buford, one of the heroes of Gettysburg, died from typhoid fever contracted in camp on the Rappahannock River. The final scrap of paper received from Buford by the adjutant general read, "I have the honor to ask for permission to proceed to Washington City for medical treatment." On December 22, at Fairfax Court House, outside Washington, Brig. Gen. Michael Corcoran died after receiving a mortal wound. Corco-ran, a celebrated Irish officer who earlier had been captured at First Bull Run and subsequently written a prison diary, had been riding with Brig. Gen. Thomas F. Meagher and a group of other officers. Corcoran raced ahead, out of sight, and when Meagher and the others caught up with him, he was found on the ground, in the midst of a convulsion, with face "purple." Pronounced dead a few minutes later, Corcoran had apparently fainted on horseback, fallen or been thrown, and fractured his skull in the process. "Genl. Corcoran died at quarter past eight o'clock this evening," read the tersely-worded telegram from Fairfax Court House, received in Washington a short time later.

WHEN IT SEEMED LIKELIEST to all that the meaning of the war remained elusive, the leading figure of the time stepped forward to define it. Abraham Lincoln had been invited to Gettysburg to deliver "a few appropriate remarks" at the dedication of the Soldiers' Cemetery, where the bodies of Union boys lay entombed in the soft Pennsylvania clay just eighteen weeks after the gigantic battle had swept across that very ground. Lincoln's invitation had essentially been an afterthought: The main speaker of the day would be the leading orator of the American nation, Edward Everett, age 69, known by all as an eminent Unitarian clergyman and statesman. Everett had seemingly done it all. He was the first professor of Greek Literature at Harvard, had been a member of the U.S. House from Massachusetts, governor of Massachusetts, minister to Great Britain, president of Harvard, secretary of state under Millard Fillmore, a U.S. senator, and a presidential candidate in 1860.

A crowd of at least 15,000 would witness a parade march from the shell-shocked town of Gettysburg up to Cemetery Hill, where several hundred people would listen to the dedicatory speeches in the new national cemetery. Lincoln would travel with the draft of his speech (written in the Executive Mansion and not as legends have it, on an envelope or while en route) by train from Washington through Baltimore and on to Hanover Junction in southern Pennsylvania, where the train would turn westward to Gettysburg. The party that accompanied Lincoln to Gettysburg included three cabinet members, William Henry Seward, Montgomery Blair, and John P. Usher. The French minister to the United States, Henri Mercier, accompanied the party as a special guest. Presidential secretaries John G. Nicolay and John M. Hay came along, as did Chief Marshal Ward Hill Lamon (Lincoln's "bodyguard") and his assistant, Benjamin B. French. Pennsylvania Governor Andrew G. Curtin was on hand. General officers were too: Darius N. Couch, Julius Stahel, and Robert C. Schenck among them. Lincoln and some of his associates stayed at the home of David Wills on Gettysburg's town square. Wills, a prominent attorney in town, had helped to organize the event and the creation of the cemetery.

On Thursday, November 19, the parade and dedication gripped the small community. On horseback Lincoln rode in the procession that moved slowly toward the hill and burying ground. Some 3,629 Union boys would end up interred within what would eventually be termed Soldiers' National Cemetery, and later Gettysburg National Cemetery, adjacent to the town's own cemetery, Evergreen. Despite the cold weather and embarrassing difficulties with his kidneys, Everett managed to rise to the speaker's platform, erected where all could see the event, and deliver his lengthy address. Everett's speech rambled along for one hour and fifty-seven minutes, filled with wordy, purple declarations aimed at the heavens, at Americans, or at the dead.

After two hours of Everett the crowd was ready for something else. Lincoln's subsequent speech was so brief, lasting only two minutes, that a photographer on hand just barely made an image of the president by the time he began to sit down. Lincoln's "few appropriate remarks," saved in five separate versions with minor variations (possibly it was the so-called second draft used for the speech), read:

> Four score and seven years ago our fathers brought forth, upon this continent, a new nation, conceived in Liberty, and dedicated to the proposition that all men are created equal.
>
> Now we are engaged in a great civil war, testing whether that nation, or any nation, so conceived, and so dedicated, can long endure. We are met here on a great battle-field of that war. We have come to dedicate a portion of it as a final resting place for those who here gave their lives that that nation might live. It is altogether fitting and proper that we should do this.
>
> But, in a larger sense we cannot dedicate—we cannot consecrate—we cannot hallow this ground. The brave men, living and dead, who struggled here, have consecrated it far above our poor power to add or detract. The world will little note, nor long remember, what we say here, but can never forget what they did here. It is for us, the living, rather to be dedicated here to the unfinished work which they have, thus far, so nobly carried on. It is rather for us to be here dedicated to the great task remaining before us—that from these honored dead we take increased devotion to that cause for which they here gave the last full measure of devotion—that we here highly resolve that these dead shall not have died in vain; that this nation shall have a new birth of freedom; and that this government of the people, by the people, for the people, shall not perish from the earth.

Lincoln could not foresee that the Gettysburg Address (in its final version) would become emblazoned on the memories of schoolchildren everywhere as one of the great speeches of history. Everett and the rest of the crowd seemed pleased with Lincoln's comments, even though they were brief and delivered in the westerner's high-pitched, shrill tenor. "I should be glad, if I came as near to the central idea of the occasion, in two hours, as you did in two minutes," Everett wrote the president the following day. Lincoln responded by writing that "I am pleased to know that, in your judgment, the little I did say was not entirely a failure. . . . The point made against the theory of the general government being only an agency, whose principals are the States, was new to me, and, as I think, is one of the best arguments for the national supremacy."

The American moment had been defined brilliantly at Gettysburg by Lincoln, with an incredible economy of language. At year's end, with a bitter war and a partisan political year ahead of him, Lincoln seemed to experience something of a revival in his confidence in the American people as well as the American government, army, and navy. "The President tonight had a dream," wrote John Hay, the day prior to Christmas Eve. "He was in a party of plain people and as it became known who he was they began to comment on his appearance. One of them said, 'He is a very common-looking man.' The President replied, 'The Lord prefers Common-looking people: that is the reason he makes so many of them.' "

CHAPTER 20

Sherman Eyes the Deep South

THE YEAR 1864 witnessed the darkest hours of America's national nightmare. The third winter of the war brought a growing acceptance of emancipation as the rationale for the war, even if many battles were yet to be fought and thousands more graves dug for local heroes. A slight increase in optimism visited the wartime psychology of the North, accompanied by a relentless press for conquest of the South. In Dixie, as the first weeks of the New Year passed, it was becoming increasingly difficult to remain upbeat about the future of the Confederacy. Still, the war was far from over, and despite the beating the South had already taken, the Southern armies and navy showed no signs of lessening their commitment to fight on.

The aggregate strength of the armies was somewhat lower during this blackest period of the war. The U.S. Army had a count of 611,250 present and 249,487 absent on January 1, 1864, resulting in an aggregate of 860,737 troops. This number was 6 percent less than the aggregate of the previous January 1, but would grow to more than one million by the war's end. The aggregate strength of the Confederate Army was reported as 472,781, up slightly from the previous January.

No one doubted that bloody battles would wash again across the American landscape in the spring. Could the country possibly hold itself together? In the Union Army, changes occurred that could answer the question affirmatively. Maj. Gen. Henry W. Halleck, who had served as general-in-chief since mid-1862, would be supplanted in the spring of 1864 by the hero of Donelson, Vicksburg, and Chattanooga, Ulysses S. Grant. Commissioned lieutenant general, the first since George Washington, Grant would be charged with command of all United States armies, and Halleck would be assigned as chief of staff to serve as a facilitator between Grant and the Lincoln administration. This was a post Halleck handled adequately, and was better suited to him than previous assignments. Though Grant commanded the entire Union Army, he was advised by his good friend Sherman to stay as far away from Washington bureaucracy as possible, and so accompanied the main eastern army, the Army of the Potomac, in the field. The doubts about Grant had by now vanished. "Now, since Vicksburg they have not a word to say against Grant's habits," recorded the Southern diarist Mary Chesnut. "He has the disagreeable habit of not retreating before irresistible veterans."

The Office of the Judge Advocate General was abolished and Brig. Gen. Joseph Holt, the judge advocate general, was assigned as chief of the Bureau of Military Justice, its successor, in June 1864. In November 1864 the Office of the Commissary General of Prisoners, under the charge of Col. William Hoffman, was divided into an eastern branch (commanded by Hoffman) and a western branch (commanded by Brig. Gen. Henry W. Wessells). At year's end Col. Benjamin F. Fisher, who had escaped from Richmond's Libby prison earlier in the year, took over the Signal Bureau (Corps). In early 1864, Brig. Gen. Montgomery C. Meigs reassumed command of the Quartermaster General's Department after spending the latter half of 1863 on an inspection tour. The Cavalry Bureau, established in 1863, was taken over briefly by Brig. Gen. Kenner Garrard and then, in late January 1864, by Brig. Gen. James H. Wilson. Brig. Gen. Amos B. Eaton commanded the Subsistence Department beginning in June 1864. Col. Benjamin W. Brice was assigned chief of the Pay Department in November 1864, overseeing the end of a year in which the army's expenditures were nearly $691 million. In the Medical Department, Brig. Gen. Joseph K. Barnes assumed permanent command as surgeon general of the army. With the death of the aged veteran Brig. Gen. Joseph G. Totten in April 1864, Brig. Gen. Richard Delafield took over as chief engineer. The superintendency of the Military Academy at West Point passed through the hands of Brig. Gen. Zealous B. Tower and, by September 1864, to Brig. Gen. George W. Cullum. Beginning in September 1864, the Ordnance Department was headed by Brig. Gen. Alexander B. Dyer. Changes with naval forces were slight. Col. Jacob Zeilen was assigned as commandant of the U.S. Marine Corps.

Though it may have needed them more than ever, the Confederate Army witnessed relatively few organizational changes in this decisive year. The largest one may have hurt more than it helped: In February, Gen. Braxton Bragg, so disliked by nearly all of the western soldiers and alienated from his subordinate commanders, was called to Richmond by Jefferson Davis. Bragg was "charged with the conduct of the military operations in the armies of the Confederacy," acting as an advisor to Davis and a *de facto* general-in-chief. Although this assignment continued on paper into January 1865, Bragg left Richmond in October 1864 again to bring his services into the field. The Confederate Engineer Bureau (Corps of Engineers) was variously commanded in 1864 by Maj. Gen. Martin L. Smith, Col. Alfred L. Rives, and Col. Jeremy F. Gilmer. Brig. Gen. John H. Winder commanded the Bureau of Prison Camps from November 1864 until his death the following February. The Confederate Navy also had few changes. Capt. Sidney S. Lee, Robert E. Lee's older brother, took charge of the Bureau of Orders and Detail. Paymaster James A. Semple was charged with the Bureau of Provisions and Clothing.

What struck most Americans during this year was the scale of the bloodshed. Of course, each escalating level of the war had shocked as never before: Shiloh, with its hideous numbers, the gruesome images displayed by photographers after the battle of Antietam, the carnage of Gettysburg. But as the armies postured for what appeared to be major spring campaigns in 1864, the scale of death appeared to be ready to leap upward again. "I have seen death in so many shapes within the last year," Rear Adm. David Dixon Porter informed his mother, "that I consider the change from life to eternity very philosophically, it is our doom." Together with Porter and other naval comrades, the two leading lights of the Federal army, Grant and Sherman, were positioned to transform war into a different and more terrible creature over the coming months. "War is simply Power unrestrained by Constitution or Compact," Sherman declared in January. Believing himself empowered by the righteous aims of the war, Sherman predicted destruction for the Confederacy and believed in it as strongly as anyone could. "All the Powers of Earth cannot restore to them their slaves," he predicted in the same letter, "any more than their dead Grandfathers."

Indeed, although the passion to protect slavery lived as angrily as ever among the Richmond government and most of the population of the South, and racism still pervaded much of the civilian North, slavery was now acknowledged as a principal factor of the war and attitudes about it were evolving. In Virginia, the Federal surgeon Daniel M. Holt wrote his wife, "After the war, when evil passions are lulled to rest, this county will be a desirable one to live in. Northern men and northern money and energy will develope [sic] its resources, and an unprecedented reign of prosperity will follow. . . . Heretofore only those of wealth, owning large plantations and a great number of Negroes, were thought much of. The poor or even small farmers were never taken into the account when the status of society was reckoned. A new era is to dawn upon the downtrodden serfs of Southern Chivalry. They are to become men, while their lords and masters will have to come down and take a back seat."

While most Southerners stuck to their cherished ideals, chinks in the philosophical armor of slavery began to appear, and only grew with the struggling military performance on the battlefield. Particularly among the poorer people, who never had been slave owners, a small but growing number of Confederate soldiers began to question the ruining of their society over slavery. "There is something wrong somewhere," Col. William H. A. Speer of the 18th North Carolina Infantry told his father. "We have as brave & great an army as ever went on a battle field, but there is some *national sin* hanging over us & I fear it is the *nigger.* So far as I am concerned, I would be glad if every drop of nigger blood was out of the Confederacy. If it was not for the nigger, this war, I think, would close in less than 60 days from today. ... And I believe that if the South was to agree to emancipate all the slaves in 30 years that the war would close at once & for my part, I am in favor of it, but this, you know, would [not] do for me to say to anyone else *yet.*"

The South had many other, more immediate woes. The increasingly successful Union blockade was beginning to strangle home life in the Confederacy, particularly deep in the countryside away from modes of transportation. A new way of life emerged on Southern tables and in Southern parlors built on shortages and substitutions of food and goods essential for daily, civilized life. "We had several substitutes for tea which were equally as palatable, and, I fancy, much more wholesome, than much that is now sold for tea," recorded Parthenia Antoinette Hague, of her homestead near Eufala, Alabama. "Prominent among these substitutes were raspberry leaves. The leaves of the blackberry bush, huckleberry leaves, and the leaves of the holly-tree when dried in the shade, also made a palatable tea."

Food shortages were paramount. Constance Cary Harrison wrote that it was impossible to eat a meal in Richmond, the population center overrun with government clerks, "without wishing there were more of it." Civilian areas near the armies, whether they be marching or in battle, were always deprived of food sources, and besieged cities like Vicksburg and (in 1864) Petersburg were depleted of practically anything edible. Fish and eggs increased in the Confederate diet, and meats, when obtainable, increasingly began to include raccoon, opossum, sheep, and, by the autumn of 1864, "rats, frogs, fried snails, young crow, snakes, locusts, earthworms, birds' nests, cats, and dogs."

A clothing shortage developed more slowly than the food problem, but was serious by war's end. All sorts of odd materials were substituted for the norm. Instead of all-leather shoes, wooden bottoms were often tacked onto leather uppers, and sometimes cloth shoes took the place of leather. Southern women spent countless hours converting old textiles into new goods, knitting, sewing, spinning, and weaving until their hands bled. Old clothes were usually turned out into new items several times during the war. Headwear often came from grasses, leaves, or straw. Raincoats were fashioned from oil cloth or rubberized piano covers. Southern ladies produced handkerchiefs from practically any material they had on hand. Substitute dyes came from all manner of improvised native plants. "Confederate candles" were made from strips of rag dipped into liquid wax. Oil lamps accustomed to kerosene often had to burn cheap commercial terebene oil, which produced great amounts of inky black smoke. In outer regions, Confederates sometimes lit their rooms with a paper wick twisted into a saucer of grease, which produced only a small, unreliable glow.

Though they were just making do with many of these items, Confederates on the home front managed to keep alive. Still, perhaps the most bothersome aspects of substitution were the little things in life that were now gone or scarce. Many Confederate magazines and newspapers either suspended publication or were hard to obtain or expensive. Books were rare, as they had chiefly come from the Northeast before the war. Southern printers in Richmond, Macon, Atlanta, Mobile, and Charleston had precious little paper, press equipment, and expertise to produce titles, and so when Confederate imprints appeared, they were cherished. They were often brown paper editions bound in wallpaper or newspaper with cheap boards glued or handstitched. Simple writing paper, account ledgers, envelopes, and wrapping paper were scarce during the war. No doubt more Confederate diaries would exist if not for this fact. Personal items such as toothbrushes, tooth powder, tobacco, perfumes, buttons, needles, pins, hair oils, combs, nails, locks, screws, cards, games, and other such items were usually unavailable or were frightfully expensive. No doubt the relative lack of amusements during the wartime South inflicted as much damage as did Sherman's army.

The paramount problem on the battlefield was a growing shortage of food even for the Confederate armies. "Short rations are having a bad effect upon the men, both morally and physically," Robert E. Lee alerted Secretary of War James A. Seddon on January 22. "Desertions to the enemy are becoming more frequent, and the men cannot continue healthy and vigorous if confined to this spare diet for any length of time. Unless there is a change, I fear the army cannot be kept together."

The soldiers in the field had a relative life of luxury, however, compared to the growing numbers of prisoners North and South. During the war the Union army captured and held about 220,000 prisoners and the Confederate army about 210,000. Nearly all of these detainees suffered ferociously in prisons North and South, and altogether some 22,600 Yankees and 26,500 Rebels died while in prison camps. The situation worsened deeply as the war dragged on. At the war's outset, prison facilities did not exist and transportation was often problematic, so numerous prisoners were released on parole. After several months, converted tobacco and shipping warehouses, forts, penitentiaries, training camps, state prisons, and even college campuses were being used as detention centers. After fierce negotiating over a prisoner exchange, a cartel was devised on July 22, 1862, between Union Maj. Gen. John A. Dix and Confederate Maj. Gen. Daniel H. Hill that provided for a system based on the parity of grades. A general or admiral would equal 60 privates; a major general or rear admiral 40 privates; a brigadier general or commodore 20 privates; a colonel or naval captain 15 privates; a lieutenant colonel or commander 10 privates; a major or lieutenant commander 8 privates; an army captain or naval lieutenant 6 privates; a lieutenant, ensign, or mate 4 privates; a cadet or midshipman 3 privates; and a noncommissioned officer or junior naval or marine officer 2 privates. The Union Army paroled and exchanged 329,963 Confederate prisoners of war, while the Confederacy paroled and exchanged about 152,015 Union prisoners of war. Commissioners of exchange refused to agree on the details, and even before the emancipation year of 1863 the whole system collapsed. Confederate authorities refused to return black Americans captured in Federal uniforms, claiming they were runaway slaves who ought to be returned to servitude. This outraged the Lincoln administration, which held they must be treated equally as soldiers fighting for their country. Largely because of the refusal of Confederate authorities to recognize black soldiers, the War Department suspended prisoner exchanges in the spring of 1863. The ranks of prisoners began to swell.

Andersonville, Georgia, dubbed the "hell hole," was the most notorious Civil War prison camp. Chosen as a site to relieve Richmond of its overcrowded prison population, the original "Camp Sumter" was chosen near Andersonville in 1863 and a stockade erected to enclose 16.5 (later 26) acres. By February 1864 the first 500 prisoners were transported to Andersonville; by July some 32,000 Union men were held at the prison, making it the fourth-largest city in the Confederacy, after New Orleans, Charleston, and Richmond. The lack of sanitation, poor food, and absence of medical treatment and supplies made life at Andersonville a nightmare. Few guards, most of them young boys or senile men, stood watch over the prisoners. Criminal "raiders" in the prison population terrorized fellow inmates. Polluted water from the only source, the trickling flow of Providence Spring, made nearly all the prisoners sick. By the end of the autumn, when Andersonville's prisoners were moved to avoid the approach of Sherman's army, 12,912 prisoners lay dead in mass trench graves. The prison's most influential commandant was Brig. Gen. John H. Winder, who was perceived by Federal authorities as being instrumental to the horrible conditions in Southern prisons, and who died in February 1865 before Union officials could catch him. Winder's successor at Andersonville, Capt. Henry Wirz, also caught an enormous share of the blame for horrible conditions at the prison, partly justifiably and partly for conditions he couldn't control. Wirz would be captured and hanged in the war's final season.

Andersonville's famous "dead line" was a barrier of wooden strips nailed to posts inside the perimeter of the stockade walls and over which prisoners could not pass lest they be shot dead. On April 9, 1864, Caleb

Coplan, a young Ohioan who had been captured at Chickamauga, became the first casualty of the dead line as he wandered into the northeastern corner of the stockade looking for material with which to patch his tent. Coplan reached under the line after a scrap of flannel and a guard shot him with .75-caliber buck-and-ball. He died the next day. Accounts of prisoners being shot inside the dead line appear with some regularity in the memoirs of Andersonville inmates. "A crazy man was shot dead an hour ago," reported John Ransom of the 9th Michigan Cavalry on May 2, 1864. "The guard dropped a piece of bread on the inside of the stockade, and the fellow went inside the dead line to get it and was killed. . . . As I write [Capt. Henry Wirz] is walking about the prison with revolver in hand, cursing and swearing. The men yell out 'Hang him up!' 'Kill the Dutch louse!' 'Buck and gag him!' 'Stone him to death!' &c., and he all the time trying to find out who is insulting him so."

In July 1864 word reached Winder that Union expeditions might be sent to liberate the Andersonville prisoners. Winder issued an order to open on the prisoners with grapeshot should any such Union forces approach the prison. "Thirty thousand prisoners, helpless, many sick, many dying, unable to take any offensive part themselves, to be opened upon with grapeshot at close range because there was danger that they might be liberated," reported Ezra Hoyt Ripple, a prisoner in the stockade. As time continued, the "raiders" terrorized their fellow prisoners increasingly. "The proceeds of these forays enabled the Raiders to wax fat and lusty, while others were dying of starvation," explained John McElroy, one of those confined. "They all had good tents, constructed of stolen blankets, and their headquarters was a large, roomy tent, with a circular top. . . . All the material for this had been wrested away from others. While hundreds were dying of scurvy and diarrhea, from the miserable, insufficient food, and lack of vegetables, these fellows had flour, fresh meat, onions, potatoes, green beans, and other things, the very looks of which were a torture to hungry, scorbutic, dysenteric men." The six raiders were eventually tried, hanged, and buried outside the stockade.

Conditions at Andersonville were so depraved that Confederate eyewitnesses sometimes caught glimpses of the horror experienced by the prisoners: "Three poor mortals breathed their last lying before the Doctor's stand waiting to be prescribed for and died while the rain splattered the sand in their faces," one Confederate officer recorded.

Andersonville was but one of many prisons holding Union boys in the South. The first Confederate prisons, those in Richmond, consisted of fifteen ship chandler and tobacco warehouses, Belle Isle (isolated in the James River), and the County Jail. As the war developed, most of the warehouses were converted into facilities to detain officers, and Belle Isle held enlisted men. Other important Confederate prisons included those at Augusta,

Georgia; Atlanta, Georgia; Cahaba, Alabama; Columbia, South Carolina; Danville, Virginia; Florence, South Carolina; Millen, Georgia (Camp Lawton); Montgomery, Alabama; Salisbury, North Carolina; Savannah, Georgia; and Tyler, Texas. Once the exchange broke down by mid-war, many of the men were sentenced to confinement for an indefinite period, and so they missed important (and sometimes tragic) personal events as if they were living on another planet. At Salisbury, Frederic Augustus James, a sailor on the USS *Housatonic* who had been captured in the night attack against Fort Sumter on September 8, 1863, wrote: "Received a letter from my wife under date of Feb. 21st bringing the sad & wholly unexpected news of the death of our darling little Mary. She was taken to her heavenly home Oct. 26 1863. . . . It would have been an unspeakable comfort & blessing to have clasped the warm & generous heart of the darling little girl once more to my own." Often values changed dramatically in the isolation of prison life—both of the loved and lost and of material things too. At the officers' prison in Macon, Georgia, Chaplain Henry S. White of the 5th Rhode Island Artillery wrote that "When Sherman was approaching, we became so eager to hear that a man offered a watch worth two hundred dollars for a newspaper, and could not get it."

At Danville prison a good many of the inmates were so committed to escape that they devised an extensive plan to tunnel out of the prison, which nearly worked. During the winter of 1864–65, the plan was discovered by a Confederate guard who fell through the ground into the tunnel. "Frightened as he was (I believe his arm was broken) he yelled murder, and the guard next to him fired off his piece," recorded 1st Lt. George H. Putnam of the 176th New York Infantry, who was confined there. "There was of course no difficulty in tracing the line of the tunnel. . . . The folding doors admitting to the cellar were closed with an iron bar, and we judged that the guards whose duty it was to hold post in the yard must have received a pretty sharp reprimand from their superiors."

But one famous escape succeeded. Second only to Andersonville as the most famous Confederate prison was Libby prison, formerly the Libby & Son Ship Chandlers & Grocers warehouse on Carey Street in Richmond, near the waterfront and the Rocketts Landing. The three-story brick building measured 150 by 100 feet and the holding area consisted of eight large rooms. By 1863 the prison swelled with captured officers, particularly following Gettysburg and Chickamauga. "Nothing but bread has, as yet, been issued to us, half a loaf twice a day, per man," scrawled Lt. Col. Frederick F. Cavada of the 114th Pennsylvania Infantry, captured at Gettysburg. "This must be washed down with James River water, drawn from a hydrant over the wash-trough. To-morrow, we are to be indulged with the luxury of bacon-soup. . . . We have tasted of the promised soup: it is boiled water sprinkled with rice, and seasoned with the rank juices of stale bacon; we must shut our eyes to eat it; the bacon, I have no doubt, might have walked into the pot of its own accord." The men slept on a hard floor and were so cramped that they had to turn over in unison. Prisoners stayed clear of the windows lest they be fired at by the guards outside.

The genesis of a sophisticated escape plot at Libby prison arose with the plans designed by Col. Thomas E. Rose (77th Pennsylvania Infantry), who had been captured at Chickamauga. Rose coordinated the digging of a hole in Libby's first-floor kitchen fireplace that allowed tunnelers to descend the chimney into the eastern section of a rat-infested cellar. Working slowly and carefully, they produced a 50-foot tunnel that stretched to the distant end of an adjacent vacant lot. Libby prison's "Great Escape" resulted on February 9, 1864, when 109 officers burrowed their way out of the prison toward freedom, including Col. Abel D. Streight, who had led the Alabama raid in April 1863. Of the 109 escapees, 48 were recaptured (including Rose), 2 drowned, and 59 eventually reached Union lines. Libby became so celebrated that it was dismantled in 1889 and rebuilt for a time as a museum in Chicago.

Great emphasis has been placed on the horrendous conditions in Southern prison camps, but life in the Northern prisons also deteriorated, particularly as Stanton and others received reports of the poor conditions of Union prisoners in the South. A soldier reported to the surgeon general that sick prisoners who were exchanged in 1863 had "their bodies and clothing covered with vermin. . . . Their pinched features, ghastly cadaveric countenances, deep sepulchral eyes, and voices that could hardly be distinguished (some could not articulate) presented a picture which could not be looked upon without its drawing out the strongest emotion of pity."

Union prisons for Southern boys included those at Alton, Illinois; Columbus, Ohio (Camp Chase); Chicago, Illinois (Camp Douglas); Elmira, New York; Fort Jefferson, Florida; Fort Lafayette (New York), New York; Fort Warren (Boston), Massachusetts; Johnson's Island, Ohio; Point Lookout, Maryland; and the Old Capitol prison, D.C. At Camp Chase, early in the war, prisoners sometimes recorded their mild impressions of a temporary lockup. "To be a prisoner of war is not such a very bad thing, were it not for the absence from loved ones and duty," claimed James Deeler, a Mississippi soldier, to his wife, Sarah. "We are in good houses, cook on stoves, and have plenty of wood, water, and wholesome food. When you hear of barbarity, cruelty, and the like, just say it is all false. I have not seen the least bit of it, and don't believe it is practiced anywhere."

But conditions went from bad to worse rapidly in the Northern prisons. Of Johnson's Island, Ohio, Capt. James Cooper Nisbet (21st Georgia Infantry) recorded that "As to health conditions, there were at all times many cases of smallpox in the pest house. Scurvy raged. It was superinduced by the everlasting—though inadequate—ration of salt white-fish. . . . It was impossible to soak or boil the salt out. Of course, what we received was devoured ravenously." Poor food plagued most of the prisons as the war dragged on. At Point Lookout, Maryland, Pvt. Bartlett Yancey Malone of the 6th North Carolina Infantry wrote home that he "spent the first day of January 64 at Point Lookout M. D. The morning was plesant but toward eavning the air changed and the nite was very coal. Was so coal that five of our men froze to death befour morning. . . . our men was so hungry to day that they caught a Rat and cooked him and eat it."

At Elmira the Southerners, unaccustomed to the Northern winters, suffered badly. "If there ever was a hell on earth Elmira prison was that hell, but it was not a hot one, for the thermometer was often 40 degrees below zero," stated Sgt. E. S. Wade of McNeill's Texas Scouts, with some degree of exaggeration. "Every day Northern ladies came in the prison, some of them followed by dogs or cats, which the boys would slip aside and choke to death. The ribs of a stewed dog were delicious, and a boiled rat was superb." The bitter pill of fear was constant along with the suffering. "The men were made to retire at sundown," recalled prisoner Thomas Head of Camp Douglas prison near Chicago, "and were not allowed to talk to one another after [they] laid down. If the Federals heard any talking at night in the barracks they would shoot into the house through the crowd." Wrote prisoner R. T. Bean: "Many a Minié ball went crashing through our barracks at night at some real or imaginary noise. It was dangerous even to snore."

RELATIVELY FEW ACTIONS marked the initial weeks of 1864, a year that would become the bloodiest of the war. In Virginia, cavalry fighting erupted at Jonesville, in the southwestern part of the state on January 3. Maj. Charles H. Beeres's battalion of the 16th Illinois Cavalry successfully drove into Jonesville and, after a skirmish, occupied it, but was attacked savagely by Brig. Gen. Samuel Jones's cavalry brigade two days later. Jones's Confederates routed the small battalion of Union horsemen and captured Beeres's men, two mountain howitzers, and a 3-inch Rodman gun. At about the same time, a Union reconnaissance ventured into Winchester, in the Valley, the town that changed hands so many times during the war. Skirmishes erupted at Flint Hill, Virginia, on January 6 and 15, near Ely's Ford on the 13th, around Petersburg two days later, and at Kelly's Ford on the 27th. In central Virginia the Army of the Potomac and the Army of Northern Virginia watched and waited, hoping to block mountain passes and other routes of attack that could give the enemy a measure of surprise. The Army of the Potomac attempted a forward movement at Morton's Ford on the Rapidan on February 6, but it immediately ran into trouble. Struck by artillery fire, the Yankees moved back north of the river at nightfall.

In West Virginia, Confederate Brig. Gen. Thomas L. Rosser led an expedition to Moorefield that produced an attack on a Union supply train. On January 29, Rosser crossed the mountain passes with a force of fewer than 1,000; he gained intelligence that the well-stocked train was headed south from New Creek to Petersburg. His Confederate horsemen approached cautiously and, near the town of Medley, located the train as it stood guarded by several Illinois, West Virginia, and Maryland regiments. Rosser placed an artillery piece in his front and sent horsemen to the flanks, attacking the train headlong and capturing it after routing the surprised Federals. Rosser took the whole train of ninety-five cars loaded with supplies. "Indeed, I believe it is the first instance during this war where cavalry attacked successfully a superior force of infantry," Rosser wrote. The spoils included 40 prisoners, including 1 major and 2 captains; loads of bacon, coffee, rice, sugar, and other commissary stores; and other goods. During the remainder of the expedition, which included another successful foray at Patterson's Creek on February 1, Rosser also brought home 1,200 cattle, 500 sheep, and 80 more prisoners.

THE WAR IN TENNESSEE began slowly with the turn of another year. Extreme cold swept as far south as Memphis, creating below-zero temperatures for thousands of miserable soldiers and freezing most plans for action. Still, slight skirmishes occurred at La Grange on January 2, around Mossy Creek on January 10–12, at Blue Springs on January 19, and at Tazewell on January 24. On January 16 and 17 cavalry units clashed near Dandridge, east of Knoxville, as Union horsemen under Brig. Gen. Samuel D. Sturgis approached a portion of Lt. Gen. James Longstreet's troops. As Sturgis moved his cavalry forward to occupy an area known as Kimbrough's Cross Roads, Col. Frank Wolford's 1st Kentucky Cavalry (USA) encountered Confederate horse soldiers who struck into the Kentuckians and offered battle but were driven back after a sharp fight. Longstreet ordered infantry up to attack the following day, and a portion of Maj. Gen. John Bell Hood's division attacked the Federals. After an afternoon's fight the Yankees withdrew to New Market and Strawberry Plains, and Longstreet's men captured some arms and ammunition. "Our infantry was not in condition to pursue," Longstreet reported, however, "half of our men being without shoes."

Again near Dandridge, this time near Kelly's Ford, Tennessee, skirmishing erupted January 26–28. As Longstreet kept most of his infantry in winter quarters at Morristown and Russellville, Confederate cavalry under Brig. Gen. John T. Morgan and Brig. Gen. Frank C. Armstrong (the commander who had fought for the Union at First Bull Run and then switched sides), and other units, attacked Sturgis's cavalry in a series of skirmishes that included Flat Creek and Muddy Creek (January 26), Kelly's Ford, McNutt's Bridge, and Fair Gardens (January 27), and Fain's Island, Indian Creek, Island Ford, Kelly's Ford, and Swann's Island (January 28). When the Union cavalry divisions of Cols. Edward M. McCook and Israel Garrard attempted to interpose themselves, Confederate infantry pushed them back, ending the affair. In his report of the several days' activities, Sturgis complained bitterly of poor supplies and suffering from the harshly cold weather. His soldiers were "almost daily engaged with the enemy," he reported, "and compelled to live mainly on parched corn, most of which has been gathered at a distance of from 6 to 15 miles."

As minor events were transpiring in Tennessee, Maj. Gen. William T. Sherman planned a winter offensive movement aimed at destroying Confederate rail lines in Mississippi and striking at the Confederate outpost of Meridian, east of Jackson and near the Alabama border. This would strengthen the Federal position at Vicksburg. Sherman had been ordered to cooperate with Maj. Gen. Nathaniel P. Banks, who would shortly launch an expedition up the Red River to recover Arkansas and Louisiana for the Union. But Banks's slow organizational start and the low water on the rivers allowed Sherman time for an interlude, and he determined to use it for an operation of his own. Sherman's Meridian expedition, as it came to be known, organized 26,000 men of the Army of the Tennessee to march from Vicksburg and 7,600 cavalry from Memphis, under Brig. Gen. William Sooy Smith (commanding the cavalry of the Military Division of the Mississippi). The opposing Confederates, in Lt. Gen. Leonidas Polk's Army of Mississippi, numbered about 20,000 and were spread across parts of the state in addition to the concentration at Meridian. Polk's army consisted of two divisions led by Maj. Gens. William W. Loring and Samuel G. French, and a cavalry corps commanded by Maj. Gen. Stephen D. Lee. Sherman's men advanced on February 3 across the battlefields of the previous summer, reaching the Big Black River Bridge the following day and marching across Champion Hill. Polk's Confederates concentrated and offered resistance on this day, as skirmishing erupted at Liverpool Heights, Champion Hill, Bolton Depot, and Edwards's Ferry. Polk abruptly called for reinforcements from Alabama and ordered his men to stand and fight the oncoming Yankees. The Federal advance consisted of two columns, the right wing led by Maj. Gen. James B. McPherson (17th Corps; divisions of Brig. Gens. Mortimer D. Leggett and Marcellus M. Crocker) and the left by Maj. Gen. Stephen A. Hurlbut (16th Corps; divisions of Brig. Gens. James M. Tuttle, Andrew J. Smith, and James C. Veatch). As Sherman's men assaulted the Confederate units along the march, dispersing them, Sooy Smith would strike at Maj.

Gen. Nathan Bedford Forrest's cavalry in northern Mississippi, keeping it out of the main fight.

At Champion Hill on February 4, Confederate cavalry commanded by Col. Robert C. Wood, Jr. (Adams's Mississippi Regiment) attacked Union cavalry, scattering it for a brief time. As it turned out, however, the resistance would be minor: Polk panicked and moved most of his force into Alabama as S. D. Lee's cavalry rode north. Skirmishes flared all along the expedition, but they were relatively minor. On February 5, Confederate cavalry again clashed with the advancing Yankees, this time at Baker's Creek, at Clinton, and near Jackson. The following day Union troops left the capital city of Jackson on their way to Meridian, and Sooy Smith's cavalry got underway from Memphis. Skirmishing broke out on February 6 at Barnett's Ford and Robertson's Ford. Now meeting almost no opposition for several days, the Union men clashed again with Rebels on February 12—Lincoln's 55th birthday—at Wall Hill, Decatur, and Chunky Station. The following day minor fighting flared around Tunnel Hill as the Yankees approached Meridian. On February 14, Sherman's men entered and captured Meridian, tearing up railroad track and supplies and destroying the value of the town as a Confederate base. "For five days 10,000 men worked hard and with a will in that work of destruction, with axes, crowbars, sledges, clawbars, and with fire," Sherman wrote. "Meridian with its depots, store-houses, arsenal, hospitals, offices, hotels, and cantonments no longer exists."

As soldiers continued destroying Meridian's military usefulness, skirmishing took place nearby at Lauderdale Springs on the 16th and at Pontotoc and Marion the following day. The campaign ended in success for Sherman, another disgraceful failure for Polk, and a stinging disappointment for Sooy Smith, who was whipped soundly during his retreat by Forrest's smaller force at West Point on February 21 and Okolona the following day. Forrest's charge scattered a Tennessee Union regiment, and then a crushing blow that employed hand-to-hand fighting rolled up the Union line. Sooy Smith's troops fled in disarray, badly demoralized, and the battle stands as one of Forrest's greatest. Smith's losses for the campaign were 54 killed, 79 wounded, and 155 missing; Forrest's casualties amounted to 25 killed, 75 wounded, and 10 captured. Among the dead was Forrest's brother Jeffrey. Federal casualties were 21 killed, 68 wounded, and 81 missing; Confederate losses were 400 killed and wounded and 200 captured—Sherman moved on to Nashville to prepare for a campaign into the Deep South, and A. J. Smith was dispatched to support Banks. At the end of the Meridian expedition, Confederates attacked and regained Yazoo City, near Vicksburg, on March 5 and 6.

Searching for a way to accelerate Reconstruction in Mississippi and the rest of the plantation South, Lincoln in January supported a policy to allow plantation owners to free their slaves and hire them immediately to continue working their plantation tracts. Military commanders were already seeing the plausibility of such a plan. "A great many of the Planters in this section desire to work their old plantations (which they never abandoned) and are willing to subscribe to all the rules and regulations which may be adopted, recognize the Freedom of the negro, etc.," McPherson informed Sherman on January 2. "Col. [John] Eaton [Jr.] Genl. Supt. of Contrabands requires that they should come to him with 'military permits' to carry on this in places, and then he will let them hire contrabands, a perfectly proper cause, but one which takes time, as each particular case has to be investigated."

SCATTERED ACTIONS flared over various points in the western theater of operations. In Missouri a shake-up occurred in the Federal army organization in late January when Maj. Gen. William S. Rosecrans was appointed commander of the Department of the Missouri, replacing Maj. Gen. John M. Schofield. The latter, who had been in Missouri since the early days of Frémont, was ousted due to the political instabilities of the hotbed state and came east to command the Army of the Ohio. Small actions and reconnaissances were the order of the day, meanwhile, as at New Bern, North Carolina, where on January 28 an expedition commenced to take the town from Union hands. Captured in March 1862, the coastal stronghold would serve as a much-needed port and base of operations in the Carolinas if it could be retaken. Accordingly, Gen. Robert E. Lee detached a portion of his inactive Army of Northern Virginia—a mixed force of Maj. Gen. George E. Pickett—to take the position. Pickett's force consisted of the division of Brig. Gen. Robert F. Hoke, which would approach from the northwest by route of Batchelder's Creek; Brig. Gen. Seth M. Barton's 3 infantry brigades, along with 600 cavalry and 14 field guns, who would move on the town from the southwest; and Col. James Dearing's 3 regiments of infantry, 300 cavalry, and 3 guns with an approach from the northeast, assigned to assault and capture Fort Anderson, across from the city on the Neuse River. Such an already complex and time-critical operation would also rely on Confederate naval Comdr. John Taylor Wood to move his 14 small boats up the Neuse to intercept Union ships and to aid the Confederate land assault by bombardment.

Pickett's North Carolina adventure began well, and by February 1 the complex plan was unfolding as Hoke crossed the creek, rebuilding bridges that had been destroyed by retreating Yankees. Barton proceeded smoothly along his southern route with great success. The naval force, meanwhile, witnessed such success that on February 2, Wood's sailors captured and destroyed the side-wheel gunboat USS *Underwriter,* which had been anchored in the Neuse. Wood, grandson of Zachary Taylor and a nephew of Jefferson

Davis, slowly moved his boats to within 100 yards of the *Underwriter* before the Union sailors detected them. Not being able to swing their guns into play so quickly, the Union sailors were attacked by Wood's Confederates, who boarded the *Underwriter* and won the ensuing hand-to-hand combat. The Confederates set the ship ablaze and fled.

Despite the promising start, however, Pickett's ambitious plan for New Bern unraveled. The Union works were formidably constructed, both at Fort Anderson and in the defensive lines to the south of the city, and both Barton and Dearing were stalled in attempting to assault them. "The citizens turned out nobly and took the place of the provost guard," claimed Federal Brig. Gen. Innis N. Palmer, commanding the District of North Carolina, headquartered at New Bern, "thus liberating an additional force for duty in the intrenchments. A force of nearly 900 negroes were also quickly armed . . . and they did excellent service." Pickett's men withdrew, and Pickett channeled his anger into court-martialing twenty-two former Confederate soldiers who were captured as Federal soldiers, at Kinston. Convicting them of desertion, Pickett hanged the soldiers.

To the south the occasional bombardment of Charleston's forts continued throughout early 1864. An unusual event occurred on February 17, when Charleston Harbor witnessed the major success of the Confederate submarine CSS *H. L. Hunley.* Following its light action and repeated sinkings under test, the *Hunley* set out to strike a significant ship in the Federal flotilla operating near Charleston. By this time 13 seamen had perished inside the *Hunley,* which had sunk and been raised twice. Still, another daring crew took its place and armed the submersible with a spar torpedo mounted far ahead of the prow. Now army Lt. George E. Dixon and his eight-man crew set out in search of the formidable Union screw sloop USS *Housatonic,* commanded by Capt. Charles W. Pickering. On this misty night with calm waters, the primitive submarine slid through the water undetected by the officers keeping watch on the *Housatonic* until the boat approached to within 100 yards, when Acting Master John K. Crosby spotted it at 8:45 P.M. "It had the appearance of a plank moving in the water," he recalled. Although officers on the Federal warship called men to quarters, it was too late. The *Hunley* slid mercilessly into the wooden hull, on the starboard side, forward of the mizzenmast, striking it with the torpedo in a deafening blast. The ship veritably exploded on contact and sank. It was the first time a submarine had ever sunk an enemy warship. Once again, however, the crew paid the price for their foray. The victorious submarine disappeared without a trace, and many years later was located on the harbor bottom, the men aboard being the last crew of drowning victims of the *H. L. Hunley.* In 2000, the ship was raised and archaeological investigations of the wreck begun.

Florida, a staunch supporter of the Confederacy and a state that thus far played little role in the war, was about to see its largest action of the con-flict. The origins of the present battle stemmed from a group of loyal Florid-ians proposing a plan to Salmon P. Chase in 1863, in which they believed that bringing Florida back into the Union might also help Chase to challenge President Lincoln in the upcoming 1864 election. Treasury Secretary Chase's supporters in Florida received the assistance of Maj. Gen. Quincy A. Gillmore, commanding the Department of the South, who ordered an expe-dition into eastern Florida to cut supply lines, enlist black soldiers, and disrupt Confederate operations in the state. By February 7 a division com-manded by Brig. Gen. Truman Seymour moved to Jacksonville, where it dis-embarked and began a march toward the Suwannee River.

As Seymour marched his 5,500 men westward, he ordered his men to destroy strategic railroads, burn Confederate supply outposts, liberate slaves, and generally wreak havoc on Confederate interests. By February 9 he met up with Gillmore at Baldwin and continued the destruction as he ap-proached the town of Olustee on February 20. The battle of Olustee, also called Ocean Pond, resulted. The town consisted of a depot on the Atlantic & Gulf Railroad and stood about fifty miles southwest of Jacksonville. There, Seymour would encounter about 5,000 Confederate soldiers under Brig. Gen. Joseph Finegan, commanding the District of East Florida, along with a small force of cavalry and 12 field guns. Although Finegan discovered the Federal approach and built trenches for his men to occupy, he grew rest-less and sent the brigade of Brig. Gen. Alfred H. Colquitt forward to assault the slowly approaching Yankees. Musketry opened around the edge of the lake known as Ocean Pond and in the pine-timbered terrain surrounding it. Seymour retaliated by thrusting Brig. Gen. Joseph R. Hawley's brigade in an assault on the Confederate batteries that were firing in the center. Two of Hawley's regiments, the 7th New Hampshire Infantry and the 8th United States Colored Troops were chopped to pieces, creating a melee of casual-ties that forced the survivors to flee in confusion and abandon a battery of Union artillery. As the battle intensified, a soldier of the 115th New York In-fantry recorded that he came across a surgeon working on about twenty men lying around in a makeshift aid station in the field. "Just then a cruel shell burst in their midst," he recalled, "and sent the mangled remains of several of them flying in all directions. . . . I next approached the quarter of our own surgeon, and found him surrounded by fifty wounded, his arms crimsoned with blood, and himself engaged in cutting out balls."

The vicious fight at Olustee continued for several hours, with incon-clusive attacks and counterattacks raging along a wide front. Colquitt's men, mostly Georgians, were reinforced by Col. George P. Harrison, Jr.'s brigade but after a time began to run out of ammunition. Sensing a golden opportu-nity, Seymour sent Col. William Barton's brigade into Harrison's men, but

Barton's Yankees were struck soundly by other regiments and taken out of the fight. As Seymour tried in vain to bolster his line, Finegan threw his reserves into the fight and sent the Union men reeling, retreating from the field and leaving scattered goods behind. Among the fleeing survivors of the fight were the members of Col. Edward N. Hallowell's 54th Massachusetts Infantry, the regiment of black soldiers who had fought so gallantly at Charleston the previous summer. Seymour's men fell back to Jacksonville while Finegan's troops repaired the damaged railroads. The casualties from Olustee were 203 killed, 1,152 wounded, and 506 missing for the Union; Confederate losses were 93 killed and 841 wounded. The Union plan for conquest of Florida was a flop. "I am now writing with a Yankee pen, Yankee ink, on Yankee paper captured on the battlefield," wrote Capt. Winston Stephens of the 2d Florida Cavalry (CSA). "We had one of the hottest contested battles of the War on yesterday. . . . I passed over the field this morning and the dead Yankees and negroes are strewn thick all over the field. . . . The enemy pressed us quite hard but our artillery and infantry opened and the boys yelled and went to work as men can only work who are in earnest, then the scene was grand and exciting."

IN FEBRUARY the first rumblings of activity erupted in northern Georgia, in what would transform into a major campaign in the spring. Following the Chattanooga campaign, Gen. Braxton Bragg had retreated to a position along the crest of Rocky Face Ridge near Dalton and Buzzard's Roost. Though major actions would not occur until May, skirmishing broke out between the Confederate Army of Tennessee, now under Gen. Joseph E. Johnston, and Maj. Gen. William T. Sherman's Army of the Tennessee. While Johnston was badgered by Jefferson Davis and Braxton Bragg in Richmond to move into Tennessee and Kentucky—a completely unreal proposition—Maj. Gen. George H. Thomas's Army of the Cumberland, which had joined Sherman in the area, moved out to reconnoiter the Confederate lines. This resulted in a skirmish from February 23 to 26, with crackles of shots and occasional booming of cannon at Rocky Face Ridge on February 24, and Dalton on February 27. Sherman and Thomas wished to move on the transportation hub at Atlanta. The skirmishes moved Confederate cavalry aside and allowed Union infantry under Maj. Gen. John M. Palmer to drive toward Dalton in a demonstration that produced firing along the lines at Catoosa Station and Tunnel Hill, northwest of Rocky Face Ridge. On the 25th, Palmer's Yankees found a strong Rebel line along Rocky Face Ridge and Palmer withdrew the following day. The final skirmish, on the 27th, was a minor affair at Stone Church near Catoosa Station. Thereafter, Georgia would see scant action until the major campaign unfolded in May. Sherman was eyeing the Deep South.

The Red River Campaign

DESPITE THE MAJOR organizational rumblings of large military movements, events remained relatively quiet as the spring of 1864 approached. In the east, Meade and Lee held on to their winter quarters and marked time along the Virginia front as Sherman and Johnston vied for position in northern Georgia, none of the forces sending out appreciable reconnoitering parties to test the enemy's strength or commitment to battle. Soldiers and civilians alike knew that major conflicts would erupt along the Virginia front and as Sherman's men attempted to strike deeper into Georgia, but they did not know how or when they would come as the warm weather arrived. The political situation was fragile on both sides: support for the Confederacy was in many areas slipping, as the cause appeared more desperate with each passing week. The Union position was delicate, too, because a presidential election was approaching. Detractors and peace advocates would attack the lanky president and the brutality of the war from all angles; in a twist of irony Lincoln's major opponent would be George B. McClellan, newly resigned from the army and running as a Democrat who would propose a quick peace.

In the midst of this potential turmoil, as we have seen, Lincoln asked Congress to confirm the appointment of Ulysses S. Grant as lieutenant general, to command all the armies of the United States. Grant informed Lincoln that he would accept the assignment if he could have a free hand in executing his plans without undue interference from Halleck and Stanton, which Lincoln promised. So on March 8, Grant arrived in Washington from the west and registered at Willard's Hotel near the Executive Mansion, accompanied by two aides and by his oldest son, 13-year-old Frederick Dent Grant. Unrecognized, he registered as "U. S. Grant and son, Galena, Illinois," and soon caused a stir after the clerk realized who stood in front of him.

Grant established his headquarters in the field with the Army of the Potomac. Although Grant has historically overshadowed George Meade, who continued in command of the great eastern army, Meade managed his army effectively and is due more credit than many historians have given him. "Grant is as good a Leader as we can find," William T. Sherman informed his brother John on April 5. "He has honesty, simplicity of character, singleness of purpose, and no hope or claim to usurp civil Power. His character more than his Genius will reconcile Armies and attach the People."

As the Union command structure was reorganizing, a curious affair unfolded amid the inactivity of the eastern theater. As we have seen, Civil War prisons held thousands of Southern and Northern soldiers in their brutal grip throughout the war. Among the most notorious prisons in the south were a group in Richmond that included Libby prison (for Yankee officers) and Belle Isle (for enlisted men). During the late winter thaws of 1864 the dashing young Union cavalry brigadier general H. Judson Kilpatrick hatched a plan to raid Richmond, free Northern prisoners, and generally wreak havoc on the city. This action was prompted by intelligence reports of horrible overcrowding in the prisons, inadequate food, and a supposed garrison force in Richmond of only 3,000. The Union high command approved of the plan, and Kilpatrick, Col. Ulric Dahlgren, and 3,584 troopers set out on the raid on February 28. Of particular value to the Yankee general was the youthful Dahlgren, just 21 years old and the son of the highly respected Union Rear Admiral John A. B. Dahlgren, a close friend of President Lincoln. Dahlgren had a reputation for hard fighting—he had lost a leg at Hagerstown, Maryland, the previous summer.

On February 29 the raiders reached Spotsylvania Court House, where Dahlgren took a detachment of 500 to attack Richmond from the south. Kilpatrick would enter the city from the north. Confederate forces lagged behind Kilpatrick, and the only nuisance on that day was a cold rain that transformed into sleet by the following night. Meanwhile, Confederate Brig. Gen. George Washington Custis Lee—Robert E. Lee's eldest son—shifted his local defense forces to block an attack from the west. Strangely, Kilpatrick, who was known for reckless bravery, halted at the outer defenses of Richmond on March 1 although only a small force met him there. By nightfall Confederate cavalry caught up with Kilpatrick and attacked him in camp. Kilpatrick retreated, aborted the plan, and left Dahlgren in the lurch. At Goochland, Dahlgren split his force and then recombined it, finally reaching a point two and a half miles south of the city on the evening of March 1. After dark, Lee's forces fought a sharp skirmish with Dahlgren. One day later, during Dahlgren's retreat, Confederates ambushed his men, capturing 92 and killing Dahlgren. Of his beloved son's death, the elder Dahlgren could only say: "How busy is death—oh, how busy indeed!"

Then came the controversy. A 13-year-old boy named William Littlepage found on Dahlgren's body papers that disclosed a plan to release 15,000 prisoners who could act as a guard until fresh Federal troops arrived. The papers also contained information about burning the city and killing Jefferson Davis and his cabinet. The papers, at the time alleged to be either forgeries or at least not in Dahlgren's hand, sparked intense debate in the South. The responses ranged from Confederate Colonel Josiah Gorgas's plan to execute all Yankee prisoners, to Robert E. Lee's more rational response of sending a letter of inquiry to the Federals. Kilpatrick issued a statement to George G. Meade that he knew nothing of the plot. Therefore, officially, the responsibility for the idea died with Dahlgren. But in a time of war and heated passions on both sides of the issue, such plots were undoubtedly contemplated more than once in both Washington and Richmond. Kilpatrick alleged that Dahlgren handed him an address that was to be read to the men of the raiding party and that it matched the one printed in the Richmond papers, except that it did not contain the phrase, printed in the papers, "exhorting the prisoners to destroy and burn the hateful city and kill the traitor Davis and his cabinet." The authenticity of the Dahlgren papers or lack thereof, particularly with regard to the inflammatory sentence, is still not resolved.

IN THE TRANS-MISSISSIPPI the spring campaign was underway. Maj. Gen. Nathaniel P. Banks, the Union general who had failed in most of his undertakings, particularly in the Shenandoah Valley in 1862, was ordered to launch his expedition up the Red River to recover Arkansas and Louisiana for the Union. The combined army-navy expedition would target the area of Shreveport, where Lt. Gen. Edmund Kirby Smith had his headquarters and which also served as a major Confederate depot and the de facto capital of Confederate Louisiana. The operation would also attempt to thwart the possible threat from the French, whose puppet emperor Maximilian I held power in Mexico, by establishing a Federal presence in Texas. Neither Grant nor Rear Adm. David D. Porter, who would command the naval force, had much confidence in the plan. The resulting Red River expedition, lasting from March 10 through May 18, would be a Federal disaster with almost no redeeming benefits in exchange for the time and lives spent on it.

Banks began the expedition with 17,000 men who would move up Bayou Teche and join another 10,000-man detachment from Sherman's forces at Alexandria. Additionally, Maj. Gen. Frederick Steele would move south from Little Rock with 15,000 men and join the expedition at Alexandria, Natchitoches, or Shreveport. The organization of the armies changed somewhat during the campaign, but began as follows: Maj. Gen. Banks's Army of the Gulf consisted of a detachment of the 13th Corps (Brig. Gen.

Thomas E. Ransom; divisions of Brig. Gen. Robert A. Cameron and Col. William J. Landram); the 19th Corps (Maj. Gen. William B. Franklin; divisions of Brig. Gens. William H. Emory and Cuvier Grover); a detached brigade of the Corps d'Afrique (Col. William H. Dickey); and a detachment of the Army of the Tennessee (Brig. Gen. Andrew J. Smith; divisions of Brig. Gens. Joseph A. Mower and Thomas Kilby Smith).

Opposing the Federal advance up the Red River would be Kirby Smith's 30,000 men in the Trans-Mississippi Department, who were scattered as follows: near Camden, Arkansas, Lt. Gen. Theophilus H. Holmes had about a third of the force; along the Texas coastline, Maj. Gen. John B. Magruder had another third; and the final third was positioned in Louisiana and commanded by Maj. Gen. Richard Taylor. Of Taylor's troops in his District of West Louisiana, Maj. Gen. John G. Walker's division was posted at Marksville and Brig. Gen. Jean J. A. A. Mouton's division south of Alexandria. Several companies of Confederate cavalrymen were scouting various positions along the Teche, particularly near Vermillionville.

The expedition commenced on March 10 when Sherman's contingent, led by A. J. Smith, departed Vicksburg and was accompanied by a large river flotilla of naval ships, comprising the ironclad gunboats USS *Carondelet*, USS *Chillicothe*, USS *Louisville*, USS *Mound City*, and USS *Pittsburg*; the converted ironclads USS *Benton*, USS *Choctaw*, USS *Eastport*, and USS *Essex*; and the river monitors USS *Neosho*, USS *Osage*, and USS *Ozark*. Accompanying the iron ships were the side-wheel gunboat USS *Lafayette*, the large tinclad USS *Ouachita*, the timberclad USS *Lexington*, the side-wheeler tinclads USS *Fort Hindman* and USS *Gazelle*, and the stern-wheeler USS *Cricket*. Porter proceeded on his flagship, the large tinclad USS *Black Hawk*.

Problems beset the Federal expedition almost from the outset, however. Shortly after embarking, Smith and the naval commanders discovered that the Confederates had obstructed the Red River at the partially built Fort De Russy, north of Marksville and Mansura. Also, they discovered that Banks was running behind schedule with the main body of troops. Despite this, Smith pushed on by transporting his men up the Atchafalaya Bayou and at Simsport commencing a march of 15,000 men and 30 field guns northward toward the fort. Walker's division was directly in the path of the Union approach and consisted of about 3,800 effectives and 12 guns—a completely inadequate force given the size of the juggernaut. Located in a small position dubbed Fort Humbug, Walker's men were immediately in danger of being overwhelmed, so they pulled back to a position that Walker believed would enable him to attack the Yankees if they moved on Fort De Russy with only a portion of the command. Walker's wishful thinking would not pay off, however. Smith marched his detachment through the swampy ground toward Fort De Russy. As the march continued, on March 14 Smith led his

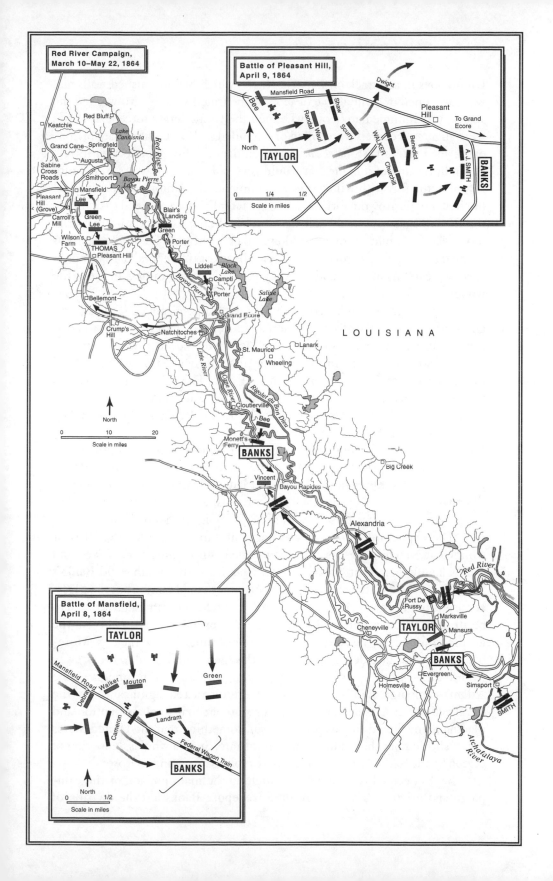

Red River Campaign, March 10–May 22, 1864

Red Bluff
Keatchie
Grand Cane Springfield
Lake Cannisnia
Augusta
Sabine Cross Roads
Smithport
Mansfield
Bayou Pierre Lake
Lee
Red River
Pleasant Hill (Grove)
Carroll's Mill
Green Lee
Blair's Landing
Green
Wilson's Farm
THOMAS Pleasant Hill
Porter
Liddell
Black Lake
Campti
Porter
Saline Lake
Bellemont
Bayou Pierre
Grand Ecore
Crump's Hill
Natchitoches
St. Maurice
Lanark
Wheeling

LOUISIANA

North
0   10   20
Scale in miles

Little River
Cane River
Rigolet du Bon Dieu
Cloutierville
Bee
Monett's Ferry
BANKS
Vincent
Bayou Rapides
Big Creek
Alexandria
Red River
Fort De Russy
Marksville
Cheneyville
TAYLOR
Mansura
BANKS
Holmesville
Evergreen
Simsport
SMITH
Atchafalaya River

Battle of Pleasant Hill, April 9, 1864

Mansfield Road
Dwight
Bee
Shaw
Randal Waul
Scurry
Pleasant Hill
Walker
To Grand Ecore
Benedict
TAYLOR
Churchill
A. J. SMITH
BANKS
North
0   1/4   1/2
Scale in miles

Battle of Mansfield, April 8, 1864

TAYLOR
Mansfield Road
Debray Walker
Mouton
Green
Cameron
Landram
Federal Wagon Train
BANKS
North
0   1/2
Scale in miles

Union boys in an attack on Fort De Russy, which had unfinished walls and was garrisoned by a tiny force of 300 poorly armed soldiers. Mower led the attack, which immediately overwhelmed the Confederate force. Casualties were slight; 38 Federals were killed or wounded and 250 Confederate prisoners taken. Porter's USS *Black Hawk* arrived near the fort shortly after its fall, at the beginning of a night that would turn cold and windy. As A. J. Smith stayed at the fort with Kilby Smith's command, the Union soldiers worked hurriedly to destroy the fort. Several days later the men planned to detonate the fort's magazine, but the job was botched as the explosion prematurely took place at night as many soldiers slept nearby. "The whole heavens seemed to be on fire," wrote one soldier, "pieces of timber and hard lumps of earth were falling in camp and even beyond. Men were running for life to the woods."

The campaign continued as Smith's detachment moved farther north and west, cutting off Walker's division and forcing Taylor to retreat to positions from which he was militarily helpless. Moving northwest along the river toward Alexandria, the Federal flotilla approached on March 15 and found the Confederates in the town had fled. The following day Union forces occupied Alexandria, its 600 remaining residents cowering in their houses. Although he was on the retreat up the Red River, Taylor dispatched the 2d Louisiana Cavalry to ride toward the Federal troops and engage them. For two days the Rebel horsemen skirmished with elements of Smith's force, most significantly on the evening of March 21 in an action termed Bayou Rapides. On this cold, rainy night, Mower led two brigades of cavalry and artillery to envelop and startle the Confederates, who were utterly routed in the darkness. Some 250 prisoners were taken, along with four field guns.

The haphazard campaign was beginning to become focused. Taylor stopped at Natchitoches, awaiting reinforcements coming from Texas, and Banks finally arrived at Alexandria on March 24. By month's end Banks's army had arrived on the scene (a full week later than planned), but the Massachusetts politician was discovering day by day that his campaign seemed to be ill timed. Low water on the river above Alexandria was a concern; the flotilla would barely be able to pass the pair of rapids above the city. Moreover, Banks was instructed that A. J. Smith's men would need to break away from the Red River campaign by April 15 to proceed east in support of the Atlanta campaign. Banks and his men were distracted significantly by the naval activity at Alexandria, which consisted of seizing bales of cotton and placing them aboard ship as prizes of war, something that the United States Navy allowed but the soldiers could not share. Such a wholesale looting of cotton by the navy turned the army participants bitter and morose.

Banks decided to gamble by launching the main portion of the campaign and ordering a movement on Shreveport. Banks left the division of

Cuvier Grover at Alexandria and set off for Grand Ecore and Natchitoches. Skirmishing erupted at Monett's Ferry on the Cane River on March 29 and, two days later, at Natchitoches as the Federals moved into the city. On April 2, Banks occupied the city as minor skirmishes, mostly involving cavalry, broke out nearby at Crump's Hill and, a day later, at Grand Ecore. Having secured the first objective, Banks now devised a complex plan that sent Kilby Smith's division by water on a 110-mile trip upriver to Springfield Landing, where Banks would reunite the land column with Kilby Smith's men on April 9. The move would be risky, since the river's water was rising only very slowly and the six ships scraped and bounced along the muddy river bottom as they went. Taylor, meanwhile, continued retreating upriver to Pleasant Hill, northwest of Natchitoches, and then to Springfield Landing, where he was joined by the Texas cavalry of Brig. Gen. Tom Green. Taylor ordered Green to command the brigades of Brig. Gens. Hamilton P. Bee and James P. Major and Col. Arthur P. Bagby, Jr., acting as rear guard. Two more divisions, those of Brig. Gens. Mosby M. Parsons and James C. Tappan, had been sent from Arkansas, and Taylor continued retreating northwest to Mansfield, arriving near the oncoming Arkansas.

As the armies marched into the new areas of potential battleground, the lay of the land changed drastically. Swampy bayous gave way to thickly forested, brushy, sandy woods. The rugged Texans, some veterans of San Jacinto, faced Smith's battle-hardened men, the westerners of Sherman's army, but also the less experienced men of Banks, who weren't used to such climates. Planning to turn and strike a blow, Taylor was frustrated with small delays and by the indecision and ambiguous orders of Kirby Smith; action finally came on April 7 when the armies clashed in a skirmish at Wilson's Farm near Pleasant Hill. Green's Texas cavalry fought a spirited engagement with Albert L. Lee's Union horsemen, who, according to Brig. Gen. William Dwight, "were not good riders. . . . [They] were infantry soldiers put on horseback." The Confederates attacked several times and kept up a hot fire between the two ranks, but finally Lee was reinforced by Landram's infantry and fought off the attack. Rather than deploying for action—and who could tell what lay out in the thick pine forest?—Banks ordered his advanced guard forward to clear the way, leaving most of his force encamped near Pleasant Hill. On April 8 the Confederate horse soldiers were pushed back to Sabine Cross Roads, three miles southwest of Mansfield, where Taylor had erected a defensive work built around the infantry of Mouton and Walker and the cavalry of Bee. Late in the afternoon, Mouton sparked the battle of Mansfield, which continued into the following day.

Taylor defended Sabine Cross Roads because it would be necessary for Banks to cross through it to continue the advance. He deployed the brigades of Walker on his right and Mouton on the left. Withdrawing in haste after their skirmish, Green's horsemen took up position in the heavy woods on Mouton's left. Approximately 5,300 infantry, 3,000 cavalry, and 500 artillerymen were spread across the battlefront. With the infantry of Landram and the cavalry of Lee reconnoitering the front, Banks ordered the divisions of Cameron and Emory up to support the front, while Taylor brought Brig. Gen. Thomas J. Churchill's two divisions into place. Both commanders were transferring forces in preparation for a battle the following day. But with Federal cavalry visible throughout the thickets, Taylor reinforced further with Col. Horace Randal's cavalry and then ordered the Confederate line forward late in the afternoon. Shortly after 4 P.M. the Federal line was struck with heavy small-arms fire and artillery in support; Mouton's men struck into the Union right as Walker crushed one flank and Green's dismounted troopers rolled up the opposite flank. As Cameron's Yankee division attempted to solidify its position around 5 P.M., most of the men within it fell back under a withering rifle fire. By 6 P.M., the Confederate advance, now spreading across the whole line, struck into Emory, who had established a line some three miles behind the first Union wave. Fighting lasted until early evening but resulted in little tactical gain. Later that night Taylor attempted to turn the Federal right, to no avail.

The morning of April 9 brought the second phase of the battle of Mansfield, often termed Pleasant Hill. Reorganizing his demoralized troops, Banks pulled back fifteen miles southeast to Pleasant Hill, hoping to reunite with A. J. Smith. Taylor pursued and during the afternoon sent the brigades of Parsons and Tappan into a line consisting of the divisions of Mower and Emory. As on the previous afternoon, the Confederate attack commenced in force at 5 P.M. Soon after the crackles of musketry began to flash across the woods, Col. Lewis Benedict's Union brigade fell back, its commander lying dead and the soldiers scattered in confusion. On the Union right, Brig. Gen. William Dwight's brigade withstood the assaults of Bee and Walker, and a counterattack by the brigade of Brig. Gen. James W. McMillan crushed Parsons's right, enabling Mower to attack the center. The Federal advance swept across the battlefield, and although Taylor pushed Brig. Gen. Camille A. J. M. Polignac's brigade up to halt the Union tide, all this did was to help coordinate a Confederate withdrawal. "The tremendous hurrahs from our side told who were victors," recalled Union 1st Lt. John Mead Gould. "In going back a shell came and exploded directly over me in such a manner that I wonder I was not stove all to pieces. . . . Artillery is dangerous sometimes but not always. The rebels are as poor off in this branch that I do not fear shells as I do the little 'zips.' " The battle, fought in two phases over two days, was a stunning blow to the momentum of both armies. Of some 12,000 engaged, Federals lost 150 killed, 844 wounded, and 375 missing; Confederate losses were 1,200 killed and wounded and 426 missing, of 12,500 engaged.

Among the dead was Mouton, who was killed on April 8 either while leading a charge or shortly after the first day's action as he was riding along the line.

The battle stopped Banks's advance; he limped back to Grand Ecore to regroup, while Kirby Smith arrived at Pleasant Hill and found the Confederates in such bad shape that he determined to leave a portion of the army in place to thwart Banks and transport the bulk of the army back to Shreveport, from which it could operate against Maj. Gen. Frederick Steele in Arkansas. By this time A. J. Smith was already late in getting back east to participate in the Atlanta campaign, and Steele would not be able to assist Banks, so the Massachusetts politician decided to break off the failed expedition. Assigned to keep Sherman abreast of the developments, Brig. Gen. John M. Corse dispatched his commander on April 8, "The tendency is to overestimate the enemy wherever I go, but I think that if we can find a crossing on the Tombigbee we can whip anything they have got." The Kilby Smith force, meanwhile, transported upriver by Porter's gunboats, dragging bottom nearly all the way, was attacked by Tom Green's horsemen on April 12 at Blair's Landing (Pleasant Hill Landing). In the brief engagement involving 750 cavalry and several guns that opened on the ships, a few casualties aboard ship were taken and Green himself was killed when the USS *Lexington* and the USS *Osage* returned fire. Shocked by Green's death, his troops broke off the engagement a short time later.

Despite the expedition's failure, scattered fighting continued. On April 21, Banks retreated from Grand Ecore, marching southeast to Cloutierville. Wharton struck into the Federal rear guard, moving it out of Natchitoches, and Bee positioned his Rebel horsemen near Monett's Ferry, six miles south of Cloutierville, to block the Union retreat. On April 23 the battle of Monett's Ferry, or Cane River, was fought when Bee assaulted the fleeing Yankees. Bee was struck by a frontal attack by Emory's infantry, and Brig. Gen. Henry W. Birge attacked from the west. Despite Bee's dismounted troopers firing solidly, and harassment from Wharton and Polignac from the rear, the Confederate assault foundered. One of the soldiers of the 153d New York Infantry who fought at Monett's Ferry was Pvt. Lyons Wakeman. Wakeman's real name was Sarah Rosetta Wakeman, a farm girl from central New York who joined the army and kept her female identity secret through two years of combat. Though she had lived through battle, Wakeman contracted chronic diarrhea and died in New Orleans in June. Rosetta Wakeman was not alone: at least 400 women dressed as men served as soldiers during the war, and possibly many more who were never discovered.

Porter's Union naval flotilla, meanwhile, was experiencing ever more serious difficulty in working its way downriver. On April 15, the USS *Eastport* struck a torpedo about eight miles below Grand Ecore, its commander, Lt. Comdr. S. Ledyard Phelps, reporting "a peculiar trembling sensation."

Phelps ran the ship aground into shoal water and for the following six days attempted to pump out the water from this largest of the ironclads on the expedition. By April 21, Phelps got the ship under way with the aid of a battery of carpenters; over the next five days the ship traveled only sixty miles downstream, grounding eight times. On April 26, Phelps transferred his crew onto the USS *Fort Hindman* and detonated more than 3,000 pounds of gunpowder that had been placed aboard the *Eastport,* blowing the ship into countless pieces. Dangerously low water levels on the river continued to make moving the other ships difficult, and to make matters worse for Porter, Confederate Col. J. H. Caudle established a blockade of the river at the confluence of the Red and Cane rivers, placing Capt. Florian Cornay's four-gun battery into position there. As Porter's last ships struggled toward Alexandria, a naval-land battle erupted on April 26 and 27 between the improvised shore batteries and the USS *Cricket,* the USS *Fort Hindman,* the stern-wheeler USS *Juliet,* and the pump steamers USS *Champion No. 3* and USS *Champion No. 5.*

Several of the Federal ships received heavy damage; the *Cricket* was hit 38 times, with 12 killed and 19 wounded, and charged by Confederates from the shore, who attempted to board the gunboat but were struck squarely by canister fire from light guns aboard the ship. By nightfall the *Cricket* finally succeeded in turning a bend of the river and moving out of range of the batteries. The *Champion No. 3* was struck squarely in the boiler, leaving it adrift, and was captured. The *Juliet's* engine was disabled by shellfire but it was towed upstream, out of range, by the *Champion No. 5,* which in the end was so heavily struck that it was grounded, wrecked, and burned. The *Juliet* made good her escape, and the *Fort Hindman,* though injured and unable to steer correctly, covered the escape of the remaining ships. The USS *Neosho* arrived on the scene to assist the operation after the damage had been done. Porter called the heavy cannonading "the heaviest fire I ever witnessed." Such a terrific stand against ships had been made by only 200 men and 4 guns on shore.

Shortly before the fight at Monett's Ferry, on April 25, Banks arrived back at Alexandria and found bleak news there. The water level on the Red River was so low at the double rapids that the Union ships would not be able to pass through. Banks and Porter were stuck with a potentially grave problem that might sacrifice the whole flotilla to Confederate guns. "I find myself blockaded by a fall of 3 feet of water," worried Porter on April 28, "... no amount of lightening will accomplish the object. . . . In the meantime, the enemy are splitting up into parties of 2,000 and bringing in the artillery." The only course of action seemed to be to destroy the ships. But then came one of the most ingenious engineering feats in military history. Lt. Col. Joseph Bailey, an engineer in the 19th Corps who had been wounded in the head at Mansfield, proposed a peculiar solution. Bailey ingeniously devised and began constructing an improvised series of wing dams to raise the water and allow the ships to pass.

After eight days of hard manual labor, Bailey, assisted by Maine and New York soldiers, finished the work of constructing his innovative dams, just below Alexandria. Hope rose that the ships might be saved. On May 9 two of the stone-laden barges composing parts of the dam collapsed under the heavy water pressure, but the wings slid into position so that a raised waterway (sluice) still flowed through the center of the river. A hasty lineup was ordered so the ships could get through with the maximum water under them, and as the water began again to fall, the *Osage* and the *Neosho,* then the *Fort Hindman* and the *Lexington,* shot over the water and into safer waters. "Thirty thousand voices rose in one deafening cheer," wrote Porter, "and universal joy seemed to pervade the face of every man present." The larger ships still remained above the dam, however, and Bailey went back to work to repair the dams. By May 13 the dams were in top form, and the last ships— the *Louisville, Chillicothe,* and *Ozark*—made their way over the rapids and into safety. "This is without a doubt the best engineering work ever performed," Porter wrote of his young engineer officer. Bailey had saved the flotilla, worth nearly $2 million, and probably saved many lives. He was commissioned a brigadier general of volunteers and later received the Thanks of Congress.

Scattered actions occurred as Banks and Porter continued retreating from Alexandria. Skirmishes flared at Mansura from May 14 to 16, at Marksville Prairie (Avoyelles Prairie) on May 15, and Belle Prairie on May 16. The last set of skirmishes in the campaign took place on May 18 at Bayou de Glaize, and once again Bailey demonstrated his engineering brilliance by bridging the 600-foot span across the Atchafalaya River at Simsport by using steamers to form a makeshift bridge. Banks moved his men, wagons, and supplies across on May 19 and 20, and the fruitless campaign was over. Banks sent his men to Donaldsonville and A. J. Smith's corps left for Vicksburg, not to be engaged in the Atlanta campaign after all.

The Red River campaign caused unhappiness and waste all the way around. Taylor bickered with Kirby Smith. Banks would not recover his reputation, now destroyed. A. J. Smith and Porter were nearly permanently embittered. Certainly, no one was angrier than the soldiers who had been put through the terrible and pointless experience, yet some tried to understand. "It was the Red River that defeated us," explained Union Private William Prentice. "Gen. Banks on the night of the 8th knew that the river had fallen so low that our transports could not proceed. . . . Banks has been blamed for not keeping his forces more concentrated, yet how could he do it on such a road & at the same time protect his train." Many believed the whole affair to be driven by cotton speculation and profiteering. In the wake of the campaign Kirby Smith burned 150,000 bales of cotton valued at $60 million.

During the time of the Red River expedition, another major military movement took place in the Trans-Mississippi—Maj. Gen. Frederick Steele's Camden expedition. Steele had performed well in the field, distinguishing himself during the Vicksburg campaign, and by the winter of 1864 was assigned to command the Department of Arkansas. Ordered to cooperate with Banks during the Red River expedition, Steele vigorously opposed the plan to move on Shreveport because roads were in such poor shape and his flanks on such a movement would be exposed. Despite his objections, Steele brought a division and two attached brigades from the 7th Corps forward out of Little Rock and planned to join Brig. Gen. John M. Thayer, another Vicksburg veteran, at Arkadelphia by the end of March. The effective force would compose an army of 10,400, mostly infantry, with which Steele could strike at the Confederates who might interfere with Banks's journey up the Red River. Just as with the Red River expedition, however, the Camden expedition almost immediately strayed from the plan, and trouble arose. By March 29, Steele reached Arkadelphia with the main force but found Thayer absent. Despite shortages of supplies, Steele determined to push forward without Thayer.

Despite the trouble, Steele initially succeeded in attracting Confederate cavalry that otherwise might have harassed Banks. On April 1, as Steele departed Arkadelphia, the Confederate horse soldiers of Brig. Gen. John S. Marmaduke approached—three brigades commanded by Brig. Gens. Jo Shelby and William L. Cabell, and Col. Colton Greene. Skirmishes erupted between the cavalrymen and soldiers on Steele's flanks, principally at Elkins's Ferry on the Little Missouri River, Arkansas, which lasted two days. By April 9 the two Union columns, Steele's and Thayer's, had found each other and united, but by then the campaign was already undersupplied and disorganized and under frequent harassment from the Confederate cavalry. On April 10, as Steele advanced into Prairie D'Ane, he struck into the Confederate force, now numbering more than 5,000, and a series of skirmishes erupted that lasted several days. Believing that Steele was targeting Washington, Arkansas, the Confederates were surprised when he turned and moved on Camden, still hoping to establish a base and gather supplies, which were now seriously lacking. To make matters worse, with his soldiers being fed half rations, Steele now learned that Banks had been defeated at Mansfield and that he was virtually isolated in hostile territory.

Steele fought a brief, sharp battle with the Confederate horsemen at Camden on April 15 and then established a base at the tiny town, sending out a foraging expedition to gather supplies for his men, who were now on the verge of starving. On April 17, Col. James M. Williams brought with him 695 infantrymen, 438 of them black soldiers of his 1st Kansas Infantry (Colored), along with 2 field guns and 198 wagons. He hoped to fill the wagons with abundant supplies of corn, which grew in the region, and any other edibles he could find. Moving out on the Prairie D'Ane-Camden Road, the men traveled fourteen miles before establishing camp and sending out half the wagons to retrieve corn. The next day he turned again toward Camden, was reinforced—bringing his strength to 1,170 men and 4 field guns—and sent another group out to retrieve more corn from various depots.

Marmaduke learned of the Union movements, meanwhile, which led to the battle of Poison Springs on April 18. Marmaduke moved 1,700 of his cavalrymen to the Lee Plantation, ten miles from Camden, and deployed them along the road. Brig. Gen. Samuel B. Maxey arrived with another 1,600 cavalry by 9:30 A.M., with Marmaduke and Maxey on the right and left and Greene's men in reserve. At 10 A.M. the unsuspecting Union scouts ran into Confederates, who opened fire, and Williams assembled an improvised defensive line. Union artillery probed the Confederate lines, but in response, Marmaduke sent forward an attack that struck hard into the Union soldiers by 10:45 A.M. Sharp crackles of musketry fire rang out in the sandy, wooded terrain, and Union artillery occasionally belched forth shots, sending back one part of the Confederate advance. But Greene's reserves plugged the gap and sent the Union troops reeling. Confederates thrust into the Federal rear guard, opening a hot, enfilading fire. The beaten and demoralized black soldiers of the 1st Kansas fled in confusion, and by early afternoon the debacle was over. Of those who were engaged on the field, Williams suffered greater than 25 percent casualties dead or wounded—204 killed and missing and 97 wounded—and the supply train and field guns were lost. Confederate losses were only 114 total. Of the Union dead, 117 were black soldiers, and credible testimony records the shooting of at least some blacks who were first wounded on the ground or attempted surrender. Tired of fighting a long war and hearing of emancipation, some Southern soldiers blamed those who they believed should remain enslaved and in the heat of battle murdered them on the ground. It was an ugly type of warfare that would occur again during this desperate year of the conflict. "Many wounded men belonging to the First Kansas Colored Volunteers fell into the hands of the enemy," decried Williams, "and I have the most positive assurances from eye-witnesses that they were murdered on the spot."

Now Steele's campaign was spiraling out of control, just as Banks's campaign had. On April 20, Steele found that Kirby Smith had moved three divisions in front of the Union movement, threatening to cut off Steele from a route of retreat back to Little Rock. Infantry of Maj. Gen. Sterling Price (commanding the District of Arkansas) also entered the operation when on April 25 they captured another supply expedition, this time at Marks's Mills.

A train consisting of 211 wagons sent from Camden toward Pine Bluff, escorted by 2,000 troops, was attacked and numerous prisoners were captured by Brig. Gen. James F. Fagan's cavalry. Union losses were 100 killed, 250 wounded, and 100 captured; Confederate losses were 41 killed, 108 wounded, and 144 missing. In a panic, Steele now ordered a withdrawal to Little Rock. But he wouldn't end the expedition without another battle, this time as he maneuvered northward. The day after Marks's Mills, Steele's men scrambled northward in a driving rain, abandoning Camden. On April 30, as Steele's men waited to cross the Saline River, a hot engagement erupted at Jenkins's Ferry.

Rainy, muddy conditions prevented professional soldiering on both sides—it was a mess. As Steele's men were astride the river, Marmaduke's advancing column struck into the rear guard of the Federal retreat about two miles from Jenkins's Ferry. For his part, at least Steele had arranged the rear of his army in a defensive position so that they could fire effectively on the attacking Confederates. Hot flashes of musketry rang out through the rain. The cries and echoes of wounded huddling in the mud characterized the late morning and afternoon as Union soldiers crossed the pontoon bridges that offered escape for Steele. Bloodied a final time, the Union expedition retreated across the river unpursued, and Steele's folly came to an end. Union casualties were 64 killed, 378 wounded, and 86 missing; Confederate losses were 86 killed, 356 wounded, and 1 missing. Among the Confederate dead was Brig. Gen. William R. Scurry, the hard-fighting Texan, who was mortally wounded and bled to death on the field, refusing to be taken to the rear.

The expedition was an utter failure. Steele's star fell. Of course, he attributed generous blame to subordinate commanders, such as Brig. Gen. Nathan Kimball, the Hoosier who had fought relatively ineffectively on the plains of Antietam and the hills of Vicksburg. "When the expedition was organized at Little Rock," Steele wrote William T. Sherman, "Genl. Kimball was absent on his own application. . . . It is necessary that I should have someone at Little Rock who will at least obey my orders. I do not want Kimball in the field, and as he asks to be relieved, I have ordered him to report to you." Ironically, Kimball was assigned temporary command of the Department of Arkansas in place of Steele.

THE WAR IN TENNESSEE merely smoldered during March and April 1864. Skirmishing, foraging expeditions, and minor raids from encampments marked the cold weather of early spring. Maj. Gen. Nathan Bedford Forrest launched a significant cavalry raid into western Tennessee and Kentucky on March 16, however, which lasted nearly a month. Forrest's 7,000 cavalrymen held as objectives capturing Yankee prisoners and supplies, destroying what they couldn't carry, and demolishing Union posts and fortifications from Paducah south to Memphis. Forrest's Cavalry Corps consisted of two divisions led by Brig. Gens. James R. Chalmers (brigades of Brig. Gen. Robert V. Richardson and Col. Robert M. McCulloch) and Abraham Buford (brigades of Cols. Tyree H. Bell and A. P. Thompson). The expedition began in earnest when Forrest sent Col. William L. Duckworth with 1,500 men to capture Union City, Tennessee, in the northwestern corner of the state. Duckworth accomplished this on March 24, after a six-hour fight with Col. Isaac R. Hawkins's 7th Tennessee Cavalry (USA). After severe skirmishing with charges and casualties mounting on both sides, Hawkins decided to surrender. "Colonel Hawkins said that it would save a great many lives if we would surrender," explained Capt. John W. Beatty of the 7th Tennessee, "and that if we renewed the fight they would kill every one that might fall into their hands. . . . The officers and men cried like a whipped child."

Forrest, meanwhile, took the bulk of his force north to Paducah, which he approached on March 25, pushing the Federal garrison, the 40th Illinois Infantry, into Fort Anderson, an earthwork on the western edge of town. Some 650 Yankees huddled in the fort and were fired on by many of Forrest's troopers, scattered throughout nearby houses. After half an hour's fight Forrest sent a demand for surrender, but Col. Stephen G. Hicks refused. Forrest's impetuous brigade commander, Col. Thompson, led a hellfire assault toward the fort (apparently wanting to recapture his hometown at any cost) and was struck and killed by a shell. As the Yankees remained in the fort and in gunboats along the Mississippi, Forrest's men moved into town and destroyed vast quantities of supplies, wrecking one steamer, the *Dacotah,* burning 60 bales of cotton, and capturing 50 prisoners. After destroying most of the useful supplies in town during ten hours of occupation, Forrest's men left.

Other skirmishes marked the trail of Forrest's raid: Columbus, Kentucky, on March 27 and April 11; Bolivar, Tennessee, on March 29; Raleigh, Tennessee, on April 3 and 9. But Forrest's men still needed supplies, and the best place for restocking was Fort Pillow, which stood overlooking the Mississippi River some 40 miles north of Memphis, west of the town of Covington. As Forrest planned to move on Fort Pillow, Brig. Gen. Benjamin Grierson at Memphis dispatched Col. Fielding Hurst with Federal cavalry to harass and stop Forrest. Hurst was turned back, however, at the skirmish at Bolivar, and Yankees did not again march out of Memphis until April 3. At Raleigh, the Yankees were again defeated and sent on the retreat to Memphis. "There is a Federal force of 500 or 600 at Fort Pillow," Forrest wrote on April 4, "which I shall attend to in a day or two, as they have horses and supplies which we need."

As a detachment of his command under Buford was striking again at

Paducah, Forrest targeted Fort Pillow. Standing on a high bluff, the fort consisted of three lines of entrenchments, arranged in a near semicircle, with dirt thrown 6 to 8 feet high to form a protective parapet surrounded by a ditch; the face of Pillow stretched about 125 yards, and the fort's rear was essentially open to the steep drop-off to the river. Once evacuated by Confederate forces in 1862, the fort had been under Federal use to protect the water approach to Memphis. About 600 men, approximately half black and half white, composed the garrison at Fort Pillow. The black soldiers were members of the 2d U.S. Colored Light Artillery and the 6th U.S. Colored Heavy Artillery and were commanded by Maj. Lionel F. Booth. Most of them were former slaves and knew well the danger they would be in if captured by Confederates. The white soldiers were members of the 13th Tennessee Cavalry (USA), commanded by Maj. William F. Bradford. They were loyal eastern Tennessee Unionists, and virtually all new recruits. Booth was in overall command.

Chalmers arrived in force with his Rebel cavalry on the morning of April 12, and by the time Forrest arrived at 10 A.M. the fort was surrounded, the Union garrison vastly outnumbered. Stray Federal fire struck Forrest's horse, and the general fell and was bruised, putting him in a disagreeable mood. He shifted sharpshooters onto some high ground surrounding the fort from which the Confederates could strike most of the occupants inside. Confederate sniping escalated during the morning, and Booth was one of those killed by sharpshooting, struck in the chest. Bradford assumed command.

By 11 A.M. the Confederates had captured two rows of barracks about 150 yards from the southern edge of the fort; a murderous fire poured out from this position, which the Yankees had failed to destroy before the Rebel onslaught. Flashes of musketry lit the surrounding woods and artillery boomed forth clouds of smoke from both sides, but it was soon apparent that the Confederate fire was winning the day. By 3:30 P.M. a soldier carrying a white flag appeared, approaching the fort, bearing a message from Forrest. As usual, Forrest demanded surrender, writing to Booth: "I now demand the unconditional surrender of your forces, at the same time assuring you that you will be treated as prisoners of war. . . . I have received a new supply of ammunition and can take your works by assault, and if compelled to do so you must take the consequences." After an hour to consult with his officers, Bradford replied, in Booth's name (wishing to conceal the fact that Booth was dead), "I will not surrender."

While the Union officers were considering their options and delivering a message back to Forrest, the Confederates shifted troops into a ravine that they had been fighting to possess. On the refusal of surrender, a tremendous Confederate charge was instantly started into the fort, firing hotly, and driving the black soldiers of the 6th U.S. Heavy Artillery out of their position, fleeing down toward the river, many of them shot in the back. The defense of the fort collapsed in a flash, the Union men throwing down their weapons and surrendering en masse, with many of the Confederates still firing and howling the Rebel yell. Then came one of the most infamous scenes of the Civil War. The so-called Fort Pillow massacre took place between 4 P.M. and dusk, as various surrendered and injured Union men, most of them black Americans, were shot as prisoners. Though the extent of the crimes at Fort Pillow have long been debated, the historical record clearly shows that war crimes were committed. Confederate losses at Fort Pillow were 14 killed and 86 wounded; casualties among the Union troops were reported as 277 to 297 dead of the 585 to 605 men present. The record does not describe exactly how many men were killed after their surrender, but clearly the sight of black troops in uniform and the initial refusal of some troops to surrender (many of the black troops believed they would only be killed if they surrendered in Federal blue), caused Confederate soldiers at the fort to kill Union soldiers in large numbers on the evening of April 12. Not all those killed were black: Bradford was among those shot after he was taken prisoner. And although he was an extreme racist, Forrest is not necessarily to blame for the event at Fort Pillow; some evidence suggests that he actually intervened to stop the random shootings. But however one argues the evidence, it's clear that a massacre did occur at Fort Pillow, with dozens of soldiers—possibly more than 200—murdered after the military action of the afternoon. Fort Pillow marked one of the bleakest, saddest events of American military history.

THE FINAL SIGNIFICANT ACTION before the large armies began to move for the spring campaigns occurred along the North Carolina shoreline at Plymouth. Gen. Braxton Bragg, military advisor to Jefferson Davis, concocted a plan to capture the seaport, located southwest of Albemarle Sound and northwest of Pamlico Sound, by using the newly completed ironclad ram CSS *Albemarle* in a combined operation with army troops commanded by Brig. Gen. Robert F. Hoke. Hoke attacked at 4 P.M. on April 17, employing his brigade with those of Brig. Gens. Matt W. Ransom and James L. Kemper. Four infantry regiments with attached artillery and cavalry opposed the Confederate attack, the garrison commanded by Brig. Gen. Henry W. Wessells. Cries for assistance from Wessells went largely unheeded, and on April 19, the *Albemarle* appeared and in a sharp naval contest rammed and sank the small side-wheel combatant USS *Southfield,* disabled the side-wheel gunboat USS *Miami,* and sank the steamer USS *Bombshell.*

With the destruction of his support from the Navy, Wessells issued a white flag and surrendered at 10 A.M. on April 20, giving Plymouth to Hoke's

Confederates. The Yankees lost 2,834, many of them prisoners (including Wessells), and a vast quantity of stores. Hoke's impressive victory netted a base from which Carolina operations could commence for the South.

As LINCOLN GAVE immense power to Grant, the president reassured the new commanding general that he would have a free hand, unshackled by the politics of Washington, even in this election year. "The particulars of your plans I neither know, or seek to know," announced the president. "You are vigilant and self-reliant; and, pleased with this, I wish not to obtrude any constraints or restraints upon you. . . . If there is anything wanting which is within my power to give, do not fail to let me know it." Lincoln further held that throughout Grant's strategy of coordinated, simultaneous movements— here, finally, came a coordination in time—"those not skinning can hold a leg." Lincoln's humor did not fail in what appeared to be the most perilous hour of the war thus far. "Today the President loafing into my room picked up a paper and read the Richmond *Examiners* recent attack on Jeff. Davis," recounted John Hay in the Executive Mansion. "It amused him. 'Why,' said he 'the *Examiner* seems abt. as fond of Jeff as the World is of me.' " Still, the dark undercurrent of the war rose day by day. "If slavery is not wrong, nothing is wrong," Lincoln wrote Albert G. Hodges, editor of the Frankfort (Kentucky) *Commonwealth*. "I cannot remember when I did not so think, and feel. And yet I have never understood that the Presidency conferred upon me an unrestricted right to act officially upon this judgment and feeling. . . . I claim not to have controlled events, but confess plainly that events have controlled me. . . . If God now wills the removal of a great wrong, and wills also that we of the North as well as you of the South, shall pay fairly for our complicity in that wrong, impartial history will find therein new cause to attest and revere the justice and goodness of God."

Grant Moves into the Wilderness

As WARM WEATHER washed over American men and boys in the fourth year of civil war, 1864, eyes North and South invariably focused on Ulysses S. Grant. The newly appointed commander of the United States Army—about 533,000 men in the field—was a westerner, like his commander-in-chief, and had a reputation for hard fighting and tenacious pursuit of the enemy. All the while, this softspoken man was accustomed to spending time alone and coolly writing out dispatches under a tree as the battle raged nearby. Though he had acquired a reputation for hard drinking, which undoubtedly he did out of loneliness in the prewar frontier army, Grant certainly did not drink often during the Civil War, but he did suffer from migraine headaches, the symptoms of which mimicked hangovers to a number of sporadic eyewitnesses. Grant drank alcohol rarely during the war—far less than many or even most general officers North and South (outrageous examples of drinking during the war, even during battles, exist in the cases of such officers as William H. Carroll, George B. Crittenden, John Dunovant, Nathan G. Evans, Edward Ferrero, James H. Ledlie, Thomas F. Meagher, Thomas A. Rowley, and John H. H. Ward). Of course, the rumors about Grant's habitual drunkenness existed during the war, as evidenced by Halleck's insinuations during the early war years and by Lincoln's acknowledgment that whatever Grant was drinking should be distributed to other generals, too. But Grant's detractors cited his behavior from before the war to fuel their assertions, and postwar writers added to the image by relying on such unreliable works as Sylvanus Cadwallader's *Three Years with Grant*.

Whatever reservations Northerners had about Grant were partly erased when he captured Fort Donelson, were reduced further when he captured Vicksburg, and were eliminated when he was commissioned lieutenant general and assigned command of the armies. "Everybody has faith in Grant," proclaimed Maj. Charles P. Mattocks to his mother, "as they have previously had in McDowell, McClellan, Burnside, or Hooker and as *we now* have in Meade. . . . It is not high treason to say that Genl. Lee is a hard man to compete with for the honors of war." Though the country swelled with confidence in Grant, easterners were more reserved in their enthusiasm; after all, he was not a product of the Army of the Potomac. Charles Francis Adams, Jr., now a captain, wrote his father, U.S. minister to Britain: "The feeling about Grant is peculiar—a little jealousy, a little dislike, a little envy, a little want of confidence. . . . If he succeeds, the war is over." For his own part, Grant, though given great latitude by Lincoln, was equally gracious with the president. "Should my success be less than I desire, and expect," he told Lincoln on May 1, "the least I can say is, the fault is not with you."

With Grant in charge and Lee readying his men for war, a new campaign was certain to commence in Virginia; Lee's men huddled in their lines, inadequately supplied and far less numerous than Meade's army—but Lee had the tactical advantage of defending against an attack and operating over interior lines. Where Meade would strike, and when, remained an open question. Other battlefronts would surely see imminent action, too. Sherman was positioned in northern Georgia for an attack deep into the state. Butler, with his Army of the James, including many black soldiers, aimed to assault Confederate positions along the James River. The North would likely strike into the Shenandoah Valley to further deplete the dwindling resources of the South. Attacks might come at Mobile or other seaport cities. Lincoln, meanwhile, faced the unrelenting approach of the election, complicated by the sensitive issue of expanding emancipation, and Davis faced increasing criticism of what appeared to a growing number of Southerners to be a failing war effort.

The great eastern campaign of 1864 would indeed begin with a thunderclap. On the eastern front Grant had a total of 118,700 men in the field and 316 guns. Of these, 99,400 men belonged to Meade's Army of the Potomac and 19,300 to Burnside's 9th Corps, which was dispersed along the Orange & Alexandria Railroad from Rappahannock Station to Manassas Junction. Lee's Army of Northern Virginia comprised about 64,000 men in the field and 274 field guns. The campaign that commenced during the first days of May was termed the Wilderness, or Overland, campaign. The battles that resulted during the following weeks as Grant and Meade maneuvered their way into Virginia would be among the costliest and most brutal of the war. The organization of the armies was significantly different than it had been when they last clashed some five months before, at Mine Run. Now Meade's Army of the Potomac consisted of four army corps commanded by Maj. Gen. Winfield Scott Hancock (2d Corps; divisions of Maj. Gen. David B. Birney and Brig. Gens. Francis C. Barlow, John Gibbon, and Gershom Mott); Maj. Gen. Gouverneur K. Warren (5th Corps; divisions of Brig. Gens. Charles Griffin, John C. Robinson, Samuel W. Crawford, and James S. Wadsworth); Maj. Gen. John Sedgwick (6th Corps; divisions of Brig. Gens. Horatio G. Wright, George W. Getty, and James B. Ricketts); and Maj. Gen. Philip H. Sheridan (Cavalry Corps; divisions of Brig. Gens. Alfred T. A. Torbert, David M. Gregg, and James H. Wilson). Additionally, Burnside's 9th Corps would be involved in the Wilderness campaign, although it belonged to the Army of the Ohio until May 24, when it was reassigned to the Army of the Potomac. The 9th Corps contained the divisions of Brig. Gens. Thomas G. Stevenson, Robert B. Potter, Orlando B. Willcox, and Edward Ferrero. Lee's Army of Northern Virginia was recomposed as a four-corps organization that contained units commanded by Lt. Gen. James Longstreet (1st Corps; divisions of Maj. Gen. Charles W. Field and Brig. Gen. Joseph B. Kershaw); Lt. Gen. Richard S. Ewell (2d Corps; divisions of Maj. Gens. Jubal A. Early, Edward Johnson, and Robert E. Rodes); Lt. Gen. A. P. Hill (3d Corps; divisions of Maj. Gens. Richard H. Anderson, Henry Heth, and Cadmus M. Wilcox); and Maj. Gen. Jeb Stuart (Cavalry Corps; divisions of Maj. Gens. Wade Hampton, Fitzhugh Lee, and William Henry Fitzhugh Lee).

The reorganization of the Federal army left some soldiers with unhappy attitudes heading into what seemed a vital campaign. Eliminating the 1st and 3d corps combined veterans and recruits into units with little in common, lowering morale. Although Grant would accompany the Army of the Potomac, he left Meade to make tactical decisions, and although the relationship was at times strained, it worked reasonably well. Sheridan became a major player by commanding the Cavalry Corps, and Burnside at first simply guarded the railroads until he was brought into the campaign more directly after the first few weeks. Grant's idea, communicated effectively to Lincoln, of simultaneously moving on the two largest remaining Confederate armies—Lee's in Virginia and Johnston's in Georgia—was sound, and a number of other simultaneous operations assisted the two primary ones. The secondary operation in the east assigned Butler to move toward Richmond along the James; the Shenandoah Valley would be threatened by Maj. Gen. Franz Sigel. Out west, the discredited Banks would again try to recover his reputation by moving against Mobile.

At the outset of the campaign Grant understood what it would take to win the war. To move against and subjugate the two large Confederate armies would require a heavy price in time, money, supplies, and human lives. At the time, and in more recent simplistic discussions of the Wilderness and subsequent campaigns, Grant has often been criticized as insensitive to the deaths and suffering of so many men that would take place over the bloody year of 1864, which has been dubbed "Simply Murder." Contemporaneously, Grant was labeled "the Butcher" by Southern and anti-administration Northern newspapers. Grant has also been criticized tactically because he did not strike into Lee frontally and defeat him in repeated, large-scale battles. Yet these criticisms fail to perceive that Grant understood what it would take to defeat Lee *strategically*, and his analysis of course was borne out in the end.

Lee positioned the main body of his force as follows: Ewell's corps was near Mine Run, scene of the previous maneuver; Hill concentrated at Orange Court House, to Ewell's southwest; Longstreet was near Mechanicsburg and Gordonsville, south of Hill; and Stuart's horsemen were scattered along a front from Fredericksburg in the east to Gordonsville. The broad, heavily defended front was far too strong to attack frontally, and by now enough foolish Civil War commanders had learned their lessons about frontal attacks that the idea seemed poor to the dullest private. Clearly, Lee had to be maneuvered out of his earthworks and onto ground that would favor the Northern army.

Now, Grant determined, was the time for a large enveloping movement. Turning Lee's left would enable Grant's soldiers to utilize outstanding countryside in which to march and fight, but it would endanger the Federal lines of communications. Turning Lee's right flank, however, would force the Army of Northern Virginia to retreat southward to preserve its lines of communications and enable Butler to strike into Lee's army from the southeast. It would also preserve the Federal lines of communications intact. But it would require fighting on unfriendly ground, the sinister region dubbed the Wilderness, Hooker's nemesis. Grant decided to risk fighting through the underbrush of the Wilderness. He aligned his corps at Germanna Ford (5th and 6th corps) and Ely's Ford (2d Corps) on May 3, preparing to cross the following day. Alerted to the action, Lee swung his three infantry corps northward and eastward to counter the assault. The stage was set for the battle of the Wilderness. As Lee consulted with some of his subordinates at Clark's Mountain, wondering about Grant's moves, Longstreet—who knew Grant as his cousin-in-law—summarized what the Confederates were facing. "That man will fight us every day and every hour till the end of this war," said the 1st Corps commander.

Soldiers and officers alike were uneasy at the potential scale of the bloodshed. In the Federal 2d Corps, the officer of the day held a special honor on such a momentous day as one when the army was organizing for a major attack. "Brig. Genl. A. Hays, Commanding Brigade, 3d Division, is announced as General Officer of the Day for the Corps, May 3d to 4th, 1864," read a circular sent by Francis A. Walker, the 2d Corps assistant adjutant general. Less than two days later Hays would fall dead, shot through the head. Confederate papers of the day included an urgent letter of Robert E. Lee to

Jefferson Davis. "You will already have learned that the army of Gen Meade is in motion," stated Lee, "and is crossing the Rapidan on our right, whether with the intention of attacking, or moving towards Fredericksburg, I am not able to say. But it is apparent that the long threatened effort to take Richmond has begun, and that the enemy has collected all his available force to accomplish it." As his army was set into motion, Meade issued an address to his men: "Soldiers! the eyes of the whole country are looking with anxious hope to the blow you are about to strike in the most sacred cause that ever called men to arms."

The Union advance began at midnight on May 3, Grant hoping for surprise and speed. He and Meade planned to move quickly to penetrate the Wilderness and pass southward before Lee could shift enough troops eastward to offer stiff opposition. Although it traveled light, leaving artillery and other heavy supplies behind, Meade's army still brought with it a supply train that stretched 70 miles, creating a vulnerable situation. His soldiers found partly opened graves that contained bleached skeletons of fallen soldiers from the Chancellorsville campaign, which unnerved them. Many were swept by a "sense of ominous dread" and wondered if Meade would simply repeat the poor tactical thinking that Hooker had displayed. Because of the disposition of the cavalry, a division moving out with each column and Torbert's division acting as a rear guard, the Union cavalry was unable to screen the infantry's advance to the west, the direction from which defending Confederates would come. Because of the inextricable tangle of vegetation, the long supply train, and the scattered cavalry, Grant and Meade's foray into the Wilderness went from a thunderclap to a crawl. Rather than quickly moving through the countryside, the army was slowed and Hancock's 2d Corps stopped its march at the Chancellorsville Tavern, the same crossroads where they had been stunned by Lee and Jackson the previous year. Warren's 5th Corps halted at Wilderness Tavern, west of Chancellorsville, at the intersection of the Orange Turnpike and the Germanna Plank Road. With two corps in fixed position and supply trains halted in the rear, Lee had an opportunity to strike on the early afternoon of May 4.

But just as Grant and Meade failed to make the start of their march as forceful as possible, Lee failed to set up for a counterattack on the Union right flank. Scattering his army along the winter entrenchments enabled him to procure food and supplies for the army more easily than concentrating them. But now this dispersion meant that Stuart's cavalry was not in position to reconnoiter the Union lines efficiently and Ewell's corps was the only one approaching on the Orange Turnpike. Hill was located to Ewell's south on the Orange Plank Road near New Verdierville, and Longstreet was forty-two miles away at Gordonsville.

Once again, a major Civil War battle would unfold without either commander wishing it. With the 5th Corps bivouacked at Wilderness Tavern and its headquarters at the J. Horace Lacy House, Ellwood—on the same ground in which Stonewall Jackson's arm lay buried—elements of Ewell's corps encountered the Federals at 7 A.M. on May 5. Warren's men had commenced a movement southward toward Parker's Store as Ewell's men moved eastward along the Orange Turnpike. The battle of the Wilderness had begun. Cavalry reconnaissance in the scrub woodland was almost impossible, and neither commander wished to bring on a major fight. Meade wanted to move southward through the Wilderness, and Lee did not want to engage until Longstreet was in position. Believing that Warren was encountering a division rather than a corps, which might be guarding most of Lee's army, still concentrated along Mine Run, Meade directed Warren to attack; Sedgwick would cover Warren's right flank, and Hancock should hold at Todd's Tavern, east of Parker's Store on the Brock Road.

The initial clash occurred in Saunders's Field, a patch of corn measuring about 400 by 800 yards, west of the Lacy House, through which the Orange Turnpike ran. Meade was close to the scene, issuing orders to Warren; he had ironically guessed correctly that Lee was trying to delay the Federal advance, but he aided Lee's plan by halting his army for battle. As the engagement began to spread across Saunders's Field and the armies approached, visual observations were limited to a few yards. "Here were two great armies," noted one soldier, "forming line of battle for a desperate struggle, within half a mile of each other, scarcely a movement of either . . . could be observed by the other." By early morning Warren dispatched Griffin westward along the turnpike, Wadsworth to his left, and Crawford south of Wadsworth toward the vicinity of the Chewning Farm. From Sedgwick's corps, Wright's division moved south along the Germanna Plank Road to support Warren's movement. Ewell's corps approached with the divisions of Rodes on the right, Johnson in the center, and Early on the left. Griffin struck into Johnson in Saunders's Field. At first the Confederates were thrust back, but vigorous fighting escalated all along both fronts and gunfire rang out from the brush, many boys falling in and near the field throughout the morning. Logistical difficulties slowed the Federal advances; Wright found the roads nearly impassable, and Wadsworth lost direction and sent his men marching northwest, away from supporting Griffin and exposing his flank to enemy fire. In a vigorous counterassault Ewell retook the ground originally forfeited by Johnson. He then stubbornly entrenched his men after receiving orders to await the arrival of Longstreet.

By 10:15 A.M. a courier rode up to Meade with a shocking message. Southern cavalry, spotted earlier to the south along the Orange Plank Road, were not merely part of a scattered reconnoitering force. Instead, Crawford, near the Chewning Farm, had spotted Confederate infantry in force approaching from the west toward Parker's Store, opening a second major route of attack from the Army of Northern Virginia. It was A. P. Hill's corps, and Hill allegedly told his men to drive into the Yankees, blurting out "Face the fire and go where it is hottest" when a captain asked him where to proceed. Hill's men encountered the Union cavalry of James H. Wilson, who deployed with repeating carbines and stalled Hill's vigorous march long enough for Meade to assess the situation. The Federal commander immediately concentrated on the Brock Road and sent Getty's division to move toward the Orange Plank Road and push Hill's Confederates back to Parker's Store. Confederate capture of the Brock Road would split Meade's army, isolating Hancock and Wilson to the south.

As noon approached, the situation was fluid: Johnson, Rodes, and Early were stacked up west of Saunders's Field; Hill's divisions of Heth and Wilcox were advancing eastward along the Orange Plank Road, Wilcox near Parker's Store and Heth passing the Widow Tapp Farm to his east; the main Federal battle line stretched north-south from Griffin (east of Saunders's Field) to Wadsworth to Crawford (at the Chewning Farm), with Robinson in reserve near the Lacy House; and Getty was marching south on the Brock Road to attack Heth. Getty sent Brig. Gen. Frank Wheaton's brigade forward to hold the crossroads of the Brock and Orange Plank roads. A quickly fired volley of Union muskets blazed through the thick underbrush and struck the lead Confederate skirmishers approaching from the west, and for the time being Getty's men held the intersection. But could he hold the roads until Hancock arrived? He hastily prepared crude entrenchments after learning from prisoners that two Confederate divisions were approaching in his front (little could be seen, and the smoke of battle only made matters worse). Hill's vanguard was still lightly engaged with elements of Wilson's cavalry.

After noon, attacks and counterattacks characterized the fight along the turnpike. Saunders's Field became a bloodbath, as did the ground to its south, stretching past the Higgerson Farm. A Union line moved out as if on parade into the field, the brigades of Brig. Gens. Romeyn B. Ayres and Joseph J. Bartlett confronting the brigades of Brig. Gens. George H. Steuart, John M. Jones, and Leroy A. Stafford. As a withering Confederate fire opened, whole groups of the blueclad soldiers fell at once. As the attack continued, the 140th New York Infantry pushed forward and fired at Confederates who had retreated into the woods, attempting to extricate themselves from tangles of wild grapevines. The Rebels regrouped and fired a stinging volley into the New Yorkers, and "the regiment melted away like snow. Men disappeared as if the earth had swallowed them." Simultaneously, a fight raged in Higgerson's Field between the Federal brigades of Brig. Gen. James C. Rice and Col. Roy Stone, which held the ground around the farmhouse (after stumbling through a swamp), and the Confederate brigades of Brig. Gens. Junius Daniel and George P. Doles.

By 2 P.M. Hancock's men began to arrive at the junction of the Brock and Orange Plank roads—Getty had held out and the Confederates had stopped pressing an attack, still awaiting Longstreet. Getty's men continued to build up their line of fortifications as Hancock took control of the area. Already bloodied, both sides now reorganized and attempted to make sense of the strange character of the fight thus far: the poor roads made marching very difficult and the thickets everywhere made visibility practically nonexistent. Numbers of troops were insignificant because large units could not be deployed in battle lines; the Wilderness fight thus far had almost been characterized by sporadic, small-unit fighting. "Friendly-fire" casualties would be higher on this battlefield than other Civil War grounds. Moreover, inadequate maps caused confusion among the Union commanders, a problem surmounted by the Confederates, who knew the land thoroughly.

As midafternoon arrived, Lee pondered his choices and wished that he could capture the Brock Road without bringing on a wholesale engagement. He dispatched Heth to attempt this feat, but by 3 P.M., Federal assaults began. Along the turnpike, Sedgwick's long-due divisions of the 6th Corps arrived north of Saunders's Field. Wright commanded the renewal of fighting around the field until 3:30 P.M., when Sedgwick arrived. Confederate artillery posted along the woods line opened fire and a spirited musketry fight flared north of Saunders's Field as Louisiana soldiers pounded the Yankees. New Jersey troops counterattacked, stinging Harry Hays's Louisianans and the Virginia soldiers belonging to the Stonewall Brigade. Col. Thomas W. Hyde, a Sedgwick staff officer, was knocked from his horse, struck in the face by a decapitated head. As he wiped the gore from his face, it took him a moment to realize that the blood and tissue were not his. Brig. Gen. Leroy Stafford, a Louisianan, was struck by a Minié bullet that lodged in his spine. In excruciating pain Stafford was carried off the field and died four days later.

As the action continued along the northern part of the field, Getty was ordered to attack along the Orange Plank Road, supported by Hancock. Meade wisely ordered this assault at once so that Longstreet could not come up to reinforce Hill; Hancock, however, unwisely completed the line of earthworks his men were constructing before deploying for the attack. So Getty's movement did not begin until 4:15 P.M., by which time he ran into stiff opposition along Heth's front, the lead elements of which were now east of the Widow Tapp Farm. Desperate fighting erupted along this line and lasted until nightfall. Many units flushed back and forth through the tangle of brush along both sides of the road; at first Getty, Wheaton, and the brigades of Brig. Gen. Henry L. Eustis and Cols. Robert McAllister, Thomas A.

Smyth, and William R. Brewster assaulted the Confederate brigades of Brig. Gens. Henry H. Walker and John R. Cooke, and Col. John M. Stone (Davis's brigade). Perfect chaos prevailed for several hours as wagons and artillery limbers cluttered the narrow roads, shells screeched overhead, patchwork barriers of logs and dirt were thrown up in helter-skelter fashion to protect the embattled, and Minié bullets plowed into the ground. Multiple attacks and counterattacks surged across the landscape, and the Confederates grimly held on to their line as they suffered monstrous casualties. Getty was handsomely reinforced by Hancock's men, and Heth was bolstered by Wilcox. Still the attacks came as the daylight slowly died and evening approached. An attack late in the evening by Barlow's division partly collapsed the Confederate right flank, and Hill's Southern boys were running low on ammunition. Still, they held their ground. The organizers of the defense were Heth and Wilcox, as Hill himself was sick (with the advancing debilitation of gonorrhea). Casualties were piling up rapidly on both sides, and hastily constructed aid stations were erected at various points in the Wilderness. Among the casualties of the evening was Confederate Brig. Gen. John M. Jones, who was killed along with an aide. Many bodies were now heaped in the trenches. Meade was not inactive; he dispatched Wadsworth to support Hancock's right, but the latter commander was slowed in his attempts to cross through the woods and could not get into position to attack before nightfall. A fire erupted throughout parts of the Wilderness battlefield, burning some of the wounded who were helpless on the ground.

"All up and down Wilderness Run," penned 1st Lt. Morris Schaff, an Ohio soldier, "over the once tilled fields of the Lacy farm and the old, gullied, pine and brier-tufted ones uplifting east of the run, little fires are blinking as they burn low. . . . There is no moon, the stars are dim, and all is hushed. The night air is permeated with the odor of freshly burnt-over woods, for the fire spread widely and is still slumbering and smoking in chunks and fallen trees." During the night, both commanders planned for attacks the following morning. Lee's plan was to bring up Longstreet, still hurrying forward, and turn the Union left, pinning Meade against the Rapidan River. To support the Union line, Burnside's 9th Corps (minus Fererro's division) was speeding toward the field from Germanna Ford, and Meade, in consultation with Grant, ordered an attack all along his line for 5 A.M. on May 6. As dawn broke in the morning, the Union attack commenced. Ewell was still positioned astride the Orange Turnpike and Hill, to his south, in a semicircular shape east of the Widow Tapp Farm. Longstreet was on the rapid approach behind him, coming quickly on the Orange Plank Road. Sedgwick opposed Ewell; Hancock, with the divisions of Wadsworth, Birney, and Mott (and Getty and Gibbon in the rear), lunged into Hill. Warren was placed in the center, with Burnside, at Wilderness Tavern, maneuvering

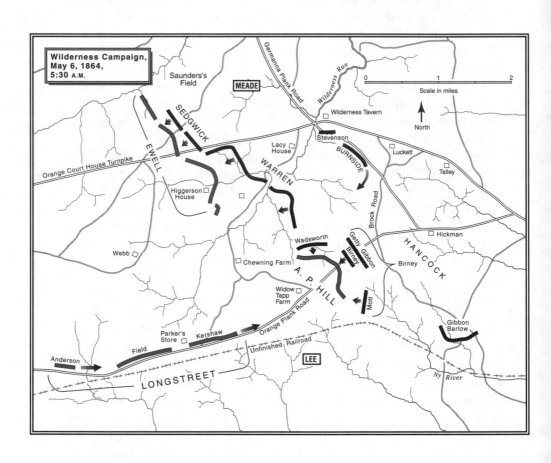

Wilderness Campaign, May 6, 1864, 5:30 A.M.

Saunders's Field

MEADE

Germanna Plank Road

Wilderness Run

Scale in miles

0   1   2

North

SEDGWICK

EWELL

Orange Court House Turnpike

Lacy House

Wilderness Tavern

Stevenson

BURNSIDE

Luckett

Talley

WARREN

Higgerson House

Brock Road

Hickman

Wadsworth

Getty Gibbon

Birney

HANCOCK

Webb

Chewning Farm

A. P. HILL

Birney

Widow Tapp Farm

Mott

Gibbon Barlow

Parker's Store

Kershaw

Field

Orange Plank Road

Unfinished Railroad

LEE

Anderson

LONGSTREET

Ny River

toward the southern fight in support of Hancock. Along the Orange Plank Road front, the battle sparked as the Federal brigades of Brig. Gens. John H. H. Ward and Alexander Hays and Col. Robert McAllister led the way into the brigades of Brig. Gens. James H. Lane, Alfred M. Scales, and Edward L. Thomas. Brisk fighting commenced across a wide front as flashes from gun barrels illuminated the early morning darkness through the thickets. To the north Ewell fought well and repulsed Sedgwick's attacks and those of Warren, inflicting many casualties in the Yankee regiments. As the southern attack continued, Hill's men were overpowered by the musketry and artillery of Hancock, and Lee found his right crumbling, slowed only by the effective fire of well-placed Confederate guns firing across the Widow Tapp Farm. Just as Lee found his right flank in dire trouble, his "war horse," Longstreet, arrived with the 1st Corps behind the Tapp Farm.

By 6 A.M. Longstreet had his men in formation and launched a counterattack, bringing the fresh brigades of Brig. Gens. John Gregg and Goode Bryan and Col. John W. Henagan (Kershaw's brigade) into the lead. The central arch of the Union attack now consisted of the brigades of Brig. Gens. Alexander Hays, Henry Baxter, and Ward. Heavy small-arms fire flared for two hours over this ground, with Barlow's division ordered forward on the flank. Among the dead was Hays, who was shot through the head while fighting near the intersection of the Brock and Orange Plank roads. Confusion in the Federal command now emerged as Union officers withheld most of Barlow's men because they felt that Maj. Gen. George E. Pickett's division must have been hanging in reserve and possibly committed to attacking the Union left; in reality, Pickett and his division had been reassigned to Richmond duty. Fighting blind, unable to see more than a few yards in many locations, the men continued their crazed fighting. Yankees mistook Stuart's cavalry for Federal soldiers when they appeared near Todd's Tavern. Lost Union troops attempting to rejoin their unit were mistaken for Confederate soldiers and were fired on by bluecoats. Sheridan, commanding the Union cavalry, failed to protect the army's flanks.

By 11 A.M. most of the energy had left both sides, the survivors exhausted, some beginning to run low on ammunition, and the cries of the wounded echoing through the bleak forest. At this hour Longstreet launched a flank attack that sent the brigades of Brig. Gens. William T. Wofford, George T. Anderson, and William Mahone and Col. John M. Stone into the Union left. The attack was precipitated by Lee's chief engineer, Maj. Gen. Martin L. Smith, who suggested Birney's flank could be turned by marching along the unfinished railroad bed that ran parallel to the plank road, and Longstreet ordered a staff officer, Lt. Col. Gilbert Moxley Sorrel, to lead the attack. Longstreet himself would direct an advance along the road itself, achieving a simultaneous bit of surprise. Mahone took actual command of the expedition, which pushed Birney's men back. By midday the Confederate push had broken the Union line, which was regrouped by the surefire soldiering of Hancock, who reorganized the line and ordered the men into trenches. In the attack one of the wealthiest and most educated men in a Union general's uniform, Wadsworth, was mortally wounded, shot in the head and left slumping from his saddle. Unconscious, he died two days later.

Longstreet took a leading role in pushing the Confederate attack, and at one point he rode out onto the Orange Plank Road accompanied by Kershaw, a group of staff officers, and Brig. Gen. Micah Jenkins, who commanded a brigade of South Carolinians. As Mahone's 12th Virginia Infantry returned to their position on the north side of the plank road, the remainder of Mahone's troops confused them for Yankees in the hazy gray of the forest and fired into the indistinct forms. Longstreet's headquarters group was caught in the "friendly" crossfire. Although several officers including Kershaw yelled fiercely, "They are friends!" it was too late. Jenkins was shot and tumbled from his horse; paralyzed, he lingered for about five hours. Longstreet rode forward to quell the musket volleys, and his assistant adjutant general, Sorrel, saw the big man "lift up" in his saddle and then come back down, with blood flowing freely from his neck and shoulder. He had been struck near the throat and the ball exited his right shoulder. "General Jenkins . . . rode up, his face flushed with joy, and, shaking hands with Longstreet, congratulated him on the result of the fight," recalled Capt. Francis Dawson of Longstreet's staff. ". . . Longstreet, who had stood there like a lion at bay, reeled as the blood poured down over his breast, and was evidently badly hurt."

Temporarily, Longstreet's command passed to Maj. Gen. Charles W. Field, and after a day, to Maj. Gen. Richard H. Anderson. Lee took over direction of the attack along the Orange Plank Road, but he discovered that the troops were too disorganized and the visibility too poor to continue the assaults. By late afternoon the brigade and regimental organizations were restored, but by then it was becoming too late to press the attack, and Hancock's line stiffened considerably. Ewell did not fare as well as he had during the earlier part of the battle. Historians have often cited his peculiarities and compared him harshly with Stonewall Jackson. Some writers have suggested that Ewell may have had severe mental problems and cite legends that he hallucinated that he was a bird, that he sat chirping in his tent, and that he sometimes only accepted sunflower seeds or grains of wheat at mealtimes. But Ewell was arguably careful, not insane, about his actions on the second day at the Wilderness. On Ewell's left Brig. Gen. John B. Gordon's brigade attempted to take advantage of a weakly supported Union right flank, but Early stubbornly declined aiding Gordon with an attack. By late afternoon, when

Lee visited Ewell, Gordon got the commanding general's attention by revealing his plan and sidestepping Early, and the attack was launched early in the evening. The attack struck the Union flank southwest of the Spotswood House, as Gordon's own brigade and those of Brig. Gens. Robert D. Johnston and John Pegram sent the brigades of Brig. Gens. Truman Seymour and Alexander Shaler reeling. Though it came too late in the day to affect the battle's result, the attack damaged Union morale on the right flank, piled up considerable casualties, and was stopped only by Sedgwick's sure leadership.

In the center of the field Burnside advanced at 2 P.M. The brigades of Cols. John F. Hartranft, Zenas R. Bliss, Simon G. Griffin, and Benjamin C. Christ attacked the Southern boys of Brig. Gens. Edward A. Perry and Abner M. Perrin and Col. William F. Perry, who were supported by Brig. Gen. Nathaniel H. Harris and Col. John M. Stone. Ultimately, the attack amounted to nothing, as Hill's Confederates repulsed it.

The two-day battle of the Wilderness thus drew to a close. Both armies were badly hurt and substantially depleted of resources. On May 7, they dug in and were separated in many positions by only half a mile. The Wilderness had been a terribly costly ordeal as well as an almost inhuman place to fight. Of the approximately 100,000 Union troops engaged, casualties were 2,246 killed, 12,037 wounded, and 3,383 missing; Confederate losses, of the 60,000 engaged, were not well known but ranged from 7,750 to 11,400. Following the battle, wounded soldiers were littered over a wide area stretching all across the lines of battle. Getting to them was not as easy as it might have been on other, more open fields. To make matters worse, on the evening of May 6, another substantial fire took hold in the dense undergrowth of the Wilderness. "The blaze ran sparkling and crackling up the trunks of the pines," recorded Maine soldier Henry C. Houston, "till they stood a pillar of fire from base to topmost spray." The fires that raged through the pine forest burned many wounded men to death, and the hideous shrieks of their suffering echoed throughout the alien landscape.

The battle had not enough direction or coordination on either side— and this was largely dictated by the physical limitations of fighting in the Wilderness. But neither side had used its cavalry effectively and had committed to piecemeal attacks that lacked a larger strategy. Lee might well have expected Meade and Grant to turn around and retreat like their predecessors. But during the day on May 7 it became clear that no such withdrawal to the Rapidan would occur. "If we were under any other General except Grant I should expect a retreat," exclaimed Elisha Hunt Rhodes, "but Grant is not that kind of a soldier, and we feel that we can trust him."

Grant would attempt to turn Lee's right, shifting his troops southeastward, to threaten Lee's lines of communications, increasingly endanger Richmond, and force Lee to come out and fight on ground of Grant's choosing. On the evening of May 7, after concluding that the Confederate positions were too strong to attack, Grant ordered the army to move southward via the Brock Road. He ordered Sedgwick and Warren to march toward Spotsylvania Court House, a crossroads on the Brock, and sent Burnside toward Aldrich, northeast of Todd's Tavern. Hancock served as rear guard and then proceeded to Todd's Tavern. A hauntingly dark, still night, poor maps, and general confusion resulted in an inefficient march. On the Brock Road, Maj. Gen. Fitzhugh Lee's cavalry caught up with horsemen commanded by Brig. Gen. Wesley Merritt and some of Warren's infantry, and on the advanced front Wilson's cavalry pushed the Rebels under Brig. Gen. Thomas L. Rosser away from Spotsylvania, opening the possibility of holding the junction as soon as the infantry arrived.

As Warren's 5th Corps pushed southward along the Brock Road at 8:30 A.M. on May 8, near the Widow Alsop House, it was struck by Anderson's 1st Corps, the soldiers who had until now fought under Longstreet. Spurred on by Lee, Anderson had started his men in the footrace for Spotsylvania Court House before midnight the previous evening and pressed on hard partly to escape the smoldering fires along the Orange Plank Road. Anderson had brought his artillery south from Parker's Store past Shady Grove Church, and then eastward. His infantry had marched along a dirt path called Pendleton's Road over Corbin's Bridge (north of Shady Grove Church) to rejoin the artillery. Only a frantic message from Jeb Stuart's cavalry prevented Anderson from stopping before he moved all the way south to the Alsop Farm. Warren's initial attack into the mostly South Carolina troops near the Spindle Farm at Laurel Hill was weak, and by early afternoon Meade organized an attack by Warren to be supported by Sedgwick. A second attack at 10:30 A.M. also failed. With Wilson's cavalry holding fast at Spotsylvania Court House, the Confederate cavalry of Fitz Lee and Rosser moved in and threatened the Yankee position, so Wilson, as ordered by Sheridan, retreated.

Warren's regrouped attack was tricky enough to set up that it didn't occur until early evening. In the meantime, Hancock, having grouped his corps into a semicricle around Todd's Tavern, dispatched the brigade of Col. Nelson A. Miles westward to reconnoiter Corbin's Bridge, but around 5 P.M., after Miles had moved along the Catharpin Road, he was attacked by Mahone's infantry and the cavalry of Rosser and Brig. Gen. Pierce M. B. Young. By 6:30 P.M. the action flared again to the south, at Laurel Hill, as Meade renewed the attack across the Spindle Farmstead. A long arc of units that commenced the attack contained Col. Henry W. Brown's brigade in the center, with the troops of Brig. Gens. James B. Ricketts, Samuel W. Crawford, Henry L. Eustis, and Col. Emory Upton, to the northeast, and those of Brig. Gens. Charles Griffin, Lysander Cutler, and David A. Russell to the west over a mile-wide front. The Confederate line was held fast by the troops of Field on the left, between Laurel Hill and the Po River, and Kershaw and Rodes on the right, from Laurel Hill to the McCoull House. The attack was repulsed with heavy losses along the front, characterized by particularly savage fighting in the center and the Confederate right flank (where Upton attacked). Ewell arrived and reinforced the Confederate line, and during the night the armies dug in and adjusted their lines as best they could. Though the several battles that raged on May 8 went by the names Alsop's Farm, Laurel Hill, and Todd's Tavern, these events began the battle and campaign of Spotsylvania Court House, which would in effect transform into a two-week stalemate. "About dark the firing gradually ceased, both sides apparently holding their own, and our division was faced to the right," reported Confederate Sgt. McHenry Howard of Ed Johnson's staff, on May 8. "The voices of Generals Johnson and Steuart were heard for some time in the night, but in the thicket and darkness the men could not see them, nor could they see each other, and staff officers could not well ride through, so that, tired, hungry, and sleepy, they finally sank down where each one happened to find himself."

Early in the afternoon on May 8, while the first battles for Spotsylvania were raging, Meade dispatched his cavalry, commanded by Sheridan, on a peculiar raid that would occupy him for sixteen days. Embarrassed and angry over the poor performance of the cavalry during the Wilderness campaign (which could be attributed to Meade's own lack of direction, Sheridan's inexperience as a cavalry commander, and Wilson's background as an engineer), Meade sent Sheridan on a mission to move around Lee's left and attack Stuart's cavalry from the rear, to cut the rail lines south of Lee's army, and to resupply, if possible, from Butler's Army of the James south of Richmond. Angered at Sheridan for his poor performance, Meade brusquely reported to Grant that Sheridan wanted to be "left alone" to destroy Stuart. "Did Sheridan say that?" Grant inquired. "Well, he generally knows what he's talking about. Let him start right out and do it." At 6 A.M. on May 9, Sheridan began moving his 10,000 cavalrymen north to Todd's Tavern and then circled southward across the North and South Anna rivers. Sheridan's corps included the divisions of Merritt, Gregg, and Wilson. Stuart divided his command on May 10, bringing 4,500 troopers to pursue Sheridan—the division of Fitz Lee (brigades of Brig. Gens. Lunsford L. Lomax and Williams C. Wickham) and the brigade of Brig. Gen. James B. Gordon.

Cries of alarm rang out in Richmond as word of the Yankee approach reached the city, reminding residents of the previous winter's Kilpatrick-Dahlgren raid. The military resources of the Confederacy were thin. A paltry 4,000 local troops, mostly boys and convalescents, manned the city's fortifications. Reinforcements were ordered north from the James River defenses that held Butler's men at bay. On May 10, along the Virginia Central Railroad south of the North Anna River, Brig. Gen. George A. Custer's brigade destroyed a large number of railroad cars and ten miles of track and freed 375 Union prisoners. On that day Jeb Stuart, in hot pursuit, sent what would be his final message to Robert E. Lee. "Should [the enemy] attack Richmond I will certainly move to his Rear and do what I can at the Same time I hope to be able to Strike him if he endeavors to escape. His force . . . will be principally as dismounted Cavalry which fights better than . . . infantry."

The next day Stuart caught up with Sheridan at Yellow Tavern, six miles north of Richmond, and a lively skirmish erupted between the horse soldiers. In a sharp action with brisk firing from carbines, Sheridan's men pushed back the Confederates and in the flash of a gun barrel, Jeb Stuart fell from his horse, mortally wounded, shot in the abdomen with a .44-caliber bullet. Placed against a tree, Stuart went into shock but remained conscious; he was moved to Richmond, where he died the next day. "I must be prepared for another world," he told staff officer Henry B. McClellan. For the South the loss of yet another of its paramount heroes—with Longstreet, too, ailing from his serious wound—seemed almost too much to bear. "Soon the mournful strains of the Dead March, the solemn procession of military mourners, the funeral carriage, the coffin draped with the Confederate banner, the saddened citizens who with tearful eyes gazed upon the melancholy pageant, told but truly the story of the departure of another hero of the South," Richmonder Sallie Putnam lamented of Stuart's funeral.

Sheridan's Richmond raid continued as the Yankee cavalry commander found the inner defenses of the city too strong to penetrate. He shifted eastward along the Chickahominy River, bridging it under fire, and moved south to Haxall's Landing. After resupplying with Butler, Sheridan moved back to Grant at Chesterfield Station on May 24. The raid accomplished relatively little aside from mortally wounding Stuart, but it did infuse the new Union cavalry command with confidence.

Meanwhile, near Spotsylvania Court House the standoff was heating up. The Confederate lines were drawn in a huge semicircle, with Anderson's corps on the left, Ewell's corps in the center, and Early's corps on the right. (Early took command of Hill's corps because of the latter's illness.) In the middle, Ewell's corps plunged out in a looped salient that came to be called the "Mule Shoe." Lee wisely drew his lines in and placed artillery along them to form a thick barrier and almost immediately began constructing a second line behind the first. As Union forces approached on May 9, they had great difficulty getting close enough to see what was happening; Sedgwick surrounded the area of the Alsop Farm, Warren marched to his south, approaching Anderson, and Hancock marched southward toward the Confederate left flank. Burnside, meanwhile, approached from the northeast, moving toward the town of Spotsylvania Court House, where Heth anchored the Confederate right. Ironically, the town contained the Court House where for a time Lee's wayward father, Light-Horse Harry, had spent time in prison. But Lee now rested easy, strengthening his lines and sending out skirmishing parties in his front, one of which killed the most beloved leader of the Army of the Potomac, John Sedgwick. Despite his staff officers' protestations about Sedgwick standing exposed to enemy sharpshooters, the major general responded with the famous line, "They couldn't hit an elephant at this distance," and moments later was struck below the left eye by a Minié bullet. Union Surg. Daniel Holt described the feeling: "This is an awful loss to us. We had learned to love and obey him as faithful, dutiful children. . . . I fear *no one* will receive the support and confidence that *'Uncle John'* has with his Corps."

Meade worked on strengthening his line as Burnside approached. The latter, still a foolish officer, encountered a small force of Confederate cavalry and believed that a large enemy infantry force lay ahead of him. In the communications to Grant that ensued, without the benefit of Sheridan's cavalry for reconnaissance, Grant believed that Lee might be preparing to move toward the Union supply base at Fredericksburg. He thus ordered Hancock to move south quickly to turn Lee's left (held by Mahone, near Blockhouse Bridge), but Hancock's abortive effort on May 9 ran out of steam as darkness fell. The following morning, however, Hancock sent Col. John R. Brooke's brigade across the Po River and turned Lee's flank, endangering the Confederate lines of communications. Rather than exploiting that opportunity, however, Grant and Meade recalled Hancock and prepared for a frontal assault planned for the late afternoon of May 10. Alerted to the Yankee movements, Heth had maneuvered around to the west and marched north to strike the exposed flank of Barlow's division, on the Union right, west of the Blockhouse Bridge. Skirmishing resulted in the early afternoon, with the brigades of Brig. Gens. Joseph R. Davis and William W. Kirkland slicing into Brooke and pushing the Union soldiers back. The promising Union foray was recalled as casualties were piling up west of the Po River. "Ambulances and army wagons with two tiers of flooring, loaded with wounded and drawn by four and six mule teams, pass along the . . . road to Fredericksburg," inscribed Capt. Augustus Brown of the 4th New York Heavy Artillery. "Many of the wounds are full of maggots. . . . and several poor fellows were holding stumps of legs and arms straight up in the air so as to ease the pain."

The major Federal attack of May 10 crystallized as Warren, in the late afternoon, reported that he believed a frontal attack would score a major victory. Meade moved it forward and by 4 P.M. Warren marched his divisions forward, toward Anderson's line, with Wright on his left and Hancock on his right. Lee's well-placed artillery now came into play; as the waves of Union attackers came toward his lines, Southern gunners opened fire and raked the Union lines. Few survived, and those who did scrambled to the rear. Wright, stunned by the initial disaster, planned a special attack force to strike at the exposed Mule Shoe salient and assigned Col. Emory Upton to the task. Upton formed four lines containing three regiments each, and the attack, which commenced at 6:10 P.M., was preceded by a bombardment of the position by heavy Union guns. Of the day's massive attack, only this portion succeeded; Upton's men scurried over the Confederate entrenchments and captured more than 1,000 Rebel prisoners. Brig. Gen. Gershom Mott's division supported Upton's force but was soon beaten back by heavy Confederate artillery fire. Hancock attacked along the western front again but without success, and by nightfall Upton was forced to withdraw. Burnside, who drew closer to Early's line, dug in south of the Ny River.

The following day, May 11, was quiet, masking a grim determination on Grant's part to engineer the end of the war. "I am now sending back to Bell Plaines [*sic*] all my wagons for a fresh supply of provisions, and Ammunition, and propose to fight it out on this line if it takes ~~me~~ all summer," he wrote Halleck. Grant concluded that the Brown House, where Mott had commenced his abortive effort to reinforce Upton, would make a fine point from which to assemble a massive attack on the Mule Shoe salient that still stuck out from the Confederate front around the McCoull and Harrison houses. Staff officers including Lt. Cols. Cyrus B. Comstock and Orville E. Babcock, and Maj. William G. Mitchell, set off under a heavy rain to, in Mitchell's words, "examine the ground in front of Spotsylvania as close to the enemy's lines as practicable . . . where it was intended to make an assault with the Second Corps [the next] morning at daybreak." Not only did the rain continue, but a dense fog formed during the night. Still, Grant instructed Meade to initiate a strong attack that began at 4:35 A.M. on May 12, when daylight made an advance possible. Lee had withdrawn his artillery, falsely believing that Grant planned a withdrawal toward Fredericksburg. When Confederates inside the Mule Shoe heard the rumbles ahead of their line, they quickly requested the return of the heavy guns.

As the cold, drenched Confederates huddled inside the Mule Shoe and awaited the return of the artillery, Hancock and Wright launched the massive frontal assault, from the Brown House and over the grounds of the Landram (Landrum) House, straight into the salient. A heavy, loud cheer from the Federal soldiers rang through the woods, and musketry blazed along the entire line. McAllister's brigade struck into the angle at the center; Ward and Crocker led the assault on the brigades of Daniel, Hays, Walker, and Stafford in the east angle, and Brooke, Brown, and Smith struck first into the brigades of Steuart and Col. William Witcher in the west angle. Throngs of Union

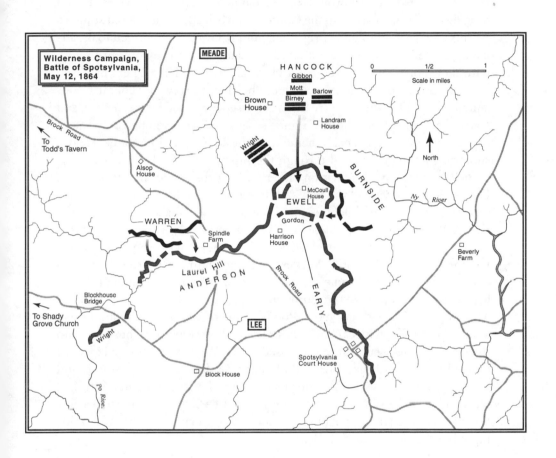

Wilderness Campaign,
Battle of Spotsylvania,
May 12, 1864

MEADE

HANCOCK
Gibbon
Mott
Birney   Barlow

0   1/2   1
Scale in miles

Brown
House

Landram
House

Brock Road
To
Todd's Tavern

Wright

Alsop
House

North

Ny   River

BURNSIDE

McCoull
House

EWELL

WARREN

Spindle
Farm

Gordon

Harrison
House

Beverly
Farm

Laurel Hill
ANDERSON

Brock Road

EARLY

Blockhouse
Bridge

To Shady
Grove Church

Wright

LEE

Spotsylvania
Court House

Block House

Po River

soldiers poured into the densely packed salient, and small-arms fire was so brisk that a twenty-two-foot oak tree was felled by rifle fire alone (it now resides in the National Museum of American History), giving the site the nickname Bloody Angle. As a hand-to-hand melee erupted, with soldiers clubbing each other with musket stocks, nearly the whole of the Confederate garrison in the salient was captured, including generals Steuart and Alleghany Johnson (both would be exchanged in August). More Union brigades followed, tearing up the Confederate brigades that offered support. As this chaos was unfolding, Brig. Gen. John B. Gordon attempted to organize a counterassault, and Lee offered to lead it but was escorted to safety with shouts of "Lee to the rear" as a Virginia officer led Traveller's bridle.

Gordon's counterattack worked. The dense array of Federal troops jammed into the Mule Shoe created a confused mass, and between 5 A.M. and 6 A.M. the Army of Northern Virginia—Gordon supported by Early—succeeded in moving Hancock's men out of the McCoull House area. Heavy, sporadic fighting continued through the misty morning. By 6:30 A.M. Brig. Gen. Thomas H. Neill's division of Wright's Corps joined the battle on the Confederate left, west of the McCoull House. Successful as Gordon's counterattack was, the Confederates could not drive the Yankees back out of the rim of the original Mule Shoe, and vicious musketry volleys and sharpshooting rang through the clearing at a frenetic pace. Fearing such a firestorm, Brig. Gen. Abner M. Perrin, commanding a brigade in Early's corps, had said, "I shall come out of this fight a live major general or a dead brigadier." Indeed, before the morning was up, he was dead, pierced by seven Minié bullets. The fighting at the Bloody Angle raged on throughout the day and into the night, with casualties piling up on both sides. Wright struck into the Confederates again but was repulsed. Later, Warren was ordered forward but fell back with heavy losses. Both sides reinforced their positions and were separated by very short distances along the line. Burnside attacked with limited success. As the action continued, Lee began constructing a new line south of the Harrison House, in back of the previous salient. After midnight the bruised armies fell silent.

On May 13 the armies were too bloodied and short of supplies to continue the ferocious fighting. It was clear to both sides now that Grant would not back away. Frontal attacks had been costly in terms of lives and matériel, and Sheridan was still riding around the countryside. Grant determined to move against Lee's right, and so Meade ordered Warren to form for an attack at 4 A.M. on May 14, striking into Early at Spotsylvania Court House. Wright would attack in support on a parallel road. But the giant clockwise motion of Warren and Wright's movements would take them across wide swaths of forested ground without roads. After rain, fog, and mud forestalled this attack, it was forgotten. From May 14 to 17, scattered fighting involving infantry and cavalry erupted, which alerted Lee and enabled him to extend his line southward. Two potentially significant operations designed to help Meade, the actions of Sigel in the Shenandoah Valley and Butler down on the James, amounted to little. Nearly continuous firing exhausted the troops surrounding Spotsylvania Court House, and the origin of another aspect of modern warfare, a trench stalemate, was emerging. Grant ordered Hancock's corps out of action to rest, and Wright proposed striking the Confederate left, so an assault was planned for dawn on May 18. The sniping and skirmishing that transpired in the meantime was awful on both sides.

The attack on the 18th was expected by Confederates, who had discovered the plan. The thunderous movement stalled with heavy casualties again, and by 10 A.M. Grant aborted the action. "We were under terrific shelling yesterday for two hours with very little damage," Confederate solider Lewis Warlick wrote of the assault. "Ewell repulsed the enemy yesterday three times making great slaughter in his [the enemy's] ranks. To-day so far everything is quiet the skirmishers dont even fire at each other but seem to be quite friendly, meet each other and exchange papers and have a talk over the times." Meade now reformed his Union line, which resembled a north-south configuration east of Spotsylvania Court House, with Hancock held in reserve farther east at Anderson. On the night of May 19, Grant wanted Hancock to march quickly southward, drawing Lee from his heavily fortified trenches, and the rest of the Union army would follow and strike Lee in the open plain. Seeking to allow Meade to interpose the Union army between his own force and Richmond, Lee sent Ewell forward to "feel" the enemy and report back. Ewell moved with a small force devoid of artillery (which would have trouble moving on the muddy roads) at 3 P.M. on May 19. Ewell and the rightmost elements of Warren's corps struck each other squarely and fought throughout a portion of the afternoon, and Ewell, assisted by Wade Hampton's cavalry, escaped as Union reinforcements approached. The following evening Hancock would begin his march and finally draw the armies away from Spotsylvania Court House and into a new phase of the Wilderness campaign. The fighting at Spotsylvania had been hellish and brutal. Of some 110,000 Union men engaged, casualties amounted to 17,500; Lee had more than 50,000 engaged and lost an unrecorded number—possibly 10,000. Among the dead or mortally wounded were Confederate Brig. Gens. Junius Daniel, shot through the abdomen on May 12, and James B. Gordon, mortally wounded on the same day at Meadow Bridge, near Richmond (fighting Sheridan). Among the Union commanders killed or mortally wounded were Brig. Gens. James C. Rice, shot in the thigh on May 10, who lost his leg and died the same day, and Thomas G. Stevenson, killed when he was shot in the head, also on May 10.

Lee was somewhat perplexed by the Federal commander's tactical movements and stubbornness. He had not seen this kind of determination. As Grant sent Hancock marching south, he was again turning the Confederate right and continuing to force Lee ever closer toward Richmond, threatening his communications and supply lines. It was a new tactic, and about to become more unusual. Yet despite the horrendous casualties, Confederate soldiers remained determined to fight. "Old Grant is a tough customer but Lee is an overmatch for him," asserted Marion Hill Fitzpatrick of the 45th Georgia Infantry. "There is no telling when the fight will end. The prisoners say that Grant says he is going to Richmond or Hell, before he quits, and has no idea of recrossing the river as long as he has a man left." The changing aspect of the war was transforming into a wearing experience for soldiers on both sides. "From Orange Court House to Richmond," a Mississippi soldier observed of the Overland campaign, "the country is made up of holes, each dug by hand (laboriously), sometimes with shovels but usually with bayonets or sharpened sticks and flattened canteens. We seldom charge 'gloriously' as we did 3 years ago. Instead we build fortifications and try to flank the enemy. The enemy does the same."

While the battles raged at the Wilderness and Spotsylvania, Maj. Gen. Ben Butler and his Army of the James attempted to move his 39,000 men into a base near the James River, disrupt lines of Confederate communications, scatter the Confederate forces left near Richmond and Petersburg, and possibly even capture the capital city. Poorly planned and even more poorly executed, the campaign was a fiasco from the outset. Butler was abruptly defeated and, as writers who have enjoyed attacking the bumbling commander over the years have stated, was "bottled up" at a base on the peninsula between the James and Appomattox rivers, between Petersburg and Richmond, known as Bermuda Hundred. The fault may not have been as squarely Butler's as historians have generally made out, but the curious campaign was indeed a study in inefficiency.

Butler's Army of the James consisted of the army corps of Maj. Gen. Quincy A. Gillmore (10th Corps, divisions of Brig. Gens. Alfred H. Terry, John W. Turner, and Adelbert Ames) and Maj. Gen. William F. Smith (18th Corps, divisions of Brig. Gens. William T. H. Brooks, Godfrey Weitzel, and Edward W. Hinks—it was Hinks's division that consisted almost entirely of black soldiers—plus a cavalry division of Brig. Gen. August V. Kautz). Opposing the Yankees in the Richmond area were less than 10,000 men, who were scattered, disorganized, and undergoing a transfer of command from Maj. Gen. George E. Pickett to Gen. P. G. T. Beauregard as the campaign began. The hero of Sumter and Shiloh would have four depleted divisions commanded by Maj. Gens. Robert Ransom, Jr., Robert F. Hoke, and William H. C. Whiting, and Brig. Gen. Alfred H. Colquitt. Richmond itself contained only four infantry brigades and a small garrison of local militia artillery.

Butler's soldiers landed on the banks of the James, disembarking transports, unopposed. As the black troops under Hinks occupied the wharves at
City Point Landing, the main body of the army hastily began constructing
trenches across the three-mile-wide front on Bermuda Hundred. This position was ideal, Butler reasoned, because it offered the opportunity to strike
at either Richmond to the north or Petersburg to the south. On May 6, Butler initiated the campaign by dispatching the brigade of Brig. Gen. Charles
A. Heckman forward toward Petersburg. Heckman's Massachusetts boys
struck into North Carolina soldiers under Col. Robert F. Graham at Port
Walthall Junction, where two railroads joined. Heckman was stopped by the
brigades of Brig. Gen. Johnson Hagood and Bushrod R. Johnson, and the
Confederates further reinforced their garrison and defenses at Drewry's
Bluff (with Brig. Gen. Archibald Gracie's brigade), the main river defense of
Richmond to its south. On May 7 the fighting at Port Walthall Junction intensified as an afternoon attack pushed Confederates away from the railroad,
enabling the Union soldiers to destroy 500 yards of track and cut the telegraph wires. By late afternoon, however, the Yankees were forced to withdraw, and one Union soldier, in frustration, wondered on paper, "How long
will it take to get to Richmond if you advance two miles every day and come
back to your starting point every night[?]"

From May 5 to 10 the Union cavalryman Kautz conducted a raid that
commenced at Suffolk, capturing and burning the 110-foot Weldon Railroad
bridge at Stony Creek, south of Petersburg, on May 8. Kautz's cavalrymen also destroyed the 210-foot span of the Nottoway Bridge farther to the
south, and these operations hampered Confederate support from the south.
Butler finally moved again on May 8–9, heading toward Petersburg via the
Richmond-Petersburg Turnpike but encountering stiff resistance from entrenched Confederates along the south bank of Swift Creek on May 9. Smith
and Gillmore strongly suggested laying a pontoon bridge across the Appo-
mattox and turning Beauregard's right (much as Meade was now turning
Lee's right), but Butler refused. After a brief skirmish at Chester Station on
May 10, north of Port Walthall Junction, Butler moved his troops back to
Bermuda Hundred. Along the line, skirmishing flared at Ware Bottom
Church on May 9. After the halfhearted demonstration toward Petersburg,
Butler advanced northward on May 12 toward Drewry's Bluff, site of the
well-defended position Union soldiers had called Fort Darling during the
1862 Peninsular campaign. The position was now strongly defended by Hoke.
Butler placed Smith's corps on the right, Gillmore on the left, and left Hinks
behind at City Point. To block a Confederate movement from Petersburg,
Kautz initiated a second raid, this time lasting from May 12 to 18, and employed a large, counterclockwise movement from Bermuda Hundred along
the Richmond & Danville Railroad southwest of Richmond, to the South-

side Railroad west of Petersburg, to the Nottoway Bridge south of Petersburg, and up to Bermuda Hundred again. Kautz's raiders were less successful this time, but they did inflict some destruction on the railroads, destroy Confederate stores, and free slaves along their route.

As Butler approached Drewry's Bluff, his men pushed the Confederate defenders into their inner works, but the sharp musketry fire stiffened as the Army of the James drew near, and, because of low water, naval support could not move upriver far enough to bombard the fort. Butler first planned to attack the fort on May 15 but then suspended his order. Curiously, to strengthen the Federal line in front of the fort, Baldy Smith found telegraph wire from the turnpike and had his men string it between tree stumps along his line, and this marked another one of the many "modern" battlefield developments that emerged during the year 1864. With Butler temporarily abandoning the initiative, Beauregard seized it and ordered an attack for 4:45 A.M. on May 16. Under a dense fog the brigades of Gracie and Col. William G. Lewis marched into Heckman's line, closely followed by the brigades of Cols. William R. Terry and Birkett D. Fry (Barton's brigade). Under heavy fire the Union line broke in disarray, and Heckman was captured (he was exchanged the following September). In the center Weitzel and Brooks repulsed heavy attacks. On the Union left Hoke attacked Gillmore's front only at 6:30 A.M., delayed by the fog. Bushrod Johnson was attacked severely and needed reinforcement by other Confederate brigades; Ransom began a sweeping envelopment and heavy, disorganized fighting continued through the morning. The density of the fog led to utter chaos amid the lines; a horse and rider departing with a message might disappear after only fifteen yards. Butler found his right flank in jeopardy. By late morning he began to withdraw and was fortunate not to be struck from the south by Whiting, who was ordered to do so but found himself stalled at Port Walthall Junction by Ames. By the following morning Butler retreated again to Bermuda Hundred and found himself "bottled up" there, after suffering casualties of 390 killed, 2,380 wounded, and 1,390 missing of the 16,000 engaged; Confederate losses were 355 killed, 1,941 wounded, and 210 missing of 18,000 engaged.

Scattered fighting erupted again along the Bermuda Hundred line at Harris's Farm and Ware Bottom Church but amounted to little; Butler's campaign thus far had only stumbled. Fighting rumbled along the lines there for some weeks to come. The presence of black soldiers particularly riled the Confederates who faced the Army of the James.

As Butler sat back in Bermuda Hundred, utterly dazed, Grant and Meade continued their flank movements toward the southeast. The North Anna River campaign resulted. Hancock departed Spotsylvania on May 20 and marched rapidly to Guinea's Station, moving south to Chesterfield Station and an approach to the North Anna River near month's end. His movements were paralleled by those of Burnside, Warren, and Wright. Lee withdrew his army quickly and raced southward, too, with the ailing A. P. Hill resuming command of his corps and taking it past New Market and to the southern bank of the North Anna River, north of Hanover Junction, by May 22. Ewell and Anderson moved their troops likewise to form a new line near Hanover Junction. Along these marches a skirmish was fought at Guinea's Station on May 21.

For four days the armies straddled the North Anna at Ox Ford, the Federal battle line consisting of Wright on the right, Warren, Burnside, and Hancock on the left. Lee's line featured Hill on the left, Anderson in the center, and Ewell on the right at Hanover Junction. When Warren arrived on May 23, he found the ford open at Jericho Mill, northwest of Ox Ford, and crossed his corps but was attacked by Hill about 6 P.M. Hill's push initially succeeded but became so disorganized that the Rebels were pushed back and Warren crossed with relative ease. Hancock attacked at Chesterfield Bridge, east of Ox Ford, and captured the position and crossed, although the Confederates burned the railroad bridge nearby. In the center Burnside did not attack at Ox Ford, for he felt the position was too strong, and he remained on the northern bank of the river. On May 24 Hancock moved the rest of his corps to the southern bank and Burnside attempted to cross at Quarles's Mill, between Ox Ford and Jericho Mill, but again was thwarted. When Sheridan's cavalry rejoined the army from his ride, Grant and Meade had dispersed their corps into a dangerous position. Fortunately for them Lee was sick and unable to coordinate a counterattack; skirmishing characterized the final two days of the campaign. By May 26, as night fell across the battlefields, Grant and Meade withdrew their men southeast once again, this time toward Cold Harbor, with Wilson's cavalry acting as a rear guard.

As the armies maneuvered toward Cold Harbor, a crossroads ten miles northeast of Richmond, skirmishes occurred at Totopotomoy Creek, Hanovertown, Hanover Junction, Jericho Mill, Salem Church, and along the Pamunkey River (May 27); at Haw's Shop and Enon Church (May 28), and at Jones's Farm, Old Church, Atlee's Station, and Ashland (May 29). Visions of great success began to form in Grant's mind as he moved so close to Richmond. "Lees Army is really whipped," he wrote Halleck on May 26. "The prisoners we now take show it, and the actions of the Army shows it unmistakeably. A battle outside of intrenchments, cannot be had. Our men feel that they have gained morale over the enemy and attack with confidence. I may be mistaken but I feel that our success over Lees Army is already insured."

As the armies maneuvered southeastward yet again, skirmishing erupted on May 30 along the Totopotomoy River, near the old battlefield of Gaines's Mill, at Hanover, and at Bethesda Church, north of Gaines's Mill

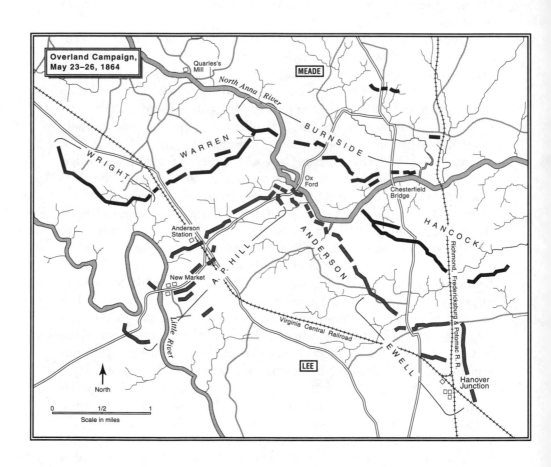

Overland Campaign, May 23–26, 1864

Quarles's Mill

MEADE

North Anna River

BURNSIDE

WARREN

WRIGHT

Ox Ford

Chesterfield Bridge

Anderson Station

A. P. HILL

ANDERSON

HANCOCK

New Market

Richmond, Fredericksburg & Potomac R. R.

Little River

Virginia Central Railroad

EWELL

LEE

Hanover Junction

North

0   1/2   1
Scale in miles

and Cold Harbor. In the fighting near Bethesda Church, Confederate Brig. Gen. James B. Terrill was killed—shot in the head—and buried on the battlefield. Sheridan strengthened his position at Old Cold Harbor on the night of May 31 and June 1. The crossroads at Old Cold Harbor stood two miles east of Gaines's Mill, where such savage action had unfolded two years prior during the Peninsular campaign. A mile and a half southwest of Old Cold Harbor was New Cold Harbor, another crossroads, which was a mile southeast of Gaines's Mill. Meade's force of 108,000 was attempting to form a hasty line in a north-south orientation along the Bethesda–Cold Harbor front to face Lee's interior line of about 59,000, who protected Richmond by stretching from the Totopotomoy River in the north to Grapevine Bridge in the south. Grant sent Wright's corps forward to occupy Old Cold Harbor by June 1, but the march became confused over unfamiliar roads in the darkness. Baldy Smith's corps (transferred from the Army of the James) disembarked at White House Landing and made its way toward the front, but errors of direction transmitted by Grant's staff sent him northward rather than westward toward Old Cold Harbor.

Despite the battlefront's inching closer to Richmond, Lee was reinforced by the divisions of Pickett, Hoke, and Maj. Gen. John C. Breckinridge, and he was determined to seize the initiative to force Grant and Meade to receive rather than initiate attacks. He had a smaller force at hand but also had the advantage of interior lines and would maneuver on ground familiar to his army. With Sheridan's cavalry divisions in possession of Old Cold Harbor, Lee sent Anderson's corps (bolstered by Hoke) to retake the crossroads on June 1. Despite the numerical inferiority of the Federal cavalry, the horse soldiers defended their ground well by using repeating carbines against the infantry muskets of the attackers. The Confederate attack collapsed, but no Federal counterattack was forthcoming. Wright and Smith didn't reach the Union line until 6 P.M., at which time they were exhausted, but they were ready for an attack the next morning. On the northern end of the line, Early sent a terrific attack forward that achieved only temporary success. The assault did capture some prisoners.

The armies shifted toward Cold Harbor and entrenched heavily, their lines constructed very close to one another in fields and woods. The planned attack of June 2 did not occur, for a hot day, afternoon rain showers, shortages of ammunition, and troop organizational gaffes caused a delay until the following day. Grant had now discovered that Lee's line between the Totopotomoy and Chickahominy rivers would be impossible to outflank; the Federal strategy of shoving Lee backward by repeatedly turning his right had come to a geographical end. Grant, therefore, determined to attack Lee frontally, break and dislodge him, and force the Southerners back into the Chickahominy. It was a risky maneuver that would certainly be costly in terms of casualties, but its success could break the line and possibly end the war in Virginia. On June 3, Grant ordered the great charge of the Overland campaign as Hancock's, Wright's, and Smith's corps formed and at 4:30 A.M. thrust into the heavily entrenched Confederate lines. Waves of musketry and the booming of well-placed field guns responded. The Union infantry had no chance. In under an hour 7,000 Union boys fell on the field as some 1,500 Confederate fell dead or wounded. It was one of the most violent hours in American history, and Grant's charge fell back, a failure. None of the Federal commanders had reconnoitered the lines properly, and the attack was not well supported. The decision to order the charge was the one military decision that Grant later wrote he always regretted. The Union attackers dug in perilously close to the Confederate lines, and thus began a round of trench warfare that witnessed nearly continuous sniping and suffering for the next ten days. The total casualties at Cold Harbor are not well known, but probably amount to 12,000 out of 50,000 Union men engaged and a few thousand out of the 30,000 Confederates engaged. Among the Confederate dead was Brig. Gen. George P. Doles, shot through the chest at Bethesda Church on June 2.

In the wake of the bloody charge the Cold Harbor battlefield was a gruesome spectacle. "The dead and dying lay in front of the Confederate lines in triangles, of which the apexes were the bravest men who came nearest to the breastworks under the withering, deadly fire," exclaimed Lt. Col. Charles S. Venable, one of Lee's staff officers, of the attack. "Lieut. Hobson of our battery walked up and down on the top of our breastworks and gave their orders calmly and deliberately," penned Confederate Pvt. Henry Robinson Berkeley, "while the death storm raged around them. The tears trickled down Hobson's cheeks as he saw one after another of his brave men go down before this terrible iron hail. Among the bravest of our battery, who fell yesterday, was [John] Christian, a boy of fifteen, who came to us six weeks ago. Poor boy, a shell took off his head while he was bravely doing his duty like an old vet."

The next move in either commander's mind was not as sure as earlier ones had been; where the campaign could go from here was a difficult proposition. Meade wanted to prevent Lee from reinforcing Confederates in the Shenandoah Valley, which meant keeping Lee's troops occupied with a fight. Sheridan was again dispatched, this time to the Valley, to rendezvous with Maj. Gen. David Hunter, who was starting a campaign there to move on Charlottesville. Lee responded quickly. He sent Breckinridge's infantry to face Hunter and sent Hampton's cavalry in pursuit of Sheridan. He dispatched Early to chase the Union infantry from Charlottesville and then break off to threaten Washington. Butler remained essentially inactive.

Faced with a pointless stalemate at the Cold Harbor trenches with the advantage to Lee if the armies sat inactive, Grant determined to make a bold move on June 12. The major supply lines providing the Confederate army were the railroads from the South, and they all converged on Petersburg, south of Richmond. So Grant determined to shift his base south of the James River to operate against Petersburg. This would not only cripple Lee's supply and communication lines but release Butler from his "bottled up" condition at Bermuda Hundred by pressuring Beauregard. With the Federal army inching along the rail lines into Richmond, Lee would be forced to retreat into a siege at the Confederate capital or abandon the area entirely and march westward into an unknown future. But the plan was wildly audacious—as risky and farsighted as the Vicksburg campaign had been—as Grant and Meade would have to move their entire army from the front directly opposing Lee's lines and cross the James River in a hostile countryside.

On June 12 the movement commenced as some men fell back to a shortened line of trenches while the bulk of the army moved south. Smith's corps moved briskly to the White House and then southward toward Charles City Court House. Hancock and Wright acted as a rear guard. Wilson's cavalry sprinted off to the Chickahominy and moved westward, establishing a screen to block Confederate advances. Warren moved swiftly in Wilson's wake and established a position east of Riddell's Shop, just north of Malvern Hill. Here, on June 13, a skirmish took place, as did scattered musket firing along the White Oak Swamp. Hancock's corps crossed the James on ferries on June 14 and 15, and Butler's engineers were busy erecting a pontoon bridge. By midnight the bridge, built south of Charles City Court House, at the northward bend in the James, was finished—2,100 feet long and one of the most impressive bridges completed to that time. The rest of the army hurried across, with Baldy Smith turning sharply westward under orders to cross the Appomattox and move toward Petersburg at daylight on June 15.

Lee took the bait. He found the Union trenches empty on the morning of June 13 but believed that Grant was again simply trying a turning movement. Lee thus shifted Anderson's and Hill's corps southward to a line near Riddell's Shop, Malvern Hill, and the White Oak Swamp, and simply erected a new line of trenches. Wilson's vigorous cavalry work, riding furiously up and down the lines, blocking Confederate reconnaissances and making demonstrations, prevented the Rebels from discovering that the cavalry division was all that confronted them. The change of base was a complex operation that was handled skillfully and with complete deception. An entirely new phase of the campaign was about to begin.

Smith's attack force consisted of his own division, the black troops of Hinks, and the cavalry division of Kautz. The Petersburg defenses were formidable. Consisting of a semicircular wall of redans south of the Appomat-

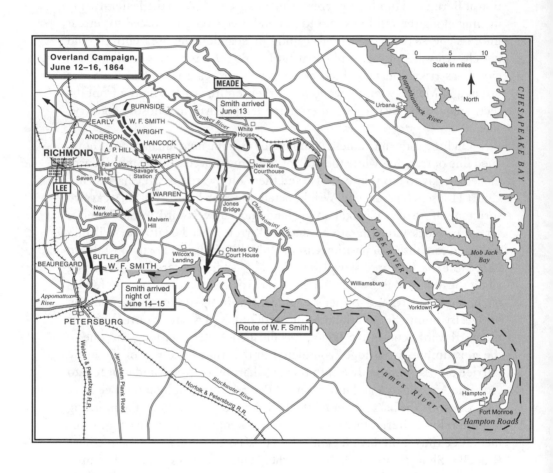

Overland Campaign,
June 12–16, 1864

MEADE

Smith arrived
June 13

BURNSIDE

EARLY   W. F. SMITH

WRIGHT

ANDERSON   HANCOCK

A. P. HILL

RICHMOND   WARREN

Fair Oaks

LEE   Savage's
Station

Seven Pines

WARREN

New
Market

Malvern
Hill

BUTLER

BEAUREGARD   W. F. SMITH

Smith arrived
night of
June 14–15

PETERSBURG

Route of W. F. Smith

Appomattox
River

Weldon & Petersburg R.R.

Jerusalem Plank Road

Blackwater River

Norfolk & Petersburg R.R.

Pamunkey River

White
House

New Kent
Courthouse

Jones
Bridge

Chickahominy River

Wilcox's
Landing

Charles City
Court House

Urbana

Rappahannock River

0   5   10
Scale in miles

North

CHESAPEAKE BAY

YORK RIVER

Mob Jack
Bay

Williamsburg

Yorktown

James River

Hampton

Fort Monroe

Hampton Roads

tox River, the defense line offered many outposts from which to strengthen gun emplacements or to offer enfilading as well as head-on fire, and crude but effective breastworks consisting of trees and tangled brush as well as ditches separated the redans from potential attackers. Haunted by the bloody frontal attack at Cold Harbor, Smith reconnoitered the Petersburg defenses with some caution on June 15, and confusion with his artillery commanders delayed any movement until 7 P.M., by which time he captured redans 5 and 6. The black troops of Hinks's division savagely attacked the line and captured a mile-wide swath of fortifications as far south as redan 11, and so due east of the city a breach in the Confederate defenses was opened.

But now Smith faltered. The "what ifs" in military history are irrelevant, but one can't help wonder what might have happened had Smith and Union reinforcements pressed an immediate westward attack into Petersburg. As it happened, Smith received reports that the Confederate line was about to be heavily reinforced, that Lee was swinging his army southward. He thus halted the attack until he could be reinforced by Hancock's 2d Corps, which was marching rapidly westward along the Jordan Point Road. Lee had sent the troops of Hoke's division southward, and Bushrod Johnson's division was about to arrive from Bermuda Hundred. The odds were evened as Smith sat inactive.

Hancock followed his orders to the letter, but a series of misadventures plagued his movement. He crossed the James and waited for supplies that never came. He received orders that failed to mention his role as a participant in the Petersburg attack, due to a miscommunication between Grant and Meade. He marched his men to an imaginary location and then countermarched back toward Petersburg, the mishap caused by a poor map at army headquarters. Finally, by 5:30 P.M., Hancock learned of his critical mission of the day, to help Smith with the Petersburg attack. By the time he reached Smith, however, Baldy was so shaken by the reinforcement of the Confederate line that he suggested that no attack take place and that Hancock's men simply relieve Smith's exhausted troops.

The first major attack at Petersburg occurred on June 16 at 6 P.M., as the majority of the Federal army arrived and aligned for battle. On this day approximately 48,000 Union troops clashed with about 14,000 Confederate defenders. Baldy Smith's men struck into those of Hoke along the Petersburg & City Point Railroad east of the city; Hancock attacked the Confederate center (consisting of Johnson's men) east of the Norfolk & Petersburg Railroad; and Burnside attacked to Hancock's south. Most of the Confederate troops from Bermuda Hundred were now pouring into the Petersburg defenses. The attack succeeded in capturing four more redans. Beauregard's counterattacks, though marked by heavy cannonading and musketry, failed. Union forces at Bermuda Hundred overran the Confederate positions, but

Lee sent Pickett northward to stop that movement and the Federal troops were recalled from their new position.

Federal attacks continued, with the goal of opening a breach in the Confederate lines east of the city. On June 17, Burnside sent a division forward to capture the ridge along the Shand House, just west of redans 14 and 15, but the supporting attacks were beaten back. Grant and Meade ordered a major attack along the whole front for June 18, which they put into motion at 4 A.M. The attack proceeded with the divisions of Brig. Gens. Thomas H. Neill and John H. Martindale on the north, Birney's corps (the 2d Corps was temporarily assigned to David B. Birney, as Hancock was bothered by a flare-up from his Gettysburg wound) and Burnside's corps in the center, and Warren's 5th Corps on the south. On this day Grant and Meade had about 67,000 men engaged, and Beauregard had 20,000 engaged in the morning and 38,000 in the afternoon. As the Yankees advanced, however, they found that Beauregard had pulled his men back into a newly constructed set of trenches a mile closer to the city, much of it paralleling the Norfolk & Petersburg Railroad, and that Lee was rapidly shifting more forces southward into the line. Heavy volleys of artillery blasted away as smoke hung over the field and the staccato of musketry inflicted heavy casualties on both sides.

One of the victims on the 18th was the celebrated Col. Joshua L. Chamberlain, hero of Gettysburg, who was shot through the hips. "I am lying mortally wounded the doctors think, but my mind & heart are at peace Jesus Christ is my all-sufficient savior," he wrote his wife Fanny, "I go to him. . . . We shall all soon meet Live for the children Give my dearest love to Father & mother & Sallie & John Oh how happy to feel yourself forgiven God bless you evermore precious precious one." Chamberlain not only survived, however, but was recommended for a brigadier general's grade by Grant himself and later commissioned to rank from the date of his wounding.

Heavy losses resulted and the Federals captured only minor areas. As the Confederate lines strengthened, it was clear that a siege of Petersburg would result. It would continue for ten months until the very end of the war in Virginia. Grant and Meade decided to halt their attacks against the siege lines and operate against Lee's lines of communications. They deployed Birney's and Wright's corps south of the city, along the Jerusalem Plank Road near the Weldon Railroad. On June 22 and 23, A. P. Hill took the divisions of Bushrod Johnson and Mahone and slammed into the Federal advance, creating the actions at the Weldon Railroad, Jerusalem Plank Road, Reams's Station, Davis's Farm, and Williams's Farm. The two Federal corps became separated, suffered in the wooded fighting, and withdrew. Casualties again were significant. Simultaneously, the cavalry of Wilson and Kautz was sent toward Burkeville to break the Southside Railroad, resulting in little gain, and Sheridan escorted the Federal wagon train southward across the James, harassed by Confederate cavalry at several points.

Frustration now began to set in among the Yankee soldiers as it became clear that long operations against Petersburg awaited them. "The feeling here in the army is that we have been absolutely butchered," stated Col. Stephen Minot Weld, Jr., of the 56th Massachusetts Infantry, to his father, "that our lives have been periled to no purpose, and wasted." The commander of the Army of the Potomac saw things in a different light, however. "I believe these two armies would fraternize and make peace in an hour, if the matter rested with them," Meade informed his wife on June 24, "not on terms to suit politicians on either side, but such as the world at large would acknowledge as honorable, and which would be satisfactory to the mass of people on both sides." Despite the end of major attacks on the Petersburg front, casualties mounted during the sniping and trench warfare that was developing. Among the numerous dead from the first phase of the campaign was Union Brig. Gen. James St. Clair Morton, who was killed on the Petersburg front on June 17, struck in the chest with a Minié bullet.

DURING THE SPOTSYLVANIA AND PETERSBURG campaigns other actions also unfolded in Virginia. At Cloyd's Mountain, on May 9, Brig. Gen. George Crook attempted to support the major campaigns by taking three brigades (6,155 men) on a raid into the rugged Allegheny Mountains to attack and destroy the Virginia & Tennessee Railroad. The battle of Cloyd's Mountain, also called New River Bridge, resulted. Hampered by cold rains and snowstorms, the Union raiders ran into a Confederate defensive line established by Brig. Gen. Albert G. Jenkins, 2,400 men deployed on a high bluff. About 11 A.M. Col. Carr B. White unleashed a flanking maneuver as Cols. Rutherford B. Hayes and Horatio G. Sickel attempted a frontal attack. A tremendous gun battle erupted, centered on the Southerners' log rail works, and hand-to-hand combat ensued as the Rebels fell back. Among the 538 Confederate casualties was Jenkins, who was shot in the left arm, shattering the bone. Captured, Jenkins had his arm amputated but infection set in and he died on May 21. Crook lost 688 men, but the Union forces burned New River Bridge before turning back for safety.

Another part of the simultaneous Union operations sent Maj. Gen. Franz Sigel, commander of the Department of West Virginia, with 6,500 men into the Shenandoah Valley. Lee ordered Maj. Gen. John C. Breckinridge, titular commander of the Trans-Allegheny Department, to stop him. Breckinridge, the former vice president of the United States, hastily assembled a force of about 5,000 that included both old men and the cadet corps of the Virginia Military Institute, from nearby Lexington, some 258 young boys. Sigel left Winchester on May 2 and marched southward along the Valley Turnpike, impeded by Brig. Gen. John D. Imboden's cavalry. By May 14, Sigel's soldiers reached Mount Jackson, and the following day he crossed the north fork of the Shenandoah River and approached Breckinridge. As the two armies neared each other at the little town of New Market, a tremendous cannonade commenced the battle on May 15. Breckinridge's men passed through the town and were cheered by the inhabitants; Sigel fell back and deployed his men on a ridge near the Bushong Farm. He established a line for his seventeen field guns. As the Confederates approached, sheets of canister fire belched from the Union cannon. The VMI cadets, most of whom had lost their shoes after scurrying across a muddy creek, charged the Federal position amid volleys of musketry and captured a Federal cannon. "The cadets, many of them old enough to be in the army, behaved very gallantly, considering they had never before been under fire, but I was told by an actor on the scene, Charles Anderson of Richmond, that the little fellows, mere children in size and years, behaved as well as the rest, and were even more eager to join the fray," recorded Confederate diarist Cornelia Peake McDonald. "He said that after the battle they were collecting the dead, that he picked up the body of a little fellow who he knew. . . . He found him lying in a fence corner as if asleep, his musket at his side, and he picked him up as easily as he would have done an infant."

After the war, the charge of the VMI cadets became legendary in the South, a victorious moment from a war that was growing ever gloomier. "Not the devoted few who stood in the pass at Thermopylae," echoed one oration, "the noble six hundred that charged at Balaklava, nor Pickett's men, who stormed the blazing crest of Gettysburg, deserve more praise than that Cadet Battalion which, amid a storm of shot and shell, won that glorious day at New Market."

As the battle continued, the Union line collapsed. "Sigel seemed in a state of excitement and rode here and there with [Julius] Stahel and [Augustus] Moor, all jabbering in German," reported David Hunter Strother, of Sigel's staff. "In his excitement he seemed to forget his English entirely, and the purely American portion of his staff were totally useless to him." After a futile effort to hold his line, Sigel retreated to Strasburg. The Yankees lost 93 killed, 482 wounded, and 256 missing; Confederate casualties were 42 killed, 522 wounded, and 13 missing. The foolishness of Sigel as a commander was as important as the gallantry of the VMI cadets in the Confederate victory at New Market.

In the wake of New Market, Sigel was reassigned from the campaign in the Shenandoah Valley and replaced with Maj. Gen. David Hunter, who was located at Strasburg and had the divisions of Brig. Gen. Jeremiah C. Sullivan (infantry) and Maj. Gen. Julius Stahel (cavalry). Hunter would also command the force at Lewisburg, which consisted of the divisions of Brig. Gens. George Crook (infantry) and William W. Averell (cavalry). The combined forces of Hunter's Army of the Shenandoah comprised 11,000 infantry and 5,000 cavalry and would be met by Brig. Gen. William E. "Grumble" Jones's force of 3,500 infantry and 5,000 horsemen.

On May 26, Hunter began a movement to Staunton and ordered Crook forward by Covington and Warm Springs. Skirmishing broke out at the former place on June 2; as Hunter reached Harrisonburg on June 4, musketry erupted near where Col. Turner Ashby, the promising Virginia cavalryman, had been killed two years prior, in a small action known as Harrisonburg or Second Port Republic. Jones had established a defensive line blocking a direct approach to Staunton, detaching cavalry to thwart Crook while his main force turned on Hunter's column. Hunter's army reached the Confederate skirmish line at 6 A.M. on June 5, pushing it into a defensive posture near Piedmont, southwest of Port Republic. The battle of Piedmont resulted. By 9 A.M. the Federal artillery opened a terrific fire, and a short time later Col. Augustus Moor's infantry pushed forward on Jones's left. Union Col. Joseph Thoburn's brigade captured a ridge on the opposite flank, and the Confederate line began to waver.

Shortly before noon the Federal attack succeeded to such an extent that the Confederate artillery was captured or withdrew. Assaults and counterassaults marked the early afternoon hours at Piedmont, with little success achieved on either side. By midafternoon Moor led an attack that pushed back the withering Rebels and, with the aid of Col. John E. Wynkoop's cavalry brigade, triggered a rout. Many of the Confederates "threw up their hands . . . and begged for mercy" as the battle ended. Grumble Jones was killed, shot in the head with a Minié bullet that knocked him from his horse. The Union army marched into Staunton and joined with Crook's men to continue their journey into the Valley. Losses at Piedmont were about 780 for the Yankees and 1,600 Confederates, 1,000 of the latter being taken prisoner.

As Hunter advanced, he targeted Lexington and Lynchburg, the former town being home of the Virginia Military Institute and Washington College. Hunter now earned the name "Black Dave" among outraged Virginians. On June 10 some of Breckinridge's scattered forces attempted to block Hunter's march, and minor actions ensued at Middlebrook, Brownsburg, and Waynesborough. The following day Hunter's men skirmished with local forces, entered Lexington, and burned the VMI buildings. "The plunderers came running out, their arms full of spoils," wrote Col. David Hunter Strother, Hunter's cousin and chief of staff. ". . . Most of them were loaded with the most useless and impracticable articles. Lieutenant Meigs came out with fine mathematical instruments, and Dr. Patton followed with a beautiful human skeleton. . . . My only spoil was a new gilt button marked 'V.M.I.' and a pair of gilt epaulettes which some of the clerks had picked up and handed to me. The burning of the Institute made a grand picture, a vast volume of black smoke rolled above the flames and covered half the horizon."

On the same day as Hunter's famous visit to Lexington, Maj. Gen. Sheridan's cavalry endeavored to link with Hunter at Charlottesville to destroy the Virginia Central Railroad between there and Hanover Junction and the James River Canal. This would serve as a distraction as Grant began his change of base. Sheridan's horsemen, 6,000 strong, moved northwest from Cold Harbor toward Hunter as Confederate Maj. Gen. Wade Hampton, with 5,000 horsemen, pursued. The forces converged near Trevilian Station at 5 A.M. on June 11, in what became the largest all-cavalry engagement of the war. Fighting along a section of forest marked by dense thickets, Sheridan and Hampton each dismounted a division and sent it forward to fight blindly, in conditions of poor visibility that echoed those of the Wilderness. Sharp fire from the cavalry weapons, including many repeating breechloaders, escalated as Sheridan committed a second division to the fight. The Confederates retreated in disorder and, at Trevilian Station, encountered Brig. Gen. George A. Custer's Michigan brigade after it had captured a portion of Hampton's wagon train. A bloody action occurred at the station as Confederate horsemen charged and fired, and under hot conditions the troopers, caked with powder, finally fought their way out of envelopment by the Confederates and escaped.

The battle of Trevilian Station flared again on the morning of June 12 when Sheridan's men attacked the railroad and were subsequently struck by a huge counterattack that stunned the Yankee horsemen. By nightfall Sheridan's men retreated toward Cold Harbor. The Union casualties amounted to 102 killed, 470 wounded, and 435 missing; Confederate losses were reported as 612, but these records were incomplete.

As Hunter and Crook continued their march to the rail center of Lynchburg, they found stiff resistance. Hunter attacked the town on June 17 and 18 but was repulsed by Breckinridge and a portion of Jubal Early's corps. "We attracted the combined forces of Hunter and Crook last Sunday evening near Lynchburg and after not more than one hours engagement Hunter Commenced a retreat in the direction of Salem," wrote Cpl. Henry C. Carpenter of the 45th Virginia Infantry. "In the fight yesterday we Captured twelve pieces of Artillery and about 200 horses and a great many Prisoners. I don't think old Hunter and Crook will stop running." Hunter retreated via Salem and the West Virginia towns of Lewisburg, Charleston, Parkersburg, and finally to Martinsburg, abandoning his Valley campaign. The opportunity for Early to launch a raid of his own would come shortly.

MAY AND JUNE witnessed another raid of the celebrated Brig. Gen. John Hunt Morgan, who this time moved into Kentucky to relieve the tightening pressure against Joe Johnston in Georgia by attacking Sherman's distant lines of communications. On May 31, Morgan's raiders skirmished at Abingdon, Virginia, and the following day at Pound Gap as they moved into Kentucky. On June 8–9, Morgan's men captured Mount Sterling, overwhelming the Federal garrison and taking $18,000 from the local bank. Two days later Morgan's men, now charged with so much spirit that they were transforming into riotous looters, moved into Lexington, torched the Federal horse stables, and let loose about 7,000 horses. After an action at Kellar's Bridge, the raiders entered Cynthiana on June 11 and captured about 300 Union soldiers. On June 12 the raiders were attacked and beaten back, forced to retreat to Abingdon, which they did by June 20. For months Brig. Gen. Edward H. Hobson had chased Morgan across Kentucky and was almost always a day or three behind him. In the melee at Cynthiana, Hobson and his staff were captured after Hobson was wounded. "They gave no parole," reported Capt. J. Bates Dickson. "In the meantime Morgan's army was routed and dispersed. We do not consider Genl. Hobson and staff as prisoners and they are now expected here."

Many other scattered actions peppered the American landscape and even foreign locations during the early summer. On May 26, Montana Territory was organized as settlement of the west continued. On June 6 fighting erupted in Arkansas at Lake Chicot. On June 19 the celebrated naval battle was fought between the screw sloop USS *Kearsarge* (Capt. John A. Winslow) and the cruiser CSS *Alabama* (Capt. Raphael Semmes) off the coast of Cherbourg, France. Launched in England on May 15, 1862, the *Alabama* had cruised through a two-year raiding party throughout the Atlantic, sinking 65 ships totaling $6.5 million in damages. By the end of 1863, routine cruising and plundering created a tranquil demeanor among Semmes and his men. "I passed the island of St. Paul on the 12th of October, and on the 22nd lost the west winds in the calm belt of the southern tropic, having made a run of 4,410 miles in twenty-four and three fourths days," Semmes wrote on December 22, 1863, "a very satisfactory run for a steamer under sail alone. The rough tumbling that my ship got in this passage caused her to complain somewhat, and even to take a little more water than usual, and in one of the gales a quarter boat was swept from one of the davits."

The worn-out *Alabama* was badly in need of repairs, and Semmes brought the ship into the French harbor for maintenance. Winslow's *Kearsarge* approached, and Semmes sailed the *Alabama*, with its 8 guns which would fire 360-pound shells, out into the calm waters to face the Federal ship, which had 7 guns throwing 430-pound projectiles. A large crowd of European spectators watched the action from the shore, about three miles away from the two ships. About 11 A.M. Semmes opened fire, and the *Kearsarge* replied in kind. After a relatively short bombardment the *Alabama*'s sides were splintered by the Union shells and she withdrew toward the shoreline, striking her flag. "She was severely hulled between her main and mizzen masts and settled by the stern," recorded Surg. John M. Browne aboard the *Kearsarge*. An English yacht, the *Deerhound,* took on some of the surviving Confederates, including Semmes. Aboard the *Alabama,* 9 were killed and 21 wounded before the ship sank (in about 15 minutes); the *Kearsarge* had only 3 wounded. Aboard the *Kearsarge,* a prisoner from the *Alabama* mistook Winslow for a steward and asked him for a drink. Winslow passed the Confederate sailor a drink of whiskey, pointed toward the Stars and Stripes, and said simply, "That is the flag you should have been under." "It is true that we have lost our ship," wrote Confederate Capt. Samuel Barron, "the ubiquitous gallant *Alabama* is no more, but we have lost no honor." Semmes could only write that "no one who is not a seaman can realize the blow that falls upon the heart of a commander, upon the sinking of his ship."

AND THEN CAME SHERMAN. After Bragg retreated to Rocky Face Ridge between Chattanooga and Atlanta (west of Dalton, Georgia), Sherman readied his army for a pursuit and drive into middle Georgia the following spring. Gen. Joseph E. Johnston had taken command of the Army of Tennessee. This army, about 50,000 strong, consisted of the corps of Lt. Gen. William J. Hardee (divisions of Maj. Gens. Benjamin F. Cheatham, Patrick R. Cleburne, William H. T. Walker, and William B. Bate); Lt. Gen. John Bell Hood (divisions of Maj. Gens. Thomas C. Hindman, Carter L. Stevenson, and Alexander P. Stewart); Maj. Gen. Joseph Wheeler (Cavalry Corps, divisions of Maj. Gen. William T. Martin and Brig. Gens. John H. Kelly and William Y. C. Humes); Lt. Gen. Leonidas Polk (also called the Army of Mississippi; divisions of Maj. Gens. William W. Loring and Samuel G. French); and the Cavalry Division of Brig. Gen. William H. Jackson. Sherman, commanding the Military Division of the Mississippi, had approximately 98,500 men as follows: Maj. Gen. George H. Thomas's Army of the Cumberland comprised the corps of Maj. Gen. Oliver O. Howard (4th Corps; divisions of Maj. Gen. David S. Stanley and Brig. Gens. John Newton and Thomas J. Wood); Maj. Gen. John M. Palmer (14th Corps; divisions of Brig. Gens. Richard W. Johnson, Jefferson C. Davis, and Absalom Baird); Maj. Gen. Joseph Hooker (20th Corps; divisions of Brig. Gens. Alpheus S. Williams, John W. Geary, and Maj. Gen. Daniel Butterfield); and Brig. Gen. Washington L. Elliott (Cavalry Corps; divisions of Brig. Gens. Edward M. McCook, Kenner Garrard, and H. Judson Kilpatrick). The second great Federal army, Maj. Gen. James B. McPherson's Army of the Tennessee, comprised the corps of Maj.

Gen. John A. Logan (15th Corps; divisions of Brig. Gens. Peter J. Osterhaus, Morgan L. Smith, John E. Smith, and William Harrow); Maj. Gen. Grenville M. Dodge (16th Corps; divisions of Brig. Gens. Thomas W. Sweeny and James C. Veatch); and Maj. Gen. Frank P. Blair, Jr. (17th Corps, which joined the army on June 8 and contained the divisions of Brig. Gens. Mortimer D. Leggett and Walter Q. Gresham). Also present was the Army of the Ohio, commanded by Maj. Gen. John M. Schofield (23d Corps; divisions of Brig. Gens. Alvin P. Hovey, Henry M. Judah, and Jacob D. Cox, plus a cavalry division commanded by Maj. Gen. George Stoneman).

Despite the fact that Sherman had a vastly larger number of men in the field, he would be attacking southward into fortified positions over unfamiliar ground, and furloughs had temporarily depleted his army so that many of the men were "present" only on paper. Moreover, poor weather and terrible logistical problems in moving supplies delayed Sherman's advance until early May. Johnston, meanwhile, was nagged to move into Tennessee by Davis and Bragg to cut Federal lines of communications, but by now these suggestions were all but ridiculous in practical terms. Grant had ordered Sherman to "move against Johnston's Army, to break it up and to get into the interior of the enemy's country as far as you can, inflicting all the damage you can against their War resources." Sherman focused on moving against Atlanta, population 9,554, a town that was vitally important as a rail center, as it connected the Western & Atlantic Railroad (to the north), the Macon Railroad (to the south), the Georgia Railroad (to the east), and the Atlanta & Western Railroad (to the southwest). The citizens of the small city knew its strategic importance, too. "Atlanta is the great strategic point," editorialized the *Atlanta Daily Constitutionalist* on May 1, "The approaches to the Gate City—every one of them—must be made a second Thermopylae."

Light skirmishing in Georgia erupted on May 4 and continued for three days along Rocky Face Ridge, at Varnell's Station north of Dalton, at Mill Creek Gap, and at Tunnel Hill, where two years earlier the *General* had raced toward Chattanooga. On May 7, Sherman set his army into motion, sending McPherson (24,000 men) south from the area of the old Chickamauga battlefield through Snake Creek Gap to cut Johnston's rail lines, screened by Kilpatrick's cavalry; Thomas (61,000) would move south from Ringgold toward Tunnel Hill and Buzzard Roost, creating a demonstration against Johnston's center; and Schofield (13,500) would cut south from Red Clay, Tennessee, along the railroad line toward Varnell's Station, with cavalry under Stoneman and McCook screening the front. Johnston's Confederates were now situated along Rocky Face Ridge across Buzzard Roost and Tunnel Hill, and his men to the south had retreated from Snake Creek Gap into Resaca. Sherman wished to cut Johnston's lines of supply and communications but also, believing his fortified position too strong to attack, aimed

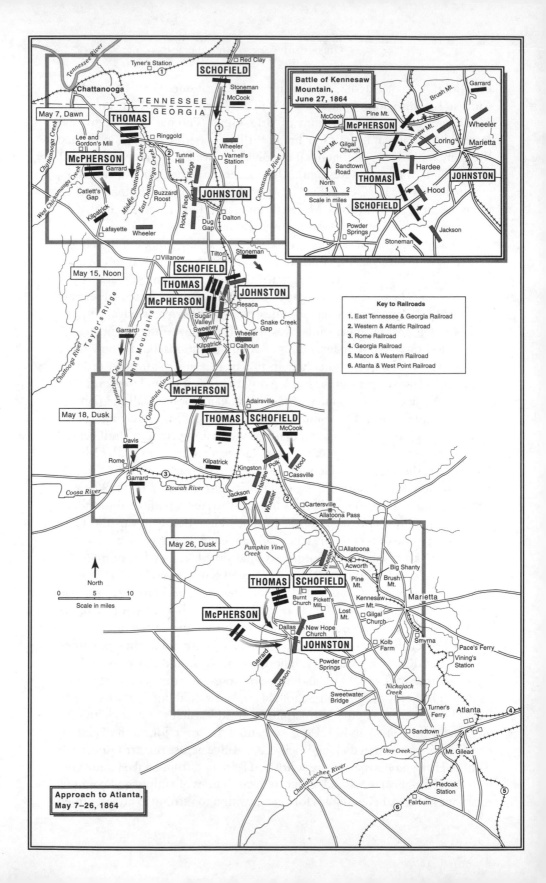

Battle of Kennesaw Mountain, June 27, 1864

Key to Railroads
1. East Tennessee & Georgia Railroad
2. Western & Atlantic Railroad
3. Rome Railroad
4. Georgia Railroad
5. Macon & Western Railroad
6. Atlanta & West Point Railroad

Approach to Atlanta, May 7–26, 1864

to turn Johnston's left flank. On May 8, as the armies drew closer, fighting erupted at Buzzard Roost, Mill Creek Gap, Dug Gap, and Snake Creek Gap. On May 9, Thomas's and Schofield's men pushed into the Confederate line at Buzzard Roost and Rocky Face Gap, and by midafternoon McPherson worked his way through Snake Creek Gap and toward Johnston's rear, hoping to strike toward Resaca. After initial skirmishing with musketry and artillery rounds, McPherson determined that the position was too well fortified and pulled back to Snake Creek Gap. Sherman was irritated and disappointed at the apparent loss of will over McPherson's stall before Johnston's line. Cavalry skirmishes flared at Varnell's Station and around the perimeter of the armies.

On May 10, Johnston discovered the plan to turn his left and, over the following day, skirmishes again lit the rocky hills with the flashes of gunfire around Rocky Face Ridge. Still disappointed by the failure to turn Johnston's left, Sherman wrote Halleck on May 11, "I shall pass through Snake Creek Gap to where General McPherson now holds its outlet. Johnston will then have to retreat below Resaca, or we shall interpose between him and [Atlanta]." Sherman ordered a movement on Resaca for May 12, which developed smoothly, forcing Johnston to withdraw from Dalton and retreat to a new line near Resaca, facing the Yankee army. The following day fighting erupted at Resaca and at Sugar Valley and along the Oostanaula River, which grew into a considerable battle by May 14. The battle of Resaca flared as Sherman tried to break the new Confederate line. Cox's division attacked and made progress on the Federal left; to his south, Judah's division received heavy casualties after a hazardous movement over hard terrain. Palmer's division attacked gallantly after crossing Camp Creek under fire but unraveled and was struck by heavy musketry fire as it approached the Confederate defenses. About 6 P.M. Hood sent the divisions of Stewart and Stevenson into Cox's Yankees, and he ordered similar counterattacks for the following morning, May 15. The fighting was severe on both sides, a Confederate officer recalling that "There were some brave spirits . . . who continued to pour it into the enemy from behind trees while the Federals occupied the crest of the ridge. We stopped all the men we could and put them in our line. I said to one fellow: 'Halt! What are you running for?' He answered, 'Bekase I kain't fly!' " Sherman, meanwhile, began constructing a pontoon bridge at Lay's Ferry on the Oostanaula River and ordered Sweeny's division forward to Calhoun, east of the ferry. An enveloping movement evolved as Garrard's cavalry sped forward to Rome. Again forced into moving his line by the flanking movement, Johnston pulled out and moved south toward Dallas.

On May 16, Sherman pressed a pursuit of the retreating Johnston, who moved his divisions south to Cassville with cavalry screening to the west at Kingston. The following day skirmishing erupted at Adairsville; by May

18–19 scattered fighting broke out along the Cassville line. On the second day at Cassville, Johnston ordered an attack by Hood on Schofield, but the latter grew anxious over rumors of a Federal encirclement and failed to attack. Johnston established a defensive position south of Cassville and Federal artillery, on the approach, opened fire. Alarmed by the Yankee advance, Hood and Polk pleaded with Johnston to again withdraw, while Hardee opposed such a move. After weighing the options briefly, Johnston again retreated, this time through Cartersville and on to the Etowah River, with his command structure again fragmented. Sherman pressed for an attack before the fleeing Confederates could reach the river.

Johnston now maneuvered his army through Allatoona Pass, south of Cartersville, and established a defensive line along the crest of mountains south of the pass, while Sherman remained steady at Kingston, resupplying and working on the railroad lines. Once resupplied, he abandoned his supply line of the railroad and again turned Johnston's left, marching rapidly toward Dallas, forcing Johnston to abandon his strong position and move out into the open to block Sherman's army at New Hope Church. On May 24 skirmishing occurred at Cass Station, Burnt Hickory (Huntsville), and near Dallas.

The New Hope Church campaign, a temporary stall in the movements of the armies and a resumption of fighting, occurred from May 25 to June 4. At 11 A.M. on May 25, Geary's division struck into the Confederate line near Dallas as he sent Col. Charles Candy's brigade forward through Owen's Mill and across a burning bridge at Pumpkin Vine Creek. The brigades of Candy and Cols. Adolphus Buschbeck and David Ireland attacked in the afternoon toward New Hope Church but were struck by a monstrous artillery fire. Hood's men fired hotly into Geary's re-formed attack and stopped it again. Hood brought together sixteen Confederate guns and fired canister repeatedly into the oncoming Yankees, giving rise to the name Hellhole for the region of ground the soldiers fought over this day.

On May 26 scattered light skirmishing occurred in the area; the next major assaults came the following afternoon. At 5 P.M. on May 27, Howard sent Hazen's brigade into the Confederate line held by two regiments of Cleburne's division at Pickett's Mill, northeast of Dallas. The Federal battle plan called for support from Richard W. Johnson's division and from Wood's division; Col. Benjamin F. Scribner's brigade moved in support but other brigades did not, and Scribner's men were struck by a heavy fire from the left, after which Cleburne mounted a vicious counterattack, drawing away the Union support. The fighting raged through a cornfield and adjacent wheat field, and Union losses were significant, including Johnson's receiving a glancing bruise from a shell. Darkness ended the battle and the stricken lay in the fields, in an "opening in the forest, faint fires here and there revealing men wounded, armless, legless and eyeless; some with heads bound up with cotton strips, some standing and walking nervously around, some sitting with bended forms, some prone on the earth."

A Confederate attack also struck the brigades of Brig. Gens. Nathan Kimball and George D. Wagner but was repulsed as Col. Daniel McCook's brigade occupied a critical pass near the Confederate center and held it against several Confederate small-arms attacks. Hood planned a major attack on May 28 but found the position of Johnson's division too strong and so canceled his plan. This time Sherman had difficulty executing the flanking maneuver and so backed away toward the railroad to be nearer his supply base. Skirmishes took place along the Dallas line until June 1, at Allatoona and Burnt Church on May 30, and at Allatoona Pass on June 1. But on the first day of June heavy rains began to thwart all the planned operations on both sides. Skirmishes flared at Acworth on June 3 and at Big Shanty, where the Yankees began to build up a base of supplies, from June 4 to 9. Sherman maneuvered rapidly back to the rail line and Johnston established a new position amid the mountains northwest of Marietta, along Lost Mountain, Pine Mountain, and Brush Mountain. Kennesaw Mountain, more formidable than the others, stood between Johnston's new line and Marietta. Skirmishes erupted on June 5 at Pine Mountain and the following day at Raccoon Creek.

Sherman had plenty to worry about. His supply lines were long and tenuous, as his men were encamped ninety miles from Chattanooga, and both Wheeler's cavalry and Forrest's men were operating to break those lines in his rear. Higher security along the railroad lines would be necessary for a prolonged campaign, and Sherman ordered forces in Tennessee to intercept and break up Forrest's command. Brig. Gen. Samuel D. Sturgis drew the assignment to track down the troublesome Confederate raider. Sturgis assembled 4,800 infantry, 3,000 cavalry, and 18 guns from Memphis to attack Forrest's cavalry, which consisted of between 3,500 and 4,000 troopers. On June 10, Sturgis caught up with Forrest at Brice's Cross Roads, Mississippi (in the northeastern part of the state), in a battle alternatively termed Guntown or Tishomingo Creek. The Union horse soldiers contacted the Rebels at 9:30 A.M. on a road crossing a swampy area that rose along a defile near the crossroads.

Union Brig. Gen. Benjamin H. Grierson, who had led the spectacular diversionary raid during the Vicksburg campaign, halted his men and dispatched a reconnoitering party. After moving a mile to the southeast, toward Guntown, the horsemen encountered Confederate pickets; Grierson dismounted and deployed his men to hold the wooded area until Sturgis's infantry arrived. The Yankees received light fire from the troops of Col. Hylan

B. Lyon late in the morning; by 1 P.M. Forrest's reinforcements arrived and he attacked the Yankees headlong. Over the next hour Grierson's men found themselves pushed back under heavy fighting, and they struggled to establish a second battle line. Conditions echoed those of the Wilderness: heat and dense undergrowth made visibility poor and organization next to impossible. Forrest struck both flanks of the Union line simultaneously, and confusion and bloody casualties turned into outright panic along the Yankee line. The Federals broke and fled, among them the 59th USCT, who certainly feared for their lives, recalling Fort Pillow. Clogged bridges and a breakdown of unit cohesiveness led to outright chaos as the Yankees crossed Tishomingo Creek. Everywhere "were evidence that the 'skeer' was still on the Federals," bragged a Confederate captain. "Knapsacks, guns, belts, and various articles of superfluous clothing lined the road. The bushes were trampled down for twenty feet on each side, and, as the morning broke, many prisoners were captured in the woods, having lost their way." Forrest completely routed the Yankees, whose casualties were 223 killed, 394 wounded, and 1,623 missing; Confederate losses were 96 killed and 396 wounded. Sherman was exasperated and looked for another commander to control the wily Confederate. "Say to General [Joseph A.] Mower that I want him advanced," Sherman wrote on June 23, "and if he will whip Forrest I will pledge him my influence for a Major General, and will ask the Secretary of War as a personal favor to hold a vacancy for him."

In Georgia, rains continued as Sherman strengthened his supply situation at Big Shanty. Skirmishes erupted at McAfee's Crossroads on June 12. An action two days later at Pine Mountain cast a long shadow on Confederate command in the west. As the Confederate high command stood atop Pine Mountain, watching Union movements, Johnston, Hardee, and Polk discussed the situation. The Confederate commanders spotted Federal artillery taking notice of their position and began to move from the summit as Polk was struck. A Parrot shell had passed through Polk's left arm, body, and right arm, emerged, and exploded against a nearby tree. The "Fighting Bishop" was suddenly gone and, although he wasn't a great field general, his influence in the command structure was lost as Loring assumed command of his corps. In shock at the bloody explosion, Johnston cried at length and repeatedly told his comrades, "We have lost so much! I would rather have anything but this." Found in Polk's pockets were four copies of Confederate Chaplain Charles T. Quintard's *Balm for the Weary and the Wounded*, three of which had been inscribed by Polk to Johnston, Hardee, and Hood, each of which was spattered with Polk's blood.

Sherman continued as much pressure as he could toward the Confederate line, with frequent heavy rains still plaguing the operations. Johnston contracted his line to form an arc along Kennesaw Mountain and southward. During the uneventful last half of June minor actions flared, and on June 22, Hood's corps made a strong attack at Peter Kolb's Farm near Kennesaw Mountain, which failed.

Sherman now faced a difficult situation. Rains hampered his moving supplies along the roads. Schofield could not move supplies from the railroad to his army. The railroad did not allow moving supply stations farther south because Johnston's fortified position along the mountains controlled the area. A movement around Johnston's left thus seemed impractical. McPherson needed to remain in place to guard against a Confederate attack toward the supply depot at Big Shanty. Sherman thus determined to attack Johnston at Kennesaw Mountain, in a risky and dangerous strategy. At 9 A.M. on June 27, Sherman sent a poorly planned attack forward into the Confederate center, with the divisions of Martin L. Smith, Jeff C. Davis, and Newton striking deeply toward the Rebel lines. Smith's men captured the outer defensive line under a withering Rebel fire but could not move into the second line. Newton was beaten back with murderous losses; a second attack by Brig. Gen. Charles G. Harker's brigade, comprising Newton's right, was met with heavy artillery and small-arms fire and withered away when Harker was shot. He died a few hours later. The brigades of Kimball and Wagner were also repulsed with heavy casualties. Davis's attack did not work any better, as the brigades of Col. Dan McCook shuddered and broke under volleys of Confederate musketry, one of which mortally wounded McCook in the right lung. He died three weeks later in Ohio.

The Davis attack at Kennesaw Mountain foundered after the most vicious fighting of the battle, which occurred at what is now called Cheatham Hill. The blistering heat and dust, rough terrain, and heavily reinforced Confederate defensive positions rendered an attack by the Union troops futile. The brunt of the attacks was received by the divisions of Cheatham, Cleburne, and Brig. Gen. Winfield Scott Featherston. Union infantry dug in perilously close to the Confederate lines and even attempted to tunnel into those lines for a time before aborting that maneuver. On June 29, Confederate soldiers attempted to dislodge Davis from his position to no avail. Kennesaw Mountain ended with a stalemate after the bloody losses of the 27th, suffered mostly by the Union brigades that attacked. Union casualties were 1,999 killed and wounded and 52 missing; Confederate losses were 270 killed and wounded and 172 missing. "It is enough to make the whole world start at the awful amount of death and destruction that now stalks abroad," Sherman wrote his wife on June 30. "Daily for the past two months has the work progressed and I see no signs of a remission til one or both and all the armies are destroyed when I suppose the balance of the People will tear each other up.

. . . I begin to regard the death & mangling of a couple thousand men as a small affair, a kind of morning dash—and it may be well that we become so hardened."

As THE WAR DRAGGED ON, an increasing number of officers and soldiers encountered varied problems. On June 29, in Washington, Brig. Gen. Joseph Pannell Taylor, Zachary Taylor's brother, uncle-in-law of Jefferson Davis, commissary general of subsistence, and former member of Lincoln's War Board, died of diarrhea and partial paralysis. Taylor died with family and officers close at hand. Others were not so lucky. One day in the middle of June 1864, Mrs. Melissa J. Hartley, of Gibson's Station, Ohio, whose husband James was fighting in the war with the 122d Ohio Infantry, received an envelope. Inside a letter read: "It is with the deepest regret I inform you of the death of Lt. James Hartley. He was killed by a cannon ball this morning about 7 A.M. Back of head torn off. Was buried by our men and grave marked." In an instant, worlds turned upside down.

Lincoln, meanwhile, faced an uncertain future in the summer of 1864, with clouds of doubt over his reelection. On June 8 he was nominated for a second term at Baltimore during the National Union party convention. Andrew Johnson, military governor of Tennessee, became the vice presidential candidate. In his reply to the National Union League of June 9, Lincoln explained, "I have not permitted myself, gentlemen, to conclude that I am the best man in the country; but I am reminded, in this connection, of a story of an old Dutch farmer, who remarked to a companion once that 'it was not best to swap horses when crossing streams.' "

Action at Atlanta and Petersburg

DESPITE THE FEDERAL SETBACK at Kennesaw Mountain, Maj. Gen. William T. Sherman was determined to press on with his movement against Joe Johnston. With hot, dry weather again spreading over Georgia during the first days of July, the Yankees found the roads improved and supplies transportable. So Sherman's army returned to a strategic game of maneuver. Schofield, Stoneman, and McPherson were sent south along the Sandtown Road to once again turn Johnston's left flank, and on July 2 the Confederate commander withdrew his men from the fortified entrenchments on Kennesaw Mountain, retreating to another previously worked line south of Marietta, along the western bank of the Chattahoochie River and Nickajack Creek. With six brigades, Johnston had a formidable force in place, but he chose a dangerous position with his back against the river. On July 3 the Yankees pursued, passing through Marietta and past Kennesaw Mountain and engaging in light skirmishes at Big Shanty, Sweetwater Bridge, Kingston, and Ruff's Mills as Confederate cavalry operated to slow them down. Minor actions erupted at Vining's Station and along a portion of Nickajack Creek.

On July 4 citizens of the United States celebrated the nation's 88th Independence Day in muted fashion. On Sherman's right McPherson moved so far south that he halted at the Chattahoochie River and found himself closer to Atlanta than Johnston was. The actions for the Chattahoochie began and would last until July 10, as Johnston again pulled back and consolidated his force along the river. Sherman dispatched Garrard's cavalry to hold a river crossing at Roswell, far to the north, and the Yankee commander was alarmed and puzzled when he found that Johnston had arrayed his troops along the western bank of the Chattahoochie not expecting him to defend the river. Many small actions flared as the armies maneuvered, at

Vining's Station, Burnt Hickory, Rottenwood Creek, and Mitchell's Cross-roads. The following day Sherman's men probed the Southern position, seeking a weak spot, and clashes erupted at Pace's Ferry, Turner's Ferry, and Isham's Ford. Cavalry operations continued for the next two days, during which Jefferson Davis wrote Johnston, declaring, "The announcement that your army has fallen back to the Chattahoochie renders me more apprehensive for the future," and, without offering further troops from Richmond, concluding that "I cannot judge of your condition or the best method of averting calamity."

On July 8, Schofield's army crossed the Chattahoochie near the mouth of Soap Creek, pushing ahead with Brig. Gen. Edward M. McCook's cavalry division facing Wheeler's cavalry. The opposition was light, and the task ahead of the Confederate forces, though they were defending and had interior lines, seemed daunting. Gov. Joe Brown of Georgia did not seem to be able to provide much help with state militia, either. Schofield's breakthrough forced a surprising turning movement that would require Johnston to fall back yet again, this time closer to Atlanta. On July 9, Johnston moved his army out of its entrenchments and crossed the river, this time halting at the city's gates. Skirmishing took place again at Vining's Station and Nickajack Creek. Sherman also ordered Maj. Gen. Lovell H. Rousseau to command a cavalry raid using soldiers primarily from Kilpatrick to depart Decatur, Alabama, and operate on the railroads between Montgomery and Columbus, Georgia. On July 9, Rousseau and 2,500 horsemen marched to Blountsville, Ashville, Talladega, and finally Opelika on July 17. Rousseau's raiders destroyed vast stretches of track before returning to Marietta.

During the Atlanta campaign, Maj. Gen. Nathan Bedford Forrest, fresh from his victory at Brice's Cross Roads, searched for ways to harass the Union effort. To counter the threat, Sherman dispatched Maj. Gen. Andrew J. Smith on an expedition after the cavalryman. Smith's 14,000 men pursued Forrest, occupying Tupelo, Mississippi, on July 13. Confederates under Lt. Gen. Stephen D. Lee moved quickly to assault Smith, resulting in the battle of Tupelo. On July 14, Lee attacked at 7 A.M., sending Kentucky and Tennessee troops forward into battle lines and stinging the Union brigades with a heavy fire. Forrest, who had been assigned command of most of the troops by Lee, shifted among his brigades and found the Kentuckians moving to the rear under a heavy fire. Forrest rallied his troops, seizing the colors, and reorganized them to attack again. On Forrest's left, Confederates were falling back because of the terrific Union fire and oppressive heat. By 1 P.M. Lee withdrew Forrest and his battle line to a new position near the Sample House. Forrest saddled Col. Edmund W. Rucker's brigade and at dusk sent it to envelop the Union left. Union soldiers fought off the movement under heavy fire, however. Those troops included the black soldiers of Col. Edward Bouton.

On July 15, Brig. Gen. Abraham Buford moved against Smith's left and attempted to turn it again, but the sweltering heat and lack of water for the battle's participants stalled the efforts on both sides. Brig. Gen. James R. Chalmers drove into the other Union flank and found the Yankees retreating; a rearguard action at Old Town Creek ended without conclusive results. The two-day losses for Smith were 77 killed, 559 wounded, and 38 missing; Confederate casualties were about 1,347 out of 9,500 men engaged. Forrest himself was wounded, hit in the right foot, during the rearguard action at Old Town Creek, and the Yankees retained the field. The results of Tupelo were mixed on both sides and strategically fruitless, but both sides put a positive spin on the action. "Allow me to congratulate you on your recent successful movement on Tupelo," Stephen A. Hurlbut wrote Smith on July 23. "The disaster which occurred in that neighborhood under [Samuel D.] Sturgis had no doubt largely inspirited the enemy in North Mississippi. . . . I have had no opportunity of either seeing or writing you since we parted at Vicksburgh, but I assure you I have watched your career with great interest." Despite the ambiguous results, everyone seemed impressed with the character of the western soldiers. "With regard to the general appearance of the Westerners," reflected John Chipman Gray of such fighters, "it is not so different from our own as I had supposed, but certain it is that discipline is most astonishingly lax."

Knowing that he had to both invest Atlanta and occupy Johnston's army, Sherman built up supplies during the period of July 10 to 17. At this time Jefferson Davis, who had never liked Johnston (ever since the argument at the war's outset over Johnston's relative rank as a general), sent his friend Braxton Bragg to Georgia to discern what Johnston intended to do. Davis also wrote Lee in a panic on July 12, asking what he should do about Johnston and wondering about Lt. Gen. John Bell Hood as a replacement. On July 17, Davis replaced Johnston with Hood, who was a hard-nosed fighter (but also minus a leg and without the use of an arm) and would certainly do more than be outflanked all across the state. "Hood has 'gone up like a rocket,' " proclaimed Maj. Gen. William H. T. Walker to his wife. "It is to be hoped . . . that 'he will not come down like the stick.' " Sherman welcomed the change because he knew of Hood's reputation for recklessness.

On July 18, Sherman finished supplying his army; the Yankee forces began to wheel southeastward toward Atlanta. A ring of fortified lines encircled the city about one and a quarter miles in diameter. Hood at first deployed Stewart and Hardee north of the city, Cheatham to its east, and Wheeler's cavalry to the southeast. Sherman initially deployed Thomas's men along Peachtree Creek, facing Stewart and Hardee, with the corps of Palmer, Hooker, and Howard in battle line. East of Thomas were the armies of Schofield (along the south fork of Peachtree Creek) and McPherson (near Decatur). Given a mandate of holding Atlanta and its rail connections, Hood had no choice but to attack. As Thomas's men crossed Peachtree Creek and headed southward, Hood made his move, resulting in the battle of Peachtree Creek on July 20 (Hood's First Sortie). Hood's movement was not well planned or executed; he attacked first with Hardee and then with Stewart, enabling Thomas to control the Hardee attack with Howard's corps before shifting reinforcements to repulse the second assault. Confederate charges lasted for nearly two hours and were fought off stoutly by the boys in blue. Of some 20,000 Yankees engaged, 1,779 were casualties of the action; Confederate losses were 4,796 of 20,000 in action. Skirmishing also erupted at Bald Hill (or Leggett's Hill, an alternative name given it for Mortimer D. Leggett, who led an attack here), near Decatur, at Flint Hill Church, and at Howard House.

Having been bloodied by attacking directly, Hood next sent Hardee's Corps on a fifteen-mile march throughout the night south and east of the city to attack McPherson's south flank; he withdrew the rest of his army into the city's defensive perimeter. On July 21, as Hardee moved against him, McPherson approached Atlanta from the east. Action again flared on Bald Hill, and after heavy volleys of musketry, intense heat, and blinding artillery fire, Yankees under Maj. Gen. Frank Blair, Jr., captured the position despite the heroic defensive work by Maj. Gen. Pat Cleburne. The Union attackers could now see the whole city of Atlanta spread before them.

July 22 brought the battle of Atlanta (Hood's Second Sortie). After their exhausting march, Hardee's men finally struck McPherson's corps between Decatur and Atlanta. Cheatham was ordered to follow up with a second wave. Wheeler's cavalry sped northward around the flank, meanwhile, to strike into Garrard's cavalry. By happenstance, two divisions of Maj. Gen. Grenville M. Dodge's corps had been sent on a reconnaissance during the night and occupied the ground where Hardee intended to strike. Flights of artillery shells and volleys of Minié bullets were exchanged through the hot, dry air.

Casualties in this heavy action were tremendous; of 30,000 Yankees engaged, 430 were killed, 1,559 wounded, and 1,733 missing; Confederate losses were as high as 10,000 of the 40,000 engaged—a price that Hood's army could hardly afford to pay. Hood responded with anger at Hardee after the battle of Atlanta, declaring that the latter was both late in attacking and failed to move his men far enough out before swinging into McPherson. Both armies were considerably stunned after the action and needed to regroup. Among the dead were William H. T. Walker, who had expressed won-

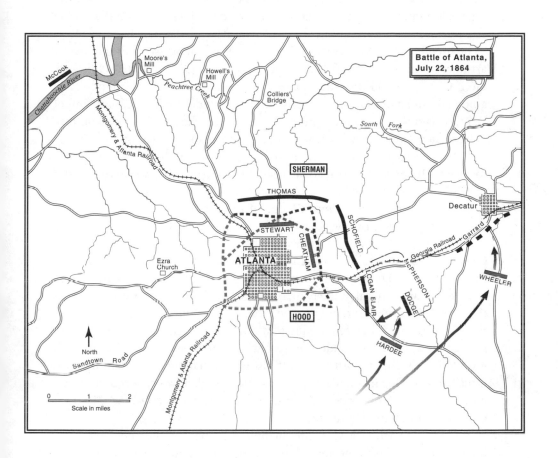

Battle of Atlanta,
July 22, 1864

McCook

Moore's Mill

Howell's Mill

Peachtree Creek

Colliers Bridge

Chattahoochie River

Montgomery & Atlanta Railroad

South Fork

SHERMAN

THOMAS

Decatur

STEWART

CHEATHAM

SCHOFIELD

ATLANTA

Ezra Church

LOGAN BLAIR

McPHERSON

Georgia Railroad

Garrard

WHEELER

DODGE

HOOD

HARDEE

North

Sandtown Road

Montgomery & Atlanta Railroad

0   1   2
Scale in miles

der over his friend Hood's appointment. On the Federal side Maj. Gen. James B. McPherson was killed during the opening minutes of the battle, struck in the back by a ball that punctured his lung before exiting through his chest. McPherson thus became one of the highest-ranking officers to die during the war, and was much lamented by both Grant and Sherman, who regarded him as one of the brightest young officers of the war. "Gen. McPherson was killed yesterday," read the terse announcement from the army's headquarters in Chattanooga. "His body will be in Nashville on the 24 or 25th. Please have an escort to convey it to his home." Back in Ohio: "The friends of late Maj. Gen. McPherson ask me for an escort of infantry & artillery for his funeral at or near Clyde, Sandusky Co.," reported Ohio Adj. Gen. Charles W. Hill. "They expect his remains tomorrow night." Also among the dead or mortally wounded were Confederate Brig. Gens. Samuel Benton, who was struck by a piece of shell in the chest and expired on July 28, and Clement H. Stevens, who was hit in the head and died on July 25.

In the wake of McPherson's death Sherman asked the War Department to assign Oliver O. Howard to succeed McPherson. "I have . . . received a dispatch from Halleck," Sherman instructed Howard on July 26. "You are assigned to command the Army & Dept. of the Tenn. . . . If you will come to my HeadQrs. I will ride with you and explain my wishes." This came as a rude surprise to the still egocentric Hooker. "I have just learned that Maj. Genl. Howard my junior has been assigned to the command of the Army of the Tennessee," Hooker complained to Brig. Gen. William D. Whipple, assistant adjutant general of the Department of the Cumberland, on July 27. "If this is the case I request that I may be relieved from duty with this army. Justice & self-respect alike require my removal from an army in which rank and service are ignored. I should like to have my personal staff relieved with me." Hooker's unpopularity and self-absorption had finally caught up with him: The War Department accepted his offer. Hooker was relieved, replaced with Maj. Gen. Alpheus S. Williams, and his letter was docketed, "Relieve Genl. Hooker at his own request."

On July 27, with the Confederate defenders back in the lines surrounding the city, Sherman determined to lay siege to Atlanta. He dispatched two cavalry raids—one led by McCook and the other by Stoneman—who would converge on Jonesboro, south of the city, cutting the last railroad link into the fortress. Howard moved his newly acquired army out of its position east of Atlanta and swung around counterclockwise toward Ezra Church, west of the city. Hood now sent Lt. Gen. Stephen D. Lee and Stewart forward to attack Howard in Hood's Third Sortie, resulting in the battle of Ezra Church on July 28. The Federal troops took up a good defensive position and repeated Confederate attacks could not dislodge them. "Hood had suffered so severely in the battles at Peachtree Creek," recalled Union Brig. Gen. Jacob

D. Cox, "and on the east of Atlanta, that his troops were losing their stomach for assaulting intrenchments." The battle lasted from early afternoon through darkness, after which the beaten Confederates withdrew into the Atlanta lines. The Yankee losses were about 600 and the Confederates lost a stunning 5,000 casualties. Indeed Hood was proving to be coming down "like the stick."

The cavalry raids continued as McCook blazed from Lovejoy's Station near Jonesboro to Campbellton at the Chattahoochie River and finally south to Newnan by July 30, well southwest of the city, destroying railroad lines and equipment and capturing supplies. At Fayetteville, McCook captured a Rebel wagon train. Near Newnan the raiders fought a skirmish at Brown's Mill, where they fled toward the Chattahoochie in "a zigzag direction through thick woods, miry swamps, and over rough hills." Wheeler struggled to keep up with the raiders and to harass them as best he could. Stoneman proceeded well south to Macon, to Hillsboro, and then to Jug Tavern by August 3. In a skirmish at Macon on July 30, the Federal horsemen approached infantry under Maj. Gen. Howell Cobb and were dispersed after heavy fire from Fort Hawkins and its surrounding ridges. A skirmish at Sunshine Church the following day resulted when Brig. Gen. Alfred Iverson blocked the Yankee advance. Wheeler finally interposed between the two cavalry raiders at Jonesboro, and Stoneman went off on another mission—to liberate the Andersonville prisoners far to the south (he failed and was captured with 700 troopers).

With the noose firmly tightening around Atlanta, Southerners could still deceive themselves about the eventuality of what was happening. "Sherman's army is *doomed*," war clerk John B. Jones confided to his diary on August 2. Sherman, meanwhile, had his hands full with more squabbles. "The question of rank has arisen by accident," Maj. Gen. John M. Palmer wrote on August 4, "and I agree with you that it is better for the interest of all parties that it should be decided, but I cannot recognize the correctness of the decision made. I therefore respectfully ask that a named officer be designated to whom I may turn over the command of the 14th Army Corps." Palmer disputed the assertion that Schofield ranked him: he was the sixty-first-ranking major general of volunteers, while Schofield was number sixty. Palmer asked to be relieved and lost his corps command to Brig. Gen. Richard W. Johnson. Sherman, however, thought little of Johnson. "If you are willing to make General Johnson your chief of cavalry," Thomas suggested to Sherman on August 19, "he might be disposed of in that way. [John H.] King has asked for a leave of absence and I understand [William P.] Carlin will ask to be relieved from duty . . . as soon as [Jefferson C.] Davis is assigned. . . . Johnson ought to make a good officer to superintend the arrangement of cavalry and I have no doubt would be delighted to get the situation."

Indeed, they disposed of Johnson into the cavalry command and placed Jeff C. Davis, the old officer who had shot Bull Nelson in Kentucky and arisen to acclaim by the westerners, into the high status of corps command.

Though the Atlanta campaign devolved into a siege, the battle of Utoy Creek occurred on August 5–6 as Sherman once more tried to envelop Hood's left. Schofield planned to force a crossing of Utoy Creek southwest of the city near Heron's Mill. An advance by Brig. Gen. Absalom Baird commenced two hours late because he did not wish to be ordered by Schofield. Confederate defenses strengthened, but Baird, when he finally left, drove into the skirmish line and captured 140 prisoners. Supporting divisions moved up into position but were not aggressive enough to attack. Hood reinforced the line with Hardee's Corps, and Federal troop movements continued until the morning of August 6. Jacob Cox's brigade pushed forward that morning and reconnoitered the line, stopped finally by heavy crossfire and abatis. Other units pushed forward and drove the Confederates back into the city's inner defenses. But Sherman failed to crack the line at Utoy Creek and so resumed his siege operation, although the Yankee troops held their ground.

Hood now dispatched Wheeler to disrupt Sherman's lines of communications. Wheeler commenced from Covington, Georgia, and his raid lasted until September 9, resulting in skirmishes near Dalton (August 14–15), Lovejoy's Station (September 2–6), and Tuscumbia, Alabama (September 10). On August 18, Kilpatrick left Sandtown on a raid to Lovejoy's Station, operating against Confederate supply lines, and resulting in minor affairs at Jonesboro (August 18), Lovejoy's Station and McDonough (August 20), Latimer and Decatur (August 21), and Decatur and Buckhead (August 22).

On August 26, Sherman determined to take the city, having lobbed numerous shells into it for days, and moved his forces out of their Utoy Creek lines, swinging Schofield rapidly southward to Rough-and-Ready, Thomas between that position and Jonesboro, and Howard directly to Jonesboro. The Federal forces reached the Macon Railroad by August 31, forcing Hood to pull out of his trenches and attempt to block the Federal movement. (Initially, Hood had believed that Sherman was withdrawing, but soon the truth dawned on him.) Hardee sped southward to block Howard's approach but was beaten back in a series of attacks and counterattacks that comprised the battle of Jonesboro. A strong attack by Hardee during midafternoon initially succeeded before crumbling away. Of the 25,000 weary Southern troops on hand, 1,725 were killed or wounded; the 25,000 Yankees lost 170 men. At Rough-and-Ready, Schofield cut the railroad, and soon Hood received the news that the city was going to fall.

Sherman kept up the pressure by ordering Slocum forward to enter the city and others to operate against the railroads. On September 1 the battle of

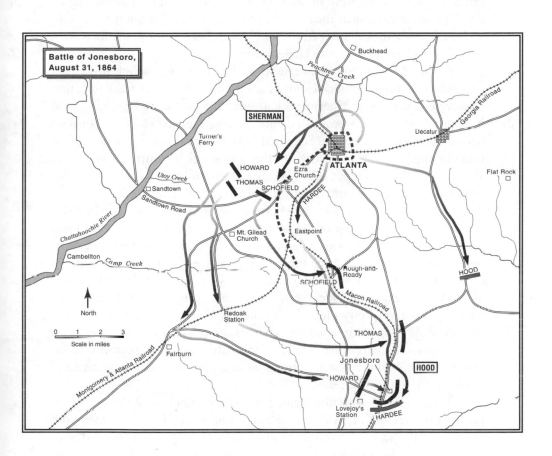

Battle of Jonesboro, August 31, 1864

Buckhead

Peachtree Creek

SHERMAN

Georgia Railroad

Turner's Ferry

Decatur

Flat Rock

HOWARD

Ezra Church

ATLANTA

THOMAS

Utoy Creek

SCHOFIELD

Sandtown

HARDEE

Sandtown Road

Eastpoint

Chattahoochie River

Mt. Gilead Church

Cambellton

Camp Creek

Rough-and-Ready

SCHOFIELD

HOOD

North

Macon Railroad

0   1   2   3
Scale in miles

Redoak Station

THOMAS

Jonesboro

Fairburn

HOWARD

HOOD

Montgomery & Atlanta Railroad

Lovejoy's Station

HARDEE

Jonesboro continued, but Atlanta's fate was sealed. Hood maneuvered Lee's corps back toward the city, but it was stalled at Rough-and-Ready; Hardee was stuck in position at Jonesboro. The battle renewed throughout this day, but the Confederates were battered by heavy musketry volleys and considerable artillery fire, leaving them unable to continue by nightfall. Hardee abandoned his position and joined Hood at Lovejoy's Station, where the remnants of his army were organizing. The following day Hood strengthened his concentration at the station as Sherman sent Slocum into the city and the terrified inhabitants came under Yankee occupation. "Atlanta is ours, & fairly won," Sherman wrote Halleck on that day.

For the moment, Sherman essentially let Hood slip away. He had captured the vital rail junction, destroyed eighty miles' worth of track (creating numerous examples of "Sherman's hairpins," the heated, twisted rails), and had further plans of his own to execute. Fleeing the city, Hood had burned his ammunition train and the Schofield & Markham Rolling Mill to prevent their capture, as well as destroying the "car shed" in central Atlanta, the Western & Atlantic Depot. The resulting fire from Hood's explosion of his ordnance stores raged out of control and burned portions of the city. That didn't stop the celebration in the Union army, however. "I telegraphed you the thrice glorious tidings of the capture of this far-famed city," Maj. Gen. John W. Geary boasted to his wife on September 3, "and now from one of its most stately mansions, I have the honor to address you. . . . The rebels in their haste burned a large number of houses containing stores of various kinds. We also captured 3 locomotives and 7 partly burned, with many cars. The city is a very pretty place, built much in northern taste and stile, and contained about 15,000 inhabitants. There is scarcely a house that does [not] exhibit in some degree the effects of the battle which so fearfully raged around it. Many of the best are utterly ruined, and many of the ornamental trees are cut down by our shells."

As far as the destruction went, Sherman did not care if the destroyed property offered military value for the opposing army. (The most celebrated example of this fact is a famous photograph taken by George Barnard after the city's fall, which shows a bank building in ruins beside a billiard parlor that stands unscathed.) As he routinely stated, the quickest way to end the war was to make it as objectionable as possible to the enemy. So he planned to evacuate the city of Atlanta. "If the people raise a howl against my barbarity & cruelty, I will answer that War is War & not popularity seeking," Sherman wrote Halleck on September 4. "If they want Peace, they & their relations must stop War." Far to the north, Ulysses S. Grant celebrated the fall of Atlanta even as he oversaw the Petersburg trench operation without initial success. "In honor of your great victory I have ordered a salute to be fired with shotted guns from every battery bearing upon the enemy," Grant dispatched his comrade on September 4. "The salute will be fired within an hour amidst great rejoicing."

FOLLOWING HUNTER'S RAID on the Shenandoah Valley, Maj. Gen. Jubal A. Early was dispatched to launch a raid into West Virginia and Maryland, and to consider threatening the Washington defenses. The "terror" value of such a raid skirting by Washington would be terrific in the still-volatile election year of the North. Writers have vastly exaggerated the danger of Early's force to Washington itself—recall that Washington was the most heavily fortified city in the world at the time, and an army of 10,000 men such as Early's could hardly "capture" the capital. After Hunter's repulse at Lynchburg on June 18, Early organized his 2d Corps, Army of Northern Virginia (temporarily termed the "Army of the Valley") into the divisions of Maj. Gens. Robert E. Rodes and Stephen Dodson Ramseur, the "corps" of Maj. Gen. John C. Breckinridge (divisions of Maj. Gen. John B. Gordon and Brig. Gen. John Echols), and the cavalry division of Maj. Gen. Robert Ransom.

As Hunter withdrew into West Virginia, Early approached the Shenandoah Valley from Lynchburg on June 23. Passing through Staunton on June 26, Early and his men then reached Winchester on July 2, sending forward men to drive in the Federal outposts at Bolivar Heights, near Harpers Ferry. Maj. Gen. Franz Sigel, at Martinsburg, was now warned of Early's approach. Brig. Gen. John D. Imboden's brigade of cavalry rode quickly to cut the Baltimore & Ohio Railroad, and skirmishing erupted all over on July 3—at Martinsburg, Leetown, Darkesville, and Buckton. Sigel found himself pushed back onto Maryland Heights, concentrating the available troops, as Early brought Confederate infantry once again marching past Harpers Ferry, on July 4. Early readied his men to cross the Potomac River, which they did at Shepherdstown, then marching to Hagerstown by July 6; skirmishing took place at Antietam, Maryland, near the site of the old Antietam Creek battlefield. At Hagerstown, Brig. Gen. John McCausland levied the city and its occupants $20,000 in retaliation for Hunter's destruction in the Valley. Two days later Early marched into Frederick and levied that city $200,000. Union troops were shifted into Baltimore and gathered at the Washington forts to defend against Early if he moved closer to the capital. Near Frederick, Maj. Gen. Lew Wallace, commanding the Federal 8th Corps (of the Middle Department), assembled forces to attack the Confederates.

Wallace's 6,000 men blocked Early's advance toward Washington from Frederick. On July 9, Early's 10,000 men moved toward the Yankees and struck into them at the battle of Monocacy, along the Monocacy River and a rail junction south of the town. Early found one brigade each of cavalry and infantry along the river plus the division of Brig. Gen. James B. Ricketts, dispatched from the Army of the Potomac. McCausland attacked with cavalry

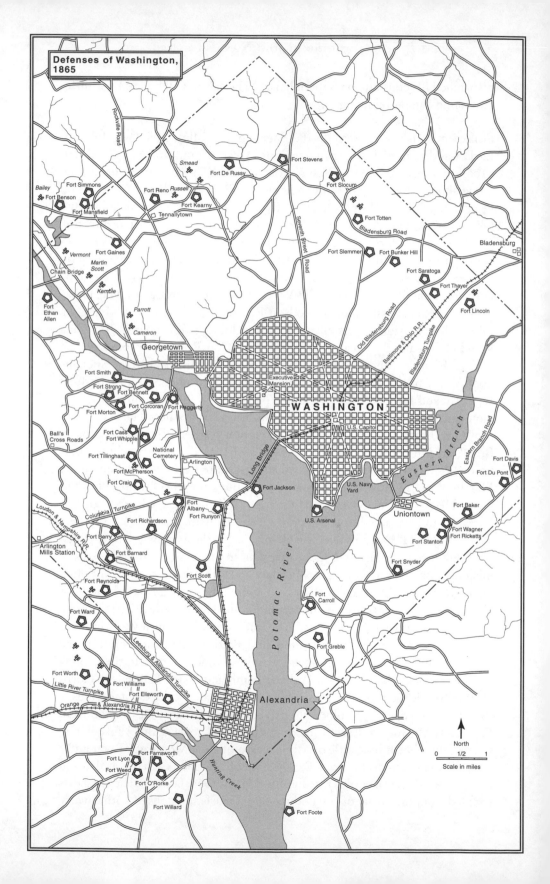

Defenses of Washington, 1865

Rockville Road

Smead
Fort Stevens
Fort De Russy
Bailey
Fort Simmons
Fort Benson
Russell
Fort Reno
Fort Mansfield
Fort Kearny
Tennallytown
Fort Slocum
Seventh Street Road
Fort Totten
Bladensburg Road
Vermont
Fort Gaines
Martin Scott
Chain Bridge
Fort Slemmer
Fort Bunker Hill
Bladensburg
Kemble
Fort Saratoga
Fort Ethan Allen
Parrott
Old Bladensburg Road
Fort Thayer
Cameron
Baltimore & Ohio R.R.
Bladensburg Turnpike
Fort Lincoln

Georgetown

Executive Mansion
WASHINGTON

Fort Smith
Fort Strong
Fort Bennett
Fort Corcoran
Fort Haggerty
Fort Morton
U.S. Capitol
Eastern Branch
Ball's Cross Roads
Fort Cass
Fort Whipple
Fort Tillinghast
National Cemetery
Eastern Branch Road
Fort McPherson
Arlington
Fort Craig
Fort Jackson
U.S. Navy Yard
Fort Davis
Fort Du Pont
Loudon & Hampshire R.R.
Columbia Turnpike
Fort Albany
Fort Runyon
Uniontown
Fort Baker
Fort Richardson
U.S. Arsenal
Arlington Mills Station
Fort Berry
Fort Wagner
Fort Ricketts
Fort Barnard
Fort Stanton
Fort Scott
Fort Snyder
Fort Reynolds
Fort Carroll
Fort Ward
Potomac River
Leesburg & Alexandria Turnpike
Fort Greble
Fort Worth
Little River Turnpike
Fort Williams
Fort Ellsworth
Orange & Alexandria R.R.

Alexandria

Fort Lyon
Fort Farnsworth
Fort Weed
Fort O'Rorke
Hunting Creek
Fort Willard
Fort Foote

North
0   1/2   1
Scale in miles

across the river and into the Federal infantry before Early initiated an over-all tactical plan, so Early was forced to send Gordon after McCausland in support. Despite the false start, Gordon's men fought valiantly, uphill, through fields with improvised fence-rail obstructions, and succeeded in pushing back the Yankees nonetheless. Grain stacks dotted the fields. Hard fighting erupted across the landscape. "Don't fire until you see the C.S.A. on their waist belts and then give it to 'em," declared Union Col. William Henry to his Vermont soldiers. As Union men rushed a fence line between the Union and Confederate positions, some of Gordon's men dashed for the position without orders, beating back the Yankees. Ramseur's division attacked at the railroad bridge as Rodes brought his men around from the north to press the attack. Of 6,050 men engaged, the Yankees lost 1,880 men; Confederate losses were 700 of the 14,000 men present at the battle. Although Wallace had been beaten and retreated to Baltimore, he slowed Early's attack so that more defensive measures could be taken to strengthen the Washington perimeter.

Early moved more slowly toward Washington over the next day. On July 11 his Confederates entered the city's suburbs, causing alarm in the populace that was spread and exaggerated by the local newspapers. At Silver Spring, Maryland, Early's men burned the Francis P. Blair family home. Skirmishing erupted at Fort Stevens, D.C., north of the city, resulting in the Federal government's calling for militia and even arming office personnel to bolster defensive measures against a force of unknown size. More than 20,000 men were now placed into the area, and Early's threat to Washington would soon come to an end. But not before a spirited engagement at Fort Stevens, which the president himself witnessed. On this first day of the Fort Stevens attack, Lincoln and his wife Mary traveled from the city to the fort and were briefly under fire. Skirmishing at the fort resumed the next day and again Lincoln rode out to see the action. Soldiers undoubtedly cautioned Lincoln to remove himself from the scene, although the fighting was sporadic and not very heavy, and a curious Lincoln eventually left. Here the legend arose that future Supreme Court Justice (and then Capt.) Oliver Wendell Holmes, Jr., shouted at Lincoln, "Get down, you damn fool, before you get shot!" But this was probably apocryphal, as Holmes did not make his claim until some sixty years later. Other accounts attribute similar remarks to a whole host of spectators or participants.

Determining that he lacked the strength to press on, Early retreated after the second day of skirmishing at Fort Stevens. This gave rise to the often-quoted statement of Capt. Elisha Hunt Rhodes, who said that "Early should have attacked early in the morning. Early was late." As for the rush of Rebels to the city, Halleck at last found a humorous reaction to a dangerous event, writing, "We have five times as many generals here as we want, but are greatly in need of privates. Anyone volunteering in that capacity will be thankfully received."

Early's men moved toward the Potomac, passing through Tenallytown, Maryland, on July 13 and crossing the river at Leesburg the following day. Maj. Gen. Horatio G. Wright, with portions of the 6th, 8th, and 19th corps, only sluggishly pursued to Poolesville and then watched the Confederates cross. "If the enemy has left Maryland, as I suppose he has," Grant wrote Halleck, "he should have upon his heels, veterans, Militiamen, men on horseback and everything that can be got to follow, to eat out Virginia clear and clean as far as they go, so that Crows flying over it for the balance of the season will have to carry their provender with them." Early moved toward Strasburg as Wright was joined by Brig. Gen. George Crook to continue a pursuit. Brig. Gen. William W. Averell threatened Early's supply trains by way of Martinsburg. On July 20 the armies converged and fought a sharp action at Stephenson's Depot, a little red-brick building north of Winchester. Union infantry and Averell's horse soldiers fired hotly into the soldiers of Ramseur's division, routing them and capturing 250 prisoners, accelerating Early's main force southward toward Strasburg. Some 73 lay dead on the field and 130 wounded were left behind. Four days later another battle at Winchester erupted in which Early's men encountered Crook along the Valley Turnpike. Cavalry skirmishes on the 23d preceded the main action the following day. Breckinridge supervised the main attack, which was accomplished by Echols's men. Crook's horsemen fled toward Bunker Hill and were joined by the scattered infantry by 9 P.M., the Yankee commander crossing the Potomac into Williamsport and rallying his men there. Yankees lost about 1,200 casualties and the Confederate loss was slight.

Early next captured the rail junction at Martinsburg, destroying much of the property, and sent the cavalry of McCausland and Col. Bradley T. Johnson to Chambersburg, Pennsylvania, to burn the town in reprisal for Hunter's Shenandoah Valley raid. The Confederate raiders accomplished this on July 30. McCausland and Johnson levied $100,000 in gold or $500,000 in currency against the citizens, who could not pay that amount, of course, and at 9 A.M. McCausland ordered the town's 3,000 citizens evacuated as he torched its structures. Oddly, Col. William E. Peters (21st Virginia Cavalry) refused the order and was arrested. Before the fires smoldered out, more than two-thirds of the town was destroyed. "Just a week this morning the rebels turned up in our devoted town again," lamented Rachel Bowman Cormany. "They demanded 500,000 dollers in default of which the town would be burned. . . . when they were informed of the impossibility they deliberately went from house to house to house & fired it. The whole heart of the town is burned. they gave us no time for people to get anything out."

On his return from Chambersburg, McCausland engaged the Yankees at Cumberland, Maryland, on August 1. He now found Yankee cavalry closing in and sped back to safety. At Moorefield, West Virginia, on August 7, McCausland and Johnson established camp only to receive a surprise attack from Averell that completely routed them. The Yankees captured 420 troopers, 4 field guns, and 400 horses. Among the prisoners was Johnson, who later escaped. Early's Washington raid came to an end as Phil Sheridan was placed in command of the Middle Military Division. Skirmishing between these forces continued through August, most notably at Front Royal (Guard Hill or Cedarville) on August 16 and Martinsburg again on August 31.

AT PETERSBURG the siege continued. Frustrations in nearby Richmond loomed large, as political divisions separated the officials (Davis and Stephens were not even speaking), supplies became ever harder to come by, and morale was disintegrating. Not only did Confederate soldiers marvel that Union boys would continue to fight so stubbornly, but bothersome concerns about the Confederate state of the war spawned a great religious revival in the armies at the same time that it accentuated doubts about the righteousness of their cause. How could God be for the Confederacy if it were to lose? There were also monetary worries in Richmond. "The treasury has been offered to and declined by Mr. [James A.] Seddon, Judge [T. Butler] King, Mr. [R. R.] Cuyler, Mr. [George A.] Trenholm, and indirectly Judge [John A.] Campbell," wrote Robert G. H. Kean, chief of the Bureau of War. "Trenholm, who was the last, replied that the legislation of Congress had been so irreconcilably opposite to the ideas he has on the subject that he could not think of it; yet he was telegraphed to come on to Richmond. There remains not over $60,000,000 of the new issue to put out. It will last, say six weeks. At the end of that time there will be no resource." In the ranks, even if the money and supplies arrived, the numbers of Yankees besieging the sons of the South seemed overwhelming. "Once, under McClellan," recalled John Esten Cooke, former staff officer of Jeb Stuart, "they seemed only bent on fighting big battles, and making a treaty of peace. Now they seem determined to drive us to the last ditch, and *into* it, the mother earth to be shovelled over us. Virginia is no longer a battlefield, but a living, shuddering body, upon which is to be inflicted the *immedicable vulnus* of all-destroying war." The food and clothing provided were week by week worse in quality and smaller in quantity. "It is hard to maintain one's patriotism on ashcake and water," moaned Confederate soldier Charles Minor Blackford. Southerners on the home front could still afford an illusion of invincibility. "Grant is not even spoken of in the papers with his grand 'On to Richmond,[']" confided pro-Confederate Floride Clemson in Beltsville, Maryland. "I suppose he is stuck in a swamp down there."

All along the Petersburg front inaction was the norm as trench warfare dragged on day by day (which would be practiced on a larger scale during World War I). "We are still before Petersburg," Brig. Gen. Adelbert Ames wrote. "We keep the rebel communications south cut, and I hope by this plan we may succeed in starving him out." Not only were the Southern defensive lines too strong to attack, but both armies were absolutely exhausted from the nearly continuous marching and fighting that began in May. So the troops lived in their trenches, waited, rested, sniped, lobbed shells into the enemy works, and thought of home. "Our bomb proofs consisted of an excavation about six feet square by six deep, covered with earth, under which were logs, and a little back cellar way was left on the side away from the enemy," recalled Pvt. Robert Goldthwaite Carter of the 22d Massachusetts Infantry. "Our shelter tents we pitched on top the bomb proof." "We are making heavy works and have miles of covered way in which we can walk and even ride in comparative security," recorded Col. Robert McAllister in a letter to his wife Ellen. "In fact, we are fixing it so we can live under the iron hail of the enemy's guns. We are preparing to send them over a storm of the same material."

As the armies developed their trench activities, many incidents occurred. Brig. Gen. Marsena R. Patrick, provost marshal general of the Army of the Potomac, described the execution of two condemned soldiers named Gordon and Geary: "They mounted the Scaffold & there I read the Order of the Court & Sentence—The Clergy talked with them a few moments & at their request, Rammell Said for them, that they died hoping for mercy thro' Jesus Christ & acknowledging the justice of the Sentence about to be executed— Rammell made a short prayer & both Clergymen took leave of the condemned & left the Scaffold— The feet were tied, the eyes bandaged, the ropes adjusted, the tap upon the drum & the drop fell! They hung, perhaps 5 minutes, when I remounted the Scaffold & said with words of warning, of reproof & of correction as seemed proper in the presence of Such a Mass of life as stood before & around me, with the dead hanging beneath my feet."

While this matrix of oddities was occurring, Lt. Col. Henry Pleasants of the 48th Pennsylvania Infantry, a regiment consisting largely of coal miners, proposed a daring plan to his superiors, and Burnside approved it. Pleasants and his men would tunnel beneath the Confederate works opposite the 9th Corps, constructing an adit stretching 511 feet, pack it with four tons of black powder, and detonate it—the resulting explosion would cause such chaos that Yankee soldiers could pour through the breach and toward Petersburg, ending the siege. The coal miners began their enterprise and Burnside chose Brig. Gen. Edward Ferrero's division of black troops to lead the assault, as they were fresh. Ferrero's men were to break through the gap and immediately wheel right and left to allow the remainder of the 9th Corps to charge in support of the attack. The spearheading column would move along the

Jerusalem Plank Road into the town. Grant and Meade halfheartedly approved of the idea and the attack was scheduled for July 30. (Confederate soldiers, meanwhile, had heard strange noises, suspected the mining work, and commenced a countermine of their own.)

Grant sent Hancock's division along with Sheridan's cavalry toward Richmond on July 26, drawing strength away from the Confederate line at the Petersburg mine. From July 27 to 29 a series of skirmishes occurred during this movement at Deep Bottom (north of Bermuda Hundred). Action also flared at Malvern Hill. On July 29, Grant recalled the diversionary expedition, massed heavy artillery batteries to support the mine explosion attack, swung Sheridan's cavalry counterclockwise south of the city to support the attack from the west (he reached Poplar Springs Church by the early morning of July 30), and ordered the other corps to prepare to help with the assault once Burnside's 9th Corps commenced it.

Before the attack, however, confusion reigned in the Federal high command. Meade altered the plan, asking for a division of white troops to lead the assault. He chose that of Brig. Gen. James H. Ledlie. Both commanders chosen to lead the assault were problematic: Ledlie served unmemorably up to this point and Ferrero was dissatisfied with the army, having only a month prior resigned, complaining of his health (the resignation was not accepted), and then had his nomination as brigadier general fail before the Senate. Both Ferrero and Ledlie drank alcoholic beverages freely. Yet both would be asked to oversee the critical attack.

At 4:40 A.M. on July 30, Union soldiers set off the blast and the chaotic battle of the Crater resulted. Huge clouds of dirt, equipment, men, everything in the area violently thrust into the air and the detonation was like nothing ever heard before by any of the men on either side. "I finally fell into a sound sleep and was awakened in the morning by the explosion of the mine under the fort," wrote Henry Matrau of the 6th Wisconsin Infantry, "which just made the earth tremble and started every man to his feet instanter. This was the signal at which the whole artillery and mortar batteries opened." Some 170 feet of the Confederate trenches had been instantly disintegrated, and 500 yards of the Confederate works were deserted as the surviving defenders fled the area. The crater at the site of the explosion measured 170 feet long, 60 to 80 feet wide, and 30 feet deep (its remnants, though eroded, are still visible today). Ledlie's men vainly struggled to get over the parapets— no one had thought about the logistics of fighting through a bomb crater. Ferrero and Ledlie, in one of the more shameful acts of Union officer irresponsibility, hid in a bombproof, drinking rum. The two were eventually disgraced over the affair. Perhaps 278 Confederate soldiers were killed instantly; their stunned survivors soon rallied and launched a counterattack against the Union forces, who amounted to about 15,000 in the vicinity of the

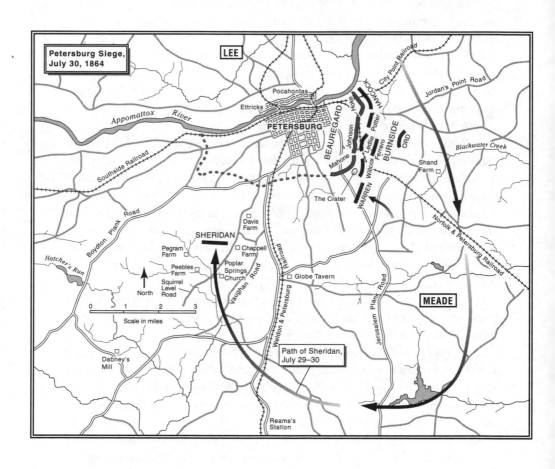

Petersburg Siege,
July 30, 1864

LEE

Appomattox River

Pocahontas

Ettricks

PETERSBURG

BEAUREGARD

Mahone

Johnson

Hoke

HANCOCK

City Point Railroad

Jordan's Point Road

Ledlie

Potter

Ferrero

BURNSIDE

ORD

Blackwater Creek

Shand Farm

Willcox

WARREN

The Crater

Southside Railroad

Norfolk & Petersburg Railroad

Boydton Plank Road

Hatcher's Run

Pegram Farm

Davis Farm

Chappell Farm

SHERIDAN

Peebles Farm

Poplar Springs Church

Squirrel Level Road

Vaughan Road

Globe Tavern

Jerusalem Plank Road

MEADE

North

0   1   2   3
Scale in miles

Weldon & Petersburg Railroad

Path of Sheridan,
July 29–30

Dabney's Mill

Reams's Station

Crater by 8:30 A.M. "The Confederates soon recovered from their confusion and concentrated their batteries upon us," reported Capt. Robert K. Beecham of the 23d USCT. ". . . there was the whole Ninth Corps crowded into a space where there was barely enough room for one division to operate, and there we stood from 5 o'clock in the morning, hour after hour, under a plunging fire from the Confederate guns, until the blistering July sun was high up in the sky."

The Confederate counterassault was effectively organized by Brig. Gen. William Mahone, reoccupying the rim of the Crater. In the rear, Confederates rained down mortar shells on the trapped Federals, and many were shot in the mire of the Crater, tangled with a morass of debris and equipment. Under Mahone's direction, Col. David A. Weisiger's Virginians furiously attacked the Yankees before them, enraged that black troops were present in uniform. By 10 A.M. hundreds of Yankees were stuck in the Crater and Mahone moved his men to batter them relentlessly. Two Coehorn mortars were moved so close to the Crater that they used one and a quarter ounces of powder to lob heavy shells into the pit. It was a scene of rampant slaughter. The fire was so hot through a gap in the Crater's rim that Brig. Gen. Joseph J. Bartlett ordered the wall reinforced; lumps of dirt were thrown into the breach and then soldiers yelled, "Put in the dead men. . . . Cartridges were running low, and we searched the boxes of all the dead and wounded," recorded one soldier.

Meade called off the attack and withdrew everyone he could as quickly as possible, but the disastrous battle of the Crater was a low point of the war for the Union. Some 4,400 casualties resulted during the morning. Grant could only write Halleck from his base at City Point, "It was the saddest affair I have witnessed in this war."

The Petersburg war in August settled back into a regular siege operation. Frustrated by the blockage of Federal gunboats on the James, Maj. Gen. Benjamin F. Butler now commenced another of his harebrained ideas by enlisting his soldiers in the digging of an immense canal at Dutch Gap. On August 10 the work began, the goal being to cut across the neck of land 174 yards wide to enable ships to bypass Confederate batteries at Trent Reach and move upriver to attack Chaffin's and Drewry's bluffs. Capt. Peter S. Michie, an accomplished engineer, was placed in command of the project, which would last for months. Grant, meanwhile, was also transforming the Virginia countryside. He had established a base at City Point on the James, where a railroad spur connected the City Point Landing with the Petersburg front. Preferring the simple, Grant gave the elegant Eppes House on the waterfront, Appomattox Manor, to his quartermaster, Brig. Gen. Rufus Ingalls, and had a simple cabin constructed in the house's yard for himself. Staggering amounts of supplies were brought into City Point by ship and transferred to the battlefront, transforming the quiet waterfront into the world's busiest seaport over the summer and autumn of 1864. On August 9, City Point also became the target of Confederate sabotage when two Confederate agents smuggled a box containing a bomb aboard a transport; the resulting explosions rocked the harbor front, killing 43 and injuring 126. Grant, sitting in front of his cabin, was struck by light debris but was uninjured.

Worried over Early's continued threat in the Valley and believing that Anderson's corps was sent to reinforce him, Grant decided to test the Confederate lines north of the James. He dispatched Hancock with the 2d and 10th corps and Brig. Gen. David M. Gregg's cavalry against these lines on August 13, commencing a week of strong demonstrations against a series of positions north of the James. Actions flared again at Deep Bottom, at Fussell's Mill, along the Charles City Road and New Market Road, at White's Tavern, Bailey's Creek, and Gravel Hill. Among the casualties from these sometimes sharp fights were two high-ranking Confederate officers. Brig. Gen. John R. Chambliss, Jr., was wounded and captured on August 16 near Deep Bottom; he died later the same day. Col. Victor J. B. Girardey, often claimed to be a brigadier general (but who was never confirmed as such), was killed at Fussell's Mill on August 16.

Grant seemed more determined than ever to press attacks and end the war as soon as possible. "They have robbed the cradle and the grave equally to get their present force," he observed of Lee's army on August 16. "Besides what they lose in frequent skirmishes and battles they are now loosing [*sic*] from desertions and other causes at least one regiment per day. With this drain upon them the end is visible if we will but be true to ourselves." He next sent Warren to capture a position along the Weldon Railroad south of Petersburg, near the Globe Tavern. This initiated a two-day action along that front on August 18 and 19. Warren's 5th Corps aimed to destroy the railroad line as far south as they could and to harass and attack any Confederate troops in the area. On August 18, Warren's men moved out and occupied a mile-long stretch of the railroad, taking the ground at Globe Tavern, Yellow House, Blick's Station, and Six Mile House. Although the dense woods made visibility difficult as his men moved, Warren efficiently began to destroy the rail lines but was attacked suddenly by Heth's division on the 18th. The resulting battle was brief before Heth retreated. At 4:30 A.M. the following day, A. P. Hill renewed the attack with a far larger mass of infantry. Mahone struck into Warren's right, separating it from the 9th Corps, now commanded by Maj. Gen. John G. Parke (Burnside had been reassigned after the Crater debacle). Heth attacked Warren's front, but a counterattack drove him away. Warren fell back on August 20 and entrenched, having suffered during the battle of the Weldon Railroad 926 killed and wounded and a staggering 2,810 missing, many of them prisoners. Hill again attacked on August 21 but was beaten back. Among the dead from this day was Confederate Brig. Gen. John C. C. Sanders, one of the war's youngest general officers, who was just 24 when he was shot through both thighs in the attack on the 21st and bled to death within a few minutes.

The Union dead littered portions of the ground along the rail line. "Two rows of men, several deep, extending far into the dense forest, formed a passage through which their comrades were now borne on stretchers," explained Thomas Morris Chester, a black soldier and correspondent for the *Philadelphia Press.* "As each fallen hero was carried along this passage of brave men, even the solemnity of the scene could not restrain the indignation of the soldiers, as they witnessed the Union dead returned to them stripped of their shoes, coats, pants, and, in some instances, of their shirts. Those who were returned in their pants gave unmistakable evidence of having their pockets rifled." Chester continued by describing his fellow black soldiers' role in the campaign: "In General Butler's army there are many regiments of colored troops, who, thus far, have inspired confidence in their officers by the discipline and bearing which they have evinced under the incessant fire of the enemy, along the lines, and the handsome manner in which they have borne themselves whenever opportunity placed them in front of the rebels. . . . The colored troops have cheerfully accepted the conditions of the Confederate Government, that between them no quarter is to be shown. Those here have not the least idea of living after they fall into the hands of the enemy, and the rebels act very much as if they entertained similar sentiments with reference to the blacks. Even deserters fear to come into our lines where colored troops may be stationed. . . . Such has been the effect of Jeff Davis's proclamation for the wholesale massacre of our colored troops, and such it will continue to be until the rebels shall treat all the defenders of the Union as prescribed by the rules of civilized warfare."

Warren, having succeeded in cutting the Weldon Railroad, dug in. The Confederate line still operated to a position south of Globe Tavern, at which point supplies were transferred to wagons and moved west of the Yankee lines, continuing to supply the city and army. To interfere with the new supply line, Grant next sent Hancock to destroy the railroad far to the south, where it crossed Rowanty Creek, three times as far south of Petersburg as Globe Tavern. Hancock brought the divisions of Maj. Gen. John Gibbon and Brig. Gen. Nelson A. Miles and Gregg's cavalry, and by August 24 reached a position three miles south of Reams's Station (itself four miles south of Globe Tavern). Hill struck into Hancock's men on August 25, and Hampton's cavalry flanked the Yankees, sending them into a disordered retreat. Confederates held fast at Reams's Station and maintained a usable rail link to Petersburg, aided by the network of wagons. The Federal casualties were 2,372, many of whom were prisoners; Confederate losses were 720. Skirmishing continued along the Petersburg lines on August 28 (Fort Gilmer, Fort Harrison, Laurel Hill, New Market Heights, and Chaffin's Farm) and August 29 (Poplar Springs Church, Jones's House, Chappell's House, Vaughan Road, Watt's Farm, Pegram's Farm, and Peebles's Farm).

Grant continued with grim determination, laying the groundwork for new plans in Sheridan's future. "If the War is to last another year," he wrote the cavalry commander, "we want the Shenandoah valley to remain a barren waste." The bodies of slain men and boys were already littering Virginia in alarming numbers. The work of memorializing the war dead began early. Encamped near Richmond, William W. Blackford, a former staff officer of Jeb Stuart's, got to work to have the world remember his fallen commander. "While in this camp I had a large cross sixteen feet high made of cedar with the inscription cut on it in neat large letters, *'Here fell Gen. J. E. B. Stuart, May 12th, 1864,'* "he wrote.

UNION ARMIES AND NAVIES had not forgotten about the important seaport city of Mobile, Alabama. With its population of 29,258, Mobile was the largest city in Alabama and its open port aided the Confederacy greatly as a supply base. Rear Adm. David G. Farragut began planning operations against Mobile in January 1864; by August his flotilla of four monitors and fourteen other ships was ready for battle and would attempt an assault on the position in combination with Maj. Gen. Gordon Granger's 13th Corps. Not only would the combined Federal force face the heavy guns of three powerful forts that protected entrance into the harbor—Forts Morgan, Gaines, and Powell—but also a small Confederate squadron commanded by Confederate Adm. Franklin Buchanan. The Federal ships included Farragut's flagship, the screw sloop USS *Hartford;* the ironclad monitors USS *Tecumseh,* USS *Manhattan,* USS *Chickasaw,* and USS *Winnebago;* the ironclad gunboat USS *Galena;* the screw sloops USS *Brooklyn,* USS *Lackawanna,* USS *Monongahela,* USS *Oneida,* USS *Ossipee,* USS *Richmond,* and USS *Seminole;* the sidewheel gunboats USS *Metacomet,* USS *Octorora,* and USS *Port Royal;* and the screw gunboats USS *Itasca* and USS *Kennebec.* Buchanan's ships were his flagship, the ironclad ram CSS *Tennessee;* and the gunboats CSS *Gaines,* CSS *Morgan,* and CSS *Selma.*

Mobile Bay was a formidable area for ships. The city itself stood near the northern end of the nearly rectangular bay, which stretched nearly forty miles long. Fort Tracy stood northeast of the city proper. Closing the Confederate port and capturing the city and the area would mean running by the batteries at Morgan, Gaines, and Powell, located along the southern end of the harbor entrance. The main shipping channel passed between two long islands guarded by Forts Morgan and Gaines; the former stood at the western end of Mobile Point and the latter on the eastern end of Dauphin Island.

Fort Powell stood northwest of Dauphin Island at Grant's Pass and protected the secondary shipping channel. Pile obstructions and minefields helped to cover the water approaches to the city. The forts mounted heavy guns and the ram *Tennessee* was a fearsome opponent within the bay; still, Farragut needed to speed forward with an attack on the position to prevent other ironclads, then under construction near the city, from being completed. The Confederate garrison in the city and spread around its forts was under Maj. Gen. Dabney H. Maury, who commanded the Military District of the Gulf; Brig. Gen. Richard Lucian Page, cousin of Robert E. Lee, commanded the troops at Morgan and Gaines. Granger assembled about 5,500 troops for the expedition and by August 3 landed 1,500 men on the western end of Dauphin Island. The following day his men moved against Fort Gaines.

The battle of Mobile Bay erupted in the waters on August 5 as Farragut attempted to run the guns at the forts. Shortly after 6 A.M. the Yankee ships slid across the bar and into the harbor. The monitors formed a column east of the wooden ships so that they would absorb most of the fire from Fort Morgan, which would need to be encountered at close range to move northward into the bay. The seven smallest ships were lashed to the screw sloops to enable the whole flotilla to pass through quickly. Shortly before 7 A.M. the USS *Tecumseh* opened fire on Fort Morgan, and the fort responded with heavy salvos toward the Yankee warships. Buchanan's ships quickly moved out to engage the enemy, and aboard the *Tecumseh,* Comdr. Tunis A. M. Craven brought his ship toward the CSS *Tennessee.* A huge explosion shuddered through the *Tecumseh* as the ship struck a large torpedo (mine) and sank in seconds. Dozens of the sailors aboard *Tecumseh* struggled in chaos to escape the ship as it quickly filled with water; Craven himself told the pilot, John Collins, "After you, pilot," and then could not escape, drowning along with 90 of his officers and men out of the 114-man crew.

Commanding the USS *Brooklyn,* Capt. James Alden stared in horror at his sister ship's demise and then suddenly ordered his pilot to back away from suspicious looking "buoys" in the water. The whole line of Union ships stalled right in range of the guns of Fort Morgan. It was at that moment that Farragut, lashed to the rigging aboard Hartford so that he could observe the action well, allegedly uttered the celebrated phrase, "Damn the torpedoes— full speed ahead!" The *Hartford* sped ahead of the *Brooklyn,* and sailors aboard the flagship could hear the torpedoes banging against the ship's hull, but none exploded.

Now Buchanan seized the initiative and attempted to ram the *Hartford* with the ironclad *Tennessee.* The *Hartford* passed the slower *Tennessee* but was pounded by her guns and those of the CSS *Selma,* exchanging fire at a mad rate, the gunners already caked with powder. Buchanan also attempted to ram the *Brooklyn* and was assisted by the gunboat CSS *Gaines* until the latter

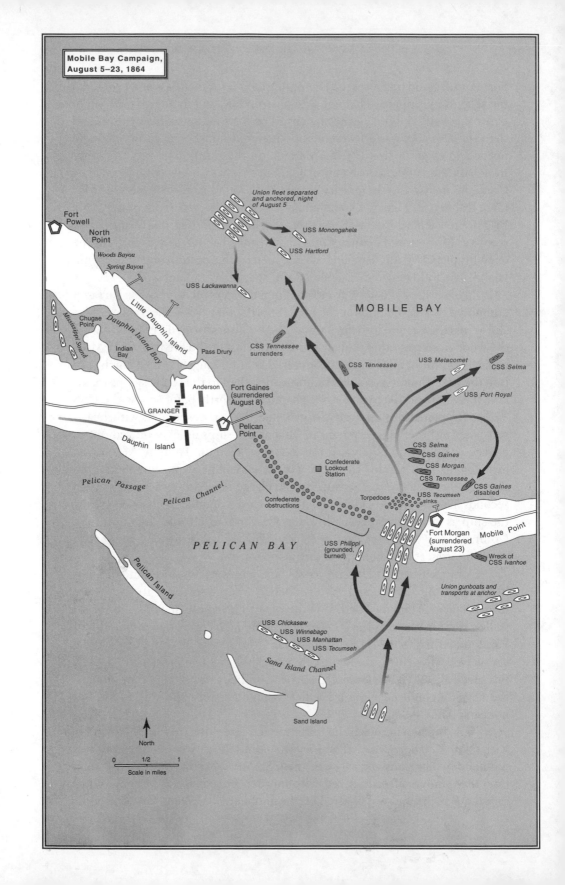

Mobile Bay Campaign,
August 5–23, 1864

Fort
Powell

North
Point

Woods Bayou

Spring Bayou

Chugae
Point

Mississippi Sound

Little Dauphin Island

Dauphin Island Bay

Indian
Bay

Pass Drury

Anderson

Fort Gaines
(surrendered
August 8)

GRANGER

Pelican
Point

Dauphin   Island

Pelican Passage

Pelican Channel

Confederate
obstructions

Confederate
Lookout
Station

Union fleet separated
and anchored, night
of August 5

USS Monongahela

USS Hartford

USS Lackawanna

MOBILE BAY

CSS Tennessee
surrenders

CSS Tennessee

USS Metacomet

CSS Selma

USS Port Royal

CSS Selma
CSS Gaines
CSS Morgan
CSS Tennessee

CSS Gaines
disabled

Torpedoes
USS Tecumseh
sinks

Fort Morgan
(surrendered
August 23)

Mobile Point

Wreck of
CSS Ivanhoe

PELICAN BAY

USS Philippi
(grounded,
burned)

Union gunboats and
transports at anchor

Pelican Island

USS Chickasaw
USS Winnebago
USS Manhattan
USS Tecumseh

Sand Island Channel

Sand Island

North

0   1/2   1

Scale in miles

ship suddenly encountered a steering problem and was forced to run aground near Fort Morgan. A nearby ship not belonging to Farragut's flotilla, the side-wheeler USS *Philippi*, attempted to assist the movement but grounded near Fort Morgan and became a hot target for the Confederate artillerists, who riddled the vessel with heavy shot; she soon was torched by Confederate sailors and ended her career as a smoldering wreck. The CSS *Morgan* was nearly cut off and captured. Buchanan then brought the *Tennessee* out to finish the fight on his own, and for nearly an hour one of the greatest, most savage naval battles in American history raged in the bay.

At close quarters the ironclad ram engaged many of the Union ships: the *Monongahela* and the *Lackawanna* struck into the Confederate ram but damaged themselves more than their opponent. The *Manhattan* soon floated alongside the *Tennessee* and opened with her 15-inch gun. "A moment after a thunderous report shook us all," recalled Confederate Lt. Arthur D. Wharton, "while a blast of dense, sulphurous smoke covered our port-holes, and 440 pounds of iron, impelled by sixty pounds of powder, admitted daylight through our side, where, before it struck us, there had been over two feet of solid wood, covered with five inches of solid iron. . . . I was glad to find myself alive after that shot."

The Federal ships now kissed bows with the *Tennessee* and relentlessly pounded away. The *Hartford* poured broadside shots into the ram; the *Chickasaw* and others contributed a firestorm at point-blank range. Buchanan was badly injured, his right leg fractured, and he assigned command of the beleaguered ship to Comdr. James D. Johnston. A merciless pounding of shot and shell tore into the *Tennessee* and disabled the ship's steering, making it a sitting duck. Finally, by 10 A.M. the ironclad ram hoisted a white flag, overcome by numbers and by the fierce firing of the Union monitors. Buchanan and his crew were captured. After a shaky start Farragut had transformed the naval battle into a complete victory that gave him control of Mobile Bay. "In the success which has attended your operations you have illustrated the efficiency and irresistible power of a naval force led by a bold and vigorous mind, and insufficiency of any batteries to prevent the passage of a fleet thus led and commanded," Gideon Welles congratulated Farragut, hearing of the great victory.

After being attacked by the four guns aboard the *Chickasaw*, the 140 Confederate soldiers at Fort Powell abandoned their work on the night of August 5. Granger, meanwhile, attacked Fort Gaines, assisted by the Union ships. On the morning of August 8 the fort's commander, Charles DeWitt Anderson, surrendered his garrison of 818 men after a halfhearted attempt to defend the position. Some 400 Confederate defenders were left in Fort Morgan, the largest and best equipped of the three forts. Granger moved his infantry toward the position, which was again shelled by the gunboats. "I am prepared to sacrifice life, and will only surrender when I have no means of defense," wrote Page inside the fort. Granger received a siege train from New Orleans on August 17. Five days later the Federal artillerists and the ships from the gunboats opened a blistering fire upon the fort, and Granger's infantry dug in within a short distance of the fort's walls. At 6 A.M. on August 23, Page finally raised a white flag, after a severe, punishing bombardment that battered the fort's walls and left its casements crumbling. "We landed at Fort Morgan and went over the place," recorded journalist FitzGerald Ross. "I confess I did not like it at all. It is built in the old style. . . . when bricks fly about violently by tons' weight at a time, which is the case when they come in contact with 15-inch shells, they make themselves very unpleasant to those who have trusted them for protection." Farragut was angered at the destruction he found in the fort. "General Page and his officers, with childish spitefulness," he wrote, "destroyed the guns which they said they would defend, but which they never defended at all. . . . If you send General Page to me now, I shall put him in irons in the coal bunker." The fort's fall left the Federal army and navy in full control of Mobile Bay and gave them a valuable victory in the Deep South.

THE SUMMER OF 1864 was a dangerous time for the Lincoln administration, especially prior to the victories at Atlanta and Mobile Bay. The peace movement was gaining steam, and the seemingly still popular George McClellan was running against Lincoln. The most remarkable thing about the election of 1864, according to one prominent historian, "is that it occurred." Deciding such an issue in the midst of civil war was unprecedented. Lincoln's many critics could use every angle to attack him and promote alternatives to a bloody, heart-rending war. No president since Andrew Jackson had won reelection with a war going on. Lincoln had sound reasons to create a memorandum on August 23 that reads: "This morning, as for some days past, it seems exceedingly probable that this Administration will not be re-elected. Then it will be my duty to so co-operate with the President elect, as to save the Union between the election and the inauguration; as he will have secured his election on such ground that he cannot possibly save it afterwards." Lincoln folded the document and asked his cabinet members to sign it without knowing its content. This occurred six days before the Democrats met in Chicago to nominate McClellan, who took as his running mate George H. Pendleton. In Cleveland, "radical Democrats" met and nominated another ex-Lincoln general officer, John C. Frémont, who had been the first Republican nominee for president in 1856. Lincoln dropped Hannibal Hamlin and ran with Tennessee's Andrew Johnson as his vice presidential candidate on the National Union ticket. The reelection of Lincoln seemed tenuous indeed until it became clear that the Republican strategy of publicizing

Democrats as treasonous Copperheads and downplaying the race and Reconstruction issues was popular and until Sherman's capture of Atlanta bolstered confidence that the North would someday win the war.

But the suffering and dying continued. In Oskaloosa, Iowa, Union Brig. Gen. Samuel A. Rice died on July 8 after lingering with an infection in his right ankle, where he had been shot at the battle of Jenkins's Ferry. In Key West on August 15, Union Brig. Gen. Daniel P. Woodbury succumbed to yellow fever. Other officers suffered much and looked for escape. "The condition of my health disables me, for the time being, from the performance of field duty," reads a note from Brig. Gen. August Willich on August 11, which is written in another hand and signed with a shaky, almost unreadable signature. Willich was suffering with paralysis of his right arm after being shot at the battle of Resaca. Also suffering much was Brig. Gen. Mortimer D. Leggett, who had fought so hard during the Atlanta campaign. During his service at Vicksburg, Leggett had been struck by wooden splinters and suffered a painful hernia. The condition affected him for the rest of his life. "I hardly know what to do," he wrote. "I am almost helpless. My disease is getting worse instead of better. The least exercise in riding or walking brings on excessive discharges of blood that prostrate me rapidly. It is the first time in my life that I have felt that I was in the hand of disease. I am really 'powerful weak.' It seems as though I would rather die than to give up my command at this time—this crisis of our campaign—but I feel it a duty to acquaint you with my condition."

"My affairs imperatively require my resignation," said Brig. Gen. John B. Turchin, the "Russian Thunderbolt." The architect of pillaging expeditions in Alabama, which were considered militarily "normal" by his standards, Turchin had narrowly escaped court-martial. Suffering from a sunstroke that gave him violent headaches whenever he saw bright lights, Turchin had had enough. "If in time every one of us will have to fight I will not remain behind. At present I must resign." He was mustered out by October. Still suffering from his Petersburg wound but wanting to remain "in" was Joshua Chamberlain, who dutifully wrote the adjutant general, "I have the honor to report that I am under treatment in this hospital, to which I was sent from the field on the 20th of June 1864, having been severely wounded in battle before Petersburg, June 18th." Others were not actually wounded, but temporarily out of service nonetheless. "Gen[.] [Thomas F.] Meagher got up this morning & drank about a quart of whiskey & went to bed again & has been there all day drunk[,]" wrote Col. Thomas B. Gates, at City Point, on August 16. "Mrs. Paine bro't me home from Paducah, Ky. and my health is improved," stated Brig. Gen. Eleazar A. Paine, also wanting to resign. "I hope my resignation will be accepted as my body is mostly worn out, although my desire to subdue the enemies of my country is as strong as the day I enlisted."

Paine suffered from chronic irritability of the bowels, and also faced charges of appropriating goods falsely. "The conduct of Genl. E. A. Paine and command in the western part of this state is intolerable," wrote Bvt. Maj. Gen. Stephen G. Burbridge from Missouri. "I respectfully request you allow me to relieve him, to report at any point you may direct." Paine resigned ingloriously by the spring of 1865.

Bitter controversies, charges, and countercharges continued throughout this complex year of war. "I have been informed that a few days since," recorded Col. Robert H. G. Minty, "in the presence of Captain McLaughlin, 4th U.S. Cav., and Captain [Charles C.] McCormick, 7th Pa. Cav. AAG on General Elliott's staff, and many other officers, Brig. Genl. E. M. McCook Comdg. 1st Div. Cav. Dept. of the Cumberland made use of the following language: 'The 2 Div. is composed of a set of damned cowards and thieves, they never have fought, and never will fight, and I will tell General Garrard so the first time I meet him.' " The document was endorsed by Kenner Garrard and Edward M. McCook, who alleged that no such event took place. McCook wrote: "No such language as that indicated in this communication was ever made use of by me." Brig. Gen. James G. Spears was not so fortunate. He was brought up on charges of "using disloyal language" by talking to several different officers with disrespect to the administration's policies against slavery. Spears allegedly said that "[the administration] just intended to abolish slavery," that "he would show them they could not interfere with a sovereign people," and that if the Administration pursued emancipation to the full extent, "God damn the government; let her go to hell, and I'll be found in the ranks fighting against her." Spears was found guilty on this and similar charges and dismissed from the army.

Many commands were shifted as districts and subdistricts were created and shuffled by the U.S. military all over the map. "In compliance with Special Orders No. 233, current series, 'Department of the Missouri,' I hereby relinquish the command of this District to Brigadier General John McNeil, U.S. Vols.," wrote militia Brig. Gen. Odon Guitar on August 28. "In quitting the District, it is a source of the highest pleasure to know that it enjoys a condition of peace and repose unknown since the inception of the rebellion. I trust it may continue under the administration of my successor, and that the day is not far distant when the 'Constitution,' rebaptized in the best blood of the nation, shall resume its peaceful sway over the whole land." The Lincoln administration worried over the activities of the anti-Republican Copperheads in Illinois and established a careful watch over their activities. "You have been detailed . . . to command the District of Illinois," read a letter received by Brig. Gen. Halbert E. Paine, cousin of the recently disgraced Eleazer Paine and a war casualty who had lost his left leg after Port Hudson. "Recent disclosures have shown a secret organization whose object is no less than the overthrow of the government. You will keep yourself advised of their movements and take such measures as you may deem necessary and proper to thwart their intentions."

Mostly, however, the common soldiers suffered through battles and disease and inadequate food and clothing, all the while waiting for the war to end. "It was impossible for a well man to keep rid of vermin," wrote Pvt. William H. H. Clayton, to his brother, "and a sick man after he became unable to help himself would actually become alive with lice. I have seen them so thick on a dead body that you could not touch it with your finger without touching one." The sick were piling up in hospitals all across America, as with the 2d Division hospital at City Point. Here nurse Cornelia Hancock recorded that "we have had as high as ten thousand here at one time. Gettysburg was a skirmish comparatively speaking. The cannonading was most severe last night and it seems sickening when you know what a scene it must bring to us. . . . I assure you if it was not for the sea breeze from the James River we should die here; the dust is shoe top deep, the sun just pours down, the smell is almost intolerable, and we have had no rain for nearly three weeks."

Still, those who suffered most were the prisoners. "There is no such thing as delicacy here," recorded John L. Ransom in his Andersonville diary. "Nine out of ten would as soon eat with a corpse for a table as any other way. In the middle of last night I was awakened by being kicked by a dying man. He was soon dead. In his struggles he had floundered clear into our bed. Got up and moved the body off a few feet, and again went to sleep to dream of the hideous sights." One week later he scribbled simply, "Ain't dead yet." At the Confederate prison in Elmira, New York, Berry Benson of the 1st South Carolina Infantry and many others began to tunnel outside as the Yankees had done at Libby, but the word spread too quickly. "We had worked only three nights, when strange men were seen going in and out under the adjoining hospital, and we suspected that another tunnel was being dug . . . [we] decided to abandon one of the three tunnels, continuing the other two. Both should be opened on the same night just as the sentinel on the fence called 11 o'clock. The night agreed upon came (Aug. 28/64). Going early to the scene, I was surprised to see so many men about. There must have been scores lounging around—all talking about the tunnel and the prospect of its early completion. The chance of escape grew wonderfully small to me all at once. A few men might get out without discovery, but not scores!"

Very few Civil War prisoners escaped. Nearly all would have to wait until war's end or, in the case of Northern prisoners held in the South, until liberating armies could reach them. In 1864 the Northern composer George F. Root produced a song with those suffering in prisons in mind, reminding them that blueclad liberators were on the way. Called "Tramp! Tramp!

Tramp!," the song resonated throughout the home front and on the march during the year, despite its syrupy sentimentality. "In the prison cell I sit / Thinking, mother dear, of you / And our bright and happy home so far away / And the tears they fill my eyes / Spite of all that I can do / Tho' I try to cheer my comrades and be gay / Tramp! Tramp! Tramp! the boys are marching / Cheer up comrades they will come / And beneath the starry flag / We shall breathe the air again / Of the freeland in our own beloved home."

CHAPTER 24

Sheridan Raids the Valley

THE FALL OF ATLANTA changed the psychology of the autumn of 1864. No longer was the South putting political pressure on Lincoln in the coming election over what appeared to be two stalled fronts. Southerners now found themselves with one of those fronts collapsed—Lt. Gen. John Bell Hood reeling in retreat and Sherman cutting deeper into Georgia. The destruction of Hood's effort was symbolized majestically by his own torching of the Confederate supply trains and the car shed in Atlanta. "I heard a terrible roar, immediately ahead of me, down the railroad," reported Robert Patrick of the 4th Louisiana Infantry on September 2. "Gen Hood had ordered a train loaded with ammunition to be destroyed to prevent its falling into the hands of the enemy. I could see how to walk for a long distance by the light of the shells and the burning cars. . . . As I approached nearer and nearer the burning train, the sound became perfectly deafening, and the fragments of shells, hurtled through the midnight darkness over my head with an ominous rushing sound. . . . After walking about two miles, the explosion of the shells suddenly ceased, and I knew that the train had been totally destroyed."

Hood spent several days gathering his beaten veterans at Lovejoy's Station, and Sherman, uncharacteristically, let him remain there without attacking. Hood therefore concocted a plan to force Sherman to abandon Atlanta by working against the Union supply lines. The Federal commander now allowed his armies to rest, and many of the key general officers dispersed for various reasons—Schofield returned to Cincinnati, Blair and Logan went on political missions. Sherman was developing a plan to work not against Hood's army but against the military usefulness of the whole Deep South. During the first two weeks of September he chiefly engaged in a letter-writing campaign with Hood and Atlanta officials. "I have deemed it to the interest of the United States that the citizens now residing in Atlanta should remove," Sherman wrote Hood on September 7, "those who prefer it to go South and the rest north." Hood wasn't pleased. "And now, sir, permit me to say that the unprecedented measure you propose transcends, in studied and ingenious cruelty, all acts ever before brought to my attention in the dark history of war," he wrote Sherman two days later. "In the name of God and humanity I protest . . . you are expelling from their homes and firesides the wives and children of a brave people."

The war of words continued. Sherman pointed out that Johnston had himself removed the families from their homes between Dalton and Atlanta for their own safety. "You who in the midst of Peace and prosperity," Sherman continued, "have plunged a nation into War . . . Expelled Union families by the thousands, burned their houses and declared by an act of your Congress the confiscation of all debts due northern men for goods had and received."

And so between September 11 and 20 the families of Atlanta left their city, some 446 families totaling about 1,600 people. "It is a pleasant, breezy afternoon in September," wrote Union Maj. James A. Connolly on the day the civilians began leaving town, "and as I sit here in my tent, on a beautiful grassy hill in the suburbs of the fallen city, and watch our National colors floating gaily from its spires, I feel profoundly thankful that God has permitted me to pass safely through all the stern struggles of this long campaign, and that mine eyes are permitted to see the old flag floating over still another stronghold of the enemy."

Petitioned by Atlanta Mayor James M. Calhoun to revoke the orders for the city's evacuation, Sherman flashed back at Calhoun and the Atlanta city council. "You cannot qualify war in harsher terms than I will," Sherman wrote on September 12. "War is cruelty, and you cannot refine it. . . . You might as well appeal against the thunder storm as against these terrible hardships of war." Though the exact scheme of how Sherman's next maneuver would aid the overall Federal strategy was yet to be developed, Grant was enormously pleased with his chief lieutenant. "You have accomplished the most gigantic undertak[ing] given to any General in this War," he wrote on September 12, "and with a skill and ability that will be acknowledged in history as unsurpassed if not unequaled. It gives me as much pleasure to record this in your favor."

Hood, meanwhile, moved his army westward to Palmetto on September 21. He planned to reequip his army and then move it into Alabama to operate against the Federal supply lines. Jefferson Davis paid Hood and his soldiers a visit on September 27, attempting to devise a new strategy. The groundwork for Hood's Tennessee campaign, or Franklin and Nashville campaign, now developed as Davis and Hood agreed that the Army of Tennessee should move toward Chattanooga to disrupt Sherman's lines of communication. "Sherman is weaker now than he will be in [the] future, and I as strong as I can expect to be," Hood informed Bragg on September 21. Hood was to be supplied from rail lines in Alabama and would improvise depending on what Sherman did next, but apparently neither Davis nor Hood prepared a coherent response in case Sherman should move across Georgia.

On September 16, Hood and Davis launched their campaign of harassment against Sherman's rear by sending Maj. Gen. Nathan Bedford Forrest on a raid into northern Alabama and middle Tennessee with about 4,500 troopers. On September 23–24, Forrest's men captured 600 Union men at Athens, Alabama (north of Decatur), and commenced to raid along the railroad lines, capturing more men, guns, and horses. Sherman countered by sending the division of Brig. Gen. John M. Corse north to Rome and that of Brig. Gen. John Newton back to Chattanooga. By September 29, as Forrest's raid continued, Sherman dispatched Thomas back to Nashville to command all the troops in Tennessee— the Southern strategy of disruption was working splendidly. Back in Atlanta, the bulk of the Northern soldiers sat tight and wondered about their next maneuvers. "Atlanta is situated on high and very undulating ground, and why it was ever selected as a site for a town, has not yet occurred to my imagination," Brig. Gen. John W. Geary wrote his wife. "I suppose it was the result of some accidental start. . . . Northern capitalists came here and built it up with taste. The situation is high and healthful, being 1050 feet above tide water."

Sherman now urged Grant to consider a plan he had concocted of striking out across Georgia to Savannah, destroying what he could of military value and emerging on the seacoast to turn north into the Carolinas. As Grant pondered this, Hood on September 29 crossed the Chattahoochie River, with Forrest still raiding and Wheeler's cavalry rejoining the main body of the army. Hood's 40,000 men moved north toward the railroads and a skirmish flared on October 1 at Salt Springs between the horsemen of both armies. Sherman was somewhat alarmed and confused by Hood's movements, but he did not want to allow them to distract his armies from their main mission. Sherman pursued and Hood, with the initiative, worked his first portion of the campaign cleverly. On October 3, Sherman left Slocum behind and moved out of Atlanta, 55,000 men marching toward Marietta, near the old Kennesaw Mountain battleground. As his advanced units arrived in Marietta, they learned that Hood's army was moving along the railroads toward Allatoona. Sherman immediately alerted Corse, at Rome, to reinforce the garrison at Allatoona, and he succeeded in getting 1,000 troops there by the early morning of October 5.

Hood sent the division of A. P. Stewart along the rail line and the remainder of his army to Dallas, west of Marietta. Stewart destroyed the railroad line from Big Shanty to Acworth and by October 5 moved back to Dallas, sending Maj. Gen. Samuel G. French to attack Corse at Allatoona Pass. The supply depot at Allatoona contained "one million" bread rations for the Federal army in Atlanta and was vital to future Union operations. The garrison consisted of 860 Yankees commanded by Lt. Col. John E. Tourtelotte and was joined by Corse's reinforcements. By 3 A.M. on October 5, French's Confederates drove in the Federal pickets, and by 8:30 A.M. the Southerners had cut the routes of retreat and reinforcement—Allatoona was surrounded. French sent a note demanding surrender to avoid a "needless effusion of blood." "Your communication demanding surrender of my command I acknowledge receipt of," replied Corse, "and respectfully reply that we are prepared for the 'needless effusion of blood' whenever it is agreeable to you."

From the crest of Kennesaw Mountain, thirteen miles to the south, Sherman could see that Corse was surrounded and could also see the glow of Hood's campfires around Dallas. The telegraph lines had been cut and so any communications had to be made by courier or signal flags. At 2 P.M. on October 4 the signal officer on Kennesaw waved flags to send the following message: "Sherman is moving in force. Hold out." At 6:30 P.M. the additional message was sent: "General Sherman says hold fast. We are coming." There was no reply. Additional messages were sent on the morning of the 5th, together giving rise to the hymn and later the expression, "Hold the fort!" Accompanied by Sherman, the signal officer at last caught a glimpse of a signal flag atop Allatoona Pass, signaling "C.R.S.E.H.E.R." The message was translated as "Corse is here."

Heavy fighting ensued along the ridge, with the brigades of Brig. Gens. Claudius W. Sears and William H. Young savagely attacking Illinois and Iowa soldiers holding the crest. Driven back by 11 A.M., the Federals nonetheless delayed the surge of Rebels long enough to secure the main fort on the northwestern rim of Allatoona Pass. Because of heavy casualties, French halted the attack in the early afternoon and regrouped. Yankee losses were 142 killed, 352 wounded, and 212 missing out of about 2,000 engaged; Confederate casualties were 122 killed, 443 wounded, and 234 missing out of some 2,000 in action. Among the badly wounded was Corse, who had been shot in the face about 1 P.M. "Corse has just signaled from Allatoona, had his right cheek and ear shot off, but is able to whip hell out of rebels yet," relayed Lt. Col. Henry W. Perkins the following day. "Enemy made two assaults on works, repelled with heavy loss. . . . No heavy fighting to-day. Genl. Sherman is well pleased."

French marched off to rejoin Hood, who crossed the Coosa River and headed for Resaca. Sherman arrived at Allatoona Pass on October 9, and three days later, as Hood demanded the surrender of a small garrison at Resaca, Sherman arrived at Rome as his army moved on Kingston. The division of Lt. Gen. Stephen D. Lee broke off his plan to attack Resaca and marched northward as Stewart reached Tunnel Hill to destroy the railroad line. Sherman's army arrived at Resaca on October 13, and the major battle that might have erupted between the two forces did not materialize. Hood had drawn Sherman north out of the city but, resting his army at Cross Roads, south of Chattanooga, determined not to offer battle but to move quickly into Tennessee to strike Thomas before Sherman could unite with Thomas's army, creating an overwhelmingly powerful force. Speed was called for because Hood would need to strike out before Sherman either joined Thomas or returned to Atlanta. By October 21, Beauregard approved Hood's plan.

Sherman, believing that Thomas had been sufficiently reinforced to handle Hood, planned his daring march across Georgia. "Until we can re-populate Georgia it is useless to occupy it," he wrote Grant, "but the utter destruction of its roads, houses, and people will cripple their military resources. By attempting to hold the roads we will lose a thousand men monthly and will gain no result. I can make the march and make Georgia howl." On October 20 he wrote Thomas: "I propose to demonstrate the vulnerability of the South, and make its inhabitants feel that war and individual ruin are synonymous terms." The basis for Sherman's March to the Sea was established.

TRENCH WARFARE, occasional bursts of action, and raids continued to characterize the Petersburg front. Actions flared on occasion both north and south of the James River, mostly amounting to skirmishes. Though supplies could still be laboriously brought through to the Confederate army by rail and then by long wagon journeys, the situation was worsening considerably week by week. Much of the food the Confederates did have was poor in quality, and some of Lee's soldiers were nearly starving. During early September, Confederates reported a large concentration of cattle held at a camp at Coggin's Point, six miles south of City Point, opposite Harrison's Landing. Maj. Gen. Wade Hampton determined to make a raid on this cattle pen and capture the beef for the Confederate army. Departing on September 11, Hampton encountered the 13th Pennsylvania Cavalry at Sycamore Church. He fought through that unit and the 1st District of Columbia Cavalry, pushing them back to Coggin's Point. On September 16 horsemen of the 7th Virginia Cavalry dismounted and attacked Union cavalry and were assisted by Hampton's other troops; the Federals responded by breaking down the corral fences and stampeding the cattle with well-timed pistol shots. But Hampton's men rounded up the beef and herded 2,486 cattle back to the Petersburg lines, capturing 300 prisoners in the process while suffering 61 casualties. Hampton's "Beefsteak raid" brought desperately needed high-quality food into the Confederate trenches and remained a legendary feat long after the war.

Although a lull continued on the front, Grant planned and executed a two-pronged drive that commenced on September 28 and lasted more than a week as he sent Maj. Gens. Edward O. C. Ord and David B. Birney driving toward Forts Harrison and Gilmer, Confederate strongholds on the James, and Warren advancing toward Petersburg from his position along the Weldon Railroad. The three-day action of Ord and Birney was termed New Market Heights, Chaffin's Farm, Laurel Hill, and Forts Harrison and Gilmer. Grant's primary goal with this action was to prevent reinforcement of Jubal Early, who was again launching a campaign into the Shenandoah Valley. Ord commanded the 18th Corps (divisions of Brig. Gens. George J. Stannard and Charles A. Heckman); Birney the 10th Corps (divisions of Brig. Gens. Alfred H. Terry, Adelbert Ames, and Charles J. Paine). Ord was assigned to cross the James on a pontoon bridge and assault the works at Chaffin's Bluff while Birney approached over the Deep Bottom Bridge and pressed toward Richmond.

The Yankees found stiff resistance at Chaffin's Farm near Fort Harrison, where Brig. Gen. Hiram Burnham's troops attacked strongly although they were raked with fire over a long, open field. They pushed on, opening repeated volleys of musketry, and Burnham's attack succeeded in capturing Fort Harrison, although the Maine-born general was shot in the abdomen and died within minutes. Heckman sent an enveloping attack from the right while Ord pushed toward Chaffin's Bluff. Ord's attack failed, however, and the corps commander himself received a disabling leg injury. This confusion allowed time for the Confederates to reinforce Fort Gilmer, Heckman's attack on the position being swept away by heavy gunfire from Confederate muskets and artillery batteries.

As Birney pressed to attack the Confederates to the east, Grant sent Terry's division along with the cavalry of Brig. Gen. August V. Kautz to attack on the northern flank; heavy assaults by the divisions of Ames and the black soldiers of Brig. Gen. William Birney's brigade failed miserably under a withering Confederate fire. David Birney's forces withdrew to Laurel Hill and dug in while the Federal troops that captured Fort Harrison prepared for a counterattack. On September 29, Maj. Gen. Richard H. Anderson's Confederate Corps (Longstreet's corps) attacked with heavy force, but the movement was poorly coordinated and failed. Of the assault, Col. James R. Hagood (1st South Carolina Infantry) recalled, "No musketry was used until we got within 200 yards of the fort; but now there issued forth from the frowning parapet a furious storm of bullets such as would appal the stoutest heart." Stannard's men helped to beat back two additional assaults, and the Vermont general lost his right arm near the battle's conclusion. It would be the last major attempt of the Yankees to capture Richmond from north of the James River. During the two-plus days of fighting, the 20,000 Yankees had suffered 383 killed, 2,299 wounded, and 645 missing; Confederate losses were unrecorded but may have totaled 2,000 of 10,000 engaged.

On September 30, meanwhile, Warren set his 5th Corps into motion south of Petersburg to envelop the right flank of Lee's lines, which had been reduced in strength because of the fighting in the Valley and north of the James. Warren's westward movement resulted in the battle of Poplar Springs Church from September 30 through October 2. On the morning of the 30th, Warren brought the divisions of Brig. Gens. Charles Griffin and Romeyn B. Ayres toward the church, west of the Globe Tavern, and was followed by Maj. Gen. John G. Parke's 9th Corps (divisions of Brig. Gens. Orlando B. Willcox and Robert B. Potter). The flanks were protected by the cavalry corps of Brig. Gen. David M. Gregg.

At Peebles's Farm, Griffin's men quickly captured a Confederate redoubt along with 100 Southerners. Moving along the left flank, Potter's division encountered stiff resistance in the afternoon as the divisions of Maj. Gens. Henry Heth and Cadmus M. Wilcox struck back to recapture ground they had lost near Pegram's Farm. Potter commenced an attack of considerable force, expecting to be supported by Griffin, but found himself isolated and had to fight off a Confederate counterattack under chaotic conditions. Griffin eventually did come to Potter's support and the Federals entrenched along Squirrel Level Road, holding Peebles's Farm.

On October 2, Gregg's cavalry came under attack and he, along with Warren, fought off Confederate assaults along the line. Parke advanced on this day and heavy skirmishing erupted, after which the 9th Corps commander developed a new line of entrenchments only a mile east of the Confederate line, connecting the Union works with those at Hatcher's Run to the west and the Globe Tavern to the east, advancing the siege lines about three miles to the west altogether. The Federal casualties from the heaviest day of action, September 30, were 187 killed, 900 wounded, and 1,802 missing; Confederate losses are unknown but may have totaled 900.

North of the James, the next action flared along the Darbytown Road on October 7, an action also called New Market Road, Johnson's Farm, and Four Mile Run. Following the earlier action at New Market Heights, Kautz's Union cavalry held the former Confederate line near Johnson's Farm along the Darbytown Road. Angered by this condition, Lee planned an attack to recapture the position for the 7th. He ordered Brig. Gen. Edward A. Perry's brigade of Floridians, supported by dismounted cavalry commanded by Brig. Gen. Martin W. Gary, to turn Kautz's left, while Maj. Gen. Charles W. Field's division would attack the position frontally. The initial push worked well as stinging volleys of musketry and booming cannon drove the Yankees back, but a second attack faltered as Union guns answered and Maj. Gen. Robert F. Hoke failed to support the movement. Total casualties amounted to 399 Union and 1,350 Confederate, including Confederate Brig. Gen. John Gregg, who was shot dead while leading his Texas brigade along the Charles City Road during the attack. Union forces again tried to penetrate the new Confederate defensive works around Johnson's Farm on October 13 but were driven back with an additional loss of 337 men. For many of the soldiers in the trenches, a war of boredom, poor supplies, and occasional bouts of fighting lay ahead.

Actions did again flare up at the end of October as Grant determined to cut the Southside Railroad. The resulting engagement came to be known as Burgess's Mill, Hatcher's Run, Boydton Plank Road, Stony Creek, Southside Railroad, and Vaughan Road. It unfolded as Hancock was ordered to cross Hatcher's Run with his 2d Corps and move north along the Vaughan Road to the intersection with the Boydton Plank Road. Parke's 9th Corps would attack the Confederate line north of Hatcher's Run. Warren's 5th Corps would support Parke's attack. It was a massive attack that employed 43,000 men against Lee's 28,000 defenders.

The morning of October 27 was a dreary one along the Petersburg front, with dark clouds hanging overhead and rains pouring down. Despite the inclement weather, Hancock succeeded in reaching the Boydton Plank Road by noon, but Parke and Warren found stiff resistance along the Confederate line north of Hatcher's Run, with particularly heavy fighting emerging from Cadmus Wilcox's division. Warren ordered the division of Brig. Gen. Samuel W. Crawford to ford Hatcher's Run, but the muddy creek and heavy brush along the banks of the stream made this impractical. Fighting intensified in the late afternoon as A. P. Hill sent forward his three divisions to strike into Hancock's veterans, and the battle line quaked with firing for several hours until darkness brought a halt to the slaughter. Hill's Confederates alternately gained ground and then fell back; because of the heavy fighting, the Federal objective could not be reached. Hancock and the others withdrew. Actions also flared in front of Forts Morton and Sedgwick, the latter termed "Fort Hell" by the troops for the ferocity of the musketry fire. Of 42,823 Yankees engaged, 166 were killed, 1,028 wounded, and 564 missing; about 20,324 Confederates were engaged and their losses are not known.

ON AUGUST 7, Maj. Gen. Philip H. Sheridan assumed command of the Army of the Shenandoah, consisting of the 6th Corps (at Harpers Ferry), the 19th Corps, and two divisions of Brig. Gen. George Crook's West Virginia infantry. Soon at Harpers Ferry the cavalry was organized into a corps commanded by Brig. Gen. Alfred T. A. Torbert. Organizing all the available forces for a coming autumn campaign against Early and against the military resources of the Shenandoah Valley gave Sheridan a command totaling about 48,000. Maj. Gen. Jubal A. Early, on the other hand, commanded the Valley District and the 2d Corps of the Army of Northern Virginia, which had been detached, and encamped near Bunker Hill, Virginia. Reinforced by troops commanded by Maj. Gen. Richard H. Anderson, Early had a combined strength of 23,000 in August, although the Yankees believed it was much higher.

Sheridan's campaign in the Shenandoah Valley began in earnest during the first days of September. On the first day of that month, with Sheridan apparently not advancing, Early was ordered to return Anderson's force to the main body of the army at Petersburg. Anderson began moving his men and on September 3 struck into Crook's infantry at Berryville. Both sides were completely taken by surprise and entered into a brisk engagement, after which the Confederates withdrew westward across Opequon Creek, and Crook did not pursue. Skirmishing flared again two days later along the Opequon when musketry rattled the landscape near Stephenson's Depot, north of Winchester. Each side sent parties out to probe and reconnoiter but would not commit to a major attack, wary of the other force and its capabilities. By September 14, Anderson departed the scene for Front Royal to rejoin the bulk of the Army of Northern Virginia while Sheridan failed to pursue or to attack Early's force. The cavalry of Maj. Gen. Fitzhugh Lee remained in position to support Early, bringing the Southern force to 12,000 infantry and 6,500 cavalry. Sheridan had not attacked while Anderson's men hovered nearby because he was ordered specifically not to; the apparent sluggishness of the Yankees as viewed by Early swelled the latter's confidence, and the Southern commander sent two divisions north to Bunker Hill, less fearful of the Northern threat.

By September 18, Early moved part of his force north to Martinsburg, driving away the Yankee cavalry, but by nightfall pulled back to Bunker Hill. Sheridan planned to attack Early by feinting toward Charlestown while moving the bulk of his army from Berryville toward Winchester, and Grant approved this plan. The result was the third battle of Winchester (the seventh engagement that had occurred inside the beleaguered town), which took place on September 19. Sheridan's army now consisted of the army corps commanded by Maj. Gen. Horatio G. Wright (6th Corps; divisions of Brig. Gens. David A. Russell, George W. Getty, and James B. Ricketts); Brig. Gen. William H. Emory (19th Corps; divisions of Brig. Gens. William Dwight and Cuvier Grover); attached troops of the Army of West Virginia, commanded by Crook (divisions of Cols. Joseph Thoburn and Isaac H. Duval); and the cavalry corps commanded by Torbert (divisions of Brigs. Gen. Wesley Merritt, William W. Averell, and James H. Wilson). Early's force now consisted of the infantry divisions of Maj. Gens. Stephen D. Ram-

seur and John B. Gordon and Brig. Gens. John Pegram and Gabriel C. Wharton, and the cavalry divisions of Maj. Gen. Lunsford L. Lomax and Brig.
Gen. Thomas L. Rosser. Maj. Gen. John C. Breckinridge was in temporary
command of the divisions of Gordon and Wharton.

Sheridan decided to strike because on September 16 he had learned that
Maj. Gen. Joseph B. Kershaw's division was detached from Early's force, offering the opportunity to strike into a scattered force. Early, moreover, badly
misjudged Sheridan, believing the Federal commander did not attack earlier
with his superior force due to "excessive caution" and "timidity." On September 19, Early's force of 8,500 infantry and 2,900 cavalry was dispersed
north and east of Winchester while Sheridan's 33,600 infantry and 6,400 cavalry approached from Charlestown, forded Opequon Creek, and attacked
from the north and east. Merritt and Averell were ordered to strike southward along the Martinsburg Pike into Early's left flank while Wilson would
strike westward with cavalry along the Berryville Pike, to be followed by the
infantry, enabling Wilson to shift southward to cut off a retreat along the
Valley Turnpike.

In the main morning attack Federal infantry struck hard into Ramseur's
division, and Early engineered a plan to reinforce him. By 10 A.M. Gordon
and Rodes moved their men up to reinforce the position. As Wright's 6th
Corps pressed forward, shooting wildly with volleys of musketry, the corps's
wagon train stood on the road blocking the way for the 19th Corps. Feeling an
opportunity to counterattack because of this lull in the Union support,
Rodes and Gordon sent their men charging ahead at 11 A.M., fighting through
fields and woods and trying to press toward Sheridan's headquarters at the
J. A. Eversole House. During this attack the Georgians in Brig. Gen.
Clement A. Evans's brigade were struck hard by small-arms and artillery fire
and sent reeling in confusion. Rodes, a veteran of the Army of Northern Virginia and close friend of Gordon, was struck in the back of the head and
killed by a shell fragment as he finished a conversation with Gordon.

The counterattack was renewed in force by Brig. Gen. Cullen A.
Battle's brigade, which struck into the divisions of Ricketts and Grover. The
movement was assisted by heavy Confederate gunning by the Virginia battery of Lt. Col. Carter M. Braxton. To help reinforce the gap that was widen-
ing between Ricketts and Grover, Col. J. Warren Keifer shifted his men to fill
the position and Col. Jacob Sharpe repositioned his 156th New York Infantry
to support the action.

At first the Confederate counterdrive excelled, driven by sheets of fire
from Southern muskets. At this time Russell struck into the deepest Confederate penetration, hoping to stem the tide of the Confederate attack. He sent
the brigade of Brig. Gen. Emory Upton forward, and Upton, who had shone
with his attack at Spotsylvania's Mule Shoe, pushed hard into the Confeder-

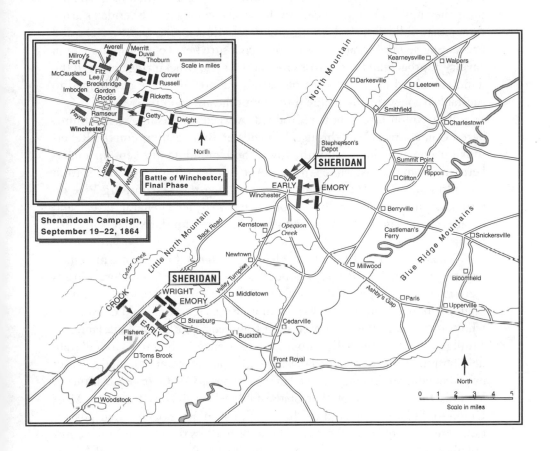

Battle of Winchester, Final Phase

Shenandoah Campaign, September 19–22, 1864

ate units and unraveled the attack. Almost simultaneously, Russell was struck by a ball, leaned forward onto his horse, but resumed riding. Soon afterward, he was struck in the chest with a shell fragment and killed instantly. A friend and favorite of Sheridan, Russell represented a huge loss to the Army of the Shenandoah.

The Confederate counterattack failed but did succeed in buying time for Early and preventing Crook's men from being used for their original purpose: they now had to be placed on the weakened right of Sheridan's army rather than following Wilson on the attack. Enveloping Early's right and preventing a withdrawal now was not such a sure bet. To oppose the Union cavalry approaching from across Opequon Creek, Breckinridge entered the fight. He joined the main force of Early's infantry by 2 P.M. and helped to reestablish a new defensive line throughout the afternoon.

The Union forces, now regrouped, worked on pushing the outnumbered Confederates back through Winchester. By late afternoon the Rebels took up a position just east of the town; the Union infantry kept up a musketry fire from the east while Crook moved down against Breckinridge from the north and the Yankee cavalry pushed along the Martinsburg Pike on Crook's right. Early had no option other than to order a general retreat, and by afternoon's end he began to withdraw his army up the Valley Turnpike toward Strasburg.

The cost of Third Winchester had been high. Of the 37,711 Union men engaged, 697 were killed, 3,983 wounded, and 338 missing; Confederate losses were 276 killed, 1,827 wounded, and 1,818 missing (many of whom were prisoners). Among the dead were Confederate Brig. Gen. Archibald C. Godwin, who was struck in the head by a shell fragment, and Union Col. James A. Mulligan, who was mortally wounded, captured, and died in a Confederate field hospital three days later. He was posthumously commissioned a brevet brigadier general. Among the dead in the town was Col. George S. Patton (2d Virginia Infantry), grandfather of the fabled World War II general. Most Union soldiers remembered the battle with absolute glory in their postaction letters and diaries. "We drove the Rebs not less than ten (10) miles," remembered Louis N. Beaudry, chaplain of the 5th New York Cavalry. "Their demoralization must be very great. They left caissons and ambulances burning behind them with many of their dead falling into our hands. With each victory, we can endure the sad losses we sustain with mournful satisfaction."

Early retreated to a defensive position near Strasburg, and Sheridan pursued, skirmishing with the rear guard near Middletown, Strasburg, and Cedarville on September 20. Early formed a defensive line at Fishers Hill, and skirmishing erupted on the 21st near Fishers Hill, at Strasburg, and at Front Royal, as Sheridan prepared for an attack on September 22. Following the fighting at Front Royal, Lucy Rebecca Buck, age 21, recorded a diary entry on her plantation outside the town. "Well the close of this most miserable day is at last here and we breathe again. . . . There was such an incessant firing that we thought our poor boys must be murdered by the wholesale. . . . Expected the Yankees would have commenced pillaging and burning first thing upon their entrance but on the contrary they have behaved quite decorously."

By now Breckinridge had been detached from Early, further weakening the Confederate force. But Early held a manageable front along Tumbling Run, southwest of Strasburg, and he stretched Lomax to the west, Ramseur to his right, then Pegram, Gordon, and Wharton on the right flank, along Fishers Hill itself and the Valley Turnpike. Sheridan devised a plan that would send Crook westward to Little North Mountain, from which he could strike Lomax and the Confederate left flank. Although the Federal plan occupied nearly the whole day with marching, Crook launched his surprise attack by sunset and scattered Lomax's dismounted troopers. The Yankee infantry next attacked headlong into Pegram and Gordon, and despite the long odds against such an attack, it worked. Sheridan was on the scene shouting, "Forward! Forward everything! . . . Go on, don't stop! Go on!" The Confederate defenders scurried from their trenches and fled southward, again to be pursued by Sheridan. The Federal losses at Fishers Hill were 8 killed, 153 wounded, and 1 missing; Confederate casualties were reported as 1,235, including 1,000 prisoners, and in the scramble the Southerners left behind 12 field guns. Among the mortally wounded was Lt. Col. Alexander "Sandie" Pendleton, son of Brig. Gen. William N. Pendleton and much admired former staff member to Stonewall Jackson.

The following day skirmishing erupted again as Sheridan continued the pursuit. On September 23 cavalry fighting raged briefly at Woodstock, near Edinburg, and at Mount Jackson. The pursuit slowed as Sheridan reorganized his cavalry; Wilson was ordered to Sherman's army and Averell was relieved for timidity on the field. "I do not advise rashness, but I do desire resolution and actual fighting, with necessary casualties, before you retire," Sheridan scolded Averell in a dispatch on September 23. "Since I have been in this department I have unfortunately incurred the displeasure of a few small politicians, and they have left no stone unturned to injure me publicly and privately," Averell replied. Custer and Col. William Powell were assigned command of the cavalry divisions. Grant requested Sheridan to abandon the pursuit of Early and to move on Charlottesville to destroy the Virginia Central Railroad, but Sheridan persuaded Grant to allow him to retire to Winchester en route to reinforcing Grant.

Scattered actions occurred through the last days of September. Skirmishing erupted at Port Republic on the 26th and 27th, and on the 29th, as Sheridan pulled out of the upper Valley, actions flared at Waynesboro. Although Sheridan had moved north, it seemed clear to all that the Federals, greatly outnumbering and outfighting Early, controlled the Valley. "These stories of our defeats in the Valley fall like blows upon a dead body," penned the diarist Mary Boykin Chesnut. "Since Atlanta I have felt as if all were dead within me, forever." "To-morrow I will continue the destruction of wheat, forage, etc., down to Fisher's Hill," Sheridan wrote Grant from Woodstock on October 7. "When this is completed the Valley, from Winchester up to Staunton, ninety-two miles, will have little in it for man or beast."

The utter destruction of much of the Valley's infrastructure was too much for some of the Confederate soldiers to bear. "These are times calling for great sacrifices," Ramseur wrote his wife, in the field near Staunton, on October 5. "We must bear separation, hardship, and danger for the sake of our Country. . . . We will do our duty leaving the result to God."

Although Sheridan's withdrawal took place without major incident, Lomax's Southern cavalry harassed the army's rear guard in the Luray Valley sufficiently that Sheridan ordered Torbert to attack the Southern horsemen, Torbert in turn sending Merritt off to do the work. This resulted in the battle of Tom's Brook on October 8 and 9. Over two hours on the 9th, the cavalry fought stubbornly in a region along the brook visible from Round Top Mountain, where Sheridan watched, and the Northerners of Custer and Merritt struck hard into their Southern counterparts of Rosser and Lomax. After serious fighting with small arms along the battlefront, the Confederate line broke and the victorious Yankees charged down the Valley Pike, sending the Rebels into an utter rout and forcing them to ride hard for miles to escape. Merritt's horsemen pursued Lomax for twenty miles to Mount Jackson and captured 5 field guns while Custer pursued Rosser to Columbia Furnace and took 6 guns; altogether, some 300 Confederate prisoners were captured and another 100 casualties inflicted, while Yankee losses were just 9 killed and 48 wounded. It was an utter destruction of the cavalry forces harassing Sheridan's maneuvers.

Sheridan believed he had cleared the Valley of harassing Southern forces, but that was not the case. He pulled back to Middletown and sent Wright's 6th Corps to rejoin Grant at Petersburg. Early moved back onto the scene by October 13, however, marching to Strasburg, and Sheridan suddenly requested Wright's presence again. Near Strasburg skirmishing occurred on October 13 and 14 as the third battle of Strasburg. The majority of Sheridan's force entrenched along Cedar Creek, near Middletown, and Early planned another attack. Sheridan, called away to Washington to confer with Lincoln and Stanton, proceeded along on the 16th, escorted by Merritt's cavalry, when he was informed of an intercepted communication. He learned that Longstreet was to reinforce Early, but quickly considered the message a ruse, and it was. Merritt's division nonetheless headed back to the Valley rather than joining Grant, and Wright had overall command of the Army of the Shenandoah at Middletown, headquartered in the classic plantation house Belle Grove southwest of the town.

Early had established a signal station at the summit of Three Top Mountain from which Confederate scouts could view the whole Federal line along Cedar Creek. From this station Gordon and topographical engineer Jedediah Hotchkiss (who had served Stonewall Jackson so well in the 1862 Valley campaign) devised a plan to attack the Yankee line. Early approved the plan as follows: at Fishers Hill engineers would bridge the north fork of the Shenandoah River, march south of the river, and recross at Bowman's Ford south of Middletown. Wharton would move north along the Valley Turnpike, reinforced by Kershaw's division, which was now with the army. Early's force would then strike the exposed left flank of the Federal army by surprise.

On the 18th, Early set his plan into motion, having placed Ramseur, Pegram, and Gordon in place to attack Crook by dawn. The accompanying cavalry force was charged with capturing Sheridan in retaliation for the destruction levied on the Valley. The next morning came the battle of Cedar Creek. Blindsided without warning, Crook's men were scattered in confusion and driven backward from their position south of Belle Grove. The sudden, sharp reports of musketry and thundering booms of cannon left no doubt with the surprised Yankees that a major battle was upon them. "Thus I was at General Grover's quarters (hungry and glad to breakfast with him) at the moment when the battle opened," recalled Capt. John William De Forest. "The 'awful rose of dawn,' veiled and softened by thick morning mist, had just begun to bloom over an eastern crest of hill, when, a mile away on our left front, a shrill prolonged wail of musketry broke forth, followed by scream on scream of the Rebel yell. . . . Grover . . . in his usual gentle, monotonous voice, said to his aide, 'Tell the brigade commanders to move their men into the trenches.' "

Stunned, Wright attempted to form the fleeing infantry of the 6th and 19th corps along the Valley Turnpike but failed to organize them. Elements of the 6th Corps made a brief fight but then withdrew to the rolling fields west of the town and attempted to regroup. Although it was being attacked frontally and from the left flank, the 6th Corps dug in and held on between 8 and 9 A.M., fighting stubbornly against the Minié bullets. Getty's division separated from the rest of the corps through utter confusion and retreated to a ridge north of the town to recommence its firing. Cavalry assembled on another ridge nearby, and most of the Yankee infantry scattered farther north along the turnpike, hoping to get away from the beehive of small-arms and cannon fire that had caught them so unaware. By late morning the Union

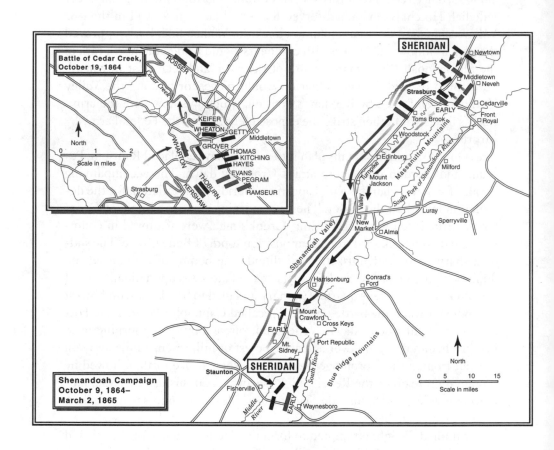

**Battle of Cedar Creek,
October 19, 1864**

ROSSER

Cedar Creek

KEIFER
WHEATON
GETTY
GROVER
THOMAS
KITCHING
HAYES
EVANS
PEGRAM
RAMSEUR
THOBURN
KERSHAW
WHARTON

Middletown

Strasburg

North

0   1   2

Scale in miles

SHERIDAN

Newtown

Middletown
Neveh

Strasburg

Cedarville

EARLY

Front
Royal

Toms Brook

Woodstock

Edinburg

Mount
Jackson

Turnpike

Massanutten Mountains

South Fork of Shenandoah River

Milford

Luray

Sperryville

Valley

New
Market

Alma

Shenandoah Valley

Harrisonburg

Conrad's
Ford

Mount
Crawford

Cross Keys

EARLY

Mt.
Sidney

Port Republic

Blue Ridge Mountains

North

Staunton

SHERIDAN

0   5   10   15

Scale in miles

Fisherville

South River

**Shenandoah Campaign
October 9, 1864–
March 2, 1865**

Middle
River

EARLY

Waynesboro

forces had abandoned 18 field guns and lost more than 1,300 taken prisoner, not to mention vast quantities of supplies.

Early now pulled up on his attacks, although Gordon urged him to press the assault as far as it could go. The Confederate commander believed the Yankees would simply abandon the field, and indeed by 10 A.M. Southern troops began to wander across the fields at random, looting the Union camps of everything they could carry. The stunned and beaten Union forces were given time to begin to recover.

Sheridan, meanwhile, had spent the night sleeping in Winchester and awoke to the sound of distant battle with a great and rising concern. He mounted his horse Rienzi (or Winchester) and galloped for the battlefield, reaching it by about 10:30 and ordering his men to reform for an attack. As his men cheered the return of their short, feisty commander, now universally known as "Little Phil," huzzahs rose along the turnpike. He encountered officers who told him what he could already see: "The army's whipped!" Sheridan replied, "You are, but the army isn't." He further shouted to the broken troops along the road such phrases as "Come on back boys"; "Give 'em hell, God damn 'em!"; and "Men, by God, we'll whip them yet! We'll sleep in our old tents tonight!"

When Sheridan reached Wright, he found the field commander had been struck by a bullet on the chin and was dripping blood onto his uniform, utterly disheartened by the day's events. Sheridan ordered his infantry to form along the ridge west of Getty's position and, when Gordon finally made a probing attack, it was repulsed in great force. Another lull throughout the afternoon permitted Sheridan to strengthen his lines further and by 4 P.M. he launched a blistering counterattack, driving Early's soldiers back in confusion to Fishers Hill. The Southern soldiers had not expected any such movement and were celebrating and looting before their time. Early's Confederates withdrew to New Market the following day, stunned by their reversal of fortune. "The enemy subsequently made a stand on the pike and in turn attacked my line and my left gave way and the rest of the troops took a panic and could not be rallied, retreating in confusion," Early explained to Walter Taylor, Lee's assistant adjutant general. "But for their bad conduct I should have defeated Sheridan's whole force."

Sheridan's ride from Winchester to Cedar Creek became the stuff of legend when it was immortalized in 1865 by the poet Thomas Buchanan Read. For decades it was standard fare for Northern schoolchildren to learn "Sheridan's Ride." "Up from the South, at break of day / Bringing to Winchester fresh dismay / The affrighted air with a shudder bore / Like a herald in haste, to the chieftain's door / The terrible grumble, rumble, and roar / Telling the battle was on once more / And Sheridan twenty miles away." As Sheridan inched closer to the field and saved the day, the poem elevated him to the elite rank of Federal commanders who were winning the war for the Union. All three were Ohioans, Grant, Sherman, and now Sheridan. For his part, Little Phil summarized for Assistant Secretary of War Dana: "I long ago made up my mind that it was not a good plan to fight battles with paper orders—that is, for the commander to stand on a hill in the rear and send his aides-de-camp with written orders to the different commanders. My practice has always been to fight in the front rank."

The casualties at Cedar Creek were substantial. Union losses were 644 killed, 3,430 wounded, and 1,591 missing; Confederate casualties were vaguely reported, but were around 320 killed, 1,540 wounded, and 1,050 missing. Among the mortally wounded was Ramseur; the young North Carolinian was struck in the chest and captured, lingering for a day at Belle Grove in the company of his West Point friends Custer and Merritt before dying. Two celebrated Union general officers were among the casualties. Brig. Gen. Daniel D. Bidwell, a New Yorker who had risen from private soldier early in the war, was knocked from his horse by a shell and died within a few hours. Brig. Gen. Charles R. Lowell, Jr., Massachusetts-born nephew of the poet James Russell Lowell, was mortally wounded, struck in the arm and lungs, and expired the next day.

The pesky Confederate raider Lt. Col. John S. Mosby added a punctuation mark to the campaign. In a sour mood and recovering from a gunshot wound of his own, Mosby had helped to harass Sheridan's campaign by hit-and-run nighttime attacks with his 43d Virginia Cavalry Battalion, burning wagons and disrupting Federal communications, sniping at unwary Union columns from long distances. The "Gray Ghost" and his band of raiders came to be labeled as a "quasi-military pest" by the Union operatives in the theater. The guerrilla tactics employed by Mosby and his men angered Grant, who ordered Sheridan to "hang without trial" any of Mosby's men who might be captured. In late September, Mosby's battalion clashed with a brigade of Federal cavalry near Front Royal, during which Lt. Charles McMaster, a Federal cavalryman, was shot and killed as his horse strayed into the opposing line. Seething Yankee horsemen captured six of Mosby's men and dragged them into Front Royal. Two of the men, David L. Jones and Lucien Love, were shot while behind the Methodist Church; two others, Thomas E. Anderson and Henry Rhodes, were shot later, and the last two, William T. Overby and a ranger named Carter, were strangled. The Federal cavalry left the dead men, one of them with a placard on his chest, "Such is the fate of all Mosby's men." The executions had been approved by Torbert; Custer and Merritt were also involved with the decision.

Mosby, learning of the murders, immediately sought retribution. On October 3 he found it when Lt. John R. Meigs, topographical engineer and son of Union Quartermaster General Montgomery C. Meigs, was returning to his camp near Harrisonburg. In a dark rainstorm, Meigs and two orderlies encountered several horsemen who they believed were Federal cavalry when suddenly shots rang out and Meigs fell dead, shot by the mounted Confederates. One of the surviving Confederates, captured by the orderlies, told Sheridan that Meigs had been murdered in cold blood. (The act inspired Meigs's father, Montgomery, U.S. quartermaster general, to establish the soldiers' cemetery in Lee's former garden at Arlington.) Enraged, Sheridan ordered the town of Dayton, near where the incident occurred, burned. "One village, *Dayton*, has been burned," wrote Holt, "and every house within five miles of it, in retaliation of the murder. . . . Thousands of head of cattle, horses, sheep, &c., are being driven off, and such as cannot be thus conveyed away, are shot upon the spot. The inhabitants look on like doomed culprits while their property is destroyed before their eyes. . . . It is hard to look upon this wholesale destruction—laying waste the most beautiful Valley the sun ever shone upon in a tract a hundred and twenty miles in length from six to twelve in breadth."

Despite the Front Royal murders and the killing of Meigs, who died at 22, Mosby's activities really accomplished relatively little in a military sense. On October 13 the raider struck out at the Baltimore & Ohio Railroad at Harpers Ferry and launched perhaps his most celebrated raid of the war, the so-called Greenback raid. At 2:30 A.M. on the 14th, Mosby and his raiders derailed a passenger train some eight miles northwest of Harpers Ferry. The act was calculated simply to harass, to achieve a measure of terrorism against the supposedly secure rail line. Mosby's men found mostly a contingent of confused German-speaking Americans, but they also discovered two paymasters carrying $173,000 in greenbacks, which they took. A few weeks later, however, the Confederacy struck again with retaliatory measures. "I am directed by the Secretary of War to inform you, your instructions to Lt. Col. Mosby, to hang an equal number of General Custar's [*sic*] men in retaliation for those of his command executed by Genl. C, are cordially approved by the Department," the War Department informed Robert E. Lee. "He instructs me to say, in addition, that if any citizens are found exposed upon any captured train, signal vengeance shall be taken upon all conductors and citizens on it, and every male passenger of the enemy's country should be treated as a prisoner."

Another minor affair with disturbing overtones occurred in Virginia in early October. The village of Saltville, standing on the Virginia & Tennessee Railroad in the mountains of southwestern Virginia, was home to the most important salt works in the state, perhaps the Confederacy. Salt was a vital commodity for the soldiers—without it beef could not be preserved. Brig. Gen. Stephen G. Burbridge launched a raid on Saltville that included 400 black soldiers in the 5th U.S. Colored Cavalry and comprised a force of 3,600 altogether. Some 2,800 Confederate defenders had hastily assembled log and rock breastworks to protect the saltworks, and Col. Felix H. Robertson's brigade contained a company of bushwhackers commanded by Capt. Champ Ferguson.

Burbridge's attack failed, and by dusk he withdrew his men and left casualties on the field. The next morning Robertson and Ferguson led their Confederates over the field, and they ruthlessly slaughtered wounded black soldiers lying on the ground. Accounts from soldiers of both sides place the number of murdered blacks in uniform at more than 100. For his part, Ferguson was eventually captured, tried, and hanged. One Confederate soldier, George D. Mosgrove, wrote, "Hearing more firing in front, I cautiously rode forward and came upon a squad of Tennesseeans, mad and excited to the highest degree. They were shooting every wounded negro they could find. ... The poor, unfortunate negroes had overslept themselves and found that they had been deserted by their comrades and left to be massacred—a fate that Burbridge must have known would befall them should they fall into Confederate hands."

WHILE THE SHENANDOAH ACTIONS transpired, the war on the border was once again heating up. Gen. Edmund Kirby Smith determined to operate against Missouri, hoping to recover the state for the Confederacy by sending Maj. Gen. Sterling Price on a raid into the state with a huge force of cavalry. The realism of attaining the objective in mind could be seriously questioned, but this was late in the war and time was running out for the Confederacy. Desperate times called for desperate measures. At the end of August, Price assembled his Army of Missouri, which consisted of some 12,000 men (about a third of whom were unarmed), with the divisions of Maj. Gen. James F. Fagan (brigades of Brig. Gen. William L. Cabell and Cols. Archibald S. Dobbin, William F. Slemons, and Thomas H. McCray); Maj. Gen. John S. Marmaduke (brigades of Brig. Gen. John B. Clark, Jr., and Col. Thomas R. Freeman); and Brig. Gen. Jo Shelby (brigades of militia Brig. Gen. M. Jeff Thompson and Cols. Sidney D. Jackman and Charles H. Tyler).

Price departed with his men at Princeton, Arkansas, on August 29. He wound his way through Arkansas to Batesville and Pocahontas, where Shelby joined the main force. Daily minor skirmishes broke out, none amounting to much. By September 19, Price entered Missouri and for the last time in the war an invasion disrupted the Trans-Mississippi theater. At Cabin Creek, Indian Territory, Brig. Gen. Stand Watie and Col. Richard M. Gano attacked a Federal wagon train, capturing or destroying 202 wagons, 5 ambulances, 40 horses, and 1,253 mules. The following day Price skirmished at Ponder's Mill and occupied the town of Keytesville.

Affairs and skirmishes continued almost daily as loyal Missouri militia units sprang to action in a panic. By September 26–27, Price attempted his first major action of the expedition when he attacked Fort Davidson near Pilot Knob. "Price arrived before Pilot Knob in the afternoon of September 26th," wrote Wiley Britton of the 6th Kansas Cavalry (USA), "and skirmished until night with detachments of Federal cavalry. . . . Price opened the attack on [Fort Davidson] at daylight on the 27th, and kept it up all day with great resolution." In a bloody fight, 1,200 Union soldiers occupying the fort, under command of Brig. Gen. Thomas Ewing, Jr., peppered the Confederate attackers with musketry and artillery fire before secretly evacuating during the night, blowing up the post with rigged explosives set around the fort. The casualties were approximately 200 Federals and 1,500 Confederates. Alarm was escalating among Federal authorities in the region as Price now directly threatened St. Louis. A band of guerrillas led by 1st Lt. William "Bloody Bill" Anderson (an associate of Col. William C. Quantrill), including Jesse and Frank James, sacked and burned Centralia. Missouri was once again transforming into a land of carnage as it had been before the war even commenced.

The Federal reaction now shifted into high gear. Maj. Gen. Andrew J. Smith's corps was brought back into the theater, protecting St. Louis. Ewing was reinforced by Maj. Gen. Alfred Pleasonton's cavalry, amounting to some 7,000 troopers. In response, Price turned sharply westward, following the Missouri River and working along the Pacific Railroad. Price's expedition skirmished and occupied a whole array of Missouri towns, from Cuba and Potosi to Ridgely.

The Union effort to oust Price was increasing. Pleasonton pursued from behind as A. J. Smith's men and Missouri militia commanded by Col. John E. Phelps harassed Price's left flank and Kansas and Colorado troops commanded by Maj. Gen. James G. Blunt moved into the state. On October 18 the forces finally came together near Waverly, twenty miles east of Lexington, when Blunt slammed into Price's men. The following day heavy skirmishing broke out as Price's men attacked and pushed Blunt's command back through Lexington to the Little Blue River. Price had brought his weakly armed force deep into Missouri but, just as Lee had been disappointed during the Maryland campaign, Price was startled to find a lack of enthusiasm among the locals to join his army. The skirmishing was increasing in severity each day. His men, nevertheless, fought a well-conceived action on October 21 along the Little Blue, and the Yankees evacuated nearby Independence.

The Union concentration only continued, however. Maj. Gen. Samuel R. Curtis approached with still more Federal troops, fought an action with Price's men along the Big Blue River on October 22, and pushed Price back to Westport, now a portion of Kansas City. Price now planned to send his trains southward and dispatched Fagan and Shelby to attack Curtis's Army of the Border as Marmaduke protected the Confederate rear from attacks by Pleasonton's cavalry. Curtis's Army of the Border consisted of the divisions of Blunt (Provisional Cavalry Division; brigades of Cols. Charles R. Jennison, Thomas Moonlight, and Charles W. Blair); Maj. Gen. George W. Deitzler (Kansas Militia Division; mixed, unbrigaded units); the division of Pleasonton's cavalry, unattached from Rosecrans's Army of Missouri (brigades of Brig. Gens. Egbert B. Brown, John McNeil, and John B. Sanborn, and Col. Edward F. Winslow); and two divisions detached from Smith's 16th Corps (those of Cols. Joseph J. Woods and David Moore).

During the night of October 22–23, Curtis organized a line along Brush Creek, south of Kansas City, and prepared for action. At dawn on the 23d the largest battle in Missouri, called Westport, erupted as Price attacked Curtis's line. Price sent his men forward to defeat Curtis so they could then turn back to attack Pleasonton's cavalry. It was a bold, perhaps foolish move for an army so small and poorly armed, and the results were disastrous. Shelby and Fagan initially achieved success by sending brisk attacks forward and pushing back elements of the Union line, but the Union men counterattacked and defeated the Rebels, and Pleasonton's men swept Marmaduke's cavalry away in defeat. After two hours of heavy combat, the Confederate troops limped back across Brush Creek; Curtis ordered a pursuit and the battle raged for two more hours, during which Curtis's men found an opportunity to turn the Confederate left. About 20,000 Union troops participated in the action, perhaps 8,000 Confederates. Casualties are not known but may have been about 1,500 on each side. "The battlefield exhibited evidences of the fiercest contest," reported the *Kansas City Western Journal of Commerce*. "The enemy had fled in such haste that he had been forced to leave his dead and many of his severely wounded. . . . Striking the open prairie beyond [Wornell's House], the evidences of the fight were visible all about." Many of the visitors to the battlefield were shocked at the sights because it was starkly apparent that the majority of the dead Confederates were boys, most of whom were 16 or 17 years old. The desperation of the Confederate military effort was becoming evident to the western civilians.

Pleasonton next attacked in a vicious fight on October 25 at the Marais des Cygnes River and Mine Creek, Kansas, as the retreating Confederates turned to fight a delaying action. Union forces captured a portion of the wagon train, and about 1,000 prisoners and 10 field guns were captured by Pleasonton's horsemen. Among the prisoners were Marmaduke and Cabell. Shelby's men came to the assitance of the battered column, but Price was forced to torch about a third of his remaining wagons and scatter southward at a fast clip. Three days later Price again turned and fought a delaying action at Newtonia, his command running low on supplies and stamina. He turned to avoid Fort Smith and marched arduously through Indian Territory before crossing back into Arkansas with 6,000 weary survivors. The expedition had been a fruitless waste of time, although Price attempted to put a good face on it by reporting that he "marched 1,434 miles, fought forty-three battles and skirmishes, captured and paroled over 3,000 Federal officers and men, captured 18 pieces of artillery." He did not emphasize what he had lost.

ON OCTOBER 19 the war struck another odd place when Lt. Bennett H. Young and some 25 fellow Confederate soldiers launched a raid on St. Albans, Vermont. The architect of a "terrorist" operation that would also produce a fire-bomb attack on New York City, Young moved his band out of Canada in an operation that aspired to burn and loot a variety of Vermont towns. At St. Albans the Southerners struck quickly, taking $200,000 from three banks, and after civilians struggled with the raiders, a civilian was mortally wounded. After a half hour of chaos, the Southern soldiers fled back over the border with the money; Young and 12 of his men were captured along with $75,000.

A curious naval action occurred on October 27, at Plymouth, North Carolina. On the Roanoke River, Lt. William B. Cushing led a boat expedition to seek and destroy the large Confederate ironclad ram CSS *Albemarle*. Cushing, age 21, was the brother of Lt. Alonzo H. Cushing, who had been killed defending his battery at the Angle at Gettysburg. He devised two plans to capture the *Albemarle*; he wanted to avoid destroying the vessel unless there was no other option. Cushing outfitted two 32-foot steam picket boats with a 12-pounder howitzer in the bow of each and a 14-foot spar torpedo. One of the boats was lost in moving south; the other arrived in place on October 24. Seven men volunteered for the attack and accompanied Cushing. On the very dark night of the 27th, with a stinging rain falling, Cushing and his men moved out in their picket boat over their eight-mile journey from Albemarle Sound to Plymouth. With its engine muffled by a thick tarpaulin, Cushing's boat glided past the captured USS *Southfield* undetected and approached the ram. An alert picket aboard the *Albemarle* spotted the oncoming boat and a heavy fire opened upon the Union attackers. Cushing turned the boat around to maneuver his way closer to the ram. "As I turned the whole back of my coat was torn out by buck shot and the sole of my shoe was carried away," he recalled.

The Confederate officer on board shouted for an identification of the boat, Cushing reported, and his men "all gave a comical answer." Cushing shot a load of canister from the boat's howitzer, then allegedly shouted, "Leave the ram, or I'll blow you to pieces!" He then lowered the torpedo boom and struck squarely into the *Albemarle*'s hull, and "a dense mass of water rushed in from the torpedo, filling the launch and completely disabling her." The *Albemarle* began to sink. The *Albemarle* was commanded by Lt. Alexander P. Warley. Warley reported that "the water gained on us so fast that all exertions were fruitless, and the vessel went down in a few moments." Cushing became an instant hero, although only he and one other comrade escaped death or capture.

THE POLITICAL CLIMATE was changing rapidly in the last weeks before the election. On September 8, George McClellan formally accepted the Democratic nomination for president. "There is a fatuity in nominating a general and warrior in time of war on a peace platform," observed Navy Secretary Gideon Welles. Nine days later John C. Frémont withdrew from the race, considering Lincoln a failure and McClellan a potential disaster but himself unelectable. As Lincoln's reelection now seemed more likely, even his adversaries, such as Salmon P. Chase, wondered about the Kentuckian's legacy. "Talk[ed] with gentleman who thought Lincoln very wise," he wrote on September 13, "if more radical would have offended conservatives—if more conservative the radicals—will this be the judgment of history?" Lincoln continued to worry about his administration and his war policies continuing for another few months. "The State election of Indiana occurs on the 11th of October," Lincoln cautioned William T. Sherman. "And the loss of it, to the friends of the Government would go far toward losing the whole Union cause. . . . Anything you can safely do to let her soldiers, or any part of them, go home and vote at the State election will be greatly in point."

Even many Southerners were caught up in the election forecasting. "Yankee politics have simplified themselves very much," recorded Robert G. H. Kean in Richmond. "McClellan stepped off his platform in his letter of acceptance, and is as strong a war man as Lincoln. He would be a much more formidable one to us because he would constantly offer peace and reconstruction on the basis of the Constitution, which would rapidly develop a reconstruction party in the South. Such a party is now beginning to form under the stress of disaster." Robert E. Lee approached President Davis with the notion of arming blacks as soldiers in the Confederacy, an unthinkable idea until desperation set in. "[I'm calling] your attention to the importance of immediate and vigorous measures to increase the strength of our armies," Lee wrote Davis on September 2. "It seems to me that we must choose between employing negroes ourselves and having them employed against us." Nothing would come of such an idea, however, at least not yet. As the Southern armies could seem only to lose territory, the Union added it not only by capture but by proclamation. On October 31, Nevada was admitted to the Union as the thirty-sixth state.

Some notable figures were about to get their comeuppance. As Joe Wheeler raided the Federal communications near Franklin, Tennessee,

Confederate Brig. Gen. John H. Kelly, only 24 years old, was shot through the chest on September 2. He lingered for two days at the Harrison House south of town before dying. Elsewhere in the state, the celebrated raider Brig. Gen. John Hunt Morgan finally met his match on the same day Kelly died. At Greeneville, Morgan was surrounded by Yankee troops and dashed into a garden before being shot in the chest and back. He died instantly.

The spy Rose O'Neal Greenhow, a Confederate who had informed Richmond about McDowell's movements at First Bull Run, allegedly had had an affair with U.S. Senator Henry Wilson, spent time in the Old Capitol Prison in Washington, escaped to Europe, and returned on a steamer in the autumn of 1864. Sailing on a blockade runner, the *Condor*, she made for the mouth of the Cape Fear River near Wilmington, North Carolina, when the ship was chased and run aground on October 1. She escaped with two companions in a lifeboat but was found dead, her body washed ashore, weighted with $2,000 in gold stuffed into her clothes. Her funeral in Wilmington was a major event of sorrow for the Confederacy in this bleak period. "It was a solemn and imposing spectacle, reported an unknown newsperson of the event. "The profusion of wax lights round the corpse, the quality of choice flowers . . . the silent mourners . . . paying the last tribute of respect to the departed heroine. On the bier, draped with a magnificent Confederate flag, lay the body, so unchanged as to look like a calm sleeper . . . passing through the dark waters of the river of death."

Soldiers and civilians alike on the Confederate side were showing signs of fear that their world might be crashing to an end. "We are going to be wiped off the face of the earth," wrote the diarist Mary Chesnut on September 21. "We have but two armies. And Sherman is between them now." "Many of the privates in our armies are fast becoming what is termed machine soldiers," recorded the war clerk John B. Jones, "and will ere long cease to fight well—having nothing to fight for." "The courage of the rebs has been marvelous," wrote Henry Brooks Adams, "but human nature has its limits and unless the sun shines a little, the devil himself would lose heart in such a case."

While the Confederacy appeared to be collapsing, a personality cult was building around Robert E. Lee as the one man who could salvage the situation, the population having lost Stonewall Jackson and abandoned Jefferson Davis. In the Petersburg lines, Lee continued to bolster the defense, pleading for more troops and supplies that couldn't come, and traveling to Richmond to meet with officials. The changing public reaction to Lee was recorded by his adjutant Walter Taylor. "The Genl proposed that we should go to Mr. Gibson's [church]," recorded Taylor on September 11. "It is quite trying to accompany the General to Church or any public place. Everybody crowds the way and stops on the pavements to have a look."

Sherman's March to the Sea

As 1864 WANED and Americans prepared for the eventuality of a fifth calendar year of civil war, relatively few actions played out in the cold weather. Attention focused on the election in the North, which would include for the first time in history armies of a significant nation voting during a war. Lincoln and his administration members still had much to fear, as McClellan's Democrats had played the Republican weaknesses for all they could, although the fall of Atlanta and Sheridan's victory in the Shenandoah, along with strong showings in the October state elections, bolstered Lincoln's confidence in his possible reelection. Southerners were absorbed in the election campaign as well, some believing that McClellan would give them a better chance at suing for peace to end the war. Although a fair number of Confederates had now become tired of the destruction and loss of life, a core constituency was still in place to fight on at any cost.

The lines at Petersburg, close as they were, remained relatively stagnant during November and December, with brief skirmishing and sniping characterizing the unfriendly and tiresome atmosphere in the trenches. Inside Petersburg, civilians were living with a rapidly increasing crime rate and scarcity of food. To keep spirits high the residents held "starvation parties." "With all our starvation we never ate rats, mice or mule-meat," Sarah Pryor reported. "We managed to exist on peas, bread, and sorghum." With her husband in a Yankee prison, Pryor remained cheerful. "It is passing strange," she later asserted, "this disposition to revel in times of danger and suffering. I think all who remember the dark days of the winter of 1864–1865 will bear witness to the unwritten law enforcing cheerfulness."

Despite the inactivity, real dangers lurked for anyone near battle. On December 2, Confederate Brig. Gen. Archibald Gracie, Jr., was peering through a telescope over the lines, his head exposed over a parapet. A shell suddenly exploded nearby and Gracie was struck by fragments, his neck fractured and his shoulder perforated. He died instantly, the day after his daughter was born, which had also been his thirty-second birthday.

There were small spurts of fighting along the Petersburg front. On November 5 minor skirmishes took place at Forts Morton and Haskell. A minor engagement flashed across Hatcher's Run on November 27. From December 7 to 11, Maj. Gen. Gouverneur K. Warren's 5th Corps launched an expedition along the Weldon Railroad that destroyed the track as far south as Hicksford, some forty miles south of Petersburg. Warren's men were reinforced by Brig. Gen. David M. Gregg's cavalry and Brig. Gen. Gershom Mott's division of infantry. Although Warren lost 100 men, he succeeded in destroying significant stretches of the track before being stopped by Lt. Gen. A. P. Hill. Simultaneously, a diversion of infantry was dispatched along Hatcher's Run on December 8–9. In the harshness of the winter weather, with both armies ill and exhausted, the warfare at Petersburg was growing less "civil." "Many of our soldiers are getting very mien [sic]," recorded Virginia private Isaac Hite. "They shoot down stock, break into their meet [sic] houses, and take any thing that they want in present of the owner. They frequently shoot where the owners make any show of defence for their property. Not long since a child was shot and killed by one of this band who aimed to shoot the lady of the house who had reproached them for taken [sic] some of her property." Confederate bushwhackers had harassed Union operations off and on near the Petersburg lines, including murdering isolated Union soldiers by cutting their throats; by mid-December retaliatory strikes had been made. One of them forced Brig. Gen. Joshua L. Chamberlain's men to burn houses and outbuildings within half a mile of the line of Union march, leaving women and children on the run. "I am willing to fight men in arms," Chamberlain informed his sister Sarah on December 14, "but not *babes in arms.*"

Other minor actions occurred in Virginia away from the Petersburg front. On November 28 a skirmish occurred at Fair Oaks, near the old battleground of 1862. On that same day Brig. Gen. Thomas L. Rosser led his Southern cavalrymen on a raid near New Creek, West Virginia. Brig. Gen. William H. F. Payne advanced his brigade along the Baltimore & Ohio Railroad, west of Cumberland, Maryland, attacking the Federal pickets. Rosser pushed into New Creek, capturing several hundred prisoners at Fort Kelly, destroying the railroad bridge, and bringing back a large store of provisions and supplies. Estimates of the number of prisoners taken range from 400 to 700. The real action during the winter cold would take place in the western theater.

DURING THE FIRST DAYS of November, Maj. Gen. William T. Sherman set into motion his celebrated March to the Sea. Sherman would depart Atlanta to commence an overland campaign devoid of supply and communication, plunging his nearly 62,000 men (55,000 infantry, 5,000 cavalry, and 2,000 artillery comprising 64 guns) with twenty days' rations moving toward Savannah and the Atlantic Ocean. Sherman's "bummers," as they came to be known, would subsist in part from the farmland and plantations along the way as they destroyed the rail lines linking the coast with Atlanta and wrecked industry of use to the war effort. Sherman had a force consisting of two columns, the right wing being the Army of the Tennessee, commanded by Maj. Gen. Oliver O. Howard, and the left wing the Army of Georgia under Maj. Gen. Henry W. Slocum. Howard's army consisted of the corps of Maj. Gen. Peter J. Osterhaus (15th Corps; divisions of Brig. Gens. Charles R. Woods, William B. Hazen, John E. Smith, and John M. Corse) and Maj. Gen. Frank Blair, Jr. (17th Corps; divisions of Maj. Gen. Joseph A. Mower and Brig. Gens. Mortimer D. Leggett and Giles A. Smith). Slocum's army contained the corps of Brig. Gen. Jefferson C. Davis (14th Corps; divisions of Brig. Gens. William P. Carlin, James D. Morgan, and Absalom Baird) and Brig. Gen. Alpheus S. Williams (20th Corps; divisions of Brig. Gens. Nathaniel J. Jackson, John W. Geary, and William T. Ward). The attached cavalry division was commanded by Brig. Gen. Judson Kilpatrick.

Following Hood's departure for Tennessee, only a meager Confederate force of about 13,000 remained at Lovejoy's Station to oppose Sherman's advance. It consisted of about 3,050 of Maj. Gen. Gustavus W. Smith's Georgia militia, some of whom were old men and boys, and the cavalry corps of Maj. Gen. Joe Wheeler. Reinforced by a brigade of Brig. Gen. William H. Jackson's horsemen, this cavalry force probably amounted to 10,000 troopers despite Wheeler's claim that it was much smaller. As Sherman moved eastward, a panicked Confederate War Department attempted to shift more troops to resist, and men were ordered to report from the Carolinas and Florida, but the lack of organization, cooperation, and supply limited to no more than 13,000 the number of men facing Sherman at any given time.

Sherman was becoming a legendary figure, much as Jackson had been. "General Sherman is the most American looking man I ever saw," observed Maj. John Chipman Gray, a Federal staff officer, "tall and lank, not very erect, with hair like a thatch, which he rubs up with his hands, a rusty beard trimmed close, a wrinkled face, sharp, prominent, red nose, small, bright eyes, coarse red hands; black felt hat slouched over the eyes." "He impresses me as a man of power more than any man I can remember," concluded Maj. Henry Hitchcock, an assistant adjutant general on Sherman's staff. "Not general intellectual power, not Websterian, but the sort of power which a flash of lightning suggests,—as clear, as intense, and as rapid."

In a series of orders for his men, Sherman spelled out the radical nature of the march, which in some ways echoed Grant's plunge into Mississippi yet demanded that soldiers live off the land even more; they would also be out of touch with the North until they reached Savannah. "The army will forage liberally on the country during the march," Sherman wrote. "Soldiers must not enter the dwellings of the inhabitants, or commit any trespass. . . . In districts and neighborhoods where the army is unmolested, no destruction of such property should be permitted; but should guerrillas or bushwhackers molest our march, or should the inhabitants burn bridges, obstruct roads, or otherwise manifest local hostility, then army commanders should order and enforce a devastation more or less relentless, according to the measure of such hostility." In his memoirs Sherman wrote of the commencement of the march. "We stood upon the very ground whereon was fought the bloody battle of July 22d, and could see the copse of wood where McPherson fell. Behind us lay Atlanta, smouldering and in ruins, the black smoke rising high in the air, and hanging like a pall over the ruined city. Away off in the distance on the McDonough Road, was the rear of Howard's column . . . and right before us the Fourteenth Corps, marching steadily and rapidly, with a cheery look and a swinging pace. . . . Some band, by accident, struck the anthem of 'John Brown's soul goes marching on'; the men caught up the strain, and never before or since have I heard the chorus of 'Glory, glory, hallelujah!' done with more spirit, or in better harmony of time and place."

Georgians were horrified at the potential destruction and the seeming inability of Confederate armies to do anything about Sherman. The Southern press viciously attacked him. "It would seem as if in him all the attributes of man were merged in the enormities of the demon, as if Heaven intended in him to manifest depths of depravity yet untouched by a fallen race," editorialized the *Macon Telegraph*. "Unsated still in his demoniac vengeance he sweeps over the country like a simoom of destruction."

As the soldiers marched, they sang a wide variety of songs, not including the one that would define the March to the Sea in later minds, "Marching Through Georgia," written by Henry Clay Work in 1865. That song was allegedly despised by Sherman himself; it became such a universal anthem that Japanese troops sang it as they entered Port Arthur and the British sang it in India; it was hugely popular during World War II. All this despite the fact that it underreported the Union strength by 20 percent. "Bring the good old bugle, boys, we'll sing another song / Sing it with a spirit that will start the world along / Sing it as we used to sing it, fifty thousand strong / While we were marching through Georgia / Hurrah! Hurrah! we bring the jubilee! / Hurrah! Hurrah! the flag that makes you free! / So we sang the chorus from Atlanta to the sea / While we were marching through Georgia."

The two Federal wings departed Atlanta on November 15 with deception in mind, misleading the Confederates as to their destination. Howard's

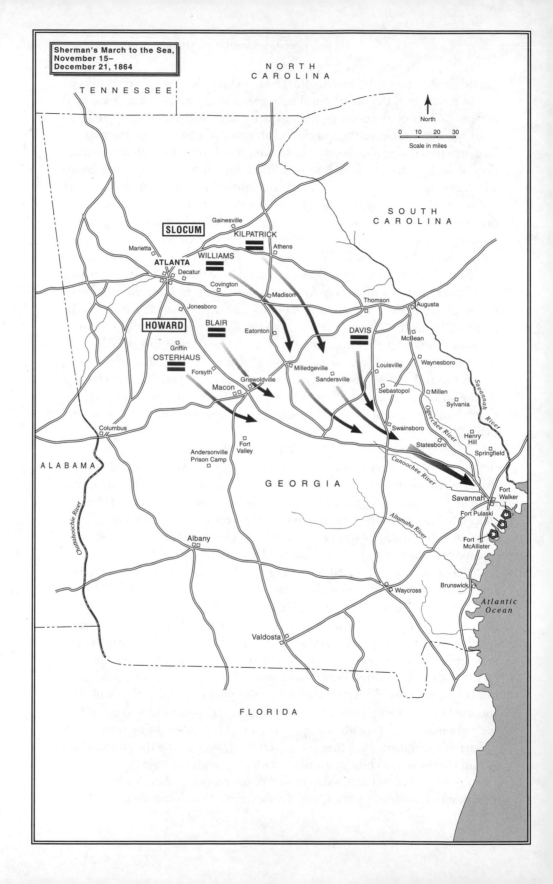

Sherman's March to the Sea,
November 15–
December 21, 1864

TENNESSEE

NORTH
CAROLINA

SOUTH
CAROLINA

North

0 10 20 30

Scale in miles

SLOCUM

KILPATRICK

Gainesville

WILLIAMS

Marietta

Athens

ATLANTA   Decatur

Covington

Madison

Thomson   Augusta

Jonesboro

McBean

HOWARD   BLAIR

Eatonton

DAVIS

Louisville   Waynesboro

Griffin

OSTERHAUS

Forsyth

Milledgeville

Sandersville

Sebastopol   Millen

Griswoldville

Sylvania

Macon

Swainsboro

Henry
Hill

Columbus

Fort
Valley

Statesboro

Springfield

ALABAMA

Andersonville
Prison Camp

GEORGIA

Canoochee River

Savannah   Fort
Walker

Fort Pulaski

Albany

Altamaha River

Fort
McAllister

Chattahoochie River

Ogeechee River

Savannah River

Atlantic
Ocean

Brunswick

Waycross

Valdosta

FLORIDA

wing marched southward along the railroad to Lovejoy's Station, led by Kilpatrick's cavalry. The bulk of the small Confederate force retreated to Macon as two remaining brigades fought a rearguard action on November 16 at Lovejoy's Station (the fifth action there). Dismounting, the 8th Indiana Cavalry attacked the Rebel line and captured two guns before the Union cavalry brigade of Col. Eli H. Murray scattered the Confederates in haste. Pursuing to Bear Creek Station, the Yankees captured 2 more guns and 50 prisoners. Kilpatrick continued on to Forsyth while Howard's infantry turned southeast at the old battleground of Jonesboro and marched to Gordon, southwest of the state capital, Milledgeville. Slocum, meanwhile, moved some seventy miles eastward along the rail line toward Macon, accompanied by Sherman. Slocum destroyed the bridge across the Oconee River and then abruptly turned south.

    With the Confederate military and Georgia civilians now fully panicking, Sherman deceived them over whether he would march on Macon, Augusta, or Savannah. Gen. P. G. T. Beauregard telegraphed frantically for reinforcements, bringing Lt. Gen. Richard Taylor into Georgia. Taylor came himself but without any troops from Alabama, as there were none to bring. In Macon, Taylor, Georgia Gov. Joseph E. Brown, Maj. Gen. Howell Cobb, and Brig. Gen. Robert A. Toombs conferred on what to do and did nothing. Beauregard called for citizens to "obstruct and destroy all roads in Sherman's front, flank, and rear," and the desperate Georgia legislature, at Milledgeville, attacked Sherman's character and called for Georgians to "die freemen rather than live [as] slaves." Shortly after passing that act, legislators fled the state capitol. On November 20 a day of skirmishes occurred at Clinton, Walnut Creek, East Macon, Griswoldville, and along the Ocmulgee River.

    On the same day Lt. Gen. William J. Hardee, commanding the Department of South Carolina, Georgia, and Florida, arrived from Savannah and realized that Sherman was not moving on Macon but had Savannah as his target. Hardee sent Wheeler to heighten the pressure on the Federal's rear and flanks while Smith's militia went scurrying eastward to protect the seaport. Near Milledgeville, Sherman's bummers helped themselves to supplies at Howell Cobb's deserted plantation. At the state capitol, on November 23, officers of Sherman's staff explored the second-story room where the state assembly met and held a mock legislature, "voting Georgia back into the Union," and playing cards inside the room.

    Howard's right wing ran into resistance on November 21–22 at Griswoldville as the Georgia militia tried to block the Yankees. On the 21st, Kilpatrick's cavalry captured a thirteen-car train loaded with military stores and commenced to burn the station and nearby factory warehouses. Wheeler's cavalry struck into the Federal horsemen on the 22d, capturing 18 men and killing 3 Yankees. The subsequent arrival of Brig. Gen. Charles C. Walcutt's brigade disrupted the Confederate attack and then established a defensive line at Duncan's Farm. A division of Georgia militia, ill equipped, poorly trained, and led by militia Brig. Gen. Pleasant J. Phillips, attacked the Federal position. After several hours of badly coordinated assaults, Phillips retreated, having suffered at least 51 dead, 472 wounded, and possibly as many as 600 missing. Union casualties were fewer than 100.

Wheeler, moving quickly to block the Union advance, struck alongside infantry in the rearguard action at Ball's Ferry on November 24–25. Howard's wing was delayed crossing the Oconee River near Ball's Bluff, and the 1st Alabama Cavalry (Federal) commenced a firefight with Confederate pickets. During the night Union engineers constructed a bridge some two miles away from the bluff and 200 soldiers crossed and endangered the Confederate position. Some 21 Yankees and 9 Confederates were killed or wounded before Howard's men erected a pontoon bridge. Another action flared again on November 25–26 at Sandersville as Wheeler struck at Slocum's advance guard. Musketry erupted on the 25th; the next day Col. Ezra A. Carman's brigade fought briskly with Confederates commanded by Maj. Alfred L. Hartridge. The 9th Illinois Mounted Infantry broke open the Confederate line, and Carman's infantry then pushed the Rebels away, enabling the Union occupation of Sandersville.

Moving eastward, Kilpatrick next fought a series of cavalry engagements with Wheeler's troopers. Kilpatrick was ordered to make a northward feint toward Augusta before destroying the railroad bridge at Brier Creek and moving on the important prison camp at Millen to liberate Union prisoners. Wheeler established a defensive line near Brier Creek, but Kilpatrick slipped by him; a series of actions from November 26 to 29 ensued. On the night of the 26th, Wheeler attacked the 8th Indiana Cavalry and 2d Kentucky Cavalry at Sylvan Grove, driving them away from their camps. Harassed by Wheeler, Kilpatrick abandoned the plan to destroy the railroad bridge and subsequently learned that the Millen prisoners had been moved. He rejoined the army at Louisville. The series of skirmishes fought on November 27 were termed Waynesboro, Buckhead Creek, and Brier Creek. At Buckhead Creek the following day, Kilpatrick was surprised and nearly captured. The 5th Ohio Infantry halted Wheeler's advance at Buckhead Creek, and Kilpatrick, at Reynolds's Plantation, stopped Wheeler decisively.

Though deep within the tangle of the Georgia countryside and out of communication, Sherman was about to be helped. Maj. Gen. John G. Foster dispatched a force to assist Sherman's planned arrival near Savannah by securing the Charleston Railroad. The plan soon went awry, however. One of Foster's district commanders, Brig. Gen. John P. Hatch, brought a force of 5,500 men and 10 field pieces from Hilton Head. Three miles south of Grahamville Station, South Carolina, at Honey Hill, Hatch attacked and fought a bloody action against Gustavus Smith's 1,400 Georgia militia troops on November 30. Smith's tattered but valiant local troops fought off the Yankee attacks and by nightfall Hatch withdrew his men by boat after suffering 88 killed, 623 wounded, and 44 missing; Smith's losses were 8 killed and 42 wounded.

Wheeler continued attempting to engage the oncoming Federals, and minor actions flared. By December 10, Sherman's men were bearing down on Savannah, ending the marching component of the campaign. Though Sherman's men were almost within sight of the ocean, Hardee now had 10,000 men entrenched in well-defended positions; his soldiers flooded the surrounding rice fields, leaving only narrow causeways for approaches to the city. The Union Navy, waiting offshore to meet Sherman's men, could not link up with them. Sherman determined to lay siege to Savannah. Sherman dispatched cavalry to ride down to Fort McAllister, which guarded the Ogeechee River, to open it as an avenue by which he could connect with the Federal fleet.

By December 12, Sherman's men were preparing to attack Fort McAllister and to invest the city, though they had not cut off a path of Confederate retreat to the north. Momentarily stalled, with a large army running out of food and with horses and other animals suffering from lack of forage, Sherman determined to attack the fort. He sent Hazen's division to capture the small garrison of 250 soldiers commanded by Maj. George W. Anderson. After a relatively brief fight, Hazen's men captured the fort, but only after some of the attackers were killed and injured by torpedoes, primitive land mines set around the position. Hazen's casualties were 134 total. Capt. Louis M. Dayton, another aide of Sherman's, wrote Slocum of the capture: "The fort was carried at 4:30 P.M., the assault lasting but fifteen minutes." Sherman now established contact with the Union fleet commanded by Rear Adm. John A. B. Dahlgren, reestablishing his lines of communications. The Lincoln administration and the Northern populace were triumphant after hearing that Sherman had emerged from his "rabbit hole" before Savannah. Sherman immediately sent for siege guns from Port Royal and planned to blast Hardee out of the city. "I have already received guns that can cast heavy and destructive shot as far as the heart of your city," he told the Southern commander on December 17. "I am therefore justified in demanding the surrender of the city of Savannah and its dependent forts, and shall await a reasonable time your answer before opening with heavy ordnance.... Should I be forced to resort to assault, and the slower and surer process of starvation, I shall then feel justified in resorting to the harshest measures, and shall make little effort to restrain my army."

The route to Charleston still open, Hardee decided to escape. On December 20 with his 10,000 men he fled across the Savannah River using a makeshift pontoon bridge constructed of rice flats, leaving the city in the hands of the Yankees. Sherman's soldiers moved in the next day, unopposed. Geary's division of the 20th Corps led the march into the city, finding its elegant squares and neoclassic buildings in good order. Though Sherman has often been criticized for allowing Hardee to slip away, Hardee was gone as soon as the northern route was threatened. On December 22, Sherman wrote Lincoln, informing him of the occupation. "I beg to present you as a Christmas gift the City of Savannah with 150 heavy guns & plenty of ammunition & also about 25,000 bales of cotton," he wrote the president. "No City was ever occupied with less disorder, or more system than . . . Savannah," Sherman informed his foster father Thomas Ewing, "and it is a subject of universal Comment that though an army of 60,000 men lay camped around it, women & children of an hostile People walk its Streets with as much security as they do in Philadelphia."

Sherman had accomplished an amazing task. He had defied military principles by operating deep within enemy territory and without lines of supply or communication. He destroyed much of the South's potential and psychology to wage war. His casualties were relatively light, about 2,200 overall. With Hardee scrambling northward, the question of a campaign in the Carolinas now lay ahead. "The truth is the whole army is burning with an insatiable desire to wreak vengeance upon South Carolina," Sherman wrote Halleck on Christmas Eve. "I almost tremble at her fate, but feel that she deserves all that seems in store for her."

Sherman's destruction in rural Georgia, though vastly exaggerated in much of the wartime literature, was real. Most of the operations were limited to foraging, but considerable destruction and pillaging did take place. Not only were houses in Atlanta burned (though with the potential for outright disaster in loss of life minimized due to the city's partial evacuation), orders had been issued to avoid burning structures. The men were also told to limit the destruction of goods to those of military value—but soldiers during the march stepped across the bounds and took matters into their own hands. The real hatred and vengeance, however, would be focused on South Carolina. Still, enough destruction occurred that an officer from New Jersey recorded in his diary that "in spite of orders, & the utmost efforts of officers, houses, in Some way, get on fire & nearly all we have passed thus far are I think in ashes."

Sherman became Georgia's archvillain. "This last campaign of Sherman's has almost disemboweled the rebellion," exclaimed Geary to his wife Mary from near Savannah. "The state of Georgia is about as badly destroyed as some of the tribes of the land of Canaan were by the Israelitish army, according to the Biblical record. . . . We are in sight of the 'promised land,' after a pilgrimage of three hundred miles."

SHERMAN'S MARCH did not take place in a vacuum. All the while, Lt. Gen. John Bell Hood (he was not confirmed in his acting grade as general) was busy with his own campaign north of Georgia. After the fall of Atlanta, Hood remained at Lovejoy's Station until September 18, when he initiated plans to move into Tennessee to threaten Nashville. His plan of striking at the Union lines of communications and drawing Sherman northward again failed, of course, but much larger strategic disasters were awaiting Hood's Army of Tennessee. Hood's 39,000 men constituted the second-largest remaining army of the Confederacy, ranking in strength after only the Army of Northern Virginia. Battle-scarred Hood was almost certainly taking opiates as pain medicine, which may have clouded his judgment. The Army of Tennessee at this time consisted of the corps of Maj. Gen. Benjamin F. Cheatham (divisions of Maj. Gens. Patrick R. Cleburne, John C. Brown, and William B. Bate); Lt. Gen. Stephen D. Lee (divisions of Maj. Gens. Edward Johnson, Carter L. Stevenson, and Henry D. Clayton); and Lt. Gen. Alexander P. Stewart (divisions of Maj. Gens. William W. Loring, Samuel G. French, and Edward C. Walthall); the cavalry was commanded by Maj. Gen. Nathan Bedford Forrest (divisions of Brig. Gens. Abraham Buford, James R. Chalmers, and William H. Jackson).

Beauregard approved Hood's plan only if Wheeler were left behind, and the latter thus constituted most of the defense against Sherman. So Forrest was brought forward to join his cavalry with the Hood operation into Tennessee. Rather than being drawn north and abandoning his March to the Sea, Sherman simply ordered Maj. Gen. George H. Thomas, commanding the Army of the Cumberland, to come forward from Nashville and halt Hood's advance, and Sherman sent the 4th and 23d Corps to bolster Thomas's force. Thomas seemed not to appreciate the urgency of the moment, however, failing to unite all the forces in the area, and Hood also encountered problems in commencing the campaign because on arriving at Decatur he found that Forrest had been delayed. Hood moved west to Tuscumbia by early November and awaited the organization of the campaign. Forrest conducted an operation against Johnsonville, Tennessee, from November 3 to 5, moving in on this supply depot and bombarding it, destroying supplies, wrecking steamboats and barges, and panicking the garrison. Finally, on November 17, as Sherman's men were marching eastward, Forrest joined Hood and the latter ordered an advance for the following day.

Thomas continued his apparent lack of response by failing to organize the troops in his department. He dispatched Maj. Gen. John M. Schofield's

Army of the Ohio to Johnsonville, west of Nashville, to counteract a raid by Forrest; he left forces under Brig. Gen. Robert S. Granger at Decatur, Alabama, and Maj. Gen. Lovell Rousseau at Tullahoma, Tennessee, neither of which was involved in the campaign.

Hood's strategy called for advancing northward from Florence, Alabama, to capture the Duck River crossing at Columbia, Tennessee, thereby perhaps separating Schofield from Thomas. He planned to defeat each in detail. Schofield's Army of the Ohio constituted some 34,000 troops, with the corps of Maj. Gen. David S. Stanley (4th Corps; divisions of Brig. Gens. Nathan Kimball, George D. Wagner, and Thomas J. Wood); Brig. Gen. Jacob D. Cox (23d Corps; divisions of Brig. Gens. Thomas H. Ruger and James W. Reilly); and a cavalry corps commanded by Maj. Gen. James H. Wilson (divisions of Brig. Gens. Edward M. McCook, Edward Hatch, Richard W. Johnson, and Joseph F. Knipe). Thomas had another 26,000 troops at Nashville and scattered around his department.

The campaign began on November 21 as Hood moved out from Florence. The following day, as Hood's men marched to Lawrenceburg, Tennessee, they skirmished with advance guards, causing Schofield to retreat from Pulaski northward toward Columbia. One of the divisions Schofield sent north arrived in time to prevent Forrest's cavalry from seizing the bridges there; by November 24, Schofield's army was encamped along a defensive line at Columbia. Two days later Hood brought his whole army into position facing this line. As the armies concentrated, skirmishes erupted throughout central Tennessee. Schofield established his line south of the Duck River, citing orders from Thomas to hold the bridges there. But by November 27, Hood threatened to turn Schofield's flank, so the latter abandoned his lines and ordered the Yankee soldiers north of the river. This played into Hood's scheme perfectly; the Southern commander left Lee's corps at Columbia and crossed the remainder of his army at Davis's Ford on November 29. Forrest, meanwhile, had occupied Wilson's Union cavalry by forcing them northeast to Hurt's Corner, making them unavailable to assist Schofield.

With the Confederates moving northward, Schofield dispatched Stanley with the divisions of Wagner and Kimball to march on Spring Hill, north of Columbia on the Columbia Pike. With Hood's forces moving in and with the increasing possibility of being enveloped, Schofield nonetheless retained Cox, Wood, and Ruger at Columbia. On his northward march Stanley left Kimball's division along Rutherford's Creek, midway between Columbia and Spring Hill, and moved forward to Spring Hill just in time to face Forrest, who had swung up from the east. Wagner rapidly deployed his men and fought a brief action with Forrest, who was driven off by the Union infantry.

Forrest's men retreated to Thompson's Station, north of Spring Hill, his troopers utterly exhausted and running low on ammunition.

The battle of Spring Hill now unfolded between infantry units on November 29. Hoping to cut off Schofield from rejoining Thomas at Nashville, Hood sent Cheatham squarely into the Union lines by midafternoon, led by Pat Cleburne. Sometimes called the "Stonewall of the West," Cleburne was one of the most admired division commanders in the Confederate army. Born in County Cork, Ireland, Cleburne was a lawyer who had moved to Arkansas and served admirably during the whole war, suffering a severe wound in 1862 at Richmond, Kentucky. At first the Confederate attacks drove the Yankees back, but superb artillery firing from Union batteries and uncoordinated, piecemeal attacks by the Confederate units eliminated any hope of a decisive outcome. By darkness, as the last flashes of musket barrels illuminated the woods and fields, the Union army had managed to maintain possession of the road and keep open their route of retreat. Firing had also occurred between scattered Union forces and Stewart's corps, which Hood had left south along Rutherford's Creek (another product of his unclear thinking). In one of the more astonishing acts of the war, not only did Stanley's men fight off the Confederate attack at Spring Hill, but during the night Schofield managed to pull all his men from the whole Duck River corridor, assemble them along the Turnpike, and escape past Hood's entire army without a fight—wagon trains and all.

Numerous arguments have raged over how this Spring Hill fiasco happened. Poor communications and personal failure marked the whole affair at Spring Hill, characterized by Hood's alarm over the inaccurate map used to plan his operation and his ghostly fears about being attacked while marching—another aspect of his clouded thinking. His failure in keeping Stewart's corps out of the action as the campaign unfolded is key, but so was Cheatham's poor performance as a corps commander, forming his men haphazardly and allowing uncoordinated attacks. Many laid most of the blame for the Union army's escape on Cheatham, who made one cautious attempt to block the road and then withdrew when he heard an erroneous report that no Union troops were seen. Stephen D. Lee noted that "his excuse being that he was outflanked on the right and did not wish to bring on a night attack" was unacceptable. Forrest, also, had failed miserably by coming into action only after dark. Schofield moved quickly to reassemble his army in Franklin, and as Ruger pushed Forrest back at midnight, at Thompson's Station, the road was fully open for the whole Federal army. By 6 A.M. the following morning the whole force was north of Spring Hill and Hood was forced to continue a pursuit, his golden opportunity vanished.

This established the bloody battle of Franklin, which occurred on November 30. Although Cox's men were tired from days of fighting and marching, the Federals constructed impressively large earthwork fortifications south of Franklin on their arrival. By noon the Union defensive line was established, stretching in a semicircle south and east of the town and bordered to the north by the Harpeth River. Kimball's division was on the western side, Ruger in the center, and Cox to the left, with Wagner detached to the south; and Col. Emerson Opdycke's brigade acted as the rear guard. Wood's division had crossed the river and taken up a position along the northern bank, occupying Fort Granger east of the city, and Schofield accompanied it, not knowing whether Hood would fight at Franklin or flank the Federal army, so that Cox was left in command of the forces in the city.

Hood approached the city cautiously and marched Cheatham's corps on the left and Stewart's on the right, with most of Forrest's cavalry screening out to the east, where they once again encountered Wilson. Hood passed by the Harrison House south of town (where Confederate Brig. Gen. John H. Kelly had died in September) and took up an observation post on Winstead Hill south of town. Marching right up into the Federal line and attacking frontally might seem insane in hindsight, as it did to some of the officers and men as it happened. But Hood also knew that Schofield had destroyed his pontoon bridges at Columbia and therefore had a limited ability to put his army across the Harpeth; somehow he reverted from exceeding cautiousness back to his characteristic recklessness. He ordered an all-out assault on the Union position, perhaps not appreciating how well constructed the log breastworks were.

Schofield's 32,000 men were mostly in the trenches south of town. Hood's 38,000 approached by midafternoon as Schofield planned for a withdrawal at 6 P.M. if not attacked by Hood. The center of the Federal line cut through the Fountain Branch Carter property, on which a fine brick house, several clapboard outbuildings, and a gin mill stood. Prior to the action, Cox used the house as a headquarters. By 3:30 P.M. the Confederates attacked frontally and in heavy force. Wagner, who had been ordered to withdraw if attacked, remained in position in the face of an enormous Confederate advance. As musketry fire opened, Wagner's boys momentarily held in check the divisions of Cleburne and Brown, but then the overwhelming fire from a long Confederate line erupted and Wagner's men retreated in a hurry. "A rush and a yell followed," reported Cox, "and the two hapless brigades came streaming to the rear in a disorganized crowd, running rapidly to reach the parapets behind them. Orders were quickly sent down the line to withhold the fire at the centre till our own men should be in."

The Union center at Carter House and on both sides of the Columbia Pike was smashed by an initial charge, but Opdycke counterattacked with his reserves and some of the hottest fighting of the western theater ensued,

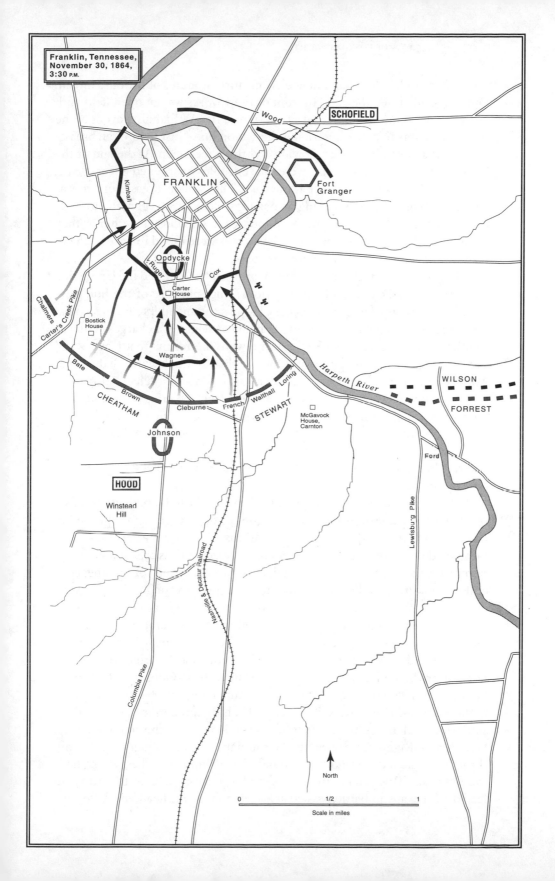

Franklin, Tennessee,
November 30, 1864,
3:30 P.M.

SCHOFIELD

Wood

FRANKLIN

Fort
Granger

Kimball

Chalmers

Carter's Creek Pike

Opdycke

Ruger

Cox

Carter
House

Bostick
House

Wagner

Bate

Brown

CHEATHAM

Cleburne

French

Walthall

Loring

STEWART

Harpeth River

WILSON

FORREST

Johnson

McGavock
House,
Carnton

HOOD

Ford

Winstead
Hill

Lewisburg Pike

Nashville & Decatur Railroad

Columbia Pike

North

0   1/2   1

Scale in miles

much of it in a hand-to-hand melee. After thirty minutes of furious combat, Opdycke had closed the gap. "In front of their works was an open field with not a tree or ravine for a mile and a half," wrote Pvt. William E. Bevens of the the 1st Arkansas Infantry, describing the Union line. "Just before the breastworks was an open ditch six feet wide and three feet deep. At the end of the ditch next to the breastworks, were placed poles sharpened spear-shape. Their main works were six feet at the base. The cannon-breast portion was cut down so that the guns, resting on oak logs, were on a level with our bodies. Behind the whole was a thicket of locust trees, as close together as they could possibly grow. After the battle these trees were found to have been cut level with the breastworks by Confederate balls."

Confederate attacks captured eight guns and penetrated the Union line before being pushed back in heavy action. Other portions of the line were assaulted with only temporary success. Hood's commanders sent piecemeal attacks forward many times, making as many as seventeen charges, with casualties resulting each time. So fearsome were the results that Capt. R. W. Banks of the 37th Mississippi Infantry wrote that "so thick were the dead and wounded in the ditch there, it became a sort of out-door 'chamber of horrors.' When night came down, the groans and frenzied cries of wounded on both sides of the earthworks were awe-inspiring. . . . Some pleadingly cried out, 'Cease firing! Cease firing!' while others agonizingly were shouting, 'We surrender! We surrender!' " If the lessons of Malvern Hill and Gettysburg had taught many Rebel commanders to avoid frontal attacks, they had not convinced Hood.

By 9 P.M., watching in horror from Winstead Hill, Hood halted the attacks, which had been made over two miles of open ground (as opposed to one mile at Gettysburg) and cost frightful casualties. By 11 P.M. the sporadic firing died down and the battle of Franklin ceased. Of its 27,000 men in action, Hood's army suffered 1,750 killed, 3,800 wounded, and 702 missing; Federal losses were 189 killed, 1,033 wounded, and 1,104 missing of about 27,000 engaged. Hood had in effect mortally wounded his army at Franklin, losing a vast number of officers among the casualties. Six generals were killed or mortally wounded. Brig. Gen. John Adams, a Tennesseean, was first hit in the right arm and subsequently struck by nine bullets as he tried to jump his horse over the Union works; he died instantly. Brig. Gen. John C. Carter, Georgia-born and only 26, was mortally wounded in the abdomen and died at the Harrison House on December 10. Cleburne, the much beloved division commander, was killed when he, too, was struck in the abdomen. Brig. Gen. States Rights Gist, a South Carolinian who had fought stubbornly throughout the war, was mortally wounded when hit in the chest, dying later the same day. Brig. Gen. Hiram B. Granbury, Mississippian by birth and leader of Texans in battle, was struck in the face and head and killed instantly. He sank down to his knees with his hands clutched at his face and remained in that position in death until his body was taken from the field. Ohio-born Brig. Gen. Otho F. Strahl, who had moved to Tennessee and sided with the South, was shot three times in the neck and head and killed instantly. Four of the six—Adams, Cleburne, Granbury, and Strahl—were laid out on the porch of the John McGavock mansion, Carnton, south of town in the wake of the battle, forming one of the gruesome, memorable sights of the war in the minds of many soldiers. Oddly, another of the Confederate dead was Capt. Theodrick "Tod" Carter, a staff officer of Brig. Gen. Thomas B. Smith in Cheatham's corps, who was mortally wounded and died on his own property—he was Fountain Branch Carter's son. Dozens of dead soldiers littered the Carter House grounds, and even today the clapboard structures—particularly those of the Farm Office building—show dozens of bullet holes from that afternoon.

Hood could never accept responsibility for the decision to attack at Franklin. "We carried the enemy's entire line of temparary [*sic*] works," he informed Secretary of War Seddon on December 11, "but failed to carry the interior line. During the night I had our Artillery brought forward and placed in position to open upon them in the morning when the attack should be renewed, but the enemy retreated rapidly during the night on Nashville, leaving their dead and wounded in our hands. . . . Our loss in officers was severe. . . . Our entire loss was four thousand five hundred (4500)." The morale among Hood's survivors was dwindling. "A [local lady] who saw the rebel army passing, told me that she saw General Hood standing on an elevated place by the roadside as the soldiers marched by," reported Union Lt. Col. William G. Le Duc. "[She] heard them curse him awfully, and say: 'You damned old fool—when are you going to have another killing? The Yanks have got one of your legs—I wish they had your whole damned body.' "

As Hood fought against Schofield and Cox, Union Maj. Gen. George Stoneman, recently exchanged from a Rebel prison, commenced a raid into eastern Tennessee and southwestern Virginia. Confederate Maj. Gen. John C. Breckinridge had been harassing Union forces in the vicinity of Knoxville. Stoneman brought Federal cavalry into the region, thwarted Breckinridge's threat, and fought a brisk skirmish at Beans's Station on December 1. Over the course of the next month he moved into Virginia, occupying Saltville and Wytheville, destroying the salt works that had been so valuable to the Confederacy and vast quantities of other military goods.

If Hood mortally wounded his army at Franklin, he would kill it two weeks later at Nashville. The Federals retreated northward after the battle, entering the city's defensive works by December 1. The following day Hood arrived in front of the capital city, discovering that Thomas's men occupied fortified lines considerably more formidable than those at Franklin. Maj.

Gen. Andrew J. Smith's corps (the 16th Corps, arrived from Missouri) occupied the line on the Union right, abutting the Cumberland River west of the city; Brig. Gen. Thomas J. Wood's corps (the 4th Corps, ex-Stanley, who was wounded at Franklin) the center, and Schofield's the left, with Maj. Gen. James B. Steedman's division anchoring the left along the southeastern edge of the city at the river. Wilson's cavalry was north of the river at Edgefield. Thomas organized his forces and slowly developed plans to defend the city. The Lincoln administration and Grant, still stalled at Petersburg, were in a panic, meanwhile, angered over Hood's apparent success in closing in on Thomas. The latter prepared to attack several times, slowly and methodically, first wanting to reorganize Wilson's cavalry before assaulting and then hampered by a driving snow and sleet storm that blanketed the landscape with ice on December 9. (Prior to this the weather had been unseasonably warm.) Meanwhile, on December 7, Forrest's horsemen struck into the Federal garrison at Murfreesboro, without significant results.

Thomas's delay was nearly too much for Grant and Halleck. "I have as much confidence in your conducting a battle rightly as I have in any other officer," Grant assured Thomas on December 9, "but it has seemed to me that you have been slow, and I have had no other explanation of affairs to convince me otherwise." Thomas curtly replied that "I can only say . . . that I could not concentrate my troops and get their transportation in order in shorter time than it has been done." Dissatisfied, Grant requested Halleck to draw up orders relieving Thomas of command. Schofield would assume command, but the orders were delayed. On December 13, the soldiers of both armies attempted to live through the bitter cold that followed the sleet storm. Maj. Gen. John A. Logan was sent to assume command of Nashville, reaching Louisville by December 15. On that same day, Thomas saved his job and destroyed Hood by plunging into the Southern army with a devastating attack.

The battle of Nashville was decisive in the west. In cold weather and under a heavy fog, Thomas's men moved out from their defensive works with a brilliant plan. It called for A. J. Smith and Wood to strike at Stewart's corps while Schofield was held in reserve to support the attack. Steedman would launch a diversionary attack against Cheatham's right flank. Wilson's cavalry screened the flank, meanwhile, keeping Chalmers's horsemen at bay during the operation. Hood's men were poorly placed, by contrast, stretched thinly over a long line that angled unnecessarily, depriving the Confederates of effective interior lines as the battle unfolded. Forrest was out of place and Hood provided for no reserves to reinforce weak points along the line. His army, moreover, was battered, undersupplied, and not ready to meet a superior enemy force at Nashville.

Steedman moved out at 6 A.M., attacking Cheatham's right two hours later along the Nashville & Chattanooga Railroad and the Nolensville Pike. The Yankees struck into a lunette on a hill beside the railroad near Rains's Hill. Muddy, messy roads delayed Smith's attack on the Confederate left; by 10 A.M. the division of Brig. Gen. John McArthur opened a route along the Hardin Pike so that Hatch's cavalry could deploy on the Federal right. The Yankees attacked strongly and pushed back Col. David Coleman's (Ector's) brigade, capturing some of the Confederate works under heavy fire. Across Smith's front, Union soldiers fired rapidly at Stewart's men, putting the divisions of Walthall and Loring under heavy pressure. Hard fighting raged along Brown's Creek, around the Felix Compton House, and along the western edge of Granny White Pike as the attacks continued. Several redoubts in the area became the targets of Union attack. Charges resulted in screaming, occasional hand-to-hand fighting, and rounds of close-range musket fire. The cavalry and infantry forces were intermingled "like a crowd of schoolboys," Hatch reported, the cavalrymen firing deadly bursts from their Spencer carbines. Facing a possible envelopment, Hood rushed forward reserves from Lee's corps, the brigades of Lt. Col. William L. Butler (Manigault's brigade) and Brig. Gen. Zachariah C. Deas. Finding comfort behind the stone wall along the Hillsboro Pike, the brigades no sooner got into position than they were attacked, broke, and retreated in utter chaos.

The Union envelopment of the Rebel left continued as Schofield sent Maj. Gen. Darius N. Couch's division forward. In short order Brig. Gen. Joseph A. Cooper's brigade sped forward and captured a ridge west of the Granny White Pike; the remainder of Schofield's command went forward in support. As the heavy fighting of the afternoon continued, the Federals solidified their gains. Cox's division sent troops forward to occupy the ground south of Couch, and Col. Israel N. Stiles's brigade remained along Richland Creek to protect the Federal right. By nightfall the advances of these units isolated Coleman's brigade of Confederates, who pulled together on a hilltop later to be called Shy's Hill. On Smith's left, meanwhile, Wood had assaulted in a southward plunge at 1 P.M., capturing Montgomery Hill, west of the Granny White Pike and closer to the city. By repeated volleys of musketry and effective artillery bombardment, Kimball's division pushed the core of Walthall's division southward, moving the Confederate center.

Hood, alerted to the attack on his left, ordered Cheatham to support the position, but the movement was slow and clumsy. In the darkness, amid the chaotic resupplying of ammunition and food, the cries of the wounded, and the attempts to stay warm, Hood established his new line in the Brentwood Hills, extending from Shy's Hill to Overton Hill, covering his two main routes of retreat—the Granny White Pike and the Franklin Pike. Although the battle would continue on December 16, neither commander at first seemed sure of whether he wanted to bring it on again. At first light the

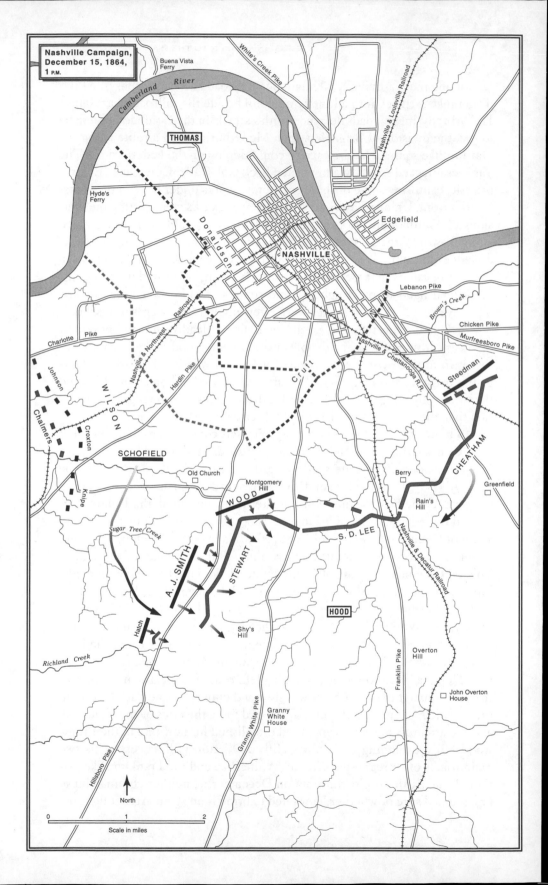

Nashville Campaign,
December 15, 1864,
1 P.M.

Union division commanders began to probe the new lines, and Steedman emerged northeast of Overton Hill and established his line adjacent to Wood. Wilson now swung his entire cavalry force southeast to Schofield's right and dismounted his troopers, as Chalmers had been removed from the scene to protect the Confederate left flank.

At 3:30 P.M. Steedman attacked the Confederate right at Overton Hill, a position well defended by Brig. Gen. Marcellus A. Stovall's brigade. Black troops of the 12th, 13th, and 100th USCT were instrumental in the assault. Although Col. Philip S. Post, a brigade commander in Wood's corps, believed the position could be taken, it was strongly defended. The Yankees were driven back with devastating losses, Post himself taken down by a grapeshot in the arm (he recovered). Success would come to the west on the other hill, however. By 4 P.M. a concerted attack on Shy's Hill was underway, despite the position's strong defense by Cheatham, Bate, and Walthall. As Wilson's cavalry attacked Chalmers, driving him back, Hood was forced to move Brig. Gen. Daniel C. Govan's brigade to help Chalmers and Coleman's brigade from Shy's Hill to replace Govan's. Bate's division was then thinned out to hold the position atop the hill. This worked for a time before heavy Union cannonading made Bate's position impossible to hold.

Hood's line began to collapse from the severity of the attack. Bate's division and the brigade of Brig. Gen. Mark P. Lowrey were cut to pieces by an attack from the rear. Lt. Col. William M. Shy, commanding the consolidated remnants of the 2d, 10th, 20th, and 37th Tennessee infantries, fought valiantly before being shot above the right eye. Shy's body became the focus of an iron coffin burial study 113 years after its internment when relic hunters vandalized his grave in a rural family cemetery in Tennessee. The shattered skull separated from the torso when the vandals pulled out the body, but the colonel's pink tissue was still visible and his clothing was remarkably intact. Initially believed to be a recent murder victim, the corpse was found to be a Civil War casualty in a remarkable state of preservation (and subsequently identified as Shy) by forensic scientists who analyzed the remains.

By nightfall the Confederate collapse was universal and the Southerners scrambled on the retreat. A heavy rain set in after dark and allowed Hood to collect his men and make good their escape. Wilson had to collect his mounts before a pursuit could be organized. Hood scrambled for Franklin. "The battle of Nashville is ended," recorded Pvt. Owen J. Hopkins of the 182d Ohio Infantry. "Hood's demoralized and badly whipped Rebels are flying towards the south. The victory is complete.... Thank God for the courage He has given to our army. He is a God of battles, and has again decided with justice and the right."

The casualties were relatively low for a two-day battle, but they were destructive for Hood's dwindling army nonetheless. Thomas's army consisted of about 55,000 men. Of these, 387 were killed, 2,562 wounded, and 112 missing. Confederate losses are not well known; of Hood's 30,000 men, about 1,500 were killed and wounded and 4,500 were captured. The Army of Tennessee would never fight as a formidable army again, and Hood was ruined. Many of his soldiers sang on the retreat to the tune of "The Yellow Rose of Texas," which had been sung by Hood's Texas brigade throughout the war, a song that jabbed at their own commander and longed for Joe Johnston. "And now I'm going Southward / For my heart is full of woe / I'm going back to Georgia / To find my 'Uncle Joe' / You may sing about your dearest maid / And sing of Rosalie / But the gallant Hood of Texas / Played hell in Tennessee."

THE MAJOR POLITICAL EVENT of the year transpired in the midst of the twin campaigns in Tennessee and Georgia. Despite his trepidation over being reelected, Abraham Lincoln found himself a huge winner in the polls on Tuesday, November 8. Republican candidate Lincoln and running mate Andrew Johnson received 2,330,552 popular votes; Democrat George McClellan and mate George H. Pendleton won 1,835,985, giving the Lincoln-Johnson ticket a plurality of nearly 56 percent. The electoral vote heavily favored the Republican ticket. Lincoln won 212 to McClellan's 21, who only won Delaware, New Jersey (McClellan's home state), and, ironically, Lincoln's birth state of Kentucky. "Election day was dull, gloomy, and rainy," Noah Brooks recorded of the fateful hour, "and, as if by common consent, the White House was deserted, only two members of the Cabinet attending the regular meeting of that body. . . . [On hearing good news from Indiana and from Baltimore, Lincoln] only smiled good-naturedly and said that was a fair beginning. [Later, after hearing good returns from Massachusetts and from Pennsylvania, Lincoln] looked solemn, as he seemed to see another term of office looming before him. [After hearing of a sweeping victory in New York, Lincoln said] I don't believe that. By midnight the few gentlemen in the office had had the pleasure of congratulating the President on his re-election. He took it very calmly—said that he was free to confess that he felt relieved of suspense, and was glad that the verdict of the people was so likely to be clear, full, and unmistakable." Lincoln triumphed among the soldiers, receiving 116,887 to the formerly popular McClellan's tally of 33,748. McClellan resigned from the army and wrote of the election, "For my country's sake I deplore the result."

"It has long been a grave question whether any government, not *too* strong for the liberties of its people, can be strong *enough* to maintain its own existence, in great emergencies," Lincoln said in responding to a postelection serenade at the Executive Mansion. "We can not have free government without elections; and if the rebellion could force us to forego, or postpone a national election, it might fairly claim to have already conquered and ruined us."

Lincoln had been reelected decisively but with an increasing air of risk in the capital city as the foundation of the Confederacy began to shudder. "I regret that you do not appreciate what I have repeatedly said to you in regard to the proper police arrangements connected with your household and your own personal safety," Lincoln's friend and bodyguard Ward Hill Lamon warned on December 10. "You are in danger. . . . To-night, as you have done on several occasions, you went unattended to the theatre. When I say unattended, I mean that you went along with Charles Sumner and a foreign minister, neither of whom could defend himself against an assault from any able-bodied woman in this city. And you know, or ought to know, that your life is sought after, and will be taken unless you and your friends are cautious for you [have] many enemies within our lines." A month after the election, Lincoln effectively removed one of his chief critics in the cabinet by naming Salmon P. Chase chief justice of the U.S. Supreme Court, succeeding Roger B. Taney, who had died.

Lincoln continued to grieve over the war and its daily cost in lives and goods. In late November he wrote the famous "Bixby letter," often quoted as one of his most sensitive missives. "I have been shown in the files of the War Department a statement of the Adjutant General of Massachusetts, that you are the mother of five sons who have died gloriously on the field of battle," Lincoln wrote Mrs. Lydia Bixby of Boston on November 21. "I feel how weak and fruitless must be any words of mine which should attempt to beguile you from the grief of a loss so overwhelming. But I cannot refrain from tendering to you the consolation that may be found in the thanks of the Republic they died to save. I pray that our Heavenly Father may assuage the anguish of your bereavement, and leave you only the cherished memory of the loved and lost, and the solemn pride that must be yours, to have laid so costly a sacrifice upon the altar of Freedom." The letter has been bathed in some controversy because the original was never found, only forgeries (amid claims that John Hay may have actually composed the letter), but the transcript was published contemporaneously in the *Boston Transcript,* and so the authorship appears to have been genuinely Lincoln's. The circumstances of the sons were confused within the Adjutant General's Office records, however: two sons were killed, Sgt. Charles N. Bixby and Pvt. Oliver C. Bixby, while Pvt. George W. Bixby was captured and either deserted or died in prison, Pvt. Edward Bixby deserted, and Cpl. Henry C. Bixby was discharged a month after the letter was written.

A day before the national election, the Confederate Congress met in Richmond to open its second (and last) session. President Davis, in his message, was adopting the tone that many Southerners now held, one of unrealistic optimism. "There are no vital points on the preservation of which the continued existence of the Confederacy depends," he said of the fall of Atlanta. Davis suggested that the Confederate government purchase slaves for employment in the army (but not yet as soldiers), a notion so shocking to many Southern citizens and legislators that it shouted desperation through the otherwise calm rhetoric. Davis repeated earlier declarations that the Confederacy would stand for a negotiated peace with the North only if the terms included independence as a nation. Of the Confederate situation, diarist Mary Chesnut could only record, "Through the deep waters we wade."

THE MILITARY SITUATION ground on. On November 25, a day when military actions flared in such remote locations as Adobe Wells, Texas, Confederate agents attempted to burn New York City. After plotting the operation in Canada, the terrorists set fire to ten hotels and to P. T. Barnum's Museum. "The bottles of Greek fire having been wrapped in paper were put in our coat pockets," explained John W. Headley, one of the agents. "Each man took ten bottles. . . . I reached the Astor House . . . after lighting the gas jet I hung the bedclothes loosely on the headboard and piled the chairs, drawers of the bureau and washstand on the bed. Then stuffed some newspapers about among the mass and poured a bottle of turpentine over it all. . . . I opened a bottle carefully and quickly and spilled it on the pile of rubbish. It blazed up instantly and the whole bed seemed to be in flames, before I could get out." The fires were handled quickly, however, and amounted to little damage. Few Copperhead supporters of the Confederate agents helped; one of the agents, R. C. Kennedy, was later hanged for setting the Barnum fire.

Four days later one of the American tragedies of the war unfolded at Sand Creek in Colorado Territory. Arapaho and Cheyenne Indians had for months been taking advantage of the sparse U.S. troops in the Denver area by committing numerous acts of violence against citizens, raiding and plundering. In September, Maj. Edward Wynkoop arranged a peace meeting between the territorial governor, John Evans, and the chiefs, but before the meeting took place Maj. Gen. Samuel R. Curtis declared that no peace could be established before the Indians had been punished for their previous acts.

Some 500 to 1,000 members of the two tribes were encamped along Sand Creek, some forty miles northeast of Fort Lyon, in late November. Col. John M. Chivington brought 950 troopers of the 3d Colorado Cavalry, 1st Colorado Cavalry, and 1st New Mexico Cavalry toward the camp in reprisal against the Indians. At sunrise on November 29, Chivington's men surrounded the camp, captured the ponies, and trained two cannon on the Indians, most of whom were sleeping. Black Kettle, chief of the Cheyenne, raised the U.S. flag to signal peace, but that was ignored and the troopers opened fire with cannon and small arms. A chaotically organized line of battle of some of the Indians collapsed after a short time from the overwhelming fire-power of Chivington's men; 400 to 600 Indians were killed, including many women and children. "The Cheyennes didn't get their lands," reported Capt. Silas Soulé of the 1st Colorado. "Or food. Or justice. What they got was slaughtered. . . . The governor sent out Colonel Chivington and a regiment of Hundred Daysers just to kill the ones that camped under our protection down at Sandy Creek. . . . The colonel cried out for vengeance, said he'd string up any son-of-a-bitch who'd bury their bodies or their bones." Sand Creek marked one of the darkest hours of the war. Ultimately, it cost Chivington his career.

In the Carolinas the final Confederate port, Wilmington, was still open. To cut off the Confederacy from the rest of the world, Grant ordered a combined operation to close the port to blockade runners. The army and navy would work together to assault Fort Fisher, the principal stronghold commanding the city's approaches. The plan had originated in the autumn of 1864 but was postponed until Wilmington's defenses were weakened by some of its troops shifting to meet the threat of Sherman's march. The attack group would consist of Maj. Gen. Benjamin F. Butler's Army of the James and a flotilla of sixty ships commanded by Rear Adm. David Dixon Porter. Grant preferred the land attack force be commanded by a fellow Ohioan and subordinate of Butler's, Maj. Gen. Godfrey Weitzel, but Butler demanded to lead the troops himself. Grant acquiesced.

Fort Fisher and its attendant land, Confederate Point, would prove a formidable target even with considerable firepower. The sprawling and heavily gunned earthwork was termed the "Gibraltar of the Confederacy" and contained more than 50 heavy cannon, including 15 heavy Columbiads and a 150-pounder Armstrong gun; the fort's 60-foot-high mound of earth near the sea face was termed the Mound Battery, and other strong points included Battery Buchanan, which commanded the Cape Fear River, and a network of bombproofs, most of which were 30 feet high along the 10-foot parapet. The fort encompassed 14,500 square feet altogether, and many obstructions were laid all around it, including land torpedoes (mines), abatis, and deep ditches. The fort's garrison, commanded by Col. William Lamb, consisted of 1,400 men. Faced with an invasion, reinforcements came from Gen. Braxton Bragg, who sent a supporting force that reached Sugar Loaf, four miles from the garrison.

Butler's plan was to soften the defenses with a naval bombardment and deliver the army troops onto the shore, where they would quickly overwhelm the beleaguered defenders. As was normally the case, Butler included an odd twist, which was loading a barge with 235 tons of black powder and exploding it on the beach near the fort by using timed fuzes. Butler failed to properly coordinate the timing with Porter, however, so that when Butler's troops departed Fort Monroe and arrived in North Carolina, Porter was nowhere to be found. When Porter arrived from Beaufort, the troops were so seasick and depleted of supplies that the expedition had to be reorganized at Beaufort.

On Christmas Eve 1864 the operation finally got underway. Porter's naval action commenced; he launched the explosive barge without Butler, and it completely failed, exploding 800 yards from the fort in a deafening crash that succeeded only in raining sand on everyone in the entire area. Butler, meanwhile, learned that Bragg had been joined by a force under Maj. Gen. Robert F. Hoke. The naval bombardment went seemingly well, pummeling the fort for twelve hours, and by 2 P.M. on Christmas Day, 2,200 of Butler's men landed to storm the fort. The advanced unit, Col. Newton M. Curtis's brigade, captured a 300-man unit of young boys outside the parapets and briefly seized the fort's colors near the wall but had to fall back under heavy cannon and small-arms fire from the still healthy garrison. Weitzel recommended aborting the mission, which Butler did by late afternoon. Butler had been ordered to lay siege to the fort if he could not carry it; when Butler retreated and informed Grant that he had done the right thing, the Union general in chief was so outraged that he replaced him as commander of the Army of the James with Maj. Gen. Edward O. C. Ord, and renewed the plan to attack Fort Fisher under Maj. Gen. Alfred H. Terry.

As THE MEN TRIED to stay warm, camped all across the American landscape in this final winter of the war, the sense that it all would be over soon emerged throughout most of the armies. In the Federal armies all hoped for a return to normalcy. In the Southern camps a great religious revival helped to enable the men to cope with what appeared to be oncoming defeat. Men on both sides embraced a new song that had been popularized during 1864 and seemed to symbolize the grim memories of the war and unknown future that lay ahead. Written by Walter Kittredge, the song was "Tenting Tonight on the Old Campground." Its familiar bars echoed cross the camps: "We're tenting tonight on the old campground / Give us a song to cheer / Our weary hearts, a song of home / And friends we love so dear / Many are the hearts that are weary tonight / Wishing for the war to cease / Many are the hearts looking for the right / To see the dawn of peace / Tenting tonight, tenting tonight / Tenting on the old campground."

Fall of the Last Confederate Port

As New Year's Day 1865 dawned, it was clear the war would soon come to an end. Hopes still hung high among the Confederate troops and civilians, but this reflected serious denial among those who believed the Confederacy could fight on for long. Reelected by a commanding majority, Lincoln now looked forward to implementing his Reconstruction policies and easing the rebelling states back into the United States. Lincoln preferred to welcome the states back with minimal disruption: radical Republicans looked to "wave the bloody shirt" and punish the states in rebellion. Congress also looked toward trying again to pass the Thirteenth Amendment, abolishing slavery, after its initial defeat. Militarily, the country was hauntingly quiet during the first two months of the year. The siege at Petersburg ground on with minor and sporadic actions; Sherman, at Savannah, looked to launch a campaign into the Carolinas. Federal troops occupied the Shenandoah Valley. Thomas had his large army intact in Tennessee. Conversely, Lee's army and the civilians in Petersburg were running low on supplies; the Army of Tennessee had been largely crushed and was unable to operate in major movements. The Union army and navy would no doubt renew combined operations to capture Wilmington, North Carolina, and presumably would move on Mobile in the west.

The armies changed relatively little during the final months of the war. At the end of 1864 the U.S. army aggregate strength stood at 959,460, with 620,924 present for duty. By the end of major military operations, on May 1, 1865, the army's strength was 1,000,516, with 797,807 present for duty. The strength of the Confederate army at the outset of 1865 was reportedly 439,675; the "last reports" figure as the war collapsed around them was 358,692. Changes in the command structure were few. In February the U.S.

Office of the Commissary General of Prisoners was restored to a single unit under the authority of Bvt. Brig. Gen. William Hoffman. In March, Congress established the Bureau of Refugees, Freedmen, and Abandoned Lands to handle problems associated with the military aspects of Reconstruction. Maj. Gen. Oliver O. Howard was assigned as the first commissioner. More changes occurred in Confederate organization. The spotlight swung fully onto Robert E. Lee. Having commanded only the Army of Northern Virginia up until now, Lee was on January 31 named general-in-chief of all Confederate armies. In February, Brig. Gen. Douglas H. Cooper assumed command of the Bureau of Indian Affairs. The same month, Brig. Gen. Isaac M. St. John took command of the Subsistence Department, leaving the Bureau of Nitre and Mining to Col. Richard Morton. In March, Maj. Gen. Daniel Ruggles took charge of the Bureau of Prison Camps; the following month Col. William Norris assumed command of the Bureau of Prisoner Exchange.

In the South all hopes now seemed to fall on Lee. "Doubtless Lee could protract the war," observed the war clerk John B. Jones, "and, by concentrating farther South, embarrass the enemy by compelling him to maintain a longer line of communication by land and by sea. Lee could have an army of 100,000 effective men for years." Most took a more realistic view, however. "I presume you have heard all the bad news that was on hand about a week ago about Sherman's taking Savannah and Hood's defeat in Tenn.," lamented Lt. Col. David Pierson of the 3d Louisiana Infantry. "It was the worst of the war, and spread gloom and dismay hereabouts. Men of sense and position were freely talking on the streets of our being whipped. Such has never been the case before. . . . If something is not done, and that speedily, all must be lost." The hardships of Confederate life were reflected by Emma LeConte in Columbia, South Carolina, who wrote about raising money at a Confederate bazaar. "Everything to eat can be had if one can pay the price—cakes, jellies, creams, candies—every kind of sweets abound," the 17-year-old confided. "A small slice of cake is two dollars—a spoonful of Charlotte Russe five dollars, and other things in proportion. Some beautiful imported wax dolls, not more than twelve inches high, raffled for five hundred dollars, and one very large doll I heard was to raffle for two thousand. 'Why,' as Uncle John says, 'one could buy a live negro baby for that.' "

The military situation for the Confederacy was growing so desperate that former slaveholders considered arming blacks. Lee suggested that emancipation was inevitable because the Confederacy could not expect slaves to fight for prospective freedom when they could get it at once by going to the enemy. Coming from Lee, the shocking idea received serious consideration. But few embraced it immediately. "You cannot make soldiers of slaves, nor slaves of soldiers," wrote Maj. Gen. Howell Cobb, who had once almost become president of the Confederacy. "If slaves will make good soldiers, our whole theory of slavery is wrong—but they won't make soldiers." As the situation grew ever more desperate, a conscription bill for black soldiers was introduced into the Confederate Senate on March 13, 1865, but was never effected. Contrary to some postwar claims that black soldiers fought for the Confederacy, they did no such thing; a few black "troops" drilled in the mostly empty streets of Richmond the day the city fell to Federal troops. That was as close as black Americans ever came to fighting as armed, conscripted Confederate soldiers.

Lee had more immediate problems to contend with, such as supplies, pay, and morale. "Every citizen who prevents a carbine or pistol from remaining unused will render a service to his country," he wrote in an appeal to the farmers of Virginia at the end of January. "Those who think to retain arms for their own defence should remember that if the army cannot protect them, the arms will be of little use." Three days later he wrote a circular to his commanders. "An impression seems to prevail among officers that the non payment of the troops proceeds from neglect . . . every effort has been made, and is now being made, to provide the necessary funds," the general-in-chief explained. "The delay arises from the legislation that has been found necessary to prevent the currency in which the troops are paid from becoming worthless, and it is better that they should wait for their pay, if by so doing, the money will be worth more, when they receive it."

The crumbling Confederate situation was the subject of endless speculation in the North. "The thinner ranks of the rebel armies show no signs of recuperation," Charles Francis Adams wrote his son and namesake. "Their paper money is dear at the price of old rags, for it does not pay for the making. And the heart that upheld them is gone. This stage of the disease cannot last any great length of time." Lincoln's Northern critics advised him to end the war as decisively as possible, with military conquest. Oddly, some of Lincoln's Southern critics began to show glimpses of backhanded respect. "Blackguard and buffoon as he is," editorialized the *Charleston Mercury,* "he has pursued his end with an energy as untiring as an Indian and a singleness of purpose that might almost be called patriotic."

IN 1861, OLIVER WENDELL HOLMES had said that if all the medical material then in use could be sunk to the bottom of the sea "it would be all the better for mankind and the worse for the fishes." This underscores one of the great tragedies of timing in the American Civil War. The understanding of disease was two steps behind the greatest explosion of disease and battlefield wounds the world had yet seen in warfare. Thus, thousands died from poor treatment, lack of treatment, or what now seems an almost medieval lack of understanding of medical science. Progress in medical and microbiological theory occurred right on the eve of the firing at Sumter. Prior to 1861 some microbes were known, but they were thought to occur from spontaneous generation, and most diseases were believed to be caused by "ill vapours" arising from the ground. Clearly, with soldiers sleeping on the ground throughout the war, with poor sanitary conditions, tainted food, and infrequent bathing, the medical departments of both armies knew they were in for a challenge. They were correct, but they were only beginning to understand why.

In 1861 the French scientist Louis Pasteur demonstrated that microorganisms are present in the air but do not generate from the air itself. It wasn't until 1864 that he developed Pasteurization and with it the "germ theory" of disease, that microbes themselves can cause illness. This led to Lister's experiments with phenol as a chemical that would kill bacteria. The new discoveries came too late to be utilized in Civil War medicine and surgery. Diseases caused by bacteria, viruses, fungi, and protozoa and other parasites devastated soldiers in the field and sailors at sea.

The most reliable reports indicate that deaths in the U.S. Army totaled 361,538. Of these, 67,058 soldiers (19 percent) were killed in action and 43,012 (12 percent) were mortally wounded. Some 224,586 men, however, died of disease—62 percent. Another 24,872 (7 percent) died of other known causes and 2,010 of unspecified causes. Confederate numbers are far less well known; records indicated about 94,000 battle deaths and about 166,000 other deaths (although Confederate losses may have been 10 to 40 percent underreported). Although many records are known to be missing, total deaths on both sides amounted to at least 621,538 dead (623,000 is a number often cited) during the war—a number approximately equal to the American deaths in all other wars combined.

As we have seen, the majority of deceased Civil War soldiers died from disease, and the commonest afflictions were diarrhea (and dysentery), measles, malaria, smallpox, bronchitis, pneumonia, influenza, scurvy, "camp itch," and "camp fever" produced by a wide range of microbes. A chronically poor diet, poor sanitary conditions (it took months for armies to learn to place latrines downriver from fellow troops, for example), poor weather, infrequent bathing, and parasitic insects fostered the majority of problems. Vast numbers of hospitals were established throughout the land and aid stations sprang up alongside battlegrounds as casualties mounted. Diseases were treated in a variety of ways with a spectrum of primitive chemicals; diarrhea, for example, most often required astringents or purgatives—often highly toxic substances containing compounds of silver, mercury, lead, bismuth, copper, antimony, or arsenic—that may have afforded some temporary relief for the original symptoms as they slowly poisoned the patients. "Blue mass," for example, contained mercury and chalk and was often used as a bowel treatment, while other diseases such as the flu called for bleeding to purge the offending vapors from the bloodstream. Such treatment, of course, weakened the patients and sometimes killed them. Opium and quinine were used for treating a wide range of ailments, and scurvy was understood and treated with fruit when available.

Within hospitals, doctors and nurses sometimes quarantined patients to limit the spread of some diseases, such as measles and smallpox. Though they did not understand the mechanism, physicians knew that somehow these diseases were communicable. Early vaccines were administered for some diseases. In the field and in hospitals, pests such as lice were omnipresent; delousing operations had to be conducted continuously. Alcohol became a preferred drug not only for the healthy but for the sick, and it sometimes did replace ether or chloroform for surgical operations, as in the celebrated images of men screaming under minimal anesthetic as they lost a limb to amputation. Whiskey and brandy, the most abundant and potent sources of ethyl alcohol, played a significant role in Civil War medicine, primarily as marginally effective analgesics and sedatives.

A small number of men influenced Civil War medicine and surgery. Surg. Gens. William A. Hammond (U.S.) and Samuel P. Moore (C.S.) were relatively ineffective as administrators; Maj. Jonathan Letterman, chief medical officer of the Army of the Potomac, helped to revolutionize the field by organizing patient care strictly and issuing well-stocked medical wagons to each brigade. Among the onboard drugs were chloroform, ether, opium, morphine, alcohols, turpentine, acids, castor oil, digitalis, and calomel. Field surgeons and doctors carried small amounts of these compounds with their surgical and medical kits. Southern officers had to rely on substances they could receive through the blockade, and consequently Confederate soldiers were more likely to endure wounds or sickness without much treatment.

Given the state of medical knowledge and the often limited supplies, Civil War medicine was a relative disaster, at least measured by the standards of a decade or two later. But at least the vast numbers of patients afforded doctors, nurses, and surgeons an incredibly wide testing ground on which to practice medicine and surgery. Unfortunately, the inescapable conclusion is that wounded soldiers often would have been better off without any treatment—even with a lead ball remaining in them, with its potential toxic effects. The first thing that happened at aid stations was typically that a cotton rag was applied to the wound—often producing the infections that killed more victims than the bullets. "We operated in old blood-stained and often pus-stained coats," recalled the surgeon W. W. Kean years later. "If a sponge or instrument fell onto the floor it was washed and squeezed in a basin of tap water and used as if it were clean."

The record of Civil War medicine and surgery is preserved in the 5,579 pages of *The Medical and Surgical History of the War of the Rebellion,* a landmark work in the history of medicine. Containing the case histories of thousands of soldiers, the work provides an unequaled view of the era; indeed, many of the specimens discussed, carefully identified and preserved, still reside in the Army Medical Museum outside Washington.

The volumes' summary of wounds and case histories show that 246,712 cases of wounds from weapons were treated during the war. Of these, 245,790 were gunshot wounds and only 922 (0.37 percent) bayonet wounds. Of the gunshot wounds, probably 5.5 percent were caused by artillery and 94 percent by small-arms fire. This demonstrates the extreme rarity of bayonet charges and hand-to-hand combat. The gunshot wounds were inflicted as follows: 26,400 in the head, face, and neck (10.7 percent); 45,184 in the torso, including the spine, chest, abdomen, pelvis, and back (18.4 percent); 87,793 in the upper extremities (35.7 percent); and 86,413 in the lower extremities (35.2 percent). These numbers probably say something not only about the relative surface areas of the body, but also about the soldier's adage to "aim low" to avoid overshooting and also to avoid exposing the torso and head to fire whenever possible.

The study's case histories form a powerful testament to the resilience of the human body. Cpl. Edson D. Bemis (12th Massachusetts Infantry), for example, was wounded thrice and survived the war. At Antietam he was shot in the left elbow, at the Wilderness a ball penetrated his abdomen, and at Hatcher's Run in February 1865 he was shot in the left temple. The third missile "entered a little outside of the left frontal protuberance, and passing backward and upward, removed a piece of the squamous portion of the temporal bone, with brain substance and membranes." When the patient entered hospital, "brain matter was oozing from the wound." Treatment consisted of removing the ball, after which the patient improved. Only light dressings were applied and after ten days of rest Bemis strengthened markedly. Although his "mental pulsations" could be felt through the thinly healed plate of skin, Bemis recovered and by 1870 could write "I am still in the land of the living. . . . My memory is affected, and I cannot hear as well as I could before I was wounded."

Gunshot wounds of the face led to some of the earliest plastic surgeries in America. Pvt. Roland Ward (4th New York Heavy Artillery) suffered a facial wound from a shell fragment at Reams's Station, Virginia, in August 1864. The fragment carried away the inferior maxillary bone, chin, and all but three teeth. Admitted to hospital in Washington, Ward improved slowly and in January 1865 underwent an operation to construct a floor for his mouth, without anesthesia. A series of flaps were constructed to attempt to reconstruct a normal face, and constant problems with evacuating saliva were encountered. In April 1865 another operation was made and the patient had a reconstructed face, albeit one without an apparent chin and with tightly sewn flaps converging into a point just below the mouth. Ward was then able to eat normally and articulate words, and a rubber button sewn into the wound prevented salival leakage.

Of course, wounds to the extremities often produced life-threatening infections. When soft tissue was mangled, bones were splintered, or gangrene threatened, amputation was often deemed the only possible course of action. Gunshot injuries caused 5,456 amputations of the arm and 5,452 of the leg, among other types. Numerous methods of extracting tissue and bone and tying flaps of skin to heal a stump were attempted, and such casualties created a small cottage industry in early artificial limbs. Mortality rates were high: in one group of 54 patients whose upper arms were amputated due to hemorrhage or gangrene, 60 percent died following the operation. Leg amputations were also highly risky. Pvt. W. J. Jones (33d Mississippi Infantry), for example, was wounded at Peachtree Creek in July 1864 and his left leg was amputated two days later. Four months later he was captured at Franklin, Tennessee, and subsequently admitted to a U.S. hospital at Louisville. Although his stump healed well, weakness and poor diet led to diarrhea, of which he died in December 1864.

The chronic diseases were the real killers. Pvt. Gibson Snodgrass (18th Kentucky Infantry) was a typical victim. Admitted to Hospital No. 9 in Louisville in May 1863, Snodgrass was suffering from chronic diarrhea, which had become dysenteric. He had free discharges of blood and mucous. The patient was emaciated. With poor food available and being unable to eat well due to weakness and dehydration, Snodgrass grew suddenly worse in late May, with thin, yellowish secretions. He began to vomit bile and died on June 7. An autopsy found the patient's intestinal tract was much ulcerated and that his stomach held bile and mucous. Such was the unhappy route by which many young Americans exited the Civil War.

THOUSANDS OF SOLDIERS spread across the Petersburg front still braved the cold winter. Though Grant had made little progress through the winter, Confederate hopes were dwindling. "[Grant's] present force is so superior to ours," Lee wrote Jefferson Davis on January 29, "that if he is reinforced to any extent, I do not see how in our present position he can be prevented from enveloping Richmond." Among the inactivity of the lines, work on the poorly conceived Dutch Gap Canal, imagined by Ben Butler as a great help in maneuvering upriver to attack Drewry's Bluff, continued. Construction on the canal, mostly accomplished by black troops from the Army of the James, continued until December 30, 1864; the next day the bulkhead on the northern side of the canal was excavated by exploding six tons of black powder. Work continued on the canal afterward to finish it and would linger until April, when it would be too late to be of any help.

Skirmishing flared at Dabney's Mill along Hatcher's Run on January 7 but amounted to little. On January 23 a minor naval action occurred at Fort Brady as eleven Confederate ships attempted to maneuver to pass downriver and attack the Union flotilla. After a short action four of the ships ran aground and nothing came of the expedition. As the war seemed to stagger toward a conclusion, on January 31 the U.S. House of Representatives passed the Thirteenth Amendment, abolishing slavery. The Senate had approved it long before. Two-thirds of the states would now be required to approve. Three days later came the Hampton Roads Peace Conference, aboard the USS *River Queen*. Confederate peace commissioners had long wanted the chance to discuss "terms" of peace. While Lincoln embraced a policy of unconditional surrender, he finally accepted the chance to talk, semiofficially, with Vice President Alexander H. Stephens, Assistant Secretary of War John A. Campbell, and Senator and former Secretary of State Robert M. T. Hunter. Accompanying Lincoln was Secretary of State William H. Seward.

The Confederates originally wanted to come to the Executive Mansion but were stopped at Fort Monroe. Lincoln made clear that recognition of the national authority of the United States within those states in rebellion was paramount. Stephens and his comrades suggested a combined movement of all the states against Maximilian in Mexico; Lincoln objected because the "Confederate States of America" legally did not exist and could not be recognized. Stephens suggested an armistice, but again Lincoln said this was not possible until there was a restoration of the United States. Stymied by the refusal of Lincoln to offer what they wanted, Stephens and friends left without preventing the probability of unconditional subjugation. The talks had been friendly, however, as Lincoln and Stephens were old acquaintances. The meeting at least accomplished the exchange of Stephens's nephew. "According to our agreement your nephew, Lieut. Stephens, goes to you bearing this note," Lincoln wrote a week later. "Please, in return, to select and send to me, that officer of the same rank imprisoned at Richmond whose physical condition most urgently requires his release."

Grant and Meade's 1865 campaign against Richmond and Petersburg began on February 5 when the general-in-chief sent Brig. Gen. David M. Gregg's cavalry against the Confederate wagon trains moving along the Boydton Plank Road. The Federal horsemen moved south via Reams's Station toward Dinwiddie Court House; infantry support for the movement came from Humphreys's 2d Corps, which established a position along Hatcher's Run near the Vaughan Road, and from Warren's 5th Corps, which established a line to the south at Monk's Neck. Cold weather and drizzle impeded the movements but succeeded in extending the Union line farther south against Lee's overstretched lines. The actions, collectively termed the battle of Hatcher's Run (the fifth such action), Dabney's Mill, Armstrong's Mill, Rowanty Creek, Vaughan Road, and Boydton Plank Road, lasted from February 5 to 7.

Confederate commanders sent troops out to meet the Federal movement along a few positions, but their musketry fire was ineffective. Gregg moved southward, captured prisoners, and moved back. On the morning of February 6 he withdrew into Warren's lines. Heavy action on this day ensued along Humphreys's line, where at 5 P.M. Maj. Gen. William Mahone's division struck hard into the position from a distance of about 1,000 yards, his men firing wildly and with reckless abandon. The brunt of the attack was stopped by the hard-fighting division of Brig. Gen. Thomas A. Smyth. To the south, Warren's men moved out toward Gravelly Run and Dabney's Mill about 1 P.M. and were soon attacked savagely by Brig. Gen. John Pegram's division. In the attack Pegram was struck in the chest and killed.

The fighting along Hatcher's Run ended as the Yankees withdrew from the Boydton Plank Road but fortified their lines along Hatcher's Run near the Vaughan Road. The Confederates' ranks were now stretched even thinner. Federal casualties for the three days amounted to 170 killed, 1,160 wounded, and 182 missing of 35,000 engaged; of the 14,000 Confederates active, the casualties are not known. Lee remained stubborn and religiously fatalistic: "The advantages of the enemy will have but little value if we do not permit them to impair our resolution," he declared in General Orders No. 2, on February 14. "Let us then oppose constancy to adversity, fortitude to suffering, and courage to danger, with the firm assurance that He who gave freedom to our fathers will bless the efforts of their children to preserve it."

As the Richmond campaign developed, Brig. Gen. Thomas L. Rosser launched a raid into West Virginia with 300 cavalrymen. Commencing on January 11 at Beverly, the raiders captured 580 Union troops and large amounts of supplies. Rosser continued the raid to Moorefield on January 29, stampeding a supply train there and capturing its 95 wagons after scattering 350 infantrymen. On February 1, at Patterson's Creek, Rosser's men captured 1,200 cattle, 500 sheep, and 80 Yankees. Such victories cheered the Confederates but were minor in light of the crumbling war effort.

WINTER CONDITIONS did not stop Maj. Gen. William T. Sherman from leading his army in a campaign focused on the Carolinas. Following his March to the Sea, Sherman began to see his place in history. "I do think that in the several grand epochs of this war, my name will have a prominent part," he predicted from Savannah on January 5. "And not least among them will be the determination I took at Atlanta to destroy that place, and march on this city, whilst Thomas, my lieutenant, should dispose of Hood." Hearing of a bill introduced into Congress to make Sherman a lieutenant general, the Ohioan confided to his foster brother Philemon Ewing, "I have written to John [Sherman] not to allow it, but to say in Committee I would not accept as it might cause a rivalry—not with us individually but on the part of mischievous friends. Again it is proposed to make the rank of General for Grant & me for Lt. General. This too I oppose. We began the war with our present system and should not alter it now."

Skirmishing occurred at Hardeeville, South Carolina, on January 1. While Sherman prepared to move his army, striking into the hated birthplace of the rebellion, a major combined operation focused again on Fort Fisher. On January 4, Federal troops departed Bermuda Hundred, this time commanded by Maj. Gen. Alfred H. Terry, the Connecticut attorney who had become one of the most competent citizen-soldiers of the war. Terry's 8,000-man force, named Terry's Provisional Corps, was a mixed unit that eventually formed the core of the consolidated 10th Corps; it was assembled from Col. Joseph C. Abbott's brigade, Brig. Gen. Adelbert Ames's division, and Brig. Gen. Charles J. Paine's division of black troops. The corps had 4 field guns and siege artillery comprising 24 guns and 20 mortars. The naval armada, one of the most impressive assembled during the war, consisted of 60 ships mounting 627 guns of the North Atlantic Blockading Squadron, commanded by Rear Adm. David Dixon Porter.

The armada rendezvoused off Beaufort, North Carolina, and proceeded to the area of Fort Fisher by January 12. The peninsula on which Fort Fisher stood was again reinforced by Gen. Braxton Bragg, who sent Maj. Gen. Robert F. Hoke with his division of 6,000 infantry and cavalry to prevent a landing of army troops; within the fort, Maj. Gen. William H. C. Whiting reinforced Col. William Lamb's garrison, bringing the total to 1,800 men manning 47 guns. "The object is to lodge the shell in the parapets, and tear away the traverses under which the bombproofs are located," Porter instructed his gunners before the bombardment began. "A shell now and then exploding over a gun en barbette may have a good effect, but there is nothing like lodging the shell before it explodes."

Shortly after midnight on January 13 the Federal ships blazed forth with a stunning bombardment, sending the garrison inside the fort huddling and responding as best they could. By 4 A.M., transports moved close to the island and began landing troops. The bombardment continued unabated as the soldiers dug in. "There would be two puffs of blue smoke about the size of a thunder cloud in June," recalled Augustus C. Buell, a Federal soldier, "and then I could see the big shell make a black streak through the air with a tail of white smoke behind it—and then would come over the water, not the quick bark of a field gun, but a slow, quivering, overpowering roar like an earth-

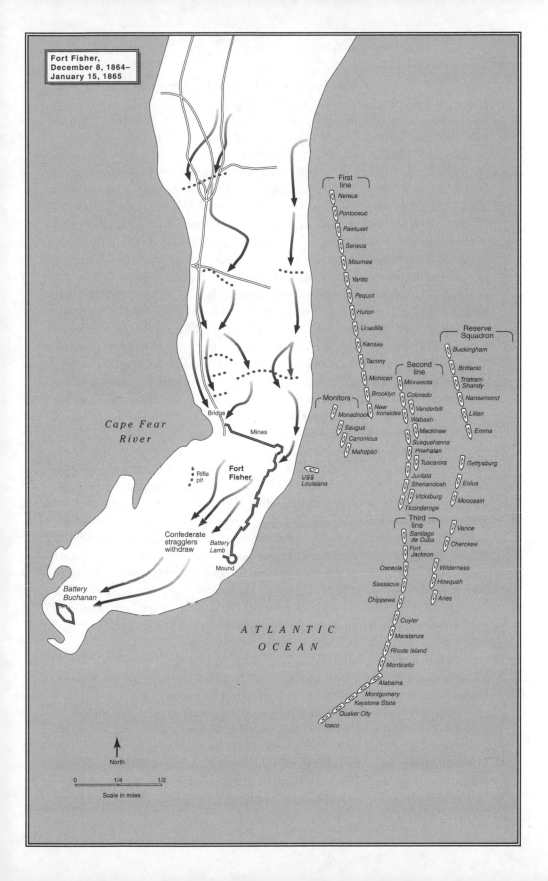

Fort Fisher,
December 8, 1864–
January 15, 1865

First
line
Nereus
Pontoosuc
Pawtuxet
Seneca
Maumee
Yantic
Pequot
Huron
Unadilla
Kansas
Tacony
Mohican
Brooklyn
New
Ironsides

Reserve
Squadron
Buckingham
Brittanic
Tristram
Shandy
Nansemond
Lilian
Emma

Second
line
Minnesota
Colorado
Vanderbilt
Wabash
Mackinaw
Susquehanna
Powhatan
Tuscarora
Juniata
Shenandoah
Vicksburg
Ticonderoga

Monitors
Monadnock
Saugus
Canonicus
Mahopac

Gettysburg
Eolus
Moccasin

Cape Fear
River

Bridge

Mines

Rifle
pit

Fort
Fisher

USS
Louisiana

Third
line
Santiago
de Cuba
Fort
Jackson
Osceola
Sassacus
Chippewa
Cuyler
Maratanza
Rhode Island
Monticello
Alabama
Montgomery
Keystone State
Quaker City
Iosco

Vance
Cherokee
Wilderness
Howquah
Aries

Confederate
stragglers
withdraw

Battery
Lamb

Mound

Battery
Buchanan

ATLANTIC
OCEAN

North

0   1/4   1/2

Scale in miles

quake, and then, away among the Rebel traverses, there would be another huge ball of mingled smoke and flame as big as a meeting house." By midafternoon the infantry troops had landed and approached Hoke's defensive line. As Whiting entered the fort and found Col. Lamb, he told the young man, "I have come to share your fate."

On January 14 heavy bombardment continued as the Yankee force prepared to assault the fort. Siege artillery brought ashore was placed opposite the Confederate lines, and Col. Newton M. Curtis's brigade occupied a work close to the front of Fort Fisher's parapets. Terry consolidated his force and planned an attack for January 15, in which he would send two columns of troops down the peninsula, one led by Ames and another, consisting of sailors and marines, led by naval Capt. Kidder R. Breese. At 8 A.M. on the 15th the Federal ships opened a blistering fire into the fort at point-blank range, deluging the land and sea faces of the fort with thousands of shells. By 2 P.M., 100 infantrymen from Curtis's brigade and the 13th Indiana Infantry attacked forward and dug in within 175 yards of the fort. The brigades of Cols. Galusha Pennypacker and Louis Bell moved in to support the attack. At 3:25 P.M. Curtis's brigade sprang forward, cutting through the palisades and attacking the parapets, all under a heavy, chaotic fire. It was "a terrific storm of death," recalled a Union chaplain; "the whole line was invisible, the men having, like worms, worked themselves into the sand."

Heavy, desperate, hand-to-hand fighting continued throughout the afternoon and evening. Blood mixed with sand and giant fountains of debris cascaded upward with each new shell that exploded inside the fort. Each gunpit and battery became a sought-after objective that was fought over for hours, with ghastly results. The column of marines and sailors, meanwhile, had far less success. In bloody, uncoordinated fighting, Breese's men were thrown back with heavy losses. Although it was a catastrophic failure, the attack of the marines served as an effective diversion. Lamb, who believed he had repulsed the main Federal attack, explained, "The heroic bravery of [the Union] officers . . . could not restrain the men from panic and retreat, and with small loss to ourselves, we witnessed what had never been seen before, a disorderly rout of American sailors and marines."

While leading a counterattack, Whiting was mortally wounded, struck by two balls in the right leg, and died a captive on March 10. Despite the debacle of the sailors and marines, the fort fell to U.S. forces on January 15 and the last Confederate port was closed. Union troops captured 1,971 men and 112 officers, including Lamb, who was also wounded. Union casualties were 266 killed, 1,018 wounded, and 57 missing; Confederate losses were about 500 killed and wounded. After the fort's capture and the closure of the Cape Fear River, Porter wrote: "The death knell of another fort is booming in the distance. Fort Caswell with its powerful batteries is in flames and being blown up, and thus is sealed the door through which the rebellion is fed." "We had lost our last blockade-running port," recalled Raphael Semmes, who would shortly be commissioned a rear admiral in the Confederate navy. "Our ports were now all hermetically sealed. The anaconda had, at last, wound his fatal folds around us."

Triumphant over the fort's fall, Terry and Ames still had questions to answer about the bungled attack of the naval and marine forces. "I am directed by the Committee on the Conduct of the War to request that you will direct Maj. Genl. Terry & Brig. Gen. Ames, if the exigencies of the service will permit, to appear before this committee to testify in relation to the attack on Fort Fisher," Senator Benjamin F. Wade wrote Edwin Stanton following the attack. Stanton, by now, knew how to protect his officers. He simply replied that they would be unable to leave their commands to testify. There was a war going on, after all.

The Carolinas campaign moved on. Sherman's army now consisted of three wings, the right (Army of the Tennessee) commanded by Maj. Gen. Oliver O. Howard, the center (Army of the Ohio) by Maj. Gen. John M. Schofield, and the left (Army of Georgia) by Maj. Gen. Henry W. Slocum. Howard's army contained the corps of Maj. Gen. John A. Logan (15th Corps; divisions of Maj. Gen. William B. Hazen and Brig. Gens. Charles R. Woods and John E. Smith); and Maj. Gen. Frank P. Blair, Jr. (17th Corps; divisions of Maj. Gen. Joseph A. Mower and Brig. Gens. Mortimer D. Leggett and Giles A. Smith). Schofield's army consisted of the corps of Maj. Gen. Alfred H. Terry (10th Corps; divisions of Brig. Gens. Henry W. Birge, Adelbert Ames, and Charles J. Paine); and the 23d Corps, commanded by Schofield himself until April 2 and Maj. Gen. Jacob D. Cox thereafter (divisions of Brig. Gens. Thomas H. Ruger, Nathaniel C. McLean, and James W. Reilly). Slocum's army consisted of the corps of Brig. Gen. Jefferson C. Davis (14th Corps; divisions of Brig. Gens. William P. Carlin, James D. Morgan, and Absalom Baird); and Brig. Gen. Alpheus S. Williams (20th Corps; divisions of Brig. Gens. Nathaniel J. Jackson, John W. Geary, and William T. Ward). On February 1, Sherman's armies contained 60,079 men; by April 1 the number had swelled to 88,948. Opposing Sherman in the Carolinas was the depleted Army of Tennessee, which had been so battered that Jefferson Davis determined to place Gen. Joe Johnston back in command. The force amounted to some 9,513 in mid-March and only 15,188 by mid-April, excluding several thousand cavalry. It was organized into three corps, commanded by Lt. Gen. William J. Hardee (divisions of Maj. Gens. John C. Brown, Robert F. Hoke, and Benjamin F. Cheatham); Lt. Gen. Alexander P. Stewart (divisions of Maj. Gens. William W. Loring, James Patton Anderson, and Edward C. Walthall); and Lt. Gen. Stephen D. Lee (divisions of Maj. Gens. D. H. Hill and Carter L. Stevenson).

During January and February, actions were scattered around the Carolinas. On January 19, Sherman ordered the northward march into South Carolina to begin, and the armies began to leave the area of Savannah. Sherman planned to reach Goldsborough, North Carolina, by March 15. As the men set out for the hotbed of rebellion, many sought vengeance. The birthplace of the war would receive retribution from the angry and exhausted soldiers of the North who had been brought into an unwanted war, they reasoned, by the irrational actions of a single state. The opposition to Sherman's armies would be weak.

By February 1 the Carolinas campaign was in full swing. Overcoming such road hazards as felled trees and wrecked bridges, Logan's and Blair's corps marched northward into South Carolina. Slocum's Army of Georgia encountered torpedoes buried in roads, many of which exploded, killing several soldiers. It then had difficulty crossing the flooded Savannah River at Sister's Ferry, South Carolina. But they moved on. As he had during the March to the Sea, Sherman confused the scattered enemy forces as to his destination, which was Columbia. Confederate cavalry and small units of militia—largely old men and young boys—harassed Howard's army along the Salkehatchie River on February 2. Skirmishing erupted at Lawtonville, Barker's Mill, and Duck Branch.

On February 5, as the battle of Hatcher's Run flared to the north, skirmishing erupted at Duncanville and along the Combahee River. The feeling that Wilmington was closed to the world was now starting to set in, both to those who wondered why supplies were not showing up and to those who had run the blockade so effectively for so long. "As we turned away from the land, our hearts sank within us," wrote Confederate Lt. John Wilkinson aboard the blockade runner *Chameleon*, "while the conviction forced itself upon us, that the cause for which so much blood had been shed, so many mistakes bravely endured, and so many sacrifices cheerfully made, was about to perish at last!" The following day skirmishes broke out at Cowpen Ford, near Barnwell, and at Fishburn's Plantation near Lane's Bridge on the Salkehatchie. Sherman's army, aided by Kilpatrick's cavalry, pressed northward. On February 7, actions flared at Blackville and at the Edisto River Bridge. The skirmishing, though light, was now daily. On the 8th, musketry crackled at Binnaker's Bridge along the South Edisto and at Holman's Bridge. On February 11, Sherman's men pressed along the railroad line from Midway to Johnson's Station. Confused, Confederate troops in the east (Charleston and Branchville) and west (Aiken and Augusta, Georgia) were separated. Though the Richmond authorities presumed Sherman would attack Charleston (and hoped that he could be defeated), he planned to pass it by. Beauregard's forces in Augusta amounted to nothing, and Hardee, in Charleston, readied to abandon the city. Cavalry commanded by Maj. Gen.

Wade Hampton, dispatched from Virginia, could only weakly harass the Yankees.

On February 14, Sherman's men crossed the Congaree River and moved on Columbia, not "wasting time" with Charleston, as Sherman termed it. Along the North Edisto River, skirmishes flared at Gunter's Bridge and Wolf's Plantation. The following day heavy fighting broke out along the Congaree, along Red Bank Creek, and near Lexington. There was no stopping the Yankees from entering Columbia, however. On the 16th they spotted the capital of South Carolina. Minor skirmishing erupted as Union officers with field glasses could see troops and civilians running around in confusion. A number of shells were lobbed into the city at the railroad depot and the enemy cavalry, and a few struck the capital (where bronze stars now mark the damage). By late afternoon the city was almost surrounded and Beauregard departed in haste, sending away the supplies he could quickly gather but leaving vast amounts behind.

On February 17, Columbia surrendered to Sherman after the city's mayor, T. J. Goodwyn, rode out in a carriage to meet the "invaders." Early in the morning a huge explosion rocked the railroad depot as a pillager inadvertently set off powder, blasting away an adjacent warehouse. During the night several piles of cotton bales were burned owing to one or more causes. Perhaps Union artillery fire ignited them, or they were torched by retreating Confederate troops, or both. An order prohibiting the burning of cotton was issued only at 7 A.M. on the 17th; prior to that, Confederate troops were instructed to burn the cotton rather than let it be captured. Hampton's cavalry troopers fled the scene after dawn, and mob rule took over as violence and plundering reigned through the streets. Wheeler's cavalry carried great quantities of goods with them as they left the city.

As Union troops entered Columbia, the situation spiraled even further out of control. Met by throngs of liberated Federal prisoners and emancipated blacks, the Union troops were overwhelmed. Supplies of liquor were soon found and large numbers of Federal soldiers began to drink. Though at first Federal troops assisted some local citizens in fighting fires, high winds swirled through the city and sent embers showering throughout the town, igniting roofs and supplies across a wide area. Dozens of buildings burned, mostly within a ten-by-four-block area of the central city, and chaos ruled as the city's fire companies attempted to combat the wild situation amid throngs of drunken Yankee soldiers, who were not about to risk their lives to play firefighter. "I began to-day's record early in the evening, and while writing I noticed an unusual glare in the sky," stated Capt. George Ward Nichols, of Sherman's staff, "and heard a sound of running to and fro in the streets, with the loud talk of servants that the horses must be removed to a safer place. Running out, I found, to my surprise and real sorrow, that the central part of the city, including the main business street, was in flames, while the wind, which had been blowing a hurricane all day, was driving the sparks and cinders in heavy masses over the eastern portion of the city."

The scene was shocking to residents. "At about seven o'clock I was standing on the back piazza in the third story," recorded Emma LeConte, age 17. "Before me the whole southern horizon was lit up by camp fires which dotted the woods. On one side the sky was illuminated by the burning of Gen. [Wade] Hampton's residence a few miles off in the county, on the other side by some blazing buildings near the river. I had scarcely gone downstairs again when Henry told me there was a fire on Main Street. Sumter Street was brightly lighted by a burning house so near our piazza that we could feel the heat."

The same day as the Columbia fire, Charleston was evacuated. "Charleston and Columbia have come into our possession without any hard fighting," proclaimed Navy Secretary Gideon Welles. "The brag and bluster, the threats and defiance which have been for thirty years the mental ailment of South Carolina prove impotent and ridiculous. They have displayed a talking courage, a manufactured bravery, but no more, and I think not so much inherent heroism as others."

On February 18, as the Columbia fire was burning itself out, Sherman destroyed railroad depots, warehouses, arsenals, machine shops, and other buildings of military value. As the evacuation of Charleston continued, Yankee troops reoccupied Fort Moultrie on Sullivans Island. Naval actions continued as Fort Anderson, up the Cape Fear River from Wilmington, was bombarded repeatedly and attacked by one of Cox's brigades, flanking the fort and necessitating surrender by Brig. Gen. Johnson Hagood on February 19. Hoke was ordered to abandon Wilmington shortly afterward because, as Bragg wrote, Cox's movements "rendered our continued occupation of the town very hazardous to the whole command." By February 22, Wilmington fell, the last major port of the South now completely in Union hands. Under command of Schofield, Federal troops captured the city after suffering 200 casualties. The destruction of railroads and depots continued as Williams's corps reached Rocky Mount on the Catawba River, skirmishing along their march. Heavy rains continued to plague the operations, but by February 25, Camden, South Carolina, on the Wateree River, fell to Yankee occupation. The Carolinas were rapidly coming back to the Union.

"Glory to God! Charleston has fallen! I feel like shouting *all over*," exclaimed Esther Hill Hawks, a Northern doctor working in Jacksonville, Florida. "A navy supply boat brings us the jubilant news. . . . And Columbia too, is ours. How can we thank God enough for these victories—brave Sherman and his army have reached the sea, and the war is virtually ended. The whole city is wild with excitement."

TIME FOR THE SOUTH seemed to be dwindling. "Everything looks like dissolution in the South," U. S. Grant wrote his old benefactor Elihu B. Washburne. "A few days more of success with Sherman will put us where we can crow loud." "Shame, disgrace, beggary, all at once," was all that Mary Chesnut could record. "Grand smash." Despite the gloom, Robert E. Lee labored on with the Confederate armies. He now issued words as if the words themselves could somehow stave off the inevitable. "They should be made to understand that discipline contributes no less to their safety than to their efficiency," he observed of the remaining Confederate troops on February 22. "Disastrous surprises and those sudden panics which lead to defeat and the greatest loss of life are of rare occurrence among disciplined troops. . . . Let officers and men be made to feel that they will most effectually secure their safety by remaining steadily at their posts, preserving order, and fighting with coolness and vigor." On the same day, he wrote his wife Mary Custis, declaring, "I shall . . . endeavor to do my duty and fight to the last."

On both sides families wondered when they would see their remaining sons return. Patrick Gilmore's song, published in 1863, took on a new importance. Its memorable strains echoed throughout marches everywhere across the land. "When Johnny comes marching home again, hurrah, hurrah! / We'll give him a hearty welcome then, hurrah, hurrah! / The men will cheer, the boys will shout / The ladies they will all turn out / And we'll all feel gay when Johnny comes marching home / And we'll all feel gay when Johnny comes marching home."

Lee's Army Crumbles

IT WAS NOW CLEAR to all that the end of the war was within sight. No one could foresee how and when it would be over, but the Confederacy was crumbling. Grant planned for offensive operations against an increasingly withered defensive line and a town full of bleary civilians at Petersburg; Sherman was likely to overwhelm the weak flow of troops available to counter him in the Carolinas. The Confederate war appeared to be on the precipice; Union movements would come against Mobile, and Wilmington had already been sealed as a resupply valve for the Petersburg lines. In Alabama, George Thomas's men were set to strike at the haggard veterans of Nathan Bedford Forrest and Dick Taylor.

Everyone wondered how the peace would come and what President Lincoln would do to ensure the smoothest transition to the Federal Union—this time without slavery. On March 4, Lincoln and his new vice president, Andrew Johnson, were inaugurated in Washington, and Lincoln delivered a brief, classic tenet of hope and forgiveness. "Fondly do we hope, fervently do we pray," Lincoln concluded, "that this mighty scourge of war may speedily pass away. . . . It must be said, 'The judgments of the Lord are true and righteous altogether.' With malice toward none, with charity for all, with firmness in the right as God gives us to see the right, let us strive on to finish the work we are in, to bind up the nation's wounds, to care for him who shall have borne the battle and for his widow and his orphan, to do all which may achieve and cherish a just and lasting peace among ourselves and with all nations."

The speech was brief and classic Lincoln, rich with biblical imagery, but it did not outline a policy for the acceleration of Reconstruction. Lincoln spoke more directly about the fall of slavery when he addressed the 140th Indiana Infantry at the Executive Mansion two weeks later. "Whenever [I] hear any one, arguing for slavery," Lincoln said, "I feel a strong impulse to see it tried on him personally." The Second Inaugural Address, destined to be recalled as one of Lincoln's great documents, stirred the public even if it failed to outline policy. "That rail-splitter lawyer is one of the wonders of the day," Lt. Col. Charles Francis Adams, Jr., told his father. "This inaugural strikes me in its grand simplicity and directness as being for all time the historical keynote of this war."

The vice president did not fare as well. Before Lincoln spoke, Johnson, who had consumed too much whiskey as medicine, stood at the dais and delivered a wandering, incoherent series of messages that stunned the crowd. It was not a strong beginning for a politician who had served well in Tennessee but who would be utterly lost in attempting to guide the nation through the aftermath of civil war.

In Richmond, Jefferson Davis (who had long ago lost the popular support of his countrymen) and the Confederate Congress went about their business as usual, approving a redesign of the national Confederate flag. A blend of helplessness and denial would keep the institutions in the Confederate capital operating and arguing over the best course of action to take across a wide range of subjects up until the very hour their government collapsed around them. Chaos ensued in different ways as the days passed. The debate on arming slaves as soldiers accelerated in the Confederate Senate. Not only were Confederates wracked with the religious dilemma of how a just God could allow them to lose the war, but now they were struck by internal contradictions of policy, born of desperation. On March 7, Robert M. T. Hunter of Virginia, the former Confederate secretary of state, declared, "If we are right in passing this measure [to arm slaves], we were wrong in denying to the old government the right to interfere with the institution of slavery and to emancipate slaves." On March 13 the Confederate Congress approved arming black soldiers, but the end of the war came too quickly for their entrance into the field. (Five days later the Congress adjourned, never to reconvene.) By April 1, Jefferson Davis could still write Lee, "I have been laboring without much progress to advance the raising of negro troops." By contrast, nearly 200,000 black soldiers and sailors would serve actively in the Union armies and navies before war's end.

ON THE PETERSBURG FRONT, Confederates readied for major Union assaults to strike at the besieged city and also to thrust into and capture Richmond. The Union cry "On to Richmond!" issued with such naïveté in 1861 now became a reality. The dwindling supplies and state of morale in the Confederate trenches made resistance for long seem almost impossible. The sense of desperation among Confederates was volatile; on March 2, Brig. Gen. Josiah Gorgas asserted that "people are almost in a state of desperation. . . . Lee is about all we have & what public confidence is left rallies around him, and he it seems to me fights without much heart in the cause." Yet despite continued criticism of Lee, Gorgas admitted hope three weeks later when he observed: "Lee seems entirely indisposed to send any portion of his force to the assistance of Johnston, yet 10,000 men so detached would enable Johnston to stop & perhaps overwhelm Sherman. No one can divine the reason of this inaction of Lee.... The confidence of the country is again rising. Stragglers from Johnston's army are said to be returning. Everything depends on his ability to meet Sherman."

On March 2 an engagement flared at Waynesborough, Virginia, as Sheridan's cavalry pushed south against the remains of Early's force in the Shenandoah Valley. Almost 5,000 men attacked under the command of Brig. Gen. George A. Custer, who defeated and scattered the smaller Rebel cavalry force of 2,000. Sheridan then turned toward Charlottesville as the beaten veterans of Early retreated to Richmond.

Only skirmishing characterized the month of March over the Petersburg battlefront. The Confederate high command would try one last, great push to reduce Grant and Meade in Virginia. The plan called for a final surprise assault, aimed at breaking out of the lines so that Lee could move south to join Joe Johnston. The lines at Petersburg would be held while the two major Confederate forces united, defeated Sherman, and then returned to fight Grant and Meade. Such a plan was ridiculous, even at the time, but there were no other apparent options left. With A. P. Hill disabled by his chronic problems with gonorrhea, Maj. Gen. John B. Gordon was placed in command of the attack. Gordon planned to strike at Fort Stedman, east of the city, only 150 yards beyond the Confederate line. If they penetrated the line here, Lee and Gordon reasoned, Grant would be forced to shorten his lines because the Federal communications would be endangered, thus enabling Lee to aid Johnston (or vice versa). At 4 A.M. on March 25, Gordon led the attack on the fort. Initially successful, the plunge captured Stedman and several surrounding positions, and the promise of sending Confederate cavalry through the gap seemed bright. Columns of infantry sent forward to find forts to the rear of Stedman could not find them and became confused; in reality, they didn't exist. In the fighting that ensued, a strong Union counterattack was launched by Brig. Gen. John F. Hartranft by 7:30 A.M., forcing the Rebels back into containment in Stedman and the adjacent Battery 10. Half an hour later the reinforced Yankees were launching murderous musketry and artillery fire into the position and Lee ordered a retreat, but it was too late, as about 1,900 Confederates surrendered. Casualties amounted to 4,000 Confederate and 1,044 Federal.

Two days after Fort Stedman, Lincoln went down to City Point to meet with Grant, Sherman, and Rear Adm. David Dixon Porter to discuss the im-

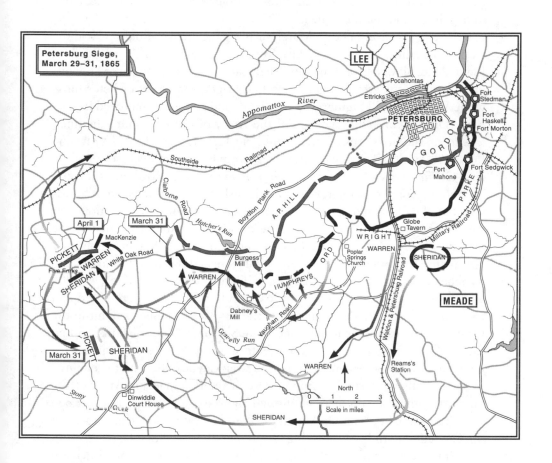

Petersburg Siege,
March 29–31, 1865

LEE

Appomattox River

Pocahontas

Ettricks

PETERSBURG

Fort Stedman

Fort Haskell
Fort Morton

GORDON

Fort Mahone

Fort Sedgwick

Southside
Railroad

PARKE

Claiborne Road

Boydton Plank Road

A. P. HILL

Hatcher's Run

Globe Tavern

Military Railroad

April 1

March 31

MacKenzie

WARREN

White Oak Road

ORD

WRIGHT

WARREN

PICKETT

Five Forks

SHERIDAN

SHERIDAN

Burgess'
Mill

Poplar
Springs
Church

WARREN

HUMPHREYS

Dabney's
Mill

Vaughan Road

Weldon & Petersburg Railroad

MEADE

PICKETT

SHERIDAN

Gravelly Run

March 31

WARREN

Reams's
Station

North

Stony

Dinwiddie
Court House

BUTLER

0   1   2   3

Scale in miles

SHERIDAN

pending end of the war. In a meeting captured by George P. A. Healy's historic painting *The Peacemakers*, Lincoln and his commanders talked for two days aboard the USS *River Queen*, the generals suggesting that one more campaign would be necessary to win the contest. Lincoln said that he wanted to grant all rights as citizens to the Rebels once they laid down arms. "I want submission and no more bloodshed," he said. "I want no one punished; treat them liberally all round. We want those people to return to their allegiance to the Union and submit to the laws."

The next action came on March 29 along the Quaker Road and had the alternative names Second Gravelly Run, Lewis Farm, and Third Boydton Plank Road. Slowed by a chilly rain, Sheridan's troopers rode out to Dinwiddie Court House, attempting to turn Lee's right, southwest of Petersburg, while Warren's and Humphreys's corps (5th and 2d Corps) marched in support. (Ord had brought a portion of the Army of the James into the lines, freeing up the two corps.) Warren sent Brig. Gen. Charles Griffin's division forward to push skirmishing parties away from Rowanty Creek, south of the city. Griffin arrived at the intersection of the Quaker Road and Gravelly Run after noon to encounter heavy skirmishing. The Yankees fought, assisted by the division of Brig. Gen. Samuel W. Crawford, to a position near Arnold's Sawmill before stopping. A fierce attack was then launched by the brigade of Brig. Gen. Joshua L. Chamberlain, which fought stubbornly against brisk Confederate musketry that ended only as the Yankees entrenched along the Boydton Plank Road. Casualties amounted to 370 killed and wounded in Warren's corps; at least 130 Confederates were killed and 200 captured. Among the wounded of the day was Chamberlain, hit in the left arm and chest. In the field Grant wrote Sheridan: "I now feel like ending the mat[ter] if it is possible to do so before going back. . . . We will act together as one Army here unt[il] it is seen what can be done with the enemy."

The following day the Union Army of the Potomac and Army of the James, together 125,000 men, intensified their actions against Lee's 57,000 men even as the rains fell. On March 30, Sheridan was poised to move against the Confederate right; skirmishing erupted on the line along Hatcher's Run and Gravelly Run and near the crossroads of Five Forks, north of Dinwiddie Court House. Lee, having detected the maneuver, sent Maj. Gen. George E. Pickett with 19,000 infantry and cavalry to Five Forks. This small and otherwise insignificant crossroads suddenly loomed large; holding it would be necessary for Lee to secure the Southside Railroad and move out to rendezvous with Johnston. Pickett, the would-be hero of Gettysburg, reemerged in the final days of the war with a very big mission.

Though the campaigns for Richmond and Petersburg were continuing, the actions that occurred between March 29 and April 1 laid the foundation for the series of events to follow, the Appomattox campaign, which would include the final pursuit of Lee. The organization of the armies, which had evolved in important ways in terms of assignments, bears another look. Grant, situated at City Point, continued to command all Federal armies. The Army of the Potomac, commanded by Maj. Gen. George G. Meade, contained the corps of Maj. Gen. Andrew A. Humphreys (2d Corps; divisions of Brig. Gens. Nelson A. Miles, William Hays, and Gershom Mott); Maj. Gen. Gouverneur K. Warren (5th Corps; divisions of Brig. Gens. Charles Griffin, Romeyn B. Ayres, and Samuel W. Crawford); Maj. Gen. Horatio G. Wright (6th Corps; divisions of Brig. Gens. Frank Wheaton, George W. Getty, and Truman Seymour); and Maj. Gen. John G. Parke (9th Corps; divisions of Brig. Gens. Orlando B. Willcox, Robert B. Potter, and John F. Hartranft). The artillery was commanded by Brig. Gen. Henry J. Hunt. The cavalry was commanded by Maj. Gen. Philip H. Sheridan (who commanded all the cavalry of the armies of the Potomac, James, and Shenandoah). The cavalry active in the campaign was that of the Army of the Shenandoah, led by Brig. Gen. Wesley Merritt. His division commanders were Brig. Gens. Thomas C. Devin and George A. Custer and Maj. Gen. George Crook). The Army of the James was commanded by Maj. Gen. Edward O. C. Ord and consisted of the Defenses of Bermuda Hundred (Maj. Gen. George L. Hartsuff) and the corps of Maj. Gen. John Gibbon (24th Corps; divisions of Brig. Gens. Robert S. Foster, Charles Devens, Jr., and John W. Turner); and Maj. Gen. Godfrey Weitzel (25th Corps; divisions of Brig. Gens. August V. Kautz and William Birney); and a cavalry division commanded by Brig. Gen. Ranald S. Mackenzie.

Lee now commanded all the Confederate armies but retained titular command of the Army of Northern Virginia. The army consisted of the corps of Lt. Gen. James Longstreet (1st Corps; divisions of Maj. Gens. George E. Pickett, Charles W. Field, and Joseph B. Kershaw); Maj. Gen. John B. Gordon (2d Corps; divisions of Maj. Gen. Bryan Grimes and Brig. Gens. James A. Walker [Early's division] and Clement A. Evans [Gordon's division]); Lt. Gen. A. P. Hill (3d Corps; divisions of Maj. Gens. Henry Heth, Cadmus M. Wilcox, and William Mahone); and Lt. Gen. Richard H. Anderson (4th Corps; division of Maj. Gen. Bushrod R. Johnson); and Maj. Gen. Fitzhugh Lee (Cavalry Corps; divisions of Col. Thomas T. Munford [Fitzhugh Lee's division] and Maj. Gens. William Henry Fitzhugh "Rooney" Lee and Thomas L. Rosser). Additionally, Maj. Gen. George Washington Custis Lee's division was attached, consisting of local brigades and a naval battalion from Richmond.

On March 30, Sheridan's cavalry stopped at Dinwiddie Court House, delayed by the heavy rains. Col. Thomas T. Munford's Confederate cavalry found the Federals there; on March 31, as the Union horsemen moved northward toward Five Forks, Pickett attacked and pushed them back slowly to

Dinwiddie. A Confederate counterstroke also slammed into Warren's 5th Corps, which was located along the White Oak Road, pushing it back. By 5 P.M. the brigade of Brig. Gen. Joseph J. Bartlett came to the aid of the exposed Sheridan, who some Federal commanders believed was in jeopardy of being wiped out. Reinforced in the evening with Brig. Gen. Ranald S. Mackenzie's cavalry brigade, Sheridan found by the morning of April 1 that elements of Warren's infantry were approaching, and Pickett backed away to Five Forks.

Pickett now found himself in dangerous isolation from the line of Confederate infantry stretched along the White Oak Road. Sheridan's cavalry fought stubbornly against the Confederate line, with Brig. Gen. Wesley Merritt commanding the divisions of both Brig. Gens. George A. Custer and Thomas C. Devin. Sheridan sent Mackenzie to strike the Confederates along the White Oak Road and then reunite with the other Yankee horsemen to the west; Warren, meanwhile, was forming for the main attack—the formation was taking seemingly forever, though, and Sheridan, who had a very short temper under any circumstance, was losing control.

Merritt's cavalry was supposed to strike toward the west flank of the Rebel line while the main attack force, under Warren, struck hard into the eastern flank. By 4 P.M. the attack finally commenced, but it was so late that the Confederate positions had shifted and the attackers found nothing; Sheridan was furious. Sheridan accompanied the division of Brig. Gen. Romeyn B. Ayres, which soon came under heavy attack itself. Sheridan quickly ordered the divisions of Crawford and Griffin to swing around to support Ayres, but a gap in the lines developed. Ayres, nonetheless, fought valiantly with his men and pushed the Confederate enfilading attack back, the other divisions striking the retreating Confederates. The brigades of Brig. Gens. Montgomery D. Corse and George H. Steuart fought stubbornly until they were forced into withdrawing by the general collapse of the line.

Rooney Lee's division of cavalry continued to put up a brisk fight. Col. Charles L. Fitzhugh's brigade of Federal cavalry charged the crossroads at Five Forks, capturing numerous prisoners and three field guns, while Mackenzie's cavalry, having reached the White Oak Road, was in a position to block a Rebel retreat. Pickett, meanwhile, accompanied by Fitzhugh Lee and Rosser, had been north of Hatcher's Run enjoying a shad bake when the musketry commenced. With the musket rounds singing through the air, Pickett rode furiously under fire to reach the battlefield at Five Forks, though Lee and Rosser stayed behind. All were negligent for being caught unprepared for the day's events. When it was over, the Federals held Five Forks, which Lee had instructed Pickett to "hold at all hazards," and the Confederates had lost 4,500 of their force of 10,000 as prisoners. Federal forces not only captured Five Forks but nearly encircled Petersburg to the south. Sheridan's 10,000 cavalry and Warren's 17,000 infantry had done most

of the fighting. Although Pickett and his men were humiliated, and jeopardized the Confederate position at Petersburg, it's usually Warren who is remembered for this day. Sheridan, hot-tempered as ever, shared his outrage
over Warren's lateness with the War Department, causing Warren to lose his
corps command and be reassigned to the Defenses of Petersburg. One of the
dead at Five Forks was Col. William R. J. Pegram, younger brother of the
slain Brig. Gen. John Pegram. The young artillerist shouted, "Fire your canister low, men," and then was hit: "Oh Gordon, I am mortally wounded, take
me off the field" were his last words.

It was now rapidly dawning on all Confederate commanders, troops,
officials, and even politicians that an evacuation of Richmond would be necessary to prevent their capture. On April 2 came the final assault at Petersburg, which placed Grant and Meade into position to completely encircle
the city. Lee's weakened defenses were stretched farther when he sent Anderson's corps to assist the remaining forces of Pickett in a reorganization
west of the city. Lee sent word to Davis that Richmond and Petersburg
would need to be evacuated, writing, "I think it is absolutely necessary that
we should abandon our position to-night." Grant learned that Lee's lines
had been weakened. He ordered an attack at 4:30 A.M. Sheridan and Griffin
(who succeeded Warren as 5th Corps commander) covered the western flank
at Five Forks while the other corps attacked. The strong fortifications and
abatis along the Confederate lines, which had been built up largely by slaves,
were never manned with sufficient strength; Wright detected weak points in
his front. Striking briskly and with heavy artillery support, Wright's men
took 1,100 casualties in only fifteen minutes but broke through a gap in the
line east of the Boydton Plank Road. Ord and Humphreys attacked savagely
on the Union left, also making headway at contracting the Confederate line,
which was defended along that position by Heth on the Claiborne Road. As
a quirk of fate, A. P. Hill was killed as he rode along, after he challenged a
Federal soldier to surrender. Armed with a pistol, Hill was nonetheless shot,
the ball carrying away his left thumb, penetrating his heart, and exiting his
back. Yet another Confederate high commander had fallen.

The stubborn fighting between Humphreys and Heth, who had dug in
to protect the Southside Railroad west of the city, continued. Aside from
Heth's determined defense, the Federal battle line pushed forward, capturing Forts Whitworth and Gregg, southwest of the city along the Boydton
Plank Road. Longstreet rushed troops forward from the James River area to
reinforce the crumbling lines; the Federal troops were now exhausted from
most of a day of heavy fighting. Grant regrouped his men to attack again
on April 3. Lee, realizing that he could not hold the lines for many more
hours, issued orders for a withdrawal. "The movements of all the troops will
commence at 8 o.c.," he wrote on April 2, "the artillery moving out first

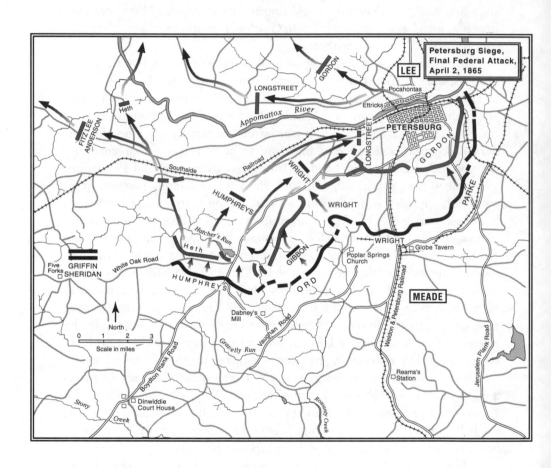

Petersburg Siege,
Final Federal Attack,
April 2, 1865

LEE

Pocahontas
Ettricks

PETERSBURG

LONGSTREET

GORDON

GORDON

LONGSTREET

Appomattox River

Heth

FITZ LEE
ANDERSON

Southside   Railroad

WRIGHT

PARKE

HUMPHREYS

WRIGHT

Hatcher's Run

Heth

WRIGHT

Globe Tavern

GIBBON

Poplar Springs
Church

Five
Forks

GRIFFIN
SHERIDAN

White Oak Road

HUMPHREYS

ORD

MEADE

North

0   1   2   3
Scale in miles

Dabney's
Mill

Vaughan Road

Weldon & Petersburg Railroad

Gravelly Run

Boydton Plank Road

Stony

Creek

Dinwiddie
Court House

Reams's
Station

Rowanty Creek

Jerusalem Plank Road

quietly, infantry following except the pickets who will be withdrawn at three o'clock—every officer is required to give his unremitting attention to cause the movement to be made successfully."

Lee would still attempt to escape to join Johnston and carry on with the war effort; Jefferson Davis, in utter shock on receiving the news from Lee, chaotically readied his government to flee, bringing with it boxcarloads of papers, goods, and materials, and destroying others. Certainly, he feared the consequences of capture; he would flee south as the Army of Northern Virginia assembled at Amelia Court House, west of Petersburg. Longstreet and Gordon took northward routes and Anderson and Fitz Lee westward (Hill's 3d Corps was merged into Longstreet's after the former's death). Davis composed a message to the people of the Confederacy that admitted "the great moral as well as material injury to our cause" that resulted from the loss of the cities, but asked them "not to despond" but to "meet the foe with fresh defiance, with unconquered and unconquerable hearts."

In Richmond, the evacuation was carried out quickly, but a mob scene followed. Looting and destruction occurred everywhere. Pandemonium resulted when Confederate officers set tobacco warehouses in the area of Rocketts Landing ablaze to prevent their capture. The fire raged out of control, burning a large portion of the city. Grant learned of the movements and occupied both Petersburg and Richmond in quick succession, restoring order and extinguishing the fires. The mayor of Richmond, Joseph Mayo, surrendered the city at 8:15 A.M. on April 3. The citizens were stunned. "We have passed through a fateful thirty-six hours," recorded Judith W. McGuire on April 3. "Yesterday morning (it seems a week ago) we went, as usual, to St. James's Church, hoping for a day of peace and quietness, as well as of religious improvement and enjoyment. How short-sighted we are, and how little do we know of what is coming, either of judgment or mercy!"

"I was wakened suddenly by four terrific explosions, one after the other, making the windows of my garret shake," exclaimed Constance Cary. "It was the blowing up, by Admiral Semmes, by order of the Secretary of the Navy, of our gunboats on the James, the signal for an all-day carnival of thundering noise and flames. Soon the fire spread, shells in the burning arsenals began to explode, and a smoke arose that shrouded the whole town, shutting out every vestige of blue sky and April sunshine. Flakes of fire fell around us, glass shattered, and chimneys fell." Even Confederate officers were shaken by the horrifying end. "We entered Richmond by the 'Rocketts' on the South side," recorded Col. Alexander Cheves Haskell, "and we entered a scene I hope never again to behold. The warehouses of Richmond, and all the Stores of the Government, were on Main and Canal Streets. . . . The Government had set fire to its warehouses, and the mob had set fire to the balance, and the streets were crammed by such a mob as can grow up in time of war at the

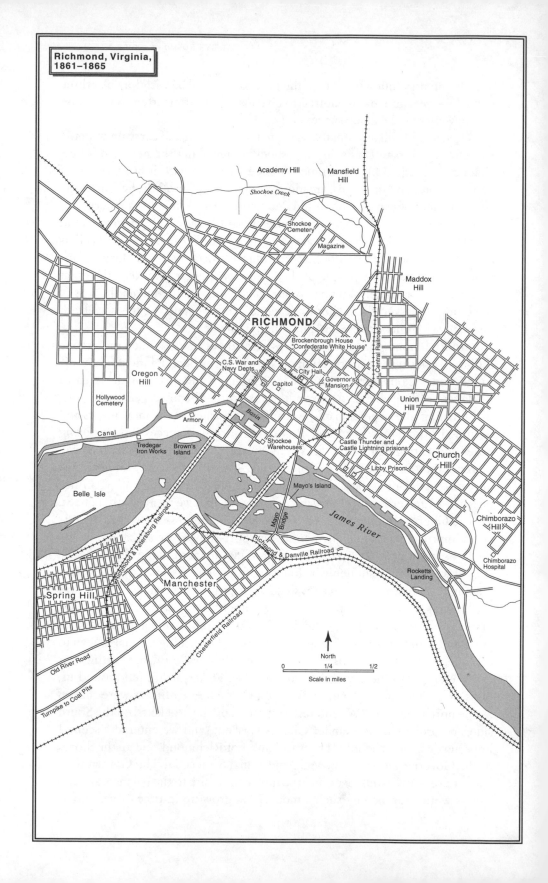

Richmond, Virginia, 1861–1865

Academy Hill
Mansfield Hill
Shockoe Creek
Shockoe Cemetery
Magazine
Maddox Hill

RICHMOND

Brockenbrough House "Confederate White House"
C.S. War and Navy Depts.
City Hall
Capitol
Governor's Mansion
Central Railroad
Union Hill

Oregon Hill

Hollywood Cemetery

Basin
Armory
Canal
Tredegar Iron Works
Brown's Island
Shockoe Warehouses
Castle Thunder and Castle Lightning prisions
Libby Prison
Church Hill

Belle Isle

Mayo's Island
Mayo Bridge
James River
Chimborazo Hill

Richmond & Petersburg Railroad
Spring Hill
Manchester
Richmond & Danville Railroad
Rocketts Landing
Chimborazo Hospital

Old River Road
Chesterfield Railroad
Turnpike to Coal Pits

North
0   1/4   1/2
Scale in miles

Capital. We did not know so many people were there.... The mob was drinking, yelling, screaming and robbing."

BY THE TIME Petersburg and Richmond fell, the Appomattox campaign was in full swing. No doubt was left that Federal forces were on the cusp of winning the war; it could have been drawn out considerably, however, with tremendous additional loss of life, had Lee been able to unite with Johnston and perhaps even carry on a prolonged guerrilla war. Lee's army raced westward to attempt to resupply and head south for Joe Johnston, and Grant and Meade pursued at high speed. Lee ordered rations and supplies sent to Amelia Court House, west of Petersburg on the Richmond & Danville Railroad, where he hoped to concentrate by April 4. The Army of Northern Virginia was now a mere shadow of the overpowering force it had been when Lee took command at Seven Pines. Now merely 30,000 infantrymen remained in the ranks, bolstered by a mixed lot of 20,000 cavalry, naval brigades, and local defense troops. The soldiers were battle-weary, underfed, poorly clothed, and exhausted. They still transported more than 1,000 wagons and 200 field guns. Lee might have capitulated when the cities fell; his innate sense of duty prevented it.

Grant and Meade anticipated Lee's possible movements and sent forces across the Richmond & Danville Railroad to block any rapid southward move. As the Southern army fled along the south bank of the Appomattox River, a rearguard action unfolded at Namozine Church and Willicomack Creek on April 3. The Union cavalry brigade of Col. William Wells struck into Brig. Gen. Rufus Barringer's horsemen along the creek and fought a stinging action along to Namozine Church, where the 8th New York Cavalry turned away a piercing Confederate attack. This led to Fitzhugh Lee and Rooney Lee separating their cavalry commands. Wells's men attacked Fitz Lee along Deep Creek under cover of darkness, and the Confederates continued their retreat. Barringer and many of his men were captured; Federal losses were 95 on the day. As Grant pushed westward toward Burkeville, Jefferson Davis and other Confederate officials arrived on the train at Danville, declaring they were not abandoning the cause.

The following day Abraham Lincoln traveled up the James River aboard the *River Queen*, transferred to the USS *Malvern*, and shortly after arrived at Richmond to visit the fallen capital. Although the city still contained groups of loud and unruly Southerners, Lincoln toured the streets with Federal officers and went through the Brockenbrough House, which Jefferson Davis had used as his "White House of the Confederacy." He sat in Davis's chair and discussed the military situation of the city with Maj. Gen. Godfrey Weitzel, assigned to command occupation forces in the city. He also met with John A. Campbell, one of the Hampton Roads commissioners, who

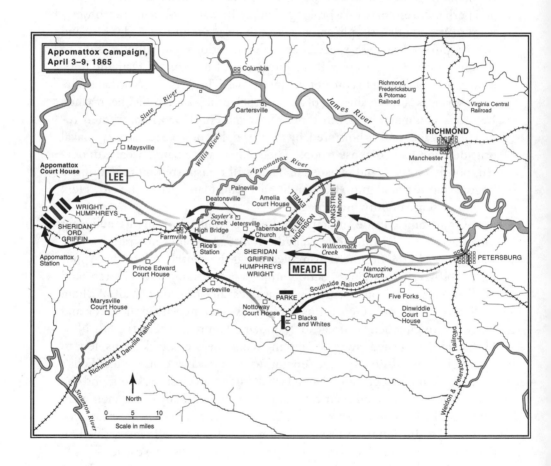

Appomattox Campaign, April 3–9, 1865

Columbia

Cartersville

Slate River

Willis River

James River

Richmond, Fredericksburg & Potomac Railroad

Virginia Central Railroad

RICHMOND

Maysville

Manchester

Appomattox River

Appomattox Court House

LEE

Paineville

Deatonsville

Amelia Court House

EWELL

LONGSTREET
Mahone

WRIGHT
HUMPHREYS

Sayler's Creek

Jetersville

SHERIDAN
ORD
GRIFFIN

High Bridge

Farmville

Tabernacle Church

F. LEE
ANDERSON

Appomattox Station

Rice's Station

Willicomack Creek

Appomattox Station

Prince Edward Court House

Burkeville

SHERIDAN
GRIFFIN
HUMPHREYS
WRIGHT

MEADE

Namozine Church

PETERSBURG

Marysville Court House

Nottoway Court House

PARKE

ORD

Southside Railroad

Five Forks

Blacks and Whites

Dinwiddie Court House

Richmond & Danville Railroad

Staunton River

North

0   5   10

Scale in miles

Weldon & Petersburg Railroad

urged Lincoln to act with moderation and magnanimity toward the Southern populace. At one point Lincoln, embarrassed as he was thronged by crowds of worshiping freed blacks, told them, "Don't kneel to me. This is not right. You must kneel to God only and thank him for the liberty you will hereafter enjoy." Despite the apparent danger from angry Southerners, Lincoln shrugged off reports of threats, one of which he received on this day via Bvt. Brig. Gen. Edward H. Ripley, one of Weitzel's brigade commanders. "I cannot bring myself to believe that any human being lives who would do me any harm," Lincoln said.

On April 4 the armies skirmished at Tabernacle Creek and Amelia Court House, with Lee's force forming at the latter place. But Lee was stunned by the lack of his supplies. On April 5 the supplies still had not come, due to disrupted communications and outright confusion that ruled the day—and not because of Davis's use of the railroads, as was sometimes alleged later. Lee now found his position worse than he expected, being blocked by Sheridan at Jetersville, which prevented use of the railroad to escape to North Carolina. Grant continued ordering his men to block the Army of Northern Virginia. "In the absence of further orders move west at 8 A.M. tomorrow morning and take position to watch the roads runing [sic] South between Burkesville [sic] and Farmville," he informed Ord on April 5. "I am strongly of opinion Lee will leave Amelia to-night to go South. He will be pursued from here at 6 A.M. if he leaves—Otherwise an advance will be made upon him where he is."

Another rearguard cavalry action occurred on this day at Amelia Springs. Sheridan dispatched the brigade of Brig. Gen. Henry E. Davies, Jr., to determine whether Lee was moving northwest from Amelia Court House. The cavalry brigade of Brig. Gen. Martin W. Gary, transporting a wagon train westward through Paineville, near Jetersville, came under attack from the 1st Pennsylvania Cavalry. The Yankees pushed through swampy land to capture a field gun and scatter the guard of 400 Rebels. Davies suggested that 200 wagons and goods, possibly including many of Lee's headquarters papers, were destroyed and 5 field guns and 11 flags captured. Some 700 prisoners were captured, half of whom were black teamsters. Confederate cavalry of Gary and Fitz Lee raced the Yankee horsemen back to Amelia Springs; 20 Yankees were killed and 96 wounded.

The pursuit had now become a running battle. On April 6 significant actions transpired, the largest at Sayler's (Saylor's or Sailor's) Creek, between Jetersville and Farmville, and just south of the Appomattox River. Lee found his army up against an impenetrable barrier of Sheridan's cavalry and Ord's and Griffith's infantry to the northeast and the infantry of Humphreys and Wright to the south; he therefore decided to move southwest to Rice's Station to resupply by Farmville and Lynchburg, which might enable him to rekindle the plan to join Johnston. A forced night march took its toll on the survivors; starving, sick men dropped out of line along the route. Grant expected a southward movement and ordered an attack toward Amelia Court House. At 8:30 A.M. Humphreys's men struck into the westward-moving column of Confederates. Gordon's corps was attempting to cover the Confederate trains; it would be overwhelmed throughout the day. Farther south along Sayler's Creek, Ewell's corps and a portion of Anderson's would be trapped and battered by Wright's corps. On the flanks Union cavalry fought savagely, forcing Ewell and Anderson to halt to regroup the wagon train. Mahone sped ahead with Longstreet, unaware of the halt, and created a gap in the column into which the wagons moved. Anderson was also delayed and found skirmishing cavalry impeding his progress; Ewell redirected the train behind him off the main road near Deatonsville, and Gordon, not informed of this change, followed the wagons rather than the southward route of the main army.

Ewell and Anderson were perplexed about a course of action to effectively dislodge Brig. Gen. George A. Custer's cavalry in their front when two divisions of infantry began attacking Ewell's rear. Along Sayler's Creek, Ewell deployed his men into a makeshift line as Federals set up batteries and began firing from a position near the James Moses Hillsman House. As Ewell attacked the center of the Union line, Brig. Gen. George W. Getty's division reinforced the position and then charged into the weak Confederates. Sheridan sent a cavalry attack forward on hearing the guns, striking Ewell's right and capturing the majority of Kershaw's division. Under heavy, sustained attack, Dick Anderson, George Pickett, and Bushrod Johnson escaped, but Ewell remained to fight as the struggle erupted into a hand-to-hand melee over parts of the field. Gordon, pushed back by Humphreys's corps to Perkinson's Mill on the creek, was completely unhinged by a forceful attack, losing some 1,700 men and regrouping his survivors along the Lynchburg railroad at High Bridge. The destruction of Lee's army was considerable at Sayler's Creek; about 7,000 to 8,000 men—about a third of those who had marched from Amelia Court House—were killed, wounded, or captured. Among the officers taken prisoner were six generals: Ewell, George W. C. Lee, Kershaw, Montgomery Corse, Dudley M. DuBose, and Eppa Hunton.

Ord advanced southward on this day, ordered to burn the railroad bridges in Lee's line of retreat. He sent a mixed force of between 500 and 1,000 men commanded by Bvt. Brig. Gen. Theodore Read, his chief of staff, to High Bridge, an impressive span resting on sixty-foot trestles that carried the Southside Railroad across the Appomattox River. Read struck into Confederate cavalry here under Maj. Gen. Tom Rosser, who was surprised but rallied his men, counterattacked, and routed the Yankees. Confederates claimed to have captured 780 men. Among the curious episodes of the last days of the eastern war was the incident between Read and Col. James Dearing. These two young high-ranking officers exchanged gunfire during the fight at High Bridge, each leading to the other's death. Dearing shot Read in the hip, killing him a few days short of his thirtieth birthday. Read shot Dearing in the chest, mortally wounding him. This Virginian, often incorrectly termed a brigadier general (his appointment as such was not confirmed), died in Lynchburg on April 23, two days shy of his twenty-fifth birthday.

It was a crushing day for the Army of Northern Virginia. "My God! Has the army been dissolved?" Lee asked Mahone at day's end. "I have been fighting heavily all day." Gordon dispatched Lee late in the afternoon. "My loss is considerable and I am still closely pressed. I fear that a portion of the train will be lost as my force is quite reduced and insufficient for its protection. So far I have been able to protect them but without assistance can scarcely hope to do so much longer. The enemy's loss has been very heavy." All now seemed to be unraveling completely. Jefferson Davis and the other Confederate executives were on the run. Richmond and Petersburg were in Federal hands. Lee's army was disintegrating. Who knew what would become of Johnston's army to the south. Other Confederate armies in the field were scattered and inconsequential.

The fighting went on. On April 7 the Confederate army concentrated fully at Farmville, and they received a scanty supply of rations for the first time since leaving Petersburg. Fighting occurred at Farmville and again at High Bridge, where Mahone, former president of the company that operated the Southside Railroad, failed to burn High Bridge, enabling the oncoming Yankees to pursue. Brig. Gen. Francis C. Barlow's division pushed forward and fought beside the bridge as a party of pioneers extinguished little fires finally set by the retreating Confederates sixty feet above the action. Humphreys pushed on toward Farmville; Brig. Gen. Thomas A. Smyth was shot in the mouth and mortally wounded in the action, dying two days later. Lee had now crossed his men north of the Appomattox River only to find his rear continually attacked by Humphreys. He established a line of battle to preserve the remaining supply train. From City Point, Lincoln wrote the famous telegram to Grant, "Gen. Sheridan says 'If the thing is pressed I think that Lee will surrender.' Let the *thing* be pressed." On this day Grant opened a correspondence with the embattled Confederate chief. "The result of the last week must convince you of the hopelessness of further resistance on the part of the Army of Northern Va. in this struggle," declared Grant. "I feel that it is so and regard it as my duty to shift from myself, the responsibility of any further effusion of blood by asking you the surrender of that portion of the C.S. Army known as the Army of Northern Va." Lee responded: "I have recd your note of this date. Though not entertaining the opinion you express of the hopelessness of further resistance on the part of the Army of Northern Virginia, I reciprocate your desire to avoid useless effusion of blood, and therefore, before considering your proposition, ask the terms you will offer on condition of its surrender."

Lynchburg now became Lee's goal. The road there led through the hamlet of Appomattox Court House, near Appomattox Station on the rail line. Sheridan approached the station on April 8, having received word that supplies had arrived there. Custer's division pushed away Confederate forces, captured the train, and moved two and a half miles northeast to Appomattox Court House, finding the Army of Northern Virginia in a defensive line southwest of the town. Sheridan readied for a major attack as the correspondence between Grant and Lee continued, as yet without resolution.

Lee now found himself trapped. As Sheridan approached from the south, backed by Ord and Griffin, the infantry of Humphreys and Wright approached from the north. On the morning of April 9, Lee sent Gordon (1,600 infantry) and Fitz Lee (2,400 cavalry) to attack Sheridan. This worked briefly, pushing back the Federal cavalry along Bent Creek Road. After an hour's fight, however, Union foot soldiers began to envelop the Confederate right and Union cavalry struck the left; by 8 A.M. Humphreys and Wright struck into Longstreet's rear guard with heavy force, and Lee realized the jig was up—there was nothing to do but surrender unconditionally. The war in the east was about to end, and the symbol of the entire Confederacy, its greatest army, would soon be no more.

Brig. Gen. Edward Porter Alexander, the brilliant artillerist, appealed to Lee to scatter the Southern forces and continue the war. Lee would not hear of it. "There are here only about 15,000 men with muskets," said Lee. "Suppose two-thirds, say 10,000, got away. Divided among the states their numbers would be too insignificant to accomplish the least good. Yes! The surrender of this army is the end of the Confederacy. . . . Their homes have been overrun by the enemy & their families need them badly. We have now simply to look the fact in the face that the Confederacy has failed."

Lee set up a plan to meet with Grant to discuss terms of surrender, uttering his famous line, "There is nothing left for me to do but to go and see General Grant, and I would rather die a thousand deaths." Grant, who had been suffering from his migraines, received a note informing him of Lee's intention. He commented to aide Horace Porter, "The pain in my head seemed to leave me the moment I got Lee's letter." In the field the Confederate soldiers were about as shocked as they could be, given the inevitability of the outcome. South Carolina Col. David G. McIntosh, riding forward with his men, noted in his diary on April 9: "Genl. Alexander stopped me and said I might halt and park, adding confidentially that the enemy was in such force in our front the march could not be resumed and it was not improbable a surrender would be the result. While I knew that things were going very badly, I was not prepared for such intelligence, and a thunderbolt from heaven could hardly have shocked me more."

It was Palm Sunday, on a clear springtime day, when Lee rode to meet Grant. The famous meeting took place about 1 P.M. in the Wilmer McLean House, the most suitable dwelling in the tiny village of Appomattox Court House. Ironically, McLean had moved west to avoid the war after Beauregard used his kitchen as a temporary headquarters during the first battle of Bull Run. Now, despite Johnston in North Carolina and Dick Taylor and Edmund Kirby Smith out west, the war would effectively come to a close in McLean's front parlor. Lee, mounted on Traveller and accompanied by Charles Marshall and Yankee Col. Orville E. Babcock of Grant's staff, rode to the house and arrived first, waiting for Grant and his remaining staff. The celebrated Union Brig. Gen. Joshua L. Chamberlain described his first vision of Lee. "Disquieted," he remarked, "I turned about, and there behind me, riding in between my two lines, appeared a commanding form, superbly mounted, richly accoutered, of imposing bearing, noble countenance, with [an] expression of deep sadness overmastered by deeper strength. It is no other than Robert E. Lee!"

Grant finally arrived toward 1:30 P.M. and the surrender interview lasted until about 3:45 P.M. Grant attempted a casual conversation based on an old encounter between the two during the Mexican War, and Lee recalled it but could not remember how Grant appeared. Finally, the Southern commander redirected the conversation toward the present situation, and they discussed all aspects of the surrender, drawing up copies of documents, and discussing details. The Federal commander allowed all Confederates to be paroled and return home, keeping their horses, sidearms, and baggage.

Later, Grant's aide Horace Porter described Lee's appearance during the interview. "Lee . . . was fully six feet in height and quite erect for one of his age, for he was Grant's senior by sixteen years. His hair and full beard were a silver-gray, and quite thick, except that the hair had become a little thin in front. He wore a new uniform of Confederate gray, buttoned up to the throat, and at his side he carried a long sword of exceedingly fine workmanship, the hilt studded with jewels."

Grant offered generous terms. "In accordance with the substance of my letter to you of the 8th inst. I propose to receive the surrender of the Army of N. Va. on the following terms: towit: Rolls of all the officers and men to be made in duplicate[.] One copy to be given to an officer designated by me, the other to be retained by such officer or officers as you designate. The officers to give their individual paroles not to take up arms against the Government of the United States until properly exchanged and each company officer or regimental commander sign a like parole for the men of his men their commands. The Arms, Artillery and public property to be parked and stacked and turned over to the officer appointed by me to receive them. This will not embrace the side Arms of the officers nor their ~~This~~ private horses or baggage.—This done each officer and man will be allowed to return to their homes not to be disturbed by United States Authority so long as they observe their parole and the laws in force where they may reside. U. S. Grant, Lt. Gn."

Following the meeting, word of the surrender formalities spread among the armies. The artillerist William T. Poague asked members of John B. Gordon's staff what was happening: " 'Surrender!' was the sententious reply. 'Surrender of what?' I asked. . . . 'General Lee's army' was the only reply I got. All at once my heart got to my throat and everything around me became dim and obscure." Carlton McCarthy, another Southern soldier, recalled, "Many of the men were sobbing and crying, like children recovering from convulsions of grief after a severe whipping. . . . Not a man was heard to blame General Lee. On the contrary, all expressed the greatest sympathy for him and declared their willingness to submit at once, or fight to the last man, as he ordered." Bryan Grimes recalled informing one of his soldiers: "Upon answering I feared it was a fact that we had been surrendered, [a soldier] cast away his musket, and holding his hands aloft, cried in an agonized voice, 'Blow, Gabriel, blow! My God, let him blow, I am ready to die!' "

Lee's parole and that of his staff was effected on this day. "We, the undersigned prisoners of war belonging to the Army of Northern Virginia," it read, "having been this day surrendered by General Robert E. Lee, C. S. Army, commanding said army, to Lieut. Gen. U. S. Grant, commanding Armies of the United States, do hereby give our solemn parole of honor that we will not hereafter serve in the armies of the Confederate States, or in any military capacity whatever, against the United States of America, or render aid to the enemies of the latter, until properly exchanged, in such manner as shall be mutually approved by the respective authorities. Done at Appomattox Court-House, Va. this 9th day of April, 1865. R. E. Lee, General."

When it was done, the General spoke to some of his men as he rode back to the Confederate lines. "I have done what I thought was best for you," he told one group as recorded by John Esten Cooke. "My heart is too full to speak, but I wish you all health and happiness." Charles Marshall remembered a scene from the following evening. "That night [April 9] the general sat with several of us at a fire in front of his tent, and . . . he told me to prepare an order to his troops."

The resulting order, the famous General Orders No. 9, was read to the troops (but not by Lee) the following day. "After four years of arduous service," it began, "marked by unsurpassed courage and fortitude, the Army of Northern Virginia has been compelled to yield to overwhelming numbers and resources. I need not tell the brave survivors of so many hard-fought battles, who have remained steadfast to the last, that I have consented to the result from no distrust of them. But, feeling that valor and devotion could accomplish nothing that could compensate for the loss that must have attended the continuance of the contest, I determined to avoid the useless sacrifice of those whose past services have endeared them to their countrymen. By the terms of the agreement officers and men can return to their homes and remain there until exchanged. You will take with you the satisfaction that proceeds from the consciousness of duty faithfully performed; and I earnestly pray that a merciful God will extend to you his blessing and protection. With an increasing admiration of your constancy and devotion to your country, and a grateful remembrance of your kind and generous considerations for myself, I bid you an affectionate farewell. R. E. Lee, General."

Elisha Hunt Rhodes simply recorded: "Well I have seen the end of the Rebellion. I was in the first battle fought by the dear old Army of the Potomac, and I was in the last. I thank God for all his blessings to me and that my life has been spared to see this glorious day. Hurrah! Hurrah!" The Southern soldiers were beaten, stunned, and starving. Immediately, provisions were made to send them rations, and Grant, for one, stunted any movement toward celebration. "The war is over," he reminded his men and officers as he rode from the McLean House, "the rebels are our countrymen again."

Grant ordered Gibbon, Griffin, and Merritt to carry into effect the surrender terms and ordered that "Brevet Brig. Gen. George H. Sharpe, Asst. Provost Marshal General, will receive and take charge of the rolls called for by the above mentioned stipulations." Arms were stacked on the Court House's "surrender triangle," akin to its town square, soldiers marched by, paid their respects, furled their flags, and the eastern war began to become a memory. The captured Confederates, 26,765 of them, were paroled. Old friendships were renewed. When Lee asked Meade, "What are you doing with all that gray in your beard?," Meade replied, "You have to answer for most of it."

As the rest of the nation began to learn of Lee's surrender, shock waves of terror and joy spread like wildfire. "It is with pain that I announce to Your Excellency the surrender of the Army of Northern Virginia," Lee informed Jefferson Davis on April 12. "Upon arriving at Amelia Court-house on the morning of the 4th with the advance of the army, . . . and not finding the supplies ordered to be placed there, nearly twenty-four hours were lost in endeavoring to collect in the country subsistence for men and horses. This delay was fatal, and could not be retrieved." In Richmond the Rebel war clerk John B. Jones wrote, "Yesterday Gen. Lee surrendered the 'Army of Northern Virginia.' . . . If Mr. Davis had been present, he never would have consented to it; and I doubt if he will ever forgive Gen. Lee." "How can I write it?" recorded North Carolina diarist Catherine Edmondston. "How find words to tell what has befallen us? *Gen Lee has surrendered!* . . . We stand appalled at our disaster! . . . [That] *Lee,* Lee upon whom hung the hopes of the whole country, should be a prisoner seems almost too dreadful to be realized!"

The war was still not over, but the heart of the Confederacy was gone. And so were many of its records. "In reply to your communication of this date calling for reports of the strength of my command on the 8th inst.," Henry Heth wrote on April 11, "such a report as I have heretofore made tri-monthly, I beg leave to state that it is impossible to make such a report—All company and regimental records and papers have been lost or destroyed." Many Confederates were still imprisoned. "I am a prisoner unwounded," reported Montgomery Corse, captured at Sayler's Creek and held in Petersburg, to his wife. "Do not know whare [*sic*] I am to be sent. Will let you know as soon as possible, when I have no doubt the Federal Authorities will let you communicate with me perhaps visit me."

All that everyone could think about was the awful death and destruction the war had brought. On hearing of the death of his wife's brother a few days after Appomattox, Meade simply wrote, "My God, what misery this dreadful war has produced, and how it comes home to the doors of almost every one!"

"I HAVE ALWAYS THOUGHT 'DIXIE' one of the best tunes I have ever heard," Abraham Lincoln said as he addressed a serenading crowd at the Executive Mansion on April 10. Nearby, the Quartermaster's band stood ready to strike the chords of the Southern anthem. "Our adversaries over the way attempted to appropriate it, but I insisted yesterday that we fairly captured it," he continued. "I now request the band to favor me with its performance." Four days later, at the height of his presidency, with the war's end virtually secured, Lincoln and Mary Todd went to the theater to get away from it all, a routine amusement.

In repeated conversations with Edwin Stanton, Thomas Eckert, Ward Hill Lamon, and others charged with his security, Lincoln was always fatalistic, believing that no one could protect him if an assassin truly wanted to take his life. As we have seen, this was the case despite the fact that caustic threats existed against Lincoln from his earliest days as president-elect, even before he left Springfield for Washington.

Nearly all of the threatening letters and "intelligence" picked up by Union officials relating to the president's security had been hollow boasts or the isolated cries of a disturbed lunatic element that didn't pose physical danger for the commander-in-chief. There was one exception, however, and that was all that was required to make history. A single confused man altered history on Good Friday, April 14, 1865, at Ford's Theatre, on 10th Street, blocks from the Executive Mansion.

The loner was John Wilkes Booth, age 26, who had been born on a farm outside Bel Air, Maryland, the son of actor Junius Brutus Booth. John had attended school in Baltimore and become an actor like his father and brothers Edwin and Junius Brutus, Jr., achieving some measure of success. Politically devoted to the South and its causes, Booth became popular on the stage, particularly in Richmond, where he garnered a considerable following. After serving as a militia soldier in the Richmond Grays in 1859 (and witnessing John Brown's hanging), he took on Shakespearean and other roles during the early war years, achieving great success with *Richard III* in New York in 1862.

Politics increasingly occupied Booth's mind during the war, and he bitterly opposed the policies of the Lincoln administration, believing them the ultimate example of despotism. Like many in the South, he disagreed with Lincoln's stand on racial issues. Increasingly frustrated at the war's direction and the possible destruction of his beloved South, Booth hatched an unlikely plot that would enable him to help to save "his country" as he enacted his greatest drama on the stage yet, securing his name in history. The notion was based on the concept of prisoner exchanges as defined by the Dix-Hill cartel of 1862. Since the April 1864 breakdown of the prisoner exchange, tens of thousands of Confederate prisoners sat in Northern pens. Booth reasoned that exchanging the ultimate hostage, the president, would release a whole army that could bolster the South's capacity to wage war.

Booth revealed the kidnapping plot to his old friends Samuel Arnold and Michael O'Laughlin in August or September 1864. Over the coming months Booth refined the plot. He spent the last weeks of 1864 looking over escape routes through Maryland; by year's end he added John H. Surratt as a coconspirator. As a Confederate mail runner, Surratt knew many disloyal citizens and Confederate agents, and his mother's boardinghouse in Washington provided a convenient base of operations. Mary E. Surratt thus became a participant in the conspiracy (her much debated role was solidified by testimony over her asking for a transfer of "shooting irons" [rifles] before the assassination night). Booth also added conspirators David E. Herold, George A. Atzerodt, Lewis Powell (alias Payne), and Edman (alias "Edward") Spangler. Arnold, O'Laughlin, and Powell had been Confederate soldiers; the others were motivated partly by adherence to secessionism, partly by the lure of becoming heroes, and partly by the magnetism of Booth himself—it was a motley crew of uneducated and rough characters. Louis J. Weichmann, a government witness at the conspiracy trial, claimed the assassins were also motivated by money promised by Booth. By the time Booth had recruited the participants, the opportunity for kidnapping was gone.

The original idea had been to abduct the president on one of his warm-weather buggy rides to the Soldiers' Home north of the city. The plot heated up again in March; eerily, Booth is visible in the background in a photograph taken of Lincoln delivering his Second Inaugural Address on the Eastern Portico of the Capitol; Powell, Atzerodt, Herold, John Surratt, and Spangler stand below the speaker's platform. On March 17, 1865, the conspirators attempted to intercept Lincoln as he ventured out to a theatrical play. But the information Booth had was erroneous and the conspirators scattered temporarily.

Recent scholarship on the Lincoln assassination has revealed compelling evidence of Booth's involvement in a plot to infiltrate Washington and blow up the Executive Mansion, killing the president and his cabinet, and that this plan was sanctioned by Jefferson Davis. How close this plan actually came to being carried off remains speculative. An explosives expert, Sgt. Thomas F. Harney of the Confederate Nitre and Mining Bureau, was to play the key role. The plot came to an end when he was captured outside Washington on April 10. The kidnapping plot, meanwhile, also had transformed. Embittered into madness by seeing the Confederacy collapse, Booth by April 3 changed the objective from hostage taking to murder.

By noon on April 14, Booth determined to murder Lincoln after hearing of his planned appearance in the box at Ford's Theatre that night to see Laura Keene and Harry Hawk in *Our American Cousin*, a farce. Booth directed the unfolding plot, as evidenced in a letter to the editor he left behind for the *National Intelligencer*. "For years I have devoted my time, my energies, and every dollar I possessed to the furtherance of an object," he explained. "I have been baffled and disappointed. The hour has come when I must change my plan. Many, I know—the vulgar herd—will blame me for what I am about to do, but posterity, I am sure, will justify me. Right or wrong, God judge me, not man. . . . This country was formed for the *white*, not for the black man. And, looking upon African slavery from the same standpoint as the noble framers of our constitution, I, for one, have ever considered it one of the greatest blessings, both for themselves and us, that God ever bestowed upon a favored nation." On this day, the last of his life, Lincoln remarked at a cabinet meeting that he had "this strange dream again last night, and we shall, judging from the past, have great news very soon." Lincoln told Gideon Welles the dream related to water, that he seemed to be in "some singular, indescribable vessel, and that he was moving with great rapidity towards an indefinite shore." Lincoln had asked the Grants to accompany him on this gala evening, with celebrations and fireworks planned throughout the city. The Grants begged off, however, to visit their sons in New Jersey. Others were invited and declined; the Lincolns were accompanied that night by Maj. Henry R. Rathbone, a branch chief in the Provost Marshal General's

Office, and his fiancée, Clara Harris, daughter of New York Senator and Lincoln friend Ira Harris.

At about 8:30 P.M. the Lincolns made their way into Ford's Theatre; as they walked toward and entered the president's box, the play halted as the orchestra struck up "Hail to the Chief" and the crowd of about 1,700 theater-goers exploded into applause for the victorious leader. The party was accompanied by a lone guard, John F. Parker of the Metropolitan Police, who soon after his arrival moved away from his chair at the hallway door leading to the box so that he could see the play. Lincoln and Mary watched the play in good cheer. Lincoln at times placed his hand on Mary's knee. It was exactly four years after the firing on Fort Sumter. The audience, transfixed by the actors on the stage, failed to notice the shadowy figure dressed in black who entered and left repeatedly, drinking next door and checking the play's progress. Booth was a familiar face around Ford's. He picked up his mail there and had the run of the place; it was a second home.

Booth carefully planned the conspiracy throughout the day, hoping to topple the Northern government. Earlier in the day, he left a calling card at Vice President Johnson's hotel room: "Don't wish to disturb you; are you at home?" About two hours before the crimes were to occur, Booth assigned the killers their roles. He ordered Atzerodt to kill Andrew Johnson and Powell to attack and murder William H. Seward. He would take the chief role by murdering Lincoln. Atzerodt lost his nerve and failed to attack Johnson; Herold lost his wits too and failed to assist Powell. Powell and Booth were committed to success.

Sometime after 10 P.M. Booth entered Ford's again, making his way up the staircase and moving past army Capt. Theodore McGowan, who moved so the little man could continue toward the president's box. He descended into the darkness of the box seats toward the right side of the theater. What happened next is unclear because of the conflicting testimony of witnesses to the same events. Probably about 10:25 P.M. Booth spoke momentarily to a man who may have been an usher adjacent to the doorway to the President's box. He then entered the door and slipped into a short narrow hallway that contained another door leading to the box itself. Booth had prepared for his crime by drilling peepholes into the door and leaving a brace in the hallway to block the door after the crime occurred. If he did speak briefly to an usher who was not the departed guard Parker, Booth talked his way in. He timed the crime perfectly. Knowing the play well, he waited for a lull that followed a particular line, leaving only one actor on stage, Harry Hawk. As Hawk said "Well, I guess I know enough to turn you inside out, old woman, you damned old sockdologizing mantrap!" laughter broke out, punctuated by a sharp bang and a waft of blue-white smoke above the president's box. The time was about 10:30 P.M. An instant of shock and confusion about whether something strange had happened that might be part of the play swiftly transformed into electric panic as Mary Todd Lincoln let out a ghastly scream. Booth jumped over the box, catching his spur in the large Treasury Guard's flag draped under the box and leaping or falling to the stage, yelling something (which may have been *"Sic semper tyrannis!"*—"Thus ever be it to tyrants," Virginia's state motto—or something else, depending on whose testimony is believed). Booth then exited into the alley, pushed down the boy who held his horse, and made a mad dash for the escape route to Maryland. Whether or not he broke or fractured a tibia or fibula during the jump or fall is a matter of dispute. (Whether or not the bone was broken, Booth's leg was very painful and, during his flight, was attended to by Dr. Samuel Mudd.)

Pandemonium reigned in the theater. Lincoln had been shot with a single homemade bullet fired from Booth's Deringer pistol, struck in the back of the head below the left ear. The bullet lodged in his brain. His breathing was slow and erratic. Rathbone, who momentarily struggled with Booth, had been slashed with a large knife and was bleeding profusely; as soon as he reopened the jammed door, Dr. Charles Leale, an army surgeon who happened to be in the audience, made his way in. Two other doctors, Charles Taft and Albert King, assisted. Leale's report of the night, preserved in the National Archives, is a critical record of the status of Lincoln after being shot.

After hearing the gun's report, Leale recorded, "I then heard cries that the 'President had been murdered,' which were followed by those of 'Kill the murderer,' 'Shoot him,' etc., which came from different parts of the audience. I immediately ran to the President's box and as soon as the door was opened was admitted and introduced to Mrs. Lincoln, when she exclaimed several times, 'O Doctor, do what you can for him, do what you can!' I told her we would do all that we possibly could. When I entered the box the ladies were very much excited. Mr. Lincoln was seated in a high backed armchair with his head leaning toward his right side supported by Mrs. Lincoln, who was weeping bitterly. Miss Harris was near her left and behind the President. While approaching the President I sent a gentleman for brandy and another for water. When I reached the President he was in a state of general paralysis, his eyes were closed and he was in a profoundly comatose condition, while his breathing was intermittent and exceedingly stertorous. I placed my finger on his right radial pulse but could perceive no movement of the artery. As two gentlemen now arrived, I requested them to assist me to place him in a recumbent position, and as I held his head and shoulders, while doing this my hand came in contact with a clot of blood near his left shoulder. Supposing that he had been stabbed there I asked a gentleman to cut his coat and shirt off from that part, to enable me if possible to check the hemorrhage, which I supposed took place from the subclavian artery or some of its branches.

"Before they had proceeded as far as the elbow I commenced to examine his head (as no wound near the shoulder was found) and soon passed my fingers over a large firm clot of blood situated about one inch below the superior curved line of the occipital bone and an inch and a half to the left of the median line of the same bone. The coagula I easily removed and passed the little finger of my left hand through the perfectly smooth opening made by the ball and found that it had entered the encephalon. As soon as I removed my finger a slight oozing of blood followed and his breathing became more regular and less stertorous. The brandy and water now arrived and a small quantity was placed in his mouth, which passed into his stomach where it was retained.

"Dr. C. S. Taft and Dr. A. F. A. King now arrived and after a moment's consultation we agreed to have him removed to the nearest house, which we immediately did, the above named with others assisting. When we arrived at the door of the box, the passage was found to be densely crowded by those who were rushing towards that part of the theatre. I called out twice 'Guards clear the passage,' which was soon done that we proceeded without a moment's delay with the President and were not in the slightest interrupted until he was placed in bed in the house of Mr. Petersen, opposite the theatre, in less than 20 minutes from the time that he was assassinated."

But no sooner was Lincoln placed in a little bed across the street from Ford's in the Petersen House than it was clear among not only the doctors but those hearing about the case that the wound was mortal. "The giant sufferer lay extended diagonally across the bed, which was not long enough for him," wrote Welles. "He had been stripped of his clothes. His large arms, which were occasionally exposed, were of a size which one would scarce have expected from his spare appearance. His slow, full respiration lifted the clothes with each breath that he took. His features were calm and striking." Mary Todd Lincoln wept inconsolably in an adjacent room, sometimes joining her wounded husband; Robert Todd Lincoln arrived, as did many military officials and politicians. Stanton arrived and set up a "command post," acting in effect as a military dictator for the night, considering the possibility that a vast conspiracy to topple the government might be underway. Seward had also been attacked as Powell, a savage, muscular figure, pushed into the Seward House, brutally wounding Frederick Seward (the Secretary's son) by battering him with a pistol, and slashed Secretary Seward with a knife. Seward had been in a carriage accident and was supported in bed by a heavy metallic brace; this may have saved his life. Others were wounded as Powell left the house, leaving a bloody, nightmarish scene behind. It was nearly miraculous that the Sewards all recovered from the attack.

The outcome would not be as good for Lincoln. The breathing became more erratic and labored throughout the night, and at 7:22 A.M. on April 15, Lincoln died. At this moment Stanton uttered the famous words, "Now he belongs to the ages." Andrew Johnson would now lead the nation through the final days of America's greatest war, and he was hardly qualified to do it. "Traitors must be made odious," said Johnson, ". . . treason must be made odious . . . traitors must be punished and impoverished." The shock over America's first political assassination of a president was chilling not only to Northerners but to intelligent Southerners as well, who realized that the result would be disastrous for Reconstruction policy. "No living man ever dreamed that it was possible that the intense joy of the nation over the recent happy deliverance from war could be or would be so soon turned to grief more intense and bitter than ever nation had before known," noted Noah Brooks. "It is hard to realize that he is gone, that we shall no more see his commanding form, hear his kind voice or touch his pure and honest hand, with its well-remembered earnestness. It is hard to take in the dreadful thought that the speaking eye is closed in death, and that the kindly, genial soul has fled, and that the head of the nation has perished by the hand of an assassin." "History furnished no parallel for the atrocity of these deeds," exclaimed Lt. Frank Dickerson of the 5th U.S. Cavalry. "President Lincoln was stricken down while in the height of glory, popularity, and personal happiness, his work was nearly completed, would to God he had been able to finish it and had been spared to complete his remaining days in quiet and peace."

Shock and grief deepened as more people discussed the chaos surrounding the assassination and the pursuit of the assassins, directed by Stanton. Lincoln, who had been both loved and deeply disliked, even by Northerners, transformed into America's martyr-hero, his assassination even coming on Good Friday. "To him our gratitude was justly due, for to him, under God, more than any other person, we are indebted for the successful vindication of the integrity of the Union and the maintenance of the power of the Republic," confided Gideon Welles. "We have had more good news in the last month than we have ever had since the war began," wrote William Babb of New Creek, West Virginia, to a friend. "Had it not been for the assassination of Lincoln we would have almost run over with good news. Wasn't that a terrible affair indeed? I have not had any thing to hurt my feelings so much since the war. But I think the Rebs cut off their nose to spite their face when they killed him. I think he would have been more lenient than Johnson will toward Rebels." Even Jefferson Davis, who had probably approved the plot to bomb Lincoln, described his feelings to Navy Secretary

Stephen Mallory. "I fear it will be disastrous for our people, and I regret it deeply."

Lincoln's remains, meanwhile, would undergo a twenty-day journey from Washington aboard a special train to Springfield, Illinois, for burial. The Lincoln lore that would dominate much of American history now began in earnest. In Washington, Walt Whitman composed his celebrated poem that emblazoned Lincoln's leadership into so many minds of the time. "O Captain! my Captain! our fearful trip is done / The ship has weather'd every rack, the prize we sought is won / The port is near, the bells I hear, the people all exulting / While follow eyes the steady keel, the vessel grim and daring / But O heart! heart! heart! / O the bleeding drops of red / Where on the deck my Captain lies / Fallen cold and dead."

Booth and Herold fled through Virginia and were hunted down at Richard H. Garrett's Farm near Port Tobacco on April 26. A few days earlier Booth attempted to make sense of his lack of acclaim as a do-gooder in his diary. "After being hunted like a dog through swamps, woods, and last night being chased by gun boats till I was forced to return wet cold and starving," he scrawled, "with every mans hand against me, I am here in despair. And why; for doing what Brutus was honored for, what made Tell a Hero. And yet I for striking down a greater tyrant than they ever knew am looked upon as a common cutthroat. . . . So ends all. For my country I have given up all that makes life sweet and Holy, brought misery upon my family, and am sure there is no pardon in Heaven for me since man condemns me so. I have only heard what has been done (except what I did myself) and it fills me with horror." The barn Booth and Herold hid in was set ablaze to force them out; Herold came out with hands in the air; Lt. Col. Everton Conger ordered Booth taken alive, but Sgt. Boston Corbett, a mentally unbalanced religious fanatic, fired on Booth in the barn, mortally wounding him. Booth died after looking hazily at his hands and uttering the phrase, "Useless, useless."

A lonely, unbalanced man had killed the president of the United States and then was himself killed. There would be a trial for the surviving conspirators that would be chastised as shabbily handled but would produce immense testimony about details of the crime. The investigation of the assassination created one of the most thorough collections of artifacts relating to a crime in history, many of which are now on display at Ford's Theatre. Yet the literature abounds with hypotheses about conspiracies involving everyone from the Confederate government to Stanton to Catholics to Jefferson Davis to foreign governments. The simple facts, extensively analyzed at a microscopic level, support the case that Booth and his cohorts were loosely connected with the Confederate authorities but pulled off the final version of their attacks essentially on their own, impelled by the collapse of the Confederacy.

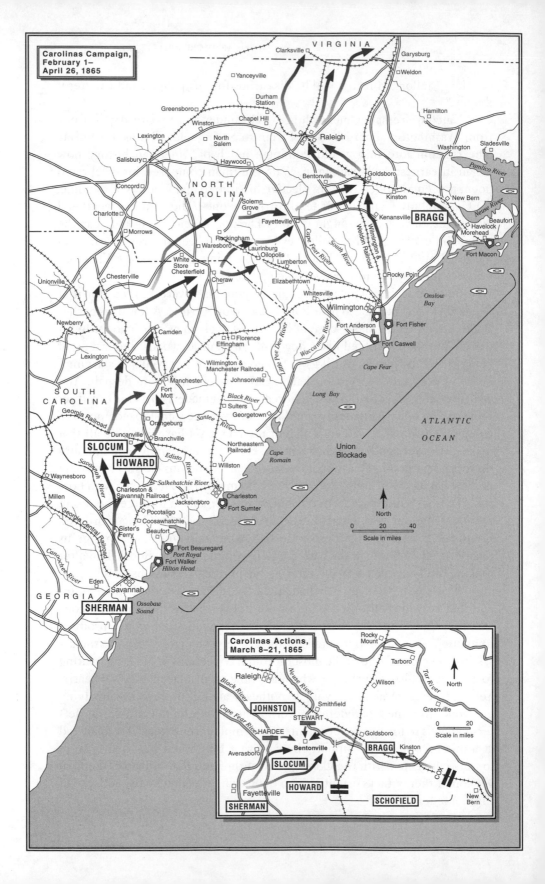

**Carolinas Campaign,
February 1–
April 26, 1865**

VIRGINIA

Clarksville
Garysburg
Yanceyville
Weldon
Durham
Station
Hamilton
Greensboro
Chapel Hill
Winston
Washington
Sladesville
Lexington
North
Salem
Raleigh
Pamlico River
Salisbury
Haywood
NORTH
CAROLINA
Bentonville
Goldsboro
New Bern
Concord
Kinston
Beaufort
Solemn
Grove
Kenansville
BRAGG
Havelock
Morehead
Charlotte
Fayetteville
Morrows
Fort Macon
Rockingham
Cape Fear River
Waresboro
Laurinburg
South River
White
Store
Oilopolis
Lumberton
Chesterfield
Cheraw
Elizabethtown
Rocky Point
Unionville
Whitesville
*Onslow
Bay*
Newberry
Camden
Florence
Wilmington
Effingham
Fort Anderson
Fort Fisher
Lexington
Columbia
Manchester
Johnsonville
Little Pee Dee River
Waccamaw River
Fort Caswell
Fort
Mott
Black River
Cape Fear
Sulters
Georgetown
Santee River
Long Bay
SLOCUM
Orangeburg
Georgia Railroad
Duncanville
Branchville
Northeastern
Railroad
*ATLANTIC
OCEAN*
HOWARD
Edisto River
Willston
*Cape
Romain*
Salkehatchie River
Waynesboro
Savannah River
Charleston &
Savannah Railroad
Jacksonboro
Charleston
Fort Sumter
Union
Blockade
Millen
Pocotaligo
Coosawhatchie
Georgia Central Railroad
Sister's
Ferry
Beaufort
North
Fort Beauregard
Port Royal
Fort Walker
Hilton Head
0   20   40
Scale in miles
Canoochee River
GEORGIA
Eden
Savannah
*Ossabaw
Sound*
SHERMAN

**Carolinas Actions,
March 8–21, 1865**

Rocky
Mount
Tarboro
Neuse River
Raleigh
Wilson
Tar River
Black River
Smithfield
Greenville
Cape Fear River
JOHNSTON
STEWART
North
HARDEE
Goldsboro
BRAGG
Kinston
0   20
Scale in miles
Averasboro
Bentonville
COX
SLOCUM
HOWARD
New
Bern
Fayetteville
SHERMAN
SCHOFIELD

As LEE'S ARMY unsuccessfully attempted to stave off Grant and Meade in Virginia, Sherman pursued Joe Johnston in the Carolinas. Johnston had relatively few troops, however, and they were badly organized. The Carolinas campaign, which would extend the last weeks of the eastern war through April 26, saw sporadic battles flare in North Carolina. Sherman's Military Division of the Mississippi consisted of the Army of the Tennessee (right wing, Maj. Gen. Oliver O. Howard), Army of the Ohio (center, Maj. Gen. John M. Schofield), and Army of Georgia (left wing, Maj. Gen. Henry W. Slocum). Howard's army consisted of the corps of Maj. Gen. John A. Logan (15th Corps; divisions of Maj. Gen. William B. Hazen and Brig. Gens. Charles R. Woods, John E. Smith, and John M. Corse); and Maj. Gen. Frank P. Blair, Jr. (17th Corps; divisions of Maj. Gen. Joseph A. Mower and Brig. Gens. Mortimer D. Leggett and Giles A. Smith). Schofield's army held the corps of Maj. Gen. Alfred H. Terry (10th Corps; divisions of Brig. Gens. Henry W. Birge, Adelbert Ames, and Charles J. Paine); and Maj. Gen. Jacob D. Cox (23d Corps; divisions of Brig. Gens. Thomas H. Ruger, Nathaniel C. McLean, and James A. Reilly). Slocum's army contained the corps of Brig. Gen. Jefferson C. Davis (14th Corps; divisions of Brig. Gens. William P. Carlin, James D. Morgan, and Absalom Baird); and Brig. Gen. Alpheus S. Williams (20th Corps; divisions of Brig. Gens. Nathaniel J. Jackson, John W. Geary, and William T. Ward). A division of cavalry was commanded by Brig. Gen. H. Judson Kilpatrick. Altogether, Sherman had 57,676 troops on March 1; by April 10 the number swelled to 88,948. Johnston, by contrast, had only 9,513 men on March 17 and by April 7 could muster a total of 18,182; he stood no chance. The remnants of the Army of Tennessee consisted of the corps of Lt. Gen. William J. Hardee (divisions of Maj. Gens. John C. Brown, Robert F. Hoke, and Benjamin F. Cheatham); Lt. Gen. Stephen D. Lee (divisions of Maj. Gens. D. H. Hill and Carter L. Stevenson); and Lt. Gen. Alexander P. Stewart (divisions of Maj. Gens. William W. Loring, James Patton Anderson, and Edward C. Walthall). Cavalry was commanded by Lt. Gen. Wade Hampton (divisions of Maj. Gens. Joseph Wheeler, Pierce M. B. Young, and Lunsford L. Lomax). Attached were Rear Adm. Raphael Semmes's naval brigade and numerous refugee units from the Department of North Carolina and Southern Virginia, and from the states of Georgia and South Carolina.

Heavy rains slowed the Federal advance. On March 2 skirmishing erupted along Thompson's Creek, South Carolina, as elements of Williams's 20th Corps entered Chesterfield. The following day Union troops occupied Cheraw. On March 4, as Lincoln and Johnson took their oaths of office, Sherman launched a movement from Cheraw to Florence that lasted several days. They focused on launching into North Carolina in the direction of

Fayetteville. On March 6, Johnston assumed command of the Department of North Carolina (which had previously been under Gen. Braxton Bragg), while Sherman's bummers crossed the Pee Dee River en route to Fayetteville. Sherman learned that Johnston had troops at Kinston on the Neuse River; the Yankees advanced between the Neuse and Trent rivers on March 7, setting up what became the battle of Kinston from March 8 to 10. Though many of the Yankee soldiers had taken delight in causing property destruction in South Carolina, they seemed glad to be departing. "We felt relieved at getting out of the most contemptible state of the Union," reported Maj. Thomas Ward Osborn, Howard's chief of artillery. "There is nothing in it or its people to place it on an equality with the meanest state of the Union, much less to place it in the van in all great movements, political and military. It has but one element of which it can boast, and that is *Treason.*"

Schofield approached Kinston with his army from New Bern, forcing Gen. Braxton Bragg, now aiding Johnston (who established headquarters at Raleigh), to send Hoke to Kinston to reinforce the place. Bragg led a force of Confederates into attack against Cox's 23d Corps, initially pushing a Yankee brigade in retreat. Although Bragg's movement was intended to thwart the Union approach from the coast, the Confederate numbers were so diminutive that after a short time Cox's men pushed the Rebels back. Schofield took command on the field and heavy skirmishing continued on March 9. The following day Bragg's Confederates attacked savagely several times before falling back, ending the fighting at Kinston. Bragg retreated to Kinston and then to Goldsboro to reunite with Johnston. The bulk of Sherman's army now approached Fayetteville, still hampered by wet weather. Kilpatrick, meanwhile, had been surprised and nearly captured in bed on the 9th near Solemn Grove, South Carolina, by Hampton's and Wheeler's horsemen. The resulting battle of Monroe's Crossroads, a brief skirmish, was given the alternative nickname "The Battle of Kilpatrick's Pants," as the Union commander fled wearing only his underclothes.

On March 11, the lightly harassed Yankee army achieved another major goal of the campaign by occupying Fayetteville. Entrance into the city came after only light skirmishing. Sherman realized that his easy successes had to a degree come by outmaneuvering Johnston and that he would soon have to face the Confederates in battle. The Yankees remained at Fayetteville until March 14, busily destroying the former U.S. Arsenal, machine shops, and buildings and property considered of military value. A Fayetteville resident recalled the shock of having unwanted enemy troops suddenly in town, writing, "The main body of Sherman's army now began to pass by in martial array with flags flying, the field officers on horseback prancing at the head of the column, the soldiers proudly keeping step to the music of the band. . . .

[A Federal officer] did all he could to comfort us, even averring that which he did not believe—that the Southern cause was not lost yet." A light skirmish erupted again on the 13th, and the following day Cox entered and occupied Kinston.

Action next transpired on March 16, when the advancing column of Sherman's left, Slocum's Army of Georgia, struck into Hardee's force that aimed to prevent passage to Goldsboro. The battle of Averasboro resulted. The divisions of Jackson and Ward, of Williams's 20th Corps, deployed to attack Hardee's men, who were strung along a narrow ridge along the Black River. Brisk musketry and artillery volleys rang out, and casualties suffered harshly on the cold, wet field. Sherman, eyeing the battlefront, sent the brigade of Col. Henry Case to cross the river and envelop the Confederate right; the soldiers fought sharply with the division of Maj. Gen. William B. Taliaferro, whose soldiers were pushed back to a rearguard line. As darkness and rain swept over the field, Hardee determined to evacuate his position. The day's casualties were 95 killed, 533 wounded, and 54 missing for the Union; Confederate losses were 865. Averasboro was a sharp action put forth by Hardee but not terribly discouraging to the oncoming Yankees. Still, it was shocking to the citizens of the area, who had never seen such an event. Jane Robeson, age 17, wrote that the battlefield scene "beggars description. The blood lay in puddles in the grove, the groans of the dying and complaints of those undergoing amputation was horrible. I can never forget it."

Minor skirmishing followed Averasboro for two days. The real counterstrike came from March 19 to 21 in the battle of Bentonville, the most significant action of the campaign. Concentrating his forces at Smithfield, Johnston assembled an army of 21,000, briefly, by absorbing Bragg's troops. Johnston determined to strike the Army of Georgia at Bentonville, hoping to destroy it before Sherman could bring reinforcements to the scene. Slocum had moved toward Bentonville following the action of the 16th. Howard moved in parallel while Kilpatrick's cavalry pursued Hardee. While Sherman moved toward Goldsboro to meet Terry and Schofield, Johnston pressed the attack on Slocum. Carlin's division of the 14th Corps encountered Hampton's Confederate troopers on the morning of March 19, which unleashed a counterattack by Johnston. Heavy, desperate fighting in the fields at Bentonville resulted before Johnston withdrew to a position along Mill Creek and entrenched. The stubborn resistance of Jeff C. Davis's men prevented a worse outcome for the Federals.

A lull washed over the field on March 20, but Sherman planned a counterattack for the following day. He ordered Mower's division forward to strike the position in front of Mill Creek to cut off Johnston's route of retreat; this action was blocked by Confederate troop positioning, however, and Johnston pulled his numerically inferior force away toward Smithfield on the night of March 21. Union casualties at the battle had been more than 1,500. They exceeded 2,600 for Johnston, many of whom were prisoners.

In the wake of Bentonville, Sherman moved to Goldsboro while Johnston concentrated at Smithfield. Terry now joined Sherman, increasing his force considerably. Sherman left the front to meet with Grant at Petersburg, in advance of a possible surrender of Johnston. "Sherman . . . is a very remarkable-looking man," said staff officer Theodore Lyman, "such as could not be grown out of America—the concentrated quintessence of Yankeedom." Johnston was now joined by Stephen D. Lee. Shortly after Lee's surrender, both army groups heard the news from Virginia and the writing seemed to be on the wall. "A little more labor, a little more toil on our part," Sherman wrote his troops, "and the great race is won, and our Government stands regenerated, after four long years of bloody war." On April 13, Sherman's men entered Raleigh under a heavy, soaking rain, and Johnston now realized the situation was hopeless. Johnston requested an armistice to discuss terms of surrender. Secretary of War Stanton halted the draft and stopped requesting war supplies. The whole war suddenly seemed to be screeching to a halt.

On April 14, as President Lincoln discussed his plans to attend the theater that night with Mary Todd, army and navy personnel participated in a ceremony at Fort Sumter, South Carolina, to again raise the U.S. flag over the battered brick structure. Federal warships fired thunderous salvos in Charleston Harbor as the ceremony commenced. Henry Ward Beecher delivered an oration that stirred the dignitaries. Robert Anderson, now a brigadier general in the regular army and placed on the retired list, raised the Stars and Stripes to the applause of all onlookers. Anderson, 59, was ill and almost feeble, but could think back to the day four years before when he had surrendered the fort to the insurgent South Carolina and Confederate forces—a day that seemed like a lifetime ago. "The ceremony began with a short prayer by the old army chaplain who had prayed when the flag was hoisted over Fort Sumter on December 27, 1860," recalled Mary Cadwalader Jones, who witnessed the event. "Next a Brooklyn clergyman [Beecher] read parts of several Psalms. . . . Then Sergeant Hart, who had held up the flag when its staff was shot through in the first attack, came forward quietly and drew the selfsame flag out of an ordinary leather mail bag. We all held our breath for a second, and then we gave a queer cry, between a cheer and a yell. . . ."

The troops and civilians in the Carolinas now received news of the Lincoln assassination and were either in mourning or dumbstruck over the magnitude of the event. In this climate Sherman and Johnston began negotiations for surrender. On April 17 the two commanders met at Bennett Place, a farmhouse near Durham Station. The following day Sherman and Johnston signed a "memorandum or basis of agreement" that called for an armistice by all armies still in the field; this infuriated Stanton and was beyond the scope of what Sherman was supposed to have agreed to with Johnston, which was simply the surrender of the latter's force. The document not only detailed how soldiers would lay down their arms and return home, not to fight against the United States, but that the president should recognize the authority of state governments when their authorities signed oaths. It further outlined the return of personal and property rights and outlined the reestablishment of Federal courts, and promised a general amnesty. Sherman had gone far beyond Grant's terms of surrender. He sent copies of the document to Halleck and Grant and when questions were immediately raised about the content, Sherman explained that he was carrying out Lincoln's wishes as he had understood them from the meeting at City Point.

Still, Stanton was outraged. Grant urged everyone to consider carefully the measures that had already been brought to light. "[Messages from Gen. Sherman] are of such importance that I think immediate action should be taken on them," he wrote Stanton on April 21, "and that it should be done by the President, in council with his whole Cabinet. I would respectfully suggest whether the President should not be notified, and all his cabinet, and the meeting take place to-night?" On April 24, Sherman learned that his terms had been rejected by Washington, and was ordered to give forty-eight hours' notice before resuming attacks on Johnston's army. Sherman wrote Johnston: "I have replies from Washington to my Communications of April Eighteenth (18th). I am Instructed to limit my operations to your Immediate Command, and not to attempt civil negotiations. I therefore demand the surrender of your army on the same terms as were given to Genl. Lee at Appomattox of April ninth (9th) Inst. purely and simply." The next day Sherman wrote Secretary Stanton, attempting to explain himself. "I admit my folly in embracing in a Military convention any Civil matters," he concluded, "but unfortunately Such is the Nature of our Situation that they Seem inextricably united and I understood from you at Savannah that the Financial State of the Country demanded Military Success and would warrant a little bending to Policy."

After much political awkwardness, Johnston finally did surrender to Sherman at Bennett Place on April 26, the same day John Wilkes Booth was hunted down and shot. By midafternoon both commanders signed terms of surrender modeled after those of Appomattox, and the remnant of the Army of Tennessee, the second great Confederate force, began to stack its arms. About 30,000 men, all those in the area, surrendered altogether. Word of the surrender spread throughout the South, and other small groups gave up in isolated places. "We have official news of the surrender of Lee's army [and of] armistice between Sherman & Johnston," reported Brig. Gen. Eugene A. Carr, in Montgomery, Alabama. "We have a rumor of the assassination of the President and Secretary Seward but I do not believe it. It would be too great a calamity."

Sherman's bummers had triumphed in their Carolinas campaign, having marched 425 miles in 50 days. It was a much rougher campaign physically than that from Atlanta to the Sea and ended the Army of Tennessee's operations. By contrast, Confederates in the Carolinas were dispirited. When Johnston and other Confederate officials met with Jefferson Davis in Greensboro in mid-April, he told the Confederate president that "our people are tired of the war, feel themselves whipped, and will not fight. Our country is overrun, its military resources greatly diminished, while the enemy's military power and resources were never greater and may be increased to any extent desired. . . . My small force is melting away like snow before the sun." As Davis listened to the old commander with whom he had enjoyed quarreling so often, he did not look up but sat with his eyes transfixed on a piece of paper, which he was "folding and unfolding abstractly."

WHILE ACTIONS were taking place in Virginia and North Carolina, a series of Union raids highlighted the other theaters. Sherman was aided by a raid of some 4,000 cavalrymen under Maj. Gen. George Stoneman, who departed Jonesboro, Tennessee, on March 20. The raid would last thirty-four days and effect a diversion that moved from Wilkesboro, North Carolina, along the Tennessee-Lynchburg Railroad between Wytheville and Salem. On April 9, Stoneman's raiders returned to North Carolina, damaging portions of the track between Danville and Greensboro. At Hendersonville the raiders discovered Johnston's surrender. Stoneman's men then captured the remnants of Lt. Gen. Jubal Early's command, holding 2,000 prisoners and 14 field-guns.

A far more significant raid commenced two days after Stoneman's, when Brig. Gen. James H. Wilson led a large cavalry force comprising three divisions southward from the Tennessee River toward Selma, Alabama, one of the only Confederate military bases remaining. Though Selma's prewar population was a mere 3,177, the town held an arsenal, a naval foundry, gun factories, warehouses containing military goods, a powder mill, and railroad shops. The war had brought more than 10,000 workers to town. Wilson's cavalry corps of the Military Division of the Mississippi was a formidable group: nearly 14,000 troopers were commanded by the divisions of Brig. Gens. Edward M. McCook, Eli Long, and Emory Upton. The movement was designed to smash the structures and goods of military value in Selma but also to operate in conjunction with the movements against Mobile. Wilson sent his horsemen forward in three separate columns to confuse the scattered cavalry forces that might intercept him, principally the 2,500 or so remaining troopers of Lt. Gen. Nathan Bedford Forrest's corps of the Department of Alabama, Mississippi, and East Louisiana, organized into two scant divisions led by Brig. Gens. James R. Chalmers and William H. Jackson, and the remains of two brigades, of Brig. Gen. Philip D. Roddey and Col. Edward Crossland. A few scattered units of militia from various states were also in the region.

After minor affairs at Houston, Alabama (March 25), and Blackwarrior River, Alabama (March 26), Wilson brought his men together at Jasper on the 27th. At Elyton, near present-day Birmingham, a skirmish occurred on March 28. Three days later the forces of Wilson and Forrest met near Montevallo, and the Confederate legend found himself routed by the larger Union army. Both places had been objectives of Wilson where he could destroy factories. Forrest had hoped to delay until Chalmers arrived but had to face Wilson's much superior, better-armed force. In the action Wilson's men captured some of Forrest's headquarters documents, which exposed Forrest's plans. Wilson immediately dispatched McCook to aid Brig. Gen. John T. Croxton's brigade at Trion and then rapidly rode toward Selma. Forrest regrouped his command at Plantersville, near Ebenezer Church, fought a final stand, and was routed and pushed toward Selma, where he deployed into a defensive line along the Alabama River.

On April 2 the battle of Selma exploded with small-arms fire as Long and Upton assaulted the works of Forrest. Heavy fighting resulted as attackers shot up to the Confederate works, resulting in brief periods of hand-to-hand struggles. Forrest watched the fight, alternately "cursing Chalmers for not coming up, or praying he might come in the night." In the afternoon the Union men finally carried the works, aided by the breakdown of militia troops, who abandoned their positions in fright. Forrest, badly beaten and without much of a force left, regrouped at Marion, where he finally joined with Chalmers. Wilson worked busily, destroying Confederate facilities at Selma for a week before marching to Montgomery, which he occupied on April 12. As the word of Lee's surrender and Lincoln's murder reached the Deep South, Wilson continued his raid, bending eastward into Georgia and going after other military facilities. On April 16, at West Point, Georgia, Col. Oscar H. La Grange's brigade attacked Fort Tyler, capturing it after a vicious fight in which the Union men had to bridge a ditch under fire of the two 32-pounder guns inside the earthwork. In the melee, the Confederate commander, Brig. Gen. Robert C. Tyler, was mortally wounded by a sharpshooter's bullet, dying an hour after being struck. He would be the last general officer killed in the war. On the same day, Upton struck into the Confederate forces at Columbus, capturing that city and its naval works and burning the ram CSS *Jackson*. Four days later Wilson's men streamed into Macon, capturing that city and learning that the war was coming to an end.

Wilson's raid had been a spectacular success, achieving all its goals, taking 6,820 prisoners, leaving 1,200 Confederate casualties and 725 Union losses behind.

Sadly, despite the winding down of the war, casualties mounted. Hundreds of Union prisoners were on their way home from Confederate prisons such as Cahaba, near Selma. Some 5,000 men had been released from that place as Wilson cleared the area. Now they were headed home by way of Vicksburg, and some 2,222 passengers—2,015 released prisoners and 207 other passengers and crew, including women and children—found themselves aboard the terrifically overcrowded side-wheel steamer *Sultana* on April 27. At 2 A.M., as the ship headed upriver, north of Memphis near Old Hen and Chickens islands, *Sultana's* defective boilers exploded, creating a tumultuous fire that spread rapidly across the ship. The explosion blew people, mules, horses, and chickens into the air, catapulting hundreds of wounded into the river. Most of the ship's pilothouse was disintegrated; the blast and fire effectively broke the ship in two above the waterline; a smoke-stack that fell forward smashed the forward hurricane deck, which fell onto the deck below. Pvt. Benjamin F. Johnson had "a rude awakening" from the blast and found a piece of red-hot coal "as large as a goose egg" flying past his right ear. He saw many passengers "hurrying hither and thither, clasping and wringing their hands . . . shrieking and groaning, and calling upon God to save them," and others "jumping into the river, to rise no more." "Everything seemed to be falling . . ." recalled Sgt. Hosea C. Aldrich. "It was all confusion. The screams of women and children mingled with the groans of wounded and dying. . . . The cries of the drowning and roaring of the flames as they leaped upward made the scene most affecting and touching."

The loss of life among the passengers aboard the *Sultana* was staggering, with a passenger list and fatality rate comparable to that of the RMS *Titanic*. Of the 2,222 persons aboard the *Sultana*, 783 to 786 were initially saved (1,439 to 1,442 died), but more than 200 of these died after rescue. Additionally, while the *Titanic* measured 882 feet in length, the *Sultana* was merely 260 feet long—the crowding was monstrous. In the end, the *Sultana* disaster was the worst mechanical accident of any type in U.S. history and one of the worst maritime accidents in world history.

As WILSON RODE TOWARD SELMA, the Federal noose was tightening on southern Alabama. Maj. Gen. Edward R. S. Canby's Army of the Military Division of West Mississippi was advancing on Mobile. This army consisted of two corps under Maj. Gen. Gordon Granger (13th Corps; divisions of Brig. Gens. James C. Veatch, Christopher C. Andrews, and William P. Benton); and Maj. Gen. Andrew J. Smith (16th Corps; divisions of Brig. Gens. John McArthur, Kenner Garrard, and Eugene A. Carr). A so-called Peninsula Column under

Maj. Gen. Frederick Steele (infantry divisions of Brig. Gens. John P. Hawkins and Joseph F. Knipe, and cavalry division of Brig. Gen. Thomas J. Lucas); and the District of South Alabama troops of Brig. Gen. Thomas Kilby Smith, yielding a total of about 45,000 men. Canby also had naval support within Mobile Bay. Defending Mobile were the forces of Maj. Gen. Dabney H. Maury's District of the Gulf, in the Department of Alabama and East Mississippi. His troops included the divisions of Brig. Gens. St. John R. Liddell and Francis M. Cockrell, and various Alabama cavalry and reserve forces.

On March 17, Canby led the main column from Forts Gaines and Morgan, hoping to approach Mobile from the east, as Steele led 13,000 from Pensacola. Smith's corps moved by water as Granger's corps marched the whole way. The march was exhausting and psychologically difficult because heavy rains drenched the coast nearly every day, but by March 25 the Yankees approached Spanish Fort, a bastion of the city's eastern defenses along the bay. Inside the fort, Confederate Brig. Gen. Randall Lee Gibson organized his 2,800 men efficiently and the earthworks were formidable and supported by heavy guns. Canby, on the other hand, had nearly 32,000 men settling in to lay siege to the city. The sheer number of attackers would be difficult to overcome. The two Federal corps reunited at Danley's Ferry and by March 27 had begun an investment of Spanish Fort. Maury added strength to Gibson's garrison, bringing it to 4,000, as Canby wheeled heavy guns into position. "In camp before 'Ft. Alexis,' or as Gen. Smith calls it 'Fort Elixir,' or as it was called before we arrived, 'Old Spanish Fort,' " Carr told his fiancée Mary, on March 31. "We are now lying before this fort which is opposite Mobile on the eastern shore of the bay. The whole is called Old Spanish Fort from an old water battery that was at the landing. It consists of several works connected by rifle pit customs all on the most commanding ground on the land side. It is flanked by some two forts on small sand islands in the bay which are so located as to fire at an enemy attacking it without hitting the fort itself."

By April 8, Canby had positioned 53 siege guns and 37 field artillery guns into position in front of Spanish Fort. At 5:30 P.M. the attack commenced; Col. James L. Geddes's brigade struck into the earthworks and broke a hole into the line. Six hours later the Confederate position was overrun, Carr's soldiers and others capturing 500 prisoners and 50 guns. Many of the other defenders escaped in a mad rush to Battery Tracy and on back to Mobile. The Confederate losses were 93 killed and 395 wounded. The next day the attack reconfigured on a nearby position in the line, Fort Blakely, which had also been undergoing siege operations since April 1.

The attack on Fort Blakely would be the last infantry battle of the war. Steele's approaching column set up siege operations against Blakely, which was defended by Cockrell's division on the left and a brigade of "boy reserves" on the right, led by Brig. Gen. Bryan M. Thomas. The commander of the fort itself was Brig. Gen. St. John R. Liddell. Siege work was dull, consisting of digging larger trenches and hiding in holes. "We fire constantly," wrote a Confederate officer, "& the men have literally nothing to wipe their rifles out with." When it came, the assault was one of the quickest of the war. On April 9, Canby assembled the whole force of 45,000 opposite Blakely and sent a major attack forward at 5:30 P.M., carrying the works in about twenty minutes. Hawkins's division, which led portions of the attack, was comprised of black assault troops, shocking the Deep Southern defenders. Among Cockrell's Missourians, officers shouted along the line, "Lay low and mow the ground—the damned niggers are coming!" The Union troops ran right up into the Confederate trenches, capturing 3,700 prisoners including Liddell, Thomas, and Cockrell. Casualties were 105 killed and 466 wounded for the Union and 116 killed, 655 wounded, and 4 missing for the Confederates.

Maury abandoned his position by destroying nearby Forts Huger and Tracy on the 11th, scattering toward Montgomery, and Canby entered and took possession of Mobile on April 12. "When I last wrote to you our batteries at this fort, and the rebel batteries 'Huger' and 'Tracy' were exchanging compliments in the shape of 100 pound balls and shells," recorded Pvt. William H. H. Clayton of the 19th Iowa Infantry. "The next day the 11th, the firing was kept up with more severity than the day previously. Our camp was in fair range, and our position was anything but pleasant. Shells fell on each side of us, but fortunately none came into our camp. A storming party was to assault the batteries that night at 2 A.M. on the 12th. The troops belonged to some brigade at Blakely. They approached them in pontoon boats and found that they had been evacuated. The next morning we learned that the 'Johnnies' had also left Mobile leaving everything in our possession. Right upon the heels of this comes the news of the surrender of Lee and his forces."

EVEN WITH THE WAR coming to an end, illness and death still stalked officers and common soldiers across the land. On April 6, Confederate Brig. Gen. John A. Wharton was shot in the chest and killed by Confederate Col. George W. Baylor during an argument at the Fannin House Hotel in Houston. Given the amount of death and suffering and the collapse of the Confederacy, Americans tried to imagine relations in the reconstructed country. Sherman, recovering from the Johnston surrender, wrote to his wife, expressing his rapidly changing feelings toward the reuniting of the sections. "The *mass* of the People South will never trouble us again. They have suffered terrifically, and now I feel disposed to befriend them."

The End of the Civil War

THE WAR WAS EFFECTIVELY OVER—in a flash, it seemed. So many things had changed so quickly, alternately shocking and relieving the nation. The surrenders of Lee and Johnston had slammed the door shut on the Confederacy; the assassination of Lincoln chilled the North and much of the South. Time seemed to be standing still, the nation existing only in paralysis, waiting for the inevitable conclusion of it all. Most Southern soldiers were simply going home, hoping to find a life there that offered something for the future. Although Confederate armies still existed in the field, it seemed a mere matter of time before they, too, would surrender. The seeds of Reconstruction chaos were being sown in Congress as the radical Republicans pushed President Johnson to punish the states in rebellion even as he proclaimed a policy that would echo the wishes of the martyred Lincoln.

Joe Johnston summarized the outlook of most Southern military leaders in his farewell circular to troops of the Army of Tennessee, issued on May 2. "In terminating our official relations," ordered Johnston, "I earnestly exhort you to observe faithfully the terms of pacification agreed upon, and to discharge the obligations of good and peaceful citizens at your homes, as well as you have performed the duties of thorough soldiers in the field. By such a course, you will best secure the comfort of your families and kindred, and restore tranquillity to our country. You will return to your homes with the admiration of our people, won by the courage and noble devotion you have displayed in this long war. I shall always remember with pride the loyal support and generous confidence you have given me. I now part with you with deep regret and bid you farewell with feelings of cordial friendship, and with the earnest wishes that you may have hereafter all the prosperity and happiness to be found in the world." Even fanatical die-hard adherents to the Confederate cause had by now had enough. "Any man who is in favor of a further prosecution of this war is a fit subject for a lunatic asylum," said Nathan Bedford Forrest, the following day, "and ought to be sent there immediately."

The largest Confederate force remaining in the field was that of Lt. Gen. Richard Taylor, whose 12,000 troops of the Department of Alabama and East Mississippi surrendered at Citronelle, Alabama, north of Mobile, on May 4. Maj. Gen. Edward R. S. Canby accepted the surrender; now the Confederate forces of Maj. Gen. Samuel Jones (in Florida), Brig. Gen. M. Jeff Thompson (in Arkansas), and Gen. Edmund Kirby Smith (in Texas) were the only significant troops left. On the day of Taylor's surrender, Abraham Lincoln was buried in Springfield, Illinois. His conspirators were standing trial for their roles in the murder.

The remnants of the Confederate government, meanwhile, were busily fleeing southward as Federal cavalry closed in. As President Davis, his wife Varina, Postmaster General John H. Reagan, Secretary of State Judah Benjamin, and others were encamped near Irwinville, Georgia, on May 10, Federal troopers rode into the camp and surprised them. In the confusion that followed, Davis and his wife, Reagan, presidential secretary Burton Harrison, and a few others were captured. In a circumstance that launched a prolonged series of derisive editorials, Davis was captured in a waterproof raincoat and shawl he had thrown on hastily. The regiment that captured Davis and his party was the 4th Michigan Cavalry, led by Lt. Col. Benjamin D. Pritchard. One of Pritchard's soldiers, Capt. Charles T. Hudson, stated that Davis was captured in woman's clothes, and the Northern press had a field day with the claim. "[Hudson] says I was dressed in female attire," Davis recalled after the war, "and said that Mrs Davis in her own justification told him 'she did dress Mr. Davis in her attire and would not deny it.' But that attire appears by his own statement to have been a water proof cloak and a shawl; now where is the hoop skirt and the petticoat and sun-bonnet, which has been the staple of so many malignant diatribes and pictorials."

Benjamin escaped; he made his way to the Bahamas, to Cuba, and then to England. Davis, however, would be incarcerated in Fort Monroe, Virginia, facing a trial that never came before eventual release. Davis was also investigated over complicity in the Lincoln assassination. "I have the honor to report in the matter of inquiry as to whether Jeff. Davis made while here expressions in approval of the assassination of President Lincoln," stated Brig. Gen. Thomas H. Ruger in Charlotte, late in May. "I cannot learn that Davis made use of expressions other than to Mr. Bates, who left this place for Washington. . . . I am satisfied that Davis did not talk on the matter in public, and that what he said was to his own immediate party or particular partisans."

On the same day as Davis's capture, President Johnson proclaimed armed resistance at an end (although it wasn't quite yet). Scattered minor skirmishing continued. Sam Jones's surrender at Tallahassee of the Districts of South Carolina and Florida in the Department of South Carolina, Georgia, and Florida also occurred on May 10. Further, on this day the 27-year-old Col. William C. Quantrill, the raider who had terrorized Lawrence, Kansas, and made savage warfare his trademark, was mortally wounded in Kentucky. The following day M. Jeff Thompson, the Swamp Fox, surrendered troops in the Northern Subdistrict of the District of Arkansas, in Chalk Bluff, Arkansas.

On May 12 came the final land battle of the war. Far out in the Trans-Mississippi, to which news traveled slowly, forces clashed near Brownsville, Texas, at Palmito Ranch (sometimes spelled Palmetto Ranch). Union men under Col. Theodore H. Barrett marched inland from Brazos Santiago and struck into the Rebels at the ranch, which stood on the Rio Grande. Barrett's force consisted of 250 troops of the 62d U.S. Colored Troops and 50 men from the 2d Texas Cavalry, dismounted. Hoosiers from the 34th Indiana Infantry also joined the expedition. The Confederate forces were led by Col. John S. Ford, known as "R.I.P. Ford" because as a judge he often penned "Rest in Peace" on his sentences. After successful attacks the Federals had to withdraw in the afternoon of the 13th under heavy fire. The last land action of the war was, ironically, a Confederate victory.

Confederates wondered about their new lives as Union military officials pondered how to keep the peace in newly occupied states. "Civil War, such as you have just passed through," advised Nathan Bedford Forrest in his farewell address, "naturally engenders feelings of animosity, hatred, and revenge. It is our duty to divest ourselves of all such feelings, and, as far as in our power to do so, to cultivate friendly feelings toward those with whom we have so long contended." Confusion over policy reigned supreme, with all eyes turning toward an eventual readmittance of the states into the Union. In Raleigh, Maj. Gen. John M. Schofield inquired of Halleck. "I have received your dispatch concerning slavery, the treatment of freed-men, &c. I will send you my orders, issued some days ago, which agree perfectly with your views on this subject. I have not recognized in any way any civil officers of the state. . . . I desire to suggest that the sooner a military governor is appointed for this state and steps taken to organize a civil government the better. The people are now in a mood to accept any thing in reason."

THE PRINCIPAL FEDERAL ARMIES, meanwhile, had been preparing for a great celebration. Over two days nearly all of Washington and thousands from other cities came out to see the Army of the Potomac and Sherman's armies of the Military Division of the Mississippi march in a grand review. Throngs of people lined the streets, mainly between the Capitol and the Executive

Mansion, bands played, children sang songs, and the armies marched as the flag over the Capitol and Executive Mansion were raised to full staff for the first time since the assassination. About 150,000 men marched over the two days; the Potomac army on May 23 and Sherman's armies the following day filed past a reviewing stand that held President Johnson, General Grant, cabinet members, dignitaries, and other commanding generals. Meade rode at the head of the first day's column and Sherman at the head of the second day's parade. Despite the death of Lincoln, Washingtonians and Americans then, it seemed, made a vow to come together for a productive and peaceful future. This event signaled the final act of the main volunteer armies, and their dissolution would commence and continue for weeks. The United States could now begin to revert to a peacetime army, a regular army that would occupy the South and see the states back into a proper relationship within the Federal Union. The volunteers would not go away as quickly as many believed, however: the final volunteer general officer was Maj. Gen. Oliver O. Howard, who was mustered out of service on January 1, 1869—and therefore it is fair to say that the war period existed until that day.

On May 29, President Johnson issued the first of several amnesty proclamations to Confederate soldiers, this one granting pardons to all persons who had directly or indirectly participated in "the existing rebellion," with the exception of the Confederate high command, significant property holders, and a few other classes. Those who accepted were required to sign an oath supporting the U.S. Constitution. The final major surrender of Confederate forces came on June 2 when Kirby Smith accepted terms that had been discussed on May 26 and surrendered the Trans-Mississippi Department. At Galveston, Canby accepted the surrender, eliminating the last significant army of the Confederacy. Some Confederates in the theater refused to surrender and scattered out west or to Mexico, but they represented a small fraction of the men who went home.

Southerners felt broken, and for some it was too much. Edmund Ruffin, the fiery secessionist who had fired one of the war's first shots near Sumter, could not bear to see it end this way. "And now, with my latest writing, and utterance," he recorded on June 18, "and with what will be near to my latest breath, I here repeat, and would willingly proclaim, my unmitigated hatred to Yankee rule. To all political, social, and business connection with the Yankees, and to the perfidious, malignant, and vile Yankee race." He then killed himself. In May, Vice President Alexander H. Stephens was imprisoned in Fort Warren, Boston Harbor. He kept an extensive journal, in which he recorded that "the horrors of imprisonment, close confinement, no one to see or to talk to, with the reflection of being cut off for I know not how long—perhaps forever—from communication with dear ones at home, are beyond description. Words utterly fail to express the soul's anguish. This day

I wept bitterly. Nerves and spirit utterly forsook me. O God, if it be possible, let this cup pass from me!" Stephens, along with Postmaster General Reagan, Treasury Secretary George A. Trenholm, Assistant Secretary of War John A. Campbell, and Governor Charles Clark of Mississippi, was paroled finally on October 11.

In late June some measure of comfort was felt by Northern civilians with the conviction of the Lincoln conspirators. On July 7, a hot, sunny day in Washington, four of them—Powell (Payne), Atzerodt, Herold, and Mary Surratt—were hanged on the grounds of the arsenal at the Old Penitentiary Building. A celebrated sequence of photographs taken by Alexander Gardner captured the event in what is one of the earliest American examples of news photography. The furor over hanging a woman, who some felt was innocent or at least less guilty than the others, lived on for years. The four surviving convicted conspirators were imprisoned at Fort Jefferson on the Dry Tortugas, where a yellow fever epidemic in 1867 killed among others Michael O'Laughlin. Samuel Mudd, the doctor who had set Booth's painful (possibly broken) ankle, was pardoned in 1868 for his help with the yellow fever patients on the island; a year later Ned Spangler and Samuel Arnold were also pardoned. John Surratt escaped to Europe unpunished and returned years later to publicize everything from the truth to weird stories of conspiracy.

Northern soldiers and sailors tried to settle into normal life again. "Render the same cheerful obedience to the civil that you have rendered to the naval law," suggested Comdr. Foxhall A. Parker to the sailors of the Potomac Flotilla. "Cast your votes as good citizens, regularly and quietly at the polls; so keeping in your hearts 'with malice toward none, with charity for all,' that after each Presidential election, whether it be with you or against you, you may be able to respond heartily to our old navy toast: 'The President of the United States: God bless him!' " Other Federals had complications to deal with because of the reoccupation of states previously in rebellion. Brig. Gen. William S. Ketcham had to reclaim a house that he owned in Tallahassee, Florida, that had been seized by the Rebel authorities when the war began. The house had subsequently been sold at auction to a Florida citizen. Numerous such transactions, not legally recognized by the United States, now had to be "undone."

Though Confederates had not accepted U.S. laws, they did accept and routinely use U.S. currency, and that was one early sign of the weakness of the Confederacy. Money is ruled by psychology: currency has value only if people are willing to accept it for goods or services. All during the war, Southerners accepted U.S. currency, but citizens of the North (and many from the South) declined to accept Confederate paper.

While the search for reasons behind the failure of the Southern war effort began (a soon-to-be cottage industry that continues today), most citizens wanted the war put behind them. "The grand mistake of the South was neglecting her navy," declared Comdr. John N. Maffit. But of course there were many causes, none more important than the eventual collapse of Southern popular support for the war once it became starkly clear that it was making life worse for Confederate civilians and offered little hope of making things better. Yet, as prominent historians have reminded readers many times in recent years, the war had to be decided on the battleground with decisive victories, and that was exactly where Grant, Sherman, and Sheridan won out.

In early July, celebrations looked toward a reunited future. "This day has been duly observed throughout the Carolinas," reported Maj. Gen. Dan Sickles on July 4, in Charleston, the former hotbed of rebellion. "Salutes have been fired at sunrise, meridian, and sunset—Business places closed and at Charleston the time honored chimes of St. Michael's Church—so long the target of Gilmore [sic] during the dark years of Rebellion—rang out the national airs. Public buildings, streets, hotels, and ships decorated with the American flag—the colored people have been out en masse parading the streets, displaying flags in profusion, bunting in great demand. . . . All quiet and orderly. Promenade concert, illumination and Fire Works at the Citadel attended by the principal citizens tonight."

Many officers seemed unclear as to their status as the volunteer army contracted. Brig. Gen. Green Berry Raum of Illinois had resigned on May 6, for example, apparently unbeknown to the Army of the Shenandoah, in which he commanded a brigade. "I do not yet know whether or not he is discharged the service, and beg that I may be informed what is his precise rank—brevet or full Brig. Gen.—and furnished a copy of his discharge, if he is out of service," requested Brig. Gen. Thomas W. Egan, his division commander. "He is reported 'absent without leave.' " Sometime later Brig. Gen. Manning F. Force of Ohio wrote from Jackson, Mississippi: "I am told there is an order discharging me (with many of the general officers) to date 15th inst. Are my acts as commanding this district, subsequent to that date, legal? Are the records and files of the district to be sent to the Adjutant General of the Army, direct, or to Department headquarters? Is the order such as to give transportation for myself, servant and horses to my residence?" Force signed the letter, "(Dubiously), Brevet Major Genl. U.S.V." Force indeed was about to be mustered out but had as yet heard only a rumor to the effect.

Though the Confederacy had ceased to exist, one particle of it, the CSS *Shenandoah*, was still on the high seas, unaware of the war's end. On August 2 the ship, en route from the Arctic to San Francisco, encountered a British ship, officers of which informed the Southern sailors that war had ceased. "We were bereft of ground for hope or aspiration, bereft of a cause for which to struggle and suffer," recalled Lt. William C. Whittle, Jr., the ship's executive officer. On November 6, 1865, the *Shenandoah* struck its flag and Lt. James Waddell, the ship's captain, surrendered her to British authorities at Liverpool, marking the final act of the Confederate States of America. Four days later retribution again reared its head when Capt. Henry Wirz, commandant of Andersonville prison, was hanged in Washington after his conviction for war crimes.

The reformulated state governments of the South spent the final weeks of 1865 ratifying the Thirteenth Amendment to the Constitution. On April 2, 1866, President Johnson proclaimed "that the insurrection which heretofore existed in the States of Georgia, South Carolina, Virginia, North Carolina, Tennessee, Alabama, Louisiana, Arkansas, Mississippi, and Florida is at an end." (Texas was excluded because its government was still being formed. Its insurrection was declared at an end in August 1865.) Slowly, the painful era of postwar Reconstruction accelerated, a traumatizing time for the South. In 1866, Tennessee would be first to be "readmitted" to the Union, on July 24. The political winds of consolidation continued in 1867: Nebraska was added to the Union on March 1; Alaska Territory was acquired from Russia on March 30 (it would be known for years as "Seward's Folly" until the value of furs, fish, gold, copper, and oil was recognized); and the Second Amnesty Proclamation was issued to all Confederate brigadier generals on September 7. In 1868, amid the impeachment chaos of the Johnson administration (sparked by the president's suspension of War Secretary Stanton), came the readmission of Florida (June 10), Arkansas (June 26), North Carolina (July 4), Louisiana (July 9), South Carolina (July 15), and Alabama (July 20); the organization of Wyoming Territory (July 25); and the Third Amnesty Proclamation, to all remaining Confederate high commanders. In 1870 the final four states were readmitted: Virginia (January 26), Mississippi (February 23), Texas (March 30), and Georgia (July 15).

"The legitimate object of war is a more perfect peace," William T. Sherman told a crowd in St. Louis in the summer of 1865. Years later, at a veterans' reunion of the Grand Army of the Republic in Columbus, Ohio, he said plainly: "There is many a boy here today who looks on war as all glory. But boys it is all hell. You can bear this warning voice to generations yet to come. I look upon war with horror, but if it has to come I am here." While Grant, Sherman, Sheridan and the other victors of the war traveled the world and made frequent speeches about the conflict, many of the vanquished retreated to a quiet life and mulled over what had gone wrong. In Lexington, Virginia, Robert E. Lee spent a great deal of time autographing photographs to raise funds for the local Presbyterian Church and writing codified messages to himself. "The gentleman does not needlessly—remind an offender of a wrong he may have committed against him," he jotted one day. "He cannot only forgive, he can forget; and he strives for that nobleness of self and mildness of character which imparts sufficient strength to let the past be but the past. A true man of honor feels humbled himself when he cannot help humbly others."

Other Southerners immediately took up the cause to continue the war on paper. In the pages of the *Southern Historical Society Papers,* published in Richmond and offering a Virginia-centric view of events, and in other outlets, they glorified Southern military heroes, rewrote the stories of each battle (in which they almost always seemed to win), and heaped glory upon the Lost Cause, as it now was becoming known. "Future years will never know the seething hell and the black infernal background of countless minor scenes and interiors of the Secession War," worried Walt Whitman in 1875. "In the mushy influences of current times the fervid atmosphere and typical events of those years are in danger of being totally forgotten." Many soldiers lectured about their war experiences, hoping that no one would forget the great struggle, and in many cases in an effort to hang on to what had been the greatest event of their lives. "Through our great good fortune in our youth our hearts were touched with fire," recalled Oliver Wendell Holmes, Jr., on Memorial Day in 1884. Certain writers, such as Ambrose Bierce, who had also been a Federal officer, worried over the accuracy of much of what appeared in print, and lamented the fallen soldiers who never saw the country reunited again—who never knew how things would be. "They were the honest and courageous foemen, having little in common with the political madmen who persuaded them to their doom and the literary bearers of false witness in the aftertime," he remarked in 1903. "They did not live through the period of honorable strife into the period of vilification—did not pass from the iron age to the brazen—from the era of the sword to that of the tongue and the pen."

THE CAUSES of Confederate failure were many. As we have seen, internal support for the Confederacy collapsed throughout the war as citizens of the South discovered the hardships of wartime life on the home front and witnessed whole communities of young men being slaughtered in battle. Slavery, at first heralded as the great cause of the war by Southerners and then denied as the root cause, created substantial problems in many ways. When the Federal armies occupied "Confederate territories," ex-slaves joined the Union armies as recruits, and as we have seen, nearly 200,000 black Americans fought for the Union during the war. Psychologically, many Southerners suffered greatly during the last year or two, when it became clear the South was losing, feeling that a just God must be punishing them for the sin of slavery. Many Southerners, in retrospect, felt duped into the war over the interests of a relatively few wealthy slave owners. "This was unjust and unnecessary," seethed Douglas J. Cater of the 19th Louisiana Infantry following surrender. "Personal ownership of slaves could have and should have been ended without the sword and musket, which caused so much sorrow and suffering, devastation and bloodshed. National questions demand fair consideration, but in this case we must conclude that personal ambition prevented it." By clinging to slavery even as the rest of the civilized world disapproved, the South relatively early on ruled out foreign intervention on its behalf, only to attempt to rush legislation to arm black soldiers in the spring of 1865, when it was too late on both practical and moral grounds.

Confederate morale was high early in the war, bolstered by Fort Sumter and First Bull Run. It slid in the spring of 1862 with the fall of Forts Henry and Donelson but climbed to an all-time high with the victories at Second Bull Run and the Kentucky and Maryland campaigns in autumn 1862. After this time the cost of the war caused morale to begin to crumble. The Federal victories of Gettysburg and Vicksburg were partly countered by Southern success at Chickamauga. The initial campaigning in the Overland campaign and Sherman's difficulty in approaching Atlanta initially favored Southern morale, but by early summer 1864, Confederate morale began a deep slide from which it would never recover. The capture of Atlanta, the reelection of Lincoln, and the disastrous adventures of Hood at Franklin and Nashville pulled the South down for good.

The poor Southern economy also made the war untenable. A treasury nearly always in danger of bankruptcy contributed to high prices, a relatively worthless currency, a scarcity of goods and an unwillingness to part with them, and the decay of the railroad system due to poor maintenance caused by lack of funds. The relative scarcity of food as the war dragged on, both for civilians and within the armies and navy, contributed greatly to declining morale. Inadequate supplies and a shortage of horses also materially contributed to Southern difficulties.

Perhaps the most damaging aspect of the Confederacy itself, as we have seen, was the lack of cooperation among politicians, officers, civilians, and common soldiers. At times every person in the Confederacy seemed to be in the war for his or her own reasons. The politicians in Richmond failed to cooperate with each other daily, a situation made worse by the stiff personality of Jefferson Davis, who was ill-suited to act as president, and the refusal of Alexander Stephens to work with him. State governors also refused to cooperate with the national government in Richmond, particularly Joe Brown in Georgia and Zeb Vance in North Carolina. State rights not only launched the war in the first place but created internal factions the Confederacy could ill afford. Military commanders opposed Davis, too, none more so than Joe Johnston.

Conversely, Northern military success came ultimately despite the grandness of the objectives in sight. As we have seen, Union armies and navies had to attack predominantly in unfamiliar territory and needed to occupy vast stretches of territory, railroads, and coastline once that territory was "retaken." The task of the Union armies was much greater than the mostly defensive strategy Confederate forces required. Certainly, the North had more matériel, money, manpower, and higher morale than the South. But whether Union armies and navies could accomplish the Herculean task before patience was exhausted among the civilians, before too many sons died to make preserving the Union seem justified, was the key question. In hindsight, peace movements never were strong enough to disrupt the war, but certainly at times public support for the seemingly unending crisis waned temporarily.

It was Grant who discovered, perhaps pioneered, the modern military concepts that had eluded other commanders during this great war. All the key principles eventually served him well—moving against and destroying armies rather than cities; using movements coordinated in time and space to affect a large-scale strategy over several theaters of operation at once; boldly using supply and communications lines or abandoning them and living off the land to face the enemy; testing possibilities for success and learning from them each time they worked or failed. Was there a single moment that decided the outcome of the Civil War? Perhaps it came when Grant, with Meade in the Wilderness, turned southward to flank Lee's right rather than retreating in the face of bloody casualties after the battle. On that day Grant put into execution everything he had learned and was determined to pursue the last remaining Southern soldier, if necessary, in order to win the war. Lincoln had unquestionably found his man.

IN SPRINGFIELD, visitors regularly came to Oak Ridge Cemetery, where Lincoln rested. So deeply traumatic was the Lincoln assassination that the martyred president had been elevated to demigod status nearly overnight, and it must be remembered that in life Lincoln was despised by many just as he had been greatly loved by a majority. In nineteenth-century America, on the heels of the war, Lincoln's death was overwhelming in a way that is hard to appreciate now, even in the wake of more recent assassinations.

Shortly after Lincoln's death an association was formed to fund and construct a proper tomb for the fallen chief. The monument would consist of an obelisk atop an elaborate tomb with bronze statuary; work began in 1869 and Lincoln's body was interred in it (transferred from a temporary tomb) in 1871. Thousands of visitors flocked to the cemetery grounds in carriages, on horseback, and on foot, many of them ex-soldiers. Flowers regularly adorned the crypt where Lincoln and three of his sons were buried. At last, Lincoln, who had come so far from the Kentucky wilderness, the prairies of Indiana and Illinois, to lead the nation through its most difficult time, was at rest. Friends of Lincoln recalled a poem, "My Childhood Home I See Again," written by the prairie lawyer at age 37, which now seemed to apply to so many American families who had lost loved ones in the war, including the Lincoln family.

> *O Memory! thou midway world*
> *'twixt earth and paradise*
> *Where things decayed and loved ones lost*
> *In dreamy shadows rise*
> *And, freed from all that's earthly vile*
> *Seem hallowed, pure, and bright*
> *Like scenes in some enchanted isle*
> *All bathed in liquid light . . .*
> *The friends I left the parting day*
> *How changed, as time has sped!*
> *Young childhood grown, strong manhood gray*
> *And half of all are dead*
> *I hear the loved survivors tell*
> *How nought from death could save*
> *Till every sound appears a knell*
> *And every spot a grave*
> *I range the fields with pensive tread*
> *And pace the hollow rooms*
> *And feel (companion of the dead)*
> *I'm living in the tombs.*

Epilogue: 1865

PVT. ROGER A. PRYOR spent the first few weeks of 1865 in a damp, dark prison cell at Fort Lafayette in New York Harbor, which was at the time called "the American Bastille." Active as a common soldier during the Petersburg campaign in 1864, Pryor had fought valiantly, even as shells landed near the house in Petersburg occupied by his wife Sara and sons (among them one-year-old Roger Jr.). At Reams's Station on August 25, 1864, the wealthy Virginia orator had displayed "coolness and courage" amid the roar of the artillery and musketry fire and refuted the claim that Confederate soldiers were all poor men waging war for the rich. In November, however, Pryor had been captured after exchanging periodicals with the Yankees near the lines; his unorthodox custody resulted from retaliation after the Confederate capture of Capt. Henry S. Burrage of the 36th Massachusetts Infantry, whom Confederate officers had taken "unfairly" as he exchanged goods.

Pryor's incarceration spurred a flurry of attempts for release in February and March 1865. Washington McLean, editor of the *Cincinnati Inquirer*, gained an audience with War Secretary Edwin M. Stanton and asked the gruff "Mars" about the celebrated prisoner, to which Stanton replied, "He shall be hanged! Damn him!" Few Unionists had forgotten how virulent a role Pryor had played in escalating secession sentiment in South Carolina and in aiding the reduction and capture of Fort Sumter in the war's first hours. McLean then journeyed to see President Lincoln and brought a letter of support from the gadfly editor Horace Greeley. McLean enlisted the support of John W. Forney, secretary of the U.S. Senate, who accompanied the editor to see the President. Lincoln, who of course knew all about Pvt. Pryor's history, produced a memorandum from young boys who had been enlisted into a Pennsylvania regiment and captured at Petersburg, after which Pryor had shared his food rations with them and procured supplies for them to increase their comfort. "The man who can do such kindness to an enemy cannot be cruel and revengeful," Lincoln allegedly said. He then produced a letter to Col. Martin Burke, commandant of Fort Lafayette, stating: "Please release General Roger A. Pryor, who will report to Colonel Forney on Capitol Hill. A. Lincoln." Pryor's kindness to the Pennsylvania boys wasn't the only reason for his release: the Virginian had paroled 5,000 Yankee prisoners in 1862 and returned them to Washington instead of to prisons; Pryor had treated prisoners in Virginia with great respect and care; and Lincoln, significantly, recalled the early journalistic skills of the writer and orator Pryor whose work had influenced Lincoln's own "House Divided" and "Irrepressible Conflict" speeches before the war came.

Pryor was sent home through the lines on February 25 with a pass signed by Lincoln himself. He had signed a parole and would no longer fight for the Confederacy. On April 2, as Petersburg fell, Pryor was arrested by Union troops but released after producing the Lincoln pass. Maj. Gen. Phil Sheridan occupied the Pryor House and Pryor moved temporarily to Nottoway County to stay with his sisters. At Petersburg, Sara Pryor found her rations of food, provided by the Federal occupational force, infested with caterpillars, and Maj. Gen. George L. Hartsuff increased the quantity and quality of food supplies after receiving a note from her. Returning to Petersburg, Roger Pryor nursed his family back to health after they each contracted malaria, then went to Richmond to look for work. He could find none, and Sara recalled, "There seemed to be no room for a rebel in all the world." The South had lost its spirit after Appomattox, and none seemingly knew how to regain it. "That war was closed on a spectacle of ruin," wrote Richmond editor Edward A. Pollard, "the greatest of modern times. There were eleven great States lying prostrate; their capital all absorbed; the fields desolate; their towns and cities ruined; their public works torn to pieces by armies; their system of labour overturned; the fruits of the toil of generations all swept into a chaos of destruction; their slave property taken away by the stroke of a pen."

As one of the vocal promoters of the rebellion, Pryor was certain to be sought as a defendant for treason. But even as correspondents were urging him to leave Virginia, to seek fortune in New York, Pryor was undergoing a rapid transformation. "We have been fairly whipped," he told his fellow Southerners after Appomattox, "and I think that such men in Lee's and Johnston's armies as do not lay down their arms and return at once to their duties as law-abiding citizens should be treated as outlaws." He decided to go to New York seeking work, and temporary freedom from prosecution, and Sara sold her watch, a diamond-laden cameo ring, and took out a $300 loan to secure her husband's passage and establishment in the city. In early summer 1865, as the war was still winding down, Pryor secured an apartment at 47 West 12th Street in Manhattan and took a position under editor Benjamin Wood on the staff of the *New York Daily News.*

Influenced by Lincoln's kindness and intolerant of those ex-Confederates who spoke badly of the fallen U.S. president, Pryor absorbed Yankeedom, a former fire-eating Rebel living among the postwar opportunity of the nation's largest city. He walked about Central Park, watched the Northern boys and girls at play, earned $25 a week, corresponded regularly with his family in Virginia, and sent money to send his boys to school. With every ounce of energy he had, Pryor studied law, sitting up late at night and learning everything he could, just as Lincoln had on the Illinois frontier years before. By year's end Pryor was admitted to the New York bar and opened a law office on Nassau Street.

This strange and delicate man who had been described as "tall; he wears long black hair, combed towards the back of his head and falling behind his ears; his countenance has a boyish expression, and his age is thirty-five years," had undergone a remarkable transformation. Celebrated and influential at a young age, the politician and orator (and, later, soldier) had so passionately backed the Confederacy that he was viewed as one of a handful of men who started the Civil War. Yet the celebrated, angry, self-absorbed man had embraced kindness and anonymity, fighting during the war both in a general's frock coat and in a private soldier's blouse and helping enemy soldiers as much as he fought them. He then urged his fellow Rebels to become good Union citizens from within its largest, most commercial city, acting as a thoroughly modern attorney and planting the seeds for a long and storied career that included service on the New York Supreme Court and friendships with a long list of ex-Union officers, including Grant, Sherman, and Sheridan.

Roger Pryor had helped to spark the greatest storm of the American nation as a savage critic of the Federal government, passed through it as an active Confederate soldier, and emerged as a staunch Union man. He had foreseen the inevitable and dropped his conservative dogmas, reinventing himself as a forward, independent thinker.

During one night in late December 1865 a bitter winter storm blew over New York City, rattling the windows. Pryor did not sleep well, and perhaps his thoughts as he tossed in bed took him back to the battlefield, to the small boat that had carried him to Fort Sumter, to the stormy speeches on the Charleston waterfront, stirring the emotions of his Southerners against the Union. The bloody, bullet-riddled bodies of young boys strewn across the Virginia Peninsula, the as yet unfulfilled aspirations of his own young sons in Virginia blew through his mind in a haze. Such a bothersome series of nightmares stirred Pryor's thoughts throughout the bleak winter storm, and yet his newfound optimism for his family and beloved Southerners, for the good of the future of the American nation, prevailed early in the morning.

Pryor dressed and felt waves of confidence as reality returned to his mind. He sipped coffee, then walked over two miles north to Central Park to see what the storm had done. Looking to the east, the clouds were separating and bright sunlight streamed down. The United States had already begun to evolve into a new, stronger nation. The longest night had come to an end.

Acknowledgments

I've spent portions of three years locked in my study revisiting my friends of the Civil War days, constructing this narrative. I have also consulted quite a few modern-day friends along the way, but any shortcomings or errors that appear in my version of history are solely my responsibility. I have to thank my wife, Lynda, and son, Chris, whose tolerance of my writing over long hours is superhuman, and my father John Eicher, Civil War authority par excellence, who has steered me free of many hangups. I owe a great debt of gratitude to Jim McPherson, who as the leading Civil War historian of this age was splendidly generous by contributing his magnificent foreword for this book. I owe much to my good friend Russell Fay, who labored for hours reading through dozens of classics and recent scholarly tomes looking for gems that could be wrapped into this story of the war. For their continual encouragement of my projects, I also wish to thank Richard A. Sauers, John Y. Simon, Lance Herdegen, and Gary W. Gallagher. Their comments are more valuable than they could possibly know.

This book would have been but a shadow of itself if not for the brilliant oversight of Bob Bender at Simon & Schuster. His reflection on many facets of the work large and small has helped to shape it into a worthwhile story. I also thank S&S's Johanna Li for her frequent help with many tasks. For their work in the production stages, I thank Fred Wiemer, who copyedited the manuscript; John Morgenstern, who checked the final pages; Peter Vabulas, who checked the final map proofs; and Gypsy da Silva, who supervised the copyediting and proofreading. My thanks, also, to Rachel Nagler in Publicity. My agent, Michael Choate of Lescher and Lescher Ltd., who enthused over the manuscript as it took shape, foresaw the need for such a volume and helped me to formulate the project in the first place. I thank Kelly Kizer Whitt for carefully proofing the whole manuscript and offering valuable suggestions. Thanks also to Bonnie Gordon and Peter Sutter for their encouragement and advice.

I owe a number of people at institutions across the country special thanks, too. I hope that I haven't left any out who went above and beyond the call to assist me: Michael Musick, Tod Butler, Becky Livingston, and Trevor Plant of the National Archives and Records Administration, Washington, D.C.; Richard J. Sommers, Tom Vossler, David A. Keough, and Pamela Cheney of the U.S. Army Military History Institute, Carlisle, Pennsylvania; Kathy Harrison and Scott Hartwig of the Gettysburg National Military Park, Gettysburg, Pennsylvania; and Ted Alexander of the Antietam National Battlefield, Sharpsburg, Maryland. They have made fighting the Civil War over again not only worthwhile, but a pleasure.

DAVID J. EICHER
Waukesha, Wisconsin

Notes

PROLOGUE: 1915

30   *"Never more will you see from Virginia"*: Holzman, *Adapt or Perish*, 124.

30   *"As an old soldier"*: New York Times, July 20, 1915.

31   *"I cannot forget the Civil War"*: Holzman, *Adapt or Perish*, 151.

31   *No ceremony that to great ones longs*: New York Times, April 19, 1914.

CHAPTER 1   THE WAR BEGINS AT SUMTER

33   *"Except that the flag was hoisted"*: James Chester, "Inside Sumter in '61," in Johnson and Buel, eds., *Battles and Leaders of the Civil War*, I, 65–66.

35   *"I looked anxiously with my glass"*: Samuel Wylie Crawford, "Diary of Brigadier-General Samuel Wylie Crawford, Fort Sumter, South Carolina, December 19, 1860–April 14, 1861," in Hewitt et al., eds., *Supplement to the Official Records of the Union and Confederate Armies*, I, 1, 11. [Hereafter, *O.R. Supplement*.]

35   *This shift occurred*: Report of James W. Ripley concerning John B. Floyd's transfer of arms to Southern arsenals, from U.S. War Department, *The War of the Rebellion: A Compilation of Official Records of the Union and Confederate Armies*, III, 1, 321. [Hereafter, *O.R.*]

36   *"In a great crisis"*: New York Times, April 3, 1861.

36   *Surrounding them, scattered about the city*: Klein, *Days of Defiance*, 408.

36   *James Louis Petigru*: Pease and Pease, *James Louis Petigru*, 156.

36   *"I thank you especially"*: Klein, *Days of Defiance*, 398.

36   *He recorded the diet as*: Crawford, in *O.R. Supplement*, I, 1, 57.

36   *The engineer Foster added*: John G. Foster, "Engineer Journal of the Bombardment of Fort Sumter," in *O.R.*, I, 1, 17.

37   *"I am ordered by the government"*: Ibid., 13.

37   *"I have the honor to acknowledge"*: Ibid.

37   *"By authority of Brigadier-General Beauregard"*: Ibid., 14.

37   *If they never again met*: Klein, *Days of Defiance*, 409.

38   *"We arose and dressed"*: Crawford, in *O.R. Supplement*, I, 1, 59.

38   *"A flash as of distant lightning"*: Chester, in Johnson and Buel, eds., *Battles and Leaders of the Civil War* (hereafter *Battles and Leaders*), I, 65–66.

38   *"A ball from Cummings's Point"*: Doubleday, *Reminiscences of Forts Sumter and Moultrie*, 142.

38   *"I do not pretend to go to sleep"*: Chesnut, *Mary Chesnut's Civil War*, 46.

41   *"Very well, gentlemen"*: Chester, in Johnson and Buel, eds., *Battles and Leaders*, I, 73.

41 *The Yankees marched out:* O.R., I, 1, 12.

42 *"A little spice of danger":* James A. Connolly, "Major Connolly's Letters to His Wife, 1862–1865," in *Transactions of the Illinois State Historical Society,* 1928.

42 *"You have long before":* Lt. Alexander C. Haskell to his parents, Light House Hills, South Carolina, April 11, 1861, from Haskell Papers, item 320.

42 *"I've often longed to see a war":* Louisa May Alcott, in Masur, ed., *Real War Will Never Get in the Books,* 21.

43 *"I wonder if it be a sin":* Chesnut, *The Private Mary Chesnut,* 42.

43 *"As it is," wrote Jefferson:* Malone, *Sage of Monticello,* 336.

44 *"A house divided against itself":* Lincoln, *Collected Works,* II, 461–469.

45 *"I John Brown am now quite certain":* Oates, *To Purge This Land with Blood,* 351.

46 *"We, the people of the State of South Carolina":* Moore, ed., *Rebellion Record,* I, 2.

46 *"All the indications":* Strong, *Diary of George Templeton Strong,* III, 95.

46 *Robert E. Lee wrote his son:* Long and Wright, eds., *Memoirs of Robert E. Lee,* 88–89.

47 *"People who are anxious":* J. I. Robertson, *Stonewall Jackson,* 206–207.

47 *"If anyone attempts to haul down":* Warner, *Generals in Blue,* 126.

47 *Such contempt for the secession movement:* A. Johnson, *Papers,* IV, 204–261.

48 *"All Montgomery had flocked":* DeLeon, *Four Years in Rebel Capitals,* 23–27.

48 *"The man and the hour have met":* W. C. Davis, *Jefferson Davis,* 307.

49 *At length, Davis continued:* Jefferson Davis, *Papers,* VII, 46–51.

49 *In short, according to one biographer:* Schott, *Alexander H. Stephens,* 20.

49 *"Our new government":* Ibid., 334.

50 *"Let me tell you what is coming":* Gallaway, *Texas,* 129.

50 *"I wish I was in de land ob cotton":* Commager, *Blue and the Gray,* 561–563.

50 *"I have never had a feeling":* Lincoln, *Collected Works,* IV, 240–241.

51 *Early in the day:* Sandburg, *Abraham Lincoln: The War Years,* I, 120.

51 *It was only the day before:* W. Scott, *Memoirs,* II, 625–628.

51 *As he rode from the Executive Mansion:* Donald, *Lincoln,* 282.

51 *"It is safe to assert that no government":* Lincoln, *Collected Works,* IV, 262–271.

51 *"When the address closed":* E. A. W. Dwight, *Life and Letters of Wilder Dwight,* 33–34.

51 *Wrote George Templeton Strong:* Strong, *Diary,* III, 106.

51 *"The cry to-day is war":* Chesnut, *The Private Mary Chesnut,* 25.

51 *"The bird of our country":* Strong, *Diary,* III, 109.

52 *"It is the strangest thing":* Hawthorne, in Masur, ed., *Real War,* 171.

52 *"Well, my dearest one":* Tyler, *Letters and Times of the Tylers,* II, 641.

53 *"Missouri can and will":* O.R., I, 1, 690.

53 *As the bombardment of Sumter raged:* J. I. Robertson, *Stonewall Jackson,* 210.

53 *At nearby Winchester:* Hearn, *Six Years of Hell,* 54.

54 *"A scene of bloody confusion":* Frederic Emory, "The Baltimore Riots," in McClure, ed., *Annals of the War,* 775.

54 *"The despot's heel is on thy shore":* Commager, *Blue and the Gray,* 567–568.

54 *"It's a notable coincidence":* Strong, *Diary,* III, 126.

54 *"Our men are not moles":* Lincoln, *Collected Works,* IV, 341–342.

55 *"With all my devotion to the Union":* Robert E. Lee, *Wartime Papers of R. E. Lee,* 8–10.

55 *"There are but two parties now":* U. S. Grant, *Papers of Ulysses S. Grant,* II, 6–7.

55 *"We thought the rebellion would be over":* Fitch, *Echoes of the Civil War as I Hear Them,* 20.

55 *"The creature has been exalted":* Jefferson Davis, *Jefferson Davis, Constitutionalist,* V, 67–84.

56 *"Undoubtedly, thousands of warm-hearted":* Hawthorne, in Masur, ed., *Real War,* 172.

CHAPTER 2   ORGANIZING THE STRUGGLE

57 *Of the total, 227,000 Northerners:* Kennedy, *Preliminary Report on the Eighth Census,* 131.

58 *On January 1, the regular army:* U.S. War Dept., *Annual Report of the Secretary of War, November 22, 1865.*

58 *At the beginning of the war:* U.S. Army, *American Military History,* 194.

58 *The patriotic response was strong:* Eicher and Eicher, *Civil War High Commands.*

58 *By year's end the number rose:* U.S. War Dept., *Annual Report of the Secretary of War, November 22, 1865.*

58 *This notwithstanding, two major calls:* Beringer et al., *Why the South Lost the Civil War,* 478.

61 *The second, the Army of the Confederate States:* Beers, *Guide to the Archives of the Government of the Confederate States of America,* 302.

62 *The fourth important Confederate:* Wallace, *Guide to Virginia Military Organizations,* 174.

62 *These were consolidated:* O.R., III, 1, 403.

63 *He suffered from bouts of vertigo:* Welsh, *Medical Histories of Union Generals,* 293–294.

63 *When in March:* Eisenhower, *Agent of Destiny,* 386–387.

65 *(This occurred after a brief stint):* O.R., I, 1, 448.

65 *The Medical Department:* Beers, *Guide to the Archives of the Confederate States,* 170.

67 *The size varied:* K. P. Williams, *Lincoln Finds a General,* II, 777.

67 *Nine new regular army regiments:* U.S. Army, *American Military History, 1607–1953,* 193.

67 *Cavalry regiments were often:* K. P. Williams, *Lincoln Finds a General,* II, 777.

67 *Comprising regiments were battalions:* Ibid.

68 *And more "modern" and influential:* Beringer et al., *Why the South Lost the Civil War,* 46.

68 *Throughout the nineteenth century:* U.S. Army, *American Military History, 1607–1953,* 4–5.

69 *Simultaneous tactical operations:* Beringer et al., *Elements of Confederate Defeat,* 59.

70 *The Union grand strategy:* A. Jones, *Civil War Command and Strategy,* 21.

70 *Winfield Scott communicated:* U.S. Navy Dept., *Civil War Naval Chronology,* I-12.

70 *Wrote Scott: "In connection with such blockade":* O.R., I, 51, 1, 369.

71 *"The first thing in the morning":* Norton, *Army Letters.*

71 *Many of the Northern troops sang:* Commager, *Blue and the Gray,* 564.

72 *"The assault on Fort Sumter":* Binney, *Life of Horace Binney,* 330.

72 *Reeve faced a force:* O.R., I, 1, 570.

73 *"I don't quite understand":* Masur, ed., *Real War,* 163–164.

73 *"Those of us who were* the last": Marszalek, *Sherman,* 149.

73 *"There is less war":* D. H. Hill, to his wife, Isabella Morrison Hill, Richmond, Virginia, May 20, 1861, from the Daniel Harvey Hill Papers, U.S. Army Military History Institute, Carlisle, Pa.

73 *Hill wrote his wife:* D. H. Hill, to his wife, Isabella Morrison Hill, Yorktown, Virginia, May 30, 1861, from the Daniel Harvey Hill Papers.

74 *One such officer wrote:* O.R., III, 1, 234.

74 *Wrote Confederate Secretary of the Navy:* U.S. Navy Dept., *Civil War Naval Chronology,* I-13.

75 *Conversely, the hero of Fort Sumter:* Jefferson Davis, *Papers of Jefferson Davis,* VII, 186–187.

75 *"As soon as real war begins":* William T. Sherman to Thomas Ewing, Jr., St. Louis, Missouri, June 3, 1861, from W. T. Sherman, *Sherman's Civil War,* 97–98.

75 *On May 1, Douglas had delivered:* Johannsen, *Stephen A. Douglas,* 868.

77 *They were all in high glee:* O.R., I, 2, 95.

77 *Confederate artillery opened:* Ibid., 85.

78 *"On turning the curve slowly":* Ibid., 126.

79 *"God damn your god damned":* Harold Holzer, *Dear Mr. Lincoln,* 340.

79 *"I have heard several persons":* Ibid., 340–341.

79 *"You are green, it is true":* W. C. Davis, *Battle at Bull Run,* 77.

CHAPTER 3   SOUTHERN JOY OVER FIRST BULL RUN

81 *"This is essentially a People's contest":* Lincoln, *Collected Works,* IV, 421–441.

83 *The casualties were few:* O.R., I, 2, 156–187.

83 *"Up to this time":* Ibid., I, 3, 18.

84   *The dead and wounded:* Hinze and Farnham, *Battle of Carthage,* 206.

84   *"Say to [Scott] . . . that I am trying to follow":* McClellan, *Civil War Papers of George B. McClellan,* 44–45.

85   *Separated by nine miles:* Newell, *Lee vs. McClellan,* 112.

85   *From Middle Fork Bridge:* O.R., I, 2, 202.

86   *They moved over the mountain:* Ibid., 214–218.

86   *On July 13, Garnett continued:* Ibid., 220–221.

86   *Garnett became the first:* Newell, *Lee vs. McClellan,* 139.

87   *McClellan had done much:* O.R., I, 2, 204.

87   *"Our generals will resolve":* J. B. Jones, *Rebel War Clerk's Diary,* I, 63.

90   *For Greenhow, however:* Fishel, *Secret War for the Union,* 57–62.

91   *"The enemy's intrenchments":* O.R., I, 1, 312–314.

91   *"A comical effect":* P. G. T. Beauregard, "The First Battle of Bull Run," in Johnson and Buel, eds., *Battles and Leaders of the Civil War,* I, 1, 196–227.

91   *"Let to-morrow be their Waterloo":* T. H. Williams, *P. G. T. Beauregard,* 77.

92   *"This is one of the most beautiful nights":* W. C. Davis, *Battle at Bull Run,* 157.

92   *As the Federal army approached:* Long and Long, *Civil War Day by Day,* 98.

94   *He sent an immediate message:* Alexander, *Fighting for the Confederacy,* 50.

94   *But he was simply ordered:* O.R., I, 2, 536.

94   *Soldiers did not pick up:* Alexander, *Fighting for the Confederacy,* 43.

94   *Before the day was out:* W. C. Davis, *Battle at Bull Run,* 204–205.

95   *"The battle is there":* Symonds, *Joseph E. Johnston,* 119.

95   *As the fighting continued:* J. I. Robertson, *Stonewall Jackson,* 264.

96   *Bartow was also struck down:* W. C. Davis, *Battle at Bull Run,* 199.

96   *"Now for a yellow sash":* Ibid., 226.

98   *"The battle was not lost":* James B. Fry, "McDowell's Advance to Bull Run," in Johnson and Buel, eds., *Battles and Leaders,* I, 167–193.

98   *"Reserve your fire":* J. I. Robertson, *Stonewall Jackson,* 266.

98   *"I perceived several wagons":* Russell, *My Diary North and South,* 223–224.

99   *He spent nearly six months:* D. J. Eicher, *Civil War in Books,* 135.

99   *In jubilation, he made:* J. H. Eicher and D. J. Eicher, *Civil War High Commands.*

99   *"Enough was done for glory":* O.R., I, 2, 507–508.

99   *"Whilst great credit is due":* M. A. Jackson, *Memoirs of Stonewall Jackson,* 178.

100   *"I have seen the great":* F. Moore, ed., *Rebellion Record,* II, 93–94.

100   *"Then for the first time":* Marszalek, *Sherman,* 154.

100   *"There is no way I can tell you":* Gaff, *If This Is War,* 213.

100   *"During the day one of the boys":* C. E. Davis, *Three Years in the Army,* 3–99.

100   *"I have no doubt":* C. F. Adams et al., *Cycle of Adams Letters,* I, 23–24.

100   *In Lynchburg, civilian Susan Blackford:* C. M. Blackford III, *Letters from Lee's Army,* 36.

100   *"Trescot says this victory":* Chesnut, *Mary Chesnut's Civil War,* 111.

100   *"Today will be known":* Strong, *Diary,* III, 169.

100   *"Scott's campaign is wholly destroyed":* C. F. Adams et al., *Cycle of Adams Letters,* I, 22–23.

101   *"By some strange operation":* McClellan, *Civil War Papers,* 70.

101   *"Who would have thought":* Ibid., 71.

101   *"I am here in a terrible place":* Ibid., 85.

101   *"The dreadful disaster":* Allen Thorndike Rice, ed., "A Page of Political Correspondence: Unpublished Letters of Mr. Stanton to Mr. Buchanan," in *North American Review* CXXIX (1879): 482–483.

102   *"If anyone had told me":* R. E. Lee, Jr., *Recollections and Letters of General Robert E. Lee,* 38–48.

102   *Magruder pushed forward:* O.R., I, 4, 567–568.

103   *But McIntosh found:* Ibid., I, 3, 51–52.

104   *As the Federals marched:* Brooksher, *Bloody Hill,* 177.

106   *He was caught falling:* Phillips, *Damned Yankee,* 254–255.

106 *According to Maj. William M. Wherry:* William M. Wherry, "Wilson's Creek, and the Death of Lyon," in Johnson and Buel, eds., *Battles and Leaders,* I, 289–297.
106 *"This mere captain of infantry":* Thomas L. Snead, "The First Year of the War in Missouri," in Johnson and Buel, eds., *Battles and Leaders,* I, 262–277.
107 *"I do not know whether":* McClellan, *Civil War Papers,* 81.
107 *"Unquestionably, Western man":* Nathaniel Hawthorne [July 1861], from "Chiefly About War Matters," *Atlantic Monthly* X (July 1862): 43–61.
107 *"We are not yet fighting":* Strong, *Diary,* III, 175.
107 *"Our enemy is so strong":* Robert E. Lee, *Wartime Papers of R. E. Lee,* 62.
107 *"I am confident from observation":* Jefferson Davis, *Papers of Jefferson Davis,* VII, 280.
108 *"Citizens of Western Virginia":* O.R., I, 5, 575–577.
108 *"I will now give a complete list":* Billings, *Hardtack and Coffee,* 110.
109 *"This was our first naval victory":* U.S. Navy Dept., *Civil War Naval Chronology,* VI-388.
109 *"The property, real and personal":* O.R., I, 3, 466–467.
109 *"Be of good cheer.":* Orville H. Browning to Abraham Lincoln, August 19, 1861, in D. Lyman, *Civil War Quotations,* 44.

CHAPTER 4   A MASSACRE AT BALL'S BLUFF

110 *Lincoln wrote Frémont:* Lincoln, *Collected Works,* IV, 506–507.
110 *"If upon reflection your better judgment":* O.R., I, 3, 477–478.
111 *Perhaps too much debate:* Gallagher, *Confederate War,* 63–111.
111 *"We are a band of brothers":* Commager, *Blue and the Gray,* 563–564.
112 *(Grant's assignment caused a stir):* Benjamin M. Prentiss, telegram to John C. Frémont, Cape Girardeau, Missouri, September 2, 1861, in the Benjamin M. Prentiss Papers.
112 *This association allowed him:* Eicher and Eicher, *Civil War High Commands.*
113 *When Grant arrived:* O.R., I, 4, 197.
113 *In distant South Carolina:* Charleston *Mercury,* September 5, 1861.
114 *"Twenty-five minutes after":* O.R., I, 5, 129–132.
114 *Benham failed to deploy:* Newell, *Lee vs. McClellan,* 208.
114 *"Disasters have come":* O.R., I, 5, 149–150.
114 *He had leaned toward holding:* D. J. Eicher, *Robert E. Lee,* 193.
115 *Donelson's men marched:* Newell, *Lee vs. McClellan,* 228.
116 *Lee's first battle:* Ibid., 231.
116 *"Our poor sick":* Robert E. Lee, *Wartime Papers,* 73–74.
116 *"I beg therefore, if not too late":* Ibid., 76.
117 *"McClellan consistently thinks no more":* Richmond *Dispatch,* September 23, 1861.
118 *Both sides employed black Americans:* Schrader, *United States Army Logistics,* 194–198.
118 *The loss of equipment:* Ibid., 199.
118 *The short ration:* Ibid., 201; U.S. War Dept., *Revised U.S. Army Regulations,* 243.
119 *During the campaigns of 1863:* Schrader, *United States Army Logistics,* 202–205.
120 *One medium-size river steamboat:* Ibid., 206.
120 *The transfer involved:* Ibid., 211.
121 *The management and protection:* Eicher and Eicher, *Civil War High Commands.*
121 *Moreover, if he had permitted:* Goff, *Confederate Supply,* 19–23.
121 *It consisted of three or four engines:* O.R., I, 38, 3, 992.
122 *"Finding, after sunset":* Ibid., I, 3, 185–188.
123 *While watching the action:* Day, *Down South,* II, 186.
123 *"Our ammunition was about gone":* James A. Mulligan, "The Siege of Lexington, Mo.," in Johnson and Buel, eds., *Battles and Leaders,* I, 307–313.
123 *"The population here":* O.R., I, 4, 429.
124 *In one of many such letters:* McClellan, *Civil War Papers,* 113–114.

124 *McClellan's record to come:* Louis Philippe Albert d'Orléans, Comte de Paris, "McClellan Organizing the Grand Army," in Johnson and Buel, eds., *Battles and Leaders,* II, 112–122.

124 *"My dear Beauty":* Orlando M. Poe, Lewinsville, September 11, 1861, to James E. B. Stuart, near Falls Church, in the James Ewell Brown Stuart Papers, Virginia Historical Society, Richmond, Reel 40, item 617–618.

125 *When he was mustered:* Eicher and Eicher, *Civil War High Commands.*

125 *Emboldened, McClellan then ordered:* O.R., I, 5, 290.

126 *At about 7 A.M. on the 21st:* Ibid., 309.

127 *"Charge, Mississippians, charge!":* Holien, *Battle at Ball's Bluff,* 70.

127 *"The Virginians and Mississippians":* Randolph Abbott Shotwell, "Three Years in Battle," in Shotwell, *Papers of Randolph Abbott Shotwell,* I, 113–119.

127 *"The first shot":* O. W. Holmes, *Touched with Fire,* 23.

127 *Capt. Robert Garlick Hill Kean:* Kean, *Inside the Confederate Government,* 13.

129 *"We have considerable power":* G. V. Fox, *Confidential Correspondence of Gustavus Vasa Fox,* I, 64–65.

CHAPTER 5   AN UNLIKELY HERO AT BELMONT

130 *The Young Napoleon himself:* McClellan, *Civil War Papers,* 123–124.

131 *He wrote his soldiers:* O.R., I, 3, 560.

131 *"The President is not equal":* C. F. Adams et al., *Cycle of Adams Letters,* I, 63–64.

131 *On leaving his old brigade:* M. A. Jackson, *Memoirs of Stonewall Jackson,* 202.

133 *Second, the exact spot of attack:* U.S. Navy Dept., *Official Records of the Union and Confederate Navies in the War of the Rebellion* (hereafter O.R.N.), I, 12, 259–261.

133 *"The fine, ordered fleet":* Du Pont, *Samuel Francis Du Pont,* I, 205.

133 *Du Pont was losing his nervousness:* Ibid., 212.

133 *In the rescue:* Ibid.

134 *The other two ships:* Silverstone, *Warships of the Civil War Navies,* 238.

134 *Ammen reported that about noon:* Daniel Ammen, "Du Pont and the Port Royal Expedition," in Johnson and Buel, eds., *Battles and Leaders,* I, 677.

134 *The following day, November 5:* Ibid.

135 *At one point:* Ibid., 678–679.

135 *As it turned out:* Ibid., 681.

135 *"There was deafening music":* Ibid., 682.

136 *"I can conceive of nothing more grand":* Ibid., 684–685.

136 *"The victory was complete":* Du Pont, *Samuel Francis Du Pont,* I, 222–226.

136 *"We have no guns that can resist":* Robert E. Lee, *Wartime Papers,* 85–86.

137 *At the outbreak of war:* Symonds, *Historical Atlas of the U.S. Navy,* 80.

137 *By 1865 about 600 naval ships:* A. Jones, *Civil War Command and Strategy,* 8; Eicher and Eicher, *Civil War High Commands.*

137 *In 1861 the* Naval Register *classified:* U.S. Navy Dept., *Official Naval Register for 1861.*

138 *During the war the Federal navy:* Eicher and Eicher, *Civil War High Commands.*

139 *The grades of vice admiral and admiral:* Ibid.

141 *During the war Confederate commerce:* Ibid.

141 *Other bureaus included the Bureau of Provisions:* Ibid.

142 *The Confederate navy's squadrons:* Ibid.

142 *The idea was to "distract the enemy":* O.R., I, 3, 269.

143 *Grant now deemed it prudent:* Hughes, *Battle of Belmont,* 51.

143 *"In order to command the approaches":* William M. Polk, "General Polk and the Battle of Belmont," in Johnson and Buel, eds., *Battles and Leaders,* I, 348.

143 *Polk's men had constructed:* Hughes, *Battle of Belmont,* 56.

144 *Sometime later he rejoiced:* Ibid., 101.

144   *Lauman told his men:* Ibid.
144   *"A strange scene followed":* Eugene Lawrence, "Grant on the Battle-Field," in *Harper's New Monthly Magazine* XXXIX (1869): 212.
144   *Grant said his soldiers:* U. S. Grant, *Personal Memoirs of U. S. Grant,* I, 274.
145   *Wounded men placed in some tents:* Hughes, *Battle of Belmont,* 131.
145   *Maj. Gen. Polk described what resulted:* Polk, "General Polk and the Battle of Belmont," in Johnson and Buel, eds., *Battles and Leaders,* I, 351.
146   *"We were all prepared":* O.R.N., I, 1, 129–131.
146   *Fairfax again asked for more:* Ibid., 134–135.
147   *It was a "most ungraceful movement":* R. M. Hunter, "The Capture of Mason and Slidell," in McClure, ed., *Annals of the War,* 794–800.
147   *"Why, this looks devilish":* O.R.N., I, 1, 135–136.
147   *Secretary Welles wrote Wilkes:* Ibid., 148.
147   *Fairfax reported that Slidell:* "Captain Wilkes's Seizure of Mason and Slidell," in Johnson and Buel, eds., *Battles and Leaders,* II, 135–142.
147   *When Mason and Slidell were freed:* H. Jones, *Union in Peril,* 99.
148   *"The painful intelligence":* *Cincinnati Commercial,* December 11, 1861.
148   *"He who does something":* Lincoln, *Collected Works,* V, 84–85.
148   *"The men are good material":* Meade and Meade, *Life and Letters of George Gordon Meade,* II, 230–231.
148   *"What are they sending me":* O.R., I, 5, 961.
149   *"This miserable scheme":* Hammond, *Secret and Sacred,* 282–283.
149   *By noon the guns:* O.R.N., I, 16, 781–782.
150   *"Their ships, both crippled":* Ibid., 783.
150   *"In general . . . the whole space":* Rosen, *Confederate Charleston,* 86.
151   *"Hour after hour of anxiety":* E. Holmes, *Diary of Miss Emma Holmes,* 105.
151   *"The enemy were totally routed":* O.R., I, 5, 461–462.
152   *"Our artillery did terrible havoc":* Ibid., 477–480.
152   *"Liberty is always won":* Jefferson Davis, *Papers of Jefferson Davis,* VII, 412–419.
152   *Lincoln, on the other hand:* Lincoln, *Collected Works,* V, 35–53.
152   *"If it were determined":* Ibid., 34–35.
152   *"All quiet along the Potomac":* Commager, *Blue and the Gray,* 565–566.

CHAPTER 6   GRANT MOVES INTO TENNESSEE

154   *By year's end the figure:* Phisterer, *Statistical Record of the Armies of the United States,* 62.
154   *By contrast, the Confederate Army:* Beringer et al., *Why the South Lost,* 478.
155   *"I am in the condition":* Ambrose, *Halleck,* 21.
155   *The board functioned:* Herman Hattaway, "The War Board: The Basis of the United States' First General Staff," in *Military Affairs* XLVI (1982): 1.
156   *"My accounts would have been rendered":* Justus McKinstry to Henry W. Halleck, Arsenal, St. Louis, Mo., February 11, 1862, in the Justus McKinstry Papers.
157   *"I state my general idea":* Lincoln, *Collected Works,* V, 98–99.
157   *"Washington was then a military camp":* Brooks, *Washington in Lincoln's Time,* 15.
157   *"Mine eyes have seen the glory":* Commager, *Blue and the Gray,* 571–573.
158   *"We are striking the guilty rebels":* Blight, *Frederick Douglass' Civil War,* 154.
158   *Stevens stood only 5 feet 1 inch:* Warner, *Generals in Blue,* 475.
159   *Instead of advancing:* O.R., I, 6, 69–71.
159   *The Federal forces crossed:* Ibid., 47–53.
159   *"Wherever his fleet can be brought":* Robert E. Lee, *Wartime Papers,* 101–102.
159   *"The importance of a rigorous blockade":* U.S. Navy Dept., *Civil War Naval Chronology,* VI-389.
160   *"With such interference":* J. I. Robertson, *Stonewall Jackson,* 317.
160   *Jackson wrote Governor Letcher:* M. A. Jackson, *Memoirs of Stonewall Jackson,* 234–235.

160   *He explained, "I am in active service":* Thomas J. Jackson to Francis McFarland, Winchester, Virginia, February 11, 1862, in the Thomas J. Jackson Papers, Virginia Military Institute, Lexington.

160   *"It was growing dark":* O.R., I, 7, 30–32.

161   *A single regiment had 350:* Edward O. Guerrant, "Marshall and Garfield in Eastern Kentucky," in Johnson and Buel, eds., *Battles and Leaders,* I, 393–397.

162   *Fry considered the placement:* R. M. Kelly, "Holding Kentucky for the Union," in Johnson and Buel, eds., *Battles and Leaders,* I, 373–392.

162   *The tree under which Zollicoffer died:* Ibid.; D. J. Eicher, *Mystic Chords of Memory,* 25.

163   *At this time a position:* O.R., I, 7, 93–94.

163   *"Perceiving the fortunes":* Ibid., 111–114.

163   *"Mud, mud":* E. H. Rhodes, *All for the Union,* 54.

163   *"This army has got to fight":* Thomas and Hyman, *Stanton,* 170.

163   *Several days later he wrote:* Ibid., 146.

163   *And by late February:* Ibid., 174.

164   *By early January:* Marvel, *Burnside,* 34.

164   *The Burnside expedition departed:* Browning, *From Cape Charles to Cape Fear,* 21.

164   *He had been warranted:* Cogar, *Dictionary of Admirals of the U.S. Navy. Vol. 1, 1862–1900,* 70.

165   *Not only was Wise:* Welsh, *Medical Histories of Confederate Generals,* 237–238.

165   *Confederate forces to the south:* Sauers, *"A Succession of Honorable Victories,"* 479–489.

165   *Fortunately for Burnside:* Browning, *From Cape Charles to Cape Fear,* 25.

166   *Seven Confederate vessels:* O.R.N., I, 6, 594–597.

166   *"Repeatedly in the course of the day":* Ibid.

167   *The ground was swampy:* Sauers, *"A Succession of Honorable Victories,"* 182–183.

167   *(Hawkins, a respected soldier):* Marvel, *Burnside,* 34.

167   *Confused by the uniforms:* Sauers, *"A Succession of Honorable Victories,"* 195.

167   *"The mission of our joint expedition":* O.R., I, 9, 363–364.

167   *"We must give up some minor points":* Roman, *Military Operations of General Beauregard,* I, 224.

168   *In summarizing his army's achievement:* Ambrose E. Burnside, "The Burnside Expedition," in Johnson and Buel, eds., *Battles and Leaders,* I, 660–669.

168   *The queer appearance:* deKay, *Monitor,* 91.

168   *"With Permission I will take":* U. S. Grant, *Papers of Ulysses S. Grant,* IV, 99–101.

171   *"Essex then necessarily dropped":* O.R.N., I, 22, 537–539.

172   *Drawing on the Nashville Union:* Ibid., 635–636.

172   *Grant advocated quick action:* Cooling, *Forts Henry and Donelson,* 116.

173   *"The ground was strewn":* James A. Connolly, "Major Connolly's Letters to His Wife, 1862–1865," *Transactions of the Illinois State Historical Society, 1928,* 220–224.

174   *During the height of the firing:* Wyeth, *Life of General Nathan Bedford Forrest,* 46–47.

174   *The suffering from this wound:* Andrew H. Foote, Autograph Letter signed (hereafter ALS), New Haven, Conn., July 17, 1862, to Charles Cullis, Boston, Mass., author's collection.

176   *He coolly told Smith:* Cooling, *Forts Henry and Donelson,* 185.

178   *He also saw the oddity:* Ibid., 198.

179   *"No terms except an unconditional":* U. S. Grant, *Papers of Ulysses S. Grant,* IV, 218.

179   *Now he replied:* O.R., I, 7, 161.

180   *"We have backed far enough":* Cooling, *Fort Donelson's Legacy,* 15.

180   *"Make Buell, Grant, and Pope major-generals":* O.R., I, 7, 628.

181   *("The Commanding General"):* J. Taylor, *Bloody Valverde,* 103.

181   *Curiously, the night before:* Ibid., 39–40.

182   *The death shook the Lincolns:* Neely, *Abraham Lincoln Encyclopedia,* 189.

182   *"The tyranny of an unbridled majority":* Long and Long, *Civil War Day by Day,* 174.

182   *An editorial in the Washington Telegraph:* Washington (Ark.) Telegraph, February 26, 1862.

CHAPTER 7   CLASH OF THE IRONCLADS

183   *"The next summer"*: James E. B. Stuart, March 2, 1862, Centreville, Va., to Flora Cooke Stuart, in James E. B. Stuart Papers, Virginia Historical Society, Richmond, Reel 40, items 836–837.

183   *"In my judgment"*: Lincoln, *Collected Works*, V, 144–146.

184   *Given this change of events*: O.R.N., I, 12, 573–575.

184   *"The victory was bloodless"*: U.S. Navy Dept., *Civil War Naval Chronology*, II-28.

185   *The men were instructed*: O.R.N., I, 12, 583.

186   *Van Dorn wished to push*: Long and Long, *Civil War Day by Day*, 179.

186   *In February, Van Dorn fell*: Welsh, *Medical Histories of Confederate Generals*, 220–221.

188   *"For God sake"*: Shea and Hess, *Pea Ridge*, 80.

188   *"The night was one of intense severity"*: Ibid., 85.

190   *Back at Oberson's Field*: Ibid., 103–104.

190   *As he reconnoitered*: Cutrer, *Ben McCulloch and the Frontier Military Tradition*, 304.

190   *Later, McCulloch's body*: Welsh, *Medical Histories of Confederate Generals*, 147–148.

190   *As the fight on Foster's Farm*: Ibid., 149.

191   *Carr had assured Curtis*: Shea and Hess, *Pea Ridge*, 151.

191   *Because the air was so cold*: Ibid., 164.

193   *"In the recent operations"*: O.R., I, 8, 786–787.

193   *Wrote Curtis in a letter*: Long and Long, *Civil War Day by Day*, 180.

193   *"The effects of an army"*: Watson, *Life in the Confederate Army*, 320–339.

195   *The CSS* Virginia: Silverstone, *Warships of the Civil War Navies*, 27, 202.

196   *"At 3:35 [P.M.]"*: O.R.N., I, 7, 21.

196   *"The shot from the* Congress": Ibid., 10–12.

196   *Jones was a Virginian*: Current et al., *Encyclopedia of the Confederacy*, II, 863.

197   *The armor plating*: Silverstone, *Warships of the Civil War Navies*, 4.

197   *Midshipman H. Beverly Littlepage*: deKay, *Monitor*, 184.

198   *Aboard the* Monitor: Keeler, *Aboard the USS* Monitor, *1862*, 37.

198   *Greene came from the turret*: S. Dana Greene, "In the 'Monitor' Turret," in Johnson and Buel, eds., *Battles and Leaders*, I, 719–729.

198   *"I cannot see"*: W. C. Davis, *Duel Between the First Ironclads*, 132.

198   *When told that it was*: deKay, *Monitor*, 198.

198   *"The* Monitor *is no more"*: Keeler, *Aboard the* USS Monitor, *1862*, 253–254.

199   *"Now comes the reign"*: U.S. Navy Dept., *Civil War Naval Chronology*, VI-386.

199   *"The contrast was that"*: O.R.N., I, 7, 10–12.

200   *Many of the transports*: Sauers, *"A Succession of Honorable Victories,"* 237.

201   *"With such soldiers"*: O.R., I, 9, 207.

202   *A correspondent*: Sauers, *"A Succession of Honorable Victories,"* 332.

203   *"I abandoned New Madrid"*: Daniel and Bock, *Island No. 10*, 66.

204   *Davis simply marked it*: O.R., I, 8, 134–135.

204   *"I congratulate you"*: Henry W. Halleck to John Pope, St. Louis, April 8, 1862, in the John Pope Papers.

204   *On the same day*: Henry W. Halleck to Edwin M. Stanton, St. Louis, April 8, 1862, in the John Pope Papers.

204   *On April 10, Lincoln replied*: Holzer, *Dear Mr. Lincoln*, 253.

207   *Slough's 844 men*: Edrington and Taylor, *Battle of Glorieta Pass*, 132.

207   *"[They were] heavily loaded"*: O.R., I, 9, 538–539.

208   *To Jackson, the Valley*: J. I. Robertson, *Stonewall Jackson*, 330.

208   *"If we cannot be successful"*: Tanner, *Stonewall in the Valley*, 104.

209   *Across the Mississippi*: Neely, *Abraham Lincoln Encyclopedia*, 277.

210   *"He ordered me to lead"*: Colt, *Defend the Valley*, 122–123.

211   *But the court-martial of Garnett*: Allan, *History of the Campaign of Gen. T. J. (Stonewall) Jackson in the Shenandoah Valley*, 54.

211 *"Our gallant little army"*: M. A. Jackson, *Memoirs of Stonewall Jackson*, 247–248.
211 *"The religious element"*: Garnet Wolseley, "A Month's Visit to Confederate Headquarters," in *Blackwood's Edinburgh Magazine* XCIII (January–June 1863): 21.
211 *"You appear much concerned"*: M. A. Jackson, *Memoirs of Stonewall Jackson*, 249.
212 *"I now proclaim"*: D. Lyman, *Civil War Quotations*, 130.
213 *The War Department was forced*: Eicher and Eicher, *Civil War High Commands*.
214 *The perceptive New Yorker*: Strong, *Diary*, III, 213–214.
214 *"At night, when it is too dark"*: Merington, ed., *Custer Story*, 27.
214 *"General Robert E. Lee"*: Samuel Cooper, General Orders No. 14, Richmond, March 13, 1862, from Robert E. Lee Papers, Virginia Historical Society, Richmond, Reel 23, item 334.
214 *"For a long time"*: McClellan, *Civil War Papers*, 211.
214 *"I have more confidence"*: Merington, ed., *Custer Story*, 27–28.
216 *A heavy object such as a wagon*: Sears, *To the Gates of Richmond*, 36.
217 *On April 6, Lincoln replied*: Lincoln, *Collected Works*, V, 182.
217 *"The country will not fail"*: Ibid., 184–185.
217 *"Some men seem born to be shot"*: C. B. Haydon, *For Country, Cause, and Leader*, 218.
217 *"I prefer Lee to Johnston"*: McClellan, *Civil War Papers*, 244–245.
217 *Privately, Lincoln repeated the comment*: Donald, *Lincoln*, 330.
217 *"No one but McClellan"*: O.R., I, 11; III, 455–456.
217 *"We are engaged in a species of warfare"*: Ibid., III, 477.

CHAPTER 8   A BLOODBATH AT SHILOH

220 *"A rumor has just reached me"*: O.R., I, 7, 682.
220 *Two days later Halleck*: Ibid., 10, 2, 15.
220 *"It has been reported"*: Lorenzo Thomas to Henry W. Halleck, Washington, March 10, 1862, in the Ulysses S. Grant Papers, Record Group 94, Adjutant General's Office Records, Generals' Papers, NARA, Washington, D.C.
220 *(In February, Sherman)*: William T. Sherman to Henry W. Halleck, Benton Barracks, Mo., February 10, 1862, in the William T. Sherman Papers, Record Group 94, Adjutant General's Office Records, Generals' Papers, NARA, Washington, D.C.
221 *"We have heard with deep regret"*: John A. McClernand, William H. L. Wallace, Leonard F. Ross, Mason Brayman, and seven lesser officers, to U. S. Grant, Pine Landing, Tenn., March 9, 1862, in the Ulysses S. Grant Papers, Record Group 94, Adjutant General's Office Records, Generals' Papers, NARA, Washington, D.C.
221 *"I return to you"*: A. Johnson, *Papers of Andrew Johnson*, V, 202–204.
221 *"To-day, at 11 o'clock A.M."*: John A. McClernand to Ulysses S. Grant, camp near Pittsburg, Tenn., March 27, 1862, in the John A. McClernand Papers.
222 *"Since your reorganization"*: John A. McClernand to Henry W. Halleck, Camp "Glades," June 1, 1862, in the John A. McClernand Papers.
223 *"I have put you in motion"*: O.R., I, 10, 1, 396–397.
223 *"I have scarsely [sic] the faintest idea"*: U.S. Grant, *Papers of Ulysses S. Grant*, V, 13–14.
224 *This gave Sherman*: Daniel, *Shiloh*, 143–144.
224 *"Suddenly, away off on the right"*: Stillwell, *Story of a Common Soldier of Army Life in the Civil War*, 42–52.
226 *Before thrusting command*: W. P. Johnston, *Life of Gen. Albert Sidney Johnston*, 582.
226 *"Fill your canteens, boys"*: F. Y. Headley, *Marching Through Georgia*, 46.
227 *Johnston had received*: Welsh, *Medical Histories of Confederate Generals*, 118–119.
228 *An Ohioan by birth*: Sword, *Shiloh*, 297.
229 *"Well, Grant, we've had the devil's own day"*: Daniel, *Shiloh*, 266.
230 *"I cannot describe the field"*: Parks, *General Leonidas Polk, C.S.A.*, 240.
231 *"If I am not too feeble"*: Charles F. Smith to Henry W. Halleck, Pittsburg Landing, Tenn., April 21, 1862, in the Charles F. Smith Papers.

231   *Four days later:* Andrew C. Kemper, AAG, General Orders No. 21, Dept. of the Missis-
       sippi, Pittsburg Landing, Tenn., April 25, 1862, in the Charles F. Smith Papers.

231   *"You have bravely fought":* O.R., I, 10, 1, 397.

231   *Grant himself remarked:* U. S. Grant, *Personal Memoirs,* I, 356.

231   *Of the western general:* McClure, *Lincoln and Men of War-Times,* 180.

232   *The fort "could not be reduced":* Quincy A. Gillmore, "Siege and Capture of Fort Pulaski,"
       in Johnson and Buel, eds., *Battles and Leaders,* II, 1–12.

233   *First Lt. Horace Porter:* Ibid.

234   *By 1 P.M., as Gillmore wrote:* Ibid.

236   *"With no car left":* William Pittenger, "The Locomotive Chase in Georgia," in Johnson
       and Buel, eds., *Battles and Leaders,* II, 709–716.

237   *They received the medals:* Angle, *Great Locomotive Chase,* 319.

238   *"I regard Butler's Ship":* O.R., I, 6, 832–834.

239   *Of this great naval calamity:* U.S. Navy Dept., *Civil War Naval Chronology,* VI-388.

241   *This after Lovell had claimed:* Hearn, *Capture of New Orleans, 1862,* 244.

241   *"A gloom has settled":* Solomon, *Civil War Diary of Clara Solomon,* 343.

241   *Another New Orleans resident:* LeGrand, *Journal of Julia LeGrand,* 39–43.

241   *Mary Chesnut, the Charleston diarist:* Chesnut, *Mary Chesnut's Civil War,* 330.

241   *Farragut recorded:* U.S. Navy Dept., *Civil War Naval Chronology,* VI-387.

241   *"This outrage will be punished":* D. Lyman, *Civil War Quotations,* 48.

241   *Warning the city's women:* Hearn, *When the Devil Came Down to Dixie,* 103.

242   *"We woo the South":* Hawthorne, in Masur, ed., *Real War,* 176.

CHAPTER 9   JACKSON'S VALLEY CAMPAIGN

250   *On April 1, 1861:* O.R., III, 3, 936–937.

250   *At war's end:* Ibid., 5, 145.

250   *The army reported:* U.S. War Dept., *Annual Report of the Secretary of War, November 14, 1866,*
       657.

250   *Grant wrote Halleck:* U. S. Grant, *Papers of Ulysses S. Grant,* V, 114–115.

250   *Of Sherman, Grant wrote:* Ibid., 110–112.

251   *Despite this, he wrote:* O.R., I, 10, 1, 801–802.

251   *He reported the Union loss:* Ibid., 839–841.

253   *As the pullout was underway:* O.R., I, 10, I, 902.

253   *"The people express a desire":* Ibid., 901.

254   *"The most painful duty":* O.R., I, 6, 660–662.

255   *Mayor L. Lindsay refused:* O.R.N., I, 18, 492.

255   *"It was interesting and sometimes exciting":* Ibid., 528–535.

255   *"The boys think it* their *duty":* Fisk, *Hard Marching Every Day,* 26–30.

255   *"Every gun fired":* New York Tribune, May 20, 1862.

257   *Second Lt. Thomas Hooton:* Brennan, *Secessionville,* 189.

257   *"Well I was in the fight":* Henry Cooley, letter to his parents, in Cooley Papers, Southern
       Historical Collection, University of North Carolina, Chapel Hill.

259   *The hill was so steep:* O.R., I, 12, I, 462–465.

259   *"Observing that some men retired":* Ibid., 484–487.

261   *When Union artillery opened:* D. C. Pfanz, *Richard S. Ewell,* 185.

261   *He wrote to the War Department:* O.R., I, 12, I, 524–525.

262   *After telling a group:* Hollandsworth, *Pretense of Glory,* 67.

263   *Ashby died instantly:* Welsh, *Medical Histories of Confederate Generals,* 11; Eicher and Eicher,
       Civil War High Commands.

263   *Jackson himself wrote:* Douglas, *I Rode with Stonewall,* 82.

265   *Three of Jackson's staff:* Krick, *Conquering the Valley,* 72.

266   *Curiously, Banks wrote:* Nathaniel P. Banks to Samuel W. Crawford, Winchester, Va., June
       10, 1862, in the Samuel Wylie Crawford Papers.
266   *"I would rather be a private":* Long and Long, *Civil War Day by Day,* 225.
267   *"Such heroism will inflame":* Corsan, *Two Months in the Confederate States,* 101.
267   *"I beg leave to tender":* James Shields to Lorenzo Thomas, Bristoe Station, Va., June 24,
       1862, in the James Shields Papers.

CHAPTER 10   THE PENINSULAR CAMPAIGN

270   *Nearby, Brig. Gen. Samuel P. Heintzelman:* Sears, *To the Gates of Richmond,* 77.
270   *"As soon as I came upon the field":* McClellan, *Civil War Papers,* 257.
272   *These operations "are regarded":* O.R., I, 11, 635.
272   *"Thus perished the* Virginia": U.S. Navy Dept., *Civil War Naval Chronology,* VI-389.
273   *Moreover, Jeffers found:* O.R.N., I, 7, 362.
273   *"Oh, the extortioners!":* J. B. Jones, *Rebel War Clerk's Diary,* I, 128.
273   *The diarist Mary Chesnut:* Chesnut, *Mary Chesnut's Civil War,* 345.
274   *"I did not think it prudent":* O.R., I, 12, I, 505–508.
274   *On May 26, Lincoln wrote:* Lincoln, *Collected Works,* V, 239–240.
276   *One Federal soldier recalled:* Robert E. L. Krick, "The Battle of Slash Church (Hanover
       Court House), May 27, 1862," in William J. Miller, ed., *The Peninsula Campaign of 1862,* II,
       1–38.
279   *"I hereby certify that":* Surg. Gideon S. Palmer, medical director, Richardson's Division,
       Fair Oaks Station, Va., June 2, 1862, in the Oliver O. Howard Papers.
279   *The same day Howard:* Oliver O. Howard to Capt. [John M.] Norvell, AAG, HQ.
       Howard's Brigade, Richardson's Division, Fair Oaks Station, Va., June 2, 1862, in the
       Oliver O. Howard Papers.
279   *"General Lee had up to this time":* Evander M. Law, "The Fight for Richmond," in *Southern
       Bivouac* (April 1867): 649.
279   *"The heroism shown":* O.R., I, 11, I, 943–946.
279   *For McClellan's part:* McClellan, *Civil War Papers,* 287–288.
287   *"Dashing across the intervening plains":* Fitz John Porter, "Hanover Court House and
       Gaines's Mill," in Johnson and Buel, eds., *Battles and Leaders,* II, 319–346.
288   *"Going on to the field":* Norton, *Army Letters,* 92.
288   *On the day of this decision:* McClellan, *Civil War Papers,* 322–323.
288   *Also on this day:* Lincoln, *Collected Works,* V, 291–292.
289   *"The army is a great place":* C. F. Adams, et al., *Cycle of Adams Letters,* I, 159–161.
291   *Among the Confederate casualties:* Welsh, *Medical Histories of Confederate Generals,* 89.
292   *"It was impossible for the enemy":* James Longstreet, " 'The Seven Days,' Including Frayser's
       Farm," from Johnson and Buel, eds., *Battles and Leaders,* II, 396–405.
296   *"Magruder's report":* Webb, *Peninsula,* 159.
296   *So costly was this advance:* D. H. Hill, "McClellan's Change of Base and Malvern Hill," in
       Johnson and Buel, eds., *Battles and Leaders,* II, 383–395.
296   *"It is not my desire to indulge":* O.R., I, 11, II, 639–645.
297   *"This fight beggars description":* J. K. Edmondson, *My Dear Emma,* 99–100.

CHAPTER 11   CONFEDERATE TRIUMPH AT SECOND BULL RUN

298   *He accompanied:* Raines, *Getting the Message Through,* 5–14.
298   *Myer also wrote:* Myer, *Manual of Signals.*
299   *Fisher gave up:* Raines, *Getting the Message Through,* 18–43.
300   *This code word:* Plum, *Military Telegraph During the Civil War,* 45.
300   *For example, Cipher No. 9:* Kahn, *Codebreakers,* 215.

300 *However, the Confederates:* Peter Maslowski, "Military Intelligence Sources During the American Civil War: A Case Study," in W. H. Hitchcock, ed., *Intelligence Revolution*, 55.

301 *Bates wrote that:* Bates, *Lincoln in the Telegraph Office*, 216.

301 *Curiously, sometime between 1858:* Edward Porter Alexander, 2d Lt. Engineers, U.S. Army [1858–1861], in Miscellaneous Signal Corps Papers, Record Group III, entry 27, NARA, Washington, D.C.

302 *Moreover, only a few key phrases:* O.R., I, 24, I, 39; Plum, *Military Telegraph During the Civil War*, 37; and O.R., I, 23, 2, 947.

302 *Transmission errors:* Kahn, *Codebreakers*, 217.

303 *"Never did such a change":* McClellan, *Civil War Papers*, 336–338.

303 *"It should not be":* Ibid., 344–345.

303 *"I think that he is":* Ibid., 354–355.

303 *(The estimate of 4,700):* Morris, *Sheridan*, 68.

303 *A withdrawal began:* O.R., I, 17; II, 62.

304 *Of the assignment:* McClellan, *Civil War Papers*, 367–368.

305 *On the Mississippi:* U.S. Navy Dept., *Civil War Naval Chronology*, II-81.

305 *Brown was commissioned:* O.R.N., I, 19, 67–68.

305 *"This is the 4th of July":* C. F. Adams et al., *Cycle of Adams Letters*, I, 161–162.

305 *Its first two:* Commager, ed., *Blue and the Gray*, 574.

306 *Among the early supporters:* F. S. Haydon, *Aeronautics in the Union and Confederate Armies*, 225; Eisenschiml, *The Celebrated Case of Fitz John Porter*, 311–312.

307 *At Tompkinsville:* O.R., I, 16, I, 766–767.

307 *"As day broke":* Ibid., 754–756.

307 *After attempting to escape:* D. A. Brown, *Bold Cavaliers*, 78.

307 *One of the riders:* E. H. Thomas, *John Hunt Morgan and His Raiders*, 40.

308 *"It is certain Morgan cannot":* O.R., I, 16, I, 734.

308 *"Morgan ought not to escape":* Ibid., 735.

308 *Morgan telegraphed Prentice:* Ibid., 780.

308 *By this time:* O.R., I, 16, I, 741.

308 *"The state is in danger":* Ibid., 747.

309 *"I must demand":* Ibid., 803–807.

309 *"It was Forrest's birthday":* Henry, ed., *As They Saw Forrest*, 40.

309 *Many, undressed:* Jordan and Pryor, *Campaigns of Lieut.-Gen. N. B. Forrest, and of Forrest's Cavalry*, 164–165.

309 *Of the surrender:* Warner, *Generals in Blue*, 101.

309 *This legendary comment:* Henry, *"First with the Most" Forrest*, 18–19.

310 *Following the raid:* B. S. Wills, *Battle from the Start*, 80.

310 *"The bearer, John S. Mosby":* James E. B. Stuart, July 19, 1862, in the John S. Mosby Papers, Virginia Historical Society, Richmond, Reel 39, item 127.

310 *"I congratulate you":* Robert E. Lee, July 24 [?], 1862, in the James E. B. Stuart Papers, Virginia Historical Society, Richmond, Reel 40, item 488.

310 *"I have the honor to report":* J. C. Davis, to Washington L. Elliott, Jacinto, Miss., August 6, 1862, from the Jefferson C. Davis Papers.

311 *As Johnson recalled it:* A. R. Johnson, *Partisan Rangers of the Confederate States Army*, 105.

311 *"The great changes of command":* McWhiney, *Braxton Bragg and Confederate Defeat*, 266.

312 *The remainder of the Yankee troops:* O.R., I, 9, 614–616.

313 *The result was:* O.R., I, 16, I, 845–847.

313 *After conducting an interview:* Ibid., 865.

314 *"The remainder":* Ibid., 885.

316 *There, according to McCray:* McDonough, *War in Kentucky*, 138.

317 *"We think you are":* New York Tribune, August 20, 1862.

317 *"My paramount object":* Lincoln, *Collected Works*, V, 388–389.

317 *"Assassination is not an American practice":* J. M. Taylor, *William Henry Seward*, 240.

317 *"I have come to you":* O.R., I, 16, III, 473–474.

318   *At the time of Pope's order:* Schutz and Trenerry, *Abandoned by Lincoln,* 103–104.

318   *On August 23:* Hennessy, *Return to Bull Run,* 82.

320   *For an hour and a half:* Krick, *Stonewall Jackson at Cedar Mountain,* 94–95.

320   *A shell fragment ripped:* Welsh, *Medical Histories of Confederate Generals,* 236–237.

321   *Of the attack:* Krick, *Stonewall Jackson at Cedar Mountain,* 123.

321   *Writing from "headquarters":* Samuel W. Crawford to George B. McClellan, "headquarters under a cedar tree," Cedar Mountain, Va., August 9, 1862, in the Samuel Wylie Crawford Papers.

324   *"What a prize it was!":* Allen C. Redwood, "Jackson's 'Foot-Cavalry' at the Second Bull Run," in Johnson and Buel, eds., *Battles and Leaders,* II, 530–538.

325   *In the action:* Welsh, Medical Histories of Union Generals, 331–332.

326   *"Our men on the left":* Gaff, *Brave Men's Tears,* 87.

326   *The cries of the wounded:* Welsh, *Medical Histories of Confederate Generals,* 63–65.

328   *"If any considerable advantages":* O.R., I, 12, II, 76.

328   *Still, he seemed outwardly confident:* Hennessy, *Return to Bull Run,* 139.

328   *Late in the afternoon:* Ibid., 509.

329   *His military career ruined:* See *O.R.,* I, 12, II, 505–536; *O.R.,* I, 12, II supplement, "The Fitz John Porter Court Martial," 821–1143; Eisenschiml, *Celebrated Case of Fitz John Porter;* and U.S. War Dept., *Proceedings and Report of the Board of Army Officers.*

333   *During the intense fighting:* Welsh, *Medical Histories of Union Generals,* 188–189.

333   *"I watched him moving":* Charles F. Walcutt, "The Battle of Chantilly," in *Papers of the Military Historical Society of Massachusetts* (1895), II: 145.

333   *"I have the honor to acknowledge":* George B. McClellan to Robert E. Lee, Headquarters, Army of the Potomac [Sharpsburg, Md.], October 5, 1862, in the Philip Kearny Papers.

333   *After passing his son:* Welsh, *Medical Histories of Union Generals,* 320.

334   *Lee stumbled and fell:* Ibid., 134–136.

334   *In response to the defeat:* Hay, *Lincoln and the Civil War in the Diaries and Letters of John Hay,* 46.

CHAPTER 12   THE WAR'S BLOODIEST DAY

335   *On hearing Lee's report:* J. B. Jones, *Rebel War Clerk's Diary,* I, 151.

335   *At the start of September:* Lincoln, *Collected Works,* V, 403–404.

336   *"We cannot afford":* Robert E. Lee, *Wartime Papers,* 292–294.

338   *"Again I have been called":* McClellan, *Civil War Papers,* 435.

338   *"I request that the Major General":* Joseph Hooker to Seth Williams, Ridgeville, Md., September 12, 1862, in the John F. Reynolds Papers.

338   *"McClellan is an intelligent engineer":* Welles, *Diary of Gideon Welles,* I, 107.

339   *"Posterity will scarcely believe":* Richmond Dispatch, October 10, 1862.

339   *"What in Heaven's name":* Small, *Road to Richmond,* 196–197.

339   *Many of the Confederate army's soldiers:* Frassanito, *Antietam,* 39.

340   *On September 11:* O.R., I, 19, II, 254–255.

340   *With so many arguments:* James A. Garfield to Harry Garfield, Washington, October 5, 1862, in James A. Garfield, *Wild Life of the Army,* 148–154.

340   *While resting with his friend:* Jamieson, *Death in September,* 31–32.

340   *By late morning:* A. Wilson Greene, " 'I Fought the Battle Splendidly': George B. McClellan and the Maryland Campaign," in Gallagher, ed., *Antietam,* 61.

340   *Suffice it to say:* Harsh, *Taken at the Flood,* 237–242.

341   *"It is evident from General Lee's movements":* Silas Colgrove, "The Finding of Lee's Lost Order," in Johnson and Buel, eds., *Battles and Leaders,* II, 603.

341   *"The marching columns extended":* Murfin, *Gleam of Bayonets,* 170.

343   *Paroled on his word of honor:* Ibid., 173.

343   *Hand-to-hand fighting ensued:* Welsh, *Medical Histories of Confederate Generals,* 76.

343   *When Brig. Gen. Samuel D. Sturgis:* Sears, *Landscape Turned Red,* 140.

344   *The farmstead of Daniel Wise:* Ibid., 157.
344   *It was a disturbing sight:* Priest, *Before Antietam,* 319.
347   *It cut so deeply:* Hearn, *Six Years of Hell,* 186.
349   *He announced an intention:* Esposito, ed., *West Point Atlas of American Wars,* I, pl. 67.
350   *Hooker himself described:* Murfin, *Gleam of Bayonets,* 213.
351   *"There is a rattling fusillade":* Dawes, *Service with the Sixth Wisconsin Volunteers,* 91.
351   *"In the time I am writing":* O.R., I, 19, I, 216–219.
352   *"The General imagined":* Lt. John Mead Gould, 10th Maine Inf., Berlin, Md., December 2, 1862, in the Joseph King Fenno Mansfield Papers, Antietam National Battlefield, Sharpsburg, Md., containing a document in the collection of the Middlesex County Historical Society, Middletown, Conn.
352   *"I have the honor to request":* Joseph Hooker to Seth Williams, Centreville, Md., September 19, 1862; in the Joseph Hooker Papers.
352   *"I go into action to-day":* Meade and Meade, *Life and Letters,* I, 310–311.
353   *"Don't be excited about it":* Hattaway, *General Stephen D. Lee,* 57.
355   *Two months after:* Alexander, *Fighting for the Confederacy,* 159.
355   *The Confederate cavalryman:* Borcke, *Memoirs of the Confederate War for Independence,* I, 234.
355   *Running out of ammunition:* Sears, *Landscape Turned Red,* 250–251.
356   *Lee, meanwhile, was visiting:* J. B. Gordon, *Reminiscences of the Civil War,* 84.
357   *He was taken back:* Welsh, *Medical Histories of Confederate Generals,* 6.
357   *"I fell forward":* J. B. Gordon, *Reminiscences of the Civil War,* 90.
357   *"I have been struck":* John B. Gordon, from the *Atlanta Constitution,* reprinted in the *National Tribune,* microfilm, Reel 1, 3-1879, 19, in the John B. Gordon Papers.
358   *He was taken to McClellan's headquarters:* Welsh, *Medical Histories of Union Generals,* 278.
358   *"I was astonished to observe":* Murfin, *Gleam of Bayonets,* 262.
360   *"The mental strain was so great":* David L. Thompson, "With Burnside at Antietam," in Johnson and Buel, eds., *Battles and Leaders,* II, 660–662.
361   *"How natural it is":* Frank Holsinger, "How Does One Feel Under Fire?" in *Papers of the Military Order of the Loyal Legion of the United States, 1887–1915* XV (1906): 301.
363   *"Here is my old war horse":* Sears, *Landscape Turned Red,* 297.
363   *When Lee asked:* Murfin, *Gleam of Bayonets,* 291.
363   *"O, why did we not attack":* E. H. Rhodes, *All for the Union,* 81–82.
363   *"To me is given the painful task":* Benjamin S. Calef, 2d U.S. sharpshooters, to "Mr. Parmalee," Keedysville, Md., September 19, 1862, in the Second United States Sharpshooters Papers, Antietam National Battlefield, Sharpsburg, Md., containing an item from the Yale University Library, New Haven, Conn.
364   *"The young man who was shot":* H. Ropes, *Civil War Nurse,* 67–69.
364   *"At last, night came on":* Shaw, *Blue-Eyed Child of Fortune,* 239–243.
364   *"The Secretary of War directs":* Peter H. Watson, Asst. Secy. of War, to John A. Dix, Washington, September 19, 1862, in the John A. Dix Papers.
365   *Secretary of State William Seward:* Neely, *Abraham Lincoln Encyclopedia,* 103–104.
365   *The preliminary proclamation:* Lincoln, *Collected Works,* V, 433–436.
366   *"I desire to express":* H. D. Hunt, *Hannibal Hamlin of Maine,* 161.
366   *"Here the people":* Pearson, ed., *Letters from Port Royal, 1862–1868,* 91–93.
366   *"The Writ of Habeas Corpus":* Lincoln, *Collected Works,* V, 436–437.
367   *"This campaign must be won":* D. Lyman, *Civil War Quotations,* 42.
370   *Helping to support:* McDonough, *War in Kentucky,* 252.
370   *He survived until nightfall:* Welsh, *Medical Histories of Union Generals,* 332–333.
371   *The investigative entries:* See *O.R.,* I, 16, I, 5–726.
371   *"Tender consideration":* Jefferson Davis, *Papers of Jefferson Davis,* VIII, 436.
372   *The battle commenced:* Cozzens, *Darkest Days of the War,* 85.
374   *Just then, a Minié bullet:* Welsh, *Medical Histories of Confederate Generals,* 141.
375   *Pvt. J. M. Vandoozer:* Cozzens, *Darkest Days of the War,* 170.
377   *He was taken:* Welsh, *Medical Histories of Union Generals,* 145.

378   *A famous wartime image:* Cockrell, ed., *Lost Account of the Battle of Corinth,* 51–52.
379   *"Do not make any calculations":* Lt. Col. Edward S. Bragg, 6th Wisconsin Inf., to his wife, Camp near Sharpsburg, Md., October 3, 1862, in the Edward S. Bragg Papers, Antietam National Battlefield, Sharpsburg, Md., containing an item from the State Historical Society of Wisconsin, Madison, Wis.
379   *"We cannot change the hearts":* D. Lyman, *Civil War Quotations,* 209.
379   *"If, as you threaten":* W. T. Sherman, *Sherman's Civil War,* 316–317.
379   *"Are you not over-cautious":* Lincoln, *Collected Works,* V, 460–462.
380   *"I have just read your despatch":* Ibid., 474.

CHAPTER 13   FREDERICKSBURG'S APPALLING LOSS

383   *"By direction of the President":* Lincoln, *Collected Works,* V, 485–486.
383   *At 11:30 P.M.:* Sears, *George B. McClellan,* 340.
383   *"Poor Burn feels dreadfully":* McClellan, *Civil War Papers,* 519–520.
383   *Of Brig. Gen. Rufus Saxton's request:* Higginson, *Army Life in a Black Regiment,* 2.
384   *"It would be grievous":* Robert E. Lee, *Wartime Papers,* 334–335.
384   *"I suppose I am to vegetate":* J. I. Robertson, *General A. P. Hill,* 157.
384   *Capt. Robert G. H. Kean:* Kean, *Inside the Confederate Government,* 31.
384   *Kean, whose sharp eye:* Ibid., 33.
385   *"Now, therefore, I, Jefferson Davis":* O.R., I, 15, 906–908.
386   *"I saw that this Rebellion":* Butler, *Private and Official Correspondence of Gen. Benjamin F. Butler,* II, 554–557.
386   *"The President is greatly dissatisfied":* O.R., I, 20; II, 123–124.
387   *The copper wires:* E. C. Bearss, *Hardluck Ironclad,* 97.
387   *The explosion under the bow:* O.R.N., I, 23, 548–550.
388   *Of the climactic moment:* O.R., I, 17, I, 555–557.
389   *"The ground was soft":* Ibid., 577–579.
389   *"General Van Dorn":* Ibid., 508–509.
390   *"Thousands will perish":* W. T. Sherman, *Sherman's Civil War,* 336–338.
391   *"Notwithstanding the destructive fire":* O.R., I, 17, I, 649–650.
391   *"The enemy left":* Ibid., 680–684.
391   *"Complete military success":* D. Lyman, *Civil War Quotations,* 210.
393   *One soldier recalled:* Banasik, *Embattled Arkansas,* 328.
393   *All was "inextricable confusion":* Ibid., 389.
398   *On December 9 he wrote:* O.R., I, 21, 64.
399   *"The pontoon bridges":* Dexter, *Seymour Dexter, Union Army,* 114–119.
400   *Pelham, age 24:* Hassler, *Colonel John Pelham,* 148.
400   *He fell from his horse:* Welsh, *Medical Histories of Confederate Generals,* 88–89.
401   *As Meagher's soldiers advanced:* George C. Rable, "It is Well that War Is So Terrible: The Carnage at Fredericksburg," in Gallagher, ed., *Fredericksburg Campaign,* 53.
401   *Watching the battle:* D. Lyman, *Civil War Quotations,* 13.
401   *Knocked to the ground:* Welsh, *Medical Histories of Confederate Generals,* 42–43.
401   *Cobb is frequently termed:* Eicher and Eicher, *Civil War High Commands.*
403   *Watching the struggle:* William N. Pendleton, *Southern Magazine,* XV (1874): 620.
403   *"The light streamed up":* D. Holt, *Mississippi Rebel in the Army of Northern Virginia,* 145.
403   *"At last, out wearied and depressed":* King and Derby, eds., *Camp-Fire Sketches and Battle-Field Echoes.*
403   *"It will scarcely be believed":* Henderson, *Civil War in the Writings of Col. G. F. R. Henderson,* 94.
405   *"I paid him much attention":* Allen, *Campaigning with "Old Stonewall,"* 195–198.
405   *Daniel E. Sickles:* Welsh, *Medical Histories of Union Generals,* 253.
405   *Duncan's wife:* Welsh, *Medical Histories of Confederate Generals,* 57.
406   *"The first thing I met":* Alcott, *Hospital Sketches,* 27.

406   *"In the course of this war":* Jefferson Davis, *Papers of Jefferson Davis,* VIII, 565–584.

406   *"This is scarcely a day for prose":* Frederick Douglass, "The Day of Jubilee Comes," in Masur, ed., *Real War,* 113.

406   *"Fellow citizens, we cannot":* Lincoln, *Collected Works,* V, 518–537.

407   *At month's end:* D. Lyman, *Civil War Quotations,* 151.

CHAPTER 14   STALEMATE AT STONES RIVER

408   *"I do order and declare":* Lincoln, *Collected Works,* VI, 28–31.

408   *(The army would report):* Eicher and Eicher, *Civil War High Commands.*

409   *The strength of the Confederate Army:* Ibid.

409   *The U.S. Ordnance Department:* U.S. War Dept., *Annual Report of the Secretary of War, November 14, 1866.*

409   *To demonstrate the type:* O.R., I, 27, I, 225–226.

410   *Various contractors aided:* Mowbray and Heroux, eds., *Civil War Arms Makers and Their Contracts,* 59–68, 160–165; Flayderman, *Flayderman's Guide to Antique American Firearms,* 450–453.

411   *Second only to the Springfield:* Bilby, *Civil War Firearms,* 62–67.

411   *Other popular rifles:* Flayderman, *Flayderman's Guide,* 84, 268–269, 502–504.

412   *"Well," said Lincoln:* Bruce, *Lincoln and the Tools of War,* 104.

412   *The battle over the breechloaders:* Flayderman, *Flayderman's Guide,* 482–505.

413   *The cavalry had a special need:* Sword, *Sharpshooter,* 64.

413   *Many other pistols:* Flayderman, *Flayderman's Guide,* 306–327.

413   *Imported revolvers:* McAulay, *Civil War Pistols of the Union,* 51–58.

414   *During the war:* Albaugh and Simmons, *Confederate Arms,* 9.

414   *Other Confederate handgun manufacturers:* Albaugh et al., *Confederate Handguns,* 157–204.

414   *The firm "prepared":* Albaugh, *Confederate Brass-Framed Colt & Whitney,* 53.

414   *Not only did Confederate arms makers:* Albaugh and Steuart, *Original Confederate Colt,* 35.

415   *But of the 246,712:* W. F. Fox, *Regimental Losses in the American Civil War, 1861–1865,* 24.

415   *Though thousands were produced:* Albaugh, *Confederate Edged Weapons,* 54–56, 93–94.

416   *In the North:* J. D. Hamilton, *Ames Sword Company,* 160.

416   *Producers and importers:* Albaugh and Steuart, *Handbook of Confederate Swords,* 13, 23–29, 35–37, 47–49, 61–63.

416   *After they refused:* O.R., I, 20, I, 153–154.

417   *"It is for you to determine":* Ibid., 135–136.

418   *There they were greeted:* Piston, *Carter's Raid,* 48.

422   *The sudden, heavy firing:* McDonough, *Stones River,* 85–86.

422   *The Minié bullet that struck:* Welsh, *Medical Histories of Union Generals,* 196.

423   *As he led a spirited counterattack:* Ibid., 304–305.

423   *"The line in advance of us":* Cozzens, *No Better Place to Die,* 139.

424   *"Never mind me":* McDonough, *Stones River,* 115.

424   *Rosecrans was shaken:* Cozzens, *No Better Place to Die,* 166.

424   *Spotting Sheridan:* McDonough, *Stones River,* 115.

424   *"The enemy now took cover":* Hazen, *Narrative of Military Service,* 71–77.

426   *Finished in 1863:* D. J. Eicher, *Civil War Battlefields,* 183.

427   *"My poor Orphan Brigade":* McDonough, *Stones River,* 202.

427   *Tennessee-born Brig. Gen.:* Welsh, *Medical Histories of Confederate Generals,* 179.

427   *Breckinridge himself:* Ibid., 92–93.

428   *"It has come to my Knowledge":* Braxton Bragg, circular to his corps and division commanders, Tullahoma, Tenn., January 11, 1863, in Frey, *In the Woods Before Dawn,* 58.

428   *"An awful battle":* N. L. Anderson, *General Nicholas Longworth Anderson,* 167.

429   *"I have heard":* Lincoln, *Collected Works,* VI, 78–79.

429   *"Well, let them come!":* J. B. Jones, *Rebel War Clerk's Diary,* I, 254–255.

429 *"Our generals, I think, have less dread"*: Thomas J. Goree, to his mother, near Fredericksburg, Va., February 4, 1863, in Goree, *Longstreet's Aide*, 102–104.
429 *"More than once"*: Robert E. Lee, *Wartime Papers*, 388–390.
430 *"You can't expect"*: U.S. Navy Dept., *Civil War Naval Chronology*, VI-388.
432 *"In no battle of the war"*: O.R., I, 17, I, 780–782.
432 *"The Jews, as a class"*: U. S. Grant, *Papers of Ulysses S. Grant*, VII, 50–56.
432 *"The mania for sudden fortunes"*: C. A. Dana, *Recollections of the Civil War*, 18–19.
432 *"The flat space"*: Boyd, *Civil War Diary of Cyrus F. Boyd*, 114.
433 *Magruder commended his troops*: O.R.N., I, 19, 467–468.
433 *When Comm. Henry H. Bell's*: Ibid., 506–508.
434 *The Confederate troops*: Ibid., 13, 635–637.
434 *Under heavy fire*: U.S. Navy Dept., *Civil War Naval Chronology*, III-36.
434 *Afterward, Porter ended*: Ibid., III-34.
435 *"I am an old soldier"*: Thomas Schrader to Samuel R. Curtis, Warrenton, Mo., January 8, 1863, in the Lewis Merrill Papers.
435 *Other officers*: B. S. Wills, *Battle from the Start*, 102.
435 *On the march*: Commager, ed., *Blue and the Gray*, 574–575.

CHAPTER 15   THE CAMPAIGN FOR VICKSBURG

436 *But the draft*: Long and Long, *Civil War Day by Day*, 325.
436 *Altogether, a total of 81,993*: Eicher and Eicher, *Civil War High Commands*.
437 *"I urge you"*: Blight, *Frederick Douglass' Civil War*, 157.
437 *"The bare sight"*: Lincoln, *Collected Works*, VI, 149–150.
437 *"Food consisted of a scanty ration"*: O.R., I, 23, 1, 85–93.
438 *Rosecrans's subsequent reports*: Ibid., 176–177.
438 *"To invest [the city]"*: William T. Sherman to Thomas Ewing, Camp Before Vicksburg, Miss., March 7, 1863, in the William T. Sherman Papers, U.S. Army Military History Institute, Carlisle, Pa.
438 *"As you say we have much to fear"*: Ibid.
440 *"Give them blizzards, boys!"*: Raab, *W. W. Loring*, 96.
440 *"The* Chillicothe *is an inglorious failure"*: O.R., I, 24, I, 380–382.
440 *In March an unknown civilian*: Anonymous, Vicksburg, Miss., March 20, 1863, in George Washington Cable, ed., "A Woman's Diary of the Siege of Vicksburg: Under Fire from the Gunboats," in *Century Illustrated Magazine*, VIII (1885): 767.
441 *"Don't duck, my son"*: L. L. Hewitt, *Port Hudson*, 77.
442 *"The ironclads," Sherman reported*: Ibid., III-47.
442 *"After working all night"*: O.R.N., I, 24, 474–478.
444 *"The contest raged"*: O.R., I, 15, 339 342.
445 *On this day Hatch*: D. A. Brown, *Grierson's Raid*, 89–90.
446 *Grant summarized the raid*: O.R., I, 24, I, 34.
446 *"Much of the country"*: Ibid., 522.
447 *"My loss in the expedition"*: Ibid., 22, 1, 285–288.
449 *They discovered that Forrest was closer*: Ibid., 23, 1, 285–293.
449 *Stoughton was appointed*: Eicher and Eicher, *Civil War High Commands*.
449 *"Unless our farmers and planters"*: *Southern Illustrated News* (Richmond), March 14, 1863.
450 *"Some malign influence"*: D. Lyman, *Civil War Quotations*, 102.
450 *"The greatest difficulty"*: Robert E. Lee, *Lee's Dispatches*, 81 83.
450 *"You can give"*: Robert E. Lee, *Wartime Papers*, 414–415.
450 *"Once I dreamed of an empire"*: D. Lyman, *Civil War Quotations*, 115.
450 *"In spite of their peculiar habits"*: Fremantle, *Three Months in the Southern States*, 60.
451 *In this action*: Mercer, *The Gallant Pelham*, 162.
451 *"The gallant Pelham"*: O.R., I, 25, 1, 59.

452 *"My men rushed forward":* Ibid., 47–53.
452 *Col. Josiah Pickett:* Ibid., 8, 187.
453 *"I am very well convinced":* August V. Kautz, "Operations South of the James River," in Johnson and Buel, eds., *Battles and Leaders,* IV, 533.
453 *"We will beat the enemy":* U.S. Navy Dept., *Civil War Naval Chronology,* VI-386.
453 *"I have never seen men":* Lamson, *Lamson of the* Gettysburg, 101–102.
453 *Never one to be accused:* O.R., I, 18, 324–326.
454 *"The attack was so sudden":* Ibid., 25, 1, 98–105.
454 *"A burning river":* Ibid., 115–121.
455 *"The monitors are not intended":* Du Pont, *Samuel Francis Du Pont,* III, 56–61.
455 *His famous epitaph:* Author's photograph collection.
455 *He died in Syracuse:* Welsh, *Medical Histories of Union Generals,* 329; Eicher and Eicher, *Civil War High Commands.*
456 *Assigned as commandant:* Welsh, *Medical Histories of Union Generals,* 76.
456 *Donelson had served:* Welsh, *Medical Histories of Confederate Generals,* 55; Eicher and Eicher, *Civil War High Commands.*
456 *So began its haunting verses:* Commager, *Blue and the Gray,* 586–587.

CHAPTER 16 LEE'S MASTER STROKE

457 *"We must live upon the enemy's country":* D. Lyman, *Civil War Quotations,* 101.
458 *Grant stood watch:* Winschel, *Triumph and Defeat,* 30.
459 *Tracy himself was struck:* Welsh, *Medical Histories of Confederate Generals,* 216.
459 *"Their artillery opened":* Winschel, *Triumph and Defeat,* 83.
462 *"He is a very able man":* C. M. Blackford, *Letters from Lee's Army,* 180.
463 *"The line was ordered forward":* O.R., I, 24, 1, 706–711.
464 *"I arrived this evening":* Symonds, *Joseph E. Johnston,* 205.
464 *"The railroads were destroyed":* O.R., I, 24, 1, 751–758.
465 *"My own views":* Ballard, *Pemberton,* 155–156.
466 *"Under a heavy charge":* Winschel, *Triumph and Defeat,* 104.
466 *Tilghman was struck:* Welsh, *Medical Histories of Confederate Generals,* 214.
469 *"Two shots entered":* O.R.N., I, 25, 42–43.
470 *"At the appointed moment":* Andrew Hickenlooper, "The Vicksburg Mine," in Johnson and Buel, eds., *Battles and Leaders,* III, 542.
470 *"Vicksburg contains many":* W. T. Sherman, *Home Letters of General Sherman,* 268–269.
471 *Although he is often claimed:* Eicher and Eicher, *Civil War High Commands.*
471 *On June 27 the Virginian:* Welsh, *Medical Histories of Confederate Generals,* 87.
471 *Of the attack on June 22:* O.R., I, 24, 1, 159–161.
471 *Disgusted with both press and public:* W. T. Sherman, *Sherman's Civil War,* 476–478.
472 *"Come on," shouted a corporal:* Hewitt, *Port Hudson,* 142.
472 *His arm dangling:* Ibid., 149.
472 *"I started out this morning":* Cunningham, *Port Hudson Campaign,* 89.
473 *He would spend the next:* Welsh, *Medical Histories of Union Generals,* 102–103; Eicher and Eicher, *Civil War High Commands.*
476 *Hooker issued General Orders No. 47:* O.R., I, 25, 1, 171.
477 *Hooker also allegedly told:* Swinton, *Campaigns of the Army of the Potomac,* 275.
477 *"This is splendid, Slocum!":* Furgurson, *Chancellorsville 1863,* 110.
477 *Some one and a half miles:* Harrison, *Chancellorsville Battlefield Sites,* 57–60.
478 *"From character of information":* O.R., I, 25, 2, 326–328.
478 *Neither of these seems to be the case:* Sears, *Chancellorsville,* 504–506.
479 *"I propose to go right around there":* Ibid., 235.
480 *In his last message to Lee:* Thomas J. Jackson, about 3 P.M., May 2, 1863, in the Thomas J. Jackson Papers, Virginia Historical Society, Richmond, Reel 17, item 617.

480   *Near the Luckett House:* Furgurson, *Chancellorsville,* 170.
482   *Despite his words of encouragement:* Ibid., 181.
482   *Though it has been described:* Andrew B. Wells, "The Charge of the Eighth Pennsylvania Cavalry," in Johnson and Buel, eds., *Battles and Leaders,* III, 187–188.
482   *Sitting atop his horse:* Furgurson, *Chancellorsville,* 202.
483   *Jackson had been shot:* Welsh, *Medical Histories of Confederate Generals,* 111–113.
483   *As described by Jackson's chaplain:* James Power Smith, "Stonewall Jackson's Last Battle," in Johnson and Buel, eds., *Battles and Leaders,* III, 211.
483   *"Could I have directed events":* Robert E. Lee, *Wartime Papers,* 452–453.
483   *"The events of the few hours":* Livermore, *Days and Events,* 203.
485   *Brig. Gen. Elisha F. "Bull" Paxton:* Welsh, *Medical Histories of Confederate Generals,* 164.
485   *"General Hooker was lying down":* Darius N. Couch, "The Chancellorsville Campaign," in Johnson and Buel, eds., *Battles and Leaders,* III, 169.
487   *"For two miles we saw":* Gary W. Gallagher, "East of Chancellorsville: Jubal A. Early at Second Fredericksburg and Salem Church," in Gary W. Gallagher, ed., *Chancellorsville,* 48.
488   *"By May 8th our wounds":* Bull, *Soldiering,* 81.
488   *Among the dead:* Welsh, *Medical Histories of Union Generals,* 28, 196, 366; Eicher and Eicher, *Civil War High Commands.*
488   *As chief engineer:* Joseph G. Totten, Engineer Order No. 5, May 11, 1863, in the Amiel W. Whipple Papers.
488   *Abraham Fulkerson summed up:* Abram Fulkerson to his wife Selina, May 18, 1863, in the Abram Fulkerson Papers.
488   *The general's last words:* J. I. Robertson, *Stonewall Jackson,* 752–753.
488   *"There was the stuff of Cromwell":* *Richmond Examiner,* May 11, 1863.
489   *"The Lord has crowned our arms":* Derastus E. W. Myers to his brother and sister, Camp near Hamilton's Crossing, Va., May 11, 1863, in the Derastus E. W. Myers Papers.
489   *"I agree with you in believing":* Robert E. Lee, *Wartime Papers,* 490.
489   *"Numbers have now no terror":* J. B. Jones, *Rebel War Clerk's Diary,* I, 318.
489   *"He who survived the thunder-burst":* Brooks, *Lincoln Observed,* 51–52.
489   *Lincoln could only utter:* Brooks, *Washington in Lincoln's Time,* 61.
490   *"There is always hazard":* Robert E. Lee, *Wartime Papers,* 504–505.
491   *"We should neglect":* Ibid., 507–509.
491   *"If the head of Lee's army":* Lincoln, *Collected Works,* VI, 273.
493   *He was sent to "Hickory Hill":* Eicher, *Robert E. Lee,* 98.
498   *The rain converted:* O.R., I, 23, 1, 538–541.
498   *Miller's regiment poured a heavy fire:* Ibid., 457–461.
498   *"It was a bright day":* Ibid., 611–614.
499   *Peters returned half an hour later:* R. G. Hartje, *Van Dorn,* 311–312.
499   *"Van Dorn has been recognized":* *Atlanta Confederacy,* quoted in the *Fayetteville Observer,* in R. G. Hartje, *Van Dorn,* 318.
499   *After encouraging his soldiers to loot:* S. B. King, *Darien,* 77.
499   *"For myself, I have gone through":* Shaw, *Blue-Eyed Child of Fortune,* 341–345.
500   *"My dear sir," said the president:* Brooks, *Lincoln Observed,* 49.
500   *"He has a face like a Hoosier":* Walt Whitman to Nat and Fred Gray, Washington, March 19, 1863, in Commager, ed., *Blue and the Gray,* 712–714.

CHAPTER 17   THREE DAYS AT GETTYSBURG

501   *At 3 A.M. on June 28:* Coddington, *Gettysburg Campaign,* 209.
502   *Among the candidates:* Ibid., 37.
502   *"By direction of the President":* George G. Meade, General Orders No. 66, Headquarters, Army of the Potomac, June 28, 1863, in the George G. Meade Papers.

504 *On that day, local citizen Jacob Hoke:* Hoke, *Great Invasion of 1863,* 123.

504 *One of the men struck:* Nye, *Here Come the Rebels!,* 245–246.

506 *"If you find that [the enemy]":* O.R., I, 27, 3, 913.

506 *In an accompanying letter:* Ibid., 915.

507 *On the evening of June 28:* Tony Trimble, "Harrison: Spying for Longstreet at Gettysburg," in *Gettysburg* magazine, no. 17 (1997): 17–19.

507 *Meade's orders from the War Department:* O.R., I, 27, 1, 61.

507 *Due to the exigencies:* Eicher and Eicher, *Civil War High Commands.*

508 *He further stated:* O.R., I, 27, 3, 458–459.

508 *"Major Gen. Reynolds will upon receipt":* Seth Williams, cipher orders, to Maj. Gen. John F. Reynolds, 1 P.M., June 30, 1863, in the John F. Reynolds Papers.

508 *The stories of Confederate expeditions:* Ibid., I, 27, 2, 637–639.

510 *By 7:30 A.M. the two forces:* Martin, *Gettysburg, July 1,* 63–64.

511 *By 9 A.M. the Federal cavalry:* Frassanito, *Early Photography at Gettysburg,* 58–59.

511 *"We were being hurried":* Martin, *Gettysburg, July 1,* 100.

512 *He spent more than a year:* Eicher and Eicher, *Civil War High Commands.*

512 *Reynolds gasped a single time:* Welsh, *Medical Histories of Union Generals,* 275.

512 *He took up arms alongside:* Frassanito, *Early Photography at Gettysburg,* 84–87.

512 *"The line of the [regiment]":* McLean, *Cutler's Brigade at Gettysburg,* 81.

513 *"My color guards were all killed":* Herdegen and Beaudot, *In the Bloody Railroad Cut at Gettysburg,* 201.

515 *"When we were in point blank range":* Robert K. Krick, "Failures of Brigade Leadership," in Gary W. Gallagher, ed., *The First Day at Gettysburg,* 133.

515 *The brigade of Brig. Gen. Gabriel R. Paul:* Welsh, *Medical Histories of Union Generals,* 253–254; Eicher and Eicher, *Civil War High Commands.*

516 *Years later Gordon:* Martin, *Gettysburg,* 291–296.

516 *"I got up and went":* Ibid., 314.

517 *There he hid between a barrel and a woodshed:* Ibid., 331–332.

517 *Inside the McClellan House:* Frassanito, *Early Photography at Gettysburg,* 119–123.

517 *Lee sent Ewell:* O.R., I, 27, 2, 313–325.

518 *In typical oversimplification:* Martin, *Gettysburg,* 514.

518 *Hancock arrived about 4:30 P.M.:* Ibid., 483.

518 *Howard allegedly replied:* Ibid., 483–487.

519 *"They seemed to fear":* Ibid., 524.

519 *They reported the enemy's line:* Ibid., 555.

520 *One of the officers:* H. W. Pfanz, *Gettysburg: The Second Day,* 42.

520 *The night remained hot:* Mark, *Red, White, and Blue Badge,* 216.

521 *He walked, discussed orders:* Welsh, *Medical Histories of Confederate Generals,* 134–136.

522 *Lee and Trimble visited:* H.W. Pfanz, *Gettysburg: The Second Day,* 111.

522 *Lee next returned:* Ibid., 112.

522 *Longstreet supposedly told Hood:* Ibid.

522 *Indeed, the written order:* Coddington, *Gettysburg Campaign,* 377.

524 *"The enemy was massed":* Sauers, *"A Caspian Sea of Ink,"* 35.

527 *With their case shot expended:* H. W. Pfanz, *Gettysburg: The Second Day,* 186.

527 *At one point:* Ibid., 187, 191.

527 *Among the dead:* Eicher and Eicher, *Civil War High Commands.*

528 *"Soon we found the enemy":* Desjardin, *Stand Firm Ye Boys from Maine,* 54.

529 *"At this moment my anxiety":* Ibid., 68.

529 *"It was imperative to strike":* Norton, *Attack and Defense of Little Round Top,* 214–215.

529 *"Suddenly, in the midst of the noise":* Spear, *Civil War Recollections of General Ellis Spear,* 34–35.

530 *Col. Strong Vincent:* Welsh, *Medical Histories of Union Generals,* 353.

530 *After the battle:* Fred T. Locke to Seth Williams, Headquarters, 5th Corps, August 7, 1863, in the Strong Vincent Papers.

530 *"I'm as dead a man as Julius Caesar":* Welsh, *Medical Histories of Union Generals,* 362–363.

530   *Additionally, the youthful artillerist:* H. W. Pfanz, *Gettysburg: The Second Day,* 240.

530   *Also dead was Paddy O'Rorke:* Bennett, *The Beau Ideal of a Soldier and a Gentleman,* 124.

531   *"Colonel Cross, this day":* H. W. Pfanz, *Gettysburg: The Second Day,* 269.

531   *"The Rebs had their slight protection":* D. Scott Hartwig, "Caldwell's Division in the Wheatfield," in Gary W. Gallagher, ed., *Second Day at Gettysburg,* 152.

531   *As Zook rode along:* Gambone, *Life of General Samuel K. Zook,* 14.

531   *Semmes, a Georgian:* Welsh, *Medical Histories of Confederate Generals,* 194.

532   *Though Antietam has been described:* H. W. Pfanz, *Gettysburg: The Second Day,* 303.

532   *"I then saw Confederates":* Bigelow, *The Peach Orchard,* 57.

533   *The knee was mangled:* Welsh, *Medical Histories of Union Generals,* 302–303; Coco, *Vast Sea of Misery,* 80–82; H. W. Pfanz, *Gettysburg: The Second Day,* 333–334.

534   *Struck above the left knee:* H. W. Pfanz, *Gettysburg: The Second Day,* 349–350; Welsh, *Medical Histories of Confederate Generals,* 13–14.

535   *"The Confederates faced toward them":* Alleman, *At Gettysburg,* 58.

536   *Hancock pointed toward Wilcox's Confederate line:* H. W. Pfanz, *Gettysburg: The Second Day,* 410–411.

537   *"Moments passed which were years":* H. W. Pfanz, *Gettysburg: Culp's Hill and Cemetery Hill,* 215.

538   *Hays's Louisianans "moved forward":* Ibid., 255–256.

538   *Alone and unrecognized:* Ibid., 258–259.

538   *The Union batteries:* Ibid., 269.

539   *When an officer mentioned:* Coddington, *Gettysburg Campaign,* 448.

539   *Its questions and answers:* Daniel Butterfield, Gettysburg, Pa., July 2, 1863, in John Gibbon, *Recollections of the Civil War,* 142–144.

541   *"At first—some of the men said":* H. W. Pfanz, *Gettysburg: Culp's Hill and Cemetery Hill,* 319–320.

542   *By one account Lee snapped:* Nesbitt, *Saber and Scapegoat,* 90.

542   *A defining moment occurred:* Wert, *General James Longstreet,* 283–284.

543   *Hunt called the display:* Coddington, *Gettysburg Campaign,* 479.

543   *Evander M. Law thought:* Evander M. Law, "The Struggle for Round Top," in Johnson and Buel, eds., *Battles and Leaders,* III, 327.

543   *To the Union artillerist:* H. W. Pfanz, *Gettysburg: Culp's Hill and Cemetery Hill,* 360.

544   *"Hunt said that he thought":* David Shultz, *"Double Canister at Ten Yards,"* 29.

544   *The attack force consisted:* Reardon, *Pickett's Charge in History and Memory,* 6.

544   *To the north, west of the Bliss Farm:* Welsh, *Medical Histories of Confederate Generals,* 98–99.

544   *Trimble was assigned:* Ibid., 166–167.

546   *At 1:35 P.M. he sent Pickett:* Alexander, *Fighting for the Confederacy,* 259–261.

546   *"Up, men, and to your posts!":* Harrison and Busey, *Nothing but Glory,* 39.

546   *"When half the valley":* Rollins, ed., *Pickett's Charge,* 172–175.

547   *"The moment I saw them":* Henry Livermore Abbott to his father, near Gettysburg, Pa., July 6, 1863, in Abbott, *Fallen Leaves,* 184–191.

547   *As Lt. Col. Edmund Rice recalled:* Edmund Rice, "Repelling Lee's Last Blow at Gettysburg," in Johnson and Buel, eds., *Battles and Leaders,* III, 389–390.

547   *Col. Frank A. Haskell:* F. A. Haskell, *Haskell of Gettysburg,* 170.

548   *The ball struck Kemper:* Welsh, *Medical Histories of Confederate Generals,* 125–126; Eicher and Eicher, *Civil War High Commands.*

548   *Garnett's sword:* Robert K. Krick, "Armistead and Garnett," in Gary W. Gallagher, ed., *The Third Day at Gettysburg and Beyond,* 122–123.

548   *Struck in the chest:* Welsh, *Medical Histories of Confederate Generals,* 10–11.

549   *Alonzo Cushing was hit:* K. M. Brown, *Cushing of Gettysburg,* 250–251.

549   *Waiting atop his horse:* G. Tucker, *Hancock the Superb,* 151.

549   *Later, Hancock was seriously wounded:* Welsh, *Medical Histories of Union Generals,* 149–151.

549   *"All this has been my fault":* D. Lyman, *Civil War Quotations,* 138.

549   *Pickett, who complained to Lee:* L. J. Gordon, *General George E. Pickett in Life and Legend,* 116.

549   *As the spotlight for failure:* " 'I Think the Union Army Had Something to Do with It': The

Pickett's Charge Nobody Knows," in Gabor S. Boritt, ed., *The Gettysburg Nobody Knows*, 122–143.

549 *Kilpatrick later wrote:* Bachelder, *John Bachelder's History of the Battle of Gettysburg*, 649–650.

550 *Reports of Farnsworth:* Welsh, *Medical Histories of Union Generals*, 113.

552 *"Strengthen your line":* Robert E. Lee to Richard S. Ewell [Hagerstown, Md.], July 11, 1863, in the Robert E. Lee Papers, U.S. Army Military History Institute, Carlisle, Pa.

552 *Amazingly, Halleck had telegraphed:* O.R., I, 27, 1, 92.

552 *"He has suggested nothing":* Welles, *Diary*, I, 372–374.

552 *Buford's cavalry detected:* Welsh, *Medical Histories of Confederate Generals*, 170–171.

552 *"I was deeply mortified":* Lincoln, *Collected Works*, VI, 341–342.

553 *On August 8 he wrote Jefferson Davis:* Robert E. Lee, *Wartime Papers*, 589–590.

553 *"Were you capable of stooping to it":* O.R., I, 29, 2, 639–640.

553 *"Our brigade moved to the front":* Donaldson, *Inside the Army of the Potomac*, 310.

553 *"I spent the night":* de Trobriand, *Our Noble Blood*, 116–118.

553 *"Their bodies were swollen":* Fisk, *Hard Marching Every Day*, 115–120.

553 *"It is impossible":* Charleston *Mercury*, July 30, 1863.

554 *"You have full account":* Thomas Henderson to Belle Edmondson, July 7, 1863, in B. Edmondson, *Lost Heroine of the Confederacy*, 52–53.

554 *"I am all right":* James E. B. Stuart, July 13, 1863, near Hagerstown, Md., to Flora Cooke Stuart, in the James E. B. Stuart Papers, Virginia Historical Society, Richmond, Reel 40, items 1031–1032.

554 *"The fury of the low Irish":* Strong, *Diary*, III, 335–337.

554 *An account from* Harper's Weekly: *Harper's Weekly*, August 1, 1863.

555 *"A certain number of the mules":* Loughborough, *My Cave Life in Vicksburg*, 109.

557 *Longhand menus for the "hotel":* Walker, *Vicksburg*, 183–184.

557 *"As soon as our troops":* Ulysses S. Grant, "The Vicksburg Campaign," in Johnson and Buel, eds., *Battles and Leaders*, III, 536.

557 *"The great Ulysses":* Vicksburg *Daily Citizen*, July 2 and 4, 1863.

557 *"It is a striking feature":* Ulysses S. Grant to John C. Kelton, report on the Vicksburg campaign, July 6, 1863, in U. S. Grant, *Papers*, VIII, 485–524.

558 *"Was ever the Nation's Birthday":* E. H. Rhodes, *All for the Union*, 117.

558 *"I wanted to hug the army":* C. F. Adams et al., *Cycle of Adams Letters*, II, 58–63.

558 *"I have no heart to write":* Catherine Ann Devereux Edmondston, Halifax County, North Carolina, July 11, 1863, in Edmondston, *"Journal of a Secesh Lady,"* 427–429.

558 *"Our home is gone":* Tryphena Blanche Holder Fox to her mother, Woodburne Plantation, Plaquemines Parish, La., July 3, 1863; in T. B. H. Fox, *A Northern Woman in the Plantation South*, 134–135.

558 *"General, allow me to observe":* Frank P. Blair to Ulysses S. Grant, Newport, R.I., August 19, 1863, from the Ulysses S. Grant Papers, Record Group 94, Adjutant General's Office Records, Generals' Papers, NARA, Washington, D.C.

559 *"The Navy under Porter":* U.S. Navy Dept., *Civil War Naval Chronology*, VI-387.

559 *"I do not remember":* Abraham Lincoln to U. S. Grant, Washington, July 13, 1863, from a typescript prepared by John G. Nicolay, in the Ulysses S. Grant Papers, Record Group 94, Adjutant General's Office Records, Generals' Papers, NARA, Washington, D.C.

559 *"The Father of Waters":* Lincoln, *Collected Works*, VI, 409.

559 *In his official report:* Hewitt, *Port Hudson*, 175–176.

560 *Morgan demanded Moore's surrender:* Ramage, *Rebel Raider*, 163.

562 *One of the farmers:* Ibid., 170.

563 *Morgan returned to Kentucky:* Ibid., 190–196.

564 *His mind "became insane":* Leslie, *Devil Knows How to Ride*, 198, 204.

564 *"Immediately the negroes and white men":* McCorkle, *Three Years with Quantrill*, 125.

565 *"Now the main question":* James Henry Gooding to Abraham Lincoln, September 28, 1863, in James Henry Gooding, *On the Altar of Freedom*, 118–120.

565 *On July 2, Shaw:* Emilio, *Brave Black Regiment*, 47–48.

566   *"The two columns now moved":* O.R., I, 28, 1, 354–355.
567   *Though the attack would be suicidal:* Emilio, *Brave Black Regiment,* 75.
568   *In one of his last letters:* Shaw, *Blue-Eyed Child of Fortune,* 373.
568   *When the rest of Strong's brigade:* Welsh, *Medical Histories of Union Generals,* 324.
568   *On July 24, Union artillery:* Manigault, *Siege Train,* 5.
569   *"The part of the Confederacy":* Kean, *Inside the Confederate Government,* 99–101.
569   *"The soldiers has a by word":* Pvt. W. Lawrence Barrett to Jesse McMahan, Camp near Richmond, July 18, 1863, in Heller and Heller, *Confederacy Is on Her Way up the Spout,* 102–103.

CHAPTER 18   VISITING THE RIVER OF DEATH

570   *(Gilmer is often misidentified):* Eicher and Eicher, *Civil War High Commands.*
570   *"To enable us to hold":* O.R., I, 28, 2, 337.
571   *"The parapet of salient":* Ibid., I, 28, 1, 482.
571   *Sgt. William H. Johnson:* William H. Johnson, Sgt., 7th Conn. Inf., to Hannah J. Johnson, his wife, Morris Island, S.C., September 15, 1863, in the William H. Johnson Papers.
571   *"The enemy now holds":* Richmond Sentinel, September 7, 1863.
571   *An observer of Fort Sumter:* U.S. Navy Dept., *Civil War Naval Chronology,* III-137.
572   *"Moultrie fired like a devil":* O.R.N., I, 14, 635–636.
573   *Asst. Engr. James H. Tomb:* Ibid., I, 15, 20–21.
574   *The Confederate Congress:* Civil War Naval Chronology, III-138.
574   *"Thus it will be seen":* O.R.N., I, 20, 559–560.
574   *(Marmaduke had on September 6):* Eicher and Eicher, *Civil War High Commands.*
574   *Dismounting, Shelby's men formed:* O.R., I, 22, 1, 670–678.
575   *The railroad blockhouse:* Ibid.
576   *"As soon as Quantrill":* Britton, *Memoirs of the Rebellion on the Border, 1863,* 418–419.
576   *"We continued the chase":* O.R., I, 22, 1, 700–701.
576   *"On looking over the ground":* Ibid., 688–690.
577   *Bragg's army comprised:* Eicher and Eicher, *Civil War High Commands.*
579   *He directed Polk:* Woodworth, *Six Armies in Tennessee,* 75.
580   *The word Chickamauga:* Woodworth, *Deep Steady Thunder,* 13; Cozzens, *This Terrible Sound,* 90.
582   *Though the Confederates:* Cozzens, *This Terrible Sound,* 131.
582   *Dr. Miller told them:* Ibid., 143.
582   *"I . . . tried to place it back":* Ibid., 162.
583   *As the 11th Ohio Infantry:* Ibid., 188–189.
584   *"Confusion reigned even before":* Ibid., 232.
585   *"For half an hour":* O.R., I, 30, 2, 153–158.
585   *Despite claims of brigadier generalship:* Welsh, *Medical Histories of Confederate Generals,* 54; Eicher and Eicher, *Civil War High Commands.*
585   *One of the rounds:* Welsh, *Medical Histories of Confederate Generals,* 201.
586   *Helm died about midnight:* Ibid., 97–98; Eicher and Eicher, *Civil War High Commands.*
588   *Rosecrans therefore sent:* Woodworth, *Deep Steady Thunder,* 80.
588   *Buell wrote that:* Cozzens, *This Terrible Sound,* 370.
589   *He had been struck:* Ibid., 387–388.
589   *"The remains of Genl. Lytle":* Alfred Pirtle to Maj. Gen. Philip H. Sheridan, Camp, 10th Ohio Inf., Chattanooga, October 13, 1863, in the William H. Lytle Papers.
590   *"There's nothing in our front":* Cozzens, *This Terrible Sound,* 440.
590   *"It was unquestionably":* Gracie, *Truth About Chickamauga,* 268–269.
590   *Of the action on the hill:* Gates P. Thruston, "The Crisis at Chickamauga," in Johnson and Buel, eds., *Battles and Leaders,* III, 664.
592   *"How many terrible scenes":* Beatty, *Citizen-Soldier,* 344.

592   *"We spread on two blankets"*: Fletcher, *Rebel Private Front and Rear,* 125–126.

592   *"The most important battle of the war"*: An anonymous Confederate private, in Heartsill, *Fourteen Hundred and 91 Days in the Confederate Army,* 155–159.

592   *"It is hard to give up"*: Brooks, *Lincoln Observed,* 72.

592   *For his part:* Hay, *Inside Lincoln's White House,* 98–99.

593   *"As we rode out"*: Cumming, *Gleanings from Southland,* 135–144.

594   *The Rebels then took:* J. P. Dyer, *From Shiloh to San Juan,* 103.

596   *As he arrived:* Welsh, *Medical Histories of Union Generals,* 138–140.

596   *"The hour now seems"*: J. B. Jones, *Rebel War Clerk's Diary,* II, 42.

597   *The Mississippi Brig. Gen. Carnot Posey:* Welsh, *Medical Histories of Confederate Generals,* 175–176.

597   *Following the debacle:* J. I. Robertson, *General A. P. Hill,* 239.

598   *His liver function was impaired:* Welsh, *Medical Histories of Union Generals,* 31–32.

598   *"The young Bloods of the South"*: William T. Sherman to Henry W. Halleck, Camp on Big Black, Miss., September 17, 1863, in W. T. Sherman, *Sherman's Civil War,* 543–550.

CHAPTER 19   THE BATTLES FOR CHATTANOOGA

600   *They became "too weak"*: Cozzens, *Shipwreck of Their Hopes,* 9.

602   *Hazen told his men:* Ibid., 65.

602   *"In Chattanooga there were but four"*: William G. Le Duc, "The Little Steamboat that Opened the Cracker Line," in Johnson and Buel, eds., *Battles and Leaders,* III, 676–678.

603   *In the process, Greene:* Welsh, *Medical Histories of Union Generals,* 140.

604   *"We gave a most unearthly yell"*: Cozzens, *Shipwreck of Their Hopes,* 98.

604   *Longstreet, outraged over the failure:* Eicher and Eicher, *Civil War High Commands.*

605   *"Flags were flying"*: Cozzens, *Shipwreck of Their Hopes,* 129.

606   *One such writer:* Sword, *Mountains Touched with Fire,* 184–185.

607   *As Geary advanced:* Ibid., 216.

609   *"No firing at the front"*: Ibid., 231.

609   *"In a moment I reflected"*: Samuel H. M. Byers, "Sherman's Attack at the Tunnel," in Johnson and Buel, eds., *Battles and Leaders,* III, 713.

610   *"Such a sight I never saw"*: Sword, *Mountains Touched with Fire,* 271.

612   *The bedazzled Grant:* Cozzens, *Shipwreck of Their Hopes,* 282.

612   *"The line ceased to be a line"*: Montgomery C. Meigs, "First Impressions of Three Days' Fighting: Quartermaster General Meigs's 'Journal of the Battle of Chattanooga,' " in Wilson and Simon, eds., *Ulysses S. Grant,* 59–76.

613   *"The disaster admits of no palliation"*: O.R., II, 52, 745.

613   *Tired of the death:* McKinney, *Education in Violence,* 303.

615   *His horse was first shot:* Welsh, *Medical Histories of Union Generals,* 287.

615   *After Campbell's Station:* House, *Very Violent Rebel,* 38–39.

616   *"For fully twenty minutes"*: Edward Porter Alexander, "Longstreet at Knoxville," in Johnson and Buel, eds., *Battles and Leaders,* III, 749.

616   *Orlando M. Poe recalled:* Orlando M. Poe, "The Defense of Knoxville," in Johnson and Buel, eds., *Battles and Leaders,* III, 743.

617   *"At 3 P.M. the enemy were driven"*: O.R., I, 29, 1, 504–508.

619   *"The country of course overrated Meade"*: "Dunn Browne," pseudonym of Capt. Samuel W. Fiske, 14th Connecticut Inf., Camp near Stevensburg, Va., December 24, 1863, from Fiske, *Mr. Dunn Browne's Experiences in the Army,* 215–216.

619   *"She deserves it all"*: Strong, *Diary,* III, 386–387.

620   *"The night was"*: Manigault, *Siege Train,* 99–103.

620   *The final scrap:* John Buford to Lt. Col. C. Ross Smith, chief of staff, Cav. Corps, Headquarters, 1st Cav. Div., November 20, 1863, in the John Buford Papers. Endorsed in the

affirmative by Surg. George L. Pancoast, Alfred Pleasonton, and medical director Jonathan Letterman.

621 *Pronounced dead:* Welsh, *Medical Histories of Union Generals,* 77–78.

621 *"Genl. Corcoran died":* Capt. William A. La Motte, AAG, telegram to Lt. Col. Joseph H. Taylor, AAG, Fairfax Court House, Va., December 22, 1863, in the Michael Corcoran Papers.

622 *Lincoln's "few appropriate remarks":* Lincoln, *Collected Works,* VII, 17–22.

623 *"I should be glad":* Ibid., 24.

623 *"The President tonight had a dream":* Hay, *Inside Lincoln's White House,* 132.

CHAPTER 20   SHERMAN EYES THE DEEP SOUTH

624 *The U.S. Army had a count:* Eicher and Eicher, *Civil War High Commands.*

625 *"Now, since Vicksburg":* Chesnut, *Mary Chesnut's Civil War,* 519–526.

625 *Bragg was "charged":* Eicher and Eicher, *Civil War High Commands.*

626 *"I have seen death":* David Dixon Porter to his mother, December 29, 1863, in D. Lyman, *Civil War Quotations,* 188.

626 *"War is simply Power unrestrained":* William T. Sherman to Maj. Roswell M. Sawyer, AAG, Army of the Tennessee, Vicksburg, Miss., January 31, 1864, in W. T. Sherman, *Sherman's Civil War,* 598–602.

626 *In Virginia, the Federal surgeon:* Daniel M. Holt to his wife, Hazel River, Va., February 7, 1864, in Daniel M. Holt, *Surgeon's Civil War,* 171–173.

627 *"There is something wrong":* William H. A. Speer to his father, February 18, 1864, in W. H. A. Speer, *Voices from Cemetery Hill,* 121–122.

627 *"We had several substitutes":* Hague, *Blockaded Family,* 102.

627 *Fish and eggs increased:* Massey, *Ersatz in the Confederacy,* 62.

628 *"Short rations are having":* Robert E. Lee to James A. Seddon, January 22, 1864, in Robert E. Lee, *Wartime Papers,* 659–660.

630 *He died the next day:* Marvel, *Andersonville,* 50.

630 *"A crazy man was shot dead":* Ransom, *John Ransom's Andersonville Diary,* 71–72.

630 *"Thirty thousand prisoners":* Ripple, *Dancing Along the Deadline,* 45.

630 *"The proceeds of these forays":* McElroy, *Andersonville,* I, 223–224.

630 *Conditions at Andersonville:* Futch, *History of Andersonville Prison,* 45.

631 *At Salisbury, Frederic Augustus James:* Frederic Augustus James, Salisbury, N.C., March 19, 1864; in James, *Frederic Augustus James's Civil War Diary,* 49–50.

631 *At the officers' prison:* Henry S. White, Wheeling, W. Va., April 24, 1865, in White, *Prison Life Among the Rebels,* 71–75.

631 *"Frightened as he was":* G. H. Putnam, *Prisoner of War in Virginia, 1864–5,* 59–60.

631 *"Nothing but bread":* Cavada, *Libby Life,* 27.

632 *A soldier reported:* Hesseltine, *Civil War Prisons,* 185.

632 *"To be a prisoner of war":* James Deeler to his wife Sarah, Camp Chase, Ohio, April 22, 1862, in Knauss, *Story of Camp Chase,* 152–153.

632 *Of Johnson's Island:* Nisbet, *Four Years on the Firing Line,* 226.

633 *At Point Lookout:* B. Y. Malone, *Whipt 'Em Everytime,* 96.

633 *"If there ever was a hell on earth":* Denney, *Civil War Prisons and Escapes,* 336.

633 *"The men were made to retire":* L. R. Speer, *Portals to Hell,* 180–182.

634 *"Indeed, I believe it is the first":* O.R., I, 33, 45–46.

634 *"Our infantry was not in condition":* Ibid., 32, I, 93–94.

635 *His soldiers were "almost daily engaged":* Ibid., 135–138.

636 *"For five days 10,000 men":* M. R. Bearss, *Sherman's Forgotten Campaign,* 192.

637 *"A great many of the Planters":* James B. McPherson to William T. Sherman, Headquarters, 17th A.C., Vicksburg, Miss., January 2, 1864, in the James B. McPherson Papers.

638 *"The citizens turned out":* O.R., I, 33, 57–59.

638   *"It had the appearance of a plank"*: U.S. Navy Dept., *Civil War Naval Chronology*, IV-21.

639   *"Just then a cruel shell burst"*: Nulty, *Confederate Florida*, 151.

640   *"I am now writing with a Yankee pen"*: Winston Stephens to Octavia Stephens, Camp Beauregard, Fla., February 21, 1864, from Blakey et al., eds., *Rose Cottage Chronicles*, 318–321.

CHAPTER 21   THE RED RIVER CAMPAIGN

642   *"Grant is as good a Leader"*: William T. Sherman to John Sherman, Nashville, Tenn., April 5, 1864, from W. T. Sherman, *Sherman's Civil War*, 612–615.

642   *Of his beloved son's death*: U.S. Navy Dept., *Civil War Naval Chronology*, VI-386.

643   *Kilpatrick alleged that Dahlgren*: O.R., I, 33, 176.

643   *The authenticity of the Dahlgren papers*: Duane Schultz, *The Dahlgren Affair*, 239–257.

646   *"The whole heavens"*: L. H. Johnson, *Red River Campaign*, 94.

647   *Green's Texas cavalry*: Ibid., 124.

648   *"The tremendous hurrahs"*: John Mead Gould, Mansfield, La., April 9, 1864, in J. M. Gould, *Civil War Journals of John Mead Gould*, 327–329.

649   *Among the dead*: Welsh, *Medical Histories of Confederate Generals*, 159–160.

649   *Assigned to keep Sherman abreast*: John M. Corse to William T. Sherman, Vicksburg, Miss., April 8, 1864, in the John M. Corse Papers.

649   *In the brief engagement*: Welsh, *Medical Histories of Confederate Generals*, 87.

649   *One of the soldiers*: Wakeman, *Uncommon Soldier*, 81–82.

649   *Rosetta Wakeman*: Leonard, *All the Daring of the Soldier*, 199–225.

650   *Porter called the heavy cannonading*: U.S. Navy Dept., *Civil War Naval Chronology*, IV-48.

650   *"I find myself blockaded"*: Ibid., IV-49.

651   *"Thirty thousand voices"*: Ibid., IV-51.

651   *"It was the Red River"*: William Prentice, a Union private, to Charles Tubbs, in Brandt, *Mr. Tubbs' Civil War*, 153.

653   *"Many wounded men"*: O.R., I, 34, 1, 743–746.

654   *Among the Confederate dead*: Welsh, *Medical Histories of Confederate Generals*, 192–193.

654   *"When the expedition was organized"*: Frederick Steele to William T. Sherman, Headquarters, Dept. of Arkansas, Camden, Ark., April 24, 1864, in the Nathan Kimball Papers.

655   *"Colonel Hawkins said"*: O.R., I, 32, 1, 542–544.

655   *"There is a Federal force"*: Wills, *Battle from the Start*, 178.

656   *As usual, Forrest demanded surrender*: O.R., I, 32, 1, 559–563.

657   *But however one argues*: Ibid., 501–623; Wills, *Battle from the Start*, 169–196; and Fuchs, *Unerring Fire*, 1–190.

658   *"The particulars of your plans"*: Abraham Lincoln to U. S. Grant, Washington, April 30, 1864, in Lincoln, *Collected Works*, VII, 324–325.

658   *"Today the President"*: John Hay, Washington, D.C., April 24, 1864, in Hay, *Inside Lincoln's White House*, 188.

658   *"If slavery is not wrong"*: Abraham Lincoln to Albert G. Hodges, Washington, April 4, 1864, in Lincoln, *Collected Works*, VII, 281–283.

CHAPTER 22   GRANT MOVES INTO THE WILDERNESS

659   *But Grant's detractors*: U. S. Grant III, "Civil War: Fact and Fiction," in *Civil War History* II (1956): 2, 29–40.

660   *"Everybody has faith in Grant"*: Charles P. Mattocks to his mother, Camp near Brandy Station, Va., May 1, 1864, in Mattocks, *"Unspoiled Heart,"* 129–133.

660   *Charles Francis Adams, Jr.*: Charles Francis Adams, Jr., to Charles Francis Adams, May 1, 1864, in Adams et al., *Cycle of Adams Letters*, II, 126–128.

660   *"Should my success"*: Ulysses S. Grant to Abraham Lincoln, Culpeper Court House, Va., May 1, 1864, in U. S. Grant, *Papers of Ulysses S. Grant*, X, 380.

662   *"That man will fight"*: Trudeau, *Bloody Roads South*, 26.

662   *"Brig. Genl. A. Hays"*: Francis A. Walker, AAG, Headquarters, 2d A.C., Cole's Hill, Culpeper Co., Va., May 2, 1864, in the Alexander Hays Papers.

663   *"You will already have learned"*: Robert E. Lee to Jefferson Davis, New Verdierville, Va., May 4, 1864, from Robert E. Lee, *Wartime Papers*, 719.

663   *"Soldiers! The eyes of the whole country"*: *O.R.*, I, 36, 2, 370.

663   *Many were swept*: McWhiney, *Battle in the Wilderness*, 42.

664   *"Here were two great armies"*: Rhea, *Battle of the Wilderness*, 105.

665   *The Rebels regrouped*: Ibid., 150.

666   *Col. Thomas W. Hyde*: Ibid., 180.

666   *Brig. Gen. Leroy Stafford*: Welsh, *Medical Histories of Confederate Generals*, 203–204.

667   *Among the casualties*: Ibid., 122–123.

667   *"All up and down Wilderness Run"*: Schaff, *Battle of the Wilderness*, 212–214.

669   *Among the dead*: Welsh, *Medical Histories of Union Generals*, 164.

670   *In the attack*: Ibid., 355.

670   *Jenkins was shot*: Welsh, *Medical Histories of Confederate Generals*, 115.

670   *Longstreet rode forward*: Ibid., 143–144.

670   *"General Jenkins . . . rode up"*: Dawson, *Reminiscences of Confederate Service*, 115.

670   *Some writers have suggested*: Peter Carmichael, "Escaping the Shadow of Gettysburg: Richard S. Ewell and Ambrose Powell Hill at the Wilderness," in Gallagher, ed., *Wilderness Campaign*, 136–159.

671   *"The blaze ran sparkling"*: Rhea, *Battle of the Wilderness*, 451.

671   *"If we were under any other General"*: E. H. Rhodes, *All for the Union*, 146–149.

673   *"About dark the firing"*: M. Howard, *Recollections of a Maryland Confederate Soldier and Staff Officer*, 284–285.

673   *"Did Sheridan say that?"*: Morris, *Sheridan*, 164.

674   *"Should [the enemy] attack"*: J. E. B. Stuart to Robert E. Lee, Richmond, Va., May 10, 1864, in Frey, *In the Woods Before Dawn*, 44.

674   *Placed against a tree*: Welsh, *Medical Histories of Confederate Generals*, 208–209.

674   *"I must be prepared"*: E. Thomas, *Bold Dragoon*, 294.

674   *"Soon the mournful strains"*: S. Putnam, *Richmond During the War*, 292.

675   *Despite his staff officers' protestations*: Martin T. McMahon, "The Death of General Sedgwick," in Johnson and Buel, eds., *Battles and Leaders*, IV, 175.

675   *Union Surg. Daniel Holt*: Daniel M. Holt, diary, May 9, 1864, in D. M. Holt, *Surgeon's Civil War*, 185.

675   *"Ambulances and army wagons"*: A. C. Brown, *Diary of a Line Officer*, 43–44.

676   *"I am now sending back"*: U. S. Grant, *Papers of Ulysses S. Grant*, X, 422.

676   *Staff officers including Lt. Cols.*: Rhea, *Battles for Spotsylvania Court House*, 217.

678   *As this chaos was unfolding*: Matter, *If It Takes All Summer*, 201–202.

678   *Fearing such a firestorm*: Welsh, *Medical Histories of Confederate Generals*, 169.

679   *"We were under terrific shelling"*: Lewis Warlick to his wife, Spotsylvania Court House, Va., May 19, 1864, in the McGimsey Papers, Southern Historical Collection, University of North Carolina, Chapel Hill, item 2680.

679   *Among the dead*: Welsh, *Medical Histories of Confederate Generals*, 51, 82–83.

679   *Among the Union commanders*: Welsh, *Medical Histories of Union Generals*, 277, 321.

680   *"Old Grant is a tough customer"*: Marion Hill Fitzpatrick, 45th Georgia Inf., to his wife, Spotsylvania Court House, Va., May 19, 1864, in Fitzpatrick, *Letters to Amanda*, 145–146.

680   *"From Orange Court House to Richmond"*: Carol Reardon, "A Hard Road to Travel: The Impact of Continuous Operations on the Army of the Potomac and the Army of Northern Virginia in May 1864," in Gallagher, ed., *Spotsylvania Campaign*, 197.

681   *By late afternoon*: W. G. Robertson, *Back Door to Richmond*, 89.

683 *"Lees army is really whipped":* Ulysses S. Grant to Henry W. Halleck, Quarles's Mills, Va., May 26, 1864, in U. S. Grant, *Papers of Ulysses S. Grant,* X, 490–491.

685 *In the fighting:* Welsh, *Medical Histories of Confederate Generals,* 212.

686 *Among the Confederate dead:* Ibid., 55.

686 *"The dead and dying":* Charles S. Venable, "General Lee in the Wilderness Campaign," in Johnson and Buel, eds., *Battles and Leaders,* IV, 245.

686 *"Lieut. Hobson of our battery":* Berkeley, *Four Years in the Confederate Artillery,* 80.

690 *"I am lying mortally wounded":* Joshua L. Chamberlain to his wife, June 19, 1864, in Chamberlain, *Through Blood and Fire,* 137.

691 *"The feeling here":* Stephen Minot Weld, Jr., to his father, Petersburg, Va., June 21, 1864, in Weld, *War Diary and Letters of Stephen Minot Weld,* 317–319.

691 *"I believe these two armies":* Meade, *Life and Letters,* II, 206–208.

691 *Among the numerous dead:* Eicher and Eicher, *Civil War High Commands.*

691 *Captured, Jenkins had his arm amputated:* Welsh, *Medical Histories of Confederate Generals,* 114–115.

692 *"The cadets, many of them":* McDonald, *Woman's Civil War,* 185.

692 *"Not the devoted few":* E. R. Turner, *New Market Campaign,* 72.

692 *"Sigel seemed in a state of excitement":* David Hunter Strother, Diary, May 15, 1864, in Strother, *Virginia Yankee in the Civil War,* 224–228.

693 *Many of the Confederates:* Duncan, *Lee's Endangered Left,* 180.

693 *Grumble Jones was killed:* Welsh, *Medical Histories of Confederate Generals,* 123–124.

693 *"The plunderers came running":* David Hunter Strother, Diary, June 12, 1864, in Strother, *Virginia Yankee in the Civil War,* 254–258.

694 *"We attracted the combined forces":* Henry C. Carpenter to his sister Elizabeth, Camp near Salem, Va., June 22, 1864, in the Henry C. Carpenter Papers.

695 *"They gave no parole":* Capt. J. Bates Dickson, AAG, Headquarters, Dist. of Kentucky, 5th Div., 23d Corps, Lexington, Ky., June 17, 1864, in the Edward H. Hobson Papers.

695 *"I passed the island":* Raphael Semmes, aboard the CSS *Alabama,* Singapore, December 22, 1863, in the Raphael Semmes Papers.

696 *"She was severely hulled":* S. C. Tucker, *Raphael Semmes and the* Alabama, 86–87.

696 *Winslow passed the Confederate:* J. M. Taylor, *Confederate Raider,* 210.

696 *"It is true that we have lost":* U.S. Navy Dept., *Civil War Naval Chronology,* VI-386.

696 *Semmes could only write:* Spencer, *Raphael Semmes,* 176.

697 *Grant had ordered:* U. S. Grant, *Papers of Ulysses S. Grant,* X, 251–254.

697 *"Atlanta is the great strategic point":* *Atlanta Daily Constitutionalist,* May 1, 1864.

699 *Still disappointed:* O.R., I, 38, 4, 133.

699 *The fighting was severe:* Secrist, *Battle of Resaca,* 41.

700 *Darkness ended the battle:* Castel, *Decision in the West,* 240.

702 *Everywhere "were evidence":* E. C. Bearss, *Forrest at Brice's Cross Roads,* 118.

702 *"Say to General [Joseph A.] Mower":* William T. Sherman to Maj. Gen. Cadwalader C. Washburn, near Kennesaw Mountain, Ga., June 23, 1864, in the Joseph A. Mower Papers.

702 *A Parrot shell:* Welsh, *Medical Histories of Confederate Generals,* 174–175.

702 *Found in Polk's pockets:* Castel, *Decision in the West,* 276–277.

703 *He died a few hours later:* Welsh, *Medical Histories of Union Generals,* 152.

703 *Davis's attack did not work:* Eicher and Eicher, *Civil War High Commands.*

703 *"It is enough to make":* W. T. Sherman, *Sherman's Civil War,* 659–661.

704 *On June 29, in Washington:* Eicher and Eicher, *Civil War High Commands.*

704 *Inside a letter read:* I. A. Sawhill, in Hartley, *Civil War Letters of the Late 1st Lieut. James J. Hartley,* 7.

704 *In his reply:* Lincoln, *Collected Works,* VII, 383–384.

CHAPTER 23   ACTION AT ATLANTA AND PETERSBURG

706   *Cavalry operations continued:* O.R., I, 38, 5, 867.

707   *Forrest himself was wounded:* Eicher and Eicher, *Civil War High Commands.*

707   *"Allow me to congratulate you":* Stephen A. Hurlbut to Andrew J. Smith, Belvidere, Ill., July 23, 1864, in the Andrew J. Smith Papers.

707   *"With regard to the general appearance":* John Chipman Gray, on board Steamboat *Bostana No. 2,* White River, Ark., July 24, 1864, in J. C. Gray and J. C. Ropes, *War Letters of John Chipman Gray and John Codman Ropes,* 364–366.

707   *"Hood has 'gone up' ":* R. K. Brown, *To the Manner Born,* 257.

708   *Among the dead:* Welsh, *Medical Histories of Confederate Generals,* 226–227.

710   *On the Federal side:* Welsh, *Medical Histories of Union Generals,* 218–219.

710   *"Gen. McPherson was killed":* John H. Munroe to Lt. Col. [Franklin] Sawyer, AAG, Chattanooga, Tenn., July 23, 1864, from the James B. McPherson Papers. The document was endorsed by Brig. Gen. Joseph D. Webster regarding the guard and escort.

710   *Back in Ohio:* Col. Charles W. Hill to Capt. C. H. Patten, AAG, Columbus, Ohio, July 25, 1864, in the James B. McPherson Papers.

710   *Also among the dead:* Welsh, *Medical Histories of Confederate Generals,* 21, 205.

710   *"I have . . . received a dispatch":* William T. Sherman to Oliver O. Howard, in the field near Atlanta, July 26, 1864, in the Oliver O. Howard Papers.

710   *"I have just learned":* Joseph Hooker to Brig. Gen. William D. Whipple, AAG, Dept. of the Cumberland; Headquarters, 20th A.C., near Atlanta, Ga., July 27, 1864, in the Joseph Hooker Papers.

710   *"Hood had suffered":* Cox, *Atlanta,* 183.

711   *Near Newnan the raiders fought:* D. Evans, *Sherman's Horsemen,* 272.

711   *"Sherman's army is* doomed": J. B. Jones, *Rebel War Clerk's Diary,* II, 259.

711   *"The question of rank has arisen":* John M. Palmer to Maj. Gen. William T. Sherman, Headquarters, 14th A.C., August 4, 1864, in the John M. Palmer Papers.

711   *"If you are willing":* George H. Thomas to William T. Sherman, Dept. of the Cumberland, August 19, 1864, in the Richard W. Johnson Papers.

714   *"Atlanta is ours, & fairly won":* W. T. Sherman, *Sherman's Civil War,* 695–696.

714   *"I telegraphed you":* John W. Geary to his wife Mary, Atlanta, Ga., September 3, 1864, in Geary, *Politician Goes to War,* 199–200.

714   *"If the people raise a howl":* W. T. Sherman, *Sherman's Civil War,* 697.

714   *"In honor of your great victory":* Ulysses S. Grant, telegram to William T. Sherman, City Point, Va., September 4, 1864, in U. S. Grant, *Papers of Ulysses S. Grant,* XII, 127.

717   *"Don't fire until you see":* Cooling, *Jubal Early's Raid on Washington, 1864,* 73.

717   *Here the legend arose:* Ibid., 143.

717   *This gave rise:* E. H. Rhodes, *All for the Union,* 169–171.

717   *As for the rush of Rebels:* Vandiver, *Jubal's Raid,* 142.

718   *"If the enemy has left Maryland":* Ulysses S. Grant to Henry W. Halleck, City Point, Va., July 14, 1864, in U. S. Grant, *Papers of Ulysses S. Grant,* XI, 242–243.

718   *"Just a week this morning":* Rachel Bowman Cormany, August 6, 1864, in Cormany and Cormany, *Cormany Diaries,* 446.

719   *"The treasury has been offered":* Kean, *Inside the Confederate Government,* 167–168.

719   *"Once, under McClellan":* Cooke, *Wearing of the Gray,* 511.

719   *"It is hard to maintain":* C. M. Blackford, *Letters from Lee's Army,* 271–272.

719   *"Grant is not even spoken of ":* Floride Clemson, Diary, Beltsville, Md., July 10, 1864, in Clemson, *Rebel Came Home,* 54.

720   *"We are still before Petersburg":* Adelbert Ames to his parents, Petersburg, Va., July 3, 1864, in Ames, *Adelbert Ames,* 169–171.

720   *"Our bomb proofs":* Robert Goldthwaite Carter, Petersburg, Va., July 19, 1864, in Carter, *Four Brothers in Blue,* 461–463.

720   *"We are making heavy works":* Col. Robert McAllister to his wife Ellen, Camp before Pe-

tersburg, Va., July 25, 1864, in McAllister, *Civil War Letters of General Robert McAllister,* 467–468.

720 *Brig. Gen. Marsena R. Patrick:* Brig. Gen. Marsena R. Patrick, Diary, Petersburg, Va., July 15, 1864, in Patrick, *Inside Lincoln's Army,* 398–399.

721 *"I finally fell":* Henry Matrau to his parents, Camp near Petersburg, Va., July 31, 1864, in Matrau, *Letters Home,* 88–91.

723 *"The Confederates soon recovered":* Capt. Robert K. Beecham, in Beecham, *As if It Were Glory,* 183.

723 *The fire was so hot:* Kinard, *Battle of the Crater,* 63.

723 *Grant could only write:* Ulysses S. Grant to Henry W. Halleck, City Point, Va., August 1, 1864, in U. S. Grant, *Papers of Ulysses S. Grant,* XI, 361–364.

724 *Col. Victor J. B. Girardey:* Eicher and Eicher, *Civil War High Commands.*

724 *"They have robbed the cradle":* Ulysses S. Grant to Elihu B. Washburne, City Point, Va., August 16, 1864, in U. S. Grant, *Papers of Ulysses S. Grant,* XII, 16–17.

725 *Among the dead:* Welsh, *Medical Histories of Confederate Generals,* 191.

725 *"Two rows of men":* Thomas Morris Chester, Petersburg, Va., August 19, 1864, in Chester, *Thomas Morris Chester,* 105–106.

725 *Chester continued:* Ibid., 108–112.

726 *"If the War is to last":* Ulysses S. Grant to Philip H. Sheridan, City Point, Va., August 26, 1864, in U. S. Grant, *Papers of Ulysses S. Grant,* XII, 96–97.

726 *"While in this camp":* W. W. Blackford, *War Years with Jeb Stuart,* 260.

727 *Dozens of the sailors:* U.S. Navy Dept., *Civil War Naval Chronology,* VI-386.

727 *It was at that moment:* C. L. Lewis, *David Glasgow Farragut,* II, 269.

729 *"A moment after":* U.S. Navy Dept., *Civil War Naval Chronology,* IV-97.

729 *"In the success":* Ibid., VI-389.

729 *"I am prepared to sacrifice life":* Ibid., VI-388.

730 *"We landed at Fort Morgan":* F. Ross, *Cities and Camps of the Confederate States,* 196–197.

730 *"General Page and his officers":* Hearn, *Admiral David Glasgow Farragut,* 299.

730 *Lincoln had sound reasons:* Lincoln, *Collected Works,* VII, 514–515.

731 *In Key West:* Welsh, *Medical Histories of Union Generals,* 277, 377.

731 *"The condition of my health":* August Willich to Samuel P. Heintzelman, Cincinnati, August 11, 1864, in the August Willich Papers.

731 *"I hardly know what to do":* Mortimer D. Leggett to Francis P. Blair, Jr., Headquarters 3d Division, 17th A.C., in the field before Atlanta, Ga., August 16, 1864, in the Mortimer D. Leggett Papers.

731 *"My affairs imperatively require":* John B. Turchin to George H. Thomas, Chicago, August 7, 1864, in the John B. Turchin Papers.

731 *Still suffering from his Petersburg wound:* Joshua L. Chamberlain to Lorenzo Thomas, Annapolis, Md., August 31, 1864, in the Joshua L. Chamberlain Papers.

731 *"Gen[.] [Thomas F.] Meagher got up":* Col. Theodore B. Gates, Diary, City Point, Va., August 16, 1864, in Gates, *Civil War Diaries of Col. Theodore B. Gates,* 152.

731 *"Mrs. Paine bro't me home":* Eleazer A. Paine to Maj. Gen. John M. Schofield, Monmouth, Ill., September 20, 1864, in the Eleazer A. Paine Papers.

732 *"The conduct of Genl. E. A. Paine":* Stephen G. Burbridge to Maj. Gen. John M. Schofield, Lexington, Ky., August 20, 1864, in the Eleazer A. Paine Papers.

732 *"I have been informed":* Col. R. H. G. Minty to Capt. Kennedy, AAG, 2d Cav. Div., near Atlanta, Ga., August 7, 1864, in the Edward M. McCook Papers.

732 *Spears allegedly said:* General Court Martial Orders No. 267, Washington, D.C., August 20, 1864, in the James G. Spears Papers.

732 *"In compliance with Special Orders":* Odon Guitar, General Orders No. 32, Rolla, Mo., August 28, 1864, in the Odon Guitar Papers.

732 *"You have been detailed":* Maj. Gen. Samuel P. Heintzelman, Headquarters, Northern Dept., to Halbert E. Paine, Columbus, Ohio, August 16, 1864, in the Halbert E. Paine Papers.

733   *"It was impossible":* Pvt. William H. H. Clayton, 19th Iowa Inf., to his brother, Fort Barrancas, Fla., August 27, 1864, in Clayton, *Damned Iowa Greyhound,* 117–120.

733   *Here nurse Cornelia Hancock recorded:* Cornelia Hancock to her sister, City Point, Va., July 1, 1864, in Hancock, *South After Gettysburg,* 124–125.

733   *"There is no such thing as delicacy":* John L. Ransom, Andersonville, Ga., July 19, 1864, in Ransom, *John Ransom's Andersonville Diary,* 124–126.

733   *"We had worked only three nights":* Berry Benson, 1st South Carolina Inf., in Benson, *Berry Benson's Civil War Book,* 129.

734   *"In the prison cell I sit":* Commager, *Blue and the Gray,* 576.

CHAPTER 24   SHERIDAN RAIDS THE VALLEY

735   *"I heard a terrible roar":* Robert Patrick, September 2, 1864, in Patrick, *Reluctant Rebel,* 204–222.

735   *"I have deemed it":* W. T. Sherman, *Sherman's Civil War,* 704.

736   *"And now, sir, permit me":* O.R., I, 39, 2, 415; Hood, *Advance and Retreat,* 230.

736   *"You who in the midst of Peace":* W. T. Sherman, *Sherman's Civil War,* 705–707.

736   *"It is a pleasant, breezy afternoon":* Maj. James A. Connolly to his wife, Atlanta, Ga., September 11, 1864, in Connolly, *Three Years in the Army of the Cumberland,* 257–260.

736   *"You cannot qualify war":* W. T. Sherman, *Memoirs of General W. T. Sherman,* II, 125–127.

736   *"You have accomplished":* Ulysses S. Grant to William T. Sherman, City Point, Va., September 12, 1864, in U. S. Grant, *Papers of Ulysses S. Grant,* XII, 154–155.

737   *"Sherman is weaker now":* John Bell Hood to Braxton Bragg, September 21, 1864, in Hood, *Advance and Retreat,* 252–253.

737   *"Atlanta is situated":* John W. Geary to his wife, Atlanta, Ga., October 1, 1864, from Geary, *Politician Goes to War,* 206–208.

738   *"Your communication demanding surrender":* O.R., I, 39, 1, 763.

738   *At 2 P.M. on October 4:* Ibid., I, 39, 3, 78.

738   *Accompanied by Sherman:* W. T. Sherman, *Memoirs,* II, 147.

738   *"Corse has just signaled":* Lt. Col. Henry W. Perkins, telegram to Alpheus S. Williams, Atlanta, Ga., October 6, 1864, in the John M. Corse Papers.

739   *"Until we can repopulate Georgia":* W. T. Sherman, *Sherman's Civil War,* 731.

739   *On October 20 he wrote:* O.R., I, 39, 3, 377–378.

740   *They pushed on:* Welsh, *Medical Histories of Union Generals,* 45.

740   *Of the assault:* Sommers, *Richmond Redeemed,* 142.

742   *Total casualties amounted to 399:* Welsh, *Medical Histories of Confederate Generals,* 88.

744   *Rodes, a veteran:* Welsh, *Medical Histories of Confederate Generals,* 188; Eicher and Eicher, *Civil War High Commands.*

746   *Soon afterward he was struck:* Welsh, *Medical Histories of Union Generals,* 285–286.

746   *He was posthumously commissioned:* Eicher and Eicher, *Civil War High Commands;* Welsh, *Medical Histories of Confederate Generals,* 81–82.

746   *"We drove the Rebs":* Louis N. Beaudry, September 19, 1864, in Beaudry, *War Journal of Louis N. Beaudry,* 170–171.

747   *"Well the close of this most miserable day":* Lucy Rebecca Buck, September 21, 1864, in Buck, *Shadows on My Heart,* 308–309.

747   *Sheridan was on the scene:* Pond, *Shenandoah Valley in 1864,* 177.

747   *"I do not advise rashness":* Sheridan, *Personal Memoirs of P. H. Sheridan,* II, 44.

747   *"Since I have been in this department":* William W. Averell, September 12, 1864, in Averell, *Ten Years in the Saddle,* 398.

748   *"These stories of our defeats":* Chesnut, *Mary Chesnut's Civil War,* 648.

748   *"To-morrow I will continue the destruction":* O.R., 43, I, 30.

748   *"These are times":* Stephen Dodson Ramseur to his wife, in the field near Staunton, Va., October 5, 1864, in Commager, *Blue and the Gray,* 1048.

749   *"Thus I was at General Grover's":* John William De Forest, *Volunteer's Adventures,* 208.

751   *He encountered officers:* Morris, *Sheridan,* 213–214.

751   *"The enemy subsequently made a stand":* Jubal A. Early to Col. Walter H. Taylor, AAG, Newmarket, Va., October 20, 1864, in Frey, *In the Woods Before Dawn,* 100.

751   *"Up from the South, at break of day":* Marius, ed., *Columbia Book of Civil War Poetry,* 184–186.

752   *For his part, Little Phil summarized:* C. A. Dana, *Recollections of the Civil War,* 250.

752   *Among the mortally wounded:* Gallagher, *Stephen Dodson Ramseur,* 165.

752   *Brig. Gen. Daniel D. Bidwell:* Welsh, *Medical Histories of Union Generals,* 29, 206.

752   *The Federal cavalry left:* Morris, *Sheridan,* 207.

753   *"One village, Dayton, has been burned":* Surg. Daniel M. Holt to his wife, Harrisonburg, Va., October 2, 1864, in Daniel M. Holt, *Surgeon's Civil War,* 261–264.

753   *"I am directed by the Secretary of War":* H. L. Clay, AAG, Richmond, November 19, 1864, to R. E. Lee, in the John S. Mosby Papers, Virginia Historical Society, Richmond, Reel 39, item 141.

754   *One Confederate soldier:* Mosgrove, *Kentucky Cavaliers in Dixie,* 206–207.

755   *"Price arrived before Pilot Knob":* Wiley Britton, "Resumé of Military Operations in Arkansas and Missouri, 1864–1865," in Johnson and Buel, eds., *Battles and Leaders,* IV, 376.

756   *"The battlefield exhibited":* Monnett, *Action Before Westport, 1864,* 123.

756   *Many of the visitors:* Castel, *General Sterling Price,* 236.

757   *The expedition had been a fruitless waste:* O.R., I, 41, 1, 640.

757   *"As I turned the whole back":* U.S. Navy Dept., *Civil War Naval Chronology,* IV-126.

757   *Cushing shot a load of canister:* Ibid.

758   *Warley reported:* O.R.N., I, 10, 624.

758   *"There is a fatuity in nominating":* Welles, *Diary,* II, 135–136.

758   *"Talk[ed] with gentleman":* Salmon P. Chase, Journal, September 13, 1864, in Chase, *Salmon P. Chase Papers,* Vol. 1, *Journals, 1829–1872,* 502.

758   *"The State election of Indiana":* Lincoln, *Collected Works,* VIII, 11.

758   *"Yankee politics have simplified themselves":* Kean, *Inside the Confederate Government,* 173–175.

758   *"[I'm calling] your attention":* Robert E. Lee, *Wartime Papers,* 847–850.

759   *He lingered for two days:* Welsh, *Medical Histories of Confederate Generals,* 124–125.

759   *At Greeneville, Morgan was surrounded:* Eicher and Eicher, *Civil War High Commands.*

759   *"It was a solemn and imposing spectacle":* Unidentified newspaper clipping reporting Rose Greenhow's funeral, ca. October 1, 1864, in the Rose O'Neal Greenhow Papers.

759   *"We are going to be wiped off":* Chesnut, *Mary Chesnut's Civil War,* 644–645.

759   *"Many of the privates":* J. B. Jones, *Rebel War Clerk's Diary,* II, 288.

759   *"The courage of the rebs":* Henry Brooks Adams to Charles Francis Adams, Jr., September 30, 1864, in Adams et al., *Cycle of Adams Letters,* II, 199–200.

759   *"The Genl proposed that we should go":* W. H. Taylor, *Lee's Adjutant,* 190–191.

CHAPTER 25   SHERMAN'S MARCH TO THE SEA

760   *"With all our starvation":* Trudeau, *Last Citadel,* 258–259.

760   *On December 2:* Welsh, *Medical Histories of Confederate Generals,* 85–86.

761   *"Many of our soldiers":* Isaac Hite, Richardson's Va. Batn., Camp near Petersburg, Va., December 10, 1864, in Jessup, *Painful News I Have to Write,* 176–177.

761   *"I am willing to fight":* Chamberlain, *Through Blood and Fire,* 143–145.

762   *"General Sherman is the most American":* John Chipman Gray, in the field near Savannah, Ga., December 14, 1864, in Roland Gray, "Memoir of John Chipman Gray," in *Proceedings of the Massachusetts Historical Society* XLIX (1915–1916): 393–394.

762   *"He impresses me":* Henry Hitchcock, Kingston, Ga., November 2, 1864, in H. Hitchcock, *Marching with Sherman,* 26–30.

763   *"The army will forage":* O.R., I, 39, 3, 713–714.

763   *"We stood upon the very ground"*: W. T. Sherman, *Memoirs*, II, 178–179.

763   *"It would seem"*: *Macon Telegraph*, December 5, 1864.

763   *"Bring the good old bugle, boys"*: Henry Clay Work, "Marching Through Georgia, 1865," in Commager, *Blue and the Gray*, 581–582.

765   *Beauregard called for citizens:* Cox, *March to the Sea*, 28–29.

767   *Capt. Louis M. Dayton:* O.R., I, 44, 704.

767   *"I have already received guns"*: Ibid., 737.

768   *"I beg to present you"*: W. T. Sherman, *Sherman's Civil War*, 772.

768   *"No City was ever occupied"*: Ibid., 782–783.

768   *"The truth is the whole army"*: Ibid., 775–778.

768   *Still, enough destruction occurred:* Glatthaar, *March to the Sea and Beyond*, 140.

768   *"This last campaign of Sherman's"*: John W. Geary to his wife Mary, near Savannah, Ga., December 1864, in Geary, *Politician Goes to War*, 217–218.

771   *Stephen D. Lee noted:* Sword, *Embrace an Angry Wind*, 154.

772   *"A rush and a yell followed"*: Cox, *March to the Sea, Franklin, and Nashville*, 88–89.

774   *"In front of their works"*: Bevens, *Reminiscences of a Private*, 207–208.

774   *So fearsome were the results:* Banks, *Battle of Franklin*, 76.

775   *Four of the six:* Eicher and Eicher, *Civil War High Commands;* Welsh, *Medical Histories of Confederate Generals*, 2–3, 35, 40–41, 80–81, 86, 207–208.

775   *Oddly, another of the Confederate dead:* Sword, *Embrace an Angry Wind*, 166, 260–261.

775   *"We carried the enemy's entire line"*: John Bell Hood to James A. Seddon, near Nashville, Tenn., December 11, 1864, in Frey, *In the Woods Before Dawn*, 194–199.

775   *"A [local lady] who saw"*: Le Duc, *Recollections of a Civil War Quartermaster*, 137.

776   *"I have as much confidence"*: O.R., I, 45, 2, 115.

776   *Thomas curtly replied:* Ibid.

777   *The cavalry and infantry:* Sword, *Embrace an Angry Wind*, 336–337.

779   *Shy's body became the focus:* Douglas W. Owsley and Bertita E. Compton, "Preservation in Late 19th Century Iron Coffin Burials," in Haglund and Sorg, *Forensic Taphonomy*, 511–526.

779   *"The battle of Nashville is ended"*: Pvt. Owen J. Hopkins, 182d Ohio Inf., to his sweetheart Julia, Nashville, Tenn., December 17, 1864, in Hopkins, *Under the Flag of the Nation*, 228–230.

780   *"And now I'm going Southward"*: Abel, *Singing the New Nation*, 212.

780   *"Election day was dull"*: Brooks, *Lincoln Observed*, 143–144.

780   *"It has long been a grave question"*: Lincoln, *Collected Works*, VIII, 100–102.

781   *"I regret that you do not appreciate"*: Ward Hill Lamon to Abraham Lincoln, Washington, December 10, 1864, in Holzer, *Lincoln Mailbag*, 195–196.

781   *"I have been shown"*: Lincoln, *Collected Works*, VIII, 116–117.

782   *Of the Confederate situation:* Chesnut, *Mary Chesnut's Civil War*, 680.

782   *"The bottles of Greek fire"*: J. W. Headley, *Confederate Operations in Canada and New York*, 274–277.

783   *"The Cheyennes didn't get their lands"*: Silas Soulé to Walter Whitman, February 12, 1865, in Cutler, *The Massacre at Sand Creek*, 114–115.

784   *Its familiar bars:* Commager, *Blue and the Gray*, 577–578.

CHAPTER 26   FALL OF THE LAST CONFEDERATE PORT

785   *At the end of 1864:* Eicher and Eicher, *Civil War High Commands*.

786   *"Doubtless Lee could protract"*: J. B. Jones, *Rebel War Clerk's Diary*, II, 418.

786   *"I presume you have heard"*: Lt. Col. David Pierson, 3d Louisiana Inf., to his father, Alexandria, La., January 11, 1865, in Pierson et al., *Brothers in Gray*, 221–222.

786   *"Everything to eat can be had"*: Emma LeConte, Columbia, S.C., January 18, 1865, in E. LeConte, *When the World Ended*, 12–14.

786   *"You cannot make soldiers of slaves":* Maj. Gen. Howell Cobb to James A. Seddon, January 8, 1865, in D. Lyman, *Civil War Quotations,* 57.

787   *"Every citizen who prevents":* O.R., I, 46, 2, 1134–1135.

787   *"An impression seems to prevail":* Robert E. Lee, circular, [this copy] to Lt. Gen. James Longstreet, January 28, 1865, in the R. E. Lee Headquarters Papers, Virginia Historical Society, Richmond, Series 8, item 138.

787   *"The thinner ranks":* Charles Francis Adams, to Charles Francis Adams, Jr., London, February 10, 1865, from Adams et al., *Cycle of Adams Letters,* II, 253–256.

787   *"Blackguard and buffoon":* Charleston Mercury, January 10, 1865.

787   *In 1861, Oliver Wendell Holmes:* Rinhart et al., *American Tintype,* 121.

788   *In 1861 the French scientist:* Tortora et al., *Microbiology,* 6–10, 14–16.

788   *The most reliable reports:* Eicher and Eicher, *Civil War High Commands.*

789   *"We operated in old":* G. W. Adams, *Doctors in Blue,* 125.

790   *The volumes' summary:* U.S. Surgeon General's Office, *Medical and Surgical History of the War of the Rebellion,* III, 2, 685ff.

790   *The study's case histories:* Ibid., II, 1, 162.

790   *Gunshot wounds of the face:* Bengtson and Kuz, *Photographic Atlas of Civil War Injuries,* 150–151.

790   *Gunshot injuries:* U.S. Surgeon General's Office, *Medical and Surgical History of the War of the Rebellion,* II, 2, 469–470.

791   *Pvt. W. J. Jones:* Ibid., III, 2, 493.

791   *The chronic diseases:* Ibid., II, 1, 230.

791   *"[Grant's] present force":* Robert E. Lee to Jefferson Davis, Petersburg, Va., January 29, 1865, in Robert E. Lee, *Lee's Dispatches,* 329–330.

792   *"According to our agreement":* Abraham Lincoln to Alexander H. Stephens, Washington, February 10, 1865, in the Abraham Lincoln Papers, University of Georgia Library, Athens.

793   *Lee remained stubborn:* D. Lyman, *Civil War Quotations,* 141.

793   *"I do think":* W. T. Sherman, *Home Letters of General Sherman,* 324–327.

794   *Hearing of a bill:* William T. Sherman to Philemon Ewing, in the field, Pocotaligo, S.C., January 29, 1865, in W. T. Sherman, *Sherman at War,* 153–158.

794   *"The object is to lodge":* O.R.N., I, 11, 425–427.

794   *"There would be two puffs":* A. C. Buell, *"The Cannoneer,"* 328–333.

796   *As Whiting entered the fort:* Gragg, *Confederate Goliath,* 121.

796   *It was "a terrific storm":* M. Moore, *Moore's Historical Guide to the Wilmington Campaign and the Battles for Fort Fisher,* 50.

796   *Although it was a catastrophic failure:* Simmons, *United States Marines,* 57.

796   *Lamb, who believed he had repulsed:* C. M. Robinson, *Hurricane of Fire,* 172.

796   *While leading a counterattack:* Welsh, *Medical Histories of Confederate Generals,* 233–234.

796   *After the fort's capture:* U.S. Navy Dept., *Civil War Naval Chronology,* VI-389.

797   *"We had lost our last":* Ibid.

797   *"I am directed by the Committee":* Benjamin F. Wade to Edwin M. Stanton, Washington, February 10, 1865, in the Alfred H. Terry Papers.

788   *"As we turned away":* U.S. Navy Dept., *Civil War Naval Chronology,* VI-390.

799   *During the night:* Lucas, *Sherman and the Burning of Columbia,* 68–69.

799   *Supplies of liquor:* Ibid., 83ff.

799   *"I began to-day's record":* Nichols, *Story of the Great March,* 160–166.

800   *"At about seven o'clock":* LeConte, *When the World Ended,* 42–52.

800   *"Charleston and Columbia":* Welles, *Diary,* II, 240–245.

800   *Hoke was ordered:* Barrett, *Civil War in North Carolina,* 283.

800   *"Glory to God! Charleston has fallen!":* Hawks, *Woman Doctor's Civil War,* 117.

801   *"Everything looks like dissolution":* Ulysses S. Grant to Elihu B. Washburne, City Point, Va., February 23, 1865, from U. S. Grant, *Papers of Ulysses S. Grant,* XIV, 30–31.

801   *"Shame, disgrace, beggary":* Chesnut, *Mary Chesnut's Civil War,* 724–725.

801   *"They should be made to understand"*: D. Lyman, *Civil War Quotations*, 141.
801   *On the same day:* Ibid.
801   *"When Johnny comes marching"*: Commager, *Blue and the Gray*, 587–588.

CHAPTER 27   LEE'S ARMY CRUMBLES

802   *"Fondly do we hope"*: Lincoln, *Collected Works*, VIII, 332–333.
802   *"Whenever [I] hear any one"*: Ibid., 360–362.
803   *"That rail-splitter lawyer"*: Adams et al., *Cycle of Adams Letters*, II, 257–258.
803   *On March 7:* D. Lyman, *Civil War Quotations*, 117.
803   *By April 1:* Ibid., 70.
803   *The sense of desperation:* Gorgas, *Journals of Josiah Gorgas*, 153–154, 157–158.
806   *"I want submission"*: Donald, *Lincoln*, 574.
806   *In the field Grant wrote:* Ulysses S. Grant to Philip H. Sheridan, in the field near Gravelly Creek, Va., March 29, 1865, in U. S. Grant, *Papers of Ulysses S. Grant*, XIV, 253–254.
809   *The young artillerist shouted:* Peter S. Carmichael, *Lee's Young Artillerist*, 163.
809   *Lee sent word:* O.R., I, 46, 3, 1378.
809   *Armed with a pistol:* Welsh, *Medical Histories of Confederate Generals*, 99–100.
809   *"The movements of all the troops"*: Walter H. Taylor, AAG, Special Orders, Headquarters, Army of Northern Virginia, April 2, 1865, in the R. E. Lee Headquarters Papers, Virginia Historical Society, Richmond, Series 8, items 469–470.
811   *Davis composed a message:* O.R., I, 46, 3, 1382–1383.
811   *"We have passed"*: Judith W. McGuire, April 3, 1865, in McGuire, *Diary of a Southern Refugee*, 342–343.
811   *"I was wakened suddenly"*: Constance Cary Harrison, *Recollections Grave and Gay*, 211.
811   *"We entered Richmond"*: Col. Alexander Cheves Haskell, April 2, 1865, in Haskell, *Alexander Cheves Haskell*, 169–170.
815   *At one point Lincoln:* Donald, *Lincoln*, 576.
815   *"I cannot bring myself to believe"*: Ibid., 577.
815   *"In the absence of further orders"*: U. S. Grant, Jetersville, Va., 10:10 P.M., April 5, 1865, to Maj. Gen. Ord, Burkeville, Va., in the R. E. Lee Headquarters Papers, Virginia Historical Society, Richmond, Series 8, items 449–450. This letter was captured by the Confederate army and marked to be allowed to pass through to Gen. Ord so that he would receive it.
817   *These two young high-ranking officers:* Eicher and Eicher, *Civil War High Commands*.
817   *"My God! Has the army"*: E. M. Thomas, *Robert E. Lee*, 358.
817   *"My loss is considerable"*: Maj. Gen. John B. Gordon, 5 P.M., April 6, 1865, to Gen. R. E. Lee, from the R. E. Lee Headquarters Papers, Virginia Historical Society, Richmond, Series 8, item 451.
817   *Humphreys pushed on:* Eicher and Eicher, *Civil War High Commands*.
817   *From City Point, Lincoln wrote:* Lincoln, *Collected Works*, VIII, 392.
817   *"The result of the last week"*: Ulysses S. Grant to Robert E. Lee, April 7, 1865, in U. S. Grant, *Papers of Ulysses S. Grant*, XIV, 361.
817   *Lee responded:* Robert E. Lee to Ulysses S. Grant, April 7, 1865, in Robert E. Lee, *Wartime Papers*, 931–932.
818   *"There are here only"*: Robert E. Lee, in E. P. Alexander, *Fighting for the Confederacy*, 532–533.
818   *Lee set up a plan:* E. M. Thomas, *Robert E. Lee*, 362.
818   *Grant, who had been suffering:* Porter, *Campaigning with Grant*, 468.
818   *"Genl. Alexander stopped me"*: David Gregg McIntosh, Diary, April 9, 1865, in the David G. McIntosh Papers, Virginia Historical Society, Richmond, Reel 25, items 37–39.
819   *"Disquieted," he remarked:* Chamberlain, *Passing of the Armies*, 246.
819   *"Lee . . . was fully six feet in height"*: Horace Porter, "The Surrender at Appomattox Court House," in Johnson and Buel, eds., *Battles and Leaders*, IV, 729–746.

819 *"In accordance with the substance":* Ulysses S. Grant to Gen. Robert E. Lee, Appomattox Court House, Va., April 9, 1865, in U. S. Grant, *Papers of Ulysses S. Grant,* XIV, 373–376.

820 *The artillerist William T. Poague:* Poague, *Gunner with Stonewall,* 124.

820 *Carlton McCarthy, another Southern soldier:* McCarthy, *Detailed Minutiae of Soldier Life,* 154.

820 *Bryan Grimes recalled:* Grimes, *Extracts of Letters of Major-General Bryan Grimes,* 119.

820 *"We, the undersigned prisoners of war":* Robert E. Lee, *Wartime Papers,* 935.

820 *"I have done what I thought":* Cooke, *Wearing of the Gray,* 562.

820 *"That night [April 9] the general sat":* Marshall, *An Aide-de-Camp of Lee,* 277–278.

820 *"After four years of arduous service":* Robert E. Lee, *Wartime Papers,* 934.

821 *Elisha Hunt Rhodes:* E. H. Rhodes, *All for the Union,* 230.

821 *"The war is over":* Porter, "The Surrender at Appomattox Court House," in Johnson and Buel, eds., *Battles and Leaders,* IV, 729–746.

821 *Grant ordered Gibbon:* Lt. Col. Ely S. Parker, AAG, Special Orders, in the field, April 9, 1865, in the R. E. Lee Headquarters Papers, Virginia Historical Society, Richmond, Series 8, item 473.

821 *When Lee asked Meade:* Theodore Lyman to his wife, aboard the *River Queen* on the Potomac, April 23, 1865, from T. Lyman, *Meade's Headquarters, 1863–1865,* 359–362.

821 *"It is with pain that I announce":* Lee, *Wartime Papers,* 935–938.

821 *In Richmond the Rebel war clerk:* John B. Jones, April 10, 1865, in J. B. Jones, *Rebel War Clerk's Diary,* II, 474–475.

822 *"How can I write it?":* Catherine Ann Devereux Edmondston, Halifax County, North Carolina, April 16, 1865, in Edmondston, *"Journal of a Secesh Lady,"* 694–696.

822 *"In reply to your communication":* Maj. Gen. Henry Heth to Lt. Col.———Latrobe, AAG, April 11, 1865, in the R. E. Lee Headquarters Papers, Virginia Historical Society, Richmond, Series 8, item 464.

822 *"I am a prisoner unwounded":* Montgomery D. Corse to his wife, Elizabeth Corse, Petersburg, Va., April 12, 1865, in the Montgomery D. Corse Papers, Alexandria Library, Alexandria, Virginia.

822 *On hearing of the death:* Meade and Meade, *Life and Letters of George Gordon Meade,* II, 272.

822 *"I have always thought 'Dixie' ":* Lincoln, *Collected Works,* VIII, 393–394.

823 *Louis J. Weichmann:* Weichmann, *True History of the Assassination of Abraham Lincoln.*

824 *Recent scholarship:* Tidwell et al., *Come Retribution;* and Tidwell, *April '65.*

824 *"For years I have devoted":* John Wilkes Booth to the editors of the *National Intelligencer,* Washington, April 14, 1865, in Booth, *"Right or Wrong, God Judge Me,"* 147–150.

824 *On this day, the last of his life:* Welles, *Diary,* II, 280–287.

825 *Earlier in the day:* Booth, *"Right or Wrong, God Judge Me,"* 146.

825 *As Hawk said "Well":* Good, *We Saw Lincoln Shot,* 15–17.

826 *After hearing the gun's report:* Charles A. Leale, Asst. Surg., USV, Executive Officer, Armory Square U.S. General Hospital, Washington, in a document titled "The Assassination and Death of Abraham Lincoln, President of the United States," in the Abraham Lincoln Assassination Papers, Record Group 94, TR 11, Special File 14, D776, NARA, Washington, D.C.

827 *"The giant sufferer lay extended":* Welles, *Diary,* II, 286–287.

828 *At this moment Stanton uttered:* Donald, *Lincoln,* 599.

828 *"Traitors must be made odious":* A. Johnson, *Papers of Andrew Johnson,* VII, 610–615.

828 *"No living man ever dreamed":* Brooks, *Lincoln Observed,* 187.

828 *"History furnished no parallel":* Lt. Frank Dickerson, 5th U.S. Cavalry, to his father, Madison, Wis., April 16, 1865, from Dickerson, *Dearest Father,* 148–151.

828 *"To him our gratitude":* U.S. Navy Dept., *Civil War Naval Chronology,* VI-389.

828 *"We have had more good news":* William J. Babb to John S. Miles, New Creek, [W. Va.], April 19, 1865, in the John S. Miles Papers.

829 *"I fear it will be disastrous":* W. C. Davis, *Jefferson Davis,* 620.

829 *"O Captain! my Captain!":* Marius, ed., *Columbia Book of Civil War Poetry,* 345–347.

829 "After being hunted like a dog": John Wilkes Booth, [April 22, 1865, near Zekiah Swamp and Nanjemoy Creek, Charles Co., Md.], from Booth, "Right or Wrong, God Judge Me," 154–157.

829 The barn Booth and Herold hid in: Bryan, Great American Myth, 266.

829 There would be a trial: Benn Pitman, Assassination of President Lincoln and the Trial of the Conspirators.

829 Yet the literature abounds: Bryan, Great American Myth; Hanchett, Lincoln Murder Conspiracies; Harrell, When the Bells Tolled for Lincoln; L. Lewis, Myths After Lincoln; and T. R. Turner, Beware the People Weeping.

832 "We felt relieved": Osborn, Fiery Trail, 170–171.

832 A Fayetteville resident: Angley et al., Sherman's March Through North Carolina, 21.

833 Janie Robeson: John G. Barrett, Sherman's March Through the Carolinas, 155.

834 "Sherman . . . is a very remarkable-looking man": T. Lyman, Meade's Headquarters, 326–327.

834 "A little more labor": O.R., I, 47, 3, 180.

834 "The ceremony began with a short prayer": Mary Cadwalader Jones, in Commager, Blue and the Gray, 1148–1149.

835 "[Messages from Gen. Sherman]": U. S. Grant, Papers of Ulysses S. Grant, XIV, 423–424.

835 Sherman wrote Johnston: W. T. Sherman, Sherman's Civil War, 876.

835 "I admit my folly": Ibid., 878–879.

835 "We have official news": Eugene A. Carr to Mary P. Maguire, his fiancée, Montgomery, Ala., April 26, 1865, in the Eugene Asa Carr Papers.

836 When Johnston and other: Symonds, Joseph E. Johnston, 354–355.

837 Forrest watched the fight: J. P. Jones, Yankee Blitzkrieg, 86.

837 In the melee: Welsh, Medical Histories of Confederate Generals, 219; Eicher and Eicher, Civil War High Commands.

838 Pvt. Benjamin F. Johnson: Salecker, Disaster on the Mississippi, 90.

838 "Everything seemed to be falling": Bryant, Cahaba Prison and the Sultana Disaster, 130.

838 The loss of life: Salecker, Disaster on the Mississippi, afterword.

839 "In camp before 'Ft. Alexis' ": Eugene A. Carr to Mary P. Maguire, Camp before Fort Alexis, Spanish Fort, Ala., March 31, 1865, in the Eugene Asa Carr Papers.

840 "We fire constantly": Bergeron, Confederate Mobile, 185.

840 Among Cockrell's Missourians: Hearn, Mobile Bay and the Mobile Campaign, 194.

840 "When I last wrote to you": Pvt. William H. H. Clayton, 19th Iowa Inf., to his brothers, Camp at Spanish Fort, Ala., April 18, 1865, in Clayton, Damned Iowa Greyhound, 162–164.

840 On April 6: Eicher and Eicher, Civil War High Commands.

840 "The mass of the People": W. T. Sherman, Sherman's Civil War, 883–884.

CHAPTER 28   THE END OF THE CIVIL WAR

841 "In terminating our official relations": J. E. Johnston, Narrative of Military Operations, 418–419.

841 "Any man who is in favor": B. S. Wills, Battle from the Start, 316.

842 "[Hudson] says I was dressed": Jefferson Davis to Rev. W. M. Green, Memphis, Tenn., August 18, 1875, in Frey, In the Woods Before Dawn, 254–255.

842 "I have the honor to report": Thomas H. Ruger to Lt. Col. Theodore Cox, AAG, 23d Corps, Charlotte, N.C., May 25, 1865, in the Thomas H. Ruger Papers.

843 "Civil War, such as you have": O.R., I, 49, 2, 1289–1290.

843 "I have received your dispatch": John M. Schofield to Henry W. Halleck, Raleigh, N.C., May 7, 1865, in the John M. Schofield Papers.

844 The volunteers would not go away: Eicher and Eicher, Civil War High Commands.

844 "And now, with my latest writing": Ruffin, Diary of Edmund Ruffin, III, 949.

844 He kept an extensive journal: A. H. Stephens, Recollections of Alexander H. Stephens, 133.

845 "Render the same cheerful obedience": U.S. Navy Dept., Civil War Naval Chronology, VI-386.

845 *Brig. Gen. William S. Ketcham:* John Beard, Receiver, Tallahassee, Fla., August 10, 1864, in the William S. Ketcham Papers.

845 *All during the war:* Roger Long, "General Orders No. 72, 'By Command of Gen. R. E. Lee,' " in *Gettysburg Magazine* (1992) 7:15.

846 *"The grand mistake of the South":* U.S. Navy Dept., *Civil War Naval Chronology,* VI-387.

846 *"This day has been duly observed":* Daniel E. Sickles to E. D. Townsend, Charleston, S.C., July 4, 1865, in the Daniel E. Sickles Papers.

846 *"I do not yet know":* Thomas W. Egan to Maj. W. Russell, Jr., AAG, Army of the Shenandoah, in the field, June 21, 1865, in the Green Berry Raum Papers.

846 *Sometime later Brig. Gen.:* Manning F. Force, Jackson, Miss., January 7, 1866, in the Manning F. Force Papers.

846 *"We were bereft of ground for hope":* U.S. Navy Dept., *Civil War Naval Chronology,* VI-390.

847 *On April 2, 1866:* A. Johnson, *Papers of Andrew Johnson,* X, 349–352.

847 *"The legitimate object of war":* W. T. Sherman, *Sherman at War,* 167.

847 *"The gentleman does not":* Robert E. Lee, ca. late 1860s, R. E. Lee Personal Papers, Virginia Historical Society, Richmond, Series 9, item 540.

848 *"Future years will never know":* Whitman, *Memoranda During the War,* 5.

848 *"Through our great good fortune":* O. W. Holmes, *Touched with Fire,* frontispiece.

848 *"They were the honest":* Ambrose Bierce, "A Bivouac of the Dead," in Bierce, *Civil War Short Stories of Ambrose Bierce,* 139.

848 *"This was unjust and unnecessary":* Cater, *As It Was,* 225.

849 *Confederate morale was high:* Wiley, *Road to Appomattox,* 1–121.

851 *"O Memory! thou midway world":* Abraham Lincoln, "My Childhood-Home I See Again," written about February 25, 1846, and sent to Andrew Johnston, a lawyer in Quincy, Ill. in Lincoln, *Collected Works,* I, 367–370.

EPILOGUE: 1865

852 *Washington McLean:* Holzman, *Adapt or Perish,* 80.

853 *"The man who can do such kindness":* Ibid., 81.

853 *He then produced:* Ibid.

853 *He could find none:* S. Pryor, *My Day,* 272.

853 *"That war was closed on a spectacle":* Pollard, *Lost Cause,* 743.

853 *"We have been fairly whipped":* New York Times, May 21, 1865.

854 *This strange and delicate man:* Holzman, *Adapt or Perish,* 78.

Bibliography

ONE INDISPENSABLE SOURCE *of Civil War history is* The War of the Rebellion: A Compilation of the Official Records of the Union and Confederate Armies (known as the *O.R.*), the 128-volume work that contains the "most important" papers of the war as they were sorted and published from 1880 to 1901. Though it has become fashionable to downplay the significance of the *O.R.* in recent years, as scholars have discovered how much manuscript material lies unresearched, the *O.R.* does contain key documents regarding the story of the war and retains priceless value relative to other published works. I have also used many "old classics" of the Civil War literature, works of high value that were published in the last three decades of the nineteenth century, and which contain resource material in the words of the participants. I've employed some seventy-seven of these works, carefully chosen to be reliable because of the high credibility of their authors, typified by such titles as Charles A. Dana's *Recollections of the Civil War,* Arthur Fremantle's *Three Months in the Southern States,* and John McElroy's *Andersonville.* I have used contemporary newspapers very sparingly. Some twenty-three newspapers and serials from the wartime period have been consulted and certain portions of them employed, but many newspapers of that era are notoriously unreliable.

Wishing to achieve as fresh an approach as possible, I have also drawn on a large amount of unpublished manuscript material, more than two hundred files altogether, from a variety of institutions. I wish to thank the staffs of the following institutions for making materials available: Alexandria Library, Alexandria, Virginia; Antietam National Battlefield, Sharpsburg, Maryland; Boston Public Library, Boston, Massachusetts; Duke University Library, Durham, North Carolina; Louisiana State University, Baton Rouge; National Archives and Records Administration, Washington, D.C.; South Caroliniana Library, University of South Carolina, Columbia; Southern Historical Collection, University of North Carolina, Chapel Hill; University of Alabama, Tuscaloosa; University of Virginia Valley of the Shadow Project Archive, Charlottesville; U.S. Army Military History Institute, Carlisle, Pennsylvania; United States Civil War Center, Louisiana State University, Baton Rouge; Virginia Historical Society, Richmond; Virginia Military Institute, Lexington; and the Virginia Polytechnic Institute and State University Library, Blacksburg. I also used documents from my own collection. Among the most curious groups of papers I went through were the Adjutant General's Office, Generals' Papers (Record Group 94) at the National Archives. Military Archivist Michael Musick described how many such officers' papers have not been examined in recent years and I have utilized dozens of documents from this collection.

I have also used many recently published scholarly battle histories, drawing on their analyses of engagements and reflecting their conclusions. I have consulted 147 such works published since the Civil War Centennial, books unpublished at the time of Catton and Foote. Similarly, I have used portions of 217 collections of period letters, diaries, and journals that have been published during the past three decades, many of them fresh sources of information about the war. Not wanting to limit the battlefield actions to male actors, I have included portions of 32 groups of letters, diaries, and journals of female participants, from the small number of female combatants to nurses, civilians, and activists. To underscore the freshness of the sources used, about 300 of the references were published in the 1990s.

Books and Papers

Abbott, Henry Livermore. *Fallen Leaves: The Civil War Letters of Major Henry Livermore Abbott.* Edited by Robert Garth Scott. Kent, Ohio: Kent State University Press, 1991.

Abel, E. Lawrence. *Singing the New Nation: How Music Shaped the Confederacy, 1861–1865.* Mechanicsburg, Pa.: Stackpole Books, 2000.

Adams, Charles Francis; Charles Francis Adams, Jr.; and Henry Brooks Adams. *A Cycle of Adams Letters, 1861–1865.* Boston: Houghton Mifflin Co., 1920.

Adams, George Worthington. *Doctors in Blue: The Medical History of the Union Army in the Civil War.* Baton Rouge: Louisiana State University Press, 1952.

Albaugh, William A., III. *The Confederate Brass-Framed Colt & Whitney.* Wilmington, N.C.: Broadfoot Publishing Co., 1993.

Albaugh, William A., III. *Confederate Edged Weapons.* Wilmington, N.C.: Broadfoot Publishing Co., 1993.

Albaugh, William A., III, and Edward N. Simmons. *Confederate Arms.* Wilmington, N.C.: Broadfoot Publishing Co., 1993.

Albaugh, William A., III, and Richard D. Steuart. *Handbook of Confederate Swords.* Wilmington, N.C.: Broadfoot Publishing Co., 1993.

Albaugh, William A., III, and Richard D. Steuart. *The Original Confederate Colt: The Story of the Leech & Rigdon and Rigdon-Ansley Revolvers.* Wilmington, N.C.: Broadfoot Publishing Co., 1993.

Albaugh, William A., III; Hugh Benet, Jr.; and Edward N. Simmons. *Confederate Handguns: Concerning the Guns and the Men Who Made Them and the Times of Their Use.* Wilmington, N.C.: Broadfoot Publishing Co., 1993.

Alcott, Louisa May. *Hospital Sketches.* Boston: J. Redpath, 1863.

————. *The Journals of Louisa May Alcott.* Edited by Joel Myerson, Daniel Shealy, and Madeleine B. Stern. Athens: University of Georgia Press, 1997.

————. *The Selected Letters of Louisa May Alcott.* Athens: University of Georgia Press, 1995.

Alexander, Edward Porter. *Fighting for the Confederacy: The Personal Recollections of General Edward Porter Alexander.* Edited by Gary W. Gallagher. Chapel Hill: University of North Carolina Press, 1989.

Allan, William. *History of the Campaign of Gen. T. J. (Stonewall) Jackson in the Shenandoah Valley of Virginia, from November 4, 1861, to June 17, 1862.* Philadelphia: J. B. Lippincott Co., 1880.

Alleman, Tillie Pierce. *At Gettysburg; or, What a Girl Saw and Heard of the Battle.* Gettysburg, Pa.: Stan Clark Military Books, and Baltimore: Butternut & Blue, 1994.

Allen, Ujanirtus. *Campaigning with "Old Stonewall": Confederate Captain Ujanirtus Allen's Let-

ters to His Wife. Edited by Randall Allen and Keith S. Bohannon. Baton Rouge: Louisiana State University Press, 1998.

Ambrose, Stephen E. *Halleck: Lincoln's Chief of Staff.* Baton Rouge: Louisiana State University Press, 1962.

Ames, Adelbert. *Adelbert Ames, 1835–1933: General, Senator, Governor.* Edited by Blanche Ames. North Easton, Mass.: Published by the editor, 1964.

————. *Chronicles from the Nineteenth Century: Family Letters of Blanche Butler and Adelbert Ames.* Edited by Jesse Ames Marshall. Clinton, Mass.: Published by the editor, 1957.

Anderson, Edward Maffitt. Papers. William Stanley Hoole Special Collections Library, University of Alabama, Tuscaloosa.

Anderson, Nicholas Longworth. *General Nicholas Longworth Anderson, Letters and Journals: Harvard, Civil War, Washington, 1854–1892.* Edited by Isabel Anderson. New York: Fleming H. Revell Co., 1942.

Andrews, Eliza Frances. *The War-Time Journal of a Georgia Girl, 1864–1865.* Lincoln: University of Nebraska Press, 1997.

Andrews, George Leonard. Papers. Louisiana State University Library, Baton Rouge.

Angle, Craig. *The Great Locomotive Chase.* Rouzerville, Pa.: Published by the author, 1992.

Angley, Wilson; Jerry L. Cross; and Michael Hill. *Sherman's March Through North Carolina: A Chronology.* Raleigh: North Carolina Division of Archives and History, 1995.

Asboth, Alexander S. Papers. Record Group 94, Adjutant General's Office Records, Generals' Papers, National Archives and Records Administration (hereafter, NARA), Washington, D.C.

Augur, Christopher C. Papers. Record Group 94, Adjutant General's Office Records, Generals' Papers, NARA, Washington, D.C.

Averell, William Woods. *Ten Years in the Saddle: The Memoir of William Woods Averell, 1851–1862.* Edited by Edward J. Eckert and Nicholas J. Amato. Novato, Calif.: Presidio Press, 1978.

Ayres, Romeyn Beck. Papers. Record Group 94, Adjutant General's Office Records, Generals' Papers, NARA, Washington, D.C.

Bachelder, John. *John Bachelder's History of the Battle of Gettysburg.* Edited by David L. Ladd and Audrey J. Ladd. Dayton, Ohio: Morningside Book Shop, 1997.

Bailey, Joseph. Papers. Record Group 94, Adjutant General's Office Records, Generals' Papers, NARA, Washington, D.C.

Ballard, Michael B. *Pemberton: A Biography.* Jackson: University Press of Mississippi, 1991.

Banasik, Michael E. *Embattled Arkansas: The Prairie Grove Campaign of 1862.* Wilmington, N.C.: Broadfoot Publishing Co., 1996.

Banks, R. W. *The Battle of Franklin, November 30, 1864.* Dayton, Ohio: Morningside Book Shop, 1982.

Barrett, John G. *The Civil War in North Carolina.* Chapel Hill: University of North Carolina Press, 1963.

————. *Sherman's March Through the Carolinas.* Chapel Hill: University of North Carolina Press, 1956.

Barry, William F. Papers. Record Group 94, Adjutant General's Office Records, Generals' Papers, NARA, Washington, D.C.

Bates, David Homer. *Lincoln in the Telegraph Office: Recollections of the United States Military Telegraph Corps During the Civil War.* New York: Century Co., 1907.

Bearss, Edwin C. *Forrest at Brice's Cross Roads and in North Mississippi in 1864.* Dayton, Ohio: Morningside Book Shop, 1979.

————. *Hardluck Ironclad: The Sinking and Salvage of the* Cairo. Baton Rouge: Louisiana State University Press, 1966.

Bearss, Margie Riddle. *Sherman's Forgotten Campaign: The Meridian Expedition.* Baltimore: Gateway Press, 1987.

Beatty, John. *The Citizen-Soldier; or, Memoirs of a Volunteer.* Cincinnati: Wilstach, Baldwin & Co., 1879.

Beaudry, Louis N. *War Journal of Louis N. Beaudry, Fifth New York Cavalry.* Edited by Richard E. Beaudry. Jefferson, N.C.: McFarland & Co., 1996.

Becker, Carl M., and Ritchie Thomas, eds. *Hearth and Knapsack: The Ladley Letters, 1857–1880.* Athens: Ohio University Press, 1988.

Beecham, Robert. *As if It Were Glory: Robert Beecham's Civil War from the Iron Brigade to the Black Regiments.* Edited by Michael E. Stevens. Madison, Wis.: Madison House, 1998.

Beers, Henry Putney. *Guide to the Archives of the Government of the Confederate States of America.* Washington, D.C.: National Archives, 1968.

Bellard, Alfred. *Gone for a Soldier: The Civil War Memoirs of Private Alfred Bellard.* Edited by David H. Donald. Boston: Little, Brown & Co., 1993.

Bengtson, Bradley, and Julian E. Kuz. *Photographic Atlas of Civil War Injuries.* Grand Rapids, Mich.: Medical Staff Press, 1996.

Benham, Henry W. Papers. Record Group 94, Adjutant General's Office Records, Generals' Papers, NARA, Washington, D.C.

Bennett, Brian A. *The Beau Ideal of a Soldier and a Gentleman: The Life of Col. Patrick Henry O'Rorke from Ireland to Gettysburg.* Wheatland, N.Y.: Triphammer Publishing Co., 1996.

Benson, Berry. *Berry Benson's Civil War Book: Memoirs of a Confederate Scout and Sharpshooter.* Edited by Susan Williams Benson. Athens: University of Georgia Press, 1992.

Bergeron, Arthur W., Jr. *Confederate Mobile.* Jackson: University Press of Mississippi, 1991.

Beringer, Richard E., et al. *The Elements of Confederate Defeat: Nationalism, War Aims, and Religion.* Athens: University of Georgia Press, 1988.

————. *Why the South Lost the Civil War.* Athens: University of Georgia Press, 1986.

Berkeley, Henry Robinson. *Four Years in the Confederate Artillery: The Diary of Private Henry Robinson Berkeley.* Edited by William H. Runge. Richmond: Virginia Historical Society, 1991.

Berlin, Ira, et al., eds. *Freedom: A Documentary History of Emancipation, 1861–1867.* New York: Cambridge University Press, 1982–1993.

Bernstein, Iver. *The New York City Draft Riots: Their Significance for American Society and Politics in the Age of the Civil War.* New York: Oxford University Press, 1990.

Bevens, William E. *Reminiscences of a Private: William E. Bevens of the First Arkansas Infantry, C.S.A.* Edited by Daniel E. Sutherland. Fayetteville: University of Arkansas Press, 1992.

Bierce, Ambrose. *The Civil War Short Stories of Ambrose Bierce.* Edited by Ernest J. Hopkins. Lincoln: University of Nebraska Press, 1988.

Bigelow, John. *The Peach Orchard, Gettysburg, July 2, 1863.* Gaithersburg, Md.: Olde Soldier Books, 1987.

Bilby, Joseph G. *Civil War Firearms: Their Historical Background, Tactical Use, and Modern Collecting and Shooting.* Conshohocken, Pa.: Combined Books, 1996.

Billings, John D. *Hardtack and Coffee; or, the Unwritten Story of Army Life.* Boston: George M. Smith & Co., 1887.

Binney, Charles Chauncey. *The Life of Horace Binney.* Philadelphia: J. B. Lippincott Co., 1903.

Birney, David Bell. Papers. Record Group 94, Adjutant General's Office Records, Generals' Papers, NARA, Washington, D.C.

Black, Harvey. *A Surgeon with Stonewall Jackson: The Civil War Letters of Dr. Harvey Black.* Edited by Glenn L. McMullen. Baltimore: Butternut & Blue, 1995.

Black, William J. Papers. Virginia Military Institute Library, Lexington.

Blackburn, Theodore W. *Letters from the Front: A Union "Preacher" Regiment (74th Ohio) in the Civil War.* Dayton, Ohio: Morningside Book Shop, 1981.

Blackford, Charles Minor, III. *Letters from Lee's Army; or, Memoirs in and out of the Army of Northern Virginia During the War Between the States.* New York: Charles Scribner's Sons, 1947.

Blackford, L. M. Papers. University of Virginia Valley of the Shadow Project Archive, Charlottesville.

Blackford, W. W. *War Years with Jeb Stuart.* New York: Charles Scribner's Sons, 1945.

Blakey, Arch Fredric; Ann Smith Lainhart; and Winston Bryant Stephens, Jr., eds. *Rose Cottage Chronicles: Civil War Letters of the Bryant-Stephens Families of North Florida.* Gainesville: University Press of Florida, 1998.

Bleser, Carol. *The Hammonds of Redcliffe.* New York: Oxford University Press, 1981.

Blight, David W. *Frederick Douglass' Civil War: Keeping Faith in Jubilee.* Baton Rouge: Louisiana State University Press, 1989.

Blunt, James G. Papers. Record Group 94, Adjutant General's Office Records, Generals' Papers, NARA, Washington, D.C.

Boatner, Mark M., III. *The Civil War Dictionary.* 2d ed. New York: David McKay Co., 1988.

Booth, John Wilkes. *"Right or Wrong, God Judge Me": The Writings of John Wilkes Booth.* Edited by John Rhodehamel and Louise Taper. Urbana: University of Illinois Press, 1997.

Borcke, Heros von. *Memoirs of the Confederate War for Independence.* Edinburgh: W. Blackwood & Sons, 1866.

Boritt, Gabor S., ed. *The Gettysburg Nobody Knows.* New York: Oxford University Press, 1997.

Bowen, Roland E. *From Ball's Bluff to Gettysburg . . . and Beyond: The Civil War Letters of Private Roland E. Bowen, 15th Massachusetts Infantry, 1861–1864.* Edited by Gregory A. Coco. Gettysburg, Pa.: Thomas Publications, 1994.

Boyd, Cyrus F. *The Civil War Diary of Cyrus F. Boyd, Fifteenth Iowa Infantry, 1861–1863.* Edited by Mildred Throne. Baton Rouge: Louisiana State University Press, 1998.

Bradley, Mark L. *The Battle of Bentonville: Last Stand in the Carolinas.* Campbell, Calif.: Savas Publishing Co., 1995.

Bragg, Edward S. Papers. Antietam National Battlefield, Sharpsburg, Md.

Branch, John; Sanford Branch; and Hamilton Branch. *Charlotte's Boys: Civil War Letters of the Branch Family of Savannah.* Edited by Mauriel Phillips Joslyn. Berryville, Va.: Rockbridge Publishing Co., 1996.

Brandegee, Charles. *Charlie's Civil War: A Private's Trial by Fire in the 5th New York Volunteers, Duryée Zouaves, and 146th New York Volunteer Infantry.* Edited by Charles Brandegee Livingstone. Gettysburg, Pa.: Thomas Publications, 1997.

Brandt, Nat. *Mr. Tubbs' Civil War.* Syracuse, N.Y.: Syracuse University Press, 1996.

Breckinridge, Lucy. *Lucy Breckinridge of Grove Hill: The Journal of a Virginia Girl, 1862–1864.* Edited by Mary D. Robinson. Columbia: University of South Carolina Press, 1994.

Brennan, Patrick. *Secessionville: Assault on Charleston.* Campbell, Calif.: Savas Publishing Co., 1996.

Brevard, Keziah Goodwyn Hopkins. *A Plantation Mistress on the Eve of the Civil War.* Edited by John Hammond Moore. Columbia: University of South Carolina Press, 1996.

Brewster, Charles Harvey. *When This Cruel War Is Over: The Civil War Letters of Charles Harvey Brewster.* Edited by David W. Blight. Amherst: University of Massachusetts Press, 1992.

Bridges, Hal. *Lee's Maverick General: Daniel Harvey Hill.* Lincoln: University of Nebraska Press, 1991.

Brinton, John H. *Personal Memoirs of John H. Brinton, Major and Surgeon, U.S.V., 1861–1865.* New York: Neale Publishing Co., 1914.

Britton, Wiley. *Memoirs of the Rebellion on the Border, 1863.* Lincoln: University of Nebraska Press, 1993.

Brooks, Noah. *Lincoln Observed: Civil War Dispatches of Noah Brooks.* Edited by Michael Burlingame. Baltimore: Johns Hopkins University Press, 1998.

———. *Washington in Lincoln's Time.* Edited by Herbert Mitgang. New York: Rinehart & Co., 1958.

Brooksher, William Riley. *Bloody Hill: The Civil War Battle of Wilson's Creek.* McLean, Va.: Brassey's, 1996.

Brown, Augustus C. *The Diary of a Line Officer.* New York: Published by the author, 1906.

Brown, Dee Alexander. *The Bold Cavaliers: Morgan's 2d Kentucky Cavalry Raiders.* Philadelphia: J. B. Lippincott Co., 1959.

———. *Grierson's Raid.* Dayton, Ohio: Morningside Book Shop, 1981.

Brown, Kent Masterson. *Cushing of Gettysburg: The Story of a Union Artillery Commander.* Lexington: University Press of Kentucky, 1993.

Brown, Russell K. *To the Manner Born: The Life of General William H. T. Walker.* Athens: University of Georgia Press, 1994.

Browning, Robert M., Jr. *From Cape Charles to Cape Fear: The North Atlantic Blockading Squadron During the Civil War.* Tuscaloosa: University of Alabama Press, 1993.

Bruce, Robert V. *Lincoln and the Tools of War.* Urbana: University of Illinois Press, 1989.

Bryan, George S. *The Great American Myth: The True Story of Lincoln's Murder.* Chicago: Americana House, 1990.

Bryant, William O. *Cahaba Prison and the Sultana Disaster.* Tuscaloosa: University of Alabama Press, 1990.

Buck, Lucy Rebecca. *Shadows on my Heart: The Civil War Diary of Lucy Rebecca Buck of Virginia.* Edited by Elizabeth R. Baer. Athens: University of Georgia Press, 1997.

Buell, Augustus C. *"The Cannoneer": Recollections of Service in the Army of the Potomac.* Washington, D.C.: National Tribune, 1890.

Buell, Don Carlos. Papers. Record Group 94, Adjutant General's Office Records, Generals' Papers, NARA, Washington, D.C.

Buford, John. Papers. Record Group 94, Adjutant General's Office Records, Generals' Papers, NARA, Washington, D.C.

Bull, Rice C. *Soldiering: The Civil War Diary of Rice C. Bull.* Edited by K. Jack Bauer. Novato, Calif.: Presidio Press, 1977.

Burge, Dolly Lunt. *The Diary of Dolly Lunt Burge, 1848–1879.* Edited by Christine Jacobson Carter. Athens: University of Georgia Press, 1997.

Burns, William W. Papers. Record Group 94, Adjutant General's Office Records, Generals' Papers, NARA, Washington, D.C.

Busey, John W., and David G. Martin. *Regimental Strengths and Losses at Gettysburg.* 3d ed. Hightstown, N.J.: Longstreet House, 1994.

Butler, Benjamin F. *Butler's Book: Autobiography and Personal Reminiscences of Major-General Benjamin F. Butler.* Boston: A. M. Thayer & Co., 1892.

———. *Private and Official Correspondence of Gen. Benjamin F. Butler, During the Period of the Civil War.* Norwood, Mass.: Plimpton Press, 1917.

Caldwell, John C. Papers. Record Group 94, Adjutant General's Office Records, Generals' Papers, NARA, Washington, D.C.

Callaway, Joshua W. *The Civil War Letters of Joshua W. Callaway.* Edited by Judith Lee Hallock. Athens: University of Georgia Press, 1997.

Camp Chase, Ohio. Papers. Virginia Historical Society, Richmond.

Carmichael, Peter S. *Lee's Young Artillerist: William R. J. Pegram.* Charlottesville: University Press of Virginia, 1995.

Carpenter, Henry C. Papers. Virginia Polytechnic Institute and State University Library, Blacksburg.

Carr, Eugene Asa. Papers. U.S. Army Military History Institute, Carlisle, Pa.

Carrington, Henry B. Papers. Record Group 94, Adjutant General's Office Records, Generals' Papers, NARA, Washington, D.C.

Carroll, Henry S. Papers. Harrisburg Civil War Round Table Collection, U.S. Army Military History Institute, Carlisle, Pa.

Carroll, Samuel S. Papers. Record Group 94, Adjutant General's Office Records, Generals' Papers, NARA, Washington, D.C.

Carter, Robert Goldthwaite. *Four Brothers in Blue; or, Sunshine and Shadows of the War of the Rebellion: A Story of the Great Civil War from Bull Run to Appomattox.* Austin: University of Texas Press, 1978.

Castel, Albert. *Decision in the West: The Atlanta Campaign of 1864.* Lawrence: University Press of Kansas, 1992.

———. *General Sterling Price and the Civil War in the West.* Baton Rouge: Louisiana State University Press, 1968.

Cater, Douglas John. *As It Was: Reminiscences of a Soldier of the Third Texas Cavalry and the Nineteenth Louisiana Infantry.* Austin, Tex.: State House Press, 1990.

Cavada, F. F. *Libby Life: Experiences of a Prisoner of War in Richmond, Va., 1863–64.* Bowie, Md.: Heritage Books, 1994.

Chamberlain, Joshua L. *The Passing of the Armies: An Account of the Final Campaign of the Army of the Potomac, Based upon Personal Reminiscences of the Fifth Army Corps.* New York: G. P. Putnam's Sons, 1915.

———. *Through Blood and Fire: Selected Civil War Papers of Major General Joshua Chamberlain.* Edited by Mark Nesbit. Mechanicsburg, Pa.: Stackpole Books, 1996.

———. Papers. Record Group 94, Adjutant General's Office Records, Generals' Papers, NARA, Washington, D.C.

Chamberlayne, John Hampden. *Ham Chamberlayne—Virginian: Letters and Papers of an Artillery Officer in the War for Southern Independence, 1861–1865.* Edited by C. G. Chamberlayne. Wilmington, N.C.: Broadfoot Publishing Co., 1992.

Chase, Salmon P. *The Salmon P. Chase Papers.* Edited by John Niven. Kent, Ohio: Kent State University Press, 1993–.

Chesnut, Mary. *Mary Chesnut's Civil War.* Edited by C. Vann Woodward. New Haven: Yale University Press, 1981.

———. *The Private Mary Chesnut: The Unpublished Civil War Diaries.* Edited by C. Vann Woodward and Elisabeth Muhlenfeld. New York: Oxford University Press, 1984.

Chester, Thomas Morris. *Thomas Morris Chester, Black Civil War Correspondent: His Dispatches from the Virginia Front.* Edited by R. J. M. Blackett. Baton Rouge: Louisiana State University Press, 1989.

Christ, Elwood. *"Over a Wide, Hot Crimson Plain": The Struggle for the Bliss Farm at Gettysburg, July 2d and 3d, 1863.* Baltimore: Butternut & Blue, 1993.

Clark, Reuben G. *Valleys of the Shadow: The Memoir of Confederate Captain Reuben G. Clark.* Edited by Willene B. Clark. Knoxville: University of Tennessee Press, 1994.

Clarke, Hermon. *Back Home in Oneida: Hermon Clarke and His Letters.* Edited by Harry F. Jackson and Thomas F. O'Donnell. Syracuse, N.Y.: Syracuse University Press, 1965.

Clayton, William Henry Harrison. *A Damned Iowa Greyhound: The Civil War Letters of William Henry Harrison Clayton.* Edited by Donald C. Elder III. Iowa City: University of Iowa Press, 1998.

Clemson, Floride. *A Rebel Came Home: The Diary and Letters of Floride Clemson, 1863–1866.* Edited by Ernest McPherson Lander, Jr., and Charles M. McGee, Jr. Columbia: University of South Carolina Press, 1989.

Cockrell, Monroe F., ed. *The Lost Account of the Battle of Corinth and the Court Martial of Gen. Van Dorn.* Wilmington, N.C.: Broadfoot Publishing Co., 1991.

Coco, Gregory A. *A Vast Sea of Misery: A History and Guide to the Union and Confederate Field Hospitals at Gettysburg, July 1–November 20, 1863.* Gettysburg, Pa.: Thomas Publications, 1988.

Coddington, Edwin B. *The Gettysburg Campaign: A Study in Command.* New York: Charles Scribner's Sons, 1984.

Coffman, Edward M. *The Old Army: A Portrait of the American Army in Peacetime, 1784–1898.* New York: Oxford University Press, 1986.

Cogar, William B. *Dictionary of Admirals of the U.S. Navy.* Vol. I; *1862–1900.* Annapolis: Naval Institute Press, 1989.

Coleman, Clayton G. Papers. Virginia Military Institute Library, Lexington.

Colt, Margaretta Barton. *Defend the Valley: A Shenandoah Family in the Civil War.* New York: Orion Books, 1994.

Commager, Henry Steele, ed. *The Blue and the Gray: The Story of the Civil War as Told by Participants.* Indianapolis: Bobbs-Merrill Co., 1950.

Comstock, Cyrus B. *The Diary of Cyrus B. Comstock.* Edited by Merlin E. Sumner. Dayton, Ohio: Morningside Book Shop, 1987.

Connolly, James A. "Major Connolly's Letters to His Wife, 1862–1865," in *Transactions of the Illinois State Historical Society,* Springfield (Publications of the Illinois State Historical Library, no. 35), 1928.

———. *Three Years in the Army of the Cumberland: The Letters and Diary of Major James A. Connolly.* Edited by Paul M. Angle. Bloomington: Indiana University Press, 1959.

Cooke, John Esten. *Wearing of the Gray: Being Personal Portraits, Scenes, and Adventures of the War.* Bloomington: Indiana University Press, 1959.

Cooley, Henry. Papers. Southern Historical Collection, University of North Carolina, Chapel Hill.

Cooling, Benjamin Franklin. *Fort Donelson's Legacy: War and Society in Kentucky and Tennessee, 1862–1863.* Knoxville: University of Tennessee Press, 1997.

———. *Forts Henry and Donelson: The Key to the Confederate Heartland.* Knoxville: University of Tennessee Press, 1987.

———. *Jubal Early's Raid on Washington, 1864.* Baltimore: Nautical & Aviation Publishing Co., 1989.

Corcoran, Michael. Papers. Record Group 94, Adjutant General's Office Records, Generals' Papers, NARA, Washington, D.C.

Cormany, Samuel, and Rachel Bowman Cormany. *The Cormany Diaries: A Northern Family in the Civil War.* Edited by James C. Mohr. Pittsburgh: University of Pittsburgh Press, 1982.

Corsan, W. C. *Two Months in the Confederate States: An Englishman's Travels Through the South.* Edited by Benjamin H. Trask. Baton Rouge: Louisiana State University Press, 1996.

Corse, John M. Papers. Record Group 94, Adjutant General's Office Records, Generals' Papers, NARA, Washington, D.C.

Corse, Montgomery D. Papers. Alexandria Library, Alexandria, Va.

Cox, Jacob D. *Atlanta.* New York: Charles Scribner's Sons, 1882.

———. *The Battle of Franklin, Tennessee, November 30, 1864.* Dayton, Ohio: Morningside Book Shop, 1983.

———. *The March to the Sea, Franklin, and Nashville.* New York: Charles Scribner's Sons, 1882.

———. Papers. Record Group 94, Adjutant General's Office Records, Generals' Papers, NARA, Washington, D.C.

Cozzens, Peter. *The Darkest Days of the War: The Battles of Iuka and Corinth.* Chapel Hill: University of North Carolina Press, 1997.

————. *No Better Place to Die: The Battle of Stones River.* Urbana: University of Illinois Press, 1990.

————. *The Shipwreck of Their Hopes: The Battles for Chattanooga.* Urbana: University of Illinois Press, 1994.

————. *This Terrible Sound: The Battle of Chickamauga.* Urbana: University of Illinois Press, 1992.

Crawford, Samuel Wylie. Papers. Record Group 94, Adjutant General's Office Records, Generals' Papers, NARA, Washington, D.C.

Crittenden, Thomas Leonidas. Papers. Record Group 94, Adjutant General's Office Records, Generals' Papers, NARA, Washington, D.C.

Crittenden, Thomas Turpin. Papers. Record Group 94, Adjutant General's Office Records, Generals' Papers, NARA, Washington, D.C.

Culver, John Oscar. Papers. U.S. Army Military History Institute, Carlisle, Pa.

Cumming, Kate. *Gleanings from Southland: Sketches of Life and Manners of the People of the South Before, During, and After the War of Secession, with Extracts from the Author's Journal and Epitome of the New South.* Birmingham, Ala.: Roberts & Son, 1895.

————. *Kate: The Journal of a Confederate Nurse.* Edited by Richard Barksdale Harwell. Baton Rouge: Louisiana State University Press, 1959.

Cunningham, Edward. *The Port Hudson Campaign, 1862–1863.* Baton Rouge: Louisiana State University Press, 1963.

Current, Richard Nelson, et al., eds. *Encyclopedia of the Confederacy.* New York: Simon & Schuster, 1993.

Curtis, Samuel R. Papers. Record Group 94, Adjutant General's Office Records, Generals' Papers, NARA, Washington, D.C.

Custer, George A. Papers. Record Group 94, Adjutant General's Office Records, Generals' Papers, NARA, Washington, D.C.

Cutler, Bruce. *The Massacre at Sand Creek: Narrative Voices.* Norman: University of Oklahoma Press, 1995.

Cutrer, Thomas W. *Ben McCulloch and the Frontier Military Tradition.* Chapel Hill: University of North Carolina Press, 1993.

Dabney, Robert L. *Life and Campaigns of Lieut.-Gen. Thomas J. Jackson (Stonewall Jackson).* New York: Blelock & Co., 1866.

Dana, Charles A. *Recollections of the Civil War: With the Leaders at Washington and in the Field in the Sixties.* New York: D. Appleton & Co., 1898.

Dana, Napoleon J. T. Papers. Record Group 94, Adjutant General's Office Records, Generals' Papers, NARA, Washington, D.C.

Daniel, Larry J. *Shiloh: The Battle that Changed the Civil War.* New York: Simon & Schuster, 1997.

Daniel, Larry J., and Lynn N. Bock. *Island No. 10: Struggle for the Mississippi Valley.* Tuscaloosa: University of Alabama Press, 1996.

Davies, Thomas A. Papers. Record Group 94, Adjutant General's Office Records, Generals' Papers, NARA, Washington, D.C.

Davis, Charles E. *Three Years in the Army: The Story of the Thirteenth Massachusetts Volunteers.* Boston: Estes & Lauriat, 1894.

Davis, Jefferson. *Jefferson Davis, Constitutionalist: His Letters, Papers, and Speeches.* Edited by Dunbar Rowland. Jackson: Mississippi Department of Archives and History, 1923.

———. *The Papers of Jefferson Davis.* Edited by Haskell M. Monroe et al. Baton Rouge: Louisiana State University Press, 1971–.

Davis, Jefferson C. Papers. Record Group 94, Adjutant General's Office Records, Generals' Papers, NARA, Washington, D.C.

Davis, William C. *Battle at Bull Run: A History of the First Major Campaign of the Civil War.* Garden City, N.Y.: Doubleday & Co., 1977.

———. *The Battle of New Market.* Garden City, N.Y.: Doubleday & Co., 1975.

———. *Duel Between the First Ironclads.* Garden City, N.Y.: Doubleday & Co., 1975.

———. *Jefferson Davis: The Man and His Hour.* New York: HarperCollins, 1991.

Dawes, Rufus R. *Service with the Sixth Wisconsin Volunteers.* Marietta, Ohio: E. R. Alderman & Sons, 1890.

Dawson, Francis W. [Austin John Reeks]. *Reminiscences of Confederate Service, 1861–1865.* Edited by Bell I. Wiley. Baton Rouge: Louisiana State University Press, 1980.

Day, Samuel P. *Down South.* London: Hurst & Blackett, 1862.

De Forest, John William. *A Volunteer's Adventures: A Union Captain's Record of the Civil War.* Edited by James H. Croushore. Baton Rouge: Louisiana State University Press, 1996.

deKay, James Tertius. Monitor: *The Story of the Legendary Civil War Ironclad and the Man Whose Invention Changed the Course of History.* New York: Walker & Co., 1997.

DeLeon, Thomas Cooper. *Four Years in Rebel Capitals: An Inside View of Life in the Southern Confederacy, from Birth to Death, from Original Notes, Collated in the Years 1861 to 1865.* Mobile, Ala.: Gossip Printing Co., 1890.

Denney, Robert E. *Civil War Prisons and Escapes: A Day-by-Day Chronicle.* New York: Sterling Publishing Co., 1993.

De Russy, Gustavus A. Papers. Record Group 94, Adjutant General's Office Records, Generals' Papers, NARA, Washington, D.C.

Desjardin, Thomas A. *Stand Firm Ye Boys from Maine: The 20th Maine and the Gettysburg Campaign.* Gettysburg, Pa.: Thomas Publications, 1995.

de Trobriand, Philippe Régis Denis de Kerenden. *Our Noble Blood: The Civil War Letters of Major-General Régis de Trobriand.* Edited by William B. Styple. Kearny, N.J.: Belle Grove Publishing Co., 1997.

Devens, Charles, Jr. Papers. Record Group 94, Adjutant General's Office Records, Generals' Papers, NARA, Washington, D.C.

Dexter, Seymour. *Seymour Dexter, Union Army: Journal and Letters, New York Volunteer Regiment of Elmira, with Illustrations.* Edited by Carl A. Morrell. Jefferson, N.C.: McFarland & Co., 1996.

Dickerson, Frank. *Dearest Father: The Civil War Letters of Lt. Frank Dickerson, a Son of Belfast, Maine.* Edited by H. Draper Hunt. Unity, Maine: North Country Press, 1992.

Dix, John A. Papers. Record Group 94, Adjutant General's Office Records, Generals' Papers, NARA, Washington, D.C.

Donald, David Herbert. *Lincoln.* New York: Simon & Schuster, 1995.

Donaldson, Francis Adams. *Inside the Army of the Potomac: The Civil War Experience of Cap-*

tain Francis Adams Donaldson. Edited by J. Gregory Acken. Mechanicsburg, Pa.: Stackpole Books, 1998.

Doubleday, Abner. *Reminiscences of Forts Sumter and Moultrie in 1860–61.* New York: Harper & Bros., 1876.

———. Papers. Record Group 94, Adjutant General's Office Records, Generals' Papers, NARA, Washington, D.C.

Douglas, Henry Kyd. *I Rode with Stonewall: Being Chiefly the War Experiences of the Youngest Member of Jackson's Staff from the John Brown Raid to the Hanging of Mrs. Surratt.* Chapel Hill: University of North Carolina Press, 1987.

Dow, Neal. Papers. Record Group 94, Adjutant General's Office Records, Generals' Papers, NARA, Washington, D.C.

Duffié, Alfred N. A. Papers. Record Group 94, Adjutant General's Office Records, Generals' Papers, NARA, Washington, D.C.

Dufour, Charles L. *The Night the War Was Lost.* Lincoln: University of Nebraska Press, 1994.

Dunaway, Wayland Fuller. *Reminiscences of a Rebel.* Baltimore: Butternut & Blue, 1996.

Duncan, Richard R. *Lee's Endangered Left: The Civil War in Western Virginia, Spring of 1864.* Baton Rouge: Louisiana State University Press, 1998.

Du Pont, Samuel F. *Samuel Francis Du Pont: A Selection from His Civil War Letters.* Edited by John D. Hayes. Ithaca: Cornell University Press, 1969.

Dwight, Elizabeth A. W., ed. *The Life and Letters of Wilder Dwight.* Boston: Ticknor & Fields, 1868.

Dwight, William. Papers. Record Group 94, Adjutant General's Office Records, Generals' Papers, NARA, Washington, D.C.

Dyer, Frederick H. *A Compendium of the War of the Rebellion: From Official Records of the Union and Confederate Armies, Reports of the Adjutant Generals of the Several States, the Army Registers, and Other Reliable Documents and Sources.* Des Moines: Dyer Publishing Co., 1908.

Dyer, John P. *From Shiloh to San Juan: The Life of "Fightin' Joe" Wheeler.* Baton Rouge: Louisiana State University Press, 1992.

Early, Jubal A. *Autobiographical Sketch and Narrative of the War Between the States.* Philadelphia: J. B. Lippincott Co., 1912.

Early, Jubal A., et al., eds. *Southern Historical Society Papers.* Richmond: Southern Historical Society and Virginia Historical Society, 1876–1959.

Edmondson, Belle. *A Lost Heroine of the Confederacy: The Diaries and Letters of Belle Edmondson.* Edited by William Galbraith and Loretta Galbraith. Jackson: University Press of Mississippi, 1990.

Edmondson, James K. *My Dear Emma: War Letters of Col. James K. Edmondson, 1861–1865.* Edited by Charles W. Turner. Verona, Va.: McClure Press, 1978.

Edmondston, Catherine Ann Devereux. *"Journal of a Secesh Lady": The Diary of Catherine Ann Devereux Edmondston, 1860–1866.* Edited by Beth Gilbert Crabtree and James W. Patton. Raleigh: North Carolina Division of Archives and History, 1995.

Edrington, Thomas S., and John Taylor. *The Battle of Glorieta Pass: A Gettysburg in the West, March 26–28, 1862.* Albuquerque: University of New Mexico Press, 1998.

Edwards, Abial H. *"Dear Friend Anna": The Civil War Letters of a Common Soldier from Maine.*

Edited by Beverly Hayes Kallgren and James L. Crouthamel. Orono: University of Maine Press, 1992.

Egan, Thomas W. Papers. Record Group 94, Adjutant General's Office Records, Generals' Papers, NARA, Washington, D.C.

Eggleston, George Cary. *A Rebel's Recollections.* Baton Rouge: Louisiana State University Press, 1996.

Eicher, David J. *Civil War Battlefields: A Touring Guide.* Dallas: Taylor Publishing Co., 1995.

———. *The Civil War in Books: An Analytical Bibliography.* Urbana: University of Illinois Press, 1997.

———. *Mystic Chords of Memory: Civil War Battlefields and Historic Sites Recaptured.* Baton Rouge: Louisiana State University Press, 1998.

———. *Robert E. Lee: A Life Portrait.* Dallas: Taylor Publishing Co., 1997.

Eicher, John H., and David J. Eicher. *Civil War High Commands.* Stanford, Calif.: Stanford University Press, 2001.

Eisenhower, John S. D. *Agent of Destiny: The Life and Times of General Winfield Scott.* New York: Free Press, 1997.

Eisenschiml, Otto. *The Celebrated Case of Fitz John Porter: An American Dreyfus Affair.* Indianapolis: Bobbs-Merrill Co., 1950.

11th Ohio Infantry. Papers. Antietam National Battlefield, Sharpsburg, Md.

Elmore, Grace Brown. *A Heritage of Woe: The Civil War Diary of Grace Brown Elmore, 1861–1868.* Edited by Marli F. Weiner. Athens: University of Georgia Press, 1997.

Emilio, Luis F. *A Brave Black Regiment: History of the Fifty-Fourth Regiment of Massachusetts Volunteer Infantry, 1863–1865.* Salem, N.H.: Ayer Co., 1990

Emory, William H. Papers. Record Group 94, Adjutant General's Office Records, Generals' Papers, NARA, Washington, D.C.

Engle, Stephen D. *Don Carlos Buell: Most Promising of All.* Chapel Hill: University of North Carolina Press, 1999.

Esposito, Vincent J., ed. *The West Point Atlas of American Wars.* Vol. I, *1689–1900.* New York: Frederick A. Praeger, 1962.

Evans, Clement A., ed. *Confederate Military History: A Library of Confederate States History Written by Distinguished Men of the South, and Edited by Gen. Clement A. Evans.* Extended ed., Wilmington, N.C.: Broadfoot Publishing Co., 1987–1989.

Evans, David. *Sherman's Horsemen: Union Cavalry Operations in the Atlanta Campaign.* Bloomington: Indiana University Press, 1996.

Ewing, George, and James Ewing. *The Ewing Family Civil War Letters.* Edited by John T. Greene. East Lansing: Michigan State University Press, 1994.

Ewing, Hugh. Papers. Record Group 94, Adjutant General's Office Records, Generals' Papers, NARA, Washington, D.C.

Ewing, Thomas, Jr. Papers. Record Group 94, Adjutant General's Office Records, Generals' Papers, NARA, Washington, D.C.

Faust, Patricia L., ed. *The Historical Times Illustrated Encyclopedia of the Civil War.* New York: Harper & Row, 1986.

Ferrero, Edward. Papers. Record Group 94, Adjutant General's Office Records, Generals' Papers, NARA, Washington, D.C.

Fishel, Edwin C. *The Secret War for the Union: The Untold Story of Military Intelligence in the Civil War.* Boston: Houghton Mifflin Co., 1996.

Fisk, Wilbur. *Hard Marching Every Day: The Civil War Letters of Private Wilbur Fisk, 1861–1865.* Edited by Emil and Ruth Rosenblatt. Lawrence: University Press of Kansas, 1992.

Fiske, Samuel W. *Mr. Dunn Browne's Experiences in the Army: The Civil War Letters of Samuel W. Fiske.* Edited by Stephen W. Sears. New York: Fordham University Press, 1998.

Fitch, Michael H. *Echoes of the Civil War as I Hear Them.* New York: R. F. Fenno & Co., 1905.

Fitzpatrick, Marion Hill. *Letters to Amanda: The Civil War Letters of Marion Hill Fitzpatrick, Army of Northern Virginia.* Edited by Jeffrey C. Lowe and Sam Hodges. Macon, Ga.: Mercer University Press, 1998.

Flayderman, Norm. *Flayderman's Guide to Antique American Firearms.* 4th ed. Northbrook, Ill.: DBI Books, 1987.

Fletcher, William A. *Rebel Private, Front and Rear: Memoirs of a Confederate Soldier.* New York: Dutton, 1995.

Foote, Andrew Hull. Papers. Author's collection.

Force, Manning F. Papers. Record Group 94, Adjutant General's Office Records, Generals' Papers, NARA, Washington, D.C.

48th Alabama Infantry. Papers. Antietam National Battlefield, Sharpsburg, Md.

47th Alabama Infantry. Papers. Antietam National Battlefield, Sharpsburg, Md.

Foster, John G. Papers. Record Group 94, Adjutant General's Office Records, Generals' Papers, NARA, Washington, D.C.

Fox, Gustavus V. *Confidential Correspondence of Gustavus Vasa Fox, Assistant Secretary of the Navy, 1861–1865.* Edited by Robert Means Thompson and Richard Wainwright. Washington, D.C.: Naval History Society, 1918.

Fox, Tryphena Blanche Holder. *A Northern Woman in the Plantation South: Letters of Tryphena Blanche Holder Fox, 1856–1876.* Edited by Wilma King. Columbia: University of South Carolina Press, 1993.

Fox, William F. *Regimental Losses in the American Civil War, 1861–1865: A Treatise on the Extent and Nature of the Mortuary Losses in the Union Regiments, with Full and Extensive Statistics Compiled from the Official Records on File in the State Military Bureaus and at Washington.* Albany, N.Y.: Albany Publishing Co., 1889.

Frassanito, William A. *Antietam: The Photographic Legacy of America's Bloodiest Day.* New York: Charles Scribner's Sons, 1978.

———. *Early Photography at Gettysburg.* Gettysburg, Pa.: Thomas Publications, 1995.

Freeman, Douglas Southall. *Lee's Lieutenants: A Study in Command.* New York: Charles Scribner's Sons, 1942–1944.

———. *R. E. Lee: A Biography.* New York: Charles Scribner's Sons, 1934–1935.

Fremantle, Arthur J. L. *Three Months in the Southern States, April–June 1863.* Lincoln: University of Nebraska Press, 1991.

French, William H. Papers. Record Group 94, Adjutant General's Office Records, Generals' Papers, NARA, Washington, D.C.

French, Winsor B. Papers. United States Civil War Center, Louisiana State University, Baton Rouge.

Frey, Jerry. *In the Woods Before Dawn: The Samuel Richey Collection of the Southern Confederacy.* Gettysburg, Pa.: Thomas Publications, 1994.

Fuchs, Richard L. *An Unerring Fire: The Massacre at Fort Pillow.* Rutherford, N.J.: Fairleigh Dickinson University Press, 1994.

Fulkerson, Abram. Papers. Virginia Military Institute Library, Lexington.

Fullam, George Townley. *The Journal of George Townley Fullam, Boarding Officer of the Confederate Sea Raider.* Edited by Charles G. Summersell. University, Ala.: University of Alabama Press, 1973.

Furgurson, Ernest B. *Chancellorsville 1863: The Souls of the Brave.* New York: Alfred A. Knopf, 1992.

Futch, Ovid L. *History of Andersonville Prison.* Gainesville: University of Florida Press, 1968.

Gaff, Alan D. *Brave Men's Tears: The Iron Brigade at Brawner Farm.* Dayton, Ohio: Morningside Book Shop, 1988.

————. *If This Is War: A History of the Campaign of Bull's Run by the Wisconsin Regiment Thereafter Known as the Ragged Ass Second.* Dayton, Ohio: Morningside Book Shop, 1991.

Gallagher, Gary W., ed. *Antietam: Essays on the 1862 Maryland Campaign.* Kent, Ohio: Kent State University Press, 1989.

————, ed. *Chancellorsville: The Battle and Its Aftermath.* Chapel Hill: University of North Carolina Press, 1996.

————. *The Confederate War: How Popular Will, Nationalism, and Military Strategy Could Not Stave Off Defeat.* Cambridge, Mass.: Harvard University Press, 1997.

————, ed. *The First Day at Gettysburg: Essays on Union and Confederate Leadership.* Kent, Ohio: Kent State University Press, 1992.

————, ed. *The Fredericksburg Campaign: Decision on the Rappahannock.* Chapel Hill: University of North Carolina Press, 1995.

————, ed. *The Second Day at Gettysburg: Essays on Union and Confederate Leadership.* Kent, Ohio: Kent State University Press, 1993.

————, ed. *The Spotsylvania Campaign.* Chapel Hill: University of North Carolina Press, 1998.

————. *Stephen Dodson Ramseur: Lee's Gallant General.* Chapel Hill: University of North Carolina Press, 1985.

————, ed. *Struggle for the Shenandoah: Essays on the 1864 Valley Campaign.* Kent, Ohio: Kent State University Press, 1991.

————, ed. *The Third Day at Gettysburg and Beyond.* Chapel Hill: University of North Carolina Press, 1994.

————, ed. *The Wilderness Campaign.* Chapel Hill: University of North Carolina Press, 1997.

Gallaway, B. P., ed. *Texas: The Dark Corner of the Confederacy.* 3d ed. Lincoln: University of Nebraska Press, 1994.

Gambone, A. M. *The Life of General Samuel K. Zook.* Baltimore: Butternut & Blue, 1996.

Garfield, James A. *The Wild Life of the Army: Civil War Letters of James A. Garfield.* Edited by Frederick D. Williams. East Lansing: Michigan State University Press, 1964.

———. Papers. Record Group 94, Adjutant General's Office Records, Generals' Papers, NARA, Washington, D.C.

Garfield, James A., and Lucretia Garfield. *Crete and James: Personal Letters of Lucretia and James Garfield.* Edited by John Shaw. East Lansing: Michigan State University Press, 1994.

Garibaldi, John. Papers. Virginia Military Institute Library, Lexington.

Gates, Theodore B. *The Civil War Diaries of Col. Theodore B. Gates, 20th New York State Militia.* Edited by Seward R. Osborne. Hightstown, N.J.: Longstreet House, 1991.

Gatewood, Andrew C. L. Papers. Virginia Military Institute Library, Lexington.

Geary, John White. *A Politician Goes to War: The Civil War Letters of John White Geary.* Edited by William Alan Blair. University Park: Pennsylvania State University Press, 1995.

Getty, George W. Papers. Record Group 94, Adjutant General's Office Records, Generals' Papers, NARA, Washington, D.C.

Gibbon, John. *Personal Recollections of the Civil War.* New York: G. P. Putnam's Sons, 1928.

———. Papers. Record Group 94, Adjutant General's Office Records, Generals' Papers, NARA, Washington, D.C.

Gillmore, Quincy A. Papers. Record Group 94, Adjutant General's Office Records, Generals' Papers, NARA, Washington, D.C.

Glatthaar, Joseph T. *The March to the Sea and Beyond: Sherman's Troops in the Savannah and Carolinas Campaigns.* New York: New York University Press, 1985.

Goff, Richard D. *Confederate Supply.* Durham, N.C.: Duke University Press, 1969.

Good, Timothy S. *We Saw Lincoln Shot: One Hundred Eyewitness Accounts.* Jackson: University Press of Mississippi, 1995.

Gooding, James Henry. *On the Altar of Freedom: A Black Soldier's Civil War Letters from the Front.* Edited by Virginia M. Adams. Amherst: University of Massachusetts Press, 1991.

Gordon, George H. Papers. Record Group 94, Adjutant General's Office Records, Generals' Papers, NARA, Washington, D.C.

Gordon, John B. *Reminiscences of the Civil War.* New York: Charles Scribner's Sons, 1903.

———. Papers. Antietam National Battlefield, Sharpsburg, Md.

Gordon, Lesley J. *General George E. Pickett in Life and Legend.* Chapel Hill: University of North Carolina Press, 1998.

Goree, Thomas J. *Longstreet's Aide: The Civil War Letters of Major Thomas J. Goree.* Edited by Thomas W. Cutrer. Charlottesville: University Press of Virginia, 1995.

Gorgas, Josiah. *The Journals of Josiah Gorgas, 1857–1878.* Edited by Sarah Woolfolk Wiggins. Tuscaloosa: University of Alabama Press, 1995.

Gorman, Willis A. Papers. Record Group 94, Adjutant General's Office Records, Generals' Papers, NARA, Washington, D.C.

Gould, John Mead. *The Civil War Journals of John Mead Gould, 1861–1866.* Edited by William B. Jordan. Baltimore: Butternut & Blue, 1997.

Gracie, Archibald, III. *The Truth About Chickamauga.* Dayton, Ohio: Morningside Book Shop, 1987.

Gragg, Rod. *Confederate Goliath: The Battle of Fort Fisher.* New York: HarperCollins, 1991.

Granger, Robert S. Papers. Record Group 94, Adjutant General's Office Records, Generals' Papers, NARA, Washington, D.C.

Grant, Ulysses S. *The Papers of Ulysses S. Grant.* Edited by John Y. Simon, et al. Carbondale: Southern Illinois University Press, 1967–.

———. *Personal Memoirs of U. S. Grant.* New York: Charles L. Webster & Co., 1885–1886.

———. Papers. Record Group 94, Adjutant General's Office Records, Generals' Papers, NARA, Washington, D.C.

Grant, Ulysses S., III. *Ulysses S. Grant: Warrior and Statesman.* New York: William Morrow & Co., 1969.

Gray, John Chipman, and John Codman Ropes. *War Letters, 1862–1865, of John Chipman Gray and John Codman Ropes.* Edited by Worthington Chauncey Ford. Boston: Houghton Mifflin Co., 1927.

Greene, William B. *Letters from a Sharpshooter: The Civil War Letters of Private William B. Greene, Co. G, 2nd United States Sharpshooters (Berdan's), Army of the Potomac.* Edited by William H. Hastings. Belleville, Wis.: Historic Publications, 1993.

Greenhow, Rose O'Neal. Papers. Duke University Library, Durham, N.C.

Gresham, Walter Q. Papers. Record Group 94, Adjutant General's Office Records, Generals' Papers, NARA, Washington, D.C.

Griffin, James B. *A Gentleman and an Officer: A Military and Social History of James B. Griffin's Civil War.* Edited by Judith N. McArthur and Orville Vernon Burton. New York: Oxford University Press, 1996.

Grimes, Bryan. *Extracts of Letters of Major-General Bryan Grimes, to His Wife, Written While in Active Service in the Army of Northern Virginia, Together with Some Personal Recollections of the War.* Edited by Gary W. Gallagher. Wilmington, N.C.: Broadfoot Publishing Co., 1986.

Grisamore, Silas T. *The Civil War Reminiscences of Major Silas T. Grisamore, C.S.A.* Edited by Arthur Bergeron, Jr. Baton Rouge: Louisiana State University Press, 1993.

Grover, Cuvier. Papers. Record Group 94, Adjutant General's Office Records, Generals' Papers, NARA, Washington, D.C.

Guitar, Odon. Papers. Record Group 94, Adjutant General's Office Records, Generals' Papers, NARA, Washington, D.C.

Haglund, William D., and Marcella H. Sorg, eds. *Forensic Taphonomy: The Postmortem Fate of Human Remains.* Boca Raton, Fla.: CRC Press, 1997.

Hague, Parthenia Antoinette. *A Blockaded Family: Life in Southern Alabama During the Civil War.* Lincoln: University of Nebraska Press, 1993.

Halsey, Thomas J. *Field of Battle: The Civil War Letters of Major Thomas J. Halsey.* Edited by K. M. Kostyal. Washington, D.C.: National Geographic Society, 1996.

Hamilton, Charles S. Papers. Record Group 94, Adjutant General's Office Records, Generals' Papers, NARA, Washington, D.C.

Hamilton, John D. *The Ames Sword Company, 1829–1935.* Lincoln, R.I.: Andrew Mowbray, 1994.

Hamilton, Schuyler. Papers. Record Group 94, Adjutant General's Office Records, Generals' Papers, NARA, Washington, D.C.

Hammond, James Henry. *Secret and Sacred: The Diaries of James Henry Hammond, a Southern Slaveholder.* Edited by Carol Bleser. New York: Oxford University Press, 1988.

Hampton Legion (South Carolina). Papers. Antietam National Battlefield, Sharpsburg, Md.

Hanchett, William. *The Lincoln Murder Conspiracies.* Urbana: University of Illinois Press, 1983.

Hancock, Cornelia. *South After Gettysburg: Letters of Cornelia Hancock, 1863–1868.* Edited by Henrietta Stratton Jaquette. New York: Thomas Y. Crowell Co., 1956.

Hancock, Winfield Scott. Papers. Record Group 94, Adjutant General's Office Records, Generals' Papers, NARA, Washington, D.C.

Hanna, John F. Papers. Virginia Military Institute Library, Lexington.

Harrell, Carolyn L. *When the Bells Tolled for Lincoln: Southern Reaction to the Assassination.* Macon, Ga.: Mercer University Press, 1998.

Harrison, Kathy Georg, and John W. Busey. *Nothing but Glory: Pickett's Division at Gettysburg.* Gettysburg, Pa.: Thomas Publications, 1993.

Harrison, Noel G. *Chancellorsville Battlefield Sites.* Lynchburg, Va.: H. E. Howard Co., 1990.

———. *Fredericksburg Civil War Sites.* Lynchburg, Va.: H. E. Howard Co., 1995.

Harsh, Joseph L. *Taken at the Flood: Robert E. Lee and Confederate Strategy in the Maryland Campaign of 1862.* Kent, Ohio: Kent State University Press, 1999.

Hartje, Robert G. *Van Dorn: The Life and Times of a Confederate General.* Nashville: Vanderbilt University Press, 1967.

Hartley, James J. *The Civil War Letters of the Late 1st Lieut. James J. Hartley, 122nd Ohio Infantry Regiment.* Edited by Garber A. Davidson. Jefferson, N.C.: McFarland & Co., 1998.

Hartsuff, George L. Papers. Record Group 94, Adjutant General's Office Records, Generals' Papers, NARA, Washington, D.C.

Hartwell, John F. L. *To My Beloved Wife and Boy at Home: The Letters and Diaries of Orderly Sergeant John F. L. Hartwell.* Edited by Ann Hartwell Britton and Thomas J. Reed. Madison, N.J.: Fairleigh Dickinson University Press, 1998.

Haskell, Alexander C. *Alexander Cheves Haskell: The Portrait of a Man.* Edited by Louise Haskell Daly. Wilmington, N.C.: Broadfoot Publishing Co., 1989.

———. Papers. Southern Historical Collection, University of North Carolina, Chapel Hill.

Haskell, Frank A. *Haskell of Gettysburg: His Life and Civil War Papers.* Edited by Frank L. Byrne and Andrew T. Weaver. Madison: State Historical Society of Wisconsin, 1970.

Hassler, William Woods. *Colonel John Pelham: Lee's Boy Artillerist.* Chapel Hill: University of North Carolina Press, 1995.

Hattaway, Herman. *General Stephen D. Lee.* Jackson: University Press of Mississippi, 1976.

———. *Shades of Blue and Gray: An Introductory Military History of the Civil War.* Columbia: University of Missouri Press, 1997.

———. "The War Board: The Basis of the United States' First General Staff," in *Military Affairs* XLVI (1982): 1.

Hattaway, Herman, and Archer Jones. *How the North Won: A Military History of the Civil War.* Urbana: University of Illinois Press, 1983.

Hawks, Esther Hill. *A Woman Doctor's Civil War: Esther Hill Hawks's Diary.* Edited by Gerald Schwartz. Columbia: University of South Carolina Press, 1984.

Hay, John M. *Inside Lincoln's White House: The Complete Civil War Diary of John Hay.* Edited by Michael Burlingame and John R. Turner Ettlinger. Carbondale: Southern Illinois University Press, 1998.

———. *Lincoln and the Civil War in the Diaries and Letters of John Hay.* Edited by Tyler Dennett. New York: Dodd, Mead & Co., 1939.

Haydon, Charles B. *For Country, Cause, and Leader: The Civil War Journal of Charles B. Haydon.* Edited by Stephen W. Sears. New York: Ticknor & Fields, 1993.

Haydon, Frederick S. *Aeronautics in the Union and Confederate Armies: With a Survey of Military Aeronautics Prior to 1861.* Baltimore: Johns Hopkins University Press, 1941.

Hayes, Joseph. Papers. Record Group 94, Adjutant General's Office Records, Generals' Papers, NARA, Washington, D.C.

Hays, Alexander. Papers. Record Group 94, Adjutant General's Office Records, Generals' Papers, NARA, Washington, D.C.

Hays, William. Papers. Record Group 94, Adjutant General's Office Records, Generals' Papers, NARA, Washington, D.C.

Hazen, William B. *A Narrative of Military Service.* Boston: Ticknor & Co., 1885.

Headley, Fenwick Y. *Marching Through Georgia: Pen Pictures of Every-Day Life in General Sherman's Army, from the Beginning of the Atlanta Campaign Until the Close of the War.* Chicago: R. R. Donnelly & Sons, 1885.

Headley, John W. *Confederate Operations in Canada and New York.* New York: Neale Publishing Co., 1906.

Hearn, Chester G. *Admiral David Glasgow Farragut: The Civil War Years.* Annapolis, Md.: Naval Institute Press, 1998.

———. *The Capture of New Orleans, 1862.* Baton Rouge: Louisiana State University Press, 1995.

———. *Mobile Bay and the Mobile Campaign: The Last Great Battles of the Civil War.* Jefferson, N.C.: McFarland & Co., 1993.

———. *Six Years of Hell: Harpers Ferry During the Civil War.* Baton Rouge: Louisiana State University Press, 1996.

———. *When the Devil Came Down to Dixie: Ben Butler in New Orleans.* Baton Rouge: Louisiana State University Press, 1997.

Heartsill, W. W. *Fourteen Hundred and 91 Days in the Confederate Army: A Journal Kept by W. W. Heartsill for Four Years, One Month and One Day; or, Camp Life, Day by Day, of the W. P. Lane Rangers from April 19, 1861 to May 20, 1865.* Edited by Bell Irvin Wiley. Wilmington, N.C.: Broadfoot Publishing Co., 1987.

Heintzelman, Samuel P. Papers. Record Group 94, Adjutant General's Office Records, Generals' Papers, NARA, Washington, D.C.

Heitman, Francis B. *Historical Register and Dictionary of the United States Army, from Its Organization, September 29, 1789, to March 2, 1903.* Washington, D.C.: U.S. Government Printing Office, 1903.

Heller, J. Roderick, III, and Carolynn Ayres Heller, eds. *The Confederacy Is on Her Way Up the Spout: Letters to South Carolina, 1861–1864.* Athens: University of Georgia Press, 1992.

Henderson, G. F. R. *The Civil War in the Writings of Col. G. F. R. Henderson, Including, Complete, The Campaign of Fredericksburg.* Edited by Jay Luvaas. New York: Da Capo Press, 1996.

Hennessy, John J. *Return to Bull Run: The Campaign and Battle of Second Manassas.* New York: Simon & Schuster, 1993.

Henry, Robert Selph, ed. *As They Saw Forrest: Some Recollections and Comments of Contemporaries.* Jackson, Tenn.: McCowat-Mercer Press, 1956.

————. *"First with the Most" Forrest.* Indianapolis: Bobbs-Merrill Co., 1944.

Herdegen, Lance J., and William J. K. Beaudot. *In the Bloody Railroad Cut at Gettysburg.* Dayton, Ohio: Morningside Book Shop, 1990.

Herron, Francis J. Papers. Record Group 94, Adjutant General's Office Records, Generals' Papers, NARA, Washington, D.C.

Hesseltine, William Best. *Civil War Prisons: A Study in War Psychology.* Columbus: Ohio State University Press, 1930.

Hewett, Janet B., Noah Andre Trudeau, and Bryce A. Suderow, eds. *Supplement to the Official Records of the Union and Confederate Armies.* Wilmington, N.C.: Broadfoot Publishing Co., 1994–.

Hewitt, Lawrence Lee. *Port Hudson: Confederate Bastion on the Mississippi.* Baton Rouge: Louisiana State University Press, 1987.

Heyward, Pauline DeCaradeuc. *A Confederate Lady Comes of Age: The Journal of Pauline De-Caradeuc Heyward, 1863–1888.* Edited by Mary D. Robertson. Columbia: University of South Carolina Press, 1992.

Higginson, Thomas Wentworth. *Army Life in a Black Regiment.* Edited by Howard Mumford Jones. East Lansing: Michigan State University Press, 1960.

Hill, Daniel Harvey. Papers. U.S. Army Military History Institute, Carlisle, Pa.

Hinze, David C., and Karen Farnham. *The Battle of Carthage: Border War in Southwest Missouri, July 5, 1861.* Campbell, Calif.: Savas Publishing Co., 1997.

Hitchcock, George A. *From Ashby to Andersonville: The Civil War Diary and Reminiscences of Private George A. Hitchcock, 21st Massachusetts Infantry.* Edited by Ronald Watson. Campbell, Calif.: Savas Publishing Co., 1997.

Hitchcock, Henry. *Marching with Sherman: Passages from the Letters and Campaign Diaries of Henry Hitchcock, Major and Assistant Adjutant General of Volunteers, November 1864–May 1865.* Edited by Mark A. DeWolfe Howe. New Haven: Yale University Press, 1927.

Hitchcock, Walter H., ed. *The Intelligence Revolution: A Historical Perspective.* Washington, D.C.: Thirteenth Military History Symposium, U.S. Air Force Academy, Office of Air Force History, 1991.

Hobson, Edward H. Papers. Record Group 94, Adjutant General's Office Records, Generals' Papers, NARA, Washington, D.C.

Hoke, Jacob. *The Great Invasion of 1863; or, General Lee in Pennsylvania.* Gettysburg, Pa.: Stan Clark Military Books, 1992.

Holien, Kim Bernard. *Battle at Ball's Bluff: The Fateful Clash of North and South at Leesburg, Virginia, October 21, 1861.* 3d ed. Leesburg, Va.: Publisher's Press, 1995.

Hollandsworth, James G., Jr. *Pretense of Glory: The Life of General Nathaniel P. Banks.* Baton Rouge: Louisiana State University Press, 1998.

Holmes, Emma. *The Diary of Miss Emma Holmes, 1861–1866.* Edited by John F. Marszalek. Baton Rouge: Louisiana State University Press, 1979.

Holmes, Oliver Wendell, Jr. *Touched with Fire: Civil War Letters and Diary of Oliver Wendell Holmes, Jr., 1861–1864.* Edited by Mark De Wolfe Howe. Cambridge, Mass.: Harvard University Press, 1947.

Holt, Daniel M. *A Surgeon's Civil War: The Letters and Diary of Daniel M. Holt, M.D.* Edited by James M. Greiner, Janet L. Coryell, and James R. Smither. Kent, Ohio: Kent State University Press, 1994.

Holt, David. *A Mississippi Rebel in the Army of Northern Virginia: The Civil War Memoirs of Private Daniel Holt.* Edited by Thomas D. Cockrell and Michael B. Ballard. Baton Rouge: Louisiana State University Press, 1996.

Holzer, Harold. *Dear Mr. Lincoln: Letters to the President.* Reading, Mass.: Addison-Wesley Publishing Co., 1993.

————. *The Lincoln Mailbag: America Writes to the President, 1861–1865.* Carbondale: Southern Illinois University Press, 1998.

Holzman, Robert S. *Adapt or Perish: The Life of General Roger A. Pryor, C.S.A.* Hamden, Conn.: Archon Books, 1976.

Hood, John Bell. *Advance and Retreat: Personal Experiences in the United States and Confederate States Armies.* New Orleans: Hood Orphan Memorial Fund, 1880.

Hooker, Joseph. Papers. Record Group 94, Adjutant General's Office Records, Generals' Papers, NARA, Washington, D.C.

Hopkins, Owen Johnston. *Under the Flag of the Nation: Diaries and Letters of Owen Johnston Hopkins, a Yankee Volunteer in the Civil War.* Edited by Otto F. Bond. Columbus: Ohio State University Press, 1998.

Hopper, George F. Papers. U.S. Army Military History Institute, Carlisle, Pa.

Hotchkiss, Jedediah. *Make Me a Map of the Valley: The Civil War Journal of Stonewall Jackson's Topographer.* Edited by Archie P. McDonald. Dallas: Southern Methodist University Press, 1988.

House, Ellen Renshaw. *A Very Violent Rebel: The Civil War Diary of Ellen Renshaw House.* Edited by Daniel E. Sutherland. Knoxville: University of Tennessee Press, 1996.

Hovey, Alvin P. Papers. Record Group 94, Adjutant General's Office Records, Generals' Papers, NARA, Washington, D.C.

Howard, McHenry. *Recollections of a Maryland Confederate Soldier and Staff Officer Under Johnston, Jackson, and Lee.* Dayton, Ohio: Morningside Book Shop, 1975.

Howard, Oliver O. Papers. Record Group 94, Adjutant General's Office Records, Generals' Papers, NARA, Washington, D.C.

Hudson, Carson O., Jr. *Civil War Williamsburg.* Mechanicsburg, Pa.: Stackpole Books, 1997.

Hughes, Nathaniel Cheairs, Jr. *The Battle of Belmont: Grant Strikes South.* Chapel Hill: University of North Carolina Press, 1991.

————. *Bentonville: The Final Battle of Sherman and Johnston.* Chapel Hill: University of North Carolina Press, 1996.

Hunt, H. Draper. *Hannibal Hamlin of Maine: Lincoln's First Vice-President.* Syracuse: Syracuse University Press, 1969.

Hunt, Henry J. Papers. Record Group 94, Adjutant General's Office Records, Generals' Papers, NARA, Washington, D.C.

Hunt, Roger D., and Jack R. Brown. *Brevet Brigadier Generals in Blue*. Gaithersburg, Md.: Olde Soldier Books, 1990.

Hunter, Alexander. *Johnny Reb and Billy Yank*. New York: Neale Publishing Co., 1905.

Hurlbut, Stephen A. Papers. Record Group 94, Adjutant General's Office Records, Generals' Papers, NARA, Washington, D.C.

Hutson, Charles Woodward. Papers. Southern Historical Collection, University of North Carolina, Chapel Hill.

Jackman, John S. *Diary of a Confederate Soldier: John S. Jackman of the Orphan Brigade*. Edited by William C. Davis. Columbia: University of South Carolina Press, 1990.

Jackson, Mary Anna. *Memoirs of Stonewall Jackson*. Louisville, Ky.: Prentice Press, 1895.

Jackson, Oscar L. *The Colonel's Diary: Journals Kept Before and During the Civil War by the Late Colonel Oscar L. Jackson of New Castle, Pennsylvania, Sometime Commander of the 63 Regiment O.V.I.* Privately printed, [1922].

Jackson, Thomas J. Papers. Virginia Historical Society, Richmond.

―――. Papers. Virginia Military Institute Library, Lexington.

James, Frederic Augustus. *Frederic Augustus James's Civil War Diary: Sumter to Andersonville*. Edited by Jefferson J. Hammer. Rutherford, N.J.: Fairleigh Dickinson University Press, 1973.

Jamieson, Perry D. *Death in September: The Antietam Campaign*. Fort Worth, Tex.: Ryan Place Publishers, 1996.

Jessup, Harlan R. *The Painful News I Have to Write: Letters and Diaries of Four Hite Brothers of Page County in the Service of the Confederacy*. Baltimore: Butternut & Blue, 1998.

Johannsen, Robert W. *Stephen A. Douglas*. New York: Oxford University Press, 1973.

Johnson, Adam Rankin. *The Partisan Rangers of the Confederate States Army*. Louisville, Ky.: G. G. Fetter, 1904.

Johnson, Andrew. *The Papers of Andrew Johnson*. Edited by LeRoy P. Graf, Ralph W. Haskins, and Paul H. Bergeron. Knoxville: University of Tennessee Press, 1967–.

Johnson, Charles F. *The Long Roll*. East Aurora, N.Y.: Roycrofters, 1911.

Johnson, Curt, and Richard C. Anderson, Jr. *Artillery Hell: The Employment of Artillery at Antietam*. College Station: Texas A&M University Press, 1995.

Johnson, Ludwell H. *Red River Campaign: Politics and Cotton in the Civil War*. Kent, Ohio: Kent State University Press, 1993.

Johnson, Mortimer. Papers. Virginia Military Institute Library, Lexington.

Johnson, Porter. Papers. Virginia Military Institute Library, Lexington.

Johnson, Richard W. Papers. Record Group 94, Adjutant General's Office Records, Generals' Papers, NARA, Washington, D.C.

Johnson, Robert Underwood, and Clarence Clough Buel, eds. *Battles and Leaders of the Civil War, Being for the Most Part Contributions by Union and Confederate Officers: Based upon "The Century" War Series*. New York: Century Co., 1887–1888.

Johnson, William H. Papers. South Caroliniana Library, University of South Carolina, Columbia.

Johnston, Joseph E. *A Narrative of Military Operations Directed, During the Late War Between the States, by Joseph E. Johnston.* Bloomington: Indiana University Press, 1959.

Johnston, William Preston. *The Life of Gen. Albert Sidney Johnston, Embracing His Services in the Armies of the United States, the Republic of Texas, and the Confederate States.* New York: D. Appleton & Co., 1878.

Jones, Archer. *Civil War Command and Strategy: The Process of Victory and Defeat.* New York: Free Press, 1992.

Jones, Howard. *Union in Peril: The Crisis over British Intervention in the Civil War.* Chapel Hill: University of North Carolina Press, 1992.

Jones, James Pickett. *Yankee Blitzkrieg: Wilson's Raid Through Alabama and Georgia.* Athens: University of Georgia Press, 1987.

Jones, John B. *A Rebel War Clerk's Diary at the Confederate States Capital.* Philadelphia: J. B. Lippincott & Co., 1866.

Jordan, Thomas, and J. P. Pryor. *The Campaigns of Lieut.–Gen. N. B. Forrest, and of Forrest's Cavalry.* New Orleans: Blelock & Co., 1868.

Kahn, David. *The Codebreakers: The Story of Secret Writing.* New York: Macmillan Co., 1967.

Kean, Robert Garlick Hill. *Inside the Confederate Government: The Diary of Robert Garlick Hill Kean.* Edited by Edward Younger. Baton Rouge: Louisiana State University Press, 1993.

Kearny, Philip. Papers. Record Group 94, Adjutant General's Office Records, Generals' Papers, NARA, Washington, D.C.

Keeler, William F. *Aboard the USS Florida, 1863–65: The Letters of Paymaster William Frederick Keeler, U.S. Navy, to His Wife, Anna.* Edited by Robert W. Daly. Annapolis, Md.: U.S. Naval Institute, 1968.

————. *Aboard the USS Monitor, 1862: The Letters of Acting Paymaster William Frederick Keeler, U.S. Navy, to His Wife, Anna.* Edited by Robert W. Daly. Annapolis, Md.: U.S. Naval Institute, 1964.

Kenly, John R. Papers. Record Group 94, Adjutant General's Office Records, Generals' Papers, NARA, Washington, D.C.

Kennedy, Joseph C. G. *Preliminary Report on the Eighth Census, 1860.* Washington, D.C.: U.S. Government Printing Office, 1862.

Kersh, Adam W. Papers. University of Virginia Valley of the Shadow Project Archive, Charlottesville.

Ketcham, William S. Papers. Record Group 94, Adjutant General's Office Records, Generals' Papers, NARA, Washington, D.C.

Kimball, Nathan. Papers. Record Group 94, Adjutant General's Office Records, Generals' Papers, NARA, Washington, D.C.

Kinard, Jeff. *The Battle of the Crater.* Fort Worth, Tex.: Ryan Place Publishers, 1995.

King, Spencer B., Jr. *Darien: The Death and Rebirth of a Southern Town.* Macon, Ga.: Mercer University Press, 1981.

King, William C., and W. P. Derby, eds. *Camp-Fire Sketches and Battle-Field Echoes of the Rebellion.* Springfield, Mass.: W. C. King & Co., 1887.

Klein, Maury. *Days of Defiance: Sumter, Secession, and the Coming of the Civil War.* New York: Alfred A. Knopf, 1997.

Knauss, William H. *The Story of Camp Chase: A History of the Prison and its Cemetery, Together with Other Cemeteries Where Confederate Prisoners Are Buried, etc.* Columbus, Ohio: The General's Books, 1994.

Krick, Robert K. *Conquering the Valley: Stonewall Jackson at Port Republic.* New York: William Morrow & Co., 1996.

————. *Stonewall Jackson at Cedar Mountain.* University of Chapel Hill: North Carolina Press, 1990.

Kunhardt, Philip B., Jr. *A New Birth of Freedom: Lincoln at Gettysburg.* Boston: Little, Brown & Co., 1983.

Lamson, Roswell H. *Lamson of the* Gettysburg: *The Civil War Letters of Lieutenant Roswell H. Lamson, U.S. Navy.* Edited by James M. McPherson and Patricia R. McPherson. New York: Oxford University Press, 1997.

Lander, Frederick W. Papers. Record Group 94, Adjutant General's Office Records, Generals' Papers, NARA, Washington, D.C.

Langhorne, J. Kent. Papers. Virginia Military Institute Library, Lexington.

Lauderdale, John Vance. *The Wounded River: The Civil War Letters of John Vancè Lauderdale, M.D.* Edited by Peter Josyph. East Lansing: Michigan State University Press, 1993.

Lawrence, Eugene. "Grant on the Battle-Field," in *Harper's New Monthly Magazine* XXXIX (1869).

Lea, George S. Papers. U.S. Army Military History Institute, Carlisle, Pa.

Leckie, William H., and Shirley A. Leckie. *Unlikely Warriors: General Benjamin Grierson and His Family.* Norman: University of Oklahoma Press, 1984.

LeConte, Emma. *When the World Ended: The Diary of Emma LeConte.* Edited by Earl Schenck Miers. Lincoln: University of Nebraska Press, 1987.

LeConte, Joseph. *'Ware Sherman: A Journal of Three Months' Personal Experience in the Last Days of the Confederacy.* Baton Rouge: Louisiana State University Press, 1999.

Ledlie, James H. Papers. Record Group 94, Adjutant General's Office Records, Generals' Papers, NARA, Washington, D.C.

Le Duc, William G. *Recollections of a Civil War Quartermaster: The Autobiography of William G. Le Duc.* St. Paul, Minn.: North Central Publishing Co., 1963.

Lee, Albert L. Papers. Record Group 94, Adjutant General's Office Records, Generals' Papers, NARA, Washington, D.C.

Lee, Elizabeth Blair. *Wartime Washington: The Civil War Letters of Elizabeth Blair Lee.* Edited by Virginia Jeans Laas. Urbana: University of Illinois Press, 1991.

Lee, Robert E. *Lee's Dispatches: Unpublished Letters of General Robert E. Lee, C.S.A., to Jefferson Davis and the War Department of the Confederate States of America, 1862–1865, from the Private Collection of Wymberley Jones de Renne, of Wormsloe, Georgia.* Edited by Douglas Southall Freeman. New York: G. P. Putnam's Sons, 1915.

————. *The Wartime Papers of R. E. Lee.* Edited by Clifford Dowdey and Louis H. Manarin. Boston: Little, Brown & Co., 1961.

————. Papers. Boston Public Library, Boston, Mass.

————. Papers. U.S. Army Military History Institute, Carlisle, Pa.

————. Papers. Virginia Historical Society, Richmond.

Lee, Robert E., Jr. *Recollections and Letters of General Robert E. Lee.* Garden City, N.Y.: Garden City Publishing Co., 1926.

Leggett, Mortimer D. Papers. Record Group 94, Adjutant General's Office Records, Generals' Papers, NARA, Washington, D.C.

LeGrand, Julia. *The Journal of Julia LeGrand: New Orleans, 1862–1863.* Edited by Kate Mason Rowland and Mrs. Morris L. Croxall. Richmond: Everett Waddey Co., 1911.

Leonard, Elizabeth D. *All the Daring of the Soldier: Women of the Civil War Armies.* New York: W. W. Norton & Co., 1999.

Leslie, Edward E. *The Devil Knows How to Ride: The True Story of William Clarke Quantrill and His Confederate Raiders.* New York: Random House, 1996.

Leuschner, Charles A. *The Civil War Diary of Charles A. Leuschner.* Edited by Charles D. Spurlin. Austin, Tex.: Eakin Press, 1992.

Lewis, Charles Lee. *David Glasgow Farragut.* Annapolis, Md.: U.S. Naval Institute, 1941.

Lewis, Lloyd. *Myths After Lincoln.* New York: Harcourt, Brace & Co., 1929.

Lincoln, Abraham. *The Collected Works of Abraham Lincoln.* Edited by Roy P. Basler. New Brunswick: Rutgers University Press, and Westport, Conn.: Greenwood Press, 1953–1990.

———. Assassination Papers. Record Group 94, TR 11, Special File 14, D776, NARA, Washington, D.C.

———. Papers. Duke University Library, Durham, N.C.

Livermore, Thomas L. *Days and Events, 1860–1866.* Boston: Houghton Mifflin Co., 1920.

Logan, David Jackson. *"A Rising Star of Promise": The Civil War Odyssey of David Jackson Logan, 17th South Carolina Volunteers, 1861–1864.* Edited by Samuel N. Thomas, Jr., and Jason H. Silverman. Campbell, Calif.: Savas Publishing Co., 1998.

Long, A. L., and Marcus J. Wright. *Memoirs of Robert E. Lee: His Military and Personal History, Embracing a Large Amount of Information Hitherto Unpublished.* New York: J. M. Stoddart & Co., 1886.

Long, E. B., and Barbara Long. *The Civil War Day by Day: An Almanac, 1861–1865.* Garden City, N.Y.: Doubleday & Co., 1971.

Longacre, Edward G. *Army of Amateurs: General Benjamin F. Butler and the Army of the James, 1863–1865.* Mechanicsburg, Pa.: Stackpole Books, 1997.

Longstreet, James. *From Manassas to Appomattox: Memoirs of the Civil War in America.* Philadelphia: J. B. Lippincott Co., 1896.

Loughborough, Mary Ann. *My Cave Life in Vicksburg, with Letters of Trial and Travel.* Wilmington, N.C.: Broadfoot Publishing Co., 1989.

Lowry, Terry. *Last Sleep: The Battle of Droop Mountain, November 6, 1863.* Charleston, W. Va.: Pictorial Histories Publishing Co., 1996.

Lucas, Marion Brunson. *Sherman and the Burning of Columbia.* College Station: Texas A&M University Press, 1976.

Lusk, William Thompson. *War Letters of William Thompson Lusk, Captain, Assistant Adjutant-General United States Volunteers, 1861–1863.* New York: Privately printed, 1911.

Lyman, Darryl. *Civil War Quotations: Including Slogans, Battle Cries, and Speeches.* Conshohocken, Pa.: Combined Publishing, 1995.

Lyman, Theodore. *Meade's Headquarters, 1863–1865: Letters of Colonel Theodore Lyman from the Wilderness to Appomattox.* Edited by George R. Agassiz. Boston: Atlantic Monthly Press, 1922.

Lytle, William H. *For Honor, Glory, and Union: The Mexican and Civil War Letters of Brig. Gen. William Haines Lytle.* Edited by Ruth C. Carter. Lexington: University Press of Kentucky, 1999.

———. Papers. Record Group 94, Adjutant General's Office Records, Generals' Papers, NARA, Washington, D.C.

Malone, Bartlett Yancey. *Whipt 'Em Everytime: The Diary of Bartlett Yancey Malone, Co. H, 6th N.C. Regiment.* Edited by William Whatley Pierson. Wilmington, N.C.: Broadfoot Publishing Co., 1991.

Malone, Dumas. *The Sage of Monticello.* Boston: Little, Brown & Co., 1981.

Manigault, Edward. *Siege Train: The Journal of a Confederate Artilleryman in the Defense of Charleston.* Edited by Warren Ripley. Columbia: University of South Carolina Press, 1986.

Mansfield, Joseph King Fenno. Papers. Antietam National Battlefield, Sharpsburg, Md.

Marius, Richard, ed. *The Columbia Book of Civil War Poetry from Whitman to Walcott.* New York: Columbia University Press, 1994.

Mark, Penrose G. *Red, White, and Blue Badge, Pennsylvania Veteran Volunteers: A History of the 93rd Regiment, Known as the "Lebanon Infantry" and "One of the 300 Fighting Regiments" from September 12th, 1861 to June 27th, 1865.* Baltimore: Butternut & Blue, 1993.

Marlin, Sidney. Papers. Virginia Military Institute Library, Lexington.

Marshall, Charles. *An Aide-de-Camp of Lee: Being the Papers of Colonel Charles Marshall, Sometime Aide-de-Camp, Military Secretary, and Assistant Adjutant General on the Staff of Robert E. Lee, 1862–1865.* Edited by Frederick Maurice. Boston: Little, Brown & Co., 1927.

Marszalek, John F. *Sherman: A Soldier's Passion for Order.* New York: Free Press, 1993.

Martin, David G. *Gettysburg, July 1.* Rev. ed. Conshohocken, Pa.: Combined Books, 1996.

Marvel, William. *Andersonville: The Last Depot.* Chapel Hill: University of North Carolina Press, 1994.

———. *Burnside.* Chapel Hill: University of North Carolina Press, 1991.

Massey, Mary Elizabeth. *Ersatz in the Confederacy: Shortages and Substitutions on the Southern Homefront.* Columbia: University of South Carolina Press, 1952.

Masur, Louis P., ed. *The Real War Will Never Get in the Books: Selections from Writers During the Civil War.* New York: Oxford University Press, 1993.

Matrau, Henry. *Letters Home: Henry Matrau of the Iron Brigade.* Edited by Marcia Reid-Green. Lincoln: University of Nebraska Press, 1993.

Matter, William D. *If It Takes All Summer: The Battle of Spotsylvania.* Chapel Hill: University of North Carolina Press, 1988.

Matthies, Charles L. Papers. Record Group 94, Adjutant General's Office Records, Generals' Papers, NARA, Washington, D.C.

Mattocks, Charles. *"Unspoiled Heart": The Journal of Charles Mattocks of the 17th Maine.* Edited by Philip N. Racine. Knoxville: University of Tennessee Press, 1994.

McAllister, Robert. *The Civil War Letters of General Robert McAllister.* Edited by James I. Robertson, Jr. Baton Rouge: Louisiana State University Press, 1998.

McArthur, John. Papers. Record Group 94, Adjutant General's Office Records, Generals' Papers, NARA, Washington, D.C.

McAuley, John D. *Civil War Pistols of the Union.* Lincoln, R.I.: Andrew Mowbray, 1992.

McCain, Thomas Hart Benton. *In Song and Sorrow: The Daily Journal of Thomas Hart Benton McCain of the Eighty-Sixth Indiana Volunteer Infantry.* Edited by Richard K. Rue and Geraldine M. Rue. Carmel: Guild Press of Indiana, 1998.

McCall, George A. Papers. Record Group 94, Adjutant General's Office Records, Generals' Papers, NARA, Washington, D.C.

McCarthy, Carlton. *Detailed Minutiae of Soldier Life in the Army of Northern Virginia, 1861–1865.* Richmond: C. McCarthy, 1882.

McClellan, George. *The Civil War Papers of George B. McClellan: Selected Correspondence, 1860–1865.* Edited by Stephen W. Sears. New York: Ticknor & Fields, 1989.

————. Papers. Record Group 94, Adjutant General's Office Records, Generals' Papers, NARA, Washington, D.C.

McClernand, John A. Papers. Record Group 94, Adjutant General's Office Records, Generals' Papers, NARA, Washington, D.C.

McClure, Alexander K., ed. *The Annals of the War Written by Leading Participants North and South: Originally Published in the Philadelphia* Weekly Times. Philadelphia: Times Publishing Co., 1879.

————. *Lincoln and Men of War-Times: Some Personal Recollections of War and Politics During the Lincoln Administration.* Philadelphia: Times Publishing Co., 1892.

McCook, Alexander M. Papers. Record Group 94, Adjutant General's Office Records, Generals' Papers, NARA, Washington, D.C.

McCook, Edward M. Papers. Record Group 94, Adjutant General's Office Records, Generals' Papers, NARA, Washington, D.C.

McCorkle, John. *Three Years with Quantrill: A True Story as Told by His Scout John McCorkle.* Edited by O. S. Barton. Norman: University of Oklahoma Press, 1992.

McDonald, Cornelia Peake. *A Woman's Civil War: A Diary, with Reminiscences of the War, from March 1862.* Edited by Minrose C. Gwin. Madison: University of Wisconsin Press, 1992.

McDonough, James Lee. *Chattanooga: A Death Grip on the Confederacy.* Knoxville: University of Tennessee Press, 1984.

————. *Stones River: Bloody Winter in Tennessee.* Knoxville: University of Tennessee Press, 1980.

————. *War in Kentucky: From Shiloh to Perryville.* Knoxville: University of Tennessee Press, 1994.

McElroy, John. *Andersonville: A Story of Rebel Military Prisons.* Toledo, Ohio: D. R. Locke, 1879.

McGuire, Hunter Holmes. Papers. Virginia Historical Society, Richmond.

McGuire, Judith W. *Diary of a Southern Refugee During the War.* New York: E. J. Hale & Son, 1867.

McIntosh, John B. Papers. Record Group 94, Adjutant General's Office Records, Generals' Papers, NARA, Washington, D.C.

McKinney, Francis F. *Education in Violence: The Life of George H. Thomas and the History of the Army of the Cumberland.* Chicago: Americana House, 1991.

McKinstry, Justis. Papers. Record Group 94, Adjutant General's Office Records, Generals' Papers, NARA, Washington, D.C.

McLean, James L. *Cutler's Brigade at Gettysburg*. Baltimore: Butternut & Blue, 1994.

———, and Judy McLean, eds. *Gettysburg Sources*. Baltimore: Butternut & Blue, 1987.

McNeil, John. Papers. Record Group 94, Adjutant General's Office Records, Generals' Papers, NARA, Washington, D.C.

McPherson, James B. Papers. Record Group 94, Adjutant General's Office Records, Generals' Papers, NARA, Washington, D.C.

McPherson, James M. *Battle Cry of Freedom: The Civil War Era*. New York: Oxford University Press, 1988.

———. *Ordeal by Fire: The Civil War and Reconstruction*. New York: Alfred A. Knopf, 1982.

McWhiney, Grady. *Battle in the Wilderness: Grant Meets Lee*. Fort Worth, Tex.: Ryan Place Publishers, 1995.

———. *Braxton Bragg and Confederate Defeat*. Vol. I, *Field Command*. New York: Columbia University Press, 1969.

Meade, George G. Papers. Record Group 94, Adjutant General's Office Records, Generals' Papers, NARA, Washington, D.C.

Meade, George G., and George G. Meade, Jr. *The Life and Letters of George Gordon Meade, Major General United States Army*. Edited by George G. Meade III. New York: Charles Scribner's Sons, 1913.

Meagher, Thomas F. Papers. Record Group 94, Adjutant General's Office Records, Generals' Papers, NARA, Washington, D.C.

Meneely, Alexander Howard. *The War Department 1861: A Study in Mobilization and Administration*. New York: Columbia University Press, 1928.

Mercer, Philip. *The Gallant Pelham*. Wilmington, N.C.: Broadfoot Publishing Co., 1995.

Meredith, Solomon. Papers. Record Group 94, Adjutant General's Office Records, Generals' Papers, NARA, Washington, D.C.

Merington, Marguerite, ed. *The Custer Story: The Life and Intimate Letters of General Custer and His Wife Elizabeth*. New York: Devin-Adair Co., 1950.

Merrill, Lewis. Papers. Record Group 94, Adjutant General's Office Records, Generals' Papers, NARA, Washington, D.C.

Miers, Earl Schenck, ed. *Lincoln Day by Day: A Chronology, 1809–1865*. Washington, D.C.: Lincoln Sesquicentennial Commission, 1960.

Miles, John S. Papers. U.S. Army Military History Institute, Carlisle, Pa.

Military Order of the Loyal Legion of the United States. *Papers of the Military Order of the Loyal Legion of the United States, 1887–1915*. Wilmington, N.C.: Broadfoot Publishing Co., 1991–1997.

Miller, Jacob D. Papers. University of Virginia Valley of the Shadow Project Archive, Charlottesville.

Miller, William J., ed. *The Peninsula Campaign of 1862: Yorktown to the Seven Days*. Campbell, Calif.: Savas Publishing Co., 1997.

Milroy, Robert H. Papers. Record Group 94, Adjutant General's Office Records, Generals' Papers, NARA, Washington, D.C.

Minor, Hubbard T. Papers. U.S. Army Military History Institute, Carlisle, Pa.

Monnett, Howard N. *Action Before Westport, 1864.* Niwot: University Press of Colorado, 1995.

Montgomery, William R. Papers. Record Group 94, Adjutant General's Office Records, Generals' Papers, NARA, Washington, D.C.

Moore, Frank, ed. *The Rebellion Record: A Diary of American Events, with Documents, Narratives, Illustrative Incidents, Poetry, etc.* New York: G. P. Putnam's Sons, 1861–1863, and New York: D. Van Nostrand Co., 1864–1868; supplemental volume, New York: G. P. Putnam's Sons and Henry Holt, 1864.

Moore, Mark. *Moore's Historical Guide to the Wilmington Campaign and the Battles for Fort Fisher.* Mason City, Iowa: Savas Publishing Co., 1999.

Morris, Roy, Jr. *Sheridan: The Life and Wars of General Phil Sheridan.* New York: Crown Publishers, 1992.

Mosby, John S. *The Memoirs of Colonel John S. Mosby.* Edited by Charles Wells Russell. Bloomington: Indiana University Press, 1959.

Mosgrove, George Dallas. *Kentucky Cavaliers in Dixie: The Reminiscences of a Confederate Cavalryman.* Edited by Bell Irvin Wiley. Wilmington, N.C.: Broadfoot Publishing Co., 1991.

Mosher, Charles. *Charlie Mosher's Civil War: From Fair Oaks to Andersonville with the Plymouth Pilgrims (85th New York Infantry).* Edited by Wayne Mahood. Hightstown, N.J.: Longstreet House, 1994.

Mowbray, Stuart C., and Jennifer Heroux, eds. *Civil War Arms Makers and Their Contracts: A Facsimile Reprint of the Report by the Commission on Ordnance and Ordnance Stores, 1862.* Lincoln, R.I.: Andrew Mowbray, 1998.

Mower, Joseph A. Papers. Record Group 94, Adjutant General's Office Records, Generals' Papers, NARA, Washington, D.C.

Murfin, James V. *The Gleam of Bayonets: The Battle of Antietam and Robert E. Lee's Maryland Campaign, September 1862.* New York: Thomas Yoseloff Co., 1965.

Musser, Charles O. *Soldier Boy: The Civil War Letters of Charles O. Musser, 29th Iowa.* Edited by Barry Popchock. Iowa City: University of Iowa Press, 1995.

Myer, Albert J. *A Manual of Signals: For the Use of Signal Officers in the Field.* New ed. New York: D. Van Nostrand Co., 1868.

Myers, Derastus E. W. Papers. Virginia Military Institute Library, Lexington.

Nagle, James. Papers. Record Group 94, Adjutant General's Office Records, Generals' Papers, NARA, Washington, D.C.

Naglee, Henry M. Papers. Record Group 94, Adjutant General's Office Records, Generals' Papers, NARA, Washington, D.C.

Neely, Mark E., Jr. *The Abraham Lincoln Encyclopedia.* New York: McGraw-Hill, 1982.

Nelson, William. Papers. Record Group 94, Adjutant General's Office Records, Generals' Papers, NARA, Washington, D.C.

Nesbitt, Mark. *Saber and Scapegoat: J. E. B. Stuart and the Gettysburg Controversy.* Mechanicsburg, Pa.: Stackpole Books, 1994.

Newell, Clayton R. *Lee vs. McClellan: The First Campaign.* Washington, D.C.: Regnery Publishing, 1996.

Newton, James K. *A Wisconsin Boy in Dixie: Civil War Letters of James K. Newton.* Edited by Stephen E. Ambrose. Madison: University of Wisconsin Press, 1961.

Newton, John. Papers. Record Group 94, Adjutant General's Office Records, Generals' Papers, NARA, Washington, D.C.

Nichols, George W. *The Story of the Great March from the Diary of a Staff Officer.* New York: Harper & Brothers, 1865.

Nisbet, James Cooper. *Four Years on the Firing Line.* Wilmington, N.C.: Broadfoot Publishing Co., 1991.

North, S. W. Papers. University of Virginia Valley of the Shadow Project Archive, Charlottesville.

Norton, Oliver W. *Army Letters, 1861–1865.* Chicago: Oliver W. Norton, 1903.

———. *The Attack and Defense of Little Round Top, Gettysburg, July 2, 1863.* Dayton, Ohio: Morningside Book Shop, 1983.

Nulty, William H. *Confederate Florida: The Road to Olustee.* Tuscaloosa: University of Alabama Press, 1990.

Nye, Wilbur Sturtevant. *Here Come the Rebels!* Dayton, Ohio: Morningside Book Shop, 1988.

Oates, Stephen B. *To Purge This Land with Blood: A Biography of John Brown.* New York: Harper & Row, 1970.

Oglesby, Richard J. Papers. Record Group 94, Adjutant General's Office Records, Generals' Papers, NARA, Washington, D.C.

Osborn, Thomas Ward. *The Fiery Trail: A Union Officer's Account of Sherman's Last Campaigns.* Edited by Richard Harwell and Philip N. Racine. Knoxville: University of Tennessee Press, 1986.

———. *No Middle Ground: Thomas Ward Osborn's Letters from the Field (1862–1864).* Edited by Herb S. Crumb and Katherine Dhalle. Hamilton, N.Y.: Edmondston Publishing Co., 1993.

Owen, Joshua T. Papers. Record Group 94, Adjutant General's Office Records, Generals' Papers, NARA, Washington, D.C.

Paine, Eleazer A. Papers. Record Group 94, Adjutant General's Office Records, Generals' Papers, NARA, Washington, D.C.

Paine, Halbert E. Papers. Record Group 94, Adjutant General's Office Records, Generals' Papers, NARA, Washington, D.C.

Palfrey, Francis Winthrop. *The Antietam and Fredericksburg.* New York: Charles Scribner's Sons, 1882.

Palmer, John M. Papers. Record Group 94, Adjutant General's Office Records, Generals' Papers, NARA, Washington, D.C.

Parks, Joseph H. *General Edmund Kirby Smith, C.S.A.* Baton Rouge: Louisiana State University Press, 1954.

———. *General Leonidas Polk, C.S.A.: The Fighting Bishop.* Baton Rouge: Louisiana State University Press, 1962.

Patrick, Marsena R. *Inside Lincoln's Army: The Diary of General Marsena Rudolph Patrick, Provost Marshal General, Army of the Potomac.* Edited by David S. Sparks. New York: A. S. Barnes & Co., 1964.

———. Papers. Record Group 94, Adjutant General's Office Records, Generals' Papers, NARA, Washington, D.C.

Patrick, Robert. *Reluctant Rebel: The Secret Diary of Robert Patrick, 1861–1865.* Edited by F. Jay Taylor. Baton Rouge: Louisiana State University Press, 1959.

Paul, Gabriel R. Papers. Record Group 94, Adjutant General's Office Records, Generals' Papers, NARA, Washington, D.C.

Pearson, Elizabeth Ware, ed. *Letters from Port Royal, 1862–1868.* Boston: W. B. Clarke Co., 1906.

Pease, William H., and Jane H. Pease. *James Louis Petigru: Southern Conservative, Southern Dissenter.* Athens: University of Georgia Press, 1995.

Pember, Phoebe Yates. *A Southern Woman's Story: Life in Confederate Richmond.* Edited by Bell Irvin Wiley. Wilmington, N.C.: Broadfoot Publishing Co., 1991.

Pender, William Dorsey. *One of Lee's Best Men: The Civil War Letters of General William Dorsey Pender.* Edited by William W. Hassler. Chapel Hill: University of North Carolina Press, 1999.

Pfanz, Donald C. *Richard S. Ewell: A Soldier's Life.* Chapel Hill: University of North Carolina Press, 1998.

Pfanz, Harry W. *Gettysburg: Culp's Hill and Cemetery Hill.* Chapel Hill: University of North Carolina Press, 1993.

———. *Gettysburg: The Second Day.* Chapel Hill: University of North Carolina Press, 1987.

Phillips, Christopher. *Damned Yankee: The Life of General Nathaniel Lyon.* Columbia: University of Missouri Press, 1990.

Phisterer, Frederick. *Statistical Record of the Armies of the United States.* New York: Charles Scribner's Sons, 1883.

Pickenpaugh, Roger. *Rescue by Rail: Troop Transfer and the Civil War in the West, 1863.* Lincoln: University of Nebraska Press, 1998.

Pierson, David; Reuben Allen Pierson; and James Pierson. *Brothers in Gray: The Civil War Letters of the Pierson Family.* Edited by Thomas W. Cutrer and T. Michael Parrish. Baton Rouge: Louisiana State University Press, 1997.

Piston, William Garrett. *Carter's Raid: An Episode of the Civil War in East Tennessee.* Johnson City, Tenn.: Overmountain Press, 1989.

Pitman, Benn, ed. *The Assassination of President Lincoln and the Trial of the Conspirators.* Cincinnati: Moore, Wilstach & Baldwin, 1865.

Pleasonton, Alfred. Papers. Record Group 94, Adjutant General's Office Records, Generals' Papers, NARA, Washington, D.C.

Plum, William R. *The Military Telegraph During the Civil War in the United States, with an Exposition of Ancient and Modern Means of Communication, and of the Federal and Confederate Cipher Systems: Also, a Running Account of the War Between the States.* Chicago: Jansen, McClurg & Co., 1882.

Plummer, Joseph B. Papers. Record Group 94, Adjutant General's Office Records, Generals' Papers, NARA, Washington, D.C.

Poague, William T. *Gunner with Stonewall: Reminiscences of William Thomas Poague.* Wilmington, N.C.: Broadfoot Publishing Co., 1989.

Pollard, Edward A. *The Lost Cause: A New Southern History of the War of the Confederates.* Baltimore: E. B. Treat & Co., 1866.

Pond, George E. *The Shenandoah Valley in 1864.* New York: Charles Scribner's Sons, 1883.

Pope, John. Papers. Record Group 94, Adjutant General's Office Records, Generals' Papers, NARA, Washington, D.C.

Porter, Horace. *Campaigning with Grant.* Bloomington: Indiana University Press, 1961.

Power, J. Tracy. *Lee's Miserables: Life in the Army of Northern Virginia from the Wilderness to Appomattox.* Chapel Hill: University of North Carolina Press, 1998.

Prentiss, Benjamin M. Papers. Record Group 94, Adjutant General's Office Records, Generals' Papers, NARA, Washington, D.C.

Price, Thomas L. Papers. Record Group 94, Adjutant General's Office Records, Generals' Papers, NARA, Washington, D.C.

Priest, John Michael. *Antietam: The Soldier's Battle.* Shippensburg, Pa.: White Mane Publishing Co., 1989.

————. *Before Antietam: The Battle for South Mountain.* New York: Oxford University Press, 1996.

Prince, Henry. Papers. Record Group 94, Adjutant General's Office Records, Generals' Papers, NARA, Washington, D.C.

Pryor, Roger Atkinson, Compiled Service Record. Record Group 109, General and Staff Officers' Papers, M331, Roll 204, NARA, Washington, D.C.

Pryor, Sara. *My Day: Reminiscences of a Long Life.* New York: Macmillan Co., 1909.

Putnam, George Haven. *A Prisoner of War in Virginia, 1864–5.* New York: G. P. Putnam's Sons, 1912.

Putnam, Sallie. *Richmond During the War: Four Years of Personal Observation.* New York: G. W. Carleton & Co., 1877.

Quinby, Isaac F. Papers. Record Group 94, Adjutant General's Office Records, Generals' Papers, NARA, Washington, D.C.

Raab, James W. *W. W. Loring: Florida's Forgotten General.* Manhattan, Kans.: Sunflower University Press, 1996.

Raines, Rebecca Robbins. *Getting the Message Through: A Branch History of the U.S. Army Signal Corps.* Washington, D.C.: Center of Military History, 1996.

Ramage, James A. *Rebel Raider: The Life of General John Hunt Morgan.* Lexington: University Press of Kentucky, 1986.

Ramseur, Stephen D. Papers. University of Virginia Valley of the Shadow Project Archive, Charlottesville.

Ransom, John. *John Ransom's Andersonville Diary.* Middlebury, Vt.: Paul S. Eriksson, 1986.

Raum, Green Berry. Papers. Record Group 94, Adjutant General's Office Records, Generals' Papers, NARA, Washington, D.C.

Reardon, Carol. *Pickett's Charge in History and Memory.* Chapel Hill: University of North Carolina Press, 1997.

Reid, James Henry. Papers. Virginia Military Institute Library, Lexington.

Reno, Jesse L. Papers. Record Group 94, Adjutant General's Office Records, Generals' Papers, NARA, Washington, D.C.

Revere, Joseph W. Papers. Record Group 94, Adjutant General's Office Records, Generals' Papers, NARA, Washington, D.C.

Reynolds, John F. Papers. Record Group 94, Adjutant General's Office Records, Generals' Papers, NARA, Washington, D.C.

Rhea, Gordon C. *The Battle of the Wilderness, May 5–6, 1864.* Baton Rouge: Louisiana State University Press, 1994.

———. *The Battles for Spotsylvania Court House and the Road to Yellow Tavern, May 7–12, 1864.* Baton Rouge: Louisiana State University Press, 1997.

Rhodes, Elisha Hunt. *All for the Union: The Civil War Diary and Letters of Elisha Hunt Rhodes.* Edited by Robert Hunt Rhodes. New York: Orion Books, 1991.

Rhodes, Richard. *The Making of the Atomic Bomb.* New York: Simon & Schuster, 1986.

Rice, Allen Thorndike, ed. "A Page of Political Correspondence, Unpublished Letters of Mr. Stanton to Mr. Buchanan," in *North American Review* CXXIX (1879).

Richardson, Israel B. Papers. Record Group 94, Adjutant General's Office Records, Generals' Papers, NARA, Washington, D.C.

Rinhart, Floyd; Marion Rinhart; and Robert W. Wagner. *The American Tintype.* Columbus: Ohio State University Press, 1999.

Rinker, Michael F. Papers. Virginia Military Institute Library, Lexington.

Ripple, Ezra Hoyt. *Dancing Along the Deadline: The Andersonville Memoir of a Prisoner of the Confederacy.* Edited by Mark A. Snell. Novato, Calif.: Presidio Press, 1996.

Ritchie, David F. *Four Years in the First New York Light Artillery: The Papers of David F. Ritchie.* Edited by Norman L. Ritchie. Hamilton, N.Y.: Edmondston Publishing Co., 1997.

Robertson, James I., Jr. *General A. P. Hill: The Story of a Confederate Warrior.* New York: Random House, 1987.

———. *Stonewall Jackson: The Man, the Soldier, the Legend.* New York: Macmillan Co., 1997.

Robertson, William Glenn. *Back Door to Richmond: The Bermuda Hundred Campaign, April–June 1864.* Baton Rouge: Louisiana State University Press, 1991.

Robinson, Charles M., III. *Hurricane of Fire: The Union Assault on Fort Fisher.* Annapolis, Md.: Naval Institute Press, 1998.

Robinson, John C. Papers. Record Group 94, Adjutant General's Office Records, Generals' Papers, NARA, Washington, D.C.

Rollins, Richard, ed. *Pickett's Charge: Eyewitness Accounts.* Redondo Beach, Calif.: Rank & File Publications, 1994.

Roman, Alfred. *The Military Operations of General Beauregard in the War Between the States, 1861 to 1865.* New York: Harper & Brothers, 1884.

Ropes, Hannah. *Civil War Nurse: The Diary and Letters of Hannah Ropes.* Edited by John R. Brumgardt. Knoxville: University of Tennessee Press, 1980.

Ropes, John Codman, and Theodore F. Dwight, eds. *Papers of the Military Historical Society of Massachusetts.* Wilmington, N.C.: Broadfoot Publishing Co., 1990.

Rosecrans, William S. Papers. Record Group 94, Adjutant General's Office Records, Generals' Papers, NARA, Washington, D.C.

Rosen, Robert N. *Confederate Charleston: An Illustrated History of the City and Its People During the Civil War.* Columbia: University of South Carolina Press, 1994.

Ross, FitzGerald. *Cities and Camps of the Confederate States.* Edited by Richard Barksdale Harwell. Urbana: University of Illinois Press, 1958.

Ross, Leonard F. Papers. Record Group 94, Adjutant General's Office Records, Generals' Papers, NARA, Washington, D.C.

Rousseau, Lovell H. Papers. Record Group 94, Adjutant General's Office Records, Generals' Papers, NARA, Washington, D.C.

Rowley, Thomas A. Papers. Record Group 94, Adjutant General's Office Records, Generals' Papers, NARA, Washington, D.C.

Ruffin, Edmund. *The Diary of Edmund Ruffin.* Edited by William K. Scarborough. Baton Rouge: Louisiana State University Press, 1972–1989.

Ruger, Thomas H. Papers. Record Group 94, Adjutant General's Office Records, Generals' Papers, NARA, Washington, D.C.

Russell, William Howard. *My Diary North and South.* New York: Harper & Bros., 1954.

Salecker, Gene Eric. *Disaster on the Mississippi: The* Sultana *Explosion, April 27, 1865.* Annapolis, Md.: Naval Institute Press, 1996.

Sandburg, Carl. *Abraham Lincoln: The War Years.* New York: Harcourt, Brace & Co., 1939.

Sanders, William P. Papers. Record Group 94, Adjutant General's Office Records, Generals' Papers, NARA, Washington, D.C.

Sandford, Charles W. Papers. Record Group 94, Adjutant General's Office Records, Generals' Papers, NARA, Washington, D.C.

Sauers, Richard A. *"A Caspian Sea of Ink": The Meade-Sickles Controversy.* Baltimore: Butternut & Blue, 1989.

———. *"A Succession of Honorable Victories": The Burnside Expedition in North Carolina.* Dayton, Ohio: Morningside House, 1996.

Saxton, Rufus. Papers. Record Group 94, Adjutant General's Office Records, Generals' Papers, NARA, Washington, D.C.

Scammon, Eliakim P. Papers. Record Group 94, Adjutant General's Office Records, Generals' Papers, NARA, Washington, D.C.

Schaff, Morris. *The Battle of the Wilderness.* Boston: Houghton Mifflin Co., 1910.

Schimmelfennig, Alexander. Papers. Record Group 94, Adjutant General's Office Records, Generals' Papers, NARA, Washington, D.C.

Schoepf, Albin F. Papers. Record Group 94, Adjutant General's Office Records, Generals' Papers, NARA, Washington, D.C.

Schofield, John M. Papers. Record Group 94, Adjutant General's Office Records, Generals' Papers, NARA, Washington, D.C.

Schott, Thomas E. *Alexander H. Stephens of Georgia: A Biography.* Baton Rouge: Louisiana State University Press, 1988.

Schrader, Charles R. *United States Army Logistics, 1775–1992, An Anthology.* Washington, D.C.: Center of Military History, U.S. Army, 1997.

Schultz, Duane. *The Dahlgren Affair: Terror and Conspiracy in the Civil War.* New York: W. W. Norton & Co., 1998.

Schurz, Carl. Papers. Record Group 94, Adjutant General's Office Records, Generals' Papers, NARA, Washington, D.C.

Schutz, Wallace J., and Walter N. Trenerry. *Abandoned by Lincoln: A Military Biography of General John Pope.* Urbana: University of Illinois Press, 1990.

Scott, Robert Garth. *Into the Wilderness with the Army of the Potomac.* Bloomington: Indiana University Press, 1985.

Scott, Winfield. *Memoirs of Lieut.–General Scott, LL.D.* New York: Sheldon & Co., 1864.

Sears, Stephen W. *Chancellorsville.* Boston: Houghton Mifflin Co., 1996.

———. *George B. McClellan: The Young Napoleon.* New York: Ticknor & Fields, 1988.

———. *Landscape Turned Red: The Battle of Antietam.* New Haven, Conn.: Ticknor & Fields, 1983.

———. *To the Gates of Richmond: The Peninsula Campaign.* New York: Ticknor & Fields, 1992.

2d United States Sharpshooters. Papers. Antietam National Battlefield, Sharpsburg, Md.

Secrist, Philip L. *The Battle of Resaca: Atlanta Campaign, 1864.* Macon, Ga.: Mercer University Press, 1998.

Sedgwick, John. *Correspondence of John Sedgwick, Major-General.* Edited by Henry D. Sedgwick. New York: De Vinne Press, 1902–1903.

Semmes, Raphael. *Memoirs of Service Afloat, During the War Between the States.* London: R. Bently & Son, 1869.

———. Papers. William Stanley Hoole Special Collections Library, University of Alabama, Tuscaloosa.

Seymour, Truman. Papers. Record Group 94, Adjutant General's Office Records, Generals' Papers, NARA, Washington, D.C.

Shackelford, James M. Papers. Record Group 94, Adjutant General's Office Records, Generals' Papers, NARA, Washington, D.C.

Shaw, Robert Gould. *Blue-Eyed Child of Fortune: The Civil War Letters of Colonel Robert Gould Shaw.* Edited by Russell Duncan. Athens: University of Georgia Press, 1992.

Shea, William L., and Earl J. Hess. *Pea Ridge: Civil War Campaign in the West.* Chapel Hill: University of North Carolina Press, 1992.

Sheridan, Philip H. *Personal Memoirs of P. H. Sheridan.* New York: D. Appleton & Co., 1888.

Sherman, Thomas W. Papers. Record Group 94, Adjutant General's Office Records, Generals' Papers, NARA, Washington, D.C.

Sherman, William Tecumseh. *Home Letters of General Sherman.* Edited by Mark A. De-Wolfe Howe. New York: Charles Scribner's Sons, 1909.

———. *Memoirs of General W. T. Sherman: Written by Himself.* New York: D. Appleton & Co., 1875.

———. *Sherman at War.* Edited by Joseph H. Ewing. Dayton, Ohio: Morningside Book Shop, 1992.

———. *Sherman's Civil War: Selected Correspondence of William T. Sherman, 1860–1865.* Edited by Brooks D. Simpson and Jean V. Berlin. Chapel Hill: University of North Carolina Press, 1999.

———. Papers. Record Group 94, Adjutant General's Office Records, Generals' Papers, NARA, Washington, D.C.

———. Papers. U.S. Army Military History Institute, Carlisle, Pa.

Sherman, William Tecumseh, and John Sherman. *The Sherman Letters: Correspondence Be-*

tween General and Senator Sherman from 1837 to 1891. Edited by Rachel Sherman Thorndike. New York: Charles Scribner's Sons, 1894.

Shields, James. Papers. Record Group 94, Adjutant General's Office Records, Generals' Papers, NARA, Washington, D.C.

Shotwell, Randolph Abbott. *The Papers of Randolph Abbott Shotwell.* Edited by J. G. Roulhac Hamilton. Raleigh: North Carolina Historical Commission, 1929.

Shultz, David. *"Double Canister at Ten Yards": The Federal Artillery and the Repulse of Pickett's Charge.* Redondo Beach, Calif.: Rank & File Publications, 1995.

Sibley, Henry H. Papers. Record Group 94, Adjutant General's Office Records, Generals' Papers, NARA, Washington, D.C.

Sickles, Daniel E. Papers. Record Group 94, Adjutant General's Office Records, Generals' Papers, NARA, Washington, D.C.

Sigel, Franz. Papers. Record Group 94, Adjutant General's Office Records, Generals' Papers, NARA, Washington, D.C.

Signal Corps, Miscellaneous Papers. Record Group 111, NARA, Washington, D.C.

Sill, Joshua W. Papers. Record Group 94, Adjutant General's Office Records, Generals' Papers, NARA, Washington, D.C.

Silverstone, Paul H. *Warships of the Civil War Navies.* Annapolis, Md.: Naval Institute Press, 1989.

Simmons, Edwin Howard. *The United States Marines: A History.* 3d ed. Annapolis, Md.: Naval Institute Press, 1999.

Simpson, Dick, and Tally Simpson. *Far, Far from Home: The Wartime Letters of Dick and Tally Simpson, 3rd South Carolina Volunteers.* Edited by Guy R. Everson and Edward H. Simpson, Jr. New York: Oxford University Press, 1994.

16th North Carolina Infantry. Papers. Antietam National Battlefield, Sharpsburg, Md.

Slough, John P. Papers. Record Group 94, Adjutant General's Office Records, Generals' Papers, NARA, Washington, D.C.

Small, Abner R. *The Road to Richmond: The Civil War Memoirs of Major Abner R. Small of the Sixteenth Maine Volunteers, Together with the Diary Which he Kept When he Was a Prisoner of War.* Edited by Harold A. Small. Berkeley: University of California Press, 1939.

Smith, Andrew J. Papers. Record Group 94, Adjutant General's Office Records, Generals' Papers, NARA, Washington, D.C.

Smith, Charles F. Papers. Record Group 94, Adjutant General's Office Records, Generals' Papers, NARA, Washington, D.C.

Smith, John Henry. Papers. Lewis Leigh Collection, U.S. Army Military History Institute, Carlisle, Pa.

Smith, William F. Papers. Record Group 94, Adjutant General's Office Records, Generals' Papers, NARA, Washington, D.C.

Solomon, Clara. *The Civil War Diary of Clara Solomon: Growing Up in New Orleans, 1861–1862.* Edited by Elliott Ashkenazi. Baton Rouge: Louisiana State University Press, 1995.

Sommers, Richard J. *Richmond Redeemed: The Siege at Petersburg.* Garden City, N.Y.: Doubleday & Co., 1981.

Sorrel, Gilbert Moxley. *Recollections of a Confederate Staff Officer.* Edited by Bell Irvin Wiley. Wilmington, N.C.: Broadfoot Publishing Co., 1991.

Spear, Ellis. *The Civil War Recollections of General Ellis Spear.* Edited by Abbott Spear, et al. Orono: University of Maine Press, 1997.

Spears, James G. Papers. Record Group 94, Adjutant General's Office Records, Generals' Papers, NARA, Washington, D.C.

Speer, Henry H. A. *Voices from Cemetery Hill: The Civil War Diary, Reports, and Letters of Colonel William Henry Asbury Speer (1861–1864).* Edited by Allen Paul Speer. Johnson City, Tenn.: Overmountain Press, 1997.

Speer, Lonnie R. *Portals to Hell: Military Prisons of the Civil War.* Mechanicsburg, Pa.: Stackpole Books, 1997.

Spencer, Warren F. *Raphael Semmes: The Philosophical Mariner.* Tuscaloosa: University of Alabama Press, 1997.

Spiegel, Marcus M. *A Jewish Colonel in the Civil War: Marcus M. Spiegel of the Ohio Volunteers.* Edited by Jean Powers Soman and Frank L. Byrne. Lincoln: University of Nebraska Press, 1985.

Stanley, David S. Papers. Record Group 94, Adjutant General's Office Records, Generals' Papers, NARA, Washington, D.C.

Stanley, Henry M. *The Autobiography of Sir Henry Morton Stanley.* Edited by Dorothy Stanley. Boston: Houghton Mifflin Co., 1909.

Stannard, George J. Papers. Record Group 94, Adjutant General's Office Records, Generals' Papers, NARA, Washington, D.C.

Steinwehr, Adolph Wilhelm August Friedrich von. Papers. Record Group 94, Adjutant General's Office Records, Generals' Papers, NARA, Washington, D.C.

Stephens, Alexander H. *Recollections of Alexander H. Stephens: His Diary Kept When a Prisoner at Fort Warren, Boston Harbour, 1865.* Edited by Myrta Lockett Avary. Baton Rouge: Louisiana State University Press, 1998.

Stephens, George E. *A Voice of Thunder: The Civil War Letters of George E. Stephens.* Edited by Donald Yacovone. Urbana: University of Illinois Press, 1997.

Stiles, Robert. *Four Years Under Marse Robert.* New York: Neale Publishing Co., 1903.

Stillwell, Leander. *The Story of a Common Soldier of Army Life in the Civil War, 1861–1865.* Kansas City, Mo.: Franklin Hudson Publishing Co., 1920.

Stone, Charles P. Papers. Record Group 94, Adjutant General's Office Records, Generals' Papers, NARA, Washington, D.C.

Stone, Kate. *Brokenburn: The Journal of Kate Stone, 1861–1868.* Edited by John Q. Anderson. Baton Rouge: Louisiana State University Press, 1955.

Stoneman, George. Papers. Record Group 94, Adjutant General's Office Records, Generals' Papers, NARA, Washington, D.C.

Stoughton, Edward H. Papers. Record Group 94, Adjutant General's Office Records, Generals' Papers, NARA, Washington, D.C.

Strong, George Templeton. *The Diary of George Templeton Strong.* Edited by Allan Nevins and Milton Halsey Thomas. New York: Macmillan Co., 1952.

Strother, David Hunter. *A Virginia Yankee in the Civil War: The Diaries of David Hunter Strother.* Edited by Cecil D. Eby, Jr. Chapel Hill: University of North Carolina Press, 1961.

Stuart, James Ewell Brown. Papers. Virginia Historical Society, Richmond.

Sturgis, Samuel D. Papers. Record Group 94, Adjutant General's Office Records, Generals' Papers, NARA, Washington, D.C.

Sullivan, Jeremiah C. Papers. Record Group 94, Adjutant General's Office Records, Generals' Papers, NARA, Washington, D.C.

Sumner, Charles. *The Selected Letters of Charles Sumner.* Edited by Beverly Wilson Palmer. Boston: Northeastern University Press, 1990.

Sumner, Edwin V., (Sr.). Papers. Record Group 94, Adjutant General's Office Records, Generals' Papers, NARA, Washington, D.C.

Swinton, William. *Campaigns of the Army of the Potomac: A Critical History of Operations in Virginia, Maryland, and Pennsylvania from the Commencement to the Close of the War, 1861–5.* New York: Charles B. Richardson, 1866.

Sword, Wiley. *Embrace an Angry Wind: The Confederacy's Last Hurrah: Spring Hill, Franklin, and Nashville.* New York: HarperCollins, 1992.

———. *Mountains Touched with Fire: Chattanooga Besieged, 1863.* New York: St. Martin's Press, 1995.

———. *Sharpshooter: Hiram Berdan, His Famous Sharpshooters, and Their Sharps Rifles.* Lincoln, R.I.: Andrew Mowbray, 1988.

———. *Shiloh: Bloody April.* New York: William Morrow & Co., 1974.

Symonds, Craig L. *The Naval Institute Historical Atlas of the U.S. Navy.* Annapolis, Md.: Naval Institute Press, 1995.

———. *Joseph E. Johnston: A Civil War Biography.* New York: W. W. Norton & Co., 1992.

Tanner, Robert G. *Stonewall in the Valley: Thomas J. "Stonewall" Jackson's Shenandoah Valley Campaign, Spring 1862.* 2d ed. Mechanicsburg, Pa.: Stackpole Books, 1996.

Taylor, John. *Bloody Valverde: A Civil War Battle on the Rio Grande, February 21, 1862.* Albuquerque: University of New Mexico Press, 1995.

Taylor, John M. *Confederate Raider: Raphael Semmes of the Alabama.* Washington, D.C.: Brassey's, 1994.

———. *William Henry Seward: Lincoln's Right Hand.* New York: HarperCollins, 1991.

Taylor, Walter H. *Lee's Adjutant: The Wartime Letters of Colonel Walter Herron Taylor, 1862–1865.* Edited by R. Lockwood Tower. Columbia: University of South Carolina Press, 1995.

Terry, Alfred H. Papers. Record Group 94, Adjutant General's Office Records, Generals' Papers, NARA, Washington, D.C.

Thomas, Benjamin P., and Harold M. Hyman. *Stanton: The Life and Times of Lincoln's Secretary of War.* New York: Alfred A. Knopf, 1962.

Thomas, Edison H. *John Hunt Morgan and His Raiders.* Lexington: University Press of Kentucky, 1985.

Thomas, Emory M. *Bold Dragoon: The Life of J. E. B. Stuart.* New York: Harper & Row, 1986.

———. *Robert E. Lee: A Biography.* New York: W. W. Norton & Co., 1995.

Tidwell, William A. *April '65: Confederate Covert Action in the American Civil War.* Kent, Ohio: Kent State University Press, 1995.

———, James O. Hall, and David Winfred Gaddy. *Come Retribution: The Confederate Secret Service and the Assassination of Lincoln.* Jackson: University Press of Mississippi, 1988.

Torbert, Alfred T. A. Papers. Record Group 94, Adjutant General's Office Records, Generals' Papers, NARA, Washington, D.C.

Tortora, Gerard J., Berdell R. Funke, and Christine L. Case. *Microbiology: An Introduction.* 4th ed. Redwood City, Calif.: Benjamin-Cummings Publishing Co., 1992.

Trudeau, Noah Andre. *Bloody Roads South: The Wilderness to Cold Harbor, May–June 1864.* Boston: Little, Brown & Co., 1989.

————. *The Last Citadel: Petersburg, Virginia, June 1864–April 1865.* Boston: Little, Brown & Co., 1991.

Tucker, Glenn. *Hancock the Superb.* Dayton, Ohio: Morningside Book Shop, 1980.

Tucker, Spencer C. *Raphael Semmes and the* Alabama. Fort Worth, Tex.: Ryan Place Publishers, 1996.

Turchin, John B. Papers. Record Group 94, Adjutant General's Office Records, Generals' Papers, NARA, Washington, D.C.

Turner, Edward Raymond. *The New Market Campaign, May 1864.* Richmond: Whittet & Shepperson, 1912.

Turner, Thomas Reed. *Beware the People Weeping: Public Opinion and the Assassination of Lincoln.* Baton Rouge: Louisiana State University Press, 1982.

Tuttle, John M. Papers. Record Group 94, Adjutant General's Office Records, Generals' Papers, NARA, Washington, D.C.

Twiggs, David E. Papers. Record Group 94, Adjutant General's Office Records, Generals' Papers, NARA, Washington, D.C.

Tyler, Lyon G. *Letters and Times of the Tylers.* Richmond, 1884.

Ullman, Daniel. Papers. Record Group 94, Adjutant General's Office Records, Generals' Papers, NARA, Washington, D.C.

Upson, Theodore F. *With Sherman to the Sea: The Civil War Letters, Diaries, and Reminiscences of Theodore F. Upson.* Edited by Oscar Osburn Winther. Baton Rouge: Louisiana State University Press, 1943.

U.S. Army. *American Military History.* Washington, D.C.: Center for Military History, U.S. Army, 1969 (revised 1973 and 1988).

————. *American Military History, 1607–1953.* (ROTC Manual No. 145-20.) Washington, D.C.: Department of the Army, 1956.

U.S. Navy Department. *Civil War Naval Chronology, 1861–1865.* Edited by Ernest M. Eller. Washington, D.C.: U.S. Government Printing Office, 1971.

————. *Official Navy Register, 1860–1865.* Washington, D.C.: U.S. Government Printing Office, 1860–1865.

————. *Official Records of the Union and Confederate Navies in the War of the Rebellion.* Washington, D.C.: U.S. Government Printing Office, 1894–1927.

U.S. Surgeon General's Office. *The Medical and Surgical History of the War of the Rebellion (1861–65), Prepared, in Accordance with the Acts of Congress, Under the Direction of Surgeon General Joseph K. Barnes, United States Army.* Washington, D.C.: U.S. Government Printing Office, 1870–1888.

U.S. War Dept. *Annual Report of the Secretary of War, November 22, 1865: 39th Congress, 1st Session, House Doc. 1, Including the Final Report of the Provost Marshal General.* Washington, D.C.: U.S. Government Printing Office, 1866.

————. *Annual Report of the Secretary of War, November 14, 1866: 39th Congress, 2d Session, Exec. Doc. 1.* Washington, D.C.: U.S. Government Printing Office, 1866.

————. *Official Army Register, 1861–1866.* Washington, D.C.: U.S. Government Printing Office, 1861–1866.

————. *Official Army Register of the Volunteer Force of the United States Army: For the Years 1861, '62, '63, '64, '65.* Washington, D.C.: U.S. Government Printing Office, 1865.

————. *Proceedings and Report of the Board of Army Officers, Convened by Special Orders No. 78, Headquarters of the Army, Adjutant General's Office, Washington, April 12, 1878, in the Case of Fitz John Porter.* Washington, D.C.: U.S. Government Printing Office, 1879.

————. *Revised Regulations for the Army of the United States, 1861.* Philadelphia: J. B. Lippincott Co., 1861.

————. *The War of the Rebellion: A Compilation of the Official Records of the Union and Confederate Armies.* Washington, D.C.: U.S. Government Printing Office, 1880–1901.

Vandiver, Frank E. *Jubal's Raid: General Early's Famous Attack on Washington in 1864.* New York: McGraw-Hill, 1960.

Vincent, Strong. Papers. Record Group 94, Adjutant General's Office Records, Generals' Papers, NARA, Washington, D.C.

Vogdes, Israel. Papers. Record Group 94, Adjutant General's Office Records, Generals' Papers, NARA, Washington, D.C.

Wagner, George D. Papers. Record Group 94, Adjutant General's Office Records, Generals' Papers, NARA, Washington, D.C.

Wainwright, Charles S. *A Diary of Battle: The Personal Journals of Colonel Charles S. Wainwright, 1861–1865.* Edited by Allan Nevins. New York: Harcourt, Brace & World, 1962.

Wakeman, Sarah Rosetta. *An Uncommon Soldier: The Civil War Letters of Sarah Rosetta Wakeman, Alias Pvt. Lyons Wakeman, 153rd Regiment, New York State Volunteers, 1862–1864.* Edited by Lauren Cook Burgess. Pasadena, Md.: Minerva Center, 1994.

Walker, Peter F. *Vicksburg: A People at War, 1860–1865.* Wilmington, N.C.: Broadfoot Publishing Co., 1987.

Wallace, Lee A., Jr. *A Guide to Virginia Military Organizations, 1861–1865.* Lynchburg, Va.: H. E. Howard, 1986.

Ward, Geoffrey C., Ric Burns, and Ken Burns. *The Civil War: An Illustrated History.* New York: Alfred A. Knopf, 1990.

Ward, John H. H. Papers. Record Group 94, Adjutant General's Office Records, Generals' Papers, NARA, Washington, D.C.

Warner, Ezra J. *Generals in Blue: Lives of the Union Commanders.* Baton Rouge: Louisiana State University Press, 1964.

————. *Generals in Gray: Lives of the Confederate Commanders.* Baton Rouge: Louisiana State University Press, 1959.

Warren, Fitz Henry. Papers. Record Group 94, Adjutant General's Office Records, Generals' Papers, NARA, Washington, D.C.

Warren, Gouverneur K. Papers. Record Group 94, Adjutant General's Office Records, Generals' Papers, NARA, Washington, D.C.

Washburn, Cadwallader C. Papers. Record Group 94, Adjutant General's Office Records, Generals' Papers, NARA, Washington, D.C.

Watson, William. *Life in the Confederate Army, Being the Observations and Experiences of an Alien in the South During the American Civil War.* London: Chapman & Hall, 1887.

Webb, Alexander S. *The Peninsula: McClellan's Campaign of 1862.* New York: Charles Scribner's Sons, 1881.

————. Papers. Antietam National Battlefield, Sharpsburg, Md.

————. Papers. Record Group 94, Adjutant General's Office Records, Generals' Papers, NARA, Washington, D.C.

Weichmann, Louis J. *A True History of the Assassination of Abraham Lincoln and the Conspiracy of 1865.* Edited by Floyd E. Risvold. New York: Alfred A. Knopf, 1975.

Weigley, Russell F. *Quartermaster General of the Union Army: A Biography of M. C. Meigs.* New York: Columbia University Press, 1959.

Welcher, Frank J. *The Union Army, 1861–1865: Organization and Operations.* Bloomington: Indiana University Press, 1989–1992.

Weld, Stephen Minot, Jr. *War Diary and Letters of Stephen Minot Weld, 1861–1865.* 2d ed. Boston: Massachusetts Historical Society, 1979.

Welles, Gideon. *The Diary of Gideon Welles.* Boston: Houghton Mifflin Co., 1911.

Welsh, Jack D. *Medical Histories of Confederate Generals.* Kent, Ohio: Kent State University Press, 1995.

————. *Medical Histories of Union Generals.* Kent, Ohio: Kent State University Press, 1996.

Wert, Jeffry D. *From Winchester to Cedar Creek: The Shenandoah Campaign of 1864.* Carlisle, Pa.: South Mountain Press, 1987.

————. *General James Longstreet: The Confederacy's Most Controversial Soldier.* New York: Simon & Schuster, 1993.

————. *Mosby's Rangers.* New York: Simon & Schuster, 1990.

Wheaton, Frank. Papers. Record Group 94, Adjutant General's Office Records, Generals' Papers, NARA, Washington, D.C.

Whipple, Amiel W. Papers. Record Group 94, Adjutant General's Office Records, Generals' Papers, NARA, Washington, D.C.

White, Henry S. *Prison Life Among the Rebels: Recollections of a Union Chaplain.* Edited by Edward D. Jervey. Kent, Ohio: Kent State University Press, 1990.

Whitman, Walt. *Memoranda During the War.* Washington, D.C.: Walt Whitman, 1875.

Wild, Edward. Papers. Record Group 94, Adjutant General's Office Records, Generals' Papers, NARA, Washington, D.C.

Wiley, Bell Irvin. *The Road to Appomattox.* Baton Rouge: Louisiana State University Press, 1994.

Williams, Alpheus S. *From the Cannon's Mouth: The Civil War Letters of General Alpheus S. Williams.* Edited by Milo M. Quaife. Detroit: Wayne State University Press and the Detroit Historical Society, 1959.

Williams, Kenneth P. *Lincoln Finds a General: A Military Study of the Civil War.* New York: Macmillan Co., 1949–1959.

Williams, T. Harry. *P. G. T. Beauregard: Napoleon in Gray.* Baton Rouge: Louisiana State University Press, 1955.

Williamson, Alice. Papers. Duke University Library, Durham, N.C.

Willich, August. Papers. Record Group 94, Adjutant General's Office Records, Generals' Papers, NARA, Washington, D.C.

Wills, Brian Steel. *A Battle from the Start: The Life of Nathan Bedford Forrest.* New York: HarperCollins, 1992.

Wills, Garry. *Lincoln at Gettysburg: The Words that Remade America.* New York: Simon & Schuster, 1992.

Wilson, David L., and John Y. Simon, eds. *Ulysses S. Grant: Essays and Documents.* Carbondale: Southern Illinois University Press, 1981.

Wilson, James H. *Under the Old Flag: Recollections of Military Operations in the War for the Union, the Spanish-American War, the Boxer Rebellion, etc.* New York: D. Appleton & Co., 1912.

———. Papers. Record Group 94, Adjutant General's Office Records, Generals' Papers, NARA, Washington, D.C.

Winschel, Terrence J. *Triumph and Defeat: The Vicksburg Campaign.* Mason City, Iowa: Savas Publishing Co., 1999.

Winthrop, Theodore. *Life in the Open Air, and Other Papers.* Boston: Ticknor & Fields, 1863.

Wolseley, Garnet. "A Month's Visit to Confederate Headquarters," in *Blackwood's Edinburgh Magazine* XCIII (January–June 1863): 21.

Woodard, William M. Papers. U.S. Army Military History Institute, Carlisle, Pa.

Woodworth, Steven E. *A Deep Steady Thunder: The Battle of Chickamauga.* Fort Worth, Tex.: Ryan Place Publishers, 1996.

———. *Six Armies in Tennessee: The Chickamauga and Chattanooga Campaigns.* Lincoln: University of Nebraska Press, 1998.

Wyeth, John Allan. *Life of General Nathan Bedford Forrest.* New York: Harper & Bros., 1899.

NEWSPAPERS AND PERIODICALS

Atlanta Confederacy
Atlanta Daily Constitutionalist
Atlantic Monthly
The Century Illustrated Magazine
Charleston Daily Courier
Charleston Mercury
Chicago Tribune
Cincinnati Commercial
Civil War History
Fayetteville Observer
Gettysburg Magazine
Macon Telegraph
National Tribune (Washington, D.C.)
New York Herald
New York Times

New York Tribune
North Carolina Historical Review
Proceedings of the Massachusetts Historical Society
Richmond Dispatch
Richmond Sentinel
Sacramento Daily Union
Southern Bivouac
Southern Illustrated News
Southern Magazine
Transactions of the Illinois State Historical Society
Vicksburg Daily Citizen
Washington Telegraph (Arkansas)

INDEX